7–3 (1) Consolidated net income, $34,000
Consolidated retained earnings, $49,000

7–4 (2) Consolidated net income, $87,700
Consolidated retained earnings, $218,500
(2) Minority interest, income statement, $3,300
Minority interest, balance sheet, $21,300

7–5 (4) Minority interest, income statement, $9,000
Consolidated net income, $212,000
Consolidated retained earnings, $912,000
Minority interest, balance sheet, $136,000

8–1 (2) Consolidated net income, $45,000
Consolidated retained earnings, $72,000

8–2 (2) Consolidated net income, $45,600
Consolidated retained earnings, $72,600

8–3 (2) Consolidated net income, $168,000
Consolidated retained earnings, $428,000

8–4 (2) Consolidated net income, $257,800
Minority interest, income statement, $10,200
Consolidated retained earnings, $217,800

8–5 (4) Consolidated net income, $87,200
Consolidated retained earnings, $228,000

9–1 (1) P Company net income, $690,000
S Company net income, $63,000
(2) Gain on extinguishment, $49,000 + $7,000

9–2 (3) Consolidated net income, $64,280
Consolidated assets, $972,050

9–3 (3) Consolidated net income, $62,100
Consolidated assets, $978,650
Minority interest, income statement, $2,280

9–4 (3) Consolidated net income, $73,200
Consolidated assets, $1,180,000

9–5 (3) Consolidated net income, $68,640
Consolidated assets, $1,206,040
Minority interest, balance sheet, $30,600

9–6 (2) Retained earnings component of analysis at Dec. 31, 19X1, $27,000
Carrying value of investment at Dec. 31, 19X1, $610,700

9–7 (2) Retained earnings component of analysis at Dec. 31, 19X1, $16,200
Carrying value of investment at Dec. 31, 19X1, $366,420

9–8 (2) Retained earnings component of analysis at Dec. 31, 19X1, $58,000
Carrying value of investment at Dec. 31, 19X1, $475,000

9–9 (2) Retained earnings component of analysis at Dec. 31, 19X1, $46,400
Carrying value of investment at Dec. 31, 19X1, $460,000

9–10 (2) Retained earnings component of analysis at Dec. 31, 19X1, $91,000
Carrying value of investment at Dec. 31, 19X1, $505,000
(6) Consolidated net income, $178,000

10–1 Carrying value of investment, $1,430,000

10–2 (1) Decrease in parent's equity interest, $360,000
(2) Goodwill element at Jan. 1, 19X6, $165,000

10–3 (1) Goodwill element at Jan. 1, 19X6, $190,000

10–4 (1) Carrying value of investment at Dec. 31, 19X4, $1,411,500
Gain on sale of shares, $32,000

10–5 (1) Carrying value of investment at Dec. 31, 19X7, $292,667
Gain on disposal, $26,500

10–6 (1) Parent's dilution, $225,000

10–7 (1) Parent's accretion, $40,000

10–8 (4) Gain on extinguishment of debt, $2,400
Minority interest, income statement, $70,050
Consolidated net income, $864,050
Consolidated assets, $4,742,100
Consolidated retained earnings, $2,764,450
Minority interest, balance sheet, $294,650

10–9 Working capital provided by operations, $120,000

11–1 (1) P Company net income, $584,000
(2) Minority interest, $30,000

11–2 (1) A Company net income, $1,080,700
(2) Minority interest, $21,800

11–3 (1) P Company net income, $687,600
(2) Minority interest, $21,400

11–4 (1) Consolidated net income, $878,000
(2) Net income accruing to controlling interests, $868,352

11–5 (1) Consolidated net income, $450,000
(3) Net income accruing to controlling interests, $430,851

11–6 (2) Alpha Company's reportable net income, $223,000
(3) 19X2 minority interest deduction, $57,000

12–1 Income tax expense recorded by parent, $80,000

Advanced Accounting

Concepts and Practice

Second Edition

Advanced Accounting

Concepts and Practice

Second Edition

Arnold J. Pahler
San Jose State University

Joseph E. Mori
San Jose State University

Harcourt Brace Jovanovich, Publishers

San Diego   New York   Chicago   Atlanta   Washington, D.C.
London   Sydney   Toronto

Dedications

To the memory of Grandma, Aunt Mabel, Aunt Pearl, and Aunt Dolly

Arnold J. Pahler

To Carol Ann Mori

Joseph E. Mori

Material from Uniform CPA Examination Questions and Unofficial Answers, copyright © 1958, 1960, 1962–1967, 1970, 1972–1979, 1982–1983 by the American Institute of Certified Public Accountants, Inc., is adapted with permission.

ISBN: 0-15-501820-5
Library of Congress Catalog Card Number: 84-81503
Printed in the United States of America

Preface

The Second Edition of *Advanced Accounting: Concepts and Practice* is noticeably different from the First Edition in many respects. Besides updating the book for new technical pronouncements, we have placed a greater emphasis on providing a thorough conceptual basis for understanding the material. In the First Edition, we used numerous examples from actual practice to make the material come alive; we have used even more examples in this edition. In many cases, the presentation of the material has been simplified.

Major changes in the second edition

(1) Consolidations—Fundamentals (Chapters 1–6):

A. **Analysis of Retained Earnings.** An analysis of retained earnings is now provided within the consolidating statement worksheet. To be consistent with actual practice, we present this analysis within the stockholders' equity section of the balance sheet. (See pages 127 and 167 for examples.)

B. **Illustrations of the Trial Balance Approach.** Although the consolidating statement worksheets within the chapters use the financial statement approach, the trial balance approach is illustrated in appendices to Chapters 4, 5, and 7.

C. **Push-Down Accounting Theory.** A discussion of push-down accounting theory (which is now required by the SEC) is included in an appendix to Chapter 3.

D. **Illustration of the Entity Theory.** Although the chapter dealing with minority interest situations is structured around the parent company theory, we have added a discussion and illustration of the entity theory in Appendix B to Chapter 5.

E. **Statement of Changes in Financial Position.** A discussion of how to prepare this statement has been added. The basics are covered at the end of Chapter 6, and additional complexities are discussed in Chapter 10.

(2) Consolidations—Special Subjects (Chapters 7–12):

A. **Tax Effects Relating to Intercompany Transactions.** The income tax effects relating to intercompany transactions (inventory transfers, fixed asset transfers, and bond holdings) are reflected in the parent company and subsidiary company columns of the worksheet. Thus, students do not have to deal with this additional complexity in preparing the consolidating statement worksheets. (For intercompany inventory transfers, the manner of dealing with the tax effects in calculating the parent's and the subsidiary's income tax expense is shown in Appendix A to Chapter 7.)

B. **Splitting Inventory and Fixed Asset Transfers into Two Chapters.** Intercompany inventory transfers are dealt with in Chapter 7, and intercompany fixed asset transfers are now dealt with in Chapter 8. (First Edition Chapters 8, 9, and 10 are now 9, 10, and 11.)

C. **Showing the Full Consolidation Process.** In the chapters on intercompany inventory transfers, intercompany fixed asset transfers, and intercompany bond holdings (Chapters 7, 8, and 9, respectively), the consolidating statement worksheets have been expanded to show the full consolidation process. The partially consolidated column was retained so that the elimination entries in these chapters could be dealt with separately from the elimination entries discussed in preceding chapters. (See pages 266–67 for an example.)

(3) Omnibus Area (Chapters 13–18):

A. **Foreign Operations and Transactions (Chapters 13 and 14).** The material, now based on *FASB Statement No. 52,* is separated into two chapters. Chapter 13 deals with translation of foreign currency financial statements, and Chapter 14 deals with translation of foreign currency transactions. In Chapter 13, a thorough discussion of the conceptual issues pertaining to translating foreign currency financial statements (using numerous easy to follow examples presented in a progressive step-by-step sequence) has been added. In Chapter 14, more emphasis has been given to protecting foreign investments.

B. **Segment Reporting (Chapter 15).** Because of the current deconglomeration trend, the discussion of segment disposals has been expanded.

C. **SEC Reporting (Chapter 17).** The chapter has been updated to reflect the simplified integrated reporting system implemented by the SEC. Much technical material has been eliminated, and the role of the SEC in relation to the FASB has been emphasized.

D. **Troubled Debt Restructurings, Bankruptcy Reorganizations, and Liquidations (Chapter 18).** This chapter has been updated to reflect the fact that *FASB Technical Bulletin No. 81-6* exempts bankruptcy reorganizations from the requirements of *FASB Statement No. 15.* The conceptual basis for the accounting in these areas has been greatly expanded.

(4) Partnerships (Chapters 19–21):

A. **Limited Partnerships.** A discussion of real estate limited partnerships and research and development limited partnerships appears in Appendix A to Chapter 19.

B. **Cash Distribution Schedule.** We have developed a simplified cash distribution schedule for installment liquidations in Chapter 21.

(5) Governmental and Nonprofit Organizations (Chapters 22–24):

A. **Adoption of GAAFR's New Terminology and Techniques.** The new journal entry terminology and techniques of the 1980 edition of *GAAFR* have been adopted. As a result, the budgetary accounts are now treated as a separate trial balance (apart from the actual operating accounts), and the presentation is simplified. (The AICPA uses this new terminology in preparing CPA examination material, as do the major CPA review courses.)

B. **Use of One Closing Procedure for Encumbrances.** The 1980 edition of *GAAFR* uses the same closing procedure for both lapsing and nonlapsing encumbrances outstanding at year-end. We have adopted this approach, whereby both budgetary accounts pertaining to encumbrances are closed at year-end. This results in a greatly simplified presentation.

C. **Nonprofit Organizations (Chapter 24).** The material in this chapter has been revised to cover separately the accounting for the following nonprofit organizations: (a) colleges and universities; (b) hospitals; (c) voluntary health and welfare organizations; and (d) all other miscellaneous nonprofit organizations.

(6) Checklist of Key Figures:
The checklist of key figures now appears on the endpapers of the book.

Consolidations template and manual for working consolidation problems on the computer

A class-tested software consolidations template and accompanying manual are available for working consolidation problems on a computer. (Any consolidation problem in the book can be worked using these materials.) To use these materials, the student must have access to one of the following electronic spreadsheet packages:

(1) VisiCalc (a trademark of VisiCorp)
(2) LOTUS 1-2-3 (a trademark of Lotus Development)
(3) SuperCalc (a trademark of Sorcim Corporation)
(4) Multiplan (a trademark of Microsoft Corporation)

In addition, access to either IBM PC (or compatible equipment) or Apple II or IIe is required.

The template has been designed so that students must perform a limited amount of spreadsheet programming. **No prior computer experience is required.** Furthermore, with the manual, students can work problems on their own **without instructor involvement** in the computer lab. Instructors who do not have one of the above combinations may contact Arnold J. Pahler to discuss the feasibility of supplying individualized materials.

Major consolidations feature:
Simplified consolidation technique based on the conceptual analysis of the investment account and use of the equity method

In preparing consolidated financial statements, we have retained the use of analyzing the investment account by its individual components, updating the analysis using the equity method of accounting, and then preparing the basic consolidation elimination entry from this updated analysis. This approach, which was received quite favorably by First Edition adopters, eliminates most of the time that otherwise would be spent developing elimination entry amounts.

Instructor-oriented features

Advanced Accounting: Concepts and Practice incorporates the following instructor-oriented features:

Chapter Discussion Cases.   Most chapters contain discussion cases designed to stimulate student thinking. A number of discussion cases are designed to push students somewhat beyond the text coverage.

Transparencies.   Transparencies of solutions to all problems are provided for Chapters 1, 3, 4, 5, 6, 7, 8, 13, and 14.

Test Booklet.   A Test Booklet containing approximately 330 true or false statements, 150 multiple choice questions, 240 completion statements (fill-ins), and 90 short problems is provided. (Because CPA examinations consistently contain excellent questions pertaining to theory, we have obtained or adapted many of the multiple choice questions from recent examinations.)

Instructor's and Solutions Manual.   To assist instructors in evaluating and selecting problem materials, each chapter in the Instructor's and Solutions Manual contains (in uninterrupted format) a description of each discussion case, exercise, and problem. The **relative difficulty** and **estimated time** for completion of problem materials is also included. In addition, **a suggested syllabus is included for a one-term course and for a two-term course.** Finally, the Instructor's and Solutions Manual contains some **teaching suggestions** and additional items instructors may want to point out or discuss with students. (The manual is perforated to facilitate the preparation of additional transparencies.)

Student-oriented features

Advanced Accounting: Concepts and Practice contains the following student-oriented features:

Table of Contents Preceding Each Chapter.   A detailed table of contents at the beginning of each chapter enables students not only to make more efficient use of the text but also to grasp readily the overall flow and development of each chapter.

Overview and Summary of Each Chapter.   Each chapter begins with an overview so that students may obtain quickly a general understanding of the nature of the chapter and the related accounting issues. Each chapter concludes with a summary.

Chapter Glossaries of New Terms.   Approximately 140 new terms are introduced in the text. New terms are defined in a glossary at the end of most chapters.

Descriptions of Discussion Cases, Exercises, and Problems.   To help students understand the nature of an assignment, an overview description is provided at the beginning of each discussion case, exercise, and problem. These descriptions also enable students desiring to do additional work to evaluate nonassigned material and select that which is most beneficial.

Vertical Format for Consolidating Statement Worksheets. Consolidating statement worksheets are presented in vertical format on a single page in chapters other than 7, 8, and 9 so that students need not continually turn the book sideways.

Checklist of Key Figures.   A checklist of key figures for most problems is included on the endpapers of the book.

Consolidations Template and Manual for Working Consolidation Problems on the Computer.   See page vii of this preface for details on this new ancillary.

Working Papers.   Working Papers are provided for problems in Chapters 1, 3, 4, 5, 6, 7, 8, 9, 13, and 19. The time saved using Working Papers in these chapters is a great advantage for students.

Acknowledgments

We are indebted to First Edition adopters who passed along suggestions for the Second Edition. The following instructors reviewed portions of the Second Edition before publication: Mary M.K. Fleming, California State University at Fullerton; George C. Mead, Michigan State University; Trini U. Melcher, California State University at Fullerton; Carl G. Orne, California State University at Hayward; and Joanne W. Rockness, North Carolina State University. We extend our heartfelt appreciation for their thorough, thoughtful, and conscientious efforts in reviewing chapters. We appreciate their many fine constructive comments and consider ourselves very fortunate to have had each of them as a reviewer for this edition.

We also thank the following First Edition users who responded to a questionnaire relating to the Second Edition: Harry Anderson, Franklin College; Leonard Bacon, California State College, Bakersfield; Virginia Bakay, University of Nevada, Las Vegas; Marianne Battista, Rider College; Edward Becker, Bucknell University; Stewart Berkshire, Jr., California State University, Long Beach; Lawrence Bezdziecki, Moravian College; Jack Borke, University of Wisconsin, Platteville; Wayne Bremser, Villanova University; Robert Campbell, Towson State University; Philip Cheng, East Carolina University; George Chorba, Villanova University; Doris Cook, University of Arkansas; William Daugherty, New Mexico State University; James Dear, University of Southern Mississippi; Donald DeRespinis, Western Connecticut State College; Donald DeSantis, St. Martin's College; Normal Dressel, Georgia State University; David Durkee, University of Wisconsin, Platteville; Dean Edmiston, Emporia State University; James Ehrenberg, Valparaiso University; John Gehman, Moravian College; Judy Harris, Worcester State College; Gary Heesacker, Central Washington University; Sharron Hoffmans, University of Texas, El Paso; Randy Huta, Utica College of Syracuse; William Kelting, SUNY at Plattsburgh; W. Lawrence Lipton, University of Maine, Machias; Gordon Louvau, John F. Kennedy University; Joseph Marcheggiani, Butler University; George Mead, Michigan State University; Richard Metcalf, University of Nebraska; Gary Michael, University of Vermont; David Mielke, Marquette University; Edward O'Malley, Western Connecticut State College; Carl Orne, California State University, Hayward; Glen Owen, University of California, Santa Barbara; Ronald Savey, Western Washington University; Richard Schmidt, California Polytechnic State University; Gene Shea, Olivet

Nazarene College; William Stevens, DePaul University; Donald Tang, Portland State University; Norman Tierney, Roger Williams College; James Volkert, Northeastern University; Charles Wagner, Gustavus Adolphus College; Lyn Wheeler, College of William and Mary; and Robert Yahr, Marquette University.

We thank Arthur Andersen & Co. for allowing us to use their professional libraries and materials. We express with appreciation our thanks to the American Institute of Certified Public Accountants, the Financial Accounting Standards Board, and the Government Finance Officers Association for their permission to quote material from their respective pronouncements and various other publications. We also thank the American Institute of Certified Public Accountants for their permission to use and adapt material from the CPA examinations.

We welcome all comments from users.

Arnold J. Pahler
Joseph E. Mori

Contents

A detailed table of contents for individual chapters appears at the beginning of each chapter.

PART ONE Consolidated Financial Statements: Fundamentals

1 Branch Accounting

OVERVIEW OF BRANCH ACCOUNTING

A substantial portion of the subject matter of advanced accounting concerns businesses that increase the number of their outlying manufacturing, retailing, or service locations to increase sales and profits. A business may establish additional outlying locations in one of the following two ways:

(1) Internal expansion. Internal expansion means that a business constructs or leases additional outlying facilities. In most instances, the additional facilities increase the company's manufacturing, retailing, or service capacities in the same line of business in which it currently operates. Much of the growth of International Business Machines Corporation, Sears, Roebuck and Company, and Bank of America occurred through such internal expansion.

(2) External expansion. External expansion takes place when two existing businesses combine into a unified larger business. Although many business combinations enable companies to increase their operations in the same line of business, an increasing proportion of business combinations occur among companies in unrelated fields. Such combinations enable companies to diversify their product lines. Much of the growth of International Telephone and Telegraph, Gulf and Western Industries, and Litton Industries came about through external expansion.

This chapter deals exclusively with the internal expansion of businesses. Subsequent chapters deal with external expansion. By discussing internal expansion first, we establish some fundamental principles of accounting for multilocation operations that will benefit us in later chapters. Accounting for outlying locations established in foreign countries through internal expansion involves special considerations; accordingly, we discuss these situations in Chapters 13 and 14, which deal with foreign operations and transactions.

Terminology

A business's outlying location established through internal expansion is not a separate legal entity but merely an extension of a legal entity. Accordingly, it cannot be referred to as a company, because it is only part of a company. Because the professional accounting pronouncements do not specify how outlying locations should be referred to, many terms have evolved over the years. Banks commonly refer to their outlying locations as **branches;** insurance companies commonly refer to them as **sales offices;** and manufacturing companies use the terms **division** and **plant.** Some companies, however, use *division* to refer to geographical area—for example, all outlying manufacturing plants in a designated eastern location might be called the East Coast Division. Some companies use the term division to refer to a particular product line. General Motors Corporation, for example, has five automobile divisions, and each division has several manufacturing plants. An outlying location of a retail establishment is a **store.** Companies in the computer-manufacturing industry often establish outlying locations to service computers; these locations may be referred to as **field engineering offices.** In some companies, the outlying locations carry only demonstration units and sales brochures—any sales that they generate are approved and filled by the home office; such outlying locations are called **sales offices** or **agencies.** In all these instances, the headquarters location of the legal entity that established the outlying location is referred to as the **home office.**

Delegation of decision-making authority

When an outlying location is established, the home office must decide the extent to which it will grant decision-making authority to management at the outlying location. While companywide policies are established by the home office, many day-to-day operating decisions can be delegated to the outlying management. The extent of delegation is part of the broad topic of centralized versus decentralized management decision making. For example, varying degrees of delegation are found in the retail industry. At one extreme are some home offices that decide all the merchandise to be carried by each outlying retail outlet, and each retail outlet must purchase all such merchandise from the home office. At the other extreme are home offices that grant managements at the outlying retail outlets complete discretion over the merchandise they may carry and from where they may buy it. Between these extremes are situations in which outlying retail outlets must carry certain merchandise specified by the home office (which often must be purchased from the home office), but local managers have complete discretion over other merchandise and where they buy it. In the banking industry, branches usually are assigned dollar limits on the amount of money they may loan to a given customer; any loan requests above the designated limits must be approved by a higher regional office or the home office. Some home offices handle national and regional advertising, allowing outlying locations to do only limited local advertising. Other home offices make each outlying location responsible for its own local advertising.

Accounting systems

The home office must decide how to account for the activities and transactions of the outlying location. This decision is based on what is most practical and economical in a given situation. Accounting systems can be categorized as either centralized or decentralized.

Centralized accounting.   Under a centralized accounting system, an outlying location does not maintain a separate general ledger in which to record its transactions. Instead, it sends source documents on sales, purchases, and payroll to the home office. Outlying locations usually deposit cash receipts in local bank accounts, which only the home office can draw upon. When the home office receives source documents, it reconciles sales information with bank deposits, reviews and processes invoices for payment, and prepares payroll checks and related payroll records. Inventory and fixed assets at each outlying location also are recorded in the home office general ledger, appropriately coded to signify the location to which they belong. Journal entries pertaining to each outlying location's transactions are then prepared and posted to the home office general ledger. These entries are usually coded so that accountants at the home office can readily prepare operating statements for each outlying location. Centralized accounting systems commonly use computers at the home office to minimize the clerical aspects of keeping records and preparing financial statements. The home office reviews operating statements for each outlying location and provides copies to outlying management. Centralized accounting systems are usually practical when the operations of the outlying location do not involve complex manufacturing operations or extensive retailing or service activities. Grocery, drug, and shoe store chains usually use centralized accounting systems. Because centralized accounting systems present no unusual accounting issues, they are not discussed any further.

Decentralized accounting.   Under a decentralized accounting system, an outlying location maintains a separate general ledger in which to record its transactions. Thus, the outlying location is a separate **accounting entity,** even though it is not a separate legal entity. It prepares its own journal entries and financial statements, submitting the latter to the home office, usually on a monthly basis. Decentralized accounting systems are common for outlying locations that have complex manufacturing operations or extensive retailing operations involving significant credit sales. In a decentralized accounting system, the following accounting issues must be resolved:

(1) The manner in which transactions between the home office and the outlying locations are recorded.
(2) The procedures by which the revenues, costs, and expenses of the outlying locations are reported for financial and income tax reporting purposes.

The remainder of this chapter deals with these two issues. As mentioned previously, many industries create outlying locations through internal expansion. We use the retail industry to illustrate the fundamental accounting principles for multilocation operations using a decentralized accounting system because retailing activities allow a complete discussion of the issues. In discussing and illustrating such issues, the outlying locations are referred to hereafter as **branches.**

BRANCH GENERAL LEDGER ACCOUNTS

Intracompany accounts

A branch is established when a home office transfers cash, inventory, or other assets to an outlying location. Because the home office views the assets transferred to the branch as an investment, it makes the entry shown at the top of page 8.

> Investment in branch xxx
>   Asset(s). xxx

This Investment in Branch account (sometimes called *Branch Current*) is used to keep track of and maintain control over (1) the assets transferred to the branch, and (2) the increase or decrease in the branch's net assets as a result of the branch's operations.

On receipt of the assets from the home office, the branch makes the following entry:

> Asset(s). xxx
>   Home office xxx

The Home Office account represents the equity interest of the home office in the branch. The use of such an account allows double-entry bookkeeping procedures to be used at the branch level. (Remember that branches are not separate legal entities and do not have Common Stock, Additional Paid-in Capital, and Retained Earnings accounts.)

The balance in the investment in Branch account on the books of the home office always equals the balance in the Home Office account on the books of the branch. In practice, these accounts are referred to as the **intracompany** or **reciprocal** accounts. At the end of each accounting period, the branch closes its income or loss to its Home Office account. Upon receipt of the branch's financial statements, the home office adjusts its Investment in Branch account to reflect the branch's income or loss, and makes the offsetting credit or debit to an income statement account called **Branch Income** or **Branch Loss,** as the case may be.

Branches are usually financed entirely by the home office and typically do not establish relations with local banks. Thus, they do not incur interest expense. If a branch has cash in excess of its immediate needs, it usually transfers it to the home office, which is responsible for investing excess cash on a companywide basis. Thus, branches do not have interest income from investments.

Income tax accounts and reporting

Because branches are not separate legal entities, they do not file individual income tax returns. The home office must include the income or loss from its branches along with its own income or loss from operations for federal income tax reporting purposes. If the home office has operations in states that impose income taxes, the home office must file individual income tax returns in those states. Federal and state income taxes are almost always computed at the home office and recorded exclusively in the home office general ledger. Few companies attempt to allocate or transfer income tax expense from the home office general ledger to branch general ledgers. This not only simplifies the tax recording procedures but also eliminates the need to make arbitrary allocation assumptions. Furthermore, the potential benefits, if any, from allocating income tax expense to the branches would be minimal in most instances.

Because branches do not have interest income, interest expense, or income tax expense, the income or loss from their operations is an **operating**

income or **loss,** not a net income or loss. Hereafter, all references to a branch's income or loss are in this context.

Home office allocations

The home office usually arranges and pays for certain expenses that benefit the branches. The most common example is insurance. In theory, some portion of the insurance expense should be allocated to the various branches, so that the home office may determine the true operating income or loss of each branch. In practice, however, allocations of home office expenses vary widely. Some home offices allocate only those expenses that relate directly to the branch operations, such as insurance and national advertising costs. Some home offices without any revenue-producing operations of their own allocate all of their expenses (including salaries of home office executives, facilities costs, legal fees, audit fees, and interest expense) to the branches. Branch managers are therefore continually aware that branch operations must cover these costs. Some home offices do not allocate any home office expenses to the branches on the theory that because the branches have no control over them, arbitrary allocations serve no useful purpose. The home office records allocations by debiting the Investment in Branch account and crediting the applicable expense accounts. The branch debits the applicable expense accounts and credits its Home Office account. The end result is the same as if the home office had transferred cash to the branch and the branch had arranged for and incurred the expenses.

Inventory transfer accounts

When inventory is transferred from the home office to a branch, all that has really happened is that inventory has physically moved from one location in the company to another. A sale has not occurred, because sales take place only between the company and outside customers. To measure the profitability of a branch, however, an intracompany billing must be prepared. The purpose of the intracompany billing is to transfer purchases from the books of the home office to the books of the branch. The branch uses a special purchases account called Shipments from Home Office to record these inventory transfers and makes the following entry:

Shipments from home office xxx
    Home office xxx

The home office uses a special contrapurchases account called Shipments to Branch to record inventory transfers. If the inventory is transferred and billed at the home office's cost, the home office makes the following entry:

Investment in branch xxx
    Shipments to branch xxx

The branch's ending inventory, cost of goods sold, gross margin, and operating profit or loss depend on the amounts of these intracompany billings. If the intracompany billing is made at the home office's cost, then these special accounts should always agree. By using these special accounts, the home office can strengthen control over branch operations. If these special accounts do not agree, then at least one of the accounting entities has made an error or a shipment is in transit. Before the month-end closing can be properly completed, an adjusting entry must be made to bring the two special accounts into agreement. Using the home office's cost in pricing intracompany inventory transfers is quite common, primarily because it does not require any special considerations in the preparation of month-end combined financial statements for the home office and its branches. The preparation of combined financial statements is discussed and illustrated later in the chapter, as are situations in which inventory transfers are made at above the home office's cost.

Fixed asset accounts

Some home offices require their branches' fixed assets to be recorded on the books of the home office instead of on the books of the branches. Such a procedure automatically ensures that uniform depreciation methods and asset lives are used for all branches. The home office usually charges the branch for the depreciation expense of its fixed assets. It does this by crediting Accumulated Depreciation and debiting the Investment in Branch account instead of debiting Depreciation Expense. The branch debits Depreciation Expense and credits the Home Office account instead of crediting Accumulated Depreciation. When fixed assets are recorded on the home office books, the fixed assets pertaining to the branch must be added to the Investment in Branch account to evaluate the profitability of branch operations in relation to the net assets invested in the branch.

Other general ledger accounts

The branch maintains the balance sheet and income statement accounts necessary to record transactions that take place between (1) the home office and the branch, and (2) the branch and its customers, creditors, and employees. The extent of the accounts required depends on the scope of the branch's operations.

Illustrative entries:
Branch formation and typical transactions

Assume Cabot Company, which prepares financial reports at the end of the calendar year, established a branch on July 1, 19X1. The following transactions occurred during the formation of the branch and its first six months of operations, ending December 31, 19X1.

(1) The home office sent $25,000 cash to the branch to begin operations.
(2) The home office shipped inventory to the branch. Intracompany billings totaled $60,000, which was the home office's cost. (Both the home office and the branch use a periodic inventory system.)
(3) The branch acquired merchandise display equipment costing $12,000 on July 1, 19X1. (Assume that branch fixed assets are not carried on the home office books.)

Illustration 1-1

Home Office Books			Branch Books		
(1) Investment in branch	25,000		(1) Cash	25,000	
Cash		25,000	Home office		25,000
(2) Investment in branch	60,000		(2) Shipments from		
Shipments to			home office . .	60,000	
branch		60,000	Home office		60,000
			(3) Equipment	12,000	
			Cash		12,000
			(4) Purchases	40,000	
			Accounts		
			payable		40,000
			(5) Cash	35,000	
			Accounts		
			receivable	85,000	
			Sales		120,000
			(6) Cash	66,000	
			Accounts		
			receivable		66,000
			(7) Accounts payable .	25,000	
			Cash		25,000
			(8) Selling expenses . .	15,000	
			Administrative		
			expenses	12,000	
			Cash		27,000
(9) Investment in branch	2,000		(9) Administrative		
Administrative			expenses	2,000	
expenses		2,000	Home office		2,000
			(10) Selling expenses . .	1,000	
			Accumulated		
			depreciation . .		1,000
(11) Cash	45,000		(11) Home office	45,000	
Investment in			Cash		45,000
branch		45,000			
(12) Investment in branch	20,000		(12) Inventory	30,000	
Branch income		20,000	Sales	120,000	
			Purchases		40,000
			Shipments from		
			home office . .		60,000
			Selling		
			expenses		16,000
			Administrative		
			expenses		14,000
			Home office . . . :		20,000

(4) The branch purchased inventory costing $40,000 from outside vendors on account.

(5) The branch had credit sales of $85,000 and cash sales of $35,000.

(6) The branch collected $66,000 on accounts receivable.

(7) The branch paid outside vendors $25,000.

(8) The branch incurred selling expenses of $15,000 and general and

administrative expenses of $12,000. These expenses were paid in cash when they were incurred and include the expense of leasing the branch's facilities.

(9) The home office charged the branch $2,000 for its share of insurance.

(10) Depreciation expense on the merchandise display equipment acquired by the branch is $1,000 for the six-month period. (Depreciation expense is classified as a selling expense.)

(11) The branch remitted $45,000 cash to the home office.

(12) The branch's physical inventory on December 31, 19X1, is $30,000. The branch prepares its closing entries, and the home office prepares its adjusting entry to reflect the increase in the branch's net assets resulting from the branch's operations.

The journal entries for these transactions as they would be recorded by the home office and the branch are presented in Illustration 1-1.

COMBINED FINANCIAL STATEMENTS: INVENTORY TRANSFERS AT HOME OFFICE COST

Month-end verification of intracompany account balances

Before the branch prepares its closing entries and submits financial statements to the home office, it must verify that its Home Office account and Shipments from Home Office account agree with the corresponding reciprocal accounts maintained by the home office. If the accounts do not agree, there are two possible explanations:

(1) A transaction initiated by one of the accounting entities has been improperly recorded by the other accounting entity. Obviously, the accounting entity that made the error must make the appropriate adjusting entry.

(2) A transaction initiated by one of the accounting entities has been recorded by the initiating entity but not yet by the receiving entity—for example, cash transfers in transit, inventory shipments in transit, and intracompany charges. Normally, the receiving accounting entity prepares the adjusting entry as if it has completed the transaction before the end of the accounting period. (It would be more disruptive to have the initiating accounting entity reverse the transaction.)

These adjusting entries to bring the intracompany accounts into agreement are absolutely necessary for the proper preparation of combined financial statements. After making any necessary adjustments, the branch submits an income statement and a balance sheet to the home office.

The primary elimination entry

The home office general ledger (after being adjusted for the branch's income or loss) reflects the overall net income earned by the home office and the branch. Generally accepted accounting principles require, however, that in reporting the results of operations to its shareholders, the home office combine the detail of the branch's income or loss with the detail of the accounts making up the net income or loss from the home office's own operations. In other words, the home office cannot report a one-line item amount called branch income or loss for the branch's operations; it must combine the sales, the cost of goods sold, and the operating expenses of both accounting entities and report the combined amounts. This is accomplished by substituting the branch's income statement for the Branch Income or Loss account in the home office general ledger. Likewise, generally accepted accounting principles require that in reporting the balance sheet amounts to its shareholders, the home office combine the individual assets and liabilities of both accounting entities and report the combined amounts. This is accomplished by substituting the individual assets and liabilities of the branch for the Investment in Branch account (which, by its nature, always equals the branch's net assets).

This substitution takes place on a worksheet, which is used to eliminate the appropriate accounts, so that the assets, liabilities, sales, cost of goods sold, and operating expenses of each accounting entity can be combined. This worksheet, called a combining statement worksheet, is shown in Illustration 1-2. Note that the Home Office account in the branch column is shown on two lines. The first line represents the branch's current-period income or loss. The remaining, or residual, balance of the Home Office account is shown on the second line. We have separated the balance in the Home Office account into these two amounts for instructional purposes only. A journal entry, which (only for instructional and ease of reference purposes) we call the **primary elimination entry,** is posted to this worksheet to eliminate the balances that exist in (1) the Investment in Branch account in the home office column; (2) the Branch Income account in the home office column; and (3) that portion of the Home Office account in the branch column that we have designated the residual balance. The entry is as follows:

Branch income	xxx	
Home office	xxx	
Investment in branch		xxx

The debit to Branch Income in the income statement section of the worksheet is totaled at the net income line and then carried forward to the first line of the Home Office account in the balance sheet section of the worksheet to eliminate the branch's current-period income or loss. Each individual account on the worksheet is then cross-totaled to arrive at the combined amounts. The amounts in the combined column are used to prepare the financial statements that are distributed to the company's stockholders.

Illustration:
Combining statement worksheet

The worksheet in Illustration 1-2 combines the financial statements of a home office with those of its branch. The financial statement amounts for the branch reflect the transactions shown in Illustration 1-1. The primary elimination entry is on page 15.

Illustration 1-2
Inventory transferred at cost

	CABOT COMPANY				
	Combining Statement Worksheet				
	For the Year Ended December 31, 19X1				
	Home Office	Branch[a]	Eliminations Dr.	Eliminations Cr.	Combined
Income Statement:					
Sales	380,000	120,000			500,000
Branch income	20,000		20,000(1)		– 0 –
Subtotal.................	400,000	120,000	20,000		500,000
Cost of goods sold:					
Beginning inventory	135,000				135,000
Purchases.................	285,000	40,000			325,000
Shipments (to) branch/ from home office..........	(60,000)	60,000			– 0 –
Less—Ending inventory......	(150,000)	(30,000)			(180,000)
Subtotal.................	210,000	70,000			280,000
Selling expenses.............	52,000	16,000			68,000
Administrative expenses	59,000	14,000			73,000
Interest expense	19,000				19,000
Subtotal.................	340,000	100,000			440,000
Income before Income Taxes ..	60,000	20,000	20,000		60,000
Income tax expense @ 40%	(24,000)				(24,000)
Net Income.................	36,000	20,000	20,000⌐		36,000
Balance Sheet:					
Cash	30,000	17,000			47,000
Accounts receivable, net	80,000	19,000			99,000
Inventory:[b]					
Acquired from vendors	150,000	6,000			156,000
Acquired from home office ...		24,000			24,000
Investment in branch	62,000			62,000(1)	– 0 –
Land.......................	22,000				22,000
Building—Cost	100,000				100,000
—Accum. depr.........	(28,000)				(28,000)
Equipment—Cost	84,000	12,000			96,000
—Accum. depr.	(32,000)	(1,000)			(33,000)
Total assets	468,000	77,000		62,000	483,000
Accounts payable and accruals	60,000	15,000			75,000
Long-term debt	200,000				200,000
Home office:					
Current-period income		20,000	20,000⌐		– 0 –
Residual balance		42,000	42,000(1)		– 0 –
Common stock	100,000				100,000
Retained earnings:					
Beginning of year	82,000				82,000
+ Net income	36,000				36,000
– Dividends declared	(10,000)				(10,000)
End of year	108,000				108,000
Total liabilities and equity ..	468,000	77,000	62,000		483,000
Proof of debit and credit postings...................			62,000	62,000	

[a] The amounts in this column reflect the activity shown in Illustration 1-1.
[b] The separation of the inventory into these two categories is not necessary if transfers are made at cost. It is shown here only for later comparison with Illustration 1-4, where transfers are made above cost.
Explanation of entry:
(1) The primary elimination entry.

(1) The primary elimination entry:

Branch income   20,000
Home office   42,000
    Investment in branch   62,000

In reviewing Illustration 1-2, the following points should be understood:

(1) The combining worksheet is started *after* the home office has made its adjusting entry concerning the branch's income and after it has provided for income taxes on the branch's income.
(2) The balance in the Retained Earnings account in the home office column includes the branch's income net of applicable income taxes. This retained earnings amount is the combined retained earnings.
(3) The balance in the Home Office account is shown on two lines for instructional purposes only.
(4) The debit balance in the eliminations column of the worksheet at the net income line is carried forward to the balance sheet—specifically, to that line of the Home Office account that shows the branch's income.
(5) The net income in the home office column is the same as the net income in the combined column.
(6) The combining worksheet is not distributed to the home office's stockholders; only the financial statements, which can be readily prepared from the combined column of the worksheet, are distributed to the stockholders. (The formal balance sheet and income statement are not shown.)
(7) The Shipments from Home Office account completely offsets the Shipments to Branch account in the combined column. This is the common procedure for eliminating these intracompany transactions, thus simplifying the combination process. If these amounts were shown on separate lines, the following elimination entry would be necessary:

Shipments to branch   60,000
    Shipments from home office   60,000

(8) The primary elimination entry is posted only to the worksheet, not to the general ledger.
(9) The primary elimination entry is the same each time the combination is performed—only the amounts differ.

COMBINED FINANCIAL STATEMENTS: INVENTORY TRANSFERS ABOVE HOME OFFICE COST

Some home offices transfer inventory to their branches at costs above their own cost. In some instances, the mark-up is designed to absorb the costs of central purchasing, warehousing, and handling, or to have those operations show a profit. In other instances, the transfer costs reflect prices that the branches would pay if they acquired the merchandise directly from the manufacturers and distributors. In theory, large volume discounts generated by the central purchasing department of the home office should not be reflected in the branch income statements. In other instances, the mark-up is designed to achieve greater companywide profits because branch personnel base the mark-up to their customers on the inflated billing prices from the home office. (Often, branch personnel are not informed of the extent of the home office's mark-up.)

In situations involving inventory transfers at above cost, it is necessary to distinguish carefully between a mark-up expressed in relation to cost versus one expressed in relation to the transfer price. For example, inventory costing $1,000 and transferred at $1,250 has a 25% mark-up based on cost ($250/$1,000) but a 20% mark-up based on the transfer price ($250/$1,250).

Procedures for transferring inventory above home office cost

Any time transfers are made at above cost, the home office must defer recognition of the mark-up until the branch sells the inventory to its customers. To do otherwise would result in the recognition of profit merely from transferring inventory from one location to another within the company. When inventory is transferred to the branch, the home office (1) credits the Shipments to Branch account at the home office's cost; (2) credits an account called Deferred Profit for the amount of the mark-up; and (3) debits the Investment in Branch account for the total intracompany billing amount. The proper journal entry is as follows:

```
Investment in branch ..........................................  xxx
    Shipments to branch ......................................        xxx
    Deferred profit ..........................................        xxx
```

The branch makes the same entry as it does when inventory transfers are made at the home office's cost. Thus, the branch debits the Shipments from Home Office account for the total intracompany billing amount and credits the Home Office account. Journal entry (2) in Illustration 1-3 records an inventory transfer above cost.

When the branch submits its month-end financial statements to the home office, it must show separately that portion of its ending inventory that was acquired from the home office. The home office can then (1) determine the amount of mark-up in the ending branch inventory; (2) adjust the Deferred Profit account to this amount; and (3) credit the Branch Income account for the recognizable mark-up. This procedure still keeps the Investment in Branch account on the home office books and the Home Office account on the branch books in agreement. However, the Shipments to Branch account on the books of the home office is always less than the Shipments from Home Office account on the books of the branch by the amount of the mark-up. As a result of the mark-up, the branch's cost of goods sold is greater and the branch reports a lower operating profit than if the transfer had been billed at the home office's cost. The lower profit reported by the branch is offset by the recognition of the deferred profit by the home office.

This procedure results in the same net income being reported on a companywide basis, just as if the inventory had been transferred at cost.

Illustrative entries:
Inventory transfers above cost

Assume that the inventory transferred to the branch from the home office in Illustration 1-1 was marked up 20% over the home office's cost of $60,000. In Illustration 1-2, we assumed that the branch had a $30,000 ending inventory, of which $6,000 represented purchases from outside vendors and $24,000 represented inventory obtained from the home office. In this case, the branch's ending inventory acquired from the home office is $28,800 ($24,000 + $4,800 mark-up). Thus, the branch's total ending inventory is $34,800 ($28,800 + $6,000 acquired from outside vendors). Illustration 1-3 shows the journal entries relating to the transfer of this inventory above cost, along with the appropriate year-end closing and adjusting entries. The journal entries are numbered to correspond to Illustration 1-1, which shows inventory transfers made at the home office's cost.

The secondary elimination entry

When inventory transfers are made above the home office's cost, an additional elimination entry must be used to prepare combined financial statements. For instructional and ease of reference purposes, we call this the **secondary elimination entry.** The purpose of the secondary elimination entry is to adjust the branch's cost of goods sold downward to the amount that it would be if the inventory were transferred from the home office at cost. The overstatement of the branch's cost of goods sold equals the amount of the deferred profit that was earned during the year and recognized by the home office. Accordingly, that portion of the credit balance in the Branch Income account pertaining to the recognition of profit from the Deferred Profit account must be reclassified to the cost of goods sold section of the

Illustration 1-3

Home Office Books			Branch Books		
(2) Investment in branch	72,000		(2) Shipments from		
Shipments to			home office	72,000	
branch..........		60,000	Home office		72,000
Deferred profit.....		12,000			
(12) Investment in branch	12,800		(12) Inventory	34,800	
Branch income		12,800	Sales.............	120,000	
			Purchases		40,000
Deferred profit.......	7,200[a]		Shipments from		
Branch income		7,200	home office		72,000
			Selling expenses .		16,000
			Administrative		
			expenses		14,000
			Home office		12,800

[a] To adjust the Deferred Profit account to the $4,800 mark-up in the ending inventory ($12,000 − $4,800 = $7,200).

income statement. Because this entry takes place entirely within the income statement section of the worksheet, it is merely a reclassification entry. When the branch has only ending inventory that was acquired from the home office, the entry is as follows:

```
Branch income  ........................................  xxx
   Ending inventory (in the income statement section
      of the worksheet) ..............................  xxx
         Shipments from home office  ...........................  xxx
```

If the branch has beginning and ending inventories acquired from the home office, the entry is as follows:

```
Branch income  ........................................  xxx
   Ending inventory (in the income statement section
      of the worksheet) ..............................  xxx
      Beginning inventory (in the income statement section
         of the worksheet) ...........................  xxx
         Shipments from home office  .......................  xxx
```

Illustration:
Combining statement worksheet

Illustration 1-4 shows a worksheet that combines the financial statements of a home office with those of a branch when inventory transfers were made above cost. The financial statements of the home office and the branch are taken from Illustration 1-2, adjusted to reflect inventory transfers at 20% above cost, as shown in Illustration 1-3.
  The following elimination entries are made:

(1) The primary elimination entry:

```
Branch income  ........................................  12,800
Home office ..........................................  54,000
   Investment in branch ...............................        66,800
```

(2) The secondary elimination entry:

```
Branch income  ........................................  7,200
Ending inventory (in the income statement section
   of the worksheet)  .................................  4,800
      Shipments from home office  .....................        12,000
```

In reviewing Illustration 1-4, the following points should be understood:

(1) The only change from Illustration 1-2 is that the merchandise shipments from the home office were billed at $72,000 instead of $60,000, with the $12,000 mark-up being initially credited to the Deferred Profit account.
(2) As in Illustration 1-2, the Shipments from Home Office account completely offsets the Shipments to Branch account in the combined column.

Illustration 1-4
Inventory transferred above cost

	Home Office	Branch	Eliminations Dr.	Eliminations Cr.	Combined
CABOT COMPANY					
Combining Statement Worksheet					
For the Year Ended December 31, 19X1					
Income Statement:					
Sales......................	380,000	120,000			500,000
Branch income	20,000		12,800(1)		– 0 –
			7,200(2)		
Subtotal	400,000	120,000	20,000		500,000
Cost of goods sold:					
Beginning inventory	135,000				135,000
Purchases	285,000	40,000			325,000
Shipments (to) branch/					
from home office	(60,000)	72,000		12,000(2)	– 0 –
Less—Ending inventory	(150,000)	(34,800)	4,800(2)		(180,000)
Subtotal	210,000	77,200	4,800	12,000	280,000
Selling expenses	52,000	16,000			68,000
Administrative expenses.....	59,000	14,000			73,000
Interest expense............	19,000				19,000
Subtotal	340,000	107,200	4,800	12,000	440,000
Income before Income Taxes.	60,000	12,800	24,800	12,000	60,000
Income tax expense @ 40%	(24,000)				(24,000)
Net Income	36,000	12,800	24,800	12,000	36,000
Balance Sheet:					
Cash	30,000	17,000			47,000
Accounts receivable, net	80,000	19,000			99,000
Inventory:					
Acquired from vendors	150,000	6,000			156,000
Acquired from home office..		28,800			28,800
Deferred profit.............	(4,800)				(4,800)
Investment in branch........	66,800			66,800(1)	– 0 –
Land	22,000				22,000
Building—Cost	100,000				100,000
—Accum. depr.	(28,000)				(28,000)
Equipment—Cost	84,000	12,000			96,000
—Accum. depr.	(32,000)	(1,000)			(33,000)
Total assets.............	468,000	81,800		66,800	483,000
Accounts payable					
and accruals	60,000	15,000			75,000
Long-term debt	200,000				200,000
Home office:					
Current-period income		12,800	24,800	12,000	– 0 –
Residual balance		54,000	54,000(1)		– 0 –
Common stock	100,000				100,000
Retained earnings:					
Beginning of year..........	82,000				82,000
+ Net income	36,000				36,000
– Dividends declared......	(10,000)				(10,000)
End of year	108,000				108,000
Total liabilities and equity	468,000	81,800	78,800	12,000	483,000
Proof of debit and credit postings..................			78,800	78,800	

Explanation of entries:
(1) The primary elimination entry.
(2) The secondary elimination entry.

(handwritten annotations: "180,000 EI" at right; "contra inv. acct", "entry" near Inventory section)

(3) The combined balances are the same in both illustrations (after the remaining deferred profit of $4,800 in Illustration 1-4 is netted against the combined inventory amounts for financial reporting purposes).
(4) Regardless of the transfer price for intracompany billing, the combined financial statements are the same for financial reporting purposes.
(5) In whichever subsequent accounting period the branch sells the remaining portion of the inventory acquired from the home office, a reclassification entry is required within the income statement section of the combining worksheet, as follows:

```
Branch income . . . . . . . . . . . . . . . . . . . . . . . . . . . . . . . . . . . . . . . . .    4,800
     Beginning inventory (in the income statement section
     of the worksheet)  . . . . . . . . . . . . . . . . . . . . . . . . . . . . . . . . . .             4,800
```

This entry reduces the branch's reported cost of goods sold to agree with the home office's cost.

OTHER MISCELLANEOUS AREAS

Perpetual inventory systems

When the home office and the branch both use perpetual inventory systems, the respective general ledger Inventory accounts are used instead of the Shipments to Branch and Shipments from Home Office accounts, as shown below:

	Transfers at Cost		Transfers above Cost	
Home office books:				
Investment in branch	60,000		72,000	
Inventory		60,000		60,000
Deferred profit				12,000
Branch books:				
Inventory	60,000		72,000	
Home office		60,000		72,000

Each accounting entity uses a Cost of Goods Sold account instead of the several accounts required to calculate cost of goods sold under a periodic system. For transfers made at cost, the primary elimination entry for preparing combined financial statements is identical with that shown previously for a periodic inventory system. For transfers above cost, the primary elimination is also identical with that shown previously, but the secondary elimination entry is as follows:

```
Branch income  . . . . . . . . . . . . . . . . . . . . . . . . . . . . . . . . . . . . . . . .    7,200
     Cost of goods sold . . . . . . . . . . . . . . . . . . . . . . . . . . . . . . . . . . .            7,200
```

Interbranch transactions

Branches often transfer inventory to one another. Each branch records the transfer using an Interbranch Receivable or Payable account and a Shipments to or from Branch account. For example, assume Branch A transfers inventory costing $5,000 to Branch B. The entries would be as follows:

Branch A books:

Interbranch receivable	5,000	
Shipments to Branch B		5,000

Branch B books:

Shipments from Branch A	5,000	
Interbranch payable		5,000

The Shipments to Branch B account offsets the Shipments from Branch A account when combined financial statements are prepared. Any unpaid interbranch receivables and payables at month-end also offset each other when combined financial statements are prepared. Some home offices do not require branches to make cash payments to one another for interbranch transfers, because this is not sound cash management on a companywide basis. Instead, company policy may require each branch to close its Interbranch Receivable or Payable accounts to its respective Home Office accounts at month-end. Assuming no other transactions occurred between branches A and B for the month, the entries to close these accounts would be as follows:

Branch A books:

Home office	5,000	
Interbranch receivable		5,000

Branch B books:

Interbranch payable	5,000	
Home office		5,000

Of course, the branch must inform the home office of the amounts that have been charged or credited to the Home Office accounts. The home office would then make the following entry:

Home office books:

Investment in Branch B	5,000	
Investment in Branch A		5,000

Freight

Freight charges incurred in acquiring inventory from the home office or from outside sources are inventoriable. When a branch acquires inventory from another branch instead of from the normal source of supply, sound accounting theory dictates that any freight charges in excess of normal should be expensed currently. If the home office is responsible for a branch having to use another branch as a supply source, then such incremental freight charges should be borne by the home office, regardless of which accounting entity makes the cash payment for the freight charges.

Start-up costs

Expenses incurred by a branch *before* it formally opens for business are start-up costs. An operating loss incurred for a period of time after the formal opening is not considered a start-up cost.

Start-up costs may be expensed as incurred or capitalized for subsequent amortization over a reasonably short period of time (usually no more than a three- to five-year amortization period). Most companies expense start-up costs as incurred.

Agencies

Some companies open outlying sales offices that carry only product samples, demonstration units, and brochures, all of which are used in obtaining sales orders. These offices are commonly referred to as agencies. Sales orders are forwarded to the home office for approval and filling.

Agency personnel are almost always paid from the home office. The home office may establish a nominal imprest cash fund for each of these outlying locations. The imprest funds, which may be in the form of petty cash or a local bank account, are used to pay for miscellaneous expenses incurred. As imprest funds are depleted, the outlying location sends invoices and receipts to the home office, which reviews them and sends a check to replenish the fund. The home office records these expenses in its general ledger, usually in accounts specially coded to signify the outlying location to which they pertain. This manner of accounting for sales offices is a predominantly centralized system.

SUMMARY

When a company establishes operations in outlying locations through internal expansion, the outlying locations can be accounted for using a centralized or a decentralized accounting system. Under a centralized accounting system, the assets, liabilities, revenues, and expenses of the outlying locations are recorded on the books of the home office. Under a decentralized accounting system, each outlying location uses its own general ledger to reflect its assets, liabilities, revenues, costs, and expenses. A decentralized accounting system requires the home office to use accounting procedures that effectively treat the outlying locations as investments to maintain control over their net assets and operations.

Management must evaluate the profitability of branch operations carefully when inventory is acquired from the home office, because intracompany billing prices established by the home office directly affect the profitability of the branches. Furthermore, the treatment of home office expenses—

none, some, or all of which may be allocated to the branches—complicates the process of evaluating the profitability of branch operations.

In preparing financial statements for stockholders, the company must combine the financial statements of the home office and the outlying locations. Combined financial statements are prepared so that intracompany transactions are eliminated and the combined financial statements reflect only those transactions that occur between the company and outside parties.

Glossary of new terms

Agency: An outlying location that carries product samples, demonstration units, and brochures for the purpose of obtaining sales orders, which are approved and filled by the home office.

Branch: An outlying manufacturing, service, or retailing location of a legal business entity.

Centralized Accounting: A system whereby the accounting for outlying locations is performed at the home office; the outlying locations do not maintain general ledgers.

Decentralized Accounting: A system whereby outlying locations maintain their own general ledgers and submit financial reports periodically to the home office.

External Expansion: The expansion of a business by combining two existing businesses into a unified larger business.

Home Office: The headquarters location of a legal business entity that establishes a branch.

Internal Expansion: The expansion of a business through the construction or leasing of additional facilities at an existing or outlying location.

Review questions

1. What is the difference between a centralized accounting system and a decentralized accounting system?
2. Why is the branch's operating income or loss not a net income or loss?
3. What is the function of the Shipments to Branch and Shipments from Home Office accounts?
4. If the intracompany accounts do not agree, what are some possible explanations? Which accounting entity must make the adjustments?
5. Why are the elimination entries not posted to any general ledger?
6. What does the primary elimination entry accomplish? The secondary elimination entry?
7. When is the secondary elimination entry necessary?
8. Why is the shipment of inventory to a branch not considered a reportable sale for combined financial reporting purposes?
9. Why does the intracompany inventory transfer price have no effect on the combined amounts for financial reporting purposes?
10. Define start-up costs.

Discussion cases

Discussion case 1–1
Treatment of intracompany billings as sales

You are the controller of a multilocation company that uses a decentralized accounting system for its many branches. The branches may purchase inventory either from the home office or from outside sources. However, purchases can be made from outside sources only if the prices are lower than those at which the home office bills. As a result, the home office bills its branches at amounts that are equivalent to what the branches would pay outside sources, which usually is greater than the home office's cost. A staff accountant at the home office has suggested to you that the home office is justified in accounting for these shipments to the branches as sales, because the intracompany billing prices are objectively determined and the branches are separate accounting entities.

Required:
How would you respond to this suggestion?

Discussion case 1–2
Mark-up of intracompany inventory transfers

You are the controller of a company that is establishing its first branch, which will use a decentralized accounting system. A substantial portion of the branch's inventory will be purchased from the home office to take advantage of the additional volume discounts that the home office can obtain. You must advise top management on the billing prices of intracompany inventory shipments to the branch. This decision is important, because the billing prices selected will directly affect the branch's operating income or loss. The branch manager has told you that all of the company's additional savings on volume discounts resulting from the formation of the branch should be passed on to the branch, since without the branch, they would not have been realized.

Required:
What considerations should be taken into account in determining the intracompany transfer pricing policy?

Discussion case 1–3
Determination and treatment of start-up costs

Balboa Furniture Company has numerous branch outlets, which operate from leased facilities. A new branch outlet historically has taken approximately two months from inception of its facility lease until it starts to generate sales and another four months before its monthly operations start showing a profit. The typical new branch incurs a loss of $80,000 during this six-month period. Near the beginning of the current year, Balboa Furniture established the Santa Cruz and Vera Cruz branches. Data for each of these branches follow.

	Santa Cruz Branch	Vera Cruz Branch
Number of months from lease inception until operations showed a profit..............................	5	11
Excess of costs and expenses over revenues until monthly operations showed a profit	$(65,000)	$(130,000)

Management intends to treat as a deferred charge $160,000 of the combined $195,000 excess of costs and expenses over revenues for the two new branches. Any amount in excess of $80,000 is considered an unfavorable start-up variance, which should be expensed as a period cost.

Required:
Evaluate the treatment proposed by the company.

Exercises

Exercise 1–1
Journal entry preparation: Periodic inventory system—
Inventory transfers at cost

The following transactions pertain to a branch's first month's operations:

(1) The home office sent $8,000 cash to the branch.
(2) The home office shipped inventory costing $40,000 to the branch; the intracompany billing is at cost.
(3) The branch purchased inventory from outside vendors for $35,000.
(4) The branch had sales of $75,000 on account.
(5) The home office allocated $1,000 in advertising expenses to the branch.
(6) The branch collected $20,000 on accounts receivable.
(7) The branch incurred operating expenses of $4,000, none of which were paid at month-end.
(8) The branch remitted $5,000 to the home office.
(9) The branch's ending inventory is $30,000.

Required:
(1) Prepare the home office and branch journal entries for these transactions, assuming a periodic inventory system is used.
(2) Prepare the month-end closing entries for the branch.
(3) Prepare the month-end adjusting entry for the home office relating to the branch's operations for the month.

Exercise 1–2
Journal entry preparation: Perpetual inventory system—
Inventory transfers at cost

Assume the transactions and data given in Exercise 1–1, except that a perpetual inventory system is used.

Required:
The requirements are the same as for Exercise 1–1.

Exercise 1–3
Journal entry preparation: Periodic inventory system—
Inventory transfers above cost

The following transactions pertain to a branch's first month's operations:

(1) The home office sent $8,000 cash to the branch.
(2) The home office shipped inventory costing $40,000 to the branch; the intracompany billing was for $50,000.
(3) Branch inventory purchases from outside vendors totaled $35,000.
(4) Branch sales on account were $75,000.
(5) The home office allocated $1,000 in advertising expenses to the branch.
(6) Branch collections on accounts receivable were $20,000.
(7) Branch operating expenses of $4,000 were incurred, none of which were paid at month-end.
(8) The branch remitted $5,000 to the home office.
(9) The branch's ending inventory (as reported in its balance sheet) is composed of:

Acquired from outside vendors	$18,000
Acquired from home office (at billing price)	15,000
Total	$33,000

Required:
(1) Prepare the home office and branch journal entries for these transactions, assuming a periodic inventory system is used.
(2) Prepare the month-end closing entries for the branch.
(3) Prepare the month-end adjusting entries for the home office relating to the branch's operations for the month.

Exercise 1–4
Journal entry preparation: Perpetual inventory system—
Inventory transfers above cost

Assume the transactions and data given in Exercise 1–3, except that a perpetual inventory system is used.

Required:
The requirements are the same as for Exercise 1–3.

Exercise 1–5
Reconciliation of intracompany accounts

On December 31, 19X1, the Home Office account on the branch's books has a balance of $42,000, and the Investment in Branch account on the home office's books has a balance of $60,000. In analyzing the activity in each of these accounts for December, you find the following differences.

(1) A $5,000 branch remittance to the home office initiated on December 27, 19X1, was recorded on the home office books on January 3, 19X2.
(2) A home office inventory shipment to the branch on December 28, 19X1, was recorded by the branch on January 4, 19X2; the billing of $20,000 was at cost.
(3) The home office allocated $5,000 of expenses to the branch on December 15, 19X1. The branch has not recorded this transaction.
(4) A branch customer erroneously remitted $3,000 to the home office. The home office recorded this cash collection on December 23, 19X1, but it did not notify the branch.
(5) Inventory costing $23,000 was sent to the branch by the home office on December 10, 19X1. The billing was at cost, but the branch recorded the transaction at $32,000.

Required:
Prepare the entries to bring the intracompany accounts into balance as of December 31, 19X1. Assume a periodic inventory system.

Exercise 1–6
Adjusting the Deferred Profit account

The Jackie Company ships candy to its How Sweet It Is branch at 125% of cost. The Deferred Profit account balance at the beginning of the year was $5,000. During the year, the branch was billed $90,000 for inventory transfers from the home office. At year-end, the branch's balance sheet shows $12,000 of inventory on hand that was acquired from the home office.

Required:
Calculate the year-end adjustment to the Deferred Profit account and show the adjusting journal entry.

Exercise 1–7
Journal entry preparation: Periodic inventory system—
Inventory transfers above cost

The following transactions pertain to branch operations:

(1) The branch purchased and paid for equipment costing $3,000. All fixed assets are recorded on the home office books.
(2) The branch received and deposited a $1,000 remittance from a customer of a nearby branch.
(3) The home office paid the monthly lease expense of $4,000 on the branch's facilities. Company policy is to allocate such expenses to the branch.
(4) A branch customer made a payment of $2,000 directly to the home office. The home office notified the branch.

(5) The home office shipped inventory to the branch. The home office's cost was $10,000, and it billed the branch $12,000.

(6) With respect to the inventory purchased from the home office in (5), assume the branch had $3,600 of this inventory on hand at month-end, as reflected in its financial statements submitted to the home office. Assume the branch had no beginning inventory of items purchased from the home office.

(7) The branch remitted $15,000 to the home office.

(8) The home office computed the monthly depreciation expense pertaining to the branch's fixed assets, which are recorded on the home office books. The depreciation expense of $4,500 was charged to the branch.

(9) The home office allocated overhead expenses of $18,000 to the branch.

(10) The home office received the branch's monthly financial statements, which showed the branch had operating income of $25,000.

Required:

Prepare the home office and branch journal entries for these transactions, assuming a periodic inventory system is used.

Exercise 1–8
Reconciliation of intracompany accounts

The following entries are reflected in the intracompany accounts of the Gleason Company and its branch in Cramdenville for June 19X2:

Home Office

			6/1	Balance..................	50,000
6/2	Remittance..............	10,000	6/8	Inventory shipment.........	30,000
6/24	Purchase of		6/10	Collection of home	
	equipment (carried on			office receivable	2,000
	home office books)	7,000	6/16	Inventory shipment.........	12,000
6/29	Remittance..............	15,000	6/24	Inventory shipment.........	17,000
6/30	Inventory returned		6/28	Advertising allocation	400
	to home office..........	1,000			
6/30	Depreciation allocation	2,000			
			6/30	Balance.................	76,400

Investment in Branch—Cramdenville

6/1	Balance..................	50,000			
6/5	Inventory shipment........	30,000	6/2	Remittance..............	10,000
6/12	Inventory shipment........	12,000	6/8	Collection of branch	
6/20	Inventory shipment........	17,000		receivable..............	1,000
6/25	Advertising allocation		6/27	Equipment purchase	
	to branch (50% of			by branch	7,000
	$8,000 incurred)	4,000			
6/28	Inventory shipment........	14,000			
6/30	Depreciation allocation	2,000			
6/30	Balance.................	111,000			

Required:

(1) Prepare a schedule to reconcile the intracompany accounts. Assume that inventory shipments to the branch are billed at 25% above the home office's cost.

(2) Prepare the adjusting journal entries to bring the intracompany accounts into balance.

Exercise 1–9
Calculating beginning inventory from selected data

The Cosmos Company transfers inventory to its Saganville branch at a 20% mark-up. During the current year, inventory costing the home office $80,000 was transferred to the branch. At year-end, the home office adjusted its Deferred Profit account downward by $18,200. The branch's year-end balance sheet shows $4,800 of inventory acquired from the home office.

Required:
Calculate the home office's cost of the branch's beginning inventory.

Problems

Problem 1–1
Preparing combining statement worksheet: Periodic inventory system— Inventory transfers at cost; initial year of branch operations

The December 31, 19X1, financial statements of a home office and its only branch (which was established in 19X1) are given below.

	Home Office	Branch
Income statement:		
Sales	$ 700,000	$200,000
Branch income	50,000	
Subtotal	$ 750,000	$200,000
Cost of goods sold:		
Beginning inventory	$ 120,000	
Purchases	540,000	$ 75,000
Shipments to branch	(100,000)	
Shipments from home office		100,000
Less—Ending inventory	(180,000)	(40,000)
Subtotal	$ 380,000	$135,000
Selling expenses	42,000	11,000
Administrative expenses	28,000	4,000
Interest expense	50,000	
Subtotal	$ 500,000	$150,000
Income before Income Taxes	$ 250,000	$ 50,000
Income tax expense @ 40%	(100,000)	
Net Income	$ 150,000	$ 50,000
Balance sheet:		
Cash	$ 90,000	$ 10,000
Accounts receivable, net	80,000	20,000
Inventory	180,000	40,000
Investment in branch	170,000	
Fixed assets, net	770,000	140,000
	$1,290,000	$210,000

	Home Office	Branch
Accounts payable and accruals	$ 200,000	$ 40,000
Long-term debt	350,000	
Home office:		
Current-period income		50,000
Residual balance		120,000
Common stock	500,000	
Retained earnings	240,000	
	$1,290,000	$210,000
Dividends declared during 19X1	$ 110,000	

Required:

Prepare a combining statement worksheet as of December 31, 19X1, assuming inventory transfers to the branch from the home office are at cost.

Problem 1–2
Preparing combining statement worksheet: Periodic inventory system— Inventory transfers above cost; initial year of branch operations

The December 31, 19X1, financial statements of a home office and its only branch (which was established in 19X1) are as follows:

	Home Office	Branch
Income statement:		
Sales	$ 700,000	$200,000
Branch income	50,000	
Subtotal	$ 750,000	$200,000
Cost of goods sold:		
Beginning inventory	$ 120,000	
Purchases	540,000	$ 75,000
Shipments to branch	(100,000)	
Shipments from home office		120,000
Less—Ending inventory	(180,000)	(46,000)
Subtotal	$ 380,000	$149,000
Selling expenses	42,000	11,000
Administrative expenses	28,000	4,000
Interest expense	50,000	
Subtotal	$ 500,000	$164,000
Income before Income Taxes	$ 250,000	$ 36,000
Income tax expense @ 40%	(100,000)	
Net Income	$ 150,000	$ 36,000
Balance sheet:		
Cash	$ 90,000	$ 10,000
Accounts receivable, net	80,000	20,000
Inventory:		
Acquired from vendors	180,000	10,000
Acquired from home office		36,000
Deferred profit	(6,000)	
Investment in branch	176,000	
Fixed assets, net	770,000	140,000
	$1,290,000	$216,000

	Home Office	Branch
Accounts payable and accruals	$ 200,000	$ 40,000
Long-term debt	350,000	
Home office:		
Current-period income.....................		36,000
Residual balance		140,000
Common stock	500,000	
Retained earnings	240,000	
	$1,290,000	$216,000
Dividends declared during 19X1.........................	$ 110,000	

Required:

Prepare a combining statement worksheet as of December 31, 19X1, assuming inventory transfers to the branch from the home office are marked up 20%.

Problem 1–3
Preparing combining statement worksheet: Perpetual inventory system—Inventory transfers above cost

Revise the financial statement information given in Problem 1–2 to reflect a perpetual inventory system.

Required:

Prepare a combining statement worksheet as of December 31, 19X1, after making the above revision.

Problem 1–4
COMPREHENSIVE   Quarter-end adjusting entries and preparing combining statement worksheet: Periodic inventory system—Inventory transfers above cost

The trial balances of Monahan Company and its only branch as of March 31, 19X5 (the end of its first reporting quarter for the current year) prior to adjusting entries are as follows:

Accounts	Monahan Company Debit	Monahan Company Credit	Aran Branch Debit	Aran Branch Credit
Cash	$ 55,000		$ 15,000	
Accounts receivable, net...............	80,000		45,000	
Inventory, January 1, 19X5:				
Acquired from vendors	230,000		30,000	
Acquired from home office			40,000	
Deferred profit.......................		$ 28,000		
Investment in branch..................	135,000			
Fixed assets, net	868,000		90,000	
Accounts payable and accruals		221,000		$ 80,000
Long-term debt		400,000		
Home office..........................				110,000
Common stock		300,000		

(handwritten annotations: "$8000 markup", "40,000 / 1.25 = 32000", "BI + shpng = 8000 + 20000", "G")

	Monahan Company		Aran Branch	
	Debit	**Credit**	**Debit**	**Credit**
Retained earnings, January 1, 19X5		350,000		
Sales................................		960,000		290,000
Purchases	800,000		120,000	
Shipments from home office			90,000	
Shipments to branch		80,000		
Selling expenses	83,000		34,000	
Administrative expenses	48,000		16,000	
Interest expense....................	40,000			
	$2,339,000	$2,339,000	$480,000	$480,000
Inventory per physical count on March 31, 19X5:				
Acquired from vendors	$ 180,000		$ 20,000	
Acquired from home office			$ 50,000	

(handwritten annotation: 90,000 ÷ 10,000 / 1.25 = 80,000 = 20,000 markup)

Additional information:

(1) Inventory transferred to Aran Branch from Monahan Company is billed at 125% of cost.

(2) Monahan Company billed its branch $10,000 for inventory it shipped to the branch on March 28, 19X5; the branch received and recorded this shipment on April 2, 19X5.

(3) Aran Branch remitted $15,000 cash to Monahan Company on March 31, 19X5; the home office received and recorded this remittance on April 4, 19X5.

(4) The Deferred Profit account is normally adjusted at the end of each reporting quarter.

(5) Income taxes at 40% are recorded at the end of each reporting quarter.

(6) No dividends were declared during the quarter.

Required:

(1) Prepare the quarter-end adjusting entries to:
    (a) Bring the intracompany accounts into agreement.
    (b) Record Aran Branch's income on Monahan Company's books.
    (c) Adjust the Deferred Profit account to the proper balance.
    (d) Provide for income taxes.

(2) Prepare a combining statement worksheet as of March 31, 19X5, after adjusting the trial balance for the entries in (1), above.

Problem 1–5
COMPREHENSIVE   Year-end adjusting entries and preparing combining statement worksheet: Periodic inventory system—Inventory transfers above cost

The preclosing trial balances of the home office and branch of the Ventura Company are as follows:

VENTURA COMPANY
Trial Balances
For the Year Ended December 31, 19X3

Accounts	Home Office Dr. (Cr.)	Branch Dr. (Cr.)
Cash	$ 17,000	$ 200
Inventory, January 1, 19X3	23,000	11,550
Inventory, Deferred profit	(11,000)	
Other assets	200,000	48,450
Branch current...	60,000	
Accounts payable and accruals............................	(35,000)	(3,500)
Home office		(51,500)
Common stock	(200,000)	
Retained earnings, January 1, 19X3	(41,170)	
Dividends declared.......................................	11,000	
Sales	(155,000)	(140,000)
Purchases..	190,000	
Shipments to branch	(100,000)	
Shipments from home office		105,000
Freight in from home office		5,500
Selling expenses...	18,170	17,000
Administrative expenses	23,000	7,300
	$ –0–	$ –0–

Additional information:

(1) The branch deposits all cash receipts in a local bank for the account of the home office. Selected deposits near year-end are as follows:

Amount	Deposited by Branch	Recorded by Home Office
$1,050	December 27, 19X3	December 31, 19X3
1,100	December 30, 19X3	January 2, 19X4
600	December 31, 19X3	January 3, 19X4
300	January 2, 19X4	January 6, 19X4

(2) The branch pays locally incurred expenses from an imprest bank account that is maintained with a balance of $2,000. Checks are drawn once a week on this imprest account, and the home office is notified of the amount needed to replenish the account. On December 31, a reimbursement check for $1,800 was mailed to the branch.

(3) The branch receives all of its goods from the home office. The home office bills the goods at cost plus a 10% mark-up. On December 31, a shipment with a billing value of $5,000 was in transit to the branch. Freight costs, which are considered inventoriable costs, are typically 5% of billed values. (Assume an independent trucking company was used.)

(4) The trial balance beginning inventories are shown at their respective costs to the home office and to the branch. The inventories at December 31, 19X3, excluding the shipment in transit, are

Home office..	$30,000
Branch, at billing amount	$10,400

(5) The Deferred Profit account is adjusted at year-end.

Required:
(1) Prepare December 31, 19X3 adjusting entries to:
    (a) Bring the intracompany accounts into balance.
    (b) Record the branch income on the home office books.
    (c) Adjust the Deferred Profit account to the proper balance.
    (d) Provide income tax expense at 40%.
(2) Prepare a combining statement worksheet at December 31, 19X3, after adjusting
    the trial balance for the entries in (1), above.

(AICPA adapted)

Problem 1–6
**COMPREHENSIVE   Year-end adjusting entries and preparing combining
statement worksheet: Periodic inventory system—Inventory transfers
above cost**

The preclosing trial balances at December 31, 19X5, for the Banshee Discount
Company and its branch office are as follows:

BANSHEE DISCOUNT COMPANY
Trial Balances
For the Year Ended December 31, 19X5

Accounts	Home Office Dr. (Cr.)	Branch Dr. (Cr.)
Cash	$ 36,000	$ 8,000
Accounts receivable, net	35,000	12,000
Inventory, January 1, 19X5	70,000	15,000
Inventory, Deferred profit	(10,500)	
Fixed assets, net	90,000	
Investment in branch	20,000	
Accounts payable	(36,000)	(13,500)
Accrued expenses	(14,000)	(2,500)
Home office		(9,000)
Common stock	(50,000)	
Retained earnings, January 1, 19X5	(53,500)	
Dividends declared	12,000	
Sales	(392,000)	(95,000)
Purchases	290,000	24,000
Shipments to branch	(40,000)	
Shipments from home office		45,000
Expenses	43,000	16,000
	$ –0–	$ –0–

Additional information:
(1) On December 23, the branch manager purchased $4,000 of furniture and
    fixtures but failed to notify the home office. The bookkeeper, knowing that all
    fixed assets are carried on the home office books, recorded the proper entry
    on the branch records. It is the company's policy not to take any depreciation
    on assets acquired in the last half of the year.

(2) On December 27, a branch customer erroneously paid his $2,000 account to the home office. The bookkeeper made the correct entry on the home office books but did not notify the branch.

(3) On December 30, the branch remitted $5,000 cash, which the home office received in January 19X6.

(4) On December 31, the branch erroneously recorded the December allocated expenses from the home office as $500 instead of $1,500.

(5) On December 31, the home office shipped merchandise billed at $3,000 to the branch. The branch received this shipment in January 19X6.

(6) The entire beginning inventory of the branch was purchased from the home office. The physical inventories on December 31, 19X5, excluding the shipment in transit, are:

Home office... $55,000
Branch (composed of $18,000 from home office and $2,000
   from outside vendors)..   20,000

(7) The home office consistently bills shipments to the branch at 20% above cost.
(8) The Deferred Profit account is adjusted at year-end.

Required:
(1) Prepare December 31, 19X5 adjusting entries to:
   (a) Bring the intracompany accounts into agreement.
   (b) Record the branch income on the home office books.
   (c) Adjust the Deferred Profit account to the proper balance.
   (d) Provide income tax expense at 40%.
(2) Prepare a combining statement worksheet at December 31, 19X5, after adjusting entries in (1), above.

(AICPA adapted)

2 Introduction to Business Combinations

OVERVIEW OF EXTERNAL BUSINESS EXPANSION

Stockholders expect management to increase a company's sales and profitability each year. Consequently, sales and profit growth is one of the major objectives of corporate management. As discussed in Chapter 1, many companies can attain this growth either by expanding their existing line of business or by entering into a new line of business through internal expansion. Internal expansion can be a lengthy and involved process, considering the problems of choosing a site location, designing facilities, dealing with architects and contractors, hiring qualified employees, developing new channels of distribution and markets, and the likely prospect of incurring operating losses for some time before revenues reach expected levels. In recent years, the need to prepare environmental impact reports, the difficulty in obtaining required government permits, and the possibility of insufficient energy allocations from energy suppliers have lessened the attractiveness of internal expansion, especially for heavy industry. Furthermore, entering into a new line of business through internal expansion generally is considered much riskier than expanding in the same line of business. This is simply because, initially at least, management's degree of expertise in the new line of business is less than that of existing competitors. Also, becoming an additional competitor in the field is bound to be risky.

The alternative to internal expansion is external expansion, whereby all or a segment of an existing business combines with the business seeking growth. Bringing together two separate businesses under common ownership is known as a business combination. Most of the problems of internal expansion are not encountered in external expansion; only the assessment of the prospects of an existing business is involved. If the assessment is favorable, then efforts can be made to combine the businesses. Most business combinations are completed in far less time than it would take to develop a new product, build manufacturing facilities to produce it, and then successfully market it. Often, the newly acquired business produces a profit from the start. The management of the newly acquired business may be retained, and no new competitor is introduced into the field.

Terminology

In the business community, business combinations are referred to as mergers and acquisitions. The company whose business is being sought is often called the **target company.** The company attempting to acquire the target company's business is referred to as the **acquiring company.** The legal agreement that specifies the terms and provisions of the business combination is known as the acquisition, purchase, or merger agreement. For simplicity, we refer to this legal agreement as the **acquisition agreement.** The process of trying to acquire a target company's business is often called a **takeover attempt.** Business combinations can be categorized as **vertical, horizontal,** or **conglomerate.** Vertical combinations take place between companies involved in the same industry but at different levels—for example, a tire manufacturer and a tire distributor. Horizontal combinations take place between companies that are competitors at the same level in a given industry—two tire manufacturers, for example. Conglomerate combinations involve companies in totally unrelated industries—such as a tire manufacturer and an insurance company. In recent years, conglomerate combinations have become much more prevalent as businesses seek to diversify their product lines and minimize the effects of cyclical sales and earnings patterns in their businesses. These categories of business combinations have no bearing on how a business combination is recorded for financial reporting purposes.

Prevalence of business combinations

External expansion is a major vehicle of corporate growth. The number of business expansions occurring in a given year is largely a function of the state of the economy: Merger activity is usually low during recession periods and high during boom periods. During boom periods, companies tend to accumulate healthy amounts of cash. Excess cash not used for dividends must be invested. Also, during boom periods, stock market prices tend to be subsequently higher, which enables an acquiring company, if using stock as consideration instead of cash, to issue fewer shares of its stock to acquire another company. The greatest number of business combinations to date for a given year was in 1969, when the Federal Trade Commission reported 4,542 mergers and acquisitions. In recent years, approximately 2,000–2,500 business combinations have occurred each year.[1] In the vast majority of cases, a large company combines with a significantly smaller company. Often such combinations enable a small company to expand more rapidly than would be possible with existing resources. Recently, however, an increasing number of business combinations have involved large companies combining with other large companies, in which the consideration given to effect the combination is in the billions of dollars. Some recent large takeover attempts that became titanic struggles between the acquiring company and the target company are discussed later in the chapter in connection with fighting a takeover attempt.

Business combinations have been criticized on the grounds that they do not create additional manufacturing, retailing, or servicing capacity and, consequently, do not create new jobs for the economy. Whereas this fact is true, it does not appear to be a valid argument. Building a plant when no additional manufacturing capacity is needed to satisfy existing demand would not be a productive use of assets either. For the most part, corporations have had little difficulty creating capacity to satisfy demand. Of greater concern is the issue of concentration of power, which is discussed later in the chapter.

Many business combinations go sour

Bringing together two companies through a business combination is not without its risks. Many acquired businesses (estimated as high as 40%) do not achieve their projected sales and profit growth, and the acquiring

---

[1] W.T. Grimm & Co., Corporate Acquisition, Mergers, & Divestitures Consultants, Chicago.

company finds that it grossly overpaid. For instance, Exxon Corporation's $1.2 billion cash payment in 1979 for Reliance Electric Company (which was developing what it considered an extremely profitable energy-saving device) has been an estimated $600 million mistake (that amount being the premium paid to acquire Reliance because it had this potentially hot product).[2]

In other instances (most notably in the electronics industry), target company top management and key engineers have left in droves because the acquired business has been seriously weakened by the acquiring company's operating policies and its unwanted involvement in the target company's daily operations. One example of this was Schlumberger Ltd.'s 1979 acquisition of Fairchild Camera & Instrument Corporation for $425 million, which has turned out to be a classic "how-not-to."[3]

In fact, many conglomerates that were created in the 1960s and 1970s have now disposed of great numbers of the companies they so eagerly acquired because things just became too unmanageable. One such example of this is Gulf & Western Industries, which embarked on a massive plan in 1983 to dispose of numerous segments comprising approximately 20% of its assets and revenues—a plan that is expected to result in write-offs of $470 million.[4] In Chapter 15, Segment Reporting, we discuss how to account for disposals of segments.

Legal restrictions on business combinations

Before discussing business combinations any further, we should note that certain combinations are prohibited. Section 7 of the Clayton Act prohibits any business combination in which "the effect of such acquisition may be substantially to lessen competition or tend to create a monopoly." The Justice Department and the Federal Trade Commission, the two federal agencies with antitrust jurisdiction, enforce this law. In 1978, these agencies issued certain precombination notification regulations: A company with assets or sales of at least $10 million that plans to acquire a manufacturing company with assets or sales of at least $10 million must file a detailed 21-page form 30 days before the planned date of consummation. (If the target company is not a manufacturing company, notification is required only if one company has at least $100 million in sales or assets and the other company has sales or assets of at least $10 million.) Such regulations enable the regulatory agencies to review proposed business combinations before they occur and, if necessary, to obtain preliminary court injunctions to block proposed combinations. Even when a proposed business combination is not challenged by the government before it is consummated, the government can later issue a divestiture order requiring the acquiring company to dispose of its acquired business. If the acquiring company appeals the divestiture order, the courts may or may not uphold it.

Although the Clayton Act apparently applies only to horizontal and vertical combinations, the regulatory agencies have challenged certain conglomerate combinations too. For the most part, these challenges have not been successful,

[2] "Exxon's $600-Million Mistake," *Fortune,* October 19, 1981, p. 69.
[3] "Oil Fields Highflier Finds Turbulent Skies in the Chip Business," *The Wall Street Journal,* August 26, 1983, p. 1.
[4] "G&W Approves Large Program of Divestitures," *The Wall Street Journal,* August 15, 1983, p. 3.

and companies expanding externally into unrelated fields generally have no problem complying with the Clayton Act. Many companies obtain a legal opinion on the application of this law to each contemplated business combination before taking steps that lead to consummation.

The increasing number of conglomerate combinations and the resultant growing concentration of power in the hands of fewer and fewer corporate officials concern many people. In recent years, the Justice Department and the Senate Judiciary Committee have addressed the necessity of legislation aimed at those effects of the conglomerate merger problem that are currently beyond the reach of existing statutes. In addition, officials have considered prohibiting combinations above a certain size unless significant competitive benefits would result. To date, no legislation along these lines has passed.

Steps leading to a business combination

Few business activities match the excitement that can be generated by an attempt to acquire a target company's business. Often an acquiring company must operate in strict secrecy until the last possible moment, so it does not attract the attention of other companies that might be interested in acquiring the business. Such secrecy minimizes the possibility of a bidding war. (Some companies, as a matter of policy, immediately cease their takeover efforts if a bidding war starts; the presumption here is that the successful bidder would probably wind up paying too much.) The acquiring company may start purchasing the common stock of the target company slowly, over a period of time, until it owns just under 5% of the target company's common stock (5% ownership requires public disclosure). Such secrecy also affects the target company: If it is opposed to the takeover, its management has less time in which to take defensive actions.

The friendly approach.   In theory, a business combination should involve only the acquiring company and the stockholders of the target company. In its simplest terms, the stockholders of the target company must decide whether or not to accept the acquiring company's offer. In evaluating an acquiring company's offer, the stockholders of the target company consider the recommendation of their directors and management. Because of this, most acquiring companies attempt to obtain a favorable recommendation from the directors and management of the target company before they present the offer to the target company's stockholders. The usual procedure for this involves negotiating an acquisition agreement with the target company's management. If successful, and the agreement is also approved by the target company's directors, the offer is then submitted to the target company's stockholders for their approval or rejection. This sequence of events is characterized as a "friendly" takeover attempt.

The refusal to be friendly.   Less friendly situations occur when (1) the approval of the target company's directors and management is not sought; (2) the target company's directors and management refuse to negotiate an acquisition agreement; and (3) negotiations do not result in an offer that the target company's directors and management feel is in the best interests of the target company's stockholders. The acquiring company must then present its offer directly to the stockholders of the target company without the approval of its directors and management. These cases are characterized as "unfriendly" takeover attempts. (Some companies have a policy of pursuing a target company only if it can be done on a friendly basis.)

Resorting to the tender offer. An offer made by an acquiring company directly to the target company's stockholders is known as a **tender offer.** Under a tender offer, the stockholders of the target company are requested to tender their shares in exchange for cash or securities offered by the acquiring company. The usual features of a tender offer are the following:

(1) The tender offer is made in newspapers.
(2) The offering price substantially exceeds the current market price of the target company's common stock.
(3) The offer must be accepted by a certain specified date, usually of short duration (such as 30 days).
(4) The acquiring company reserves the right to withdraw the offer if a specified number of shares are not tendered. (If more than the specified number of shares are tendered, the acquiring company reserves the right to reject such excess shares.)

Because the stockholders send their shares to a financial institution, which holds the shares in a fiduciary capacity until the expiration date of the offer, the shares are said to have been tendered—not sold. At the expiration date, the acquiring company then pays for the shares tendered, provided the minimum number of shares have been tendered.

Statutes governing tender offers (takeover bids)

In 1968, Congress passed the Williams Act, which provides for federal regulation of tender offers (takeover bids). The purpose of the law, which is enforced by the S.E.C., is to protect the target company's shareholders by requiring the bidder to furnish detailed disclosures to the target company and its stockholders, including the following:

(1) The number of shares being sought.
(2) Background information about the bidder.
(3) The source and amount of funds or other consideration for the acquisition of the securities for which the tender is made.
(4) The purpose of the tender offer and any plans for the target company.
(5) Recent financial statements.

Since 1968, 37 states have passed legislation ostensibly to provide further protection to stockholders of the target company. For the most part, these statutes require more detailed disclosures than the federal statutes. Furthermore, most of them do not permit a tender offer to be made until 20 days after the initial public disclosure, whereas the federal requirement is only five days. A great controversy has developed over whether these state laws are really essential to protect the stockholders or whether they merely favor the in-state targets over out-of-state bidders, since the additional disclosures and waiting period give the target company extra time to thwart the takeover bid if it so desires. The constitutionality of these laws may be questioned on the grounds that they interfere with interstate commerce and that federal statutes preempt state statutes. The courts have generally declined to enforce these laws for these reasons. As a result, bidding companies routinely file suits (at the public announcement of their takeover bids) seeking injunctions against the enforcement of these laws. Still, the states continually revise their laws hoping to exert regulation in this area. Efforts are now being directed toward a uniform model-tender-offer act.

Defensive tactics during takeover attempts

The board of directors of a target company may authorize management to take aggressive action to try to prevent a takeover. A common defensive action is the filing of lawsuits against the acquiring company on various grounds relating to probable violation of antitrust laws, violation of state takeover laws, and violation of securities laws pertaining to public disclosures. Even if a lawsuit by itself is not successful, it entangles the acquiring company in legal proceedings and usually gives management more time to fight the takeover attempt. In recent years, anti-takeover tactics have gone well beyond the standard anti-trust and regulatory challenges. Some of these newer tactics are:

(1) **Seeking a different suitor.** When the bidder is unlikely to need the management of the target company, management may seek a bidder that will need management. For instance, after Mobil Corporation sought to acquire Marathon Oil Company in 1981 for $5.1 billion, Marathon attracted U.S. Steel Corporation, which won the bidding war with a $6.4 billion offer. This tactic also is used when management of the bidder is not to the liking of the target company's management, even though management is likely to be retained.

(2) **Disposing of key segments.** When a bidder's primary interest in a target company is one or more prized segments, management may sell those segments. For instance, after Whittaker Corporation sought to acquire Brunswick Corporation in 1982 for $320 million, Brunswick sold its highly lucrative hospital products division to a different company, causing Whittaker to abandon its takeover efforts. This tactic is commonly referred to as the "sale of the crown jewel asset" defense.

(3) **Acquiring another company.** When a major reason for an attempted takeover is the target company's favorable cash position, the target company may try to use this excess cash in attempting a takeover of its own. Such an action not only uses excess cash but also may result in a combined business that the initial acquiring company is not interested in acquiring. For instance, acquiring a competitor of the initial acquiring company creates anti-trust issues.

(4) **Attempting to acquire the acquiring company.** When the target company is fairly large relative to the acquiring company, the target company may attempt to acquire the acquiring company. For instance, when Bendix Corporation sought to acquire Martin-Marietta Corporation in 1982 for $1.5 billion, Martin-Marietta then sought to acquire Bendix Corporation. Considered the most bizarre and spectacular takeover

attempt to date, the two companies exhausted their liquid assets trying to gain control of each other and be the first to oust the other's management and directors. As it became evident that the two companies would wind up owning each other and the result would be a unified but financially ailing enterprise, Bendix sought refuge by being acquired by Allied Chemical Corporation. Martin-Marietta successfully resisted the takeover attempt. This tactic is now known as the "Pac-man" defense.

(5) **Attacking the quality of the acquiring company's securities and management.** When the acquiring company offers stock instead of cash, the target company's management may try to convince the stockholders that the stock would be a bad investment. In several recent takeover attempts, the fierce attacks (commonly known as *mud-slinging*) on the integrity and ability of the acquiring company's management (in light of certain past transactions and recent performance) put the acquiring company on the defensive to such a degree that they abandoned their takeover attempts. This tactic is sometimes referred to as the "scorched earth" defense.

Whose interest is being served by resisting?   Sometimes refusing an offer or even to negotiate results in the acquiring company making a higher offer. This is clearly in the best interest of the target company's stockholders. Far too often, however, such actions by management are self-serving in that managers oppose the takeover because they want to remain top executives of an independent company rather than be top executives of a small part of a much larger company, or they fear the loss of their jobs. In some instances, management's actions in defending against takeover attempts are irresponsible, especially when their stockholders are overwhelmingly tendering their shares and thereby accepting the offer. Occasionally, stockholders of target companies have filed lawsuits against their managers and directors alleging (a) misuse of corporate resources in resisting takeover attempts (in a great number of instances, millions have been spent fighting the takeover attempt), or (b) violation of their fiduciary duty to stockholders by refusing to negotiate for the highest price possible. For the most part, the courts have been reluctant to find managements and directors guilty of these charges. Some companies attempt to protect their directors from such potential actions by dissatisfied stockholders by having stockholders require the board of directors (through an amendment to the articles of incorporation) to consider factors other than the value and type of consideration offered (such as social and economic effects on employees and communities in which the target company has operations) in determining whether to accept an offer.

Taking defensive steps to prevent a takeover attempt

Because business combinations are so prevalent, managements in fear of a potential takeover have in the last few years taken steps (colloquially known as "shark repellant") to make it more difficult for an acquiring company to effect a takeover. Some of the more routine steps involve requesting stockholders to approve such articles of incorporation, charter, and bylaw provisions as the following:

(1) Elimination of cumulative voting. Under cumulative voting, each stockholder has as many votes as the number of shares owned multiplied by the number of directors up for election. Thus, with cumulative voting, a potential acquiring company with a relatively small holding of common stock could get representation on the board of directors. (Many companies have reincorporated in Delaware, which does not require cumulative voting.)

(2) Use of staggered terms for directors. If directors have staggered terms, changes in the composition of the board of directors occur more slowly, making it impossible for a successful suitor to gain control of the board on consummation of the business combination.

(3) Use of a high percentage for shareholder approval of certain types of business combinations. For statutory mergers and acquisitions of assets (specific types of business combinations that are discussed in detail later in the chapter), imposing a stipulated percentage in excess of a simple majority (known as "supermajority" provisions) makes it more difficult to effect a takeover by either of these types of business combinations.

(4) Authorization of a class of preferred stock whose approval is necessary on any proposed merger or sale of net assets. Such authorization enables management to place the preferred stock privately in friendly hands.

Such actions by management that tend to insulate a company from acquisition have not gone unnoticed by the Securities and Exchange Commission. In recognition of the possibility that the interests of management (to stay in power) may conflict with the interests of stockholders (who might be receptive to an acquisition), the staff of the SEC has indicated that it intends to review proxy materials in detail to ensure that management has made adequate disclosure to shareholders regarding its proposals. Specifically, the staff has indicated that appropriate disclosures in proxy materials regarding such proposals should include the following:

(1) The reason(s) for the proposal and the bases of such reason(s).
(2) Whether the corporation's charter or bylaws presently contain other provisions having an anti-takeover effect, whether the ... proposal is part of a plan by management to adopt a series of such amendments, and whether management presently intends to propose other anti-takeover measures in future proxy solicitations.
(3) The overall effects of the proposal, if adopted.
(4) The advantages and disadvantages of the proposal ... both to incumbent management and to shareholders generally.
(5) Disclosure of how the proposal will operate.[5]

A continuous state of readiness. In 1982 and 1983, scores of companies that considered themselves potential takeover candidates started operating in a state of continuous readiness to fend off takeover attempts. Such steps include having

---

[5] Release No. 34-15230—Disclosure in Proxy and Information Statements, "Anti-takeover or Similar Proposals" (Washington, D.C.: SEC, October 13, 1978), pp. 7–10.

(1) Arrangements in place for investment bankers and lawyers who specialize in takeover attempts to assist them in the event of a "hostile" offer.
(2) Extensive credit resources lined up, in case funds are needed.
(3) Contracts with "stock watch" companies that closely monitor purchases of its stock to see if a "raider" is accumulating its stock.
(4) Management contracts (known as "golden parachutes"), whereby top executives are to receive substantial cash and/or other benefits (running into millions of dollars, in many instances) in the event of an unfriendly takeover or their dismissal after a takeover. Such contracts are justified by these companies on the grounds that an executive with a secure financial future can more objectively evaluate a takeover offer without regard to the impact on his or her job. Others contend that it assures management stability in a troubled time and prevents a drain of talent during an attempted takeover. Critics charge that these contracts merely allow executives to walk away rich and also make the acquisition more expensive for the acquiring company, which would effectively have to pay for these costs if the takeover is successful. (So many of these contracts were entered into in 1982 that it became known as "the year of the golden parachute.") As this book goes to print, Congress is considering a proposal to prohibit such contracts during tender offers.

ACCOUNTING METHODS

The two basic methods of accounting for business combinations are the **pooling of interests method** and the **purchase method.** These two methods are discussed in detail in *APB Opinion No. 16,* "Accounting for Business Combinations," which became effective in November 1970. When the value of the consideration given by the acquiring company is above or below the book value of the target company's net assets, these two methods produce dramatically different reporting of results of operations and financial position. Acquiring companies are fully aware of these consequences and often attempt to use the method that maximizes future earnings and earnings per share amounts. A major result of this pronouncement, however, was to eliminate the considerable latitude that previously existed in the use of either the purchase method or the pooling of interests method. If one of these specific methods is desired, then the terms and provisions of the acquisition agreement must be structured accordingly. This is a key point in that, **for a given set of terms and provisions, only one accounting method will apply.** The methods used in a given set of circumstances are no longer elective.

In this respect, company accountants must be thoroughly familiar with *APB Opinion No. 16,* so they can properly advise top management during the negotiations. Many corporate controllers follow the practice of obtaining an opinion from their certified public accountants as to whether or not a proposed set of terms and conditions will allow the use of the desired accounting method. This is practically essential, considering the complexity of this pronouncement. The objective, of course, is to prevent a combination from being completed in a manner that, it is thought, will be accounted for under a specific desired method only to have the certified public accountants later uncover something in the acquisition agreement that disallows use of that method.

The pooling of interests method

The theory underlying pooling of interests accounting is that **a sale and purchase of a business have not occurred.** Two companies have simply pooled their financial resources and managerial talents in such a manner that the owners of each of the separate businesses are now the owners of an enlarged business. This fusion of equity interests is the foundation of the pooling of interests concept. Obviously, continuity of interests exists only if the target company's shareholders receive only common stock of the acquiring company as consideration for their business. This is the most important condition of the pooling of interests method. Specifically, 12 conditions must be met for pooling of interests accounting to be allowed. These rules involve the attributes of the combining companies, the mechanics of the exchange, and transactions that are prohibited in periods subsequent to the exchange. If any one of these 12 rules is not met, then the pooling of interests method cannot be used. If all 12 rules are complied with, then the pooling of interests method must be used. These 12 rules are discussed in detail in Chapter 6, which discusses and illustrates the application of this method in detail.

When a combination qualifies for pooling of interests treatment, the recorded assets and liabilities of the separate companies are carried forward to the combined corporation at their historically recorded amounts. Goodwill is never created, and future income statements of the combined, enlarged business never include goodwill amortization expense. Furthermore, in the event future income statements are presented for periods before the combination date, the separate income statements of each constituent company are combined, restated, and then reported as income of the combined corporation.

The purchase method

If the transaction does not qualify for pooling of interests treatment, then the purchase method must be used. The underlying concept of the purchase method is that **one company has acquired the business of another company and a sale has occurred.** Under this method, the acquiring company's cost (essentially the value of the consideration given for the acquired business) must be allocated to the individual assets acquired. In most situations, the acquired assets are valued at their current values. To the extent that the acquiring company's cost exceeds the current value of the identifiable assets, then goodwill arises, which must be amortized to income over a period not to exceed 40 years. In an inflationary economy, the acquiring company usually pays in excess of the book value of the net assets of the acquired company. If this excess relates to assets other than land (a nondepreciable asset), greater depreciation and amortization charges are reflected in future income statements than if the pooling of interests method had been used. Accordingly, future earnings are lower under the purchase method. This upward revaluation of the acquired business's assets and the possible creation of goodwill are the major disadvantages of the purchase method compared with the pooling of interests method from the viewpoint of future earnings and earnings per share.

Criticism of *APB Opinion No. 16*

APB Opinion No. 16 received barely the required two-thirds majority vote. Since its issuance, it has been widely criticized for not being a sound or logical solution to the issues associated with business combinations. Specifically, the main criticism is that the results produced under the pooling of interests method often do not accurately portray the underlying economics of the business combination. For example, a company that has sales and assets of $100,000 could "pool" its resources and management with a company having sales and assets of $100,000,000. Many accountants feel that to treat such a combination as a pooling is just not sensible. In this situation, the substance of the combination is obviously the acquisition of the small business by the large business—a reality that is ignored under the pooling of interests concept.

Most accountants agree with the fundamental concept of the purchase method, except for the treatment of goodwill. Many accountants and corporate executives think that goodwill should not be shown as an asset of the acquiring company but should be charged to the equity section of the acquiring company at the acquisition. Their reasoning is that the acquiring entity has, in substance, given up some of its equity with the hope of recouping it in subsequent years through the acquired company's superior earnings (which may or may not materialize). Also criticized are the arbitrary rules relating to the amortization of goodwill, as set forth in *APB Opinion No. 17*, "Intangible Assets." Goodwill created before November 1, 1970, does not have to be amortized at all, whereas goodwill created after October 31, 1970, must be amortized over a period no longer than 40 years.

About three years after these two controversial pronouncements were issued, the rule-making authority for the accounting profession was transferred to the Financial Accounting Standards Board, with the hope that a more independent organization (whose members are not tied to the public accounting profession that serves the public corporations) would be more effective in resolving current accounting issues.

Reevaluation of issues by the FASB

In 1975, the Financial Accounting Standards Board considered the possibility of completely reevaluating the pooling of interests criteria set forth in *APB Opinion No. 16*. The Board subsequently decided to reexamine the entire issue of business combinations, and in August 1976, issued a discussion memorandum. The Board has put this project in abeyance pending the completion of its conceptual framework project for financial accounting and reporting, which encompasses (1) the objectives of financial statements; (2) the basic elements of financial statements; and (3) the qualitative characteristics and measurement aspects of financial statements. The results of the conceptual framework project are expected to benefit the business combinations project because the issues are closely related. Because almost all of the criticism is directed toward the pooling of interests method and that portion of the purchase method dealing with goodwill, any changes in accounting for business combinations will probably be made in these areas.

SPECIFIC TERMS AND PROVISIONS OF THE ACQUISITION AGREEMENT

Types of consideration given

The consideration given by the acquiring company can be the same as that used to pay for or finance internal expansions—namely, cash, other assets, or issuance of debt, preferred, or common stock. Under the purchase method, the consideration may consist of various combinations of cash, debt, and common stock. As stated earlier, substantially all of the consideration given in a transaction that qualifies for pooling of interests treatment is the acquiring company's common stock.

Types of assets acquired

A business may be acquired in one of two ways:

(1) Acquisition of assets. The acquiring company acquires the target company's assets and simultaneously assumes responsibility for paying existing, specific liabilities of the target company. If pooling of interests treatment is desired, 100% of the assets must be acquired; no such requirement exists for the purchase method.

(2) Acquisition of common stock. The acquiring company must purchase more than 50% of the target company's outstanding common stock for a business combination to have occurred. With an ownership interest greater than 50%, the acquiring company can control the target company.

Many circumstances affect the determination of whether the acquiring company should acquire assets or common stock of the target company. Some of the more common considerations are the following:

(1) Transferring stock certificates is easier than transferring assets. The transfer of assets may require the preparation of separate bills of sale for each asset or class of asset; also, state laws concerning bulk sales must be observed.

(2) If the target company's contracts, leases, franchises, or operating rights cannot be transferred through the sale of assets, common stock must be acquired.

(3) If the acquiring company does not wish to acquire all of the target company's assets, the acquisition of assets allows the acquiring company to obtain only those assets it desires. (To arrange for the acquisition of its common stock, the target company could dispose of the unwanted assets, but it may not always be feasible to do so in the time specified in the acquisition agreement.)

(4) If the target company has significant contingent liabilities, the acquiring company can best insulate itself from responsibility for these contingencies by acquiring assets. (If assets are acquired, the acquiring company usually clearly specifies in the acquisition agreement those liabilities for which it assumes responsibility.)

(5) When the sale of the target company's business to the acquiring company is treated as a taxable event (taxable versus nontaxable treatment is

discussed later in the chapter), there are several considerations from the seller's viewpoint, the most important of which are the following:

(a) If there is a taxable gain and the seller insists on structuring the transaction in such a manner that the gain is reportable on the installment basis for tax purposes, then the acquiring company must acquire common stock to accommodate the seller.

(b) A sale of assets may result in a substantial investment credit recapture liability to the target company. Investment credit recapture liabilities are created when property on which the investment credit has been taken is disposed of before the expiration of the required holding period. Acquiring common stock avoids this liability.

(c) A sale of assets may result in substantial depreciation recapture. Depreciation recapture has the effect of treating certain portions of a taxable gain as ordinary income as opposed to capital gain income. If the shareholders sell their common stock, a gain will probably be taxed entirely as a capital gain.

(6) If the acquiring company offers cash as consideration and the target company has substantial cash and short-term investment assets, the acquisition of assets makes the target company's cash and short-term investment assets available to the acquiring company to either help replenish its cash or repay loans obtained to finance the acquisition. In effect, the acquisition can be partially paid for using the funds of the target company. If common stock were acquired, the target company's cash and short-term investment assets would not be available to the acquiring company, except to the extent that the target company (as a subsidiary and a separate legal entity) could pay dividends to the acquiring company (as the parent).

RESULTING ORGANIZATIONAL FORM OF ACQUIRED BUSINESS

Accounting for business combinations focuses on **how the acquiring company initially records the transaction that brings about the combination.** The detailed accounting entries for the acquiring company require substantial explanation under both the purchase method and the pooling of interests method; these are discussed and illustrated in detail in Chapters 3 and 6, respectively. The entries made by the target company, on the other hand, are quite simple. The following discussion is general in nature, so that an overall understanding can be grasped of the organizational effects of business combinations.

Acquisition of assets

Centralized accounting.   One manner of accounting for the operations of the acquired business is called **centralized accounting,** whereby the assets acquired and the liabilities assumed are recorded in the existing general ledger of the acquiring company. This is common, however, only when the acquiring company already has similar operations that are accounted for on a centralized basis. Thus, this method would most likely be found only in a horizontal combination. When centralized accounting is used, only two general ledgers are involved in the transaction—the acquiring company's and the target company's. (Assets and liabilities merely are transferred from the target company's general ledger to the acquiring company's general ledger.)

Decentralized accounting. Another manner of accounting for the operations of the acquired business is called **decentralized accounting,** whereby the assets acquired and the liabilities assumed are recorded in a new general ledger maintained at the location of the newly acquired business. The newly acquired business is normally referred to as a **division** of the acquiring company. The difference between the assets acquired and the liabilities assumed are reflected in the division's Home Office account. The balance in this account always equals the balance in the Investment in Division account in the general ledger maintained at the acquiring company's headquarters. At this point, the division refers to the acquiring company as the home office. Accounting for a home office and a division is identical with the procedures used to account for a home office and a branch, which were discussed and illustrated in Chapter 1. Note that under this approach, three general ledgers are involved in the transaction—the two general ledgers of the acquiring company (one maintained at the home office and one maintained at the division) and the general ledger of the target company (which is still a separate legal entity). (Assets and liabilities merely are transferred from the target company's general ledger to the newly formed division's general ledger.)

Forming a wholly owned subsidiary to acquire the assets. In some cases, the acquiring company forms a wholly owned subsidiary to effect the acquisition of the target company's assets. This is done in situations in which it is not possible, practicable, or desirable to acquire the target company's common stock, but it is desirable to operate the acquired business as a separate legal entity insulated from the existing operations of the acquiring company.

Entries made by the target company. The target company, which disposes of its assets and is relieved of its liabilities, makes the following journal entries:

(1) Credit the various asset accounts for the assets that were disposed of.
(2) Debit the various liability accounts for the liabilities for which it is no longer responsible.
(3) Debit the appropriate asset accounts for the consideration received from the acquiring company—for example, cash, notes receivable, or investment in acquiring company.
(4) Record a gain or loss, depending on whether the assets are disposed of at a gain or a loss.

Removal of records. The target company must pack up its records (including its general ledger) and remove them from the location of the business that was sold.

Subsequent courses of action for the target company. If all its assets are disposed of and all its liabilities are assumed, the target company's remaining assets consist solely of the consideration received from the acquiring company. At this point, the target company (which is still a separate legal entity) is referred to as a **nonoperating company,** because it has no operating business—only passive assets. The following three courses of action are available:

(1) Continue as a nonoperating company.
(2) Use the assets to embark in a new line of business.
(3) Distribute the assets to its shareholders. (This last option is the most common one selected.)

When the last option is exercised, then the target company is referred to as a **"shell" company** because it has no operating business and no assets. However, it still is a separate legal entity until steps are taken to have its charter withdrawn (which is usually done).

Tax treatment on any gain by target company. If the disposal of the target company's assets and liabilities is pursuant to a plan of complete liquidation and all assets are distributed to its shareholders within a 12-month period, then the target company can avoid paying tax at the corporate level on any gain (with certain limitations). This rule allows the shareholders to be taxed on the gain instead of both the company and the shareholders being taxed. For tax purposes, the results are the same whether the target company disposes of assets or the shareholders dispose of stock.

Acquisition of common stock

A company owning more than 50% of the outstanding common stock of another company is referred to as the **parent** of that company. Conversely, a company whose outstanding common stock is more than 50% owned by another company is referred to as a **subsidiary** of that company. A subsidiary (as opposed to a division) is a separate legal entity that must maintain its own general ledger. Accordingly, the subsidiary's operations must be accounted for on a decentralized basis. The acquisition of the outstanding common stock of the acquired company is a personal transaction between the acquiring company and the acquired company's shareholders. For the target company, all that has happened is that the company's ownership is concentrated in the hands of significantly fewer stockholders, or even one stockholder if 100% of the outstanding common stock has been acquired. Consequently, only the acquiring company (the parent) must make an entry relating to the business combination.

Cash for stock exchange. If the acquiring company gives cash as consideration for the target company's outstanding common stock, it makes the following entry:

```
Investment in subsidiary .......................................  xxx
    Cash ......................................................         xxx
```

Stock for stock exchange.   Although any type of consideration may be given to acquire the outstanding common stock of the target company, the issuance of common stock by the acquiring company requires a discussion of what is known as the **exchange ratio.** The number of common shares to be issued by the acquiring company for each common share of the target company determines the exchange ratio. The exchange ratio is usually set forth in the acquisition agreement. An exchange ratio of 3:1, for instance, means that the acquiring company issues three shares of its common stock for each share of the target company's common stock acquired. If the target company has 200,000 shares of common stock outstanding and all of the stockholders agree to exchange their shares for shares of the acquiring company's common stock, then the acquiring company would have to issue 600,000 shares of common stock to effect the business combination. The following entry would be made by the acquiring company:

Investment in subsidiary   xxx
   Common stock (600,000 × the par value)   xxx
   Additional paid-in capital   xxx

This entry is slightly more involved if pooling of interests treatrnent applies. (More about this in Chapter 6.)

Statutory merger

A third common way of effecting a business combination is the **statutory merger.** In a statutory merger, the target company's equity securities are retired, and the corporate existence of the target company is terminated. The assets and liabilities of the target company are transferred to the acquiring company. Because the acquiring company is the only surviving legal entity, the target company is said to have been "merged" into the acquiring company. Because these combinations take place pursuant to state laws, they are called statutory mergers. The primary requirements of the state statutory merger laws are as follows:

(1) The board of directors of each company must approve the plan of proposed merger before the plan can be submitted to the shareholders of each company.
(2) The required percentage (usually a simple majority to 80%) of the voting power of each company must approve the plan of proposed merger.

The end result of a statutory merger is the same as if the acquiring company had acquired directly the target company's assets and the target company had then ceased its legal existence. The reasons for using this roundabout manner of acquiring a target company's assets are explained in the following paragraphs.

Forcing out dissenting shareholders.   In most cases in which the acquiring company acquires common stock, it desires 100% of the outstanding common stock of the target company. In some of these situations, this outcome may be unlikely because some shareholders of the target company object to the business combination. The acquiring company cannot force the dissenting shareholders to sell their shares. However, if the acquiring company acquires the required percentage of outstanding shares to approve a statutory merger, it can force out the dissenting shareholders by taking the necessary steps to liquidate the target company. (In some tender offers, the acquiring company clearly specifies that if all of the target company's shareholders do not accept the offer, the acquiring company intends to effect a statutory merger of the target company into the acquiring company, once the required ownership percentage is attained. This is a "tender your shares now or get forced out later" message.)

Note that in these cases, the business combination technically occurs when the acquiring company acquires more than 50% of the target company's outstanding common stock, which creates a parent–subsidiary relationship. Thus, the statutory merger takes place after the business combination date, a process that normally can be completed within 30 to 60 days after approval of the plan of merger.

When the statutory merger subsequently becomes effective, entries are made to: (1) transfer the target company's assets and liabilities to the acquiring company, and (2) close out the equity accounts in the target company's general ledger. In addition, it is necessary to make a settlement with the dissenting shareholders of the target company (who did not tender their shares). State laws pertaining to statutory mergers generally provide that dissenting shareholders have the right to receive (in cash) the fair value of their shares as of the day before shareholder approval of the merger. Such value may have to be established through a judicial determination as provided under state law if the dissenting shareholders and the acquiring company cannot agree on the value of these shares.

Forcing out shareholders who cannot be located. When common stock is being acquired, it is not always possible to locate a small number of the target company's shareholders. When total ownership is desired, the statutory merger route is a vehicle to liquidate these interests in the target company.

Inability to acquire assets directly. In unfriendly takeover attempts, the acquiring company is prevented from acquiring the assets directly from the target company, because the directors' refusal of the offer prevents the shareholders of the target company from voting on it. The acquiring company must then make a tender offer to the shareholders. If the acquiring company acquires the required percentage of outstanding shares through the tender offer and it does not wish to maintain a parent–subsidiary relationship, the acquiring company can then take the necessary steps to liquidate the target company via a statutory merger.

Formation of a holding company

Infrequently, two companies (generally of comparable size) combine in such a manner that a new corporate entity is established that controls the operations of both combining companies. This is done when the existing name of each corporation would not indicate the scope of operations of the combined business or it is desired to have the top-level corporation operate as a **holding company.** (A holding company has no revenue-producing operations of its own, only investments in subsidiaries.) To illustrate, assume Company A and Company B wish to combine. They form Company C, which issues its stock for the stock of Company A and Company B. Company A and Company B can now be operated as subsidiaries of Company C.

Statutory consolidation

More infrequent than the holding company route is the **statutory consolidation.** A statutory consolidation results in a new legal entity that takes over the assets and assumes the liabilities of each of the combining companies. The combining companies simultaneously cease their separate corporate existences. Because the new legal entity is the only surviving legal entity, the combining companies are said to have been "consolidated" into the new corporation. Because these combinations take place pursuant to state laws, they are called statutory consolidations. The primary requirements of the state statutory consolidation laws are the same as for statutory mergers.

Illustration:
Interrelationships of preceding areas

Illustration 2-1 presents the interrelationships of the various areas discussed up to this point.

Illustration 2-1

	Business Combinations			
	Purchase		Pooling of interests	
I. Accounting methods				
II. Type of consideration that may be given	Cash, other assets, debt, preferred stock, common stock — in any combination		Common stock — with restrictions on extent of other forms of consideration	
III. Type of asset that may be acquired	Common stock	Net assets	Common stock	Net assets (must acquire 100%)
IV. Resulting organizational form of acquired business	Subsidiary	Division[a]	Subsidiary	Division[a]
V. Type of accounting system that may be used — centralized or decentralized	Decentralized	Either	Decentralized	Either

[a] It is assumed here that a separate subsidiary is not formed for the sole purpose of acquiring the assets of the acquired business.

TAX RAMIFICATIONS

The income tax rules for business combinations are quite complex and thus more properly the topic of an advanced income tax course. However, it is important at this point that you understand the relationship and similarities between the accounting rules and the income tax rules—an understanding that does not always result when the tax rules are dealt with solely in an advanced tax course. Accordingly, the following discussion is limited, general in nature, and designed to accomplish this objective.

As explained earlier, for financial reporting purposes, the terms and provisions in the acquisition agreement determine whether the purchase method or the pooling of interests method is used to record the combination. For income tax reporting purposes, the same terms and provisions in the acquisition agreement determine whether the combination is treated as a **taxable combination** or as a **tax-deferrable combination,** the latter commonly referred to as a **tax-free combination.**

Taxable combinations

The underlying concept: A sale has occurred.   The underlying concept of purchase accounting—that one company has acquired the business of another company—is essentially the same concept as that embodied in the Internal Revenue Code with respect to taxable combinations. For income tax reporting purposes, **a taxable combination is a completed and closed transaction in that a sale is deemed to have occurred.** Accordingly, the acquired business reports, or its shareholders report, a gain or loss in the year of the transaction. The fair value of the consideration received by the acquired business or its shareholders is compared with the tax basis of the assets sold to the acquiring business to compute the taxable gain or tax-deductible loss.

The resulting change in basis.   For the acquiring company, the tax basis of the acquired property (whether assets or common stock) is the purchase price paid. Obviously, if assets are acquired for more than their carrying value as of the acquisition date, the acquired assets are stepped up in basis for tax depreciation and amortization purposes. If common stock is acquired, the assets of the acquired business can be stepped up in basis only if the acquiring company elects to treat the acquisition of the target company's common stock as an asset purchase. Accordingly, when the election is made, the basis of the common stock is effectively transferred to the assets of the acquired business. (A more detailed discussion regarding this election is contained in Chapter 12.) This allows the acquirer to be in the same position as it would be if assets had been acquired instead of common stock.

Relationship and similarities between accounting and tax rules. Although the underlying concept of the purchase method for financial reporting purposes is the same as that embodied in the Internal Revenue Code with respect to taxable combinations, it is important to recognize that the specific rules of *APB Opinion No. 16* regarding the purchase method are different from the specific rules of the Internal Revenue Code regarding taxable combinations. In other words, each set of rules is independent, so that the treatment for financial reporting purposes does not determine the treatment for tax reporting purposes and vice versa. Accordingly, some combinations that are accounted for under the purchase method for financial reporting purposes are treated as taxable combinations for income tax reporting purposes, whereas other combinations that are accounted for under the purchase method of accounting for financial reporting purposes are treated as tax-free combinations for income tax reporting purposes. Because of this sameness of concept but difference in specific rules, the only generalization that can be made is that **combinations accounted for under the purchase method for financial reporting purposes are more likely to be taxable combinations than tax-free combinations.**

Tax-free combinations

The underlying concept: No sale has occurred.   The underlying concept of pooling of interests accounting—that the two equity interests of the combining companies pool together in such a manner that there is a continuity of interest in the new, enlarged business—is essentially the same concept as that embodied in the Internal Revenue Code with respect to tax-free combinations (referred to as *tax-free reorganizations* in the Internal Revenue Code). For income tax reporting purposes, **a tax-free reorganization is not a completed or closed transaction in that a sale is not deemed to have occurred.** Accordingly, the acquired business (or its shareholders) does not report a gain or loss in the year of the transaction. Only the form of the investment has changed; the investment in the business itself is maintained even though such business is now part of a larger business. At some later time, when the property that was received in the combination (typically the acquiring company's common stock) is disposed of in a completed taxable transaction, a gain or loss is reportable for income tax reporting purposes. Accordingly, in a tax-free reorganization, income taxes are merely deferred or postponed until a later date.

No resulting change in basis.   With respect to the continuing enlarged business, the basis of the property acquired is not changed for income tax reporting purposes, regardless of whether assets or common stock is received in the exchange. The tax rules relating to tax-free reorganizations can accommodate acquisitions of assets and acquisitions of common stock. Section 368(a) of the Internal Revenue Code describes the various procedures by which tax-free combinations may be attained. Three specific procedures for accomplishing this are set forth in subsections (a)(1)(A), (B), and (C). In practice, these are referred to as "A," "B," and "C" reorganizations. Type A reorganizations pertain to statutory mergers and statutory consolidations that take place under a specific state statute. Type B reorganizations pertain to stock for stock exchanges. Type C reorganizations pertain to an exchange of stock for assets. If the combining companies agree on a tax-free reorganization, the terms and provisions of the acquisition agreement must be structured carefully around one of these three specific procedures. The requirements of the Internal Revenue Code must be fully complied with before tax-free treatment is allowed. The safest course of action is to secure a specific ruling in advance from the Internal Revenue Service. Because this is a highly specialized area of tax practice, competent tax advice should be obtained.

Relationship and similarities between accounting and tax rules.   The underlying concept of the pooling of interests method for financial reporting purposes is the same as that embodied in the Internal Revenue Code with respect to tax-free reorganizations. The same independent relationship exists between the pooling of interests method (for financial reporting purposes) and tax-free reorganizations (for income tax reporting purposes) as was explained for purchase accounting (for financial reporting purposes) in relation to taxable combinations (for income tax reporting purposes). The pooling of interests requirements, however, are much more stringent than the tax-free reorganization rules. As a result, the generalization can be made that **combinations accounted for under the pooling of interests method for financial reporting purposes almost always qualify for tax-free reorganization treatment.**

Conflicting interests of combining businesses

Conflicting interests often exist between the acquiring company and the target company or its stockholders with respect to the desired accounting and tax treatments. The most common **accounting conflict** occurs when the acquiring company desires to use pooling of interests accounting (which requires that it issue common stock to the acquired business or to its shareholders), whereas the acquired business or its shareholders may want to receive cash or other nonstock consideration.

The **tax conflicts** center around (1) whether the acquiring company desires to change the tax basis of the property received in the combination (assets or common stock) to its current value based on the consideration given by the acquiring company, and (2) whether the acquired company or its shareholders want a tax-free treatment.

The most common situation in an inflationary economy arises when the acquiring company gives consideration that is greater in value than the tax basis of the property it is to receive. In such situations, the acquiring company would prefer a taxable treatment so that it can step up the basis of the property it is to receive. Thus, it will have greater depreciation and amortization deductions for income tax reporting purposes (or a higher basis in the acquired company's stock if a parent–subsidiary relationship is to be maintained). The acquired company or its shareholders, however, may prefer a tax-free treatment to defer or postpone the recognition of a gain for income tax reporting purposes.

The roles usually are reversed in situations in which the acquiring company gives consideration that is lower in value than the tax basis of the property it is to receive. In such a situation, the acquiring company would prefer a tax-free treatment, so that the higher basis of the property it is to receive will carry over. Thus, it would have greater depreciation and amortization deductions for income tax reporting purposes (or a higher basis in the acquired company's stock if a parent–subsidiary relationship is to be maintained). The acquired company or its shareholders, however, may prefer a taxable treatment to immediately recognize a loss for income tax reporting purposes.

The ultimate resolution of these conflicting interests depends on the relative bargaining strengths and positions of each party.

SUMMARY

Business combinations are a major means of attaining corporate growth. The acquiring company may account for the acquired business using either the purchase method or the pooling of interests method. The purchase method treats the combination as a purchase of the acquired business, whereby the acquired assets of the target company are recorded at the acquiring company's cost, which is based essentially on the fair value of the consideration given. In contrast, the pooling of interests method treats the combination as a fusion of equity interests, whereby the acquired assets of the target company are recorded at the target company's historical book values as of the acquisition date. This fusion of equity interests is accomplished through the issuance of the acquiring company's common stock as consideration. Whether the acquiring company acquires the target company's assets or outstanding common stock has no bearing on the accounting treatment; only the resulting organizational form of the acquired business is different.

Business combinations are treated as either taxable or tax-free transactions. Under a taxable transaction, the acquiring company establishes a new basis for the acquired assets. Under a tax-free transaction, the basis to the acquired company carries over to the acquiring company. Tax considerations are often of primary consideration in negotiating the terms of the acquisition agreement, as is the desired accounting treatment from the acquiring company's point of view.

Glossary of new terms

Acquiring Company: A company attempting to acquire the business of another company.

Acquisition Agreement: The legal agreement that specifies the terms and provisions of a business combination.

Conglomerate Combination: A business combination that takes place between companies in unrelated industries.

Division: In this chapter, division refers to a newly acquired business that does not maintain its separate legal existence.

Exchange Ratio: The number of common shares issued by the acquiring company in exchange for each outstanding common share of the target company.

Horizontal Combination: A business combination that takes place between companies involved as competitors at the same level in a given industry.

Parent: A company that owns more than 50% of the outstanding common stock of another company.

Pooling of Interests Method: A method of accounting for a business combination whereby the assets of the acquired business are carried forward to the combined corporation at their historically recorded amounts. A fusion of equity interests is deemed to have occurred as opposed to a sale.

Purchase Method: A method of accounting for a business combination whereby the assets and liabilities of the acquired business are valued at their current values based on the consideration given by the acquiring company. A sale is deemed to have occurred.

Statutory Consolidation: A legal term referring to a specific type of business combination in which a new corporation is formed to carry on the businesses of two predecessor corporations that are liquidated.

Statutory Merger: A legal term referring to a specific type of business combination in which a newly acquired target company is liquidated into a division at the time of the business combination.

Subsidiary: A company whose outstanding common stock is more than 50% owned by another company.

Takeover Attempt: The process of trying to acquire the business of a target company.

Target Company: The company whose business a company is seeking to acquire.

Tax-free Combination: A specific type of business combination in which the acquired business or its shareholders do not report a gain or loss at the time of the business combination for income tax reporting purposes.

Tender Offer: An offer made by an acquiring company directly to the stockholders of the target company, whereby the stockholders of the target company are requested to tender their common shares in exchange for the consideration offered by the acquiring company.

Vertical Combination: A business combination that takes place between companies involved at different levels in a given industry.

Review questions

1. What is the difference between horizontal, vertical, and conglomerate combinations?
2. Contrast the purchase method with the pooling of interests method of accounting.
3. Why is the acquisition agreement so important in determining the ultimate accounting method used in recording a business combination?
4. On what grounds has *APB Opinion No. 16* been criticized?
5. What types of consideration can be given under purchase accounting and under pooling of interests accounting?
6. What types of assets can the acquiring company obtain in business combinations?
7. What various organizational forms can result from a business combination?
8. What is the difference between centralized and decentralized accounting systems?
9. How is the selling entity's gain or loss computed on the disposition of its assets?
10. Explain the relationship between *APB Opinion No. 16* and the income tax rules relating to business combinations.
11. What is meant by a tax-free combination?
12. Why does a conflict often exist between the acquiring company and the target company or its stockholders with respect to whether the combination should be treated in a taxable or nontaxable manner?

Discussion cases

Discussion case 2–1
Purchase versus pooling of interests

On July 1, 19X1, P Company acquired all of the outstanding common stock of S Company for $1,000,000 cash. P Company's controller informed you of this acquisition in August 19X1 and indicated that management has not yet decided whether to use the purchase method or the pooling of interests method to account for this business combination. The controller has asked you to assist him in evaluating the alternative accounting treatments between now and December 31, 19X1, the end of P Company's reporting period.

Required:
How would you advise the controller?

Discussion case 2–2
Accounting versus tax treatment

Expresso Company plans to embark on a business acquisition program to diversify its product lines. The controller has indicated to you that she is unclear on whether the tax treatment determines the accounting treatment or whether the accounting treatment determines the tax treatment.

Required:
How would you advise the controller?

Discussion case 2–3
Limiting legal liability and consistency

Conglomerate Company is having merger discussions with Nonglomerate Company. All of Conglomerate Company's business acquisitions to date have been acquisitions of common stock resulting in parent–subsidiary relationships. Conglomerate prefers to legally insulate each of its acquired businesses from all other operations. Nonglomerate Company has been and still is involved as a defendant in several lawsuits. As a result, Conglomerate Company plans to acquire Nonglomerate's assets to insulate itself from any current or potential legal entanglements. The controller indicates to you that if the merger is consummated in this manner, the company will not be accounting for its acquisitions consistently, which will violate a fundamental accounting principle. Furthermore, all businesses acquired to date have been consistently recorded as poolings of interests; the acquisition of Nonglomerate will not qualify for pooling of interests treatment, which means an additional inconsistency will be created.

Required:
(1) How could Conglomerate Company achieve the objective of insulating the business of Nonglomerate Company?

(2) Is the consistency principle being violated as a result of acquiring assets? Why or why not?

(3) Is the consistency principle being violated as a result of the combination not qualifying for pooling of interests treatment? Why or why not?

Exercises

Exercise 2–1
Terminology

Indicate the appropriate term(s) for each of the following:

(1) The expansion of a business by constructing a manufacturing facility.
(2) A business combination in which a company acquires one of its suppliers.
(3) A business combination in which a company acquires one of its competitors.
(4) A business combination in which a company acquires businesses to diversify its product lines.
(5) The broad terms used in business to refer to business combinations.
(6) A business combination in which the target company's corporate existence is terminated in conjunction with the transfer of its assets and liabilities to the acquiring company.
(7) A business combination in which a new corporation is formed to acquire the businesses of two existing corporations.
(8) The two methods of accounting for business combinations as set forth in *APB Opinion No. 16.*
(9) The two types of assets that can be acquired in a business combination.
(10) The expansion of a business by acquiring an existing business.
(11) An acquired business that maintains its separate legal existence.
(12) An acquiring business that acquires common stock of the acquired business, the latter maintaining its separate legal existence.
(13) An acquired business that ceases to be a separate legal entity but continues to use a separate general ledger.
(14) The primary type of consideration given in a business combination that is accounted for as a pooling of interests.
(15) The allowable types of consideration that can be given in a business combination accounted for as a purchase.

Exercise 2–2
Pooling of interests method—Acquisition of assets

Perky Company acquired all of the assets of Spry Company in a business combination that qualified for pooling of interests treatment. The current value of the common stock issued by Perky Company exceeded the book value of Spry Company's net assets by $300,000.

Required:
Explain the general accounting procedures to be followed by Perky Company in recording the acquisition of the assets.

Exercise 2–3
Purchase method—Acquisition of assets

Polk Company acquired all of the assets of Shelby Company in a business combination that did not qualify for pooling of interests treatment. Polk Company paid $800,000 cash. The book value of Shelby Company's net assets is $600,000 and their current value is $750,000.

Required:
Explain the general accounting procedures to be followed by Polk Company in recording the acquisition of the assets.

Exercise 2–4
Divestiture accounting—Sale of common stock

Patari Company acquired all of the outstanding common stock of Sente Company from its shareholders by issuing common stock.

Required:
Explain in general how Sente Company should account for this change in ownership of its outstanding common stock.

Exercise 2–5
Divestiture accounting—Sale of assets

Pepsi Company acquired all of the assets of Shasta Company by issuing common stock (and assuming Shasta's liabilities).

Required:
Explain in general how Shasta Company should account for this transaction.

Exercise 2–6
Statutory merger and statutory consolidation

Pimex Corporation is considering a merger or consolidation with Sago Corporation. Both methods of acquisition are being considered under applicable corporate statutory law. Pimex is the larger of the two corporations and is in reality acquiring Sago Corporation.

Required:
Discuss the meaning of the terms *merger* and *consolidation* as used in corporate law with particular emphasis on the legal difference between the two.

(AICPA adapted)

Problems

Problem 2–1
COMPREHENSIVE Acquisition of assets for cash

PBM Company acquired all of the assets of Sapple Computer Company by assuming responsibility for all of its liabilities and paying $1,600,000 cash. Information with respect to Sapple at the date of combination follows:

	Book Value	Current Value
Cash	$ 10,000	$ 10,000
Accounts receivable, net (including $30,000 due		
from PBM Company)......................................	90,000	90,000
Inventory..	100,000	100,000
Land	300,000	400,000
Building—Cost..	2,000,000	1,600,000
—Accum. depr.......................................	(800,000)	
Equipment—Cost	500,000	300,000
—Accum. depr.	(400,000)	
	$1,800,000	$2,500,000
Accounts payable and accruals	$ 200,000	$ 200,000
Long-term debt	900,000	900,000
Total liabilities	$1,100,000	$1,100,000
Common stock	$ 10,000	
Additional paid-in capital...............................	490,000	
Retained earnings	200,000	
Total stockholders' equity............................	$ 700,000	$1,400,000
	$1,800,000	$2,500,000

Required:
(1) Does the acquisition appear to be a horizontal, vertical, or conglomerate type of combination? *Don't know*
(2) How could PBM Company have determined the current value of Sapple Computer Company's assets and liabilities?
(3) Why did PBM Company pay $1,600,000 for a company whose net assets are worth only $1,400,000 at their current value? —
(4) Can the acquired business be accounted for on a centralized basis or a decentralized basis?
(5) Would the transaction be accounted for as a purchase or a pooling of interests?
(6) What is the probable treatment for income tax reporting purposes?
(7) From your answer in (6), what is the tax basis of the fixed assets acquired by PBM Company? *The Sapple will be tied on their Basi. PBM pays tes based on their asset*
(8) Is PBM Company the parent company of Sapple Computer Company? Why or why not? *when assets purchased there is no parent-subsidiary relation - parent owns stock in sub*
(9) Is Sapple Computer Company a separate legal entity after the transaction has been consummated? *yes - assets exchanged for (ase)-CASH*
(10) Is Sapple Computer Company a subsidiary? Why or why not? *no*
(11) Prepare the journal entry that would be made, if any, on the books of Sapple Computer Company on the date of combination.

Assets purch for cash. goodwill exists Current value above therefore must be purch.

(12) Prepare a balance sheet for Sapple Computer Company after recording the entry in (11).

Problem 2–2
COMPREHENSIVE   Acquisition of common stock for cash

Assume the same information as provided in Problem 2–1, except that PBM Company acquired all of the outstanding common stock of Sapple Computer Company instead of all of its assets.

Required:
Respond to requirements (4) through (12) in Problem 2–1.

Problem 2–3
COMPREHENSIVE   Acquisition of assets for common stock

Assume the same information as provided in Problem 2–1, except that PBM Company acquired all of the assets of Sapple Computer Company by issuing common stock with a total market value of $1,600,000 instead of paying cash.

Required:
Respond to requirements (4) through (12) in Problem 2–1.

Problem 2–4
COMPREHENSIVE   Acquisition of common stock for common stock

Assume the same information as provided in Problem 2–1, except that PBM Company acquired all of the outstanding common stock of Sapple Computer Company by issuing common stock with a total market value of $1,600,000 instead of paying cash.

Required:
Respond to requirements (4) through (12) in Problem 2–1.

3 The Purchase Method of Accounting— Date of Acquisition

Chapter 2 introduced the purchase method and the pooling of interests method of accounting for business combinations. Because these two methods are diametrically opposed conceptually, they are best discussed and illustrated separately. In this and the following two chapters, the purchase method is discussed. In Chapter 6, the pooling of interests method is discussed in detail, illustrated, and contrasted with the purchase method.

The purchase method, like the pooling of interests method, can be applied to the acquisition of assets as well as to the acquisition of common stock. One form of business combination involves acquiring assets and another form involves acquiring common stock. The form selected is of no consequence, however, when applying the purchase method of accounting. The end result is the same in terms of reporting the results of operations and the financial position of the enlarged business. To prove this point, we discuss and illustrate each form of business combination. In our illustrations, of course, we must compare a situation in which all of the assets are acquired with one in which all of the common stock is acquired. Otherwise, a comparison is not possible. Acquisition of less than 100% of the common stock requires some additional considerations that are not relevant in situations in which all of the common stock is acquired. Discussion of these more involved situations is delayed until Chapter 5.

ESSENCE OF THE PURCHASE METHOD

The underlying concept of the purchase method of accounting is that one entity has purchased the business of another entity—that is, a sale has been consummated. The acquiring company records at its cost the assets or the common stock acquired. The acquiring company's cost is based essentially on the value of the consideration given. If the acquiring company's cost is above the current value of the target company's net assets (determined by valuing its tangible assets, identifiable intangible assets, and liabilities at their current values, which may involve qualified appraisers), then goodwill exists, which must be amortized over a period not to exceed 40 years. Thus, **goodwill is determined in a residual manner.** In the far less frequent circumstances in which the acquiring company's cost is below the current value of the target company's net assets, a **bargain purchase element** exists, which must be allocated against the current value of certain noncurrent assets. If the bargain purchase element is so great that it reduces the applicable noncurrent assets to zero, the remaining amount is recorded as a **deferred credit** and amortized over a period not to exceed 40 years.

The purchase method parallels accounting for the acquisition of individual assets—that is, historical cost is used. Some assets and liabilities of the enlarged business consequently are recorded at their historical cost (the assets and liabilities of the acquiring company), whereas some assets and liabilities of the enlarged business (the assets and liabilities of the acquired business) are reported at their current values as of the acquisition date.

Of course, these current values become the acquiring company's historical cost. From the date of acquisition, the income of the acquired company is combined with the income of the acquiring company. The acquired company's preacquisition earnings are never combined with preacquisition earnings of the acquiring company.

The purchase method can be neatly divided into two specific questions:

(1) What is the total cost of the acquired business to the acquiring business?
(2) What is specifically acquired for the total cost incurred?

The rest of this chapter discusses the detailed procedures used to answer these questions. In addition, the procedures for presenting the financial position of the enlarged business as of the acquisition date are discussed and illustrated.

DETERMINING TOTAL COST OF THE ACQUIRED BUSINESS

The total cost of the acquired business equals the sum of

(1) The **fair value of the consideration given;**
(2) The **direct costs** incurred in connection with the acquisition, excluding costs of registering with the Securities and Exchange Commission any securities given as consideration by the acquiring company; and
(3) The **fair value of any contingent consideration** that is given subsequent to the acquisition date.

Each of these areas is discussed below.

Fair value of consideration given

The following three types of consideration may be given in any combination:

(1) Cash or other assets. Cost is the amount of cash or the fair value of other assets given.
(2) Debt. Cost is the present value of the debt issued, determined by applying the provisions of *APB Opinion No. 21,* "Interest on Receivables and Payables."
(3) Equity securities. Cost is the fair value of the equity securities issued. However, if the fair value of the property acquired is more clearly evident than the fair value of the equity securities issued, then the fair value of the property acquired is used to determine cost.[1]

As a practical matter, when equity securities issued are identical with the acquiring company's outstanding publicly traded securities, the fair value of the equity securities given is readily determinable and is almost always used to determine cost. If the acquiring company's equity securities are not publicly traded or a new class of stock is issued, it is usually

[1] *APB Opinion No. 16,* "Accounting for Business Combinations" (New York: AICPA, 1970), paragraph 67.

necessary to obtain either (a) an appraisal of the fair value of the equity securities issued (usually obtainable from an investment banker) or (b) an appraisal of the property acquired, the latter alternative being preferable.

Direct costs incurred

Acquiring companies commonly use outside lawyers and accountants in various capacities throughout the course of events leading to a completed acquisition. Travel costs are common during acquisiton negotiations, as are finders' fees. Such costs and fees, as well as any other direct costs, that **pertain to the acquisition** are added to the cost of the acquired business. In situations in which the consideration given is equity securities, costs and fees that **pertain to the issuance or registration of the equity securities** are not added to the cost of the acquired business. Instead, they are charged to additional paid-in capital.[2] (Recall from intermediate accounting that the costs incurred to issue and register equity securities in nonbusiness combinations are treated in this manner because they are considered a reduction of the fair value of the securities issued.) Indirect and general expenses, including salary and overhead costs of an internal acquisitions department, are not direct costs of an acquisition and are expensed as incurred.[3]

Contingent consideration

Contingent consideration is often used as a compromise when the buyer and seller disagree on the purchase price or the form of consideration to be given, or both. Contingent consideration may be divided into the following two mutually exclusive categories:

(1) **Contingencies that are currently determinable.** If it is reasonably determinable at the acquisition date that the contingent consideration will have to be paid, then the fair value of the additional consideration should be recorded at that time as part of the cost of the acquired business.[4] (Relatively few contingencies fall into this category.)

(2) **Contingencies that are not currently determinable.** If it is not determinable beyond a reasonable doubt at the acquisition date that the contingent consideration will have to be paid, the contingent consideration should be disclosed but not recorded as a liability or shown as outstanding securities until it is determinable beyond a reasonable doubt.[5] An example of appropriate footnote disclosure is given later in the chapter in the section on disclosures. (This "determinable beyond a reasonable doubt" criterion of *APB Opinion No. 16* is more demanding than the "probable" criterion set forth in *FASB Statement No. 5*, "Accounting for Contingencies," which applies only to loss and gain contingencies.) Contin-

---

[2]*APB Opinion No. 16*, paragraph 76.
[3]*APB Opinion No. 16*, paragraph 76, and Accounting Interpretation No. 33 to *APB Opinion No. 16*.
[4]*APB Opinion No. 16*, paragraph 78.
[5]*APB Opinion No. 16*, paragraph 78.

gencies that are not currently determinable can be divided into two categories.

(a) Contingencies based on other than security prices. This type of contingency often is based on sales or earnings goals for the acquired business. It is commonly used when the target company or its shareholders want to protect themselves from selling out too cheaply in the event the acquired business subsequently realizes the potential they feel it possesses and the buyer wants to protect itself from paying too much in the event the acquired business does not realize such potential. Contingent consideration is the compromise, whereby an additional amount of consideration is given to the seller(s) at a later date if the acquired business achieves certain agreed-upon sales or earnings levels within a specified

Illustration 3-1
Contingent consideration based on security prices

> **Assumed Facts:**
>   Pine Company acquires the business of Spruce Company. (Whether assets or com-
> mon stock is acquired is irrelevant.) The total consideration paid by Pine is $1,000,000
> worth of its $5 par value common stock. The market price of Pine's common stock on the
> acquisition date is $50 per share; thus, 20,000 shares are issued at that time. A condition
> of the purchase is that the common stock issued be held by the seller for two years. If, at
> the end of two years, the market price of the common stock is below $50 per share, then
> an appropriate additional number of shares must be issued so that the total value of the
> issued shares equals $1,000,000. Two years later, the market price of Pine's common
> stock is $40 per share. Thus, $1,000,000 divided by $40 per share equals 25,000 shares.
> Because 20,000 shares have already been issued, an additional 5,000 shares are issued
> at that time.
>
> Entry at the acquisition date:
>   Cost of acquired business[a]   1,000,000
>   Common stock   100,000
>   Additional paid-in capital   900,000
>   To record the issuance of 20,000 shares of
> $5 par value common stock.
>   Entries required two years later:
>   Cost of acquired business[a]   200,000
>   Common stock   25,000
>   Additional paid-in capital   175,000
>   To record the issuance of 5,000 shares of
> $5 par value common stock as additional
>   consideration.
>   Additional paid-in capital   200,000
>   Cost of acquired business[a]   200,000
>   To reflect the reduction in value of the
>   previously issued shares from
> $50 per share to $40 per share.
>   Note that the effect of the entries recorded two years after acquisition is to debit additional
> paid-in capital for $25,000 and credit common stock for $25,000. Thus, there is no effect
> on the cost of the acquired business, as initially recorded on the acquisition date.
>
> [a] Later in the chapter, a more descriptive term is used, depending on whether assets or common stock
>   is acquired.

period of time. Later, when the contingency is resolved and any additional consideration is distributable, **the current value of the additional consideration is added to the acquiring company's cost of the acquired business.**[6] (Usually, this increases the amount of goodwill.)

(b) **Contingencies based on security prices.** This type of contingency is common when the target company or its shareholders receive as consideration the acquiring company's equity securities, which must be held for a certain period of time. In this situation, the target company or its shareholders want protection in the event the market price of the securities at the expiration of the holding period is below the market price of the securities at the acquisition date. The acquiring company must issue an additional number of securities if the market price at the end of the holding period is below the market price that existed on the acquisition date. The result is to bring the total value of the holdings of the target company or its shareholders at that time up to the total value existing on the acquisition date. If additional securities are later issued, the current value of the additional consideration is added to the acquiring company's cost of the acquired business. "However, the amount previously recorded for securities issued at the date of acquisition should simultaneously be reduced to the lower current value of those securities."[7] **The net effect of this procedure is not to increase the cost of the acquired business above what was recorded at the acquisition date.** The rationale is that the initial recorded cost represents the amount that would have been paid for the business in a straight cash transaction. Illustration 3-1 gives an example of the accounting entries for this type of contingency.

TOTAL COST IN RELATION TO CURRENT VALUE AND BOOK VALUE OF ACQUIRED BUSINESS'S NET ASSETS

After determining the acquiring company's total cost of the acquired business, we must determine the current value of the acquired business's net assets. When the acquiring company's total cost is greater than the current value of the acquired business's net assets, such excess amount is considered **goodwill.** The current value of the acquired business's net assets and the residual amount determined as goodwill are reported in the financial statements of the enlarged, combined business.

If the acquiring company's total cost is below the current value of the acquired business's net assets, then a **bargain purchase element** exists. This bargain purchase element is allocated as much as possible against the current values of certain noncurrent assets. If this allocation does not extinguish the bargain purchase element, then a deferred credit exists. The current value of the acquired business's net assets (adjusted for the bargain purchase element), along with any remaining deferred credit, is reported in the financial statements of the enlarged, combined business.

[6] *APB Opinion No. 16,* paragraph 79.
[7] *APB Opinion No. 16,* paragraph 82.

Illustration 3-2 summarizes the possible situations with respect to the relationships among (1) the total cost of the investment; (2) the current value of the acquired business's net assets; and (3) the book value of the acquired business's net assets. Book value is the value recorded on the target company's books as of the acquisition date.

The rest of this chapter deals with recording business combinations and preparing combined and consolidated financial statements as of the date of business combination. In an inflationary economy, the net assets of an acquired business are usually undervalued. Thus, Situations B, E, and H of Illustration 3-2 are most common. Each of the situations in Illustration 3-2 is not individually discussed and illustrated. Instead, one situation from each major category is discussed and illustrated—namely, Situations A, E, and H—to develop the general procedures applicable to each major category. For Situations A and E, acquisition of assets and acquisition of common stock are discussed and illustrated, so that these two methods of acquisition are compared. In addition, Situation F of Illustration 3-2 is discussed for an acquisition of common stock, to explain the procedures for accounting for a situation in which the net assets are overvalued.

When assets are acquired, the procedures to record the business combination and to prepare financial statements reflecting the enlarged, combined operations are not complicated. This is because the assets acquired and liabilities assumed are recorded directly by the acquiring company in its own general ledger (or in the general ledger of a newly established division) at their current values.

When common stock is acquired, the procedures used to record the business combination are also not complicated. However, the procedures

Illustration 3-2
Summary of relationships among total cost, current value, and book value

Category	Total Cost	Net Assets of Acquired Business	
		Current Value	Book Value
I. **Neither Goodwill nor a Bargain Purchase Element Exists—Total cost equals current value:**			
A. Current value equals book value	$60,000	$60,000	$60,000
B. Current value is above book value	$80,000	$80,000	$60,000
C. Current value is below book value	$50,000	$50,000	$60,000
II. **Goodwill Exists—Total cost is above current value:**			
D. Current value equals book value	$70,000	$60,000	$60,000
E. Current value is above book value	$90,000	$80,000	$60,000
F. Current value is below book value	$55,000	$50,000	$60,000
III. **Bargain Purchase Element Exists—Total cost is below current value:**			
G. Current value equals book value	$50,000	$60,000	$60,000
H. Current value is above book value	$75,000	$80,000	$60,000
I. Current value is below book value	$45,000	$50,000	$60,000

Note: The book value column is relevant to the acquiring company only in situations in which common stock is acquired, as explained later in the chapter.

to prepare financial statements reflecting the enlarged, combined operations are somewhat involved, because the acquired subsidiary continues to account for its assets and liabilities using its recorded book values. Stated differently, the parent does not directly record the assets and liabilities of the acquired business in its own general ledger. The only account in which the parent records the cost of the acquired business is an account called Investment in Subsidiary. As a result, the parent must deal with the book value of the subsidiary's net assets (as recorded on the books of the subsidiary) in preparing financial statements that reflect the enlarged, combined operations.

ACQUISITION OF ASSETS

The acquisition of assets is merely the purchase of the target company's assets, with part of the purchase price taking the form of assuming responsibility for the target company's existing liabilities. Before the acquiring company can record the acquisition of assets, it must determine whether the operations of the acquired business will be accounted for on a centralized or decentralized basis. In most instances, decentralized accounting is most practical unless the acquisition is a horizontal combination and the acquiring company already has similar outlying operations accounted for on a centralized basis. Decentralized and centralized accounting systems are discussed in the following illustrations.

Illustration:
Neither goodwill nor a bargain purchase element exists (Total cost equals current value of net assets) and net assets are not over- or undervalued

To illustrate the recording of the acquisition and the preparation of combined financial statements as of the acquisition date when cost equals current value, and current value equals book value (Situation A of Illustration 3-2), we assume the following information:

(1) P Company acquired all of S Company's assets on January 1, 19X1, by assuming responsibility for all of its liabilities and paying $60,000 cash.
(2) Total cost $60,000
(3) Current value of net assets.................................... $60,000
(4) Book value of net assets.................................... $60,000
(5) The balance sheets for each company as of January 1, 19X1—immediately prior to the business combination—are as follows.

	P Company	S Company
Assets:		
Cash	$110,000	$ 20,000
Accounts receivable, net	120,000	30,000
Inventory	80,000	32,000
Land	80,000	30,000
Building—Cost	400,000	100,000
—Accum. depr.	(250,000)	(18,000)
Equipment—Cost	300,000	90,000
—Accum. depr.	(140,000)	(34,000)
	$700,000	$250,000

	P Company	S Company
Liabilities and stockholders' equity:		
Liabilities	$300,000	$190,000
Common stock	300,000	40,000
Retained earnings	100,000	20,000
	$700,000	$250,000

Decentralized accounting.   Under a decentralized accounting system, the individual assets acquired and liabilities assumed are recorded at their current values in a new general ledger maintained at the location of the acquired business. This location is usually referred to as a division of the acquiring company. The acquiring company, referred to as the home office, charges the cost of the acquired business to an account called Investment in Division. The entries are as follows:

Entry on home office books:

Investment in Division S	60,000	
Cash		60,000

Entry on Division S books:

Cash	20,000	
Accounts receivable	30,000	
Inventory..	32,000	
Land	30,000	
Building..	82,000	
Equipment	56,000	
Liabilities...		190,000
Home office		60,000

In reviewing these entries, the following points should be understood:

(1) Each asset and liability is recorded at its current value, which in this illustration coincides with its book value.
(2) The accumulated depreciation accounts relating to the fixed assets recorded on S Company's books do not carry over to the acquiring company. The current values of these assets are the new cost basis for P Company.
(3) At no time did P Company make any entries on S Company's books.
(4) After S Company records the receipt of the cash and the sale of its assets, its sole asset is $60,000 cash, which most likely will be distributed to its stockholders. S Company will then end its legal existence.
(5) From the acquisition date, division earnings are combined with the earnings of the home office. Any income statements presented by P Company for periods prior to the acquisition date will not include any preacquisition earnings of S Company.

Combined financial statements. Accounting for the subsequent operations of the newly established division is identical with the procedures discussed in Chapter 1 for branches. A combined balance sheet as of the acquisition date is prepared in the same manner as a combined balance sheet for a home office and a branch on the date that a branch is established. The entry to combine the two balance sheets as of the acquisition date is as follows:

(1) The primary elimination entry:

Home office 60,000
     Investment in Division S   60,000

Illustration 3-3 shows a combining statement worksheet, which combines the balance sheets of the home office and the newly established division as of the acquisition date.

Centralized accounting. Under a centralized accounting system, the acquiring company does not establish a separate general ledger at the location of the acquired business. Instead, it records the assets acquired and liabilities assumed directly in the general ledger maintained at its headquarters offices. In such situations, the preparation of combined financial statements through the use of the combining statement worksheet does not apply.

Illustration 3-3

	Home Office	Division	Eliminations Dr.	Eliminations Cr.	Combined
P COMPANY Combining Statement Worksheet As of January 1, 19X1					
Balance Sheet:					
Cash	50,000	20,000			70,000
Accounts receivable, net	120,000	30,000			150,000
Inventory	80,000	32,000			112,000
Investment in Division S.....	60,000			60,000(1)	-0-
Land	80,000	30,000			110,000
Building—Cost	400,000	82,000			482,000
—Accum. depr.	(250,000)				(250,000)
Equipment—Cost	300,000	56,000			356,000
—Accum. depr.	(140,000)				(140,000)
	700,000	250,000		60,000	890,000
Liabilities	300,000	190,000			490,000
Home office...............		60,000	60,000(1)		-0-
Common stock	300,000				300,000
Retained earnings	100,000				100,000
	700,000	250,000	60,000		890,000
Proof of debit and credit postings			60,000	60,000	

Explanation of entry:
  (1) The primary elimination entry.

Illustration:
Goodwill exists (Total cost is above current value of net assets) and net assets are undervalued

To illustrate recording the acquisition and preparing combined financial statements as of the acquisition date when cost is above current value and current value is above book value (Situation E of Illustration 3-2), we revise our assumptions of the previous illustration as follows:

(1) Total cost $90,000
(2) Current value of net assets................................. $80,000
(3) Book value of net assets...................................... $60,000
(4) The current values of S Company's assets and liabilities are assumed to equal their book values, except for the following assets:

	Book Value	Current Value	Current Value over Book Value
Inventory	$32,000	$36,000	$ 4,000
Land....................................	30,000	40,000	10,000
Building	82,000	88,000	6,000
			$20,000

Accordingly, $20,000 of the cost in excess of the book value of the net assets is attributable to these assets. The remaining $10,000 of cost in excess of the book value of the net assets represents goodwill.

Because goodwill is not deductible for income tax reporting purposes, acquiring companies often try to include in the acquisition agreement a tax-deductible feature known as a "covenant not-to-compete." Covenants not-to-compete are intangible assets similar to goodwill. Such a covenant prevents the target company from reentering the same line of business for a specified period of time.

Decentralized accounting.   Under a decentralized accounting system, the individual assets acquired and liabilities assumed are recorded in the new division's newly established general ledger at their current values. The entries are as follows:

Entry on home office books:

Investment in Division S	90,000	
Cash		90,000

Entry on Division S books:

Cash	20,000	
Accounts receivable	30,000	
Inventory......................................	36,000	
Land	40,000	
Building.......................................	88,000	
Equipment	56,000	
Goodwill	10,000	
Liabilities..		190,000
Home office		90,000

Combined financial statements. A combined balance sheet as of the acquisition date is prepared using the following entry:

(1) The primary elimination entry:

Home office 90,000
    Investment in Division S   90,000

Illustration 3-4 shows a combining statement worksheet, which combines the balance sheets of the home office and the division as of the acquisition date.

In reviewing Illustration 3-4, the following points should be understood:

(1) As in Illustration 3-3, the assets acquired and the liabilities assumed are recorded at their current values.
(2) No revaluation has been made of P Company's assets and liabilities that existed immediately before the acquisition date. They are stated at historical cost. Thus, the combined column includes some assets and liabilities recorded at historical cost and some at current values.

Centralized accounting. Under a centralized accounting system, the acquiring company records the assets acquired and liabilities assumed at their current values directly in the general ledger maintained at its own headquarters offices.

Illustration 3-4

	P COMPANY				
	Combining Statement Worksheet				
	As of January 1, 19X1				
	Home Office	Division	Eliminations Dr.	Eliminations Cr.	Combined
Balance Sheet:					
Cash	20,000	20,000			40,000
Accounts receivable, net	120,000	30,000			150,000
Inventory	80,000	36,000			116,000
Investment in Division S.....	90,000			90,000(1)	-0-
Land	80,000	40,000			120,000
Building—Cost	400,000	88,000			488,000
—Accum. depr.	(250,000)				(250,000)
Equipment—Cost	300,000	56,000			356,000
—Accum. depr.	(140,000)				(140,000)
Goodwill		10,000			10,000
	700,000	280,000		90,000	890,000
Liabilities	300,000	190,000			490,000
Home office...............		90,000	90,000(1)		-0-
Common stock	300,000				300,000
Retained earnings	100,000				100,000
	700,000	280,000	90,000		890,000
Proof of debit and credit postings			90,000	90,000	

Explanation of entry:
  (1) The primary elimination entry.

Illustration:
Bargain purchase element exists (Total cost is below current value of net assets) and net assets are undervalued

To illustrate recording the acquisition and preparing combined financial statements as of the acquisition date when cost is below current value and current value is above book value (Situation H of Illustration 3-2), we revise our assumptions of the previous illustration as follows:

(1) Total cost $75,000
(2) Current value of net assets.................................... $80,000
(3) Book value of net assets.. $60,000

The only change from the preceding situation is the lowering of the total cost from $90,000 to $75,000. Because the current value of the acquired business's assets is $80,000, a purchase price of $75,000 results in a bargain purchase element of $5,000.

Bargain purchase elements are treated arbitrarily under the provisions of *APB Opinion No. 16*. First, the bargain purchase element must be treated as a reduction of the current values assigned to any noncurrent assets acquired other than long-term investments in marketable securities. If the bargain purchase element is so large that the applicable noncurrent assets are reduced to zero (which rarely, if ever, happens), any remaining credit is recorded as a deferred credit and amortized to income over a period not more than 40 years. The rationale for attempting to eliminate the bargain purchase element is that the values assigned to the net assets as a whole should not exceed the purchase price paid. The purchase price constitutes cost under historical cost-based accounting. Were it not for this requirement, managements would have the opportunity to seek or use the highest possible appraisals for the assets to obtain the highest possible bargain purchase element. The high (artificial) bargain purchase element could then be amortized to income over a relatively short period of time in comparison with time periods assigned to the noncurrent assets. Thus, substantial opportunity for manipulating income would exist.

Because bargain purchase elements most frequently arise when the acquired business has recently experienced operating losses, this treatment results in a conservative valuation of the noncurrent assets other than long-term investments in marketable securities. This makes sense in that such noncurrent assets acquired from a company experiencing operating losses are subject to greater realization risks than if the target company had not experienced operating losses.

In this specific situation, the $5,000 bargain purchase element is allocated to the land, building, and equipment, using their relative current values, as shown below:

Appropriate Noncurrent Assets	Current Value[a]	Percentage to Total (Rounded)	Bargain Purchase Element	Percentage Times Bargain Purchase Element	Adjusted Current Value
Land	$ 40,000	22%	$5,000	$1,100	$ 38,900
Building........	88,000	48	5,000	2,400	85,600
Equipment	56,000	30	5,000	1,500	54,500
	$184,000	100%		$5,000	$179,000

[a] As given in the preceding illustration.

The entry to record the acquisition under a decentralized accounting system is as follows:

Entry on home office books:

Investment in Division S	75,000	
Cash		75,000

Entry on Division S books:

Cash	20,000	
Accounts receivable	30,000	
Inventory	36,000	
Land	38,900	
Building	85,600	
Equipment	54,500	
Liabilities		190,000
Home office		75,000

A combined balance sheet as of the acquisition date would be prepared in the same manner as shown in the preceding illustration; only the amounts would differ.

Some accountants incorrectly refer to an excess of current value over cost as *negative goodwill* rather than as a bargain purchase element. The use of this term is unfortunate and improper. Goodwill either does or does not exist; there is no such thing as a company having negative goodwill. We point this term out only because you may encounter it in practice.

ACQUISITION OF COMMON STOCK (WHOLLY OWNED SUBSIDIARY)

When common stock is acquired, the acquiring company charges its total cost to an account called Investment in Subsidiary. Assuming that the value of the consideration given by the acquiring company is $85,000 and direct costs incurred are $5,000 (that may be properly added to the cost of the acquisition), the entry to record the acquisition would be as follows:

Assuming $85,000 cash is the consideration given:

Investment in subsidiary	90,000	
Cash		90,000

Assuming 1,000 shares of $1 par value common stock (having a market value of $85,000) is the consideration given:

Investment in subsidiary	90,000	
Common stock		1,000
Additional paid-in capital		84,000
Cash		5,000

Note that if the common stock issued is registered with the SEC the following additional entry would be made for the additional direct costs incurred to register the common stock:

Additional paid-in capital   xxx
    Cash   xxx

When a parent–subsidiary relationship is established, the subsidiary retains its status as a separate legal entity. (Obviously, the subsidiary also retains ownership of its assets and responsibility for its liabilities.) The subsidiary cannot revalue its assets and liabilities to their current values merely because its outstanding common stock has changed hands and has become concentrated in the hands of significantly fewer or even a single stockholder. The obvious question, then, is: How are the subsidiary's assets and liabilities revalued to their current values as required under the purchase method of accounting? The answer requires an understanding of the major conceptual elements of the parent's total cost of the investment as reflected in its Investment in Subsidiary account.

Separating the total cost of the investment into major conceptual elements

The total cost of the investment as recorded on the parent's books must be separated into its major conceptual elements. We do this by analyzing the relationship existing among the total cost, the current value of the subsidiary's net assets, and the book value of the subsidiary's net assets. Assume the following information (Situation E of Illustration 3-2):

(1) P Company acquired all of S Company's outstanding common stock on January 1, 19X1.
(2) Total cost $90,000
(3) Current value of net assets $80,000
(4) Book value of net assets $60,000
(5) The current values of S Company's assets and liabilities are assumed to equal their book values, except for the following assets:

	Book Value	Current Value	Current Value over Book Value
Inventory	$32,000	$36,000	$ 4,000
Land	30,000	40,000	10,000
Building	82,000	88,000	6,000
			$20,000

Accordingly, $20,000 of the cost in excess of the book value of the net assets is attributable to these assets. The remaining $10,000 of cost in excess of the book value represents goodwill.

Thus, the total cost of the investment may be considered to comprise three major elements as follows:

(1) The book value element. The parent's ownership interest in the subsidiary's recorded net assets at their book value (100% of $60,000) $60,000

(2) The current value over book value element. The parent's ownership interest in the subsidiary's excess of the current value of its net assets over their book value (100% of $20,000) 20,000

(3) The goodwill element. The parent's total cost in excess of the current value of the subsidiary's net assets ($90,000 − $80,000)......................... <u>10,000</u>

Total cost of the investment .... <u>$90,000</u>

Thus, the $20,000 difference between the current value of the subsidiary's net assets and their book value is included in the parent's investment account. When the subsidiary's financial statements are combined with its parent's financial statements, this $20,000 difference is reclassified from the investment account to the specific assets with which it has been identified. (In this situation, $4,000 is identified with undervalued inventories, $10,000 is identified with undervalued land, and $6,000 is identified with an undervalued building.) The process of combining the financial statements of a parent and a subsidiary is called **consolidation,** which is discussed later in the chapter. The parent accounts for the individual items that make up this difference in the same manner that the subsidiary accounts for the specific assets that are undervalued.

The acquisition of assets—in which the assets acquired and liabilities assumed are recorded at their current values on the books of the acquiring company or its division—contrasts with parent–subsidiary situations in the following ways:

(1) The subsidiary continues to depreciate its assets at their historical cost as if the business combination had never occurred.
(2) The parent amortizes to its future income that portion of its cost in excess of book value that is attributable to depreciable or amortizable assets (in this example, $4,000 pertaining to the inventory and $6,000 pertaining to the building). The $4,000 amount relating to inventory is amortized to income as the subsidiary sells its inventory. The $6,000 amount relating to the building is amortized to income using the same remaining life that the subsidiary uses to depreciate its historical cost.
(3) The parent also amortizes that portion of its investment account that represents goodwill ($10,000 in this example).

In other words, with respect to the subsidiary's assets, depreciation and amortization take place on two sets of books instead of just one set, as when assets are acquired. These amortization procedures on the books of the parent company are necessary to charge the combined operations with the current value of the assets acquired, because the assets cannot be revalued on the subsidiary's books. In substance, the net effect on the enlarged business as a whole is the same as if the assets had been acquired instead of the common stock.

Illustration 3-5
Separating the total cost of the investment into major conceptual elements

Situation from Illustration 3-2 on page 74	Net Assets of Subsidiary		Current Value over (under) Book Value (3) (1) – (2)	Total Cost (4) (Given)	Separation of Total Cost into Its Major Conceptual Elements		
	Current Value (1) (Given)	Book Value (2) (Given)			Book Value Element (5) (2)	Current Value over (under) Book Value Element (6) (3)	Goodwill (Bargain Purchase Element) (7) (Residual)
I. Neither Goodwill nor a Bargain Purchase Element Exists—Total cost equals current value:							
A. Current value equals book value	$60,000	$60,000		$60,000 =	$60,000		
II. Goodwill Exists—Total cost is above current value:							
E. Current value is above book value	80,000	60,000	$20,000	90,000 =	60,000 +	$20,000 +	$10,000
F. Current value is below book value	50,000	60,000	(10,000)	55,000 =	60,000 +	(10,000) +	5,000
III. Bargain Purchase Element Exists—Total cost is below current value:							
H. Current value is above book value	80,000	60,000	20,000	75,000 =	60,000 +	20,000 +	(5,000)[a]

[a] This bargain purchase element must be allocated to noncurrent assets other than long-term investments. To the extent possible to noncurrent assets other than long-term investments. If all of it is allocated thus, then the amounts in the column to the left decrease by $5,000 and no deferred credit remains. (See Illustration 3-6, where all of it is allocated to the appropriate noncurrent assets.)

Illustrations:
Separating total cost of the investment
into major conceptual elements

Separating the total cost of the investment into its major conceptual elements is possible for any and all common stock investments, regardless of the price paid by the parent. In the discussion of the acquisition of net assets, three situations were presented, each with a different total cost and a different assumed current value for the net assets. Those three situations were:

(1) Neither Goodwill nor a Bargain Purchase Element Exists—Total cost equals current value of net assets (Situation A of Illustration 3-2). The total cost of $60,000 was equal to the current value of the subsidiary's net assets of $60,000, and current value was equal to the book value of the subsidiary's net assets.

(2) Goodwill Exists—Total cost is above current value of net assets (Situation E of Illustration 3-2). The total cost of $90,000 was above the current value of the subsidiary's net assets of $80,000, with certain assets undervalued. Goodwill of $10,000 was present.

(3) Bargain Purchase Element Exists—Total cost is below current value of net assets (Situation H of Illustration 3-2). The total cost of $75,000 was below the current value of the subsidiary's net assets of $80,000, with certain assets undervalued. A bargain purchase element of $5,000 was present.

Using these three situations—but assuming that all of the common stock was acquired instead of all of the assets—we would separate the total cost of the investment on the parent company's books into its major conceptual elements as shown in Illustration 3-5. In addition, Situation F of Illustration 3-2 (in which net assets are overvalued by $10,000) is shown. For simplicity, the entire overvaluation of net assets in this situation is assumed to apply to equipment. This situation does not involve any principles or procedures other than those discussed for situations in which the net assets are undervalued. It is shown only to demonstrate the conceptual view of overvalued assets.

In reviewing Illustration 3-5, the following points should be understood:

(1) In Situation A, only one major conceptual element exists because total cost equals current value and current value equals book value.

(2) In Situation E, all three major conceptual elements exist. If the total cost of the investment had been $10,000 less, no goodwill element and only two major conceptual elements would have existed.

(3) In Situation F, all three major conceptual elements exist, but the parent has a credit balance instead of a debit balance for its current value under book value element. This credit balance is identified with depreciable assets and is amortized in future periods to the parent's income statement, as are the debit balances in Situations E and H, which are identified with depreciable assets.

Displaying the major conceptual elements by their individual components

The analysis of the parent's total cost by major conceptual elements can be expanded so that the individual components of the book value element and the individual components of the current value over book value element are displayed. This expanded analysis can be used as the source of a journal entry that consolidates the financial statements of the parent with those of the subsidiary. Historically, the preparation of consolidated financial statements has been a somewhat involved process. However, the use of an expanded analysis of the total cost of the investment, **which displays the individual components of the major conceptual elements,** substantially simplifies the consolidation procedures. The procedures for expanding the analysis are explained below using Situation E of Illustration 3-5, in which total cost is above current value and current value is above book value.

Separating the book value element. This major conceptual element is easily separated into its individual components by multiplying the parent's ownership interest by the balance in each of the subsidiary's individual capital accounts—namely, Common Stock, Additional Paid-in Capital, and Retained Earnings—as of the acquisition date. The capital accounts of S Company as of the acquisition date are as follows:

Common stock	$40,000
Retained earnings	20,000
Total stockholders' equity	$60,000

Because we assume P Company acquires 100% of S Company's outstanding common stock, the $60,000 book value element comprises these two individual components.

Separating the current value over (under) book value element. As stated previously, the parent accounts for the individual components of the current value over (under) book value element—not for the total difference as a lump sum. Thus, the current value over (under) book value element can be thought of as comprising the following three components:

Inventory	$ 4,000
Land	10,000
Building	6,000
Total current value over book value	$20,000

The goodwill element and the bargain purchase element. No separation is needed for goodwill, which is a residual amount accounted for as a lump sum. When a bargain purchase element exists, the initial bargain purchase element credit must be allocated as much as possible to noncurrent assets other than long-term investments in marketable securities. Any remaining bargain purchase element is amortized to income in future periods.

Recap of conceptual elements. The analysis of the total investment cost as shown in Situation E of Illustration 3-5 is shown below by major conceptual elements and by the components of the major conceptual elements.

	Analysis of Total Investment Cost	
	By Major Conceptual Elements	By Components of Major Conceptual Elements
Book value element:		
Common stock		$40,000
Retained earnings		20,000
Total	$60,000	$60,000
Current value over book value element:		
Inventory		$ 4,000
Land		10,000
Building		6,000
Total	20,000	$20,000
Goodwill element	10,000	$10,000
Total cost...........................	$90,000	$90,000

In Illustration 3-6, the major conceptual elements for the situations in Illustration 3-5 are displayed by their individual components.

In reviewing Illustration 3-6, the following points should be understood:

(1) In Situation A, in which only the book value element exists, the parent has completed accounting for its investment under the purchase method of accounting. No additional accounting procedures are necessary because no other major conceptual elements exist.

(2) In Situations E and H, in which the current value of the net assets exceeds their book value and the parent pays more than the book value of the net assets, the amounts applicable to the building and equipment are amortized to the parent's future income over the remaining life of these assets, using the same remaining life that the subsidiary uses to depreciate these items. The amount determined for inventory is amortized in the following year, assuming the subsidiary sells its inventory. The amount determined for the land is not amortized because land is never depreciated. If the land is ever sold, the amount determined for land is charged to income at that time. In summary, the parent accounts for each individual component in a manner consistent with the way the subsidiary accounts for its historical cost. Goodwill is amortized over its expected life, up to 40 years.

(3) In Situation F, in which the current value of the net assets is below their book value, the parent has a credit amount instead of debit amounts to amortize to its subsequent income statements. Otherwise, the procedures are the same as in (2). The amortization partially offsets the depreciation expense recorded on the subsidiary's books from the viewpoint of combined operations.

(4) The expanded analysis of the investment account is maintained in a supporting schedule to the Investment in Subsidiary general ledger account.

Illustration 3-6
Displaying the major conceptual elements by their individual components

Situation from Illustration 3-2 on page 74	Total Cost =	Book Value Element		Current Value over (under) Book Value Element				Goodwill (Bargain Purchase) Element
		Common Stock +	Retained Earnings +	Inventory +	Land +	Building +	Equipment +	
I. Neither Goodwill nor a Bargain Purchase Element Exists—Total cost equals current value:								
A. Current value equals book value	$60,000 =	$40,000 +	$20,000					
II. Goodwill Exists—Total cost is above current value:								
E. Current value is above book value	90,000 =	40,000 +	20,000 +	$4,000 +	$10,000 +	$6,000		+ $10,000
F. Current value is below book value.......	55,000 =	40,000 +	20,000				+ $(10,000) +	5,000
III. Bargain Purchase Element Exists—Total cost is below current value:								
H. Current value is above book value	75,000 =	40,000 +	20,000 +	4,000 +	10,000 +	6,000		+ (5,000)^a
					(1,100)^a	(2,400)^a		5,000^a
	$75,000	$40,000	$20,000	$4,000	$ 8,900	$3,600	$ (1,500)	$ -0-

^{a} This allocation is the same as that illustrated previously in which assets were acquired at below their current value (page 80).

The next section discusses the preparation of consolidated financial statements—a process of combining the financial statements of the parent and the subsidiary (which is essentially the same as combining the financial statements of a home office and a division). The expanded analysis of the investment account illustrated in this section is used later in the chapter in the preparation of these consolidated financial statements.

CONSOLIDATED FINANCIAL STATEMENTS

Essence of consolidated financial statements

The process of preparing consolidated financial statements merely entails adding each of the balance sheet and income statement items of the parent and the subsidiary together on a worksheet. For the balance sheet, this is a substitution process whereby the asset and liability accounts of the subsidiary are substituted for the book value element of the parent's Investment in Subsidiary account. This substitution prevents the double counting of the subsidiary's net assets in arriving at the consolidated amounts. Combining the future income statements of a parent and a subsidiary is discussed in Chapter 4.

Purpose of consolidated statements

The purpose of consolidated financial statements is best expressed in *Accounting Research Bulletin No. 51:*

> The purpose of consolidated statements is to present, primarily for the benefit of the shareholders and creditors of the parent company, the results of operations and the financial position of a parent company and its subsidiaries essentially as if the group were a single company with one or more branches or divisions. There is a presumption that consolidated statements are more meaningful than separate statements and that they are usually necessary for a fair presentation when one of the companies in the group directly or indirectly has a controlling financial interest in the other companies.[8]

Consolidation policy

The decision whether or not to consolidate a subsidiary is governed by the policy set forth in *ARB No. 51:*

> The usual condition for a controlling interest is ownership of a majority voting interest, and, therefore, as a general rule ownership by one company, directly or indirectly, of over fifty percent of the outstanding voting shares of another company is a condition pointing toward consolidation. However, there are exceptions to this general rule. For example, a subsidiary should not be consolidated where control is likely to be temporary, or where it does not rest with the majority owners (as, for instance, where the subsidiary is in legal reorganization or in bankruptcy).[9]

---

[8]*ARB No. 51*, "Consolidated Financial Statements" (New York: AICPA, 1959), paragraph 1.
[9]*ARB No. 51*, paragraph 2.

ARB No. 51 also allows latitude in deciding on the consolidation policy when the nature of a subsidiary's business is substantially different from the parent company's. The criterion here is whether or not it would be more meaningful and informative to present the separate statements for a subsidiary (or combined statements for a group of subsidiaries) than to include such subsidiary (or subsidiaries) in consolidation. In this regard, the pronouncement states:

> Separate statements may be required for a subsidiary which is a bank or an insurance company and may be preferable for a finance company where the parent and the other subsidiaires are engaged in manufacturing operations.[10]

In practice, manufacturing companies usually exclude from consolidation insurance, banking, savings and loan, finance, and leasing subsidiaries. Financial statements for such subsidiaries are usually presented in notes to the consolidated financial statements (often in condensed form).

Some companies, however, do consolidate such subsidiaries. For example, Sears, Roebuck and Company consolidates (a) its Sears Roebuck Acceptance Corporation finance subsidiary; (b) its Allstate Insurance subsidiary; (c) its Allstate Savings and Loan subsidiary; (d) its Coldwell Banker real estate subsidiary; and (e) its Dean Witter financial services subsidiary.

In essence, *ARB No. 51* allows substantial latitude when there are different lines of business. In some cases, competing companies follow different consolidation policies as to their finance subsidiaries. Thus, comparability of financial statements is impaired for competing companies as well as noncompeting companies. As this book goes to print, the FASB is reexamining the consolidation policy of *ARB No. 51,* because it has been increasingly criticized in this respect. (The accounting to be followed for unconsolidated subsidiaries is discussed in Chapter 4 on page 118.)

Additional considerations for foreign subsidiaries are discussed in Chapter 13, "Translation of Foreign Currency Financial Statements."

The subsidiary's fiscal year-end should be within three months of the parent's year-end. If not, the subsidiary (or possibly even the parent) must change its fiscal year-end.

The parent must disclose its consolidation policy. A typical example of such disclosure in a note to the financial statements is as follows:

> The consolidated financial statements include the accounts of the company and its domestic and foreign subsidiaries. Significant intercompany accounts and transactions have been eliminated.

Limitations of consolidated financial statements

Consolidated financial statements have limited usefulness in assessing the future prospects of companies with significant diversified operations in more than one industry or significant foreign operations. In recognition of this fact, *FASB Statement No. 14,* "Financial Reporting for Segments of a Business Enterprise," was issued in 1976, requiring specified information on industry segments and foreign operations to be presented as supplementary in-

---

[10]*ARB No. 51,* paragraph 3.

formation to the consolidated financial statements. This pronouncement, which is discussed at length in Chapter 15, imposes extensive reporting requirements on companies with diversified or foreign operations.

The primary elimination entry

The consolidation is prepared by posting an elimination entry to a consolidating statement worksheet. The entry eliminates the Investment in Subsidiary account and the subsidiary's capital accounts, thus effecting the desired substitution. The entry is posted only to the worksheet and not to any general ledger account. (We call this entry the primary elimination entry for instructional and ease of reference purposes only. In later chapters, other types of elimination entries are encountered.) The source of the primary elimination entry is the expanded analysis of the Investment in Subsidiary account, which displays the individual components of the major conceptual elements.

The consolidating statement worksheet

Unless the business combination occurs on the last day of the parent's reporting year (which rarely happens), there is no need to prepare consolidated financial statements as of the acquisition date. They are illustrated in this chapter for instructional purposes only.

The balance sheet is the only financial statement of the subsidiary that can be consolidated with the parent's financial statement as of the acquisition date. This is a fundamental concept of the purchase method—that is, the parent company can report to its stockholders only the operations of the subsidiary that occur subsequent to the acquisition date.

Illustration:
Neither goodwill nor a bargain purchase element exists (Total cost equals current value of net assets) and net assets are not over- or undervalued

Before illustrating a consolidation of normal complexity involving a situation in which the total cost and the current value exceed the book value of the subsidiary's net assets, a simpler illustration is presented to highlight the substitution process that takes place in the consolidating statement worksheet.

Using the information in Situation A of Illustration 3-6 (in which the total cost of the investment equals the current value and the book value of the subsidiary's net assets), the expanded analysis of the total investment cost by individual components of the major conceptual elements as of the acquisition date is as follows:

| | Analysis of Total Investment Cost | | |
| | | Book Value Element | |
	Total Cost	Common Stock	Retained Earnings
Balance January 1, 19X1............................	$60,000 =	$40,000 +	$20,000

This expanded analysis is the source of the primary elimination entry, which effects the desired substitution. The total cost amount is a credit, and all other amounts in the analysis are debits. Consolidated financial statements as of the acquisition date are prepared using the following primary elimination entry:

Common stock 40,000
Retained earnings 20,000
    Investment in subsidiary 60,000

Illustration 3-7 shows a consolidating statement worksheet as of January 1, 19X1.

In reviewing Illustration 3-7, the following points should be understood:

(1) The primary elimination entry substitutes the subsidiary's assets and liabilities for the ownership interest in the net assets as represented by the Investment in Subsidiary account.
(2) The effect of the consolidation is to derive consolidated amounts that would have existed had the assets been acquired instead of the ownership interest in the assets. The amounts in the consolidated column are the same as the amounts in the combined column of Illustration 3-3, in which assets were acquired instead of common stock, except that the subsidiary has not offset its accumulated depreciation amounts against the historical cost of its assets as of the acquisition date. Theoretically,

Illustration 3-7

P COMPANY AND SUBSIDIARY (S COMPANY)
Consolidating Statement Worksheet
As of January 1, 19X1

	P Company	S Company	Eliminations Dr.	Eliminations Cr.	Consolidated
Balance Sheet:					
Cash	50,000	20,000			70,000
Accounts receivable, net	120,000	30,000			150,000
Inventory	80,000	32,000			112,000
Investment in S Company ...	60,000			60,000(1)	-0-
Land	80,000	30,000			110,000
Building—Cost	400,000	100,000			500,000
—Accum. depr.	(250,000)	(18,000)			(268,000)
Equipment—Cost	300,000	90,000			390,000
—Accum. depr.	(140,000)	(34,000)			(174,000)
	700,000	250,000		60,000	890,000
Liabilities	300,000	190,000			490,000
Common stock:					
P Company	300,000				300,000
S Company		40,000	40,000(1)		-0-
Retained earnings:					
P Company	100,000				100,000
S Company		20,000	20,000(1)		-0-
	700,000	250,000	60,000		890,000
Proof of debit and credit postings.................			60,000	60,000	

Explanation of entry:
  (1) The primary elimination entry.

this should be done to prepare consolidated financial statements, but in practice it usually is not done.

(3) The consolidating statement worksheet is not made available to the parent's stockholders—the consolidated amounts are used to prepare the consolidated balance sheet that is distributed to stockholders.

Illustration:
Goodwill exists (Total cost is above current value of net assets) and net assets are undervalued

Using the information from Situation E in Illustration 3-6 (in which cost is in excess of the current value of the subsidiary's net assets), the primary elimination entry as of the acquisition date is obtained directly from the expanded analysis of the total investment cost, which displays the individual components of the major conceptual elements. The entry is as follows:

Common stock	40,000	
Retained earnings	20,000	
Inventory	4,000	
Land	10,000	
Building	6,000	
Goodwill	10,000	
Investment in subsidiary		90,000

Illustration 3-8 shows the preparation of the consolidating statement worksheet as of the acquisition date using the above primary elimination entry.

In reviewing Illustration 3-8, the following points should be understood:

(1) The parent's investment cost in excess of the book value of the subsidiary's net assets "pops out" in the consolidation process. The excess is effectively reclassified to the balance sheet accounts with which it has been identified.
(2) The amounts in the consolidated column are composed of (a) the parent's items based on book values, and (b) the subsidiary's items based on the current value of those items as of the acquisition date.
(3) The amounts shown in the consolidated column are the same as those shown in the combined column of Illustration 3-4 (page 79), in which assets were acquired, except that the subsidiary has not eliminated its accumulated depreciation accounts. This theoretically should be done for consolidation purposes but usually is not done. Using the building as an example, the $88,000 current value shown in Illustration 3-4 is the equivalent of (a) the $82,000 book value shown in Illustration 3-8 ($100,000 cost less $18,000 accumulated depreciation), and (b) the $6,000 of undervaluation reported as a result of the consolidation process.

Illustration:
Goodwill exists (Total cost is above current value of net assets) but net assets are overvalued

When the current value of the net assets is below their book value, the consolidation procedures are the same as those illustrated for the case in which the current value is above the book value of the net assets, except

Illustration 3-8

P COMPANY AND SUBSIDIARY (S COMPANY) Consolidating Statement Worksheet As of January 1, 19X1					
	P Company	S Company	Eliminations		Consoli- dated
			Dr.	Cr.	
Balance Sheet:					
Cash	20,000	20,000			40,000
Accounts receivable, net	120,000	30,000			150,000
Inventory	80,000	32,000	4,000(1)		116,000
Investment in S Company . . .	90,000			90,000(1)	-0-
Land	80,000	30,000	10,000(1)		120,000
Building—Cost	400,000	100,000	6,000(1)		506,000
—Accum. depr.	(250,000)	(18,000)			(268,000)
Equipment—Cost	300,000	90,000			390,000
—Accum. depr. . . .	(140,000)	(34,000)			(174,000)
Goodwill			10,000(1)		10,000
	700,000	250,000	30,000	90,000	890,000
Liabilities	300,000	190,000			490,000
Common stock:					
P Company	300,000				300,000
S Company		40,000	40,000(1)		-0-
Retained earnings:					
P Company	100,000				100,000
S Company		20,000	20,000(1)		-0-
	700,000	250,000	60,000		890,000
Proof of debit and credit postings.			90,000	90,000	

Explanation of entry:
(1) The primary elimination entry.

that a net credit balance exists in the current value under book value section of the expanded analysis, which displays the individual components of the major conceptual elements. The extent of the credit balances depends on the current value of each asset and liability compared with its book value.

From the information in Situation F of Illustration 3-6 (in which the current value is below the book value of the net assets), the primary elimination entry at the acquisition date is as follows:

Common stock	40,000	
Retained earnings	20,000	
Goodwill	5,000	
Equipment		10,000
Investment in subsidiary		55,000

The preparation of consolidated financial statements for this situation is not shown, because the procedures are the same as for situations in which the current value is above the book value of the net assets.

Dealing with over- or undervalued liabilities

For simplicity, the previous discussions and illustrations dealt only with certain under- and overvalued assets. The current values of accounts payable and accrued liabilities (using present value procedures) are usually so close to their book values—because of the relatively short period until payment of the obligation—that the difference is often ignored in the interest of practicality. The current value of borrowings that have a floating interest rate always equals the book value. If the borrowings have a fixed interest rate that is different from the interest rate existing at the acquisition date, however, the present value of the debt does not equal its book value. Thus, the difference must be reflected as one of the components of the current value over (under) book value element in the conceptual analysis of the Investment in Subsidiary account. For example, assume that a subsidiary has 8% bonds payable outstanding at the acquisition date. If the current interest rate is 12%, the present value of the debt is below the book value. (The low fixed interest rate of 8% in relation to the current interest rate of 12% means that the debt appears larger than it really is.)

Reporting the debt at its present value.   To illustrate, assume that on the January 1, 19X1, acquisition date, the subsidiary has 8% bonds outstanding having a face amount of $100,000 and a maturity date of December 31, 19X2 (two years from now). If the current interest rate is 12%, the present value of the bonds would be calculated as follows:

Present value of $100,000 principal payment
  due December 31,19X2
  ($100,000 × 0.79719) $79,719
Present value of two $8,000 interest
  payments due at the end of 19X1 and 19X2
  ($8,000 × 1.69005).. 13,520
    Total $93,239

Accordingly, the $6,761 difference between the book value of the bonds ($100,000) and the present value ($93,239) would be reflected as an individual component of the current value over (under) book value element. If consolidated financial statements were prepared as of the acquisition date, the bonds would be reported in the consolidated column at their present value of $93,239 because the $6,761 amount would be debited to the Bonds Payable account in consolidation, as shown below:

	P Company	S Company	Eliminations Dr.	Cr.	Consoli- dated
Bonds payable		100,000	6,761		93,239

Subsequent treatment of the difference.   The $6,761 amount is analogous to a discount and would be amortized to interest expense over the next two years using the "interest method" of amortization. Over the next two years, interest expense would be reported at 12% of the debt's carrying value (instead of at 8% of the book value of $100,000). For 19X1, interest expense of $11,190 would be reported (12% × $93,239), and the $3,190 difference between the $11,190 and the $8,000 cash payment would be amortized out of the Investment account. At December 31, 19X1, this individual component of the Investment account would have an unamortized balance of $3,571, which results in a $96,429 carrying value of the debt in consolidation at that date. For 19X2, interest expense of $11,571 would be reported (12% × $96,429), which is made up of the $8,000 cash payment and $3,571 amortized out of the Investment account. In the following chapter, we show the actual mechanics of amortizing amounts out of the Investment account.

DISCLOSURES

Basic disclosures

The acquiring company must make the following footnote disclosures for each period in which a business combination is accounted for under the purchase method:

(1) The name and brief description of the acquired business.
(2) A statement that the purchase method has been used to record the combination.
(3) The period for which the results of operations of the acquired business are included in the acquiring company's income statement. (This period is from the acquisition date to the acquiring entity's reporting year-end, except for situations involving a subsidiary that has a reporting year-end different from the parent company's.)
(4) The cost of the acquired business, including information about the number of shares issued, issuable, and their assigned value.
(5) The life and method of amortizing any goodwill.
(6) Contingent consideration, if any, and the related proposed accounting treatment.[11]

Following is an example of this basic disclosure for an acquiring company having a calendar year-end:

> On July 1, 19X1, the Pana Company acquired all of the outstanding common stock of Sonic Corporation, a manufacturer of small computers. The acquisition has been accounted for as a purchase; therefore, the results of operations of the acquired business for the period from July 1, 19X1, through December 31, 19X1, are included in the consolidated income statement of the Pana Company. The recorded cost of the acquisition was $5,200,000 (50,000 common shares issued times their then fair market value of $100 per share, plus legal and finders' fees of $200,000). Goodwill of $1,000,000 is being amortized over 40 years using the straight-line method. Additional common shares are issuable (a maximum of 100,000 shares), depending on the cumulative sales level of the acquired business for the three years subsequent to the acquisition date. If and when any or all of these contingent shares are distributable (June 30, 19X4), the current value of the shares issuable will be recorded as an additional cost of the acquired business, which will increase goodwill. As of December

[11] APB Opinion No. 16, paragraph 95.

31, 19X1, no additional shares would be issuable based on the sales level of the acquired business for the six months then ended.

Supplemental disclosures required for publicly owned companies

In addition to basic footnote disclosures, certain information related to income statements (including revenues, net income, and earnings per share, among other items) must be disclosed by publicly owned companies as supplemental information for the following periods:

(1) Such income statement-related information that would have resulted had the combination occurred at the beginning of the current reporting period.
(2) Such income statement-related information that would have resulted had the combination occurred at the beginning of the preceding reporting period.[12]

Obviously, this supplemental disclosure notifies readers of the financial statements that some percentage of the change in revenues and net income is the result of external expansion, not just the result of internal expansion.

Following is an example of a supplemental disclosure that relates to the preceding example of basic disclosure:

Results of operations of the Pana Company combined on a pro forma basis with the operating results of Sonic Corporation for the years ended December 31, 19X1, and 19X0, as if the companies had been combined at January 1, 19X0, are as follows:

	19X1	19X0
Revenues	$53,500,000	$26,750,000
Net income	2,400,000	1,400,000
Net income per common and common equivalent share	$2.47	$1.27

Acquisition near beginning of the year.   When an acquisition occurs near the beginning of the acquiring company's reporting year, it may include the operations of the acquired business from the beginning of the current reporting year to the acquisition date, and also show as a deduction in the income statement an amount equal to the net income for these operations for this period. Assume the following information for a business acquired on March 1, 19X1 (two months after the beginning of the acquiring company's current reporting period):

	Jan. 1–Feb. 28, 19X1	Mar. 1–Dec. 31, 19X1
Revenues	$15,000	$110,000
Cost of goods sold	(9,000)	(66,000)
Expenses	(4,000)	(33,000)
Net income	$ 2,000	$ 11,000

[12] *APB Opinion No. 16*, paragraph 96. (*FASB Statement No. 79*, "Elimination of Certain Disclosures for Business Combinations by Nonpublic Enterprises," amended *APB Opinion No. 16* in 1984 by exempting nonpublic enterprises from the disclosure requirements of paragraph 96 of *APB Opinion No. 16*.)

The acquiring company automatically includes the operations of the acquired business from March 1, 19X1 through December 31, 19X1, with its own operations—this is a fundamental concept of the purchase method of accounting. The acquiring company may disclose the operations of the acquired business for January 1, 19X1 through February 28, 19X1, as supplemental information (as previously explained) or, using the more practical approach, include the following accounts and amounts with its own operations for the entire year:

Revenues	$125,000
Cost of goods sold	(75,000)
Expenses	(37,000)
Subtotal	$ 13,000
Less—Preacquisition earnings	(2,000)
Net Income	$ 11,000

This approach allows the acquiring entity to bypass the supplemental disclosure requirement for the current reporting year, but it does not violate the basic principle of purchase accounting—namely, **preacquisition earnings are not reportable as part of an acquiring company's operations.**

SUMMARY

Under the purchase method of accounting, the acquisition of either assets or common stock results in a revaluation of the assets and liabilities of the acquired business to their current values. When assets are acquired, the assets acquired and liabilities assumed are recorded at their current values directly in the books of the acquiring company or, if decentralized accounting is used, in the books of the newly established division. When common stock is acquired, however, the subsidiary cannot revalue its assets and liabilities to their current values, because it is still a separate legal entity and must comply with historical cost-based accounting principles. The revaluation of a subsidiary's assets and liabilities to their current values takes place when consolidated financial statements are prepared. Before consolidated financial statements can be prepared, the parent company must conceptually analyze the total cost of its investment in the subsidiary to determine how much of the total cost relates to under- or overvaluation of the subsidiary's net assets. The process of preparing consolidated financial statements for a parent and a subsidiary is essentially the same as preparing combined financial statements for a home office and a division.

Glossary of new terms

Bargain Purchase Element: The amount by which the total cost of the investment is below the current value of an acquired business's net assets.

Consolidation: The process of combining the financial statements of a parent and one or more subsidiaries, so that results of operations and financial position are presented as if the separate companies were a single company with one or more divisions or branches.

Contingent Consideration: Consideration that must be paid if certain future conditions are satisfied.

Controlling Interest: In general, a controlling interest exists when one company owns, either directly or indirectly, more than 50% of the outstanding voting shares of another company.

Appendix
PUSH-DOWN ACCOUNTING THEORY   *not in operation yet.*

What is it?   The push-down accounting theory maintains that the subsidiary should adjust its assets and liabilities to their current values and record any goodwill at the acquisition date, regardless of whether the parent company acquires assets or common stock. Thus, the subsidiary's net assets (as adjusted) would equal the balance in the parent company's Investment in Subsidiary account. This procedure would negate the need to (a) analyze the investment account by its individual components, and (b) make amortization entries on the parent company's books. The end result is that the consolidation process would be substantially simplified, because the primary elimination entry in all cases would be as follows:

```
Common stock ..............................................  xxx
Additional paid-in capital (if present) ...........................  xxx
Retained earnings ...........................................  xxx
    Investment in subsidiary ...................................        xxx
```

The consolidated financial statements still would be identical to those prepared when the subsidiary does not revalue its assets and liabilities at the acquisition date. Furthermore, the subsidiary's separate financial statements would be presented under this push-down accounting basis. Retained earnings as of the acquisition date would not be reported.

The rationale behind it.   The rationale for having the subsidiary adjust its assets and liabilities to their current values as of the acquisition date rests on a substance over form argument. Advocates of push-down accounting contend that the relevant factor is the acquisition itself, not the form of consummating the acquisition. Whether the parent company acquires assets or common stock is irrelevant. Recall that when assets are acquired, the individual assets and liabilities are revalued to their current values when they are recorded in the acquiring company's general ledger (or in the division's general ledger if decentralized accounting is used). With the acquisition itself being the relevant factor, a new basis of accounting has been established for the assets and liabilities. Merely because common stock is acquired instead of assets should not prevent this new basis of accounting from being reflected at the subsidiary level.

The SEC's position.   Push-down accounting had not gained significant acceptance or use prior to 1983. In 1983, the Securities and Exchange Commission required its use in the separate financial statements of a subsidiary acquired in a purchase transaction. The impetus for this position stemmed from the substantial number of subsidiaries that issued stock to the public in recent years based on financial statements that did not reflect push-down accounting. As a result, subsidiaries were not reporting their true cost of doing business, and their earnings were overstated. (When a significant minority interest, preferred stock, or outstanding public debt exists, the SEC encourages push-down accounting but does not require it.)[13]

Concluding comments.   As this book goes to print, the FASB is addressing the appropriateness of push-down accounting in connection with its project on consolidations and the equity method of accounting.

Review questions

1. What is the essence of the purchase method of accounting?
2. What two basic questions must be answered with respect to the purchase method of accounting?
3. What types of consideration can the acquiring entity give in a business combination?
4. When is it preferable in recording a business combination to use the fair value of the equity securities issued instead of the current value of the net assets of the acquired business?
5. How should direct costs incurred in a business combination be treated?
6. What is contingent consideration and how should it be accounted for?
7. What are the three major conceptual elements into which the total cost of an investment could possibly be separated?
8. In which situations would only one major conceptual element exist? In which situation would only two major conceptual elements exist?
9. What is the purpose of separating the total cost of the investment into the individual components of the major conceptual elements?
10. Why is there no separate account for goodwill on the parent company's books?
11. Why are consolidated financial statements necessary?
12. What is the usual condition for a controlling interest?
13. What is the distinction between the basic disclosures and the supplemental disclosures required for business combinations accounted for under the purchase method of accounting?
14. How are preacquisition earnings of an acquired business treated under the purchase method of accounting?

Discussion cases

Discussion case 3–1
Treatment of Goodwill

You are the controller of a company that has recently acquired a business that has substantial goodwill. In determining if the treatment prescribed by *APB Opinion No. 17*, "Intangible Assets," presents your company's financial statements fairly,

[13]*Staff Accounting Bulletin No. 54* (Washington, D.C.: SEC, 1983).

you discover that the APB considered the following alternatives prior to its issuance of *APB Opinion No. 17:*

(1) Allow goodwill to be reported as a "permanent" asset, with no amortization required unless impairment occurred.
(2) Require goodwill to be amortized.
(3) Require goodwill to be charged to stockholders' equity of the acquiring company at the acquisition date.

Required:
(1) Briefly evaluate the soundness of each of these alternatives.
(2) For alternative (2), evaluate the soundness of allowing up to 40 years to amortize goodwill.

Discussion case 3–2
Manner of reporting "cost in excess of net assets"

The December 31, 1983, consolidated balance sheet of Kidde, Inc. has the following described asset:

Excess of cost over related net assets
of businesses acquired $86,102,000

The related footnote reads as follows:

> The excess of cost over related net assets applicable to businesses acquired prior to November 1, 1970 amounts to $11,000,000 and is not amortized, as it is believed to have continuing value; the balance applicable to businesses acquired after October 31, 1970, is being amortized on a straight-line basis over forty years.

Required:
(1) Is the title of the asset accurate?
(2) Is the title of the asset informative?
(3) What does the asset represent?
(4) What is the theoretical justification for amortizing only part of this amount?

Discussion case 3–3
Treatment of bargain purchase element

You are the CPA for a company that has recently acquired all of the assets of another company at an amount below their current value. The controller has indicated to you that the bargain purchase element will be accounted for in one of the following ways:

(1) Credit it to income in the year of the acquisition, possibly classified as an extraordinary item.
(2) Amortize it to income over the two-year period needed to turn the acquired operation into a profit-making operation.

(3) Allocate it to the acquired assets based on relative current values, thereby lowering the recorded values of these items.

(4) Credit it to contributed capital.

Required:

How would you respond to these proposed treatments? Be sure to evaluate the theoretical soundness of each alternative regardless of the requirements of *APB Opinion No. 16.*

Discussion case 3–4
Treatment of cost in excess of book value
of acquired subsidiary's net assets

Proctor Company, a highly diversified company, acquired all of the outstanding common stock of three companies during the current year. In each case, Proctor Company's total cost was $100,000 in excess of book value of the net assets. The reason for paying in excess of book value of the net assets of each company is stated below:

(1) Acquisition of Digger Company. Digger mines iron ore from land it owns. Proctor acquired Digger to assure itself a continual supply of iron ore for its steel-making operation.

(2) Acquisition of Chipo Company. Chipo manufactures high-quality memory chips for computers. Few companies can manufacture high-quality memory chips of this type. Proctor acquired Chipo to assure itself of a continual supply of high-quality memory chips for its computer manufacturing operation.

(3) Acquisition of Tracto Company. Tracto Company manufactures farm machinery. Tracto earns a return on investment that is average for its industry. On this basis, Tracto was not worth acquiring. Proctor, however, feels it can bring about substantial efficiencies by integrating Tracto's operations with the operations of another subsidiary, which manufactures farm machinery. The combined results are expected to increase substantially the overall return on investment of each previously separate operation.

Required:

For each of these acquisitions, determine how you would classify the cost in excess of book value and how you would account for the cost in excess of book value in future-period consolidated financial statements.

Exercises

Exercise 3–1
Recording acquisition of assets for cash—Division

Pettle Company acquired all of the assets (except cash) and assumed all of the liabilities of Stemco Company for $1,200,000 cash. The acquired business is to be accounted for as a division with a decentralized accounting system. The assets and liabilities of Stemco Company as of the acquisition date are as follows:

	Book Value	Current Value
Cash	$ 50,000	$ 50,000
Accounts receivable, net	60,000	60,000
Inventory	90,000	100,000
Land	100,000	200,000
Building—Cost	800,000	820,000
—Accum. depr.	(200,000)	
Equipment—Cost	400,000	250,000
—Accum. depr.	(300,000)	
	$1,000,000	$1,480,000
Accounts payable and accruals	$ 100,000	$ 100,000
Long term debt	300,000	300,000
	$ 400,000	$ 400,000
Net assets	$ 600,000	$1,080,000

Required:

(1) Prepare the entry to record the acquisition on the books of the home office and on the books of the newly formed division.
(2) How would the entries be different if the accounting for the acquired business were centralized?

Exercise 3–2
Recording acquisition of assets for stock—Division

Assume the same information as in Exercise 3–1, except that Pettle Company issued 10,000 shares of its common stock ($10 par value), which was selling for $120 per share at the acquisition date, instead of giving cash to effect the business combination.

$$10\,000 * \$10 = \$100\,000 \quad CS$$
$$10\,000 * 110 = 1,100,000 \quad APIC$$

Required:

(1) Prepare the entry to record the acquisition on the books of the home office and on the newly formed division.
(2) How would the entries be different if the accounting for the acquired business were centralized?

Exercise 3–3
Recording acquisition of common stock for cash and stock

P Company acquired 100% of the outstanding common stock of S Company for $1,500,000 cash and 10,000 shares of its common stock ($10 par value), which was traded at $60 per share at the acquisition date.

$$10\,000 * 60 = 600,000$$
$$600 \quad 1500 \quad 2100$$

Required:

Prepare the entry to record the business combination on P Company's books.

Exercise 3–4
Recording direct costs

Assume the same information provided in Exercise 3–3. In addition, assume P Company incurred the following direct costs:

Legal fees, relating to preparing the acquisition agreement ...... *ok*	$ 30,000
Accounting fees, relating to the purchase investigation .... *ok*	20,000
Travel expenses, relating to meetings held with management of S Company...	10,000
Legal fees, relating to registering the common stock issued with the SEC .... *ok*	25,000
Accounting fees, relating to the review of unaudited financial statements and other data included in the registration statement .... *ok*	15,000
SEC filing fees.. *ok*	2,000
	$102,000

As of the acquisition date, $88,000 has been paid and charged to a Deferred Charges account. The remaining $14,000 has not been paid or accrued.

Required:
Prepare the journal entry to record the business combination and the direct costs.

Exercise 3–5
Contingent consideration based on future sales

Pam Company acquired all of the outstanding common stock of Sam Company for $1,000,000 cash. If the cumulative sales of Sam Company for the three years subsequent to the acquisition date exceed $10,000,000, then additional cash of $200,000 is to be paid to the former shareholders of Sam Company.

Required:
Prepare the entry to record the business combination. Explain the accounting treatment of the contingent consideration.

Exercise 3–6
Contingent consideration based on future earnings

Assume the same information provided in Exercise 3–5, except that the additional cash contingently payable is payable only if the cumulative earnings of Sam Company for the three years subsequent to the acquisition date exceed $2,000,000.

Required:
Prepare the entry to record the business combination. Be sure to explain the accounting treatment of the contingent consideration.

Exercise 3–7
Contingent consideration based on future security prices—
Existing security price to be maintained

Parton Company acquired all of the outstanding common stock of Sargo Company by issuing 80,000 shares of its common stock ($10 par value), which had a market value of $40 per share at the acquisition date. If the market value of Parton Company's common stock is below $40 per share two years after the acquisition date, then Parton Company must issue additional shares at that time to the former shareholders of Sargo Company so that the total value of the shares issued equals $3,200,000.

Required:
Note: You may want to review paragraphs 81 and 82 of *APB Opinion No. 16* before solving.

(1) Prepare the entry to record the business combination. Explain the accounting treatment of the contingent consideration.
(2) Assume the market value of Parton Company's common stock is $32 per share two years later. Prepare the entry to record the additional shares issued.

Exercise 3–8
Contingent consideration based on future security prices—
Higher security price to be attained

Pane Company acquired all of the outstanding common stock of Shane Company by issuing 60,000 shares of its common stock ($5 par value), which had a market value of $50 per share as of the acquisition date. If the market value of Pane Company's common stock is not at least $70 per share two years after the acquisition date, then additional shares must be issued to the former shareholders of Shane Company so that the total value of the shares issued equals $4,200,000.

Inv. in Shane Co. 60 000 × 50 .... 3000 000
Required:
Com. Stock 300 000
APIC 2,700,000
Note: You may want to review paragraphs 81 and 82 of *APB Opinion No. 16* before solving.

(1) Prepare the entry to record the business combination. Explain the accounting treatment of the contingent consideration.
(2) Assume the market value of Pane Company's common stock is $60 per share two years later. Prepare the entry to record the additional shares issued.

Inv in Shane Co. (20000 shares) 1200000
Com. Str 100,000
APIC 1,100,000

Exercise 3–9
Acquisition of common stock: Separating total cost
into major conceptual elements—Cost is above current value
and book value of net assets

Pump Company acquired all of the outstanding common stock of Sump Company at a total cost of $1,000,000. Sump Company's net assets have a book value of $700,000 and a current value of $900,000 as of the acquisition date.

Required:
Separate the total cost of the investment into its major conceptual elements as of the acquisition date.

Exercise 3–10
Acquisition of common stock: Separating total cost
into major conceptual elements—Cost is below current value
but above book value of net assets

Pun Company acquired 100% of the outstanding common stock of Sun Company, a manufacturing company with extensive manufacturing facilities, at a total cost of $2,000,000. The net assets of Sun Company have a book value of $1,500,000 and a current value of $2,200,000 as of the acquisition date.

Required:
Separate the total cost of the investment into its major conceptual elements as of the acquisition date.

Exercise 3–11
Acquisition of common stock: Separating total cost
into individual components of the major conceptual elements—
Cost is above current value and book value of net assets

Pert Company acquired all of the outstanding common stock of Sernie Company for $800,000 cash. (Assume there were no direct costs or contingent consideration.) Information with respect to Sernie Company as of the acquisition date is as follows:

	Book Value	Current Value
Cash	$ 50,000	$ 50,000
Accounts receivable, net	100,000	100,000
Inventory	200,000	210,000
Land	300,000	420,000
Building, net	400,000	480,000
Equipment, net	150,000	200,000
Total assets	$1,200,000	$1,460,000
Accounts payable and accruals	$ 100,000	$ 100,000
Long-term debt	600,000	625,000
Total liabilities	$ 700,000	$ 725,000
Common stock	$ 50,000	
Additional paid-in capital	300,000	
Retained earnings	150,000	
Total stockholders' equity	$ 500,000	735,000
Total liabilities and equity	$1,200,000	$1,460,000

Required:
(1) Separate the total cost of the investment into the individual components of the major conceptual elements as of the acquisition date.
(2) Explain why the current value of the long-term debt is greater than its book value.

Exercise 3–12
Calculation of goodwill

On April 1, 19X6, Prince Company paid $400,000 for all the issued and outstanding common stock of Sauper Corporation in a transaction properly accounted for as a purchase. The assets and liabilities of Sauper Corporation on April 1, 19X6, are as follows:

Cash..	$ 40,000
Inventory	120,000
Property and equipment (net of accumulated depreciation of $160,000)...	240,000
Liabilities	(90,000)

On April 1, 19X6, the current value of Sauper's inventory was determined to be $95,000, and its property and equipment (net) had a current value of $280,000.

Required:
What amount should Prince record as goodwill as a result of the business combination?

(a) 0
(b) $25,000
(c) $75,000
(d) $90,000

(AICPA adapted)

Problems

Problem 3–1
Acquisition of common stock: Separating total cost into individual components of the major conceptual elements— Cost is above current value of net assets and current value is above book value

Philip Company acquired all of the outstanding stock of Sarlowe Company for $1,600,000 cash. Information with respect to Sarlowe Company as of the acquisition date is as follows:

	Book Value	Current Value	
Cash	$ 20,000	$ 20,000	
Accounts receivable, net	80,000	70,000	<10,000>
Notes receivable	100,000	85,000	<15000>
Inventory	200,000	220,000	20000
Land	400,000	600,000	200,000
Building, net	450,000	690,000	240000
Equipment, net	150,000	210,000	60000
Patent..	20,000	105,000	85000
Goodwill	80,000	See (1) Following	
Total assets....................................	$1,500,000		
Accounts payable and accruals	$ 200,000	$200,000	
Long-term debt.......................................	500,000	475,000	<25000>
Deferred income taxes	100,000	See (2) Following	<25000>
Total liabilities	$ 800,000		
Common stock	$ 100,000		
Additional paid-in capital	400,000		
Retained earnings	200,000		
Total stockholders' equity.................	$ 700,000		
Total liabilities and equity.................	$1,500,000		

(1) The $80,000 of goodwill arose from Sarlowe Company's acquisition two years ago of the net assets of a local competitor. The goodwill is being amortized over 10 years. During the negotiations with Philip Company, the management of Sarlowe Company indicated that these acquired operations have produced superior earnings since acquisition, which are expected to continue for at least another eight years. (Refer to paragraph 88 of *APB Opinion No. 16* for treatment.)

(2) The deferred income taxes relate to accelerated depreciation on the building for income tax purposes. (Refer to paragraphs 88 and 89 of *APB Opinion No. 16* for treatment.)

Required:

(1) For other than existing goodwill and deferred income taxes, what procedures and guidelines are used to determine current values of assets acquired and liabilities assumed? (Refer to paragraphs 87 and 88 of *APB Opinion No. 16*.)

(2) Separate the total investment cost into the individual components of the major conceptual elements as of the acquisition date.

Problem 3–2
Acquisition of common stock: Separating total cost into individual components of the major conceptual elements— Cost is below current value of net assets and current value is above book value

Pointer Company acquired all of the outstanding common stock of Setter Company for $450,000 cash. Information with respect to Setter Company as of the acquisition date is as follows:

	Book Value	Current Value
Cash	$ 10,000	$ 10,000
Accounts receivable, net	20,000	20,000
Inventory	150,000	170,000
Land	90,000	150,000
Building, net	220,000	400,000
Equipment, net	210,000	250,000
Total assets	$700,000	$1,000,000
Accounts payable and accruals	$ 50,000	$ 50,000
Long-term debt	400,000	400,000
Total liabilities	$450,000	$ 450,000
Common stock	$ 10,000	
Additional paid-in capital	190,000	
Retained earnings	50,000	
Total stockholders' equity	$250,000	550,000
Total liabilities and equity	$700,000	$1,000,000

Required:

Separate the total cost of the investment into the individual components of the major conceptual elements as of the acquisition date.

Problem 3–3
Acquisition of common stock: Separating total cost
into individual components of the major conceptual elements—
Cost is below current value of net assets
and current value is below book value

Paddle Company acquired all of the outstanding common stock of Saddle Company for $65,000 cash. Information with respect to Saddle Company, which leases its manufacturing facilities and is in poor financial condition as of the acquisition date, is as follows:

	Book Value	Current Value
Cash	$ 5,000	$ 5,000
Accounts receivable, net	245,000	245,000
Inventory	400,000	380,000
Equipment, net	50,000	40,000
Total assets	$700,000	$670,000
Accounts payable and accruals	$350,000	$350,000
Long-term debt	200,000	200,000
Total liabilities	$550,000	$550,000
Common stock	$100,000	
Additional paid-in capital	400,000	
Accumulated deficit	(350,000)	
Total stockholders' equity	$150,000	120,000
Total liabilities and equity	$700,000	$670,000

Required:
Separate the total investment cost into the individual components of the major conceptual elements as of the acquisition date.

Problem 3–4
Acquisition of common stock: Preparing consolidated
financial statements—Cost equals current value of net assets
and current value equals book value

Post Company, which is a calendar-year reporting company, acquired all of the outstanding common stock of Script Company at a total cost of $800,000 (an amount equal to the current value and book value of Script Company's net assets) on December 31, 19X1. The financial statements of each company for the year ended December 31, 19X1, immediately after the acquisition are as follows:

	Post Company	Script Company
Income Statement (19X1):		
Sales	$10,000,000	$ 900,000
Cost of goods sold	(6,000,000)	(500,000)
Marketing expenses	(2,000,000)	(180,000)
Administrative expenses	(1,000,000)	(140,000)
Income tax expense @ 40%	(400,000)	(32,000)
Net Income	$ 600,000	$ 48,000

	Post Company	Script Company
Balance Sheet as of December 31, 19X1:		
Cash..	$ 1,000,000	$ 200,000
Accounts receivable, net	2,000,000	300,000
Inventory	1,200,000	600,000
Fixed assets, net..................................	7,000,000	900,000
Investment in Script Company	800,000	
	$12,000,000	$2,000,000
Accounts payable and accruals	$ 1,500,000	$ 450,000
Long-term debt	2,500,000	750,000
Common stock.....................................	1,000,000	100,000
Additional paid-in capital	2,000,000	400,000
Retained earnings	5,000,000	300,000
	$12,000,000	$2,000,000

Required:
(1) Prepare the primary elimination entry as of December 31, 19X1.
(2) Prepare a consolidating statement worksheet at December 31, 19X1.

Problem 3–5
Acquisition of common stock: Preparing consolidated
financial statements—Cost is above current value of net assets
and current value is above book value

Peanut Company, which is a calendar-year reporting company, acquired all of the outstanding common stock of Shell Company at a total cost of $250,000 on December 31, 19X1. The analysis of Peanut Company's investment in Shell Company by the individual components of the major conceptual elements as of the acquisition date is as follows:

Book value element:	
Common stock..	$ 50,000
Retained earnings	75,000
Current value over (under) book value element:	
Inventory	2,000
Land..	28,000
Building	20,000
Patent	15,000
Goodwill element..	60,000
Total cost	$250,000

The financial statements of each company for the year ended December 31, 19X1, immediately after the acquisition are as follows:

	Peanut Company	Shell Company
Income Statement (19X1):		
Sales..	$1,500,000	$450,000
Cost of goods sold	(800,000)	(240,000)
Marketing expenses	(200,000)	(95,000)
Administrative expenses...................................	(250,000)	(75,000)
Income before Income Taxes	$ 250,000	$ 40,000
Income tax expense @ 40%............................	(100,000)	(16,000)
Net Income	$ 150,000	$ 24,000
Balance Sheet (as of December 31, 19X1):		
Cash	$ 250,000	$ 18,000
Accounts receivable, net	350,000	32,000
Inventory	450,000	65,000
Land	600,000	105,000
Building—Cost	1,100,000	100,000
—Accum. depr.	(300,000)	(20,000)
Equipment—Cost	500,000	30,000
—Accum. depr.	(200,000)	(15,000)
Patent...		10,000
Investment in Shell Company	250,000	
	$3,000,000	$325,000
Accounts payable and accruals	$ 350,000	$ 50,000
Long-term debt......................................	850,000	150,000
Common stock	250,000	50,000
Additional paid-in capital	1,250,000	
Retained earnings	300,000	75,000
	$3,000,000	$325,000

Required:
(1) Prepare the primary elimination entry as of December 31, 19X1.
(2) Prepare a consolidating statement worksheet at December 31, 19X1.

Problem 3–6
Acquisition of common stock: Preparing consolidated financial statements—Cost is equal to current value of net assets and current value is below book value

Poppy Company, which is a calendar-year reporting company, acquired all of the outstanding common stock of Seed Company, at a total cost of $350,000 on December 31, 19X1. The analysis of Poppy Company's investment in Seed Company by the individual components of the major conceptual elements as of the acquisition date is as follows:

Book value element:	
Common stock..	$200,000
Retained earnings	175,000

Current value over (under) book value element:

Land...	10,000
Building	(20,000)
Equipment...	(15,000)
Total cost	$350,000

The financial statements of each company for the year ended December 31, 19X1, immediately after the acquisition are as follows:

	Poppy Company	Seed Company
Income Statement (19X1):		
Sales...	$5,000,000	$ 400,000
Cost of goods sold	(3,000,000)	(300,000)
Marketing expenses	(900,000)	(120,000)
Administrative expenses..................................	(600,000)	(80,000)
Income (Loss) before Income Taxes....................	$ 500,000	$(100,000)
Income tax expense @ 40%............................	(200,000)	
Net Income	$ 300,000	$(100,000)
Balance Sheet (as of December 31, 19X1):		
Cash..	$ 30,000	$ 5,000
Accounts receivable, net	140,000	80,000
Inventory	380,000	120,000
Land	200,000	100,000
Building—Cost	1,100,000	250,000
—Accum. depr.	(400,000)	(50,000)
Equipment—Cost	450,000	75,000
—Accum. depr.	(250,000)	(30,000)
Investment in Seed Company............................	350,000	
	$2,000,000	$ 550,000
Accounts payable and accruals	$ 275,000	$ 105,000
Long-term debt..	825,000	70,000
Common stock	40,000	200,000
Additional paid-in capital	360,000	
Retained earnings	500,000	175,000
	$2,000,000	$ 550,000

Required:
(1) Prepare the primary elimination entry as of December 31, 19X1.
(2) Prepare a consolidating statement worksheet at December 31, 19X1.

Problem 3–7
COMPREHENSIVE   Acquisition of common stock: Analyzing the investment and preparing consolidated financial statements—Cost is above current value of net assets and current value is above book value

P Company acquired all of the outstanding common stock of S Company for $700,000 cash on January 1, 19X1. P Company also incurred $42,000 of direct costs in connection with the acquisition. Financial data for each company immediately before the acquisition are as follows:

	P Company	S Company	
	Book Value	Book Value	Current Value
Cash	$1,300,000	$ 90,000	$ 90,000
Accounts receivable, net.....................	725,000	170,000	170,000
Notes receivable............................		20,000	15,000
Inventory....................................	800,000	280,000	287,000
Land	760,000	420,000	420,000
Building, net................................	1,300,000	700,000	790,000
Equipment, net	645,000	490,000	490,000
Patent	125,000	20,000	60,000
Goodwill		60,000	
	$5,655,000	$2,250,000	$2,322,000
Accounts payable and			
accrued liabilities	$ 845,000	$ 510,000	$ 510,000
Long-term debt	3,000,000	1,200,000	1,150,000
Common stock	1,000,000	250,000	
Retained earnings	810,000	290,000	
	$5,655,000	$2,250,000	

(Handwritten margin notes: Notes receivable (5000); Inventory 7000; Building, net 90 000; Patent 40 000; Goodwill (60 000); Long-term debt (50 000))

Required:
(1) Analyze the Investment account by the individual components of the major conceptual elements as of the acquisition date.
(2) Prepare the primary elimination entry as of the acquisition date.
(3) Prepare a consolidating statement worksheet as of the acquisition date.

Problem 3–8
COMPREHENSIVE   Acquisition of assets: Recording the acquisition and preparing combined financial statements—Cost is above current value of net assets

Use the same information provided in Problem 3–7, except that all of the assets were acquired instead of all of the common stock.

Required:
(1) Prepare the entries made by P Company to record the acquisition, assuming a decentralized accounting system is used.
(2) Prepare the primary elimination entry as of the acquisition date.
(3) Prepare a combining statement worksheet as of the acquisition date.

4 The Purchase Method of Accounting— Subsequent to Date of Acquisition

Chapter 3 dealt with acquisitions of assets, acquisitions of common stock, and the preparation of consolidated financial statements as of the acquisition date. Chapter 3 also explained that for business combinations in which assets are acquired, accounting for a division that uses a decentralized accounting system is the same as accounting for a branch that uses a decentralized accounting system.

In addition, when common stock is acquired, any portion of the parent's cost of the investment that relates to the subsidiary's depreciable or amortizable assets and goodwill must be charged against, or credited to, the combined future earnings of the parent and the subsidiary. The procedure for accomplishing this depends on the method the parent selects to account for its investment in the subsidiary. Two methods are available for valuing such an investment—the equity method and the cost method. Conceptually, these methods are at opposite ends of the spectrum. We will see, however, that regardless of which method the parent selects to account for its investment, the reporting of financial position and results of operations on a consolidated basis for periods subsequent to the acquisition date are the same.

This chapter discusses the equity and cost methods of accounting for investments in subsidiaries. The equity method is emphasized, as it is the predominant method in use. Furthermore, the equity method lends itself to updating the analysis of the investment account by the individual components of the major conceptual elements for all later activity in a manner that substantially simplifies the preparation of consolidated financial statements in subsequent periods. The preparation of consolidated financial statements for periods subsequent to the acquisition date is discussed and illustrated later in the chapter.

ACCOUNTING FOR THE PARENT'S INVESTMENT

Accounting for long-term investments, as covered in intermediate accounting texts, requires that investments in common stocks be accounted for as follows:

(1) **Ownership interest is below 20%.** Apply the rule of lower of cost or market in accordance with the provisions of *FASB Statement No. 12,* "Accounting for Certain Marketable Securities."

(2) **Ownership interest is at least 20% but not over 50%.** Apply the equity method of accounting in accordance with the provisions of *APB Opinion No. 18,* "The Equity Method of Accounting for Investments in Common Stock." (Note: The equity method applies here only if the investor's interest is in *voting stock.*)

(3) **Ownership interest is above 50%.** Use either the equity method or the cost method, with the two following limitations, as set forth in *APB Opinion No. 18.*

[handwritten margin note: applies to reporting for subsidiaries (50+% ownership only).]

(a) Parent company only statements. The cost method cannot be used when parent company only financial statements are issued—in such statements, the investment in <u>subsidiary</u> must be accounted for under the equity method. Parent company only financial statements do not include subsidiaries' statements. (Such statements are generally required in addition to consolidated financial statements in certain financial reports that must be submitted to the Securities and Exchange Commission.)

(b) Unconsolidated subsidiaries. The cost method cannot be used for subsidiaries that are not consolidated when the parent company issues consolidated financial statements (of itself and of other consolidated subsidiaries). In other words, in such statements, the investment in subsidiary must be accounted for under the equity method.[1]

The equity method

The equity method of valuing an investment in a subsidiary is similar to the accrual method of accounting in that it reflects the substance of the economic activity that has occurred. Under the equity method, the parent's interest in the subsidiary's earnings and losses is reflected as upward and downward adjustments, respectively, to the Investment in Subsidiary account. The offsetting credit or debit is recorded in the parent's income statement. Any dividends on common stock declared by the subsidiary are credited to the investment account at their declaration, with the offsetting debit to Dividends Receivable. Thus, **all dividends (except stock dividends) declared by the subsidiary are treated as a liquidation of the investment.**

The cost method

Under the cost method, dividends declared by the subsidiary are recorded as dividend income by the parent at their declaration, with the offsetting debit to Dividends Receivable. (When dividends subsequently declared by the subsidiary exceed **postacquisition earnings,** the parent treats such excess dividends as a **liquidating dividend** and, accordingly, credits the investment account instead of Dividend Income.) The parent's interest in the subsidiary's earnings and losses is completely ignored unless the magnitude of the subsidiary's losses is such that realization of the parent's cost is in serious doubt. In such instances, a write-down of the investment may be necessary. If such a write-down is made and, subsequently, the subsidiary's operations improve to such a degree that, in retrospect, the original write-down was not required, no adjustment is made to write up the investment to its original cost. <u>The cost method is conceptually unsound.</u> When a subsidiary continues to have profitable operations, the cost method can result in an overly conservative valuation of the investment, unless the subsidiary declares dividends equal to earnings each year. Furthermore, the parent's dividend income can be easily manipulated, because the parent controls the subsidiary's dividend policy.

---

[1] *APB Opinion No. 18,* "The Equity Method of Accounting for Investments in Common Stock" (New York: AICPA, 1971), paragraph 14.

Illustration:
Equity method compared with cost method

In this section, we illustrate the equity method and the cost method for a period of two years subsequent to the acquisition date. Assume all of the common stock of a subsidiary was acquired on January 1, 19X1, and that the earnings, losses, and dividends of the subsidiary for the following two years are as shown below:

	19X1	19X2
Net income	$15,000	$24,000
Dividends (Declared December 15, 19X1 and paid January 15, 19X2)	5,000	-0-

Before the equity method and the cost method can be illustrated, the amount of any amortization of cost over or under the book value of the subsidiary's net assets must be determined. With the information developed in Chapter 3 (Situation E of Illustration 3-6, page 88), in which the parent's total cost of $90,000 was $30,000 in excess of the $60,000 book value of the subsidiary's net assets, the amortization for the two years subsequent to January 1, 19X1, is calculated as follows:

	Current Value over Book Value Element			Goodwill Element	Total
	Inventory	Land	Building		
Remaining life:	(3 months)	(Indefinite)	(20 years)	(10 years)	
Balance, January 1, 19X1 ...	$4,000	$10,000	$6,000	$10,000	$30,000
Amortization—19X1	(4,000)		(300)	(1,000)	(5,300)
Balance, December 31, 19X1.	$ -0-	$10,000	$5,700	$ 9,000	$24,700
Amortization—19X2			(300)	(1,000)	(1,300)
Balance, December 31, 19X2.	$ -0-	$10,000	$5,400	$ 8,000	$23,400

The entries that would be made under the equity method and the cost method for the above assumed facts are presented in Illustration 4-1. The entries assume that no additional income taxes need to be recorded on amounts credited to income on the parent's books; actually, some income taxes may have to be recorded. (Income tax considerations relating to investments in subsidiaries are discussed in Chapter 12.)

In reviewing Illustration 4-1, note that the entries relating to the amortization of the parent's cost in excess of the book value of the subsidiary's net assets are shown only under the equity method. Historically, this amortization is not part of the cost method for the following reasons:

(1) When a parent company used the cost method and issued parent company only statements (which was possible before *APB Opinion No. 18* was issued), the parent company's income statement did not include the subsidiary's earnings (except dividends declared, which were usually infrequent), and thus, from a matching viewpoint, amortizing this excess on the parent's general ledger was inappropriate—that is, the amortization expense would not be matched against the parent's interest in the subsidiary's earnings.

[handwritten, circled: BOOKED ENTRIES]

Illustration 4-1
Equity method compared with cost method

Equity Method		Cost Method	
Entries for 19X1:			
(1) Subsidiary has earnings of $15,000:			
Investment in subsidiary.. 15,000		No entry.	
Equity in net income of			
subsidiary..........	15,000	*[handwritten: Proportionate share based on % ownership]*	
(2) Subsidiary declares dividend of $5,000:			
Dividends receivable 5,000		Dividends receivable 5,000	
Investment in		Dividend income.......	5,000
subsidiary..........	5,000	*[handwritten: no income from dividends - does not affect income statement.]*	
(3) Amortization of cost in excess of book value:			
Amortization of cost in			
excess of book value[a] ... 5,300		No entry.	
Investment in			
subsidiary.........	5,300		
Entries for 19X2:			
(1) Subsidiary pays dividend declared in 19X1:			
Cash 5,000		Cash 5,000	
Dividends receivable ...	5,000	Dividends receivable ...	5,000
(2) Subsidiary has earnings of $24,000:			
Investment in subsidiary.. 24,000			
Equity in net income of		No entry.	
subsidiary..........	24,000		
(3) Amortization of cost in excess of book value:			
Amortization of cost in			
excess of book value[a] ... 1,300		No entry.	
Investment in			
subsidiary.........	1,300		

[a] This is an income statement account on the parent's books.
Note: If the subsidiary had a net loss instead of a net income, the entry under the equity method would be:
Equity in net loss of subsidiary... xxx
Investment in subsidiary xxx

[handwritten left margin: Equity means after taxes - not included in Parent Co. taxable earnings]

(2) Accordingly, to satisfy the requirements of *APB Opinion No. 16* and earlier pronouncements, this amortization was made in the process of preparing the consolidated financial statements (which is done on work-sheets, not in the parent's general ledger). From a consolidated viewpoint, this produced the same results that would occur if the amortization were recorded on the parent's books. Unfortunately, this procedure complicates the consolidation process.

With the issuance of *APB Opinion No. 18,* which disallows the use of the cost method when parent company only statements are issued, it seems appropriate for companies still using the cost method to record the amortization on the general ledger, because parent company only statements cannot be issued. The preparation of consolidated financial statements would thus be simplified.

The equity method is the predominant accounting method in use, primarily because if the cost method is used, we must convert to the equity method whenever parent company only statements are issued—a needless conversion that can be avoided by using the equity method in the first place. The remainder of this chapter discusses the preparation of consolidated financial statements for periods subsequent to the acquisition date when the parent uses the equity method of accounting. Appendix A of this chapter discusses the preparation of consolidated financial statements for periods subsequent to the acquisition date when the parent uses the cost method of accounting for its investment.

Updating the expanded analysis of the investment account using the equity method

To prepare consolidated financial statements for periods subsequent to the acquisition date, we must first update the analysis of the investment account by the individual components of the major conceptual elements for the entries recorded under the equity method. In updating the analysis of the investment account, certain format modifications and assumptions are made to facilitate the preparation of consolidated financial statements, as follows:

(1) The following two additional retained earnings columns are used: (a) one column to isolate the parent company's interest in the subsidiary's current earnings, and (b) one column to isolate the parent company's share of dividends declared by the subsidiary during the current year.
(2) Columns are added to separate accumulated depreciation amounts from the initial cost assigned to depreciable assets.

Updating the analysis of the investment account in this manner allows the balances at a given date to be the source of the primary elimination entry that effects the consolidation. These techniques greatly simplify the preparation of consolidated financial statements. After the consolidated financial statements are prepared, the balances in the two additional retained earnings columns are reclassified to the "prior years" retained earnings column to facilitate the preparation of the consolidated financial statements in the following year.

Illustration:
Updating the expanded analysis of the investment account using the equity method

The balances in the investment account at January 1, 19X1, as shown in Situation E in Illustration 3-6 (page 88), are updated in Illustration 4-2 using the equity method of accounting for the parent's investment. The amounts are from Illustration 4-1.

In reviewing Illustration 4-2, the following points should be understood.

See wksheet entries p. 126
elim. " p. 126

See flow thru p. 130

Illustration 4-2
Updating the expanded analysis of the investment account using the equity method
[Wholly owned subsidiary—Total cost is above current value of subsidiary's net assets (Current value is above book value)]

	Total Cost =	Common Stock +	Book Value Element Prior Years +	Retained Earnings Current Year Earnings –	Dividends +	Inventory +	Land +	Current Value over Book Value Element Building Cost +	Accum. Depr. +	Goodwill Element
Balance, January 1, 19X1	$ 90,000	$40,000	$20,000			$ 4,000	$10,000	$6,000	$(300)	$10,000
Equity in net income	15,000			$15,000						
Dividends	(5,000)				$(5,000)					
Amortization	(5,300)					(4,000)			$(300)	(1,000)
Subtotal^a	$ 94,700	$40,000	$20,000	$15,000	$(5,000)	$ -0-	$10,000	$6,000	$(300)	$ 9,000
Reclassification^a			10,000	(15,000)	5,000					
Balance, December 31, 19X1	$ 94,700	$40,000	$30,000	$ -0-	$ -0-	$ -0-	$10,000	$6,000	$(300)	$ 9,000
Equity in net income	24,000			24,000						
Amortization	(1,300)								(300)	(1,000)
Subtotal^a	$117,400	$40,000	$30,000	$24,000	$ -0-	$ -0-	$10,000	$6,000	$(600)	$ 8,000
Reclassification^a			24,000	(24,000)						
Balance, December 31, 19X2	$117,400	$40,000	$54,000	$ -0-	$ -0-	$ -0-	$10,000	$6,000	$(600)	$ 8,000

Note (1) The beginning balances are taken from Situation E of Illustration 3-6 (page 88).
Note (2) The amounts used to update the analysis are from Illustration 4-1 (page 120).
^a This reclassification is made after the primary elimination entry is prepared and is analogous to a closing entry. No formal journal entry is recorded because the analysis of the total cost of the investment is maintained in a schedule outside the general ledger.

(1) The entries pertaining to the amortization of the current value over book value element actually expense a portion of the total cost of the investment on the parent company's books. These entries bring the investment's total carrying value closer to the book value of the subsidiary's net assets.
(2) The goodwill element is amortized to expense over 10 years. At the end of 10 years, the goodwill element will no longer exist.
(3) The inventory component of the current value over book value element was completely expensed in 19X1. Thus, this component does not exist after 19X1.
(4) The building component of the current value over book value element is amortized to expense over 20 years. At the end of 20 years, the amount in the accumulated depreciation column will equal the amount in the building cost column. Thereafter, these offsetting amounts are part of the current value over book value element until the building is disposed of.
(5) The land component of the current value over book value element is part of that element until the land is disposed of, at which time it is charged to income.
(6) All of the amortization expense is charged to a separate account on the parent company's books called Amortization of Cost in Excess of Book Value. We explain later in the chapter why and how this expense amount is reclassified in consolidation to the appropriate, traditional income statement classifications—for example, cost of goods sold and administrative expenses.

CONSOLIDATED FINANCIAL STATEMENTS SUBSEQUENT TO THE ACQUISITION DATE

The process of consolidation subsequent to the acquisition date is the same as it is at the acquisition date, except that, in addition, the parent's income statement must be combined with the subsidiary's income statement. In combining the detail of the two income statements, we must eliminate the Equity in Net Income or Loss of Subsidiary account balance in the parent's column of the worksheet. The effect of eliminating this account is to substitute for this account balance the revenue, cost, and expense accounts of the subsidiary. This substitution prevents double-counting the subsidiary's net income or loss in arriving at the consolidated net income. In substance, the process is identical with the elimination of the branch income or loss account recorded on the books of a home office when combined financial statements are prepared for a home office and a branch.

Consolidated statement of retained earnings

The consolidations illustrated here incorporate analyses of retained earnings for both the parent and the subsidiary. These analyses are contained in the balance sheet section of the worksheet, which is consistent with actual practice. Because the parent company must issue a consolidated statement of retained earnings, the analysis of the parent company's retained earnings in the worksheet readily provides the amounts for this statement. Under the equity method of accounting, the parent company's Retained Earnings account contains all the information necessary to prepare this statement. The postacquisition earnings of the subsidiary are included in the parent's retained earnings. The dividends declared by the parent, which constitute the only dividends to outsiders, are also included in this account. Any dividends declared by the wholly owned subsidiary are intercompany transactions that cannot be considered dividends from the consolidated group to outsiders. Thus, the subsidiary's dividends cannot be added to the parent's dividends in preparing the consolidated statement of retained earnings.

The primary elimination entry

The source of the primary elimination entry as of each subsequent consolidation date is the updated analysis of the investment account by the individual components of the major conceptual elements. Isolating the subsidiary's current-year earnings or losses in a separate column enables us to eliminate the Equity in Net Income or Loss of Subsidiary account balance in the parent's column of the consolidating statement worksheet by posting the balance in the current-year earnings column directly to this account on the worksheet. The posting is then totaled at the net income line and carried forward to the net income line in the analysis of the subsidiary's retained earnings in the balance sheet section of the worksheet. The dividends declared by the subsidiary are posted directly to the dividends declared line in that analysis of retained earnings. The combination of the carryforward from the income statement, the direct posting of the dividends declared, and the direct posting of the beginning of year retained earnings balance result in complete elimination of the subsidiary's retained earnings in consolidation. This entry is illustrated later in the chapter.

The secondary elimination entry

When the parent has recorded amortization of cost in excess of (or below) the book value of the subsidiary's net assets, an additional elimination entry must be made to reclassify this amortization to the appropriate traditional cost and expense accounts. For example, that portion of the amortization relating to inventory should be shown as part of cost of goods sold. That portion of the amortization relating to the building should be allocated among all departments that use the building—for example, manufacturing, marketing, and administration. Obviously, this elimination entry could be avoided if the parent initially charged the appropriate traditional cost and expense accounts when it recorded the amortization. This would not be proper, however, because the amortization account relates solely to the parent's investment in the subsidiary and not to any of its own separate operations. Accordingly, amortization is charged only to one account, which is considered a contra account to the Equity in Net Income of Subsidiary account. Combining these two accounts reveals the subsidiary's earnings in relation to the parent's investment in the subsidiary. Furthermore, because this amortization is not deductible for income tax reporting purposes, the preparation of income tax returns is simplified if the amortization is charged to only one account in the parent's general ledger, instead of scattered among several accounts.

This treatment presents a problem, however, when consolidated financial statements are prepared in that the amortization must be shown among the traditional income cost and expense classifications to which it relates. Accordingly, an additional elimination entry is made to reclassify the balance in the Amortization of Cost in Excess of or under Book Value account to the appropriate traditional cost and expense accounts. The entry does not affect net income, because it takes place entirely within the income statement section of the worksheet. For instructional and ease of reference purposes, we find it convenient to label this entry; accordingly, we call it the secondary elimination entry.

From the information in Illustration 4-1, the secondary elimination entries as of December 31, 19X1 (one year after the acquisition date) and December 31, 19X2 (two years after the acquisition date) are as follows:

	Consolidation Date	
	December 31, 19X1	December 31, 19X2
Cost of goods sold	5,300	1,300
Amortization of cost in excess of book value	5,300	1,300

For simplicity, we arbitrarily assumed that all of the goodwill amortization and all of the amortization relating to the building should be classified as part of cost of goods sold. Obviously, the amortization relating to the inventory belongs in cost of goods sold.

Illustration:
Neither goodwill nor a bargain purchase element exists (Total cost equals current value of net assets) and net assets are not over- or undervalued

Before illustrating a consolidation of normal complexity involving a situation in which the parent's cost exceeds the book value of the subsidiary's net assets, we present a simpler illustration to highlight the substitution process that takes place in the consolidating statement worksheet.

We use information in Situation A of Illustration 3-6 (page 88), in which the total cost of the investment equals the current value of the subsidiary's net assets and the net assets are not over- or undervalued. Applying the information with respect to the subsidiary's subsequent earnings and dividends as shown in Illustration 4-1 (page 120), we update the expanded analysis of the investment account for the year subsequent to acquisition, using the equity method of accounting, as follows:

			Book Value Element		
				Retained Earnings	
				Current Year	
	Total	Common	Prior		
	Cost =	Stock +	Years +	Earnings −	Dividends
Balance, January 1, 19X1	$60,000	$40,000	$20,000		
Equity in net income	15,000			$15,000	
Dividends	(5,000)				$(5,000)
Subtotal	$70,000	$40,000	$20,000	$15,000	$(5,000)
Reclassification			10,000	(15,000)	5,000
Balance, December 31, 19X1 ...	$70,000	$40,000	$30,000	$ -0-	$ -0-

Consolidated financial statements as of December 31, 19X1 (one year after the acquisition date) are prepared using the following primary elimination entry:

Common stock	40,000	
Retained earnings (beginning of year)....................	20,000	
Equity in net income of subsidiary	15,000	
Dividends declared.................................		5,000
Investment in subsidiary		70,000

A consolidating statement worksheet at December 31, 19X1, is given in Illustration 4-3. In reviewing Illustration 4-3, the following points should be understood:

(1) The primary elimination entry substitutes the subsidiary's individual income statement accounts for the Equity in Net Income of Subsidiary account.
(2) P Company's net income is the same as consolidated net income.
(3) P Company's retained earnings is the same as the consolidated retained earnings.
(4) The $15,000 debit in the elimination column is subtotaled at the net income line and then carried forward to the net income line in the analysis of the subsidiary's retained earnings in the balance sheet section of the worksheet.
(5) When the total cost equals the current value and the book value of the subsidiary's net assets, the primary elimination is essentially the same as that used to combine the financial statements of a branch or a division with those of a home office. (The only difference is in the account descriptions.)

Illustrations:
Goodwill exists (Total cost is above current value of net assets) and net assets are undervalued

From the information in Illustration 4-2 (page 122), in which the parent's cost exceeds the current value of the subsidiary's net assets and net assets are undervalued, the primary elimination entries as of December 31, 19X1 (one year after the acquisition date) and December 31, 19X2 (two years after the acquisition date) are as follows:

	Consolidation Date	
	December 31, 19X1	December 31, 19X2
Common stock	40,000	40,000
Retained earnings (beginning of year).........	20,000	30,000
Equity in net income of subsidiary	15,000	24,000
Land......................................	10,000	10,000
Building	6,000	6,000
Goodwill	9,000	8,000
Dividends declared......................	5,000	
Accumulated depreciation (building)	300	600
Investment in subsidiary	94,700	117,400

Illustration 4-3

			Eliminations		Consoli-
	P Company	**S Company**	**Dr.**	**Cr.**	**dated**
Income Statement:					
Sales	600,000	200,000			800,000
Income from subsidiary:					
Equity in net income...........	15,000		15,000(1)		-0-
Subtotal	615,000	200,000	15,000		800,000
Cost of goods sold	360,000	120,000			480,000
Marketing expenses	90,000	30,000			120,000
Administrative expenses	60,000	20,000			80,000
Interest expense	30,000	5,000			35,000
Subtotal	540,000	175,000			715,000
Income before Income Taxes.....	75,000	25,000	15,000		85,000
Income tax expense @ 40% ...	(24,000)[a]	(10,000)			(34,000)
Net Income	51,000	15,000	⌐15,000		51,000
Balance Sheet:					
Cash..........................	55,000	32,000			87,000
Accounts receivable, net	145,000	43,000			188,000
Inventory	90,000	40,000			130,000
Investment in S Company........	70,000			70,000(1)	-0-
Land..........................	80,000	30,000			110,000
Building, net	140,000	77,000			217,000
Equipment, net.................	130,000	48,000			178,000
Total assets	710,000	270,000		70,000	910,000
Liabilities	290,000	200,000			490,000
Common stock:					
P Company...................	300,000				300,000
S Company...................		40,000	40,000(1)		-0-
Retained earnings—P Company:					
Beginning of year	100,000[b]				100,000
+ Net income	51,000				51,000
- Dividends declared	(31,000)				(31,000)
End of year..................	120,000				120,000
Retained earnings—S Company:					
Beginning of year		20,000	20,000(1)		-0-
+ Net income		15,000	⌐15,000		-0-
- Dividends declared		(5,000)		5,000(1)	-0-
End of year..................		30,000	35,000	5,000	-0-
Total liabilities and equity	710,000	270,000	75,000	5,000	910,000
Proof of debit and credit postings			75,000	75,000	

P COMPANY AND SUBSIDIARY (S COMPANY)
Consolidating Statement Worksheet
For the Year Ended December 31, 19X1

Explanation of entry:
  (1) The primary elimination entry.
[a] It is assumed that no income taxes need to be recorded on the $15,000 of earnings recorded by the parent under the equity method of accounting. Accordingly, the income tax calculation is 40% of $60,000, not 40% of $75,000.
[b] This amount is the parent's retained earnings as of the acquisition date as shown in Illustration 3-7 (page 92).

Illustrations 4-4 and 4-5 show the consolidating statement worksheets using the primary elimination entries on page 126. The secondary entry is the same as that illustrated earlier. It is repeated below for convenience:

	Consolidation Date	
	December 31, 19X1	December 31, 19X2
Cost of goods sold	5,300	1,300
Amortization of cost in		
excess of book value	5,300	1,300

In reviewing Illustrations 4-4 and 4-5, the following points should be understood:

(1) The parent's cost of the investment in excess of the subsidiary's net assets at book value "pops out" in the consolidation process. In effect, the excess is reclassified to the balance sheet accounts with which it has been identified.
(2) The amounts in the consolidated column are composed of (a) the parent's items based on book values and (b) the subsidiary's items based on their current values as of the acquisition date.
(3) On full amortization of the excess relating to the building (which is the individual component with the longest remaining life other than land), the Investment in Subsidiary account balance is $10,000 (relating to the land element) over the subsidiary's net assets at book value.
(4) If the subsidiary's land is sold, this $10,000 would be amortized in full at that time, and the investment account would eventually equal the book value of the subsidiary's net assets.

Commentary:
Current value is below book value of net assets

When the current value of the subsidiary's net assets is below their book value, the net overvaluation produces a negative amount in the second major conceptual element—the current value over (under) book value element. Separating this major conceptual element into its individual components may reveal that certain assets are overvalued and certain assets are undervalued. For those depreciable and amortizable assets that are overvalued, a credit balance is amortized instead of a debit balance. Thus, the secondary elimination entry involves reclassifying the *credit* balance in the Amortization of Cost *Below* Book Value account to the appropriate traditional accounts.

The procedures for preparing consolidated financial statements for these situations are the same as when the current value of the subsidiary's net assets is above their book value.

SUMMARY

The equity method of accounting for an investment in a subsidiary results in a valuation that reflects the economic activity of the subsidiary. It is

Illustration 4-4

	P Company	S Company	Eliminations Dr.	Eliminations Cr.	Consolidated
Income Statement:					
Sales	600,000	200,000			800,000
Income from subsidiary:					
Equity in net income	15,000		15,000(1)		-0-
Amortization of cost in					
excess of book value........	(5,300)			5,300(2)	-0-
Subtotal.................	609,700	200,000	15,000	5,300	800,000
Cost of goods sold	360,000	120,000	5,300(2)		485,300
Marketing expenses	90,000	30,000			120,000
Administrative expenses	60,000	20,000			80,000
Interest expense	30,000	5,000			35,000
Subtotal.................	540,000	175,000	5,300		720,300
Income before Income Taxes	69,700	25,000	20,300	5,300	79,700
Income tax expense @ 40% ...	(24,000)[a]	(10,000)			(34,000)
Net Income....................	45,700	15,000	20,300	5,300	45,700
Balance Sheet:					
Cash	25,000	32,000			57,000
Accounts receivable, net.........	145,000	43,000			188,000
Inventory.....................	90,000	40,000			130,000
Investment in S Company	94,700			94,700(1)	-0-
Land.........................	80,000	30,000	10,000(1)		120,000
Building—Cost.................	400,000	100,000	6,000(1)		506,000
—Accum. depr.	(260,000)	(23,000)		300(1)	(283,300)
Equipment—Cost	300,000	90,000			390,000
—Accum. depr.	(170,000)	(42,000)			(212,000)
Goodwill			9,000(1)		9,000
Total assets	704,700	270,000	25,000	95,000	904,700
Liabilities.....................	290,000	200,000			490,000
Common stock:					
P Company	300,000				300,000
S Company		40,000	40,000(1)		-0-
Retained earnings—P Company:					
Beginning of year	100,000				100,000
+ Net income	45,700				45,700
− Dividends declared	(31,000)				(31,000)
End of year	114,700				114,700
Retained earnings—S Company:					
Beginning of year		20,000	20,000(1)		-0-
+ Net income		15,000	20,300	5,300	-0-
− Dividends declared		(5,000)		5,000(1)	-0-
End of year		30,000	40,300	10,300	-0-
Total liabilities and equity	704,700	270,000	80,300	10,300	904,700
Proof of debit and credit postings			105,300	105,300	

Explanation of entries:
(1) The primary elimination entry.
(2) The secondary elimination entry.

[a] It is assumed that no income taxes need to be provided on the $15,000 of earnings recorded by the parent under the equity method of accounting; also, the $5,300 of amortization of cost in excess of book value is not tax deductible. Accordingly, the income tax calculation is 40% of $60,000, not 40% of $69,700.

Illustration 4-5

	P COMPANY AND SUBSIDIARY (S COMPANY) Consolidating Statement Worksheet For the Year Ended December 31, 19X2				
	P Company	S Company	Eliminations Dr.	Eliminations Cr.	Consolidated
Income Statement:					
Sales	650,000	230,000			880,000
Income from subsidiary:					
Equity in net income	24,000		24,000(1)		-0-
Amortization of cost in					
excess of book value	(1,300)			1,300(2)	-0-
Subtotal..................	672,700	230,000	24,000	1,300	880,000
Cost of goods sold	390,000	130,000	1,300(2)		521,300
Marketing expenses	100,000	35,000			135,000
Administrative expenses	60,000	20,000			80,000
Interest expense	30,000	5,000			35,000
Subtotal..................	580,000	190,000	1,300		771,300
Income before Income Taxes	92,700	40,000	25,300	1,300	108,700
Income tax expense @ 40% ...	(28,000)[a]	(16,000)			(44,000)
Net Income....................	64,700	24,000	25,300	1,300	64,700
Balance Sheet:					
Cash	40,000	15,000			55,000
Accounts receivable, net	190,000	65,000			255,000
Inventory......................	110,000	60,000			170,000
Investment in S Company	117,400			117,400(1)	-0-
Land..........................	80,000	30,000	10,000(1)		120,000
Building—Cost	400,000	100,000	6,000(1)		506,000
—Accum. depr.	(270,000)	(28,000)		600(1)	(298,600)
Equipment—Cost	300,000	90,000			390,000
—Accum. depr.	(200,000)	(50,000)			(250,000)
Goodwill			8,000(1)		8,000
Total assets	767,400	282,000	24,000	118,000	955,400
Liabilities	329,000	188,000			517,000
Common stock:					
P Company	300,000				300,000
S Company		40,000	40,000(1)		-0-
Retained earnings—P Company:					
Beginning of year	114,700				114,700
+ Net income	64,700				64,700
− Dividends declared	(41,000)				(41,000)
End of year	138,400				138,400
Retained earnings—S Company:					
Beginning of year		30,000	30,000(1)		-0-
+ Net income		24,000	25,300	1,300	-0-
− Dividends declared		-0-			-0-
End of year		54,000	55,300	1,300	-0-
Total liabilities and equity	767,400	282,000	95,300	1,300	955,400
Proof of debit and credit postings			119,300	119,300	

Explanation of entries:
  (1) The primary elimination entry.
  (2) The secondary elimination entry.
[a] It is assumed that no income taxes need to be provided on the $24,000 of earnings recorded by the parent under the equity method of accounting; also, the $1,300 of amortization of cost in excess of book value is not tax deductible. Accordingly, the income tax calculation is 40% of $70,000, not 40% of $92,700.

conceptually superior to the cost method, which in effect ignores the economic activity of the subsidiary.

The preparation of consolidated financial statements for periods subsequent to the acquisition date is similar to the preparation of combined financial statements for a home office and a branch or division. The income statements of the parent and the subsidiary are combined in such a way that the consolidated amounts show the detailed income statement accounts of both companies. The key to straightforward preparation of consolidated financial statements is maintaining the analysis of the investment account by the individual components of the major conceptual elements in a format that facilitates the preparation of the primary elimination entry. When the parent has amortization of cost above or below the book value of the subsidiary's net assets, a secondary elimination entry is needed to reclassify the amortization to the appropriate traditional accounts. This must be done so that the subsidiary's costs and expenses reflect the parent's cost of acquiring the net assets.

Glossary of new terms

Cost Method: A method of accounting for an investment in a subsidiary whereby the carrying value of the investment is never changed, unless it is permanently impaired.

Equity Method (as applied to subsidiaries): A method of accounting for an investment in a subsidiary whereby the carrying value of the investment is (1) increased as a result of the subsidiary's earnings; (2) decreased as a result of the subsidiary's losses; (3) decreased as a result of the dividends declared on the subsidiary's common stock; and (4) adjusted for the amortization of cost over or under the book value of the subsidiary's net assets.

Parent Company Only Statements: Financial statements of a parent company that do not include the financial statements of its subsidiaries. The parent's investments in its subsidiaries are shown in these statements. (When such statements are issued, the parent's investment in its unconsolidated subsidiaries must be reported under the equity method.)

Appendix A
PREPARATION OF CONSOLIDATED FINANCIAL STATEMENTS WHEN THE PARENT ACCOUNTS FOR ITS INVESTMENT UNDER THE COST METHOD

Under the cost method of accounting for an investment in a subsidiary, the parent never changes the original cost of the investment unless either a liquidating dividend or a permanent impairment of the investment's value exists. If the same consolidated amounts are to be obtained as when the equity method is used, the consolidation elimination entries must be different from those used when the equity method is used.

This is a key concept. Whether the parent uses the equity method or the cost method, the consolidated amounts are identical—only the procedures of preparing the consolidating statement worksheet are different. The main conceptual points of the cost method are:

(1) To arrive at consolidated net income each year, the net income of the parent must be reduced for any dividend income of the subsidiary that is included. This adjusted net income is then added to the subsidiary's net income to arrive at consolidated net income.
(2) To arrive at consolidated retained earnings, the parent's retained earnings (which includes only those earnings of the subsidiary that have been remitted to the parent in the form of dividends since the acquisition date) must be added to the postacquisition earnings of the subsidiary that have not been remitted to the parent.

The primary elimination entry

The primary elimination entry is always exactly the same as the primary elimination entry made on the acquisition date. Using the assumptions of Illustrations 4-4 and 4-5, in which the parent's cost of $90,000 exceeded both the current value ($80,000) and the book value ($60,000) of the subsidiary's net assets, we determine the primary elimination for all future consolidation dates as follows:

Common stock	40,000	
Retained earnings	20,000	
Inventory	4,000	
Land	10,000	
Building	6,000	
Goodwill	10,000	
Investment in subsidiary		90,000

Obviously, if this entry is used for all future consolidation dates, then the secondary entry must be revised so that the consolidated financial statements reflect subsequent, appropriate amortization of cost over the book value of the net assets.

The secondary elimination entry

The secondary elimination entry reflects the amortization of cost over the book value of the net assets directly in the appropriate, traditional cost and expense accounts. Thus, under the cost method, the secondary elimination entry is an adjusting entry (instead of a reclassifying entry as under the equity method). This accomplishes on the consolidating statement worksheet what otherwise is accomplished in the parent's general ledger under the equity method.

For all periods after the year following the acquisition date, the credits are made to the individual components on a cumulative basis. The beginning of period cumulative amortization is charged to retained earnings. For the two years subsequent to the acquisition date, the secondary elimination entries are as follows.

	Consolidation Date	
	December 31, 19X1	**December 31, 19X2**
Cost of goods sold	5,300	1,300
Inventory	4,000	4,000
Accumulated depreciation (building)	300	600
Goodwill	1,000	2,000
Retained earnings	5,300	

The dividend income elimination entry

A third elimination entry is necessary to eliminate any dividend income recorded on the parent's books that results from dividends received from the subsidiary. This entry is necessary only in years in which the subsidiary declares a dividend. The entry is as follows:

	Consolidation Date	
	December 31, 19X1	**December 31, 19X2**
Dividend income	5,000	No entry
Dividends declared	5,000	

This entry does not affect the balance sheet because the debit is carried forward from the income statement to the retained earnings analysis of the subsidiary in the balance sheet. The sole purpose of the entry is to eliminate the dividend income from the parent's income statement.

Illustrations:
Goodwill exists (Total cost is above current value and book value of net assets) and net assets are undervalued

Illustrations 4-6 and 4-7 show the consolidating statement worksheets as of December 31, 19X1 (the year subsequent to acquisition) and December 31, 19X2 (two years subsequent to acquisition) prepared using the cost method. (The consolidating worksheet is not shown as of the acquisition date because it is identical with the one in Illustration 3-8.)

In reviewing Illustrations 4-6 and 4-7, the following points should be understood:

(1) The amounts in the parent's column are different from the amounts in Illustrations 4-4 (page 129) and 4-5 (page 130) (the comparable consolidating worksheets as of these dates when the equity method is used), whereas the amounts in the subsidiary's column and the consolidated column are the same.

(2) The parent's Retained Earnings accounts under the cost method include only those postacquisition earnings that have been remitted to the parent through dividends, whereas the parent's Retained Earnings account under the equity method includes all postacquisition earnings of the subsidiary.

(3) As under the equity method, the eliminations and adjustments made to the income statement section of the worksheet are subtotaled at the

Illustration 4-6

P COMPANY AND SUBSIDIARY (S COMPANY)
Consolidating Statement Worksheet
For the Year Ended December 31, 19X1

	P Company	S Company	Eliminations Dr.	Eliminations Cr.	Consolidated
Income Statement:					
Sales	600,000	200,000			800,000
Income from subsidiary:					
Dividends	5,000		5,000(3)		-0-
Subtotal....................	605,000	200,000	5,000		800,000
Cost of goods sold	360,000	120,000	5,300(2)		485,300
Marketing expenses	90,000	30,000			120,000
Administrative expenses	60,000	20,000			80,000
Interest expense	30,000	5,000			35,000
Subtotal....................	540,000	175,000	5,300		720,300
Income before Income Taxes	65,000	25,000	10,300		79,700
Income tax expense @ 40% ...	(24,000)[a]	(10,000)			(34,000)
Net Income....................	41,000	15,000	10,300		45,700
Balance Sheet:					
Cash	25,000	32,000			57,000
Accounts receivable, net	145,000	43,000			188,000
Inventory......................	90,000	40,000	4,000(1)	4,000(2)	130,000
Investment in S Company	90,000			90,000(1)	-0-
Land..........................	80,000	30,000	10,000(1)		120,000
Building—Cost	400,000	100,000	6,000(1)		506,000
—Accum. depr..........	(260,000)	(23,000)		300(2)	(283,300)
Equipment—Cost	300,000	90,000			390,000
—Accum. depr.	(170,000)	(42,000)			(212,000)
Goodwill			10,000(1)	1,000(2)	9,000
Total assets	700,000	270,000	30,000	95,300	904,700
Liabilities.....................	290,000	200,000			490,000
Common stock:					
P Company	300,000				300,000
S Company		40,000	40,000(1)		-0-
Retained earnings—P Company:					
Beginning of year	100,000				100,000
+ Net income	41,000				41,000
− Dividends declared	(31,000)				(31,000)
End of year	110,000				110,000
Retained earnings—S Company:					
Beginning of year		20,000	20,000(1)		-0-
+ Net income		15,000	10,300		4,700
− Dividends declared		(5,000)		5,000(3)	-0-
End of year		30,000	30,300	5,000	4,700
Total liabilities and equity	700,000	270,000	70,300	5,000	904,700
Proof of debit and credit postings.....................			100,300	100,300	

Recap of Retained Earnings
P Company .... $110,000←
S Company .... 4,700←
$114,700

Explanation of entries:
(1) The primary elimination entry.
(2) The secondary elimination entry.
(3) The dividend income elimination entry.
[a] It is assumed that no income taxes need to be provided on the $5,000 of dividend income. Accordingly, the income tax calculation is 40% of $60,000, not 40% of $65,000. The $5,300 of amortization of cost in excess of book value is not tax deductible; thus, the recorded income tax expense does not require adjustment.

Illustration 4-7

	P COMPANY AND SUBSIDIARY (S COMPANY)				
	Consolidating Statement Worksheet				
	For the Year Ended December 31, 19X2				
	P	S	Eliminations		Consoli-
	Company	Company	Dr.	Cr.	dated
Income Statement:					
Sales	650,000	230,000			880,000
Income from subsidiary:					
Dividends	-0-				-0-
Subtotal....................	650,000	230,000			880,000
Cost of goods sold.............	390,000	130,000	1,300(2)		521,300
Marketing expenses	100,000	35,000			135,000
Administrative expenses	60,000	20,000			80,000
Interest expense	30,000	5,000			35,000
Subtotal....................	580,000	190,000	1,300		771,300
Income before Income Taxes	70,000	40,000	1,300[a]		108,700
Income tax expense @ 40% ...	(28,000)	(16,000)			(44,000)
Net Income....................	42,000	24,000	⌐1,300		64,700
Balance Sheet:					
Cash	40,000	15,000			55,000
Accounts receivable, net.........	190,000	65,000			255,000
Inventory.......................	110,000	60,000	4,000(1)	4,000(2)	170,000
Investment in S Company	90,000			90,000(1)	-0-
Land..........................	80,000	30,000	10,000(1)		120,000
Building—Cost.................	400,000	100,000	6,000(1)		506,000
—Accum. depr..........	(270,000)	(28,000)		600(2)	(298,600)
Equipment—Cost	300,000	90,000			390,000
—Accum. depr.	(200,000)	(50,000)			(250,000)
Goodwill			10,000(1)	2,000(2)	8,000
Total assets	740,000	282,000	30,000	96,600	955,400
Liabilities......................	329,000	188,000			517,000
Common stock:					
P Company	300,000				300,000
S Company		40,000	40,000(1)		-0-
Retained earnings—P Company:					
Beginning of year	110,000				110,000
+ Net income	42,000				42,000
− Dividends declared	(41,000)				(41,000)
End of year	111,000				111,000⌐
Retained earnings—S Company:			5,300(2) ⌉		
Beginning of year		30,000	20,000(1) ⌡		4,700
+ Net income		24,000	↳1,300		22,700
− Dividends declared		-0-			-0-
End of year		54,000	26,600		27,400⌐
Total liabilities and equity	740,000	282,000	66,600		955,400
Proof of debit and credit postings....................			96,600	96,600	

Recap of Retained Earnings
P Company .... $111,000◄─┐
S Company ....   27,400◄─┘
         $138,400

Explanation of entries:
(1) The primary elimination entry.
(2) The secondary elimination entry.
[a] The $1,300 amortization of cost in excess of book value is not tax deductible. Accordingly, the recorded income tax expense does not require adjustment.

net income line and carried forward to the retained earnings section of the balance sheet.

(4) The two retained earnings amounts in the consolidated column are combined, and only this single combined amount is reported in the consolidated balance sheet.

(5) It was assumed that no additional income taxes are payable on the parent's dividend income received from the subsidiary. Actually, some tax may be payable. This subject is discussed in Chapter 12 on income tax considerations of investments in subsidiaries.

Appendix B
PREPARATION OF CONSOLIDATING STATEMENT WORKSHEET USING THE TRIAL BALANCE APPROACH

Some companies prepare their consolidating statement worksheets from trial balances rather than from financial statements. The same elimination entries are used as when the worksheets are prepared from financial statements. To demonstrate the preparation of the worksheet using the trial balance approach, we have reformatted the financial statements used in Illustration 4-4 on page 129 into the trial balance approach shown in Illustration 4-8 (pages 138–39). The primary and secondary elimination entries from Illustration 4-4 are repeated below for convenience:

The primary elimination entry:

Common stock	40,000	
Retained earnings (beginning of year)	20,000	
Equity in net income of subsidiary	15,000	
Land	10,000	
Building	6,000	
Goodwill	9,000	
Dividends declared		5,000
Accumulated depreciation (building)		300
Investment in subsidiary		94,700

The secondary elimination entry:

Cost of goods sold	5,300	
Amortization of cost in excess of book value		5,300

Review questions

1. Contrast the equity method of accounting with the cost method.
2. When it is inappropriate to consolidate a subsidiary's financial statements with those of its parent, how must the parent company account for its investment in the subsidiary?

3. What are parent company only statements? How must investments in subsidiaries be reported in such statements?
4. What are liquidating dividends? How are they treated under the equity method? Under the cost method?
5. Why must the consolidated amounts be the same regardless of whether the parent company uses the equity method or the cost method to account for its investment in a subsidiary?
6. In the expanded analysis of the investment account, why is a separate column used for the parent company's share of the subsidiary's current-year net income or loss?
7. What is the source of the primary elimination entry when the parent uses the equity method?
8. What is the purpose of the secondary elimination entry?

Discussion cases

Discussion case 4–1
Selection of the equity method or the cost method
for purposes of measuring return on investment

Pong Company acquired all of the outstanding common stock of Song Company on January 1, 19X1, for $1,000,000 cash. Pong views the Song operation as an investment and wants to account for its investment in a manner that will enable it to evaluate readily the profitability of the investment each year, using a return on investment approach. Assume that Song expects net income of $200,000 for 19X1 and $300,000 for 19X2, and that no dividends will be paid to the parent company during these two years.

Required:
(1) Calculate the expected return on investment for 19X1 and 19X2 assuming Pong Company uses:
  (a) the equity method.
  (b) the cost method.
(2) Which method allows the correct return on investment to be calculated?

Discussion case 4–2
Treatment of amortization of cost in excess of book value in calculating
return on investment under the equity method

Paxx Company acquired all of the outstanding common stock of Sax Company on January 1, 19X1, for $1,000,000 cash. For 19X1, Sax reported net income of $150,000. On December 31, 19X1, Sax paid a $75,000 dividend to Paxx. Paxx amortized $30,000 of cost in excess of book value during 19X1, which it recorded under the equity method of accounting.

Required:
(1) Calculate the parent company's 19X1 return on investment.
(2) Calculate the parent company's 19X1 return on investment assuming that the dividend was paid on June 30, 19X1. For simplicity, assume the declaration date of the dividend is the same as the payment date.

Illustration 4-8
Trial Balance Approach (Illustration 4-4 reformatted)

	P COMPANY AND SUBSIDIARY (S COMPANY) Consolidating Statement Worksheet For the Year Ended December 31,19X1			
	P Company		S Company	
	Dr.	Cr.	Dr.	Cr.
Cash	25,000		32,000	
Accounts receivable, net	145,000		43,000	
Inventory	90,000		40,000	
Investment in S Company	94,700			
Land	80,000		30,000	
Building—Cost	400,000		100,000	
—Accum. depr.		260,000		23,000
Equipment—Cost	300,000		90,000	
—Accum. depr.		170,000		42,000
Goodwill				
Liabilities		290,000		200,000
Common stock:				
P Company		300,000		
S Company				40,000
Retained earnings, January 1, 19X1:				
P Company		100,000		
S Company				20,000
Dividends declared:				
P Company	31,000			
S Company			5,000	
Sales		600,000		200,000
Equity in net income of subsidiary		15,000		
Amortization of cost				
in excess of book value	5,300			
Cost of goods sold	360,000		120,000	
Marketing expenses	90,000		30,000	
Administrative expenses	60,000		20,000	
Interest expense	30,000		5,000	
Income before Income Taxes				
Income tax expense	24,000		10,000	
	1,735,000	1,735,000	525,000	525,000

Consolidated net income . . . .

Consolidated retained earnings . . . .

Explanation of entries:
(1) The primary elimination entry.
(2) The secondary elimination entry.

Illustration 4-8 (continued)

Eliminations Dr.	Eliminations Cr.	Income Statement Dr.	Income Statement Cr.	Consolidated Retained Earnings (Dr.) Cr.	Balance Sheet
					57,000
					188,000
					130,000
	94,700(1)				-0-
10,000(1)					120,000
6,000(1)					506,000
	300(1)				(283,300)
					390,000
					(212,000)
9,000(1)					9,000
					904,700
					490,000
					300,000
40,000(1)					-0-
				100,000	
20,000(1)				-0-	
				(31,000)	
	5,000(1)			-0-	
			800,000		
15,000(1)			-0-		
	5,300(2)	-0-			
5,300(2)		485,300			
		120,000			
		80,000			
		35,000			
			79,700		
		34,000			
105,300	105,300				
			45,700	→ 45,700	
			114,700	→ 114,700	
					904,700

Discussion case 4–3
Treatment of subsidiary dividends in preparing the consolidated statement of retained earnings

The controller of Plair Company is preparing the consolidated statement of retained earnings. Plair Company declared dividends of $100,000 on its common stock during the year. Plair Company's wholly owned subsidiary, which was acquired at the beginning of the year, declared dividends of $20,000 on its common stock during the year ($10,000 of which was declared on the last day of the year and has not been paid). The controller wants to know whether the consolidated statement of retained earnings for the year should reflect dividends of $100,000, $110,000, or $120,000.

Required:
How would you advise the controller?

Discussion case 4–4
Subsequent accounting for "cost in excess of net assets"

Pruitt Company acquired the business of Rogers Company on January 1, 19X1, at a cost of $900,000 in excess of the current value of Rogers' net assets. Rogers' operations had been unprofitable for the two years preceding the business combination and thus, did not possess superior earning power. Pruitt paid the $900,000 so that it could readily establish itself in this high-risk industry. Pruitt expects Rogers' operations to report profits within three years. The cost in excess of current value is being amortized over 10 years.

Required:
Assume that at December 31, 19X4, Rogers' operations are still unprofitable. Management is uncertain whether Rogers' operations will ever be profitable. What are the implications of this situation?

Exercises

Exercise 4–1
Preparation of comparative entries under the equity method and the cost method: Cost is above current value of net assets and current value equals book value

Palibu Company acquired 100% of the outstanding common stock of Saguna Company at a total cost of $550,000 on January 1, 19X1. Assume the current value of Saguna Company's net assets equals their book value of $510,000. Also assume goodwill is assigned a 40-year life. The net income (loss) and dividends declared by Saguna Company for 19X1 and 19X2 are as follows:

	Net Income (Loss)	Dividends Declared (and Paid)
19X1	30,000	10,000
19X2	(12,000)	5,000

Required:
Prepare in comparative form the parent company's entries for 19X1 and 19X2 under the equity method and the cost method.

Exercise 4–2
Applying the equity method and preparing the primary elimination entry: Cost equals current value of net assets and current value equals book value

On January 1, 19X1, Pitt Company acquired 100% of the outstanding common stock of Sitters Company at a total cost of $750,000. The general ledger balances of Sitters Company's capital accounts on the acquisition date were as follows:

Common stock	$100,000
Additional paid-in capital	400,000
Retained earnings	250,000
	$750,000

Assume the current value of Sitters Company's net assets equals their book value. The net income (loss) and dividends declared by Sitters Company for 19X1 and 19X2 are as follows:

	Net Income (Loss)	Dividends Declared (and Paid)
19X1	$80,000	$25,000
19X2	(40,000)	10,000

Required:
(1) Assuming Pitt Company uses the equity method of accounting, prepare the journal entries it would make for 19X1 and 19X2 with respect to its investment in Sitters Company.
(2) Prepare an expanded analysis of the investment account as of the acquisition date and update it for the entries developed in (1).
(3) Prepare the primary elimination entry as of December 31, 19X1, and December 31, 19X2.
(4) Explain why there is no secondary elimination entry.

Exercise 4–3
Applying the equity method and preparing the primary and secondary elimination entries: Cost is above current value of net assets and current value is above book value

On January 1, 19X1, Patch Company acquired 100% of the outstanding common stock of Satchel Company at a total cost of $400,000. The analysis of Patch Company's investment in Satchel Company by the individual components of the major conceptual elements as of the acquisition date is as follows.

		Remaining Life
Book value element:		
Common stock	$100,000	
Retained earnings	60,000	
Current value over book value element:		
Inventory	5,000	3 months
Land	105,000	Indefinite
Building	90,000	15 years
Goodwill element	40,000	40 years
Total cost	$400,000	

The net income (loss) and dividends declared by Satchel Company for 19X1 and 19X2 are as follows:

	Net Income (Loss)	Dividends Declared (and Paid)
19X1	$35,000	$5,000
19X2	(10,000)	5,000

Required:

(1) Assuming Patch Company uses the equity method of accounting, prepare the journal entries it would make for 19X1 and 19X2 for its investment in Satchel Company.

(2) Prepare an analysis of the investment account by the individual components of the major conceptual elements as of the acquisition date, and update it for the entries developed in (1).

(3) Prepare the primary and secondary elimination entries as of December 31, 19X1, and December 31, 19X2.

Exercise 4–4
Applying the equity method and preparing the primary and secondary elimination entries: Cost is below current value of net assets and current value is below book value

Pimm Company acquired 100% of the outstanding common stock of Simms Company at a total cost of $310,000 on January 1, 19X1. The analysis of Pimm Company's investment in Simms Company by the individual components of the major conceptual elements as of the acquisition date (after appropriate allocation of the bargain purchase element) is as follows:

		Remaining Life
Book value element:		
Common stock	$250,000	
Retained earnings	100,000	
Current value over (under) book value element:		
Inventory	5,000	3 months
Land	30,000	Indefinite
Building	(75,000)	25 years
Total cost	$310,000	

The net income (loss) and dividends declared by Simms Company for 19X1 and 19X2 are as follows:

	Net Income (Loss)	Dividends Declared (and Paid)
19X1	$(15,000)	$1,000
19X2	30,000	5,000

Required:
(1) Assuming Pimm Company uses the equity method of accounting, prepare the journal entries it would make for 19X1 and 19X2 with respect to its investment in Simms Company.
(2) Prepare an analysis of the investment account by the individual components of the major conceptual elements as of the acquisition date and update it for the entries developed in (1).
(3) Prepare the primary and secondary elimination entries as of December 31, 19X1, and December 31, 19X2.

Exercise 4–5
Theory: Multiple choice questions

(1) What would be the effect on the financial statements if an unconsolidated subsidiary is accounted for by the equity method but consolidated statements are prepared with other subsidiaries?
  (a) All of the unconsolidated subsidiary's accounts are included individually in the consolidated statements.
  (b) The consolidated retained earnings amount does not reflect the earnings of the unconsolidated subsidiary.
  (c) The consolidated retained earnings amount is the same as it would be if the subsidiary had been included in the consolidation.
  (d) Dividend revenue from the unconsolidated subsidiary is reflected in consolidated net income.
(2) At which amount should a parent company carry its unconsolidated domestic subsidiary on its separate financial statements in periods subsequent to acquisition?
  (a) Original cost of the investment to the parent company.
  (b) Original cost of the investment adjusted for the parent's share of the subsidiary's earnings, losses, dividends, and amortization of cost over or under the book value of the subsidiary's net assets.
  (c) Current market value of the investment adjusted for dividends received.
  (d) Current market value of the investment.
(3) In a parent's unconsolidated financial statements, which accounts, other than Cash, are affected when a subsidiary's earnings and dividends are recorded?
  (a) Dividend Revenue, Equity in Earnings of Subsidiary, and Retained Earnings.
  (b) Dividend Revenue and Retained Earnings.
  (c) Investment in Subsidiary, Equity in Earnings of Subsidiary, Dividend Revenue, and Retained Earnings.
  (d) Investment in Subsidiary, Equity in Earnings of Subsidiary, and Retained Earnings.

(AICPA adapted)

Exercise for Appendix A

Exercise 4–6A
Applying the cost method and preparing the primary, secondary, and dividend income elimination entries: Cost is above current value of net assets and current value is above book value

On January 1, 19X1, Pell Company acquired all of the outstanding common stock of Sello Company at a total cost of $200,000. The analysis of Pell Company's investment in Sello Company by the individual components of the major conceptual elements as of the acquisition date is as follows:

		Remaining Life
Book value element:		
Common stock	$ 50,000	
Retained earnings..	25,000	
Current value over book value element:		
Inventory	5,000	1 month
Land..	45,000	Indefinite
Building	25,000	25 years
Equipment	10,000	5 years
Goodwill element	40,000	10 years
Total cost	$200,000	

The net income (loss) and dividends declared by Sello Company for 19X1 and 19X2 are as follows:

	Net Income (Loss)	Dividends Declared (and Paid)
19X1	$10,000	$6,000
19X2	(2,000)	2,000

Required:
(1) Assuming Pell Company uses the cost method of accounting for its investment in Sello Company, prepare the entries it would make for 19X1 and 19X2.
(2) Prepare the primary, secondary, and dividend income elimination entries, as appropriate, as of December 31, 19X1, and December 31, 19X2.
(3) Explain how your answer would change for 19X2 if $5,000 of dividends were declared and paid instead of $2,000.

Problems

Problem 4–1
Preparing consolidated financial statements:
Cost equals current value of net assets
and current value equals book value (Continuation of Problem 3–4)

On December 31, 19X1, Post Company, a calendar-year reporting company, acquired all of the outstanding common stock of Script Company at a total cost of $800,000 (an amount equal to the current value and book value of Script Company's net assets). The analysis of the investment account as of the acquisition date is as follows:

Book value element:
Common stock..	$100,000
Additional paid-in capital	400,000
Retained earnings	300,000
Total cost	$800,000

The financial statements of each company for the year ended December 31, 19X2, are as follows:

	Post Company	Script Company
Income Statement (19X2):		
Sales.......................................	$11,000,000	$ 950,000
Equity in net income of subsidiary.....................	60,000	
Cost of goods sold	(6,500,000)	(540,000)
Marketing expenses	(2,300,000)	(190,000)
Administrative expenses................................	(850,000)	(70,000)
Interest expense.......................................	(250,000)	(50,000)
Income before Income Taxes	$ 1,160,000	$ 100,000
Income tax expense @ 40%..........................	(440,000)	(40,000)
Net Income	$ 720,000	$ 60,000
Balance Sheet (December 31, 19X2):		
Cash	$ 1,100,000	$ 180,000
Accounts receivable, net	2,300,000	340,000
Inventory	1,500,000	680,000
Investment in Script Company	850,000	
Fixed assets, net	6,400,000	820,000
	$12,150,000	$2,020,000
Accounts payable and accruals	$ 1,230,000	$ 445,000
Long-term debt.......................................	2,400,000	725,000
Common stock	1,000,000	100,000
Additional paid-in capital	2,000,000	400,000
Retained earnings	5,520,000	350,000
	$12,150,000	$2,020,000
Dividends declared during 19X2.......................	$ 200,000	$ 10,000

Required:
(1) Update the analysis of the investment account through December 31, 19X2.
(2) Prepare the primary elimination entry as of December 31, 19X2.
(3) Prepare a consolidating statement worksheet at December 31, 19X2. (The parent's retained earnings as of January 1, 19X2, was $5,000,000.)

Problem 4–2
Preparing consolidated financial statements:
Cost is above current value of net assets
and current value is above book value (Continuation of Problem 3–5)

Peanut Company, a calendar-year reporting company, acquired all of the outstanding common stock of Shell Company at a total cost of $250,000 on December 31, 19X1. The analysis of Peanut Company's investment in Shell Company as of the acquisition date is as follows.

		Remaining Life
Book value element:		
Common stock	$ 50,000	
Retained earnings	75,000	
Current value over book value element:		
Inventory	2,000	3 months
Land	28,000	Indefinite
Building	20,000	20 years
Patent	15,000	5 years
Goodwill element	60,000	15 years
Total cost	$250,000	

The financial statements of each company for the year ended December 31, 19X2, are as follows:

	Peanut Company	Shell Company
Income Statement (19X2):		
Sales	$1,800,000	$600,000
Equity in net income of subsidiary	42,000	
Amortization of cost in excess of book value	(10,000)	
Cost of goods sold	(950,000)	(320,000)
Marketing expenses	(240,000)	(120,000)
Administrative expenses	(190,000)	(76,000)
Interest expense	(70,000)	(14,000)
Income before Income Taxes	$ 382,000	$ 70,000
Income tax expense @ 40%	(140,000)	(28,000)
Net Income	$ 242,000	$ 42,000
Balance Sheet (December 31, 19X2):		
Cash	$ 305,000	$ 30,000
Accounts receivable, net	420,000	45,000
Inventory	510,000	95,000
Investment in Shell Company	263,000	
Land	600,000	105,000
Building—Cost	1,100,000	100,000
—Accum. depr.	(325,000)	(25,000)
Equipment—Cost	500,000	30,000
—Accum. depr.	(250,000)	(20,000)
Patent		9,000
	$3,123,000	$369,000
Accounts payable and accruals	$ 415,000	$ 71,000
Long-term debt	800,000	150,000
Common stock	250,000	50,000
Additional paid-in capital	1,250,000	
Retained earnings	408,000	98,000
	$3,123,000	$369,000
Dividends declared during 19X2	$ 134,000	$ 19,000

Required:
(1) Update the analysis of the investment account through December 31, 19X2.
(2) Prepare the primary and secondary elimination entries as of December 31, 19X2.

(3) Prepare a consolidating statement worksheet at December 31, 19X2. (The parent's retained earnings as of January 1, 19X2, was $300,000.)

(4) Prepare a formal consolidated balance sheet and income statement to be included in the annual report to the stockholders.

Problem 4–3
Preparing consolidated financial statements:
Cost is equal to current value of net assets and current
value is below book value (Continuation of Problem 3–6)

Poppy Company, a calendar-year reporting company, acquired all of the outstanding common stock of Seed Company at a total cost of $350,000 on December 31, 19X1. The analysis of Poppy Company's investment in Seed Company as of the acquisition date is as follows:

		Remaining Life
Book value element:		
Common stock	$200,000	
Retained earnings	175,000	
Current value over (under) book value element:		
Land	10,000	Indefinite
Building	(20,000)	20 years
Equipment	(15,000)	5 years
Total cost	$350,000	

The financial statements of each company for the year ended December 31, 19X2, are as follows:

	Poppy Company	Seed Company
Income Statement (19X2):		
Sales	$5,400,000	$450,000
Equity in net loss of subsidiary	(30,000)	
Amortization of cost below book value	4,000	
Cost of goods sold	(3,100,000)	(320,000)
Marketing expenses	(950,000)	(90,000)
Administrative expenses	(550,000)	(63,000)
Interest expense	(100,000)	(7,000)
Income (Loss) before Income Taxes	$ 674,000	$ (30,000)
Income tax expense @ 40%	(280,000)	
Net Income (Loss)	$ 394,000	$ (30,000)
Balance Sheet (December 31, 19X2):		
Cash	$ 125,000	$ 12,000
Accounts receivable, net	230,000	74,000
Inventory	340,000	98,000
Investment in Seed Company	324,000	
Land	200,000	100,000
Building—Cost	1,100,000	250,000
—Accum. depr.	(430,000)	(60,000)
Equipment—Cost	450,000	75,000
—Accum. depr.	(265,000)	(39,000)
	$2,074,000	$510,000

	Poppy Company	Seed Company
Accounts payable and accruals	$ 220,000	$100,000
Long-term debt	800,000	65,000
Common stock	40,000	200,000
Additional paid-in capital	360,000	
Retained earnings	654,000	145,000
	$2,074,000	$510,000
Dividends declared during 19X2	$ 240,000	$ -0-

Required:

(1) Update the analysis of the investment account through December 31, 19X2.
(2) Prepare the primary and secondary elimination entries as of December 31, 19X2.
(3) Prepare a consolidating statement worksheet at December 31, 19X2. (The parent's retained earnings as of January 1, 19X2, was $500,000.)

Problem 4–4
CHALLENGER   Evaluating the future results under the purchase method in a business combination with a troubled savings and loan

You are the auditor for Pie-in-the-Sky Savings and Loan Association, which recently acquired all of the assets of Sinking Savings and Loan Association. The combination was structured so that the transaction did not qualify for pooling of interests treatment. Sinking S & L had incurred losses for approximately two years prior to the combination as a result of paying a higher interest rate to its depositors than it was earning on its loan portfolio. The combination was arranged by the Federal Savings and Loan Insurance Corporation to prevent the liquidation of Sinking S & L, which had exhausted its net worth. Selected data for Sinking S & L as of the combination date are as follows:

	Book Value	Current Value
Assets	$200,000,000	$160,000,000
Liabilities	200,000,000	200,000,000
Common stock	7,000,000	
Accumulated deficit	(7,000,000)	

The current value of the assets is lower than the book value because the current lending rate on home mortgages is 14%, whereas the yield on the loan portfolio (which has an average remaining life of 10 years) is only 10%. Pie-in-the-Sky S & L did not have to pay any consideration; it merely took title to the assets and assumed responsibility for the liabilities. Management intends to amortize goodwill over 40 years.

Required:

(1) Prepare an analysis of the investment account at the acquisition date.
(2) For years 1–10 (in total) and for years 11–40 (in total), determine the effect on income of amortizations made from the parent company's investment account.

(3) Evaluate the soundness of the results that are reported under the purchase method at the acquisition date and for future periods.

(4) What, if anything, should be done differently?

Problem 4–5
COMPREHENSIVE   Recording the acquisition, analyzing the investment account, applying the equity method, and preparing consolidated financial statements: Cost is above current value of net assets and current value is above book value

On January 1, 19X1, Pocono Company acquired 100% of the outstanding common stock of Sono Company by issuing 5,000 shares of $10 par value common stock (which was trading at $70 per share on that date). In addition, Pocono Company incurred direct costs of $80,000 relating to the acquisition, $30,000 of which was for the registration of the shares issued with the SEC. (All these direct costs were charged to the investment account.) The balances in the capital accounts of Sono Company as of the acquisition date are as follows:

Common stock	$200,000
Retained earnings	62,000
	$262,000

All assets and liabilities of Sono Company have a current value equal to their book value, except for the following:

	Book Value	Current Value	Remaining Life
Inventory	$ 82,000	$ 90,000	2 months
Land	60,000	175,000	Indefinite
Equipment	145,000	115,000	5 years

Assume any goodwill has a 15-year life from the acquisition date. The only entry Pocono Company has made on its books since the acquisition date was to credit the investment account for the $10,000 dividend it received from the subsidiary during 19X1.

The financial statements of each company for the year ended December 31, 19X1, are as follows:

	Pocono Company	Sono Company
Income Statement (19X1):		
Sales	$ 960,000	$420,000
Cost of goods sold	(500,000)	(220,000)
Marketing expenses	(92,000)	(65,000)
Administrative expenses	(98,000)	(40,000)
Interest expense	(20,000)	(5,000)
Income before Income Taxes	$ 250,000	$ 90,000
Income tax expense @ 40%	(100,000)	(36,000)
Net Income	$ 150,000	$ 54,000

	Pocono Company	Sono Company
Balance Sheet (December 31, 19X1):		
Cash..........	$ 85,000	$ 20,000
Accounts receivable, net	110,000	30,000
Inventory	220,000	95,000
Investment in Sono Company	420,000	
Land........	450,000	60,000
Building—Cost	725,000	255,000
—Accum. depr.	(180,000)	(133,000)
Equipment—Cost.........	570,000	190,000
—Accum. depr........	(130,000)	(74,000)
	$2,270,000	$443,000
Accounts payable and accruals	$ 260,000	$ 67,000
Long-term debt	220,000	70,000
Common stock.......	550,000	200,000
Additional paid-in capital	825,000	
Retained earnings	415,000	106,000
	$2,270,000	$443,000
Dividends declared during 19X1	$ 90,000	$ 10,000

Required:
(1) Analyze the investment account by the individual components of the major conceptual elements as of the acquisition date. Make any appropriate adjusting entries.
(2) Update the analysis of the investment account to reflect activity under the equity method of accounting through December 31, 19X1.
(3) Prepare the primary and secondary elimination entries as of December 31, 19X1.
(4) Adjust the parent company's financial statements as shown above to reflect the equity method of accounting, and then prepare a consolidating statement worksheet at December 31, 19X1.

Problem 4–6
COMPREHENSIVE CHALLENGER   Converting to the equity method from the cost method two years after the acquisition date: analyzing the investment account, and preparing consolidated financial statements: Cost is above current value of net assets and current value is above book value

Puzzle Company acquired all of the outstanding common stock of Somnia Company for $820,000 cash on January 1, 19X1. Puzzle Company also incurred $47,000 of direct costs in connection with the acquisition. Selected information on Somnia Company as of the acquisition date is as follows:

	Book Value	Current Value	Remaining Life
Inventory......	$ 280,000	$ 287,000	6 months
Building, net.....	700,000	790,000	15 years
Patent	20,000	60,000	5 years
Goodwill	60,000	- 0 -	6 years
10% Bonds payable	1,200,000	1,000,000	10 years

Puzzle Company has used the cost method since the acquisition date and has decided to change to the equity method to account for its investment in Somnia Company. Assume a 40-year life for any goodwill paid for in the transaction.

The financial statements of each company for the year ended December 31, 19X2, are as follows:

	Puzzle Company	Somnia Company
Income Statement (19X2):		
Sales	$8,500,000	$ 980,000
Cost of goods sold	(4,500,000)	(430,000)
Marketing expenses	(1,600,000)	(125,000)
Administrative expenses	(1,400,000)	(65,000)
Interest expense	(400,000)	(120,000)
Dividend income	50,000	-0-
Income before Income Taxes	$ 650,000	$ 240,000
Income tax expense @ 40%	(240,000)	(100,000)[a]
Net Income.............................	$ 410,000	$ 140,000
Balance Sheet (December 31, 19X2):		
Cash	$ 458,000	$ 118,000
Accounts receivable, net	750,000	190,000
Inventory	820,000	380,000
Investment in Somnia Company	867,000	
Land.......................................	760,000	440,000
Building—Cost	4,300,000	800,000
—Accum. depr.	(1,100,000)	(200,000)
Equipment—Cost	1,960,000	720,000
—Accum. depr.	(1,365,000)	(280,000)
Patent	100,000	12,000
Goodwill		40,000
	$7,550,000	$2,220,000
Accounts payable and accruals.......	$1,600,000	$ 370,000
Long-term debt	3,000,000	1,200,000
Common stock	2,000,000	250,000
Retained earnings......................	950,000	400,000
	$7,550,000	$2,220,000
Dividends declared during 19X2	$ 100,000	$ 50,000
Dividends declared during 19X1	$ 80,000	$ 40,000
Reported net income for 19X1	$ 200,000	$ 90,000

[a] Goodwill amortization of $10,000 is not tax deductible; thus, tax calculation is 40% of $250,000, not 40% of $240,000.

Required:
(1) Analyze the investment account by the individual components of the major conceptual elements as of the acquisition date.
(2) Update the analysis of the investment account to reflect activity under the equity method of accounting through December 31, 19X2 (a two-year period).
(3) Prepare the journal entry to convert to the equity method from the cost method.
(4) Prepare the primary and secondary elimination entries as of December 31, 19X2.

(5) Adjust Puzzle Company's financial statements to reflect the equity method of accounting, and then prepare a consolidating statement worksheet at December 31, 19X2.

Problems for Appendix A

Problem 4–7A
Preparing consolidated financial statements: Cost equals current value of net assets and current value equals book value
(Problem 4–1 revised to reflect the cost method)

On December 31, 19X1, Post Company acquired all of the outstanding common stock of Script Company at a total cost of $800,000 (an amount equal to the book value of Script Company's net assets). The financial statements of each company for the year ended December 31, 19X2, are as follows:

	Post Company	Script Company
Income Statement (19X2):		
Sales..	$11,000,000	$ 950,000
Dividend income......................................	10,000	
Cost of goods sold	(6,500,000)	(540,000)
Marketing expenses	(2,300,000)	(190,000)
Administrative expenses............................	(850,000)	(70,000)
Interest expense.......................................	(250,000)	(50,000)
Income before Income Taxes	$ 1,110,000	$ 100,000
Income tax expense @ 40%.........................	(440,000)	(40,000)
Net Income	$ 670,000	$ 60,000
Balance Sheet (December 31, 19X2):		
Cash..	$ 1,100,000	$ 180,000
Accounts receivable, net	2,300,000	340,000
Inventory	1,500,000	680,000
Investment in Script Company	800,000	
Fixed assets, net	6,400,000	820,000
	$12,100,000	$2,020,000
Accounts payable and accruals	$ 1,230,000	$ 445,000
Long-term debt..	2,400,000	725,000
Common stock	1,000,000	100,000
Additional paid-in capital	2,000,000	400,000
Retained earnings	5,470,000	350,000
	$12,100,000	$2,020,000
Dividends declared during 19X2........................	$ 200,000	$ 10,000

Required:
(1) Prepare the primary elimination entry at December 31, 19X2.
(2) Why is there no secondary elimination entry at December 31, 19X2?
(3) Prepare the dividend income elimination entry at December 31, 19X2.
(4) Prepare a consolidating statement worksheet at December 31, 19X2.
(5) Prepare a consolidated statement of retained earnings for 19X2. (The parent's retained earnings on January 1, 19X2, was $5,000,000.)

Problem 4–8A
Preparing consolidated financial statements: Cost is above current value of net assets and current value is above book value
(Problem 4–2 revised to reflect the cost method)

Peanut Company acquired all of the outstanding common stock of Shell Company at a total cost of $250,000 on December 31, 19X1. The analysis of Peanut Company's investment in Shell Company as of the acquisition date is as follows:

		Remaining Life
Book value element:		
Common stock	$ 50,000	
Retained earnings	75,000	
Current value over book value element:		
Inventory	2,000	3 months
Land	28,000	Indefinite
Building	20,000	20 years
Patent	15,000	5 years
Goodwill element	60,000	15 years
Total cost	$250,000	

The financial statements of each company for the year ended December 31, 19X2, are as follows:

	Peanut Company	Shell Company
Income Statement (19X2):		
Sales	$1,800,000	$600,000
Dividend income	19,000	
Cost of goods sold	(950,000)	(320,000)
Marketing expenses	(240,000)	(120,000)
Administrative expenses	(190,000)	(76,000)
Interest expense	(70,000)	(14,000)
Income before Income Taxes	$ 369,000	$ 70,000
Income tax expense @ 40%	(140,000)	(28,000)
Net Income	$ 229,000	$ 42,000
Balance Sheet (December 31, 19X2):		
Cash	$ 305,000	$ 30,000
Accounts receivable, net	420,000	45,000
Inventory	510,000	95,000
Investment in Shell Company	250,000	
Land	600,000	105,000
Building—Cost	1,100,000	100,000
—Accum. depr.	(325,000)	(25,000)
Equipment—Cost	500,000	30,000
—Accum. depr.	(250,000)	(20,000)
Patent		9,000
	$3,110,000	$369,000
Accounts payable and accruals	$ 415,000	$ 71,000
Long-term debt	800,000	150,000
Common stock	250,000	50,000
Additional paid-in capital	1,250,000	
Retained earnings	395,000	98,000
	$3,110,000	$369,000
Dividends declared during 19X2	$ 134,000	$ 19,000

Required:
(1) Prepare the primary elimination entry, the secondary elimination entry, and the dividend income elimination entry at December 31, 19X2.
(2) Prepare a consolidating statement worksheet at December 31, 19X2.
(3) Prepare a consolidated statement of retained earnings for 19X2. (The parent's retained earnings on January 1, 19X2, was $300,000.)

Problem 4–9A
Preparing consolidated financial statements: Cost equals current value of net assets and current value is below book value (Problem 4–3 revised to reflect the cost method)

Poppy Company acquired all of the outstanding common stock of Seed Company at a total cost of $350,000 on December 31, 19X1. The analysis of Poppy Company's investment in Seed Company as of the acquisition date is as follows:

		Remaining Life
Book value element:		
Common stock..	$200,000	
Retained earnings	175,000	
Current value over (under) book value element:		
Land	10,000	Indefinite
Building	(20,000)	20 years
Equipment...	(15,000)	5 years
Total cost	$350,000	

The financial statements of each company for the year ended December 31, 19X2, are as follows:

	Poppy Company	Seed Company
Income Statement (19X2):		
Sales	$5,400,000	$450,000
Cost of goods sold	(3,100,000)	(320,000)
Marketing expenses	(950,000)	(90,000)
Administrative expenses	(550,000)	(63,000)
Interest expense	(100,000)	(7,000)
Income (Loss) before Income Taxes	$ 700,000	$ (30,000)
Income tax expense @ 40%	(280,000)	
Net Income (Loss)	$ 420,000	$ (30,000)
Balance Sheet (December 31, 19X2):		
Cash...	$ 125,000	$ 12,000
Accounts receivable, net	230,000	74,000
Inventory	340,000	98,000
Investment in Seed Company	350,000	
Land...	200,000	100,000
Building—Cost	1,100,000	250,000
—Accum. depr.	(430,000)	(60,000)
Equipment—Cost..	450,000	75,000
—Accum. depr...............................	(265,000)	(39,000)
	$2,100,000	$510,000

	Poppy Company	Seed Company
Accounts payable and accruals	$ 220,000	$100,000
Long-term debt	800,000	65,000
Common stock	40,000	200,000
Additional paid-in capital	360,000	
Retained earnings	680,000	145,000
	$2,100,000	$510,000
Dividends declared during 19X2	$ 240,000	

Required:
(1) Prepare the primary and secondary elimination entries at December 31, 19X2.
(2) Prepare a consolidating statement worksheet at December 31, 19X2.
(3) Prepare a consolidated statement of retained earnings for 19X2. (The parent's retained earnings as of January 1, 19X2, was $500,000.)

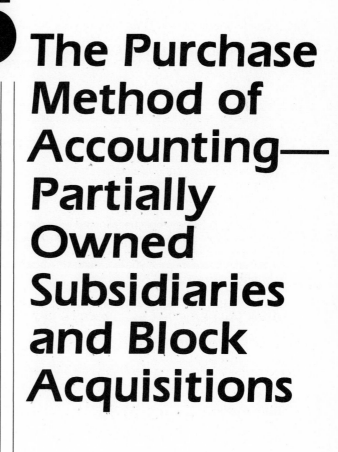

5 The Purchase Method of Accounting— Partially Owned Subsidiaries and Block Acquisitions

OVERVIEW OF ACCOUNTING
FOR MINORITY INTERESTS

Frequently, a company creates its own subsidiary through internal expansion. Internally created subsidiaries are almost always wholly owned. As shown in Chapter 4, the consolidation process for wholly owned subsidiaries is relatively straightforward: It is merely a matter of updating the expanded analysis of the total cost of the investment, preparing the primary elimination entry from the ending updated balances, and posting the primary elimination entry to the consolidating statement worksheet. When amortization of cost over or under the book value of the subsidiary's net assets exists, a secondary elimination entry is necessary to reclassify the amortization to the appropriate accounts.

When the parent owns less than 100% of the subsidiary's outstanding common stock, the consolidation process is slightly more complicated because special procedures are required to account for the interest of the subsidiary's other stockholders. We refer to this interest hereafter as the **minority interest.** Usually, a minority interest exists because (1) the parent has chosen not to purchase the minority interest; (2) the parent cannot locate a small number of stockholders; and (3) some stockholders refuse to sell their shares to the parent company at its offering price.

In this chapter, we use examples from Chapters 3 and 4, adjusted to reflect only partial ownership, to illustrate accounting for partially owned subsidiaries.

Consolidation of only the parent's interest

Accounting for the minority interest would not be necessary if the parent consolidated only its ownership interest in each of the subsidiary's financial statement items. In other words, for a 90% owned subsidiary, we would multiply the subsidiary's cash, accounts receivable, sales, and so on, by 90% to arrive at the consolidated amounts. This approach would simplify accounting for the minority interest, but generally accepted accounting principles do not permit it for the following reasons:

(1) The parent does not have a separable percentage interest in each individual asset, liability, and income statement account of the subsidiary. Its ownership interest is a percentage of the net assets and net income as a whole.
(2) The parent controls all of the subsidiary even though its ownership is less than 100%.
(3) The purpose of consolidated statements is to combine the operations of the parent and the subsidiary as if they were a single company.

Accordingly, we must consolidate the entire amount of each of the subsidiary's individual asset, liability, and income statement accounts with those of the parent company. Because the subsidiary is only partially owned, however, the primary elimination entry does not eliminate all of the subsidiary's equity account balances and its entire net income. This is demonstrated later in the chapter. The amounts that are not eliminated constitute the minority interest in these items. Therefore, the minority interest in the subsidiary's net assets and net income are reported as separate items in the consolidated financial statements.

Classification of minority interest

The following two theories have evolved concerning the treatment of the minority interest in consolidated financial statements:

(1) The parent company theory.
(2) The entity theory (applied to consolidated financial statements).

The parent company theory.   The parent company theory assumes that the reporting entity does not change as a result of the consolidation process. Consolidated reporting merely represents a different manner of reporting the parent's financial position and the results of its operations. Thus, **the parent company is still considered the reporting entity.** As a result, (1) the interest of the minority shareholders is not considered an equity interest of the consolidated reporting entity, and (2) consolidated net income equals the parent's net income (which includes its share of the subsidiary's net income through application of the equity method of accounting). Therefore, the minority interest is presented in the consolidated financial statements as follows:

(1) Consolidated balance sheet. The minority interest in the subsidiary's net assets is treated as an outside interest and is shown outside the stockholders' equity section in one of the following manners:
   (a) Between liabilities and stockholders' equity. This presentation reflects the unique nature of the minority interest. It is an equity interest, but not of the parent company, which is the reporting entity.
   (b) Among liabilities. This presentation has little, if any, supporting theory. However, if the minority interest is insignificant and a separate classification is unwarranted, companies commonly classify it among liabilities.
(2) Consolidated income statement. The minority interest in the subsidiary's net income is shown as a deduction in the consolidated income statement in arriving at the consolidated net income. For example, assuming that a 90% owned subsidiary had net income of $15,000 for the year, the minority interest deduction would be $1,500 (10% of $15,000) and would be presented as follows:

	Consolidated Income Statement
Revenues...	$800,000
Costs and expenses:	
Cost of goods sold	$480,000
Marketing expenses	120,000
Administrative expenses..	80,000
Interest expense...	35,000
Minority interest in net income of subsidiary	1,500
Subtotal	$716,500
Income before Income Taxes	$ 83,500
Income tax expense	(34,000)
Net Income	$ 49,500

The entity theory. The entity theory assumes that the reporting entity has changed as a result of the consolidation process. **A new reporting entity is deemed to exist.** This new reporting entity has two classes of equity interests—the controlling interest (the parent's shareholders) and the minority interest. Because the nature of these interests is the same, they must be treated the same way in consolidated financial statements. As a result, (1) the interest of the minority shareholders is treated as an equity interest of the consolidated reporting entity, and (2) consolidated net income equals the combined net incomes of both companies (without the application of the equity method of accounting). The minority interest is presented in the consolidated financial statements as follows:

(1) **Consolidated balance sheet.** The minority interest in the subsidiary's net assets is shown as a separate category within the stockholders' equity section.
(2) **Consolidated income statement.** The minority interest in the subsidiary's net income is shown as a portion of the total net income of the consolidated entity. Using the same amounts as in the above example, we can present the consolidated income statement as follows:

	Consolidated Income Statement
Revenues...	$800,000
Costs and expenses:	
Cost of goods sold	$480,000
Marketing expenses	120,000
Administrative expenses..	80,000
Interest expense...	35,000
Subtotal	$715,000
Income before Income Taxes	$ 85,000
Income tax expense	(34,000)
Net Income	$ 51,000
Division of net income:	
To controlling interest	$ 49,500
To minority interest	1,500
Total Net Income	$ 51,000

Whether the parent company theory or the entity theory is correct depends on whether the reporting entity is considered to have changed as a result of the consolidation process—a purely subjective evaluation. The minority shareholders do not influence the parent's operating policies. Thus, the consolidated financial statements are usually of no benefit whatsoever to the minority shareholders. This group is entitled only to the financial statements of the partially owned subsidiary. Minority shareholders who desire a set of the consolidated financial statements (for whatever reason) must make a formal request to the parent.

Accounting Research Bulletin No. 51 does not indicate how minority interest should be presented in consolidated financial statements. However, it does state that consolidated financial statements are prepared primarily for the benefit of the parent's shareholders and creditors.[1] This provision is consistent with the parent company theory but not with the entity theory. In practice, the minority interest is presented in consolidated financial statements almost exclusively in accordance with the parent company theory. For these reasons, the income statement sections of the consolidating statement worksheets presented later in this chapter are consistent with the parent company theory, under which the minority interest in the subsidiary's net income is shown as a deduction in arriving at the consolidated net income. (As this book goes to print, the FASB is addressing the minority interest presentation issue in its project on consolidations and the equity method of accounting.)

The minority interest entry

In the consolidating statement worksheet for periods subsequent to the acquisition date, the consolidated net income must not include that portion of the subsidiary's net income that does not accrue to the parent company. Because the consolidated income statement must include all of the subsidiary's sales, costs, and expenses, that portion of the subsidiary's net income that accrues to the minority interest must be shown as a deduction in consolidation. If this is not done, consolidated net income is overstated by an amount equal to the minority shareholders' interest in the subsidiary's net income. Including this deduction in the consolidated column of the worksheet makes the detail of the subsidiary's income statement accounts equal the parent's interest in the subsidiary's net income, which it has recorded under the equity method of accounting.

The minority interest deduction appears in the income statement section of the worksheet as the posting of an entry, which we call the minority interest entry. For example, assume a 90% owned subsidiary has net income of $15,000 for a given year. The minority interest deduction would equal 10% of the subsidiary's net income of $15,000, or $1,500. The entry is as follows:

Minority interest (income statement) 1,500
    Retained earnings—Subsidiary (net income line)   1,500

---

[1] *ARB No. 51,* "Consolidated Financial Statements" (New York: AICPA, 1959), paragraph 1.

The debit is posted to the income statement section of the worksheet, and the credit is posted to the subsidiary's net income line in the analysis of retained earnings in the balance sheet section of the worksheet. This entry affects only the income statement. The balance sheet is not affected, because the debit posting in the income statement is totaled at the net income line of the income statement and then carried forward to the subsidiary's net income line in the analysis of retained earnings in the balance sheet section of the worksheet. The sole purpose of the entry is to make the detail of the subsidiary's net income statement accounts equal the parent's interest in the subsidiary's net income.

Other than this additional entry, the consolidation procedures for a partially owned subsidiary are the same as those for a wholly owned subsidiary. When the subsidiary has a net loss, the debit is to Retained Earnings and the credit is to Minority Interest. As with the primary and secondary elimination entries, this minority interest entry is posted only to the consolidating statement worksheet—never to the general ledger.

Treatment of dividends paid to minority shareholders

In Chapter 4, we stated that dividend payments from the subsidiary to the parent constitute intercompany transactions and are therefore not reported as dividends in the consolidated statement of retained earnings. Such transactions do not take place between the consolidated group and outsiders.

In partially owned subsidiaries, dividends paid to minority interest shareholders do take place between the consolidated group and outsiders. Such dividends, however, cannot be added to the dividends declared by the parent in preparing the consolidated statement of retained earnings. The reason is obvious. The consolidated retained earnings include only the earnings of the subsidiary that accrue to the parent. Thus, including dividends paid to minority shareholders with dividends paid to the parent's shareholders would be inconsistent. Instead, the subsidiary's dividends that accrue to the minority shareholders are treated as a reduction of the minority interest.

NEITHER GOODWILL NOR A BARGAIN PURCHASE ELEMENT EXISTS AND NET ASSETS ARE NOT OVER- OR UNDERVALUED

When the parent's cost equals the parent's ownership interest in the current value of the subsidiary's net assets and the current value equals the book value, the analysis of the investment account as of the acquisition date is relatively simple. Because the analysis contains only the book value element, we must only separate the book value element into its individual components. We do this by multiplying the parent's ownership percentage by each of the subsidiary's existing capital account balances as of the acquisition date.

Illustration:
Preparing consolidated financial statements
as of the acquisition date

Assume the same information for P Company and S Company as provided in Chapter 3 (page 91), except assume that P Company acquired only 90% of S Company's outstanding common stock at a cost of $54,000 (instead of 100% at a cost of $60,000). The expanded analysis of the investment account as of the acquisition date is as follows:

			Book Value Element		
Date	Total Cost	=	Common Stock (90% of $40,000)	+	Retained Earnings (90% of $20,000)
January 1, 19X1	$54,000		$36,000		$18,000

From this analysis of the investment account, the primary elimination entry as of the acquisition date is as follows:

(1) The primary elimination entry:

Common stock	36,000	
Retained earnings	18,000	
Investment in subsidiary		54,000

Illustration 5-1 shows a consolidating statement worksheet as of January 1, 19X1 (the acquisition date). In reviewing Illustration 5-1, the following points should be understood:

(1) The primary elimination entry eliminates the investment account against the parent's interest in the subsidiary's net assets.
(2) The minority interest in the subsidiary's net assets is that portion of the subsidiary's capital accounts that is not eliminated by the primary elimination entry.
(3) The minority interest in each of the subsidiary's individual capital accounts is extended to the consolidated column, and the letter "M" placed next to the amount designates it as minority interest.
(4) The amounts designated as minority interest in the consolidated column are combined into one amount when the parent's consolidated balance sheet is prepared for issuance to the parent company's stockholders— that is, only one amount is disclosed as the minority interest.
(5) The total minority interest is always determinable by multiplying the minority interest ownership percentage by the total stockholders' equity of the subsidiary. In this example, it is 10% of $60,000, or $6,000.

Illustration:
Preparing consolidated financial statements
for first year subsequent to the acquisition date

Assume the subsidiary in the preceding illustration had net income of $15,000 in 19X1 and declared dividends of $5,000 in that year. Under the

Illustration 5-1

P COMPANY AND SUBSIDIARY (S COMPANY) Consolidating Statement Worksheet As of January 1, 19X1					
	P Company	S Company	Eliminations		Consoli- dated
			Dr.	Cr.	
Balance Sheet:					
Cash......................	56,000	20,000			76,000
Accounts receivable, net	120,000	30,000			150,000
Inventory	80,000	32,000			112,000
Investment in S Company ...	54,000			54,000(1)	-0-
Land	80,000	30,000			110,000
Building—Cost	400,000	100,000			500,000
—Accum. depr.	(250,000)	(18,000)			(268,000)
Equipment—Cost	300,000	90,000			390,000
—Accum. depr.	(140,000)	(34,000)			(174,000)
	700,000	250,000		54,000	896,000
Liabilities	300,000	190,000			490,000
Common stock:					
P Company	300,000				300,000
S Company		40,000	36,000(1)		4,000M
Retained earnings:					
P Company	100,000				100,000
S Company		20,000	18,000(1)		2,000M
	700,000	250,000	54,000		896,000
Proof of debit and credit postings			54,000	54,000	
Total minority interest					$6,000

Explanation of entry:
(1) The primary elimination entry.

equity method of accounting, the parent would report its share of these amounts. The expanded analysis of the investment account would be updated as follows:

			Book Value Element			
				Retained Earnings		
				Prior	Current Year	
	Total Cost	=	Common Stock	+ Years	+ Earnings	– Dividends
Balance, January 1, 19X1	$54,000		$36,000	$18,000		
Equity in net income	13,500				$13,500	
Dividends	(4,500)					$(4,500)
Subtotal.....................	$63,000		$36,000	$18,000	$13,500	$(4,500)
Reclassification				9,000	(13,500)	4,500
Balance, December 31, 19X1	$63,000		$36,000	$27,000	$ -0-	$ -0-

Consolidated financial statements as of December 31, 19X1, would be prepared using the following primary elimination entry:

Common stock	36,000	
Retained earnings	18,000	
Equity in net income of subsidiary	13,500	
Dividends declared.....................................		4,500
Investment in subsidiary		63,000

The minority interest entry is 10% of the subsidiary's $15,000 net income, as follows:

Minority interest (income statement) 1,500
     Retained earnings—Subsidiary (net income line)   1,500

The above entries are posted to the consolidating statement worksheet as of December 31, 19X1, in Illustration 5-2. In reviewing Illustration 5-2, the following points should be understood:

(1) As with the primary elimination entry, the minority interest entry is posted only to the consolidating statement worksheet—never to a general ledger.
(2) The entries in the eliminations column in the income statement section are subtotaled at the net income line, and this amount is carried forward to the net income line in the analysis of the subsidiary's retained earnings in the balance sheet section.
(3) The primary elimination entry eliminates the parent's interest in the subsidiary's retained earnings amount. The minority interest entry affects only the income statement; it has a wash effect in the balance sheet.
(4) The total minority interest in the balance sheet ($7,000) can be proved by multiplying the minority interest ownership percentage (10%) by the total stockholders' equity of the subsidiary ($70,000).
(5) The minority interest in net income in the income statement section of the consolidated column is shown below the income tax provision only on the worksheet. In the consolidated income statement that the parent prepares for its stockholders, the amount of the minority interest in net income is shown among the costs and expenses used in arriving at income before taxes.
(6) The net income in the parent's income column is identical with the consolidated net income.
(7) The analysis of retained earnings in the parent's column is identical with the analysis of consolidated retained earnings in the consolidated column.

GOODWILL EXISTS AND NET ASSETS ARE UNDERVALUED

The parent company theory

In the preceding two illustrations, the subsidiary's net assets were not over- or undervalued and goodwill did not exist. The cost to the parent of acquiring 90% of the outstanding common stock was 90% of the book value of the subsidiary's net assets. When the subsidiary has undervalued assets or goodwill, or both, the parent's cost in excess of its ownership interest in the book value of the subsidiary's net assets logically depends on the parent's ownership interest. For example, assume the subsidiary has undervalued assets worth $20,000. If the acquiring company is willing to pay $20,000 in excess of the book value of the net assets for all of the outstanding

Illustration 5-2

<table>
<tr><td colspan="7">P COMPANY AND SUBSIDIARY (S COMPANY)
Consolidating Statement Worksheet
For the Year Ended December 31, 19X1</td></tr>
<tr><td></td><td>P</td><td>S</td><td colspan="2">Eliminations</td><td colspan="2">Consoli-</td></tr>
<tr><td></td><td>Company</td><td>Company</td><td>Dr.</td><td>Cr.</td><td colspan="2">dated</td></tr>
<tr><td colspan="7">Income Statement:</td></tr>
<tr><td>Sales . . . .</td><td>600,000</td><td>200,000</td><td></td><td></td><td colspan="2">800,000</td></tr>
<tr><td>Income from subsidiary:</td><td></td><td></td><td></td><td></td><td colspan="2"></td></tr>
<tr><td>Equity in net income . . . .</td><td>13,500</td><td></td><td>13,500(1)</td><td></td><td colspan="2">-0-</td></tr>
<tr><td>Subtotal . . . .</td><td>613,500</td><td>200,000</td><td>13,500</td><td></td><td colspan="2">800,000</td></tr>
<tr><td>Cost of goods sold. . . . .</td><td>360,000</td><td>120,000</td><td></td><td></td><td colspan="2">480,000</td></tr>
<tr><td>Marketing expenses. . . . .</td><td>90,000</td><td>30,000</td><td></td><td></td><td colspan="2">120,000</td></tr>
<tr><td>Administrative expenses . . . .</td><td>60,000</td><td>20,000</td><td></td><td></td><td colspan="2">80,000</td></tr>
<tr><td>Interest expense . . . .</td><td>30,000</td><td>5,000</td><td></td><td></td><td colspan="2">35,000</td></tr>
<tr><td>Subtotal . . . .</td><td>540,000</td><td>175,000</td><td></td><td></td><td colspan="2">715,000</td></tr>
<tr><td>Income before Income Taxes
and Minority Interest . . . .</td><td>73,500</td><td>25,000</td><td>13,500</td><td></td><td colspan="2">85,000</td></tr>
<tr><td>Income tax expense @ 40%</td><td>(24,000)[a]</td><td>(10,000)</td><td></td><td></td><td colspan="2">(34,000)</td></tr>
<tr><td>Income before Minority Interest. .</td><td>49,500</td><td>15,000</td><td>13,500</td><td></td><td colspan="2">51,000</td></tr>
<tr><td>Minority interest . . . .</td><td></td><td></td><td>1,500(2)</td><td></td><td colspan="2">(1,500)</td></tr>
<tr><td>Net Income . . . .</td><td>49,500</td><td>15,000</td><td>15,000</td><td></td><td colspan="2">49,500</td></tr>
<tr><td colspan="7">Balance Sheet:</td></tr>
<tr><td>Cash . . . .</td><td>60,500</td><td>32,000</td><td></td><td></td><td colspan="2">92,500</td></tr>
<tr><td>Accounts receivable, net. . . . .</td><td>145,000</td><td>43,000</td><td></td><td></td><td colspan="2">188,000</td></tr>
<tr><td>Inventory. . . . .</td><td>90,000</td><td>40,000</td><td></td><td></td><td colspan="2">130,000</td></tr>
<tr><td>Investment in S Company . . . . . .</td><td>63,000</td><td></td><td></td><td>63,000(1)</td><td colspan="2">-0-</td></tr>
<tr><td>Land . . . .</td><td>80,000</td><td>30,000</td><td></td><td></td><td colspan="2">110,000</td></tr>
<tr><td>Building, net. . . . .</td><td>140,000</td><td>77,000</td><td></td><td></td><td colspan="2">217,000</td></tr>
<tr><td>Equipment, net . . . .</td><td>130,000</td><td>48,000</td><td></td><td></td><td colspan="2">178,000</td></tr>
<tr><td>Total assets . . . .</td><td>708,500</td><td>270,000</td><td></td><td>63,000</td><td colspan="2">915,500</td></tr>
<tr><td>Liabilities. . . . .</td><td>290,000</td><td>200,000</td><td></td><td></td><td colspan="2">490,000</td></tr>
<tr><td>Common stock:</td><td></td><td></td><td></td><td></td><td colspan="2"></td></tr>
<tr><td>P Company . . . .</td><td>300,000</td><td></td><td></td><td></td><td colspan="2">300,000</td></tr>
<tr><td>S Company . . . .</td><td></td><td>40,000</td><td>36,000(1)</td><td></td><td>4,000M</td><td rowspan="4">⎤
⎥
⎥
⎥</td></tr>
<tr><td>Retained earnings—P Company:</td><td></td><td></td><td></td><td></td><td></td></tr>
<tr><td>Beginning of year . . . .</td><td>100,000</td><td></td><td></td><td></td><td>100,000</td></tr>
<tr><td>+ Net income . . . .</td><td>49,500</td><td></td><td></td><td></td><td>49,500</td></tr>
<tr><td>− Dividends declared . . . .</td><td>(31,000)</td><td></td><td></td><td></td><td colspan="2">(31,000)</td></tr>
<tr><td>End of year . . . .</td><td>118,500</td><td></td><td></td><td></td><td colspan="2">118,500</td></tr>
<tr><td>Retained earnings—S Company:</td><td></td><td></td><td></td><td></td><td colspan="2"></td></tr>
<tr><td>Beginning of year . . . .</td><td></td><td>20,000</td><td>18,000(1)</td><td></td><td colspan="2">2,000M</td></tr>
<tr><td>+ Net income . . . .</td><td></td><td>15,000</td><td>→15,000 ·</td><td>1,500(2)</td><td colspan="2">1,500M</td></tr>
<tr><td>− Dividends declared . . . .</td><td></td><td>(5,000)</td><td></td><td>4,500(1)</td><td colspan="2">(500)M</td></tr>
<tr><td>End of year . . . .</td><td></td><td>30,000</td><td>33,000</td><td>6,000</td><td>3,000M</td><td>⎦</td></tr>
<tr><td>Total liabilities and equity . . .</td><td>708,500</td><td>270,000</td><td>69,000</td><td>6,000</td><td colspan="2">915,500</td></tr>
<tr><td>Proof of debit and credit postings . . . .</td><td></td><td></td><td>69,000</td><td>69,000</td><td colspan="2"></td></tr>
<tr><td colspan="5">Total minority interest . . . .</td><td>7,000 ←</td><td>┘</td></tr>
</table>

Explanation of entries:
(1) The primary elimination entry.
(2) The minority interest entry.
[a] The income tax calculation is 40% of $60,000, not 40% of $73,500.

common stock, then for a 90% ownership interest, the acquiring company should be willing to pay only $18,000 in excess of its ownership interest in the book value of the net assets. Similarly, if the acquiring company is willing to pay $10,000 for goodwill in acquiring all of the common stock, then it obviously should be willing to pay only $9,000 for goodwill if it acquired only a 90% ownership interest.

Separating total cost into major conceptual elements. With this understanding of the factors that enter into the determination of total cost in partial ownership situations, we may separate the total cost into its major conceptual elements using the following procedures:

(1) The book value element is determined by multiplying the parent's own-ership percentage by the book value of the subsidiary's net assets.
(2) The current value over book value element is determined by multiplying the parent's ownership percentage by the undervaluation of the sub-sidiary's net assets.
(3) The goodwill element is the cost in excess of the sum of the amounts determined in (1) and (2). Thus, the goodwill element is determined in a residual manner.

In Situation E of Illustration 3-5 (page 84), P Company acquired 100% of the outstanding common stock of S Company at a cost of $90,000, which was $30,000 in excess of the book value of the subsidiary's net assets. The $30,000 excess payment was identified as undervalued assets ($20,000) and goodwill ($10,000). Assume instead that P Company purchased only 90% of the outstanding common stock for $81,000 (90% of $90,000). The separation of the total cost into its major conceptual elements is as follows:

		Book Value Element		Current Value over Book Value Element		Goodwill Element
Total Cost	=	(90% of $60,000)	+	(90% of $20,000)	+	(Residual)
$81,000		$54,000		$18,000		$9,000

Separating the major conceptual elements into their individual com-ponents. We separate the current value over book value element into its individual components by multiplying the parent's ownership percentages by the amount that each asset is undervalued. In Illustration 3-6 (page 88), the $20,000 undervaluation was attributed to Inventory, Land, and Building accounts. This $20,000 is separated into its individual components as follows:

Asset	Total Current Value over Book Value	Parent's Ownership Percentage	Parent's Interest in Current Value over Book Value
Inventory	$ 4,000	90	$ 3,600
Land	10,000	90	9,000
Building	6,000	90	5,400
	$20,000		$18,000

The expanded analysis of the investment account by the individual components of the major conceptual elements is as follows:

Book value element:
Common stock	$36,000	
Retained earnings	18,000	$54,000
Current value over book value element:		
Inventory	$ 3,600	
Land	9,000	
Building	5,400	18,000
Goodwill element		9,000
Total cost		$81,000

The primary elimination entry obtained with this procedure revalues the subsidiary's assets to their current values **only to the extent that such undervaluation is paid for by the parent company** ($18,000 in this example). Likewise, goodwill is reflected in the consolidated financial statements only to the extent that it is paid for by the parent company ($9,000 in this example). Thus, this approach results in **partial revaluation** of the subsidiary's assets, which is consistent with the parent company theory, discussed earlier in the chapter.

A different revaluation result occurs under the entity theory, which was also discussed earlier in the chapter. Before discussing how this occurs, we illustrate the preparation of consolidated financial statements (as of the acquisition date and in years subsequent to the acquisition date) using the partial revaluation results that occur under the parent company theory.

Illustration:
Preparing consolidated financial statements
as of the acquisition date

For this example, the primary elimination entry as of the acquisition date, taken from the expanded analysis of the investment account, is as follows:

(1) The primary elimination entry:

Common stock	36,000	
Retained earnings	18,000	
Inventory	3,600	
Land	9,000	
Building	5,400	
Goodwill	9,000	
Investment in subsidiary		81,000

This primary elimination entry is used in Illustration 5-3 to prepare a consolidating statement worksheet as of January 1, 19X1 (the acquisition date) for P Company and S Company.

Illustration 5-3

	P Company	S Company	Eliminations Dr.	Eliminations Cr.	Consolidated
P COMPANY AND SUBSIDIARY (S COMPANY) Consolidating Statement Worksheet As of January 1, 19X1					
Balance Sheet:					
Cash	29,000	20,000			49,000
Accounts receivable, net	120,000	30,000			150,000
Inventory	80,000	32,000	3,600(1)		115,600
Investment in S Company . . .	81,000			81,000(1)	-0-
Land	80,000	30,000	9,000(1)		119,000
Building—Cost	400,000	100,000	5,400(1)		505,400
—Accum. depr.	(250,000)	(18,000)			(268,000)
Equipment—Cost	300,000	90,000			390,000
—Accum. depr. . . .	(140,000)	(34,000)			(174,000)
Goodwill			9,000(1)		9,000
	700,000	250,000	27,000	81,000	896,000
Liabilities	300,000	190,000			490,000
Common stock:					
P Company	300,000				300,000
S Company		40,000	36,000(1)		4,000M
Retained earnings:					
P Company	100,000				100,000
S Company		20,000	18,000(1)		2,000M
	700,000	250,000	54,000		896,000

Proof of debit and credit postings 81,000   81,000

Total minority interest   6,000

Explanation of entry:
(1) The primary elimination entry.

Illustration:
Updating the expanded analysis of the investment account using the equity method

Assume that S Company had the following earnings, losses, dividends, and amortization of cost over book value for the two years subsequent to the acquisition date:

	19X1	19X2
Net income	$15,000	$24,000
Dividends	5,000	-0-
Amortization of cost in excess of book value	4,770	1,170

Illustration 5-4 shows an expanded analysis of the investment account for two years following the acquisition date, using the above information.

Illustrations:
Preparing consolidated financial statements for first and second years subsequent to the acquisition date

The consolidated financial statements as of December 31, 19X1 (one year after the acquisition date) and December 31, 19X2 (two years after the

Illustration 5-4
Updating the expanded analysis of the investment account using the equity method
(90% owned subsidiary—Goodwill exists and net assets are undervalued)

	Total Cost =	Common Stock +	Book Value Element — Retained Earnings — Prior Years +	Current Year Earnings –	Dividends +	Current Value over Book Value Element — Inven-tory (3 Mo) +	Land (Infinite) +	Building — Cost (20 Yr) +	Accum. Depr. +	Goodwill Element (10 Yr)
Remaining life										
Balance, January 1, 19X1	$ 81,000	$36,000	$18,000			$ 3,600	$9,000	$5,400		$9,000
Equity in net income	13,500			$13,500						
Dividends	(4,500)				$(4,500)					
Amortization	(4,770)					(3,600)			$(270)	(900)
Subtotal	$ 85,230	$36,000	$18,000	$13,500	$(4,500)	$ -0-	$9,000	$5,400	$(270)	$8,100
Reclassification			9,000	(13,500)	4,500					
Balance, December 31,19X1	$ 85,230	$36,000	$27,000	$ -0-	$ -0-	$ -0-	$9,000	$5,400	$(270)	$8,100
Equity in net income	21,600			21,600						
Amortization	(1,170)								(270)	(900)
Subtotal	$105,660	$36,000	$27,000	$21,600	$ -0-	$ -0-	$9,000	$5,400	$(540)	$7,200
Reclassification			21,600	(21,600)						
Balance, December 31, 19X2	$105,660	$36,000	$48,600	$ -0-	$ -0-	$ -0-	$9,000	$5,400	$(540)	$7,200

Note: The updating of the analysis for the two years after the acquisition date uses the same income, loss, and dividend information (and the same remaining lives of the assets) as in Illustration 4-2 (page 122).

acquisition date) are prepared using the following primary, secondary, and minority interest entries:

(1) The primary elimination entry:

	Consolidation Date	
	December 31, 19X1	December 31, 19X2
Common stock	36,000	36,000
Retained earnings	18,000	27,000
Equity in net income of subsidiary..............	13,500	21,600
Land	9,000	9,000
Building—Cost	5,400	5,400
—Accum. depr.	270	540
Goodwill	8,100	7,200
Dividends declared	4,500	
Investment in subsidiary..................	85,230	105,660

(2) The secondary elimination entry:

Cost of goods sold	4,770	1,170
Amortization of cost in excess of book value	4,770	1,170

(3) The minority interest entry:

Minority interest (income statement)	1,500	2,400
Retained earnings—Subsidiary (net income line).................................	1,500	2,400

(10% of subsidiary's net income
of $15,000 for 19X1 and $24,000 for 19X2)

Illustrations 5-5 and 5-6 show consolidating statement worksheets as of December 31, 19X1, and December 31, 19X2, respectively.

In reviewing Illustrations 5-5 and 5-6, the following points should be understood:

(1) The minority interest in the consolidated balance sheet is always the minority interest ownership percentage multiplied by the total stockholders' equity of the subsidiary.
(2) The minority interest in the consolidated income statement always equals the minority interest ownership percentage multiplied by the subsidiary's reported net income or loss.

The entity theory

In the example used in the discussion of the parent company theory, the subsidiary's net assets were undervalued by $20,000 at the acquisition date, and the undervalued assets were revalued upward by $18,000 (90% × $20,000) in consolidation. Some accountants believe that the **subsidiary's identifiable assets and liabilities should be fully revalued in consolidation to 100% of their current values, regardless of the parent's ownership interest.** Thus, they would revalue the subsidiary's assets upward by $20,000

Illustration 5-5

P COMPANY AND SUBSIDIARY (S COMPANY) Consolidating Statement Worksheet For the Year Ended December 31, 19X1					
	P Company	S Company	Eliminations Dr.	Eliminations Cr.	Consolidated
Income Statement:					
Sales........................	600,000	200,000			800,000
Income from subsidiary:					
Equity in net income	13,500		13,500(1)		-0-
Amortization of cost in					
excess of book value	(4,770)			4,770(2)	-0-
Subtotal	608,730	200,000	13,500	4,770	800,000
Cost of goods sold.............	360,000	120,000	4,770(2)		484,770
Marketing expenses............	90,000	30,000			120,000
Administrative expenses	60,000	20,000			80,000
Interest expense	30,000	5,000			35,000
Subtotal	540,000	175,000	4,770		719,770
Income before Income Taxes					
and Minority Interest	68,730	25,000	18,270	4,770	80,230
Income tax expense @ 40%	(24,000)[a]	(10,000)			(34,000)
Income before Minority Interest..	44,730	15,000	18,270	4,770	46,230
Minority interest				1,500(3)	(1,500)
Net Income	44,730	15,000	19,770	4,770	44,730
Balance Sheet:					
Cash........................	33,500	32,000			65,500
Accounts receivable, net	145,000	43,000			188,000
Inventory	90,000	40,000			130,000
Investment in S Company	85,230			85,230(1)	-0-
Land	80,000	30,000	9,000(1)		119,000
Building—Cost	400,000	100,000	5,400(1)		505,400
—Accum. depr.	(260,000)	(23,000)		270(1)	(283,270)
Equipment—Cost	300,000	90,000			390,000
—Accum. depr.	(170,000)	(42,000)			(212,000)
Goodwill.....................			8,100(1)		8,100
Total assets..............	703,730	270,000	22,500	85,500	910,730
Liabilities	290,000	200,000			490,000
Common stock:					
P Company.................	300,000				300,000
S Company.................		40,000	36,000(1)		4,000M
Retained earnings—P Company:					
Beginning of year............	100,000				100,000
+ Net income	44,730				44,730
− Dividends declared........	(31,000)				(31,000)
End of year	113,730				113,730
Retained earnings—S Company:					
Beginning of year............		20,000	18,000(1)		2,000M
+ Net income		15,000	19,770	4,770 1,500(3)	1,500M
− Dividends declared........		(5,000)		4,500(1)	(500)M
End of year		30,000	37,770	10,770	3,000M
Total liabilities and equity...	703,730	270,000	73,770	10,770	910,730
Proof of debit and credit postings....................			96,270	96,270	
Total minority interest					7,000

Explanation of entries:
 (1) The primary elimination entry.
 (2) The secondary elimination entry.
 (3) The minority interest entry.
 [a] The income tax calculation is 40% of $60,000, not 40% of $68,730.

Illustration 5-6

P COMPANY AND SUBSIDIARY (S COMPANY)
Consolidating Statement Worksheet
For the Year Ended December 31, 19X2

	P Company	S Company	Eliminations Dr.	Eliminations Cr.	Consolidated
Income Statement:					
Sales.........................	650,000	230,000			880,000
Income from subsidiary:					
Equity in net income	21,600		21,600(1)		-0-
Amortization of cost in					
excess of book value	(1,170)			1,170(2)	-0-
Subtotal	670,430	230,000	21,600	1,170	880,000
Cost of goods sold	390,000	130,000	1,170(2)		521,170
Marketing expenses	100,000	35,000			135,000
Administrative expenses........	60,000	20,000			80,000
Interest expense..............	30,000	5,000			35,000
Subtotal	580,000	190,000	1,170		771,170
Income before Income Taxes					
and Minority Interest	90,430	40,000	22,770	1,170	108,830
Income tax expense @ 40%	(28,000)[a]	(16,000)			(44,000)
Income before Minority Interest	62,430	24,000	22,770	1,170	64,830
Minority interest				2,400	(2,400)
Net Income	62,430	24,000	25,170	1,170	62,430
Balance Sheet:					
Cash.........................	48,500	15,000			63,500
Accounts receivable, net	190,000	65,000			255,000
Inventory	110,000	60,000			170,000
Investment in S Company	105,660			105,660(1)	-0-
Land	80,000	30,000	9,000(1)		119,000
Building—Cost	400,000	100,000	5,400(1)		505,400
—Accum. depr.	(270,000)	(28,000)		540(1)	(298,540)
Equipment—Cost	300,000	90,000			390,000
—Accum. depr.	(200,000)	(50,000)			(250,000)
Goodwill			7,200(1)		7,200
Total assets..............	764,160	282,000	21,600	106,200	961,560
Liabilities	329,000	188,000			517,000
Common stock:					
P Company	300,000				300,000
S Company		40,000	36,000(1)		4,000M
Retained earnings—P Company:					
Beginning of year............	113,730				113,730
+ Net income	62,430				62,430
− Dividends declared........	(41,000)				(41,000)
End of year	135,160				135,160
Retained earnings—S Company:					
Beginning of year............		30,000	27,000(1)		3,000M
+ Net income		24,000	25,170	1,170	2,400M
				2,400(3)	
− Dividends declared........		-0-			-0-
End of year		54,000	52,170	3,570	5,400M
Total liabilities and equity...	764,160	282,000	88,170	3,570	961,560
Proof of debit and credit postings.................			109,770	109,770	

Total minority interest 9,400

Explanation of entries:
  (1) The primary elimination entry.
  (2) The secondary elimination entry.
  (3) The minority interest entry.
  [a] The income tax calculation is 40% of $70,000, not 40% of $90,430.

instead of $18,000. The additional $2,000 valuation would be reflected as an increase in the minority interest in the balance sheet. Such additional valuation results in additional amortization charges in future consolidated income statements. However, a corresponding reduction in the amount of consolidated net income is allocated to the minority shareholders. Thus, the amount of consolidated net income allocated to the controlling interests (the parent's shareholders) is not affected. (The mechanics of accomplishing this are illustrated in Appendix A.) This approach comes under the entity theory, which was discussed earlier in the chapter. Theoretically, the approach has substantial merit in that a partial revaluation of the subsidiary's assets and liabilities results in a hybrid valuation of such items somewhere between their historical costs and their current values. The proponents of this theory feel that it makes more sense to revalue the assets and liabilities to their current values, as this would be more informative. However, because most business combinations involve large companies acquiring significantly smaller companies, the consolidated financial statements would not be that much more meaningful under the full revaluation approach.

Under the entity theory, the value of goodwill in consolidation is based on the amount of goodwill implicit in the transaction. For example, if the parent paid $9,000 for goodwill in acquiring a 90% ownership interest, then the goodwill implicit in the transaction would be $10,000 ($9,000/90%). Thus, goodwill would be valued at $10,000 instead of $9,000, and the additional $1,000 valuation would be reflected as an increase to the minority interest in the balance sheet. As in the case of undervalued assets, this additional goodwill results in additional amortization expense in future consolidated income statements. However, a corresponding reduction in the amount of consolidated net income is allocated to the minority shareholders. Thus, the amount of consolidated net income allocated to the controlling interests (the parent's shareholders) is not affected.

The combination entity–parent company approach

A third alternative adopts certain features of both the parent company theory and the entity theory. We refer to this approach as the **combination entity– parent company approach.** Under this approach, the subsidiary's identifiable assets and liabilities are fully revalued in consolidation to 100% of their current values (as is done under the entity theory). However, goodwill is valued in consolidation only to the extent that it is paid for by the parent company (as is done under the parent company theory).

Whether the minority interest under this combination approach should be presented in the consolidated financial statements in accordance with the entity theory or the parent company theory is an arbitrary decision, because the approach is a combination of the two theories. The minority interest is rarely presented under the entity theory; apparently, companies that use this combination approach present the minority interest in accordance with the parent company theory.

Selection of valuation method

Neither *ARB No. 51* nor *APB Opinion No. 16* provides explicit guidance on which of the three valuation choices to use. Regardless of the theoretical soundness of the entity theory (as used in its entirety or in the combination entity–parent company approach), we believe that it produces results that are not consistent with the historical cost basis of accounting (which underlies the purchase method) because values are imputed above and beyond cost. The AICPA's answers to its CPA examination problems in this area support our position by showing assets and liabilities revalued and goodwill valued only to the extent of the parent company's cost over its ownership interest in the book value of the subsidiary's net assets. The entity theory and the combination entity–parent company approach make the preparation of consolidated financial statements somewhat more involved. When the parent's ownership interest is close to 100%, using the entity theory or the combination entity–parent company approach usually has no appreciable effect on the balance sheet. (In most business combinations in which common stock is acquired, the parent's ownership is more than 90%.)

The extent to which each of the three valuation techniques is actually used is not readily determinable. In 1976, the FASB attempted to make such a determination in connection with its project on accounting for business combinations and purchased intangibles. FASB staff interviews revealed that the majority of U.S. companies use either the parent company theory or the combination entity–parent company approach. The FASB surveyed 250 enterprises that apparently had business combinations accounted for as purchases and found that in the 122 usable responses, only 15 business combinations existed in which minority interests remained outstanding. The method of determining the minority interests was indicated for only 13 of these partial acquisitions. For these 13 responses, 12 companies indicated that the valuation of the minority interest in the consolidated financial statements was based on the amount shown in the acquired company's financial statements; that is, partial revaluation pursuant to the parent company theory was used. The one other response indicated that the valuation of the minority interest in the consolidated financial statements was based on the fair value of the consideration given. In other words, full revaluation pursuant to the entity theory was used. Of the 122 usable responses, approximately 70% listed their stock either on the New York Stock Exchange or the American Stock Exchange, and approximately 25% of the companies traded their stock over the counter or on a regional stock exchange.[2]

For these reasons, we used the parent company theory instead of the entity theory or the combination entity–parent company approach to illustrate the preparation of consolidated financial statements in this section of the chapter. (We also use the parent company theory in later chapters when minority interest situations are encountered.) Consequently, the minority interest presented in the consolidated balance sheet always equals the ownership percentage of the minority shareholders multiplied by the book value of the subsidiary's stockholders' equity. Likewise, the minority interest presented in the consolidated income statement (which is shown as a deduction in arriving at consolidated net income under the parent company theory) is always based on the subsidiary's net income as shown in its separate income statement.

---

[2] *FASB Discussion Memorandum,* "Accounting for Business Combinations and Purchased Intangibles" (Stamford, CT: FASB, 1976) pp. 107, E-8, and E-17.

The FASB is addressing the valuation method issue for minority interest situations in its project on consolidations and the equity method of accounting. Thus, the FASB may choose any one of the three valuation methods. Accordingly, in Appendix B, we discuss and illustrate how to deal with the additional values reported in consolidation under the entity theory and the combination entity–parent company approach.

COST IS BELOW THE PARENT'S OWNERSHIP INTEREST IN THE BOOK VALUE OF THE SUBSIDIARY'S NET ASSETS

When the parent's cost is below its ownership interest in the book value of the subsidiary's net assets, the procedures for analyzing the investment account by the individual components of the major conceptual elements are identical with those previously illustrated. The only difference is that the second major conceptual element—the current value over (under) book value element—has a negative balance instead of a positive balance. We do not illustrate preparing consolidated financial statements for these situations, because the procedures are the same as in situations in which the current value of the subsidiary's net assets exceeds their book value.

BLOCK ACQUISITIONS

All the business combinations illustrated so far (in which a parent–subsidiary relationship was formed) were assumed to result from a single acquisition of the acquired company's outstanding common stock. Often, control over an entity is accomplished by acquiring blocks of common stock over a period of time. When the acquiring company attains more than 50% ownership, the acquired company becomes a subsidiary and consolidation procedures are appropriate. Until then, the investor must account for the investment as follows:

(1) **Less that 20% ownership.** The lower of cost or market, as prescribed by *FASB Statement No. 12*.
(2) **20% through 50% ownership.** The equity method of accounting, as prescribed by *APB Opinion No. 18*.

When blocks of stock are acquired, *ARB No. 51* governs the determination of the individual components as of the control date so that consolidated financial statements can be prepared. It reads as follows:

> When one company purchases two or more blocks of stock of another company at various dates and eventually obtains control of the other company, the date of acquisition (for the purpose of preparing consolidated statements) depends on the circumstances. If two or more purchases are made over a period of time, the earned surplus [current terminology is retained earnings] of the subsidiary at acquisition should generally be determined on a step-by-step basis; however, if small purchases are made over a period of time and then a purchase is made which results in control, the date of the latest purchase, as a matter of convenience, may be considered as the date of acquisition.[3]

[3] *ARB No. 51*, paragraph 10.

In the **step-by-step** method, the cost of each block of stock acquired is separated into its individual components of the major conceptual elements using data that apply to the date the block was purchased. Cumulative amounts are then determined for each of the individual components of the major conceptual elements as of the control date, using the analysis of each block's cost by individual components. The procedures for analyzing the cost of each block of stock by the individual components of the major conceptual elements are identical with those discussed and illustrated earlier in the chapter when the purchase of a single (although large) block of stock resulted in control.

In the **date of latest purchase** method, the total carrying value of the investment, as of the control date, is separated into the individual components of the major conceptual elements using data that apply only to the date control is obtained. This approach makes the practical (although artificial) assumption that all of the acquired shares were purchased on the date control was obtained. It is identical with the procedures discussed and illustrated earlier in the chapter when control was achieved in a single purchase. Accordingly, it is not illustrated in this section.

It is important to realize that *ARB No. 51* was issued before *APB Opinion No. 18* was issued. When 20–50% ownership levels exist, *APB Opinion No. 18* requires the investor to separate its cost into the individual components of the major conceptual elements using the step-by-step approach. When less than 20% ownership exists and an additional purchase results in at least 20% ownership, the investor must adjust the investment account "retroactively in a manner consistent with accounting for a step-by-step acquisition of a subsidiary."[4] As a result of *APB Opinion No. 18,* the probability of using the date of the latest purchase as the acquisition date has been significantly reduced. In many instances, with several small purchases over a period of time, the investor must use the equity method of accounting on reaching the 20% ownership level. Any blocks acquired beyond the 20% ownership level would be accounted for using the step-by-step method. For the date of latest purchase method to be used, the investor would have to make several small purchases that, cumulatively, do not exceed the 20% ownership level, and then make a large purchase that gives more than 50% ownership—for example, 5%, 5%, 5%, and 40%. In other words, the 20–50% ownership range would have to be bypassed.

Step-by-step method

In the following illustration, an investment accounted for under the equity method is increased until control over the investee is eventually obtained. The step-by-step method is used.

Illustration:
Preparing the expanded analysis of the investment account as of the control date—Step-by-step method

Assume the following block acquisition information.

[4] *APB Opinion No. 18,* "The Equity Method of Accounting for Investments in Common Stock" (New York: AICPA, 1971), paragraph 19m.

			Information Relating to Investee		
Date of Block Acquisition	Ownership Percentage Acquired	Cost	Common Stock	Retained Earnings[a]	Net Assets Current Value over Book Value[b]
January 1, 19X1	20	$15,000	$40,000	$ 5,000	$20,000
January 1, 19X2	25	21,750	40,000	15,000	20,000
July 1, 19X2	30	33,500	40,000	35,000	20,000

[a] We assume the investee paid no dividends during the time the block acquisitions were made. Accordingly, the earnings for 19X1 and the first six months of 19X2 are $10,000 and $20,000, respectively.
[b] For simplicity, we assume that the entire undervaluation of net assets relates to a parcel of land held by the subsidiary.

In Illustration 5-7, the cost of each block of stock is separated into its individual components using the above information. In reviewing Illustration 5-7, the following points should be understood:

(1) *APB Opinion No. 18* requires investors to amortize the excess of cost over book value to the extent such excess relates to depreciable or amortizable tangible and intangible assets.

(2) The information given assumes that the investor can obtain information on the current value of the subsidiary's net assets as of each block acquisition date. Often this is not possible or practicable. In such situations, the entire excess of cost over the investor's interest in the investee's net assets at book value must be assigned to goodwill.[5]

(3) The purpose of the schedule is to determine the cumulative amounts in each individual component of the major conceptual elements as of the control date (July 1, 19X2). This has been done on a step-by-step basis.

(4) The July 1, 19X2, balances (after the acquisition of the last block) are the starting point for the procedures the parent must use to account for its investment in the subsidiary.

(5) The primary elimination entry that would be used in preparing consolidated financial statements as of July 1, 19X2, is as follows:

```
Common stock.........................................   30,000
Retained earnings....................................   26,250
Land.................................................   15,000
Goodwill.............................................    8,750
        Investment in subsidiary ..........................          80,000
```

(6) For all subsequent periods, the two additional separate retained earnings columns must be used in the analysis of the investment account to isolate the parent's share of the subsidiary's future earnings and dividends. These additional columns were not necessary in prior periods, because consolidated financial statements could not be prepared (the ownership was not more than 50%).

[5] *APB Opinion No. 18*, paragraph 19n.

Illustration 5-7
Preparing the expanded analysis of the investment account as of the control date—Step-by-step method

Ownership Percentage Acquired	Date	Total Cost	=	Book Value Element		+	Current Value over Book Value Element	+	Goodwill Element[a]
				Common Stock	Retained Earnings		Land		
20	Block purchase, January 1, 19X1	$15,000		$ 8,000	$ 1,000		$ 4,000[b]		$2,000
	Equity in 19X1 net income (20% × $10,000)	2,000			2,000				
	Amortize cost in excess of book value	(500)							(500)
20	Balance, December 31, 19X1	$16,500		$ 8,000	$ 3,000		$ 4,000		$1,500
+25	Block purchase, January 1, 19X2	21,750		10,000	3,750		5,000[c]		3,000
	Equity in net income (6 mo) (45% × $20,000)	9,000			9,000				
	Amortize cost in excess of book value:								
	Block 1 ($2,000 × ¼ × ½ yr)	(250)							(250)
	Block 2 ($3,000 × ⅓ × ½ yr)	(500)							(500)
45	Balance, June 30, 19X2	$46,500		$18,000	$15,750		$ 9,000		$3,750
+30	Block purchase, July 1, 19X2	33,500		12,000	10,500		6,000[d]		5,000
75	Balance, July 1, 19X2	$80,000		$30,000	$26,250		$15,000		$8,750

[a] A remaining life of four years from the initial acquisition date is used to amortize goodwill. Thus, the $3,000 of goodwill from the second block purchase has a three-year life.
[b] Calculated at 20% of $20,000.
[c] Calculated at 25% of $20,000.
[d] Calculated at 30% of $20,000.

SUMMARY

The procedures to consolidate the financial statements of a partially owned subsidiary are essentially the same as those in which a subsidiary is wholly owned. The primary and secondary elimination entries are determined in the same manner as when a subsidiary is wholly owned. However, an additional entry is necessary for partially owned subsidiaries. This entry makes the detail of the subsidiary's income statement accounts equal the parent's share of the subsidiary's net income or loss. Minority interest amounts reported in the consolidated financial statements are always based on amounts shown in the subsidiary's separate financial statements. Dividends accruing to minority interest shareholders are treated as a reduction of the minority interest and not as dividends of the consolidated group. In the consolidated balance sheet, the minority interest is most frequently shown between liabilities and stockholders' equity. In the consolidated income statement, minority interest in the net income of the subsidiary is usually shown as a deduction among costs and expenses.

Glossary of new terms

Block Acquisitions: Acquisitions in which blocks of an investee company's outstanding common stock are acquired over time until the ownership level exceeds 50%.

Date of Latest Purchase Method: When control over a company is achieved as a result of block acquisitions, the carrying value of the investment as of the control date is separated into the individual components of the major conceptual elements, using the current values of the subsidiary's assets and liabilities at the date control is obtained.

Entity Theory: A theory pertaining to how the assets and liabilities of partially owned subsidiaries and the related minority shareholders' interests in the subsidiary's earnings and net assets should be valued and presented in consolidated financial statements. The foundation of the theory is that a new reporting entity (other than the parent) is deemed to exist as a result of consolidation. Minority interest, therefore, is treated as an equity interest of the new consolidated reporting entity. Assets and liabilities of partially owned subsidiaries are revalued to their full current values as of the date of the business combination. Goodwill value is based on total goodwill implicit in the purchase price.

Minority Interest: The interest of the shareholders of a partially owned subsidiary, other than the parent, in the subsidiary's earnings, losses, and net assets.

Parent Company Theory: A theory pertaining to how the assets and liabilities of partially owned subsidiaries and the related minority shareholders' interests in the subsidiary's earnings and net assets should be valued and presented in consolidated finanical statements. The foundation of the theory is that the parent company is the consolidated reporting entity. Minority interest, therefore, is not treated as an equity interest of the consolidated reporting entity. Assets and liabilities of partially owned subsidiaries are revalued to their current values as of the business combination date only to the extent of the parent's cost over or under its ownership interest in the book value of the subsidiaries' net assets. Goodwill is reported only to the extent that it is paid for by the parent.

Illustration 5-8
Trial Balance Approach (Illustration 5-5 reformatted)

P COMPANY AND SUBSIDIARY (S COMPANY) Consolidating Statement Worksheet For the Year Ended December 31, 19X1					
	P Company		S Company		
	Dr.	Cr.	Dr.	Cr.	
Cash	33,500		32,000		
Accounts receivable, net	145,000		43,000		
Inventory................................	90,000		40,000		
Investment in S Company	85,230				
Land....................................	80,000		30,000		
Building—Cost...........................	400,000		100,000		
—Accum. depr....................		260,000		23,000	
Equipment—Cost	300,000		90,000		
—Accum. depr.		170,000		42,000	
Goodwill					
Liabilities...............................		290,000		200,000	
Common stock:					
P Company		300,000			
S Company				40,000	
Retained earnings, January 1, 19X1:					
P Company		100,000			
S Company				20,000	
Dividends declared:					
P Company	31,000				
S Company			5,000		
Sales		600,000		200,000	
Equity in net income of subsidiary		13,500			
Amortization of cost in excess of book value	4,770				
Cost of goods sold......................	360,000		120,000		
Marketing expenses	90,000		30,000		
Administrative expenses	60,000		20,000		
Interest expense	30,000		5,000		
Income before Income Taxes					
Income tax expense.....................	24,000		10,000		
	1,733,500	1,733,500	525,000	525,000	

Income before Minority Interest ....
Minority interest (income statement)........
Minority interest (equity column) ....
Consolidated net income...
Consolidated retained earnings ....
Total minority interest ....

Explanation of entries:
  (1) The primary elimination entry.
  (2) The secondary elimination entry.
  (3) The minority interest entry.

Illustration 5-8 (continued)

				Consolidated		
Eliminations		Income Statement		Retained Earnings	Minority Interest	Balance Sheet
Dr.	Cr.	Dr.	Cr.	(Dr.) Cr.	(Dr.) Cr.	
						65,500
						188,000
						130,000
	85,230(1)					-0-
9,000(1)						119,000
5,400(1)						505,400
	270(1)					(283,270)
						390,000
						(212,000)
8,100(1)						8,100
						910,730
						490,000
						300,000
36,000(1)					4,000	
				100,000		
18,000(1)					2,000	
				(31,000)		
	4,500(1)				(500)	
			800,000			
13,500(1)						
	4,770(2)					
4,770(2)		484,770				
		120,000				
		80,000				
		35,000				
			80,230			
		34,000				
94,770	94,770					
			46,230			
1,500(3)		1,500				
	1,500(3)				1,500	
. . . .			44,730 →	→ 44,730		
. . . .				113,730 →		→ 113,730
. . . .					7,000 →	→ 7,000M
						910,730

Step-by-Step Method: When control over a company is achieved as a result of block acquisitions, the total carrying value of the investment as of the control date is separated into the individual components of the major conceptual elements by analyzing the cost of each separate block of stock.

Appendix A
PREPARATION OF CONSOLIDATED FINANCIAL STATEMENTS USING THE TRIAL BALANCE APPROACH

To demonstrate the preparation of the worksheet using the trial balance approach when a subsidiary is partially owned, we have reformatted the financial statements used in Illustration 5-5 (page 173) into the trial balance approach shown in Illustration 5-8. The primary and secondary elimination entries and the minority interest entry used in Illustration 5-5 are repeated below for convenience:

(1) The primary elimination entry:

Common stock	36,000	
Retained earnings (beginning of year)	18,000	
Equity in net income of subsidiary	13,500	
Land	9,000	
Building	5,400	
Goodwill	8,100	
Dividends declared		4,500
Accumulated depreciation (building)		270
Investment in subsidiary		85,230

(2) The secondary elimination entry:

Cost of goods sold	4,770	
Amortization of cost in		
excess of book value		4,770

(3) The minority interest entry:

Minority interest (income statement)	1,500	
Minority interest (equity column)[a]		1,500

[a] Because a separate minority interest column is used in the trial balance approach, it is necessary to make the credit to this column rather than to retained earnings.

Appendix B
PREPARATION OF CONSOLIDATED FINANCIAL STATEMENTS USING THE COMBINATION ENTITY– PARENT COMPANY APPROACH AND THE ENTITY THEORY

The combination entity–parent company approach

Recall from the chapter that under the combination entity–parent company approach

(1) The subsidiary's net assets are revalued in consolidation to 100% of their current values as of the acquisition date.
(2) Goodwill is reported in consolidation only to the extent that it is paid for by the parent company.

In the chapter example that dealt with the parent company theory, the subsidiary's net assets were undervalued by $20,000. In consolidation, these assets were revalued upward by $18,000 (90% of $20,000). Thus, an additional $2,000 of undervaluation must be dealt with under the combination entity–parent company approach. This $2,000 is analyzed as follows:

Asset	Total Current Value over Book Value	Parent's Interest in Undervaluation (90%)	Minority Interest in Undervaluation (10%)
Inventory	$ 4,000	$ 3,600	$ 400
Land.	10,000	9,000	1,000
Building	6,000	5,400	600
	$20,000	$18,000	$2,000

One way to deal with the $2,000 in consolidation is to maintain an analysis similar to the current value over book value element of the conceptual analysis of the investment account. Such an analysis for two years subsequent to the acquisition date is shown in Illustration 5-9.

The balances in this analysis would not be entered in the parent company's general ledger (although they could be entered on a memorandum basis for improved record-keeping purposes). Thus, all entries originating from this analysis would be made only on the consolidating statement worksheet.

As of the acquisition date, the following entry would be made in consolidation:

Inventory.	400	
Land	1,000	
Building.	600	
Minority interest in undervalued		
assets (balance sheet)		2,000

Illustration 5-9
Analysis of minority shareholders' interest in subsidiary's undervalued assets

				Debit (Credit)		
				Building		Minority Interest
	Inven-				Accum.	in Undervalued
Date	tory	+ Land	+ Cost		Depr. =	Assets
Balance, January 1, 19X1	$400	$1,000	$600			$(2,000)
Amortization	(400)				$(30)	430
Balance, December 31, 19X1 . . .	$ -0-	$1,000	$600		$(30)	$(1,570)
Amortization					(30)	30
Balance, December 31, 19X2 . . .	$ -0-	$1,000	$600		$(60)	$(1,540)

For the two years following the acquisition date, the following entries would be made in consolidation:

	Consolidation Date	
	December 31, 19X1	December 31, 19X2
Amortization of cost in excess of book value	430	30
Minority interest (income statement)	430	30
To reflect additional amortization expense, which is allocable to the minority interest share of the subsidiary's income.		
Land	1,000	1,000
Building—Cost..............................	600	600
—Accum. depr........................	30	60
Minority interest in undervalued assets (balance sheet)	1,570	1,540

Illustration:
Preparing consolidated financial statements for the first and second year subsequent to the acquisition date

To illustrate the preparation of consolidated financial statements subsequent to the acquisition date under the combination entity–parent company approach, the preceding entries are used along with the parent's primary, secondary, and minority interest entries. The primary, secondary, and minority interest entries developed under the parent company theory for use in Illustration 5-5 are repeated below for convenience:

	Consolidation Date	
	December 31, 19X1	December 31, 19X2

(1) The primary elimination entry:

Common stock................................	36,000	36,000
Retained earnings (beginning of year)	18,000	27,000
Equity in net income of subsidiary	13,500	21,600
Land..	9,000	9,000
Building—Cost	5,400	5,400
—Accum. depr.	270	540
Goodwill....................................	8,100	7,200
Dividends declared	4,500	
Investment in subsidiary	85,230	105,660

(2) The secondary elimination entry
(increased by additional amortization of $430 for 19X1 and $30 for 19X2):

Cost of goods sold	5,200	1,200
Amortization of cost in excess of book value	5,200	1,200

(3) The minority interest entry:

	Consolidation Date	
	December 31, 19X1	December 31, 19X2
Minority interest (income statement)	1,500	2,400
Retained earnings—Subsidiary (net income line)	1,500	2,400
(10% of subsidiary's reported net income of $15,000 for 19X1 and $24,000 for 19X2)		

The preceding worksheet entries result in reporting in consolidation a minority interest deduction of $1,070 for 19X1 and $2,370 for 19X2. The proof of these amounts is shown in the following calculations:

		19X1	19X2
Subsidiary's reported net income		$15,000	$24,000
Minority ownership percentage		10%	10%
Minority interest in book income.............................		$ 1,500	$ 2,400
Less: Additional amortization relating to minority interest in undervalued assets:			

	19X1	19X2		
Inventory	$400	$-0-		
Building	30	30		
Total	$430	$ 30	(430)	(30)
			$ 1,070	$ 2,370

Alternate calculation:

	19X1	19X2
Subsidiary's reported net income	$15,000	$24,000
Less: Total amortization on undervalued assets:		
Inventory...	(4,000)	-0-
Building	(300)	(300)
Subtotal	$10,700	$23,700
Minority ownership percentage	10%	10%
Minority interest	$ 1,070	$ 2,370

Illustration 5-10 shows a consolidating statement worksheet as of December 31, 19X1. In reviewing Illustration 5-10, note the following points:

(1) Consolidated costs and expenses are $430 more than in Illustration 5-5 (page 173), but the minority interest deduction is $430 less. Consolidated net income is the same in both illustrations.
(2) Consolidated assets and the minority interest in the consolidated balance sheet are $1,570 greater than in Illustration 5-5. The difference relates entirely to the additional values being accounted for net of amortization.

The entity theory

Recall that under the entity theory

(1) The subsidiary's net assets are revalued in consolidation to 100% of their current values as of the acquisition date.

Illustration 5-10

P COMPANY AND SUBSIDIARY (S COMPANY)
Consolidating Statement Worksheet
For the Year Ended December 31, 19X1

	P Company	S Company	Eliminations Dr.	Eliminations Cr.	Consolidated
Income Statement:					
Sales	600,000	200,000			800,000
Income from subsidiary:					
Equity in net income	13,500		13,500(1)		-0-
Amortization of cost in					
excess of book value	(4,770)		430(4)	5,200(2)	-0-
Subtotal	608,730	200,000	13,930	5,200	800,000
Cost of goods sold	360,000	120,000	5,200(2)		485,200
Marketing expenses	90,000	30,000			120,000
Administrative expenses	60,000	20,000			80,000
Interest expense	30,000	5,000			35,000
Subtotal	540,000	175,000	5,200		720,200
Income before Income Taxes					
and Minority Interest	68,730	25,000	19,130	5,200	79,800
Income tax expense @ 40%	(24,000)[a]	(10,000)			(34,000)
Income before Minority Interest	44,730	15,000	19,130	5,200	45,800
Minority interest			1,500(3)	430(4)	(1,070)
Net Income	44,730	15,000	⌐20,630	⌐5,630	44,730
Balance Sheet:					
Cash	33,500	32,000			65,500
Accounts receivable, net	145,000	43,000			188,000
Inventory	90,000	40,000			130,000
Investment in S Company	85,230		{1,000(5) 9,000(1)}	85,230(1)	-0-
Land	80,000	30,000			120,000
Building—Cost	400,000	100,000	{5,400(1) 600(5)}		506,000
—Accum. depr.	(260,000)	(23,000)		270(1) 30(5)	(283,300)
Equipment—Cost	300,000	90,000			390,000
—Accum. depr.	(170,000)	(42,000)			(212,000)
Goodwill			8,100(1)		8,100
Total assets	703,730	270,000	24,100	85,530	912,300
Liabilities	290,000	200,000			490,000
Minority interest in					
undervalued assets				1,570(5)	1,570M
Common stock:					
P Company	300,000				300,000
S Company		40,000	36,000(1)		4,000M
Retained earnings—P Company:					
Beginning of year	100,000				100,000
+ Net income	44,730				44,730
− Dividends declared	(31,000)				(31,000)
End of year	113,730				113,730
Retained earnings—S Company:					
Beginning of year		20,000	18,000(1)		2,000M
+ Net income		15,000	→20,630	→5,630 1,500(3)	1,500M
− Dividends declared		(5,000)		4,500(1)	(500)M
End of year		30,000	38,630	11,630	3,000M
Total liabilities and equity	703,730	270,000	74,630	13,200	912,300
Proof of debit and credit postings			98,730	98,730	
Total minority interest					8,570

Explanation of entries:
(1) The primary elimination entry.
(2) The secondary elimination entry.
(3) The minority interest entry.
(4) Additional amortization entry.
(5) Additional valuation entry.
[a] The income tax calculation is 40% of $60,000, not 40% of $68,300.

(2) Goodwill is reported in consolidation based on the amount of goodwill implicit in the transaction.

The only difference between the illustration of the combination entity–parent company approach and the entity theory is that additional goodwill must be accounted for under the entity theory. In the chapter example of the parent company theory (pages 166–172), goodwill of $9,000 was determined. We also demonstrated in the discussion of the entity theory (page 175) that $10,000 is the total goodwill implicit in the transaction ($9,000/90% ownership interest). Thus, an additional $1,000 of goodwill is reported under the entity theory. Accounting for this additional goodwill presents no difficulty. We simply add a column for goodwill to Illustration 5-9 and reflect the additional amortization for this goodwill. Because Illustration 5-9 requires only this modification to go from the combination entity–parent company approach to the entity theory, a complete set of journal entries and the related consolidating statement worksheet are not presented for the entity theory.

Review questions

1. Why is it unacceptable to consolidate only the parent company's ownership interest in the subsidiary's assets, liabilities, and income statement accounts?
2. What are the three possible ways of classifying minority interest in the balance sheet? Which way is used most often?
3. What is the function of the minority interest entry? How is it determined?
4. What overall check can be used to determine that the minority interest in the balance sheet section of the consolidating statement worksheet has been properly calculated?
5. Is the minority interest entry posted to the parent company's general ledger? Why or why not?
6. How are dividends that are paid to minority shareholders treated for consolidated reporting purposes?
7. Explain the entity theory as it relates to consolidated statements.
8. How does the step-by-step method work when control is achieved after several block purchases?
9. When control is achieved after several block acquisitions, in which situations is the date of latest purchase method appropriate?

Discussion cases

Discussion case 5–1
Classification of minority interest in the consolidated balance sheet

Pegco Company's controller has requested your advice on how to classify the minority interest of the company's recently acquired partially owned subsidiary. The controller is concerned that the minority shareholders may object to (1) being classified as creditors if a liability classification is used, and (2) being classified as other than stockholders if a classification above the stockholders' equity section but below the liabilities section is used. The controller is also concerned that the parent's stockholders may object to classifying the minority interest as part of stockholders' equity.

Required:
(1) Evaluate the rationale behind each method of presentation.
(2) How would you advise the controller?

Discussion case 5–2
Miscellaneous theory questions by a new staff accountant

P Company recently hired a new staff accountant to prepare consolidated financial statements. After preparing consolidated financial statements for the first time, the new staff accountant poses the following questions to you, the company controller:

(1) Is the minority interest deduction tax deductible?
(2) Should the dividends paid to minority shareholders be added to the parent's dividends in the consolidated statement of retained earnings?
(3) Why not just buy out the minority shareholders to simplify the consolidation process?

Required:
How would you respond to these questions? Be sure to explain your answers.

Exercises

Exercise 5–1
Calculation of consolidated net income

On January 1, 19X1, Pismo Company acquired 80% of the outstanding common stock of Soohickey Company for $20,000 plus its share of Soohickey Company's net assets at carrying value. (Of this $20,000 payment over its share of the book value, $5,000 was amortized in 19X1.) Each company's 19X1 net income from its own separate operations, exclusive of earnings recorded under the equity method, is as follows:

Pismo Company $1,000,000
Soohickey Company.. 100,000

Required:
(1) Determine the amount of consolidated net income.
(2) Determine the amount of the minority interest in the subsidiary's net income.

Exercise 5–2
Calculation of consolidated net income

Pepper Company owns 80% of the outstanding common stock of Salter Company and 90% of the outstanding common stock of Shaker Company. Each company's 19X1 net income from its own separate operations, exclusive of earnings recorded under the equity method and amortization of cost over book value of net assets, is as follows:

Pepper Company	$1,000,000
Salter Company	100,000
Shaker Company	10,000

Amortization of cost over book value of net assets for 19X1 (from the acquisition date, assumed below to year-end) is $3,000 and $1,000 for Salter Company and Shaker Company, respectively.

Required:
(1) Calculate the minority interest in each subsidiary's net income and the consolidated net income for 19X1, assuming the subsidiaries were owned during the entire year.
(2) Calculate the minority interest in each subsidiary's net income and the consolidated net income for 19X1, assuming Salter Company was acquired on April 1, 19X1, and Shaker Company was acquired on July 1, 19X1. (Assume earnings occurred evenly throughout the year.)

Exercise 5–3
Determination of consolidated income statement amounts not using a consolidating statement worksheet

On January 1, 19X1, Putter Company acquired 75% of the outstanding common stock of Stroker Company at an amount equal to 75% of Stroker Company's net assets at carrying value. Each company's 19X1 income statement, exclusive of earnings recorded under the equity method, is as follows:

	Putter Company	Stroker Company
Sales	$800,000	$200,000
Cost of goods sold	(400,000)	(100,000)
Marketing expenses	(80,000)	(20,000)
Administrative expenses	(40,000)	(10,000)
Interest expense	(30,000)	(10,000)
Income before Income Taxes	$250,000	$ 60,000
Income tax expense @ 40%	(100,000)	(24,000)
Net Income	$150,000	$ 36,000

Balance sheet amounts for each company at December 31, 19X1, are purposely not furnished; accordingly, a formal consolidating statement worksheet cannot be prepared. However, the consolidated amounts still can be determined if the main concept of the chapter is understood.

Required:
(1) Determine the consolidated income statement amounts.
(2) Determine the consolidated income statement amounts assuming Putter Company amortized $2,000 of cost in excess of book value of net assets that pertains to goodwill.

Exercise 5–4
Separating total cost into individual components of major conceptual elements: Cost exceeds current value of net assets and current value exceeds book value

On January 1, 19X6, Poasis Company acquired 60% of the outstanding common stock of Sahara Company at a total cost of $225,000. Sahara's capital account balances at December 31, 19X5, are as follows:

Common stock..	$ 10,000
Additional paid-in capital	90,000
Retained earnings	160,000
	$260,000

Each of Sahara's assets and liabilities has a current value equal to its book value, except for the following items:

	Current Value	Book Value
Land.. *20,000.*	$120,000	$100,000
Building..................................... *15,000.*	95,000	80,000
Equipment .... *<.10000.>*	40,000	50,000
25000		

Required:
Prepare an expanded analysis of the investment account as of the acquisition date.

Exercise 5–5
Determining subsidiary's equity from consolidated data

Pennsyl Company acquired 70% of the outstanding common stock of Sharp Corporation. Pennsyl's separate balance sheet immediately after the acquisition and the consolidated balance sheet are as follows:

	Pennsyl	Consolidated
Current assets..	$106,000	$148,000
Investment in Sharp (cost)............................	100,000	—
Goodwill	—	8,100
Fixed assets (net)	270,000	370,000
	$476,000	$526,100
Current liabilities......................................	$ 15,000	$ 30,000
Minority interest	—	35,100
Capital stock	350,000	350,000
Retained earnings	111,000	111,000
	$476,000	$526,100

Of the excess payment for the investment in Sharp, $10,000 was attributed to undervaluation of its fixed assets; the balance was attributed to goodwill.

Required:
(1) Calculate the total stockholders' equity of the subsidiary when it was acquired.
(2) Prepare a conceptual analysis of the investment account at the acquisition date.

(AICPA adapted)

Exercise 5–6
Comparison of parent company theory and entity theory—
Tangible assets

On January 1, 19X1, Poole Company acquired 60% of the outstanding common stock of Sharkee Company for an amount equal to 60% of Sharkee Company's net assets at carrying value plus $600,000. This $600,000 cost in excess of Poole Company's share of net assets at carrying value is entirely attributable to a parcel of land owned by Sharkee Company. Sharkee Company acquired this land many years ago for $50,000; its current value is $1,050,000. (The book value of Sharkee's net assets is $2,000,000.)

Required:
(1) Under the parent company theory, at what amount would the land be reported in the consolidated balance sheet?
(2) Under the entity theory, at what amount would the land be reported in the consolidated balance sheet?
(3) Compare the results in (1) and (2). What is the effect on the stockholders' equity section and the minority interest in the subsidiary's net assets as reported in the consolidated balance sheet?

Exercise 5–7
Comparison of parent company theory and entity theory—Goodwill

Prom Company acquired 70% of the outstanding common stock of Spring Company on January 1, 19X3, for an amount equal to 70% of Spring Company's net assets at carrying value plus $2,100,000. The cost in excess of its share of book value is entirely attributable to the expected superior earnings ability of Spring Company. (The book value of Spring's net assets is $7,000,000.)

Required:
(1) Under the parent company theory, at what amount would goodwill be reported in the consolidated balance sheet?   2,100 000
(2) Under the entity theory, at what amount would the goodwill be reported in the consolidated balance sheet?   3,000,000
(3) Compare the results in (1) and (2). What is the effect on the stockholders' equity section and the minority interest in the net assets of the subsidiary as reported in the consolidated balance sheet?

Problems

Problem 5–1
Preparing consolidated financial statements as of acquisition date:
Cost equals current value of net assets
and current value equals book value

On December 31, 19X1, Post Company, a calendar-year reporting company, acquired 80% of the outstanding common stock of Script Company at a total cost of $640,000. Each of Script's assets and liabilities has a current value equal to its book value.

Each company's financial statements for the year ended December 31, 19X1, immediately after the acquisition date, are as follows:

	Post Company	Script Company
Income Statement (19X1):		
Sales..	$10,000,000	$ 900,000
Cost of goods sold	(6,000,000)	(500,000)
Marketing expenses	(2,000,000)	(180,000)
Administrative expenses..............................	(800,000)	(88,000)
Interest expense.....................................	(200,000)	(52,000)
Income before Income Taxes	$ 1,000,000	$ 80,000
Income tax expense @ 40%..........................	(400,000)	(32,000)
Net Income	$ 600,000	$ 48,000
Balance Sheet (as of December 31, 19X1):		
Cash	$ 1,160,000	$ 200,000
Accounts receivable, net	2,000,000	300,000
Inventory	1,200,000	600,000
Investment in Script Company	640,000	
Fixed assets, net	7,000,000	900,000
	$12,000,000	$2,000,000
Accounts payable and accruals	$ 1,500,000	$ 450,000
Long-term debt.....................................	2,500,000	750,000
Common stock	1,000,000	100,000
Additional paid-in capital	2,000,000	400,000
Retained earnings	5,000,000	300,000
	$12,000,000	$2,000,000

Required:
(1) Prepare the primary elimination entry as of December 31, 19X1.
(2) Prepare a consolidating statement worksheet at December 31, 19X1.
(3) What amount of income does Post Company report to its stockholders for 19X1?
(4) What is the total minority interest at December 31, 19X1?

Problem 5–2
Preparing consolidated financial statements subsequent to acquisition date: Cost equals current value of net assets and current value equals book value (Continuation of Problem 5–1)

As described in Problem 5–1, Post Company acquired 80% of Script Company for $640,000 on December 31, 19X1. Each company's financial statements as of December 31, 19X2 (one year after the acquisition date) are as follows:

	Post Company	Script Company
Income Statement (19X2):		
Sales...	$11,000,000	$ 950,000
Equity in net income of subsidiary......................	48,000	
Cost of goods sold	(6,500,000)	(540,000)
Marketing expenses	(2,300,000)	(190,000)
Administrative expenses..............................	(850,000)	(70,000)
Interest expense.....................................	(250,000)	(50,000)
Income before Income Taxes	$ 1,148,000	$ 100,000
Income tax expense @ 40%..........................	(440,000)	(40,000)
Net Income	$ 708,000	$ 60,000

	Post Company	Script Company
Balance Sheet (as of December 31, 19X2):		
Cash	$ 1,258,000	$ 180,000
Accounts receivable, net	2,300,000	340,000
Inventory	1,500,000	680,000
Investment in Script Company	680,000	
Fixed assets, net	6,400,000	820,000
	$12,138,000	$2,020,000
Accounts payable and accruals	$ 1,230,000	$ 445,000
Long-term debt	2,400,000	725,000
Common stock	1,000,000	100,000
Additional paid-in capital	2,000,000	400,000
Retained earnings	5,508,000	350,000
	$12,138,000	$2,020,000
Dividends declared during 19X2	$ 200,000	$ 10,000

Required:
(1) Prepare and update the expanded analysis of the investment account through December 31, 19X2.
(2) Prepare the primary elimination and the minority interest entries at December 31, 19X2.
(3) Prepare a consolidating statement worksheet at December 31, 19X2. (The parent's retained earnings at December 31, 19X1 was $5,000,000.)
(4) Prepare a formal consolidated balance sheet and income statement to be included in the annual report to the stockholders.

Problem 5–3
Preparing consolidated financial statements as of acquisition date: Cost is above current value of net assets and current value is above book value

On December 31, 19X1, Peanut Company, a calendar-year reporting company, acquired 75% of the outstanding common stock of Shell Company at a total cost of $187,500. The analysis of Peanut Company's investment in Shell Company as of the acquisition date is as follows:

		Remaining Life
Book value element:		
Common stock	$ 37,500	93,750
Retained earnings	56,250	
Current value over book value element:		
Inventory	1,500	3 months
Land	21,000	Indefinite
Building	15,000	20 years
Patent	11,250	5 years
Goodwill element	45,000	15 years
Total cost	$187,500	

Each company's financial statements for the year ended December 31, 19X1, immediately after the acquisition date, are as follows:

	Peanut Company	Shell Company
Income Statement (19X1):		
Sales	$1,500,000	$450,000
Cost of goods sold	(800,000)	(240,000)
Marketing expenses	(200,000)	(95,000)
Administrative expenses	(170,000)	(61,000)
Interest expense	(80,000)	(14,000)
Income before Income Taxes	$ 250,000	$ 40,000
Income tax expense @ 40%	(100,000)	(16,000)
Net Income...................................	$ 150,000	$ 24,000
Balance Sheet (as of December 31, 19X1):		
Cash	$ 312,500	$ 18,000
Accounts receivable, net	350,000	32,000
Inventory	450,000	65,000
Investment in Shell Company	187,500	
Land	600,000	105,000
Building—Cost	1,100,000	100,000
—Accum. depr.	(300,000)	(20,000)
Equipment—Cost	500,000	30,000
—Accum. depr.	(200,000)	(15,000)
Patent		10,000
	$3,000,000	$325,000
Accounts payable and accruals........	$ 350,000	$ 50,000
Long-term debt	850,000	150,000
Common stock	250,000	50,000
Additional paid-in capital	1,250,000	
Retained earnings...........................	300,000	75,000
	$3,000,000	$325,000

Required:
(1) Prepare the primary elimination entry as of December 31, 19X1.
(2) Prepare a consolidating statement worksheet at December 31, 19X1.
(3) What amount of income does Peanut Company report to its shareholders for 19X1?   #150,000
(4) What is the total minority interest at December 31, 19X1?

$$.25\left(50000 + 75000\right) = \$31,250 = 12,500 + 18,750$$

$$= .25(50,000) + .25(75,000)$$

Problem 5–4
Preparing consolidated financial statements subsequent to acquisition date: Cost is above current value of net assets and current value is above book value (Continuation of Problem 5–3)

As described in Problem 5–3, Peanut Company acquired 75% of Shell Company for $187,500 on December 31, 19X1. Each company's financial statements as of December 31, 19X2 (one year after the acquisition date) are as follows.

	Peanut Company	Shell Company
Income Statement (19X2):		
Sales	$1,800,000	$600,000
Equity in net income of subsidiary	31,500	
Amortization of cost in excess of book value...............	(7,500)	
Cost of goods sold..	(950,000)	(320,000)
Marketing expenses	(240,000)	(120,000)
Administrative expenses	(190,000)	(76,000)
Interest expense	(70,000)	(14,000)
Income before Income Taxes	$ 374,000	$ 70,000
Income tax expense @ 40%	(140,000)	(28,000)
Net Income......................................	$ 234,000	$ 42,000
Balance Sheet (as of December 31, 19X2):		
Cash	$ 362,750	$ 30,000
Accounts receivable, net..................................	420,000	45,000
Inventory	510,000	95,000
Investment in Shell Company	197,250	
Land..	600,000	105,000
Building—Cost	1,100,000	100,000
—Accum. depr.	(325,000)	(25,000)
Equipment—Cost	500,000	30,000
—Accum. depr.	(250,000)	(20,000)
Patent		9,000
	$3,115,000	$369,000
Accounts payable and accruals..........................	$ 415,000	$ 71,000
Long-term debt	800,000	150,000
Common stock	250,000	50,000
Additional paid-in capital	1,250,000	
Retained earnings..	400,000	98,000
	$3,115,000	$369,000
Dividends declared during 19X2	$ 134,000	$ 19,000

Required:

(1) Prepare and update the expanded analysis of the investment account through December 31, 19X2.

(2) Prepare the primary and secondary elimination entries and the minority interest entry at December 31, 19X2.

(3) Prepare a consolidating statement worksheet at December 31, 19X2. (The parent's retained earnings at December 31, 19X1 was $300,000.)

(4) Prepare a formal consolidated balance sheet and income statement to be included in the annual report to the stockholders.

Problem 5–5
Preparing consolidated financial statements as of acquisition date:
Cost equals current value of net assets
and current value is below book value

Poppy Company, a calendar-year reporting company, acquired 90% of the outstanding common stock of Seed Company at a total cost of $315,000 on December 31,

19X1. The expanded analysis of Poppy Company's investment in Seed Company as of the acquisition date is as follows:

		Remaining Life
Book value element:		
Common stock	$180,000	
Retained earnings	157,500	
Current value over (under) book value element:		
Land	9,000	Indefinite
Building	(18,000)	20 years
Equipment	(13,500)	5 years
Total cost	$315,000	

Each company's financial statements for the year ended December 31, 19X1, immediately after the acquisition date, are as follows:

	Poppy Company	Seed Company
Income Statement (19X1):		
Sales	$5,000,000	$ 400,000
Cost of goods sold	(3,000,000)	(300,000)
Marketing expenses	(900,000)	(120,000)
Administrative expenses	(500,000)	(70,000)
Interest expense	(100,000)	(10,000)
Income (Loss) before Income Taxes	$ 500,000	$(100,000)
Income tax expense @ 40%	(200,000)	
Net Income (Loss)	$ 300,000	$(100,000)
Balance Sheet (as of December 31, 19X1):		
Cash	$ 65,000	$ 5,000
Accounts receivable, net	170,000	80,000
Inventory	350,000	120,000
Investment in Seed Company	315,000	
Land	200,000	100,000
Building—Cost	1,100,000	250,000
—Accum. depr.	(400,000)	(50,000)
Equipment—Cost	450,000	75,000
—Accum. depr.	(250,000)	(30,000)
	$2,000,000	$ 550,000
Accounts payable and accruals	$ 275,000	$ 105,000
Long-term debt	825,000	70,000
Common stock	40,000	200,000
Additional paid-in capital	360,000	
Retained earnings	500,000	175,000
	$2,000,000	$ 550,000

Required:
(1) Prepare the primary elimination entry as of December 31, 19X1.
(2) Prepare a consolidating statement worksheet at December 31, 19X1.
(3) What amount of income does Poppy Company report to its stockholders for 19X1?
(4) What is the total minority interest at December 31, 19X1?

Problem 5–6
Preparing consolidated financial statements subsequent to
acquisition date: Cost equals current value of net assets
and current value is below book value (Continuation of Problem 5–5)

As described in Problem 5–5, Poppy Company acquired 90% of Seed Company
for $315,000 on December 31, 19X1. Each company's financial statements as of
December 31, 19X2 (one year after the acquisition date) are as follows:

	Poppy Company	Seed Company
Income Statement (19X2):		
Sales...	$5,400,000	$ 450,000
Equity in net loss of subsidiary..........................	(27,000)	
Amortization of cost below book value	3,600	
Cost of goods sold	(3,100,000)	(320,000)
Marketing expenses	(950,000)	(90,000)
Administrative expenses................................	(550,000)	(63,000)
Interest expense.......................................	(100,000)	(7,000)
Income (Loss) before Income Taxes....................	$ 676,600	$ (30,000)
Income tax expense @ 40%...........................	(280,000)	
Net Income (Loss).....................................	$ 396,600	$ (30,000)
Balance Sheet (as of December 31, 19X2):		
Cash..	$ 160,000	$ 12,000
Accounts receivable, net	230,000	74,000
Inventory	340,000	98,000
Investment in Seed Company..........................	291,600	
Land	200,000	100,000
Building—Cost	1,100,000	250,000
—Accum. depr.	(430,000)	(60,000)
Equipment—Cost	450,000	75,000
—Accum. depr.	(265,000)	(39,000)
	$2,076,600	$ 510,000
Accounts payable and accruals	$ 220,000	$ 100,000
Long-term debt.......................................	800,000	65,000
Common stock	40,000	200,000
Additional paid-in capital	360,000	
Retained earnings	656,600	145,000
	$2,076,600	$ 510,000
Dividends declared during 19X2.........................	$ 240,000	

Required:
(1) Prepare and update the expanded analysis of the investment account through
December 31, 19X2.
(2) Prepare the primary and secondary elimination entries and the minority interest
entry at December 31, 19X2.
(3) Prepare a consolidating statement worksheet at December 31, 19X2. (The
parent's retained earnings at December 31, 19X1 was $500,000.)
(4) Prepare a formal consolidated balance sheet and income statement to be
included in the annual report to the stockholders.

Problem 5–7
CHALLENGER   Preparing consolidated financial statements subsequent to acquisition date and preparing entries to convert from cost method to equity method four years after the acquisition date

On December 31, 19X2, Parr Company, a wholesaler, purchased 80% of the issued and outstanding common stock of Subb Company for $120,000. At that date, Subb had one class of common stock outstanding at a stated value of $100,000 and retained earnings of $30,000. Parr Company had a $50,000 deficit balance in Retained Earnings.

Parr purchased the stock from Subb's major stockholder primarily to acquire control of signboard leases owned by Subb. The leases expire on December 31, 19X7, and Parr Company executives estimate the nonrenewable leases are worth at least $20,000 more than their book value when the stock was purchased.

Parr has carried its investment at cost since the acquisition date and now desires to convert to the equity method. The financial statements for both companies for the year ended December 31, 19X6, are as follows:

PARR COMPANY AND SUBSIDIARY (SUBB COMPANY)
Financial Statements
For the Year Ended December 31, 19X6

	Parr Company	Subb Company
Balance Sheet:		
Cash	$ 29,200	$ 37,500
Accounts receivable, net	88,000	76,000
Inventories	54,800	85,600
Investment in Subb Company	120,000	
Land	25,000	10,500
Plant and equipment	200,000	40,000
Accumulated depreciation	(102,000)	(7,000)
Signboard leases		42,000
Amortization to date		(33,600)
	$415,000	$251,000
Accounts payable	$ 35,500	$ 56,000
Notes payable	24,500	20,000
Common stock	300,000	100,000
Retained earnings	55,000	75,000
	$415,000	$251,000
Income Statement:		
Sales	$416,000	$300,000
Dividend income	4,000	
Cost of goods sold	(315,000)	(240,000)
Expenses	(65,000)	(35,000)
Net Income	$ 40,000	$ 25,000
Dividends declared in 19X6	$ 7,000	$ 5,000

Required:
(1) Prepare the entry to convert to the equity method of accounting for the investment. (Ignore income tax considerations.)
(2) Prepare the primary and secondary elimination entries and the minority interest entry at December 31, 19X6.

(3) Prepare a consolidating statement worksheet for 19X6. (Parr's income statement for 19X6 should reflect the equity method on the consolidating statement worksheet.)

(AICPA adapted)

Problem 5–8
REVIEW   Analyzing the investment; applying the equity method; computing minority interest and consolidated retained earnings

On January 1, 19X6, Pitch Corporation made the following investments:

(1) Acquired 80% of the outstanding common stock of Sanders Corporation for $80 cash per share. The stockholders' equity of Sanders on January 1, 19X6, consisted of the following:

Common stock, $50 par value	$50,000
Retained earnings	20,000

(2) Acquired 70% of the outstanding common stock of Trapp Corporation for $40 cash per share. The stockholders' equity of Trapp on January 1, 19X6, consisted of the following:

Common stock, $20 par value	$60,000
Paid-in capital in excess of par value	20,000
Retained earnings	40,000

The current values of each subsidiary's net assets equal their book values except for a parcel of land owned by Sanders which has a current value of $5,000 *less* than its book value. At the time of these acquisitions, Pitch expected both companies to have superior earnings for the next 10 years. Pitch has accounted for these investments using the cost method. An analysis of each company's retained earnings for 19X6 is as follows:

	Pitch	Sanders	Trapp
Balance, January 1, 19X6	$240,000	$20,000	$40,000
Net income (loss)	104,600	36,000	(12,000)
Cash dividends paid	(40,000)	(16,000)	(9,000)
Balance, December 31, 19X6	$304,600	$40,000	$19,000

Required:
(1) Under the equity method, what entries should have been made on the books of Pitch during 19X6 to record the following (ignore income taxes and deferred tax considerations)?
  (a) Investments in subsidiaries.
  (b) Parent's share of subsidiary income or loss.
  (c) Subsidiary dividends received.
  (d) Amortization of cost in excess of (under) book value, if any.
(2) Compute the amount of minority interest in each subsidiary's stockholders' equity at December 31, 19X6.

(3) What were Pitch's earnings from its own operations for 19X6, excluding accounts relating to its ownership in these subsidiaries?

(4) What amount should Pitch Corporation and subsidiaries report as consolidated retained earnings as of December 31, 19X6?

(AICPA adapted)

Problem 5–9
Block acquisitions: Step-by-step method

Pine Company acquired blocks of stock of Sapp Company over a period of several years. Information regarding such purchases along with pertinent information relating to the investee as of each purchase date is as follows:

Date of Block Acquisition	Ownership Percentage Acquired	Cost	Information on Investee		
			Common Stock	Retained Earnings[a]	Net Assets Current Value over Book Value[b]
January 1, 19X1	20	$23,000	$50,000	$15,000	[c]
January 1, 19X2	20	37,000	50,000	35,000	[c]
December 31, 19X2	25	60,000	50,000	70,000	$10,000[d]

[a] Sapp Company declared cash dividends on common stock of $5,000 per year during 19X1 and 19X2.
[b] Assume Pine Company uses maximum allowable amortization lives for any goodwill acquired; also, assume goodwill associated with each block acquisition has its own separate life.
[c] It was impractical to obtain specific information from the investee as to the current value of its individual assets and liabilities at the time of this block purchase.
[d] This amount is identified entirely with land.

Required:

(1) Using the step-by-step approach, determine the balances that should exist in the investment account by the individual components of the major conceptual elements as of the control date (December 31, 19X2). *Hint:* Refer to paragraph 19n of *APB Opinion No. 18* for treatment of cost over investor's share of the investee's net assets at book value that cannot be identified with specific assets or liabilities.

(2) Prepare the primary elimination entry at December 31, 19X2.

Problem 5–10
Block acquisitions: Step-by-step method

On January 1, 19X3, Picadilly Company acquired 25% of the outstanding common stock of Square Company at a total cost of $245,000. At that time, Square Company's capital accounts were as follows:

Common stock	$100,000
Additional paid-in capital	400,000
Retained earnings	320,000
	$820,000

On April 1, 19X3, Picadilly acquired 50% of the outstanding common stock of Square at a cost of $544,000. Earnings and dividend information for Square for 19X3 is as follows.

	First Quarter	Remainder of Year
Net income	$48,000	$160,000
Dividends......................................	20,000	60,000

Assume that Picadilly uses a 10-year life for goodwill associated with each block of stock. Assume also that none of Square's recorded assets or liabilities is over- or undervalued at either block acquisition date.

Required:
(1) Using the step-by-step method, determine the balances that should exist in the investment account by the individual components of the major conceptual elements as of the control date (April 1, 19X3).
(2) Update the analysis of the investment account through December 31, 19X3, assuming Picadilly intends to include only the revenue and expense items of Square for the period April 1, 19X3 to December 31, 19X3, in preparing the consolidated income statement for 19X3.
(3) Prepare the primary elimination entry at April 1, 19X3.
(4) Prepare all the elimination entries required at December 31, 19X3.
(5) Explain the two methods available to the parent in reporting the subsidiary's earnings for 19X3. Specifically, explain how the earnings recorded under the equity method of accounting for the first quarter are presented.

Problem 5–11
Block acquisitions: Comparison of date of latest purchase method with step-by-step method

Parker Company acquired two blocks of stock of Soccer Company. Information regarding each purchase along with pertinent information about the investee as of each purchase date is as follows:

Date of Block Acquisition	Ownership Percentage Acquired	Cost	Information on Investee		Net Assets Current Value over Book Value
			Common Stock	Retained Earnings[a]	
January 1,19X4	10	$ 80,000[b]	$500,000	$100,000	$12,000[c]
December 31, 19X6	70	650,000	500,000	340,000	18,000[c]

[a] Soccer Company declared cash dividends on common stock of $20,000 per year in 19X4, 19X5, and 19X6.
[b] The carrying value of this block on Parker Company's books has never been below cost from the date it was acquired.
[c] This amount is identified entirely with land.

Required:
(1) Using the date of latest purchase method, determine the balances that should exist in the investment account by the individual components of the major conceptual elements as of the control date (December 31, 19X6).
(2) Using the step-by-step method, determine the balances that should exist in the investment account by the individual components of the major conceptual elements as of the control date (December 31, 19X6).

6 The Pooling of Interests Method of Accounting

OVERVIEW OF THE POOLING OF INTERESTS METHOD

In this chapter, the pooling of interests method of accounting for a business combination is discussed, illustrated, and contrasted with the purchase method. Recall from Chapter 2 that the terms and provisions of the acquisition agreement determine whether the purchase method or the pooling of interests method is used to record a business combination. The terms and provisions that qualify a business combination as a pooling of interests are reviewed in general and then in detail.

Paragraphs 27–65 of *APB Opinion No. 16* deal with the pooling of interests method. Throughout these paragraphs, the terms "acquiring company" and "acquired company" are purposely not used because the word "acquiring" describes the purchase method of accounting in paragraphs 66–96. Instead, the discussion uses the terms "combining company," "combined company," and "company issuing stock to effect the combination." This language is consistent with the underlying concept of pooling of interests accounting that a combining, or pooling, of the equity interests occurs as opposed to an acquisition. The latter term refers to a situation in which one company acquires the business of another company for which purchase accounting is appropriate.

However, the distinction is moot. Most business combinations that are accounted for under the pooling of interests method are, in substance, acquisitions in the sense that one entity acquires the business of another entity, and the acquiring entity is completely dominant. This is how the parties involved see the transaction from other than an accounting viewpoint. In other words, the transaction is viewed as an acquisition that is merely recorded as a pooling of interests. Accordingly, except in the section that discusses the specific pooling of interests conditions (which are quoted from *APB Opinion No. 16*), we refer to a company that issues common stock to effect a business combination as the acquiring company and a company that gives up its assets (or whose stockholders give up their common stock) as the target company or the acquired business.

Essence of the pooling of interests method

Under the pooling of interests method, each company's stockholders are presumed to have combined or fused their ownership interests in such a manner that each group becomes an owner of the combined, enlarged business. To accomplish this fusing of ownership interests, the acquiring company must issue common stock as consideration for the business that it acquires. Under this pooling of interests concept, the fair value of the consideration given and the current value of the acquired company's net assets are completely irrelevant. Instead, the book value of the acquired company's net assets is used as the basis for recording the "cost" of the investment to the acquiring company. This approach is completely the opposite of that under the purchase method. As a result, the assets and liabilities of the acquired company are reported at their historical costs in the consolidated financial statements. Furthermore, goodwill is never created. In an inflationary economy, the assets of companies are usually undervalued. Thus, the pooling of interests method is popular because the acquired company's assets do not have to be reflected at their current values, along with any goodwill, in the future financial statements. Future charges to income are thereby avoided. The disadvantage—an understatement of the consolidated stockholders' equity—is almost always of secondary importance compared with the advantages that result in the income statement.

When financial statements are presented for periods prior to the combination date, the earnings of each company are combined as if the combination had occurred at the beginning of the earliest period presented. In presenting dividend information for periods before the combination date, dividends of each company are combined to the extent of the ownership interest acquired. This is just the opposite of the purchase method, which disallows presenting the two companies' operations results and dividend information together for preacquisition periods.

Conceptual basis for pooling of interests

The fusion of equity interests through the issuance of common stock by one of the combining companies in exchange for the assets or common stock of the other combining company is the cornerstone of pooling of interests accounting. Proponents of pooling view such a combination as a combining of equity interests instead of a buy-out of one company's shareholders. Accordingly, they conclude that purchase accounting is inappropriate because a buy-out does not occur.

Critics of pooling contend that for most combinations treated as pooling of interests, the fusion of the equity interests is irrelevant. They maintain that what is relevant is whether or not one company has acquired or obtained control over the business of another company. If this control is the substance of the transaction, then purchase accounting is appropriate, regardless of the type of consideration given. This is the primary conclusion of *Accounting Research Study No. 5,* "A Critical Study of Accounting for Business Combinations," by Arthur R. Wyatt, which the AICPA published in 1963. (Research studies do not constitute the official position of the AICPA; they are for discussion purposes only.) This group would allow poolings of interests only when the companies involved are of comparable size and it is evident that a buy-out is not occurring. Because most transactions accounted for as poolings of interests involve companies of significantly disproportionate sizes, few business combinations would be treated as poolings of interests with this approach.

In summary, each group views the economic substance of a business combination involving the issuance of common stock differently. As mentioned in Chapter 2, *APB Opinion No. 16* is a controversial pronouncement, which has received such substantial criticism since its issuance that the FASB is expected to reexamine the accounting issues involved in business combinations in the near future.

Pooling of interests criteria—General discussion

Before *APB Opinion No. 16* was issued, only general guidelines determined when a business combination should be treated as a pooling of interests. Because the guidelines could not be logically supported for the most part, in practice they were often ignored or broadly interpreted. The relative looseness of accounting principles in this area resulted in substantial criticism of the accounting profession, which led to the issuance of a pronouncement that contained specific pooling of interests criteria. In addition, *APB Opinion No. 16* substantially narrowed management's ability to choose between accounting alternatives for a given set of terms and conditions, because the opinion

(1) Specifically defines the criteria under which a business combination is treated as a pooling of interests.
(2) Requires all business combinations meeting each of these specific criteria to be accounted for as a pooling of interests.
(3) Requires all business combinations failing to meet any one of the specific criteria to be accounted for using purchase accounting.

Twelve specific conditions must be met before pooling of interests accounting is permitted. In many respects, the conditions are arbitrary and not totally clear or comprehensive. As a result, the AICPA and the FASB have issued numerous interpretations. With the possible exception of accounting for leases, more interpretations have been issued for this pronouncement than for any other professional pronouncement. In practice, it has been one of the most difficult professional pronouncements with which to work. Many large public accounting firms have prepared lengthy booklets for internal use, explaining how certain areas of the pronouncement are to be interpreted for uniform application within their firms.

The 12 conditions generally allow pooling of interests treatment only when a combination of independent equity interests occurs as opposed to a buy-out of one of the common shareholder equity interests. As a result, a great deal of emphasis is placed on the form and manner of accomplishing the combination, so that the two stockholder groups "pool" their equity resources. Most of the conditions pertain to the manner of effecting the combination. The more salient points of the criteria are as follows:

(1) Common stock must be the primary consideration given by the acquiring company.
   (a) If assets are acquired, 100% of the assets must be acquired solely in exchange for the acquiring company's common stock.
   (b) If common stock is acquired, at least 90% of the outstanding common shares must be acquired solely in exchange for the acquiring company's common stock. (Cash or other consideration may be given to dissenting stockholders of the target company, as long as this group does not hold more than 10% of the target company's outstanding common stock.)
(2) The common stock issued must have the same rights and privileges as the already issued and outstanding common stock of the acquiring

company. In other words, the acquiring company's new stockholders must be full-fledged stockholders of the enlarged business.

(3) There can be no arrangements to reacquire the common stock issued as consideration for the assets or common stock acquired.

Interestingly enough, the stockholders receiving common stock from the acquiring company can, immediately after the combination is consummated, sell the common stock received if they do not want to continue as owners in the combined business. No continuity of ownership interest is required whereby the new stockholders must remain shareholders of the combined business for any specified period of time. Thus, the "fusion" of equity interests need only be for an instant.

POOLING OF INTERESTS CRITERIA—
SPECIFIC CONDITIONS

The 12 conditions for the pooling of interests method fit into three broad categories:

(1) Attributes of the combining companies,
(2) Manner of combining equity interests, and
(3) Absence of planned transactions.

Each condition is listed under the appropriate category and discussed in detail. Note that many of the conditions are designed to prevent companies from circumventing the basic concept of having to combine substantially all common shareholder equity interests.

Attributes of the combining companies

Two conditions pertain to the attributes that the combining companies must possess.

(A) "Each of the combining companies is autonomous and has not been a subsidiary or division of another corporation within two years before the plan of combination is initiated" (Paragraph 46a of *APB Opinion No. 16*).

This condition presumes that the pooling of interests concept applies only to independent companies. For the most part, this condition is sound in that most divestitures of subsidiaries or divisions are intended disposals of interests as opposed to an intended pooling of equity interests.

A subsidiary that is spun off pursuant to a governmental divestiture order or a new company that acquires assets it must dispose of is an arbitrary exception to this condition and is deemed an autonomous company. This exception does not appear to be based on logic, and its inclusion is apparently an accommodation to the disposing company for purposes of facilitating the disposal.

When a portion of a business is spun off to certain stockholders in exchange for some or all of their stock, the stockholders of the newly established corporation may wish to combine their equity interests with another company in the true sense of the pooling of interests concept. Such a combining of equity interests could not be accounted for as a pooling of interests unless two years had elapsed from the spin-off date. Thus, a portion of a business cannot be spun off in this manner and then pooled with another company shortly thereafter. This is because the spinning off and subsequent combination are viewed as mere steps of a single transaction, the substance of which is a disposal of an interest.

(B) "Each of the combining companies is independent of the other combining companies" (Paragraph 46b of *APB Opinion No. 16*).

This condition means that at the initiation date and until the business combination is consummated, the combining companies cannot hold more than 10% of the outstanding voting common stock of any combining company. Voting common stock that is acquired during this time interval in exchange for voting common stock issued in connection with the terms of the business combination agreement is excluded in the percentage computation.

This condition is intended to prevent a combining company from altering the equity interests of the other combining company. (Paragraph 47c, which is discussed later in the chapter, prohibits each combining company from altering the equity interest of its own voting common stock in contemplation of a pooling.) If this condition were not imposed, a combining company could circumvent the intended purpose of paragraph 47c by buying out a large group of dissenting shareholders of the other combining company and then effecting a pooling of interests with its remaining shareholders.

Independence based on net worth invested.   Usually, each combining company is independent of the other if neither company owns more than 10% of the outstanding voting common stock of the other. Occasionally, however, neither company owns more than 10% of the outstanding common stock of the other and independence still does not exist. This can occur when the smaller company has a significant investment—**in terms of its own net worth**—in the acquiring company. For instance, assume that Mini-Computer Company (the target company) owns 6% of IBMM Company's outstanding common stock. If this investment constitutes more than 10% of Mini-Computer's net worth, then the companies are not independent. The calculation to determine if the 10% figure is exceeded is shown using the following facts:

(1) IBMM Company has 400,000 common shares outstanding.
(2) Mini-Computer Company has 100,000 common shares outstanding.
(3) IBMM will issue two shares of its common stock for each share of Mini-Computer's outstanding common stock—in other words, a 2 for 1 exchange ratio.
(4) Mini-Computer owns 24,000 IBMM common shares, which is 6% of IBMM's outstanding common shares.

Because Mini-Computer's shareholders will receive 200,000 shares of IBMM common stock, Mini-Computer's net worth can be thought of as the equivalent of 200,000 shares of IBMM common stock. Because it holds an investment in IBMM of 24,000 shares, more than 10% of its net worth is invested in IBMM (24,000/200,000 = 12%). (In an alternate approach, the

24,000 shares of IBMM are adjusted for the combination's exchange ratio to 12,000 shares, and the 12,000 shares are compared with the 100,000 outstanding shares of Mini-Computer. The same 12% answer results.) In this situation, the companies are not independent because the 10% level has been exceeded. In summary, independence is evaluated not only from the perspective of how much of the other combining company's outstanding common stock is owned but also from the perspective of how much of a company's own net worth is invested in the other combining company.

Smaller company issues the common stock.   In the preceding illustration, the larger of the two companies issued common stock to bring about the combination (the typical case). In a stock-for-stock exchange, the relative holdings of each group of stockholders can be the same regardless of which company issues the common stock to effect the pooling of interests. Let us change the facts of the preceding illustration to make Mini-Computer the issuing company. The same relative holdings of each group of stockholders is maintained if Mini-Computer issues one share for each two shares of IBMM outstanding common stock (a 1 for 2 exchange ratio). In this case, the issuing company has the intercorporate investment. However, the companies are still not independent, for the reasons discussed in the preceding paragraph. The smaller of the two companies issues the common stock (and thereby becomes the parent company) when it is more desirable to use the smaller company's name than the larger company's name. For example, the larger company may have an unfavorable public image, or the smaller company may have a wider investor following.

Dual intercorporate investments.   The 10% independence test must be performed in a cumulative manner when each company has an investment in the other. To illustrate, assume the following facts:

(1) IBMM Company has 400,000 common shares outstanding.
(2) Mini-Computer Company has 100,000 common shares outstanding.
(3) IBMM will issue two shares of its common stock for each share of Mini-Computer's outstanding common shares—a 2 for 1 exchange ratio.
(4) Mini-Computer owns 16,000 IBMM outstanding common shares, which is 4% of IBMM's outstanding common shares.
(5) IBMM owns 3,000 shares of Mini-Computer's outstanding common shares, which is 3% of Mini-Computer's outstanding common shares.

Although neither company owns more than 10% of the other company's outstanding common stock and neither company has more than 10% of its own net worth invested in the other company, the *combination* of intercorporate investments exceeds the 10% level, as shown by the following calculation:

Percent of Mini-Computer's common stock owned by IBMM	3%
Percent of Mini-Computer's net worth invested in IBMM	
[16,000 shares/200,000 common shares to be received in the exchange, or alternately, 8,000 shares (adjusted for the 2 for 1 exchange ratio)/100,000 outstanding shares]	<u>8%</u>
	<u>11%</u>

In *APB Opinion No. 16,* the manner of dealing with an investment in the company issuing the common stock is explained in connection with paragraph 47b. The approach treats shares owned in the issuing company (adjusted for the exchange ratio) as a reduction of the target company's outstanding shares to determine if 90% of the target company's outstanding common stock has been acquired in exchange for the issuing company's common stock. We illustrate this as follows:

Mini-Computer's outstanding common shares	100,000
Less: Shares owned by IBMM	(3,000)
Equivalent number of shares invested in IBMM by Mini-Computer (16,000/2)	(8,000)
	89,000
Shares needed to reach the 90% level	90,000

Thus, the 90% level has not been reached. This analysis is difficult to understand. Because the issue is independence, we presented the discussion of dealing with investments in the issuing company from paragraph 46b instead of paragraph 47b.

Manner of combining equity interests

Seven conditions pertain to the manner of effecting the combination, as follows:

(A) "The combination is effected in a single transaction or is completed in accordance with a specific plan within the year after the plan is initiated" (Paragraph 47a of *APB Opinion No. 16*).

George C. Watt, who was chairman of the APB subcommittee for business combinations when *APB Opinion No. 16* was issued, explained why this condition was included as follows:

> The transaction should be consummated within a reasonable time. We thought it was fair to permit an offer and a reasonable time for each side to look at the resources of the other, but that the deal ought to go through within a reasonable period of time—one year. Actually, since the resources are changing rapidly, the offer information isn't fair after a while, and in the meantime there is a cloud over each company's separate existence.[1]

(B) "A corporation offers and issues only common stock with rights identical to those of its outstanding voting common stock in exchange for substantially all of the voting common stock interest of another company at the date the plan of combination is consummated" (Paragraph 47b of *APB Opinion No. 16*).

The fundamental requirement for effecting a pooling of interests, this condition means that the company issuing common stock must acquire at

---

[1] "Accounting Principles for Pooling of Interests: A Panel Discussion Sponsored by the Section on Taxation of the American Bar Association in May 1971," *Tax Lawyer,* Fall 1971, p. 33.

least 90% of the other combining company's outstanding common stock subsequent to the initiation date in exchange for its own common stock. Thus, shares acquired prior to the initiation date—no matter how acquired—cannot be used to determine if the 90% requirement has been met. To illustrate how the 90% rule is applied, assume the following facts:

(1) P is the company issuing common stock.
(2) S has 102,000 common shares issued, of which 2,000 shares are held in treasury. Thus, S has 100,000 common shares outstanding.
(3) P acquires common shares of S as follows:
      (a) Prior to the initiation date   3,000
      (b) Between the initiation date and the consummation date:
            For cash   4,000
            For its common stock pursuant to the terms of
            the combination agreement   5,000
      (c) At the consummation date by exchanging its own
            common stock pursuant to the terms of the combination
            agreement   84,000
                  Total shares owned   96,000

Although P owns more than 90% of S's outstanding common shares, it did not acquire at least 90,000 shares (90% of S's 100,000 outstanding shares) after the initiation date by exchanging common stock. Only 89,000 were obtained after the initiation date through an exchange of common stock (5,000 + 84,000). Therefore, the combination must be accounted for as a purchase instead of a pooling of interests.

The 90% rule does not allow the issuing company to give any cash to the 90% group of shareholders. (An exception pertains to cash given for fractional shares.) Dissenting shareholders, which as a group cannot hold more than 10% of the acquired company's outstanding common shares, may be given cash or other consideration in acquiring their shares.

This condition implies a stock-for-stock exchange. However, assets of a combining company can be exchanged, providing 100% of the assets are exchanged. In these situations, the acquired company can retain assets to settle liabilities, contingencies, or disputed items that are not assumed by the acquiring company, providing any assets remaining after settlement are transferred to the acquiring company.

(C) "None of the combining companies changes the equity interest of the voting common stock in contemplation of effecting the combination either within two years before the plan of combination is initiated or between the dates the combination is initiated and consummated; changes in contemplation of effecting the combination may include distributions to stockholders and additional issuances, exchanges, and retirements of securities" (Paragraph 47c of *APB Opinion No. 16*).

The concept of a pooling of interests does not allow a change in or alteration of the equity interests of the voting common stock of either combining company; only a fusing of the existing ownership interests occurs. Thus, this condition is necessary so that the fundamental concept is not violated.

Above-normal dividend distributions to common shareholders would be considered a "change in the equity interest." The spin-off of a subsidiary or division to certain existing shareholders in exchange for some or all of their common stock is an example of a distribution and retirement of outstanding securities. (This condition does not pertain to the disposal of a subsidiary or division by other means, such as an outright sale.)

(D) "Each of the combining companies reacquires shares of voting common stock only for purposes other than business combinations [to be accounted for as poolings of interests], and no company reacquires more than a normal number of shares between the dates the plan of combination is initiated and consummated" (Paragraph 47d of *APB Opinion No. 16*).

This condition has a twofold purpose:

(1) It prevents a target company from buying out a large group of its own dissenting shareholders (more than 10%) so that its remaining shareholders can effect a combination as a pooling of interests in the manner set forth in paragraph 47b.
(2) Sometimes an acquiring company desires to effect a combination as a pooling of interests and yet does not want to increase the number of its outstanding common shares at all or beyond a certain number. This condition prevents the acquiring company from using cash or other assets or incurring liabilities to reacquire common shares, and then using such reacquired shares to effect a combination as a pooling of interests. This would clearly be an alteration of the equity interest, which is prohibited by paragraph 47c.

The phrase "for purposes other than business combinations" as used in paragraph 47d seems to allow substantial subjective interpretation as to the purpose of acquiring shares. For example, an acquiring company could assert that it reacquired some of its shares because the company was overcapitalized or the price of its stock was at an attractive level. On the surface, such reacquisitions would not appear to be for purposes of business combinations. Thus, the intended purpose of the condition could be easily circumvented. As a result, the AICPA issued the following interpretation to this condition:

> In the absence of persuasive evidence to the contrary . . . it should be presumed that all acquisitions of treasury stock during the two years preceding the date a plan of combination is initiated . . . and between the initiation and consummation were made in contemplation of effecting business combinations to be accounted for as a pooling of interests. Thus, lacking such evidence, this combination would be accounted for by the purchase method regardless of whether treasury stock or unissued shares or both are issued in the combination.
>
> The specific purposes for which treasury shares may be reacquired prior to consummation of a "pooling" include shares granted under stock option or compensation plans, stock dividends declared (or to be declared as a recurring distribution), and recurring distributions as provided in paragraph 47d. Likewise, treasury shares reacquired for issuance in a specific "purchase" or to resolve an existing contingent

share agreement from a prior business combination would not invalidate a concurrent "pooling." Treasury shares reacquired for these purposes should be either reissued prior to consummation or specifically reserved for these purposes existing at consummation.[2]

Assessing the purpose of the reacquisition of treasury shares by an acquiring company generally involves evaluating the subsequent distribution of such shares. In most instances, a systematic pattern of reacquisitions for specified distribution purposes must be established at least two years before the combination plan is initiated to constitute "persuasive evidence to the contrary."

(E) "The ratio of the interest of an individual common stockholder to those of other common stockholders in a combining company remains the same as a result of the exchange of stock to effect the combination" (Paragraph 47e of *APB Opinion No. 16*).

Each shareholder of the target company who exchanges common stock for voting common stock of the acquiring company must receive that voting common stock in exact proportion to his or her relative common stock interest in the target company before the combination is effected. Thus, a shareholder who owns 20% of the target company's outstanding common stock must receive 20% of the voting common shares that the acquiring company issues to effect the combination.

Watt explained why this condition was essential as follows:

> Suppose that 20% of the stock of acquired Company B was in the initial proprietor's hands and he wanted to accept more or less shares than Company B's other shareholders in the negotiation of the deal. This did not seem to the Board to be a pure combining of interests but also to involve a reshuffling of shareholders' interests in the process. This is what the . . . condition is designed to prevent.[3]

(F) "The voting rights to which the common stock ownership interests in the resulting combined corporation are entitled are exercisable by the stockholders; the stockholders are neither deprived of nor restricted in exercising those rights for a period" (Paragraph 47f of *APB Opinion No. 16*).

Any limitations on voting rights would obviously be inconsistent with the pooling of interests concept.

(G) "The combination is resolved at the date the plan is consummated and no provisions of the plan relating to the issue of securities or other considerations are pending" (Paragraph 47g of *APB Opinion No. 16*).

---

[2] *Accounting Interpretation No. 20 to APB Opinion No. 16*, "Accounting for Business Combinations" (New York: AICPA, 1971). Copyright © 1971 by the American Institute of Certified Public Accountants, Inc.
[3] "Accounting Principles for Pooling of Interests," p. 34.

This condition is intended primarily to prohibit poolings of interests when contingent consideration is issuable based on future sales, earnings, or market prices. Such contingencies are incompatible with the mutual sharing of risks and rewards, which underlies the pooling of interests concept. An interpretation says the following:

> The only contingent arrangement permitted under paragraph 47g is for settlement of a contingency pending at consummation, such as the later settlement of a lawsuit. A contingent arrangement would also be permitted for an additional income tax liability resulting from the examination of "open" income tax returns.[4]

Absence of planned transactions

Three conditions pertain to certain types of postcombination transactions that cannot be included either explicitly or implicitly in either the negotiations or the terms of the combination agreement. The conditions are as follows:

(A) "The combining corporation does not agree directly or indirectly to retire or reacquire all or part of the common stock issued to effect the combination" (Paragraph 48a of *APB Opinion No. 16*).

only says no promise may be made - does not say can't re-acquire stock.

This condition prevents an acquiring company from circumventing the intended purpose of paragraph 47b. Obviously, issuing common shares to effect a combination and subsequently repurchasing the shares issued would not be, in substance, a combining of equity interests.

APB Opinion No. 16 does not prohibit an acquiring company from reacquiring shares issued in a pooling of interests (or an equivalent number of shares issued). It is prohibited only from making an agreement to repurchase the shares issued. In this area, the Securities and Exchange Commission has taken the following position:

> In specific fact situations, subsequent reacquisitions may be so closely related to the prior combination that they should be considered part of the combination plan. Thus, significant reacquisitions closely following a plan of combination which otherwise qualified as a pooling of interests may invalidate the applicability of that method. . . .[5]

> The Commission does not intend to establish an additional criterion for determining the accounting treatment of a business combination. Rather it intended simply to caution registrants and auditors that the substance of reacquisitions closely following consummation of a combination should not be ignored. . . .[6]

---

[4] *Accounting Interpretation No. 14 to APB Opinion No. 16*, "Accounting for Business Combinations" (New York: AICPA, 1971).

[5] *Accounting Series Release No. 146*, "Effect of Treasury Stock Transactions on Accounting for Business Combinations," tenth paragraph (Washington, D.C.: SEC, 1973). [This release is now part of *Financial Reporting Release No. 1* (Section 201.02), which was issued in 1982 and is a codification of all accounting-related leases in effect at that time.]

[6] *Accounting Series Release No. 146-A*, "Statement of Policy and Interpretations in Regard to Accounting Series Release No. 146, paragraph 3 (Washington, D.C.: SEC, 1974). [Section 201.02 of *Financial Reporting Release No. 1.*]

(B) "The combined corporation does not enter into other financial arrangements for the benefit of the former stockholders of a combining company,
such as a guaranty of loans secured by stock issued in the combination,
which in effect negates the exchange of securities" (Paragraph 48b of
APB Opinion No. 16).

Arrangements of this nature are considered "bail outs" of former stockholders of the acquired company. Such provisions are inconsistent with
the pooling of interests concept.

(C) "The combined corporation does not intend or plan to dispose of a
significant part of the assets of the combining companies within two
years after the combination other than disposals in the ordinary course
of business of the formerly separate companies and to eliminate duplicate
facilities or excess capacity" (Paragraph 48c of *APB Opinion No. 16*).

The apparent purpose of this condition is to prohibit acquiring companies
from effecting pooling of interests with companies having substantially undervalued assets, when the intent is to sell the undervalued assets shortly
after consummation and thereby report immediate profits from the sale.
(Such widely criticized practices existed before the issuance of *APB Opinion
No. 16*.)

RECORDING A POOLING OF INTERESTS

Acquisition of assets

When assets are acquired, the acquiring company records the assets
acquired and the liabilities assumed at their book values on the acquired
company's books. As in purchase accounting, a centralized or a decentralized
accounting system may be used subsequently to account for the acquired
business. The entries that would be made under centralized and decentralized
accounting systems are not illustrated, because the account descriptions
for the recording of assets acquired and liabilities assumed are the same
as those illustrated for the purchase method in Chapter 3. That portion of
the entry relating to the consideration given by the acquiring company is determined in the same manner as in situations in which common stock is
acquired. These situations are illustrated in the following section.

Acquisition of common stock

Recording a business combination under the pooling of interests method
is drastically different from recording it under the purchase method. As a
result, significant differences can occur in the subsequent reporting of
financial position and results of operations. The pooling of interests method
is best illustrated by comparing it with the purchase method.

Assume the following information:

(1) P Company and S Company have agreed to combine under terms that provide for P Company to issue common stock in exchange for all of S Company's outstanding common stock.
(2) Information with respect to each company as of the combination date is as follows:

	P Company	S Company
Common stock, $10 par value	$ 50,000	
Common stock, $1 par value		$ 5,000
Additional paid-in capital	8,000	20,000
Retained earnings	100,000	35,000
Total stockholders' equity	$158,000	$60,000
Market price of stock on combination date	$50	Irrelevant
Current value of net assets	Irrelevant	$100,000

(3) All conditions for pooling have been met. In illustrating the entries under the purchase method, we assume that the combination does not qualify for pooling in one minor respect, but that the terms and conditions relating to the exchange of stock are the same.

Illustration:
Comparison of entries under the pooling of interests method and the purchase method—100% of outstanding common stock acquired

Illustration 6-1 compares recording a business combination under the pooling of interests method with the purchase method, using the above information. In reviewing Illustration 6-1, the following points should be understood:

(1) The pooling of interests method ignores both the fair value of the consideration given and the current value of the subsidiary's net assets in determining the "cost" of the investment.
(2) The purchase method uses the fair value of the consideration given (the number of shares issued multiplied by the market price on the date of the combination) to determine the cost of the investment.
(3) Under the pooling of interests method, the investment account has only one major element—the book value element. Thus, there is no cost above or below book value to amortize against the combined income of future periods.
(4) Under the purchase method, the current value over or under the book value element exists in all four situations, with the goodwill element existing only in Situations C and D and a bargain purchase element existing in Situation A.
(5) The given information purposely assigned a low amount to P Company's additional paid-in capital to show the extreme situation of reducing P Company's Additional Paid-in Capital account to zero. In practice, this

[handwritten margin notes: B 50 MKT   P CO PAR #10   5 CO PAR #1   TTL equity 5 CO #60,000   RE · 5 CO 35000   CN 5 CO 100,000]

Illustration 6-1
Comparison of the pooling of interests method
with the purchase method—100% of common stock acquired

Situation:	A		B		C		D	
Shares assumed to be issued:	1,000		2,000		3,000		4,000	
	Dr.	Cr.	Dr.	Cr.	Dr.	Cr.	Dr.	Cr.
Pooling of interests:								
(1) Investment in								
S Company .. 60,000			60,000		60,000		60,000	
(4) Additional paid-								
in capital					5,000		8,000	
(2) Common stock.... 10,000				20,000		30,000		40,000
(4) Additional paid-								
in capital 15,000				5,000				
(3) Retained								
earnings 35,000				35,000		35,000		28,000
Purchase method:								
(5) Investment in								
S Company .. 50,000			100,000		150,000		200,000	
(2) Common stock.... 10,000				20,000		30,000		40,000
(6) Additional paid-								
in capital 40,000				80,000		120,000		160,000

(1) This amount always equals the parent's ownership interest in the subsidiary's net assets at book value.
(2) This amount always equals the number of shares issued multiplied by the par value of the issuing company's common stock.
(3) This amount always equals (a) the parent's ownership interest in the subsidiary's Retained Earnings account less (b) any amount that cannot be charged to the parent's Additional Paid-in Capital account, inasmuch as a debit balance would be created.
(4) This amount is a plug to balance the entry; a debit plug cannot be greater than the Additional Paid-in Capital account balance on the parent's books. (Any additional debit is charged to Retained Earnings.)
(5) This amount always equals the number of shares issued multiplied by the market price on the date of the combination.
(6) This amount is always the difference between the amounts determined in (5) and (2).

would rarely occur because companies usually assign a very low par value to their common stock.

Illustration:
Comparison of entries under the pooling of interests method and the purchase method—90% of outstanding common stock acquired

Illustration 6-2 compares the recording of a business combination under both methods using the information given above, but assuming only 90% of the outstanding common stock is acquired in exchange for 10% fewer shares issued by P Company.

In reviewing Illustration 6-2, note that the manner of determining the amounts recorded is the same as that used in Illustration 6-1, except that

Illustration 6-2
Comparison of the pooling of interests method
with the purchase method—90% of common stock acquired

Situation:	A		B		C		D	
Shares assumed								
to be issued:	900		1,800		2,700		3,600	
	Dr.	Cr.	Dr.	Cr.	Dr.	Cr.	Dr.	Cr.
Pooling of interests:								
(1) Investment in								
S Company .. 54,000	54,000		54,000		54,000		54,000	
(4) Additional paid-								
in capital					4,500		8,000	
(2) Common stock.... 9,000				18,000		27,000		36,000
(4) Additional paid-								
in capital 13,500				4,500				
(3) Retained								
earnings 31,500				31,500		31,500		26,000
Purchase method:								
(5) Investment in								
S Company .. 45,000	45,000		90,000		135,000		180,000	
(2) Common stock.... 9,000				18,000		27,000		36,000
(6) Additional paid-								
in capital 36,000				72,000		108,000		144,000

(1) This amount always equals the parent's ownership interest in the subsidiary's net assets at book value.
(2) This amount always equals the number of shares issued multiplied by the par value of the issuing company's common stock.
(3) This amount always equals (a) the parent's ownership interest in the subsidiary's Retained Earnings account less (b) any amount that cannot be charged to the parent's Additional Paid-in Capital account, inasmuch as a debit balance would be created.
(4) This amount is a plug to balance the entry; a debit plug cannot be greater than the Additional Paid-in Capital account balance on the parent's books. (Any additional debit is charged to Retained Earnings.)
(5) This amount always equals the number of shares issued multiplied by the market price on the date of the combination.
(6) This amount is always the difference between the amounts determined in (5) and (2).

90% instead of 100% is used to determine the amount of the investment in S Company and the credit to retained earnings.

Purchase of shares from dissenting shareholders

Occasionally, some shareholders of the target company refuse to take common stock of the acquiring company as consideration. These shareholders are known as **dissenting shareholders.** To acquire these shares, the acquiring company must usually offer other types of consideration—cash is the most common. As long as the dissenting shareholders do not hold more than 10% of the target company's outstanding shares, consideration other than the acquiring company's common stock may be given to dissenting shareholders, and pooling of interests treatment is allowed.

The purchase of these shares is similar to the purchase of a block of stock as discussed and illustrated in the preceding chapter. Accordingly, the manner of acquiring these shares seems to dictate that purchase accounting be used to account for their acquisition. However, *APB Opinion No. 16* provides that when shares are acquired from dissenting shareholders at the same time the business combination is consummated "a single method should be applied to an entire combination."[7] Thus, the purchase method cannot be used to account for the cost of acquiring these shares from the dissenting shareholders; the pooling of interests method is used to account for all of the shares acquired. In other words, **the combination cannot be recorded as part pooling, part purchase.**

Illustration:
Dissenting shareholders bought out with cash
at combination date

In Situation B of Illustration 6-2, we assumed that P Company issued 1,800 shares of its common stock in exchange for 9,000 shares of S Company's outstanding common stock (90% of the outstanding shares). Let us assume P Company acquired the remaining 1,000 shares from the dissenting shareholders at the combination date by paying $10,000 cash. The entry to record the entire transaction as a pooling of interests is as follows:

Investment in S Company (100% of $60,000)	60,000	
Additional paid-in capital (plug)	3,000	
Cash		10,000
Common stock (1,800 shares × $10)		18,000
Retained earnings (100% of $35,000)		35,000

Treatment of direct costs and registration expenses

Accounting treatment.   Under the purchase method of accounting, direct costs relating to the acquisition of the common stock or the assets are included in the cost of the investment. In contrast, under the pooling of interests method, direct costs are charged to income in the period in which they are incurred. In addition, the costs of registering equity shares issued by the acquiring company are charged to income as incurred instead of being charged to additional paid-in capital as under the purchase method. The rationale is that no new capital is raised—only a "pooling" of the existing capital occurs.[8] In practice, these costs and expenses are customarily deferred until the combination is consummated, so that the costs and expenses are charged against the first period in which income from the newly combined business is included in net income.

Income tax treatment.   We mentioned in Chapter 2 that a combination that qualifies for pooling of interests treatment for financial reporting purposes is almost always treated as a tax-free reorganization for income tax reporting purposes. In almost all instances, direct costs are not currently deductible for income tax reporting purposes. The acquisition of assets is treated as a capital expenditure that results in the creation of a capital asset with an indeterminable useful life. This asset remains intact until it is totally

---

[7] *APB Opinion No. 16*, paragraph 43.
[8] *APB Opinion No. 16*, paragraph 58.

worthless or is disposed of, at which time a tax deduction may be obtained. When common stock is acquired, direct costs are treated as an upward adjustment to the basis of the common stock received by the acquiring company. If the subsidiary is ever sold, these costs are effectively deducted against the proceeds from the sale.

PREPARING CONSOLIDATED FINANCIAL STATEMENTS

Illustration:
Preparing consolidated financial statements as of acquisition date and first year subsequent to acquisition date—Wholly owned subsidiary

Assume that for 19X1, S Company had net income of $15,000 and declared dividends of $5,000. Using the information given in Illustration 6-1, we analyze P Company's investment account by the individual components of the book value element as of the combination date (January 1, 19X1), and then update the analysis for the subsequent year's activity (under the equity method of accounting) as follows:

Analysis of Investment Account

	Total Cost	Common Stock	Additional Paid-In Capital	Retained Earnings Prior Years	Current Year Earnings	Current Year Dividends
Balance, January 1, 19X1	$60,000 =	$5,000 +	$20,000 +	$35,000		
Equity in net income	15,000				$15,000	
Dividends	(5,000)					$(5,000)
Subtotal..............	$70,000 =	$5,000 +	$20,000 +	$35,000 +	$15,000	$(5,000)
Reclassification				10,000	(15,000)	5,000
Balance, December 31, 19X1	$70,000 =	$5,000 +	$20,000 +	$45,000 +	$ -0-	$ -0-

Note that this analysis is the same as to the number of shares issued by P Company, regardless of which situation is used.

The primary elimination entries as of January 1, 19X1 (the combination date) and December 31, 19X1 (one year subsequent to the combination date) are as follows:

	Consolidation Date	
	January 1, 19X1	December 31, 19X1
Common stock	5,000	5,000
Additional paid-in capital.........................	20,000	20,000
Retained earnings (beginning of year)	35,000	35,000
Equity in net income of subsidiary		15,000
Dividends declared...........................		5,000
Investment in S Company	60,000	70,000

Because the book value element is the only major element under pooling of interests accounting, there is no cost over or under book value to amortize, and thus no secondary elimination entry is necessary.

Illustrations 6-3 and 6-4 show consolidating statement worksheets as of the above dates, assuming that 3,000 shares were issued (Situation C in Illustration 6-1) to effect the combination. In reviewing Illustrations 6-3 and 6-4, the following points should be understood:

(1) The primary elimination entry is developed in exactly the same way as in purchase accounting, except that the updating of the expanded analysis of the investment account is simpler because only the book value element is involved.
(2) The amounts in the consolidated column are composed of (a) the parent's items based on book values and (b) the subsidiary's items based on book values. No revaluation to current values has been made.
(3) A secondary elimination entry is not needed when pooling of interests accounting is used.
(4) The use of the equity method to account subsequently for the parent's investment maintains the investment account balance equal to the subsidiary's net assets at book value, which simplifies the consolidation process.
(5) When ownership of the subsidiary is less than 100% (it must be at least 90% to qualify for pooling of interests treatment), the necessary minority

Illustration 6-3

<table>
<tr><td colspan="6">P COMPANY AND SUBSIDIARY (S COMPANY)
Consolidating Statement Worksheet
As of January 1, 19X1</td></tr>
<tr><td></td><td>P</td><td>S</td><td colspan="2">Eliminations</td><td>Consoli-</td></tr>
<tr><td></td><td>Company</td><td>Company</td><td>Dr.</td><td>Cr.</td><td>dated</td></tr>
<tr><td>Balance Sheet:</td><td></td><td></td><td></td><td></td><td></td></tr>
<tr><td>Cash ....</td><td>10,000</td><td>5,000</td><td></td><td></td><td>15,000</td></tr>
<tr><td>Accounts receivable, net ....</td><td>15,000</td><td>12,000</td><td></td><td></td><td>27,000</td></tr>
<tr><td>Inventory ....</td><td>25,000</td><td>18,000</td><td></td><td></td><td>43,000</td></tr>
<tr><td>Investment in S Company ...</td><td>60,000</td><td></td><td></td><td>60,000(1)</td><td>-0-</td></tr>
<tr><td>Land ....</td><td>60,000</td><td>15,000</td><td></td><td></td><td>75,000</td></tr>
<tr><td>Building, net ....</td><td>110,000</td><td>30,000</td><td></td><td></td><td>140,000</td></tr>
<tr><td>Equipment, net ....</td><td>40,000</td><td>20,000</td><td></td><td></td><td>60,000</td></tr>
<tr><td></td><td>320,000</td><td>100,000</td><td></td><td>60,000</td><td>360,000</td></tr>
<tr><td>Liabilities ....</td><td>102,000</td><td>40,000</td><td></td><td></td><td>142,000</td></tr>
<tr><td>Common stock:</td><td></td><td></td><td></td><td></td><td></td></tr>
<tr><td>P Company ....</td><td>80,000</td><td></td><td></td><td></td><td>80,000</td></tr>
<tr><td>S Company ....</td><td></td><td>5,000</td><td>5,000(1)</td><td></td><td>-0-</td></tr>
<tr><td>Additional paid-in capital:</td><td></td><td></td><td></td><td></td><td></td></tr>
<tr><td>P Company ....</td><td>3,000</td><td></td><td></td><td></td><td>3,000</td></tr>
<tr><td>S Company ....</td><td></td><td>20,000</td><td>20,000(1)</td><td></td><td>-0-</td></tr>
<tr><td>Retained earnings:</td><td></td><td></td><td></td><td></td><td></td></tr>
<tr><td>P Company ....</td><td>135,000</td><td></td><td></td><td></td><td>135,000</td></tr>
<tr><td>S Company ....</td><td></td><td>35,000</td><td>35,000(1)</td><td></td><td>-0-</td></tr>
<tr><td></td><td>320,000</td><td>100,000</td><td>60,000</td><td></td><td>360,000</td></tr>
<tr><td>Proof of debit and credit postings ....</td><td></td><td></td><td>60,000</td><td>60,000</td><td></td></tr>
<tr><td colspan="6">Explanation of entry:
(1) The primary elimination entry.</td></tr>
</table>

Illustration 6-4

P COMPANY AND SUBSIDIARY (S COMPANY)
Consolidating Statement Worksheet
For the Year Ended December 31, 19X1

	P Company	S Company	Eliminations Dr.	Eliminations Cr.	Consolidated
Income Statement:					
Sales	400,000	160,000			560,000
Income from subsidiary:		–			
Equity in net income	15,000		15,000(1)		-0-
Subtotal	415,000	160,000	15,000		560,000
Cost of goods sold.	240,000	100,000			340,000
Marketing expenses.	80,000	20,000			100,000
Administrative expenses	20,000	10,000			30,000
Interest expense	10,000	5,000			15,000
Subtotal	350,000	135,000			485,000
Income before Income Taxes . . .	65,000	25,000	15,000		75,000
Income tax expense @ 40% . .	(20,000)[a]	(10,000)			(30,000)
Net Income	45,000	15,000	⌐15,000		45,000
Balance Sheet:					
Cash	25,000	15,000			40,000
Accounts receivable, net.	55,000	25,000			80,000
Inventory.	35,000	30,000			65,000
Investment in S Company	70,000			70,000(1)	-0-
Land	60,000	15,000			75,000
Building, net.	100,000	28,000			128,000
Equipment, net	35,000	17,000			52,000
Total assets	380,000	130,000		70,000	440,000
Liabilities.	144,000	60,000			204,000
Common stock:					
P Company	80,000				80,000
S Company		5,000	5,000(1)		-0-
Additional paid-in capital:					
P Company	3,000				3,000
S Company		20,000	20,000(1)		-0-
Retained earnings—P Company:					
Beginning of year	100,000				100,000
+ Effect of pooling	35,000				35,000
+ Net income.	45,000				45,000
– Dividends declared	(27,000)				(27,000)
End of year	153,000				153,000
Retained earnings—S Company:					
Beginning of year		35,000	35,000(1)		-0-
+ Net income.		15,000	⌐→15,000		-0-
– Dividends declared		(5,000)		5,000(1)	-0-
End of year		45,000	50,000	5,000	-0-
Total liabilities and equity . . .	380,000	130,000	75,000	5,000	440,000
Proof of debit and credit postings			75,000	75,000	

Explanation of entry:
 (1) The primary elimination entry.
[a] The income tax calculation is 40% of $50,000, not 40% of $65,000.

interest entry is computed in the same manner as shown in the preceding chapter for situations in which purchase accounting is used.

(6) Assuming P Company declared dividends of $27,000 during 19X1, the consolidated statement of retained earnings would reflect the following activity:

Balance, January 1, 19X1, as reported at December 31, 19X0	$100,000
Effect of pooling of interests with S Company..................	35,000[a]
Balance, January 1, 19X1, as restated	$135,000
Net income for the year	45,000
Subtotal..	$180,000
Dividends	(27,000)
Balance, December 31, 19X1	$153,000

[a] This amount always equals the subsidiary's retained earnings as of the beginning of the year, regardless of the actual business combination date. (This is because the subsidiary's earnings for the entire year are combined with the parent's regardless of when during the year the combination occurs.) Also, dividends declared by the subsidiary prior to the combination date (other than amounts applicable to minority shareholders) would be combined with the parent's dividends in this statement.

The preceding illustration assumed that the parent company used the equity method to account for its investment in the subsidiary. The parent company may, however, account for its investment in the subsidiary using the cost method. The cost method is not illustrated, because the procedures are the same as those shown in Appendix A to Chapter 4.

Comparative income statements—Pooling of interests versus purchase accounting

In Illustration 6-4, we assumed that 3,000 shares of common stock were issued to effect the combination (Situation C in Illustration 6-1). The fair value of the consideration given in Situation C was $150,000. If the combination did not qualify for pooling of interests treatment, then under purchase accounting, the $150,000 total cost would consist of the following major conceptual elements:

(1) The book value element (100% of $60,000)..................	$ 60,000
(2) The current value over book value element ($100,000 − $60,000)	40,000
(3) The goodwill element ($150,000 − $100,000)...............	50,000
	$150,000

Assuming that the undervaluation of net assets relates to equipment with a remaining life of 10 years, then $4,000 of amortization related to this element would be recorded in 19X1 under the purchase method. Assuming the goodwill was assigned a 10-year life, then $5,000 of amortization related to this element would be recorded in 19X1 under the purchase method. Income statements for 19X1 are shown under both methods for comparison.

	Pooling of Interests (Per Illus. 6-4)	Purchase Method
Revenues...	$560,000	$560,000
Costs and expenses:		
Cost of goods sold	$340,000	$349,000
Marketing expenses	100,000	100,000
Administrative expenses.................................	30,000	30,000
Interest expense.......................................	15,000	15,000
Subtotal	$485,000	$494,000
Income before Income Taxes	$ 75,000	$ 66,000
Income tax expense @ 40%...............................	(30,000)	(30,000)[a]
Net Income	$ 45,000	$ 36,000

[a] The $9,000 of amortization of cost in excess of book value is not deductible for income tax reporting purposes. Thus, income taxes are calculated on $75,000, not $66,000.

Conforming accounting methods

Under the purchase method of accounting, a new valuation basis is established for the assets and liabilities of the acquired business. In these situations, the acquiring company's accounting methods can be imposed on the acquired business at the consummation date to have uniform accounting methods on a combined or consolidated basis. However, uniform accounting methods are not required. Thus, a parent using straight-line depreciation that acquires a subsidiary using an accelerated depreciation method has the following options:

(1) Allow the subsidiary to use accelerated depreciation.
(2) Direct the subsidiary to use straight-line depreciation.

Obviously, the second alternative is more desirable, because the consolidated financial statements are presented using uniform accounting methods.

Under the pooling of interests method of accounting, a new valuation basis is not established for the assets and liabilities of the acquired business. The AICPA, however, recognized the merits of presenting combined or consolidated financial statements that use uniform accounting methods. Accordingly, it included the following provision pertaining to conforming accounting methods for situations involving pooling of interests.

> The separate companies may have recorded assets and liabilities under differing methods of accounting and the amounts may be adjusted to the same basis of accounting if the change would otherwise have been appropriate for the separate company. A change in accounting method to conform the individual methods should be applied retroactively, and financial statements presented for prior periods should be restated.[9]

This statement does not make conformity of accounting methods mandatory. It states that the amounts "**may be adjusted** to the same basis of

---

[9] *APB Opinion No. 16*, paragraph 52.

accounting." Thus, conforming accounting methods is optional, as in purchase accounting.

DISCLOSURES

The acquiring entity must make the following disclosures for each period in which a business combination accounted for under the pooling of interests method occurs.

Disclosure in the financial statements

The financial statements must indicate that a business combination accounted for under the pooling of interests method has occurred. This indication may be either by captions or by references to notes to the financial statements.[10]

Disclosure in the notes to the financial statements

The following footnote disclosures, among others, are required:

(1) The name and description of the business combined.
(2) The fact that the pooling of interests method is used to account for the combination.
(3) The number of shares issued and a description thereof.
(4) Income information (including revenues and net income) for preacquisition periods of the acquired business that are included in the current combined income statement.
(5) Reconciliations of revenues and earnings to amounts previously reported by the acquiring entity.[11]

CONSOLIDATED STATEMENT OF CHANGES IN FINANCIAL POSITION

When a consolidated balance sheet and income statement are presented, a consolidated statement of changes in financial position is also necessary. A few additional areas require special consideration when the statement of changes in financial position is prepared on a consolidated basis versus when it is prepared on a separate company only basis. These areas of special consideration are discussed later in this chapter.

The two approaches

Two approaches can be used to prepare the consolidated statement of changes in financial position. Regardless of which approach is taken, a parent company usually requires each subsidiary to submit a statement of changes in financial position to facilitate its preparation of the consolidated statement. Thus, information is readily provided for each company within the consolidated group as to property additions, retirements, depreciation expense, borrowings, and repayments—items commonly set out separately in a statement of changes in financial position.

[10] *APB Opinion No. 16*, paragraph 63.
[11] *APB Opinion No. 16*, paragraph 64.

Consolidating statement worksheet approach. A multi-column worksheet can be used to consolidate the separate company statements of changes in financial position. The worksheet columnar headings would be as follows:

P Company	S Company	Eliminations		Consolidated
		Dr.	Cr.	

This approach is practical when no intercompany inventory, fixed asset, or bond transactions (topics dealt with in Chapters 7, 8, and 9) have occurred. Elimination entries are needed only for (1) eliminating intercompany dividends; (2) eliminating the parent's interest in the subsidiary's net income (to prevent double-counting); and (3) reflecting the minority interest as a charge that did not require the use of funds (we explain (3) more fully later).

Analyzing the changes in the consolidated balance sheets approach. A company can use its consolidated balance sheets for the beginning and end of a year to prepare a statement of changes in financial position. The change in each individual account balance for the year is analyzed in terms of sources and uses of funds. (You learned this approach in intermediate accounting.) When intercompany inventory, fixed asset, or bond transactions have occurred, this method is much quicker because these intercompany transactions have been eliminated (as shown in later chapters) in preparing the consolidated balance sheet and income statement. Thus, these intercompany transactions are not dealt with again in preparing the consolidated statement of changes in financial position, as would be necessary under the consolidating statement worksheet approach.

Areas requiring special consideration

In preparing the consolidated statement of changes in financial position, the following areas require special consideration:

(1) Goodwill amortization.
(2) Minority interest.
(3) Subsidiary with preferred stock.
(4) Changes in the parent's ownership interest.

Items (3) and (4) are covered in Chapters 9 and 10. Accordingly, we now discuss only items (1) and (2).

Goodwill amortization. Preparation of the consolidated statement of changes in financial position begins with consolidated net income (obtained from the consolidated income statement). Recall from intermediate accounting that charges to income that do not require the use of funds (working capital or cash, depending on a firm's concept of funds) are added back to net income in the statement of changes in financial position to arrive at funds provided from operations. Because goodwill amortization is a charge that does not require the use of funds, it is added back to consolidated net income (along with depreciation expense and any other charges that do not require the use of funds) to arrive at funds provided from operations.

Minority interest.   Recall that the minority interest in a subsidiary's net income is shown in the consolidated income statement as a deduction in arriving at consolidated net income. This minority interest deduction, however, does not require the use of funds. Accordingly, it is added back to consolidated net income to arrive at funds provided from operations. Dividends paid to minority shareholders constitute a use of funds and are shown as such in the consolidated statement of changes in financial position, along with dividends paid to the parent's stockholders.

SUMMARY

Under the pooling of interests method, a business combination is viewed as a combining of equity interests. This combining of equity interests is possible only in situations in which the acquiring company issues substantially all common stock as consideration for the acquired business. In addition, numerous secondary conditions must be met before pooling of interests treatment may be used. If all conditions for pooling of interests treatment are met, then pooling of interests accounting must be used. If any one condition is not met, then purchase accounting must be used.

A business combination that qualifies for pooling of interests treatment is recorded based on the book value of the acquired company's net assets. The acquired company's assets and liabilities are reported at their historical amounts in the future financial statements of the combined businesses. Consequently, goodwill is never created under pooling of interests accounting. The pooling of interests method is conceptually opposed to the purchase method because it completely ignores the fair value of the consideration given and the current value of the acquired company's net assets. The pooling of interests method is popular primarily because it usually results in reporting greater earnings and earnings per share amounts in future periods than would be reported under the purchase method.

Glossary of new terms

Dissenting Shareholders: Target company shareholders who refuse to exchange their common shares for only common stock of the acquiring company.

Spin-Off: A divestiture of a portion of a business whereby certain assets, liabilities, or common stock holdings of a subsidiary are given to certain shareholders of a company in exchange for some or all of their outstanding common stock holdings in the company.

Review questions

1. Why is the term *acquired business* not used in the discussion of pooling of interests accounting in *APB Opinion No. 16?*
2. What is the underlying premise of pooling of interests accounting?

3. How is the value of the consideration given by the acquiring company accounted for in a business combination that qualifies as a pooling of interests?
4. What is the major criticism of the pooling of interests concept?
5. What determines whether a business combination is treated as a pooling of interests?
6. What primary consideration is given in a business combination that qualifies as a pooling of interests?
7. How many major elements exist in the investment account for a business combination accounted for as a pooling of interests?
8. Can cash be given to the shareholders of the acquired company in a business combination that is accounted for as a pooling of interests?
9. When the acquisition of a subsidiary has been accounted for as a pooling of interests, is a secondary elimination entry required in preparing a consolidating statement worksheet? Why or why not?
10. To what extent are the subsidiary's net assets reflected at their current values in a business combination accounted for as a pooling of interests?
11. What is the primary reason for the popularity of pooling of interests accounting?
12. How are preacquisition earnings of the acquired business treated in income statements for periods before the acquisition date when the combination has been accounted for as a pooling of interests?
13. What fundamental disclosures are required when a business combination accounted for as a pooling of interests has occurred?
14. When assets have been acquired, may pooling of interests accounting be used?

Discussion cases

Discussion case 6–1
Pooling of interests criteria

Perch Company is negotiating a business combination with Sardinee Company. In discussing the business combination with Perch Company's controller at a lunch meeting, you, the certified public accountant for Perch Company, learn the following:

(1) Perch Company will issue common stock to effect the combination. (The book value of Sardinee's net assets is 1% of the book value of Perch's net assets; the same relationship exists on a current value basis.) After the combination, the former shareholders of Sardinee will hold approximately 4% of Perch Company's total outstanding common shares. As a result, these shareholders cannot significantly influence the operations of the combined companies.
(2) There will be no specified holding period during which the former Sardinee Company shareholders must not sell the Perch Company shares that they receive in the transaction.
(3) Sardinee Company is an industry leader, has remarkably high profits, and has a price–earnings ratio of 60 to 1 (indicating that it has substantial goodwill).
(4) Perch Company's management intends to acquire Sardinee's business at any cost, regardless of whether or not pooling of interests treatment can be used. In other words, the objective is to acquire the business; the form of consideration to be given is of secondary importance.

(5) Immediately after the combination, approximately 20% of Sardinee's former stockholders plan to sell the Perch Company common stock they receive in the combination, because they need the cash.

Required:
How does this information affect your opinion on whether pooling of interests accounting treatment is appropriate?

Discussion case 6–2
Pooling of interests criteria—Substantial undervaluation of acquired company's net assets and nonoperating status

PDQ Company recently acquired all of the outstanding common stock of Sern County Realty Company in a transaction structured to qualify for pooling of interests treatment. Sern County Realty Company has substantial land holdings that were acquired many years ago. The current value of these land holdings is several million dollars in excess of book value. The fair value of the consideration given to the shareholders of Sern County Realty Company equaled the current value of Sern's net assets. PDQ Company's controller has indicated to you that they structured the transaction as a pooling of interests to prevent the revaluation of these land holdings to their current values, as would be done under purchase accounting. In this way, PDQ Company can start selling these land holdings after the combination date and report substantial profits at that time.

Required:
(1) How do these comments affect your opinion on whether the pooling of interests accounting treatment is appropriate?
(2) Assuming the 12 specific conditions for pooling of interests treatment are met, would the fact that Sern has been relatively inactive for the preceding few years—that is, it had no activities or operations other than these existing land investments—raise any other issues that would preclude pooling of interests treatment?

Discussion case 6–3
Review of specific pooling of interests conditions

The boards of directors of Parento Corporation, Alpha Company, Beta, Inc., and Camma Corporation are meeting jointly to discuss plans for a business combination. Each corporation has one class of common stock outstanding; Alpha also has one class of preferred stock outstanding. Although terms have not been settled, Parento will be the acquiring or issuing corporation. Because the directors want to conform to generally accepted accounting principles, they have asked you to attend the meeting as an advisor.

Required:
Consider each of the following questions independently of the others and answer each in accordance with generally accepted accounting principles. Explain your answers.

(1) Assume that the combination will be consummated August 31, 19X3. Explain the philosophy underlying the accounting and how the balance sheet accounts of the four corporations will appear on Parento's consolidated balance sheet on September 1, 19X3, if the combination is accounted for as
  (a) A pooling of interests.
  (b) A purchase.
(2) Assume that the combination will be consummated August 31, 19X3. Explain how the income statement accounts of the four corporations will be accounted for in preparing Parento's consolidated income statement for the year ended December 31, 19X3, if the combination is accounted for as
  (a) A pooling of interests.
  (b) A purchase.
(3) Some of the directors believe that the terms of the combination should be settled immediately and that the method of accounting to be used (whether pooling of interests, purchase, or a mixture) may be chosen at some later date. Others believe that the terms of the combination and the accounting method are closely related. Which position is correct?
(4) Parento and Camma are comparable in size; Alpha and Beta are much smaller. How do these facts affect the choice of accounting method?
(5) Beta was formerly a subsidiary of Tucker Corporation, which is not related to any of the four companies discussing combination. Eighteen months ago, Tucker voluntarily spun off Beta. How do these facts affect the choice of accounting method?
(6) Mrs. Victor Camma, Sr., who holds 5% of Camma's common stock, will almost certainly object to the combination. Assume that Parento can acquire only 95% (rather than 100%) of Camma's stock, issuing Parento common stock in exchange.
  (a) Which accounting method is applicable?
  (b) If Parento can acquire the remaining 5% at some future time—in five years, for instance—in exchange for its own common stock, which accounting method will be applicable to this second acquisition?
(7) Because the directors feel that one of Camma's major divisions will not be compatible with the combined company's operations, they expect to sell it as soon as possible after the combination is consummated. They expect to have no trouble finding a buyer. What effect, if any, do these facts have on the choice of accounting methods?

(AICPA adapted)

Discussion case 6–4
Pooling of interests—Lawsuit alleging deception

In January 19X5, Plotter Company entered into a business combination transaction with Sleeper Company. Plotter issued the common stock to effect the transaction. The 12 conditions for pooling of interests treatment were met, so the transaction was recorded as a pooling of interests. Sleeper Company had a substantial amount of undervalued assets as of the combination date.

Through December 31, 19X7, Plotter reported six consecutive years of increased profits and had attracted a wide following on Wall Street. In 19X8, the company's earnings from operations were down slightly from 19X7. To show a continued trend of higher profits, management sold at a substantial profit (throughout 19X8) Sleeper Company's undervalued assets. In 19X9, earnings from operations were the same as in 19X8, but the company had no undervalued assets to sell. Accordingly, 19X9 earnings were substantially below those of 19X8 and 19X7.

As a result of reporting lower profits in 19X9, the price of the company's common stock dropped sharply, and many investors lost substantial amounts of money. A class action lawsuit was filed against the company shortly after earnings were reported for 19X9, alleging that the company had conspired to issue false and misleading financial statements for 19X8. The focal point of the lawsuit was that the use of the pooling of interests method in 19X5 resulted in deceptive financial reporting in 19X8 and that the purchase method of accounting should have been used instead. (Only a nominal gain would have been reported on the sale of the assets in 19X8 if the purchase method had been used.)

The parties named in the lawsuit are Plotter's top management, including the controller, and the certified public accountants for Plotter (Arthur, Waterwick, Toupers, and Sernst).

Required:

(1) Does the company have an adequate defense if they used generally accepted accounting principles?
(2) To use the pooling of interests method, did Plotter's controller have to believe personally that it results in a fair presentation?
(3) How might the lawyer for the plaintiffs use *Accounting Research Study No. 5*? What impact might its use have on the jury?
(4) In reading *APB Opinion No. 16,* the lawyer for the plaintiffs found that one of the dissenting members of the Accounting Principles Board was a partner in the CPA firm named in the lawsuit. Further research revealed that this CPA firm was vehemently against the pooling of interests concept prior to the issuance of *APB Opinion No. 16.* Of what use might this information be?

Exercises

Exercise 6–1
Pooling of interests criteria

Indicate whether each of the following conditions or terms negates pooling of interests accounting treatment:

(1) Acquisition of 90% of the assets. *no*
(2) Acquisition of 85% of outstanding common stock. *Yes*
(3) Pro rata distribution of cash and common stock to acquired company's shareholders. *Yes - unless cash for fractional shares*
(4) Additional common stock to be issued by the acquiring company if its common stock has a fair market value below $50 per share two years after the combination date. *yes*
(5) The acquired subsidiary is to be liquidated into a division. *Yes*
(6) After acquisition of 100% of the division's assets, its accounting is to be centralized. *no*
(7) Acquisition of 90% of outstanding common stock. *no*

(8) The common stock issued to the acquired company's shareholders has certain voting restrictions. *Yes*
(9) Additional common shares are to be issued by the acquiring company, depending on the subsequent sales level of the acquired business for three years after the acquisition date. *Yes*
(10) The acquiring company agrees to purchase for cash less than 10% of the shares issued within three years of the acquisition date. *Yes*

Exercise 6–2
Testing for independence

Pennant Company and Series Company are contemplating a business combination structured to qualify as a pooling of interests. Common stock information is as follows:

	Pennant Company	Series Company
Outstanding common shares	300,000	100,000
Pennant Company common stock owned by Series Company		15,000

Required:
(1) Determine if the companies are independent. Assume Pennant will issue three shares for every one outstanding share of Series Company.
(2) Determine if the companies are independent, but assume that Pennant will issue one share for every one outstanding share of Series Company.
(3) Explain why the answers in requirements (1) and (2) are different.

Exercise 6–3
Testing for independence—dual intercorporate investments

Pulsar Company and Starr Company are contemplating a business combination structured to qualify as a pooling of interests. Common stock information is as follows:

	Pulsar Company	Starr Company
Outstanding common shares	600,000	100,000
Starr Company common stock owned by Pulsar Company	5,000	
Pulsar Company common stock owned by Starr Company........................		4,000

Pulsar will issue one common share for each two outstanding common shares of Starr Company.

Required:
(1) Determine if the companies are independent.
(2) If Starr were the company issuing the common stock, what exchange ratio would it use to maintain the relative holdings between the two stockholder groups?

Exercise 6–4
Recording a pooling of interests—
100% of outstanding common stock acquired

On January 1, 19X1, Port Company acquired 100% of the outstanding common stock of Sea Company by issuing 20,000 shares of its $5 par value common stock. Selected information as of the acquisition date is as follows:

	Port Company	Sea Company
Common stock, $5 par value	$1,000,000	$200,000
Additional paid-in capital	3,000,000	400,000
Retained earnings	2,000,000	250,000
	$6,000,000	$850,000
Fair market value per share	$50	$25
Net assets at current value	$7,000,000	$900,000

Assume the business combination qualifies for pooling of interests treatment.

Required:
(1) Prepare the entry to record the business combination.
(2) Prepare an expanded analysis of the investment account as of the acquisition date.
(3) Prepare the primary elimination entry at January 1, 19X1.

Exercise 6–5
Recording a pooling of interests—
100% of outstanding common stock acquired

On January 1, 19X1, Pops Company acquired 100% of the outstanding common stock of Siedler Company by issuing shares of its common stock. Each company's equity accounts as of the acquisition date are as follows:

	Pops Company	Siedler Company
Common stock, $20 par value	$1,000,000	
Common stock, $5 par value		$ 50,000
Additional paid-in capital	30,000	50,000
Retained earnings	200,000	40,000
	$1,230,000	$140,000

Assume the business combination qualifies for pooling of interests accounting.

Required:
(1) Prepare the entry to record the business combination, assuming Pops Company issued
  (a) 4,000 shares.
  (b) 5,000 shares.
  (c) 6,000 shares.
  (d) 7,000 shares.

(2) Prepare the primary elimination entry as of the acquisition date for each situation in part (1).

Exercise 6–6
Recording a pooling of interests—
90% of outstanding common stock acquired

Assume the information provided in Exercise 6–5, except that Pops Company acquired only 90% of the outstanding common stock of Siedler Company.

Required:
(1) Prepare the entry to record the business combination, assuming Pops Company issued
  (a) 3,600 shares.
  (b) 4,500 shares.
  (c) 5,400 shares.
  (d) 6,300 shares.
(2) Prepare the primary elimination entry as of the acquisition date for each situation in part (1).

Exercise 6–7
COMPREHENSIVE   Recording a pooling of interests:
applying the equity method; preparing primary elimination entries—
100% of outstanding common stock acquired

On January 1, 19X1, Poll Company acquired 100% of the outstanding common stock of Survey Company by issuing 20,000 shares of its common stock. Each company's equity accounts as of the acquisition date are as follows:

	Poll Company	Survey Company
Common stock, $1 par value	$ 100,000	
Common stock, $5 par value		$ 5,000
Additional paid-in capital	900,000	95,000
Retained earnings	500,000	60,000
	$1,500,000	$160,000

For the year ended December 31, 19X1, Survey Company had net income of $40,000 and declared cash dividends of $10,000. Assume the business combination qualifies for pooling of interests accounting.

Required:
(1) Prepare the entry to record the business combination.
(2) Prepare the primary elimination entry as of the acquisition date.
(3) Prepare the entries for 19X1 required under the equity method of accounting.
(4) Update the analysis of the investment account for 19X1, and prepare the primary elimination entry as of December 31, 19X1.

Exercise 6–8
COMPREHENSIVE   Recording a pooling of interests: applying the equity method; preparing primary elimination entries— 90% of outstanding common stock acquired

Assume the information provided in Exercise 6–7, except that Poll Company acquired only 90% of the outstanding common stock of Survey Company on January 1, 19X1, by issuing 18,000 shares of its common stock.

Required:
The requirements are the same as those in Exercise 6–7.

Exercise 6–9
Theory of pooling of interests—Determining consolidated retained earnings and consolidated net income in acquisition year

On June 30, 19X5, Paxel, Inc. acquired Selle, Inc. in a business combination properly accounted for as a pooling of interests. Paxel exchanged six of its shares of common stock for each share of Selle's outstanding common stock. June 30 was the fiscal year-end for both companies. No intercompany transactions occurred during the year. The balance sheets immediately before the combination are as follows:

	Paxel Book Value	Selle Book Value	Selle Fair Value
Current assets	$ 40,000	$ 30,000	$ 45,000
Equipment (net)	150,000	120,000	140,000
Land	30,000		
	$220,000	$150,000	$185,000
Current liabilities	$ 35,000	$ 15,000	$ 15,000
Notes payable	40,000		
Bonds payable		100,000	100,000
Common stock ($1 par value)	75,000		
Common stock ($5 par value)		50,000	
Retained earnings	70,000	(15,000)	
	$220,000	$150,000	

(Handwritten annotations: "25,000" and "10,000" near common stock lines; "135000" and "45000" and "180—" near Selle fair value column)

Required:
(1) What was the Retained Earnings account balance on the combined balance sheet at June 30, 19X5?
   (a) $45,000
   (b) $55,000
   (c) $70,000
   (d) $80,000

(Handwritten: "env. in Selle Co. 35000"; "Addt'l Pd in Cap 25000 60000"; "Comm. Stk 25000"; "Retained Earn")

(2) How should the combined net income for the year be computed?
   (a) Use only Paxel's income because the combination occurred on the last day of the fiscal year.
   (b) Use only Selle's income because the combination occurred on the last day of the fiscal year.

(c) Add together both companies' incomes even though the combination occurred on the last day of the fiscal year.

(d) Add together both companies' incomes and subtract the annual amortization of goodwill.

(AICPA adapted)

Exercise 6–10
Theory of pooling of interests—Determining consolidated net income in acquisition year

On January 1, 19X7, Pilson, Inc. issued 100,000 additional shares of $10 par value voting common stock in exchange for all of Somson Company's voting common stock in a business combination appropriately accounted for as a pooling of interests. Net income for the year ended December 31, 19X7, was $400,000 for Somson and $1,300,000 for Pilson, exclusive of any consideration of Somson. During 19X7, Pilson paid $900,000 dividends to its stockholders, and Somson paid $250,000 dividends to Pilson. *400000 + 1300000 = 1 700 000 NI*

Required:
Determine the consolidated net income for the year ended December 31, 19X7.

(AICPA adapted)

Exercise 6–11
Theory of pooling of interests—Determining effect on parent's stockholders' equity

Poke Corporation issued voting common stock with a $90,000 stated value in exchange for all of the outstanding common stock of Shasta Company. The combination was properly accounted for as a pooling of interests.

The stockholders' equity section in Shasta Company's balance sheet at the combination date was as follows:

Common stock	$ 70,000
Capital contributed in excess of stated value	7,000
Retained earnings	50,000
	$127,000

Required:
What should be the increase in stockholders' equity of Poke Corporation at the acquisition date as a result of this business combination?

(a) $-0-
(b) $37,000
(c) $90,000
(d) $127,000

Inv. in S   127000
APIC Common Stock   13000
RE   90000
*   50 000*

(AICPA adapted)

Exercise 6–12
Theory of pooling of interests—Determining
effect on parent's stockholders' equity

In a business combination accounted for as a pooling of interests, the combined corporation's retained earnings usually equals the sum of the retained earnings of the individual combining corporations.

Required:
Assuming there is no contributed capital other than capital stock at par value on each company's books, which of the following describes a situation in which the combined retained earnings must be increased or decreased?

(a) Increased if the par value dollar amount of the outstanding shares of the combined corporation exceeds the total capital stock of the separate combining companies.

(b) Increased if the par value dollar amount of the outstanding shares of the combined corporation is less than the total capital stock of the separate combining companies.

(c) Decreased if the par value dollar amount of the outstanding shares of the combined corporation exceeds the total capital stock of the separate combining companies.

(d) Decreased if the par value dollar amount of the outstanding shares of the combined corporation is less than the total capital stock of the separate combining companies.

(AICPA adapted)

Problems

Problem 6–1
Recording a pooling of interests; preparing consolidated financial
statements as of acquisition date—100% of outstanding
common stock acquired

On December 31, 19X2, Patter Company acquired 100% of the outstanding common stock of Sprinkles Company by issuing 1,000 shares of its common stock. The financial statements of each company for the year ended December 31, 19X2, *before the business combination,* are as follows:

	Patter Company	Sprinkles Company
Income Statement (19X2):		
Sales	$400,000	$120,000
Cost of goods sold	(200,000)	(70,000)
Marketing expenses	(60,000)	(30,000)
Administrative expenses	(90,000)	(10,000)
Interest expense	(35,000)	(5,000)
Income before Income Taxes	$ 15,000	$ 5,000
Income tax expense @ 40%	(6,000)	(2,000)
Net Income	$ 9,000	$ 3,000

	Patter Company	Sprinkles Company
Balance Sheet (as of December 31, 19X2):		
Cash	$ 50,000	$ 33,000
Accounts receivable, net	60,000	20,000
Inventory	80,000	27,000
Fixed assets, net	610,000	120,000
	$800,000	$200,000
Accounts payable and accruals	$ 90,000	$ 25,000
Long-term debt	360,000	65,000
Common stock, $10 par value	100,000	
Common stock, $2 par value		20,000
Additional paid-in capital	200,000	80,000
Retained earnings	50,000	10,000
	$800,000	$200,000
Dividends declared in 19X2.	$ 5,000	$ 1,000

Assume the business combination qualifies for pooling of interests treatment. (Note that the combination occurred at the end of the year, not at the beginning of the year as illustrated in the text. Thus, the equity method is not applied during 19X2.)

Required:
(1) Prepare the entry to record the business combination.
(2) Prepare the primary elimination entry at December 31, 19X2.
(3) Prepare a consolidating statement worksheet at December 31, 19X2.
(4) Prepare a consolidated statement of retained earnings for 19X2. (Patter Company's retained earnings at December 31, 19X1, was $46,000.) *Hint:* Use an analysis of the subsidiary's retained earnings for 19X2 to assist you.

Problem 6–2
Recording a pooling of interests; preparing consolidated financial statements as of acquisition date—90% of outstanding common stock acquired

Assume the information provided in Problem 6–1, except that Patter Company acquired 90% of the outstanding common stock of Sprinkles Company on December 31, 19X2, by issuing 900 shares of its common stock.

Required:
The requirements are the same as for Problem 6–1. In addition, a minority interest entry is necessary.

Problem 6–3
Determining the entry used to record a pooling of interests; updating analysis of investment account for year subsequent to combination; preparing consolidated financial statements subsequent to acquisition date—100% of outstanding common stock acquired

Pike Company acquired 100% of the outstanding common stock of Smith Company on January 1, 19X4, by issuing 4,000 shares of its common stock. The financial statements of each company for the year ended December 31, 19X4, are as follows:

	Pike Company	Smith Company
Income Statement (19X4):		
Sales.	$ 800,000	$100,000
Equity in net income of subsidiary	6,000	
Cost of goods sold.	(500,000)	(50,000)
Marketing expenses.	(110,000)	(20,000)
Administrative expenses	(90,000)	(15,000)
Interest expense	(50,000)	(5,000)
Income before Income Taxes	$ 56,000	$ 10,000
Income tax expense @ 40%	(20,000)	(4,000)
Net Income	$ 36,000	$ 6,000
Balance Sheet (as of December 31, 19X4):		
Cash	$ 60,000	$ 10,000
Accounts receivable, net.	90,000	20,000
Inventory.	150,000	60,000
Investment in subsidiary	133,000	
Fixed assets, net	567,000	110,000
	$1,000,000	$200,000
Accounts payable and accruals	$ 76,000	$ 17,000
Long-term debt	300,000	50,000
Common stock, $10 par value	100,000	
Common stock, $1 par value		20,000
Additional paid-in capital.	400,000	80,000
Retained earnings	124,000	33,000
	$1,000,000	$200,000
Dividends declared in 19X4.	$ 10,000	$ 1,000

Assume the business combination qualifies for pooling of interests accounting.

Required:
(1) Prepare an expanded and updated analysis of the investment account for 19X4, using the equity method of accounting. (*Hint:* It is necessary to work backwards.)
(2) Determine the entry Pike Company made on January 1, 19X4, to record the business combination.
(3) Prepare the primary elimination entry at December 31, 19X4.
(4) Prepare a consolidating statement worksheet at December 31, 19X4.
(5) Prepare a consolidated statement of retained earnings for 19X4. (Pike Company's retained earnings at December 31, 19X3, was $70,000.)

Problem 6–4
COMPREHENSIVE   Recording a pooling of interests: Dissenting shareholders; direct costs; updating analysis of investment account; preparing consolidated financial statements subsequent to acquisition date—100% of outstanding common stock acquired

On December 31, 19X2, Pace Company acquired all of the outstanding common stock of Strider Company by issuing 45,000 shares of its common stock to holders of 9,000 shares of Strider Company common stock, and by giving $100,000 cash to holders of 1,000 shares of Strider Company common stock (the dissenting shareholders). Direct costs incurred in connection with the business combination were $120,000. An additional $80,000 cost was incurred in registering the common stock issued with the SEC. Each company's financial statements for the year ended December 31, 19X2, *before the business combination* are as follows:

	Pace Company	Strider Company
Income Statement (19X2):		
Sales	$8,000,000	$ 800,000
Cost of goods sold	(4,000,000)	(400,000)
Marketing expenses	(600,000)	(60,000)
Administrative expenses	(500,000)	(50,000)
Interest expense	(400,000)	(40,000)
Income before Income Taxes	$2,500,000	$ 250,000
Income tax expense @ 40%	(1,000,000)	(100,000)
Net Income.........................	$1,500,000	$ 150,000
Balance Sheet (as of December 31, 19X2):		
Cash	$ 650,000	$ 100,000
Accounts receivable, net	1,450,000	200,000
Inventory.................................	2,400,000	300,000
Fixed assets, net	3,500,000	1,200,000
	$8,000,000	$1,800,000
Accounts payable and accruals............	$1,800,000	$ 340,000
Long-term debt	3,000,000	600,000
Common stock, $1 par value..............	700,000	
Common stock, $10 par value.............		100,000
Additional paid-in capital	800,000	400,000
Retained earnings........................	1,700,000	360,000
	$8,000,000	$1,800,000
Dividends declared in 19X2	$ 800,000	$ 90,000

Assume the business combination qualifies for pooling of interests accounting. Assume the $200,000 of direct costs were paid in cash when the business combination was consummated—that is, they are not reflected in the above financial statements.

Required:
(Note that the combination occurred at the end of the year, not at the beginning of the year as illustrated in the text. Thus, the equity method is not applied during 19X2.)

(1) Prepare the entry to record the business combination.
(2) Prepare the primary elimination entry at December 31, 19X2.
(3) Prepare a consolidating statement worksheet at December 31, 19X2.
(4) Prepare a consolidated statement of retained earnings for 19X2. (Pace Company's retained earnings at December 31, 19X1, was $1,000,000.) *Hint:* Use an analysis of the subsidiary's retained earnings for 19X2 to assist you.

Problem 6–5

COMPREHENSIVE Recording a pooling of interests: Direct costs; updating analysis of investment account; preparing consolidated financial statements subsequent to acquisition date—90% of outstanding common stock acquired

Assume the information provided in Problem 6–4, except that Pace Company acquired 90% of the outstanding common stock of Strider Company by issuing 45,000 shares of its common stock. Pace did not acquire the shares of the dissenting shareholders.

Required:

The requirements are the same as those for Problem 6–4. In addition, a minority interest entry is necessary.

Problem 6–6

COMPREHENSIVE CHALLENGER Recording a pooling of interests: Conforming accounting methods; updating analysis of investment account; preparing consolidated financial statements subsequent to acquisition date—100% of outstanding common stock acquired

On September 30, 19X4, Pozo Company obtained a 100% interest in Seco Company through an exchange of its common stock for Seco common stock on a 1 for 4 basis. Pozo's common stock was selling on the market for $8 per share at the time, and the investment was recorded on this basis using the following journal entry:

Investment in Seco	80,000	
Common stock		50,000
Additional paid-in capital		30,000

The transaction qualified for pooling of interests treatment.

No market price was available for Seco's common stock when it was acquired by Pozo. The book value of Seco's common stock was $1.60 per share at the combination date. Pozo's board of directors justified the premium paid for the Seco stock on the grounds that the fixed assets and inventory were undervalued.

Each company's financial statements for the year ended December 31, 19X4, are as follows:

	Pozo Company	Seco Company
Income Statement:		
Sales	$450,000	$200,000
Cost of goods sold	(250,000)	(110,000)
Marketing expenses	(75,000)	(33,000)
Administrative expenses	(45,000)	(17,000)
Interest expense	(10,000)	(8,000)
Net Income	$ 70,000	$ 32,000
Balance Sheet:		
Cash	$ 50,000	$ 12,000
Accounts receivable, net	110,000	68,000
Inventory	177,000	22,000
Fixed assets, net	318,000	180,000
Investment in Seco Company	80,000	
	$735,000	$282,000

	Pozo Company	Seco Company
Accounts payable and accruals	$117,000	$ 98,000
Long-term debt	140,000	106,000
Common stock, $5 par value	200,000	
Common stock, $1 par value		40,000
Additional paid-in capital	160,000	
Retained earnings	118,000	38,000
	$735,000	$282,000
Dividends declared in 19X4	$ 55,000	$ -0-

These financial statements reflect the use of the FIFO method of valuing inventories for Pozo and the use of the LIFO method for Seco. Pozo desires to conform Seco's inventory method to its own as of the combination date. Seco has developed the following information pertaining to its inventory:

Date	LIFO	FIFO
December 31, 19X3	$18,000	$27,000
September 30, 19X4	20,000	30,000[a]
December 31, 19X4	22,000	34,000

[a] Assume this amount is equal to current value on this date.

Required:
(1) Prepare Seco's December 31, 19X4 entry to conform its inventory accounting practice to Pozo's. Ignore income tax considerations. (*Hint:* Refer to paragraph 27 of *APB Opinion No. 20,* "Accounting Changes" and paragraph 52 of *APB Opinion No. 16.*)
(2) Prepare the adjusting entry to reflect the combination as a pooling of interests at September 30, 19X4.
(3) Prepare the entry resulting from the application of the equity method of accounting from September 30, 19X4, through December 31, 19X4.
(4) Prepare an expanded analysis of the investment account as of September 30, 19X4, and update it through December 31, 19X4.
(5) Prepare the primary elimination entry at December 31, 19X4.
(6) Prepare a consolidating statement worksheet for 19X4 [after adjusting the financial statements for entries in parts (1), (2), and (3)].
(7) Prepare a consolidated statement of retained earnings for 19X4. (Pozo Company's retained earnings at December 31, 19X3, was $103,000.)

(AICPA adapted)

Problems comparing pooling of interests method with purchase method

Problem 6–7
Calculation of consolidated net income—
pooling of interests method versus purchase method

Continental Conglomerates Company acquired several businesses during 19X1. Information relating to each business is as follows:

Company	Date Acquired	Percentage Acquired	Net Income (Loss) for 19X1
Able Company	1/1/X1	100	$90,000
Baker Company	4/1/X1	90	80,000
Charley Company	7/1/X1	100	20,000
Delta Company.....................	11/1/X1	95	60,000
Echo Company.....................	12/31/X1	90	(10,000)

Assume all earnings and losses occurred evenly throughout the year. Assume Continental Conglomerates Company had net income of $500,000 from its own separate operations, exclusive of earnings or losses recorded under the equity method of accounting.

Required:

(1) Determine the amount of consolidated net income for 19X1, assuming all business combinations qualified for pooling of interests accounting.

(2) Determine the amount of consolidated net income for 19X1, assuming none of the business combinations qualified for pooling of interests accounting. Assume Continental Conglomerates amortized $17,000 cost in excess of book value, which is not reflected in the $500,000 amount given above.

Problem 6–8
Comparing purchase method with pooling of interests method:
Preparing consolidated balance sheets under both methods

Sterling Corporation merged into Pound Corporation on August 31, 19X4, and Sterling Corporation ceased to exist. Both corporations had fiscal years ending on August 31, and Pound Corporation will retain this fiscal year. The worksheet (page 247) contains a balance sheet for each corporation and a combined balance sheet as of August 31, 19X4, immediately before the merger, and net income figures for each corporation for the fiscal year ended August 31, 19X4.

Additional information:
As of the date of the merger:

(1) The fair value of each corporation's assets and liabilities on August 31, 19X4, was as follows:

	Pound	Sterling
Current assets	$ 4,950,000	$ 3,400,000
Plant and equipment, net..............................	22,000,000	14,000,000
Patents...	570,000	360,000
Market research	150,000	40,000
Total assets..	$27,670,000	$17,800,000
Liabilities	(2,650,000)	(2,100,000)
Net assets	$25,020,000	$15,700,000

(2) Pound Corporation capitalized its fiscal year 19X4 market research costs, which it amortizes over five years, beginning with the year of expenditure. All Pound's market research costs have been appropriately capitalized and amortized for the current and preceding years. Sterling Corporation incurred $50,000 in market research costs, which were expensed during the fiscal year ended August 31, 19X4. Sterling did not have any market research costs in any year before 19X4. Sterling will adopt Pound's method of accounting for market research costs.

(3) Internally generated general expenses incurred because of the merger were $25,000, which are included in Pound's current assets as a prepaid expense.
(4) No intercompany transactions occurred during the year.
(5) Before the merger, Pound had 3,000,000 shares of common stock authorized; 1,200,000 shares issued; and 1,100,000 shares outstanding. Sterling had 750,000 shares of common stock authorized, issued, and outstanding.

Required:
On the worksheet below, prepare the balance sheet and determine the amount of net income under each of the following independent situations. Include explanations of adjustments on the worksheet. Cross-reference the explanations to the adjustments. (Do not prepare formal journal entries.)

(1) Pound Corporation exchanged 400,000 shares of previously unissued common stock and 100,000 shares of treasury stock for all the outstanding common stock of Sterling Corporation. All the conditions for pooling of interests accounting enumerated in *APB Opinion No. 16* ("Business Combinations") were met.
(2) Pound Corporation purchased the assets and assumed the liabilities of Sterling Corporation by paying $3,100,000 cash and issuing debentures of $16,900,000 at face value.

(AICPA adapted)

POUND CORPORATION AND STERLING CORPORATION
Consolidating Statement Worksheet for Pooling of Interests
and Purchase Accounting
August 31, 19X4

	Pound Corporation	Sterling Corporation	Combined
Assets:			
Current assets	$ 4,350,000	$ 3,000,000	$ 7,350,000
Plant and equipment, net.............	18,500,000	11,300,000	29,800,000
Patents............................	450,000	200,000	650,000
Market research	150,000	—	150,000
	$23,450,000	$14,500,000	$37,950,000
Liabilities and stockholders' equity:			
Liabilities	$ 2,650,000	$ 2,100,000	$ 4,750,000
Common stock, $10 par value	12,000,000	—	12,000,000
Common stock, $5 par value	—	3,750,000	3,750,000
Paid-in capital in excess of par value.....................	4,200,000	—	4,200,000
Paid-in capital in excess of par value.....................	—	3,200,000	3,200,000
Retained earnings	5,850,000	—	5,850,000
Retained earnings	—	5,450,000	5,450,000
	$24,700,000	$14,500,000	$39,200,000
Less treasury stock, at cost, 100,000 shares...................	(1,250,000)	—	(1,250,000)
	$23,450,000	$14,500,000	$37,950,000
Net income (no extraordinary items) for fiscal year ended August 31, 19X4	$ 2,450,000	$ 1,300,000	

The format for the right side of the worksheet is as follows:

(1) Adjustments		Pooling of	(2) Adjustments		
Debit	Credit	Interests	Debit	Credit	Purchase

Problem 6–9
COMPREHENSIVE REVIEW   Pooling of interests method versus purchase method

(1) In a business combination, how should the acquired corporation's plant and equipment generally be reported under each of the following methods?

Pooling of interests	Purchase
a. Current value	Recorded value
b. Current value	Current value
c. Recorded value	Recorded value
d. Recorded value	Current value

(2) Perkins Company incurred a $20,000 finder's and consultation fee and $7,000 of SEC registration costs in acquiring Sayco Company. Of these costs, how much should be reported in the income statement as business combination expenses in the year of the acquisition under each of the following methods?
   a. Pooling of interests
   b. Purchase

(3) Using the information in the preceding question, how much would be capitalized as part of the acquisition cost?
   a. Pooling of interests
   b. Purchase

(4) How would the retained earnings of a subsidiary acquired in a business combination usually be treated in a consolidated balance sheet prepared immediately after the acquisition under each of the following methods?

Pooling of interests	Purchase
a. Excluded	Excluded
b. Excluded	Included
c. Included	Included
d. Included	Excluded

(5) A subsidiary may be acquired by issuing common stock in a pooling of interests transaction or by paying cash in a purchase transaction. Which of the following items would be reported in the consolidated financial statements at the same amount regardless of the accounting method used?
   a. Minority interest.
   b. Goodwill.
   c. Retained earnings.
   d. Capital stock.

(6) Ownership of 51% of the outstanding voting stock of a company would usually result in
   a. The use of the cost method.
   b. The use of the lower of cost or market method.

c. A pooling of interests.

d. A consolidation.

(7) A supporting argument for the pooling of interests method of accounting for a business combination is that

    a. One company is clearly the dominant and continuing entity.

    b. Goodwill is generally a part of any acquisition.

    c. It was developed within the boundaries of the historical cost system and is compatible with it.

    d. A portion of the total cost is assigned to individual assets acquired on the basis of their current value.

(8) What minimum amount of an investee's common stock must be exchanged during the combination period for the investor's common stock under the following methods?

    a. Pooling of interests

    b. Purchase

(9) If all other conditions for consolidation are met, how should subsidiaries acquired in a business combination be shown under each of the following methods?

Pooling of interests	Purchase
a. Consolidated	Not consolidated
b. Consolidated	Consolidated
c. Not consolidated	Consolidated
d. Not consolidated	Not consolidated

Problem involving consolidated statement of changes in financial position

Problem 6–10
Consolidated statement of changes in financial position

The 19X1 separate company statements of changes in financial position for Pittsville Company and its 90% owned subsidiary, Seedsburg Company, follow:

Statement of Changes in Financial Position (19X1):	Pittsville Company	Seedsburg Company
Working capital provided by:		
Operations:		
Net income	$127,000	$30,000
Charges (credits) not affecting working capital:		
Depreciation expense	14,000	6,000
Goodwill amortization	4,000	
Equity in net income of subsidiary	(27,000)	
	$118,000	$36,000
Sale of common stock	50,000	
Sale of preferred stock	40,000	
Sale of bonds at par		20,000
Dividends from subsidiary	9,000	
	$217,000	$56,000

	Pittsville Company	Seedsburg Company
Working capital used for:		
Dividends on common stock	$ 60,000	$10,000
Dividends on preferred stock	2,000	
Purchase of equipment	71,000	19,000
Retirement of debt	30,000	15,000
	$163,000	$44,000
Increase in working capital	$ 54,000	$12,000

Additional information:

(1) The only intercompany transaction during 19X1 was the payment of dividends to the parent.

(2) The parent acquired the 90% interest in the subsidiary two years ago.

Required:

Prepare a consolidated statement of changes in financial position. Use a worksheet with the following column headings:

Pittsville Company	Seedsburg Company	Eliminations		Consoli- dated
		Dr.	Cr.	

Note: Even though the preparation of such a worksheet is not demonstrated in the chapter, you should be able to prepare it using your basic understanding of consolidated statements and the explanatory material in the chapter.

PART TWO Consolidated Financial Statements: Specialized Subjects

7 Intercompany Inventory Transfers

OVERVIEW OF INTERCOMPANY TRANSACTIONS

As stated in Chapter 3, consolidated financial statements present the financial position and results of operations of a parent and its subsidiaries as if the group were a single entity with one or more branches or divisions. Therefore, transactions among companies within the consolidated group should be eliminated during the process of consolidation. Such eliminations cause the consolidated financial statements to reflect only transactions between the consolidated group and outside parties. Unless intercompany transactions are eliminated, companies would report profits on "sales" to themselves.

This chapter discusses (1) the conceptual aspects of eliminating inter-company transactions, and (2) the manner of accomplishing the eliminations in the consolidating statement worksheets.

Format of the consolidating statement worksheet

To focus attention on the elimination entries covered in this chapter and the following two chapters, we arrange the format of the consolidating statement worksheets as follows:

P Company	S Company	Non-intercompany Transaction Eliminations		Partially Consoli-dated	Intercompany Transaction Eliminations		Consoli-dated
		Dr.	Cr.		Dr.	Cr.	
		(Entries relating to Chapters 3–6)			(Entries relating to Chapters 7–9)		

In this way, we may more easily understand the impact of the entries that eliminate intercompany transactions. In practice, when numerous intercompany transactions exist, preparing the consolidating statement worksheet in this manner significantly reduces the possibility of errors.

The financial statements and elimination entries needed for "partial consolidation" were obtained, to the extent possible, from illustrations in previous chapters, appropriately modified to reflect intercompany transactions. In dealing with the entries in Chapters 7–9, it is important to understand that the method of acquisition (purchase or pooling of interests) is irrelevant. The entries are the same regardless of how the acquisition of the subsidiary was accounted for. The intercompany transactions discussed in Chapters 7–9 constitute separate transactions that are not affected by the manner of recording the acquisition of the subsidiary.

Types of intercompany transactions

Intercompany transactions among parent companies and subsidiaries consist of the following types:

(1) Sales of inventory. This transaction is most common in vertically integrated operations in which a customer–supplier relationship exists.

Because the selling and buying entities are separate legal entities, the transfer prices almost always approximate outside market prices. Consequently, the selling entity usually records a gross profit at the time of sale.

Inventory sales from a parent to one of its subsidiaries are referred to as **downstream** sales. Inventory sales from a subsidiary to its parent are referred to as **upstream** sales. Inventory sales between subsidiaries of a common parent are referred to as **lateral** sales. Because lateral sales are less frequent than upstream or downstream sales, they are not illustrated. The principles and procedures of eliminating intercompany transactions in lateral sales, however, are the same as those that are discussed and illustrated for downstream and upstream sales.

(2) Transfers of long-lived assets. Far less common than inventory transfers is the transfer of long-lived assets. This transaction most often occurs when one entity has surplus assets or when one entity manufactures assets usable by another entity. In the latter situation, the consolidated group has widely diverse operations. The procedures to account for intercompany fixed asset transfers are discussed in Chapter 8.

(3) Loans. Subsidiaries often do not have local banking relationships, because treasury functions are usually centralized at the parent's headquarters. This allows the parent to monitor closely the cash positions of its subsidiaries, which obtain needed cash from the parent. Practice varies widely as to the charging of interest on loans to subsidiaries.

(4) Services. A parent may charge its subsidiaries for top management services, including centralized research and development services, central computer services, and legal and advertising expenses.

(5) Dividends. When a parent uses the equity method to account for its investment in a subsidiary, no elimination entry is necessary because the dividend reduces the investment account. However, when a parent uses the cost method, the dividend is recorded as dividend income, which must be eliminated in preparing consolidated financial statements, as shown in Appendix A to Chapter 4.

(6) Bond investments. Infrequently, an entity within a consolidated group purchases bonds of another entity within the group. The procedures to account for these intercompany bond holdings in consolidation are discussed in Chapter 9.

Intercompany transactions are normally recorded in separate general ledger accounts, to the extent practicable, to facilitate and simplify the consolidation process.

With respect to all of these types of intercompany transactions, *Accounting Research Bulletin No. 51* states:

> In the preparation of consolidated statements, intercompany balances and transactions should be eliminated. This includes intercompany open account balances, security holdings, sales and purchases, interest, dividends, etc. As consolidated statements are based on the assumption that they represent the financial position and operating results of a single business enterprise, such statements should not include gain or loss on transactions among the companies in the group. Accordingly, any intercompany

profit or loss on assets remaining within the group should be eliminated; the concept usually applied for this purpose is gross profit or loss.[1]

CONCEPTUAL ISSUES

Elimination of gross profit, operating profit, or profit before income taxes

As indicated in the preceding section, when inventory and fixed assets are transferred from one company to another within a consolidated group, *ARB No. 51* designates the amount of profit to be eliminated in consolidation as the selling entity's **gross profit.** In selecting gross profit as the amount to be eliminated, other measures of profit—such as **operating profit** and **profit before income taxes**—were rejected to prevent the effect of capitalizing the selling entity's marketing, administrative, and borrowing expenses. Such expenses are period costs on a separate company basis, and no justification exists for treating them otherwise on a consolidated basis. From a consolidated viewpoint, the sale of inventory or equipment among entities within a consolidated group is considered merely the physical movement of the items from one location to another, and a bona fide transaction does not occur. When the entire gross profit is eliminated, the cost basis of the selling entity is reported in consolidation.

Transportation costs

ARB No. 51 does not specifically address the consolidation treatment of transportation costs incurred in transferring inventory among entities of a consolidated group. Because normal transportation costs are inventoriable costs, there is no sound reason to treat them otherwise in consolidated financial statements.

When the buying entity incurs the transportation costs and treats them as inventoriable costs, the elimination of all the selling entity's gross profit makes the transportation costs part of inventory cost on a consolidated basis. (Thus, no special procedures or elimination entries are needed in consolidation relating to transportation costs.) However, when the selling entity incurs the transportation costs—which are marketing costs for the selling entity—the elimination of the selling entity's gross profit results in expensing the transportation costs on a consolidated basis. Accordingly, in consolidation an additional elimination entry must be made in these latter cases to (1) eliminate the transportation costs being reported as marketing expenses and (2) charge the transportation costs to inventory.

For the sake of simplicity, the illustrations pertaining to inventory transfers assume transportation costs are insignificant. Such costs are therefore treated as period costs on a separate company and on a consolidated basis.

---

[1] *Accounting Research Bulletin No. 51,* "Consolidated Financial Statements" (New York: AICPA, 1959), paragraph 6.

Income tax considerations

ARB No. 51 requires elimination of any income taxes that have been provided on gross profit eliminated in consolidation.[2]

Consolidated income tax returns.   In most cases, parent companies and their domestic subsidiaries file consolidated income tax returns. (The Internal Revenue Code specifies the conditions that must be met to file consolidated returns.) Consolidated income tax returns are discussed in detail in Chapter 12. Briefly, consolidated income tax returns allow a parent and a subsidiary to defer reporting intercompany gross profit on assets remaining within the group in the same manner that such gross profit is deferred for consolidated financial reporting purposes. In these situations, no timing differences exist between consolidated financial reporting and consolidated income tax reporting. The parent calculates the income tax expense for consolidated reporting purposes using the consolidated income before tax amount. Any difference between this calculated amount and the combined income tax expense already recorded by the parent and the subsidiary is recorded as an adjusting entry in the general ledger of the parent or the subsidiary. The entry adjusts the total income tax expense and the related income tax liability accounts and effectively defers the taxes on the intercompany gross profit. For simplicity and because this is a general ledger entry—as opposed to a "worksheet only" entry—we assume in our illustrations that this year-end adjusting entry has already been recorded in the general ledger of the parent or the subsidiary. Thus, a separate entry dealing with the tax effects of gross profit deferred in consolidation is not required on the consolidating statement worksheet. Appendix A deals with just the opposite situation, in which the tax effect is shown as an adjusting entry on the consolidating worksheet.

Separate company income tax returns.   A parent and its subsidiaries may file separate income tax returns. This situation is most common when the parent has foreign subsidiaries, because consolidated returns may only be filed for domestic subsidiaries. In these cases, the gross profit deferred in consolidation for financial reporting purposes is a timing difference between financial reporting and income tax reporting. In other words, the selling entity reports the gross profit for income tax reporting purposes before the gross profit is reported for consolidated financial reporting purposes. The deferral of the related income taxes must be shown as an adjusting entry on the consolidating worksheet. Such situations are also discussed in Appendix A.

Minority interest situations

When a subsidiary is partially owned, the parent may question whether to eliminate (a) all of the gross profit, or (b) only that portion of the gross profit that accrues to the parent company. We address this issue later in the chapter when dealing with partially owned subsidiaries.

---

[2] *ARB No. 51*, paragraph 16.

INTERCOMPANY LOANS AND MANAGEMENT FEES

Intercompany loans

When interest is charged on intercompany loans, the interest income on the parent's books equals the interest expense on the subsidiary's books. The following elimination entry is made on the consolidating statement worksheet:

Intercompany interest income xxx
     Intercompany interest expense   xxx

When a loan remains unpaid as of the consolidation date, the intercompany loan receivable on the parent's books equals the intercompany loan payable on the subsidiary's books. The following elimination entry is made on the consolidating statement worksheet:

Intercompany loan payable xxx
     Intercompany loan receivable   xxx

Intercompany management charges

When management fees have been charged to the subsidiary, the intercompany management fee income on the parent's books equals the intercompany management fee expense on the subsidiary's books. The following elimination entry is made on the consolidating statement worksheet:

Intercompany management fee income......................... xxx
     Intercompany management fee expense   xxx

Elimination accomplished by rearrangement

Each of the above elimination entries takes place entirely within one of the financial statements. Most companies arrange the individual accounts on the consolidating statement worksheet so that these entries do not have to be made there. All that is necessary is to show in parentheses the intercompany accounts of one of the entities in the corresponding section of the worksheet. For example, by putting the subsidiary's intercompany loan payable amount, in parentheses, on the same line as the parent's intercompany loan receivable in the asset section of the balance sheet, the balances add across to zero in the consolidated column. Of course, the intercompany accounts should agree before the consolidation process. Elimination by rearrangement reduces the number of required elimination entries. An example of elimination by rearrangement follows:

	P Company	S Company	Eliminations Dr.	Cr.	Consolidated
Intercompany interest income (expense) ..	1,000	(1,000)			-0-
Intercompany receivable (payable)........	10,000	(10,000)			-0-

INTERCOMPANY INVENTORY TRANSFERS

Intercompany inventory transfers are usually recorded at amounts approximating outside market prices; thus, the selling entity records a profit at the time of sale. This is usually necessary to facilitate management's review of the operating performance of the individual companies. To illustrate the first basic principle of the elimination of intercompany inventory transactions, the first several examples are of transfers at cost.

Downstream transfers at cost

The illustrations in this section show how the double-counting of sales and cost of goods sold is prevented in arriving at consolidated amounts.

100% resold by subsidiary.   Assume that inventory costing $50,000 is sold to a subsidiary for $50,000 and that the subsidiary has resold all of this inventory for $100,000 in the same period in which it was acquired from the parent. The appropriate consolidating statement worksheet accounts would reflect the following with respect to these transactions only:

	P Company	S Company
Sales:		
To third parties...		100,000
Intercompany	50,000	
Cost of goods sold:		
To third parties...		50,000
Intercompany	50,000	

If no elimination entry is made, both consolidated sales and consolidated cost of goods sold would be overstated by $50,000. Accordingly, the following elimination entry is necessary.

| Intercompany sales .... 50,000 | |
| Intercompany cost of goods sold .... | 50,000 |

The elimination entry prevents the double-counting of these accounts and allows the consolidated amounts to reflect only transactions with third parties. After this entry is posted, the appropriate worksheet accounts would appear as follows:

	P Company	S Company	Eliminations Dr.	Eliminations Cr.	Consolidated
Sales:					
To third parties..............		100,000			100,000
Intercompany	50,000		50,000		-0-
Cost of goods sold:					
To third parties..............		50,000			50,000
Intercompany	50,000			50,000	-0-
Net income			50,000	50,000	

None resold by subsidiary.   Assume the facts in the preceding illustration, except that none of the inventory acquired from the parent has been resold by the subsidiary. The appropriate consolidating statement

worksheet accounts would reflect the following with respect to these transactions only:

	P Company	S Company
Sales:		
To third parties		
Intercompany	50,000	
Cost of goods sold:		
To third parties		
Intercompany	50,000	
Inventory (balance sheet).....................................		50,000

Because these transactions did not generate sales to third parties, no
sales or cost of goods sold amounts should appear in the consolidated
column of the consolidating statement worksheet. Accordingly, the following
elimination entry is necessary:

Intercompany sales 50,000
    Intercompany cost of goods sold   50,000

80% resold by subsidiary. Assume the facts in the preceding illustrations, except that the subsidiary has resold 80% of the inventory for
$80,000. The appropriate consolidating statement worksheet accounts would
reflect the following with respect to these transactions only:

	P Company	S Company
Sales:		
To third parties		80,000
Intercompany	50,000	
Cost of goods sold:		
To third parties		40,000
Intercompany	50,000	
Inventory (balance sheet).....................................		10,000

The only amounts that should appear in the consolidated column are
the sales to third parties, the cost of those sales at the parent company's
cost, and the remaining unsold inventory at the parent company's cost.
Accordingly, the following elimination entry is necessary:

Intercompany sales 50,000
    Intercompany cost of goods sold   50,000

After this entry is posted, the appropriate worksheet accounts would appear
as follows:

	P Company	S Company	Eliminations Dr.	Eliminations Cr.	Consolidated
Sales:					
To third parties		80,000			80,000
Intercompany	50,000		50,000		-0-
Cost of goods sold:					
To third parties		40,000			40,000
Intercompany	50,000			50,000	-0-
Net income			50,000	50,000	
Inventory		10,000			10,000

Concluding observations.   Obviously, whenever inventory is transferred at cost, the elimination entry is the same regardless of the percentage of the inventory that has been resold by the subsidiary. In each of the three preceding illustrations, the debit in the income statement section of the consolidating statement worksheet equals the credit, and there is no net effect on the income statement.

Downstream transfers above cost

In this section, we illustrate the second basic principle of the elimination of intercompany inventory sales: Any profit on transfers that have not been resold by the acquiring entity must be deferred.

100% resold by subsidiary.   Assume that inventory costing $50,000 is sold to a subsidiary for $75,000 and that the subsidiary has resold all of this inventory for $100,000 in the same period in which it was acquired from the parent. The appropriate consolidating statement worksheet accounts would reflect the following with respect to these transactions only:

	P Company	S Company
Sales:		
To third parties		100,000
Intercompany	75,000	
Cost of goods sold:		
To third parties		75,000
Intercompany	50,000	

Without the elimination entry, both consolidated sales and consolidated cost of goods sold would be overstated by $75,000. Because the only amounts that should be reflected in the consolidated column are the sales to the third parties and the cost of those sales at the parent company's cost, the following elimination entry is necessary:

Intercompany sales	75,000	
Intercompany cost of goods sold		50,000
Cost of goods sold to third parties		25,000

This elimination entry not only prevents the double-counting of sales and cost of goods sold, but it also reduces the subsidiary's cost of goods sold to the parent's cost to obtain the same results as if the inventory had been sold to the subsidiary at cost. After this entry is posted, the appropriate worksheet accounts would appear as follows:

	P Company	S Company	Eliminations Dr.	Eliminations Cr.	Consolidated
Sales:					
To third parties		100,000			100,000
Intercompany	75,000		75,000		-0-
Cost of goods sold:					
To third parties		75,000		25,000	50,000
Intercompany	50,000			50,000	-0-
Net income			75,000	75,000	

Because the entry takes place entirely within the income statement section of the worksheet, there is no net effect on the income statement.

None resold by subsidiary. Assume the facts in the preceding illustration, except that none of the inventory acquired from the parent has been resold by the subsidiary. The appropriate consolidating statement worksheet accounts would reflect the following with respect to these transactions only:

	P Company	S Company
Sales:		
To third parties...		
Intercompany	75,000	
Cost of goods sold:		
To third parties..		
Intercompany	50,000	
Inventory (balance sheet)....................................		75,000

Because these transactions did not generate sales to third parties, no amounts should appear in the income statement section of the consolidated column. Accordingly, the following elimination entry is used:

Intercompany sales	75,000	
Intercompany cost of goods sold		50,000
Inventory...		25,000

The entry eliminates the intercompany sales and the intercompany cost of goods sold and it reduces the inventory in the balance sheet to the parent's cost to obtain the same results as if the inventory had been sold to the subsidiary at cost.

After this entry is posted, the appropriate worksheet accounts would appear as follows:

	P Company	S Company	Eliminations Dr.	Eliminations Cr.	Consolidated
Sales:					
To third parties..............					
Intercompany	75,000		75,000		-0-
Cost of goods sold:					
To third parties..............					
Intercompany	50,000			50,000	-0-
Net income			75,000	50,000	
Inventory		75,000		25,000	50,000

In the eliminations column, the debit total at the net income line is $75,000 and the credit total is $50,000. Thus, the reporting of $25,000 of gross profit is deferred until the inventory is resold by the subsidiary to third parties. These debit and credit totals at the net income line are carried forward to the net income line in the analysis of retained earnings in the balance sheet section of the worksheet. The net debit of $25,000 to retained earnings has the effect of deferring the $25,000 of gross profit, which is included in the parent's Retained Earnings account.

80% resold by subsidiary.   Assume the facts in the preceding illustrations, except that the subsidiary has resold 80% of the inventory for
$80,000. The appropriate consolidating statement worksheet accounts would
reflect the following with respect to these transactions only:

	P Company	S Company
Sales:		
To third parties...		80,000
Intercompany	75,000	
Cost of goods sold:		
To third parties...		60,000
Intercompany	50,000	
Inventory (balance sheet).................................		15,000

The only amounts that should appear in the consolidated column are
the sales to third parties, the cost of those sales at the parent company's
cost, and the remaining unsold inventory at the parent's cost. Because
80% of the inventory has been resold, 80% of the $25,000, or $20,000, of
intercompany gross profit is included in cost of goods sold to third parties.
Likewise, because 20% of the inventory is still on hand, 20% of the $25,000,
or $5,000, of intercompany gross profit is included in inventory. Accordingly,
the following elimination entry is necessary:

Intercompany sales	75,000	
Intercompany cost of goods sold		50,000
Cost of goods sold to third parties (80% of $25,000)		20,000
Inventory (balance sheet) (20% of $25,000)		5,000

After this entry is posted, the appropriate worksheet accounts would
appear as follows:

	P Company	S Company	Eliminations Dr.	Eliminations Cr.	Consoli- dated
Sales:					
To third parties..............		80,000			80,000
Intercompany	75,000		75,000		-0-
Cost of goods sold:					
To third parties..............		60,000		20,000	40,000
Intercompany	50,000			50,000	-0-
Net income			75,000	70,000	
Inventory		15,000		5,000	10,000

In the eliminations column, the debit total at the net income line is $75,000
and the credit total is $70,000. Thus, the reporting of $5,000 of intercompany
gross profit is deferred until the inventory is resold by the subsidiary to
third parties. These debit and credit totals at the net income line are carried
forward to the net income line in the analysis of retained earnings in the
balance sheet section of the worksheet. The net debit of $5,000 to retained
earnings has the effect of deferring the $5,000 of intercompany gross profit,
which is included in the parent's Retained Earnings account.

In this illustration, 80% of the inventory was resold by the subsidiary, leaving 20% as still on hand. In practice, the appropriate percentages can only be determined by ascertaining the amount of inventory still on hand, either by making a physical count or referring to perpetual inventory records. Usually a formal analysis, as shown below, is prepared to show how the intercompany gross profit is divided between cost of goods sold to third parties and inventory still on hand.

Analysis of intercompany sales

	Total (Given)	Resold	On Hand
Intercompany sales	$75,000	$60,000	$15,000
Intercompany cost of goods sold	(50,000)	(40,000)	(10,000)
Gross profit	$25,000	$20,000	$ 5,000

The first line of the analysis shows what portion of the year's total intercompany purchases have been charged to cost of goods sold by the subsidiary and what portion remains on hand at year-end. This separation is made by determining the amount of intercompany inventory purchases on hand at year-end ($15,000) and then subtracting this amount from the total intercompany sales for the year ($75,000) to arrive at the amount charged to cost of goods sold ($60,000).

The second line of the analysis shows what amount would have been charged to cost of goods sold and at what amount the ending inventory would be stated had the intercompany transfer been at the selling entity's cost. The percentage of inventory resold and the percentage of inventory still on hand (determined using the amounts on the first line) are applied to the total intercompany cost of goods sold ($50,000) to determine the amounts in the resold and on hand columns.

The difference between the first and second lines shows the amount by which cost of goods sold and ending inventory are overstated, as to the consolidated entity, because the inventory transfer was made above cost.

Illustration:
Preparing consolidated financial statements—
Downstream sales above cost

The information in the preceding example is used in Illustration 7-1 to get from the partially consolidated column to the consolidated column of the worksheet. The P Company and S Company financial statements presented in Illustration 4-4 on page 129, along with the primary and secondary elimination entries in that illustration, are used to obtain the partially consolidated amounts. Of course, the P Company and S Company columns were appropriately modified to reflect the intercompany inventory transactions shown in the preceding example. [In addition, the income tax expense and related income tax liability in the P Company column were reduced $2,000 (40% of $5,000) for the income tax effect of the $5,000 gross profit deferred in consolidation at December 31, 19X1. Recall that we assumed the filing of a consolidated income tax return and the recording of the tax effects

Illustration 7-1

P COMPANY AND SUBSIDIARY (S COMPANY)
Consolidating Statement Worksheet
For the Year Ended December 31, 19X1

	P Company	S Company	Non-intercompany Transaction Eliminations Dr.	Non-intercompany Transaction Eliminations Cr.	Partially Consolidated	Intercompany Transaction Eliminations Dr.	Intercompany Transaction Eliminations Cr.	Consolidated
Income Statement:								
Sales:								
To third parties	525,000	200,000			725,000			725,000
Intercompany	75,000				75,000	75,000(3)		-0-
Income from subsidiary:								
Equity in net income	15,000		15,000(1)		-0-			-0-
Amortization of cost in excess of book value	(5,300)			5,300(2)	-0-			-0-
Subtotal	609,700	200,000	15,000	5,300	800,000	75,000		725,000
Cost of goods sold:								
To third parties	310,000	120,000	5,300(2)		435,300		20,000(3)	415,300
Intercompany	50,000				50,000		50,000(3)	-0-
Marketing expenses	90,000	30,000			120,000			120,000
Administrative expenses	60,000	20,000			80,000			80,000
Interest expense	30,000	5,000			35,000			35,000
Subtotal	540,000	175,000	5,300		720,300		50,000	650,300
Income before Income Taxes	69,700	25,000	20,300	5,300	79,700	75,000	70,000	74,700
Income tax expense	(22,000)	(10,000)			(32,000)			(32,000)
Net Income	47,700	15,000	20,300	5,300	47,700	75,000	70,000	42,700

Balance Sheet:

	P Company	S Company	Elim. Dr.	Elim. Cr.	Consolidated	(3)	Consolidated
Cash	25,000	32,000			57,000		57,000
Accounts receivable	145,000	43,000			188,000		188,000
Inventory:							
From vendors	90,000	25,000			115,000		115,000
Intercompany		15,000			15,000	5,000(3)	10,000
Investment in S Company	94,700			94,700(1)	-0-		-0-
Land	80,000	30,000	10,000(1)		120,000		120,000
Building—Cost	400,000	100,000	6,000(1)		506,000		506,000
—Accum. depr.	(260,000)	(23,000)		300(1)	(283,300)		(283,300)
Equipment—Cost	300,000	90,000			390,000		390,000
—Accum. depr.	(170,000)	(42,000)			(212,000)		(212,000)
Goodwill			9,000(1)		9,000		9,000
Total assets	704,700	270,000	25,000	95,000	904,700	5,000	899,700
Liabilities	288,000	200,000			488,000		488,000
Common stock:							
P Company	300,000				300,000		300,000
S Company		40,000	40,000(1)		-0-		-0-
Retained earnings—P Company:							
Beginning of year	100,000				100,000		100,000
+ Net income	47,700		→75,000	→70,000	47,700		42,700
− Dividends declared	(31,000)				(31,000)		(31,000)
End of year	116,700		75,000	70,000	116,700		111,700
Retained earnings—S Company:							
Beginning of year		20,000	20,000(1)		-0-		-0-
+ Net income		15,000	→20,300	→5,300 / 5,000(1)	-0-		-0-
− Dividends declared		(5,000)		5,000(1)	-0-		-0-
End of year		30,000	40,300	10,300	-0-		-0-
Total liabilities and equity	704,700	270,000	75,000	75,000	904,700		899,700
Proof of debit and credit postings			105,300	105,300		75,000	75,000

Explanation of entries:
(1) The primary elimination entry.
(2) The secondary elimination entry.
(3) The current-year intercompany inventory transactions elimination entry.

as a general ledger year-end adjusting entry.] The elimination entries used in Illustration 7-1 are repeated below for convenience:

(1) The primary elimination entry:

Common stock	40,000	
Retained earnings (beginning of year)	20,000	
Equity in net income of subsidiary	15,000	
Land	10,000	
Building	6,000	
Accumulated depreciation		300
Goodwill	9,000	
Dividends declared		5,000
Investment in subsidiary		94,700

(2) The secondary elimination entry:

Cost of goods sold	5,300	
Amortization of cost in		
excess of book value		5,300

(3) The current-year intercompany inventory transactions elimination entry:

Intercompany sales	75,000	
Intercompany cost of goods sold		50,000
Cost of goods sold to third parties		20,000
Inventory		5,000

In reviewing Illustration 7-1, the following points should be understood:

(1) The net income in the consolidated column is $5,000 lower than the net income in the partially consolidated column. The difference is entirely attributable to the elimination entry, which effectively defers the reporting of the $5,000 of gross profit included in S Company's ending inventory.
(2) The retained earnings in the consolidated column is $5,000 less than the retained earnings in the partially consolidated column for the reason given in (1), above.
(3) The postings to the income statement section of the worksheet are always totaled at the net income line and carried forward to the net income line in the analysis of retained earnings in the balance sheet section of the worksheet.
(4) The objective of the intercompany inventory transaction elimination entry is (a) to report as sales and cost of goods sold only the transactions between the consolidated group and outside parties, and (b) to compute amounts in the consolidated column as if the intercompany inventory transfers were made at cost.
(5) The elimination entry is posted only to the consolidating statement worksheet, never to a general ledger.

Subsequent year treatment of unsold inventory

In this section, we explain the accounting treatment in 19X2 of the 20% of the intercompany inventory transfer that was unsold at December 31, 19X1. We cover separately the possibilities that the inventory is not resold by December 31, 19X2 or that it is resold.

Not resold at the end of 19X2. If the inventory is still on hand at the end of 19X2, the following elimination entry is required in consolidation at December 31, 19X2:

```
Retained earnings—P Company (beginning of year) . . . . . . . . . . .  5,000
     Inventory . . . . . . . . . . . . . . . . . . . . . . . . . . . . . . . . . . . . . . . . . . . . . .       5,000
```

The credit brings the $15,000 S Company inventory down to a $10,000 amount in consolidation, just as the $5,000 credit did in consolidation at December 31, 19X1 ($10,000 is the parent's cost). The $5,000 debit to retained earnings eliminates the gross profit recorded in the general ledger in 19X1 that is still not reportable from a consolidated viewpoint. (This entry is made at every consolidation date after December 31, 19X1 until the inventory is resold by the subsidiary.) Note that this entry does not involve the Intercompany Sales or Intercompany Cost of Goods Sold accounts. The intercompany sales relating to this inventory took place in 19X1, and those accounts were eliminated in consolidation in 19X1.

Resold by the end of 19X2. If the inventory has been resold by the end of 19X2, then the gross profit deferred at the end of 19X1 is now reportable. In consolidation at December 31, 19X2, the following entry would be made:

```
Retained earnings—P Company (beginning of year) . . . . . . . . . . .  5,000
     Cost of goods sold to third parties . . . . . . . . . . . . . . . . . . . . . . .       5,000
```

The $5,000 credit reduces cost of goods sold to the parent's cost. Because this credit posting is subtotaled at the net income line and carried forward to the net income line in the analysis of retained earnings in the balance sheet section of the worksheet, it exactly offsets the debit posting made to retained earnings. Thus, it has the desired wash effect on retained earnings. In other words, we want the $5,000 of gross profit recorded in the general ledger in 19X1 to flow across and be reported in the consolidated column.

Dealing with beginning inventory and current-year transfers

In a normal consolidation involving intercompany inventory transactions, intercompany sales of inventory usually occur each year. Accordingly, entries are required both (1) to recognize the profit on the beginning intercompany inventory, and (2) to eliminate the current-year intercompany transactions. In this regard, it is simplest to separate these entries, and not try to handle them as a single, combined elimination entry.

Some of the beginning inventory may be physically part of the ending inventory. However, by assuming that the beginning inventory has been sold and that the ending inventory all came from the current-year intercompany inventory transactions, the consolidation effort is simplified. As long as the gross profit rates are the same (or very close) year to year, the assumption is a safe one.

Minority interest considerations

For downstream inventory transfers, accountants agree that all of the gross profit on assets remaining within the group should be eliminated, regardless of the parent's ownership interest in the subsidiary. This is because all of the gross profit accrues to the parent.

When inventory transfers are upstream from a wholly owned subsidiary, accountants agree that all of the gross profit on assets remaining within the group should be eliminated for the same reason. However, when the upstream inventory sales are from a partially owned subsidiary, two schools of thought differ on the amount of gross profit that should be eliminated. In discussing these schools of thought, we assume that the subsidiary is 90% owned and the parent company has on hand at year-end $15,000 of intercompany-acquired inventory, which cost the subsidiary $10,000. Thus, a total intercompany gross profit of $5,000 exists, of which $4,500 accrues to the parent company and $500 accrues to the minority interest. The two schools of thought are as follows:

(1) Complete elimination. Under this approach, all of the gross profit is eliminated on the grounds that to do otherwise would be inconsistent with the underlying purpose of consolidated financial statements, which is to report activities as if a single entity existed. As a result, consolidated net income and consolidated retained earnings would be reduced $4,500, and the minority interest would be reduced $500. (Mechanically, a $500 adjustment is made to the minority interest on the worksheet so that the $5,000 deferral is shared in this manner.)

(2) Partial elimination. Under this approach, only the portion of the gross profit that accrues to the parent is eliminated. The portion of the profit that accrues to the minority interest is not eliminated on the grounds that it has been realized from the viewpoint of the minority interest shareholders. It is irrelevant to whom the subsidiary sells as far as the subsidiary's minority shareholders are concerned. As a result, consolidated net income and consolidated retained earnings would be reduced $4,500. The minority interest would not be reduced $500.

In *Accounting Research Bulletin No. 51,* the AICPA chose the first alternative, whereby all of the gross profit is eliminated. This pronouncement states:

> The amount of intercompany profit or loss to be eliminated . . . is not affected by the existence of a minority interest. The complete elimination of the intercompany profit or loss is consistent with the underlying assumption that the consolidated statements represent the financial position and operating results of a single business

enterprise. The elimination of the intercompany profit or loss may be allocated proportionately between the majority and minority interests.[3]

This position is reaffirmed in *Accounting Interpretation No. 1 to APB Opinion No. 18,* as follows:

> When an investor controls an investee through majority voting interest and enters into a transaction with an investee which is not on an "arm's length" basis, none of the intercompany profit or loss from the transaction should be recognized in income by the investor until it has been realized through transactions with third parties.[4]

The interpretation also states that:

> In other cases, it would be appropriate for the investor to eliminate intercompany profit in relation to the investor's common stock interest in the investee.[5]

However, this latter statement is immediately followed by an example of a 30% investment in an investee. The "in other cases" obviously refers to situations in which less than majority ownership exists. Accordingly, all of the profit recorded on intercompany transactions with subsidiaries must be deferred until it has been realized through transactions with third parties. (All transactions with controlled companies are considered to be on less than an "arm's length" basis.)

Upstream transfers above cost (90% owned subsidiary)

By requiring the elimination of all of the gross profit in consolidation regardless of whether or not a minority interest exists, the only difference between upstream and downstream inventory transfers is that an additional worksheet adjustment is made to the minority interest in an upstream transfer to allocate a portion of the deferred intercompany gross profit to the minority interest. Without this adjustment, the consolidated net income and consolidated retained earnings would be reduced by the total amount of the deferred intercompany gross profit (rather than just the portion that accrues to the parent company).

Using the intercompany inventory transaction information given for Illustration 7-1, but assuming that the intercompany sales are upstream and the subsidiary is 90% owned, the appropriate elimination entries are as follows:

Intercompany sales	75,000	
Intercompany cost of goods sold		50,000
Cost of goods sold to third parties....................		20,000
Inventory (balance sheet)		5,000

To eliminate the intercompany transactions and
defer the recognition of $5,000 of intercompany
gross profit.

---

[3] *ARB No. 51,* paragraph 14.
[4] *Accounting Interpretation No. 1 to APB Opinion No. 18* (New York: AICPA, 1971), paragraph 4.
[5] *Accounting Interpretation No. 1 to APB Opinion No. 18,* paragraph 5.

Retained earnings—S Company (net income line)   500
   Minority interest (income statement)   500
   To allocate to the minority interest $500 of the $5,000
   deferred intercompany gross profit.

In the latter entry, the debit to Retained Earnings reduces the minority interest in the balance sheet by $500. The credit to the minority interest deduction in the income statement reduces that deduction and thereby results in consolidated net income being reduced by $4,500 ($5,000 from the first entry less the $500 in the second entry) instead of by $5,000.

Illustration:
Preparing consolidated financial statements—
Upstream sales above cost (90% owned subsidiary)

The preceding two elimination entries are used in Illustration 7-2 to get from the partially consolidated column of the worksheet to the consolidated column. The worksheet starts with the P Company and S Company financial statements presented in Illustration 5-5 (page 173). The following modifications were necessary because the transaction is upstream:

(1) The intercompany sales and cost of goods sold have been reflected in the S Company column.
(2) The $2,000 tax effect of the $5,000 intercompany gross profit deferred at the end of 19X1 (40% of $5,000) is reflected in S Company's general ledger, because we are dealing with the subsidiary's deferred gross profit. By lowering the tax expense $2,000, S Company's net income is now $17,000 instead of $15,000.
(3) The additional $2,000 of income reported by S Company has been reflected under the equity method of accounting. Accordingly, the primary elimination entry has been modified. Similarly, the minority interest entry—based on the reported net income—is now $1,700 instead of $1,500.

Modified primary, secondary, and minority interest entries are shown below:

(1) The primary elimination entry:

Common stock   36,000
Retained earnings (beginning of year)   18,000
Equity in net income of subsidiary
   (90% of $17,000)   15,300
Land   9,000
Building   5,400
   Accumulated depreciation   270
Goodwill   8,100
   Dividends declared   4,500
   Investment in subsidiary   87,030

(2) The secondary elimination entry:

Cost of goods sold   5,300
    Amortization of cost in
       excess of book value   5,300

(3) The minority interest entry:

Minority interest (income statement)   1,700
    Retained earnings—Subsidiary (net income line)   1,700
    (10% of $17,000 book income)

In reviewing Illustration 7-2, the following points should be understood:

(1) From the partially consolidated column to the consolidated column, net income and retained earnings have been reduced by $4,500 (90% of $5,000).
(2) Likewise, the minority interest deduction has been reduced by $500 as well as the minority interest in the balance sheet (10% of $5,000).
(3) The $1,200 minority interest deduction in the consolidated column is equal to 10% of $12,000. The $12,000 figure is the subsidiary's recorded net income of $17,000 less the $5,000 intercompany gross profit deferred in consolidation.

Subsequent year treatment of unsold inventory

Not resold at the end of 19X2. If the intercompany-acquired inventory is still on hand at the end of 19X2, the following elimination entry is required in consolidation at December 31, 19X2:

Retained earnings—P Company (beginning of year)   4,500
Retained earnings—S Company (beginning of year)   500
    Inventory   5,000

Note that the $500 debit to the subsidiary's Retained Earnings account is effectively a debit to the minority interest in the balance sheet. This is because the subsidiary's retained earnings that have not been eliminated in posting the primary elimination entry are part of the minority interest. (This entry is made at every consolidation date after December 31, 19X1 until the inventory is resold by the parent.)

Resold by the end of 19X2. If the intercompany-acquired inventory has been resold by the end of 19X2, then the gross profit deferred at the end of 19X1 is now reportable. In consolidation at December 31, 19X2, the following entry would be made:

Retained earnings—P Company (beginning of year)   4,500
Minority interest (income statement)   500
    Cost of goods sold to third parties   5,000

This entry in the income statement effectively reports $4,500 more consolidated net income ($5,000 − $500). The $500 debit and the $5,000

Illustration 7-2

P COMPANY AND SUBSIDIARY (S COMPANY)
Consolidating Statement Worksheet
For the Year Ended December 31, 19X1

	P Company	S Company	Non-intercompany Transaction Eliminations Dr.	Non-intercompany Transaction Eliminations Cr.	Partially Consolidated	Intercompany Transaction Eliminations Dr.	Intercompany Transaction Eliminations Cr.	Consolidated
Income Statement:								
Sales:								
To third parties	600,000	125,000			725,000			725,000
Intercompany		75,000			75,000	75,000(4)		-0-
Income from subsidiary:								
Equity in net income	15,300		15,300(1)		-0-			-0-
Amortization of cost in excess of book value	(4,770)			4,770(2)	-0-			-0-
Subtotal	610,530	200,000	15,300	4,770	800,000	75,000		725,000
Cost of goods sold:								
To third parties	360,000	70,000	4,770(2)		434,770		20,000(4)	414,770
Intercompany		50,000			50,000		50,000(4)	-0-
Marketing expenses	90,000	30,000			120,000			120,000
Administrative expenses	60,000	20,000			80,000			80,000
Interest expense	30,000	5,000			35,000			35,000
Subtotal	540,000	175,000	4,770		719,770		70,000	649,770
Income before Income Taxes and Minority Interest	70,530	25,000	20,070	4,770	80,230	75,000	70,000	75,230
Income tax expense	(24,000)	(8,000)			(32,000)			(32,000)
Income before Minority Interest								
Interest	46,530	17,000	20,070	4,770	48,230	75,000	70,000	43,230
Minority interest			1,700(3)		(1,700)		500(5)	(1,200)
Net Income	46,530	17,000	21,770	4,770	46,530	75,000	70,500	42,030

Balance Sheet:

	P Company	S Company	Elim. Dr	Elim. Cr	Consolidated	Minority Interest	Consolidated
Cash	33,500	32,000			65,500		65,500
Accounts receivable, net	145,000	43,000			188,000		188,000
Inventory:							
From vendors	75,000	40,000			115,000		115,000
Intercompany	15,000				15,000	5,000(4)	10,000
Investment in S Company	87,030			87,030(1)	-0-		-0-
Land	80,000	30,000	9,000(1)		119,000		119,000
Building—Cost	400,000	100,000	5,400(1)		505,400		505,400
—Accum. depr.	(260,000)	(23,000)		270(1)	(283,270)		(283,270)
Equipment—Cost	300,000	90,000			390,000		390,000
—Accum. depr.	(170,000)	(42,000)			(212,000)		(212,000)
Goodwill			8,100(1)		8,100		8,100
Total assets	705,530	270,000	22,500	87,300	910,730	5,000	905,730
Liabilities	290,000	198,000			488,000		488,000
Common stock:							
P Company	300,000				300,000		300,000
S Company		40,000	36,000(1)		4,000M		4,000M
Retained earnings—P Company:							
Beginning of year	100,000				100,000		100,000
+ Net income	46,530			4,500(1)	46,530	→75,000	42,030
− Dividends declared	(31,000)				(31,000)		(31,000)
End of year	115,530			→70,500	115,530	70,500	111,030
Retained earnings—S Company:							
Beginning of year		20,000	18,000(1)	→4,770	2,000M		2,000M
+ Net income		17,000	→21,770	1,700(3)	1,700(3)	500(5)	1,200M
− Dividends declared		(5,000)		500(5)	(500)M		(500)M
End of year		32,000	4,500(1)		3,200M	500	2,700M
Total liabilities and equity	705,530	270,000	75,770	10,970	910,730	75,500	905,730
Proof of debit and credit postings			98,270	98,270		75,500	

Total minority interest. 6,700M

Explanation of entries:
(1) The primary elimination entry.
(2) The secondary elimination entry.
(3) The minority interest entry.
(4) The current-year intercompany inventory transactions elimination entry.
(5) The adjustment to minority interest for deferral of profit on intercompany inventory transactions.

credit are subtotaled at the net income line and carried forward to the net income line in the analysis of the parent's retained earnings in the balance sheet section of the worksheet. These carryforward amounts offset the $4,500 direct posting to the parent's Retained Earnings account, resulting in a wash effect. This allows the $4,500 in the parent's Retained Earnings account—in the general ledger—to flow across to the consolidated column and be reported for consolidated reporting purposes.

Lower of cost or market adjustments

Occasionally, the buying entity makes a lower of cost or market adjustment in its general ledger relating to intercompany-acquired inventory. The write-down must be reversed in consolidation, but only to the extent of intercompany gross profit. To illustrate, assume a parent company transfers inventory costing $10,000 to its subsidiary at a transfer price of $15,000. If at year-end the subsidiary determines the market value of the inventory is $14,000, it would enter a $1,000 market adjustment in its general ledger. By reversing the $1,000 write-down in consolidation and then making the normal $5,000 intercompany gross profit elimination entry, the inventory would be reported in consolidation at $10,000, which is the parent's cost (and which is below the $14,000 market value).

Let us change the facts to assume the subsidiary determined the market value as $8,000 and entered a $7,000 market adjustment. By reversing only $5,000 of the market adjustment and then making the normal $5,000 intercompany gross profit elimination entry, the inventory would be reported at $8,000 in consolidation, which is below the parent's cost of $10,000.

UNCONSOLIDATED SUBSIDIARY AND PARENT COMPANY ONLY STATEMENTS

Situations are commonly encountered in which (1) a subsidiary is not con-solidated or (2) parent company only statements are issued in addition to the consolidated financial statements. For convenience, we refer to the parent's separate financial statements in each of these situations as the **parent company financial statements.**

Obviously, it would be nonsensical for a parent company that has in-tercompany transactions to report a greater profit merely by not consolidating a subsidiary. In such cases, the parent should reflect any unrealized in-tercompany gross profit in its parent company financial statements in one of two ways:

(1) By making adjustments on a worksheet (not a consolidating statement worksheet).
(2) By making adjustments in the general ledger.

Assuming a parent company has $5,000 of unrealized intercompany gross profit at December 31, 19X1 relating to a downstream transfer, the following entry would be made:

Deferral of gross profit on intercompany sales
   (income statement) 5,000
      Deferred gross profit (balance sheet)   5,000

To defer the recognition of unrealized gross
profit on intercompany inventory sales.

This entry could be posted to the general ledger or on a worksheet as an adjustment to the parent's financial statements.

If the intercompany transfer were upstream, the parent company could direct the subsidiary to make such an entry in its general ledger. (The parent would then apply the equity method of accounting to a lower net income amount.) Alternately, the parent could make the following entry (either in its general ledger or on a worksheet):

Equity in net income of subsidiary   5,000
    Deferred gross profit (balance sheet)   5,000
  To defer the recognition of unrealized gross
  profit on intercompany inventory sales.

Such adjustments are required pursuant to *APB Opinion No 18,* "The Equity Method of Accounting for Investments in Common Stock." Recall from Chapter 4 that the parent must account for its investment in a subsidiary under the equity method whenever parent company financial statements are issued.

SUMMARY

Consolidated financial statements present the financial position and the results of operations of all companies within the consolidated group as if a single entity exists. Consequently, the consolidated financial statements should reflect only transactions that take place between the consolidated group and outside parties. All open intercompany account balances and intercompany transactions that affect the income statement must be eliminated.

Transfers of inventory between companies within a consolidated group at amounts other than the transferring entity's cost require that the recorded intercompany profit or loss not be reported on a consolidated basis until the acquiring entity has disposed of the inventory. We accomplish this by preparing elimination entries, which are posted to the consolidating statement worksheet. Thus, profit or loss recorded by the transferring entity is deferred on the consolidating statement worksheet until such profit or loss is properly reportable. The concept of profit or loss for these purposes is gross profit or loss. In deferring any gross profit or loss pertaining to unsold intercompany-acquired inventory as of a consolidation date, the appropriate income tax effect on the amount deferred must be given.

Glossary of new terms

Arm's Length Transaction: Transactions that take place between completely independent parties.
Downstream Sale: The sale of an asset from a parent to one of its subsidiaries.
Lateral Sale: The sale of an asset between subsidiaries of a common parent.
Upstream Sale: The sale of an asset from a subsidiary to its parent.

Appendix A
INCOME TAX CONSIDERATIONS

In the chapter illustrations, we assumed the following facts concerning income taxes:

(1) The parent and subsidiary file a consolidated income tax return.
(2) The tax effects of the gross profit deferred in consolidation have already been accounted for by the parent (in downstream sales) or the subsidiary (in upstream sales) in making the year-end tax provision.

Accordingly, the income tax calculations for Illustrations 7-1 and 7-2 were as follows:

Calculations used in Illustration 7-1

	P Company	S Company	Consoli- dated
Income before Income Taxes	$69,700	$25,000	$74,700[a]
Permanent differences:			
Equity in net income	(15,000)		
Amortization of cost in excess of book value	5,300		5,300
Intercompany gross profit not reportable for tax or financial reporting purposes......................	(5,000)		
Taxable income	$55,000	$25,000	$80,000
Income tax rate assumed	40%	40%	40%
Income tax expense	$22,000	$10,000	$32,000

[a] This amount is already net of the $5,000 intercompany gross profit deferred in consolidation.

Calculations used in Illustration 7-2

	P Company	S Company	Consoli- dated
Income before Income Taxes	$70,530	$25,000	$75,230[a]
Permanent differences:			
Equity in net income	(15,300)		
Amortization of cost in excess of book value	4,770		4,770
Intercompany gross profit not reportable for tax or financial reporting purposes......................		(5,000)	
Taxable income	$60,000	$20,000	$80,000
Income tax rate assumed	40%	40%	40%
Income tax expense	$24,000	$ 8,000	$32,000

[a] This amount is already net of the $5,000 intercompany gross profit deferred in consolidation.

If the income tax effects of the $5,000 of deferred intercompany gross profit were not taken into consideration in the year-end general ledger income tax adjustments, the tax effects (40% of $5,000, or $2,000) would have to appear on the consolidating statement worksheet. Accordingly, the following entry would be made.

Income taxes currently payable............................	2,000	
Income tax expense....................................		2,000

Obviously, the consolidation effort is simpler if the income tax effect is taken into consideration in making the year-end general ledger income tax adjustment. Furthermore, the effect requires recognition in the general ledger, so the entry is best made as a general ledger entry separate from the consolidation elimination entries (which are not general ledger entries).

Separate income tax return situations

When the parent and subsidiary file separate income tax returns, timing differences result from deferred intercompany gross profit. Such intercompany gross profit is reportable for income tax reporting purposes but not for consolidated financial reporting purposes. As a result, prepaid income taxes exist in consolidation. In this situation, the tax effects must be dealt with on the consolidating statement worksheet instead of in the general ledger. Accordingly, the following worksheet entry would be made:

Prepaid income taxes	2,000	
Income tax expense.....................................		2,000

If the intercompany-acquired inventory is still on hand at subsequent consolidation dates, the prepaid tax position would still exist and would have to be reflected in consolidation by the following worksheet entry:

Prepaid income taxes	2,000	
Retained earnings—P Company (beginning of year)	3,000	
Inventory...		5,000

If the intercompany-acquired inventory is sold subsequent to 19X1, the prepaid tax position would cease to exist. The following entry would be made in consolidation to recognize the gross profit and provide income taxes thereon:

Income tax expense.......................................	2,000	
Retained earnings—P Company (beginning of year)	3,000	
Cost of goods sold to third parties......................		5,000

Note that the Prepaid Income Taxes account is now Income Tax Expense. It was not necessary to credit Prepaid Income Taxes to debit Income Tax Expense, because the prepaid income taxes existed only on the worksheet and not in the general ledger.

Appendix B
THE COMPLETE EQUITY METHOD

In Illustrations 7-1 and 7-2, the consolidated net income and consolidated retained earnings amounts in the partially consolidated column were the same as the net income and retained earnings amount, respectively, in the P Company column. Because the amounts are the same, any difference automatically means an error has been made in going from the separate financial statements to the partially consolidated column. Thus, this section of the worksheet contains a built-in checking feature. In going from the partially consolidated column to the consolidated column, however, the consolidated net income and consolidated retained earnings amounts were lower in the consolidated column than in the partially consolidated column. Thus, no built-in checking feature exists in this section of the worksheet.

Under the **complete equity method,** entries are made in the general ledger relating to the unrealized intercompany gross profit. In this approach, the built-in checking feature is maintained in going from the partially consolidated column to the consolidated column of the worksheet. (The final consolidated amounts are the same as when these entries are not made in the general ledger.) Although this feature is desirable, it is mechanically more complicated, and therefore, not as widely used in practice. For these reasons, we based the chapter illustrations on a modified equity method, whereby unrealized intercompany gross profit is dealt with entirely on the consolidating statement worksheet and no general ledger entries are made. The complete equity method is theoretically sound, however, and for this reason, we discuss it in this appendix.

Conceptual basis of the complete equity method

APB Opinion No. 18 describes the equity method of accounting as follows:

> The difference between consolidation and the equity method lies in the details reported in the financial statements. Thus, an investor's net income for the period and its stockholders' equity at the end of the period are the same whether an investment in a subsidiary is accounted for under the equity method or the subsidiary is consolidated.[6]

This means that, technically, any unrealized intercompany gross profit being deferred should be reflected in the general ledger, not merely on the worksheet. The parent's net income and retained earnings are the same as that reported upon consolidation of the subsidiary only after this general ledger adjustment is made. The following sections illustrate the appropriate general ledger entries.

Downstream transfers above cost

We use the intercompany inventory transfer information given in Illustration 7-1, which included $5,000 of unreportable intercompany gross profit at December 31, 19X1. The parent company would make the following general ledger entry at December 31:

Deferral of gross profit on intercompany
   sales (income statement) 5,000
      Deferred gross profit (balance sheet) 5,000
  To defer the reporting of unrealized intercompany
  gross profit on inventory transfers.

---

[6] *APB Opinion No. 18,* "The Equity Method of Accounting for Investments in Common Stock" (New York: AICPA, 1971), paragraph 19.

Thus, the parent's net income and retained earnings would be $5,000 lower. In consolidation at December 31, 19X2, this entry would be reversed and the normal intercompany inventory transaction elimination entry would be made, as follows:

Deferred gross profit (balance sheet)	5,000	
Deferral of gross profit on intercompany		
sales (income statement)		5,000
To reverse in consolidation the year-end		
general ledger entry deferring intercompany gross		
profit.		

Intercompany sales	75,000	
Intercompany cost of goods sold		50,000
Cost of goods sold to third parties....................		20,000
Inventory..		5,000
To eliminate current-year intercompany		
transactions.		

Note that in consolidation these two entries post equal debits and credits to the income statement ($75,000). As a result, no net effect is carried forward to retained earnings. The $5,000 of gross profit deferred has already been reflected in the general ledger Retained Earnings account.

Compared with the approach used in the chapter, the complete equity method requires two additional journal entries—a general ledger entry and the reversal of this entry on the worksheet. Thus, the approach used in the chapter is considered a shortcut approach because these two additional entries are bypassed.

Inventory not resold in 19X2. If the inventory is still on hand at the end of 19X2, no entries are needed in consolidation relating to the unrealized intercompany gross profit. The deferral is already reflected in the general ledger.

Inventory resold in 19X2. If the inventory has been resold by the end of 19X2, the following entry would be made in the parent's general ledger at the time of the sale:

Deferred gross profit (balance sheet)	5,000	
Recognition of gross profit on intercompany		
inventory sales (income statement)		5,000
To recognize the gross profit on prior year's		
intercompany sales deferred in the prior year.		

In consolidation at December 31, 19X2, the following elimination entry would be made on the worksheet:

Recognition of gross profit on intercompany		
inventory sales (income statement)	5,000	
Cost of goods sold to third parties.....................		5,000
To reclassify the credit balance in the		
Recognition of Gross Profit account to		
Cost of Goods Sold to Third Parties.		

Upstream transfers above cost

When the subsidiary sells inventory to the parent, a strict application of the equity method (as described in paragraph 6b of *APB Opinion No. 18*) calls for the investor to adjust the investee's reported net income to eliminate any unrealized intercompany gross profit before applying the equity method. This adjustment is simply made by having the subsidiary make the following general ledger entry:

Deferral of gross profit on intercompany sales (income statement)	5,000	
Deferred gross profit (balance sheet)		5,000
To defer the reporting of unrealized intercompany gross profit on inventory transfers.		

(The parent booked the same entry in its general ledger when the intercompany transfer was downstream.) Thus, the subsidiary's net income and retained earnings would be $5,000 lower. Accordingly, the equity method of accounting would then be applied to the lower net income amount. In consolidation at year-end, this entry would be reversed and the normal intercompany inventory transaction elimination entry would be made. These entries are not shown here as they are identical to the entries shown for a downstream inventory transfer.

In summary, the procedures for upstream transfers are identical to those used for downstream transfers, except that the general ledger entry to defer the reporting of the unrealized intercompany gross profit at year-end is made in the subsidiary's general ledger instead of the parent's general ledger.

Appendix C
THE TRIAL BALANCE APPROACH

To demonstrate the trial balance approach to the preparation of the worksheet when intercompany inventory transfers exist, the financial statements used in Illustration 7-2 (page 274) have been reformatted for the trial balance approach and are shown in Illustration 7-3 (pages 284–85). The elimination entries used in Illustration 7-2 are repeated below for convenience. The two minority interest entries have been combined into a single entry ($1,700 − $500) because a partially consolidated column is not used in the trial balance approach.

(1) The primary elimination entry:

Common stock	36,000	
Retained earnings (beginning of year)	18,000	
Equity in net income of subsidiary	15,300	
Land	9,000	
Building	5,400	
Goodwill	8,100	
Dividends declared		4,500
Accumulated depreciation (building)		270
Investment in subsidiary		87,030

(2) The secondary elimination entry:

Cost of goods sold	4,770	
Amortization of cost in excess of book value		4,770

(3) The minority interest entry:

Minority interest (income statement)	1,200	
Minority interest (equity column)[a]		1,200

[a] Because a separate minority interest column is used in the trial balance approach, the credit is made to this column rather than to retained earnings. (The amount here is 10% of the subsidiary's book income of $17,000, net of the $5,000 of intercompany gross profit deferred at December 31, 19X1.)

(4) The current-year intercompany inventory transaction elimination entry:

Intercompany sales	75,000	
Intercompany cost of goods sold.....................		50,000
Cost of goods sold to third parties		20,000
Inventory		5,000

Review questions

1. List five types of intercompany transactions.
2. Why are intercompany transactions usually recorded in separate general ledger accounts?
3. Why are intercompany sales not considered arm's length transactions?
4. Why must intercompany transactions be eliminated?
5. Which intercompany accounts can be eliminated by the rearrangement process?
6. How much profit on an intercompany sale of inventory must be eliminated in consolidation?
7. If intercompany profit is deferred in consolidation, must income taxes that have been provided on that profit be deferred also? Why or why not?
8. What is a downstream sale? an upstream sale?
9. Why are intercompany inventory transfers usually recorded at amounts in excess of cost?
10. When may the profit on an intercompany inventory sale be recognized for financial reporting purposes?
11. Are elimination entries relating to intercompany inventory transactions recorded in the general ledger? Why or why not?
12. If a parent company sells inventory to a subsidiary at prices equal to competitive market prices, has a bona fide sale occurred? Why or why not?

Discussion cases

Discussion case 7–1
Evaluation of manner of determining intercompany transfer prices and accounting ramifications of pricing disparities

Profitto Company manufactures a standard line of minicomputers. A substantial portion of the domestic manufacturing output is marketed in numerous foreign

Illustration 7-3
Trial Balance Approach (Illustration 7-2 reformatted)

	P Company		S Company		
	Dr.	Cr.	Dr.	Cr.	
Cash	33,500	32,000	32,000		
Accounts receivable, net	145,000		43,000		
Inventory—From vendors	75,000		40,000		
—Intercompany.................	15,000				
Investment in S Company	87,030				
Land......................................	80,000		30,000		
Building—Cost.........................	400,000		100,000		
—Accum. depr...................		260,000		23,000	
Equipment—Cost	300,000		90,000		
—Accum. depr.		170,000		42,000	
Goodwill					
Liabilities		290,000		198,000	
Common stock:					
P Company		300,000			
S Company				40,000	
Retained earnings, January 1, 19X1:					
P Company		100,000			
S Company				20,000	
Dividends declared:					
P Company	31,000				
S Company			5,000		
Sales—To third parties		600,000		125,000	
—Intercompany				75,000	
Equity in net income of subsidiary		15,300			
Amortization of cost in excess of book value	4,770				
Cost of goods sold—To third parties	360,000		70,000		
—Intercompany.........			50,000		
Marketing expenses	90,000		30,000		
Administrative expenses	60,000		20,000		
Interest expense	30,000		5,000		
Income before Income Taxes					
Income tax expense.....................	24,000		8,000		
	1,735,300	1,735,300	523,000	523,000	

Income before Minority Interest..
Minority interest (income statement)..
Minority interest (equity column) ....
Consolidated net income...
Consolidated retained earnings ....
Total minority interest ....

Explanation of entries:
  (1) The primary elimination entry.   (4) The current-year intercompany
  (2) The secondary elimination entry.   inventory transactions
  (3) The minority interest entry.   elimination entry.

Illustration 7-3 (continued)

				Consolidated		
Eliminations		Income Statement		Retained Earnings	Minority Interest	Balance Sheet
Dr.	Cr.	Dr.	Cr.	(Dr.) Cr.	(Dr.) Cr.	
						65,500
						188,000
						115,000
	5,000(4)					10,000
	87,030(1)					-0-
9,000(1)						119,000
5,400(1)						505,400
	270(1)					(283,270)
						390,000
						(212,000)
8,100(1)						8,100
						905,730
						488,000
						300,000
36,000(1)					4,000	
				100,000		
18,000(1)					2,000	
				(31,000)		
	4,500(1)				(500)	
			725,000			
75,000(4)			-0-			
15,300(1)			-0-			
	4,770(2)	-0-				
4,770(2)	20,000(4)	414,770				
	50,000(4)	-0-				
		120,000				
		80,000				
		35,000				
			75,230			
		32,000				
171,570	171,570					
			43,230			
1,200(3)		1,200(3)				
	1,200(3)				1,200	
....		42,030	→ 42,030			
....				111,030	→	111,030
....					6,700 →	6,700 M
						905,730

countries through wholly owned foreign subsidiaries. The foreign subsidiaries purchase the minicomputers from the domestic parent, which has only one foreign subsidiary in any foreign country. You have recently been assigned the task of preparing the monthly consolidating statement worksheet, and you notice that the parent's gross profit rates are quite high for intercompany sales to foreign subsidiaries with high income tax rates (higher than the U.S. income tax rate) and quite low to foreign subsidiaries with low income tax rates (lower than the U.S. income tax rate). Considering that the product is highly standardized, this seems unusual. You query the vice-president of marketing who informs you of the following facts.

(1) The transfer prices are negotiated by the marketing personnel at the parent's location and the individual managements of the foreign subsidiaries, and
(2) The parent could impose transfer prices, but company policy is to negotiate transfer prices so that meaningful evaluations of each separate company can be made.

Required:
(1) What other reason might account for this disparity?
(2) What are the potential ramifications, if any, of this disparity?

Exercises

Exercise 7–1
Downstream transfers at cost (three different assumptions)

In 19X1, Pyler Company sold inventory costing $40,000 to its wholly owned subsidiary, Stacker Company, for $40,000.

Required:
Prepare the elimination entry required in consolidation at the end of 19X1, 19X2, and 19X3 relating to this intercompany inventory transfer under each of the following assumptions:

(a) All of the inventory was resold by the subsidiary in 19X1 for $60,000.
(b) All of the inventory was resold by the subsidiary in 19X3 for $60,000.
(c) In 19X1, 75% of the inventory was sold for $45,000, and the remaining 25% was sold in 19X3 for $15,000.

Exercise 7–2
Downstream transfers above cost (three different assumptions)

In 19X1, Posmos Company sold inventory costing $60,000 to its wholly owned subsidiary, Sagan Company, for $80,000.

Required:
(1) Prepare the elimination entry required in consolidation at the end of 19X1, 19X2, and 19X3 relating to this intercompany inventory transfer under each of the following assumptions:

(a) All of the inventory was sold by the subsidiary in 19X1 for $112,000.
(b) All of the inventory was sold by the subsidiary in 19X3 for $112,000.

(c) In 19X1, 75% of the inventory was sold for $84,000, and the remaining
   25% was sold in 19X3 for $28,000.
(2) For assumptions (b) and (c), determine the amount at which the inventory is
   reported in consolidation at the end of 19X1 and 19X2.

Exercise 7–3
Downstream transfers above cost

In 19X1, Pivingston Company sold inventory costing $20,000 to its wholly owned
subsidiary, Stanley Company, for $30,000. As of December 31, 19X1, Stanley had
resold 90% of this inventory for $45,000. In 19X3, Stanley resold the remaining
10% for $6,000.

Required:
(1) Prepare the elimination entry required in consolidation at the end of 19X1, 19X2,
   and 19X3 relating to this intercompany inventory transfer.
(2) Determine the amount at which the inventory is reported in consolidation at the
   end of 19X1 and 19X2.

Exercise 7–4
Downstream transfers above cost (to partially owned subsidiary)

Assume the information provided in Exercise 7–3, except that Stanley Company
is only 80% owned by Pivingston Company.

Required:
The requirements are the same as for Exercise 7–3.

Exercise 7–5
Upstream transfers above cost

In 19X1, Pluto Company acquired inventory from its 75% owned subsidiary, Saturn
Company, for $100,000. Saturn's cost was $80,000. At December 31, 19X1, Pluto
Company had resold 60% of this inventory for $78,000. The remaining 40% was
resold in 19X3 for $52,000.

Required:
(1) Prepare the elimination entries required in consolidation at the end of 19X1,
   19X2, and 19X3 relating to this intercompany inventory transfer.
(2) Determine the amount at which the inventory is reported in consolidation at the
   end of 19X1 and 19X2.

Exercise 7–6
Upstream transfers above cost (three different assumptions)

Pace Company owns 80% of the outstanding common stock of Swift Company.
During 19X1, Pace Company acquired inventory from Swift Company for $100,000.
Swift's cost was $60,000.

Required:
(1) Prepare the elimination entries required in consolidation at the end of 19X1, 19X2, and 19X3 relating to this intercompany inventory transfer under each of the following assumptions:
  (a) All of the inventory was sold by the parent in 19X1 for $116,000.
  (b) All of the inventory was sold by the parent in 19X3 for $116,000.
  (c) In 19X1, 75% of the inventory was sold for $87,000, and the remaining 25% was sold in 19X3 for $29,000.
(2) For assumptions (b) and (c), determine the amount at which the inventory is reported in consolidation at the end of 19X1 and 19X2.

Exercise 7–7
Transfers above cost (Downstream and upstream)

A parent company and its subsidiary had intercompany inventory transactions in 19X1. The following information has been obtained from the individual financial statements of each company:

	Total	Resold	On Hand
Intercompany sales	$240,000	204000	$36,000
Intercompany cost of goods sold	180,000	153000	27000
Gross profit	$ 60,000	5 1000	9000

Required:
(1) Complete the analysis.
(2) Prepare the elimination entry required in consolidation at the end of 19X1, assuming the transfers are downstream.
(3) Prepare the elimination entries required in consolidation at the end of 19X1, assuming the transfers are upstream, and the subsidiary is 90% owned.

Exercise 7–8
Lower of cost or market adjustment

In 19X1, P Company sold inventory costing $60,000 to its subsidiary, S Company, for $70,000. At the end of 19X1, the subsidiary recorded a lower of cost or market adjustment relating to this inventory, 60% of which had been sold during 19X1.

Required:
(1) Prepare the elimination entries required in consolidation at the end of 19X1, assuming the adjustment was
  (a) $3,000.
  (b) $6,000.
(2) Determine the amount at which the inventory should be reported in consolidation under each of the above assumptions.

Exercise 7–9
Downstream transfers above cost;
Two years of intercompany sales

The following information relates to sales from Post Company to its wholly owned subsidiary, Stake Company.

	19X1	19X2
Intercompany sales	$100,000	$130,000
Intercompany cost of goods sold	$ 60,000	$ 80,000
Intercompany inventory purchases on hand at year-end	20%	25%

Assume that all of the intercompany inventory on hand at December 31, 19X1 was resold in 19X2.

Required:
(1) Prepare the elimination entry required in consolidation at December 31, 19X1 relating to the 19X1 intercompany inventory transaction.
(2) Prepare the elimination entries required in consolidation at December 31, 19X2 relating to the 19X1 and 19X2 intercompany inventory transactions.

Exercise 7–10
Upstream transfers above cost;
Two years of intercompany sales

Assume the information provided in Exercise 7–9, except that Stake Company is a 90% owned subsidiary and the sales are upstream—that is, the subsidiary sells to the parent.

Required:
The requirements are the same as in Exercise 7–9.

Problems

Problem 7–1
Completing the consolidating statement worksheet; Downstream transfers above cost—Profit in beginning and ending inventory

The partially consolidated financial statements of Pebble Company and its wholly owned subsidiary, Stoner Company, for the year ended December 31,19X2, are as follows:

	Partially Consolidated
Income Statement (19X2):	
Sales:	
To third parties	$699,000
Intercompany	100,000
Subtotal..	$799,000
Cost of goods sold:	
To third parties	$400,000
Intercompany	60,000
Expenses	240,000
Subtotal..	$700,000
Income before Income Taxes	$ 99,000
Income tax expense...............................	(44,000)
Net Income.......................................	$ 55,000

	Partially Consolidated
Balance Sheet (December 31, 19X2):	
Cash	$120,000
Accounts receivable, net	180,000
Inventory:	
From vendors	190,000
Intercompany	10,000
Fixed assets, net	440,000
Total Assets	$940,000
Liabilities	$400,000
Common stock—Pebble Company	$300,000
Retained earnings—Pebble Company:	
Beginning of year	$210,000
+ Net income	55,000
− Dividends declared	(25,000)
End of year	$240,000
Total Liabilities and Equity	$940,000

Stoner Company's December 31, 19X1 inventory included inventory it had acquired from Pebble Company in 19X1 at a cost of $40,000; Pebble's cost was $25,000. (Assume that all of this inventory was resold by Stoner Company in 19X2.)

Required:
(1) Complete the consolidating statement worksheet at December 31, 19X2. (Assume that the acquisition of Stoner was recorded as a purchase.)
(2) How would the elimination entries for requirement (1) be different if pooling of interests accounting had been used when Stoner Company was acquired?

Problem 7–2
Preparing the consolidating statement worksheet; Downstream transfers above cost—Profit in beginning and ending inventory

On January 1, 19X1, Player Company acquired all of the outstanding common stock of Spectator Company for $100,000 cash. The following information concerns Spectator Company at that date:

Common stock	$10,000
Retained earnings	80,000

The entire cost in excess of book value was assigned to goodwill, which was deemed to have a 10-year life. Financial statements for 19X2 and at December 31, 19X2 follow.

	Player Company	Spectator Company
Income Statement (19X2):		
Sales:		
To third parties	$200,000	$147,000
Intercompany	70,000	
Income from subsidiary:		
Equity in net income	12,000	
Amortization of cost in excess of		
book value	(1,000)	
Subtotal	$281,000	$147,000
Cost of goods sold:		
To third parties	$110,000	$ 82,000
Intercompany	40,000	
Expenses	56,000	45,000
Subtotal	$206,000	$127,000
Income before Income Taxes	$ 75,000	$ 20,000
Income tax expense	(28,000)	(8,000)
Net Income	$ 47,000	$ 12,000
Balance Sheet (December 31, 19X2):		
Inventory:		
From vendors	$ 55,000	
Intercompany		$ 14,000
Investment in Spectator Company	108,000	
Other assets	337,000	286,000
Total Assets	$500,000	$300,000
Liabilities	$170,000	$200,000
Common stock	150,000	10,000
Retained earnings	180,000	90,000
Total Liabilities and Equity	$500,000	$300,000
Dividends declared—19X2	$ 23,000	$ 7,000
—19X1	17,000	4,000

During 19X1, Player Company sold inventory costing $35,000 to Spectator for $65,000. At December 31, 19X1, Spectator's balance sheet showed $26,000 of this inventory still on hand. All of this inventory was resold in 19X2. $30,000 * \frac{26}{65} = 12000$

Required:
(1) Prepare the entries required in consolidation at December 31, 19X2.
(2) Prepare a consolidating statement worksheet at December 31, 19X2.
(3) How would the elimination entries pertaining to the intercompany transfers be different if the acquisition of the subsidiary had qualified for pooling of interests treatment?

Problem 7–3
Completing the consolidating statement worksheet; Upstream transfers above cost from 80% owned subsidiary—Profit in ending inventory

The partially consolidated financial statements of P Company and its 80% owned subsidiary, S Company, for the year ended December 31, 19X2, are as follows.

	Partially Consolidated
Income Statement (19X2):	
Sales:	
To third parties	$157,000
Intercompany	48,000
Subtotal	$205,000
Cost of goods sold:	
To third parties	$ 73,000
Intercompany	32,000
Expenses	35,000
Subtotal	$140,000
Income before Income Taxes	$ 65,000
Income tax expense	(24,000)
Income before Minority Interest	$ 41,000
Minority interest	(3,000)[a]
Net Income	$ 38,000
Balance Sheet (December 31, 19X2):	
Cash	$ 5,000
Accounts receivable, net	10,000
Inventory:	
From vendors	25,000
Intercompany	15,000
Fixed assets, net	95,000
Total Assets	$150,000
Liabilities	$ 40,000
Common stock:	
P Company	$ 50,000
S Company	$ 2,000M
Retained earnings—P Company:	
Beginning of year	$ 25,000
+ Net income	38,000
− Dividends declared	(10,000)
End of year	$ 53,000
Retained earnings—S Company:	
Beginning of year	$ 4,000M
+ Net income	3,000M
− Dividends declared	(2,000)M
End of year	$ 5,000M
Total Liabilities and Equity	$150,000

[a] Based on the subsidiary's book income of $15,000.

Note: No intercompany-acquired inventory was on hand at December 31, 19X1

Required:
(1) Complete the consolidating statement worksheet at December 31, 19X2. (Assume that the acquisition of S Company was recorded as a pooling of interests.)
(2) How would the elimination entries for requirement (1) be different if purchase accounting had been used when S Company was acquired?

Problem 7–4
Preparing the consolidating statement worksheet; Upstream transfers above cost from 90% owned subsidiary—Profit in ending inventory

On January 1, 19X1, Pinn Company acquired 90% of the outstanding common stock of Stripes Company for $310,000 cash. Information regarding Stripes Company on that date is:

Common stock	$120,000
Retained earnings	80,000
Land—Book value	85,000
—Current value	185,000

Goodwill was assigned a 20-year life. Separate company financial statements for 19X1 and at December 31, 19X1 follow:

	Pinn Company	Stripes Company
Income Statement (19X1):		
Sales:		
To third parties	$330,000	$ 70,000
Intercompany		250,000
Income from subsidiary:		
Equity in net income	43,200	
Amortization of cost in		
excess of book value	(2,000)	
Subtotal	$371,200	$320,000
Cost of goods sold:		
To third parties	$175,000	$ 30,000
Intercompany		200,000
Expenses	55,000	20,000
Subtotal	$230,000	$250,000
Income before Income Taxes	$141,200	$ 70,000
Income tax expense	(40,000)	(22,000)
Net Income	$101,200	$ 48,000
Balance Sheet (December 31, 19X1):		
Inventory:		
From vendors	$ 80,000	$ 40,000
Intercompany	75,000	
Land	200,000	85,000
Other assets	111,800	275,000
Investment in Stripes Company	333,200	
Total Assets	$800,000	$400,000
Liabilities	$168,000	$172,000
Common stock	400,000	120,000
Retained earnings	232,000	108,000
Total Liabilities and Equity.............................	$800,000	$400,000
Dividends declared in 19X1................................	$ 66,000	$ 20,000

Required:

(1) Prepare the entries required in consolidation at December 31, 19X1.

(2) Prepare a consolidating statement worksheet at December 31, 19X1.

(3) How would the elimination entry pertaining to the intercompany inventory transfer be different if the acquisition of the subsidiary had qualified for pooling of interests treatment?

Problem 7–5

COMPREHENSIVE   (Chapters 3–7) Preparing consolidated statements: Upstream transfers above cost from 75% owned subsidiary—Profit in ending inventory; Intercompany loans and management fees; Adjustment of statements to the equity method at the end of the acquisition year

On June 30, 19X3, Plume Company acquired 75% of the outstanding common stock of Starling Company for $533,000 cash. At the purchase date, each of Starling's recorded assets and liabilities had a current value equal to its book value, except for the following items:

	Book Value	Current Value
Inventory..	$ 90,000	$ 70,000
Machinery and equipment	240,000	320,000

As of June 30, 19X3, Starling's machinery and equipment had an estimated remaining life of five years. (Starling uses straight-line depreciation.) Plume's policy is to amortize intangibles over 10 years. By December 31, 19X3, Starling's inventory on hand at June 30, 19X3 had been charged to cost of goods sold.

No intercompany transactions had occurred between Plume and Starling prior to the acquisition date. During the six months ended December 31, 19X3, the following intercompany transactions occurred:

(1) Starling sold inventory to Plume for $150,000, none of which has been paid for at December 31, 19X3.

(2) On October 1, 19X3, Plume loaned Starling $200,000 for internal expansion. The borrowing is in the form of a note bearing interest at 10%. (No interest or principal payments have been made to Plume.)

(3) Certain Starling management functions are now performed by Plume. As a result, Plume charges Starling a management fee of $3,000 per month. (All intercompany management fees have been paid.)

(4) On December 28, 19X3, Starling declared a $36,000 dividend payable on January 15, 19X4. The only entry Plume has made with respect to the dividend is to record the receipt of its share of the dividend on January 17, 19X4.

The financial statements of Plume for the year ended December 31, 19X3 and the financial statements of Starling for the six months ended December 31, 19X3 are as follows.

	Plume Company	Starling Company July 1, 19X3–Dec. 31, 19X3
Income Statement (19X3):		
Sales:		
To third parties..........................	$3,500,000	$ 710,000
Intercompany		150,000
Management fees	18,000	
Subtotal	$3,518,000	$ 860,000
Cost of goods sold:		
To third parties..........................	$2,100,000	$ 450,000
Intercompany		90,000
Marketing expenses	650,000	165,000
Administrative expenses...................	233,000	70,000
Interest expense.........................	240,000	
Intercompany interest expense.............		5,000
Intercompany interest (income).............	(5,000)	
Subtotal	$3,218,000	$ 780,000
Income before Income Taxes	$ 300,000	$ 80,000
Income tax expense	(120,000)	(24,000)
Net Income	$ 180,000	$ 56,000
Balance Sheet (December 31, 19X3):		
Cash	$ 365,000	$ 50,000
Accounts receivable, net	290,000	125,000
Intercompany receivables..................		145,000
Intercompany note receivable	200,000	
Inventory:		
From vendors	402,000	205,000
Intercompany	50,000	
Investment in Starling Company............	533,000	
Land and building, net	2,900,000	325,000
Machinery and equipment	1,680,000	460,000
Accumulated depreciation	(270,000)	(140,000)
Total Assets	$6,150,000	$1,170,000
Accounts payable........................	$ 625,000	$ 370,000
Dividend payable		36,000
Intercompany payables....................	145,000	
Intercompany note payable		200,000
Long-term debt..........................	2,500,000	
Common stock	2,000,000	400,000
Retained earnings	880,000	164,000
Total Liabilities and Equity..............	$6,150,000	$1,170,000
Dividends declared in 19X3................	$ 110,000	$ 36,000

Plume desires to account for its investment in Starling using the equity method; however, it has not made any entries to the investment account since the acquisition date.

Required:
(1) Prepare an expanded analysis of the investment account as of the acquisition date. Update it through December 31, 19X3 using the equity method.
(2) Prepare the primary, secondary, and minority interest entries at December 31, 19X3.

(3) Prepare the elimination entries relating to intercompany transactions.
(4) Adjust Plume's financial statements to reflect the equity method, and then prepare a consolidating statement worksheet.
(5) Prepare a consolidated statement of retained earnings for 19X3. (Plume Company's reported retained earnings was $810,000 at December 31, 19X2.)
(6) How would your answers in requirement (3) be different if the acquisition of Starling Company had qualified for pooling of interests treatment?

8 Intercompany Fixed Asset Transfers

OVERVIEW OF INTERCOMPANY FIXED ASSET TRANSFERS

Fixed assets are occasionally transferred among entities of a consolidated group. If the transfers are made at the carrying values of the assets, then no entries are necessary in consolidation because no intercompany profit or loss is recorded. If transfers are made above or below the carrying value, special procedures are required in consolidation to defer recognition of the gain or loss. The reason for deferring the gain or loss is the same as in the case of inventory transfers—no gain or loss is reportable on intercompany transactions from a consolidated viewpoint.

Because intercompany gain or loss is deferred in consolidation, fixed assets are reported at the cost to the selling entity. Likewise, depreciation (for depreciable assets) is reported in consolidation based on this cost to the selling entity. Obviously, from a consolidated viewpoint, the reported amount for a fixed asset cannot change merely because the asset has been moved to a different location within the consolidated group or because legal ownership within the consolidated group has changed.

Basic approach for developing the elimination entries

In this chapter, the approach used to develop the elimination entries required in consolidation parallels the approach used to make correcting entries. The classic approach to correcting entries is to (1) determine the entry that was made; (2) determine the entry that should have been made; and (3) compare the accounts and amounts in (1) and (2); the differences constitute the correcting entry.

In this chapter, to develop elimination entries, we

(1) Determine the actual general ledger account balances of the selling and acquiring entities as a result of the transfer.
(2) Determine the balances that would exist (a pro forma determination) had the intercompany transfer taken place at no gain or loss.
(3) Compare the accounts and amounts in (1) and (2) at each consolidation date; the differences constitute the elimination entry.

TRANSFERS OF NONDEPRECIABLE ASSETS

When land is transferred at above its carrying value, the selling entity records a gain. In preparing the consolidated financial statements, the gain is not reportable and must be deferred until the acquiring entity resells the land. For example, assume land costing $20,000 is sold in 19X1 to a subsidiary for $30,000. The entry necessary to eliminate the gain and reduce the land to the parent's carrying value at the transfer date is as follows:

```
Gain on sale of land .....................................  10,000
    Land  .............................................          10,000
```

On posting this entry to the worksheet, the appropriate worksheet accounts would appear as follows:

	P Company	S Company	Intercompany Transaction Eliminations Dr.	Cr.	Consoli- dated
Gain on sale of land	10,000		10,000		-0-
Net income.......................			⌐10,000		
Land............................		30,000		10,000	20,000
Retained earnings—P Company					
(net income line)................	10,000		└→10,000		-0-

Land not resold at the end of 19X2. If the subsidiary still owns the land at the end of 19X2, the following elimination entry would be necessary:

```
Retained earnings—P Company (beginning of year) .........  10,000
    Land  .........................................          10,000
```

On posting this entry to the worksheet, the appropriate worksheet accounts would appear as follows:

	P Company	S Company	Intercompany Transaction Eliminations Dr.	Cr.	Consoli- dated
Land............................		30,000		10,000	20,000
Retained earnings—P Company					
(beginning of year)	10,000		10,000		-0-

The entry does not involve the income statement accounts because the income statement activity occurred in 19X1. This entry would be made in all periods subsequent to 19X1 until the land is sold by the subsidiary.

Land resold by the end of 19X3. If the subsidiary subsequently sells the land in 19X3 for $32,000, it would report a $2,000 gain ($32,000 − $30,000). However, the reportable gain in consolidation is $12,000 ($32,000 − $20,000). Accordingly, the entry required in consolidation to recognize the previously deferred gain of $10,000 is as follows:

```
Retained earnings—P Company (beginning of year) .........  10,000
    Gain on sale of land  ..............................          10,000
```

On posting this entry, the appropriate worksheet accounts would appear as follows.

	P Company	S Company	Intercompany Transaction Eliminations		Consoli- dated
			Dr.	Cr.	
Gain on sale of land		2,000		10,000	12,000
Net income				10,000	
Retained earnings—P Company:					
Beginning of year	10,000		10,000		-0-
+ Net income	2,000[a]			10,000	12,000
End of year	12,000		10,000	10,000	12,000

[a] The parent has recorded this amount under the equity method of accounting.

Income tax effects. For simplicity, we ignored income tax effects in this example. Assuming a consolidated income tax return is filed, the tax effects would be recorded in the general ledger only in the year the subsidiary resold the land. In that year, the parent would record income taxes on its $10,000 gain, and the subsidiary would record income taxes on its $2,000 gain.

Transfers below cost and upstream transfers. When land is transferred below cost, the loss must be deferred. The principle is the same as that for a transfer above cost; only the debits and credits are reversed.

When the transfer is upstream, the procedures are exactly the same as for a downstream sale only if the subsidiary is wholly owned. If the subsidiary is partially owned, then an additional adjustment is necessary for the minority interest. Upstream transfers are discussed and illustrated in the next section on transfers of depreciable assets.

TRANSFERS OF DEPRECIABLE ASSETS

Downstream transfers above cost

When a depreciable asset is transferred downstream at above its carrying value, the gain recorded by the parent must be deferred in consolidation in the same manner that a gain on the transfer of a nondepreciable asset is deferred.

Because the subsidiary uses the transfer price as its cost, its depreciation expense in future periods is greater than it would have been had the parent transferred the asset at its carrying value. This additional depreciation expense in future periods must be eliminated, because from a consolidated viewpoint, depreciation expense must be based on the parent's carrying value at the transfer date.

This additional depreciation expense on the subsidiary's books eventually offsets the initial gain recorded on the parent's books. As a result, the parent's general ledger Retained Earnings account balance is the reportable retained earnings in consolidation, but not until the subsidiary has fully depreciated the asset.

After the elimination entries, the parent's cost and accumulated depreciation (based on that cost) are reported in consolidation in the fixed assets section of the balance sheet.

Illustration:
Downstream transfer above cost

Let us assume the following facts:

Sales price of equipment sold to subsidiary on January 1, 19X1..................		$18,000
Carrying value on parent's books:		
Cost...	$50,000	
Accumulated depreciation..........................	(35,000)	15,000
Gain recorded by parent..............................		$ 3,000
Remaining life		3 years

Note: For simplicity, we assumed that the equipment is used by an administrative department of the subsidiary. Thus, the acquiring entity's depreciation expense on this equipment is included in its administrative expenses.

The subsidiary bases its periodic depreciation expense on the $18,000 transfer price. As a result, the subsidiary records $6,000 of depreciation expense per year over the next three years rather than $5,000 per year (which is based on the parent company's $15,000 carrying value).

Consolidation at January 1, 19X1. Immediately after the transfer, the appropriate accounts of the parent and the subsidiary would be as follows:

	P Company	S Company
Gain on sale of equipment...............................	3,000	
Equipment		18,000
Accumulated depreciation.................................		-0-
Retained earnings—P Company (net income line)	3,000	

If a consolidating statement worksheet is prepared on January 1, 19X1 (the transfer date), the following elimination entry is made to (1) eliminate the gain and (2) report the equipment at the parent's cost, along with the related accumulated depreciation based on this cost:

Gain on sale of equipment................................	3,000	
Equipment ($50,000 − $18,000)	32,000	
Accumulated depreciation ($35,000 − $0).....................................		35,000

On posting this entry, the appropriate worksheet accounts would appear as follows:

	P Company	S Company	Intercompany Transaction Eliminations Dr.	Cr.	Consolidated
Gain on sale of equipment..........	3,000		3,000		-0-
Net income........................			3,000		
Equipment		18,000	32,000		50,000
Accumulated depreciation...........		-0-		35,000	(35,000)
Retained earnings—P Company (net income line).................	3,000		3,000		-0-

The equipment is reported in consolidation as if it had been transferred at the parent's $15,000 carrying value and the subsidiary had recorded $50,000 and $35,000 as its cost and accumulated depreciation, respectively, instead of $18,000 and $0.

Consolidation at December 31, 19X1.   At the end of 19X1, the appropriate accounts of the parent and subsidiary would be as follows:

	P Company	S Company
Gain on sale of equipment	3,000	
Depreciation expense		6,000
Equipment		18,000
Accumulated depreciation		(6,000)
Retained earnings—P Company (net income line)	2,000[a]	

[a] This amount is the $3,000 gain − $1,000 incremental depreciation expense as a result of applying the equity method.

If a consolidating statement worksheet is prepared at December 31, 19X1, the following elimination entry is made to (1) eliminate the gain; (2) eliminate the incremental depreciation expense; and (3) report the equipment at the parent's cost, along with the related accumulated depreciation based on this cost:

Gain on sale of equipment	3,000	
Equipment ($50,000 − $18,000)	32,000	
Accumulated depreciation ($35,000 + $5,000 = $40,000; $40,000 − $6,000 = $34,000)		34,000
Depreciation expense ($6,000 − $5,000)		1,000

On posting this entry, the appropriate worksheet accounts would appear as follows:

	P Company	S Company	Intercompany Transaction Eliminations Dr.	Cr.	Consolidated
Gain on sale of equipment	3,000		3,000		-0-
Depreciation expense		6,000		1,000	5,000
Net income			−3,000	−1,000	
Equipment		18,000	32,000		50,000
Accumulated depreciation		(6,000)		34,000	(40,000)
Retained earnings—P Company (net income line)	2,000		→3,000	→1,000	-0-

Note that consolidated depreciation expense is $5,000, which is the $15,000 carrying value of the equipment at the transfer date divided by the three-year remaining life.

Consolidation at December 31, 19X2. At the end of 19X2, the appropriate accounts of the parent and subsidiary would be as follows:

	P Company	S Company
Depreciation expense		6,000
Equipment		18,000
Accumulated depreciation		(12,000)
Retained earnings—P Company:		
Beginning of year	2,000	
+ Net income (loss)	(1,000)	
End of year	1,000	

If a consolidating statement worksheet is prepared at December 31, 19X2, the following elimination entry is made:

Equipment ($50,000 − $18,000)	32,000	
Retained earnings—P Company (beginning of year)	2,000	
Accumulated depreciation ($35,000 + $10,000		
= $45,000; $45,000 − $12,000 = $33,000)		33,000
Depreciation expense ($6,000 − $5,000)		1,000

On posting this entry, the appropriate worksheet accounts would appear as follows:

	P Company	S Company	Intercompany Transaction Eliminations Dr.	Cr.	Consolidated
Depreciation expense		6,000		1,000	5,000
Net income				−1,000	
Equipment		18,000	32,000		50,000
Accumulated depreciation		(12,000)		33,000	(45,000)
Retained earnings—P Company:					
Beginning of year	2,000		2,000		-0-
+ Net income (loss)	(1,000)			1,000	-0-
End of year	1,000		2,000	1,000	-0-

Effect on parent's retained earnings at the end of 19X3. There is no need to show a consolidation at December 31, 19X3. However, we should realize that at December 31, 19X3 (the date the equipment is fully depreciated by the subsidiary), there will be no net effect on the parent's general ledger Retained Earnings account as a result of the intercompany equipment transfer at above carrying value. The $3,000 gain recorded by the parent in 19X1 has been completely offset by the $3,000 incremental depreciation expense recorded on the subsidiary's books, which under the equity method of accounting, the parent has recorded as a reduction to its retained earnings.

Master analysis. For a depreciable asset sold to a subsidiary at above carrying value, a company often prepares an overall analysis that readily develops the elimination entries necessary over the asset's remaining life. Such an analysis is shown in Illustration 8-1.

Illustration 8-1
Analysis of equipment sold to subsidiary at above carrying value

	Asset		Annual	Unreportable
	Cost	Accum. Depr.	Depreciation Expense	Retained Earnings
I. Balances that would have existed if transferred at carrying value:				
January 1, 19X1	$50,000	$35,000		
19X1		5,000	$5,000	
December 31, 19X1	$50,000	$40,000		
19X2		5,000	5,000	
December 31, 19X2	$50,000	$45,000		
19X3		5,000	5,000	
December 31, 19X3	$50,000	$50,000		
II. Balances that will exist since transferred at above carrying value:				
January 1, 19X1	$18,000			
19X1		$ 6,000	$6,000	
December 31, 19X1	$18,000	$ 6,000		
19X2		6,000	6,000	
December 31, 19X2	$18,000	$12,000		
19X3		6,000	6,000	
December 31, 19X3	$18,000	$18,000		
III. Differences between I and II (basis for intercompany elimination entry):				
January 1, 19X1	$32,000	$35,000		$3,000
19X1			$1,000	
December 31, 19X1	32,000	34,000		2,000
19X2			1,000	
December 31, 19X2	32,000	33,000		1,000
19X3			1,000	
December 31, 19X3	32,000	32,000		-0-

IV. Entry required in consolidation:

	Jan. 1, 19X1		Dec. 31, 19X1		Dec. 31, 19X2		Dec. 31, 19X3	
	Dr.	Cr.	Dr.	Cr.	Dr.	Cr.	Dr.	Cr.
Gain on sale	3,000		3,000					
Equipment	32,000		32,000		32,000		32,000	
Accumulated depreciation		35,000		34,000		33,000		32,000
Depreciation expense				1,000		1,000		1,000
Retained earnings—P Company (beginning of year)						2,000[a]		1,000[a]

[a] The unreportable retained earnings at the beginning of the year.
Note: The entry after December 31, 19X3 (until the asset is sold or retired) is as follows:

Equipment	32,000
Accumulated depreciation	32,000

Section I of the analysis (the pro forma part) shows the balances and activity that would have existed if the asset had been transferred at its $15,000 carrying value. In preparing this part of the analysis, companies assume that the subsidiary recorded the asset at the parent's cost ($50,000) less the related accumulated depreciation on the parent's books at the transfer date ($35,000).

Section II of the analysis shows the balances and activity that will occur in the subsidiary's general ledger as a result of the transfer at $18,000. In preparing sections I and II of the analysis, companies must use the assets **new, remaining assigned life,** if different from the old remaining life. The old remaining life is no longer relevant.

Section III is merely the differences between the amounts in sections I and II. The balances produced in this section are the amounts used in the elimination entries at each consolidation date. Section IV shows these elimination entries for each consolidation date.

Income tax considerations.   In the preceding illustration, no entries were made in consolidation concerning income tax effects. If we assume that a consolidated income tax return is filed, no such entries are necessary. The parent does not treat the $3,000 gain as a taxable item when it provides income taxes in its general ledger for 19X1. Likewise, the subsidiary does not treat the incremental depreciation expense of $1,000 per year as a tax-deductible item when it provides income taxes in its general ledger for 19X1, 19X2, and 19X3. In other words, because no tax effects have been recorded in the general ledgers on these items, no income tax amounts require elimination or deferral on the worksheet.

Concluding comments.   An illustration of the full consolidation process for financial statements (as shown in Chapter 7) is not presented for downstream equipment transfers. In the following section, which deals with an upstream transfer, the full consolidation process for financial statements is illustrated. The only additional consideration is dealing with the minority interest.

Upstream transfers above cost

When depreciable assets are transferred from the subsidiary to the parent (upstream), the entries required in consolidation are the same as those previously shown for a downstream transfer, but only if the subsidiary is wholly owned. When the subsidiary is partially owned, the entries are modified slightly to reflect the minority shareholders' share of the gain in the transaction.

Using the facts in Illustration 8-1, except that the sale is upstream from a 90% owned subsidiary, we determine the minority interest in the subsidiary's gain as $300 (10% of $3,000). This $300 is reportable as an increase to the minority interest, but not at the transfer date. Instead, it is reported over the period that the parent depreciates the equipment. The subsidiary's gain is realized in the same manner as far as the minority interest is concerned. [Note that the net effect of the upstream transfer on the parent's general ledger Retained Earnings account is a decrease of $300, which is the total incremental depreciation expense of $3,000 recorded by the parent less its $2,700 share of the subsidiary's reported gain of $3,000 (90% of $3,000) that the parent records under the equity method of accounting.]

Illustration 8-2 shows the entries presented in Illustration 8-1, modified for the minority interest. The entries assume that the minority interest—based on the subsidiary's reported net income—has already been established at the partially consolidated column of the worksheet.

Illustration:
Preparing consolidated financial statements—
Upstream transfer above cost

The December 31, 19X1 elimination entry in Illustration 8-2 is used in Illustration 8-3 in going from the partially consolidated column to the consolidated column. The worksheet starts with the P Company and S Company financial statements presented in Illustration 5-5 (page 173). These financial statements were modified as follows:

(1) The subsidiary's financial statements reflect a $3,000 gain on the equipment transfer.
(2) The parent's financial statements reflect the $1,000 incremental depreciation expense.
(3) The parent's financial statements reflect an additional $2,700 (90% of $3,000) recorded under the equity method of accounting.

Illustration 8-2
Journal entries for upstream transfer

	Jan. 1, 19X1		Dec. 31, 19X1		Dec. 31, 19X2		Dec. 31, 19X3	
Consolidation Date	Dr.	Cr.	Dr.	Cr.	Dr.	Cr.	Dr.	Cr.
Gain on sale.............	3,000		3,000					
Equipment...............	32,000		32,000		32,000		32,000	
Accumulated								
depreciation		35,000		34,000		33,000		32,000
Depreciation								
expense...........				1,000		1,000		1,000
Retained earnings—								
S Company:								
Beginning of year					100[a]		-0-[a]	
Net income line	300[a]		200[a]			100		
Minority interest								
(income statement)					100		100	
Minority interest								
(income statement)		300		200				
Retained earnings—								
P Company:								
Beginning of year					1,800[b]		900[b]	

[a] The unreportable minority interest at this consolidation date.
[b] The unreportable retained earnings at the beginning of the year.

Illustration 8-3

P COMPANY AND SUBSIDIARY (S COMPANY)
Consolidating Statement Worksheet
For the Year Ended December 31, 19X1

Income Statement:	P Company	S Company	Non-intercompany Transaction Eliminations Dr.	Cr.	Partially Consolidated	Intercompany Transaction Eliminations Dr.	Cr.	Consolidated
Sales	600,000	200,000			800,000	3,000(4)		800,000
Intercompany gain		3,000			3,000			-0-
Income from subsidiary:								
Equity in net income	16,200		16,200(1)		-0-			-0-
Amortization of cost in excess of book value	(4,770)			4,770(2)	-0-			-0-
Subtotal	611,430	203,000	16,200	4,770	803,000	3,000		800,000
Cost of goods sold	360,000	120,000	4,770(2)		484,770			484,770
Marketing expenses	90,000	30,000			120,000			120,000
Administrative expenses	61,000	20,000			81,000		1,000(4)	80,000
Interest expense	30,000	5,000			35,000			35,000
Subtotal	541,000	175,000	4,770		720,770		1,000	719,770
Income before Income Taxes	70,430	28,000	20,970	4,770	82,230	3,000	1,000	80,230
Income tax expense	(24,000)	(10,000)			(34,000)			(34,000)
Income before Minority Interest	46,430	18,000	20,970	4,770	48,230	3,000	1,000	46,230
Minority interest			1,800(3)		(1,800)		200(5)	(1,600)
Net Income	46,430	18,000	22,770	4,770	46,430	3,000	1,200	44,630

Balance Sheet:

	P Company	S Company	Elim. Dr	Elim. Cr	Combined	Min. Dr	Min. Cr	Consolidated
Current assets	265,500	118,000			383,500			383,500
Investment in S Company	87,930			87,930(1)	-0-			-0-
Land	80,000	30,000	9,000(1)		119,000			119,000
Building—Cost	400,000	100,000	5,400(1)		505,400			505,400
—Accum. depr.	(260,000)	(23,000)		270(1)	(283,270)			(283,270)
Equipment—Cost	303,000	90,000			393,000	32,000(1)		425,000
—Accum. depr.	(171,000)	(42,000)			(213,000)		34,000(4)	(247,000)
Goodwill			8,100(1)		8,100			8,100
Total assets	705,430	273,000	22,500	88,200	912,730	32,000	34,000	910,730
Liabilities	290,000	200,000			490,000			490,000
Common stock:								
P Company	300,000				300,000			300,000
S Company		40,000	36,000(1)		4,000M			4,000M
Retained earnings—P Company:								
Beginning of year	100,000				100,000			100,000
+ Net income	46,430				46,430	3,000	1,200	44,630
− Dividends declared	(31,000)				(31,000)			(31,000)
End of year	115,430				115,430	3,000	1,200	113,630
Retained earnings—S Company:								
Beginning of year		20,000	18,000(1)		2,000M			2,000M
+ Net income		18,000	22,770	4,770 1,800(3)	1,800M	200(5)		1,600M
− Dividends declared		(5,000)		4,500(1)	(500)M	200		(500)M
End of year		33,000	40,770	11,070	3,300M	200		3,100M
Total liabilities and equity	705,430	273,000	76,770	11,070	912,730	3,200	1,200	910,730
Proof of debit and credit postings			99,270	99,270		35,200	35,200	

Total minority interest.......... 7,100M

Explanation of entries:
(1) The primary elimination entry.
(2) The secondary elimination entry.
(3) The minority interest entry.
(4) The intercompany equipment transfer elimination entry.
(5) The adjustment to the minority interest for the deferral of the gain on the equipment transfer.

Modified primary, secondary, and minority interest entries follow:

(1) The primary elimination entry:

Common stock	36,000	
Retained earnings (beginning of year)	18,000	
Equity in net income of subsidiary (90% of $18,000)	16,200	
Land	9,000	
Building—Cost	5,400	
—Accumulated depreciation		270
Goodwill	8,100	
Dividends declared		4,500
Investment in subsidiary		87,930

(2) The secondary elimination entry:

Cost of goods sold	4,770	
Amortization of cost in excess of book value		4,770

(3) The minority interest entry:

Minority interest (income statement)	1,800	
Retained earnings—S Company (net income line)		1,800
(10% of $18,000 book income)		

In reviewing Illustration 8-3, note the following items:

(1) The $1,600 minority interest deduction in the consolidated column can be determined as follows:

Subsidiary's reported net income	$18,000
Less—Intercompany gain not deemed realized	
as far as the minority interest is concerned	
($3,000 total gain − $1,000 deemed realized in 19X1)	(2,000)
	$16,000
Minority ownership percentage	10%
Reportable minority interest deduction	$ 1,600

(2) The net effect at the net income line in the intercompany transaction eliminations column is $1,800 ($3,000 − $1,200). This $1,800 (which is the net effect on the parent's retained earnings via the carryforward process) can be viewed as follows:

Total intercompany gain	$3,000
Less—Incremental depreciation recorded	
through December 31, 19X1	(1,000)
	$2,000
—Minority interest in unrealized gain (10% of $2,000)	(200)
Unreportable retained earnings at December 31, 19X1	$1,800

SUMMARY

Transfer of a fixed asset between companies within a consolidated group cannot result in a reportable gain or loss from a consolidated viewpoint. Any recorded gain or loss on the transfer is eliminated in consolidation. In a situation involving a depreciable asset, the recorded depreciation expense must be adjusted in consolidation to obtain an amount based on the selling entity's carrying value at the transfer date. In the consolidated balance sheet, the transferred asset must be reported at the selling entity's cost, with accumulated depreciation, if appropriate, based on this cost. For transfers from a partially owned subsidiary, additional adjustments are required in consolidation to reflect the minority interest share in any gain or loss on the transfer.

Discussion cases

Discussion case 8–1
Review of procedures for consolidation—
Upstream sale of equipment

Silver Company, a wholly owned subsidiary of Platinum Company, manufactures and installs industrial air conditioning systems. All of Silver's sales are normally to outside parties. During the current year, Silver sold for $600,000 an air conditioning system to Platinum, which constructed a new corporate headquarters. (Silver's manufacturing cost was $400,000.) In addition, Silver charged Platinum an installation fee of $90,000. (Silver's installation costs were $65,000.)

Required:
Explain the procedures for preparing consolidated financial statements for the current year and in future years with respect to this transaction.

Discussion case 8–2
Review of procedures for consolidation—
Lateral sales; unconsolidated subsidiary

Serrox Company is a wholly owned subsidiary of Parma Company, which is a conglomerate. Serrox manufactures office copiers, and all of its sales are normally to outside parties. At the beginning of the current year, a wholly owned insurance subsidiary of Parma acquired several office copiers from Serrox for its sales offices at a cost of $800,000. (Serrox's manufacturing cost was $500,000.) Only the insurance subsidiary is not consolidated with Parma. Companywide policy is to take a full year of depreciation in the year of acquisition.

Required:
Explain Parma's procedures in preparing its financial statements for its stockholders for the current year and future years with respect to this transaction.

Exercises

Exercise 8–1
Land transfer above cost—Downstream

On January 1, 19X1, Patch Company sold land costing $40,000 to its wholly owned subsidiary, Sew Company, for $100,000.

Required:
(1) Prepare the elimination entry required in consolidation as of January 1, 19X1, December 31, 19X1, and December 31, 19X2.
(2) Prepare the entry required in consolidation at December 31, 19X3, assuming Sew subsequently sold the land for $120,000.

Exercise 8–2
Land transfer above cost—Upstream from 90% owned subsidiary

Assume the information in Exercise 8–1, except that Sew Company is a 90% owned subsidiary and the transfer is upstream—that is, the subsidiary sold the land to the parent.

Required:
The requirements are the same as in Exercise 8–1.

Exercise 8–3
Equipment transfer above carrying value—Downstream

On January 1, 19X1, Picke Company sold equipment to its wholly owned subsidiary, Shovelle Company, for $800,000. The equipment cost Picke Company $1,000,000; accumulated depreciation at the time of the sale was $400,000. Picke has depreciated the equipment over 10 years using the straight-line method and no salvage value.

Required:
Determine the amounts at which the cost and accumulated depreciation should be reported in the consolidated balance sheet at December 31, 19X1 under each of the following assumptions:

(1) The subsidiary does not revise the estimated remaining life.
(2) The subsidiary estimates the remaining life as eight years.

Exercise 8–4
Equipment transfer above carrying value—Downstream

On January 1, 19X1, Placid Company sold machinery to its wholly owned subsidiary, Sereno Company. Information related to the sale is as follows:

Sales price		$16,000
Cost	$40,000	
Less—Accumulated depreciation	(30,000)	10,000
Gain		$ 6,000

Original life used by Placid Company . . . . 8 years
Remaining life assigned by Sereno Company . . . . 3 years

Required:
Prepare the entries required in consolidation as of January 1, 19X1; December 31, 19X1; December 31, 19X2; December 31, 19X3; and December 31, 19X4.

Exercise 8–5
Equipment transfer above carrying value—Upstream from 90% owned subsidiary

Assume the information in Exercise 8–4, except that Sereno Company is a 90% owned subsidiary and the sale is upstream—that is, the subsidiary sold the machinery to the parent.

Required:
The requirements are the same as in Exercise 8–4.

Problems

Problem 8–1
Completing the consolidating statement worksheet:
Equipment transfer above carrying value—Downstream

The partially consolidated financial statements of Pert Company and its 80% owned subsidiary, Savvy Company, for the year ended December 31, 19X2, are as follows:

	Partially Consolidated
Income Statement (19X2):	
Sales.	$282,000
Gain on sale of equipment	4,000
Subtotal	$286,000
Cost of goods sold	$140,000
Marketing expenses	30,000
Administrative expenses.	23,000
Interest expense.	10,000
Subtotal	$203,000
Income before Income Taxes	$ 83,000
Income tax expense	(32,000)
Income before Minority Interest	$ 51,000
Minority interest	(3,000)[a]
Net Income	$ 48,000
Balance Sheet (December 31, 19X2):	
Equipment	$ 60,000
Accumulated depreciation	(40,000)
Other assets	190,000
Total Assets	$210,000
Liabilities	$ 25,000
Common stock:	
Pert Company.	$100,000
Savvy Company.	$ 2,000M

	Partially Consolidated
Retained earnings—P Company:	
Beginning of year.	$ 42,000
+ Net income	48,000
− Dividends declared.	(15,000)
End of year.	$ 75,000
Retained earnings—S Company:	
Beginning of year.	$ 6,000M
+ Net income	3,000M
− Dividends declared.	(1,000)M
End of year.	$ 8,000M
Total Liabilities and Equity.	$210,000

ª Based on the subsidiary's book income of $15,000.

On July 1, 19X2, Pert Company sold a piece of office equipment to Savvy Company. Information pertaining to this transfer follows:

Sales price.		$12,000
Carrying value:		
Cost.	$30,000	
Accumulated depreciation through July 1, 19X2.	(22,000)	(8,000)
Gain recorded by parent.		$ 4,000
Remaining life.		2 years

Required:
(1) Prepare the required elimination entry at December 31, 19X2.
(2) Complete the preparation of the consolidating statement worksheet at December 31, 19X2.

Problem 8–2
Completing the consolidating statement worksheet: Equipment transfer above carrying value—Upstream from 80% owned subsidiary

Assume the information in Problem 8–1 regarding the intercompany sale of office equipment, except that the sale is upstream from Savvy Company to Pert Company.

Required:
The requirements are the same as in Problem 8–1.

Problem 8–3
Mini-consolidation using condensed financial statements: Equipment transfer above carrying value—Downstream

On January 1, 19X1, Prism Company acquired all of the outstanding common stock of Spectrum Company for $90,000 cash. Spectrum's book value was $70,000 at that date ($45,000 common stock + $25,000 retained earnings). The entire cost in excess of book value was assigned to goodwill, which was deemed to have a four-year life. On January 2, 19X1, Prism Company sold equipment to Spectrum Company. Information related to the sale is as follows.

Sales price..		$35,000
Cost...	$50,000	
Less—Accumulated depreciation	(30,000)	20,000
Gain...		$15,000
Original life used by Prism Company		10 years
Remaining life assigned by Spectrum Company..........................		5 years

Condensed financial statement information for 19X1 and at December 31, 19X1 follows:

	Prism Company	Spectrum Company
Income Statement (19X1):		
Operating profit (excluding items		
listed below).......................................	$200,000	$ 50,000
Depreciation expense	(60,000)	(20,000)
Equity in net income of subsidiary	30,000	
Amortization of cost in excess		
of book value..	(5,000)	
Gain on sale of equipment..............................	15,000	
Net Income (income taxes are ignored)	$180,000	$ 30,000
Balance Sheet (December 31, 19X1):		
Investment in Spectrum Company	$103,000	
Equipment	250,000	$ 75,000
Accumulated depreciation...............................	(100,000)	(24,000)
Other assets	597,000	59,000
Total Assets.......................................	$850,000	$110,000
Liabilities...	$110,000	$ 22,000
Common stock	300,000	45,000
Retained earnings.....................................	440,000	43,000
Total Liabilities and Equity	$850,000	$110,000
Dividends declared.....................................	$ 80,000	$ 12,000

Required:
(1) Prepare the elimination entries required in consolidation at December 31, 19X1.
(2) Prepare a consolidating statement worksheet at December 31, 19X1.

Problem 8–4
Mini-consolidation using condensed financial statements: Equipment transfer above carrying value—Upstream from 80% owned subsidiary

On January 1, 19X1, Prop Company purchased 80% of the outstanding common stock of Stage Company for $143,000 cash. At that date, Stage Company had (1) a book value of $150,000 ($100,000 common stock + $50,000 retained earnings) and (2) land that was undervalued by $10,000. Goodwill in the transaction was assigned a five-year life. On January 3, 19X1, Stage Company sold equipment to Prop Company. Information related to the sale is as follows:

Sales price...		$22,000
Cost..	$25,000	
Less—Accumulated depreciation	(15,000)	10,000
Gain..		$12,000
Original life used by Stage Company *Sub*................................		5 years
Remaining life assigned by Prop Company *Parent*........................		4 years

Use 4yr life for what would have been dep. as usual

Condensed financial statements for the year ended December 31, 19X1 follow:

	Prop Company	Stage Company
Income Statement (19X1):		
Operating profit (excluding items listed below)	$300,000	$ 78,000
Depreciation expense	(80,000)	(30,000)
Equity in net income of subsidiary.........................	48,000	
Amortization of cost in excess of book value	(3,000)	
Gain on sale of equipment		12,000
Net Income (income taxes are ignored)	$265,000	$ 60,000
Balance Sheet (December 31, 19X1):		
Investment in Stage Company	$172,000	
Equipment—Cost	130,000	$ 44,000
—Accumulated depreciation	(40,000)	(14,000)
Other assets	238,000	165,000
Total Assets	$500,000	$195,000
Liabilities	$ 75,000	$ 5,000
Common stock	200,000	100,000
Retained earnings	225,000	90,000
Total Liabilities and Equity.............................	$500,000	$195,000
Dividends declared	$135,000	$ 20,000

Required:
(1) Prepare the elimination entries required in consolidation at December 31, 19X1.
(2) Prepare a consolidating statement worksheet at December 31, 19X1.

Problem 8–5
COMPREHENSIVE (Chapters 7 and 8)   Preparing consolidating statement worksheet: Downstream inventory transfers above cost—Profit in beginning and ending inventory; Upstream equipment transfer above carrying value from wholly owned subsidiary

On January 1, 19X1, Pane Company acquired 100% of the outstanding common stock of Sill Company for $290,000 cash. An additional $10,000 of direct costs were incurred. The analysis of the investment account by the individual components of the major conceptual elements as of the acquisition date is as follows:

		Remaining Life
Common stock...	$200,000	
Retained earnings	25,000	
Land..	30,000	Indefinite
Equipment..	25,000	5 years
Goodwill..	20,000	10 years
	$300,000	

Many of the management functions of the two companies have been consolidated since the acquisition date. Pane Company charges Sill Company a management fee of $2,000 per month.

On January 3, 19X2, Sill Company sold office equipment to Pane Company. Information related to this transfer is as follows:

Sales price		$25,000
Cost	$45,000	
Accumulated depreciation	(30,000)	15,000
Gain		10,000
Original life used by Sill Company		9 years
Remaining life assigned by Pane Company		5 years

The financial statements of each company for the year ended December 31, 19X2 are as follows:

	Pane Company	Sill Company
Income Statement (19X2):		
Sales:		
To third parties	$890,000	$400,000
Intercompany	50,000	
Gain on sale of equipment		10,000
Income from subsidiary:		
Management fee	24,000	
Equity in net income	40,000	
Amortization of cost in excess of book value	(7,000)	
Subtotal	$997,000	$410,000
Cost of goods sold:		
To third parties	$570,000	$200,000
Intercompany	30,000	
Marketing expenses	130,000	80,000
Administrative expenses	110,000	70,000
Interest expense	20,000	
Subtotal	$860,000	$350,000
Income before Income Taxes	$137,000	$ 60,000
Income tax expense	(42,800)	(20,000)
Net Income	$ 94,200	$ 40,000
Balance Sheet (December 31, 19X2):		
Cash	$ 40,000	$ 20,000
Accounts receivable, net	100,000	70,000
Intercompany receivable	70,000	
Inventory:		
From vendors	120,000	80,000
Intercompany		10,000
Investment in Sill Company	312,000	
Land and building, net	223,000	115,000
Equipment	155,000	140,000
Accumulated depreciation	(50,000)	(55,000)
Total Assets	$970,000	$380,000
Intercompany payable		$ 70,000
Liabilities	$330,000	59,000
Common stock:		
Pane Company	400,000	
Sill Company		200,000
Retained earnings:		
Pane Company	240,000	
Sill Company		51,000
Total Liabilities and Equity	$970,000	$380,000
Dividends declared:		
19X1	$ 30,000	$ 5,000
19X2	49,000	25,000

Sill Company's December 31, 19X1 inventory included inventory costing $15,000 that had been acquired from Pane Company in 19X1. Pane Company's cost was $10,000. Assume that all of this inventory was resold by the subsidiary in 19X2.

Required:
(1) Prepare an expanded analysis of the investment account as of the acquisition date and update it through December 31, 19X2 using the equity method.
(2) Prepare the primary and secondary elimination entries at December 31, 19X2.
(3) Prepare the elimination entries related to intercompany transactions.
(4) Prepare a consolidating statement worksheet at December 31, 19X2.

9 Intercompany Bond Holdings and Subsidiary with Preferred Stock

INTERCOMPANY BOND HOLDINGS

A parent or a subsidiary that has outstanding bonds may want to retire some or all of the bonds before their maturity dates. This is common when interest rates have declined significantly since the original issue date and new bonds can be issued at a lower interest rate, or when excess cash has been accumulated beyond foreseeable needs. The entity that issues the bonds (hereafter referred to as the *issuing entity*) may not have the cash available to retire the bonds or it may be impracticable to issue new bonds to retire the old bonds. In these situations, another company within the consolidated group that has available cash or the ability to issue debt can purchase some or all of the outstanding bonds in the open market. Although it is not unusual for a parent to purchase a subsidiary's bonds, a subsidiary purchases a parent's bonds only if directed to do so by the parent.

When bonds are acquired within a consolidated group, no amounts are owed to any party outside the consolidated group. Therefore, the purchase by one entity within the group of any or all of the outstanding bonds of another entity represents a retirement of the bonds. Any imputed gain or loss on this deemed retirement of acquired bonds must be reported in the income statement in the period of the purchase, as required by *APB Opinion No. 26,* "Early Extinguishment of Debt." If the gain or loss is material, it must be reported as an extraordinary item, as required by *FASB Statement No. 4,* "Reporting Gains and Losses from Extinguishment of Debt."

The accounting in consolidation is complicated by the fact that the issuing entity continues to account for the bonds as outstanding, which they are from its viewpoint. The acquiring entity continues to account for the bonds as an investment until the issuing entity actually retires them. Accordingly, with respect to intercompany bond holdings, the objective of the consolidation procedures is to make the necessary adjustments on the consolidating statement worksheets to reflect, in the consolidated financial statements, amounts that would have existed if the issuing entity had acquired the bonds rather than the acquiring entity. These adjustments must be made from the acquisition date of the bonds to the date that they are actually retired.

Determination of gain or loss on extinguishment of debt

The amount of the *imputed* gain or loss on the extinguishment of debt that is reported in the period in which the affiliate's bonds are purchased is determined by comparing the acquisition cost to the applicable percentage of the carrying value of the bonds payable as of the bond purchase date. For example, assume P Company acquired in the open market 40% of the outstanding 10% bonds of its wholly owned subsidiary, S Company, for $19,400 on January 1, 19X4. (The assumed maturity date of the bonds is December 31, 19X6, which is three years later.) Interest is payable on July

1 and January 1. Thus, none of the purchase cost relates to interest. The gain or loss is calculated at that date as follows:

Calculation of gain or loss on extinguishment of debt at January 1, 19X4

	Face Amount	Unamortized Premium (S Co.)	Unamortized Discount (P Co.)	Carrying Value
Bonds payable....................	$50,000	$3,750		$53,750
Percent acquired..................	40%	40%		40%
Amount deemed retired..............	$20,000	$1,500		$21,500
Investment in bonds...............	20,000		$600	19,400
Unrecorded gain on extinguishment of debt		$1,500	$600	$ 2,100

The gain is attributable to the applicable percentage (40%) of the unamortized premium on the subsidiary's books and all of the discount on the parent's books. At the bond purchase date, the subsidiary would make the following entry in its general ledger to reflect the fact that the parent company now holds a portion of the bonds:

Bonds payable	20,000	
Bond premium...	1,500	
Intercompany bonds payable.........................		20,000
Intercompany bond premium		1,500

If consolidated financial statements are prepared on January 1, 19X4 (the bond acquisition date), the following elimination entry is required in consolidation to (1) reflect this deemed retirement of the bonds and (2) report the gain on extinguishment:

Intercompany bonds payable.............................	20,000	
Intercompany bond premium	1,500	
Investment in S Company bonds		19,400
Gain on extinguishment		2,100

This entry produces the same results as if the subsidiary had acquired and retired the bonds. Usually, there is no need to prepare consolidated financial statements on a bond acquisition date unless it coincides with a normal consolidation preparation date.

The preceding example involved a premium on the issuing company's books and a discount on the acquiring company's books. This combination always results in a gain. If the issuing company has the discount and the acquiring company has the premium, a loss on early extinguishment of debt always results. When each company has a discount or each company has a premium, the net effect is a gain or a loss, depending on which company has the greater discount or premium. In all of these situations, the correct procedures for preparing consolidated financial statements can be determined by carefully applying the principles discussed and illustrated for the example used in this chapter.

Dealing with subsequent amortization of bond premium and discount

In the preceding example, the substance of the deemed bond retirement is to accelerate reporting the $1,500 intercompany bond premium and the $600 bond discount as income. In other words, instead of the $1,500 bond premium being reported as income over the remaining life of the bonds (as a reduction of interest expense through the amortization process), it is reported as income in consolidation at the bond acquisition date. Likewise, instead of the $600 bond discount being reported as income over the remaining life of the bonds (as additional interest income through the amortization process), it is reported as income in consolidation at the bond acquisition date.

Because the $1,500 intercompany bond premium and the $600 discount are reported as income in consolidation at the bond acquisition date, the parent's consolidated retained earnings balance is $2,100 greater than its general ledger Retained Earnings account balance. The parent's general ledger Retained Earnings account balance equals the consolidated retained earnings balance only through the complete amortization of the $1,500 bond premium and $600 discount that takes place in the general ledgers over the remaining life of the bonds. At December 31, 19X6 (the bond maturity date), the entire intercompany bond premium of $1,500 and the discount of $600 have been amortized in the general ledgers. As a result, the parent's general ledger Retained Earnings account balance is $2,100 greater than at January 1, 19X4 (the bond acquisition date).

If nothing is done in consolidation at the end of 19X4, 19X5, and 19X6 concerning this amortization, then the $2,100 has been reported as income twice:

(1) First, as a $2,100 gain on extinguishment in 19X4 as a result of the elimination entry made in consolidation to eliminate the bond investment and the related intercompany bond payable and premium accounts.
(2) Second, as additional interest income ($600) and lesser interest expense ($1,500) from January 1, 19X4 to December 31, 19X6 as a result of amortizing the $600 discount and the $1,500 intercompany bond premium to income in the general ledgers.

Obviously, the $2,100 can be reported as income only once. Thus, in periods subsequent to the bond acquisition date, elimination entries are needed in consolidation to eliminate this income resulting from the amortization process. This, of course, is consistent with the consolidated viewpoint that the bonds are deemed to be retired at the bond acquisition date. Thus, future-period consolidated income statements cannot report any interest income or expense with respect to these bonds.

Entries recorded in books subsequent to bond acquisition date

Assume that P Company and S Company use the straight-line method of amortizing bond premium and discount (the results from the straight-line method are not materially different from results under the interest method).

The entries that would be recorded in each company's general ledger during 19X4, 19X5, and 19X6 relating to the bonds are as follows:

	P Company	S Company
Intercompany interest expense	2,000	
Interest expense	3,000	
Intercompany interest payable/cash		2,000
Interest payable/cash		3,000
To record interest expense (10% of		
$50,000, 40% of which is intercompany).		
Intercompany interest receivable/cash 2,000		
Intercompany interest income	2,000	
To record interest income (10% of $20,000).		
Intercompany bond premium	500	
Bond premium..................................	750	
Intercompany interest expense		500
Interest expense		750
To amortize bond premium.		
Investment in S Company bonds 200		
Intercompany interest income	200	
To amortize bond discount.		

At the end of each of these years, the balances in the Intercompany Interest Expense and Intercompany Interest Income accounts would be as follows:

P Company		S Company	
Intercompany		Intercompany	
Interest Income		Interest Expense	
	2,000	2,000	
	200		500
	2,200	1,500	

The difference between the two accounts is a net credit of $700, which is the result of the amortization of the intercompany bond premium of $500 and the bond discount of $200. Because three such years of amortization occur, the cumulative three-year difference is $2,100 (equal to the gain on extinguishment of debt reportable at January 1, 19X4). As explained in the preceding section, these account balances must be eliminated in consolidation at the end of 19X4, 19X5, and 19X6.

Illustration:
Preparing consolidated financial statements at the end of the bond acquisition year—Wholly owned subsidiary

Assuming P Company is a calendar year-end reporting company, the elimination entries that would be made in consolidation at December 31, 19X4 (one year after the bond acquisition date) are as follows:

(1) The elimination of intercompany interest income and intercompany interest expense:

Intercompany interest income..........................	2,200	
Intercompany interest expense		1,500
Gain on extinguishment of debt....................		700

(2) The elimination of the investment in the bonds and the related bond liability and premium accounts:

Intercompany bonds payable	20,000	
Intercompany bond premium ($1,500 −		
$500 19X1 amortization)	1,000	
Investment in bonds ($19,400 +		
$200 19X1 amortization)		19,600
Gain on extinguishment of debt......................		1,400

The combination of the two entries results in a $2,100 credit to the Gain on Extinguishment of Debt account, which was the amount of gain determined on January 1, 19X1 (the date the bond investment was made). Because of the actual $700 amortization that was recorded in the general ledgers during 19X1, only $1,400 of premium and discount remain "locked into" the balance sheet at the end of 19X1.

The two preceding entries are posted to the December 31, 19X4, consolidating statement worksheet in Illustration 9-1. The following assumptions were made for simplicity:

(1) P Company acquired all of the outstanding common stock of S Company on January 1, 19X1 at an amount equal to book value of S Company's net assets. Accordingly, no secondary elimination entry is made for cost over or under book value. In 19X4, S Company had net income of $29,600 and declared dividends of $10,000. The primary elimination entry (assuming P Company uses the equity method of accounting) is as follows:

The primary elimination entry:

Common stock..	40,000	
Retained earnings (beginning of year)	64,000	
Equity in net income of subsidiary	29,600	
Dividends declared		10,000
Investment in subsidiary		123,600

(2) Intercompany interest payable of $1,000 at December 31, 19X4 ($2,500 × 40%) is eliminated against intercompany interest receivable of $1,000 using the rearrangement procedure discussed in Chapter 7. S Company's intercompany payable is shown among its assets in parentheses. Accordingly, no elimination entry is needed for these accounts.

In reviewing Illustration 9-1, the following points should be understood:

(1) Both consolidated net income and consolidated retained earnings are $1,400 greater than the corresponding account balances in the partially consolidated column. The difference is attributable to P Company's

Illustration 9-1

P COMPANY AND SUBSIDIARY (S COMPANY)
Consolidating Statement Worksheet
For the Year Ended December 31, 19X4

	P Company	S Company	Non-intercompany Transaction Eliminations Dr.	Non-intercompany Transaction Eliminations Cr.	Partially Consolidated	Intercompany Transaction Eliminations Dr.	Intercompany Transaction Eliminations Cr.	Consolidated
Income Statement:								
Sales	680,000	280,000			960,000			960,000
Equity in net income of subsidiary	29,600		29,600(1)		-0-			-0-
Subtotal	709,600	280,000	29,600		960,000			960,000
Cost of goods sold	378,000	120,000			498,000			498,000
Marketing expenses	118,000	85,000			203,000			203,000
Administrative expenses	81,200	21,250			102,450			102,450
Interest expense	30,000	2,250			32,250			32,250
Intercompany interest expense		1,500			1,500		1,500(2)	-0-
Intercompany interest (income)	(2,200)				(2,200)	2,200(2)		-0-
Gain on extinguishment of debt							700(2) 1,400(3)	(2,100)
Subtotal	605,000	230,000			835,000	2,200	3,600	833,600
Income before Income Taxes	104,600	50,000		29,600	125,000	2,200	3,600	126,400
Income tax expense	(30,160)	(20,400)			(50,560)			(50,560)
Net Income	74,440	29,600		29,600	74,440		3,600	75,840

Balance Sheet:	P Company	S Company	Eliminations Dr	Eliminations Cr	Combined	Eliminations Dr	Eliminations Cr	Consolidated
Investment in S Company:								
Common stock	123,600			123,600(1)	-0-			-0-
Bonds	19,600				19,600		19,600(3)	-0-
Intercompany interest receivable (payable)	1,000	(1,000)			-0-			-0-
Other assets	591,000	320,000			911,000			911,000
Total assets	735,200	319,000		123,600	930,600		19,600	911,000
Accounts payable and accruals	248,760	142,900			391,660			391,660
Bond payable		30,000			30,000			30,000
Bond premium		1,500			1,500			1,500
Intercompany bonds payable		20,000			20,000	20,000(3)		-0-
Intercompany bond premium		1,000			1,000	1,000(3)		-0-
Common stock:								
P Company	300,000				300,000			300,000
S Company		40,000	40,000(1)		-0-			-0-
Retained earnings—P Company:								
Beginning of year	163,000				163,000			163,000
+ Net income	74,440				74,440	2,200	3,600	75,840
− Dividends declared	(51,000)				(51,000)			(51,000)
End of year	186,440				186,440	2,200	3,600	187,840
Retained earnings—S Company:								
Beginning of year		64,000	64,000(1)		-0-			-0-
+ Net income		29,600	29,600(1)		-0-			-0-
− Dividends declared		(10,000)		10,000(1)	-0-			-0-
End of year		83,600	93,600	10,000	-0-			-0-
Total liabilities and equity	735,200	319,000	133,600	133,600	930,600	23,200	23,200	911,000
Proof of debit and credit postings			133,600	133,600		23,200	23,200	

Explanation of entries:

(1) The primary elimination entry.

(2) The elimination of intercompany interest income and intercompany interest expense.

(3) The elimination of the bond investment and related bond liability and premium accounts.

unamortized discount of $400 at December 31, 19X4 and S Company's unamortized intercompany bond premium of $1,000 at December 31, 19X4. (Under the equity method of accounting, the subsidiary's unamortized intercompany bond premium of $1,000 that is recognized in consolidation in 19X4 accrues to the parent and is properly reportable as part of consolidated net income and consolidated retained earnings.)

(2) The $2,100 gain on extinguishment in the consolidated column is less than 2% of income before income taxes. Accordingly, the gain is not reported as an extraordinary item because it is immaterial.

(3) We assume that a consolidated income tax return is filed. Thus, the parent's unamortized discount of $400 at December 31, 19X4 is taxable in 19X4. Likewise, the subsidiary's unamortized intercompany bond premium of $1,000 at December 31, 19X4 is taxable in 19X4. Because the income taxes on these amounts must be recorded in the general ledgers, an additional $160 of income tax expense (40% assumed income tax rate × $400) is provided in the P Company column. Likewise, an additional $400 of income tax expense (40% × $1,000) is provided in the S Company column. Consequently, no tax effects are dealt with in the eliminations columns.

Bond elimination entries for periods subsequent to the bond acquisition year

For periods subsequent to the bond acquisition year, the bond-related elimination entries required in consolidation are nearly identical to the two bond elimination entries shown for Illustration 9-1. The differences are as follows:

(1) The elimination entry pertaining to the bond investment and related intercompany bond payable and premium accounts contains updated amounts because of the amortization that was recorded in the general ledgers during the year.

(2) Retained Earnings—P Company (beginning of year) is credited in each of these elimination entries rather than Gain on Extinguishment of Debt. The gain was reported in 19X4 as part of consolidated retained earnings at December 31, 19X4. Thus, the credits to Retained Earnings merely re-establish on the worksheet the portion of the gain on extinguishment that had not yet been recorded in the parent's Retained Earnings account (through the amortization process) at the beginning of the year.

The bond-related elimination entries that would be made in consolidation at December 31, 19X5 and December 31, 19X6 are as follows:

	December 31, 19X5		December 31, 19X6	
Intercompany interest income	2,200		2,200	
Intercompany interest expense		1,500		1,500
Retained earnings—P Company (beginning of year)		700		700
Intercompany bonds payable	20,000		20,000	
Intercompany bond premium	500			
Investment in bonds		19,800		20,000
Retained earnings—P Company (beginning of year)		700		

Minority interest considerations at bond acquisition date

In the preceding discussion, we assumed that S Company was a wholly owned subsidiary. When the subsidiary is partially owned, the entries made in consolidation in connection with intercompany bonds require an adjustment to the minority interest if part of the gain or loss on early extinguishment of debt is attributable to the subsidiary's unamortized discount or premium. No adjustment is necessary if the subsidiary issued or acquired bonds at their face amount.

Let us change our example to reflect a 90% ownership in S Company. Of the $2,100 gain on extinguishment of debt, we know that $1,500 is a result of the premium on the subsidiary's books. Only 90%, or $1,350, of this $1,500 accrues to the parent company. The remaining $150 accrues to the minority interest shareholders. In consolidation, this $150 is reflected as additional minority interest in the subsidiary's net income. Accordingly, if consolidated financial statements are prepared at January 1, 19X4, an additional entry is required to adjust the minority interest. This worksheet entry is as follows:

```
Minority interest (income statement) ...........................   150
      Retained earnings—S Company (posted to
      the net income line in the analysis
      of retained earnings) ....................................        150
```

As a result of a 10% minority interest in the subsidiary, the consolidated net income is greater by $1,950 ($1,350 + $600 discount) rather than by $2,100.

Minority interest considerations at the end of the bond acquisition year

The normal minority interest entry that is made at December 31, 19X4 (one year after the purchase of the bonds by the parent) is based on the subsidiary's $29,600 recorded net income for 19X4. This $29,600 includes one year's amortization of the bond premium of $500 (intercompany portion only). However, the amortization of the remaining premium of $1,000 (intercompany portion only) must be accelerated for consolidated reporting purposes. Of this amount, 10%, or $100, accrues to minority shareholders. Consequently, an additional $100 minority interest deduction must be made in consolidation at December 31, 19X4, as follows:

```
Minority interest (income statement) ..........................   100
      Retained earnings—S Company (posted to
      the net income line of the analysis of
      retained earnings) .......................................        100
```

Illustration:
Preparing consolidated financial statements at the end of the bond acquisition year—partially owned subsidiary

Illustration 9-2 shows Illustration 9-1 revised to reflect 90% ownership of the subsidiary. The preceding minority interest entry is used in going from the partially consolidated column to the consolidated column of the worksheet.

Illustration 9-2

P COMPANY AND SUBSIDIARY (S COMPANY)
Consolidating Statement Worksheet
For the Year Ended December 31, 19X4

	P Company	S Company	Non-intercompany Transaction Eliminations Dr.	Non-intercompany Transaction Eliminations Cr.	Partially Consolidated	Intercompany Transaction Eliminations Dr.	Intercompany Transaction Eliminations Cr.	Consolidated
Income Statement:								
Sales	680,000	280,000			960,000			960,000
Equity in net income of subsidiary	26,640		26,640(1)		-0-			-0-
Subtotal	706,640	280,000	26,640		960,000			960,000
Cost of goods sold	378,000	120,000			498,000			498,000
Marketing expenses	118,000	85,000			203,000			203,000
Administrative expenses	81,200	21,250			102,450			102,450
Interest expense	30,000	2,250			32,250			32,250
Intercompany interest expense		1,500			1,500		1,500(3)	-0-
Intercompany interest (income)	(2,200)				(2,200)	2,200(3)		-0-
Gain on extinguishment of debt							700(3) 1,400(4)	(2,100)
Subtotal	605,000	230,000			835,000	2,200	3,600	833,600
Income before Income Taxes	101,640	50,000	26,640		125,000	2,200	3,600	126,400
Income tax expense	(30,160)	(20,400)			(50,560)			(50,560)
Income before Minority								
Interest	71,480	29,600			74,440	2,200	3,600	75,840
Minority interest			2,960(2)		(2,960)	100(5)		(3,060)
Net Income	71,480	29,600	29,600		71,480	2,300	3,600	72,780

Balance Sheet:

Account	P Company	S Company	Elim. Dr	Elim. Cr	Consolidated	M.I. Dr	M.I. Cr	Consolidated Balance Sheet
Investment in S Company:								
Common stock	111,240			111,240(1)	-0-			-0-
Bonds	19,600				19,600		19,600(4)	-0-
Intercompany interest receivable (payable)	1,000	(1,000)			-0-			-0-
Other assets	595,500	320,000			915,500			915,500
Total assets	727,340	319,000		111,240	935,100		19,600	915,500
Accounts payable and accruals	248,760	142,900			391,660			391,660
Bond payable		30,000			30,000			30,000
Bond premium		1,500			1,500			1,500
Intercompany bonds payable		20,000			20,000	20,000(4)		-0-
Intercompany bond premium		1,000			1,000	1,000(4)		-0-
Common stock:								
P Company	300,000				300,000			300,000
S Company		40,000	36,000(1)		4,000M			4,000M
Retained earnings—P Company:								
Beginning of year	158,100				158,100			158,100
+ Net income	71,480				71,480	2,300	3,600	72,780
– Dividends declared	(51,000)				(51,000)			(51,000)
End of year	178,580				178,580	2,300	3,600	179,880
Retained earnings—S Company:								
Beginning of year		64,000	57,600(1)		6,400M			6,400M
+ Net income		29,600	29,600(1)	2,960(2)	2,960M		100(5)	3,060M
– Dividends declared		(10,000)		9,000(1)	(1,000)M			(1,000)M
End of year		83,600	87,200	11,960	8,360M		100	8,460M
Total liabilities and equity	727,340	319,000	123,200	11,960	935,100	23,300		915,500
Proof of debit and credit postings			123,200	123,200		23,300	23,300	

Total minority interest.......... 12,460

Explanation of entries:
(1) The primary elimination entry.
(2) The minority interest entry (based on book income).
(3) The elimination of intercompany interest income and intercompany interest expense [entry (2) in Illus. 9-1].
(4) The elimination of the bond investment and related bond liability and premium accounts [entry (3) in Illus. 9-1].
(5) The adjustment to the minority interest.

The following worksheet entries would be made to go from the P Company and S Company columns to the partially consolidated column:

(1) The primary elimination entry:

Common stock	36,000	
Retained earnings—S Company (beginning of year)	57,600	
Equity in net income of subsidiary (90% of $29,600)	26,640	
Dividends declared (90% of $10,000)		9,000
Investment in subsidiary		111,240

(2) The minority interest entry:

Minority interest (income statement)	2,960	
Retained earnings—S Company (posted to the net income line in the analysis of retained earnings)		2,960
(10% of $29,600 book income.)		

In reviewing Illustration 9-2, note the following items:

(1) The $3,060 minority interest deduction in the consolidated column is determined as follows:

Subsidiary's reported net income	$29,600
Plus—Unamortized intercompany bond premium at December 31, 19X4 recognized in consolidation in 19X4	1,000
	$30,600
Minority interest ownership percentage	10%
Reportable minority interest deduction	$ 3,060

(2) If a partially consolidated column is not used, then the minority interest deduction is established using a single minority interest entry in the amount of $3,060.

Bond elimination entries for periods subsequent to the bond acquisition year—Minority interest situations

When a minority interest is involved, the following bond-related elimination entries are required in consolidation for periods subsequent to the bond acquisition year.

	December 31,			
	19X5		19X6	
Intercompany interest income	2,200		2,200	
Intercompany interest expense		1,500		1,500
Minority interest (income statement)				
(10% of the $500 intercompany bond				
premium amortized during the year)		50		50
Retained earnings—P Company				
(beginning of year).		650		650
Intercompany bonds payable.	20,000		20,000	
Intercompany bond premium	500			
Investment in bonds		19,800		20,000
Retained earnings—S Company				
(beginning of year).		50		
Retained earnings—P Company				
(beginning of year).		650		

These entries assume that the minority interest deduction in the income statement—based on the subsidiary's reported net income—has already been established at the partially consolidated column of the worksheet.

The credits to the parent's Retained Earnings account merely re-establish on the worksheet the portion of the gain on extinguishment that had not yet been recorded in the parent's retained earnings (through the amortization process) at the beginning of the year. Likewise, the credit to the subsidiary's Retained Earnings account merely re-establishes on the worksheet the portion of the gain on extinguishment that accrues to the minority interest but that has not yet been recorded in the subsidiary's retained earnings (through the amortization process) at this consolidation date; the amount here is 10% of the $500 unamortized intercompany bond premium at December 31, 19X5.

Purchase between interest payment dates

In the preceding examples, we assumed for simplicity that bond purchases occurred on an interest payment date. When an affiliate's bonds are acquired between interest dates, the only other element to account for is the additional amount that would be paid by the acquiring entity for interest from the last interest payment date to the purchase date. This additional amount is charged to interest receivable at the purchase date. The procedures to determine and account for imputed gains and losses in consolidation do not change.

Reissuance of intercompany bond holdings

Infrequently, an acquiring entity sells some or all of the intercompany bonds to an outside party instead of holding them until their maturity date. In these cases, the bonds sold by the acquiring entity are considered to be reissued from a consolidated viewpoint. The consolidation procedures are modified as follows:

(1) Any difference between the carrying value of the bonds sold at the time of sale and the face value is treated as previously reported in consolidation.
(2) Any difference between the proceeds (other than amounts that relate to interest income) and the face value is treated as a premium or discount, as the case may be, and amortized to income over the remaining term of the bond.

These procedures produce the same results as if the issuing entity redeemed the bonds at their face value and then reissued them to an outside party.

Summary of accounting for intercompany bond holdings

The acquisition of an affiliated company's outstanding bonds is accounted for in consolidation as a retirement of those bonds, even though the bonds are not actually retired. When the bonds are retired, a gain or loss on early extinguishment of debt exists to the extent of the combined unamortized premium or discount (intercompany portion only) existing at the bond acquisition date, as reflected on each company's books. Such gain or loss is reportable in the income statement in the period in which the bond acquisition occurs.

With repect to the acquired bonds, the consolidation procedures report the appropriate unamortized bond premium or discount in the period in which the bonds are acquired. In subsequent periods, steps must be taken to prevent the reporting of bond premium and discount amortization that is actually recorded in subsequent separate company income statements. Thus, amounts that are reported as interest income or interest expense in later periods in each company's general ledger are reported as a gain or loss on early extinguishment of debt in the bond acquisition period. When a partially owned subsidiary has a premium or a discount, special adjustments are made to the minority interest.

SUBSIDIARY WITH PREFERRED STOCK

In consolidated financial statements, a subsidiary's preferred stock—to the extent it is not held by the parent company—is treated as part of the minority interest. However, the amount recorded on the subsidiary's books relating to its preferred stock is not necessarily the amount that is added to the minority interest in consolidation. The amount added to the minority interest in consolidation depends on the features of the preferred stock—that is, whether it is cumulative or noncumulative, whether it is participating or nonparticipating, and whether it is callable at amounts other than its par value. Additional amounts above the recorded amount of the preferred stock that need to be added to the minority interest are taken from the subsidiary's recorded retained earnings. The parent must use an amount other than the subsidiary's recorded retained earnings to calculate the amount initially assigned to this individual component in its expanded analysis of the Investment in Subsidiary account.

Parent companies do not usually invest in the preferred stock of their subsidiaries. Accordingly, we discuss the subject in the following order:

(1) Determination of minority interest **as of the acquisition date,** assuming the parent does not have or make an investment in the subsidiary's preferred stock.
(2) Determination of minority interest **subsequent to the acquisition date,** assuming the parent **does not invest** in the subsidiary's preferred stock in such subsequent period.
(3) Determination of minority interest **subsequent to the acquisition date,** assuming the parent **does invest** in the subsidiary's preferred stock subsequent to the acquisition date.

Determination of minority interest as of the acquisition date:
Parent owns none of subsidiary's preferred stock

The preferred stock amount used to ascertain the minority interest as of the parent's acquisition date is determined using procedures for calculating the book value of preferred stock that are discussed in intermediate accounting texts. Briefly, the recorded amount of the preferred stock is increased for any of the following, as applicable:

(1) For cumulative preferred stock. Add any dividends in arrears through the acquisition date.
(2) For participating preferred stock. Add any unpaid participation amounts through the acquisition date.
(3) For callable preferred stock. Add any premium relating to the call feature.

To the extent that any or all of these three features apply, the subsidiary's retained earnings amount as of the acquisition date is reclassified and attributed to the preferred stock to calculate the parent's interest in the retained earnings applicable to common stock. (No entry is made on the subsidiary's books, of course.)

For example, assume that $3,000 in dividends are in arrears on S Company's 6% **cumulative** preferred stock on January 1, 19X1, the date P Company acquired 90% of the outstanding common stock of S Company. The calculation of the minority interest as of January 1, 19X1 follows, assuming S Company's capital accounts on the acquisition date are as follows:

	Total	Parent's Interest	Minority Interest
6% Preferred stock, cumulative	$ 50,000		$50,000
Common stock	40,000	$36,000	4,000
Retained earnings:			
Allocable to preferred stock..................	3,000		3,000
Allocable to common stock	17,000	15,300	1,700
Total stockholders' equity.................	$110,000	$51,300	$58,700

Accordingly, the parent assigns $15,300 to the retained earnings component in its expanded analysis of the Investment in Subsidiary account as of the acquisition date. These added features of the preferred stock effectively force the parent company to separate the subsidiary's retained earnings into two amounts—the portion that is allocable to the preferred stock and the residual, which is allocable to the common stock. Even if the allocation to the preferred stockholders results in a negative balance for the common stockholders, the retained earnings are still separated in this manner.

Determination of minority interest subsequent to the acquisition date:
Parent owns none of subsidiary's preferred stock

In periods subsequent to acquisition, the subsidiary's net income must be allocated between the preferred stockholders' and the common stockholders' interests. Assuming S Company had net income of $10,000 for 19X1 and paid no dividends on its preferred stock, the allocation of the net income for 19X1 is as follows:

Total net income	$10,000
Less—Preferred stock dividend requirement	(3,000)
Residual allocable to common stockholders	$ 7,000

The parent company applies the equity method of accounting to the $7,000 and records $6,300 (90% of $7,000) of the subsidiary's earnings. This procedure is in accordance with *APB Opinion No. 18,* which states:

> When an investee has outstanding cumulative preferred stock, an investor should compute its share of earnings (losses) after deducting the investee's preferred dividends, whether or not such dividends are declared.[1]

As of December 31, 19X1 (one year after the acquisition date), the minority interest would be calculated as follows:

	Total	Parent's Interest	Minority Interest
6% Preferred stock, cumulative	$ 50,000		$50,000
Common stock	40,000	$36,000	4,000
Retained earnings:			
Allocable to preferred stock	6,000[a]		6,000
Allocable to common stock	24,000	21,600	2,400
Total stockholders' equity	$120,000	$57,600	$62,400

[a] Two years of dividends are assumed to be in arrears.

Determination of minority interest subsequent to the acquisition date:
Parent subsequently acquires some of subsidiary's preferred stock

Using the data in the preceding example, assume P Company acquired 40% of the subsidiary's outstanding preferred stock on January 1, 19X2 for $21,000. As with an intercompany bond purchase, for consolidated

---

[1] *APB Opinion No. 18,* "The Equity Method of Accounting for Investments in Common Stock" (New York: AICPA, 1971), paragraph 19k.

reporting purposes the preferred stock acquired is treated as retired. The total book value of the preferred stock on that date is $56,000 ($50,000 + $6,000 dividends in arrears); 40% of this total book value is $22,400. Thus, the parent's cost of the preferred stock is less than its share of book value by $1,400. The issue now raised is how the parent should account for its cost under book value when consolidated financial statements are prepared. Two apparent possibilities exist:

(1) Treat the cost under book value the same as an acquisition of a common stock minority interest, applying the purchase method of accounting. Under this approach, the preferred stock label is ignored. The substance of the transaction is the acquisition of minority interest, the class of which is irrelevant. This approach is not sanctioned by any official pronouncement.
(2) Treat the cost under book value the same as if the preferred stock were that of the parent company, in which case, any amount by which cost is below book value is credited to additional paid-in capital. (If cost exceeds the applicable share of book value, such excess would be charged to additional paid-in capital to the extent available, with any remaining difference charged to retained earnings.) The argument here is that although the preferred stock is classified as part of minority interest, it is distinctively different from the common stock minority interest. Any difference between cost and book value is unrelated either to the difference between asset values and book values or to expected superior earnings. This approach makes the most sense.

Under this second approach, P Company makes the following worksheet elimination entry in consolidation as long as it holds the subsidiary's preferred stock:

Preferred stock (40% of $50,000)	20,000	
Retained earnings—S Company (40% of $6,000)[a]	2,400	
Investment in S Company preferred stock		21,000
Additional paid-in capital		1,400

[a] On the acquisition date, $6,000 of preferred dividends are in arrears.

To the extent that the $6,000 of preferred stock dividends, in arrears as of the acquisition date, are paid in subsequent periods, the debit to the subsidiary's Retained Earnings account decreases and is offset by a debit to the parent's Retained Earnings account. That portion of the subsidiary's retained earnings has been transferred to the parent.

Preferred stock dividends received by the parent company are recorded as dividend income but are eliminated in consolidation, inasmuch as they constitute intercompany transactions. The worksheet entry to eliminate intercompany preferred stock dividends in consolidation is as follows:

Dividend income	xxx	
Retained earnings (posted to the		
net income line in the analysis		
of retained earnings)		xxx

Illustration:
Preparing consolidated financial statements;
parent holds subsidiary's preferred stock

Assume the information in the preceding example concerning the parent company's acquisition of the subsidiary's preferred stock on January 1, 19X2, as well as the following additional information:

(1) S Company had net income of $24,000 for 19X2. Because $3,000 of these earnings relate to the preferred stock dividend requirement, only $21,000 is available for common shareholders. Consequently, the parent's share of this $21,000 is $18,900 (90% of $21,000).

(2) S Company paid preferred stock dividends of $6,000 in 19X2, which leaves one year of dividends in arrears as of December 31, 19X2. (No dividends have been paid on common stock since the parent acquired it.)

(3) P Company acquired its 90% interest in S Company on January 1, 19X1 for $60,000, with the excess of cost over the book value of the subsidiary's net assets attributable entirely to land. Thus, no amortization entry appears on P Company's books nor is any secondary reclassification entry required in consolidation.

The parent's investment account is analyzed from January 1, 19X1 through December 31, 19X2 in Illustration 9-3. The December 31, 19X2 primary elimination entry obtained from this analysis is as follows:

Common stock	36,000	
Retained earnings—S Company (beginning of year)	21,600	
Equity in net income of subsidiary	18,900	
Land	8,700	
Investment in subsidiary		85,200

Illustration 9-3
Updating the expanded analysis of the investment in S Company's common stock from January 1, 19X1 through December 31, 19X2 using the equity method

	Total Cost	Common Stock	Book Value Element — Retained Earnings Prior Years	Book Value Element — Retained Earnings Current Year	Current Value over Book Value Element Land
Balance, January 1, 19X1	$60,000	$36,000	$15,300(1)		$8,700
Equity in net income—					
19X1	6,300			$ 6,300	
Subtotal	$66,300	$36,000	$15,300	$ 6,300	$8,700
Reclassification			6,300	(6,300)	
Balance, December 31, 19X1	$66,300	$36,000	$21,600	$ -0-	$8,700
Equity in net income—					
19X2	18,900			18,900	
Subtotal	$85,200	$36,000	$21,600	$18,900	$8,700
Reclassification			18,900	(18,900)	
Balance, December 31, 19X2	$85,200	$36,000	$40,500	$ -0-	$8,700

(1) This amount was determined in the example on page 335.

Illustration 9-4
Memorandum analysis of subsidiary's retained earnings
from January 1, 19X1 through December 31, 19X2

	Total Subsidiary Retained Earnings	Allocable To: Preferred Stockholders	Common Stockholders	Common Stockholders' Interest in Retained Earnings Minority Interest (10%)	Parent's Interest (90%)
Balance, January 1, 19X1	$20,000	$3,000	$17,000	$1,700	$15,300
Net income—19X1..............	10,000	3,000	7,000	700	6,300
Balance, December 31, 19X1	$30,000	$6,000	$24,000	$2,400	$21,600
Net income, 19X2	24,000	3,000	21,000	2,100	18,900
Dividends paid on					
preferred stock	(6,000)	(6,000)			
Balance, December 31, 19X2	$48,000	$3,000	$45,000	$4,500	$40,500

Amount of 19X2 net income that accrues to minority interest:

60% of $3,000 earnings that accrue to preferred stockholders	$1,800
10% of $21,000 residual earnings that accrue to common stockholders	2,100
	$3,900

The subsidiary's retained earnings is analyzed on a memorandum basis from January 1, 19X1 through December 31, 19X2 in Illustration 9-4. This schedule separates the subsidiary's retained earnings into the amount allocable to the subsidiary's preferred stockholders and the residual amount, which is allocable to the common stockholders. On the consolidating statement worksheet, the subsidiary's retained earnings is shown in these two amounts to facilitate the consolidation process.

The amount of the minority interest deduction is readily determinable from this schedule, and the minority interest entry is as follows:

Minority interest (income statement) 3,900
      Retained earnings—S Company (posted
      to the net income line in the
      analysis of retained earnings) 3,900

Because the parent owns 40% of the subsidiary's outstanding preferred stock, 40% of the $3,000 of earnings that accrue to the preferred stockholders ($1,200) is reportable by the parent as part of consolidated net income. However, because the parent does not record this income under the equity method of accounting, the $1,200 is not included in the parent's general ledger Retained Earnings account. Accordingly, this $1,200 must be re-classified in consolidation from the subsidiary's retained earnings (specifically, from the portion of the subsidiary's retained earnings that is allocable to preferred stockholders) to the parent's retained earnings. The following worksheet entry accomplishes this:

Retained earnings—S Company (allocable to
    preferred stockholders) 1,200
      Retained earnings—P Company (posted to
      the net income line in the analysis
      of retained earnings) 1,200

The worksheet entry to eliminate the preferred stock investment is the same as shown previously, except that the debit to retained earnings is to the parent's retained earnings rather than to the subsidiary's retained earnings. This is because the dividends that were in arrears when the parent acquired the preferred stock were subsequently paid.

The worksheet entry to eliminate the preferred stock dividend income recorded by the parent company is as follows:

Dividend income 2,400
      Retained earnings (posted to the net
      income line in the analysis of
      retained earnings)[a] 2,400

[a] When a partially consolidated column is used on the worksheet and this entry is posted to the second set of elimination columns (the intercompany transactions elimination column), this credit would be posted to the parent's Retained Earnings account (because the debit posting is totaled at the net income line and then carried forward to the parent's retained earnings line). Technically, this is the proper way to deal with this elimination entry. When a partially consolidated column is not used (as in the example later in the chapter), this credit must be posted to the subsidiary's Retained Earnings account (inasmuch as the debit posting is one of several debit postings to the income statement, the total of which at the net income line is carried forward to the subsidiary's retained earnings line). The result in consolidation is the same, regardless of whether a partially consolidated column is used, because this entry has a wash effect on retained earnings.

The preceding five worksheet entries are used in Illustration 9-5 to prepare consolidated financial statements as of December 31, 19X2. (We assume that no other intercompany transactions require elimination.)

Summary of accounting for subsidiary's preferred stock

A subsidiary's preferred stock is treated as additional minority interest in the consolidated financial statements. The special features of a subsidiary's preferred stock may require that a portion of the subsidiary's retained earnings be shown as part of the minority interest in the consolidated financial statements. When a parent acquires some or all of a subsidiary's outstanding preferred stock, the acquired preferred stock is treated as retired for consolidated reporting purposes. A gain on retirement of preferred stock is credited to additional paid-in capital; a loss is charged to additional paid-in capital to the extent available, with any remaining loss charged to retained earnings. Dividend income recorded by the parent is also eliminated in consolidation.

Review questions

1. From a consolidated viewpoint, what is the substance of an intercompany bond purchase?
2. How is the gain or loss on the extinguishment of debt determined?
3. Are gains and losses on extinguishment of debt extraordinary items?
4. If appropriate entries are made in consolidation to effect the retirement of intercompany bonds in the year that they are acquired, why are entries in consolidation necessary in subsequent years?

Illustration 9-5

P COMPANY AND SUBSIDIARY (S COMPANY)					
Consolidating Statement Worksheet					
For the Year Ended December 31, 19X2					
	P	S	Eliminations		Consoli-
	Company	Company	Dr.	Cr.	dated
Income Statement:					
Sales	650,000	230,000			880,000
Income from subsidiary:					
Equity in net income	18,900		18,900(1)		-0-
Dividend income on					
preferred stock	2,400		2,400(4)		-0-
Subtotal	671,300	230,000	21,300		880,000
Cost of goods sold	390,000	130,000			520,000
Marketing expenses	100,000	35,000			135,000
Administrative expenses	60,000	20,000			80,000
Interest expense	30,000	5,000			35,000
Subtotal	580,000	190,000			770,000
Income before Income Taxes . . .	91,300	40,000	21,300		110,000
Income tax expense @ 40% . .	(28,000)	(16,000)			(44,000)
Income before Minority Interest . .	63,300	24,000	21,300		66,000
Minority interest				3,900(3)	(3,900)
Net Income	63,300	24,000	25,200		62,100
Balance Sheet:					
Investments in S Company:					
Preferred stock	21,000			21,000(2)	-0-
Common stock	85,200			85,200(1)	-0-
Land	80,000	30,000	8,700(1)		118,700
Other assets	576,400	246,000			822,400
Total assets	762,600	276,000	8,700	106,200	941,100
Liabilities	329,000	138,000			467,000
Preferred stock		50,000	20,000(2)		30,000M
Common stock:					
P Company	300,000				300,000
S Company		40,000	36,000(1)		4,000M
Additional paid-in capital				1,400(2)	1,400
Retained earnings—P Company:					
Beginning of year	111,300				111,300
+ Net income	63,300		2,400(2)	1,200(5)	62,100
− Dividends declared	(41,000)				(41,000)
End of year	133,600		2,400	1,200	132,400
Retained earnings—S Company:					
Allocable to preferred		3,000	1,200(5)		1,800M
Allocable to common					
Beginning of year		24,000	21,600(1)		2,400M
+ Net income		21,000	25,200	3,900(3) 2,400(4)	2,100M
End of year		45,000	48,000	6,300	4,500M
Total liabilities and equity . . .	762,600	276,000	106,400	8,900	941,100
Proof of debit and credit postings			115,100	115,100	
			Total minority interest		40,300

Explanation of entries:
  (1) The primary elimination entry.
  (2) The preferred stock investment elimination entry.
  (3) The minority interest entry.
  (4) The dividend income elimination entry.
  (5) The parent's equity in earnings that accrue to the preferred stockholders entry.

5. If a subsidiary acquires a parent company's bonds, is a minority interest entry required in connection with the entry made in consolidation to treat the bonds as retired? Why or why not?
6. Is interest income earned on an affiliate's bonds considered an intercompany transaction? Must all intercompany transactions be eliminated?
7. Is the book value of a company's common stock computed differently solely because it is a subsidiary?
8. What reasons might explain why a portion of a subsidiary's retained earnings is considered not allocable to common shareholders?
9. Under the equity method of accounting, are preferred stock dividends always deducted from net income?
10. How is the acquisition of an 80% owned subsidiary's preferred stock similar to the acquisition of 10% of the subsidiary's common shares? How is it different?
11. How is the analysis of a parent company's investment account by the individual components of the major conceptual elements prepared differently as a result of an acquired subsidiary having preferred stock with dividends in arrears that is callable at above par value?
12. When a partially owned subsidiary has preferred stock that is shown as additional minority interest in the consolidated financial statements, should the acquisition of some or all of the preferred stock above book value be treated as cost in excess of book value in accordance with the purchase method of accounting?

Discussion cases

Discussion case 9–1
Decision whether or not to use excess cash
to purchase subsidiary's bonds

P Company owns all of the outstanding common stock of S Company. S Company has outstanding $500,000 of 25-year, 10% debenture bonds, which it issued five years ago at a discount of $50,000. P Company has excess cash and is considering purchasing these bonds, which are currently selling at their face value. P Company's controller has indicated to the treasurer that a loss will be reflected in consolidation when these bonds are purchased. The treasurer has subsequently indicated to the controller that it might be best to avoid this loss by investing the excess cash elsewhere.

Required:
Evaluate the validity of these comments.

Discussion case 9–2
Decision whether or not to purchase subsidiary's bonds
to report a gain on extinguishment of debt

P Company owns all of the outstanding common stock of S Company. S Company has outstanding $1,000,000 of 15-year, 10% debenture bonds, which it issued five years ago at a premium of $75,000. P Company's management anticipates that consolidated earnings for this year will be lower than expected. Accordingly, management is evaluating ways to increase earnings for the remainder of this year.

The controller has suggested that P Company issue $1,000,000 of bonds and use the proceeds to acquire the outstanding bonds of S Company. S Company's bonds are currently selling at 90. Thus, a $150,000 gain can be generated and reported. P Company's anticipated borrowing rate is approximately 14%.

Required:
Evaluate the validity and merits of the controller's idea.

Discussion case 9–3
Reissuance of intercompany bond holdings

In 19X1, Procton Company acquired for $480,000 bonds of its wholly owned subsidiary, Silex Company. The acquired bonds were initially issued at their face value of $500,000. In 19X4, Procton Company needed cash and sold all of the bonds for $505,000, when the carrying value of the bond investment was $483,000. (The above purchase price and proceeds exclude amounts pertaining to interest income.)

Required:
Using the amounts determinable from the above information, explain the procedures that should be used in consolidation in 19X4 and later years to account for the reissuance of these bonds. Indicate why the procedures you recommend are appropriate.

Exercises

Exercise 9–1
Intercompany bonds: Preparing elimination entries—Wholly owned subsidiary (Parent–acquirer has discount and subsidiary–issuer has premium)

Pam Company owns 100% of the outstanding common stock of Sam Company. On January 1, 19X4, Pam Company acquired in the open market 20% of Sam Company's outstanding 10% bonds at a cost of $160,000. On January 1, 19X4, the carrying value of all of the bonds ($1,000,000 face amount) was $1,020,000, and the maturity date is December 31, 19X7. (Assume each company uses straight-line amortization for bond premium or discount.)

Required:
(1) Determine the gain or loss from early extinguishment of debt reported in con-solidation for 19X4.
(2) Determine the entry required in consolidation at January 1, 19X4.
(3) Determine the entries required in consolidation at December 31, 19X4.
(4) Determine the entries required in consolidation at December 31, 19X5.

Exercise 9–2
Intercompany bonds: Preparing elimination entries—Partially owned subsidiary (Exercise 9-1 revised to reflect partial ownership)

Assume the information in Exercise 9–1, except that Pam Company owns only 75% of the outstanding common stock of Sam Company.

Required:
The requirements are the same as for Exercise 9–1.

Exercise 9–3
Intercompany bonds: Preparing elimination entries—Wholly owned subsidiary (Parent–acquirer has premium and subsidiary–issuer has premium)

Pladd Company owns 100% of the outstanding common stock of Shane Company. On January 1, 19X3, Pladd Company acquired in the open market 60% of Shane Company's outstanding 10% bonds at a cost of $620,000. On January 1, 19X3, the carrying value of all of the bonds ($1,000,000 face amount) was $1,050,000, and their maturity date is December 31, 19X7. (Assume each company uses straight-line amortization for bond discount.)

Required:
(1) Determine the gain or loss from early extinguishment of debt reported in consolidation for 19X3.
(2) Determine the entry required in consolidation at January 1, 19X3.
(3) Determine the entries required in consolidation at December 31, 19X3.
(4) Determine the entries required in consolidation at December 31, 19X4.

Exercise 9–4
Intercompany bonds: Preparing elimination entries—Partially owned subsidiary (Exercise 9–3 revised to reflect partial ownership)

Assume the information in Exercise 9–3, except that Pladd Company owns only 80% of the outstanding common stock of Shane Company.

Required:
The requirements are the same as for Exercise 9–3.

Exercise 9–5
Intercompany bonds: Preparing elimination entries—Wholly owned subsidiary (Parent–acquirer has premium and subsidiary–issuer has discount)

Palance Company owns 100% of the outstanding common stock of Syker Company. On January 1, 19X1, Syker Company issued $10,000,000 of five-year, 10% bonds at 95. On January 1, 19X3, (2 years later) Palance Company acquired in the open market 30% of these bonds at 101. (Assume each company uses straight-line amortization for bond premium.) The maturity date of the bonds is January 1, 19X6.

Required:
(1) Determine the gain or loss from early extinguishment of debt reported in consolidation for 19X3.
(2) Determine the entry required in consolidation at January 1, 19X3.
(3) Determine the entries required in consolidation at December 31, 19X3.
(4) Determine the entries required in consolidation at December 31, 19X4.
(5) Determine the entries required in consolidation at December 31, 19X5.

Exercise 9–6
Intercompany bonds: Preparing elimination entries—Partially owned
subsidiary (Exercise 9–5 revised to reflect partial ownership)

Assume the information in Exercise 9–5, except that Palance Company owns only 90% of the outstanding common stock of Syker Company.

Required:
The requirements are the same as for Exercise 9–5.

Exercise 9–7
Preferred stock: Determining parent's share of retained earnings—
Wholly owned subsidiary (Parent owns none of subsidiary's
preferred stock)

On January 1, 19X1, Pogart Company acquired 100% of the outstanding common stock of Sergman Company for $350,000 cash. Assume that the total current value of Sergman Company's net assets equals the total book value. The equity structure of Sergman Company as of January 1, 19X1 is as follows:

50% Preferred stock, cumulative, callable at 103	
(dividends of $5,000 in arrears)	$100,000
Common stock	10,000
Additional paid-in capital	190,000
Retained earnings	80,000
	$380,000

Required:
Prepare an analysis of the investment account by the individual components of the major conceptual elements as of January 1, 19X1.

Exercise 9–8
Preferred stock: Determining parent's share of retained earnings—
Partially owned subsidiary (Exercise 9–7 revised to reflect partial
ownership)

Assume the information in Exercise 9–7, except that Pogart Company acquired only 60% of the outstanding common stock of Sergman Company for $210,000.

Required:
The requirement is the same as for Exercise 9–7.

Exercise 9–9
Preferred stock: Determining parent's share of retained earnings—
Wholly owned subsidiary (Parent owns none of subsidiary's
preferred stock)

On January 1, 19X1, Photo Company acquired 100% of the outstanding common stock of Snapco Company for $1,650,000 cash. Assume the total current value of Snapco Company net assets equals the total book value. The capital structure of Snapco Company as of January 1, 19X1 is as follows.

5% Convertible bonds	$ 500,000
10% Convertible bonds	1,000,000
4% Convertible preferred stock, cumulative, callable at 103 (dividends of $12,000 in arrears)	100,000
8% Preferred stock, cumulative, callable at 102 (dividends of $16,000 in arrears)	200,000
Common stock, $1 par value	300,000
Additional paid-in capital	700,000
Retained earnings	400,000

Note: Assume that the 5% convertible bonds are common stock equivalents under *APB Opinion No. 15.*

Required:
Prepare an expanded analysis of the investment account as of January 1, 19X1.

Exercise 9–10
Preferred stock: Determining parent's share of retained earnings— Partially owned subsidiary (Exercise 9–9 revised to reflect partial ownership)

Assume the information in Exercise 9–9, except that Photo Company acquired only 80% of the outstanding common stock of Snapco Company for $1,320,000.

Required:
The requirement is the same as for Exercise 9–9.

Problems

Problem 9–1
Intercompany bonds: Completing separate company income statements in year of acquisition—Wholly owned subsidiary (Parent–acquirer has discount and subsidiary–issuer has premium)

The partially completed income statements of P Company and its wholly owned subsidiary, S Company, for the year ended December 31, 19X6, are as follows:

	P Company	S Company
Sales	$5,500,000	$1,200,000
Equity in net income of S Company		
Cost of goods sold	(3,000,000)	(700,000)
Marketing expenses	(800,000)	(200,000)
Administrative expenses	(700,000)	(100,000)
Operating income		$ 200,000
Intercompany interest income		
Intercompany interest expense		
Interest expense		
Income before Income Taxes		
Income tax expense @ 40%		
Net Income		

Additional information:
(1) Assume P Company's cost for S Company's common stock equals its share of S Company's net assets at book value.

(2) On January 1, 19X6, P Company acquired 40% of S Company's outstanding 10% bonds ($1,000,000 face amount) at 90. S Company had initially issued these 10-year bonds on January 1, 19X4 at 105.
(3) Assume that neither company had any other investments or indebtedness that would give rise to interest income or interest expense.
(4) Assume each company uses straight-line amortization for bond premium or discount.
(5) Assume no additional income taxes need to be provided on the parent company's equity in the subsidiary's net income.

Required:
(1) Fill in the blanks in the above income statements.
(2) Prepare the entries required in consolidation at December 31, 19X6 relating to the intercompany bond holding.

Problem 9–2
Intercompany bonds: Preparing consolidated financial statements in year of acquisition—Wholly owned subsidiary (Parent–acquirer has discount and subsidiary–issuer has premium)

Pollo Company acquired 100% of the outstanding common stock of Star Company on January 1, 19X1. The cost of the investment was $10,000 in excess of the $60,000 book value of the net assets. This excess was assigned to goodwill and is being amortized over 10 years. On January 1, 19X6, Pollo Company acquired in the open market 75% of Star Company's outstanding 10% bonds at a total cost of $73,800. Information regarding Star's bonds as of the bond acquisition date is as follows:

Total face amount	$100,000
Unamortized bond premium.................................	$ 6,000
Maturity date	December 31,19X8
Interest payment dates	July 1 and January 1

The financial statements of each company for the year ended December 31, 19X6 are as follows:

	Pollo Company	Star Company
Income Statement (19X6):		
Sales..	$550,000	$370,000
Equity in net income of subsidiary	19,800[a]	
Amortization of cost in excess of book value	(1,000)[b]	
Cost of goods sold.......................................	(280,000)	(190,000)
Marketing expenses.......................................	(95,000)	(75,000)
Administrative expenses	(96,900)	(62,000)
Interest expense...	(16,000)	(2,000)
Intercompany interest expense		(6,000)
Intercompany interest income	7,900	
Income before Income Taxes	$ 88,800	$ 35,000
Income tax expense	(28,320)	(15,200)
Net Income	$ 60,480	$ 19,800

	Pollo Company	Star Company
Balance Sheet (December 31, 19X6):		
Current assets..	$291,800	$ 85,000
Investments in Star Company:		
Common stock	134,000	
Bonds	74,200	
Fixed assets, net	400,000	195,000
Total Assets.......................................	$900,000	$280,000
Current liabilities.....................................	$170,000	$ 46,000
Long-term debt (including premium)	200,000	26,000
Intercompany bonds payable.........................		75,000
Intercompany bond premium		3,000
Common stock	400,000	50,000
Retained earnings	130,000	80,000
Total Liabilities and Equity	$900,000	$280,000
Dividends declared.....................................	$ 10,000	$ -0-

[a] Assumed to be nontaxable.
[b] Not tax deductible.

Required:
(1) Prepare an analysis of the appropriate accounts as of January 1, 19X6 that shows how the gain or loss on early extinguishment of debt is determined.
(2) Prepare the entries required in consolidation at December 31, 19X6.
(3) Prepare a consolidating statement worksheet at December 31, 19X6.

Problem 9–3
Intercompany bonds: Preparing consolidated financial statements in year of acquisition—Partially owned subsidiary
(Problem 9–2 revised to reflect partial ownership)

Assume the information in Problem 9–2, except that Pollo Company acquired only 90% of the outstanding common stock of Star Company at a cost of its share of book value plus $9,000. The financial statements of each company for the year ended December 31, 19X6, revised to reflect 90% ownership in the subsidiary, are as follows:

	Pollo Company	Star Company
Income Statement (19X6):		
Sales..	$550,000	$370,000
Equity in net income of subsidiary	17,820[a]	
Amortization of cost in excess of book value ...	(900)[b]	
Cost of goods sold......................................	(280,000)	(190,000)
Marketing expenses.....................................	(95,000)	(75,000)
Administrative expenses	(96,900)	(62,000)
Interest expense	(16,000)	(2,000)
Intercompany interest expense		(6,000)
Intercompany interest income	7,900	
Income before Income Taxes	$ 86,920	$ 35,000
Income tax expense	(28,320)	(15,200)
Net Income	$ 58,600	$ 19,800

	Pollo Company	Star Company
Balance Sheet (December 31, 19X6):		
Current assets..	$298,800	$ 85,000
Investment in Star Company:		
Common stock	120,600	
Bonds	74,200	
Fixed assets, net	400,000	195,000
Total Assets..	$893,600	$280,000
Current liabilities......................................	$170,000	$ 46,000
Long-term debt (including unamortized premium).............	200,000	26,000
Intercompany bonds payable................................		75,000
Intercompany bond premium		3,000
Common stock	400,000	50,000
Retained earnings	123,600	80,000
Total Liabilities and Equity	$893,600	$280,000
Dividends declared....................................	$ 10,000	$ -0-

[a] Assumed to be nontaxable.
[b] Not tax deductible.

Same as prior with of $450
Min int of 300 M
_300 M_

Required:
(1) Prepare an analysis of the appropriate accounts as of January 1, 19X6 that shows how the gain or loss on early extinguishment of debt is determined.
(2) Prepare the entries required in consolidation at December 31, 19X6.
(3) Prepare a consolidating statement worksheet at December 31, 19X6.

Problem 9–4
Intercompany bonds: Preparing consolidated financial statements in year of acquisition—Wholly owned subsidiary (Parent–acquirer has discount and subsidiary–issuer has discount)

Poise Company acquired 100% of the outstanding common stock of Sascade Company on January 1, 19X5. The cost of the investment was $30,000 in excess of the $150,000 book value of the net assets. All of this excess was assigned to land. Also on January 1, 19X5, Poise Company acquired in the open market 60% of Sascade Company's outstanding 10% bonds at a total cost of $175,000. Information regarding Sascade's bonds as of the bond acquisition date is as follows:

Total face amount	$300,000
Unamortized bond discount	$ 25,000
Maturity date	December 31, 19X9
Interest payment dates	January 1 and July 1

The financial statements of each company for the year ended December 31, 19X5 are as follows.

	Poise Company	Sascade Company
Income Statement (19X5):		
Sales.	$625,000	$360,000
Equity in net income of subsidiary	34,800[a]	
Cost of goods sold	(305,000)	(175,000)
Marketing expenses	(118,000)	(62,000)
Administrative expenses	(91,000)	(38,000)
Interest expense	(50,000)	(14,000)
Intercompany interest expense		(21,000)
Intercompany interest income	19,000	
Income before Income Taxes	$114,800	$ 50,000
Income tax expense	(33,600)	(15,200)
Net Income	$ 81,200	$ 34,800
Balance Sheet (December 31, 19X5):		
Current assets	$139,000	$230,000
Investments in Sascade Company:		
Common stock	195,000	
Bonds	176,000	
Fixed assets, net	470,000	320,000
Total Assets	$980,000	$550,000
Current liabilities	$125,000	$105,000
Long-term debt (net of discount)	520,000	112,000
Intercompany bonds payable		180,000
Intercompany bond discount		(12,000)
Common stock	200,000	50,000
Retained earnings	135,000	115,000
Total Liabilities and Equity	$980,000	$550,000
Dividends declared	$ 15,000	$ 19,800

[a] Assumed to be nontaxable.

Required:
(1) Prepare an analysis of the appropriate accounts as of January 1, 19X5 that shows how the gain or loss on early extinguishment of debt is determined.
(2) Prepare the entries required in consolidation at December 31, 19X5.
(3) Prepare a consolidating statement worksheet at December 31, 19X5.

Problem 9–5
Intercompany bonds: Preparing consolidated financial statements in year of acquisition—Partially owned subsidiary
(Problem 9–4 revised to reflect partial ownership)

Assume the information in Problem 9–4, except that Poise Company acquired only 80% of the outstanding common stock of Sascade Company. The cost of the investment was $24,000 in excess of its share of the $150,000 book value of the net assets. All of this excess is assigned to land.

The revised amounts in Poise Company's 19X5 financial statements are as follows (all other amounts, except subtotals and totals, stay the same):

Equity in net income of subsidiary	$ 27,840
Investment in common stock of subsidiary	156,000

Current assets	$171,040
Retained earnings	128,040

Required:
The requirements are the same as for Problem 9–4.

Problem 9–6
**Preferred stock: Determining parent's share of retained earnings—
Wholly owned subsidiary (Parent owns none of subsidiary's
preferred stock)**

On January 1, 19X1, Paltese Company acquired 100% of the outstanding common
stock of Salcon Company for $600,000 cash. All cost in excess of book value is
allocable to goodwill, which has a 10-year life. Salcon Company's capital structure
as of January 1, 19X1 is as follows:

5% Convertible bonds	$1,000,000
6% Convertible preferred stock, callable at 105,	
cumulative (dividends of $18,000 in arrears)	100,000
Common stock, $10 par value	500,000
Retained earnings	30,000

During 19X1, Salcon Company had net income of $26,000. It declared and paid
cash dividends of $12,000 on its preferred stock.

Required:
(1) Prepare an analysis of the investment account as of January 1, 19X1.
(2) Update the analysis of the investment account for 19X1 activity under the equity
    method of accounting.

Problem 9–7
**Preferred stock: Determining parent's share of retained earnings—
Partially owned subsidiary (Problem 9–6 revised to reflect partial
ownership)**

Assume the information in Problem 9–6, except that Paltese Company acquired
only 60% of the outstanding common stock of Salcon Company for $360,000 cash.

Required:
The requirements are the same as for Problem 9–6.

Problem 9–8
**Preferred stock: Determining parent's share of retained earnings
and preparing preferred stock elimination entry—Wholly owned
subsidiary (Parent acquires some of subsidiary's preferred stock
subsequent to business combination date)**

On January 1, 19X1, Preenstreet Company acquired all of the outstanding common
stock of Sorre Company for $450,000 cash. All cost in excess of the book value
of the net assets is allocable to land. Sorre Company's capital structure at January
1, 19X1 is as follows.

5% Preferred stock, cumulative, callable at 102	
(dividends of $15,000 in arrears)	$100,000
Common stock, $10 par value	350,000
Retained earnings	50,000
	$500,000

On December 31, 19X1, Preenstreet Company acquired 20% of Sorre Company's outstanding preferred stock for $17,000. During 19X1, Sorre Company had net income of $30,000 and declared cash dividends of $5,000 on its preferred stock.

Required:
(1) Prepare an analysis of the investment account at January 1, 19X1.
(2) Update the analysis of the investment account through December 31, 19X1.
(3) Determine the entry required in consolidation at December 31, 19X1 relating to the preferred stock.

Problem 9–9
Preferred stock: Determining parent's share of retained earnings and preparing preferred stock elimination entry—Partially owned subsidiary (Problem 9–8 revised to reflect partial ownership)

Assume the information in Problem 9–8, except that Preenstreet Company acquired only 80% of the outstanding common stock of Sorre Company for $360,000 cash.

Required:
The requirements are the same as for Problem 9–8.

Problem 9–10
Preferred stock: Preparing consolidated financial statements; parent acquires some of subsidiary's preferred stock subsequent to business combination date—Wholly owned subsidiary

On January 1, 19X1, P Company acquired 100% of the outstanding common stock of S Company for $450,000 cash. All cost in excess of book value is allocable to land. S Company's capital structure on January 1, 19X1 is as follows:

5% Preferred stock, cumulative, callable at 104	
(dividends of $10,000 in arrears)	$100,000
Common stock, $100 par value	350,000
Retained earnings	50,000
	$500,000

Also on January 1, 19X1, P Company acquired 60% of S Company's outstanding preferred stock for $65,000. During 19X1, S Company declared cash dividends of $10,000 on its preferred stock. The financial statements for each company for the year ended December 31, 19X1 are as follows.

	P Company	S Company
Income Statement (19X1):		
Sales......	$750,000	$350,000
Equity in net income of S Company	55,000	
Dividend income (on S Company preferred stock)	6,000	
Cost of goods sold	(400,000)	(200,000)
Marketing, administrative, and interest expenses......	(150,000)	(50,000)
Income before Income Taxes	$261,000	$100,000
Income tax expense @ 40%......	(80,000)	(40,000)
Net Income	$181,000	$ 60,000
Balance Sheet (December 31, 19X1):		
Investments in S Company:		
Common stock	$505,000	
Preferred stock......	65,000	
Other assets	380,000	$585,000
Total Assets	$950,000	$585,000
Liabilities	$300,000	$ 35,000
Preferred stock......		100,000
Common stock	400,000	350,000
Retained earnings	250,000	100,000
Total Liabilities and Equity......	$950,000	$585,000
Dividends declared on common stock	$100,000	$ -0-

Assume no additional income taxes need to be provided on the parent company's equity in the subsidiary's earnings or the preferred stock dividend income.

Required:
(1) Prepare an analysis of the investment in common stock of the subsidiary as of January 1, 19X1.
(2) Update the analysis of the investment in common stock of the subsidiary through December 31, 19X1 under the equity method of accounting.
(3) Prepare the primary elimination entry at December 31, 19X1.
(4) Prepare the elimination entry related to preferred stock at December 31, 19X1.
(5) Prepare the entry to eliminate the preferred stock dividend income at December 31, 19X1.
(6) Prepare a consolidating statement worksheet for the year ended December 31, 19X1.

10 Changes in Parent's Ownership Interest and Other Changes in Subsidiary's Capital Accounts

CHANGES IN PARENT'S OWNERSHIP INTEREST

Changes in a parent's ownership interest in a subsidiary occur infrequently with respect to each parent–subsidiary relationship. The procedures used to account for some of these changes are based on principles discussed in earlier chapters. Other changes involve such new issues as how to determine and account for the effect of a change in the ownership interest. Although variations of certain types of changes can occur, only the basic principle involved in each type is discussed and illustrated.

Acquisition of minority interest

APB Opinion No. 16 allows only the use of the purchase method to account for the acquisition of minority interests. It states:

> The acquisition . . . of some or all of the stock held by minority stockholders of a subsidiary—whether acquired by the parent, the subsidiary itself, or another affiliate— should be accounted for by the purchase method rather than by the pooling of interests method.[1]

Acquisition of minority interest by parent.   The parent's acquisition of any or all of the minority interest is merely a block acquisition. The cost of the block of stock acquired must be separated into its individual components in the same manner that the initial investment cost of a partially owned subsidiary is separated into its individual components (illustrated in Chapter 5). Thus, the parent's acquisition of any or all of the minority interest presents no new accounting issues. The acquisition of any or all of the minority interest by the subsidiary is also a block acquisition from a consolidated viewpoint, but the procedures for this treatment must be explained.

Acquisition of minority interest by subsidiary.   When the subsidiary acquires any or all of the minority interest and retires the acquired shares (which it does only if directed to do so by the parent), the accounting in consolidation must reflect the purchase method of accounting with respect to the shares acquired. The entries made by the subsidiary are the same as those made by any corporation acquiring and retiring its outstanding shares—that is, debit the capital accounts and credit Cash (assuming cash is the consideration given). The parent does not adjust the total carrying

---

[1] *APB Opinion No. 16*, ''Accounting for Business Combinations'' (New York: AICPA, 1970), paragraph 43.

value of its Investment in Subsidiary account regardless of the price paid by the subsidiary to acquire the minority interest. However, if the subsidiary pays more or less than book value per share, the parent's total dollar interest in the subsidiary's net assets at their book value decreases or increases, respectively. Accordingly, the expanded analysis of the investment account by individual components must be adjusted to reflect that the parent's interest in the subsidiary's net assets at book value has changed. To the extent that the parent's total dollar interest decreases (when the subsidiary pays more than book value), the book value element must be decreased and the current value over book value element and/or goodwill element must be increased by an offsetting amount. The reverse occurs when the subsidiary pays less than book value. Because this adjustment within the expanded analysis does not change the total carrying value of the investment, it is essentially a *reclassification* of amounts between the individual components.

Illustration:
Acquisition of entire minority interest by subsidiary at above book value

Assume the following information:

	Percent	Shares
Parent's ownership in subsidiary:		
Before acquisition of minority interest by subsidiary.............	80	800
After acquisition of minority interest by subsidiary	100	800
Purchase price paid by subsidiary to acquire all 200 outstanding		
shares held by minority interest shareholders	$40,000	

This information is used in Illustration 10-1 to calculate the decrease in the parent's interest in the subsidiary's net assets. (The procedure is the same when the parent's equity in the subsidiary's net assets increases.)

In reviewing Illustration 10-1, the following points should be understood:

(1) The minority shareholders received an additional $11,000 in excess of their ownership interest in the subsidiary's net assets at book value.
(2) This excess payment to the minority shareholders dilutes the parent's interest in the subsidiary's net assets at book value by $11,000.
(3) The $11,000 excess payment must be treated as cost in excess of book value by the parent. From a consolidated viewpoint, it is irrelevant that the subsidiary acquired the minority interest rather than the parent.

To reflect the $11,000 excess payment as cost in excess of book value, the parent adjusts its expanded analysis of the investment account by the individual components of the major conceptual elements. Assuming the parent had $50,000 of unamortized cost in excess of its share of the subsidiary's net assets at book value as of the minority interest acquisition date, the required reclassification is determined as follows on page 360.

Illustration 10-1
Calculation of decrease in parent's interest in subsidiary's net assets as a result of subsidiary's acquisition of entire minority interest at amount in excess of book value

	Subsidiary's Equity Accounts	Book Value per Share	Parent's Interest		Minority Interest	
			Percent	Amount	Percent	Amount
Before acquisition of minority interest:						
Common stock	$ 70,000		80	$ 56,000	20	$ 14,000
Retained earnings	75,000		80	60,000	20	15,000
	$145,000	$145		$116,000		$ 29,000
After acquisition of minority interest:						
Common stock	$ 56,000[a]		100	$ 56,000		—
Retained earnings	49,000		100	49,000		—
	$105,000	$131.25		$105,000		—
Decrease in equity	$ (40,000)			$ (11,000)		$(29,000)

[a] For simplicity, we assume that the $40,000 payment for the shares acquired and retired was properly charged to the subsidiary's capital accounts as follows:

Common stock (20% of $70,000)	$14,000
Retained earnings (residual)	26,000
	$40,000

Note: The parent's new ownership percentage is derived by dividing the shares owned by the parent (800 shares) by the outstanding shares of the subsidiary (800 shares). In other words, the parent's holdings remain constant—only the outstanding shares of the subsidiary (the denominator used in calculating the parent's ownership percentage) decrease.

| | Book Value Element | | Cost in |
	Common Stock	Retained Earnings	Excess of Book Value[a]
Balances immediately *before the acquisition* of the minority interest	$56,000[b]	$60,000[b]	$50,000
Required reclassification to treat the $11,000 excess payment as cost in excess of book value.............................		(11,000)[c]	11,000[d]
Balances immediately *after the acquisition* of the minority interest......................	$56,000[b]	$49,000[b]	$61,000

[a] The breakdown of this cost into its individual components is not shown, because it is not necessary with respect to the principle involved.
[b] This amount was obtained from the analysis in Illustration 10-1.
[c] This change of interest in this individual component element is determined by using the balances *before* and the balances *after* the acquisition of the minority interest.
[d] This is the $11,000 excess payment. It equals the total dilution of the parent's interest in the subsidiary's net assets at book value.

The required reclassification takes place entirely within the expanded analysis of the investment account by the individual components of the major conceptual elements. The total carrying value of the parent's investment account is unchanged. This reclassification prevents the parent from reporting a loss on the acquisition of the minority interest related to the dilution of the parent's interest in the subsidiary's net assets at book value. Of course, the $11,000 cost in excess of book value must be separated into its individual components in accordance with the purchase method of accounting. After the required reclassification is made within the expanded analysis of the investment account, the analysis is updated in the normal manner. The ending balances as of any future consolidation date are the sources for the primary elimination entry, as illustrated in Chapters 4 and 5.

The following is a "before and after" presentation of the applicable accounts on the consolidating statement worksheet:

Immediately before the acquisition of the minority interest (thousands of dollars)

	P Company	S Company	Eliminations Dr.	Eliminations Cr.	Consolidated
Cash		40			40
Investment in S Company	166			166	—
Cost in excess of book value			50		50
Common stock		70	56		14M
Retained earnings		75	60		15M

Immediately after the acquisition of the minority interest (thousands of dollars)

	P Company	S Company	Eliminations Dr.	Eliminations Cr.	Consolidated
Cash		—			—
Investment in S Company	166			166	—
Cost in excess of book value			61		61
Common stock		56	56		—
Retained earnings		49	49		—

Reviewing this "before and after" presentation, we can see that the effect on the consolidated financial statements is as if the following entry had been made from a consolidated viewpoint:

Minority interest..	29,000	
Cost in excess of book value	11,000	
Cash		40,000

(handwritten margin note: not a book or a worksheet — Entry — just a demonstration entry.)

Acquisition of part of the minority interest by the subsidiary. In the preceding example, the subsidiary acquired all of the minority interest. When the subsidiary acquires only a portion of the minority interest at more or less than book value per share, both the parent's and the remaining minority shareholders' total dollar interests in the subsidiary's net assets at book value decrease or increase, respectively. Only the parent's decrease or increase, as the case may be, results in an increase or decrease, respectively, of the current value over book value element and/or goodwill element.

Disposal of interest in a subsidiary

A parent may dispose of a portion or all of its common stock investment in a subsidiary. The former often occurs when the parent wants to raise cash, whereas the latter usually occurs when the parent decides either to dispose of a line of business or to contract operations.

100% Disposals. The complete disposal of the investment in a subsidiary's common stock fits into two categories:

(1) Disposals of a segment. This category includes subsidiaries whose activities represent a separate major line of business or class of customer. Special reporting requirements pertaining to disposals of segments are set forth in paragraphs 13–18 of *APB Opinion No. 30,* "Reporting the Results of Operations." These requirements are discussed in Chapter 15, "Segment Reporting."

(2) All other disposals. This category includes disposals that constitute a contraction of operations—that is, the consolidated group remains in the line of business in which the subsidiary is engaged but at a reduced manufacturing, retailing, or service capacity. Such disposals do not fit the definition of extraordinary events; although infrequent, business contractions are not unusual. The reporting for disposals in this category is governed by the provisions of paragraph 26 of *APB Opinion No. 30,* which states:

> A material event or transaction that is unusual in nature or occurs infrequently but not both, and therefore does not meet both criteria for classification as an extraordinary item, should be reported as a separate component of income from continuing operations.[2]

Partial disposals. When a parent sells a portion of its common stock holdings in a subsidiary, the accounting problem is that of determining the

---

[2] *APB Opinion No. 30,* "Reporting the Results of Operations" (New York: AICPA, 1973), paragraph 26.

amount of the reduction to the investment account. This amount is compared with the proceeds from the sale to determine the reportable gain or loss. The two categories of partial disposal are as follows:

(1) Shares acquired in a single acquisition. When all of the shares owned were acquired at one time, the investment account should be reduced using the average cost of all shares owned.

(2) Shares acquired in block acquisitions. When the shares owned were acquired at more than one time (in block acquisitions or when the minority interest was subsequently acquired), three methods of reducing the investment account are available:
(a) The average cost method.
(b) The specific identification method.
(c) The first-in, first-out method.

Our preference is the average cost method, because the other two methods introduce an artificial element. For instance, under the specific identification method, the gain or loss reported could be partially determined by the particular block of stock selected for sale; whereas under the first-in, first-out method, we use an assumed flow concept initially intended for inventory pricing. Furthermore, the manner of acquiring the shares is irrelevant to the accounting for the disposal of shares—the issue is the amount of the total ownership interest that is disposed of. This percentage answer should also apply to the carrying value of the cost of the investment. (Although only the specific identification and the first-in, first-out methods are allowed for federal income tax reporting purposes, this has no bearing on which method should be used for financial reporting purposes.)

Regardless of the method selected to reduce the investment account, it must be applied to each individual component in the expanded analysis of the investment account. Before the investment account is reduced, however, it must be adjusted in accordance with the equity method of accounting up to the date of sale.

Illustration:
Partial disposal using average cost method

Assume the following information:

	Percent	Shares
Parent's ownership in subsidiary:		
Before partial disposal	80	800
After partial disposal	60	600
Shares sold		200
Subsidiary's net income:		
Jan. 1, 19X8–June 30, 19X8	$20,000	
July 1, 19X8–Dec. 31, 19X8	10,000	
Total	$30,000	
Disposal date	July 1, 19X8	
Proceeds from sale	$40,000	
Subsidiary's dividends:		

On the last day of the first three quarters, dividends of $5,000 were declared; no dividends were declared in the fourth quarter of the year.

In Illustration 10-2, the expanded analysis of the investment account is updated for the year in which a disposal of a portion of shares held in a subsidiary takes place. In reviewing Illustration 10-2, the following points should be understood:

(1) The reportable gain on the disposal of the shares sold is determined as follows:

Proceeds from sale	$40,000
Average cost of shares sold	(28,625)
Gain	$11,375

(2) The following journal entry on the parent's books records this disposal:

Cash	40,000	
Investment in S Company		28,625
Gain on sale of subsidiary's stock		11,375

(3) The December 31, 19X8 balance in the Equity in Earnings of Subsidiary account in the parent's general ledger is as follows:

Equity in earnings Jan. 1, 19X8–June 30, 19X8	$16,000
Equity in earnings July 1, 19X8–Dec. 31, 19X8	6,000
Total	$22,000

(4) The primary elimination entry used to prepare the December 31, 19X8 consolidated financial statements is from the analysis of the investment account as of December 31, 19X8 (shown in Illustration 10-2). The entry is as follows:

Common stock	24,000	
Retained earnings	31,500	
Equity in earnings of subsidiary	18,000	
Land	6,000	
Building	15,000	
Accumulated depreciation		2,250
Goodwill	4,500	
Dividends declared		9,000
Investment in subsidiary		87,750

(5) The primary elimination entry does not totally eliminate the $22,000 balance in the Equity in Earnings of Subsidiary account. The remaining $4,000 represents the equity interest of the shares sold in the first six months' earnings of the subsidiary (20% of $20,000).

(6) This remaining $4,000 must also be eliminated to prevent an overstatement of consolidated earnings. The appropriate elimination entry is as follows:

Equity in earnings of subsidiary	4,000	
Retained earnings—S Company (net income line)		4,000

Illustration 10-2

Updating the expanded analysis of the investment account for a partial disposal using the average cost method

	Total Cost =	Common Stock +	Book Value Element — Retained Earnings: Prior Year +	Current Year: Earnings −	Current Year: Dividends +	Land +	Building: Cost +	Building: Accum. Depr. +	Goodwill Element
Remaining life as of Jan. 1, 19X8:						(Indef.)	(18 yr)		(4 yr)
Balance, Jan. 1, 19X8	$108,000	$32,000	$42,000			$8,000	$20,000	$(2,000)	$8,000
Equity in net income (80% of $20,000)	16,000			$16,000					
Dividends—first and second quarters	(8,000)				$(8,000)				
Amortization of cost over book value	(1,500)							(500)[b]	(1,000)[c]
Balance, June 30, 19X8	$114,500	$32,000	$42,000	$16,000	$(8,000)	$8,000	$20,000	$(2,500)	$7,000
Disposal, July 1, 19X8[a]	(28,625)	(8,000)	(10,500)	(4,000)	2,000	(2,000)	(5,000)	625	(1,750)
Balance, July 1, 19X8	$85,875	$24,000	$31,500	$12,000	$(6,000)	$6,000	$15,000	$(1,875)	$5,250
Equity in net income (60% of $10,000)	6,000			6,000					
Dividends—third quarter	(3,000)				(3,000)				
Amortization of cost over book value	(1,125)							(375)	(750)
Balance, December 31, 19X8	$87,750	$24,000	$31,500	$18,000	$(9,000)	$6,000	$15,000	$(2,250)	$4,500

[a] Each individual component is reduced by 25%, the ratio of the shares sold to total shares held (200/800 = 25%).

[b] $18,000 carrying value/18 years = $1,000/yr; ½ year = $500. (A 17½-year remaining life is used to compute the amortization expense for the last half of 19X8).

[c] $8,000/4 years = $2,000/yr; ½ year = $1,000. (A 3½-year remaining life is used to compute the amortization expense for the last half of 19X8.)

As in the case of the minority interest entry, this entry affects only the income statement. It has a wash effect on the balance sheet.

(7) The minority interest deduction for the year is determined as follows:

	Jan. 1, 19X8– June 30, 19X8	July 1, 19X8– Dec. 31, 19X8	Total
Subsidiary's net income	$20,000	$10,000	$30,000
Minority interest ownership percentage.............................	20%	40%	
Minority interest	$ 4,000	$ 4,000	$ 8,000

Accordingly, the minority interest would be as follows:

Minority interest (income statement) 8,000
      Retained earnings—S Company (net income line)   8,000

(8) By updating the investment account analysis as illustrated, the disposal of a portion of the holdings in a subsidiary's common stock does not affect the basic procedures used to prepare consolidated financial statements.

In Illustration 10-3, a consolidating statement worksheet for the year ended December 31, 19X8 is prepared using the above elimination entries and minority interest entry. The secondary elimination entry is as follows:

The secondary elimination entry:

Cost of goods sold.. 2,625
      Amortization of cost in excess of book value   2,625
(We assume that all depreciation expense and all goodwill amortization is properly classifiable to cost of goods sold.)

Issuance of additional common stock by subsidiary

Rather than disposing of a portion of its stock holdings in a subsidiary to raise funds for the consolidated group, a parent may direct the subsidiary to issue additional common stock to the public.

If the shares issued to the public are sold below the current book value per share of the subsidiary's common stock as of the issuance date, the parent's total dollar interest in the subsidiary's net assets at book value is diluted and thus decreases. On the other hand, when the subsidiary issues shares above the existing book value of its common stock as of the issuance date, the parent's total dollar interest in the subsidiary's net assets at book value increases. The issue is how to account for an increase or a decrease in the parent's interest in the subsidiary's net assets at book value as a result of the issuance of the additional shares.

Accountants agree that an increase or a decrease in the parent's interest in the subsidiary's net assets at book value should result in an increase or decrease, respectively, to the carrying value of the investment. Accountants

Illustration 10-3

	P Company	S Company	Eliminations Dr.	Eliminations Cr.	Consolidated
P COMPANY AND SUBSIDIARY (S COMPANY)					
Consolidating Statement Worksheet					
For the Year Ended December 31, 19X8					
Income Statement:					
Sales..........................	615,000	350,000			965,000
Gain on sale of subsidiary's stock................	11,375				11,375
Income from subsidiary:					
Equity in net income.........	22,000		18,000(1)		-0-
			4,000(3)		
Amortization of cost in excess of book value......	(2,625)			2,625(2)	-0-
Subtotal	645,750	350,000	22,000	2,625	976,375
Cost of goods sold	305,375	180,000	2,625(2)		488,000
Marketing expenses	145,000	70,000			215,000
Administrative expenses........	60,000	42,000			102,000
Interest expense...............	16,000	8,000			24,000
Subtotal	526,375	300,000	2,625		829,000
Income before Income Taxes and Minority Interest........	119,375	50,000	24,625	2,625	147,375
Income tax expense @ 40%..	(40,000)	(20,000)			(60,000)
Income before Minority Interest	79,375	30,000	24,625	2,625	87,375
Minority interest				8,000(4)	(8,000)
Net Income	79,375	30,000	32,625	2,625	79,375
Balance Sheet:					
Current assets	311,000	109,000			420,000
Investment in S Company	87,750			87,750(2)	-0-
Land	80,000	30,000	6,000(1)		116,000
Building	400,000	100,000	15,000(1)		515,000
Accum. depreciation	(330,000)	(58,000)		2,250(1)	(390,250)
Equipment, net	260,000	70,000			330,000
Goodwill			4,500(1)		4,500
Total assets...............	808,750	251,000	25,500	90,000	995,250
Liabilities	278,750	143,500			422,250
Common stock:					
P Company	300,000				300,000
S Company		40,000	24,000(1)		16,000M
Retained earnings—P Company:					
Beginning of year.............	211,625				211,625
+ Net income	79,375				79,375
− Dividends declared........	(61,000)				(61,000)
End of year	230,000				230,000
Retained earnings—S Company:					
Beginning of year.............		52,500	31,500(1)		21,000M
+ Net income		30,000	32,625	2,625	12,000M
				4,000(3)	
				8,000(4)	
− Dividends declared........		(15,000)		9,000(1)	(6,000)M
End of year		67,500	64,125	23,625	27,000M
Total liabilities and equity...	808,750	251,000	88,125	23,625	995,250
Proof of debit and credit postings			113,625	113,625	

Explanation of entries:
(1) The primary elimination entry.
(2) The secondary elimination entry.
(3) The elimination of equity in subsidiary's net income from shares held January 1, 19X8 to July 1, 19X8, which were sold.
(4) The minority interest entry.

do not agree on the treatment of the offsetting credit or debit. The two alternative accounting treatments are as follows:

(1) Record as an adjustment to the parent's additional paid-in capital. (This treatment carries through to the consolidated balance sheet.)
(2) Record as a gain or loss in the parent's income statement. (The gain or loss **is not eliminated in consolidation.**)

Rationale for additional paid-in capital treatment. Under the first alternative, the issuance of additional common stock by the subsidiary is a capital-raising transaction for the consolidated group. Because capital-raising transactions do not cause either a gain or a loss on a separate company basis, they should not cause either a gain or a loss on a consolidated basis. In consolidation, an increase in the parent's interest in the subsidiary's net assets at book value is deemed to be a capital contribution from the minority shareholders to the parent. Similarly, a decrease in the parent's interest in the subsidiary's net assets at book value is treated in consolidation as a capital contribution from the parent to the minority shareholders. This approach fits under the entity theory, which (as discussed in Chapter 5) maintains that a new reporting entity with two classes of common shareholders results from the consolidation process.

Rationale for income statement treatment. Under the second alternative, the parent gains or loses when a subsidiary issues additional common stock above or below, respectively, the book value of its existing outstanding common stock. As a result, the gain or loss should be reflected in the income statement. The advocates of this approach also contend that substantively the sale of a subsidiary's shares by the parent (pursuant to a partial disposal)—whereby a gain or loss is recorded in the income statement—is no different from the issuance of additional common shares by a subsidiary. This approach fits under the parent company theory, which (as discussed in Chapter 5) views the parent as the reporting entity in consolidation.

Position of the Securities and Exchange Commission. In 1983, the staff of the SEC issued *Staff Accounting Bulletin No. 51,* which expresses the SEC's views concerning the subsidiary's issuance of additional common stock. According to the SEC staff, companies may recognize gains or losses resulting from these transactions when the subsidiary's sale of shares is not a part of a corporate reorganization contemplated or planned by the parent company. (The staff had previously required, without benefit of any ruling or publication, that these transactions be accounted for in consolidated financial statements as capital transactions.) Companies must show any such gain or loss as a separate item in the consolidated income statement, without regard to materiality. Furthermore, the gain or loss must be clearly designated as nonoperating. Companies also should include an appropriate description of the transaction in the notes to the financial statements.

Concluding comments. The choice between these alternative treatments is purely subjective, depending on whether the parent company theory or the entity theory is used. The journal entry in the following illustration reflects the second alternative, to be consistent with the parent company theory, which we used in Chapter 5 illustrations.

Illustration:
Issuance of additional shares at below book value

Assume the following information:

	Percent	Shares
Parent's ownership in subsidiary:		
Before subsidiary issues additional shares to the public	80	800
After subsidiary issues additional shares to the public	$66\frac{2}{3}$	800
Minority ownership in subsidiary:		
Before subsidiary issues additional shares to the public	20	200
After subsidiary issues additional shares to the public	$33\frac{1}{3}$	400
Proceeds from issuance of 200 additional shares of the		
subsidiary's no-par common stock at $100 per share........	$20,000	

In Illustration 10-4, the above information is used to calculate the loss to the parent. (The procedure is the same when there is a gain.) In reviewing Illustration 10-4, the following points should be understood:

(1) The entry to record the loss on the parent's books is as follows:

Loss resulting from dilution of interest in subsidiary's net assets.................................	6,000	
Investment in subsidiary		6,000

This loss is not eliminated in consolidation.

(2) The individual components within the book value element in the expanded analysis of the investment account are adjusted as follows as a result of the entry in (1), above.

	Individual Components within the Parent's Analysis of the Investment Account	
	Common Stock	Retained Earnings
Balance immediately *before* issuance of additional shares	$56,000[a]	$60,000[a]
Adjustment as a result of dilution of interest in subsidiary......................................	4,000	(10,000)
Balance immediately *after* issuance of additional shares	$60,000[a]	$50,000[a]

[a] Per Illustration 10-4.

(3) After the adjustment is made for the dilution of the parent's interest in the subsidiary's net assets, the analysis of the investment account is updated in the normal manner. The ending balances as of any future consolidation date are the sources of the primary elimination entry, as illustrated in earlier chapters.

Illustration 10-4
Calculation of parent's dilution of equity in net assets of subsidiary—
Subsidiary sells additional common stock below book value

	Subsidiary's Equity Accounts	Book Value per Share	Parent's Interest		Minority Interest	
			Percent	Amount	Percent	Amount
Before issuance of additional shares:						
Common stock	$ 70,000		80	$ 56,000	20	$14,000
Retained earnings	75,000		80	60,000	20	15,000
	$145,000	$145		$116,000		$29,000
After issuance of additional shares:						
Common stock	$ 90,000[a]		66⅔	$ 60,000	33⅓	$30,000
Retained earnings	75,000		66⅔	50,000	33⅓	25,000
	$165,000	$137.50		$110,000		$55,000
Difference	$ 20,000			$ (6,000)		$26,000
Proceeds from issuance	(20,000)	$100				(20,000)
Parent's dilution/minority interest accretion[b]	$ -0-			$ (6,000)		$ 6,000

[a] For simplicity, we assume that the subsidiary's common stock is no-par. Thus, the $20,000 proceeds have been credited to the Common Stock account.
[b] The dilution suffered by the parent is offset by the accretion that accrues to the minority interest.

OTHER CHANGES IN SUBSIDIARY'S CAPITAL ACCOUNTS

Stock dividends

The treatment of stock dividends is set forth in *ARB No. 51* as follows:

> Occasionally, subsidiary companies capitalize earned surplus [retained earnings] arising since acquisition, by means of a stock dividend or otherwise. This does not require a transfer to capital surplus [additional paid-in capital] on consolidation, inasmuch as the retained earnings in the consolidated financial statements should reflect the accumulated earnings of the consolidated group not distributed to the shareholders of, or capitalized by, the parent company.[3]

In other words, a stock dividend by a subsidiary has no effect on the parent's books or in consolidation. The subsidiary has merely reshuffled amounts within its equity accounts by reducing retained earnings and increasing common stock and additional paid-in capital in accordance with procedures discussed in intermediate accounting texts. Although no entry is required to adjust the carrying value of the Investment in Subsidiary account, the parent must adjust these accounts as they exist within the expanded analysis of their investment account by individual components. Assume the following information:

	Subsidiary's Books	
	Common Stock	Retained Earnings
Balances immediately *before* stock dividend	$70,000	$75,000
Capitalization of retained earnings as a result of stock dividend	25,000	(25,000)
Balances immediately *after* stock dividend	$95,000	$50,000

If the parent holds an 80% interest in the subsidiary, the balances in the expanded analysis of the investment account by individual components are adjusted as follows:

	Individual Components within the Parent's Analysis of the Investment Account	
	Common Stock	Retained Earnings
Balances immediately *before* stock dividend	$56,000	$60,000
Reclassification as a result of stock dividend	20,000	(20,000)
Balances immediately *after* stock dividend	$76,000	$40,000

The reclassification within the parent's expanded analysis of the investment account by individual components is necessary so that the posting of the primary elimination entry used to prepare consolidated financial statements properly eliminates the subsidiary's equity accounts.

If the capitalization of retained earnings exceeds the total retained earnings as of the acquisition date, an interesting problem results. Under the equity

---

[3] *Accounting Research Bulletin No. 51*, "Consolidated Financial Statements" (New York: AICPA, 1959), paragraph 18.

method of accounting, the parent has included amounts in its Retained Earnings account that it cannot obtain from the subsidiary as a result of the capitalization. If material, this restriction on dividend availability should be disclosed in the consolidated financial statements.

Stock splits

As with stock dividends, when a stock split occurs, no entry is required on the parent's books to adjust the carrying value of its investment in the subsidiary. However, the parent does not make any reclassifications within the expanded analysis of the investment account by individual components, because no changes were made to the subsidiary's capital accounts at the time of the stock split. The parent company makes only a memorandum notation of the stock split.

Changes from par value to no-par and vice versa

When a subsidiary changes the par value of its common stock to no-par or vice versa, changes are made on its books in the Common Stock and Additional Paid-in Capital accounts. As a result, the parent makes an adjustment within the expanded analysis of the investment account by individual components. The carrying value of the investment itself does not change.

Appropriation of retained earnings

Inasmuch as the amount of the subsidiary's retained earnings existing as of the acquisition date is eliminated in consolidation, any appropriation of retained earnings by the subsidiary that does not exceed the total amount of retained earnings existing as of the acquisition date (including any amount that accrues to minority interests) has no effect on the parent's books or the consolidated financial statements. However, when appropriations of retained earnings exceed this amount, the restriction on dividend availability must be disclosed in the consolidated financial statements, if material.

CONSOLIDATED STATEMENT OF CHANGES IN FINANCIAL POSITION (ADDITIONAL CONSIDERATIONS)

In Chapter 6, we discussed the preparation of the consolidated statement of changes in financial position in terms of the types of transactions covered to that point. We now discuss the preparation of this statement in terms of the transactions discussed in Chapters 7–10.

Recall that when intercompany inventory transactions concerning inventory, fixed assets, or bond holdings occur, it is usually quicker and more practical to prepare this statement using the "analyzing the consolidated balance sheets" approach rather than trying to consolidate the separate company statements of changes in financial position. The former approach does not deal with these intercompany transactions a second time, but the latter approach does. Thus, when these types of transactions occur, no special problems exist in preparing this statement, as long as the former approach is used.

Subsidiary with preferred stock

When a subsidiary issues preferred stock, the proceeds are reported as a source of funds in the consolidated statement of changes in financial position. (We discussed in Chapter 9 that such preferred stock is classified as part of the minority interest in the consolidated balance sheet.) The purchase of the preferred stock by the parent or the retirement of the preferred stock by the subsidiary is treated as a use of funds. Any dividends paid on the preferred stock are shown as a use of funds in the consolidated statement of changes in financial position.

Changes in parent's ownership interest

When the parent (or the subsidiary) acquires some or all of a minority interest, the amount paid is reported as a use of funds in the consolidated statement of changes in financial position.

When a subsidiary issues additional common stock, the proceeds are reported as a source of funds in the consolidated statement of changes in financial position.

SUMMARY

The acquisition of any or all of a subsidiary's minority interest is treated as an acquisition of a block of stock for which purchase accounting must be used. This holds true whether the parent or the subsidiary acquires the minority interest shares. When the subsidiary acquires minority interest shares above or below book value, the decrease or increase in the parent's interest in the book value of the subsidiary's net assets must be determined. The total dollar dilution of the parent's interest is treated as cost in excess of book value and must be assigned to the appropriate individual components. Any increase in the parent's interest is treated as a reduction to any existing cost in excess of the book value element.

For the partial disposal of a parent's interest in a subsidiary, the parent must select a method of determining the cost to be removed from the investment account. Conceptually, the average cost method is the soundest method. Each component of the investment account should be appropriately relieved to avoid disrupting the normal procedures used to determine the primary elimination entry for future consolidation purposes. Any gain or loss on partial disposal is reported currently in the income statement.

The sale of additional common stock to the public by a subsidiary above or below book value results in either an increase or a decrease, respectively, in the parent's interest in the subsidiary's net assets at book value. Under the entity theory, the increase or decrease is a shift of equity interests between the controlling interests and the minority interests; accordingly, no gain or loss is reported. Under the parent company theory, the parent has realized a gain or suffered a loss, which should be reported.

Review questions

1. When some or all of a minority interest is acquired, is the purchase method or the pooling of interests method of accounting used?

2. Does the accounting method used for the acquisition of some or all of a minority interest depend on whether the parent or the subsidiary acquires the minority interest?

3. When a subsidiary has acquired some or all of its outstanding minority interest at an amount in excess of book value, has the parent's interest in the subsidiary's net assets increased or decreased?

4. Is a parent's sale of all of its common stock holdings in a subsidiary a disposal of a segment?

5. When a parent's interest in a subsidiary was acquired in blocks, and a portion of such holdings is sold, what three methods may be used to relieve the investment account?

6. Which of the three methods in Question 5 are acceptable for federal income tax reporting purposes?

7. When a parent disposes of a portion of its common stock holdings in a subsidiary, why must the equity method of accounting be applied up to the date of sale?

8. In which situations does a parent "lose" when a subsidiary issues additional common shares to the public?

9. Does a parent make a general ledger entry when a subsidiary declares a stock dividend?

10. Does a parent make a general ledger entry when a subsidiary effects a stock split?

Discussion cases

Discussion case 10–1
Acquisition of minority interest by parent—Pooling of interests versus purchase method

The controller of Piper Company has indicated to you that the company plans to acquire the entire minority interest of its 92% owned subsidiary, Strauss Company, by issuing common stock. The terms of the acquisition are identical to those that were used to obtain the 92% interest in Strauss Company two years ago. The business combination qualified for pooling of interests accounting treatment at that time. The controller has asked your advice as to how to account for this acquisition.

Required:
How would you advise the controller? State your reasons.

Discussion case 10–2
Manner of acquiring minority interest—
By parent or by subsidiary

Patte Company owns 70% of the outstanding common stock of Sheehan Company. Patte Company desires to purchase one-half of the minority interest shares. The purchase price of the shares will be in excess of book value. Patte Company can purchase the shares itself or direct the subsidiary to acquire the shares.

Required:
Which course of action, if either, is more beneficial to Patte Company?

Discussion case 10–3
Statutory merger to eliminate minority shareholders—
Rights of minority shareholders

Several years ago, Picklaus Company acquired 80% of the outstanding common stock of Sutton Company. Picklaus has now decided to merge with Sutton. Under state law, the merger required approval of only two-thirds of Sutton's shareholders. Picklaus voted its 80% of Sutton's stock in favor of the merger, which provided that each of Sutton's minority stockholders receive one share of Picklaus stock in exchange for three shares of Sutton stock. Your examination of Picklaus's financial statements has revealed that some of the minority stockholders voted against the merger. You are concerned that Picklaus properly disclose in its financial statements the liability, if any, to the minority stockholders voting against the merger.

Required:
(1) What are the rights of Sutton's stockholders who oppose the merger?
(2) What steps must minority stockholders ordinarily take to protect their rights in these circumstances?

(AICPA adapted)

Discussion case 10–4
Partial disposal of interest in a subsidiary—
Treatment of gain on disposal

Palmer Company sold a portion of its common stock holdings in one of its subsidiaries at a gain of $80,000. The controller is considering the following options:

(1) Crediting this gain to the investment account to reduce the remaining $240,000 of unamortized goodwill.
(2) Reporting the gain as an extraordinary item, because this is the first such disposal.
(3) Reporting the gain as a partial disposal of a segment under the special reporting provisions of *APB Opinion No. 30* applicable to disposals of segments, because neither the parent nor its other subsidiaries are in the same line of business.

Required:
Evaluate the theoretical merits of these three options.

Discussion case 10–5
Sale of additional common stock to the public by subsidiary—
Treatment of parent's dilution

Snead Company is a partially owned subsidiary of Pogan Company. In 19X8, Snead Company issued additional shares of its common stock to the public at an amount below book value.

In consolidation, Pogan Company is considering the following options:

(1) Computing the minority interest of these new shareholders based on the amounts they paid for their interest plus their share of earnings minus their share of dividends since the date the additional shares were issued.

(2) Computing total minority interest by multiplying the total minority interest ownership percentage by the subsidiary's net assets at book value.
(3) Treating the dollar effect of the parent's decrease in interest in the subsidiary's net assets as additional cost in excess of book value.
(4) Treating the dollar effect of the parent's decrease in interest in the subsidiary's net assets as a loss in the current period.

Required:
Evaluate the theoretical merits of these four options.

Exercises

Exercise 10–1
Acquisition of minority interest by parent

Pratt Company owns 80% of the outstanding common stock of Switney Company. The expanded analysis of the parent's investment account by individual components of the major conceptual elements at January 1, 19X6 is as follows:

Book value element:	
Common stock	$ 80,000
Retained earnings	72,000
Current value over book value element:	
Land	40,000
Goodwill element	28,000
	$220,000

On January 2, 19X6, Pratt Company acquired 15% of the outstanding common stock of Switney Company from its minority shareholders for $45,000 cash. All assets and liabilities of Switney Company have a current value equal to their book value at January 2, 19X6, except land, which is worth $60,000 in excess of its book value.

Required:
Update the expanded analysis of the parent's investment account to reflect this acquisition of a portion of the minority holdings.

Exercise 10–2
Acquisition of minority interest by subsidiary—
Determination of parent's increase or decrease in net assets

Penney Company owns 75% of the outstanding common stock of Sears Company. On January 1, 19X6, Sears Company acquired 15% of its outstanding common stock from the minority shareholders for $300,000 cash. These shares were immediately retired (the Common Stock account was charged $15,000, the Additional Paid-in Capital account was charged $135,000, and the Retained Earnings account was charged $150,000). The subsidiary's capital accounts immediately before the acquisition are as follows:

Common stock, $1 par value	$ 100,000
Additional paid-in capital	900,000
Retained earnings	600,000
	$1,600,000

Required:
(1) Calculate the total change in the equity in the subsidiary's net assets for the parent and the remaining minority interests as a result of the acquisition of a portion of the minority interest.
(2) Determine the changes that must be reflected in the expanded analysis of the investment account.

Exercise 10–3
Complete disposal of interest in certain subsidiaries— Manner of reporting disposal

Ponglom Company is a holding company that has all of its investments in its subsidiaries. Each subsidiary operates in one of the following four major business segments: electronic products (television sets, radios, fire and smoke detectors, and burglar alarms); specialty metal products (high-speed and alloy steels, tungsten, and molybdenum); meatpacking (cattle, lamb, and hogs); and wood products (primarily plywood). In 19X6, the company sold one of its three television manufacturing subsidiaries (to bring its capacity into line with current market demand) and all of its wood products subsidiaries.

Required:
How would these disposals be reported in the 19X6 financial statements?

Exercise 10–4
Stock dividend by subsidiary—Effect on parent's investment

On April 1, 19X7, Puget Company, a 75% owned subsidiary of Sound Company, declared a 10% common stock dividend on its 10,000 outstanding shares of $20 par value common stock. Puget recorded the following entry:

Retained earnings	160,000	
Common stock		20,000
Additional paid-in capital		140,000

Required:
Determine the appropriate changes that the parent company should make to its expanded analysis of the investment account by individual components as a result of the stock dividend.

Exercise 10–5
Stock split by subsidiary—Effect on parent's investment

On January 1, 19X3, Splitter Company, a 60% owned subsidiary of Pike Company, split its $10 par value common stock 4 for 1. At the time of the stock split, Splitter Company's capital accounts were as follows:

Common stock	$ 100,000
Additional paid-in capital	900,000
Retained earnings	400,000
	$1,400,000

Required:
Determine the appropriate changes that the parent company should make to its expanded analysis of the investment account by individual components as a result of the stock split.

Problems

Problem 10–1
Acquisition of minority interest by parent

On January 1, 19X3, Pebble Company acquired all of the minority interest shares of its 90% owned subsidiary, Stoner Company, by issuing 10,000 shares of its $5 par value common stock. Pebble Company's common stock had a fair market value of $17 per share on January 1, 19X3. The business combination with Stoner Company was recorded as a pooling of interests at the time of the combination. The capital accounts of Stoner Company on December 31, 19X2 are as follows:

Common stock.	$1,000,000
Retained earnings	400,000
	$1,400,000

All of Stoner Company's assets and liabilities have a current value equal to their book value at January 1, 19X3, except for its building, which is worth $70,000 in excess of book value.

Required:
Prepare and update the expanded analysis of the parent's investment account to reflect the acquisition of the minority interest.

Problem 10–2
Acquisition of minority interest by subsidiary—
Determination of parent's increase or decrease in net assets

Possi Company owns 60% of the outstanding common stock of Sandee Company. On January 1, 19X6, Sandee Company acquired 20% of its outstanding common stock from its minority interest shareholders for $360,000 cash. (These shares were immediately retired by debiting Common Stock for $20,000, debiting Additional Paid-in Capital for $80,000, and debiting Retained Earnings for $260,000.) The expanded analysis of Possi Company's investment account by individual components at December 31, 19X5, is as follows:

Book value element:	
Common stock	$ 60,000
Additional paid-in capital	240,000
Retained earnings	420,000
Current value over book value element:	
Land	60,000
Goodwill element	90,000
	$870,000

All of Sandee Company's assets and liabilities have a current value equal to their book value on January 1, 19X6, except for land, which has a current value $100,000 over its book value.

Required:
(1) Calculate the amount of the decrease in the parent's interest in the subsidiary's net assets.
(2) Update the expanded analysis of the investment account by individual components to reflect this acquisition of a portion of the minority interest.

Problem 10–3
Acquisition of minority interest by parent
(Problem 10–2 revised to reflect parent's purchase of minority interest)

Assume the information provided in Problem 10–2, except that the parent acquired 20% of the subsidiary's outstanding common stock from the minority interest shareholders for $360,000 cash.

Required:
(1) Update the expanded analysis of the investment account by individual components to reflect this acquisition of a portion of the minority interest.
(2) Explain why the parent suffered dilution in Problem 10–2 but not in Problem 10–3.
(3) Explain why the parent's cost in excess of book value increased by a greater amount in Problem 10–3 than in Problem 10–2.

Problem 10–4
Partial disposal of investment in a subsidiary—Updating analysis
of investment account and preparing year-end elimination entries

On October 1, 19X4, Ponzi Company (a calendar year reporting company) sold 25% of its common stock holdings in its 80% owned subsidiary, Swindilly Company, for $500,000 cash. All of Swindilly Company's shares owned were acquired on January 1, 19X1 in a business combination that was accounted for as a purchase. The expanded analysis of the investment account by individual components as of January 1, 19X4 is as follows:

		Remaining Life as of January 1, 19X4
Book value element:		
Common stock	$1,200,000	
Retained earnings	400,000	
Current value over book value element:		
Land	200,000	Indefinite
Equipment—Cost	48,000	5 years
—Accum. depr.	(18,000)	
Goodwill element	24,000	12 years
	$1,854,000	

During 19X4, Swindilly Company had net income of $85,000 ($25,000 of which was earned in the fourth quarter) and declared dividends of $10,000 at the end of each quarter.

Required:
(1) Update the parent company's expanded analysis of the investment account through December 31, 19X4, assuming Ponzi Company uses the equity method.
(2) Prepare the primary elimination entry as of December 31, 19X4.
(3) Prepare the entry to eliminate the remainder of the earnings recorded under the equity method of accounting.
(4) Determine the minority interest deduction for 19X4.
(5) Prepare the entry to record the partial disposal by the parent.

Problem 10–5
Partial disposal of investment in a subsidiary—Updating analysis of investment account and preparing year-end elimination entries

On July 1, 19X7, Price Company (a calendar year reporting company) sold 3,000 of the 9,000 Selle Company common shares it held for $170,000 cash. The 9,000 common shares of Selle Company (a 90% interest) were acquired on January 1, 19X1 in a business combination that was accounted for as a purchase. The expanded analysis of the investment account by individual components as of January 1, 19X7, is as follows:

		Remaining Life as of January 1, 19X7
Book value element:		
Common stock	$ 90,000	
Retained earnings	135,000	
Current value over book value element:		
Land	75,000	Indefinite
Building—Cost	108,000	6 years
—Accum. depr.	(54,000)	
Goodwill element	50,000	5 years
	$404,000	

During 19X7, Selle Company had the following:

	Net Income	Dividends Declared
Jan. 1, 19X7–June 30, 19X7	$50,000	$10,000
July 1, 19X7–Dec. 31, 19X7	30,000	10,000

Required:
(1) Update the parent's expanded analysis of the investment account through December 31, 19X7, assuming the parent uses the equity method.
(2) Prepare the primary elimination entry as of December 31, 19X7.
(3) Prepare the entry to eliminate the remainder of the earnings recorded under the equity method.
(4) Determine the minority interest deduction for 19X7.
(5) Prepare the entry to record the sale of the 3,000 shares by the parent.

Problem 10–6
Issuance of additional common shares by subsidiary

On July 1, 19X5, Stewart Company, a 90% owned subsidiary of Payne Company, issued 20,000 shares of its $10 par value common stock to the public for $1,200,000. The balances in Stewart Company's equity accounts immediately prior to the issuance are as follows:

Common stock..	$1,000,000
Additional paid-in capital	4,000,000
Retained earnings	2,500,000
	$7,500,000

Required:
(1) Determine the "gain" or "loss" that the parent incurs as a result of the issuance.
(2) How should the gain or loss be reported?

Problem 10–7
Issuance of additional common shares by subsidiary

On April 1, 19X8, Silver Company, an 80% owned subsidiary of Pewter Company, issued 10,000 shares of its $1 par value common stock to the public for $360,000. The balances in Silver Company's equity accounts immediately prior to the issuance are as follows:

Common stock..	$ 50,000
Additional paid-in capital	450,000
Retained earnings	1,000,000
	$1,500,000

Required:
(1) Determine the "gain" or "loss" that the parent incurs as a result of the issuance.
(2) How should the gain or loss be reported?

Problem 10–8
COMPREHENSIVE (Chapters 7, 9, and 10)
Inventory transfers, bond holdings, and changes in ownership;
Preparing consolidated financial statements

On January 3, 19X3, Patson Company acquired 80% of the outstanding common stock of Sherlock Company by paying $400,000 cash to Jonathon Sherlock, the company's sole stockholder. In addition, Patson Company acquired a patent from Jonathon Sherlock for $40,000 cash. Patson Company charged the entire $440,000 to the Investment in Sherlock Company Common Stock account.

Additional information:
(1) The book value of Sherlock Company's common stock on the acquisition date was $500,000. The book values of the individual assets and liabilities equaled their current values.
(2) The patent had a remaining legal life of four years as of January 3, 19X3. No amortization has been recorded since the acquisition date.

(3) During 19X4, Sherlock Company sold merchandise to Patson Company for $130,000, which included a markup of 30% over Sherlock's cost. At December 31, 19X4, $52,000 of this merchandise remained in Patson's inventory. In February 19X5, Patson sold this merchandise at an $8,000 profit.

(4) On July 1, 19X5, Patson reduced its investment in Sherlock to 75% of Sherlock's outstanding common stock by selling shares to an unaffiliated company for $70,000, a profit of $16,000. Patson recorded the proceeds as a credit to its investment account.

(5) In November 19X5, Patson sold merchandise to Sherlock for the first time. Patson's cost for this merchandise was $80,000, and the sale was made at 120% of cost. Sherlock's December 31, 19X5 inventory contained $24,000 of the merchandise that was purchased from Patson.

(6) On December 31, 19X5, a $40,000 payment was in transit from Sherlock Company to Patson Company. Accounts receivable and accounts payable include intercompany receivables and payables. (Sherlock still owes Patson $12,000.)

(7) In December 19X5, Sherlock declared and paid cash dividends of $100,000 to its stockholders.

(8) Sherlock Company had $140,000 of net income for the six months ended June 30, 19X5 and $160,000 of net income for the six months ended December 31, 19X5.

(9) On July 1, 19X5, Patson paid $56,000 for 50% of the outstanding bonds issued by Sherlock Company. The bonds mature on June 30, 19X9 and were originally issued at a discount. At December 31, 19X5, the unamortized discount on Sherlock Company's books is $2,800. (Interest at 10% is due on June 30 and December 31 of each year.) The December 31, 19X5 interest payment was made on time. (Both companies use the straight-line method of discount amortization.)

(10) The financial statements of each company for the year ended December 31, 19X5, are as follows:

	Patson Company	Sherlock Company
Income Statement:		
Sales.....................................	$4,000,000	$1,700,000
Dividend income (Sherlock)........................	75,000	
Equity in net income of subsidiary...................	232,000	
Interest income......................................	3,500	
Subtotal..	$4,310,500	$1,700,000
Cost of goods sold................................	$2,985,000	$1,015,000
Operating expenses................................	400,500	372,200
Interest expense....................................		12,800
Subtotal..	$3,385,500	$1,400,000
Net Income.......................................	$ 925,000	$ 300,000
Balance Sheet:		
Cash..	$ 487,500	$ 249,600
Accounts receivable, net...........................	235,000	185,000
Inventory...	475,000	355,000
Fixed assets, net..................................	2,231,000	530,000
Investments in Sherlock Company:		
Common stock...................................	954,000	
Bonds..	56,500	
Total assets....................................	$4,439,000	$1,319,600

	Patson Company	Sherlock Company
Accounts payable....................................	$ 384,000	$ 62,400
Bonds payable		$ 120,000
Unamortized discount on bonds		$ (2,800)
Common stock:		
Patson Company	$1,200,000	
Sherlock Company		$ 250,000
Additional paid-in capital		$ 50,000
Retained earnings—Patson:		
Beginning of year................................	$2,100,000	
+ Net income	925,000	
− Dividends declared............................	(170,000)	
End of year	$2,855,000	
Retained earnings—Sherlock:		
Beginning of year................................		$ 640,000
+ Net income		300,000
− Dividends declared............................		(100,000)
End of year		$ 840,000
Total liabilities and equity.......................	$4,439,000	$1,319,600

Required:

For all requirements, ignore income tax consideratons.

(1) Prepare the appropriate adjusting entries required at December 31, 19X5.

(2) Adjust the financial statements for the entries developed in requirement (1). Modify the financial statements to reflect the use of intercompany accounts.

(3) Prepare the appropriate elimination entries in consolidation at December 31, 19X5.

(4) Prepare a consolidating statement worksheet at December 31, 19X5, using the partially consolidated column format demonstrated in Chapters 7, 8, and 9. [Parent and subsidiary columns should reflect the adjustments made in requirement (2).]

(AICPA adapted)

Problem 10–9
Consolidated statement of changes in financial position

The following consolidated income statement and comparative balance sheets are for Parker Company and its 80% owned subsidiary, Schaeffer Company:

	19X1
Sales	$ 600,000
Cost of goods sold	(350,000)
Marketing and administrative expenses	(103,000)
Gain on sale of equipment	3,000
Minority interest	(6,000)
Income before Income Taxes	$ 144,000
Income tax expense	(60,000)
Net Income	$ 84,000

	December 31,	
	19X1	**19X0**
Cash	$ 75,000	$ 60,000
Receivables, net.	90,000	70,000
Inventory	200,000	170,000
Fixed assets—Cost	506,000	465,000
—Accum. depr.	(103,000)	(100,000)
Goodwill	32,000	35,000
Total assets.	$800,000	$700,000
Accounts payable.	$180,000	$164,000
Bonds payable—Current	20,000	20,000
—Long-term	160,000	180,000
Minority interest	66,000	36,000
Common stock	250,000	200,000
Retained earnings	124,000	100,000
Total liabilities and equity.	$800,000	$700,000

Additional information:

(1) On January 1, 19X1, Parker increased its ownership in Schaeffer from 70% to 80% by paying $17,000 cash to certain minority shareholders. (The cost in excess of book value was designated as goodwill.)

(2) On December 31, 19X1, Schaeffer issued preferred stock at par totaling $40,000 (shown as part of the minority interest in the December 31, 19X1 consolidated balance sheet). Schaeffer had no preferred stock outstanding prior to this issuance.

(3) As of January 1, 19X1, goodwill has a five-year remaining life (including the goodwill paid for on January 1, 19X1).

(4) On July 1, 19X1, Parker issued 5,000 shares of common stock for $10 per share.

(5) During 19X1, dividends on common stock were declared and paid as follows:

Parker Company	$60,000
Schaeffer Company	20,000

(6) On January 2, 19X1, Parker sold equipment to Schaeffer for $21,000. The equipment had cost Parker $30,000 and was 60% depreciated at the time of the intercompany transfer. Schaeffer assigned a three-year life to the equipment. In consolidation at December 31, 19X1, the following elimination entry was made as a result of this transfer:

Gain on sale of equipment	9,000	
Equipment.	9,000	
Depreciation expense.		3,000
Accumulated depreciation		15,000

(7) The only fixed asset retirement during 19X1 was a machine that had cost $33,000, had accumulated depreciation of $22,000, and was sold for $14,000.

Required:

Prepare a consolidated statement of changes in financial position for 19X1 using the working capital concept of funds.

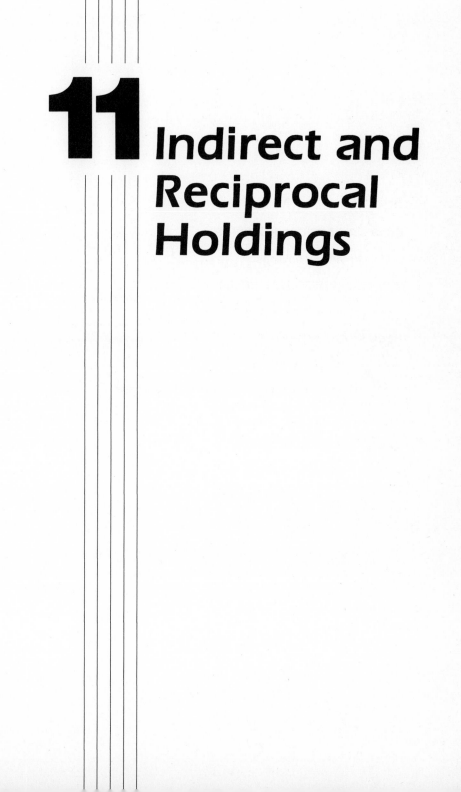

11 Indirect and Reciprocal Holdings

The most common intercompany relationship is the parent company's direct investment in a subsidiary's common stock. Other types of relationships are encountered less frequently; they can be categorized as follows:

(1) Indirect vertical holdings.
(2) Indirect horizontal holdings.
(3) Reciprocal (mutual) holdings.

These various relationships are shown in Illustration 11-1. The three categories are not mutually exclusive—any combination of relationships

Illustration 11-1
Affiliation diagrams

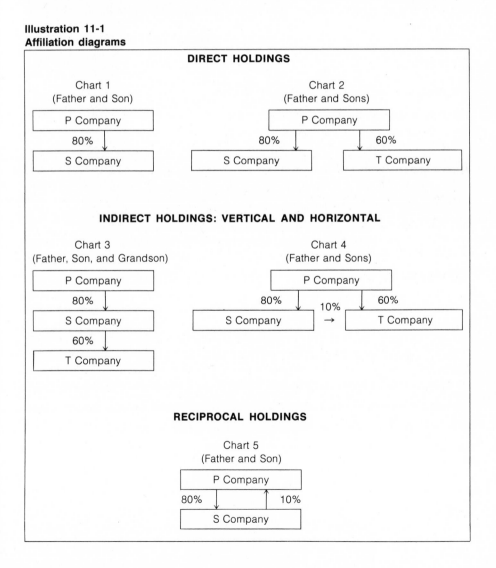

may exist. This chapter discusses each category independently of the others. Accounting for special corporate relationships involving combinations of indirect vertical holdings, indirect horizontal holdings, and reciprocal holdings can be developed from a careful application of the principles discussed in this chapter.

The accounting procedures for indirect vertical holdings and indirect horizontal holdings follow the principles discussed in earlier chapters with respect to accounting for the investment and preparing consolidated financial statements. In these relationships, the **sequence** of procedures in the consolidation process is of paramount importance.

For reciprocal holdings involving a partially owned subsidiary, two methods have evolved for presenting the combined earnings in the consolidated income statement. Each method is discussed and illustrated in detail. Selecting the method that **presents the most meaningful financial information** is important.

Discussion of the ramifications of unrealized intercompany profits on asset transfers is delayed until the end of the chapter.

INDIRECT VERTICAL HOLDINGS

An indirect vertical holding occurs when P Company, for example, owns more than 50% of S Company, and S Company owns more than 50% of T Company. In such relationships, commonly referred to as chains, S Company, although a subsidiary of P Company, is a parent with respect to T Company.

The procedures used to consolidate the financial statements of the three companies are as follows:

(1) T Company is consolidated into S Company.
(2) S Company, which is now consolidated with T Company, is consolidated into P Company.

When minority interests exist at each level, the minority interest deduction in the income statement section and the minority interest in the balance sheet section of the consolidating statement worksheet increase at each higher level of consolidation.

Net income for P Company (the top-level parent) can be determined without consolidation by successive application of the equity method of accounting, starting with the lowest-level parent within the chain. For example, assume the following information for 19X1:

(1) P Company owns 80% of S Company, and S Company owns 60% of T Company. The affiliation can be diagramed as follows.

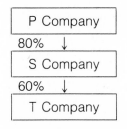

(2) Net income from each company's operations, excluding equity in net income of subsidiary and amortization of cost in excess of book value, is as follows:

P Company	$1,000,000
S Company	100,000
T Company	10,000

(3) All of P Company's $10,000 cost in excess of book value was allocable to land. All of S Company's $6,000 cost in excess of book value was allocable to goodwill—$1,000 was amortized during 19X1.

The successive application of the equity method of accounting is as follows:

S Company's income from its own operations	$100,000
S Company's equity in T Company's net income	
(60% of $10,000)	6,000
Less—Amortization of cost in excess of book value	(1,000)
Net income of S Company	$105,000

P Company's income from its own operations	$1,000,000
P Company's equity in S Company's net income	
(80% of $105,000)	84,000
Net income of P Company	$1,084,000

Note that only 48% of T Company's $10,000 net income is reflected in P Company's net income under the equity method of accounting [80% (60% × $10,000)]. Of the $1,000 amortization of cost in excess of book value expense recorded by S Company, 80%, or $800, accrues to P Company. Thus, the net amount that accrues to P Company is $4,000 ($4,800 − $800). Even though a majority of T Company's net income does not accrue to the consolidated group, successive consolidation is still appropriate, because T Company is controlled indirectly through S Company.

Illustrations:
Preparing consolidated financial statements;
Indirect vertical holdings

Companies S and T are consolidated as of December 31, 19X1 in Illustration 11-2, and companies P and S are subsequently consolidated as of December 31, 19X1 in Illustration 11-3. The ownership and income information is from the preceding example. (We assume that no intercompany transactions requiring elimination occurred.) The primary and secondary elimination entries and the minority interest entries for these illustrations are given as follows:

	Consolidation of			
	Companies S and T		Companies P and S	
(1) The primary elimination entry:				
Common stock.........................	24,000		240,000	
Retained earnings (beginning of year)....	12,000		80,000	
Equity in net income of subsidiary	6,000		84,000	
Land......................................			40,000	
Goodwill.................................	5,000			
Dividends declared		3,000		28,000
Investment in subsidiary		44,000		416,000
(2) The secondary elimination entry:				
Cost of goods sold	1,000			
Amortization of cost in excess				
of book value		1,000		
(3) The minority interest entry:				
Minority interest (income statement)	4,000		21,000	
Retained earnings—Subsidiary (net				
income line)		4,000		21,000
(40% of $10,000)				
(20% of $105,000)				

In reviewing Illustrations 11-2 and 11-3, the following points should be understood:

(1) At each higher level of consolidation, the minority interest deduction increases, as does the minority interest in the balance sheet.
(2) S Company treats the amortization of cost in excess of book value on its books as a normal expense, thereby reducing its net income, which in turn reduces the minority interest deduction when S Company is consolidated with P Company. In other words, the amortization of cost in excess of book value by S Company is considered a bona fide expense in determining S Company's net income, and the minority interest deduction is based on this net income.
(3) The consolidation process starts at the lowest parent–subsidiary level and then works upward.

INDIRECT HORIZONTAL HOLDINGS

Indirect horizontal holdings occur when one subsidiary holds an investment in another subsidiary of a common parent—for example, P Company owns more than 50% of companies S and T, and S Company has an investment in T Company, which obviously must be less than 50%.

Consolidating the financial statements of the three companies is accomplished as follows:

(1) S Company (an investor) applies the equity method of accounting with respect to the earnings of T Company (an investee).
(2) P Company applies the equity method of accounting to each of its subsidiaries and then consolidates S Company.
(3) P Company then consolidates T Company.

Illustration 11-2

S COMPANY AND SUBSIDIARY (T COMPANY) Consolidating Statement Worksheet For the Year Ended December 31, 19X1					
			Eliminations		S and T Consoli- dated
	S Company	T Company	Dr.	Cr.	
Income Statement:					
Sales......................	790,000	200,000			990,000
Income from subsidiary:					
Equity in net income.........	6,000		6,000(1)		-0-
Amortization of cost in					
excess of book value	(1,000)			1,000(2)	-0-
Subtotal	795,000	200,000	6,000	1,000	990,000
Cost of goods sold	360,000	120,000	1,000(2)		481,000
Marketing expenses	90,000	30,000			120,000
Administrative expenses........	60,000	20,000			80,000
Interest expense...............	30,000	5,000			35,000
Subtotal	540,000	175,000	1,000		716,000
Income before Income Taxes and Minority Interest	255,000	25,000	7,000	1,000	274,000
Income tax expense @ 60%	(150,000)	(15,000)			(165,000)
Income before Minority Interest....	105,000	10,000	7,000	1,000	109,000
Minority interest			4,000(3)		(4,000)
Net Income	105,000	10,000	11,000	1,000	105,000
Balance Sheet:					
Current assets	338,000	115,000			453,000
Investment in T Company	44,000			44,000(1)	-0-
Fixed assets, net	350,000	155,000			505,000
Goodwill			5,000(1)		5,000
Total assets..............	732,000	270,000	5,000	44,000	963,000
Liabilities	262,000	205,000			467,000
Common stock:					
S Company	300,000				300,000
T Company		40,000	24,000(1)		16,000M
Retained earnings—S Company:					
Beginning of year............	100,000				100,000
+ Net income	105,000				105,000
− Dividends declared........	(35,000)				(35,000)
End of year	170,000				170,000
Retained earnings—T Company:					
Beginning of year............		20,000	12,000(1)		8,000M
+ Net income		10,000	11,000	1,000	4,000M
				4,000(3)	
− Dividends declared........		(5,000)		3,000(1)	(2,000)M
End of year		25,000	23,000	8,000	10,000M
Total liabilities and equity...	732,000	270,000	47,000	8,000	963,000
Proof of debit and credit postings			52,000	52,000	
Total minority interest					26,000

Explanation of entries:
(1) The primary elimination entry.
(2) The secondary elimination entry.
(3) The minority interest entry.
We assume that no income taxes need to be provided on earnings recorded under the equity method. The amortization of cost in excess of book value is not tax deductible.

Illustration 11-3

	P Company	S and T Consolidated[a]	Eliminations Dr.	Eliminations Cr.	P + S + T Consolidated
P COMPANY AND SUBSIDIARY (S COMPANY) Consolidating Statement Worksheet For the Year Ended December 31, 19X1					
Income Statement:					
Sales.........................	7,500,000	990,000			8,490,000
Income from subsidiary:					
Equity in net income	84,000		84,000(1)		-0-
Subtotal	7,584,000	990,000	84,000		8,490,000
Cost of goods sold	4,000,000	481,000			4,481,000
Marketing expenses	600,000	120,000			720,000
Administrative expenses........	300,000	80,000			380,000
Interest expense...............	100,000	35,000			135,000
Subtotal	5,000,000	716,000			5,716,000
Income before Income Taxes and Minority Interest	2,584,000	274,000	84,000		2,774,000
Income tax expense @ 60%	(1,500,000)	(165,000)			(1,665,000)
Income before Minority Interest	1,084,000	109,000	84,000		1,109,000
Minority interest		(4,000)	21,000(3)		(25,000)
Net Income	1,084,000	105,000	─105,000		1,084,000
Balance Sheet:					
Current assets	2,068,000	453,000			2,521,000
Investment in S Company	416,000			416,000(1)	-0-
Fixed assets, net	2,600,000	505,000	40,000(1)		3,145,000
Goodwill......................		5,000			5,000
Total assets...............	5,084,000	963,000	40,000	416,000	5,671,000
Liabilities	1,000,000	467,000			1,467,000
Minority interest in T Company		26,000			26,000M
Common stock:					
P Company.................	2,000,000				2,000,000
S Company		300,000	240,000(1)		60,000M
Retained earnings—P Company:					
Beginning of year............	1,700,000				1,700,000
+ Net income	1,084,000				1,084,000
− Dividends declared........	(700,000)				(700,000)
End of year	2,084,000				2,084,000
Retained earnings—S Company:					
Beginning of year............		100,000	80,000(1)		20,000M
+ Net income		105,000	↳105,000	21,000(3)	21,000M
− Dividends declared........		(35,000)		28,000(1)	(7,000)M
End of year		170,000	185,000	49,000	34,000M
Total liabilities and equity...	5,084,000	963,000	425,000	49,000	5,671,000
Proof of debit and credit postings			465,000	465,000	
Total minority interest					120,000

[a] Per Illustration 11-2.

Explanation of entries:
  (1) The primary elimination entry.
  (2) (There is no secondary elimination entry.)
  (3) The minority interest entry.
We assume that no income taxes need to be provided on earnings recorded under the equity method.

When the three companies are consolidated in this sequence, the individual investments in T Company by companies P and S are added together when companies P and S are consolidated. This combined investment in T Company is then eliminated in a single step when T Company is consolidated with P Company, which is already consolidated with S Company. When eliminating the combined investment in T Company, the individual components of P Company's investment account must be combined with the individual components of S Company's investment account.

Regardless of one subsidiary's ownership percentage in another subsidiary, the equity method of accounting should be used by the investor subsidiary (even if the percentage is less than 20%), because the parent exercises significant influence over the investee subsidiary.

P Company's net income can be determined without consolidation by successive application of the equity method of accounting, starting with the lowest-level investor. Assume the following information for 19X1:

(1) P Company owns 80% of S Company and 60% of T Company, and S Company owns 10% of T Company. The affiliations are diagramed as follows:

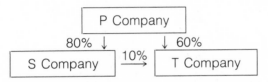

(2) Income from each company's operations, excluding the equity in net income of any subsidiary or investee, is as follows:

P Company	$1,000,000
S Company	100,000
T Company	10,000

(3) For simplicity, we assume that all cost in excess of book value was allocable to land. Thus, there is no amortization of cost in excess of book value.

The successive application of the equity method of accounting is as follows:

S Company's income from its own operations	$ 100,000
S Company's equity in T Company's net income	
(10% of $10,000)	1,000
Total net income of S Company	$ 101,000
P Company's income from its own operations	$1,000,000
P Company's equity in S Company's net income	
(80% of $101,000)	80,800
P Company's equity in T Company's net income	
(60% of $10,000)	6,000
Total net income of P Company	$1,086,800

Illustrations:
Preparing consolidated financial statements;
Indirect horizontal holdings

From the ownership and income information in the preceding example, companies P and S are consolidated as of December 31, 19X1 in Illustration 11-4, and P Company (now consolidated with S Company) is consolidated with T Company as of December 31, 19X1 in Illustration 11-5. (We assume that no intercompany transactions occurred requiring elimination.) The primary elimination entries along with the minority interest entries are given as follows:

	Consolidation of	
	Companies P and S	Companies P and T (See below for source of these amounts)
(1) The primary elimination entry:		
Common stock	240,000	28,000
Retained earnings (beginning of year)....	80,000	14,000
Equity in net income		
of subsidiary	80,800	7,000
Land	40,000	9,500
Dividends declared.................	28,000	3,500
Investment in subsidiary	412,800	55,000

The primary elimination entry to consolidate companies P and T is obtained by combining the individual components of the major conceptual elements of P Company's investment in T Company and S Company's investment in T Company as shown below:

	Analysis of the Investment Accounts by the Individual Components of the Major Conceptual Elements		
	P Company's Investment in T Company	S Company's Investment in T Company	Total
Common stock	$24,000	$ 4,000	$28,000
Retained earnings (beginning of year)	12,000	2,000	14,000
Equity in net income of T Company	6,000	1,000	7,000
Dividends declared	(3,000)	(500)	(3,500)
Land	6,000	3,500	9,500
	$45,000	$10,000	$55,000

(2) The minority interest entry:		
Minority interest (income statement)	20,200	3,000
Retained earnings—Subsidiary (net income line).....	20,200	3,000
(20% of $101,000 for S Company)		
(30% of $10,000 for T Company)		

Illustration 11-4

<table>
<tr><td colspan="6" align="center">P COMPANY AND SUBSIDIARY (S COMPANY)
Consolidating Statement Worksheet
For the Year Ended December 31, 19X1</td></tr>
<tr>
<th></th>
<th>P
Company</th>
<th>S
Company</th>
<th colspan="2">Eliminations</th>
<th>P + S
Consoli-
dated</th>
</tr>
<tr>
<th></th>
<th></th>
<th></th>
<th>Dr.</th>
<th>Cr.</th>
<th></th>
</tr>
<tr><td>Income Statement:</td><td></td><td></td><td></td><td></td><td></td></tr>
<tr><td>Sales.......................</td><td>7,500,000</td><td>790,000</td><td></td><td></td><td>8,290,000</td></tr>
<tr><td> Equity in net income—S......</td><td>80,800</td><td></td><td>80,800(1)</td><td></td><td>-0-</td></tr>
<tr><td> Equity in net income—T......</td><td>6,000</td><td>1,000</td><td></td><td></td><td>7,000</td></tr>
<tr><td>   Subtotal ....</td><td>7,586,800</td><td>791,000</td><td>80,800</td><td></td><td>8,297,000</td></tr>
<tr><td>Cost of goods sold ....</td><td>4,000,000</td><td>360,000</td><td></td><td></td><td>4,360,000</td></tr>
<tr><td>Marketing expenses ....</td><td>600,000</td><td>90,000</td><td></td><td></td><td>690,000</td></tr>
<tr><td>Administrative expenses.......</td><td>300,000</td><td>60,000</td><td></td><td></td><td>360,000</td></tr>
<tr><td>Interest expense..............</td><td>100,000</td><td>30,000</td><td></td><td></td><td>130,000</td></tr>
<tr><td>   Subtotal ....</td><td>5,000,000</td><td>540,000</td><td></td><td></td><td>5,540,000</td></tr>
<tr><td>Income before Income Taxes
  and Minority Interest.........</td><td>2,586,800</td><td>251,000</td><td>80,800</td><td></td><td>2,757,000</td></tr>
<tr><td> Income tax expense @ 60%</td><td>(1,500,000)</td><td>(150,000)</td><td></td><td></td><td>(1,650,000)</td></tr>
<tr><td>Income before Minority Interest....</td><td>1,086,800</td><td>101,000</td><td>80,800</td><td></td><td>1,107,000</td></tr>
<tr><td> Minority interest ....</td><td></td><td></td><td></td><td>20,200(2)</td><td>(20,200)</td></tr>
<tr><td>Net Income ....</td><td>1,086,800</td><td>101,000</td><td>101,000</td><td></td><td>1,086,800</td></tr>
<tr><td>Balance Sheet:</td><td></td><td></td><td></td><td></td><td></td></tr>
<tr><td>Current assets ....</td><td>2,029,000</td><td>368,000</td><td></td><td></td><td>2,397,000</td></tr>
<tr><td>Investment in Subs:</td><td></td><td></td><td></td><td></td><td></td></tr>
<tr><td> S Company.................</td><td>412,800</td><td></td><td></td><td>412,800(1)</td><td>-0-</td></tr>
<tr><td> T Company.................</td><td>45,000</td><td>10,000</td><td></td><td></td><td>55,000</td></tr>
<tr><td>Fixed assets, net ....</td><td>2,600,000</td><td>350,000</td><td>40,000(1)</td><td></td><td>2,990,000</td></tr>
<tr><td>   Total assets..............</td><td>5,086,800</td><td>728,000</td><td>40,000</td><td>412,800</td><td>5,442,000</td></tr>
<tr><td>Liabilities ....</td><td>1,000,000</td><td>262,000</td><td></td><td></td><td>1,262,000</td></tr>
<tr><td>Common stock:</td><td></td><td></td><td></td><td></td><td></td></tr>
<tr><td> P Company.................</td><td>2,000,000</td><td></td><td></td><td></td><td>2,000,000</td></tr>
<tr><td> S Company.................</td><td></td><td>300,000</td><td>240,000(1)</td><td></td><td>60,000M</td></tr>
<tr><td>Retained earnings—P Company:</td><td></td><td></td><td></td><td></td><td></td></tr>
<tr><td> Beginning of year............</td><td>1,700,000</td><td></td><td></td><td></td><td>1,700,000</td></tr>
<tr><td> + Net income ....</td><td>1,086,800</td><td></td><td></td><td></td><td>1,086,800</td></tr>
<tr><td> − Dividends declared........</td><td>(700,000)</td><td></td><td></td><td></td><td>(700,000)</td></tr>
<tr><td> End of year................</td><td>2,086,800</td><td></td><td></td><td></td><td>2,086,800</td></tr>
<tr><td>Retained earnings—S Company:</td><td></td><td></td><td></td><td></td><td></td></tr>
<tr><td> Beginning of year...........</td><td></td><td></td><td>100,000</td><td>80,000(1)</td><td>20,000M</td></tr>
<tr><td> + Net income ....</td><td></td><td></td><td>101,000</td><td>101,000</td><td>20,200M</td></tr>
<tr><td></td><td></td><td></td><td></td><td>20,200(2)</td><td></td></tr>
<tr><td> − Dividends declared........</td><td></td><td></td><td>(35,000)</td><td>28,000(1)</td><td>(7,000)M</td></tr>
<tr><td> End of year................</td><td></td><td></td><td>166,000</td><td>181,000</td><td>33,200M</td></tr>
<tr><td>   Total liabilities and equity...</td><td>5,086,800</td><td>728,000</td><td>421,000</td><td>48,200</td><td>5,442,000</td></tr>
<tr><td>Proof of debit and credit postings ....</td><td></td><td></td><td>461,000</td><td>461,000</td><td></td></tr>
<tr><td>Total minority interest ....</td><td></td><td></td><td></td><td></td><td>93,200 ←</td></tr>
</table>

Explanation of entries:
(1) The primary elimination entry.
(2) The minority interest entry.
We assume that no income taxes need to be provided on earnings recorded under the equity method.

Illustration 11-5

P AND S COMPANIES (Consolidated) AND SUBSIDIARY (T COMPANY)
Consolidating Statement Worksheet
For the Year Ended December 31, 19X1

	P and S Consoli-dated[a]	T Company	Eliminations Dr.	Eliminations Cr.	P + S + T Consoli-dated
Income Statement:					
Sales.........................	8,290,000	200,000			8,490,000
Equity in net income—T......	7,000		7,000(1)		-0-
Subtotal	8,297,000	200,000	7,000		8,490,000
Cost of goods sold	4,360,000	120,000			4,480,000
Marketing expenses	690,000	30,000			720,000
Administrative expenses........	360,000	20,000			380,000
Interest expense...............	130,000	5,000			135,000
Subtotal	5,540,000	175,000			5,715,000
Income before Income Taxes and Minority Interest	2,757,000	25,000	7,000		2,775,000
Income tax expense @ 60%	(1,650,000)	(15,000)			(1,665,000)
Income before Minority Interest....	1,107,000	10,000	7,000		1,110,000
Minority interest	(20,200)			3,000(2)	(23,200)
Net Income	1,086,800	10,000	10,000		1,086,800
Balance Sheet:					
Current assets	2,397,000	115,000			2,512,000
Investment in T Company	55,000			55,000(1)	-0-
Fixed assets, net	2,990,000	155,000	9,500(1)		3,154,500
Total assets..............	5,442,000	270,000	9,500	55,000	5,666,500
Liabilities	1,262,000	205,000			1,467,000
Minority interest in S Company...............	93,200				93,200M
Common stock:					
P Company	2,000,000				2,000,000
T Company		40,000	28,000(1)		12,000M
Retained earnings—P Company:					
Beginning of year............	1,700,000				1,700,000
+ Net income	1,086,800				1,086,800
− Dividends declared........	(700,000)				(700,000)
End of year	2,086,800				2,086,800
Retained earnings—T Company:					
Beginning of year............		20,000	14,000(1)		6,000M
+ Net income		10,000	10,000(1)	3,000(2)	3,000M
− Dividends declared........		(5,000)		3,500(1)	(1,500)M
End of year		25,000	21,000	3,500	7,500M
Total liabilities and equity...	5,442,000	270,000	49,000	3,500	5,666,500
Proof of debit and credit postings			58,500	58,500	

Total minority interest 112,700

[a] Per Illustration 11-4.
Explanation of entries:
(1) The primary elimination entry.
(2) The minority interest entry.
We assume that no income taxes need to be provided on earnings recorded under the equity method.

In reviewing Illustrations 11-4 and 11-5, the following points should be understood:

(1) For the percentage investment held in T Company, S Company's cost in excess of book value was greater than P Company's cost in excess of book value. We assumed that (1) S Company made its investment in T Company after P Company made its investment in T Company, and (2) the land appreciated in value during that interval.
(2) The consolidation can also be performed using one consolidation work-sheet in which companies S and T are simultaneously consolidated with P Company. This is the common procedure in practice; separate consolidations of each company are used for instructional purposes.

RECIPROCAL HOLDINGS

Reciprocal holdings occur when a subsidiary invests in its parent company's common stock. Two accounting questions are raised by such holdings:

(1) How should the subsidiary individually account for the investment in the parent company?
(2) How should the investment in the parent company be accounted for in consolidation?

Accounting by the subsidiary

An investment by a subsidiary in its parent's common stock must be con-sidered a long-term investment. Because such investments rarely, if ever, reach the 20% level, in the typical situation, ownership in the parent's common stock is less than 20%. In this situation, the subsidiary must account for the investment under the lower of cost or market method, as prescribed by *FASB Statement No. 12,* "Investments in Certain Marketable Securities."

Remember that a subsidiary, as a separate legal entity, must follow generally accepted accounting principles without regard to the fact that it is a subsidiary. Many subsidiaries must issue separate financial statements pursuant to loan indenture agreements. When contingent consideration based on the subsidiary's postcombination sales or earnings amounts is a provision of the business combination agreement, separate audited financial statements are often required.

Accounting in consolidation

The subsidiary's method of accounting for its investment in the parent when preparing consolidated financial statements is prescribed by *ARB No. 51* as follows:

> Shares of the parent held by a subsidiary should not be treated as outstanding stock in the consolidated balance sheet.[1]

---

[1] *Accounting Research Bulletin No. 51,* "Consolidated Financial Statements" (New York: AICPA, 1959), paragraph 13.

If the parent had acquired its own shares, then the cost would be treated as a cost of treasury shares. Because the parent directed the subsidiary to acquire the shares, which is usually the way such investments are made, should not matter. If the subsidiary is wholly owned, this treatment makes sense. However, if the subsidiary is partially owned, the requirement to treat all of the shares it owns as not outstanding ignores the reality that the subsidiary's minority shareholders are indirectly shareholders of the parent. This requirement can cause a misleading earnings per share amount to be reported, as demonstrated later in the chapter.

This *ARB No. 51* requirement, therefore, means that in consolidation, the cost of the investment in the parent's common stock is treated as a cost of treasury shares. Accordingly, a reclassification must be made in the balance sheet section of the consolidating statement worksheet as follows:

Cost of treasury stock XXX
    Investment in parent company's common stock XXX

When a subsidiary has lowered the carrying value of its investment in its parent through a valuation allowance, the offsetting charge to its stockholders' equity section (required under *FASB Statement No. 12*) must be reclassified in consolidation as part of the total cost of the treasury shares. Until the subsidiary disposes of some or all of its investment in its parent, the balance of the cost of the treasury shares, as reported in the consolidated financial statements, remains unchanged.

When a subsidiary is wholly owned, consolidated net income obviously is the sum of (1) the parent's earnings from its own operations, exclusive of earnings on its investment in the subsidiary and (2) the subsidiary's earnings from its own operations, exclusive of earnings on its investment in the parent. These situations present no accounting issues in preparing consolidated financial statements.

When a subsidiary is partially owned, the accounting issue is how to report the combined earnings for financial reporting purposes in view of the fact that the subsidiary's minority shareholders are indirectly shareholders of the parent. *ARB No. 51* does not specify the procedures for these situations. Two schools of thought explain how the combined earnings should be reported—one advocating the treasury stock method and the other advocating the traditional allocation method. Each of these methods is best discussed using an example. Assume the following information:

	P Company	S Company
Number of common shares outstanding	100,000	20,000
Ownership interest in the other—		
Percentage	70%	10%
Number of shares	14,000	10,000
Net income for the year (from own separate		
operations, exclusive of earnings on		
investments in the other)	$1,000,000	$500,000

The affiliation diagram is as follows:

```
┌─────────────────────┐
│     P Company       │
└─────────────────────┘
  70% ↓      ↑ 10%
┌─────────────────────┐
│     S Company       │
└─────────────────────┘
```

The treasury stock method. The treasury stock method essentially comes under the parent company theory, which is discussed in Chapter 5. Recall that under the parent company theory the parent is the reporting entity. The consolidation process is merely the substitution of the subsidiary's assets and liabilities for the parent's Investment in Subsidiary account. From this perspective, consolidated net income should be the sum of:

(1) The parent's earnings from its own separate operations, and
(2) The parent's share of the subsidiary's earnings from its own separate operations.

From the above data, consolidated net income under this method is $1,350,000 [$1,000,000 + (70% × $500,000)]. Thus, the minority interest deduction is based solely on the minority interest ownership percentage of the subsidiary's earnings from its own separate operations, exclusive of earnings on its investment in the parent. From the preceding data, the minority interest deduction would be $150,000 (30% of $500,000).

The consolidated net income, therefore, is the amount by which the parent's retained earnings would increase if the subsidiary distributed as dividends all of its earnings from its own separate operations, exclusive of its earnings on its investment in the parent. Of course, dividend distributions to the parent's stockholders are ignored in calculating the amount of this increase. Whether the parent uses the equity method or the cost method to account for its investment in the subsidiary is irrelevant.

When the parent accounts for its investment in the subsidiary under the equity method of accounting, it merely applies its ownership percentage in the subsidiary to the subsidiary's earnings from its own separate operations, exclusive of the subsidiary's earnings on its investment in the parent. In the example, this would be $350,000 (70% of $500,000). As a result, the parent's $1,350,000 recorded net income equals the $1,350,000 consolidated net income. Recall from Chapter 7 that this equality is required by the equity method of accounting, which states:

> The difference between consolidation and the equity method lies in the details reported in the financial statements. Thus, an investor's net income for the period and its stockholders' equity at the end of the period are the same whether an investment in a subsidiary is accounted for under the equity method or the subsidiary is consolidated . . .[2]

---

[2] *APB Opinion No. 18,* "The Equity Method of Accounting for Investments in Common Stock" (New York: AICPA, 1971), paragraph 19.

The amount of earnings per share on a consolidated basis (assuming no other dilutive securities) is computed by dividing the consolidated net income of $1,350,000 by the 90,000 shares deemed outstanding (100,000 shares issued − 10,000 shares held by the subsidiary treated as not outstanding). This computation gives $15 per share. However, treating all 10,000 shares of the parent's stock held by the subsidiary as not outstanding results in a meaningless earnings per share amount. If the parent distributed as dividends all of its $1,350,000 consolidated net income, this amount would not be distributed solely to the holders of the 90,000 shares. Because 10,000 shares of the parent's stocks are held by the subsidiary and because the subsidiary is only 70% owned by the parent, the subsidiary's minority shareholders are effectively indirect shareholders of the parent to the extent of 3,000 shares (30% of 10,000). Assume that the subsidiary was liquidated immediately after it distributed as dividends its net income from its own separate operations. The 10,000 shares held as an investment in the parent would be distributed to the subsidiary's shareholders—7,000 to the parent and 3,000 to the minority shareholders. Thus, the parent's consolidated net income of $1,350,000 would be distributed to holders of 93,000 shares, not 90,000 shares. Dividing $1,350,000 by 93,000 gives $14.52 per share. In terms of dollars, the holders of the 90,000 shares would receive (90,000/93,000) of the consolidated net income of $1,350,000, or $1,306,452. The minority interest shareholders would receive (3,000/93,000) of the consolidated net income cf $1,350,000, or $43,548. The $14.52 earnings per share amount is therefore more meaningful.

The traditional allocation method. The traditional allocation method essentially comes under the entity theory, which is discussed in Chapter 5. Recall that under the entity theory a "new reporting entity" is deemed to exist as a result of consolidation. This new reporting entity has two classes of shareholders:

(1) The controlling interests (in the example, holders of 90,000 shares of the parent's outstanding common stock).
(2) The subsidiary's minority shareholders (who indirectly own 3,000 shares of the parent's outstanding common stock in the example).

From this perspective, the combined earnings of the parent and the subsidiary should appear in the consolidated income statement so that the amount that accrues to each class of shareholders is shown. As demonstrated in the discussion of the treasury stock method, the holders of the 90,000 shares are entitled to $1,306,452 of the combined earnings of $1,500,000 ($1,000,000 + $500,000), and the minority shareholders are entitled to $193,548. The amount that accrues to the minority shareholders can be thought of as comprising two amounts, as follows:

(1) The minority shareholders' interest in the subsidiary's
earnings from its own separate operations, exclusive
of earnings from its investment in the parent
(30% of $500,000) $150,000

(2) The minority shareholders' interest in:
  (a) The parent's earnings from its separate
      operations $1,000,000
  (b) The parent's share of the subsidiary's
      earnings of $500,000 from its own
      separate operations (70% of $500,000) . . . . . .   <u>350,000</u>
                                                            $1,350,000

  As shown in the discussion of the treasury
  stock method, the minority interest in these
  amounts is in the ratio of 3,000 shares to
  93,000 shares (3,000/93,000) × $1,350,000 = ...   <u>43,548</u>
  Portion of combined earnings that accrues
  to the minority shareholders . . . .   <u>$193,548</u>

Recall from Chapter 5 that under the entity theory, the combined earnings
of the parent and the subsidiary are reported in the consolidated income
statement as follows:

Earnings accruing to controlling interests $1,306,452
Earnings accruing to minority interests . . . .   <u>193,548</u>
  Consolidated net income . . . .   <u>$1,500,000</u>

Some accountants advocate an alternative presentation, which deducts the
amount accruing to the minority interests from the combined earnings of
$1,500,000, to arrive at a consolidated net income of $1,306,452. In our
opinion, this presentation is inconsistent with the underlying premise of the
traditional allocation method, in which the parent is not viewed as the
reporting entity.

Presenting the combined earnings using either of the above methods
is obviously inconsistent with the requirements of *APB Opinion No. 18* with
respect to the equality that should exist between the parent's recorded net
income under the equity method of accounting and the amount reported
as consolidated net income. In a strict application of the equity method,
the parent would record $350,000 as its share of the subsidiary's earnings
(70% of $500,000). Thus, the parent's net income under the equity method
would be $1,350,000, which is not reported using either of the above
methods of presenting the combined earnings. Whether this provision of
APB Opinion No. 18 was intended to reject the traditional allocation method
is not known.

The amount of earnings per share on a consolidated basis (assuming
no other dilutive securities) is computed by dividing the $1,306,452 earnings
that accrue to the controlling interests by 90,000 shares deemed outstanding
(100,000 issued shares − 10,000 shares held by the subsidiary treated
as not outstanding). This computation gives $14.52 per share, which is a
meaningful amount to the holders of the 90,000 shares. (The same earnings
per share amount was calculated under the treasury stock approach using
93,000 as the denominator.)

Mathematically, the amount of the combined earnings that accrues to
each class of shareholders is usually determined under this approach using

Illustration 11-6
Application of simultaneous equations to traditional allocation method

---

Let P equal P Company's net income from its own separate operations plus its share of S Company's net income that would accrue to it on S Company's liquidation.
Let S equal S Company's net income from its own separate operations plus its share of P Company's net income that would accrue to it on P Company's liquidation.
Thus:

$$P = \$1,000,000 + (70\% \times S)$$
$$S = \$500,000 + (10\% \times P)$$

Substituting for P:

$$S = \$500,000 + 10\%(\$1,000,000 + 70\% \times S)$$
$$S = \$500,000 + \$100,000 + 0.07S$$
$$0.93S = \$600,000$$
$$S = \$645,161$$

S Company's minority shareholders would be entitled to $193,548 (30% of $645,161). Subtracting $193,548 from the combined earnings of $1,500,000 gives earnings of $1,306,452, which accrue to the controlling interests.

Alternatively, the earnings that accrue to the controlling interests can be computed by solving the equation for P by substituting for S as follows:

$$P = \$1,000,000 + 70\%(\$500,000 + 10\% \times P)$$
$$P = \$1,000,000 + \$350,000 + 0.07P$$
$$0.93P = \$1,350,000$$
$$P = \$1,451,613$$

Because P Company's existing shareholders (other than S Company) own 90% of its outstanding common stock, they would be entitled to $1,306,452 (90% of $1,451,613) in the event of a double liquidation.

---

simultaneous equations. In Illustration 11-6, the data from the example in this section are used with simultaneous equations to arrive at these amounts.

Whether to use the treasury stock method or the traditional allocation method depends on whether the parent company theory or the entity theory produces the more meaningful form of reported combined earnings. This purely subjective evaluation revolves around whether or not the reporting entity is transformed into a new reporting entity by the consolidation process. The treasury stock method is widely practiced, whereas the traditional allocation method is not, partly because of the simplicity of the treasury stock method and management's reluctance to treat part of the parent's earnings as accruing to the minority shareholders.

INTERCOMPANY PROFIT ON ASSET TRANSFERS

Regardless of the degree of complexity of the relationship among the entities within the consolidated group, all unrealized profit on intercompany asset transfers must be eliminated when preparing consolidated financial statements. In consolidation, intercompany transactions are eliminated using the procedures shown in Chapters 7–9. With respect to the special intercorporate relationships discussed in this chapter, this elimination process is used only when the unrealized intercompany profit is shared with minority shareholders. In these cases, the problem is to determine how much of the total unrealized intercompany profit must be allocated to the minority shareholders. We do this by carefully analyzing individual intercompany asset transfers that remain within the consolidated group to determine how much of each entity's unrealized intercompany profit accrues to the minority shareholders.

In most instances, the unrealized intercompany profit pertains to inventory transfers. When all unrealized intercompany profit pertains to inventory transfers and the intercorporate relationship is complex, the following procedures can be used to determine the amount of unrealized intercompany inventory profit to allocate to the minority shareholders on an overall basis:

(1) Complete the consolidation process through the partially consolidated column as illustrated in Chapters 7–9. Remember that the consolidated net income at this point is what would be reported if intercompany transactions were not eliminated.

(2) Determine the amount of unrealized intercompany profit recorded on each entity's books. Add these amounts to obtain a total amount of unrealized intercompany profit for all entities within the consolidated group.

(3) Determine each entity's income from its own separate operations— excluding earnings recorded under the equity method, but including any amortization of cost over or under book value. Subtract the amount of any unrealized intercompany profit recorded by that entity.

(4) Calculate the *reportable* consolidated net income through application of the equity method using the adjusted income amounts determined in (3).

(5) Subtract the reportable consolidated net income determined in (4) from the consolidated net income determined in (1). The difference represents the portion of the total unrealized intercompany profit, calculated in (2), that is treated as a deferral of the consolidated net income determined in (1).

(6) Subtract the amount determined in (5) from the amount determined in (2). The difference represents the amount of unrealized intercompany profit to be allocated to the minority shareholders.

The above procedures do not apply in cases involving reciprocal holdings in which the traditional allocation method is used. In these cases, the adjusted income amounts calculated in (3) are used in the simultaneous equations.

SUMMARY

Indirect vertical holdings are chain holdings in which one company has more than 50% ownership interest in another company; the second company, in turn, has more than 50% ownership interest in a third company. In applying the equity method of accounting to these situations, the lowest-level parent must apply the equity method before it is applied at the next higher level in the chain.

In indirect horizontal holdings, a subsidiary has an ownership interest in another subsidiary of its parent. In applying the equity method of accounting to these situations, the investor–subsidiary must apply the equity method of accounting to its investee's earnings before the parent applies the equity method to the investor–subsidiary's earnings.

Reciprocal holdings are formed when a subsidiary invests in its parent company's common stock. When the subsidiary is partially owned, there are two theories concerning how the combined earnings of the parent and the subsidiary should be presented in the consolidated financial statements—the treasury stock method and the traditional allocation method. Under the treasury stock method, the minority interest deduction is based solely on the subsidiary's earnings from its own separate operations, excluding earnings on its investment in the parent. Under the traditional allocation method, the portion of the combined earnings that accrues to the minority shareholders includes a portion of the parent's earnings from its own separate operations.

Glossary of new terms

Indirect Horizontal Holdings: An intercorporate relationship in which a subsidiary has a common stock investment in another subsidiary of their common parent.

Indirect Vertical Holdings: An intercorporate relationship in which a subsidiary has a controlling common stock interest in another company.

Reciprocal Holdings: An intercorporate relationship in which two entities of an affiliated group of companies have common stock investments in each other.

Treasury Stock Method: A procedure whereby the combined earnings of companies having reciprocal holdings (the controlled company being partially owned) are presented in a manner that portrays the parent as the reporting entity in consolidation. Under this method, the fact that the subsidiary's minority shareholders are indirectly shareholders of the parent is considered irrelevant.

Traditional Allocation Method: A procedure whereby the combined earnings of companies having reciprocal holdings (the controlled company being partially owned) are presented in a manner that implies the existence of a new reporting entity from the consolidation process. Under this method, the combined earnings are divided between amounts that accrue to the controlling interests and amounts that accrue to the minority interests, based on their respective interests in the new reporting entity.

Review questions

1. What is the difference between an indirect vertical holding and an indirect horizontal holding?
2. What are the two methods of accounting for reciprocal holdings?
3. Can a group of affiliated companies simultaneously have indirect vertical holdings, indirect horizontal holdings, and reciprocal holdings?
4. When indirect vertical holdings exist, what is the sequence of the consolidation process?
5. When indirect horizontal holdings exist, what is the sequence of the consolidation process?
6. How should a subsidiary account for an investment in its parent company?
7. From a consolidated viewpoint, are shares of a parent company that are held by a subsidiary considered issued stock or outstanding stock?

8. In consolidated financial statements, how is the cost of a subsidiary's investment in its parent's stock treated?
9. Under the traditional allocation method, is the parent viewed as the reporting entity in consolidation? Why or why not?
10. Under the treasury stock method, why is it misleading to treat all of the parent's common shares held by a partially owned subsidiary as not outstanding when computing consolidated earnings per share?

Discussion cases

Discussion case 11–1
Reciprocal holdings: Selection of accounting method

During 19X1, P Company acquired 80% of S Company's outstanding common stock, and S Company acquired 10% of P Company's outstanding common stock. P Company's top management has indicated to its controller that the minority interest shareholders of S Company will probably not share in P Company's earnings for many years to come, because P Company does not expect to pay any dividends on its common stock inasmuch as it intends to retain earnings for growth.

Required:
You must decide whether to use the treasury stock method or the traditional allocation method. How does this dividend policy influence your decision?

Discussion case 11–2
Reciprocal holdings: Determining dividends to be reported
in consolidated statement of retained earnings—Treasury stock method

Perez Company (which has an 80% owned subsidiary, which in turn owns 10% of the parent company's outstanding common stock) uses the treasury stock method to determine consolidated net income. Perez declared and paid cash dividends of $100,000 on its outstanding common stock during 19X1, $10,000 of which went to its 80% owned subsidiary. Perez Company's controller is uncertain whether the consolidated statement of retained earnings for 19X1 should show dividends declared of $100,000, $90,000, or $92,000.

Required:
How would you advise the controller?

Discussion case 11–3
Reciprocal holdings: Theory

P Company has a partially owned subsidiary, which recently acquired some of the parent company's outstanding common stock. You are the staff accountant in charge of preparing the consolidated financial statements for the first year after the reciprocal investment was established. P Company's controller has indicated that you should calculate the minority interest deduction by using the traditional allocation method.

Required:
How would you respond to this instruction?

Discussion case 11–4
Reciprocal holdings: Ramifications of dual intercorporate control

P Company owns 100% of S Company's outstanding common stock. S Company owns 100% of P Company's outstanding common stock.

Required:
What are the ramifications of such intercorporate holdings?

Exercises

Exercise 11–1
Indirect vertical holdings: Cost equals book value of net assets

X Company owns 90% of Y Company's outstanding common stock, and Y Company owns 80% of Z Company's outstanding common stock. Each company earned $100,000 during 19X1 from its own operations, exclusive of earnings on its investment in its subsidiary. (Assume there was no cost in excess of or below book value to amortize.)

Required:
(1) Determine consolidated net income for X Company in 19X1 through successive application of the equity method of accounting.
(2) Determine the minority interest deduction shown in X Company's consolidated income statement for 19X1.
(3) Indicate the sequence of the consolidation process.

Exercise 11–2
Indirect vertical holdings: Cost equals book value of net assets

On January 1, 19X1, Delta Company acquired 80% of the outstanding common stock of Echo Company. On January 1, 19X2, Echo Company acquired 80% of the outstanding common stock of Fox Company. On January 1, 19X3, P Company acquired 75% of the outstanding common stock of Delta Company. Each company's earnings for 19X3 (exclusive of earnings on investments in affiliates) are as follows:

P Company	$400,000
Delta Company	300,000
Echo Company	200,000
Fox Company	100,000

Each company declared cash dividends on its common stock of $10,000 during 19X1, 19X2, and 19X3. (Assume there was no cost in excess of or below book value to amortize.)

Required:
(1) Determine the net income of P Company and its subsidiaries for 19X3 through successive application of the equity method of accounting.
(2) Determine the total minority interest deduction shown in P Company's consolidated income statement for 19X3.
(3) Indicate the sequence of the consolidation process.

Exercise 11-3
Indirect horizontal holdings: Cost equals book value of net assets

On January 1, 19X1, X Company acquired 80% of Y Company's outstanding common stock and 70% of Z Company's outstanding common stock. On July 1, 19X1, Y Company acquired 10% of Z Company's outstanding common stock. (Assume all investments were made at a cost equal to the applicable share of net assets at book value.) For 19X2, the following amounts were reported:

	Income from Own Operations (exclusive of earnings on investments in affiliates)	Dividends Declared
X Company	$300,000	$50,000
Y Company	100,000	20,000
Z Company	50,000	10,000

Required:
(1) Determine the consolidated net income of X Company and its subsidiaries for 19X2 through successive application of the equity method of accounting.
(2) Determine the total minority interest deduction shown in X Company's consolidated income statement for 19X2.
(3) Indicate the sequence of the consolidation process.

Exercise 11-4
Several indirect horizontal holdings: Cost equals book value of net assets

P Company, a nonoperating holding company, is a parent of the following subsidiaries with the indicated ownership percentages:

Subsidiary Company	Ownership Percentage
B	90
C	80
D	70
E	60

In addition, B Company owns 10% of the outstanding common stock of C Company, D Company, and E Company; D Company owns 20% of the outstanding common stock of E Company. (Assume all investments were made at a cost equal to the applicable share of net assets at book value.)

Each company's net income from its own operations (exclusive of earnings on investments in affiliates) is as follows for 19X1:

P Company...	$ -0-
B Company...	10,000,000
C Company	1,000,000
D Company	100,000
E Company...	10,000

Required:
(1) Determine P Company's 19X1 net income through successive application of the equity method of accounting.
(2) Determine the total minority interest deduction shown in P Company's consolidated income statement for 19X1.
(3) Indicate the sequence of the consolidation process.

Exercise 11–5
Reciprocal holdings: Parent's cost equals book value of net assets

Alpha Company owns 80% of the outstanding common stock of Zebra Company, which in turn owns 10% of the outstanding common stock of Alpha Company. During 19X1, Alpha earned $500,000 from its own operations, exclusive of earnings on its investment in Zebra. (Assume the cost of the parent company's investment equals its share of the net assets at book value.) Zebra earned $100,000 from its own separate operations in 19X1. Neither company declared dividends during 19X1.

Required:
(1) Compute the consolidated net income and the minority interest deduction for 19X1 under the treasury stock method.
(2) Compute the amount of the combined earnings that accrues to the controlling interests and the minority interests for 19X1 under the traditional allocation method.

Problems

Problem 11–1
Indirect vertical holdings: Cost exceeds book value of net assets

On January 1, 19X1, P Company acquired 80% of S Company's outstanding common stock at a cost of $40,000 in excess of its share of net assets at book value. Assume that this excess is allocable to goodwill, which has a 10-year life.

On January 1, 19X2, S Company acquired 60% of T Company's outstanding common stock at a cost of $20,000 in excess of its share of net assets at book value. Assume that this excess is allocable to goodwill, which has a 10-year life.

For 19X2, the companies reported the following.

	Income from Own Operations (exclusive of earnings and amortization on investments in affiliates)	Dividends Declared
P Company	$500,000	$100,000
S Company	100,000	50,000
T Company	20,000	10,000

Required:
(1) Determine the consolidated net income of P Company and its subsidiaries for 19X2 using successive application of the equity method of accounting.
(2) Determine the total minority interest deduction shown in P Company's consolidated income statement for 19X2.
(3) Indicate the sequence of the consolidation process.

Problem 11–2
Indirect horizontal holdings: Cost exceeds book value of net assets

On January 1, 19X1, A Company acquired 80% of B Company's outstanding common stock at a cost of $100,000 in excess of its share of net assets at book value. Assume that this excess is allocable to goodwill, which has an estimated 20-year life.

On January 1, 19X2, A Company acquired 65% of C Company's outstanding common stock at a cost of $20,000 in excess of its share of net assets at book value. Assume that this excess is allocable to goodwill, which has an estimated 10-year life.

On January 1, 19X3, B Company acquired 20% of C Company's outstanding common stock at a cost of $5,000 in excess of its share of net assets at book value. Assume that this excess is allocable to goodwill, which has an estimated 10-year life.

Each company reported the following amounts during 19X3:

	Income from Own Operations (excluding income and amortization on investments in affiliates)	Dividends Declared
A Company	$1,000,000	$500,000
B Company	100,000	50,000
C Company	10,000	5,000

Required:
(1) Determine the amount of consolidated net income for A Company and its subsidiaries for 19X3 through successive application of the equity method of accounting.
(2) Determine the total minority interest deduction shown in A Company's consolidated income statement for 19X3.
(3) Indicate the sequence of the consolidation process.

Problem 11–3
Indirect horizontal holdings: Cost exceeds book value of net assets

On January 1, 19X1, P Company acquired 80% of the outstanding common stock of S Company and 70% of the outstanding common stock of T Company. On January 2, 19X1, S Company acquired 20% of the outstanding common stock of T Company. The analysis of the investment accounts by the individual components of the major conceptual elements for each acquisition at the acquisition date is as follows:

	P Company's Investment		S Company's Investment
	S Company	T Company	T Company
Book value element:			
Common stock	$ 16,000	$ 7,000	$ 2,000
Additional paid-in capital	144,000	63,000	18,000
Retained earnings	40,000	21,000	6,000
Current value over book value element:			
Land	20,000	7,000	4,000
Goodwill element	40,000	10,000	5,000
	$260,000	$108,000	$35,000

Assume goodwill has a five-year life from the purchase date. Data for 19X1 for each company are as follows:

	Income from Own Operations (exclusive of earnings and amortization on investments in affiliates)	Quarterly Dividends Declared
P Company	$600,000	$100,000
S Company	80,000	30,000
T Company	40,000	10,000

Assume earnings for each company occurred evenly during the year.

Required:
(1) Calculate the amount of P Company's consolidated net income for 19X1 through successive application of the equity method of accounting.
(2) Determine the minority interest deduction shown in P Company's consolidated income statement for 19X1.
(3) Indicate the sequence of the consolidation process.

Problem 11–4
Reciprocal holdings: Parent's cost exceeds book value of net assets

Pronto Company owns 90% of Speedee Company's outstanding common stock. Speedee Company owns 10% of Pronto Company's outstanding common stock. Data for each company for 19X1 are as follows.

	Income from Own Operations (exclusive of earnings on investments in affiliates)	Dividends Declared
Pronto Company............................	$800,000	$200,000
Speedee Company	100,000	30,000

In addition, Pronto had $12,000 amortization of cost in excess of book value during 19X1, which is not reflected in Pronto's separate earnings of $800,000.

Required:
(1) Calculate the consolidated net income and the minority interest deduction for 19X1 using the treasury stock method.
(2) Calculate the amount of combined earnings that accrues to the controlling interests and the minority interests under the traditional allocation method.

Problem 11–5
CHALLENGER Reciprocal holdings: Parent's cost exceeds book value; preparing consolidated statement of retained earnings in year subsequent to acquisition

Proctor Company acquired 60% of Sample Company's outstanding common stock on January 1, 19X1. On January 2, 19X1, Sample Company acquired 10% of Proctor Company's outstanding common stock. Data for each company for 19X1 are as follows:

	Proctor Company	Sample Company
Retained earnings, January 1, 19X1..........................	$900,000	$300,000
Income from own operations for 19X1, exclusive of earnings on investments in affiliates and amortization of cost in excess of book value	400,000	100,000
Amortization of cost in excess of book value	10,000	
Dividends declared in 19X1.....................................	150,000	30,000
Common shares outstanding.....................................	100,000	20,000

Required:
(1) Calculate the consolidated net income and the minority interest deduction for 19X1 under the treasury stock method.
(2) Prepare a consolidated statement of retained earnings for 19X1 assuming the parent uses the treasury stock method.
(3) Calculate the amount of combined earnings that accrues to the controlling interests and the minority interests for 19X1 under the traditional allocation method.
(4) Prepare a consolidated statement of retained earnings for 19X1 assuming the parent uses the traditional allocation method.

Problem 11–6
Indirect vertical holdings: Intercompany inventory profit in ending inventory from upstream sale

Alpha Company acquired 75% of Bravo Company's outstanding common stock on January 1, 19X1, and Bravo Company acquired 80% of Charley Company's outstanding common stock on January 1, 19X2. The cost of these acquisitions was at the applicable percentage of net assets at book value.

During 19X2, each company reported $100,000 of income (after income taxes) from its own operations, exclusive of earnings on investments in affiliates. At December 31, 19X2, Bravo Company's ending inventory included merchandise it had acquired from Charley Company at a cost of $50,000. Charley Company's cost was $30,000.

Required:
(1) Determine the consolidated net income that Bravo Company reports to its parent company for 19X2 through successive application of the equity method of accounting.
(2) Determine the consolidated net income that Alpha Company reports to its stockholders for 19X2 through successive application of the equity method of accounting.
(3) Determine the total minority interest deduction for 19X2.

12 Income Taxes and Earnings per Share

INCOME TAXES

In the first section of this chapter, we discuss accounting for income taxes for financial reporting purposes related to parent company investments in both domestic and foreign subsidiaries. Income tax considerations for investments in which control does not exist but significant influence does exist (20% through 50% ownership situations) are also discussed.

For income tax reporting purposes, investor companies must pay income taxes on dividends *received* from investee companies. (Some exceptions to this requirement are discussed later in the chapter.) In this respect, the income tax rules are on the cash basis. The financial reporting issue is determining whether investor companies should record such income taxes in their books on the cash basis (consistent with income tax reporting) or on the accrual basis, whereby income taxes on an investor's share of an investee's net income are recorded in the year the investee reports its earnings. For investments in subsidiaries, the Accounting Principles Board compromised between the cash basis and the accrual basis. For investments in which the ownership level is in the 20% through 50% range, the APB requires a strict application of the accrual basis. The rationale for this position is discussed in detail. The procedures for calculating income taxes to be recorded by an investor company on its share of an investee company's net income are also explained and illustrated.

Consolidated income tax return situations

A parent company and its **domestic** subsidiaries may file a consolidated federal income tax return if the parent owns a specified percentage of each subsidiary included. The primary condition is that the parent own at least 80% of the voting power of all classes of stock of each subsidiary included in the consolidated return.[1] Filing a consolidated income tax return relieves each subsidiary of the responsibility of filing a separate federal income tax return.

The process of preparing a consolidated federal income tax return is similar to preparing a consolidated income statement for financial reporting purposes. Often, only an appropriate adjustment is needed to the consolidated income statement that was prepared for financial reporting purposes to arrive at consolidated taxable income. Other similarities are as follows:

(1) Losses of companies within the consolidated group that do not generate profits can offset the earnings of the other members of the consolidated group.
(2) Intercompany profits and losses recorded on the sale of assets between entities are deferred until such assets are either sold (for inventory transfers) or depreciation occurs (for equipment transfers).

---

[1] The detailed requirements are set forth in the U.S. Internal Revenue Code of 1954, Code Sec. 1504(a).

(3) Intercompany dividends are **not taxable** to the parent at all. However, when a **domestic** subsidiary files a separate federal income tax return, dividends paid by a subsidiary to its parent **are taxable** to the parent. (However, an 85% "dividends received deduction" is allowed; thus, only 15% of the dividend is taxed.)

For financial reporting purposes, the obvious implication of a consolidated income tax return is that no income taxes need to be recorded by a parent with respect to the subsidiary's **net income.** This holds true whether or not the subsidiary actually makes dividend payments to the parent. Thus, from a consolidated viewpoint, these situations involve no accounting issues. From a separate company viewpoint, the total consolidated income tax expense must be allocated among the companies included in the consolidated income tax return. Any separate company financial statements issued by such companies must include full disclosure regarding the fact that the income tax expense is an allocated amount because the company is included in a consolidated income tax return.

The following section focuses on situations in which subsidiaries file separate federal income tax returns. These situations involve accounting issues from a consolidated viewpoint.

Separate income tax return situations

The accounting issue. Subsidiaries that file separate federal income tax returns record the income taxes they will pay individually. Parent companies include in their tax return only **dividends received** from their subsidiaries, not their full share of subsidiary earnings. The accounting issue is determining if and when income taxes should be recorded by the parent on the subsidiary's **net income** for financial reporting purposes. The following two obvious possibilities exist:

(1) The cash basis. Under the cash basis, income taxes are recorded in the year in which the parent *receives the dividends.* Thus, for a wholly owned domestic subsidiary with net income of $300,000, paying dividends of $100,000 in a given year, the parent would record income taxes of $6,000, assuming a 40% income tax rate and the application of the 85% dividends received deduction [40%(1 − 0.85) × $100,000]. No income taxes would be recorded on the undistributed earnings of $200,000. (Of course, under the equity method of accounting, the parent would record $300,000 earnings.)

(2) The accrual basis. Under the accrual basis, income taxes are recorded in the year in which the subsidiary *reports income,* as opposed to the year in which it pays dividends. Timing differences result between financial reporting and tax reporting when current earnings are not distributed. Compared with the preceding example using the cash basis, the parent would record income taxes of $18,000 under the accrual approach [40%(1 − 0.85) × $300,000]. (Although the 85% dividends received deduction is an income tax provision applicable only to dividends actually received, we apply the concept to the full $300,000 of earnings in computing income tax expense for financial reporting purposes, not just to the $100,000 of dividends actually received. Hereafter, for financial reporting purposes, we refer to the 85% dividends received deduction as the 85% **dividend exclusion** to signify that the 85% is not applied solely to dividends received.)

To be consistent with the accrual basis of accounting, the apparent solution would have the parent record any required federal income taxes in the period in which the subsidiary reports the income. However, some practical considerations must be dealt with in determining sound accounting principles in this area. The major consideration is that a subsidiary may not distribute all of its earnings because funds are needed to finance internal growth. This situation is most common for newly established foreign subsidiaries, when parent companies desire to limit the amount of equity capital the subsidiary obtains directly from the parent. Thus, the parent views all or a large portion of the subsidiary's retained earnings as *permanent capital.* From this viewpoint, no U.S. income taxes would ever be paid on the amount deemed permanent capital, because it would never be distributed as dividends. Consequently, the parent would not record any income taxes on that portion of a subsidiary's earnings that is invested in the subsidiary indefinitely. This consideration is reinforced by U.S. federal income tax laws that allow a subsidiary to remit its undistributed earnings to its parent in a tax-free liquidation, providing certain conditions are met.

Requirements of *APB Opinion No. 23.* These practical considerations were given substantial weight when the Accounting Principles Board issued *APB Opinion No. 23,* "Accounting for Income Taxes—Special Areas." This pronouncement specifies the accounting treatment for financial reporting purposes of income tax considerations related to investments in subsidiaries. It requires parent companies to provide income taxes on their share of their subsidiaries' net incomes unless evidence shows that **some** or **all** of the undistributed subsidiary earnings

(1) Have been or will be invested indefinitely, or
(2) Will be remitted in a tax-free liquidation.[2]

If either of these two conditions is satisfied, the parent records no income taxes on the applicable portion of the undistributed subsidiary earnings. Of course, appropriate income taxes must always be recorded on subsidiary earnings that are distributed or are expected to be distributed. (Calculations are shown later in the chapter.) Note that the word "indefinitely" in (1), above, does not mean "permanently." In other words, parent companies are not required to invest the undistributed earnings of their subsidiaries forever—only for the foreseeable future. Two examples of evidence required to satisfy either of the conditions listed above are **experience** and **future programs of operations.**[3]

---

[2] *APB Opinion No. 23,* "Accounting for Income Taxes—Special Areas" (New York: AICPA, 1972), paragraph 12.
[3] *APB Opinion No. 23,* paragraph 12.

In essence, income taxes are recorded by the parent only to the extent that their payment is reasonably expected. Thus, in addition to the extreme cases of (1) 100% reinvestment on an indefinite basis, and (2) no intention to reinvest any earnings on an indefinite basis, possible hybrid situations exist in which a percentage of current earnings has been or is expected to be distributed as dividends and the remainder is reinvested indefinitely. With respect to changing circumstances, the pronouncement states

(1) If circumstances change and it becomes apparent that some or all of the undistributed earnings of a subsidiary will be remitted in the foreseeable future but income taxes have not been recognized by the parent company, it should accrue as an expense of the current-period income taxes attributable to that remittance; income tax expense for such remittance should not be accounted for as an extraordinary item.

(2) If it becomes apparent that some or all of the undistributed earnings of a subsidiary on which income taxes have been accrued will not be remitted in the foreseeable future, the parent company should adjust income tax expense of the current period; such adjustment of income tax expense should not be accounted for as an extraordinary item.[4]

Situation (1) typically occurs when a parent company anticipates either (a) a significant decrease in the direct exchange rate of the currency of the country in which its subsidiary is located (whether from an expected weakening of the foreign currency or a strengthening of the dollar), or (b) the foreign government's imposition of currency transfer restrictions. Situation (2) typically occurs during a continuing increase in the direct exchange rate of the currency of the country in which the subsidiary is located or when the foreign government encourages the expansion of existing operations by granting inducements.

When subsidiaries' earnings are not reinvested indefinitely, the calculation of income taxes recorded by the parent on the earnings of a subsidiary is different for a domestic subsidiary than for a foreign subsidiary. The following sections illustrate these separate calculations.

Illustration: Computing and recording income taxes; domestic subsidiary—Earnings not invested indefinitely. For domestic subsidiaries, income taxes recorded on the parent's equity in the subsidiary's net income are calculated using the 85% dividend exclusion. For a 90% owned subsidiary with net income of $100,000, the calculation is as follows:

Net income of subsidiary	$100,000
Parent's ownership percentage	90%
Parent's equity in earnings of subsidiary	$ 90,000
Less—dividend exclusion @ 85%	(76,500)
Net income subject to taxation	$ 13,500
Assumed income tax rate	40%
Income taxes	$ 5,400

---

[4] *APB Opinion No. 23*, paragraph 12. Copyright © 1972 by the American Institute of Certified Public Accountants, Inc.

To the extent that all of the current earnings are not distributed in the current year, timing differences result, and the Deferred Income Taxes account must be credited for the income taxes relating to the undistributed current earnings. Assuming the subsidiary paid total dividends of $20,000 (20% of its net income) during the year, the parent company's entries with respect to the subsidiary's operations for the year are as follows:

(1) To record equity in earnings of subsidiary:

Investment in subsidiary	90,000	
Equity in net income of subsidiary		90,000
(90% of $100,000)		

(2) To record dividend received from subsidiary:

Cash..	18,000	
Investment in subsidiary		18,000
(90% of $20,000)		

(3) To record income tax expense on equity in earnings of subsidiary:

Income tax expense	5,400	
Income taxes currently payable		
[($18,000/$90,000) × $5,400].....................		1,080
Deferred income taxes		
[($72,000/$90,000) × $5,400].....................		4,320

Foreign subsidiaries: General discussion of tax rules. A foreign subsidiary files an income tax return in the country in which it is domiciled. Dividends paid to a U.S. parent are not eligible for the 85% dividends received deduction. However, the parent pays U.S. federal income taxes on these dividends only if the subsidiary's foreign income tax credits cannot offset amounts otherwise payable to the U.S. government. For foreign subsidiaries, the income taxes recorded on the parent's equity in the subsidiary's net income are calculated as follows:

(1) The subsidiary's net income is irrelevant; instead, the subsidiary's pretax income is treated as if it had been earned in the United States.
(2) U.S. income taxes are calculated on this foreign pretax income using regular income tax rates.
(3) Foreign tax credits are subtracted from the taxes calculated in (2). If a positive balance exists, then that amount of U.S. income tax is payable. If a zero or negative balance exists, no U.S. income tax is payable. The following two kinds of foreign tax credits exist:
  (a) Foreign income taxes.
  (b) Dividend withholding taxes. These taxes are withheld by the foreign government when a dividend is remitted.

A list of statutory income tax rates for several countries appears in Illustration 12-1.

Illustration 12-1
Examples of foreign income tax rates

	Statutory Income Tax Rate[a] (percent)	Dividend Withholding Tax Rate[b] (percent)
Brazil	25–40	25
Canada—Manufacturing	30	15
—Other	36	15
France	50	5–15
Ireland (Republic of)—Manufacturing	10	Nil
—Other	45	Nil
Italy	36	5–30
Japan	46–56	10–15
Mexico	25–42	21
Middle Eastern countries (an average of Iran, Iraq, Israel, Kuwait, Lebanon, Saudi Arabia, and Syria)	50	Nil
Switzerland	23–36	5–15
United Kingdom	40–52	Nil
United States	15–46	15–30
Venezuela	50	15
West Germany	36–56	15–25

SOURCE: Latest available published statutory rates.
[a] For countries that have a range of income tax rates indicated, the exact rate is a function of one or more of the following factors: amount of income, amount of capitalization, whether earnings are distributed or retained, type of business, and whether the corporation is a resident or nonresident company.
[b] For foreign countries, the withholding tax rate indicated is that existing under tax treaties with the United States.

In addition to any U.S. income taxes, the parent must record on its books the dividend withholding tax payable.[5] The dividend withholding tax is a tax to the recipient; accordingly, it is never recorded as an expense on the foreign subsidiary's books.

Illustration: Computing and recording income taxes; foreign subsidiaries—Earnings not invested indefinitely. The amount of income taxes recorded on the parent's books for a wholly owned foreign subsidiary whose earnings are **not invested indefinitely** is calculated in the following examples:

	Country A	Country B
Assumed foreign income tax rate	30%	50%
Assumed foreign dividend withholding rate	10%	15%
Foreign subsidiary's pretax income	$200,000	$200,000
Foreign income tax expense	(60,000)	(100,000)
Foreign subsidiary's net income	$140,000	$100,000
U.S. income taxes at assumed rate of 46% on pretax income	$ 92,000	$ 92,000
Less foreign tax credits—		
Foreign income taxes (per above)	(60,000)	(100,000)
Dividend withholding taxes (10% and 15%, respectively, of subsidiary's net income)	(14,000)	(15,000)
U.S. income taxes recorded by the parent company	$ 18,000	$ -0-

[5] *APB Opinion No. 23,* paragraph 10.

Timing differences result when all current earnings are not distributed in the current year, and the Deferred Income Taxes account must be credited for taxes on the undistributed current earnings. Assuming each subsidiary paid $20,000 total dividends during the year ($\frac{1}{7}$ and $\frac{1}{5}$ of their respective net incomes), the parent's entries with respect to each subsidiary's operations for the year are as follows:

(1) To record equity in earnings of subsidiary:

Investment in subsidiary	140,000		100,000	
Equity in net income of subsidiary		140,000		100,000
(100% of $140,000 and $100,000, respectively.)				

(2) To record the dividend withholding tax:

Income tax expense	14,000		15,000	
Income taxes payable ($\frac{1}{7}$ and $\frac{1}{5}$, respectively).........		2,000		3,000
Deferred income taxes ($\frac{6}{7}$ and $\frac{4}{5}$, respectively).........		12,000		12,000
(100% of $14,000 and $15,000, respectively.)				

(3) To record dividend received from subsidiary:

Cash..............................	18,000		17,000	
Income taxes payable	2,000		3,000	
Investment in subsidiary		20,000		20,000

Note: Income taxes payable equal the taxes withheld at the time of remittance.

(4) To record U.S. income taxes on equity in earnings of subsidiary:

Income tax expense	18,000	
Income taxes payable ($\frac{1}{7}$)		2,571
Deferred income taxes ($\frac{6}{7}$)		15,429

Obviously, the greater the foreign income tax and dividend withholding tax rates, the greater are the credits against the U.S. income taxes otherwise payable. The preceding examples assumed no limitations on the credit amount allowable against U.S. income taxes otherwise payable. However, on a per country basis and on an overall basis, the Internal Revenue Code does limit the credit amount allowable against U.S. income taxes otherwise payable. The specific limitations are beyond the scope of this text, but you should be aware that they exist.

Disclosures required—Earnings invested indefinitely. When a parent has not recorded income taxes on all or a portion of its share of a subsidiary's undistributed earnings or dividend withholding taxes, *APB Opinion No. 23* requires disclosure in the notes to the financial statements as follows:

(1) A declaration of an intention to reinvest undistributed earnings of a subsidiary to support the conclusion that remittance of those earnings has been indefinitely postponed, or a declaration that the undistributed earnings will be remitted in the form of a tax-free liquidation, and

(2) The cumulative amount of undistributed earnings on which the parent company has not recognized income taxes.[6]

The usefulness of the latter disclosure requirement is questionable because of the complexities involved in computing the additional income taxes potentially payable on the undistributed earnings. It would be more informative to disclose the income taxes that have not been recorded on the earnings of the current year and on a cumulative basis.

Investments in which control does not exist but significant influence does exist (20–50% ownership)

Investments in the 20–50% ownership range are accounted for under the equity method of accounting as prescribed by *APB Opinion No. 18,* "The Equity Method of Accounting for Investments in Common Stock." The Internal Revenue Code does not have corresponding rules relating to the equity method of accounting. Accordingly, as the equity method of accounting is applied to record an investor's share of an investee's net income, the income recorded by the investor does not constitute taxable income for federal income tax reporting purposes until such income is paid out by the investee as dividends. As with a subsidiary paying dividends to a parent company, the federal income tax rules use the cash basis of accounting for taxation of this income.

Requirements of *APB Opinion No. 24.* Unless all of the investee's net income is paid out as dividends each year, timing differences result between financial reporting and income tax reporting. *APB Opinion No. 24,* "Accounting for Income Taxes," governs the income tax treatment, for financial reporting purposes, of investments in common stock when control does not exist but significant influence does exist. This pronouncement requires that income taxes be recorded on these timing differences in one of two ways, depending on how the ultimate realization of the investor's equity in the investee's undistributed earnings is expected. This depends on all of the facts and circumstances of each individual investment. The two ways in which realization may be expected are as follows:

(1) Realization through dividends. If realization is expected through receipt of dividends, then the income recorded under the equity method of accounting should have regular income taxes recorded thereon, considering the following provisions:

   (a) Investments in domestic corporations. The available 85% dividend exclusion should be taken into account.

---

[6] *APB Opinion No. 23,* paragraph 14.

(b) Investment in foreign corporations.   Any available foreign tax credits should be taken into account.

(2) Realization through disposition (sale).   If realization is expected through the sale of the investment, then the income recorded under the equity method of accounting should have capital gain taxes (or other appropriate rates) recorded thereon, taking into consideration all available deductions and credits.[7] (The presumption here is that because undistributed earnings increase the book value per share, the market price per share of the stock should also increase, enabling the investor to sell at a gain.)

No percentage guidelines exist concerning when regular income tax rates should be used as opposed to capital gain tax rates. The question we must answer is: Why was the investment made? In general, the higher the ownership percentage, the less likely it is that realization of the investor's equity in the investee's earnings is expected through disposition.

Accounting rules for common stock investments in this ownership range require that income taxes be recorded even if the investee has invested or will invest its undistributed earnings indefinitely. As was the case in the preceding section dealing with a subsidiary, an investee company may not distribute some or all of its earnings to have funds to finance internal growth. Consequently, income taxes may never be paid by the investee's investors, because dividends presumably would never be paid on this deemed amount of permanent capital. The APB concluded, however, that these situations were substantially different from situations in which the investor is a parent. In a parent–subsidiary relationship, the parent controls the dividend policies of its subsidiaries. In an investor–investee relationship in which the ownership level is not over 50%, the investor does not control the dividend policy of the investee. This key factor influenced the APB to require investors to record income taxes on all earnings that are recorded under the equity method of accounting, regardless of the investee's reinvestment intentions.

Illustration: Computing and recording income taxes.   To illustrate the entries that would be made in the above situations, assume P Company owns 30% of the outstanding common stock of S Company, which is a domestic company. Also assume S Company had net income of $100,000 for 19X1 and paid dividends of $40,000. P Company intends to hold the investment for a long time. P Company's entries that would be recorded during 19X1, using a regular income tax rate of 40%, are as follows.

(1) To record equity in earnings of investee:

Investment in investee	30,000	
Equity in net income of investee		30,000
(30% of $100,000)		

---

[7] *APB Opinion No. 24,* "Accounting for Income Taxes—Investments in Common Stock Accounted for by the Equity Method (Other than Subsidiaries and Corporate Joint Ventures)" (New York: AICPA, 1972), paragraphs 7–8.

(2) To record dividend received from investee:

```
Cash.............................................. 12,000
    Investment in investee ............................    12,000
    (30% of $40,000)
```

(3) To record income taxes on equity in earnings of investee:

```
Income tax expense ...................................  1,800
    Income taxes payable (40%) ........................       720
    Deferred income taxes (60%)........................     1,080
    [40%(1 − 0.85) × $30,000]
```

Note: The nature of the investment dictates the use of the 85% dividend exclusion.

Tax treatment of parent's amortization of cost above or below its interest in subsidiary's net assets at book value

Chapters 4 and 5 illustrated the amortization procedures appropriate for that portion of a parent's cost that is in excess of or below its interest in the subsidiary's net assets at book value. For income tax reporting purposes, the amortization of cost in excess of book value is not tax deductible. This holds true even if some amortization relates to depreciable, tangible assets. Likewise, when a parent's cost is below book value, the amortization (which is a credit to income in these situations) is not taxable. Thus, the amortization for financial reporting purposes is a permanent difference. (Recall from the illustrations in Chapters 4 and 5, in which amortization of cost was in excess of book value, that the amortization was treated as a permanent difference in calculating the parent's income tax expense for financial reporting purposes.)

Under Section 338 of the Internal Revenue Code, an acquiring company may treat the acquisition of a target company's common stock as an asset purchase. If this election is made, the tax basis of the assets is "stepped up" based on the purchase cost of the target company's common stock, just as if the assets had been acquired instead of common stock. (As discussed in Chapter 2, certain nontax reasons may exist for acquiring common stock instead of assets.) Some finer points and other information concerning Section 338 include the following:

(1) The subsidiary must be 80% owned. (The 80% ownership level must have been obtained within a 12-month period.)
(2) The election must be made within 75 days after obtaining 80% ownership of the target company's common stock.
(3) Amounts assigned to goodwill are not tax deductible.
(4) Section 338 is a new section enacted as part of the Tax Equity and Fiscal Responsibility Act of 1982. It replaces Section 334(b)(2), which required that the target company be liquidated to obtain the step-up in tax basis.

Note that when control does not exist and an investor must account for its investment under the equity method of accounting (20–50% ownership situations), any required amortization made pursuant to the provisions of paragraph 19n of *APB Opinion No. 18* is neither tax deductible nor taxable. No special tax provisions allow tax deductibility as they do in situations in which ownership is at least 80% and other conditions are satisfied as discussed above.

Summary

A parent company may have to pay U.S. income taxes on the net incomes of its subsidiaries. These income taxes are above and beyond the income taxes recorded on each subsidiary's separate books. In general, these additional income taxes are recorded by the parent in the period in which the subsidiary reports the related earnings, as opposed to the period in which the dividends are received. However, if it is reasonably expected that some or all of a subsidiary's earnings will remain undistributed indefinitely, then a parent company need not record income taxes that otherwise would be payable if these earnings were distributed. When income taxes on a subsidiary's net income have not been recorded by the parent, complete disclosure is required to explain why income taxes have not been recorded.

EARNINGS PER SHARE

Fundamentally, consolidated earnings per share is simply consolidated net income (income accruing to the benefit of the parent's shareholders) divided by the average number of parent company common shares outstanding (adjusted for the parent's common equivalent shares and its other potentially dilutive securities, if any).

Most subsidiaries are wholly owned and do not have outstanding any potentially dilutive securities such as stock options, warrants, convertible bonds, and convertible preferred stocks. The parent's calculation of earnings per share on a consolidated basis presents no special problems in these cases. To make the calculations, the parent company merely uses the income it has recorded under the equity method of accounting with respect to the subsidiary's earnings, along with the net income from its own operations.

When a subsidiary is partially owned and has no potentially dilutive securities outstanding, the procedures are identical to situations in which a subsidiary is wholly owned and has no potentially dilutive securities outstanding. The subsidiary's earnings that accrue to the minority shareholders and the minority interest shares outstanding are excluded in the calculation of consolidated earnings per share.

When a subsidiary has potentially dilutive securities outstanding (whether the subsidiary is wholly owned or partially owned), the above procedures are not proper. A parent company must follow different procedures to determine the amount of a subsidiary's earnings that may be included with a parent company's net income for purposes of computing earnings per share on a consolidated basis.

At this point, you should have a solid understanding of the procedures used to compute earnings per share as discussed in *APB Opinion No. 15,*

"Earnings per Share." This pronouncement is discussed in detail in intermediate accounting texts.

Requirements of *APB Opinion No. 15*

APB Opinion No. 15 specifies the accounting procedures used to compute earnings per share on a consolidated basis as follows:

> If a subsidiary has dilutive warrants or options outstanding or dilutive convertible securities which are common stock equivalents from the standpoint of the subsidiary, consolidated . . . primary earnings per share should include the portion of the subsidiary's income that would be applicable to the consolidated group based on its holdings and the subsidiary's primary earnings per share.
>
> If a subsidiary's convertible securities are not common stock equivalents from the standpoint of the subsidiary, only the portion of the subsidiary's income that would be applicable to the consolidated group based on its holdings and the fully diluted earnings per share of the subsidiary should be included in consolidated . . . fully diluted earnings per share.[8]

The procedures for determining "the portion of the subsidiary's income that would be applicable to the consolidated group based on its holdings and the subsidiary's primary/fully diluted earnings per share" are explained in the next section.

Basic approach

When a subsidiary has potentially dilutive securities outstanding, the effect of their potential dilution must be considered when computing earnings per share on a consolidated basis. This is done by substituting an earnings amount (the calculation of which is explained and illustrated later in this chapter) for the subsidiary's earnings that the parent has recorded under the equity method of accounting, the latter amount being usable for calculating consolidated earnings per share only when the subsidiary has no potentially dilutive securities outstanding.

This substitution effectively adjusts the numerator that the parent uses to calculate the primary and fully diluted earnings per share on a consolidated basis. Because this adjustment to the numerator is made only to compute earnings per share, it is accomplished on a worksheet outside the general ledger—the Equity in Earnings of Subsidiary account recorded on the parent company's books is not adjusted.

The denominator that the parent uses to calculate the primary and fully diluted earnings per share on a consolidated basis is determined using only the parent's outstanding common stock and potentially dilutive securities.

To determine how a subsidiary's potentially dilutive securities affect earnings per share on a consolidated basis, the subsidiary must calculate its own individual primary and fully diluted earnings per share. The actual amount of a subsidiary's earnings per share need not be determined, but the numerator and denominator used in the calculation are necessary. The numerator represents the earnings for purposes of earnings per share. The objective is to determine how much of this numerator accrues to the parent

---

[8] *APB Opinion No. 15*, "Earnings per Share" (New York: AICPA, 1969), paragraphs 66–67. Copyright © 1969 by the American Institute of Certified Public Accountants, Inc.

company so that earnings per share on a consolidated basis can be calculated.

This is done by developing a percentage from the denominator used to compute the subsidiary's earnings per share; this percentage is then applied to the numerator. The percentage is developed from the following ratio:

$$\frac{\text{Number of shares in denominator that are owned by or accrue to the parent}}{\text{Total number of shares in denominator}} = \text{Percentage}$$

This is the percentage of the numerator in the subsidiary's primary earnings per share and fully diluted earnings per share calculations that accrues to the parent company.

This approach produces the same results illustrated in an unofficial accounting interpretation of *APB Opinion No. 15* issued by the American Institute of Certified Public Accountants.[9] However, the illustration in that unofficial interpretation uses a different and somewhat more involved mechanical procedure than we have illustrated here.

Illustration:
Computing earnings per share on a consolidated basis when subsidiary has potentially dilutive securities outstanding

Assume the following information with respect to P Company and its 90% owned subsidiary, S Company, for 19X1:

(1) Information related to P Company:

Income data:

Income from its own separate operations	$150,000
Equity in net income of subsidiary (90% of $80,000)	72,000
Amortization of cost in excess of book value	(12,000)
Consolidated net income	$210,000

Securities data:

Average number of common stock shares outstanding during the year	250,000
Common equivalent shares deemed outstanding, net of shares assumed repurchased under the treasury stock method	50,000
Denominator for purposes of computing consolidated primary earnings per share	300,000
Other potentially dilutive securities	None

(On the basis of the structure of P Company's securities, fully diluted earnings per share on a consolidated basis is not necessary because P Company has no other potentially dilutive securities outstanding.)

---

[9] *Unofficial Accounting Interpretations of APB Opinion No. 15*, "Computing Earnings per Share" (New York: AICPA, 1970), *Definitional Interpretation No. 93.*

(2) Information related to S Company:

Income data:

Net income	$100,000
Less—Preferred stock dividend requirement	(20,000)
Net income allocable to common stock	$ 80,000

Securities data:

Average number of common stock shares outstanding during the year	60,000
Common equivalent shares deemed outstanding (stock options and warrants), net of shares assumed repurchased under the treasury stock method (P Company owns 40% of these outstanding securities)	20,000
Denominator for purposes of computing primary earnings per share	80,000

Other potentially dilutive securities:

Preferred stock, convertible into 40,000 shares of common stock, annual cumulative dividend requirement is $20,000 (P Company owns none of these preferred shares)	40,000
Denominator for purposes of computing fully diluted earnings per share	120,000

S Company's primary and fully diluted earnings per share are calculated as follows:

Calculation of primary earnings per share—S Company

Net Income	$100,000
Less—Preferred stock dividend requirements	(20,000)
Numerator	$ 80,000
Denominator	80,000 shares
Primary earnings per share	$1.00

Calculation of fully diluted earnings per share—S Company

Net Income (Numerator)	$100,000
Denominator	120,000 shares
Fully diluted earnings per share	$0.83

The calculation of the earnings per share amounts above is unnecessary. The numerator and denominator used in each calculation, however, are needed to determine the amount of the subsidiary's earnings that may be included with the parent's own separate earnings when computing consolidated earnings per share. This amount is calculated as follows:

	Shares Owned by or That Accrue to P Company	Total
Average number of common stock shares outstanding during the year	54,000	60,000
Common stock equivalents deemed outstanding, net of shares assumed repurchased under the treasury stock method	8,000 (40%)	20,000
	62,000	80,000

The ratio (62,000/80,000) is equivalent to 77.5%, which is multiplied by the numerator used by S Company to compute its primary earnings per share as follows:

Numerator used by S Company to compute its primary earnings per share	$80,000
Percentage calculated above	77.5%
Amount of S Company earnings that P Company must use to compute consolidated primary earnings per share	$62,000

The consolidated primary earnings per share is calculated as follows:

Calculation of consolidated primary earnings per share

Amount of S Company's earnings that P Company can include in computing consolidated primary earnings per share (per preceding calculation)	$ 62,000
P Company's earnings from its own separate operations	150,000
Less—Amortization of cost in excess of book value	(12,000)
Numerator for purposes of computing consolidated primary earnings per share	$200,000
Denominator	300,000 shares
Primary earnings per share (consolidated)	$0.67

The amount of the subsidiary's earnings that P Company can include in its numerator for purposes of computing consolidated fully diluted earnings per share is computed as follows:

	Shares Owned by or That Accrue to P Company	Total
Average number of common stock shares outstanding during the year	54,000	60,000
Common stock equivalents deemed outstanding, net of shares assumed repurchased under the treasury stock method	8,000 (40%)	20,000
Other potentially dilutive securities (preferred stock)		40,000
	62,000	120,000

The ratio (62,000/120,000) is equivalent to 51.67%, which is multiplied by the numerator used by S Company to compute its fully diluted earnings per share as follows:

Numerator used by S Company to compute its fully diluted earnings per share	$100,000
Percentage calculated above	51.67%
Amount of S Company's earnings that P Company must use to compute consolidated fully diluted earnings per share	$ 51,667

The consolidated fully diluted earnings per share is calculated as follows:

Calculation of consolidated fully diluted earnings per share

Amount of S Company's earnings per share that the parent can include to compute consolidated fully diluted earnings per share (per preceding calculation)............................	$ 51,667
P Company's earnings from its own separate operations.............	150,000
Less—Amortization of cost in excess of book value	(12,000)
Numerator for purposes of computing consolidated fully diluted earnings per share	$189,667
Denominator (same as in primary earnings per share because P Company has no other potentially dilutive securities outstanding)	300,000 shares
Consolidated fully diluted earnings per share	$0.63

In reviewing the preceding illustration, the following points should be understood:

(1) The equity in the subsidiary's earnings recorded by P Company was calculated after the preferred stock dividend requirement was subtracted from S Company's net income, as required by paragraph 19k of *APB Opinion No. 18*.

(2) The $72,000 equity in the subsidiary's earnings, recorded by P Company under the equity method of accounting, was greater than both the $62,000 used to compute consolidated primary earnings per share and the $51,667 used to compute consolidated fully diluted earnings per share.

(3) Initially, P Company did not have to calculate a fully diluted earnings per share amount inasmuch as it does not have any "other potentially dilutive securities" outstanding. The subsidiary, however, does have "other potentially dilutive securities" outstanding, which significantly reduce the parent's interest in the subsidiary's net income. Accordingly, a fully diluted earnings per share amount must be calculated on a consolidated basis.

(4) We assumed that no unrealized profit existed pertaining to intercompany transactions that required eliminations in arriving at consolidated net income. Any unrealized profit deferred in consolidation would have to be subtracted from the numerators used above to compute consolidated primary and fully diluted earnings per share.

Summary

When a subsidiary has common stock equivalents or other potentially dilutive securities, the parent company cannot use the earnings it has recorded in its general ledger under the equity method of accounting to compute consolidated primary and fully diluted earnings per share. Instead, another amount that reflects the parent's interest in the subsidiary's earnings must be used, assuming the subsidiary's common stock equivalents and other potentially dilutive securities had been exercised or converted into common stock. To determine this other amount involves analyzing the number of shares that the subsidiary uses as its denominators to compute its individual primary and fully diluted earnings per share amounts. This analysis produces a ratio, which when applied to the numerators used by the subsidiary to compute its individual primary and fully diluted earnings per share amounts, produces the proper amount the parent must use to compute consolidated primary and fully diluted earnings per share amounts.

Review questions

1. For investments in which control does not exist, in what two ways may the investee's earnings be realized by the investor?
2. Is the 85% dividends received deduction applicable only to dividends received from domestic corporations?
3. Does the term *invested indefinitely* mean the same thing as *invested permanently*?
4. What types of evidence satisfy the indefinite investment criterion?
5. When a subsidiary's earnings are considered to be invested indefinitely, what disclosures are required?
6. In general, how are the earnings of foreign subsidiaries taxed in the United States?
7. On whose books is the dividend withholding tax recorded? Why?
8. In what situations do deferred income taxes arise?
9. When a parent company's cost is in excess of its share of its subsidiary's net assets at book value, and such excess may be assigned to depreciable assets, is that excess deductible for income tax reporting purposes?
10. What steps are necessary to make cost in excess of book value deductible for income tax reporting purposes?
11. Summarize the basic approach to calculating consolidated earnings per share when a subsidiary has potentially dilutive securities outstanding.
12. When a subsidiary has potentially dilutive securities outstanding, is the denominator used by a parent company adjusted to compute consolidated earnings per share? Why or why not?

Discussion cases

Discussion case 12–1
Income taxes: Planning

On January 1, 19X1, Paul Company acquired all of Saul Company's outstanding common stock in such a manner that the business combination did not qualify either as a pooling of interests for financial reporting purposes or as a tax-free reorganization for income tax reporting purposes. The value of the consideration given by Paul Company greatly exceeded the book value of Saul Company's net assets. The cost in excess of book value was assignable to land, depreciable fixed assets, and goodwill.

Required:
What important income tax consideration should be addressed?

Discussion case 12–2
Income taxes: Determining if and when to record

Edwin Company is establishing a foreign subsidiary. The plans call for investing $500,000 to establish initial operations. The subsidiary will retain all earnings for the first five years to finance internal growth. At the end of the five-year period, future internal growth is expected to be more moderate, and all of the future earnings will not be needed to finance additional internal growth.

Required:
Evaluate if and when Edwin Company should record income taxes on the foreign subsidiary's earnings, assuming foreign income tax credits will not offset income taxes that would otherwise be payable.

Discussion case 12–3
Income taxes: Determining if and when to record

Decker Company is a multinational corporation with numerous foreign subsidiaries. During each year, Decker Company employs the following dividend strategy with respect to each of its foreign subsidiaries:

(1) If a foreign currency is weakening, then dividends are declared quarterly by the foreign subsidiary as profits are earned.
(2) If a foreign currency is strengthening, then dividends are not declared until the strengthening has subsided. This strategy is followed if cash held by a foreign subsidiary must be invested in liquid investments.

Required:
Evaluate if and when Decker Company should record income taxes on its foreign subsidiaries' earnings, assuming foreign income tax credits will not offset income taxes that would otherwise be payable.

Exercises

Exercise 12–1
Income taxes: Controlling interest—Domestic subsidiary

PDQ Company owns 100% of the outstanding common stock of Sprint Company, a domestic company that had net income of $100,000 in 19X1. Sprint Company's earnings are not intended to be retained in the business indefinitely. In 19X1, Sprint Company paid cash dividends of $25,000 on its common stock. Assume a 40% income tax rate and a 25% capital gain rate.

Required:
Prepare PDQ Company's 19X1 entries with respect to its investment in Sprint Company.

Exercise 12–2
Income taxes: Controlling interest—Domestic subsidiary

Assume the information in Exercise 12–1, except that all of Sprint Company's earnings are intended to be retained in the business for internal expansion and that Sprint has not paid any dividends on its common stock since its inception.

Required:
The requirement is the same as for Exercise 12–1.

Exercise 12–3
Income taxes: Controlling interest—Foreign subsidiary

Pike Company owns 100% of the outstanding common stock of Shonty Company, a foreign subsidiary that had net income of $65,000 in 19X1. Shonty Company consistently declares no dividends on its common stock, because the earnings are used each year for internal expansion, which is expected to continue into the foreseeable future. Assume a 46% domestic income tax rate, a 35% foreign income tax rate, and a 10% withholding tax rate.

Required:
Prepare Pike Company's 19X1 entries with respect to its investment in Shonty Company.

Exercise 12–4
Income taxes: Less than a controlling interest—Domestic investee

On January 1, 19X1, Pence Company acquired 40% of the outstanding common stock of Schilling Company, a domestic company. Schilling Company had net income of $100,000 in 19X1 and has not paid a dividend since its inception six years ago. Schilling Company's 19X1 annual report stated that management planned to reinvest its earnings for the foreseeable future. Pence Company is currently considering acquiring enough additional shares to give it control over Schilling Company. Assume a 40% income tax rate and a 25% capital gain rate.

Required:
Prepare Pence Company's 19X1 entries related to its investment in Schilling Company.

Exercise 12–5
Income taxes: Less than a controlling interest—Domestic investee

On January 1, 19X1, Pozelle Company acquired 20% of Spencer Company's outstanding common stock. Spencer Company had $100,000 of net income in 19X1 and paid cash dividends of $40,000 on its common stock in 19X1. Pozelle Company plans to sell this stock in the near future. Assume a 40% income tax rate and a 25% capital gain rate.

Required:
Prepare Pozelle Company's 19X1 entries with respect to its investment in Spencer Company.

Exercise 12–6
Income taxes: Less than a controlling interest—Domestic investee

Baker, Inc. owns 35% of the outstanding common stock of Cable, Inc. During the

19X4 calendar year, Baker's Investment in Cable, Inc. account appeared as follows:

Balance, January 1, 19X4	$650,000
Equity in Cable's 19X4 earnings	100,000
Dividends received from Cable—19X4	(20,000)
Balance, December 31, 19X4	$730,000

Baker feels that its equity in Cable's undistributed earnings will be realized in future dividends. Assuming a 40% income tax rate, by how much should these facts affect deferred taxes?

(a) $4,800
(b) $6,000
(c) $7,200
(d) $9,000   (AICPA adapted)

Exercise 12–7
Income taxes: Less than a controlling interest—Foreign investee

Francisco Company owns 25% of the common stock of an overseas corporation that has consistently operated profitably since the investment was made. Because the foreign corporation needs capital for growth, the foreign interests that own a majority of its stock have declared no dividends and evidently will not change this policy in the foreseeable future. In light of these facts, Francisco Company, which uses the equity method to account for its investment,

(a) need not make any provision now for taxes on the foreign profits.
(b) must accrue a provision for taxes on the foreign profits.
(c) can, on a discretionary basis, provide for taxes on the foreign profits.
(d) should recognize taxes only when and as foreign profits are remitted as dividends (with a resultant prior-period adjustment).

                                                            (AICPA adapted)

Exercise 12–8
Income taxes: Controlling interest—Foreign subsidiary

In 19X5, the Angeles Company formed a foreign subsidiary. Income before U.S. and foreign income taxes for this wholly owned subsidiary was $500,000 in 19X5. The income tax rate in the foreign subsidiary's country is 40%. None of the foreign subsidiary's earnings have been remitted to Angeles; however, nothing indicates that these earnings will not be remitted to Angeles in the future.

The foreign country in which the subsidiary is located does not impose a tax on remittances to the United States. A tax credit is allowed in the United States for taxes payable in the foreign country.

Assuming the income tax rate in the United States is 46%, what total amount of income taxes related to the foreign subsidiary should be shown in Angeles Company's 19X5 income statement?

(a) $0
(b) $30,000
(c) $200,000
(d) $230,000   (AICPA adapted)

Exercise 12–9
Earnings per share: Partially owned subsidiary with warrants; parent with simple capital structure

Powell Company owns 75% of Somas Company's outstanding common stock. Income and securities data for each company for 19X1 are as follows:

	Powell Company	Somas Company
Income from own operations....................................	$500,000	$100,000
Average number of common stock shares outstanding during 19X1..	200,000	20,000
Common equivalent shares:		
Warrants—		
Average number of warrants outstanding during 19X1........		15,000
Shares assumed repurchased under the treasury stock method		10,000

Required:
(1) Calculate primary earnings per share on a consolidated basis assuming:
   (a) The parent company owns none of the subsidiary's warrants.
   (b) The parent company owns 20% of the subsidiary's warrants.
(2) Determine consolidated net income.

Exercise 12–10
Earnings per share: Wholly owned subsidiary with convertible preferred stock; parent with simple capital structure

Press Company owns 100% of Stamp Company's outstanding common stock. Income and securities data for each company for 19X1 are as follows:

	Press Company	Stamp Company
Income from own operations	$1,000,000	$500,000
Average number of common stock shares outstanding during 19X1	100,000	75,000
Common equivalent shares:		
Convertible preferred stock—		
Shares outstanding during 19X1		5,000
Dividends per share (cumulative)		$10
Number of common shares obtainable on conversion		25,000

Required:
(1) Calculate primary earnings per share on a consolidated basis assuming:
   (a) The parent company owns none of the subsidiary's convertible preferred stock.
   (b) The parent company owns 40% of the subsidiary's convertible preferred stock.
(2) Determine consolidated net income.

Exercise 12–11
Earnings per share: Wholly owned subsidiary with convertible bonds; parent with simple capital structure

Piker Company owns all of Skinflint Company's outstanding common stock. Income and securities data for each company for 19X1 are as follows:

	Piker Company	Skinflint Company
Income from own operations	$600,000	$ 200,000
Average number of common stock shares outstanding during 19X1	300,000	100,000
Preferred stock (nonconvertible)—		
Average number of shares outstanding during 19X1	25,000	
Dividends per share (cumulative)	$4	
Common equivalent shares:		
Convertible bonds—		
Face amount outstanding during 19X1		$1,000,000
Interest rate		10%
Assumed income tax rate		40%
Number of common shares obtainable on conversion		50,000

Required:
(1) Calculate primary earnings per share on a consolidated basis assuming:
    (a) The parent company owns none of the subsidiary's convertible bonds.
    (b) The parent company owns 60% of the subsidiary's convertible bonds.
(2) Determine consolidated net income.

Problems

Problem 12–1
Income taxes: Controlling interest—Foreign subsidiary

Pinelle Company owns 100% of the outstanding common stock of Spruance Company, a foreign subsidiary that had net income of $300,000 in 19X1. The foreign country in which Spruance Company is domiciled has a 30% corporate income tax rate and a 10% dividend withholding tax. Assume a 46% U.S. income tax rate. Spruance Company consistently pays cash dividends on its common stock. Pinelle Company instructs this foreign subsidiary to remit dividends to the maximum extent possible, considering cash requirements for normal operations that are not expected to expand. No dividends were declared in 19X1.

Required:
Prepare Pinelle Company's 19X1 entries related to its investment in Spruance Company.

Problem 12–2
Income taxes: Controlling interest—Foreign subsidiary (Problem 12–1 revised to reflect partial indefinite reinvestment of earnings)

Assume the information in Problem 12–1, except that Spruance Company consistently pays cash dividends on its common stock equal to 20% of annual net income. The remaining 80% of net income is retained each year for internal expansion, which is expected to continue for the foreseeable future.

Required:
The requirement is the same as for Problem 12–1.

Problem 12–3
Income taxes: Controlling interest—Foreign subsidiary

On January 1, 19X1, Poem Company formed a wholly owned foreign subsidiary, Storey. Storey is domiciled in a foreign country that has a 30% corporate income tax rate and a 10% dividend withholding rate. Assume a 46% U.S. income tax rate. Poem expects Storey to be operational for 5–10 years, after which its total accumulated earnings will be remitted to Poem Company in a tax-free liquidation. The subsidiary had a net income of $200,000 in 19X1.

Required:
Prepare Poem Company's 19X1 entries related to its investment in Storey Company.

Problem 12–4
Income taxes: Controlling interest—Foreign subsidiary

Pimitz Company owns 100% of the outstanding common stock of Shippy Company, a foreign subsidiary domiciled in a foreign country that imposes a 25% corporate income tax and a 15% dividend withholding tax. Assume a 46% U.S. income tax rate. Shippy Company had net income of $150,000 in 19X1. Shippy Company's earnings are not being reinvested indefinitely; Shippy paid cash dividends of $60,000 on its common stock in 19X1.

Required:
Prepare Pimitz Company's 19X1 entries related to its investment in Shippy Company.

Problem 12–5
Income taxes: Less than a controlling interest—Domestic investee

On January 1, 19X1, Perfecto Company acquired 50% of the outstanding common stock of Summers Company, a domestic company. Summers Company had net income of $100,000 in 19X1. Summers Company's dividend policy is to declare cash dividends on its common stock equal to 20% of its annual net income. In 19X1, $20,000 in cash dividends were declared on its common stock. The remaining earnings are retained to finance internal expansion, which is consistent with prior years. Assume a 40% income tax rate and a 25% capital gain rate.

Required:
Prepare Perfecto Company's 19X1 entries with respect to its investment in Summers Company.

Problem 12–6
Earnings per share: Partially owned subsidiary with warrants; parent with warrants

Powers Company owns 80% of Sanders Company's outstanding common stock. Income and securities data for each company for 19X1 are as follows:

	Powers Company	Sanders Company
Income from own operations	$2,000,000	$600,000
Average number of common stock shares outstanding during 19X1	1,450,000	200,000
Common equivalent shares:		
Warrants—		
Average number of warrants outstanding during 19X1 ...	200,000	45,000
Shares assumed repurchased under the treasury stock method	150,000	25,000

Required:
(1) Calculate primary earnings per share on a consolidated basis assuming:
  (a) The parent company owns none of the subsidiary's warrants.
  (b) The parent company owns 75% of the subsidiary's warrants.
(2) Determine consolidated net income.

Problem 12–7
Earnings per share: Partially owned subsidiary with convertible preferred stock; parent with convertible preferred stock

Plain Company owns 60% of Selva Company's outstanding common stock. Income and securities data for each company for 19X1 are as follows:

	Plain Company	Selva Company
Income from own operations	$700,000	$250,000
Average number of common stock shares outstanding during 19X1	800,000	200,000
Common equivalent shares:		
Convertible preferred stock—		
Shares outstanding during 19X1	20,000	50,000
Dividends per share (cumulative)	$5	$1
Number of common shares obtainable on conversion	200,000	80,000

Required:
(1) Calculate primary earnings per share on a consolidated basis assuming:
  (a) The parent company owns none of the subsidiary's convertible preferred stock.
  (b) The parent company owns 25% of the subsidiary's convertible preferred stock.
(2) Determine consolidated net income.

Problem 12–8
Earnings per share: Partially owned subsidiary with warrants and convertible bonds; parent with warrants and convertible preferred stock

Parker Company owns 80% of Sheldon Company's outstanding common stock. Income and securities data for each company for 19X1 are as follows:

	Parker Company	Sheldon Company
Income from own operations	$1,500,000	$480,000
Average number of common stock shares outstanding during 19X1	900,000	200,000
Common equivalent shares:		
Warrants—		
Average number of warrants outstanding during 19X1 ...	250,000	80,000
Shares assumed repurchased under the treasury stock method	150,000	50,000
Convertible bonds—		
Face amount outstanding during 19X1		$500,000
Interest rate		10%
Assumed income tax rate		60%
Number of common shares obtainable on conversion		20,000
Other potentially dilutive securities:		
Convertible preferred stock—		
Shares outstanding during 19X1	80,000	
Dividends per share	$2.50	
Number of common shares obtainable on conversion	300,000	

Required:

(1) Calculate primary and fully diluted earnings per share on a consolidated basis assuming:
   (a) The parent company owns none of the subsidiary's warrants or convertible bonds.
   (b) The parent company owns 75% of the subsidiary's warrants and none of the convertible bonds.
(2) Determine consolidated net income.

PART THREE Omnibus Area

13 Translation of Foreign Currency Financial Statements

OVERVIEW OF FOREIGN OPERATIONS
AND TRANSACTIONS

The expansion of international business in the last 40 years has been phenomenal. Total U.S. exports and imports are each nearly $300 billion. Investments overseas by U.S. companies total nearly $200 billion (up from approximately $12 billion in 1950), producing over $40 billion in earnings per year. As a result, export sales and foreign operations now constitute a significant part of the overall activities of a considerable number of domestic corporations. For many of these companies, foreign activities are limited to such operations as importing goods from unaffiliated foreign suppliers and exporting goods to unaffiliated foreign customers.

The accounting issues

Foreign operations.   Through internal or external expansion, some companies build or acquire overseas manufacturing or marketing organizations, which may conduct import or export activities with the domestic operation. Such foreign operations may be conducted through branches, divisions, or subsidiaries, but the most common form of organization is the subsidiary, because it best insulates legally the foreign operation from the domestic operation. For foreign operations of a domestic parent, the accounting issues are:

(1) How should the earnings and losses of the foreign units be determined in dollars?
(2) What additional risks must be considered in reporting earnings from foreign operations? Is consolidation appropriate?
(3) Should supplemental information disclose the extent of a company's foreign operations?

Foreign currency transactions.   Importing and exporting situations that require settlement (payment) in a foreign currency raise the following accounting issues:

(1) How should the transaction be recorded in dollars at the transaction date?
(2) If credit terms are granted and used, how should the accounting consequences of the decision to grant or use credit be recorded?

In this chapter, we lay the groundwork for dealing with currency exchange rates and discuss how to translate foreign currency financial statements. In Chapter 14, we discuss how to translate foreign currency transactions.

The governing pronouncements

Regarding translation.   The principles and procedures to be followed in accounting for the translation of foreign operations and transactions are set forth in *FASB Statement No. 52,* "Foreign Currency Translation." Issued in 1981 after three years of intensive research and extensive participation by professionals in industry, public accounting, academe, and finance, *FASB Statement No. 52* addresses what is widely recognized as one of the most complex and controversial accounting issues. *FASB Statement No. 52* replaces *FASB Statement No. 8,* "Accounting for the Translation of Foreign Currency Transactions and Foreign Currency Financial Statements," which was issued in 1975. *FASB Statement No. 8* outlined uniform accounting procedures for an area previously characterized by numerous practices that often produced widely different results. However, the results under the uniform treatment prescribed by *FASB Statement No. 8* were widely criticized as not reflective of economic changes, and the business community's strong opposition to and continued criticism of the pronouncement resulted in the 1979 FASB decision to reconsider the entire translation issue. Later in this chapter (and in Chapter 14), we examine *FASB Statement No. 52* in detail.

Regarding additional risks and the appropriateness of consolidation. *Accounting Research Bulletin No. 43* addresses the additional risks associated with foreign operations and the appropriateness of consolidation. We discuss these aspects at the end of this chapter.

Regarding supplemental disclosures. The issue of presenting in financial statements supplemental information pertaining to the extent of a company's foreign operations is addressed in *FASB Statement No. 14,* "Financial Reporting for Segments of a Business Enterprise." We discuss this pronouncement in detail in Chapter 15, which covers segment reporting.

CURRENCY EXCHANGE RATES

Conversion versus translation

Actually changing one currency into another currency is called **conversion.** Foreign currencies are usually purchased through commercial banks. Likewise, when payment is received in a foreign currency, the foreign currency may be converted into dollars at such institutions. Conversion must be differentiated from **translation,** which is the process of expressing amounts stated in one currency in terms of another currency by using the appropriate **currency exchange rates.**

Methods of expressing exchange rates

The ratio of the number of units of one currency needed to acquire one unit of another currency constitutes the exchange rate between the two currencies. The exchange rate may be expressed in two ways:

(1) Indirect quotation. The number of units of the foreign currency needed to acquire one unit of the domestic currency is the **indirect** quotation of the exchange rate (for example, 1 dollar = 0.625 pounds). To determine the dollar equivalent of an amount stated in a foreign currency, the foreign currency is **divided** by the exchange rate. (Professional traders in foreign currencies use the indirect quotation rate.)

(2) **Direct quotation.**   The number of units of the domestic currency needed to acquire one unit of the foreign currency is a **direct** quotation of the exchange rate (for example, 1 pound = $1.60). To determine the dollar equivalent of an amount stated in a foreign currency, the foreign currency amount is **multiplied** by the exchange rate. (Travelers prefer the direct quotation rate.)

In the United States, banks and daily newspapers quote exchange rates indirectly and directly. Translation of amounts stated in foreign currencies is usually performed using direct quotations. In all examples and illustrations in this chapter, we use the direct quotation of the exchange rate. Direct quotations of the exchange rates between the dollar and several major foreign currencies are as follows:

Country (currency)	Dollar Equivalent of One Unit of Foreign Currency			Percent Change	
	12/31/78	12/31/82	12/31/83	1 yr	5 yr
Brazil (cruzeiro)	$0.0491	$0.0039	$0.0011	−72	−98
Britain (pound)	2.0435	1.6200	1.4525	−10	−29
Canada (dollar).......	0.8435	0.8098	0.8038	−1	−5
France (franc)	0.2404	0.1485	0.1200	−19	−50
Italy (lira)	0.0012	0.0007	0.0006	−14	−50
Japan (yen)..........	0.0051	0.0043	0.0043	-0-	−16
Mexico (peso)........	0.0441	0.0068	0.0059	−13	−87
Switzerland (franc)....	0.6203	0.4988	0.4587	−26	−8
West Germany (mark)	0.5510	0.4199	0.3676	−12	−33

The exchange rate system— Floating versus fixed exchange rates

Today, currency exchange rates are a function of market conditions, which, in turn, are a function of changing economic and political conditions, such as the balance of payments surplus or deficit, the internal spending surplus or deficit, the internal inflation rate, and the imminence of various civil disorders. Exchange rates determined by market conditions are either **floating** or **free** rates.

Before 1974, the dollar was tied to gold, and most currencies were tied to the dollar. As a result, **fixed** or **official** exchange rates existed. When fixed rates no longer reflected economic conditions, governments were forced to devalue or revalue their currencies (as the U.S. government did in 1973 when it announced a 10% devaluation). Although devaluations of certain currencies were often expected, it was impossible to determine exactly when they would occur or the amount of the devaluation. This major drawback and the fact that the system could not deal with rapid inflation made the system unsustainable. In 1974, the dollar was taken off the gold standard (that is, the dollar was no longer backed by gold), and most currencies that had not already been allowed to float were allowed to do so. As a result, changing international economic conditions are reflected in the currency exchange rates on a daily basis.

Even under the floating exchange rate system, governments may intervene in the exchange markets by buying and selling currencies (as the U.S. government did in the late 1970s to bolster the dollar). An extreme example of intervention is the Mexican peso. After nearly 25 years of stability, the Mexican government allowed the peso to float in 1976. It promptly declined 50% in value against the dollar. In theory, the peso became a floating currency in the international money markets at that time. However, by buying and selling dollars, the central bank of Mexico tried to control the value of the peso at a fairly fixed level against the dollar. In early 1982, the central bank's reserves of U.S. dollars were nearly exhausted, and the government announced that it would withdraw temporarily from the foreign exchange markets. The peso promptly declined nearly 40% in value against the dollar. Two subsequent interventions and temporary withdrawals occurred in 1982; the peso declined approximately 85% in value against the dollar in 1982.

A change in a floating exchange rate is appropriately referred to as a **strengthening** or **weakening** of one currency in relation to another.

Strengthening currencies.   A foreign currency that is strengthening in value in relation to the dollar requires more dollars to obtain a unit of the foreign currency; accordingly, the direct exchange rate increases. A weakening of the dollar has the same effect on the direct exchange rate as does the strengthening of the foreign currency.

Weakening currencies.   A foreign currency that is weakening in value in relation to the dollar requires fewer dollars to obtain a unit of the foreign currency; accordingly, the direct exchange rate decreases. A strengthening of the dollar has the same effect on the direct exchange rate as does the weakening of the foreign currency.

Spot and forward exchange rates.   Exchange rates at which currencies could be converted immediately (for settlement in two days) are termed **spot rates.** Exchange rates also exist for transactions whereby conversion could be made at some stipulated date (normally up to 12 months) in the future. **Future,** or **forward,** rates are discussed in Chapter 14.

Exchange rates used in translation

Before we discuss the specific issues and procedures for translating foreign currency transactions and foreign currency financial statements into dollars, we must define the currency exchange rates that are used in these translation processes.

Current exchange rate.   For **transactions,** the current exchange rate is the rate at which one unit of currency can be exchanged for another currency. For **translation** of a foreign unit's financial statements into dollars, *FASB Statement No. 52* requires the use of a current exchange rate in most situations. Specifically, a company must use (a) the exchange rate existing at the balance sheet date for assets and liabilities and (b) the exchange rates in effect at the time of recognition of revenues, cost of goods sold, expenses, gains, and losses in the income statement.[1]

Average exchange rates.   Because it is impractical to translate the various income statement items at the numerous exchange rates that could exist throughout a period, *FASB Statement No. 52* allows firms to use appropriately weighted average exchange rates for the period.

Historical exchange rate.   *FASB Statement No. 52* requires the use of both the current exchange rate and the historical exchange rate (depending on the individual item) when the current rate method of translation is not appropriate. For example, the exchange rate in effect last year when a building was acquired (the current rate at that time) is now the historical exchange rate, which is used in translation instead of the current exchange rate existing at the balance sheet date. Likewise, the historical exchange rate would be used in translating depreciation expense related to the building rather than the rate in effect when the depreciation was recognized in the income statement.

Multiple exchange rates.   In addition to the floating rates, many countries declare one or more official rates for certain types of currency conversions. For example, to discourage the repatriation of dividends to a foreign parent company, a country would use a rate whereby the parent company would receive a lesser amount of its own currency than it otherwise would receive had the free rate been used. When such multiple rates exist, *FASB Statement No. 52* requires:

a. *Foreign Currency Transactions*—The applicable rate at which a particular transaction could be settled at the transaction date shall be used to translate and record the transaction. At a subsequent balance sheet date, the current rate is that rate at which the related receivable or payable could be settled at that date. [Transactions are discussed in Chapter 14.]
b. *Foreign Currency Statements*—In the absence of unusual circumstances, the rate applicable to conversion of a currency for purposes of dividend remittances shall be used to translate foreign statements.[2]

GETTING IN STEP WITH U.S. GAAP

Companies establish foreign operations with the expectation that the foreign units will generate profits on the investments made. Domestic companies, therefore, want to know the profit or loss generated by their foreign units. Each foreign unit keeps its books and records in its own local currency. However, the profit or loss of a foreign unit as stated in the foreign currency is not meaningful to the domestic parent or home office. Domestic companies

---

[1] *FASB Statement No. 52*, "Foreign Currency Translation" (Stamford, CT: FASB, 1981), paragraph 12.

[2] *FASB Statement No. 52*, paragraph 27. Copyright by Financial Accounting Standards Board, High Ridge Park, Stamford, Connecticut 06905, USA. Reprinted with permission. Copies of the complete document are available from the FASB.

must be able to determine the profit or loss of each of their foreign units in dollars. This is done by translating the foreign currency financial statements into dollars, using appropriate currency exchange rates. However, translating profit or loss amounts of foreign units into dollars is complicated by the fact that foreign units use the accounting principles of the countries in which they are located—not U.S. generally accepted accounting principles.

Diversity of worldwide accounting principles

Accounting principles are not uniform worldwide. Different national laws, different tax laws, and varying degrees of formalization of accounting and reporting practices by private sector standard-setting bodies are the main reasons for these differences. The major differences involve the following four areas:

(1) LIFO inventory costing. Although widely used in the United States, this method has virtually no acceptance in other countries.
(2) Interperiod income tax allocation. Although mandatory in the United States, only a handful of other countries require it.
(3) Pooling of interests. Although required in the United States when the specified criteria are met, it is allowed in only a few other countries and then only under rigid constraints. Pooling of interests is unheard of in many countries.
(4) Goodwill amortization. Amortization is mandatory in the United States, but most foreign countries do not require amortization, allowing goodwill to appear on the balance sheet practically forever.

The following examples demonstrate the range and diversity of accounting practices in foreign countries.

Australia
- Land and buildings are reported at either cost or appraised values (or a mixture of both), less depreciation.
- Certain nonmanufacturing assets may not be depreciated.
- Usually, all cost in excess of an acquired business's net assets at book value is deemed to be goodwill. Goodwill may be shown as a deduction from capital or charged to capital.

Brazil
- All fixed assets are written up once a year, using indexes published by the federal government that are based on the percentage of inflation that occurred during the year. Depreciation for financial and tax reporting purposes is based on the revalued amounts.
- A provision for "maintenance of working capital" may be recorded to remove from profit the effect of inflation on current and long-term assets (excluding fixed assets) and liabilities. This provision is also deductible for tax reporting purposes.

France
- Pension costs are provided only to the extent that such provisions are deductible for income tax purposes.

Germany
- Certain inventory valuation methods may result in a valuation lower than that produced by applying the lower of cost or market rule.

Italy
- Periodically, the national legislative body authorizes companies to revalue their fixed assets to reflect inflation.

Japan
- Goodwill may be expensed as incurred or amortized over no more than five years.
- Research and development costs may be deferred over a maximum of five years.
- Losses generally are not provided on obsolete or slow-moving inventory.

Mexico
- Most industrial and retail firms revalue their fixed assets annually to current appraised value.
- Some companies report income tax expense on the cash basis.
- All cost in excess of an acquired business's net assets at book value is deemed to be goodwill.

Switzerland
- The equity method is not used to account for long-term investments.
- Machinery and equipment may be expensed at the time of purchase.

Just as it does not make sense to add together financial statement amounts in dollars and foreign currencies, it would not be meaningful financial reporting to report worldwide operations using one set of accounting principles for domestic operations and a variety of accounting principles for foreign operations. Accordingly, when foreign currency financial statements are prepared using accounting principles and practices that are materially different from U.S. generally accepted accounting principles, such statements must be restated to reflect U.S. generally accepted accounting principles **before they are translated into dollars.**

Obviously, the lack of worldwide uniform accounting principles and practices is unfortunate. Some international accounting organizations are seeking to promote worldwide uniform accounting principles and practices. The problem is not only one of reaching agreement on what the worldwide accounting principles should be but also of getting countries to adopt uniform accounting principles. Both aspects of the problem are monumental, and efforts to date have not produced significant results.

CONCEPTUAL ISSUES

The process of translating foreign currency financial statements into dollars is merely a mechanical process, once the exchange rate for each account has been determined. However, for many years a raging controversy has existed over the following two conceptual issues.

(1) Which exchange rates should be used to translate the foreign currency financial statements into dollars?
(2) How should the effect of a change in the exchange rate be reported?

In this section of the chapter, we devote considerable attention to the substance of this controversy and the solutions that have been tried and rejected. This background is a solid base for understanding the rationale for and the requirements of *FASB Statement No. 52*. More importantly, this section emphasizes thinking rather than memorization of detailed rules and requirements, thereby enabling you to evaluate the requirements of *FASB Statement No. 52*.

Conceptual Issue (1): Which Exchange Rates to Use?

Criteria used as a frame of reference

The first conceptual issue is determining the appropriate exchange rates for translating the individual assets and liabilities in the balance sheet. The translation of the stockholders' equity accounts is not part of the issue, because the total translated stockholders' equity is a forced residual amount that is the difference between the total translated assets and the total translated liabilities. Once the appropriate exchange rates have been determined for the assets and liabilities, consistency and logic dictate the appropriate exchange rates for translating the income statement accounts.

Balance sheet accounts may be conveniently grouped into **monetary** and **nonmonetary** classifications (the same classification scheme used in constant dollar accounting). Monetary items include cash and accounts that are contractually obligated to be settled in cash—namely, receivables and payables. All other accounts—inventory, fixed assets, and the equity accounts, for example—are nonmonetary. This first conceptual issue is easily discussed as to each of these categories.

Accountants have used the following criteria as a frame of reference for determining the appropriate exchange rates:

(1) Does the exchange rate selected for a specific account result in a meaningful dollar amount?
(2) Does the exchange rate selected for a specific account change the basis of accounting in translation? (For example, is the historical cost basis for fixed assets in the foreign currency retained when translation is made into dollars?)
(3) When a change has occurred in the exchange rate, do the translated results reflect the economic impact of the change?

The first two criteria require no explanation. For the last criteria, we should understand that when a U.S. company has invested money in a foreign country, an increase in the direct exchange rate is a favorable economic event, which should result in a positive report. Likewise, a decrease in the direct exchange rate is an unfavorable economic event, which should result in an adverse report. For example, assume you invested $1,000 in a savings account in a Mexican bank when the direct exchange rate was $0.08 (as many U.S. citizens did in 1975–1976 because of the high interest rates). The bank would credit your account for 12,500 pesos ($1,000/$0.08). Assume that the direct exchange rate then dropped to $0.04 (as it did in 1976). If you then withdrew your 12,500 pesos and converted them into dollars, you would have only $500 (12,500 pesos × $0.04). Thus, this decrease in the direct exchange rate was indeed an adverse economic event that caused your net worth to decrease by $500.

In the discussion of the first conceptual issue, we refer to the effect of a change in the exchange rate as a **translation adjustment.** How to report a change in the exchange rate is a controversial issue that we address in our discussion of the second conceptual issue.

Translating monetary accounts

Most accountants agree that the only sensible way to translate monetary items is to use the exchange rate in effect at the balance sheet date (a current exchange rate). This procedure effectively values these items on a current-value basis, which is considered the ultimate reporting basis. To illustrate, assume the following information:

(1) A domestic company formed a West German subsidiary on December 1, 19X1.
(2) The domestic company acquired the subsidiary's common stock for $450,000 on that date when the direct exchange rate was $0.45. (The subsidiary immediately converted the $450,000 into 1,000,000 marks.)
(3) The subsidiary had no other transactions from its inception to December 31, 19X1 (the parent's and its year-end).
(4) The direct exchange rate at December 31, 19X1 was $0.60. Thus, either the mark strengthened or the dollar weakened during this period—it does not matter which occurred.

What is the appropriate exchange rate to translate the 1,000,000 marks at December 31, 19X1 into dollars? The only meaningful dollar amount is the dollar equivalent of the marks—that is, the number of dollars into which the 1,000,000 marks could be converted. Obviously, only the $0.60 direct exchange rate at December 31, 19X1 gives a meaningful answer ($600,000). Using the $0.45 exchange rate that existed at December 1, 19X1 would give $450,000, an amount that has absolutely no meaning or usefulness. Accordingly, the translation process for the Cash and the Common Stock accounts as of December 1, 19X1 and December 31, 19X1 would be as follows:

	Amount (marks)	December 1, 19X1		December 31, 19X1	
		Rate	Amount	Rate	Amount
Cash	1,000,000	$0.45	$450,000	$0.60	$600,000
Common Stock	1,000,000	0.45	450,000	0.45[a]	450,000
Translation adjustment (the effect of the change in the exchange rate)					150,000

[a] The historical exchange rate of $0.45 must be used here to isolate the effect of the change in the exchange rate.

If the parent liquidated the foreign subsidiary on December 31, 19X1, it would receive $600,000, not the $450,000 it initially invested. The parent's investment actually increased in value during December 19X1 by $150,000. The use of the $0.60 exchange rate existing at the balance sheet date reflects the economics of what has transpired, and the increase in the direct exchange rate is a favorable economic event. In summary, all three criteria listed on page 452 are satisfied.

Monetary items other than cash.   To translate the remaining monetary items (receivables and payables), we use the logic that was applied to cash. Because receivables are one step away from cash, the only meaningful dollar amount is the dollar equivalent of the receivables. Likewise, payables require the use of cash, so the only meaningful dollar amount is the dollar equivalent that would be needed to settle the payables. The direct exchange rate existing at the balance sheet date is the only exchange rate that produces meaningful dollar amounts. Furthermore, the use of the exchange rate existing at the balance sheet date does not change the valuation basis of these accounts in translation. (For example, the valuation basis of receivables in a foreign currency is *net realizable value,* and the use of the exchange rate existing at the balance sheet date produces the dollar equivalent of the net amount expected to be realized.) Finally, as with cash, the use of the exchange rate existing at the balance sheet date reflects the economic impact of any change in the exchange rate. Thus, all three criteria listed on page 452 are satisfied.

Translating nonmonetary accounts— An introduction to the controversy

Accountants do not agree on the appropriate exchange rates to translate nonmonetary accounts at the balance sheet date. Two schools of thought have evolved concerning the appropriate exchange rate to use at the balance sheet date to translate nonmonetary accounts into dollars—the **parent company perspective** and the **foreign perspective.**

Is the monetary–nonmonetary distinction relevant?   Under the parent company approach, the distinction between monetary and nonmonetary items is crucial, and therefore the use of the exchange rate existing at the balance sheet date (a current exchange rate) is deemed inappropriate for nonmonetary accounts. Under the foreign approach, the distinction between monetary and nonmonetary items is irrelevant, and the exchange rate existing at the balance sheet date may be used for nonmonetary accounts.

In deciding whether a distinction between monetary and nonmonetary is relevant, it is important to realize that a foreign unit's machinery and equipment (although classified as nonmonetary items) are actually transformed from nonmonetary assets into monetary assets. Nonmonetary assets generate a cash flow, part of which constitutes a recovery of the cost of these assets. Of course, the process takes as long as the depreciation lives selected, and the transformation is not as evident as when nonmonetary assets are sold (disposed of) outright for cash. Because of this transformation process, when the exchange rate changes, the cash flow generated by these nonmonetary assets is worth a greater number of dollars (when the direct exchange rate increases) or a lesser number of dollars (when the direct exchange rate decreases). Thus, in determining the appropriate exchange rate to translate nonmonetary items into dollars, we may view nonmonetary assets as being on the road to becoming monetary assets.

The parent company perspective

To illustrate the parent company perspective, let us change slightly the facts from the example used in the discussion of monetary accounts by assuming the foreign subsidiary used the 1,000,000 marks from the issuance of the common stock to purchase a parcel of land on December 1, 19X1. Thus, at December 31, 19X1, it has land reported at 1,000,000 marks in its balance sheet instead of cash of 1,000,000 marks.

The rationale behind it.   From the parent company perspective, foreign operations are viewed as extensions of the parent company. Therefore, **all transactions must be translated in a manner that produces the dollar equivalent of the transaction at the time the transaction occurred.** From this perspective, the historical cost of the land in dollars is the amount of dollars that were needed to acquire it on December 1, 19X1. Because we know this amount is $450,000, the only exchange rate that translates the 1,000,000 marks into this amount is the historical exchange rate of $0.45 (the rate in effect on December 1, 19X1). Using the historical exchange rate not only expresses the cost of the land in dollars, but it also **changes the "unit of measure" from the foreign currency to the dollar.** Thus, the cost of the land has been **"remeasured" and expressed in dollars.** (This concept is difficult to grasp at this point; you should understand it fully after you have read the foreign perspective, under which the foreign currency is retained as the unit of measure in the translation process.) Obviously, the historical exchange rate retains or preserves the historical cost measurement basis in dollars. Fixed assets of the domestic parent and its foreign units are therefore reported in consolidation on the same historical cost basis in terms of the reporting currency (dollars). Proponents of this approach claim that the results are clearly meaningful dollar amounts.

Its shortcoming.   The shortcoming of the parent company perspective is that **it completely disregards how changes in the exchange rate affect the nonmonetary accounts.** Changes in the exchange rate are economic events that have considerable impact on the U.S. parent company, which has invested money in the foreign unit. This fact holds true regardless of whether the foreign unit holds all monetary assets, all nonmonetary assets, or any combination of the two. When the effects of a change in the exchange rate are not reflected in the reporting results, the parent is effectively pretending that the exchange rate did not change.

To illustrate this shortcoming, we first deal with a situation in which the exchange rate changes and nonmonetary assets are financed entirely by a capital (common stock) investment by the parent. In a second situation, the nonmonetary assets are financed entirely by a local loan in the foreign country, and the parent has a nil investment in the subsidiary.

Situation (1): Parent company financing of nonmonetary assets. Let us continue with the example in the preceding discussion to see how a favorable economic event (an increase in the direct exchange rate) is not reported because the historical exchange rate is used to translate the nonmonetary accounts into dollars. Using the information presented so far, we know the translation process for the Land and Common Stock accounts as of December 1, 19X1 and December 31, 19X1 would be as follows:

	Amount (marks)	December 1, 19X1 Rate	December 1, 19X1 Amount	December 31, 19X1 Rate	December 31, 19X1 Amount
Land	1,000,000	$0.45	$450,000	$0.45	$450,000
Common stock	1,000,000	0.45	450,000	0.45	450,000

This presentation clearly shows that the economic impact of the change in the exchange rate is not reported under this approach. However, from an economic viewpoint, the parent's $450,000 initial investment has increased in value to $600,000, because the direct exchange rate has increased from $0.45 at December 1, 19X1 to $0.60 at December 31, 19X1. (Of course, the $150,000 increase would be considered an unrealized increase in value.)

We may more easily understand this concept if we assume that the land was sold on December 31, 19X1 for cash of 1,000,000 marks, its book value on that date. On the date of sale, cash of 1,000,000 marks would be translated at $0.60, resulting in $600,000. This translated amount is $150,000 more than the Land account would show if the land were still owned. (Note that we do not assume that the land has appreciated in value in marks—the value in marks holds constant at 1,000,000.) However, because historical exchange rates are used to translate nonmonetary accounts, this favorable economic event (the increase in the direct exchange rate) is never reported. What is equally misleading is that if the land is sold on January 1, 19X2 (instead of December 31, 19X1) for cash of 1,000,000 marks (its book value), a $150,000 favorable result would be reportable at that time (assuming the exchange rate did not change from December 31, 19X1), even though nothing happened economically on January 1, 19X2. [Likewise, a decrease in the exchange rate in December 19X1 from $0.45 to $0.30 (an unfavorable economic event) would be ignored in the reporting process, even though from an economic viewpoint the parent's $450,000 initial investment has decreased in value by $150,000 to $300,000.]

Situation (2): Foreign financing of nonmonetary assets. To minimize the risk of investing in foreign companies (including the risk that the exchange rate could change adversely), U.S. companies commonly finance foreign operations through foreign borrowings to the extent possible, thereby keeping their investments in the foreign units as small as possible. To illustrate this situation, let us change the example in the preceding discussion as follows:

(1) The foreign subsidiary was so thinly capitalized by the parent on December 1, 19X1 that we can ignore the translation of the Common Stock account.
(2) The foreign subsidiary borrowed 1,000,000 marks from a local bank

on December 1, 19X1, and used the proceeds to purchase the parcel of land. (The loan is payable in marks.)

(3) For simplicity, interest expense on the loan is ignored.

(4) No principal payments were made on the loan in December 19X1.

Using this information, we determine the translation process for the Land and Notes Payable accounts (the loan is a monetary item) as of December 1, 19X1 and December 31, 19X1 as follows:

	Amount (marks)	December 1, 19X1 Rate	December 1, 19X1 Amount	December 31, 19X1 Rate	December 31, 19X1 Amount
Land	1,000,000	$0.45	$450,000	$0.45	$450,000
Notes payable.................	1,000,000	0.45	450,000	0.60	600,000
Translation adjustment (the effect of the change in the exchange rate).......					(150,000)

Under this translation approach, an adverse result of $150,000 would be reported. We might conclude from this result that it would take $150,000 more to pay off the loan at December 31, 19X1 than were needed at December 1, 19X1. However, the adverse result under this approach exactly offsets the $150,000 increase in value of the land, which is completely ignored because of the use of the historical exchange rate of $0.45 for the land at December 31, 19X1.

We may more easily understand why nothing adverse has actually occurred from an economic viewpoint by assuming the land was sold on December 31, 19X1 for cash of 1,000,000 marks, its book value on that date. On the date of sale, cash of 1,000,000 marks would be translated at $0.60 into $600,000 rather than at $0.45 into $450,000. The translated cash amount of $600,000 equals the translated note payable amount of $600,000, and no translation adjustment is needed. Interestingly, if the land is sold on January 1, 19X2 (instead of on December 31, 19X1) for cash of 1,000,000 marks (its book value), a favorable result of $150,000 would be reportable at that time (assuming the exchange rate does not change from December 31, 19X1), even though nothing happened economically on January 1, 19X2. Note also that this $150,000 favorable result for 19X2 completely offsets the $150,000 unfavorable result reportable for 19X1.

In this example, the most convincing proof that nothing adverse has happened during December 19X1, as far as the parent's investment in the subsidiary is concerned, is the fact that the parent's investment is negligible. It had nothing invested and therefore nothing at risk. To report a $150,000 adverse result for 19X1 under these conditions makes no sense. (The same logic would be applied if the exchange rate decreased during December from $0.45 to $0.30, but the reporting results would be reversed.) Accordingly, when the parent can finance the foreign unit's nonmonetary assets with foreign borrowings that are repayable in the foreign currency, a change in the exchange rate has no economic impact on the parent. In this situation, the reporting of favorable and unfavorable results is viewed as mere paper gains and losses that are reversed in later periods—in other words, timing differences. From this viewpoint, it is not sensible to report adverse results in one period that are offset by favorable results in later periods and vice versa.

The two translation methods that fit under the parent company theory.   Two translation methods fit under the parent company perspective— the **temporal method** and the **monetary–nonmonetary** method. The temporal method can accommodate any measurement basis (historical cost, current replacement price, or current market price). Under the temporal method, a foreign currency measurement is changed into a dollar measurement without changing the measurement basis. Thus, **the accounting principles are not changed** (even though the unit of measure has been changed to the dollar). The measurement basis of an asset or liability determines the exchange rate used in translating that asset or liability. Accordingly, different exchange rates are used for different measurement bases (for example, historical exchange rates for fixed assets and a current exchange rate for receivables). The monetary–nonmonetary method is merely a classification scheme, whereby all monetary assets and liabilities are translated at the exchange rate existing at the balance sheet date, and all nonmonetary assets and liabilities are translated at historical exchange rates. As generally accepted accounting principles now exist, the results of the temporal method coincide with the results of the monetary–nonmonetary method. However, if accounting principles change so that nonmonetary assets (such as marketable equity securities) are measured at current prices instead of at historical prices or at the lower of cost or market, the results would be different. The temporal method conceptually could accommodate such accounting principles, whereas the monetary–nonmonetary method could not, because the measurement basis would not be maintained in the translation process.

The focus: Net monetary position.   Under both the temporal and the monetary–nonmonetary translation methods, the monetary or nonmonetary composition of the individual assets and liabilities is critical in determining whether a favorable or unfavorable result is reported as a consequence of a change in the exchange rate. In this respect, the focus is on the net monetary position. An excess of monetary assets over monetary liabilities is referred to as a **net monetary asset position;** an excess of monetary liabilities over monetary assets is referred to as a **net monetary liability position.** If the direct exchange rate has increased since the beginning of the period (a favorable economic event), a company in a net monetary asset position reports a favorable result, whereas in a net monetary liability position, a company reports an unfavorable result. On the other hand, if the direct exchange rate has decreased since the beginning of the period (an unfavorable economic event), a company in a net monetary asset position reports an unfavorable result, but in a net monetary liability position, the company reports a favorable result.

The FASB's first attempt.   In 1975, the FASB adopted the parent company perspective by requiring the temporal method of translation in all cases. The unusual results that occur under the parent company perspective led to a reconsideration of the entire translation issue in 1979. In 1981, *FASB Statement No. 52* superseded *FASB Statement No. 8,* and the parent company perspective is called for now only in certain situations (which are discussed later in the chapter).

The foreign (or local) perspective

The rationale behind it. From the foreign perspective, a foreign operation is a separate business unit whose only factual financial statements are those prepared in its foreign currency. From this premise, we reason that **the relationships of items must be maintained in the translation process.** The only way to maintain the relationships of items in translation is to use a single exchange rate for all assets and liabilities. The exchange rate existing at the balance sheet date (a current exchange rate) is presumably the single most meaningful exchange rate. For translation using a single exchange rate, **the foreign currency is the "unit of measure"** in the dollar financial statements. **Thus, the nonmonetary accounts are not translated to produce the dollar equivalent of the nonmonetary accounts when the transactions were recorded.** Consequently, **the nonmonetary accounts are not remeasured in dollars—they are only expressed in dollars.** The use of the exchange rate existing at the balance sheet date clearly overcomes the objections raised for the parent company perspective— namely, that the economic impact of the change in the exchange rate is completely ignored in the translation of the nonmonetary accounts. As a result, the proponents of the foreign perspective assert that the translated amounts are obviously meaningful dollar amounts.

Is the translated amount historical cost? The most difficult result to understand under the foreign perspective is whether the amount expressed in dollars should be considered historical cost or some form of current value. Let us continue with the example of translating the value of land that we used in discussing the parent company perspective. Under the foreign approach, the foreign subsidiary's Land and Common Stock accounts would be translated into dollars at December 1, 19X1 and December 31, 19X1 as follows:

	Amount (marks)	December 1, 19X1 Rate	December 1, 19X1 Amount	December 31, 19X1 Rate	December 31, 19X1 Amount
Land	1,000,000	$0.45	$450,000	$0.60	$600,000
Common stock	1,000,000	0.45	450,000	0.45[a]	450,000
Translation adjustment (the effect of the change in the exchange rate)........					150,000

[a] The historical exchange rate of $0.45 must be used here to isolate the effect of the change in the exchange rate.

Obviously, the $600,000 translated amount for the land at December 31, 19X1 is not historical cost in terms of the equivalent number of dollars that were needed to acquire the land on December 1, 19X1 (that is, $450,000). Advocates of the foreign perspective claim that **the $600,000 is the historical cost of the land using the foreign currency as the unit of measure rather than the dollar.** If the direct exchange rate were $0.70 at December 31, 19X2 (one year later), then the historical cost "using the foreign currency as the unit of measure" would be $700,000 (1,000,000 marks × $0.70). Thus, the land would be reported in the consolidated financial statements at a different amount every year as the exchange rate changed each year. Critics of the foreign perspective contend that, in substance, this is merely an abandonment of historical cost and a change to a form of current-value accounting.

Is the translated amount current value? Let us continue with the preceding example dealing with land but assume that the land appreciated in value by 100,000 marks during December 19X1. Thus, its current value in marks at December 31, 19X1 is 1,100,000 marks. To obtain the land's current value in dollars at that date, this amount would have to be multiplied by the $0.60 exchange rate existing at December 31, 19X1, which gives us $660,000. However, nonmonetary accounts are not adjusted for inflation prior to translation. Accordingly, the use of the exchange rate existing at the balance sheet date would result in current value only if the nonmonetary account were restated for the effects of inflation. Furthermore, when dealing with depreciable assets, the amounts expressed in dollars would approximate current value only if the depreciation lives and methods used gave results that closely corresponded to the decline in the assets' values.

The disappearing plant problem. About 15 countries (primarily in South America) currently have highly inflationary economies (approximately 100% or more over a three-year period). The use of the foreign perspective can result in meaningless figures in these situations. To illustrate, consider the following example of a manufacturing plant in Argentina that cost 10,000,000 pesos when it was purchased on December 31, 1974:

| | Amount | December 31, 1974 | | December 31, 1983 | |
	(pesos)	Rate	Amount	Rate	Amount
Plant	10,000,000	$0.20	$2,000,000	$0.0000048	$48

Obviously, the application of the December 31, 1983 current exchange rate to the historical cost in pesos produces an amount that bears no relationship to current value or a reasonable historical cost amount. The use of the current exchange rate would produce a meaningful amount only if it were applied to the inflation-adjusted historical cost in pesos. However, this procedure would depart from historical cost in the foreign currency. Accordingly, operations in highly inflationary economies require special consideration. Later in the chapter, we see how *FASB Statement No. 52* deals with these situations.

The current-rate method of translation. Only one translation method fits under the foreign perspective—the **current-rate** method. Under the current-rate method, an increase in the direct exchange rate results in a favorable translation adjustment, and a decrease in the direct exchange rate results in an unfavorable translation adjustment.

The focus: The net investment. The current-rate method focuses on the parent's net investment (total assets — total liabilities), not on the composition of the individual assets and liabilities. In other words, the monetary or nonmonetary classification of the individual assets and liabilities is irrelevant. This approach emphasizes that the foreign operation's net assets are at risk (described as a **net investment** view as opposed to the individual asset and liability view under the temporal method).

The FASB's second attempt.   *FASB Statement No. 52* adopted the foreign perspective in addition to the parent company perspective. However, the foreign company perspective is the dominant perspective because its use is required far more often than the parent company perspective. After we discuss the second conceptual issue, we address the factors to consider in determining which perspective to use for a particular foreign operation.

Conceptual Issue (2): How to Report the Effect of a Change in the Exchange Rate

This issue centers around whether or not the effect of a change in the exchange rate (the translation adjustment) should be reported in the income statement in the period in which the exchange rate changes.

Arguments for reporting it immediately in the income statement

The following list contains the principal arguments for including the translation adjustment immediately in the income statement:

(1) The possibility of exchange rate changes is a risk of investing in a foreign country. The effects of this possibility can be economically favorable or unfavorable. Favorable effects are gains; unfavorable effects are losses. Gains and losses should be recognized in the period in which they occur.
(2) Recognizing in the income statement the effects of changes in the exchange rate is consistent with the all-inclusive income statement approach that has prevailed in accounting in recent years.
(3) Past exchange rate changes are historical facts, and each accounting period should reflect the economic events that occurred during that time frame.
(4) Exchange rates fluctuate. Not including the effects of such fluctuations in net income when they occur gives the impression that exchange rates are stable.

Arguments for not reporting it immediately in the income statement

The following list contains the principal arguments for excluding the translation adjustment from the income statement:

(1) If exchange rates are likely to reverse, the effect should be deferred. (This argument presumes that managements are reasonably adept at predicting future exchange rates; in reality, a high degree of uncertainty exists with future exchange rates.)
(2) Exchange rate changes often reverse, causing unnecessary fluctuations in net income. (This argument implies that a function of accounting is to minimize the reporting of fluctuations.)
(3) The following arguments apply to the parent company perspective when monetary liabilities exceed monetary assets (nonmonetary assets thus financed to some degree by borrowings).

    a. The sacrifice view.   The effect should be treated as an adjustment to the cost of the related assets on the theory that the cost of the related assets should equal the total sacrifice required to discharge all related liabilities.

    b. The cover view.   Because the use of historical exchange rates for nonmonetary assets ignores the economic impact of exchange rate changes on such assets, the translation adjustment should be deferred to offset (a) the unrecognized decrease in value on these assets (when the direct exchange rate decreases), and (b) the unrecognized increase in value of these assets (when the direct exchange rate increases). (This approach would eliminate some of the unusual reporting results that occur under the parent company perspective; however, it is merely a disguised manner of revaluing the nonmonetary assets upward or downward. As a result, these items are translated at exchange rates that are between the historical exchange rate and the exchange rate existing at the balance sheet date, depending on the amount of borrowings to finance these nonmonetary assets.)

(4) For many foreign operations, translation adjustments do not affect the operations or cash flows of the foreign unit. They arise only in translation and thus do not affect directly the cash flows of the reporting currency (dollars). The effects of changes in the exchange rate are unrealized until the investment is disposed of or liquidated. Translation adjustments do not possess the characteristics of items normally included in determining net income.[3] (Comments in the following two paragraphs relate to this argument.)

    The dual approach of *FASB Statement No. 52.*   In *FASB Statement No. 52,* how to report the effect of a change in the exchange rate is a function of the perspective used for each foreign operation. When the foreign perspective is used (requiring the use of the current-rate method of translation), the effect of a change in the exchange rate is called a **translation adjustment** (in *FASB Statement No. 52*), and it is **reported as a separate component of stockholders' equity,** bypassing the income statement until disposal or liquidation of the investment. [Argument (4), above, which was first presented in *FASB Statement No. 52,* is the basis for this position.] When the parent company perspective is used (requiring the use of procedures that are nearly identical to the temporal method of translation), the effect of a change in the exchange rate is called a **foreign currency transaction gain or loss** (in *FASB Statement No. 52*), and it is **reported currently in the income statement.**

    Why the separate component of stockholders' equity?   We mentioned earlier that the foreign perspective is now required more often than the parent company perspective. Thus, we might think that the criticisms of *FASB Statement No. 8* (which required the parent company perspective in all cases) have been addressed. A major part of the business community's dissatisfaction with *FASB Statement No. 8* was not only the results produced under the parent company perspective but the requirement to report the

---

[3] *FASB Statement No. 52,* paragraphs 111 and 117.

effects of the change in the exchange rate currently in the income statement when subsequent reversals were expected (the paper gain and loss conclusion discussed earlier). Wild gyrations in adjustments often resulted on a quarter-to-quarter basis. Even under the foreign perspective (which requires the use of the current-rate method of translation), significant fluctuations in translation adjustments occur as long as exchange rates continue to change back and forth significantly, which is possible under the current floating exchange rate system. In fact, the fluctuations may be even greater under the foreign perspective—the only requirement is that a foreign operation's net asset position be greater than its net monetary asset or liability position. Thus, while having a method available that produces results that reflect the economics, the business community opposes the reporting of translation adjustments currently in the income statement because of the significant fluctuations that occur. The FASB's decision to require companies to report translation adjustments resulting from the use of the current-rate method as a separate component of stockholders' equity may have been partly attributable to the practical aspects of the environment in which the FASB operates.

THE FUNCTIONAL CURRENCY CONCEPT

Objectives of translation

FASB Statement No. 52 states the following objectives for translation of foreign currency financial statements:

> a. Provide information that is generally compatible with the expected economic effects of a rate change on an enterprise's cash flows and equity.
> b. Reflect in consolidated statements the financial results and relationships of the individual consolidated entities as measured in their *functional currencies* in conformity with U.S. generally accepted accounting principles.[4]

The first objective merely states that the selected exchange rate and the reporting of the effect of a change in the exchange rate should reflect the economics of what has transpired. The second objective allows for the use of both the parent company perspective (when the dollar is the foreign unit's functional currency) and the foreign perspective (when the foreign currency is the foreign unit's functional currency), the latter situation being most prevalent. To achieve these two objectives, a **functional currency** concept was developed.

Basis for the functional currency concept

FASB Statement No. 52 presumes that an enterprise's foreign operations may be conducted in one or more economic and currency environments. The primary economic environment must be determined for each separate foreign operation. However, the pronouncement does not specifically define the economic environment concept. Each foreign country obviously has its

---

[4] *FASB Statement No. 52*, paragraph 4.

own economic environment composed of taxation policies, currency controls, government policies toward intervention in the international currency markets, economic instability, and inflation. The primary economic environment concept, however, pertains to the manner in which the foreign operation conducts its operations—namely, the currency it primarily uses to generate and expend cash.[5] (This concept presumes that each foreign operation has a primary currency.)

The currency of the primary economic environment is then designated as that foreign operation's functional currency. FASB has developed some economic factors that are to be considered individually and collectively in determining the functional currency for each foreign operation of an enterprise. A list of these economic factors appears in Illustration 13-1. The functional currency so determined for each foreign operation is the basis for the method of translation into dollars. When the foreign currency is designated the functional currency (which occurs most of the time), the foreign perspective must be used; thus, the current-rate method is used to translate the foreign currency financial statements into dollars. When the dollar is designated the functional currency, the parent company perspective must be used; thus, translating foreign currency financial statements into dollars is accomplished using procedures that are nearly identical to the temporal method (which *FASB Statement No. 8* required for all situations).[6]

Two categories of foreign operations.   In reviewing Illustration 13-1, we must realize that most foreign operations conveniently fit into one of two categories. The **first category** includes foreign operations that are **relatively self-contained and independent of the parent's operations.** These operations primarily generate and expend the foreign currency of the country in which they are located. Earnings may be reinvested or distributed to the parent. In these cases, the foreign currency is obviously the functional currency. (An example in this category would be a foreign subsidiary that manufactures automobiles for sale in the foreign country, with no parts being purchased from the parent's operations.) The **second category** includes foreign operations that are **not relatively self-contained and independent of the parent's operations.** These operations may be viewed as a direct extension or integral component of the parent's operations. The day-to-day operations of these units impact directly on the parent company's dollar cash flows. In these cases, the dollar is the functional currency. (An example would be a foreign subsidiary that manufactures automobile transmissions, which are shipped to the parent for inclusion in cars produced domestically.)[7]

No arbitrary selection allowed.   The determination of the functional currency should be based on the economic facts—it cannot be an arbitrary selection. Because significant differences in reported net income can occur as a result of choosing the foreign currency or the dollar as the functional currency, managements must be prevented from arbitrarily choosing their accounting principles. When the economic factors listed in Illustration 13-1 do not clearly indicate a foreign operation's functional currency, man-

---

[5] *FASB Statement No. 52*, paragraphs 5 and 78.
[6] *FASB Statement No. 52*, paragraphs 5, 10, 12, 47, and 48.
[7] *FASB Statement No. 52*, paragraphs 79–81.

Illustration 13-1

Economic factors to be considered in determining functional currency

Type of Factor	Factors Pointing to a Foreign Functional Currency	Factors Pointing to a Dollar Functional Currency
Cash flows	Cash flows related to the foreign entity's individual assets and liabilities are primarily in the foreign currency and do not directly impact the parent company's cash flows.	Cash flows related to the foreign entity's individual assets and liabilities directly impact the parent's cash flows on a current basis and are readily available for remittance to the parent company.
Sales prices	Sales prices for the foreign entity's products are not primarily responsive on a short-term basis to changes in exchange rates but are determined more by local competition or local government regulation.	Sales prices for the foreign entity's products are primarily responsive on a short-term basis to changes in exchange rates; for example, sales prices are determined more by worldwide competition or by international prices.
Sales market	An active local sales market exists for the foreign entity's products, although significant amounts of exports might also be available.	The sales market is mostly in the parent's country, or sales contracts are denominated in the parent's currency.
Costs and expenses	Labor, materials, and other costs for the foreign entity's products or services are primarily local costs, even though imports from other countries might also be available.	Labor, materials, and other costs for the foreign entity's products or services, on a continuing basis, are primarily costs for components obtained from the country in which the parent company is located.
Financing	Financing is primarily denominated in foreign currency, and funds generated by the foreign entity's operations are sufficient to service existing and normally expected debt obligations.	Financing is primarily from the parent or other dollar-denominated obligations, or funds generated by the foreign entity's operations are not sufficient to service existing and normally expected debt obligations without the infusion of additional funds from the parent company. Infusion of additional funds from the parent company for expansion is not a factor, provided funds generated by the foreign entity's expanded operations are expected to be sufficient to service that additional financing.
Intercompany transactions and arrangements	There is a low volume of intercompany transactions, and an extensive interrelationship does not exist between the operations of the foreign entity and the parent company. However, the foreign entity's operations may rely on the parent's or affiliates' competitive advantages such as patents and trademarks.	There is a high volume of intercompany transactions, and an extensive interrelationship exists between the operations of the foreign entity and the parent company. Additionally, the parent's currency generally would be the functional currency if the foreign entity is a device or shell corporation for holding investments, obligations, intangible assets, and so on, that could readily be carried on the parent's or an affiliate's books.

Source: Adapted from *FASB Statement No. 52,* Appendix A, paragraph 42.

agement can weigh the individual economic factors and use its judgment, considering the stated objectives of translation.[8]

Highly inflationary economies. An exception to the approach of determining the functional currency from economic facts is made for operations in highly inflationary economies. *FASB Statement No. 52* defines an inflationary economy as "one that has cumulative inflation of approximately 100 percent or more over a 3-year period."[9] In these cases, the dollar is used as the functional currency. The purpose of the exception is to deal with the "disappearing plant" problem discussed on page 460. Recall that applying the current exchange rate to historical cost amounts in foreign currency financial statements can produce meaningless dollar amounts for fixed assets in such economies. The problem, of course, is the foreign currency's lack of stability, which makes it completely unsuitable for use as a functional currency. In the exposure draft that preceded the issuance of *FASB Statement No. 52,* the FASB proposed restating the historical cost amounts for inflation prior to translation (and then allowing the use of the current-rate method). However, the proposal was dropped because of the conceptual objections to mixing historical cost with inflation-adjusted amounts and the inadequacy of published indices for several countries. As a practical alternative, which is an acknowledged conceptual compromise, the FASB designated the dollar as the functional currency (whereby the historical cost amounts are translated at historical exchange rates). The results are more reasonable dollar amounts for the fixed assets of these foreign operations.

Illustration 13-2 lists the countries whose cumulative inflation rates have recently exceeded 100% over three-year periods; countries approaching this 100% threshold are also listed. Although 100% may seem high, an

---

[8] *FASB Statement No. 52,* paragraphs 8 and 82.
[9] *FASB Statement No. 52,* paragraph 11.

Illustration 13-2
Countries having high inflation rates

Recent three-year inflation rate exceeds 100%	Recent three-year inflation rate approaches 100%
Argentina	Jamaica
Bolivia	Korea
Brazil	Mexico
Chile	Sudan
Colombia	Tanzania
Ghana	
Iceland	
Peru	
Somalia	
Turkey	
Uruguay	
Yugoslavia	
Zaire	

Source: *International Financial Statistics,* Bureau of Statistics, International Monetary Fund.

annual inflation rate of only 26% results in 100% inflation cumulatively over a three-year period. The use of 100% is obviously arbitrary, but the use of the modifier "approximately" in the pronouncement allows management some latitude in judgment. Thus, a cumulative inflation rate of 90%, for example, could be sufficient grounds for using the dollar as the functional currency, whereas a foreign unit operating with a cumulative inflation rate of 110% could still use the foreign currency as the functional currency. We must also consider management's latitude when the economic facts do not clearly indicate the functional currency. In such a case and when the cumulative inflation rate is high but below 100%, management may lean toward using the dollar as the functional currency.

Distinguishing "translation" from "remeasurement"

For simplicity, we have referred to the process of applying exchange rates to a foreign operation's financial statements to arrive at dollar amounts as *translation.* Historically, this has been the definition of this term. The use of the functional currency concept, however, has resulted in a narrower definition of this term in *FASB Statement No. 52.*

Translation.   In *FASB Statement No. 52,* **translation** refers to the process of **expressing functional currency amounts in the reporting currency.** Accordingly, the term is restricted to situations in which the foreign currency is the functional currency. Recall that when the foreign currency is the functional currency, the current-rate method is required, and it merely *expresses* the foreign currency financial statements in dollars. (It does not "remeasure" the nonmonetary accounts to obtain their dollar equivalents at the time the transactions were recorded.) The effect of a change in the exchange rate in these "translation" situations is called a **translation adjustment.** Translation adjustments are reported separately in stockholders' equity (a less closely monitored section of the financial statements, unfortunately) pending sale or liquidation of the investment.[10]

Remeasurement.   In *FASB Statement No. 52,* **remeasurement** is the process of applying exchange rates to a foreign operation's financial statements when they are not stated in the functional currency. **Thus, amounts in a different currency are expressed in the functional currency.** The most common example occurs when the functional currency of the foreign operation is the dollar. Of course, foreign operations normally maintain their books and prepare their financial statements in the currency of the foreign country in which they are located, regardless of whether the dollar is their functional currency. Recall that when the dollar is the functional currency, a combination of current and historical exchange rates is used whereby the nonmonetary accounts are remeasured in dollars to obtain the dollar equivalent of the transactions at the time they were recorded. Thus, the remeasurement process in *FASB Statement No. 52* refers to the remeasuring in the functional currency. Note that when the dollar is the functional currency, translation (as narrowly defined in the preceding paragraph) is not necessary

[10] *FASB Statement No. 52,* paragraphs 12–14.

because the functional currency is also the reporting currency. The effect of a change in the exchange rate from the remeasurement process is called a **foreign currency transaction gain or loss,** which must be reported currently in the income statement.[11]

Remeasurement and translation situations. Infrequently, a foreign operation's functional currency is a foreign currency that is different from the currency it uses to maintain its books and prepare its financial statements. An example would be a Swiss operation that keeps its books in Swiss francs (most likely because of tax laws) but uses the French franc as its functional currency. In such a case, the Swiss financial statements must be "remeasured" and expressed in French francs. Then, the French franc financial statements must be "translated" into dollars. Thus, a two-step process is required to obtain amounts in dollars. However, most foreign operations require only a one-step process—the "translation" process or the "remeasurement" process.

Comparison comment. The "translation" process is relatively simple because of the use of the current-rate method. In comparison, the "remeasurement" process is slightly more involved because of the use of current and historical exchange rates. When the remeasurement process is illustrated later in the chapter, we list the accounts to be remeasured using historical exchange rates. (For now, merely understand that these accounts are nonmonetary accounts and their amortizations.)

THE TRANSLATION PROCESS

In this section, we deal with the actual translation of foreign currency financial statements into dollars. Recall that in the "translation" process, the foreign currency is the functional currency.

Basic procedures before translation

Certain fundamental procedures must be performed before the financial statements of foreign subsidiaries or branches may be translated into dollars.

Adjustments to conform to U.S. generally accepted accounting principles. Operations conducted in a foreign country must be accounted for using that country's accounting principles. When foreign currency financial statements use accounting principles that are different from U.S. generally accepted accounting principles, appropriate adjustments must be made to the foreign currency financial statements before translation so that such statements conform to U.S. generally accepted accounting principles. These adjustments, which are **made on a worksheet,** are never posted to the general ledger of the foreign accounting entity. The adjustments are necessary regardless of (1) the organizational form through which foreign operations are conducted, and (2) whether or not the foreign operation's statements are consolidated (if a subsidiary) or combined (if a division or a branch) with the financial statements of the domestic accounting entity.

---

[11] *FASB Statement No. 52,* paragraph 15.

Similarly, when a domestic company has a 20–50% interest in a foreign operation, which must be accounted for under the equity method of accounting, the investee's foreign statements must be adjusted to conform to U.S. generally accepted accounting principles before translation into dollars. The equity method is then applied after the translation process in accordance with *FASB Statement No. 52.*

Adjustments to receivables and payables.   A foreign operation's receivables or payables in other than its local currency must be adjusted to reflect the current rate between the local currency (of the foreign country) and the currency in which the receivable or payable is stated. Chapter 14 covers how to make and account for such adjustments. (In the illustration of the translation process in this section, we assume that any such adjustments have already been made.)

Reconciliation of inter- or intracompany receivable and payable accounts.   Inventory and cash are commonly transferred between domestic and foreign operations. Such transactions (other than dividend remittances) are usually recorded in separate inter- or intracompany receivable and payable accounts by each accounting entity. Such accounts must be reconciled to each other before translation to ensure that no clerical errors or unrecorded in-transit items exist. Only by performing this reconciliation will these inter- or intracompany accounts completely offset each other after translation.

Furthermore, when the inter- or intracompany account is to be settled in dollars (rather than in the foreign unit's local currency), the foreign unit's accounts must be adjusted as described in the preceding section. (If settlement is to be made in the foreign unit's local currency, the domestic operation must adjust its books.) Such adjustments are illustrated in Chapter 14, where the intricacies of intercompany transactions with foreign subsidiaries are discussed.

Translating branch Home Office account.   Most foreign operations are conducted using subsidiaries. When branches are used, the Home Office account on the books of the branch replaces the equity accounts otherwise used by a subsidiary. The simplest technique is to have the branch maintain its Home Office account in three categories and to have the home office maintain its Investment in Branch account in three categories. The first category is the amount of the preceding period's ending balances of all three categories. This amount is translated at the combined amount shown for the Home Office account in the translated financial statements of the preceding period. The second category reflects all current-year transactions with the home office and is, in substance, a combination intracompany account (as discussed in the preceding paragraph) and quasi-capital account. Although the activity in this category must be reconciled with that period's activity in the corresponding category of the home office's Investment in Branch account, no adjustments are made for changes in the exchange rate. If each accounting entity has recorded all current-period transactions properly, this category is readily translated into dollars using the amount in the corresponding category on the home office's books. The third category represents the branch's current-year income; the translated amount in dollars is obtained from the translation of the branch's income statement.

Specific translation procedures

In the translation process using the foreign perspective, current exchange rates are used.

Balance sheet accounts. The following procedures are used to translate the individual balance sheet accounts:

(1) All assets and liabilities are translated at the exchange rate existing at the balance sheet date.
(2) Common stock and additional paid-in capital are translated at historical exchange rates (to isolate the effect of the change in the exchange rate for the current period).
(3) Beginning retained earnings is the dollar balance in the Retained Earnings account at the end of the prior period. (Dividend payments, if any, reduce this balance using the exchange rate in effect at the time of the declaration.)

Revenue, cost of goods sold, and expense accounts. All revenues, costs of sales, and expenses are translated using exchange rates that were in effect when these items were **recognized** in the income statement. Thus, exchange rates in effect during the current period are used. The following paragraphs explain how this process can be simplified.

The use of average exchange rates. When translating income statement accounts, average exchange rates may be used, provided that approximately the same results can be obtained from translating each individual transaction into dollars using the exchange rate that was in effect when the transaction occurred. If the item being translated occurred evenly throughout the period (month, quarter, or year), a simple average is sufficient. Otherwise, a weighted average is necessary. (Most publicly owned companies achieve a weighted average result by multiplying each individual month's amount by each month's average exchange rate.) Average exchange rates must be calculated using the direct exchange rates that existed during the period; indirect exchange rates would not give the proper translated amounts.

The substitution technique. A simplifying technique commonly used to translate income statement accounts that arise from activity with the parent or home office is to **substitute the amount in the domestic company's account for the subsidiary's or branch's account.** For example, the Intercompany Interest Expense account on the foreign subsidiary's books would be translated at the amount recorded in the Intercompany Interest Income account on the parent company's books. Likewise, the Intercompany Sales account on the foreign subsidiary's books would be translated at the amount recorded in the Intercompany Purchases account on the parent's books. This procedure automatically translates these items at the rates in effect on each transaction date, thus negating the need to use average rates. (This technique cannot be used in the translation process for downstream sales because it would result in a cost of goods sold amount based on exchange prices in existence when the inventory was acquired by the foreign unit rather than when the foreign unit sold the inventory. The latter is required under the translation process.)

In most cases, inter- or intracompany revenue and expense accounts need not be reconciled before doing the substitution. By reconciling the inter- or intracompany receivable and payable accounts before this substitution is made (as discussed on page 469), any clerical errors or unrecorded in-transit items affecting these income statement accounts would have been detected.

Forcing out the translation adjustment.   Recall that in the translation process, the effect of a change in the exchange rate is called a translation adjustment (which must be reported in a separate category of stockholders' equity). Under the fixed exchange rate system, translation adjustments could be calculated by multiplying the foreign operation's net asset position existing at the time of a devaluation or revaluation by the change in the exchange rate. Under the current floating exchange rate system, exchange rates change daily, and no such calculation is possible. The only practical alternative is to "force out" the translation adjustment, as follows (the amounts used are from Illustration 13-3, page 473):

(1)	Translated assets.....................................	$300,000
(2) Less	Translated liabilities	(208,000)
(3) Equals	Total stockholders' equity...........................	$ 92,000
(4) Less	Translated common stock and additional paid-in capital accounts.................	(50,000)
(5) Equals	Total retained earnings and the cumulative translation adjustment	$ 42,000
(6) Less	Beginning retained earnings in dollars as reported in the prior period's translated financial statements (reduced for any dividends declared)	(33,000)
(7) Less	Translated net income (determined from translating the individual revenue and expense accounts)	(25,200)
(8) Equals	The cumulative translation adjustment	$ (16,200)
(9) Less	The cumulative translation adjustment as of the beginning of the period	(6,400)
(10) Equals	The current-period translation adjustment	$ (9,800)

Illustration:
Translation of foreign currency financial statements

Assume the following information for a wholly owned subsidiary located in West Germany.

(1) **Conformity with U.S. generally accepted accounting principles.** The financial statements in marks have been adjusted to conform with U.S. generally accepted accounting principles. No adjustments are necessary on the worksheet before translation.

(2) **Intercompany receivable and payable accounts.** The parent company and the subsidiary have no intercompany transactions (other than dividends declared by the subsidiary). Accordingly, no intercompany receivable and payable accounts exist, and no adjustments must be made at the balance sheet date prior to the translation process relating to changes in the exchange rate.

(3) **Exchange rates.** The direct exchange rate at the beginning of the year was $0.45. The mark weakened or the dollar strengthened during the year such that the direct exchange rate at year-end was $0.40. The average rate for the year was $0.42.

(4) **Common stock.** The subsidiary was formed several years ago when the direct exchange rate was $0.50. No additional capital stock changes have occurred since then.

(5) **Retained earnings—Beginning of year.** No dividends were declared during 19X1. The translated amount of retained earnings at the end of the prior year was $33,000.

(6) **Sales, costs, and expenses.** All sales, costs, and expenses occurred evenly throughout the year.

(7) **Cumulative translation adjustment—Beginning of year.** The amount of the cumulative translation adjustment at the end of the prior year was a debit balance of $6,400.

The above information is used in Illustration 13-3 to translate the foreign subsidiary's financial statements.

In reviewing Illustration 13-3, note the following items:

(1) The $300,000 translated amount for the assets was inserted at the total liabilities and equity line (the first step in the "forcing" process).

(2) The $25,200 translated net income amount was then inserted into the balance sheet to force out the current-period translation adjustment.

(3) Because the exchange rate decreased from $0.45 at the beginning of the year to $0.40 at year-end—a decrease of $0.05—the subsidiary's average net asset position during the year was approximately 196,000 marks ($9,800 translation adjustment/$0.05).

(4) No amounts are shown for the income tax consequences relating to the translation adjustments. Such adjustments, if any, would be made to the dollar amounts on a worksheet prior to the consolidation process.

(5) *APB Opinion No. 18* provides that "an investor's net income for the period and its stockholders' equity at the end of the period are the same whether an investment in a subsidiary is accounted for under the equity method or the subsidiary is consolidated."[12] The parent company would make the following entry to meet this requirement:

Investment in subsidiary	15,400	
Cumulative translation adjustment	9,800	
Equity in net income of subsidiary		25,200

---

[12] *APB Opinion No. 18*, paragraph 19.

Illustration 13-3
Translation of foreign subsidiary's financial statements
for the year ended December 31, 19X1

	Marks	Exchange Rates Code	Exchange Rates Rate	Dollars
Balance Sheet:				
Cash	50,000	C	$0.40	$ 20,000
Accounts receivable, net	150,000	C	0.40	60,000
Inventory	200,000	C	0.40	80,000
Fixed assets	400,000	C	0.40	160,000
Accumulated depreciation	(50,000)	C	0.40	(20,000)
Total assets.	750,000			$300,000
Accounts payable.	230,000	C	0.40	$ 92,000
Income taxes payable	40,000	C	0.40	16,000
Long-term debt	250,000	C	0.40	100,000
Total liabilities	520,000			$208,000
Common stock	100,000	H	0.50	$ 50,000
Retained earnings:				
Prior years.	70,000		(1)	33,000
Current year	60,000	(Per net income below)		25,200
Cumulative translation adjustment, net:				
Prior years.			(1)	(6,400)
Current year		(Forced amount)		(9,800)
Total equity	230,000			$ 92,000
Total liabilities and equity. . . .	750,000	(Per above)		$300,000
Income Statement:				
Sales.	800,000	A	0.42	$336,000
Cost of goods sold	(500,000)	A	0.42	(210,000)
Depreciation expense	(20,000)	A	0.42	(8,400)
Operating expenses	(180,000)	A	0.42	(75,600)
Income before income taxes	100,000			$ 42,000
Income tax expense @ 40%.	(40,000)	A	0.42	(16,800)
Net income	60,000			$ 25,200

(1) The amount in dollars is given in the introduction to the illustration on page 472.
Code:
  C = Current rate existing at the balance sheet date.
  A = Average rate, as given in the introduction to the illustration on page 472.
  H = Historical rate.

This entry always maintains the investment account balance at the difference between the subsidiary's assets and liabilities.

Disposition of translation adjustments

The translation adjustments reported as a separate component of stock-holders' equity are removed from that separate component (along with any related income taxes) and reported in the income statement on (a) complete or substantially complete liquidation or (b) sale of the investment.[13] (*FASB Interpretation No. 37* requires such treatment on a pro rata basis when only

[13] *FASB Statement No. 52*, paragraph 14.

part of the ownership interest in a foreign operation is sold.[14]) Further interpretations are needed in this area to address the following questions:

(1) Does the conversion of all operating assets into cash constitute a liquidation?
(2) Does the conversion of all operating assets into passive investments constitute a liquidation?
(3) What percentage of the operating assets would have to be sold to constitute a substantially complete liquidation?

A company that has foreign operations in more than one foreign country must, of course, maintain the separate translation component of equity for each such foreign operation that has translation adjustments.

Income tax consequences of rate changes

FASB Statement No. 52 does not amend APB Opinions 11, 23, or 24, which deal with income taxes. These pronouncements must be followed to the extent their provisions apply to foreign operations. Because translation adjustments (as defined in *FASB Statement No. 52*) are not specifically addressed in APB Opinions 11, 23, and 24, paragraph 23 of *FASB Statement No. 52* states that (1) translation adjustments are accounted for as **timing differences** in accordance with the provisions of those APB opinions and (2) any income taxes provided on such translation adjustments are allocated to the separate component of equity.[15]

Recall from Chapter 12 that under the provisions of *APB Opinion No. 23,* "Accounting for Income Taxes—Special Areas," companies need not provide for taxes on subsidiaries' undistributed earnings under certain conditions—if earnings are invested indefinitely or will be remitted in a tax-free liquidation.

THE REMEASUREMENT PROCESS

In this section, we deal with the actual remeasurement of a foreign operation's financial statements into dollars, which is the foreign unit's functional currency. The basic procedures required before translation that were discussed in the preceding section on the "translation" process also apply to the remeasurement process—namely, making adjustments to conform to U.S. GAAP, adjusting foreign currency receivable and payable accounts, and reconciling inter- or intracompany accounts.

Specific remeasurement procedures

Earlier in the chapter, we said that the intent of the remeasurement process is to produce the same results as if the foreign unit's transactions had been recorded in the functional currency (dollars, in this case) using the exchange rates in effect when the transactions occurred. Thus, a combination of

---

[14] *FASB Interpretation No. 37,* "Accounting for Translation Adjustments upon Sale of Part of an Investment in a Foreign Entity" (Stamford, CT: FASB, 1983), paragraph 2.
[15] *FASB Statement No. 52,* paragraphs 22–24.

current and historical exchange rates is used. To achieve this objective, the FASB specified which accounts are remeasured using historical exchange rates (the current rate is used for all other accounts). These accounts are listed in Illustration 13-4.

   Forcing out the foreign currency transaction gain or loss from re-measurement.   Recall that the effect of the change in the exchange rate under the remeasurement process is reported in the income statement as a foreign currency transaction gain or loss. Because of the floating exchange rate system, this amount must be forced out in the income statement, as follows (amounts used are from Illustration 13-5, page 478):

(1)		Remeasured assets	$336,000
(2)	Less	Remeasured liabilities	(208,000)
(3)	Equals	Total stockholders' equity	$128,000
(4)	Less	Remeasured common stock and additional paid-in capital	(50,000)
(5)	Equals	Total retained earnings	$ 78,000
(6)	Less	Beginning retained earnings in dollars as reported in the prior period's remeasured financial statements (reduced for any dividends declared)	(46,400)
(7)	Equals	Current-period net income	$ 31,600
(8)	Less	Remeasured revenues and expenses	(16,600)
(9)	Equals	The current-period foreign currency transaction gain from remeasurement	$ 15,000

Illustration:
Remeasurement of a foreign operation's financial statements into dollars

To compare the results of the remeasurement process with the results of the translation process illustrated in the previous section, we use the financial statements for the same West German foreign subsidiary in the following illustration. In addition, we reflect an intercompany payable account of 50,000 marks (long-term debt was reduced by 50,000 marks). The assumptions for this illustration (some of which are identical to those used in the translation process) are as follows:

(1) Conformity with U.S. generally accepted accounting principles.   The financial statements in marks have been adjusted to conform with U.S. generally accepted accounting principles. No adjustments are necessary on the worksheet before remeasurement.

(2) Intercompany receivable and payable accounts.   The parent company and the subsidiary have considerable intercompany transactions (involving mainly inventory transfers). The subsidiary's intercompany payable ac-

Illustration 13-4
Accounts remeasured using historical exchange rates

Assets:
  Marketable securities carried at cost:
    Equity securities
    Debt securities not intended to be held until maturity
  Inventories carried at cost
  Prepaid expenses, such as insurance, advertising, and rent
  Property, plant, and equipment
  Accumulated depreciation on property, plant, and equipment
  Patents, trademarks, licenses, and formulas
  Goodwill
  Other tangible assets

Liabilities:
  Deferred income

Equity:
  Common stock
  Preferred stock carried at issuance price

Revenues, costs, and expenses (examples of accounts related to
    nonmonetary items):
  Cost of goods sold
  Depreciation of property, plant, and equipment
  Amortization of intangible items, such as goodwill, patents,
    licenses, and so on
  Amortization of deferred charges or credits, except deferred income
    taxes and policy acquisition costs for life insurance companies

Source: *FASB Statement No. 52*, paragraph 48.

Comments:
(1) **Additional Paid-in Capital.** Although not listed above, this account would be remeasured at historical exchange rates. (The Common Stock account listed above was obviously intended to include this account.)
(2) **Retained Earnings.** This account is not listed above, not because the current rate is used, but because it is a "forced out" amount.
(3) Note that the above list excludes deferred income taxes; they would be remeasured using the current rate.

---

count is payable in marks. Accordingly, the parent company has a foreign currency transaction and is the entity that must adjust its intercompany receivable account at year-end to reflect the exchange rate existing at the balance sheet date. (Chapter 14 discusses how to make adjustments to intercompany payables and receivables.)

(3) Exchange rates. The direct exchange rate at the beginning of the year was $0.45. The mark weakened or the dollar strengthened during the year such that the direct exchange rate at year-end was $0.40. The average rate for the year was $0.42.

(4) Inventory. The beginning inventory was remeasured at $46,000 in last year's financial statements. Ending inventory cost was below market in marks, resulting in no adjustment in marks for valuation purposes. The subsidiary determines that its ending inventory was acquired when the exchange rates were as follows:

Marks	Rate	Dollars
20,000	$0.42	$ 8,400
60,000	0.41	24,600
120,000	0.40	48,000
200,000		$81,000

(5) Fixed assets. All fixed assets were acquired in prior years when the exchange rate was $0.50. No fixed assets were retired during the year.

(6) Common stock. The subsidiary was formed several years ago when the exchange rate was $0.50. No additional capital stock changes have occurred since then.

(7) Retained earnings—Beginning of year. No dividends were declared during 19X1. The translated retained earnings amount at the end of the prior year was $46,400.

(8) Sales, purchases, and expenses. All sales, purchases, and expenses occurred evenly throughout the year.

The above information is used in Illustration 13-5 to remeasure the foreign subsidiary's financial statements into dollars.

In reviewing Illustration 13-5, note the following items:

(1) The $336,000 translated amount for the assets was inserted at the total liabilities and equity line (the first step in the "forcing" process). As a result, current-period net income can be forced out in the equity section.

(2) The net income forced out in the equity section was then inserted at the bottom of the income statement (the second step in the forcing process). This allows the transaction gain from remeasurement to be forced out in the income statement.

(3) The exchange rate decreased from $0.45 at the beginning of the year to $0.40 at year-end—a decrease of $0.05—and a $15,000 transaction gain from remeasurement was reported. Therefore, the foreign subsidiary was in an average net monetary liability position of 300,000 marks during the year ($15,000/$0.05). In other words, monetary liabilities exceeded monetary assets by 300,000 marks on the average during the year. [This average net monetary liability position approximates the December 31, 19X1 net monetary liability position, which is 320,000 marks (520,000 − 200,000).]

(4) The decrease in the direct exchange rate was an adverse economic event; however, a $15,000 favorable result was reported for the effect of the change in the exchange rate. (This unusual result situation was discussed in detail in the conceptual issues section of this chapter.)

(5) The $15,000 transaction gain from remeasurement would not have resulted if the company had kept monetary assets and monetary liabilities at approximately the same level throughout the year. Doing this merely to minimize transaction gains and losses from remeasurement, however, counteracts the long-standing principle of minimizing the risks associated with foreign operations by financing them with foreign borrowings (payable in the foreign currency of the foreign operation) to the maximum extent possible. Obviously, companies must carefully weigh these conflicting

Illustration 13-5
Remeasurement of foreign subsidiary's financial statements into dollars for the year ended December 31, 19X1

	Marks	Code	Rate	Dollars
		Exchange Rates		
Balance Sheet:				
Cash	50,000	C	$0.40	$ 20,000
Accounts receivable, net	150,000	C	0.40	60,000
Inventory *valued at rate when purchased*	200,000	H	(1)	81,000
Fixed assets	400,000	H	0.50	200,000
Accumulated depreciation	(50,000)	H	0.50	(25,000)
Total assets.	750,000			$336,000
Accounts payable.	230,000	C	0.40	$ 92,000
Income taxes payable	40,000	C	0.40	16,000
Intercompany payable	50,000	C	0.40	20,000
Long-term debt	200,000	C	0.40	80,000
Total liabilities	520,000			$208,000
Common stock	100,000	H	0.50	50,000
Retained earnings:				
Prior years.	70,000		(1)	46,400
Current year	60,000	(Forced amount)		31,600
Total equity	230,000			$128,000
Total liabilities and equity. .	750,000	(Per above)		$336,000
Income Statement:				
Sales.	800,000	A	0.42	$336,000
Cost of goods sold:				
Beginning inventory	100,000		(1)	46,000
Purchases	600,000	A	0.42	252,000
Goods available for sale . .	700,000			298,000
Less: Ending inventory	(200,000) (500,000)	(Per balance sheet)		(81,000) (217,000)
Depreciation expense	(20,000)	H	0.50	(10,000)
Operating expenses	(180,000)	A	0.42	(75,600)
Income before income taxes . . .	100,000			$ 33,400
Income tax expense @ 40%. . .	(40,000)	A	0.42	(16,800)
Income before transaction gain from remeasurement . . .	60,000			$ 16,600
Transaction gain from remeasurement.		(Forced amount)		15,000
Net income	60,000	(Per balance sheet)		$ 31,600

(1) The amount in dollars is given in the introduction to the illustration on pages 476–77.
Code:
C = Current rate existing at the balance sheet date.
H = Historical rate.
A = Average rate, as given in the introduction to the illustration on page 476.

objectives. (In Chapter 14, we discuss other means of minimizing gains and losses resulting from remeasurement.)

(6) Total assets and total equity are both higher by $36,000 in Illustration 13-5 than in Illustration 13-3, in which the "translation" process was shown. This difference is the result of using historical exchange rates in Illustration 13–5 for inventory (a $1,000 difference) and fixed assets (a $35,000 difference) rather than the rate existing at the balance sheet date (a current rate).

Income tax consequences of rate changes

Foreign currency transaction gains or losses from the remeasurement process that are not currently reported for tax purposes should be treated as **timing differences** for which interperiod tax allocation is necessary. (If the conditions set forth in *APB Opinion No. 23,* "Accounting for Income Taxes—Special Areas," are met, deferred income taxes need not be provided.)[16]

Basic procedures after remeasurement

Because of the use of historical exchange rates for most nonmonetary assets, the results of the remeasurement process create a special problem that does not arise with the "translation" process. Nonmonetary assets remeasured at historical exchange rates are not necessarily realizable in dollars (even though no realizability problem exists in the foreign currency). Thus, the foreign operation's remeasured nonmonetary assets must be reviewed and evaluated concerning their realizability in dollars. Prior to consolidation, the dollar amounts of such assets on the worksheet must be adjusted to the extent that they are not realizable in dollars. *FASB Statement No. 52* discusses the realization of inventory in dollars in great detail; however, it only briefly touches on the realization of fixed assets, which may be an even greater problem.

Inventory.   The lower of cost or market test must also be performed in dollars, to ensure that the realizable value in dollars is not less than remeasured historical cost. Such situations usually arise when ending inventory is acquired before the direct exchange rate decreases significantly, and the inventory is thus priced at historical cost and remeasured at the historical rate. In applying the lower of cost or market test in dollars, we determine current replacement cost, net realizable value, and net realizable value reduced for a normal profit margin (a percentage concept) in the foreign currency and then express each one in dollars using the exchange rate existing at the balance sheet date. (These are current value concepts; thus, the exchange rate existing at the balance sheet date is the only sensible exchange rate.)

To illustrate this procedure, we must use a more drastic exchange rate decrease than the one assumed in Illustration 13-5. Let us assume the 85% decline in the value of the Mexican peso that occurred in 1982. Assume ending inventory was acquired for 1,000,000 pesos before the decrease

---

[16] *FASB Statement No. 52,* paragraphs 22–24.

in the direct exchange rate. The exchange rate before the decrease was $0.04, and the exchange rate after the decrease was $0.006. The lower of cost or market calculation in dollars is as follows:

	Pesos	Rate	Dollars
Historical cost	1,000,000	$0.04	$40,000
Replacement cost	1,000,000	0.006	6,000
Net realizable value	1,200,000	0.006	$ 7,200 (ceiling)
Net realizable value reduced for a normal profit margin	1,000,000	0.006	6,000 (floor)

Accordingly, the inventory must be valued at $6,000, a write-down of $34,000. This write-down is made to the dollar column; it would never be posted to the peso general ledger. This process is necessary regardless of whether a write-down was needed in applying the lower of cost or market test in pesos. In an alternative view of the rationale for performing the lower of cost or market test in dollars, we assume that the inventory was sold on the last day of the year for 1,200,000 pesos. The 1,200,000 pesos (cash or receivables) would be remeasured to $7,200, which is below the re-measured historical cost of $40,000.

This example assumed that selling prices and purchase prices did not advance after the weakening of the peso. When selling prices neither advance nor decline, replacement cost always equals the floor. If selling prices had advanced in pesos after the weakening of the peso, the ceiling and floor would have been higher, thus necessitating a lower write-down. (Inflation often increases after a sharp decline in the value of a foreign currency.) The process of performing a lower of cost or market test for inventory in dollars is discussed at length in paragraphs 49–53 of *FASB Statement No. 52*.

Assets other than inventory. Fixed assets may be realizable in the foreign currency, but the future cash flow that such assets generate (including that portion of the future cash flow that presumably represents a recovery of the investment in fixed assets) is worth significantly less (in dollars) as a result of a weakening of the foreign currency. Surprisingly, the use of historical rates in remeasuring assets other than inventory and the potential realization problems that may arise are given only footnote attention in *FASB Statement No. 52*. Footnote 5 to paragraph 49 states:

> An asset other than inventory may sometimes be written down from historical cost. Although that write-down is not under the rule of cost or market, whichever is lower, the approach described in this paragraph might be appropriate. . . .[17]

If a substantial decline in the direct exchange rate occurs (such as the 85% devaluation of the Mexican peso in 1982), the realization of fixed assets in dollars represents a major problem that could be a much greater problem than the realization of inventory in dollars.

In practice, write-downs of fixed assets are rare. However, when an operation is losing money and the prospects of improving the situation are

---

[17] *FASB Statement No. 52*, paragraph 49, footnote 5.

not good, such operations are often sold. If the operation is sold for less than book value, as could be expected, the loss in value of the fixed assets is reported as a loss on disposal of a segment (if a segment is being disposed of) or as a loss on disposal of fixed assets if the disposal does not qualify as a disposal of a segment. (Disposals of segments are discussed in Chapter 15.)

In Illustration 13-5, the direct exchange rate decreased during the year, and a $15,000 transaction gain resulted from the remeasurement process. Because of the decline in the exchange rate, the inventory and fixed assets must be reviewed as to their realization in dollars. A write-down would offset (partially or fully) the transaction gain from remeasurement. Depending on the extent of the write-down, this procedure either minimizes or eliminates the reporting of a current-period transaction gain from remeasurement that will only be offset by the reporting of future-period transaction losses from remeasurement.

If the direct exchange rate had increased rather than decreased in Illustration 13-5, a transaction loss from remeasurement would have resulted; however, no provisions exist for revaluing inventory and fixed assets upward to obtain the offsetting effect discussed in the preceding paragraph. Accordingly, the reporting of a current-period transaction loss from remeasurement is offset in later periods as the nonmonetary assets are realized (transformed into monetary assets).

MANNER OF REPORTING FOREIGN OPERATIONS

Disclosures concerning translation and remeasurement

Pertaining to the translation process. For the separate component of stockholders' equity containing the cumulative translation adjustments, the FASB requires an analysis of the following changes during the period:

a. Beginning and ending amount of cumulative translation adjustments.
b. The aggregate adjustment for the period resulting from translation adjustments and gains and losses from certain hedges and intercompany balances [the latter items are discussed in Chapter 14].
c. The amount of income taxes for the period allocated to translation adjustments.
d. The amounts transferred from cumulative translation adjustments [including all items above] and included in determining net income for the period as a result of the sale or complete or substantially complete liquidation of an investment in a foreign subsidiary.[18]

This analysis may be shown (1) in a separate financial statement, (2) in notes to the financial statements, or (3) as part of a statement of changes in stockholders' equity.

Pertaining to the remeasurement process. The total of all transaction gains and losses from remeasurement (along with other foreign currency transaction gains and losses that are reported in the income statement—

---

[18] *FASB Statement No. 52,* paragraph 31.

such as those resulting from importing and exporting transactions) is disclosed as a net amount either in the income statement or in notes to the financial statements.[19] (Transaction gains and losses are not considered extraordinary items, no matter how material they might be.)

Additional risks in reporting earnings from foreign operations

An asset held in a foreign country is not the same as an asset held domestically. This is true for monetary assets (such as cash, receivables, or any other asset that will be settled by the payment of currency) and non-monetary assets (such as land, buildings, equipment, and inventory). Assets held in foreign countries entail the following additional risks:

(1) Expropriation, or the seizure of assets.
(2) Devaluation, or the diminution of value of both monetary assets and the cash flows from future operations.
(3) Currency transfer restrictions, or the limitation on repatriation of foreign profits and invested capital.
(4) Wars and civil disorders.

These risks must be considered in determining the earnings reported from foreign operations, regardless of the amounts determined under the procedures called for in *FASB Statement No. 52.* Of course, these factors also influence whether or not consolidation is appropriate. In practice, for example, a domestic company usually does not consolidate foreign operations located in a country that imposes currency exchange restrictions, because the assets are no longer under the domestic company's complete control.

Nonconsolidation of a foreign operation.   If a foreign subsidiary is not consolidated, then the parent company's investment in the subsidiary must be accounted for under the equity method of accounting, as required by *APB Opinion No. 18,* "The Equity Method of Accounting for Investments in Common Stock." Thus, regardless of whether or not a foreign subsidiary is consolidated, the parent company must determine the foreign subsidiary's net income or loss in the manner explained earlier in the chapter. The parent must then consider the additional risks. In some cases, the parent may need to write down the investment. (Note that the need to consider the additional risks is not eliminated merely by not consolidating.)

Disclosures concerning foreign assets, revenues, and profitability

FASB Statement No. 14, "Financial Reporting for Segments of a Business Enterprise," requires disclosures of foreign assets, revenues, and profitability of consolidated foreign operations if specific tests are met. We discuss these tests and the disclosure requirements in Chapter 15, which deals with segment reporting.

---

[19] *FASB Statement No. 52,* paragraph 15.

CONCLUDING COMMENTS

Knowledgeable people, many with substantial experience in assessing and dealing with foreign operations, draw completely different conclusions concerning how to account for the effects of changes in the exchange rate in reporting foreign operations. For example, *FASB Statement No. 52* was passed by a mere 4 to 3 vote. We summarize the views of the dissenting members of the FASB below.

Views of the dissenting FASB members

The substantial objections and views of the three dissenting FASB members are presented in pages 15–23 of *FASB Statement No. 52.* They basically objected to allowing the use of a foreign currency as the unit of measure (when the dollar is not the functional currency). (This objection essentially rejects the functional currency concept as a relevant factor in determining how foreign operations should be expressed in dollars.) In their view, the dollar should be used as the unit of measure in all cases. Furthermore, dissenting members felt that the translation adjustments should not be reported directly in stockholders' equity. In their view, translation adjustments are gains and losses from a dollar perspective that should be currently reported in the income statement. In summary, these members felt that *FASB Statement No. 8* was conceptually sound and that the temporal method of translation should be used in all cases. (They would have allowed a practical modification for inventory; locally acquired inventory could be translated at the current exchange rate.)

Has the controversy ended?

Whether *FASB Statement No. 52* is the last chapter concerning the foreign currency translation issue or merely the latest chapter remains to be seen. An adequate assessment of the reporting results from using the functional currency concept and not reporting translation adjustments currently in the income statement will probably require a fairly long period of time. Considering the extensive monumental effort that the FASB and its staff devoted to *FASB Statement No. 52,* they will likely not want to readdress this issue for quite a while.

SUMMARY

The cornerstone of *FASB Statement No. 52* is the functional currency concept. The functional currency for each foreign operation must be determined. The currency in which the foreign operation primarily generates and expends cash is its functional currency, and this currency is not necessarily the one in which it maintains its books and prepares its financial statements. Illustration 13-6 contains a summary of accounting for the translation of foreign currency financial statements once the functional currency has been determined.

Illustration 13-6
**Summary of accounting for the translation
of foreign currency financial statements**

	Functional Currency	
	Foreign Currency	U.S. Dollar
Perspective taken.........................	Foreign	Parent Company
Name given to process....................	Translation	Remeasurement
Exchange rates to be used for:		
Assets and liabilities	Current rate[a]	Combination of current[a] and historical rates
Income statement accounts	Current rate[b]	Combination of current[b] and historical rates
Term used to describe the effect of a change in the exchange rate	Translation adjustment	Foreign currency transaction gain or loss
Treatment to be accorded the effect of a change in the exchange rate	Accumulate in separate component of stockholders' equity (pending liquidation or disposal of the investment)	Report currently in the income statement

[a] Current rate here means the exchange rate existing at the balance sheet date.
[b] Current rate here means the exchange rate existing when the items were recognized in the income statement.
Note: For operations located in countries that have highly inflationary economies, the dollar is deemed to be the functional currency.

Glossary of new terms

Conversion: The exchange of one currency for another.
Current Exchange Rate: The current exchange rate is the rate at which one unit of a currency can be exchanged for (converted into) another currency. For purposes of translation . . ., the current exchange rate is the rate as of the end of the period covered by the financial statements or as of the dates of recognition in those statements in the case of revenues, expenses, gains, and losses.[20]
Foreign Currency Translation (broad definition):   The process of expressing in the reporting currency of the enterprise those amounts that are denominated or measured in a different currency.[20] (This definition encompasses both the "translation" process and the "remeasurement" process.)
Foreign Operation: An operation (for example, subsidiary, division, branch, joint venture, and so on) whose financial statements (a) are prepared in a currency

---

[20] Taken directly from *FASB Statement No. 52*, Appendix E, pp. 75–78.

other than the reporting currency of the reporting enterprise and (b) are combined or consolidated with or accounted for on the equity basis in the financial statements of the reporting enterprise.[20]

Monetary Accounts: Cash and receivables and payables to be settled in currency.

Nonmonetary Accounts: All balance sheet accounts that are not monetary accounts.

Net Monetary Asset Position: Having monetary assets in excess of monetary liabilities.

Net Monetary Liability Position: Having monetary liabilities in excess of monetary assets.

Remeasurement: The process of measuring in the functional currency amounts denominated or stated in another currency.

Translation (distinguished from remeasurement):   The process of expressing functional currency measurements in the reporting currency.

Translation Adjustments: Translation adjustments result from the process of translating financial statements from the entity's functional currency into the reporting currency.

Unit of Measure: The currency in which assets, liabilities, revenues, expenses, gains, and losses are measured.[20]

Review questions

1. Differentiate between conversion and translation.
2. What is the direct quotation rate? the indirect quotation rate?
3. What is meant when a currency is said to be strengthening? weakening?
4. What is meant by the current exchange rate? historical exchange rate?
5. What is meant by the term *monetary accounts?*
6. Summarize the parent company perspective.
7. Summarize the foreign (or local) perspective.
8. What is meant by the term *functional currency?*
9. How are highly inflationary economy situations dealt with in *FASB Statement No. 52?*
10. Differentiate between translation and remeasurement.
11. How are the effects of changes in the exchange rate treated in translation situations? in remeasurement situations?
12. List the basic procedures required before the translation or remeasurement process begins.

Discussion cases

Discussion case 13–1
Functional currency determination

The All-Cheery Company manufactures soap domestically and in a foreign country, which has low labor costs. The foreign operation (conducted through a wholly owned subsidiary) purchases all of its raw materials from the parent company, which can obtain volume discounts because of its size. (Were it not for the volume

[20] Taken directly from *FASB Statement No. 52,* Appendix E, pp. 75–78.

discount, the foreign subsidiary would purchase the raw materials directly from suppliers.) The foreign subsidiary's purchases from the parent company are de-nominated in dollars.

All of the subsidiary's sales are in its local currency, the mun, and all employees are paid in muns. The parent company has established that the subsidiary's dividend policy is to convert its available funds into dollars as quickly as possible each month for current or near-term distribution to the parent.

Required:
Determine whether the functional currency is the dollar or the mun.

Discussion case 13–2
Evaluation of the impact of a weakening foreign currency

Assume you are the controller of a domestic company that established operations in Mexico two years ago. These foreign operations are conducted through a Mexican subsidiary. The subsidiary has three operational manufacturing plants, all of which cost approximately the same amount and were financed as follows:

(1) The first plant was financed entirely from a capital stock investment made by the parent in the subsidiary.
(2) The second plant was financed entirely from a long-term loan from a local Mexican bank, none of which has been repaid.
(3) The third plant was financed entirely from an interest-bearing, long-term loan from the parent, none of which has been repaid. (The loan is payable in dollars.)

During the month preceding the annual shareholders' meeting, the Mexican peso declined approximately 30% in value. You are sure a question will arise at the shareholders' meeting concerning the financial consequences of this decline.

Required:
(1) Without regard to whether the functional currency is the dollar or the peso, prepare a brief summary of the impact of the decline in the value of the peso on the company's foreign operations.
(2) Indicate the effect of the change in the exchange rate that will be reported for the current year for each of the plants assuming that the functional currency is
a. the peso.
b. the dollar.

Discussion case 13–3
Evaluation of the impact of a weakening dollar

Forester Corporation is a domestic company that established a manufacturing subsidiary in West Germany four years ago. In establishing this foreign operation, Forester minimized the number of dollars taken out of the United States by financing the subsidiary's manufacturing plant through a loan obtained from a West German financial institution. This loan is being repaid over 25 years. As a result, the subsidiary is thinly capitalized.

During the current year, the dollar weakened approximately 20% against the mark, as concerns arose over the sizable U.S. foreign trade deficit, the federal spending deficit, and the inability to control inflation. (The mark held steady against the other major currencies of the world.) In marks, the subsidiary had a profit for the current year comparable to the prior year. In dollars, the subsidiary had a loss for the current year, compared with a profit for the prior year.

Required:
Forester's president has asked you, the controller, to respond to the following questions:
(1) How is it possible to report a loss on the foreign operation for the current year, considering
  (a) The parent minimized its dollars at risk by financing the foreign plant with local borrowings?
  (b) The operation was run as efficiently this year as in the prior year?
(2) Is this an economic loss or a paper loss? Explain your answer.
(3) Is there any way the loss could have been avoided?

Discussion case 13–4
Criteria for consolidation of foreign subsidiary

J & R Products Company was incorporated in the state of Texas 15 years ago to manufacture medical supplies and equipment. Since incorporating, J & R has doubled in size about every three years and is now considered one of the leading medical supply companies in the country.

During January 19X1, J & R established a subsidiary, Ross, Ltd., in the emerging nation of Ewinga. J & R owns 90% of Ross's outstanding capital stock; the remaining 10% of Ross's outstanding capital stock is held by Ewinga citizens, as required by Ewinga constitutional law. The investment in Ross, which J & R accounts for using the equity method, represents about 18% of J & R's total assets at December 31, 19X4, the close of the accounting period for both companies.

Required:
What criteria should J & R Products Company use in determining whether to prepare consolidated financial statements with Ross, Ltd., for the year ended December 31, 19X4? Explain.

(AICPA adapted)

Exercises

Exercise 13–1
Exchange rates

On January 1, 19X1, 100,000 Mexican pesos could be converted into $400. On December 31, 19X1, 100,000 pesos could be converted into $500.

Required:
(1) Express the relationship between the two currencies at each date directly and indirectly.

(2) Did the peso strengthen or weaken during 19X1? Did the dollar strengthen or weaken during 19X1?

Exercise 13–2
Selection of proper exchange rate—balance sheet accounts

The following accounts exist in a foreign subsidiary's books:

 (1) Allowance for doubtful accounts
 (2) Inventory (carried at cost)
 (3) Inventory (carried at market, which is below cost)
 (4) Marketable equity securities (carried at cost)
 (5) Marketable equity securities (carried at market, which exceeds historical cost)
 (6) Patents
 (7) Equipment
 (8) Accumulated depreciation
 (9) Intercompany payable
(10) Long-term debt
(11) Income taxes payable
(12) Deferred income taxes
(13) Common stock
(14) Additional paid-in capital
(15) Retained earnings

Required:
(1) Assuming the subsidiary's local currency is its functional currency, determine whether the historical exchange rate, the current exchange rate, an average exchange rate, or some other procedure should be used to translate the above accounts.
(2) Assuming the dollar is the subsidiary's functional currency, determine whether the historical exchange rate, the current exchange rate, an average exchange rate, or some other procedure should be used to remeasure the above accounts in dollars.

Exercise 13–3
Selection of proper exchange rate—income statement accounts

The following accounts exist in a foreign subsidiary's books:

 (1) Revenues
 (2) Intercompany sales to parent company
 (3) Purchases
 (4) Intercompany purchases from parent company
 (5) Cost of goods sold
 (6) Selling expenses
 (7) Depreciation expense
 (8) Income tax expense
 (9) Goodwill amortization
(10) Gain on sale of equipment

(11) Intercompany interest expense
(12) Depreciation expenses (incremental amount resulting from adjusting assets for inflation)

Required:
The requirements are the same as those in Exercise 13–2.

Exercise 13–4
Determining the financial position of foreign operations from effect and direction of exchange rate changes

Various information for Far-Flung Corporation's overseas subsidiaries for 19X1 is presented below:

	Country	Functional Currency	Direction of Direct Exchange Rate in 19X1	Effect of Change in Exchange Rate
(1)	Brazil	Dollar	Decreased	Favorable
(2)	Mexico	Dollar	Decreased	Unfavorable
(3)	Sweden	Krona	Increased	Favorable
(4)	Belgium	Franc	Increased	Unfavorable
(5)	Ireland	Punt	Decreased	Unfavorable
(6)	Spain	Peseta	Decreased	Favorable
(7)	Saudi Arabia	Dollar	Increased	Favorable
(8)	Japan	Dollar	Increaesd	Unfavorable

Required:
Determine the appropriate financial position that each of the above foreign operations was in during the year for the above listed effect to have resulted.

Exercise 13–5
Translation of depreciation expense

The Melcher Company owns a foreign subsidiary with 3,600,000 local currency units (LCU) of property, plant, and equipment before accumulated depreciation at December 31, 19X5. Of this amount, 2,400,000 LCU were acquired in 19X3 when the exchange rate was 5 LCU to $1; 1,200,000 LCU were acquired in 19X4 when the exchange rate was 8 LCU to $1.

The exchange rate in effect at December 31, 19X5, was 10 LCU to $1. The weighted average of exchange rates that were in effect during 19X5 was 12 LCU to $1. Assume that the property, plant, and equipment are depreciated using the straight-line method over a 10-year period with no salvage value.

Required:
Determine the dollar amount of depreciation expense for 19X5 assuming that the foreign operation's functional currency is
a. the LCU.
b. the dollar.

(AICPA adapted)

Exercise 13–6
Calculating the effect of a change in the exchange rate

The Fleming Corporation has a foreign subsidiary in a country in which the direct exchange rate has decreased from $0.25 at January 1, 19X1 to $0.20 at December 31, 19X1. The average balances of the individual assets and liabilities during the year were as follows:

	Units of Foreign Currency
Cash	80,000
Accounts receivable	220,000
Inventory	275,000
Fixed assets, net	425,000
	1,000,000
Accounts payable and accruals	325,000
Current portion of long-term debt	25,000
Intercompany payable	100,000
Long-term debt	300,000
Deferred income taxes	50,000
	800,000

Required:
Determine the effect of the change in the exchange rate for 19X1 assuming the foreign operation's functional currency is
a. the foreign currency.
b. the dollar.

Problems

Problem 13–1
Three special translation situations

The following selected information is provided in connection with the translation of a Mexican subsidiary's December 31, 19X1 financial statements:

(1) The subsidiary must adjust its fixed assets annually for inflation. Amounts of these adjustments are maintained in separate general ledger accounts. The balances in these accounts at year-end are as follows:

	Debit	Credit
Land—revaluation	500,000	
Building—revaluation	800,000	
Accumulated depreciation—revaluation		200,000
Depreciation expense—revaluation (19X1)	40,000	

The depreciation expense increment is deductible for Mexican federal tax purposes. Assume the tax rate is 40%.
(2) The December 31, 19X1 inventory was acquired when the following exchange rates existed:

Pesos	Direct Rate
1,000,000	$.009
3,000,000	.008
7,000,000	.007
10,000,000	.006
15,000,000	.005
36,000,000	

The replacement cost of the inventory is 38,000,000 pesos; the net realizable value is 60,000,000 pesos; and the net realizable value less a normal profit margin is 40,000,000 pesos.

(3) Equipment acquired in prior years costing 4,000,000 pesos was sold on April 1, 19X1 for 2,500,000 pesos when the exchange rate was $0.008. (The exchange rate existing when the equipment was purchased several years ago was $0.04.) A 1,000,000 peso gain relating to this disposal is recorded in the general ledger.

The exchange rate at December 31, 19X1 is 200 pesos to $1; however, the average relationship for 19X1 was 150 pesos to $1.

Required:
(1) For item (1), prepare the adjusting entry necessary to convert to U.S. GAAP.
(2) For item (2), perform a lower of cost or market test in dollars assuming
    a. the peso is the functional currency.
    b. the dollar is the functional currency.
(3) For item (3), determine the amount of the gain in dollars assuming
    a. the peso is the functional currency.
    b. the dollar is the functional currency.

Problem 13–2
Translation of financial statements: Subsidiary
(foreign currency is the functional currency)

The financial statements of the Danielle Company, a foreign subsidiary domiciled in France, for the year ended December 31, 19X2 are as follows:

	Francs
Balance Sheet:	
Cash	200,000
Accounts receivable, net..	1,000,000
Inventory..	2,000,000
Property, plant, and equipment	6,300,000
Accumulated depreciation.......................................	(500,000)
Total assets	9,000,000
Accounts payable	2,500,000
Income taxes payable	200,000
Long-term debt	2,800,000
Total liabilities	5,500,000

	Francs
Common stock	1,500,000
Retained earnings:	
Prior years	1,400,000
Current year	600,000
Total equity	3,500,000
Total liabilities and equity	9,000,000

Income Statement:

Sales		10,000,000
Cost of goods sold:		
Beginning inventory	1,500,000	
Purchases	6,000,000	
	7,500,000	
Less: Ending inventory	(2,000,000)	(5,500,000)
Depreciation expense (total)		(200,000)
Operating expenses		(3,300,000)
Income before Income Taxes		1,000,000
Income tax expense		(400,000)
Net Income		600,000

Additional information:

(1) Conformity with U.S. GAAP. Assume the financial statements in francs have been adjusted to conform with U.S. generally accepted accounting principles.

(2) Exchange rates:

	Direct Rate
Current rate at December 31, 19X1	$0.15
Average rate for 19X2	0.12
Current rate at December 31, 19X2	0.10

(3) Inventory. The ending inventory is valued at the lower of cost or market in francs; however, no write-down to market was necessary on the subsidiary's books. Assume that the inventory at December 31, 19X2 was acquired when the exchange rate was $0.11. Inventory at December 31, 19X1 was acquired when the exchange rate was $0.16.

(4) Property, plant, and equipment. All were acquired in prior years when the exchange rate was $0.16, except equipment costing 300,000 francs, which was acquired in late December 19X2 when the exchange rate was $0.11. (No depreciation was recorded on this equipment for 19X2.)

(5) Sales, purchases, and operating expenses. All occurred evenly throughout the year.

(6) Common stock. The subsidiary was formed two years ago when the direct exchange rate was $0.16. No additional capital transactions have occurred since then.

(7) Retained earnings—Beginning of year. The subsidiary did not declare any dividends during the year.

Required:

(1) Translate the financial statements into dollars assuming that
   a. the franc is the functional currency.
   b. retained earnings at December 31, 19X1 (per the translated financial statements) was $217,000.
   c. the cumulative translation adjustment at December 31, 19X1 was $(22,000).

(2) Calculate the average financial position that the subsidiary was in during the year to have the translation adjustment that resulted for 19X2.
(3) Prepare the parent company's entry at December 31, 19X2 relating to the equity method of accounting.

Problem 13–3
Remeasurement of financial statements:
Subsidiary (dollar is the functional currency)

Assume the information provided in Problem 13–2.

Required:
(1) Remeasure the financial statements into dollars assuming that
    a. the dollar is the functional currency.
    b. retained earnings at December 31, 19X1 (per the dollar financial statements) was $260,000.
(2) Calculate the average financial position that the subsidiary was in during the year to have the transaction gain or loss from remeasurement that occurred for 19X2.
(3) Prepare the parent company's entry at December 31, 19X2 relating to the equity method of accounting.
(4) After you have completed the remeasurement process, evaluate whether any other important areas should be addressed.

Problem 13–4
Translation of financial statements: Branch
(foreign currency is the functional currency)

The financial statements of Rockness Company's Coventry, England, branch for the year ended December 31, 19X6 are as follows:

		Pounds
Balance Sheet:		
Cash		10,000
Accounts receivable		12,000
Allowance for doubtful accounts		(2,000)
Inventory (FIFO)		30,000
Equipment		15,000
Accumulated depreciation		(5,000)
Total assets		60,000
Notes payable		5,000
Accrued liabilities		4,000
Income taxes payable		6,000
Home office:		
Balance, January 1, 19X6	22,000	
Current-year intercompany transactions	11,000	
Current-year earnings	12,000	45,000
Total liabilities and equity		60,000

Income Statement:		Pounds
Sales.....		200,000
Cost of goods sold:		
Beginning inventory.....	40,000	
Purchases	140,000	
	180,000	
Less: Ending inventory	(30,000)	(150,000)
Depreciation expense (total)		(4,000)
Operating expenses		(16,000)
Income before Income Taxes		30,000
Income tax expense @ 60%.....		(18,000)
Net Income		12,000

Additional information:

(1) Conformity with U.S. GAAP. Assume the financial statements in pounds are in accordance with U.S. generally accepted accounting principles; thus no adjustments are required.

(2) Exchange rates:

	Direct Rate
Current rate at December 31, 19X5	$1.62
Average rate for 19X6	1.55
Current rate at December 31, 19X6	1.50

(3) Inventory. The ending inventory is valued at the lower of cost or market in pounds; however, no write-down to market was necessary on the branch's books. Assume that the inventory at December 31, 19X6 was acquired in December 19X6 when the direct exchange rate was $1.50, except inventory costing 5,000 pounds, which was acquired when the direct exchange rate was $1.52. The inventory at December 31, 19X5 was acquired when the exchange rate was $1.65, and no market adjustment in pounds was necessary.

(4) Equipment. The equipment was acquired in prior years when the direct exchange rate was $1.70.

(5) Home Office account. The Investment in Branch account on the home office books has increased $18,000 as a result of current-year transactions with the branch.

(6) Sales and operating expenses. Assume sales and expenses occurred evenly throughout the year.

(7) Purchases. All inventory purchases were from the home office at the home office's cost. The 19X6 balance in the home office's Shipments to Branch account is $217,000.

Required:

(1) Translate the financial statements into dollars assuming that
   a. the pound is the functional currency (regardless of the inventory acquired from the home office).
   b. the total balance in the Home Office account at December 31, 19X5 was $37,000 (per the translated financial statements).
   c. the cumulative translation adjustment at December 31, 19X5 was $(1,360).

(2) Calculate the average financial position that the subsidiary was in during the year to have the translation adjustment that resulted for 19X6.

(3) Prepare the home office's entry with respect to the branch's income or loss.

Problem 13–5
Remeasurement of financial statements: Branch (dollar is the functional currency)

Assume the information provided in Problem 13–4.

Required:
(1) Remeasure the financial statements into dollars assuming that
    a. the dollar is the functional currency.
    b. the total balance in the Home Office account at December 31, 19X5 was $38,000 (per the dollar financial statements).
(2) Calculate the average financial position that the subsidiary was in during the year to have the transaction gain or loss from remeasurement that resulted for 19X6.
(3) Prepare the home office's entry with respect to the branch's income or loss.

14 Translation of Foreign Currency Transactions

In this chapter, we discuss accounting for (1) importing and exporting transactions that require settlement in a foreign currency; (2) transactions entered into to protect against adverse exchange rate changes on the transactions in (1); (3) transactions a domestic company may enter into to protect its investment in a foreign operation against adverse exchange rate changes; and (4) transactions a domestic company may have with its foreign operation. Categories (1) and (2), above, require an understanding only of pages 446–49 in Chapter 13. Categories (3) and (4) require a complete understanding of Chapter 13.

TRANSLATION OF FOREIGN CURRENCY TRANSACTIONS—BASICS

Measured versus denominated

The currency in which a transaction is to be settled must be stipulated. When the transaction is to be settled by the receipt or payment of a fixed amount of a specified currency, the receivable or payable, respectively, is said to be **denominated** in that currency. When the transaction is to be settled by the receipt or payment of a fixed amount of a currency other than the U.S. dollar, from the perspective of a U.S. reporting entity, the receivable or payable is denominated in a foreign currency. A party to a transaction **measures** and records the transaction in the currency of the country in which that party is located. A transaction may be measured and denominated in one currency, or it may be measured in one currency and denominated in another currency. The following examples illustrate this process:

(1) A U.S. importer purchases goods on credit from a Swiss exporter, with payment to be made in a specified number of Swiss francs. The domestic importer measures and records the transaction in dollars, and the Swiss exporter measures and records the transaction in Swiss francs. The domestic importer's liability is denominated in a foreign currency—the Swiss franc. The Swiss exporter's receivable is denominated in Swiss francs. (If the terms of the transaction called for payment to be made in dollars, the transaction would be measured and denominated in dollars, from the perspective of the importer.)
(2) A Swiss subsidiary of a U.S. company purchases goods on credit from another Swiss company, with payment to be made in a specified number of Swiss francs. The Swiss subsidiary measures the asset acquired and the liability incurred in Swiss francs. The Swiss subsidiary's liability is not denominated in a foreign currency, because the liability is denominated in Swiss francs. From the perspective of the U.S. parent, however, the Swiss subsidiary's liability is denominated in a foreign currency, because the liability is not payable in dollars.

(3) A Swiss subsidiary of a U.S. company purchases goods on credit from an Italian company, with payment to be made in Italian lira. The Swiss subsidiary measures the asset acquired and liability incurred in Swiss francs. The Swiss subsidiary's liability is denominated in a foreign currency. From the perspective of the U.S. parent, the Swiss subsidiary's liability is denominated in a foreign currency, because the liability is not payable in dollars.

Foreign transactions versus foreign currency transactions

For each foreign transaction, only one party has a foreign currency transaction, because payment is usually specified in only one currency. The party that must make or receive payment in other than its own local currency has the **foreign currency transaction.** For example, a domestic importer who pays for goods in the supplier's currency has a foreign currency transaction, whereas the supplier has only a **foreign transaction.** Likewise, a domestic exporter who receives payment in the customer's currency has a foreign currency transaction, whereas the customer has only a foreign transaction.

When the domestic company makes or receives payment in dollars, no special accounting procedures are necessary because no accounting issues exist. When the domestic company pays or receives in the foreign currency, however, several accounting issues arise. Before discussing these issues, we must define the following three dates that may be involved in a foreign currency transaction:

(1) **The transaction date.** The transaction date is the date on which the transaction is initially recordable under generally accepted accounting principles.
(2) **Intervening balance sheet dates.** Intervening balance sheet dates occur between the transaction date and the settlement date. Thus, a transaction recorded on August 20, 19X5 and settled on January 10, 19X6 would have five intervening balance sheet dates, assuming monthly financial statements are prepared. Intervening balance sheet dates exist only for transactions in which credit terms are granted and used.
(3) **The settlement date.** Payment is made on the settlement date. On this date, one currency is **converted** into the other currency. (When credit terms are not granted, the transaction date and the settlement date coincide.)

Conceptual issues

In foreign currency transactions, the first accounting issue pertains to how the transaction should be recorded in dollars at the transaction date. Accountants generally agree that the transaction should be recorded at the transaction date using the exchange rate in effect at that date. For an import transaction, therefore, the acquired asset is initially recorded at the dollar amount needed to purchase the amount of foreign currency that would settle the transaction at the transaction date. For an export transaction, the export sale is recorded at the dollar amount that would be received from converting the foreign currency into dollars if full payment were made at the transaction date.

If credit terms are not granted, no other accounting issues exist. If credit terms are granted and used, the following additional accounting issues arise:

(1) If the exchange rate used to record the transaction at the transaction date has changed between the transaction date and an intervening balance sheet date, should the receivable or payable pertaining to the unsettled portion of the transaction be adjusted to reflect the current rate at such intervening balance sheet date?
(2) If the transaction is settled at an amount different from that at which it was initially recorded, how should the difference be recorded?

With respect to the first issue, most accountants agree that any unsettled portion of the transaction represented by a payable or receivable should be adjusted at intervening balance sheet dates to reflect the exchange rate in effect at those dates. It makes sense to carry the receivable or payable at the amount of dollars that would be received or paid, respectively, if the transaction were settled on that date. (This is essentially current-value accounting.) The following two viewpoints exist with respect to the second issue:

(1) **The one-transaction perspective.** Under the one-transaction perspective, all aspects of the transaction are viewed as part of a single transaction. A company's commitment to pay or receive foreign currency is considered a necessary and inseparable part of the transaction to purchase or sell goods, respectively. The amount initially recorded at the transaction date is considered an estimate until the final settlement. As a result, the initially recorded cost of goods acquired or revenue is subsequently adjusted for any difference between the amount recorded at the transaction date and the amount at which the transaction is ultimately settled.
(2) **The two-transaction perspective.** Under the two-transaction perspective, the commitment to pay or receive foreign currency is considered a separate transaction from the purchase or sale of goods. The decision to grant or use credit is considered a separate decision from that of purchasing or selling goods. As a result, any difference between the amount initially recorded at the transaction date and the amount at which the transaction is ultimately settled is considered a foreign currency transaction gain or loss—no adjustment is made to the initially recorded cost of goods acquired or revenues recorded pertaining to goods sold, as the case may be.

From either perspective, the risk in a foreign currency transaction from potential adverse exchange rate changes can be eliminated by not granting or using credit or by using a forward exchange contract (discussed later in the chapter).

FASB adopts the two-transaction perspective. The FASB rejected the one-transaction approach in *FASB Statement No. 52* (as it did in *FASB Statement No. 8*) on the grounds that the consequences of the risks associated with foreign currency transactions should be accounted for separately from the purchase or sale of goods. Thus, the requirements of *FASB Statement No. 52* reflect the two-transaction perspective, and a domestic importer or exporter would account for such transactions as follows:

(1) At the **transaction date,** measure and record in dollars each asset, liability, expense, or gain arising from the transaction using the exchange rate in effect at that date.
(2) At each **intervening balance sheet date,** adjust the recorded balances of any foreign currency receivable or payable to reflect the current exchange rate.
(3) Report in the income statement a **foreign currency transaction gain or loss** resulting from (a) adjustments made at any intervening balance sheet dates, and (b) any adjustments from settling the transaction at an amount different from that recorded at the latest intervening balance sheet date (or the transaction date when there are no intervening balance sheet dates).[1]

In summary, the cost or the revenue arising from a transaction should be determined only once—when the transaction is initially recorded. The fact that credit terms are granted should not result in a later adjustment to the asset or service acquired, or to the revenue initially recorded, if the exchange rate changes between the transaction date and the settlement date. Any additional or lesser amount than that initially recorded represents a gain or loss that could have been avoided had the transaction been fully paid for when it occurred. Thus, any additional or lesser amount payable involves a decision to grant or exercise credit, which should be charged or credited to income in the period in which the exchange rate changes.

Illustration:
Import and export transactions

Assume a domestic company has the following import and export transactions with suppliers and customers in Britain:

(1) On December 11, 19X1, inventory is acquired from Vendor A for 100,000 pounds. Payment is due in pounds on January 10, 19X2.
(2) Inventory is sold to Customer X for 200,000 pounds on December 21, 19X1. Payment is due in pounds on January 20, 19X2.

Illustration 14-1 shows these transactions as initially recorded and as adjusted at the intervening balance sheet date (December 31, 19X1). Payments are made as required. The direct exchange rates (spot rates) for the applicable dates in December 19X1 and January 19X2 (when the pound was strengthening) are as follows:

---

[1] *FASB Statement No. 52,* paragraphs 15 and 16.

December 11, 19X1	$1.50
December 21, 19X1	1.52
December 31, 19X1	1.55
January 10, 19X2	1.57
January 20, 19X2	1.60

In reviewing Illustration 14-1, the following points should be understood:

(1) When its payments are due in pounds, the domestic company has a foreign currency transaction, not a foreign transaction.
(2) Adjustments for the foreign currency transactions were necessary at December 31, 19X1 because the exchange rates had changed since the dates the transactions were initially recorded. Such adjustments would have been avoided if full payment had been made when the transactions were initially recorded.

Illustration 14-1
Recording foreign currency transactions

Entries Related to Vendor A
December 11, 19X1:

Inventory (or Purchases)	150,000	
Foreign currency payable		150,000
To record purchase of inventory.		
(100,000 pounds × $1.50 = $150,000)		

December 31, 19X1:

Foreign currency transaction loss	5,000	
Foreign currency payable		5,000
To adjust foreign currency payable to the		
current spot rate.		
($1.55 − $1.50 = $0.05)		
($0.05 × 100,000 pounds = $5,000)		

January 10, 19X2:

Foreign currency transaction loss	2,000	
Foreign currency payable		2,000
To adjust foreign currency payable to the		
current spot rate.		
($1.57 − $1.55 = $0.02)		
($0.02 × 100,000 pounds = $2,000)		
Foreign currency	157,000	
Cash		157,000
To record purchase of foreign currency.		
Foreign currency payable	157,000	
Foreign currency		157,000
To record payment to vendor.		

In an alternative (shortcut) approach at January 10, 19X2, the foreign currency payable is not adjusted, but the following entry is made (instead of the first and third entries shown above for January 10, 19X2):

Foreign currency payable	155,000	
Foreign currency transaction loss	2,000	
Foreign currency		157,000

Illustration 14-1 (continued)

Entries Related to Customer X:
December 21, 19X1:

Foreign currency receivable	304,000	
Sales		304,000

To record sale.
(200,000 pounds × $1.52 = $304,000)

December 31, 19X1:

Foreign currency receivable	6,000	
Foreign currency transaction gain		6,000

To adjust foreign currency receivable to
the current spot rate.
($1.55 − $1.52 = $0.03)
($0.03 × 200,000 pounds = $6,000)

January 20, 19X2:

Foreign currency receivable	10,000	
Foreign currency transaction gain		10,000

To adjust foreign currency receivable to
the current spot rate.
($1.60 − $1.55 = $0.05)
($0.05 × 200,000 pounds = $10,000)

Foreign currency	320,000	
Foreign currency receivable		320,000

To record collection from customer.
(200,000 pounds × $1.60 = $320,000)

Cash	320,000	
Foreign currency		320,000

To convert foreign currency into U.S. dollars.

In the alternative (shortcut) approach at January 20, 19X2, the foreign currency receivable is not adjusted, but the following entry is made (instead of the first two entries shown above for January 20, 19X2):

Foreign currency	320,000	
Foreign currency receivable		310,000
Foreign currency transaction gain		10,000

(3) The 19X1 net foreign currency transaction gain is $1,000 ($6,000 gain on receivable − $5,000 loss on payable). The net foreign currency transaction gain is credited to income in 19X1.

(4) Foreign currency transaction gains are almost always taxable; thus, income taxes must be provided on the net foreign currency transaction gain. (Likewise, net foreign currency transaction losses are almost always tax deductible.)

(5) When one of the parties to a foreign transaction incurs a foreign currency transaction gain or loss, the other party does not incur an opposite, offsetting foreign currency transaction gain or loss. Foreign currency transaction gains and losses, therefore, are one-sided.

TRANSLATION OF FOREIGN CURRENCY TRANSACTIONS—SPECIAL AREAS

In addition to the basic importing and exporting transactions settled in a foreign currency, companies often enter into foreign currency transactions with foreign currency dealers to (a) hedge an existing foreign currency transaction (exposure), and (b) speculate. By hedging, a company can avoid a loss that may arise from an existing foreign currency transaction; the idea is to have a counterbalancing gain on the hedging transaction if a loss occurs on the existing foreign currency transaction. Three types of hedging transactions exist.

(1) A hedge of a **recorded but unsettled** foreign currency transaction (such as from importing or exporting inventory).
(2) A hedge of an **identifiable foreign currency commitment** (such as an order for inventory or equipment from a foreign company); in other words, a transaction that is **not yet recordable.**
(3) A hedge of a **net investment** in a foreign operation or a hedge of a **net monetary position.**

The most common hedging or speculating transactions involve a forward exchange contract. (Other less frequently used methods are discussed along with forward exchange contracts.)

Forward exchange contracts

A **forward exchange contract** is an agreement to buy or sell a foreign currency at a specified future date (usually within 12 months) at a specified exchange rate, commonly called the **forward rate.** Invariably, the forward rate is slightly above or slightly below the spot rate. The difference is primarily attributable to the difference in interest rates obtainable on the two currencies in the international money market for the duration of the contract.

When the interest rate obtainable on the dollar is higher than the interest rate obtainable on the foreign currency, the forward exchange rate is higher than the spot rate, and the foreign currency is said to be selling at a **premium** on the forward market. On the other hand, when the interest rate obtainable on the dollar is lower than the interest rate obtainable on the foreign currency, the forward exchange rate is lower than the spot rate, and the foreign currency is said to be selling at a **discount** on the forward market. The premium or discount rate multiplied by the units of foreign currency to be received or delivered under the contract equals the total amount of premium or discount on the forward exchange contract. This interest parity system, in effect, prevents the transfer of money between international money markets merely to obtain a higher interest rate relatively risk-free through the use of a forward exchange contract.

When a currency is strengthening or weakening to a limited extent, the difference between the spot rate and the forward rate may also be attributable somewhat to expectations of what the spot rate will be at the specified future date. When a currency is strengthening or weakening to a greater extent and substantial economic or political uncertainties exist, the risks may be significant enough to cause the futures market to cease temporarily until stability is achieved.

Accounting for forward exchange contracts is different for the three types of hedging transactions and for speculative transactions. We discuss each of these areas separately.

Hedge of a recorded but unsettled foreign currency transaction

A company that has a liability in a foreign currency is said to be in an **exposed liability position.** A company that has a receivable in a foreign currency is said to be in an **exposed asset position.** Because accounting for these situations is symmetrical, we illustrate only the first situation.

Exposed liability position. In Illustration 14-1 (pages 503–4), the domestic company agreed to pay Vendor A 100,000 pounds for inventory on January 10, 19X2; the domestic company is in an exposed liability position. To avoid the risk of an exchange rate increase during the period from the transaction date (December 11, 19X1) to the settlement date (January 10, 19X2), the domestic company could enter into a 30-day forward exchange contract on December 11, 19X1, whereby it agreed to **purchase 100,000 pounds on January 10, 19X2 at the currently existing forward exchange rate.** Thus, the domestic company can determine now, rather than on January 10, 19X2, how many dollars are needed to obtain 100,000 pounds.

Entering into a forward exchange contract is an immediately recordable transaction. The domestic company has (1) a fixed dollar liability to the foreign currency dealer that is determined by multiplying the forward rate by the number of units of foreign currency to be acquired; and (2) a foreign currency receivable that is initially valued at the spot rate multiplied by the number of units of foreign currency to be acquired. At subsequent balance sheet dates before the forward contract expiration date, the foreign currency receivable is adjusted to reflect **the spot rate on that date.**[2] The difference, if any, between the amounts initially recorded at (1) and (2) represent either a premium or discount that must be amortized over the life of the contract.[3]

At the end of the contract, the fixed liability to the foreign currency dealer is extinguished by the payment of cash (dollars) to the dealer, and the foreign currency receivable is extinguished by receipt of the foreign currency from the foreign currency dealer. The latter part of the exchange requires a debit to a Foreign Currency account. When the foreign currency is delivered to Vendor A, the Foreign Currency account is credited and the Foreign Currency Payable account is debited.

By valuing the foreign currency receivable at the current spot rate (both initially and subsequently), the foreign currency receivable always equals the amount payable to Vendor A, because the amount payable to Vendor

[2] *FASB Statement No. 52*, paragraph 18.
[3] *FASB Statement No. 52*, paragraph 18.

A is always adjusted to the current spot rate, as shown in Illustration 14-1. Accordingly, any exchange loss on the payable to Vendor A exactly offsets an exchange gain on the foreign currency receivable—such is the purpose of the forward exchange contract. The shifting of risk to the foreign currency dealer also involves a commission charge that would be amortized over the life of the contract.

Illustration:
Hedge of a recorded but unsettled
foreign currency transaction

Illustration 14-2 shows the entries that would be made under a forward exchange contract entered into to protect the exposed liability position of the 100,000 pound purchase transaction with Vendor A. (For simplicity, we ignore commission charges.) The direct exchange rates for the applicable dates in December 19X1 and January 19X2 (when the pound was strengthening were the following:

	Spot Rate	Forward Rate
December 11, 19X1 (the date the forward exchange contract was entered into)	$1.50	$1.54
December 31, 19X1 (the intervening balance sheet date)	1.55	n/a
January 10, 19X2 (the expiration date of the forward exchange contract)	1.57	n/a

In reviewing Illustration 14-2, the following points should be understood:

(1) During the 30-day period of the forward exchange contract, the pound strengthened from $1.50 to $1.57. Without the forward exchange contract, the $7,000 additional amount payable to Vendor A would not have been offset by the $7,000 foreign currency transaction gain.
(2) Inasmuch as the foreign currency transaction loss on the amount payable to Vendor A is offset by the foreign currency transaction gain on the forward exchange contract, the net cost of the forward exchange contract is the $4,000 premium.
(3) The forward exchange contract is an independent transaction in relation to the transaction with Vendor A. Accounting for one is independent of accounting for the other.

Exposed asset position. An exposed asset position most often results from an exporting transaction, with payment to be received in the foreign currency. In these situations, the domestic exporter agrees to **sell a specified number of foreign currency units at a specified future date.** Because the domestic company is selling foreign currency under the forward exchange contract, it has a fixed receivable amount from the foreign currency dealer and a foreign currency payable (which is valued at the spot rate) to the foreign currency dealer. Any premium or discount is amortized to income over the life of the contract, along with the commission.

Illustration 14-2
Hedge of a recorded but unsettled transaction

December 11, 19X1:		
Foreign currency receivable ($1.50 × 100,000 pounds)	150,000	
Deferred premium on forward exchange contract	4,000	
Liability to foreign currency dealer		
($1.54 × 100,000 pounds)		154,000
To record initially the forward exchange contract.		
December 31, 19X1:		
Foreign currency receivable	5,000	
Foreign currency transaction gain		5,000[a]
To adjust the foreign currency receivable to the		
current spot rate.		
($1.55 − $1.50 = $0.05)		
($0.05 × 100,000 pounds = $5,000)		
Premium amortization expense	2,667	
Deferred premium on forward exchange contract		2,667
To amortize the premium on the contract.		
[(20/30) × $4,000 = $2,667]		
January 10, 19X2:		
Foreign currency receivable	2,000	
Foreign currency transaction gain		2,000[b]
To adjust the foreign currency receivable to the		
current spot rate.		
($1.57 − $1.55 = $0.02)		
($0.02 × 100,000 pounds = $2,000)		
Premium amortization expense	1,333	
Deferred premium on forward exchange contract		1,333
To amortize the premium on the contract.		
(10/30 × $4,000 = $1,333)		
Liability to foreign currency dealer	154,000	
Cash.		154,000
Foreign currency	157,000	
Foreign currency receivable		157,000
To pay the foreign currency dealer in exchange for		
the receipt of 100,000 pounds.		

[a] This gain offsets the $5,000 foreign currency transaction loss on the importing transaction; see the journal entry on page 503.
[b] This gain offsets the $2,000 foreign currency transaction loss on the importing transaction; see the journal entry on page 503.
Note: In addition to the preceding entries (which relate only to the forward exchange contract), the following entry is necessary to discharge the liability to Vendor A:

Foreign currency payable	157,000	
Foreign currency.		157,000

Hedge of an identifiable foreign currency commitment

Commitment to purchase. A domestic company often enters into an agreement with a foreign company, whereby the domestic company purchases goods to be delivered and paid for in the future in the foreign currency. In such situations, the future transaction date may be known or reasonably determinable, but the exchange rate cannot be known. Accordingly, the domestic company may desire to protect itself from the risks of exchange rate fluctuations by entering into a forward exchange contract under which the domestic importer agrees to **purchase a specified number of foreign currency units at a specified future date.** In these situations, any gain or loss that arises from the forward exchange contract must be deferred until the transaction is recorded. The gain or loss is then subtracted from or added to the cost of the goods acquired. In addition, the premium or discount on the forward exchange contract may be either amortized over the life of the contract (as is required in exposed asset or exposed liability situations) or treated the same as a gain or loss arising from the forward exchange contract—that is, it may be deferred and added to or subtracted from, respectively, the cost of the goods acquired.[4]

The rationale for deferring the foreign currency transaction gain or loss is that of the one-transaction perspective discussed on page 501. In this situation, the one-transaction perspective makes sense because we are dealing with a commitment instead of a recorded purchase or sales transaction in which the cost or revenue has already been determined. This rationale also allows the premium or discount to be treated the same as a foreign currency transaction gain or loss. (While not specifically addressed in *FASB Statement No. 52* because of their immateriality, commission costs could also be treated in this manner under the one-transaction perspective.)

Illustration:
Hedge of an identifiable foreign currency commitment (purchase commitment)

Assume a domestic company with a calendar year-end entered into the following transactions on October 10, 19X1:

(1) Ordered equipment built to its specifications from a French manufacturer. The purchase price is 1,000,000 francs. Delivery is to be in 90 days (January 8, 19X2), and the payment is due then.
(2) Contracted with a foreign currency dealer to purchase 1,000,000 francs on January 8, 19X2 at the forward exchange rate of $0.098 plus a commission of $750.

Illustration 14-3 shows these transactions as initially recorded and as adjusted at the intervening balance sheet date (December 31, 19X1). Delivery and payments are made as required. The direct exchange rates for the applicable dates were the following:

	Exchange Rates	
	Spot	Forward
October 10, 19X1	$0.100	$0.098
December 31, 19X1	0.105	n/a
January 8, 19X2	0.104	n/a

In reviewing Illustration 14-3, note the following points.

[4] *FASB Statement No. 52*, paragraph 21.

Illustration 14-3
Hedge of an identifiable foreign currency commitment

October 10, 19X1:		
Foreign currency receivable (1,000,000 francs × $0.10)	100,000	
Deferred commission costs	750	
Liability to foreign currency dealer		
(1,000,000 francs × $0.098 + $750 commission)		98,750
Deferred discount on forward exchange contract		
(1,000,000 francs × $0.002)		2,000
To record initially the forward exchange contract.		
December 31, 19X1:		
Foreign currency receivable	5,000	
Deferred foreign currency transaction gain		5,000
To adjust the foreign currency receivable to the		
current spot rate.		
($0.105 − $0.100 = $0.005)		
($0.005 × 1,000,000 francs = $5,000)		

Note: The deferred discount and deferred commission costs need not be amortized, as it is assumed that they will be treated as adjustments to the purchase price of the equipment at the time of delivery.

January 8, 19X2:		
Deferred foreign currency transaction gain	1,000	
Foreign currency receivable		1,000
To adjust the foreign currency receivable to the		
current spot rate.		
($0.105 − $0.104 = $0.001)		
($0.001 × 1,000,000 francs = $1,000)		
Liability to foreign currency dealer	98,750	
Cash		98,750
Foreign currency	104,000	
Foreign currency receivable		104,000
To pay the foreign currency dealer in exchange for		
the receipt of 1,000,000 francs.		

Note: In addition to the preceding entries (which relate only to the forward exchange contract), the following entry would be made to record the purchase of the equipment on January 8, 19X2 (when delivery and payment were made):

Deferred discount on forward exchange contract	2,000	
Deferred foreign currency transaction gain	4,000	
Equipment	98,750	
Deferred commission costs		750
Foreign currency		104,000

(1) The capitalized cost of the equipment ($98,750) is determined as follows:

Dollar equivalent of foreign currency		
paid to supplier (1,000,000 francs × $0.104)		$104,000
Less—Deferred transaction gain on forward		
exchange contract		(4,000)
Deferred discount on forward exchange		
contract		(2,000)
Plus—Deferred commission costs		750
		$ 98,750

(2) If the forward exchange contract had not been entered into, the capitalized cost would have been $104,000.
(3) The $4,000 foreign currency transaction gain can be treated as an adjustment to the $104,000 purchase price because the company's expected purchase price was $100,000 (based on the exchange rate existing when the equipment was ordered). The forward exchange contract merely locks in this price.
(4) The discount and commission cost can be treated as adjustments to the locked-in purchase price of $100,000 because these items are necessary and incidental costs to protect or lock in the $100,000 purchase price.

Commitment to sell. Parallel accounting procedures are used when (1) the domestic company has entered into an agreement to sell goods to a foreign company in the future, with payment to be received in the foreign currency, and (2) the domestic company wishes to protect itself from the risk of exchange rate fluctuations by entering into a forward exchange contract to **sell a specified number of foreign currency units at a specified future date.**

Qualifying conditions. The following two conditions must be met for a forward exchange contract (or other foreign currency transaction) to qualify as a hedge of an identifiable foreign currency commitment:

    a. The foreign currency transaction is designated as, and is effective as, a hedge of a foreign currency commitment.
    b. The foreign currency commitment is firm.[5]

The designation part of the first condition merely means that the company must **identify the intent of the hedge with the foreign currency commitment.** Whether or not a hedge transaction is **effective** is an **after-the-fact determination.** Obviously, the hedge is effective if (1) the forward exchange contract is in the same currency as the transaction being hedged, and (2) the gain or loss on the hedging transaction is in the **opposite direction** to the loss or gain on the transaction being hedged.

The second condition is not defined in *FASB Statement No. 52.* However, it implies that the foreign currency commitment is either noncancelable or that the probability of cancellation is remote because of a severe monetary penalty.

Transactions other than forward exchange contracts. The preceding two conditions are sufficiently broad that foreign currency transactions other than forward exchange contracts may qualify as hedges of foreign currency commitments. The following examples are other types of transactions that could qualify as hedges of foreign currency commitments.

(1) A U.S. company committed to constructing a building in France and receiving payment in francs could borrow francs to finance the construction and designate the borrowing as a hedge of the commitment.

---

[5] *FASB Statement No. 52,* paragraph 21.

(2) A U.S. company committed to purchasing inventory or equipment from a Japanese company could convert dollars into yen, hold or invest the yen, and designate them as a hedge of the commitment.

(3) A U.S. company, or its Spanish subsidiary, could designate a foreign currency receivable in Italian lira as a hedge against a foreign currency purchase commitment in Italian lira.

Other technical points. The hedging transaction need not be entered into at the same time as the foreign currency commitment; nor must it extend from the foreign currency commitment date to the anticipated transaction date. Other technical points include the following:

(1) If the hedging transaction extends **beyond the foreign currency commitment transaction date,** any gain or loss on the hedging transaction that occurs after that date cannot be deferred; it must be reported in the income statement as it arises.

(2) If the hedging is terminated **before the foreign currency transaction commitment date,** any deferred gain or loss on the hedging transaction up to that point is still deferred and treated as part of the cost of the asset acquired or as an adjustment to the sales price of the asset sold.

(3) If the hedging transaction amount **exceeds the foreign currency transaction commitment amount,** only the gain or loss on the hedging transaction up to the foreign currency transaction commitment amount may be deferred and included as an adjustment to the cost of the asset acquired or as an adjustment to the sales price of the asset sold.

(4) Losses on hedging transactions related to a foreign currency transaction commitment cannot be deferred (but must be reported currently in the income statement) if such deferral would lead to recognizing losses in a later period.[6]

Speculating in foreign currency

When a company enters into a forward exchange contract that does not relate to a foreign currency exposure, the forward exchange contract is intended to produce an investment gain. Any gains or losses on such contracts are recognized currently in the income statement as they arise (no special deferral provisions exist for this type of hedging). In calculating gains and losses, the foreign currency receivable or payable must be **carried in the balance sheet at the current forward exchange rate for the remaining life of the forward exchange contract** (rather than at the current exchange rate existing at each intervening balance sheet date).[7] The current forward exchange rate is presumably a better indicator of the ultimate amount that will be received or paid when the contract expires. Because the foreign currency receivable or payable is initially recorded at the fixed liability to or receivable from the foreign currency dealer, no accounting recognition is given to premiums and discounts.

---

[6] *FASB Statement No. 52,* paragraph 21.
[7] *FASB Statement No. 52,* paragraph 19.

Illustration:
Speculating in foreign currency

Assume a domestic company with a calendar year-end concludes that the Swiss franc will strengthen within 90 days. Accordingly, it contracts with a foreign currency dealer on November 11, 19X1 to purchase 100,000 Swiss francs at the 90-day forward rate of $0.49. (For simplicity, we ignore the commission charge, which would be amortized over the life of the contract.) Illustration 14-4 shows the entries that would be made for this contract using the following assumed direct exchange rates:

	Spot Rate	Forward Rate for February 9, 19X2
November 11, 19X1 (the date the forward exchange contract was entered into)	n/a	$0.049
December 31, 19X1 (the intervening balance sheet date)	n/a	0.052
February 9, 19X2 (the expiration date of the forward exchange contract)	$0.57	n/a

Illustration 14-4
Speculating in foreign currency

November 11, 19X1:		
Foreign currency receivable	49,000	
Liability to foreign currency dealer		49,000
To record initially the forward exchange contract. (100,000 francs × $0.49 = $49,000)		
December 31, 19X1:		
Foreign currency receivable	3,000	
Foreign currency transaction gain		3,000
To adjust the foreign currency receivable to the forward rate available at the expiration of the contract. ($0.52 − $0.49 = $0.03) (100,000 francs × $0.03 = $3,000)		
February 9, 19X2:		
Foreign currency receivable	5,000	
Foreign currency transaction gain		5,000
To adjust the foreign currency receivable to the spot rate at the expiration of the contract. ($0.57 − $0.52 = $0.05) (100,000 francs × $0.05 = $5,000)		
Liability to foreign currency dealer	49,000	
Cash		49,000
Foreign currency	57,000	
Foreign currency receivable		57,000
To pay the foreign currency dealer in exchange for the 100,000 francs.		

Note: At this point, the company could convert the foreign currency of 100,000 francs into $57,000.

In reviewing Illustration 14-4, note the following:

(1) The ultimate gain on the contract depends on the spot rate existing when the contract expires.
(2) If the spot rate were used to value the foreign currency receivable at December 31, 19X1 (instead of the forward rate available for February 9, 19X2) the $8,000 total gain would have been reported differently than as shown in the illustration.

Hedging a net investment

Companies with foreign operations normally have a person or department responsible for monitoring foreign currency changes and handling foreign currency operations. Because of the potentially substantial economic losses from adverse exchange rate changes, the person in charge is often a vice-president.

Forward exchange contracts and other foreign transactions (such as borrowings in a foreign currency) are also commonly used to hedge a net investment in a foreign operation. For example, in 1982 (when the Mexican peso declined sharply in value), some domestic companies with operations in Mexico correctly concluded that a decline was imminent. Accordingly, the parent company or the Mexican subsidiary borrowed pesos to hedge some or all of the company's net asset position. (The borrowings were immediately converted into dollars.) When the direct exchange rate then declined, the adverse effect on the net asset position was partially or fully offset by the fewer number of dollars required to buy pesos to repay the loan. Accounting for the gain or loss on these transactions depends on whether the foreign currency or the dollar is the foreign operation's functional currency.

Foreign currency is the functional currency. When the foreign currency is the functional currency, the gain or loss on the hedging transaction (net of the related tax effect) must be **accumulated in the separate component of equity.** This requirement allows a foreign currency translation adjustment to be offset partially or fully by the effect of a rate change on the hedging transaction. For the gain or loss to be deferred in this manner, however, **the transaction must be designated as a hedge of the net investment** and **it must be effective** (go in the opposite direction to the translation adjustment).[8]

Illustration:
Hedging a net investment position—
Foreign currency is the functional currency

Assume a domestic company with a calendar year-end and a $500,000 investment in a wholly owned Japanese subsidiary expects the Japanese yen to weaken considerably within six months. Accordingly, it contracts with a foreign currency dealer on July 10, 19X1 to sell 100,000,000 yen in 180 days at the forward rate of $0.0049. Illustration 14-5 shows the accounting treatment for this contract. (For simplicity, we ignore commission costs and

---

[8] *FASB Statement No. 52*, paragraph 20.

Illustration 14-5
Hedging a net investment position

July 10, 19X1:		
Receivable from foreign currency dealer		
(100,000,000 yen × $0.0049)	490,000	
Deferred premium on forward exchange contract	10,000	
Foreign currency payable (100,000,000 yen × $0.005)		500,000
To record initially the forward exchange contract.		
December 31, 19X1:		
Foreign currency payable	70,000	
Foreign currency transaction gain		70,000
To adjust the foreign currency payable to the current		
spot rate.		
($0.0050 − $0.0043 = $0.0007)		
(100,000,000 yen × $0.0007 = $70,000)		
Premium amortization expense	9,667	
Deferred premium on forward exchange contract		9,667
To amortize the premium on the contract.		
(174/180 × $10,000 = $9,667)		
January 6, 19X2:		
Foreign currency payable	10,000	
Foreign currency transaction gain		10,000
To adjust the foreign currency payable to the		
current spot rate.		
($0.0043 − $0.0042 = $0.0001)		
(100,000,000 yen × $0.0001 = $10,000)		
Premium amortization expense	333	
Deferred premium on forward exchange contract		333
To amortize the premium on the contract.		
(6/180 × $10,000 = $333)		
Foreign currency	420,000	
Cash		420,000
To record purchase of 100,000,000 yen.		
(100,000,000 × $0.0042 = $420,000)		
Foreign currency payable	420,000	
Foreign currency		420,000
Cash	490,000	
Receivable from foreign currency dealer		490,000
To collect the amount due from the foreign currency		
dealer in exchange for the 100,000,000 yen.		

assume that the only intervening balance sheet date is December 31, 19X1.)
The following direct exchange rates are assumed:

	Spot Rate	Forward Rate for January 6, 19X2
July 10, 19X1 (the date the forward		
exchange contract was entered into)	$0.0050	$0.0049
December 31, 19X1 (the intervening		
balance sheet date)	0.0043	n/a
January 6, 19X2 (the expiration of the		
forward exchange contract)	0.0042	n/a

In reviewing Illustration 14-5, the following points should be understood:

(1) The following amount may be deferred and accumulated in the separate component of equity at December 31, 19X1:

Foreign currency transaction gain $70,000
Less—Premium amortization expense . . . .   (9,667)
    Net deferrable amount $60,333

(2) Assuming a $68,000 unfavorable translation adjustment for 19X1 (determined by using the translation procedures discussed in Chapter 13), the net charge to the separate component of equity for 19X1 (ignoring income tax effects) would be $7,667 ($68,000 − $60,333). Obviously, the hedge was effective.

The dollar is the functional currency.   When the dollar is the functional currency, the gain or loss on the hedging transaction is **reported in the income statement.**[9] Recall that when the dollar is the functional currency, the remeasurement process is required (instead of the "translation" process), and any gains or losses from remeasurement are reported currently in the income statement. Hedging a net asset position when the dollar is the functional currency may or may not cause an offsetting effect, which occurs when the foreign currency is the functional currency. The gain or loss resulting from the remeasurement process is **not based on the net asset position but on the net monetary position.** Being in a net monetary asset position causes an offsetting effect in the income statement. However, being in a net monetary liability position does not cause an offsetting effect in the income statement. Instead, two gains or two losses are reported—such as a gain on the hedging transaction and a gain resulting from the remeasurement process (or a loss on each). Some companies with foreign operations that use the dollar as its functional currency hedge the net asset position, wisely realizing that the gain or loss from remeasurement (in net monetary liability situations) is merely a paper gain or loss that will reverse itself in the future as the nonmonetary assets are financially transformed into monetary assets. (The amount of the gain or loss on the hedging transaction could be more, less, or equal to the gain or loss from remeasurement, depending on the amount of the net investment hedged and the amount of the net monetary position.)

Hedging a net monetary position

When the dollar is the foreign unit's functional currency, a company may decide to hedge the net monetary position instead of the net asset position to ensure an offsetting effect in the income statement. An interesting dilemma occurs when the foreign operation is in a net monetary liability position and the foreign currency is expected to strengthen or the dollar is expected to

---

[9] *FASB Statement No. 52,* paragraphs 15 and 17.

weaken. To prevent the reporting of a transaction loss from remeasurement if the direct exchange rate increases, the company may decide to enter into a forward exchange contract (or other type of hedging transaction) to purchase foreign currency to the extent of the net monetary liability position. If the direct exchange rate increases as expected, the transaction loss from remeasurement offsets the gain on the forward exchange contract. However, if the direct exchange rate decreases, a loss on the forward exchange contract and a transaction gain from the remeasurement process occur. As explained previously, the transaction gain from remeasurement (in net monetary liability position situations) may be viewed as a paper gain that will reverse itself in later periods. The loss on the forward exchange contract, however, is an actual loss that will not reverse in later periods.

One of the criticisms leveled at the temporal method of translation required under *FASB Statement No. 8* was that companies focused their attention on hedging net monetary positions to minimize the impact of currency exchange rate changes on consolidated income. (From an economic viewpoint, the net assets should be the focus of the hedging.) Because the remeasurement process procedures are nearly identical to the temporal method, this problem continues to exist when the dollar is the functional currency.

Summary illustration

Illustration 14-6 summarizes the accounting treatment of the special foreign currency transactions discussed so far.

SUMMARY

A foreign currency transaction involves a commitment to receive or purchase foreign currency in settlement of the transaction. When the transaction involves credit, the party engaging in the foreign currency transaction assumes the risk that the currency exchange rate may change between the transaction date and the settlement date. The effect of exchange rate changes that occur between these two dates is called a foreign currency transaction gain or loss. Such gains or losses are accounted for separately from the purchase or sale of goods, as recorded on the transaction date. Transaction gains or losses are reported in the income statement in the period in which they occur.

A company usually enters into special foreign currency transactions to protect its exposure to exchange rate changes. (Illustration 14-6 on page 518 summarizes how to account for gains and losses on such transactions.)

Glossary of new terms

Discount or Premium on Forward Exchange Contract: The foreign currency amount of the contract multiplied by the difference between the contracted forward rate and the spot rate at the date of inception of the contract.[10]

---

[10] Taken directly from *FASB Statement No. 52,* Appendix E, pp. 75–78.

Illustration 14-6
**Summary of accounting for special
foreign currency transactions**

	Accounting Treatment Accorded Gains and Losses	
Type of Transaction	Recognize Currently in the Income Statement	Special Treatment
A. Hedge of a recorded but un-settled foreign currency transaction	X	
B. Hedge of an identifiable for-eign currency commitment		Defer and treat as an adjustment to cost of item acquired or sales price of item sold.
C. Speculation in foreign currency	X	
D. Hedge of a net investment:		
a. Foreign currency is func-tional currency		Accumulate in the special com-ponent of stockholders' equity.
b. Dollar is functional currency	X	
E. Hedge of a net monetary po-sition (occurs when the dollar is the functional currency)	X	

Other considerations pertaining to foreign currency transactions involving forward exchange contracts include the following:

(1) In determining the gain or loss on the contract, the foreign currency receivable or payable is carried at the current (spot) rate (except in speculation situations, for which the available forward rate is used).

(2) Premiums and discounts on forward exchange contracts are recognized currently in the income statement if the gain or loss on the contract is treated in that manner. If the gain or loss is given special treatment (as shown above), the premium or discount *may be given the same special treatment* or be recognized currently in the income statement. (Premiums and discounts are not recognized in speculation situations.)

Foreign Currency Transactions: Transactions whose terms are denominated in a currency other than the entity's functional currency.[10]

Settlement Date: The date at which a receivable is collected or a payable is paid.

Spot Rate: The exchange rate for immediate delivery of currencies exchanged.[10]

Transaction Date: The date at which a transaction (for example, a sale or purchase of merchandise or services) is recorded in accounting records in conformity with generally accepted accounting principles.[10]

Transaction Gain or Loss: Transaction gains or losses result from a change in exchange rates between the functional currency and the currency in which a foreign currency transaction is denominated. They represent an increase or decrease in (a) the functional currency cash flows realized upon settlement of foreign currency transactions and (b) the expected functional currency cash flows on unsettled foreign currency transactions.[10]

[10] Taken directly from *FASB Statement No. 52*, Appendix E, pp. 75–78.

Appendix:
INTERCOMPANY TRANSACTIONS WITH FOREIGN UNITS

This appendix discusses the specific reporting requirements pertaining to intercompany transactions between a parent company and a foreign subsidiary.

Adjusting intercompany receivables and payables

When intercompany receivables and payables exist, the entity that makes or receives payment in the foreign currency (that is, in other than its own currency) must adjust its intercompany receivable or payable to reflect the new exchange rate. In Illustration 13-5 (page 478), which dealt with the remeasurement process, the foreign subsidiary had an intercompany payable to the parent company. The payable was denominated in marks; thus, the parent company had the foreign currency transaction and was the entity that made the adjustment to reflect the current rate. Let us assume that the payable of 50,000 marks arose when the direct exchange rate was $0.45 (the parent's receivable was therefore $22,500). The direct exchange rate at December 31, 19X1 was $0.40, making the receivable worth only $20,000 (50,000 marks × $0.40). Accordingly, the parent would make the following adjustment:

Foreign currency transaction loss	2,500	
Intercompany receivable		2,500
To adjust intercompany receivable to		
reflect the new exchange rate of $0.40.		
($22,500 − $20,000 = $2,500)		

If the intercompany payable had been repayable in dollars instead of marks, the foreign subsidiary would have made the adjustment at December 31, 19X1 ($22,500/$0.40 = 56,250 marks):

Foreign currency transaction loss	6,250 (marks)	
Intercompany payable		6,250 (marks)
To adjust the intercompany payable		
to reflect the new exchange rate of $0.40.		
(56,250 marks − 50,000 marks = 6,250 marks)		

When expressing the foreign subsidiary's financial statements in dollars, the parent company must use the direct exchange rate to which the intercompany payable was adjusted ($0.40) in dealing with the foreign currency transaction loss of 6,250 marks. This calculation gives $2,500 (6,250 marks × $0.40), which equals the amount of loss the parent company would have recorded if the payable had been repayable in marks instead of dollars. (Alternatively, we could obtain this answer by multiplying the 50,000 marks by the $0.05 change in the direct exchange rate.)

Of course, if the appropriate adjusting entries are not made at the balance sheet date, the intercompany receivable and payable accounts would not agree and would not eliminate in consolidation.

The wash effect.   The preceding entries indicate that a $2,500 transaction loss would be reported as a result of adjustments to the intercompany receivable or payable accounts. **However, the parent company's equity is never affected by adjustments to the intercompany accounts.** This fact holds true whether the amounts are denominated in the dollar or in the foreign operation's local currency. The zero net answer results from the translation process or the remeasurement process, as the case may be. When the dollar is the foreign operation's functional currency, a $2,500 transaction gain from remeasurement arises on the 50,000 mark intercompany payable (50,000 marks × $0.05 decrease in direct exchange rate). This amount offsets the $2,500 transaction loss in the income statement. When the foreign currency is the functional currency, a $2,500 translation adjustment arises on the 50,000 mark intercompany payable. This $2,500 translation adjustment, however, is reported in the translation adjustment component of stockholders' equity. Thus, the income statement contains no offsetting entry, but stockholders' equity does.

Long-term intercompany receivables and payables.   A long-term intercompany receivable on the parent company's books is, in substance, an addition to its investment. Likewise, a long-term intercompany payable on the parent company's books is, in substance, a reduction of its investment. When such receivables and payables exist **and settlement is not planned or anticipated in the foreseeable future,** *FASB Statement No. 52* requires that transaction gains and losses resulting from adjusting these accounts (as a result of exchange rate changes) should be treated as translation adjustments. They are **accumulated in the separate component of stockholders' equity** rather than reported currently in the income statement.[11] This provision ensures that the entire effect of a rate change on the true net investment in a foreign unit is shown as part of the separate component of stockholders' equity. This requirement applies **only when the "translation" process is involved, that is, when the foreign currency is the functional currency.**

Intercompany profits

An intercompany profit from intercompany transactions must, of course, be eliminated. Under *FASB Statement No. 52,* no special problems are involved when the foreign unit has the dollar as its functional currency, because all foreign unit account balances are remeasured into the equivalent dollar amounts. However, when the foreign unit has a foreign currency as its functional currency, the translated cost of any remaining intercompany-acquired inventory or fixed assets does not equal the parent's selling price if the exchange rate has changed since the transfer date. The difference between the translated cost at the transfer date and translated cost at the balance sheet date is treated as part of the effect of the change in the exchange rate—that is, as part of the translation adjustment accumulated in the special component of stockholders' equity. *FASB Statement No. 52* requires that **any intercompany profit be eliminated using the exchange**

---

[11] *FASB Statement No. 52,* paragraph 20.

rate existing at the time of the transfer. The gross profit determined at the time of the transfer is used for subsequent eliminations, regardless of any subsequent exchange rate changes.[12]

Intercompany dividends

The parent company uses **the exchange rate existing when dividends are declared** to record a dividend receivable. Any changes in the exchange rate between the declaration date and the remittance date result in a foreign currency transaction gain or loss recorded by one of the entities. Such gains and losses can be avoided if dividends are remitted at their declaration.

Summary

Gains or losses from adjusting intercompany receivable and payable balances for exchange rate changes are reported currently in the income statement unless (1) the adjustment pertains to long-term receivables and payables, and (2) the foreign unit's functional currency is *not* the dollar. When intercompany asset transfers occur, the gross profit eliminated is based on the gross profit determined at the time of the transfer. Subsequent changes in the exchange rate have no bearing in this respect.

Review questions

1. What does denominated mean?
2. What is the difference between a foreign transaction and a foreign currency transaction?
3. Summarize the two-transaction perspective.
4. Summarize the one-transaction perspective.
5. Why would a company enter into a forward exchange contract?
6. How does a company treat gains and losses on forward exchange contracts related to hedges of identifiable foreign currency commitments?
7. What two conditions must be met to qualify a forward exchange contract as a hedge of an identifiable foreign currency commitment?
8. Distinguish between hedging a net investment and hedging a net monetary position.
9. How are gains and losses on hedging a net investment treated?

Exercises

Exercise 14–1
Basic understanding of foreign currency exposure

The Flipp Company has many importing and exporting transactions with companies located in a foreign country that has the koine as its currency. Credit terms are granted and used.

---

[12] *FASB Statement No. 52*, paragraph 25.

Required:

(1) Flipp Company should be concerned about whether the direct exchange rate
    a. goes up.
    b. goes down.
(2) Indicate in the following table what the foreign currency exposure concern
    should be:

Trans-action	Billing Currency	Whether the Dollar Will		Whether the Koine Will	
		Strengthen	Weaken	Strengthen	Weaken
Importing	Dollar	_____	_____	_____	_____
Importing	Koine	_____	_____	_____	_____
Exporting	Dollar	_____	_____	_____	_____
Exporting	Koine	_____	_____	_____	_____

Exercise 14–2
Basic understanding of forward exchange contracts

The Boggle Company has foreign operations and importing and exporting transactions
that require settlement in a foreign currency. The company often enters into forward
exchange contracts to hedge its foreign currency exposure and occasionally to
speculate. Boggle must determine whether it should contract to buy or sell a foreign
currency in each of the following situations:

Area of Foreign Currency Exposure	Future Expectation		Buy	Sell
	Direct Rate or Currency	Direction		
(1) Importing	Direct Rate	Up	____	____
	Direct Rate	Down	____	____
	U.S. Dollar	Strengthen	____	____
	U.S. Dollar	Weaken	____	____
	Foreign	Strengthen	____	____
	Foreign	Weaken	____	____
(2) Exporting	Direct Rate	Up	____	____
	Direct Rate	Down	____	____
	U.S. Dollar	Strengthen	____	____
	U.S. Dollar	Weaken	____	____
	Foreign	Strengthen	____	____
	Foreign	Weaken	____	____
(3) Net investment in a foreign subsidiary	U.S. Dollar	Strengthen	____	____
	U.S. Dollar	Weaken	____	____
	Foreign	Strengthen	____	____
	Foreign	Weaken	____	____
(4) Net monetary asset position of a foreign subsidiary	U.S. Dollar	Strengthen	____	____
	U.S. Dollar	Weaken	____	____
	Foreign	Strengthen	____	____
	Foreign	Weaken	____	____

(5) Net monetary liability	U.S. Dollar	Strengthen	——	——
position of a	U.S. Dollar	Weaken	——	——
foreign subsidiary	Foreign	Strengthen	——	——
	Foreign	Weaken	——	——
(6) n/a—Speculation	Foreign	Strengthen	——	——
	Foreign	Weaken	——	——

Required:

Put an X in the appropriate buy or sell column in the table.

Exercises for appendix

Exercise 14–3
Adjusting intercompany accounts

The New Horizons Company formed a foreign subsidiary on December 30, 19X1. The parent company lent the subsidiary $90,000 at that time when the direct exchange rate between the dollar and the widgetta (the foreign country's currency) was $0.10. The subsidiary immediately converted the $90,000 into widgettas and used the entire amount to purchase land on December 30, 19X1. At December 31, 19X1, the year-end of the parent company and the subsidiary, the direct exchange rate was $0.09.

Required:
(1) Make the appropriate adjustments at December 31, 19X1, assuming the loan is denominated in widgettas.
(2) Make the appropriate adjustments at December 31, 19X1, assuming the loan is denominated in dollars.
(3) Express in dollars the effect of the adjustments made in requirement (2). (Show the calculations for the two ways of determining this amount.)

Exercise 14–4
Accounting for dividend from foreign subsidiary

For the year ended December 31, 19X5, MBI Corporation's foreign subsidiary had net income of 60,000,000 local currency units (LCU), which was appropriately translated into $2,900,000. On July 25, 19X5, when the exchange rate was 20 LCU to $1, the foreign subsidiary declared a dividend to MBI of 30,000,000 LCU. The dividend represented the foreign subsidiary's net income for the six months ended June 30, 19X5, during which time the weighted average of the exchange rate was 21 LCU to $1. The dividend was paid on August 3, 19X5, when the exchange rate was 19 LCU to $1. The exchange rate existing at December 31, 19X5 was 18.5 LCU to $1. MBI uses the equity method of accounting for the foreign subsidiary.

Required:
(1) Prepare the parent company's entry to record the dividend receivable.
(2) Prepare the entry related to the receipt of the dividend on August 3, 19X5.

Problems

Problem 14–1
Importing and exporting transactions:
No intervening balance sheet date

During July 19X5, the Bippy Company had the following transactions with foreign businesses:

Date	Nature of Transaction	Billing Currency	Exchange Rate (Direct)
Vendor A:			
July 1, 19X1	Imported merchandise costing 1,000,000 pesos from Acapulco wholesaler	Pesos	$0.0070
July 10, 19X1	Paid 50% of amount owed	Pesos	0.0071
July 31, 19X1	Paid remaining amount owed	Pesos	0.0066
Customer A:			
July 15, 19X1	Sold merchandise for 50,000 francs to French wholesaler	Francs	$0.130
July 20, 19X1	Received 50% payment	Francs	0.120
July 30, 19X1	Received entire payment	Francs	0.125

Required:
Prepare journal entries for the above transactions.

Problem 14–2
Importing and exporting transactions:
Intervening balance sheet date

During June and July of 19X1, the Bunky Company (which reports on a calendar year basis and issues quarterly financial statements) had the following transactions with foreign businesses:

Date	Nature of Transaction	Billing Currency	Exchange Rate (Direct)
Vendor A:			
June 15, 19X1	Imported merchandise costing 100,000 Canadian dollars from Canadian manufacturer........	Canadian Dollars	$0.80
July 15, 19X1	Paid entire amount owed.............	Dollars	0.77
Customer A:			
June 20, 19X1	Sold merchandise for 10,000 pounds to London retailer	Pounds	$1.55
June 30, 19X1	Received 50% payment	Pounds	1.52
July 10, 19X1	Received remaining amount owed.....	Pounds	1.54

The exchange rate on June 30, 19X1 for Canadian dollars was $0.79.

Required:
Prepare journal entries for the above transactions. (Be sure to prepare journal entries at June 30, 19X1 when necessary.)

Problem 14–3
Hedge of an exposed liability position:
Intervening balance sheet date

On October 17, 19X1, Bretton Company purchased merchandise costing 40,000,000 lira from the Rossi Company of Italy. The spot rate (direct) on that date was $0.00063. Payment is due in lira in 90 days.

Concurrently, Bretton Company entered into a foreign exchange contract, whereby it agreed to purchase 40,000,000 lira for delivery in 90 days at $0.00065 (the forward rate). On December 31, 19X1, the spot rate was $0.00068, and on January 15, 19X2 (the date the Rossi Company was paid in full), the spot rate was $0.00066. Bretton Company has a June 30 fiscal year-end and issues quarterly financial reports.

Required:
Prepare the journal entries to record the above transactions. (Be sure to prepare journal entries at December 31, 19X1 when necessary.)

Problem 14–4
Hedge of an exposed asset position:
Intervening balance sheet date

On April 1, 19X3, Smith Company, a calendar-year reporting company that issues quarterly financial reports, sold merchandise to a Canadian company for 100,000 Canadian dollars. The spot rate (direct) on April 1, 19X3 was $0.81. Payment is due in 120 days.

Concurrently, Smith Company entered into a forward exchange contract to sell 100,000 Canadian dollars at $0.80 (the forward rate). The spot rate on July 30, 19X3 was $0.82. Assume payment was made on July 30, 19X3. (The spot rate on June 30, 19X3 was $0.825.)

Required:
Prepare the entries related to the above transactions, including appropriate June 30, 19X3 adjustments.

Problem 14–5
Hedge of an identifiable foreign currency commitment:
Intervening balance sheet date

On October 1, 19X1, Summit Company, a calendar-year reporting company, entered into a noncancelable contract with a Swiss company, whereby the Swiss company would manufacture a custom-built aerial tram for 1,000,000 francs, with delivery to be in 180 days and payment to be in Swiss francs. On October 1, 19X1, the exchange rate (direct) was $0.47.

Concurrently, Summit Company entered into a forward exchange contract (at a commission cost of $1,000) to acquire 1,000,000 Swiss francs in 180 days at $0.48. At December 31, 19X1 (the only intervening balance sheet date for purposes of this problem), the current exchange rate was $0.463. Assume delivery and payment were made in 180 days and that Summit Company desires to maximize earnings in 19X1. Assume the spot rate on March 30, 19X2 was $0.45.

Required:

Prepare the entries related to the above transactions, including appropriate adjustments at the intervening month-end.

Problem 14-6
Hedging a net investment position

The functional currency for Haytko Company's foreign subsidiary is its local currency, the debita. For 19X1, the subsidiary's net income was 100,000 debitas, which translated into $35,000. (Earnings occurred evenly throughout the year and were remitted to the parent monthly.) An unfavorable translation adjustment of $75,000 resulted for 19X1.

On January 5, 19X1, in expectation that the debita would weaken throughout 19X1, management entered into a 360-day forward exchange contract with a foreign currency dealer to sell 600,000 debitas (which approximates its net investment in the subsidiary) on December 31, 19X1 at the forward rate of $0.41 plus a commission of $850. The following exchange rates are for 19X1:

		Exchange Rates	
	Spot	Forward (for 12/31/X1)
January 1, 19X1	$0.401	n/a
January 5, 19X1	0.400	$0.410
June 30, 19X1 (assumed to be the only intervening balance sheet date)	0.360	0.340
December 31, 19X1	0.300	n/a
Average rate for 19X1	0.350	n/a

Required:
(1) Prepare the journal entries pertaining to the forward exchange contract.
(2) Determine the amount to be charged or credited to the special component of stockholders' equity for 19X1.

Problem 14-7
Hedging net investments and net monetary positions

Laurabelle Company's foreign subsidiary had the following average account balances for 19X1 (expressed in its local currency, the smurf):

Monetary assets	400,000	Monetary liabilities	300,000
Nonmonetary assets	400,000	Stockholders' equity	500,000

Net income for 19X1 was 100,000 smurfs, earned evenly throughout the year and remitted to the parent monthly. During 19X1, the smurf weakened 25%, the direct (spot) rate going from $0.40 to $0.30. Various assumptions for different situations follow:

Situation	Functional Currency	Item Hedged
A	Smurf	Net investment
B	Smurf	Net monetary asset position
C	U.S. dollar	Net investment
D	U.S. dollar	Net monetary asset position
E	U.S. dollar	Net monetary liability position
		(For situation E, assume average monetary liabilities were 500,000 smurfs and average stockholders' equity was 300,000 smurfs.)

For situations A, B, C, and D, assume management expected the smurf to weaken during 19X1 and it hedged the item indicated using forward exchange contracts entered into on January 1, 19X1 and terminated December 31, 19X1. For situation E, assume management expected the smurf to strengthen during 19X1 and it hedged accordingly. (For simplicity, assume that the forward rate on January 1, 19X1 for a one-year forward exchange contract was $0.40.)

Required:
For each situation, determine the following and indicate how the amounts should be reported for 19X1:
(1) The hedging gain or loss.
(2) The translation adjustment or the gain or loss from the remeasurement process, as appropriate.

Problems for appendix

Problem 14–8
Determining the net effect of adjustments to intercompany account

A domestic company formed a foreign subsidiary on December 1, 19X1. On that date, the parent company lent the foreign subsidiary $180,000; the subsidiary converted the $180,000 into gismos (its local currency) and used all of the gismos to purchase land. The direct exchange rate was $0.40 at December 1, 19X1 and $0.45 at December 31, 19X1. For simplicity, assume the subsidiary was so thinly capitalized that we can ignore the Common Stock account.

Required:
(1) Make the appropriate December 31, 19X1 adjusting entry, assuming the loan is denominated in dollars.
(2) Translate the subsidiary's December 31, 19X1 financial statements into dollars, assuming the gismo is the foreign subsidiary's functional currency.

(3) Remeasure the subsidiary's December 31, 19X1 financial statements in dollars, assuming the dollar is the foreign subsidiary's functional currency.
(4) Considering the effect of the adjustment made for requirement (1), determine the net effect of the change in the exchange rate in the 19X1 consolidated statements assuming:
   a. the gismo is the functional currency.
   b. the dollar is the functional currency.

Problem 14–9
Determining the net effect of adjustments to intercompany account

Assume the information in Problem 14–8, except that the subsidiary used the money from the loan to open a checking account rather than buying land.

Required:
The requirements are the same as in Problem 14–8.

15 Segment Reporting

OVERVIEW OF SEGMENT REPORTING

The foregoing chapters deal with the preparation of combined and consolidated financial statements, which are important to investors and lenders
in evaluating the overall performance and condition of an enterprise. Historically, financial statements have also been used by investors and lenders
to prepare trends and ratios that are useful in assessing the future prospects
of an enterprise. For companies that have expanded into different industries
or geographic areas, this task is usually more complicated because of
different opportunities for growth, degrees and types of risk, and return on
investments among the various segments. As discussed in Chapter 13,
significant additional risks arise in conducting operations in foreign countries.
Even when a company has only domestic operations, substantial differences
in future prospects may exist among the industry segments.

Because of two major events, accountants feel that lenders and investors
would be better served if combined or consolidated financial statements
were supplemented with information concerning the industries and geographic
areas in which an enterprise operates. The first major event was the substantial
foreign investment that occurred after World War II. The second major
event was the substantial product diversification carried out by scores of
companies beginning in the 1960s and continuing unabated to the present.
In 1976, the FASB issued *Statement No. 14*, "Financial Reporting for Segments
of a Business Enterprise," in response to these events. This pronouncement
requires the disclosure of information in addition to the basic financial
statements. This additional information fits into three broad categories, as
follows:

(1) Different industries
(2) Foreign operations and export sales
(3) Major customers[1]

If a complete set of the basic financial statements is presented for more
than one year (for comparative purposes), then the information that must
be disclosed under *FASB Statement No. 14* is presented for each such
year.[2]

The reporting requirements of this pronouncement are substantial for
companies obliged to comply (certain companies are exempted from this
pronouncement's reporting requirements). Before *FASB Statement No. 14*
was issued, the Securities and Exchange Commission had imposed line
of business reporting requirements on publicly owned companies. The
current SEC reporting requirements in Regulation S-K (an integrated disclosure

---

[1] *FASB Statement No. 14*, "Financial Reporting for Segments of a Business Enterprise" (Stamford, CT:
FASB, 1976), paragraph 3. Copyright by Financial Accounting Standards Board, High Ridge Park, Stamford,
CT 06905, USA. Reprinted with permission. Copies of the complete document are available from the
FASB.
[2] *FASB Statement No. 14*, paragraph 3.

regulation adopted in 1977, which is discussed in detail in Chapter 17) are closely patterned after *FASB Statement No. 14.*

Applicability of *FASB Statement No. 14*

Nonpublic enterprises. As initially issued, *FASB Statement No. 14,* applied to all enterprises. Subsequently, however, it was evident that (1) the reporting requirements of this pronouncement burdened small, closely held enterprises, and (2) the benefit to nonmanagement investors and creditors was too limited. Consequently, *FASB Statement No. 21,* "Suspension of the Reporting of Earnings per Share and Segment Information by Nonpublic Enterprises," was issued, suspending the requirements of *FASB Statement No. 14* for nonpublic enterprises. *FASB Statement No. 21* defines a nonpublic enterprise as follows:

> For purposes of this Statement, a nonpublic enterprise is an enterprise other than one (a) whose debt or equity securities trade in a public market on a foreign or domestic stock exchange or in the over-the-counter market (including securities quoted only locally or regionally) or (b) that is required to file financial statements with the Securities and Exchange Commission. An enterprise is no longer considered a nonpublic enterprise when its financial statements are issued in preparation for the sale of any class of securities in a public market.[3]

Interim financial statements. As initially issued, *FASB Statement No. 14* required that segment information be included in interim financial reports that constituted a complete set of financial statements—containing statements of financial position, results of operations, and changes in financial position in conformity with generally accepted accounting principles. However, *FASB Statement No. 18,* "Financial Reporting for Segments of a Business Enterprise—Interim Financial Statements," subsequently rescinded this requirement.[4]

Financial statements presented in another enterprise's financial report. Many situations arise in which a complete set of an entity's financial statements is presented in another enterprise's financial report. The three most common such situations are the following:

(1) "Parent company only" statements are presented in addition to the consolidated financial statements.
(2) The financial statements of an unconsolidated subsidiary are presented in footnotes to the parent's financial statements (which may be consolidated with the financial statements of other subsidiaries).
(3) The financial statements of a 50%-or-less owned investee are presented in the footnotes to the investor's financial statements.

---

[3] *FASB Statement No. 21,* "Suspension of the Reporting of Earnings per Share and Segment Information by Nonpublic Enterprises" (Stamford, CT: FASB, 1978), paragraph 13. Copyright by Financial Accounting Standards Board, High Ridge Park, Stamford, CT 06905, USA. Reprinted with permission. Copies of the complete document are available from the FASB.
[4] *FASB Statement No. 18,* "Financial Reporting for Segments of a Business Enterprise—Interim Financial Statements" (Stamford, CT: FASB, 1977), paragraph 7.

In a literal interpretation of paragraph 7 of *FASB Statement No. 14*, the separate "additional" set of financial statements described in the above three situations must include the information required by *FASB Statement No. 14*. *FASB Statement No. 24*, "Reporting Segment Information in Financial Statements That Are Presented in Another Enterprise's Financial Report" subsequently amended this paragraph to delete this reporting requirement in certain situations. With respect to the three situations listed above, the *FASB Statement No. 24* provisions are as follows:

(1) The disclosure requirements of *FASB Statement No. 14* do not apply to "parent company only" statements (because such statements are included in the consolidated statements).
(2) The disclosure requirements of *FASB Statement No. 14* apply to the financial statements of unconsolidated subsidiaries "if that information is significant in relation to the financial statements of the primary reporting entity in that financial report."[5]
(3) The disclosure requirements of *FASB Statement No. 14* in these situations depend on whether the 50%-or-less owned investee is a domestic or foreign entity.
   (a) **Domestic entity.** The requirements of *FASB Statement No. 14* apply to a domestic entity's financial statements "if that information is significant in relation to the financial statements of the primary reporting entity in that financial report."[6]
   (b) **Foreign entity.** The requirements of *FASB Statement No. 14* do not apply to a foreign entity's financial statements "unless that foreign entity's *separately issued* financial statements disclose the information required by *FASB Statement No. 14*."[7]

In summary, the disclosure requirements of *FASB Statement No. 14* currently pertain to **annual** financial statements of **publicly held** companies. When the financial reports of these companies also include a complete set of financial statements of an unconsolidated subsidiary or a 50%-or-less owned entity, then the requirements of *FASB Statement No. 14* may also apply to the investee's financial statements (as included in the financial report of the investor), depending on the individual circumstances.

Principles used to present segment information

Recall that a basic principle in the preparation of consolidated financial statements is that all intercompany transactions (and intracompany transactions when divisions are used) are completely eliminated just as if the transactions had never occurred. This principle is also used in the preparation of segment information, with the modification that any **intersegment** sales should be separately **disclosed** but then also **eliminated** in reconciling to the consolidated revenues—this disclosure and elimination are shown to-

---

[5] *FASB Statement No. 24*, "Reporting Segment Information in Financial Statements That Are Presented in Another Enterprise's Financial Report" (Stamford, CT: FASB, 1978), paragraph 5.
[6] *FASB Statement No. 24*, paragraph 5.
[7] *FASB Statement No. 24*, paragraph 5.

gether. Any **intrasegment** sales (such as those within a vertically integrated operation) need not be disclosed.

With respect to reporting information by geographic areas, the modified basic principle requires separate disclosure of transfers between geographic areas with the elimination of these transfers in reconciling to consolidated revenues; this disclosure and elimination also are shown together. The word "transfer" means shipments of inventory, whether or not accounted for as a sale by the shipping organization. (The statement ignores the organizational structure of companies—that is, whether divided into branches, divisions, or subsidiaries.)

The Appendix to this chapter contains a comprehensive illustration of the type of disclosure required by *FASB Statement No. 14.* Before proceeding, you should lightly review this appendix to obtain a general understanding of the disclosure required under this pronouncement. You will be referred to specific sections of the appendix later in the chapter as the material is discussed.

INFORMATION ABOUT DIFFERENT INDUSTRIES

FASB Statement No. 14 specifies detailed mathematical tests for determining the components of a business that must disclose certain information regarding their operations. Components that meet these tests are "reportable industry segments." Before discussing these mathematical tests, we present the information that must be disclosed for each "reportable industry segment" and the manner of reporting this information.

Information presented for reportable industry segments

The following information must be presented for each reportable industry segment and in total for all nonreportable industry segments:

(1) *Revenue.*   Sales to unaffiliated customers and sales or transfers to other industry segments. . . .

(2) *Profitability.*   Operating profit or loss . . . [along with an explanation of] the nature and amount of any unusual or infrequently occurring items . . . that have been added or deducted in computing the operating profit or loss. . . .

(3) *Identifiable assets.*   The aggregate carrying amount of identifiable assets. . . .

(4) *Other related disclosures:*
  (a) The aggregate amount of depreciation, depletion, and amortization expense. . . .
  (b) The amount of . . . capital expenditures, i.e., additions to its property, plant, and equipment. . . .
  (c) The . . . equity in the net income from and investment in the net assets of unconsolidated subsidiaries and other equity method investees whose operations are vertically integrated with the operations of that segment. . . .
  (d) The effect . . . on the operating profit [of a change in accounting principle].[8]

The pronouncement defines items (1), (2), and (3) as follows:

Revenue.   The revenue of an industry segment includes revenue both from sales to unaffiliated customers (i.e., revenue from customers outside the enterprise as

[8] *FASB Statement No. 14,* paragraphs 22–27.

reported in the enterprise's income statement) and from intersegment sales or transfers, if any, of products and services similar to those sold to unaffiliated customers. . . .

Operating Profit or Loss. The operating profit or loss of an industry segment is its revenue as defined . . . minus all operating expenses. As used herein, operating expenses include expenses that relate to both revenue from sales to unaffiliated customers and revenue from intersegment sales or transfers. . . .

Identifiable Assets. The identifiable assets of an industry segment are those tangible and intangible enterprise assets that are used by the industry segment, including (1) assets that are used exclusively by that industry segment and (2) an allocated portion of assets used jointly by two or more industry segments. . . .[9]

The identifiable assets of segments that were acquired in a business combination accounted for as a purchase include the amount of the parent's cost of an investment in excess of its interest in a subsidiary's net assets. This is necessary so that the amount of a segment's identifiable net assets is the same whether assets or common stock was acquired.

Methods of presenting information on reportable segments

The required information pertaining to reportable segments must be included in the financial statements in one of the following ways:

(1) Within the body of the financial statements, with appropriate explanatory disclosures in the footnotes to the financial statements.
(2) Entirely in the footnotes to the financial statements.
(3) In a separate schedule that is included as an integral part of the financial statements.[10]

The information that must be presented for individual reportable industry segments and in the aggregate for industry segments not deemed reportable must be reconciled to the consolidated financial statements as follows:

(1) Revenue shall be reconciled to revenue reported in the consolidated income statement. . . .
(2) Operating profit or loss shall be reconciled to pretax income from continuing operations (before gain or loss on discontinued operations, extraordinary items, and cumulative effect of a change in accounting principle) in the consolidated income statement. . . .
(3) Identifiable assets shall be reconciled to consolidated total assets, with assets maintained for general corporate purposes separately identified in the reconciliation.[11]

Reconciling items (2) and (3) to consolidated amounts requires the use of procedures discussed and illustrated in Chapters 7 and 8 concerning the recognition and deferral of gross profit or gain on intercompany asset transfers.

Transfer pricing

The definition of revenue includes revenues from intersegment sales and transfers, if any, of products and services similar to those sold to unaffiliated

[9] *FASB Statement No. 14*, paragraph 10.
[10] *FASB Statement No. 14*, paragraph 28.
[11] *FASB Statement No. 14*, paragraph 30.

customers. Accordingly, the reported profitability of each segment is directly affected by the sales or transfer prices used. Because such sales or transfers are not determined on an arm's length basis from a consolidated viewpoint, substantial latitude exists for top management to shift profits between the selling and buying segments.

It would be impractical for the FASB to try to establish a basis to set prices for sales or transfers between segments. Instead, the Board requires companies to use the same transfer prices (for reporting purposes under the pronouncement) as those used internally to price the intersegment sales or transfers.[12] Because transfer pricing has historically been associated with vertically integrated operations (which need not be disaggregated), the potential for shifting profits is of less apparent concern.

Furthermore, when sales or transfers take place between segments, most often the organizational structures of the segments are similar to profit centers. This organizational structure is a substantial motivating factor for each segment to sell or transfer at no more or no less than independent market prices, as the case may be. The basis of accounting for sales or transfers between industry segments and between geographic areas must be disclosed. If the basis is changed, the nature and effect of the change must be disclosed in the period of change.[13]

Allocation of common costs

When determining an industry segment's operating profit or loss, the operating expenses subtracted from revenue (as defined in the pronouncement) include expenses related to both revenue from sales to unaffiliated customers and revenue from intersegment sales or transfers. Operating expenses not directly traceable to an industry segment are allocated on a reasonable basis among those industry segments for whose benefit the expenses were incurred.[14]

The methods used to allocate operating expenses among industry segments must be consistently applied from period to period. If the methods are changed, however, the nature of the change and the effect on the operating profit or loss of reportable segments must be disclosed in the period of change.[15]

Because many items would have to be allocated on an arbitrary basis, *FASB Statement No. 14* specifies that the following items are neither added nor deducted, as the case may be, in computing an industry segment's operating profit or loss:

(1) Revenue earned at the corporate level and not derived from the operations of any industry segment.
(2) General corporate expenses.
(3) Interest expense.
(4) Domestic and foreign income taxes.

---

[12] *FASB Statement No. 14,* paragraph 10.
[13] *FASB Statement No. 14,* paragraphs 23 and 35.
[14] *FASB Statement No. 14,* paragraph 10.
[15] *FASB Statement No. 14,* paragraph 24.

(5) Equity in income or loss from unconsolidated subsidiaries and other unconsolidated investees.
(6) Gain or loss on discontinued operations.
(7) Extraordinary items.
(8) Minority interest.
(9) The cumulative effect of a change in accounting principle.[16]

Note that items (3)–(9) appear below the operating income or loss line as that term is customarily used in income statements. Thus, the meaning of operating profit or loss for a segment is consistent with the customary definition of operating profit or loss.

In the Appendix to this chapter, Exhibits A and B and the Note to Exhibit B contain the industry segment information discussed up to this point.

Determination of industry segments

An industry segment is defined as follows:

> A component of an enterprise engaged in providing a product or service or a group of related products and services primarily to unaffiliated customers (i.e., customers outside the enterprise) for a profit. By defining an industry segment in terms of products and services that are sold primarily to unaffiliated customers, the Statement does not require the disaggregation of the vertically integrated operations of an enterprise.[17]

The products and services that are sold to outside customers must be grouped by industry lines to arrive at industry segments. Because the available classification systems are not entirely suitable, the grouping of products and services into appropriate industry segments is left to management's judgment, with the following considerations:[18]

(1) The nature of the product.
(2) The nature of the production process.
(3) Markets and marketing methods.[19]

> Broad categories such as *manufacturing, wholesaling, retailing,* and *consumer products* are not per se indicative of the industries in which an enterprise operates, and those terms should not be used without identification of a product or service to describe an enterprise's industry segments.[20]

The underlying philosophy is to disaggregate the total business into segments with distinct markets and thus different profitability, growth potential, and/or risk patterns. The enterprise's internal data by organizational, divisional, or parent–subsidiary lines *may* be used, but only if consistent with this philosophy.

---

[16] *FASB Statement No. 14,* paragraph 10.
[17] *FASB Statement No. 14,* paragraph 10.
[18] *FASB Statement No. 14,* paragraph 12.
[19] *FASB Statement No. 14,* paragraph 100.
[20] *FASB Statement No. 14,* paragraph 101.

Determination of reportable industry segments

A reportable industry segment is

> an industry segment (or, in certain cases, a group of two or more closely related industry segments . . .) for which information is required to be reported by this Statement.[21]

An industry segment is "reportable" simply if it is big enough. Any industry segment that satisfies one or more of the following criteria is considered a reportable segment for which specific information should be disclosed:

(1) Its revenue (including both sales to unaffiliated customers and intersegment sales or transfers) is 10% or more of the combined revenue (sales to unaffiliated customers and intersegment sales or transfers) of all of the enterprise's industry segments.

(2) The absolute amount of its operating profit or operating loss is 10% or more of the greater, in absolute amount, of:

  (a) The combined operating profit of all industry segments that did not incur an operating loss, or

  (b) The combined operating loss of all industry segments that did incur an operating loss.

(3) Its identifiable assets are 10% or more of the combined identifiable assets of all industry segments.[22]

To illustrate the application of the second test, assume that a company has eight industry segments, which are grouped as follows:

Industry Segment	Operating Profit	Operating Loss
A	$ 100,000	
B	300,000	
C	400,000	
D	200,000	
E		$ 290,000
F		600,000
G		100,000
H		110,000
	$1,000,000	$1,100,000

The total of the operating losses is greater than the total of the operating profits. Applying the 10% test to the total of the operating losses gives $110,000. Any segment that has an operating profit or loss equal to or above $110,000 satisfies the test and is a reportable segment. In this situation, only segments A and G do not pass the test. Segments that do not satisfy the tests of a reportable segment are shown as a combined group of segments, appropriately described.

After applying the three 10% tests, an enterprise must exercise judgment

[21] *FASB Statement No. 14*, paragraph 10.
[22] *FASB Statement No. 14*, paragraph 15.

in evaluating the results of the tests. In this respect, it may be appropriate to:

(1) Exclude a segment that satisfies one of the tests if the result is a freak occurrence, such as an abnormally high revenue or operating profit or loss for the segment.
(2) Include a segment that does not meet one of the tests if the result is a freak occurrence, such as an abnormally low revenue or operating profit or loss.

This latitude was granted so that interperiod comparability could be maintained. When a "reportable" segment is excluded or a "nonreportable" segment is included, appropriate disclosure of such circumstances is required.[23]

Enough individual segments must be shown so that at least 75% of the combined revenues (from sales to unaffiliated customers of all industry segments) is shown by reportable segments.[24] To illustrate how the 75% test is applied, assume a company with eight industry segments has the following revenues:

Industry Segment	Sales to Unaffiliated Customers	Intersegment Sales	Total
A	$ 100,000		$ 100,000
B	200,000		200,000
C	310,000	$ 40,000	350,000
D	340,000		340,000
E	550,000		550,000
F	600,000	60,000	660,000
G	700,000		700,000
H	800,000	300,000	1,100,000
	$3,600,000	$400,000	$4,000,000
	75%		
	$2,700,000		

Assume that the operating profit or loss test and the identifiable assets test do not result in any reportable segments other than those determined below in the 10% of total revenues test.

Industry Segment	Sales to Unaffiliated Customers
E	$ 550,000
F	600,000
G	700,000
H	800,000
	$2,650,000

---

[23] FASB Statement No. 14, paragraph 16.
[24] FASB Statement No. 14, paragraph 17.

An additional segment must be selected so that at least $2,700,000 of sales to unaffiliated customers is shown by individual segments. This 75% requirement is determined after the three tests pertaining to revenues, operating profit or loss, and identifiable assets have been performed.

Situations may exist in which a substantial number of segments must be presented to comply with the 75% test. No specific limit is imposed on the number of segments for which information is reported. However, for practical reasons, the Board has indicated that if more than 10 industry segments are reportable segments, a company may combine "the most closely related industry segments into broader reportable segments."[25]

INFORMATION ABOUT FOREIGN OPERATIONS AND EXPORT SALES

Definition of foreign operations

Foreign operations are defined as revenue-producing operations (except for unconsolidated subsidiaries and other unconsolidated investees) that

> (a) are located outside of the enterprise's home country (the United States for U.S. enterprises) and (b) are generating revenue either from sales to unaffiliated customers or from intraenterprise sales or transfers between geographic areas.[26]

Determination of reportable foreign operations

Information about foreign operations must be presented if either of the following criteria is met:

> (1) Revenue generated by the enterprise's foreign operations from sales to unaffiliated customers is 10% or more of consolidated revenue as reported in the enterprise's income statement.
> (2) Identifiable assets of the enterprise's foreign operations are 10% or more of consolidated total assets as reported in the enterprise's balance sheet.[27]

These two tests are based on the consolidated amounts, whereas the revenue and identifiable assets tests used to determine reportable industry segments are based on total industry segment amounts. Note that the 10% operating profit or loss test used for industry segments is not used for geographic segments. This test was apparently excluded because potential misinterpretations could occur as a result of significant differences in tax structures among geographic areas.

Determination of geographic areas

Disclosures required for foreign operations are presented in total or by geographic area. The grouping of foreign countries into geographic areas is left to the judgment of management, which should consider the following

---

[25] *FASB Statement No. 14*, paragraph 19.
[26] *FASB Statement No. 14*, paragraph 31.
[27] *FASB Statement No. 14*, paragraph 32.

factors: "proximity, economic affinity, similarities in business environment, and the nature, scale, and degree of interrelationship of the various countries."[28] These factors could create differing patterns of risk, profitability, and growth.

Determination of reportable geographic areas

When foreign operations are conducted in more than one geographic area, information must be presented for any geographic area meeting one of the following conditions:

(1) If its revenues from sales to unaffiliated customers are 10% or more of consolidated revenues.
(2) If its identifiable assets are 10% or more of consolidated total assets.[29]

Information presented about foreign operations

The following information must be presented in total (when only one foreign geographic area exists) or for each reportable geographic area, and in the aggregate for all other foreign geographic areas that individually are not reportable geographic areas:

> (1) Revenue . . . with sales to unaffiliated customers and sales or transfers between geographic areas shown separately. . . .
> (2) Operating profit or loss . . . or net income, or some other measure of profitability between operating profit or loss and net income. . . .
> (3) Identifiable assets. . . .[30]

With respect to item (2), a wide range of profitability can be used in lieu of operating profit and loss (as required for industry segment reporting). There are two apparent reasons for allowing this flexibility.

(1) Companies already must disclose the incomes and losses of their foreign operations pursuant to the provisions of *ARB No. 43* (discussed in Chapter 13). Thus, the use of a net income or loss level would satisfy both reporting requirements.
(2) When significant differences exist among tax structures of foreign countries and the United States, misleading conclusions could possibly result if the operating income or loss level alone were imposed.

A multinational company that has diversified operations may have to disclose both industry segment information *and* information about its foreign operations.

Information presented about export sales

When sales to unaffiliated foreign customers by a domestic company (export sales) are 10% or more of total revenue from sales to unaffiliated customers

---

[28] *FASB Statement No. 14*, paragraph 34.
[29] *FASB Statement No. 14*, paragraph 33.
[30] *FASB Statement No. 14*, paragraph 35.

as reported in the consolidated income statement, the total export sales must be separately reported, in total, and by geographic areas.[31]

Methods of presenting foreign operations and export sales information

Foreign operations and export sales information may be presented in any of the ways shown previously for presenting industry segment information. The information presented for foreign operations, however, must be presented with the same information for domestic operations. The domestic operations information and the foreign operations information must then be reconciled to the related amounts in the consolidated financial statements in a manner similar to that described for industry segment information.[32]

Information regarding export sales may have to be presented even though segment data need not be disclosed. In these cases, the information would normally be presented in a simple narrative footnote rather than as part of a more complex schedule dealing with segment data.

In the Appendix to this chapter, Exhibit C and the Note to Exhibit C illustrate the type of disclosure required with respect to foreign operations and export sales.

INFORMATION ABOUT MAJOR CUSTOMERS

Some enterprises rely heavily on major customers. *FASB Statement No. 14,* as amended by *FASB Statement No. 30,* "Disclosure of Information about Major Customers," requires enterprises having revenues from any single customer in excess of 10% of total revenues to disclose the following information:

(1) The fact that the enterprise has revenues from one or more single customers in excess of 10% of total revenues.
(2) The amount of revenues from each such customer, but not the identity of each such customer.
(3) The industry segment making the sales to each such customer.[33]

The federal government (including its agencies), a state government, a local governmental unit (such as a county or a municipality), a foreign government, and a group of entities under common control are each considered a single customer.[34] As in the case of export sales, information about major customers may have to be presented even though segment data need not be disclosed. A simple narrative footnote usually suffices in these cases.

---

[31] *FASB Statement No. 14,* paragraph 36.
[32] *FASB Statement No. 14,* paragraphs 37–38.
[33] *FASB Statement No. 30,* "Disclosure of Information about Major Customers" (Stamford, CT: FASB, 1979), paragraph 6. Copyright by Financial Accounting Standards Board, High Ridge Park, CT 06905, USA. Reprinted with permission. Copies of the complete document are available from the FASB.
[34] *FASB Statement No. 30,* paragraph 6.

REPORTING THE DISPOSAL
OF A SEGMENT OF A BUSINESS

The professional management approach.   In the 1960s and 1970s, a professional management approach became exceedingly popular. Under this approach, it was thought that acquired businesses could be managed by professional managers, whose skills could be applied successfully to almost any acquired business. Managing a diverse group of acquired businesses was likened to managing a portfolio of investments. This thinking contributed to the rapid rise in the number of conglomerates during this period (discussed in Chapter 2).

The reversal of the professional management approach and the deconglomeration trend.   By the early 1980s, it was evident that this approach had not been that successful. After an acquisitions binge, many companies found that they had bitten off more than they could chew. Many companies had bought into the wrong industry, or they just did not have the managerial talent to manage a diverse group of industries effectively. In fact, of the 14 companies identified as having supremely excellent management by Peters and Waterman in their 1982 best selling book *In Search of Excellence: Lessons from America's Best-Run Companies,* not one was a conglomerate.

In recent years, scores of top managements have undone much of the external expansion of previous top managements because the acquired businesses had lower than expected rates of return or continuous operating losses. Of course, such undoings are referred to as "divestiture programs" rather than "selling your losers." In the 1980s, the number of disposals of unwanted businesses per year has increased dramatically (approaching 1,000 for 1983). Clearly, there is a trend away from "making deals" and toward "operating businesses that managements know best." Recent notable divestiture programs include the following:

(1) From 1978–1980, International Telephone & Telegraph Corporation (ITT), a giant conglomerate that grew by leaps and bounds through external expansion in the 1960s and 1970s, sold approximately 40 of its businesses, which had estimated annual sales of $1 billion.[35] (After these disposals, ITT still had approximately 230 profit centers for its remaining businesses.)

(2) In 1983, Beatrice Foods Company sold 18 of the 52 subsidiaries it had targeted to sell.[36]

(3) In 1984, Gulf & Western Industries, Inc. (a conglomerate) announced that it was close to selling the remaining seven units out of 51 that it had marked for divestiture in early 1983.[37]

---

[35] "ITT's Araskog Reverses Geneen Formula, Sheds Units to Improve Company Fortunes," *The Wall Street Journal,* April 1, 1981, p. 29.

[36] "Recovery Stirs Large Number of Divestitures," *The Wall Street Journal,* November 2, 1983, p. 29.

[37] "G&W Chief Nears Goal of Reshaping Firm Through Sale of Units and Stock Holdings," *The Wall Street Journal,* August 2, 1984, p. 10.

Results of divestitures. Divesting companies are leaner and healthier after divesting unwanted units. New management may run the divested units more effectively. If existing management buys the business, it may be entrepreneur-oriented and able to make decisions faster than allowed in a major corporation's rigid and stifling reporting structure.

Manner of divesting. Companies commonly employ investment advisers (at substantial fees) to assist them in their divestitures. Divestitures can take the following forms: (a) selling segments to other companies (a business combination for the acquiring company); (b) selling segments to managers or employees of the units (increasingly common in recent years); (c) spinning segments off as separate companies (distributing the common stock of the subsidiary to the parent company's shareholders); and, when all else fails, (d) liquidating the business.

Accounting issues

The following accounting issues are associated with the disposal of a segment of a business:

(1) How should a gain or loss on the disposal of a segment be measured and classified in the income statement?
(2) How should the results of operations of the discontinued operation be reported in the income statement?

The reporting and accounting for the disposal of a segment of a business are governed by *APB Opinion No. 30*, "Reporting the Results of Operations." This pronouncement introduced the idea that the results of operations of a discontinued segment and any gain or loss on the disposal should be reported separately from continuing operations. Before *APB Opinion No. 30* was issued, losses on the disposals of segments were commonly reported as extraordinary items, whereas gains were not commonly shown as extraordinary items; the results of operations of the discontinued segments were not separated from the continuing operations.

Manner of reporting a disposal of a segment

APB Opinion No. 30 specifies the manner of reporting the disposal of a segment as follows:

> For purposes of this Opinion, the term "discontinued operations" refers to the operations of a segment of a business . . . that has been sold, abandoned, spun off, or otherwise disposed of or, although still operating, is the subject of a formal plan for disposal. . . . The Board concludes that the results of continuing operations should be reported separately from discontinued operations and that any gain or loss from disposal of a segment of a business . . . should be reported in conjunction with the related results of discontinued operations and not as an extraordinary item. Accordingly, operations of a segment that has been or will be discontinued should be reported separately as a component of income before extraordinary items and the cumulative effect of accounting changes (if applicable) in the following manner:

Income from continuing operations before income taxes . . . . $xxxx
Provision for income taxes xxx
    Income from continuing operations . . . . $xxxx
Discontinued operations (Note _____):
    Income (loss) from operations of discontinued Division X
      (less applicable income taxes of $ _____) . . . . $xxxx
    Loss on disposal of Division X, including provision of
      $ _____ for operating losses during phase-out
      period (less applicable income taxes of $ _____) xxxx   xxxx
          Net Income . . . . $xxxx

Amounts of income taxes applicable to the results of discontinued operations and the gain or loss from disposal of the segment should be disclosed on the face of the income statement or in related notes. Revenues applicable to the discontinued operations should be separately disclosed in the related notes.[38]

If prior-period income statements are presented for comparative purposes, such statements are **restated** to report the results of operations of the segment being disposed of as a separate component of income before extraordinary items, net of taxes.[39]

Definition of a segment of a business

The precise definition of a segment of a business in *APB Opinion No. 30,* which is different from the definition in *FASB Statement No. 14,* is as follows:

> For purposes of this Opinion, the term "segment of a business" refers to a component of an entity whose activities represent a separate major line of business or class of customer. A segment may be in the form of a subsidiary, a division, or a department, and in some cases a joint venture or other nonsubsidiary investee, provided that its assets, results of operations, and activities can be clearly distinguished, physically and operationally and for financial reporting purposes, from the other assets, results of operations, and activities of the entity. . . . The fact that the results of operations of the segment being sold or abandoned cannot be separately identified strongly suggests that the transaction should not be classified as the disposal of a segment of the business. The disposal of a segment of a business should be distinguished from other disposals of assets incident to the evolution of the entity's business, such as the disposal of part of a line of business, the shifting of production or marketing activities for a particular line of business from one location to another, the phasing out of a product line or class of service, and other changes occasioned by technological improvements.[40]

This definition is apparently narrower than the definition used in *FASB Statement No. 14* in that the disposal of a discrete operation within a vertically integrated operation would be considered a disposal of a segment. (Actually, this would be a disposal of a portion of a segment as that term

---

[38] *APB Opinion No. 30,* "Reporting the Results of Operations" (New York: AICPA, 1973), paragraph 8. Copyright © 1973 by the American Institute of Certified Public Accountants, Inc.
[39] *APB Opinion No. 30,* paragraph 13.
[40] *APB Opinion No. 30,* paragraph 13.

is used in *FASB Statement No. 14.*) This interpretation is consistent with the intent of *FASB Statement No. 14,* because an appendix to the statement illustrates the disposal of a portion of a segment (as that term is defined in *FASB Statement No. 14*), which is reported in accordance with the procedures set forth in *APB Opinion No. 30.*

Definition of measurement and disposal dates

APB Opinion No. 30 distinguishes between the operations of a segment that occur before a decision to dispose of that segment and operations that occur after that time. The particular point in time, referred to as the **measurement date,** is defined as follows:

> The "measurement date" of a disposal is the date on which management, having authority to approve the action, commits itself to a formal plan to dispose of a segment of the business, whether by sale or abandonment. The disposal should include, as a minimum, identification of the major assets to be disposed of, the expected method of disposal, the period expected to be required for completion of the disposal, an active program to find a buyer if disposal is by sale, the estimated results of operations of the segment from the measurement date to the disposal date, and the estimated proceeds or salvage to be realized by disposal.[41]

The **disposal date** as used in the preceding definition is defined as follows:

> The "disposal date" is the date of closing the sale if the disposal is by sale or the date that operations cease if the disposal is by abandonment.[42]

The format for reporting the discontinued operations of a business includes two categories. The first category (the income or loss from operations of a discontinued segment of a business) includes all operations up to the measurement date. The second category (the gain or loss on disposal of a segment of a business) includes the following:

(1) The income or loss from operations **during the phase-out period** (from the measurement date to the disposal date).
(2) The gain or loss on the sale or abandonment of the segment.

The amount reported in the second category **as of the measurement date** depends on the relative amounts determined for items (1) and (2), above, and whether the amounts are positive or negative. The pronouncement requires companies to recognize losses currently and to recognize income and gains only when realized, but some offsetting is also required. Thus, an anticipated loss on the sale or abandonment of the segment is recognized as of the measurement date, whereas an anticipated gain is recognized when realized. However, estimated losses from operations during the phase-out period are included in this calculation. Estimated income from operations during the phase-out period is included only to the extent of the estimated

---

[41] *APB Opinion No. 30,* paragraph 14.
[42] *APB Opinion No. 30,* paragraph 14.

Illustration 15-1
Determining amount reported for category 2: — *Know* —
Loss or gain on disposal (thousands of dollars)

	Estimated Income (Loss) from Operations during the Phase-Out Period (Oct. 1, 19X1 to Mar. 31, 19X2)			Estimated Gain (Loss) on Sale of Segment	Category 2 Gain (Loss) to Be Reported	
	19X1	19X2	Total	Mar. 31, 19X2	19X1	19X2
A.	$(30)	$(70)	$(100)	$(140)	$(240)[a]	
B.	(30)	(70)	(100)	80	(20)[a]	
C.	(30)	(70)	(100)	130		$ 30[b]
D.	30	70	100	(140)	(40)[a]	
E.	30	70	100	(90)		10[b]
F.	30	70	100	160	30[b]	230[b]

[a] Reported as of the measurement date (October 1, 19X1).
[b] Reported when realized.
Note: For simplicity, income tax effects were not considered.

loss on the sale or abandonment of the segment (with any remaining amount to be recognized when realized).[43]

To illustrate, assume that on October 1, 19X1 a company with a calendar year-end decides to dispose of a segment of its business. The expected sales date is March 31, 19X2. Illustration 15-1 shows the amounts reported for 19X1 and 19X2 under various assumptions.

Guidelines in determining gain or loss on disposal

APB Opinion No. 30 specifies the following guidelines to determine the amount of the gain or loss:

> Estimated amounts of income or loss from operations of a segment between measurement date and disposal date included in the determination of loss on disposal should be limited to those amounts that can be projected with reasonable accuracy. In the usual circumstance, it would be expected that the plan of disposal would be carried out within a period of one year from the measurement date and that such projections of operating income or loss would not cover a period exceeding approximately one year.
>
> Gain or loss from the disposal of a segment of a business should not include adjustments, costs, and expenses associated with normal business activities that should have been recognized on a going-concern basis up to the measurement date, such as adjustments of accruals on long-term contracts or write-down or write-off of receivables, inventories, property, plant, and equipment used in the business, equipment leased to others, . . . or other intangible assets. However, such adjustments, costs, and expenses which (a) are clearly a "direct" result of the decision to dispose of the segment and (b) are clearly not the adjustments of carrying amounts or costs, or expenses that should have been recognized on a going-concern basis prior to the measurement date should be included in determining the gain or loss on disposal.

[43] *APB Opinion No. 30*, paragraph 15.

Results of operations before the measurement date should not be included in the gain or loss on disposal.

Costs and expenses "directly" associated with the decision to dispose include items such as severance pay, additional pension costs, employee relocation expenses, and future rentals on long-term leases to the extent they are not offset by sublease rentals.[44]

Disclosure

In addition to the manner of reporting in the income statement gains or losses on the disposal of a segment, the notes to the financial statements for the period encompassing the measurement date should disclose the following:

(1) The identity of the segment of business that has or will be discontinued.
(2) The expected disposal date, if known.
(3) The expected manner of disposal.
(4) A description of the remaining assets and liabilities of the segment at the balance sheet date, and
(5) The income or loss from operations and any proceeds from disposal of the segment during the period from the measurement date to the date of the balance sheet.[45]

SUMMARY

Consolidated financial statements have limited usefulness in enabling investors and lenders to assess the future prospects of enterprises with diversified operations. Supplemental data on industry segments and foreign operations are considered necessary to assist financial statement users to assess future prospects.

The process of supplying information by industry involves (1) identifying the various industry segments in which the enterprise operates; (2) applying three tests to each industry segment to determine if it is considered a reportable industry segment; and (3) presenting financial information for each reportable industry segment and all other industry segments combined in such a manner that the amounts shown tie in to the consolidated financial statements. The basic criterion for determining whether a component of a business is an industry segment is whether or not that component sells products or provides services primarily to unaffiliated customers for a profit. The three major disclosures for a reportable industry segment pertain to revenues, operating profit or loss, and identifiable assets used by the segment. In addition, a fourth category of miscellaneous disclosures relates primarily to capital investments, depreciation, and effects of changes in accounting principles.

The process of disclosing information about foreign operations involves (1) grouping the various foreign countries in which the enterprise operates into meaningful, related geographic areas; (2) applying two tests to each geo-

---

[44] *APB Opinion No. 30*, paragraphs 15–17. Copyright © 1973 by the American Institute of Certified Public Accountants, Inc.

[45] *APB Opinion No. 30*, paragraph 18.

graphic area to determine if it is reportable; and (3) presenting financial information and data for each reportable geographic area and all other geographic areas combined in such a manner that the amounts shown tie in to the consolidated financial statements. The three major disclosures for geographic areas pertain to revenues, operating profit or loss, and identifiable assets used by each segment.

Disposals of segments (or part of a segment) are reported in the income statement separately from all other operations that are referred to as the continuing operations.

Glossary of new terms

Disposal Date: The disposal date is the date of closing the sale if the disposal is by sale or the date that operations cease if the disposal is by abandonment.[46]

Identifiable Assets: The identifiable assets of an industry segment are those tangible and intangible enterprise assets that are used by the industry segment, including (1) assets that are used exclusively by that industry segment and (2) an allocated portion of assets used jointly by two or more industry segments.[47]

Industry Segments: A component of an enterprise engaged in providing a product or service or a group of related products and services primarily to unaffiliated customers (i.e., customers outside the enterprise) for a profit. By defining an industry segment in terms of products and services that are sold primarily to unaffiliated customers, the Statement does not require the disaggregation of the vertically integrated operations of an enterprise.[47]

Measurement Date: The measurement date of a disposal is the date on which management, having authority to approve the action, commits itself to a formal plan to dispose of a segment of the business, whether by sale or abandonment.[46]

Operating Profit or Loss: The operating profit or loss of an industry segment is its revenue as defined . . . minus all operating expenses. Operating expenses include expenses that relate to both revenue from sale to unaffiliated customers and revenue from intersegment sales or transfers.[47]

Reportable Segments: An industry segment (or, in certain cases, a group of two or more closely related industry segments . . .) for which information is required to be reported by the Statement.[47]

Revenue: The revenue of an industry segment includes revenue both from sales to unaffiliated customers (i.e., revenue from customers outside the enterprise as reported in the enterprise's income statement) and from intersegment sales or transfers, if any, of products and services similar to those sold to unaffiliated customers.[47]

Appendix
COMPREHENSIVE ILLUSTRATION

This Appendix contains illustrations of the type of information required by *FASB Statement No. 14,* as follows:

---

[46] Definition quoted from *APB Opinion No. 30,* paragraph 14.
[47] Definition quoted from *FASB Statement No. 14,* paragraph 10.

Exhibit A

X COMPANY Consolidated Income Statement For the Year Ended December 31, 19X1 (thousands of dollars)		
Sales		$4,700
Cost of sales	$3,000	
Selling, general, and administrative expense	700	
Interest expense	200	(3,900)
		$ 800
Equity in net income of X Company (25% owned)		100
Income from continuing operations before income taxes.............		$ 900
Income taxes		(400)
Income from continuing operations		$ 500
Discontinued operations:		
Loss from operations of discontinued farm machinery manufacturing business (net of $50 income tax effect)	$ 70	
Loss on disposal of farm machinery manufacturing business (net of $100 income tax effect)	130	(200)
Income before extraordinary gain and before cumulative effect of change in accounting principle..........................		$ 300
Extraordinary gain (net of $80 income tax effect)		90
Cumulative effect on prior years of change from straight-line to accelerated depreciation (net of $60 income tax effect)		(60)
Net income		$ 330

Exhibit A   Consolidated income statement of a hypothetical company for the year ended December 31, 19X1.

Exhibit B   Information about operations in different industries and sales to major customers.

Exhibit C   Information about operations in different geographic areas and export sales.

The consolidated income statement in Exhibit A is not required pursuant to *FASB Statement No. 14;* it is included so that amounts in Exhibits B and C can be identified in the consolidated income statement.

Exhibits A, B, and C were adapted from *FASB Statement No. 14,* "Financial Reporting for Segments of a Business Enterprise" (Stamford, CT: FASB, 1976), Appendix F.

Note to Exhibit B

X Company operates principally in three industries—computers, food processing, and can manufacturing. Operations in the computer industry include the design, development, manufacture, and marketing of large computers. Operations in the food-processing industry include the cleaning, cooking, canning, and marketing of vegetables. Operations in the can-manufacturing industry include the production and sale of aluminum and steel cans for the canning industry. Total revenue by industry includes both sales to unaffiliated customers, as reported in the company's consolidated income statement, and intersegment sales, which are accounted for at negotiated

Exhibit B

X COMPANY
Information about the Company's Operations in Different Industries
(thousands of dollars)

	Computers	Food Processing	Can Manufacturing	Other Industries	Adjustments and Eliminations	Consolidated
Sales to unaffiliated customers	$1,200	$2,000	$1,300	$ 200		$ 4,700
Intersegment sales			700	200	$(700)	
Total revenue	$1,200	$2,000	$2,000	$ 200	$(700)	$ 4,700
Operating profit	$ 200	$ 290	$ 600	$ 50	$ (40)[a]	$ 1,100
Equity in net income of Z Company						100
General corporate expenses						(100)
Interest expense						(200)
Income from continuing operations before income taxes						$ 900
Identifiable assets at December 31, 19X1	$2,000	$4,050	$6,000	$1,000	$ (50)	$13,000
Investment in net assets of Z Company						400
Corporate assets						1,600
Total assets at December 31, 19X1						$15,000

See accompanying note.

[a] $10,000 of intersegment operating profit in beginning inventory, net of $50,000 of intersegment operating profit in ending inventory.

prices between the segments. The company feels these negotiated prices approximate outside market prices.

Operating profit is total revenue less operating expenses. In computing operating profit, none of the following items has been added or deducted: general corporate expenses, interest expense, income taxes, equity in income from unconsolidated investee, loss from discontinued operations of the farm machinery manufacturing business (which was a separate industry), extraordinary gain (which relates to the company's operations in the computer industry, and the cumulative effect of the change from straight-line to accelerated depreciation, of which $30 relates to the company's operations in the computer industry, $10 to the food-processing industry, and $20 to the can-manufacturing industry). Depreciation for these three industries was $80, $100, and $150, respectively. Capital expenditures for the three industries were $100, $200, and $400, respectively.

Changing from straight-line to accelerated depreciation reduced the 19X1 operating profit of the computer industry, the food-processing industry, and the can-manufacturing industry by $40, $30, and $20, respectively.

Identifiable assets by industry are assets that are used in the company's operations in each industry. Corporate assets are principally cash and marketable securities.

The company has a 25% interest in Z Company, whose operations are in the United States and are vertically integrated with the company's operations in the computer industry. The equity in Z Company's net income was $100; the investment in Z Company's net assets was $400.

To reconcile industry information with consolidated amounts, the following eliminations have been made: $700 of intersegment sales; $40 from the net change in intersegment operating profit in beginning and ending inventories; and $50 intersegment operating profit in inventory at December 31, 19X1.

Contracts with a U.S. government agency account for $1,000 of the sales to unaffiliated customers of the food-processing industry.

Note to Exhibit C

Transfers between geographic areas are accounted for at prices negotiated between the buying and selling units. The company feels such prices approximate outside market prices. Operating profit is total revenue less operating expenses. In computing operating profit, none of the following items has been added or deducted: general corporate expenses, interest expense, income taxes, equity in income from unconsolidated investee, loss from discontinued operations of the farm machinery manufacturing business (which was part of the company's domestic operations), extraordinary gain (which relates to the company's operations in Western Europe), and the cumulative effect of the change from straight-line to accelerated depreciation (which relates entirely to the company's operations in the United States).

The company's identifiable assets are identified with the operations in each geographic area. Corporate assets are principally cash and marketable securities.

Of the $3,000 U.S. sales to unaffiliated customers, $1,200 were export sales, principally to South America.

Exhibit C

X COMPANY
Information about the Company's Operations
in Different Geographic Areas
For the Year Ended December 31, 19X1
(thousands of dollars)

	United States	Western Europe	South America	Adjustments and Eliminations	Consolidated
Sales to unaffiliated customers..	$3,000	$1,000	$ 700		$ 4,700
Transfers between geographic					
areas......................	1,000			$(1,000)	
Total revenue	$4,000	$1,000	$ 700	$(1,000)	$ 4,700
Operating profit...............	$ 800	$ 400	$ 100	$ (200)	$ 1,100
Equity in net income of					
Z Company					100
General corporate expenses					(100)
Interest expense..............					(200)
Income from continuing operations before income					
taxes.....................					$ 900
Identifiable assets at					
December 31, 19X1	$7,300	$3,400	$2,450	$ (150)	$13,000
Investment in net assets of					
Z Company					400
Corporate assets					1,600
Total assets at					
December 31, 19X1					$15,000

See accompanying note.

Review questions

1. Why are consolidated financial statements alone considered insufficient and inadequate financial reports?
2. What three basic disclosures relate to industry segment reporting?
3. Define *industry segment* according to *FASB Statement No. 14.*
4. Distinguish between an industry segment and a reportable segment.
5. What tests determine if an industry segment is a reportable segment?
6. What amounts for industry segments must be reconciled to consolidated amounts?
7. Under *FASB Statement No. 14,* how should prices be determined for transfers between segments?
8. Name five items that cannot be allocated to industry segments in computing a segment's operating profit or loss.
9. What two tests determine whether foreign operations are reportable?
10. Under *FASB Statement No. 14,* how are foreign countries grouped into geographic areas?
11. What three types of information must be disclosed for a reportable geographic area?

12. Explain the difference between the definition of an industry segment under *FASB Statement No. 14* and the definition under *APB Opinion No. 30*.
13. Distinguish between the measurement date and the disposal date as those terms are used in *APB Opinion No. 30*.
14. How are revenues, cost of goods sold, and operating expenses from the beginning of the year to the measurement date reported for a segment being disposed of?

Discussion cases

Discussion case 15–1
Procedures used to determine industry segments

Bordley Company has the following operations: (1) planting and growing trees; (2) harvesting trees; (3) processing cut trees into building materials (lumber and plywood); (4) manufacturing paper and paper products; and (5) manufacturing container and packaging products.

The controller has asked your advice on determining industry segments.

Required:
(1) How would you determine which operations constitute industry segments?
(2) Make several possible assumptions as to the key determinant, and proceed accordingly.

Discussion case 15–2
Treatment of central research and development costs

Farr Company operates in four industries, each of which is conducted through subsidiaries. The operations of these subsidiaries are located some distance from the parent's headquarters location. Each subsidiary conducts research and development at its separate location. In addition, the parent maintains a central research department at its own headquarters location, which benefits all of the segments in the same manner that top management at the headquarters location benefits all segments.

Required:
Evaluate the treatment used to record the facilities and expenses of the central research department in preparing segment information disclosures.

Discussion case 15–3
Manner of reconciling segment information to consolidated amounts

Tripple Company operates in three industry segments—A, B, and C. Industry Segment A comprises three companies (X, Y, and Z), which constitute a vertically integrated operation. Company X sells solely to Company Y, which sells solely to Company Z, which sells solely to unaffiliated customers. In addition, Segment B sells about 10% of its production output to Segment C. Segments B and C are not vertically integrated operations. All of these intercompany sales are at prices approximating outside market prices. Assume Company Y, Company Z, and Segment C have intercompany inventory purchases on hand at the beginning and end of the current reporting year.

Required:
How are intercompany sales and intercompany profits on such intercompany inventory sales presented in disclosing industry segment information? Be specific as to effect on presenting revenues, operating profit or loss, and identifiable assets.

Exercises

Exercise 15–1
Segment reporting: Multiple choice

(1) Select the items that are part of the additional information disclosure requirements of *FASB Statement No. 14.*
  (a) Major customers
  (b) Different industries
  (c) Imports
  (d) Major suppliers
  (e) Export sales
  (f) Foreign operations

(2) Select the items that are used in one of the three 10% tests for determining reportable industry segments.
  (a) Total revenues
  (b) Operating profit or loss
  (c) Segment net income
  (d) Revenues to unaffiliated customers
  (e) Identifiable assets
  (f) Nonidentifiable assets

(3) Select the items that are to be disclosed for reportable industry segments.
  (a) Identifiable assets
  (b) Capital expenditures
  (c) Pretax accounting income
  (d) Depreciation expense
  (e) Operating profit or loss
  (f) Total revenues
  (g) Revenues from sales to unaffiliated customers and sales or transfers to other industry segments

(4) Select the items reportable by industry segment that must be reconciled to consolidated amounts.
  (a) Net income
  (b) Identifiable assets
  (c) Cost of goods sold
  (d) Operating profit or loss
  (e) Intersegment sales
  (f) Revenues

(5) Select the items that cannot be added or deducted, as the case may be, in computing the operating profit or loss of an industry segment.
  (a) Income taxes
  (b) General corporate expenses
  (c) Interest expense
  (d) Property taxes
  (e) Research and development expenses
  (f) Gain on early extinguishment of debt
  (g) Extraordinary items

Exercise 15–2
Segment reporting: True or false

Indicate whether the following statements are true or false.
  (1) The definition of revenue under *FASB Statement No. 14* includes revenues from intersegment sales or transfers.

(2) The FASB has established a basis that should be used to set prices for intersegment sales.
(3) The FASB has allowed management to determine the procedures for allocating general corporate expenses to individual segments.
(4) *FASB Statement No. 14* applies to companies having consolidated sales under $100,000,000.
(5) The emphasis of *FASB Statement No. 14* is on organizational structures—that is, branches, divisions, and subsidiaries.
(6) An industry segment is the component of a business that sells only to unaffiliated customers.
(7) The operating profit or loss of an industry segment is its revenue as defined . . . minus all operating expenses.
(8) The definition of operating expenses does not include expenses related to both revenues from sales to unaffiliated customers and revenues from inter-segment sales or transfers.
(9) Identifiable assets of an industry segment may include an allocated portion of assets used jointly by two or more segments.
(10) Management determines the grouping of products and services into appropriate industry segments.

Exercise 15–3
Segment reporting: Fill-in

Fill in the blanks with the appropriate word or phrase.
(1) If more than _____ reportable industry segments exist, a company may appropriately combine the most closely related segments into broader segments.
(2) Enough individual segments must be presented so that at least _____ % of the combined revenues (from sales to _____ _____ of all industry segments) is shown by reportable segments.
(3) An industry segment is a component of an enterprise engaged in providing a _____ or _____ or a group of related _____ and _____ primarily to _____ customers for a _____.
(4) Segment reporting is not required for _____ companies.
(5) The percentage used in the three tests for determining if an industry segment is reportable is _____.
(6) The revenues test used to determine if an industry segment is reportable is based on _____ _____, which includes sales to _____ customers and _____ sales.
(7) The revenues test and the identifiable assets test used to determine if a geographic area is separately reportable are based on _____ amounts.
(8) The three basic types of information provided for a reportable geographic area are _____, _____, and _____ _____.

Exercise 15–4
Segment reporting: Treatment of common costs

Tracey Company operates in three different industries, each of which is appropriately regarded as a reportable segment. Segment 1 contributed 60% of Tracey Company's total sales. Sales for Segment 1 were $900,000 and traceable costs were $400,000. Total common costs for Tracey were $300,000. Tracey allocates common costs based on the ratio of a segment's sales to total sales, an appropriate method of allocation. Assume a 40% income tax rate.

Required:
Determine the operating profit presented for Segment 1.

(AICPA adapted)

Exercise 15–5
Segment reporting: Determining reportable segments—
Revenues test

Harbrace Company has the following revenues (stated in thousands of dollars) for its industry segments:

Segment	Sales to Unaffiliated Customers	Intersegment Sales	Total Sales
A	$ 170		$ 170
B	150		150
C	75		75
D	300	$125	425
E	80		80
F	125		125
G	200	175	375
	$1,100	$300	$1,400

Required:
(1) Determine the reportable segments based on the revenues test.
(2) Assuming the other two 10% tests based on operating profit or loss and identifiable assets do not result in any additional reportable segments, perform the 75% test.

Exercise 15–6
Segment reporting: Determining reportable geographic areas—
Revenues test

Novich Company earns revenues (in thousands of dollars) in the following geographic areas:

Geographic Area	Sales to Unaffiliated Customers	Transfers between Geographic Areas	Total
Western Europe	$ 100	$100	$ 200
Africa	200	150	350
South America	300		300
Australia	400	100	500
Middle East	500		500
United States	1,000	150	1,150
	$2,500	$500	$3,000

Required:
Determine which foreign geographic areas are reportable areas based on the revenues test.

Exercise 15–7
Disposal of a segment: Determining amounts to be reported

The following condensed income statement for Shredder Corporation, a diversified company, is presented for the two years ended December 31, 19X7 and 19X6:

	19X7	19X6
Net sales	$5,000,000	$4,800,000
Cost of goods sold	(3,100,000)	(3,000,000)
Gross profit	$1,900,000	$1,800,000
Operating expenses	(1,100,000)	(1,200,000)
Operating income	$ 800,000	$ 600,000
Gain on sale of division	450,000	
Income before Income Taxes	$1,250,000	$ 600,000
Provision for income taxes	(625,000)	(300,000)
Net Income	$ 625,000	$ 300,000

On January 1, 19X7, Shredder entered into an agreement to sell for $1,600,000 the assets and product line of one of its separate operating divisions. The sale was consummated on December 31, 19X7, and resulted in a pretax gain on disposition of $450,000. This division's contribution to Shredder's reported pretax operating income for each year was as follows: 19X6, $(250,000) loss; 19X7, $(320,000) loss. Assume an income tax rate of 50%.

Required:
Determine the following amounts that Shredder should report in its comparative income statements for 19X7 and 19X6:
a. Income from continuing operations (after income taxes).
b. Discontinued operations.
c. Net income.

(AICPA adapted)

Exercise 15–8
Disposal of a segment: Determination of loss related
to discontinued operations

The Dangerfield Company is disposing of a segment of its business. With respect to this disposal, the following information is given:

Estimated operating loss from the measurement date to the end of the current year	$200,000
Severance pay	100,000
Relocation costs (for employees)	50,000
Actual operating loss from the beginning of the year to the measurement date	300,000
Estimated operating loss from the end of the current year to the estimated disposal date	400,000
Estimated loss on the sale of the segment's assets in the following year	500,000

The severance pay and the employee relocation costs are directly associated with the decision to dispose of this segment. Assume a 40% income tax rate.

Required:
Prepare the discontinued operations section of the income statement for the current year.

Problems

Problem 15–1
Segment reporting: Determining reportable segments—
Revenues test, operating profit or loss test, and identifiable assets test

Information (in thousands of dollars) with respect to Percento Company's industry segments for 19X1 follows:

Segment	Total Revenue	Operating Profit (Loss)	Identifiable Assets
A	$ 60	$ (10)	$ 75
B	210	100	400
C	80	(40)	125
D	190	20	100
E	170	(60)	250
F	40	10	100
G	250	110	450
	$1,000	$130	$1,500

The only intersegment revenues were $60,000 from Segment E to Segment D.

Required:
(1) Determine which industry segments are reportable segments.
(2) Perform the 75% test.

Problem 15–2
Segment reporting: Presenting industry segment information—
Intersegment inventory sales (Intercompany profit
in ending inventory)

Continental Company operates in five major industry segments, all of which are reportable segments. Financial information for each segment for 19X8 follows:

	Segment				
	A	B	C	D	E
Total revenues	$70,000	$60,000	$50,000	$40,000	$30,000
Operating profit	30,000	25,000	20,000	15,000	10,000
Indentifiable assets	40,000	35,000	30,000	25,000	20,000

Intersegment sales (included in the above total revenues) were as follows:

(1) Segment C sold inventory costing $5,000 to Segment D for $8,000. At December 31, 19X8, all of this inventory had been sold by Segment D.

(2) Segment A sold inventory costing $6,000 to Segment B for $10,000. At December 31, 19X8, 20% of this inventory had not been sold by Segment B.

Assume no intercompany inventory was on hand at December 31, 19X7, and assume a consolidated income tax return is filed. Data related to the corporate offices are as follows:

Corporate expenses	$12,000
Interest expense	18,000
Interest income	5,000
Corporate assets	15,000
Overall corporate income tax rate	40%

Required:
Prepare a report presenting industry segment information, reconciling, when required, to amounts that would appear in the consolidated financial statements. (Use the illustration in the appendix to this chapter as a guide.)

Problem 15–3
Segment reporting: Presenting industry segment information—Intrasegment and intersegment sales (Intercompany profit in beginning and ending inventories)

Pioneer Products Company has three industry segments—A, B, and C. Data (in thousands of dollars) for these segments for 19X2 are as follows:

	Revenues		Operating Profit	Identifiable Assets
	Inter-company	Unaffiliated Customers		
Segment A:				
Company X	$100		$ 30	$240
Company Y		$700	170	660
Segment B:				
Company M		300	80	310
Company N	50	560	120	490
Segment C:				
Company T		300	50	200

Additional information:
(1) Segment A is a vertically integrated operation. Company X sells all of its output to Company Y.
(2) Segments B and C are not vertically integrated operations. Company N's intercompany sales are to Company T.
(3) All intercompany sales are at prices that approximate outside market prices. Assume a 40% gross profit margin on all intercompany sales.
(4) At the end of the current reporting year, each company has 10% of its current-year intercompany inventory purchases on hand.
(5) Data relating to the corporate offices are as follows:

Corporate expenses	$35,000
Interest expense	29,000
Corporate assets	40,000

(6) Assume a consolidated federal income tax return is filed and a 40% income tax rate.

Required:
(1) Present the above data in a schedule that satisfies the disclosure requirements of *FASB Statement No. 14*, assuming no intercompany inventory purchases were on hand at the beginning of the year.
(2) Present the above data in a schedule that satisfies the disclosure requirements of *FASB Statement No. 14*, assuming (a) Company Y had $25,000 of intercompany inventory on hand at the beginning of the year, and (b) Company T had $4,000 of intercompany inventory on hand at the beginning of the year. (Assume a 40% gross profit rate for the prior year.)

Problem 15–4
Segment reporting: Presenting geographic area information— Intrageographic and intergeographic transfers (Intercompany profit in ending inventory)

Energy Enterprises has operations in the United States, Mexico, and England. Data (in thousands of dollars) with respect to these areas for 19X3 are as follows:

| | Revenues | | Operating | Identifiable |
	Inter-company	Unaffiliated Customers	Profit	Assets
United States:				
Company A		$800	$200	$300
Company B	$150	450	150	200
Company C	60	600	240	350
Mexico:				
Company X	100		30	180
England:				
Company S		280	110	90

Additional information:
(1) Company X is part of a vertically integrated industry and sells all of its output to Company B.
(2) Company B is part of a vertically integrated industry and sells part of its output to Company S.
(3) Company C's intercompany sales are to Company A.
(4) All intercompany sales are at prices that approximate outside market prices. Assume a 40% gross profit margin on all intercompany sales.
(5) At the end of the current reporting year, each company has 10% of its current-year intercompany inventory purchases on hand.
(6) Data as to the corporate offices are as follows:

General corporate expenses	$37,000
Interest expense.	28,000
Corporate assets	65,000

(7) Assume a 40% income tax rate.

Required:

Present the above data in a schedule that satisfies the disclosure requirements of *FASB Statement No. 14*, assuming no intercompany inventory purchases were on hand at the beginning of the year.

Problem 15–5
Disposal of a segment: Determining amounts to report

On June 30, 19X1, Sanchez Enterprises (a calendar year-end reporting company) announced plans to dispose of several of its segments. Data gathered at that time for these segments follow:

Seg- ment	Year-to-Date Income (Loss) from Operations	Estimated Future Income (Loss) from Operations through the Disposal Date 19X1	19X2	Estimated Gain (Loss) on Disposal	Estimated Disposal Date
A	$(400)	$(300)	$(200)	$(100)	2/1/X2
B	(100)	(400)	(300)	800	2/1/X2
C	200	(500)	100	300	2/1/X2
D	(300)	(400)		200	10/1/X1
E	(300)	(200)		400	10/1/X1
F	300	200		(400)	10/1/X1
G	200	200	200	300	3/1/X2
H	200	400	200	(300)	3/1/X2
I	600	300	(100)	(300)	3/1/X2

These amounts do not reflect income taxes.

Required:

Determine the amounts to be reported in the two categories of the discontinued operations section of the income statement for each of the above segments. Use the following reporting periods:

First and Second Quarters—19X1	Third and Fourth Quarters—19X1	First Quarter— 19X2

For simplicity, assume future operations and sales of the segments proceed according to plan. Ignore income tax effects.

Problem 15–6
Disposal of a segment: Preparing income statement and statement of retained earnings—Variety of events and transactions

Reeling Company had the following events and transactions in 19X5:

Sales...	$10,000,000[a]
Cost of goods sold (as corrected for inventory pricing error at December 31, 19X4)	5,700,000[a]

Understatement of December 31, 19X4 inventory	
(pricing error)	250,000
Marketing and administrative expenses	2,000,000[a]
Operating loss for 19X5 related to Gismo Division,	
$150,000 of which occurred after the decision	
to dispose of the division	500,000
Estimated 19X6 operating loss for Gismo Division	300,000[b]
Estimated loss on sale of Gismo Division's net assets (a separate	
industry segment), disposal to be completed in 19X6...............	550,000
Gain on early extinguishment of debt	600,000
Flood loss, uninsured	700,000[b]
Settlement of lawsuit related to 19X3	
activity (not accrued in prior years)	400,000[c]

[a] Excludes Gismo Division.
[b] The last major flood in the area was 60 years ago.
[c] From the time the lawsuit was filed in 19X3, legal counsel felt that the company would not win the lawsuit. Legal counsel could not estimate either the ultimate settlement amount or a likely range within which the settlement amount would fall. Future such lawsuits are possible.

Assume a combined federal and state income tax rate of 40%. Assume that no timing or permanent differences exist between pretax accounting income and taxable income. Retained earnings were $2,000,000 on January 1, 19X5, and cash dividends of $100,000 were declared during 19X5.

Required:
Prepare an income statement and a statement of retained earnings for 19X5.

16 Interim Reporting

OVERVIEW OF INTERIM REPORTING

Applicability

Users of financial data need continuous, timely information about the performance of an enterprise to make investment or credit-related decisions. Although it has the benefit of an independent audit, an annual report is inadequate by itself in meeting these needs. Accordingly, the reporting of quarterly financial data has become a basic part of the corporate reporting process. Quarterly periods are sufficiently short to reveal business turning points, which may be obscured in annual reports. For companies that have significant seasonal variations in their operations, quarterly financial reports may give investors a better understanding of the nature of the business.

Quarterly financial reporting is not required by any official accounting pronouncement of the FASB or any of its predecessor organizations. However, the New York Stock Exchange and the American Stock Exchange require their listed companies to furnish interim quarterly operating results to their stockholders. Companies not subject to these stock exchange listing requirements usually furnish such reports voluntarily. In fact, many privately owned companies furnish financial information to their stockholders as often as monthly.

SEC Requirements. Publicly owned companies that are subject to the continuous reporting requirements of the Securities and Exchange Commission (SEC) must file interim financial statements with the SEC on Form 10-Q. This form must be filed for each of the first three quarters of each fiscal year within 45 days after the end of each such quarter.[1] Furthermore, the SEC requires specified quarterly financial data pertaining to operations for the latest two years to be presented in the annual report sent to stockholders and in the annual financial statements that must be filed with the SEC on Form 10-K.[2] (Forms 10-Q and 10-K are discussed in detail in Chapter 17.) Such disclosures inform investors of the pattern of corporate activities throughout the year.[3]

Official accounting pronouncements

The first and still current pronouncement specifically dealing with interim reports is *APB Opinion No. 28,* "Interim Financial Reporting," which was issued in 1973. This pronouncement has been amended by *FASB Statement No. 3,* "Reporting Accounting Changes in Interim Financial Statements," and interpreted by *FASB Interpretation No. 18,* "Accounting for Income

---

[1] Companies whose securities are listed on a stock exchange and companies meeting certain size tests whose securities are traded in the over-the-counter market are subject to the continuous reporting requirements of the SEC.

[2] Proxy and Information Statement Rule 14a-3(b)(3); Form 10-K, Item 8; and Regulation S-K, Item 302 (a); (Washington, D.C.: SEC).

[3] *Accounting Series Release No. 177* (Washington, D.C.: SEC, 1975).

Taxes in Interim Periods." *APB Opinion No. 28* is divided into the following two major parts:

(1) Part I does not require interim financial reports to be issued, but sets forth accounting standards to be used in preparing them.
(2) Part II sets forth minimum disclosures to be included in interim financial reports issued by publicly owned companies.

Interim financial statements filed with the SEC on Form 10-Q must be prepared in accordance with the provisions of *APB Opinion No. 28* and any amendments. Before discussing the detailed requirements of this pronouncement and the related amendment and interpretation, we discuss the conceptual issues associated with interim reporting.

CONCEPTUAL ISSUES

The fundamental conceptual issue concerning interim financial statements (whether complete or condensed) is whether or not they should be prepared in accordance with the same accounting principles and practices used to prepare annual financial statements. This issue pertains almost solely to the recognition of costs and expenses, because accountants generally agree that for interim reporting purposes no sensible alternatives exist to the long-established practice of recognizing revenue when it is earned. The following examples of costs and expenses illustrate the problems associated with their treatment for interim reporting purposes:

(1) Major advertising expenditures. Suppose that a major advertising campaign is launched early in the year. For interim reporting purposes, should the cost be deferred as an asset and amortized throughout the year, even though no portion of advertising costs can be deferred and reported as an asset at the end of the annual reporting period?

(2) Seasonal repairs. Suppose a company historically makes major annual repairs late in the year. Accruing liabilities for future repair costs (other than warranty-related costs) is not proper at the end of an annual reporting period. Is it proper, therefore, to spread total estimated repairs throughout the year by accruing such costs in interim periods prior to their incurrence?

(3) Depreciation and rent. In most cases, depreciation and rent expenses are computed for annual reporting purposes based on the passage of time. Should a year's depreciation and rent expense be assigned to interim periods for interim reporting purposes on this same basis, or should some other basis (such as sales) be used?

(4) Social Security taxes. Social Security taxes are paid by the employer only during a portion of the year for employees who have incomes greater than the maximum amount on which employer Social Security taxes must be paid. Should the employer's Social Security taxes for these employees be charged to expense over the entire year, using deferrals?

(5) Year-end bonuses. Should year-end bonuses be anticipated and accrued for interim reporting purposes?

Three schools of thought exist concerning the approach used in interim reporting—the discrete view, the integral view, and the combination discrete–integral view.

The discrete view

Under the discrete view, an interim period is a discrete, self-contained segment of history, just as an annual period is a discrete, self-contained segment of history. Therefore, an interim period must stand on its own. From this perspective, the results of operations for each interim period are determined using the same accounting principles and practices used to prepare annual reports. No special deferral or accrual practices are used for interim reporting purposes that cannot be used for annual reporting purposes. As a result, the components of assets, liabilities, revenues, expenses, and earnings are defined for interim reporting purposes the same way as they are defined for annual reporting purposes. Under the discrete view, the function of accounting is to record transactions and events as they occur. Thus, the period of time for which results of operations are determined should not influence how such transactions and events are reported.

This approach is unacceptable to most accountants because it does not allow accruals, deferrals, and estimations at interim dates for annual items.

The integral view

Under the integral view, an interim period is an integral part of an annual period. From this perspective, the expected relationship between revenues and expenses for the annual period should be reflected in the interim periods so that reasonably constant operating profit margins can be reported throughout the year. Under this "pure form" of the integral view, annual expenses are estimated and assigned to interim periods in proportion to revenues recognized. Special deferral and accrual practices are used for interim reporting purposes that may not be used for annual reporting purposes. As a result, the components of assets, liabilities, revenues, expenses, and earnings are defined differently for interim reporting purposes than for annual reporting purposes. The costs of unforeseen events and certain other nonoperating items—such as settlement of litigation, discontinued operations, and asset disposals—are recorded in the interim period in which they occur.

This approach is also unacceptable to most accountants because of the artificial assumption that each dollar of revenue attracts the same rate of operating profit margin. Such an assumption is no more appropriate for periods within a year than it is over a company's entire life cycle.

The combination discrete–integral view

Between the extremes of the discrete view and the pure form of the integral view are various combination discrete–integral approaches. Under these approaches, the integral view is used for some costs and the discrete view is used for the remaining costs. All methods of deciding which costs are treated with integral techniques and which are treated under the discrete view are arbitrary. The remainder of this chapter discusses *APB Opinion No. 28,* which prescribes a combination discrete–integral approach.

REQUIREMENTS OF *APB OPINION NO. 28*

Revenues

> Revenue from products sold or services rendered should be recognized as earned during an interim period on the same basis as followed for the full year.[4]

This provision, which requires that each interim period be viewed as an annual period, produces the following results:

(1) Companies that have seasonal revenues must report such revenues in the interim period in which they are earned as opposed to allocating them over the full year.
(2) When receipts at an interim date precede the earnings process, the revenues are deferred until the interim period in which the product is delivered or the service is rendered.
(3) Companies using the percentage-of-completion method for long-term construction-type contracts must recognize revenues in interim periods using the same procedures that are used at the end of the annual period.

Costs associated with revenues (Product costs)

> Those costs and expenses that are associated directly with or allocated to the products sold or to the services rendered for annual reporting purposes (including for example, material costs, wages and salaries and related fringe benefits, manufacturing overhead, and warranties) should be similarly treated for interim reporting purposes. . . . Companies should generally use the same inventory pricing methods and make provisions for write-downs to market at interim dates on the same basis as used at annual inventory dates . . .[5]

Although this provision appears to treat each interim period as if it were an annual period, the following four specified exceptions allow each interim period to be viewed as part of an annual period:

(1) Estimated gross profit rates may be used to determine the cost of goods sold during interim periods. This procedure is merely a practical modification, as complete physical inventories are usually not taken at interim dates.
(2) Liquidation at an interim date of LIFO base-period inventories that the company expects to replace by the end of the annual period does not affect interim results; that is, cost of goods sold for the interim reporting

---

[4] *APB Opinion No. 28,* "Interim Financial Reporting" (New York: AICPA, 1973), paragraph 11.
[5] *APB Opinion No. 28,* paragraphs 13–14.

period should include the expected cost of replacing the liquidated LIFO base.

(3) Declines in market price at interim dates that will probably be recovered by the end of the annual period (temporary declines) "need not" be recognized at the interim date. If inventory losses from market declines are recognized at an interim date, any subsequent recoveries should be recognized as gains in those periods, but only to the extent of previously recognized losses.

(4) For companies using standard cost accounting systems, purchase price variances or volume or capacity variances of costs that are inventoriable "should ordinarily" be deferred at interim reporting dates, providing such variances are planned and expected to be absorbed by the end of the annual period.

With respect to the third exception discussed above, assume that a company has on hand at the beginning of the year 15,000 units of a particular inventory item, which are valued at their historical FIFO cost of $20 per unit. For simplicity, we assume that no additional purchases of this item are made during the year. Assumed sales for each quarter and replacement costs (assumed to be market) at the end of each quarter are as follows:

Quarter	Units Sold During Quarter	Replacement Cost at End of Quarter
1	1,000	$16 (Not considered a temporary decline)
2	2,000	14 (Considered a temporary decline)
3	3,000	17
4	4,000	21

Illustration 16-1 shows the adjustments that would be made to the Inventory account for this item during the year for market changes.

In reviewing Illustration 16-1, note that no market adjustment was made at the end of the second quarter. The market decline during that quarter was considered a temporary decline that was reasonably expected to disappear by the end of the annual period.

Note also that the use of the language "need not" in the pronouncement (as opposed to the mandatory term "should") permits companies to recognize temporary market declines in the interim period in which they occur if they choose to do so. Thus, alternative treatments for temporary market declines are sanctioned.

With respect to the fourth exception that deals with companies using standard cost accounting systems, the use of the language "should ordinarily" in the pronouncement (as opposed to an unqualified "should") permits alternative treatments for purchase price and volume variances that are planned and expected to be absorbed by year-end. In summary, *APB Opinion No. 28* allows substantial leeway in dealing with certain aspects of inventory costing and manufacturing cost variances in interim reports.

Illustration 16-1
Analysis of the Inventory account for the year

	Units		Amount
Balance, January 1	15,000 ×	$20	= $300,000
First quarter sales	(1,000) ×	20	= (20,000)
			$280,000
First quarter market adjustment	14,000 ×	(4) [$20 − $16] =	(56,000)
Balance, March 31	14,000 ×	16	= $224,000
Second quarter sales	(2,000) ×	16	= (32,000)
Balance, June 30.........................	12,000 ×	16	= $192,000
Third quarter sales	(3,000) ×	16	= (48,000)
			$144,000
Third quarter market adjustment	9,000 ×	1 [$17 − $16] =	9,000
Balance, September 30	9,000 ×	17	= $153,000
Fourth quarter sales	(4,000) ×	17	= (68,000)
			$ 85,000
Fourth quarter market adjustment	5,000 ×	3 [$20 − $17] =	15,000
Balance, December 31.....................	5,000 ×	20	= $100,000

All other costs and expenses

The Accounting Principles Board developed the following standards for all costs and expenses other than product costs:

   (a) Costs and expenses other than product costs should be charged to interim periods as incurred, or be allocated among interim periods based on an estimate of time expired, benefit received or activity associated with the periods. Procedures adopted for assigning specific cost and expense items to an interim period should be consistent with the bases followed by the company in reporting results of operations at annual reporting dates. However, when a specific cost or expense item charged to expense for annual reporting purposes benefits more than one interim period, the cost or expense item may be allocated to those interim periods.

   (b) Some costs and expenses incurred in an interim period, however, cannot be readily identified with the activities or benefits of other interim periods and should be charged to the interim period in which incurred. Disclosure should be made as to the nature and amount of such costs unless items of a comparable nature are included in both the current interim period and in the corresponding interim period of the preceding year.

   (c) Arbitrary assignment of the amount of such costs to an interim period should not be made.

   (d) Gains and losses that arise in any interim period similar to those that would not be deferred at year end should not be deferred to later interim periods within the same fiscal year.[6]

These standards do the following:

(1) Prohibit the "normalizing" or "spreading" of expenditures over a fiscal year on a revenue basis as under a pure integral approach.

(2) Require that most expenditures be treated as if each interim period were an annual reporting period.

[6] *APB Opinion No. 28,* paragraph 15. Copyright © 1973 by the American Institute of Certified Public Accountants, Inc.

(3) Permit certain expenditures that clearly benefit more than one interim period to be allocated among the interim periods benefited. Note that this treatment is **permissive—not mandatory.** Some examples of expenditures that may qualify for allocation among interim periods are major annual repairs, costs of periodic advertising campaigns. Social Security taxes, and charitable contributions.

In addition to the preceding standards, the pronouncement requires that estimation procedures be used at interim dates for items that historically have resulted in year-end adjustments (usually charges to income) or that can be reasonably approximated at interim dates. Examples are allowances for uncollectible accounts, inventory shrinkage, quantity discounts, and accruals for discretionary year-end bonuses.[7] This requirement clearly attempts to prevent the reporting of material fourth-quarter adjustments that cast a shadow on the reliability of prior interim reports and undermine the integrity of the interim reporting process.

Seasonal revenues, costs, and expenses

Many businesses—such as amusement parks, professional sports teams, farming corporations, department stores, and toy manufacturers—receive all or a major portion of their revenues in one or two interim periods. As a result, these companies report wide fluctuations in revenues and profitability in their interim reports. Such companies must disclose the seasonal nature of their activities to avoid misleading inferences about revenues and profitability for the entire year. Furthermore, these companies should consider providing supplemental financial information for the 12-month periods ended at the interim date for the current and prior years.[8]

Income tax provisions

The basic provision for the computation of income taxes for interim periods is as follows:

> At the end of each interim period the company should make its best estimate of the effective tax rate expected to be applicable for the full fiscal year. The rate so determined should be used in providing for income taxes on a current year-to-date basis. The effective tax rate should reflect anticipated investment tax credits, foreign tax rates, percentage depletion, capital gains rates, and other available tax planning alternatives.[9]

The following points concerning this provision should be understood:

(1) Each interim period is *not* a separate taxable period.
(2) If the estimated tax rate for the year changes as the year proceeds, the effect of the change is included in the appropriate interim period as a change in estimate. No retroactive restatement of prior interim

---

[7] *APB Opinion No. 28,* paragraph 17.
[8] *APB Opinion No. 28,* paragraph 18.
[9] *APB Opinion No. 28,* paragraph 19.

periods is made. The provision for income taxes for the third quarter of a company's fiscal year, for example, is the result of applying the expected tax rate to year-to-date earnings and subtracting the provisions reported for the first and second quarters.

The basic provision as stated above is supplemented for the tax effects of unusual or extraordinary items as follows.

Illustration 16-2
Calculation of estimated effective annual income tax rate and interim tax provisions

I. Assumptions:

Income before income taxes for 19X1:

First quarter (actual)	$100,000
Remainder of the year (estimated)	$500,000
Federal income tax rate	46%
State income tax rate	5%
Estimated federal investment tax credits for 19X1 (flow-through method)	$ 15,000
Estimated officers' life insurance premiums not deductible for state or federal income tax	$ 10,000

II. Calculation of Estimated Effective Annual Income Tax Rate and First Quarter Income Tax Provision:

Calculation of estimated state income taxes for 19X1:

Estimated annual income before income taxes ($100,000 + $500,000)	$600,000
Add—Officers' life insurance premiums	10,000
Estimated state taxable income for 19X1	$610,000
State income tax rate	5%
Estimated state income taxes for 19X1	$ 30,500

Calculation of estimated federal income taxes for 19X1:

Estimated annual income before income taxes ($100,000 + $500,000)	$600,000
Add—Officers' life insurance premiums	10,000
Less—State income taxes	(30,500)
Estimated federal taxable income for 19X1	$579,500
Federal income tax rate	46%
	$266,570
Less—Investment tax credits	(15,000)
Estimated federal income taxes for 19X1	$251,570

Calculation of estimated effective annual income tax rate for 19X1:

Combined estimated federal and state income taxes for 19X1 ($251,570 + $30,500)	$282,070
Estimated income before income taxes for 19X1	$600,000
Estimated effective annual income tax rate ($282,070/$600,000)	47%

Calculation of income tax provision for the first quarter:

Income before income taxes for first quarter	$100,000
Estimated effective annual income tax rate	47%
Income tax provision	$ 47,000

Illustration 16-2 (continued)

III. Calculation of Second Quarter Income Tax Provision:
At the end of the second quarter, another calculation would be made of the estimated effective annual income tax rate for 19X1 using the same procedures used at the end of the first quarter. Assume that the calculation at the end of the second quarter produces an estimated effective annual income tax rate of 45%. The calculation of the income tax provision to be reported for the second quarter, assuming second quarter income before income taxes of $180,000, is as follows:

Income before income taxes for the first six months ($100,000 + $180,000)	$280,000
Estimated effective annual income tax rate (calculated at the end of the second quarter)	45%
Cumulative income tax provision	$126,000
Less—Income tax provision reported for the first quarter	(47,000)
Income tax provision for second quarter	$ 79,000

Note that 45% of $180,000 is $81,000. The difference between this amount and the $79,000 amount calculated above is the 2% change in the estimated annual tax rate multiplied by the first quarter income before income taxes of $100,000.

> However, in arriving at this effective tax rate no effect should be included for the tax related to significant unusual or extraordinary items that will be separately reported or reported net of their related tax effect in reports for the interim period or for the fiscal year.[10]

Illustration 16-2 shows how to calculate the estimated effective annual income tax rate at interim periods and how to determine the income tax provision for the first interim quarter and subsequent interim quarters. For simplicity, the assumed facts do not involve any unusual or extraordinary items. Computing interim period income taxes is more involved when one or more of the following items is present:

(1) Unusual items reported separately.
(2) Extraordinary items reported net of related tax effects.
(3) Losses in one or more interim periods.
(4) Prior year operating loss carryforwards available.
(5) Discontinued operations.
(6) Changes in accounting principles.
(7) Effects of new tax legislation.

A discussion and illustration of each of these items is beyond the scope of this chapter. However, item (3)—losses in one or more interim periods—deserves some attention here as it relates to seasonal businesses that may have losses during early interim periods but that are expected to be profitable for the entire year. In these cases, the tax effects of losses arising in the early portion of a fiscal year are recognized only if (1) the carryback of such losses to prior years is possible; or (2) realization is assured beyond

---

[10] APB Opinion No. 28, paragraph 19

Illustration 16-3
Income tax expense or benefit to be reported for a seasonal business—
Loss in the first interim reporting period but profitable for the entire year
(in thousands of dollars)

| | Reporting Quarter | | | | Fiscal |
	1	2	3	4	Year
Income (loss) before income taxes	$(200)	$100	$150	$950	$1,000
Income tax benefit (expense) @ 40%	80	(40)	(60)	(380)	(400)
Net income (loss)	$(120)	$ 60	$ 90	$570	$ 600

reasonable doubt as a result of profitable operations expected for the entire year. A historical pattern of losses in early interim periods that have been offset by profits in later interim periods normally constitutes sufficient evidence that realization is assured beyond a reasonable doubt, unless other facts indicate that the historical pattern will not repeat.[11]

Illustration 16-3 shows the income tax expense or benefit reported in each interim reporting period for an enterprise engaged in a seasonal business that shows a loss for the first interim reporting period. We assume that the enterprise anticipates being profitable for the entire year and that this expectation proves to be correct. Established seasonal patterns ensure realization of the tax benefit related to the loss in the first interim reporting period. For simplicity, we also assume that (1) the estimated annual effective tax rate is 40%; (2) this rate does not change during the year; and (3) no unusual or extraordinary items are present.

FASB Interpretation No. 18, "Accounting for Income Taxes in Interim Periods," clarifies the application of *APB Opinion No. 28* with respect to accounting for income taxes. This interpretation, containing more than 20 detailed examples spread over more than 40 pages, shows how to compute interim period income taxes involving the more complex areas listed on page 575. You should refer to that pronouncement for a complete discussion and related examples.

Disposal of a segment of a business and extraordinary, unusual, infrequently occurring, and contingent items

The effects of the disposal of a segment of a business and extraordinary, unusual and infrequently occurring items are reported in the period in which they occur. If the effects are material in relation to the operating results of the interim period, they are reported separately.[12]

The basic thrust of *APB Opinion No. 28* concerning contingencies is a discrete approach; that is, disclosures are made in interim reports in the same manner as they are made in annual reports, except that the significance of a contingency should be judged in relation to annual financial statements.[13] *FASB Statement No. 5,* "Accounting for Contingencies," was issued after *APB Opinion No. 28.* The application of *FASB Statement No. 5* provisions to interim periods as if each interim period were an annual period is consistent with the basic thrust of *APB Opinion No. 28* in this area. Thus, the **probable**

---

[11] *APB Opinion No. 28,* paragraph 20.
[12] *APB Opinion No. 28,* paragraph 21.
[13] *APB Opinion No. 28,* paragraph 22.

and **reasonably estimatable** criteria of *FASB Statement No. 5* would be used to determine in which interim period a loss contingency should be accrued.

Accounting changes

Interim financial reports must disclose any changes in accounting principles or practices. The basic provisions of *APB Opinion No. 20,* "Accounting Changes," apply to interim reporting. Changes in accounting principles that require **retroactive restatement** of previously issued annual financial statements result in the similar restatement of previously issued interim financial statements when such accounting changes are made in other than the first interim reporting period.[14] (*APB Opinion No. 20* specifically sets forth the few changes that can be accorded retroactive restatement, such as a change in the method of accounting for long-term construction contracts.)

The **cumulative effect** of a change in accounting principles is reported as an adjustment in the current-year income statement as prescribed by *FASB Statement No. 3,* an amendment to *APB Opinion No. 28.* If such a change is made during the *first* interim reporting period, the cumulative effect as of the beginning of that year is included in the net income of that first interim reporting period. If such a change is made in *other than the first* interim reporting period, however, the prior interim reporting periods of the current year are restated by applying the new accounting principles, and the cumulative effect as of the beginning of that year is included in the restated net income of the first interim reporting period of the current year.[15] The end result, therefore, is as if all such changes had been made in the first interim reporting period.

Changes in accounting estimates must be accounted for in the interim period in which the change is made on a prospective basis, regardless of the interim period of the change. Thus, restatement of previously reported interim information is prohibited for such changes.[16]

Previously issued interim reports may be restated for corrections of an error just as previously issued annual financial statements may be restated for such items.[17]

Disclosures of summarized interim financial data by publicly owned companies

The following minimum disclosures must be furnished to stockholders in interim reports (including fourth-quarter reports):

    (a) Sales or gross revenues, provision for income taxes, extraordinary terms (including related income tax effects), cumulative effect of a change in accounting principles or practices, and net income.
    (b) Primary and fully diluted earnings per share data for each period presented . . .
    (c) Seasonal revenue, costs or expenses.
    (d) Significant changes in estimates or provisions for income taxes.

---

[14] *APB Opinion No. 28,* paragraph 25.
[15] *FASB Statement No. 3,* "Reporting Accounting Changes in Interim Financial Statements" (Stamford, CT: FASB, 1974), paragraphs 9–10.
[16] *APB Opinion No. 28,* paragraph 26.
[17] *APB Opinion No. 28,* paragraph 25.

(e) Disposal of a segment of a business and extraordinary, unusual or infrequently occurring items.
(f) Contingent items.
(g) Changes in accounting principles or estimates.
(h) Significant changes in financial position.[18]

Most publicly owned companies exceed these requirements by furnishing either a condensed or a complete income statement. These income statements (condensed or complete) are usually presented in comparative form. For reports other than the first quarter, quarterly data and **year-to-date** amounts are usually presented. Many companies also furnish complete or condensed balance sheets (usually in comparative form) in their interim reports. In addition to financial data, these interim reports usually contain a narrative discussion of interim period highlights. Illustration 16-4 is an example of an interim quarterly report.

[18] *APB Opinion No. 28*, paragraph 30.

Illustration 16-4
Example of an interim quarterly report[a]

Letter to Shareholders
for Quarterly Report

Revenues in the second quarter of 1983 were at an all-time high for the third consecutive quarter. Earnings also increased substantially over the comparable period of 1982 as well as the previous quarter in 1983. These improved financial results reflect customer acceptance of the new processor, storage, and communications products introduced in the latter half of 1982. These results are gratifying in light of the investment we have made in research and development over the last several years. We plan to continue our commitment to research and development in 1983 as these expenditures reach an all-time high.

The Company made several new product announcements during the quarter. The Model 5840, the lowest priced model of the 580 Series of large-scale computers, was announced for delivery in the fourth quarter of 1983. New 580 Series extensions and enhancements were also announced, together with the availability dates for supporting IBM's latest operating system releases (MVS/XA) for both 470 and 580 Series of large scale processors.

Amdahl was the successful bidder for a large procurement by the Australian Department of Social Security. The contract calls for us to supply various models of the 580 processor series and the 4705 communication processor. The initial equipment award is in excess of $21,000,000 over the next few years.

In May, we announced a two-for-one stock split effective June 13, 1983 for shareholders of record May 27. In June, the issuance of 1,975,000 new shares of common stock was authorized, and the public offering was completed in July by issuing 1,350,000 shares to the public and 625,000 to Fujitsu Ltd. of Japan. The net proceeds to the Company, of approximately $50,000,000, were used to reduce indebtedness under the Company's revolving credit agreements.

We look forward to a very favorable remainder of the year and beyond. The expected product cost improvements, coupled with expanding volumes on our new products, should result in continuing favorable comparisons to the prior quarters.

John C. Lewis
President and
Chief Executive Officer

Eugene R. White
Chairman of the Board

---

[a] Reprinted by permission of Amdahl Corporation.

Illustration 16-4 (continued)
Highlights

	Second Quarter		Year-to-Date	
	1983	1982†	1983	1982†
Revenues................	$180,831,000	$106,845,000	$352,451,000	$216,580,000
Income before tax and extraordinary credit ..	14,949,000	1,629,000	23,531,000	5,827,000
Income before extraordinary credit ..	8,849,000	961,000	13,831,000	3,463,000
Net income	9,649,000	961,000	17,031,000	3,463,000
Earnings per share:				
Income before extraordinary credit ..	0.20	0.02	0.31	0.09
Net income	0.22	0.02	0.38	0.09
Stockholders' equity			292,639,000	267,804,000

Amdahl Corporation
Condensed statements of consolidated operations
(dollars in thousands, except per share amounts)

	Quarter Ended		Six Months Ended	
	7/1/83	6/25/82†	7/1/83	6/25/82†
Revenues................	$ 180,831	$ 106,845	$ 352,451	$ 216,580
Cost of revenues	$ 105,455	$ 59,157	$ 212,034	$ 119,211
Engineering and development	23,754	19,393	48,087	40,498
Marketing, general, and administrative	34,901	30,361	66,197	58,916
Interest expense (income), net..........	1,772	(3,695)	2,602	(7,872)
	$ 165,882	$ 105,216	$ 328,920	$ 210,753
Income before income taxes and extraordinary credit	$ 14,949	$ 1,629	$ 23,531	$ 5,827
Provision for income taxes.................	6,100	668	9,700	2,364
Income before extraordinary credit	$ 8,849	$ 961	$ 13,831	$ 3,463
Extraordinary credit—Tax benefit of net operating loss carryforwards	800	—	3,200	—
Net income	$ 9,649	$ 961	$ 17,031	$ 3,463
Earnings per common share:				
Primary				
Income before extraordinary credit	$0.20	$0.02	$0.32	$0.09
Net income	$0.22	$0.02	$0.40	$0.09
Average outstanding shares............	43,286,000	39,355,000	42,881,000	39,744,000
Fully diluted				
Income before extraordinary credit	$0.20	$0.02	$0.31	$0.09
Net income	$0.22	$0.02	$0.38	$0.09
Average outstanding shares............	44,544,000	39,355,000	44,327,000	39,744,000

† Per share amounts and average shares outstanding have been restated to reflect a two-for-one stock split effective June 13, 1983.

Amdahl Corporation
Condensed consolidated balance sheets
(dollars in thousands)

Assets	7/1/83	12/31/82	Liabilities	7/1/83	12/31/82
Cash and short-			Current debt	$ 41,155	$ 17,320
term investments..	$ 6,756	$ 4,997	Accounts payable...	63,066	76,128
Receivables........	222,639	154,273	Accrued liabilities ...	74,524	68,152
Inventories.........	146,821	158,519			
Other current			Total current		
assets...........	24,155	21,969	liabilities	$178,745	$161,600
Total current					
assets.......	$400,371	$339,758	Long-term debt.....	122,317	78,053
			Deferred income tax		
Long-term			and tax credits ...	56,364	55,245
receivables	43,454	42,429			
Property and equip-			Stockholders'		
ment, net	206,240	183,133	equity	292,639	270,422
	$650,065	$565,320		$650,065	$565,320

The condensed statements of consolidated operations and condensed consolidated balance sheets are unaudited but include all adjustments which, in management's opinion, are necessary for a fair presentation.

Many publicly traded companies do not issue a separate report covering fourth-quarter interim results. Such companies often disclose fourth-quarter results (as outlined in paragraph 30 of *APB Opinion No. 28*) in the annual report. If the results of the fourth quarter are not furnished in a separate report or in the annual report, a company must disclose the following items recognized in the fourth quarter in a note to the annual financial statements:

(1) Disposals of segments.
(2) Extraordinary items.
(3) Unusual or infrequently occurring items.
(4) The aggregate effect of year-end adjustments that are material to the results of the fourth quarter.[19]

In addition, the effects of accounting changes made during the fourth quarter are disclosed in a note to the annual financial statements in the absence of a separate fourth-quarter report or disclosure in the annual report.[20]

Requirements of *APB Opinion No. 28* compared with the requirements of Form 10-Q

The disclosure requirements of SEC Form 10-Q are more extensive than those of *APB Opinion No. 28*. Form 10-Q requires that the following condensed financial statements be included in interim reports filed with the SEC:

(1) **Balance sheets.** Balance sheets are presented as of the end of the most recent fiscal quarter and for the end of the preceding fiscal year.

[19] *APB Opinion No. 28*, paragraph 31.
[20] *FASB Statement No. 3*, paragraph 14.

(2) **Income statements.** Income statements are presented for the most recent fiscal quarter, for the period between the end of the last fiscal year and the end of the most recent fiscal quarter (year-to-date amounts in second- and third-quarter reports), and for corresponding periods of the preceding fiscal year.

(3) **Statements of changes in financial position.** Statements of changes in financial position are presented for the period between the end of the last fiscal year and the end of the most recent fiscal quarter, and for the corresponding period of the preceding fiscal year.

As stated earlier, financial statements included in Form 10-Q reports are prepared in accordance with *APB Opinion No. 28* provisions and any amendments to the opinion that may be adopted by the FASB. Disclosures must be complete enough so that none of the information presented is misleading. Furthermore, management must provide an analysis of the quarterly results of operations. Information required in Form 10-Q may be omitted from that form if such information is contained in a quarterly report to the stockholders and a copy of that quarterly report is filed with Form 10-Q.

INVOLVEMENT OF CERTIFIED PUBLIC ACCOUNTANTS IN INTERIM REPORTING

Audited interim financial reports are virtually nonexistent. For many years prior to 1975, common deficiencies in unaudited reports included a preponderance of unusual charges and, less often, credits to income late in the year and corrections to previously issued interim financial data. In recognition of such significant, continuing deficiencies and abuses in the interim reporting process, the SEC took steps in 1975 to improve the quality of interim financial reports by effectively forcing the accounting profession to accept auditor involvement in the interim reporting process. At that time, most members of the profession did not want to be associated with interim financial reports on anything less than a complete audit basis, fearing potential lawsuits in the event interim financial report data proved to be false or misleading. The SEC obtained auditor involvement in quite an interesting way. First, it passed a rule, requiring that quarterly financial data appear in a note to the annual financial statements included in the annual 10-K report filed with the SEC. This requirement caused auditors to be "associated" with these data by virtue of reporting on the financial statements in which the note was included. This occurred even though the SEC allowed the note to be labeled "unaudited" and the auditors had not audited the data in the note.

Second, the SEC passed a rule informing auditors that the SEC presumed that auditors applied "appropriate professional standards and procedures with respect to the data in the note." Thus, auditors had to perform some form of "review" of the data included in this note. Furthermore, the SEC indicated that unless the AICPA developed professional standards and procedures in connection with reviewing the data in this note, the SEC would do so. The AICPA chose to do so, and these standards and procedures are contained in *Statement on Auditing Standards No. 36,* "Review of

Interim Financial Information."[21] Because this pronouncement is the subject of an auditing course, it is not discussed in detail here. Briefly, auditors must perform certain procedures that are **substantially less than an audit.**

Auditors are not specifically required as part of the interim reporting process to perform these review procedures during the year. Thus, the review can be made at year-end. The SEC took these steps, however, in the belief that companies would have the reviews made as part of the interim reporting process for the following reasons:

(1) The likelihood of having to revise quarterly data when the annual statements are published should be less.
(2) The likelihood of discovering needed adjustments on a timely basis should be greater, so that unusual charges and credits are less frequent in the last month of the year.
(3) The added expertise of professional accountants increases the quality of the interim reporting process.[22]

To encourage auditors to be more involved in the interim reporting process, the SEC adopted a rule in 1979 that exempts interim financial reports from a federal securities law provision automatically making certified public accountants liable for a client's false and misleading financial statements unless such accountants can prove they were diligent. (Certified public accountants are not exempted, however, from the section of the federal securities law that deals with fraud.) Even before the adoption of this rule, the opposition of auditors to involvement in the interim reporting process had, for the most part, dissipated. Most auditors of publicly held companies now encourage their clients to have the review performed as part of the interim reporting process instead of at year-end.

In 1980, the SEC revised its reporting requirements, so that (a) quarterly financial data may be presented outside of the notes to the annual financial statements, and (b) auditors must follow the AICPA's review standards and procedures regardless of the placement of the quarterly financial data.[23]

SUMMARY

Interim reporting raises the fundamental issue of whether or not interim financial statements should be prepared using the same accounting principles and practices used in preparing annual financial statements. Under the discrete view, each interim period must stand on its own without regard to the fact that it is part of an annual reporting period. Under the integral view, the fact that an interim period is part of an annual reporting period is a basis for assigning the total estimated annual costs and expenses to interim periods based on revenues to report reasonably constant operating margins. *APB Opinion No. 28* adopted a combination discrete–integral approach, whereby revenues, extraordinary items, gains or losses from the

---

[21] *Statement on Auditing Standards No. 36,* "Review of Interim Financial Information" (New York: AICPA, 1981). (This pronouncement supersedes *Statement on Auditing Standards No. 24,* which was issued in 1979.)
[22] *Accounting Series Release No. 177* (Washington, D.C.: SEC, 1975).
[23] Regulation S-K, Item 302(a)(1) and (4) (Washington, D.C.: SEC, 1980).

disposal of a segment, unusual items, and infrequently occurring items are treated under the discrete view. For costs associated with revenue (product costs), the discrete view is used. (Four specified exceptions to this rule produce integral results.) The discrete view must be used for all other costs and expenses, unless an item meets specified standards for integral treatment. If the standards are met, the company may use integral techniques. For income taxes, the integral view is prescribed.

Glossary of new terms

Discrete View: A manner of measuring interim period earnings by viewing each interim period as an independent period that must stand on its own.

Integral View: A manner of measuring interim period earnings by viewing each interim period as an integral part of an annual reporting period. Under this view, each interim period should bear part of the annual expenses that are incurred in generating revenues for the entire year.

Combination Discrete–Integral View: A manner of measuring interim period earnings by accepting the integral view for certain costs and expenses and using the discrete view for all other costs and expenses.

Review questions

1. Do the principles and practices that apply to interim reporting apply only to publicly owned companies?
2. What is the fundamental issue pertaining to interim reporting?
3. Are the issues associated with interim reporting primarily related to revenues or to costs and expenses?
4. Name the three schools of thought that exist concerning the approach to interim reporting.
5. Under which approach must each interim period stand on its own?
6. Does *APB Opinion No. 28* impose integral techniques for costs and expenses not associated with revenue? Explain.
7. What factors could cause the estimated annual income tax rate to change from quarter to quarter?
8. If fourth-quarter results are not furnished in a separate report or in the annual report, which items recognized in the fourth quarter must be disclosed in a note to the annual financial statements?

Discussion cases

Discussion case 16–1
Treatment of annual furnace relining costs

The Kole Company was formed in 19X1 to produce steel. Production commenced in October 19X2, and sales began in November 19X2. The company expects to close down its furnaces each September to reline them, which takes about a month.

Members of the controller's staff disagree on how the costs of relining the furnaces should be reported. The following approaches are advocated:

(1) Expense the costs in the period in which they are incurred.
(2) Expense the costs over the company's calendar reporting year.
(3) Expense the costs over a period from September to August of the following year.

Required:
Evaluate the theoretical soundness of these proposed treatments and comment on their conformity with the provisions of *APB Opinion No. 28.*

Discussion case 16–2
Treatment of accounting and legal fees related to reporting to stockholders

Quartex Company reports on a calendar year-end. The accounting firm that performs the annual year-end audit renders approximately one-third of its audit-related services in the fourth quarter of each calendar year and approximately two-thirds of its audit-related services in the first quarter of each calendar year. (The accounting firm renders an interim billing in the fourth quarter for services performed during that quarter.)

The legal firm that assists the company in preparing its annual 10-K report, which must be filed with the SEC within 90 days after year-end, renders all of its 10-K related services in the first calendar quarter of each year. (The legal firm renders its billing sometime in the second quarter.)

Required:
Determine how these accounting and legal fees should be reported in the quarterly financial statements.

Discussion case 16–3
Material year-end physical inventory adjustment

The Surprise Company uses a periodic inventory system and takes an annual physical inventory at year-end. Historically, the company's book to physical inventory adjustments have been insignificant. Current-year sales and production increased substantially over the prior year, and a material book to physical inventory adjustment (a shortage) occurred. Management has not determined the cause of the physical inventory adjustment.

The market price of the company's common stock rose during the year due to the favorable sales and earnings pattern reported for the first three quarters. The market price declined sharply when the company announced that the annual earnings would be below estimated amounts as a result of the large physical inventory adjustment.

Required:
(1) How should the physical inventory adjustment be reported?
(2) What are the possible consequences of large fourth-quarter adjustments?

Discussion case 16–4
Revising previously issued quarterly results

In November 1982, Tandem Computers, Inc. announced results for its fourth quarter (ended September 30, 1982) prior to the completion of its annual audit. (The company assumed that its outside auditors would not have any proposed adjustments.) In December 1982, after the auditors had completed their work, the company announced a restatement of third- and fourth-quarter results because (a) recorded sales included shipments that had occurred after the end of these quarters, and (b) previously recorded sales did not have sufficient documentation. Reported results (in millions of dollars) follow:

	Initially Reported	Restated	Decrease Amount	Percent
Sales..........	$336.9	$312.1	$(23.8)	(7)
Net income	37.3	29.9	(7.4)	(20)

After this announcement, the price of the company's common stock immediately fell 6 points, a 20% decline.[24]

Required:
(1) What are the ramifications of restating results for these quarters?
(2) If the auditors reviewed quarterly information at the end of each quarter, why did they not discover this problem at the end of the third quarter?

Discussion 16–5
Treatment of unresolved item

During its second quarter, Gambolle Company entered into a new type of transaction, which will result in the immediate reporting of substantial income. The company feels that its proposed accounting treatment is in accordance with GAAP. However, its outside auditors have been noncommittal as to whether the company's interpretation of the applicable FASB accounting standard is proper. At the end of the second quarter, the auditors indicate that they need more time to study the issue and do research. (Assume the auditors review quarterly results at year-end.)

Required:
(1) Should the company record the transaction and report the income in the second quarter? State your reasons for your position.
(2) What steps might the outside auditors take in doing research?
(3) What other steps should the auditors consider?

Exercises

Exercise 16–1
Inventory loss from market decline

An inventory loss of $420,000 from market declines occurred in April 19X6. At that time, the market decline was not considered temporary. Of this loss, $100,000 was recovered in the fourth quarter ended December 31, 19X6.

---

[24] *The San Jose Mercury,* December 9, 1982, pp. 1F and 2F.

Required:
How should this loss be reflected in the quarterly income statements for 19X6?

(AICPA adapted)

Exercise 16–2
Annual major repairs and property taxes

On January 1, 19X6, Kamm Company paid property taxes of $40,000 on its plant for calendar year 19X6. In March 19X6, Kamm made its annual major repairs to its machinery amounting to $120,000. These repairs benefit the entire calendar year's operations.

Required:
How should these expenditures be reflected in the quarterly income statements for 19X6?

(AICPA adapted)

Exercise 16–3
Year-end bonuses

In January 19X7, Milburn Company estimated that its 19X7 year-end bonuses to executives would be $240,000. The actual amount paid for 19X6 year-end bonuses was $224,000. The 19X7 estimate is subject to year-end adjustment.

Required:
What amount, if any, of expense should be reflected in the quarterly income statement for the three months ended March 31, 19X7?

(AICPA adapted)

Exercise 16–4
Percentage-of-completion method on long-term contracts

For annual reporting purposes, LBN Company appropriately accounts for revenues from long-term construction contracts under the percentage-of-completion method. In December 19X5, for budgeting purposes, LBN estimated that these revenues would be $1,600,000 for 19X6. As a result of favorable business conditions in October 19X6, LBN recognized revenues of $2,000,000 for the year ended December 31, 19X6. If the percentage-of-completion method had been used for the quarterly income statements on the same basis as followed for the year-end income statement, revenues would have been as follows:

Three months ended March 31, 19X6	$ 300,000
Three months ended June 30, 19X6	400,000
Three months ended September 30, 19X6	200,000
Three months ended December 31, 19X6	1,100,000
Total	$2,000,000

Required:
What amount of revenues from long-term construction contracts should be reflected in the quarterly income statement for the three months ended December 31, 19X6?

(AICPA adapted)

Exercise 16–5
Severance pay

During the second quarter of its current reporting year, National Scissors Company announced that it would trim its work force by 7% as a result of below-normal demand for its products. Employees being laid-off are given 3–6 weeks severance pay, depending on their length of employment.

Required:
Assuming the severance pay was paid in the second quarter, how should it be accounted for in the quarterly reports for the current year?

Problems

Problem 16–1
Income tax provision—Change in estimated rate

Dimex Company had the following pretax income for the first two reporting quarters of 19X2:

First quarter	$500,000
Second quarter	700,000

Dimex's actual annual effective income tax rate for 19X1 was 40%. For budgeting purposes, Dimex estimated that the effective annual income tax rate for 19X2 would also be 40%. Near the end of the second quarter, Dimex ordered a substantial amount of equipment, on which it can claim an investment tax credit this year. The equipment will be delivered during the third quarter and will become operational during the fourth quarter. The investment credit applicable to this equipment purchase will reduce the estimated effective income tax rate for 19X2 to 35%. Dimex issues its quarterly reports within 45 days of the end of the quarter.

Required:
Determine the amount of income tax expense reported for the first and second quarters of 19X2.

Problem 16–2
Incentive compensation plan for sales personnel

Selmore Company uses an incentive system for its sales personnel whereby each salesperson receives:

(1) A base salary of $1,000 per month.
(2) A commission of 2% of the individual salesperson's sales.
(3) A bonus of 10% on the individual salesperson's annual sales in excess of $1,200,000. (This bonus is paid in the first quarter of the year following the year on which the bonus is based.)

The company's sales do not occur in a seasonal pattern. Sales generated by certain sales personnel for the first and second quarters of 19X3 are as follows:

	First Quarter	Second Quarter	Cumulative
Arlo	$ 400,000	$ 350,000	$ 750,000
Guthrie	340,000	220,000	560,000
Seeger	260,000	380,000	640,000
Weaver.................................	280,000	290,000	570,000
Total	$1,280,000	$1,240,000	$2,520,000

Payments made during the first quarter of 19X3 for bonuses based on total 19X2 sales are as follows:

Arlo..	$24,000
Weaver	3,000

Required:
Determine the amount of compensation reported as expense for the first and second quarters of 19X3 using two different approaches for the bonuses.

Problem 16–3
Calculation of estimated effective annual income tax rate and interim tax provisions

Datamex Company has developed the following data for 19X2 at the end of its first reporting quarter:

Income before income taxes:	
First quarter (actual)	$200,000
Remainder of year (estimated).......................................	$800,000
Federal income tax rate...	50%
State income tax rate	10%
Estimated federal investment tax credits	$ 70,500
Officers' life insurance premiums not deductible for state or federal purposes	$ 10,000
Excess of accelerated depreciation over straight-line depreciation for state and federal purposes	$ 50,000

Required:
(1) Calculate the estimated effective annual income tax rate at the end of the first quarter.
(2) Calculate the income tax provision for the first quarter.
(3) Calculate the estimated effective annual income tax rate at the end of the second quarter assuming:
   (a) Income before income taxes for the second quarter was $400,000.
   (b) The estimated income before income taxes for the third and fourth quarters is $500,000 in total.
(4) Calculate the income tax provision for the second quarter.

Problem 16–4
COMPREHENSIVE   Identifying weaknesses in an interim report and evaluating treatment of selected items

The Miller Manufacturing Company, which is listed on the American Stock Exchange, budgeted activities for 19X5 as follows:

	Amount	Units
Net sales	$6,000,000	1,000,000
Cost of goods sold	3,600,000	1,000,000
Gross margin	$2,400,000	
Selling, general, and administrative expenses	1,400,000	
Operating income.....	$1,000,000	
Nonoperating revenue and expenses	-0-	
Income before Income Taxes	$1,000,000	
Estimated income taxes (current and deferred)	550,000	
Net Income	$ 450,000	
Earnings per share of common stock	$4.50	

The company has operated profitably for many years and has experienced a seasonal pattern of sales volume and production similar to the ones forecasted for 19X5. Sales volume is expected to follow a quarterly pattern of 10%, 20%, 35%, and 35%, respectively, because of the seasonality of the industry. Because of production and storage capacity limitations, production is expected to follow a pattern of 20%, 25%, 30%, and 25% per quarter, respectively.

At the conclusion of the first quarter of 19X5, the controller prepared and issued the following interim report for public release:

	Amount	Units
Net sales	$ 600,000	100,000
Cost of goods sold	360,000	100,000
Gross margin	$ 240,000	
Selling, general, and administrative expenses	275,000	
Operating loss	$ (35,000)	
Loss from warehouse fire	(175,000)	
Loss before Income Taxes	$(210,000)	
Estimated income taxes	-0-	
Net Loss	$(210,000)	
Loss per share of common stock.....	$(2.10)	

The following additional information is available for the first quarter just completed but was not included in the information released to the public:

(a) The company uses a standard costing system, in which standards are set annually at currently attainable levels. At the end of the first quarter, an underapplied fixed factory overhead (volume variance) of $50,000 was treated as an asset at the end of the quarter. Production during the quarter was 200 000 units, of which 100,000 units were sold.

(b) The selling, general, and administrative expenses were budgeted on a basis of $900,000 fixed expenses for the year plus $0.50 variable expenses per unit of sales.

(c) Assume that the warehouse fire loss met the conditions of an extraordinary loss. The warehouse had an undepreciated cost of $320,000; $145,000 was recovered from insurance on the warehouse. No other gains or losses are anticipated this year from similar events or transactions, nor has the company had any similar losses in preceding years; thus, the full loss is deductible as an ordinary loss for income tax purposes.

(d) The effective income tax rate, for federal and state taxes combined, is expected to average 40% of earnings before income taxes during 19X5. No permanent differences exist between pretax accounting earnings and taxable income.

(e) Earnings per share were computed on the basis of 100,000 shares of capital stock outstanding. Miller has only one class of stock issued, no long-term debt outstanding, and no stock option plan.

Required:

(1) Without reference to the specific situation described above, what standards of disclosure exist for interim financial data (published interim financial reports) for publicly traded companies? Explain.

(2) Identify the form and content weaknesses of the interim report without reference to the additional information.

(3) Indicate for interim reporting purposes the preferable treatment for each of the five items of additional information and explain why that treatment is preferable.

(AICPA adapted)

17 Securities and Exchange Commission Reporting

OVERVIEW OF SEC REPORTING

Historical background

The nature of securities is such that their purchase and sale can create substantial opportunities for misrepresentation, manipulation, and other fraudulent acts. In reaction to a rapidly increasing number of flagrant abuses in this area, all but one state enacted some form of legislation between 1911 and 1933 to regulate the purchase and sale of corporate securities. Commonly referred to as the **blue sky laws,** these laws vary widely among the states. In addition, because these laws apply only to intrastate transactions, from an overall standpoint in protecting the public, they have proved to be ineffective. The stock market crash of 1929, testimonial to the inadequacy of this type of regulation, was preceded by (1) the issuance of billions of dollars of securities during the preceding decade that proved to be worthless; (2) the excessive use of credit to purchase stocks on margin; (3) the extensive manipulation of stock prices by various means; (4) the extensive use of inside information by officers and directors for purposes of self-enrichment; and (5) lax standards governing the solicitation of votes from shareholders whereby managements were often able to perpetuate themselves in power. The magnitude of the inadequate financial reporting and questionable ethical standards that led to this financial collapse substantially undermined the integrity of the capital markets and thus raised serious questions concerning the survival of our system of free capital markets.

To restore investor confidence and reestablish integrity in the capital markets, Congress passed the Securities Act of 1933 (the 1933 Act) and the Securities Exchange Act of 1934 (the 1934 Act). These two Acts do not replace the intrastate regulation provided by the blue sky laws but merely supplement them. The 1933 Act applies to the initial distribution of securities to the public. The purpose of the Act, as expressed in its preamble, is

> To provide full and fair disclosure of the character of securities sold in interstate and foreign commerce and through the mails, and to prevent frauds in the sale thereof . . .

This required disclosure is accomplished by "registering" securities with the Securities and Exchange Commission (the SEC) before they may be offered to the public. The registration procedure involves filing specified financial and nonfinancial information with the SEC for examination.

The 1934 Act applies to the subsequent trading in outstanding securities that are listed on organized stock exchanges and in the over-the-counter markets. The purpose of the Act, as expressed in its preamble, is

> To provide for the regulation of securities exchanges and of over-the-counter markets operating in interstate and foreign commerce and through the mails to prevent inequitable and unfair practices on such exchanges and markets . . .

Companies that come under the provisions of the 1934 Act must file periodic reports with the SEC of specified financial and nonfinancial information. In addition, certain practices are prohibited.

Because each Act constitutes a major piece of legislation, we cannot discuss them in great detail in one chapter. Accordingly, this chapter provides you with a general familiarity with (1) selected portions of each Act, and (2) the means of complying with the financial reporting requirements established by the SEC.

Functions of the SEC

Before discussing the two Acts, we must discuss the functions and organizational structure of the Securities and Exchange Commission. The SEC is a quasi-judicial agency of the U.S. government that was created in 1934 to administer the 1933 Act and the 1934 Act, the 1933 Act having been administered for one year by the Federal Trade Commission. Since that time, the SEC's responsibilities have broadened so that it now administers and enforces the following additional Acts:

(1) **The Public Utility Holding Company Act of 1935.** This Act requires geographic integration of operations and simplification of unduly cumbersome and complex capital structures of public utility holding companies. Because these objectives were accomplished many years ago through the registration process, current efforts are directed toward maintaining the status quo.

(2) **The Trust Indenture Act of 1939.** This Act requires the use of a trust indenture that meets certain requirements for debt securities offered to the public to protect the rights of investors in such securities. Although a separate Act, it is substantively an amendment to the 1933 Act.

(3) **The Investment Company Act of 1940.** This Act regulates investment companies, that is, companies engaged primarily in the business of investing, reinvesting, owning, holding, or trading in securities. Mutual funds are the most visible investment companies. Regulation is effected through the registration process.

(4) **The Investment Advisers Act of 1940.** This Act regulates the conduct of investment advisers similarly to the manner in which the conduct of brokers and dealers is regulated under the 1934 Act. Regulation is effected through the registration process.

Organizational structure of the SEC

The Securities and Exchange Commission is composed of five members appointed by the President, with the advice and consent of the Senate, for a five-year term, with one term expiring each year. No more than three members may be of the same political party. An extensive professional staff—comprising primarily lawyers, accountants, and financial analysts—has been organized into the following separate offices and divisions.

Offices	**Divisions**
Administrative Law Judges	Corporate Regulation
Opinions and Review	Investment Management
The Secretary	Corporation Finance
The Chief Accountant	Enforcement
The Chief Economic Adviser	Market Regulation
The General Counsel	
The Executive Director	

The following additional offices report to the Executive Director:
- Consumer Affairs
- Public Affairs
- Reports and Information Services
- Comptroller
- Data Processing
- Administrative Services
- Personnel

These offices and divisions are responsible to the Commission and carry out its orders and legal responsibilities. In addition to this bureaucracy located in Washington, D.C., nine regional offices and eight branch offices are located in major cities throughout the country.

The roles of the Office of the Chief Accountant and the Division of Corporation Finance are pertinent to this chapter. The Chief Accountant is the Commission's chief accounting officer for all accounting and auditing matters in connection with the administration of the various Acts. The Chief Accountant advises the Commission of accounting problems and recommends courses of action. Administratively, the Chief Accountant drafts rules and regulations governing the form and content of the financial statements that must be filed with the Commission under the various Acts.

The Division of Corporation Finance reviews the registration statements and reports that registrants file with the SEC. The review determines (1) that all required financial statements and supporting schedules have been included, and (2) that such financial statements apparently have been prepared in accordance with generally accepted accounting principles, as well as the rules, regulations, and policies issued by the SEC. Because the SEC does not perform audits of registrants' financial statements, it cannot absolutely determine whether they have been prepared in accordance with generally accepted accounting principles. For this, it relies on the reports of registrants' outside certified public accountants (we discuss this later in the chapter).

ROLE OF THE SEC IN RELATION TO THE FASB

Statutory authority of the SEC

Under the 1933 Act and the 1934 Act, the SEC has the power to

(1) Adopt, amend, and rescind rules and regulations as necessary to carry out the provisions of these Acts.
(2) Prescribe the form or forms on which required information is filed with the SEC.

(3) Prescribe the accounting methods to be followed in the financial statements filed with the SEC.
(4) Prescribe the items or details to be shown in the financial statements filed with the SEC.

In item (3), the SEC has the statutory authority to prescribe accounting principles for companies falling under its jurisdiction. In recognition of the expertise and substantial resources of the public accounting profession, however, the SEC historically has looked to the accounting profession's standard-setting bodies to establish and improve accounting and reporting standards. When the FASB was established in 1973, for instance, the SEC specifically announced that

> principles, standards and practices promulgated by the FASB in its Statements and Interpretations will be considered by the Commission as having substantial authoritative support and those contrary to such FASB promulgations will be considered to have no such support. [*Accounting Series Release No. 150, 1973*][1]

This policy of looking to the private sector in establishing and improving standards is by no means an abdication of its responsibilities or authority. When the SEC has concluded that such bodies were moving too slowly or in the wrong direction, it has not hesitated to take one of the following courses of action:

(1) Establish its own additional financial reporting requirements (calling for additional disclosures).
(2) Impose a moratorium on accounting practices.
(3) Overrule a pronouncement of the FASB.

Concerning items (1) and (2), the SEC, in most instances, has subsequently rescinded its own action as a result of the passage of new or revised accounting principles or disclosure requirements by the profession's standard-setting bodies. The following two paragraphs contain examples of the most recent major actions of the SEC along these lines.

Examples of additional disclosures required.   The SEC imposed line-of-business disclosure requirements long before the 1976 issuance of *FASB Statement No. 14,* "Financial Reporting for Segments of a Business Enterprise." Shortly after the statement was issued, the SEC modified its previous line-of-business disclosure requirements to conform in most respects with the requirements of *FASB Statement No. 14.* In 1976, the SEC required certain large companies to disclose replacement cost data (*Accounting Series Release No. 190*). After *FASB Statement No. 33,* "Financial Reporting and Changing Prices," was issued in 1979, the SEC rescinded its requirements in this area.

---

[1] In April 1982, *Accounting Series Release No. 150* was codified in *SEC Financial Reporting Release No. 1,* Section 101.

Examples of prohibiting accounting practices. In 1974, the SEC imposed a moratorium on the capitalization of interest (*Accounting Series Release No. 163*). The SEC had noted with concern an increase in the number of companies changing their accounting methods to a policy of capitalizing interest cost. Because no authoritative statement on this subject existed at that time (except for two specific industries), this action stopped a developing trend until the FASB could deal with the issue. In 1979, after the FASB issued *FASB Statement No. 34,* "Capitalization of Interest Cost," the SEC rescinded its moratorium. In 1983, the SEC moved to halt the spread of a controversial accounting method that more than a dozen computer software companies were using to increase their earnings. The SEC had noticed a trend in the industry toward capitalization without adequate criteria— the accounting standards and related interpretation that existed then were somewhat fuzzy. Therefore, the SEC imposed a moratorium on the capitalization of software development costs for companies that had not publicly disclosed the practice of capitalizing those costs prior to April 14, 1983. The SEC will reconsider the moratorium after the FASB has considered the issue and developed adequate guidance (*Financial Reporting Release No. 12*).

Overruling the FASB. Only once has the SEC overruled a pronouncement of the FASB. This ruling occurred in 1978 when the SEC rejected the standards set forth in *FASB Statement No. 19,* "Financial Accounting and Reporting for Oil and Gas Producing Companies." The SEC favored developing a new system of "reserve recognition accounting" (RRA). The conflict between the requirements of *FASB Statement No. 19* and those of the SEC (as set forth in *Accounting Series Release No. 253*) resulted in an untenable situation. (Privately owned companies were subject to *FASB Statement No. 19* and publicly owned companies were subject to *ASR No. 253.* Lack of comparability resulted.) Accordingly, the FASB voluntarily (and to be practical) issued *FASB Statement No. 25,* which suspended the effective dates of most requirements in *FASB Statement No. 19.* In 1981, the SEC abandoned its effort to develop RRA and announced it would support FASB efforts to develop disclosure requirements for oil and gas producers. In 1982, the FASB issued *FASB Statement No. 69,* "Disclosures about Oil and Gas Producing Activities," which amended *FASB Statements No. 19* and *No. 25.* Shortly thereafter, the SEC amended its disclosure requirements for oil and gas producers to require compliance with the provisions of *FASB Statement No. 69.*

Current working relationship. The SEC and the FASB now try to maintain a close working relationship to prevent any future conflicts. FASB members meet with SEC Commissioners on a regular basis to exchange information on the status of projects and plans, and to discuss other matters of mutual interest. Members of the Chief Accountant's staff are responsible for keeping track of the development of specific FASB technical projects. SEC staff members participate in advisory task force meetings on those projects and frequently observe FASB meetings. When the SEC proposes changes to its rules and regulations, the FASB has occasionally expressed its views on such proposals. In summary, both organizations strive for a climate of mutual cooperation and non-surprise.

Enforcement role

In reviewing financial statements filed with it, the SEC does not hesitate to question the accounting and reporting practices used, regardless of whether a registrant's outside auditors concur with the registrant's accounting treatment. Unlike the FASB, the SEC can order companies to revise their financial statements if it concludes a particular accounting treatment is not proper. The following are examples of such SEC actions taken in 1983 and 1984:

(1) Financial Corporation of America had to restate its net income for the first half of 1984 to a loss of $(79.9) million from the previously reported profit of $75.3 million. The SEC required the company to change its method of accounting for its reverse repurchase agreement transactions.
(2) BankAmerica Corporation had to reclassify as an extraordinary item a $30.8 million gain from a debt-equity exchange that it previously reported as part of operating income.
(3) Aetna Life & Casualty Company was prohibited from giving tax effects to items through the use of the operating loss carryforward provisions of *APB Opinion No. 11.*

During economically troubled times, the SEC usually scrutinizes financial reports closely, because fraudulent and deceptive practices are much more likely when companies attempt to conceal their financial difficulties. Overall, the SEC is given high marks and has won the reputation as a tough police officer of corporate conduct.

SEC PROMULGATIONS

To carry out its responsibilities, the SEC issues various rules, Regulations (a group of Rules), releases, and staff accounting bulletins, and prescribes certain forms that companies must use in filing registration statements and reports. The 1933 Act and the 1934 Act each has its own individual regulations, rules, releases, and forms. In addition, certain regulations and releases apply to both the 1933 Act and the 1934 Act. The Staff Accounting Bulletins also apply to both Acts. An understanding of all of these items is essential to comply with the registration and reporting requirements of these Acts. Accordingly, we now define and discuss these various items.

The general rules and regulations; forms; releases

The general rules and regulations. The Securities Act of 1933 is divided into 26 sections, and the 1934 Act is divided into 35 sections. The SEC has adopted rules pertaining to the 1933 Act, which are assigned three-digit numbers starting with 100. The rules are grouped into various categories, most of which are designated regulations. For example, Rules 400–494 make up Regulation C, which deals with the mechanics of registering securities with the SEC.

Rules and regulations pertaining to the 1934 Act are assigned numbers that correspond to the section of the Act to which they relate. The major sections of the Act are referred to as regulations, and the detailed rules within each regulation are rules. For example, Section 10(b) of the Act is called Regulation 10B, and the individual rules within that section are referred to as Rule 10b-1 through Rule 10b-17.

Forms.   The forms are enumerations of the form and content of the information included in registration statements and reports. (They are not blank forms to be filled out, as the term is used by the Internal Revenue Service and other taxing authorities.) Each Act has its own forms.

Releases.   Releases are announcements pertaining to the various rules, regulations, and forms. Releases are numbered sequentially as issued. To date, approximately 6,500 releases have been issued under the 1933 Act and approximately 20,000 under the 1934 Act. A release is formally designated as follows: Securities Act of 1933, Release No. 5307. A release is informally referred to simply as Release 33-5307, for example, under the 1933 Act, and Release 34-9310, for example, under the 1934 Act. Some SEC releases under the 1934 Act also apply under the 1933 Act. In these cases, a release is assigned a number under the 1933 Act and a different number under the 1934 Act. Except for Interpretative Releases, they are subject to the Administrative Procedures Act and must be exposed for public comment before becoming effective. The primary matters to which these releases pertain are as follows:

(1) Proposals to amend or adopt new rules and forms. Changes are often necessary to keep up with the times. In some instances, better ways of disclosure are found. For example, to improve the readability of information provided to investors, the SEC issued Release 33-5164, which proposed certain amendments to Rules 425A and 426 of the Securities Act of 1933.

   Interested companies and certified public accountants usually make comments and suggestions to the SEC. The final adopted amendment or new rule or form probably reflects many of these comments and suggestions. Sometimes, a proposed item is not adopted for various reasons.

(2) Adoption of amendments or new rules and forms. To continue with the preceding example, the proposals contained in Release 33-5164 were revised to reflect the comments and suggestions that the SEC considered significant and were subsequently adopted in Release 33-5278.

Regulation S-K and Regulation S-X

In 1983, the SEC concluded its efforts to integrate the disclosure requirements of the 1933 Act and the 1934 Act. At that time, the SEC outlined (a) all nonfinancial statement disclosure requirements in Regulation S-K and (b) all financial statement disclosure requirements in Regulation S-X. Previously, each form (under the 1933 Act and the 1934 Act) contained its own specific, detailed financial and nonfinancial statement disclosure requirements. The specific disclosures are now centralized in Regulations S-K and S-X. Each Form under the 1933 Act and the 1934 Act now merely specifies the disclosures contained in Regulations S-K and S-X that are to be made for that form.

Regulation S-K (Nonfinancial statement disclosure requirements). The major disclosure requirements contained in Regulation S-K deal with (a) a description of the company's business; (b) a description of the company's properties; (c) a description of the company's legal proceedings; (d) selected financial data for the last five years (including sales, income from continuing operations, cash dividends per common share, total assets, and long-term obligations); (e) supplementary financial information (quarterly financial data and information on the effects of changing prices); (f) information about the company's directors and management (including management remuneration); and finally (g) management's discussion and analysis (commonly referred to as the "MDA") of financial condition and results of operations.

Regulation S-X (Financial statement disclosure requirements). Regulation S-X, which accountants deal with most often, not only lists the **specific financial statements** that must be filed under all Acts administered by the SEC but also details the **form and content of such financial statements.** The term **financial statements** as used in this Regulation includes all notes to the financial statements and all related financial statement supporting schedules. The financial statements filed under Regulation S-X are (a) audited balance sheets as of the end of the two most recent fiscal years, and (b) audited statements of income and changes in financial position for the three fiscal years preceding the date of the most recent audited balance sheet being filed. (Variations from these requirements are permitted for certain specified filings.) In addition, the regulation gives requirements for filing interim financial statements. A detailed discussion of Regulation S-X is presented later in the chapter.

Accounting Series Releases (ASRs) and Staff Accounting Bulletins (SABs)

Accounting series releases (ASRs). The Accounting Series Releases, numbered sequentially, pertain solely to accounting matters. Until their discontinuance in 1982, over 300 Accounting Series Releases were issued. These releases pertain to the following major areas of accounting:

(1) Adoption of amendment or revision of Regulation S-X. Many ASRs include financial reporting requirements that go beyond the pronouncements of the FASB and its predecessor organizations. In addition to setting forth an amendment or revision to Regulation S-X, such ASRs also discuss (a) the purpose of the new reporting requirements, and (b) comments received in response to the SEC's proposed revisions to Regulation S-X (including the SEC's reaction to those comments).

In some cases, an ASR contains exhibits and examples to assist companies in understanding and complying with the new reporting requirements of Regulation S-X.

Many ASRs have been rescinded as a result of the issuance of subsequent accounting pronouncements. However, the SEC rescinds such requirements only when it concurs with an accounting pronouncement.

(2) Policy/interpretive statements regarding particular accounting areas. *Accounting Series Releases 130, 135, 146,* and *146A,* for example, deal with how the SEC interprets certain provisions of *APB Opinion No. 16,* "Accounting for Business Combinations." Thus, accountants must be familiar with such releases in addition to the provisions of the professional pronouncements. (Recall that *Accounting Series Releases 146* and *146A* were discussed in Chapter 6 in connection with pooling of interests accounting.)

(3) Disciplinary proceedings against certified public accountants. Approximately 75 releases have dealt with substandard auditing procedures by certified public accountants. In some instances, the certified public accountants have been barred from practicing before the SEC or accepting new publicly owned companies as clients for a stipulated period of time. In other instances the SEC has required accounting firms to improve their audit procedures and practices.

In June 1982, the SEC separated these releases into two distinct categories, creating the following two new series of releases:

(1) Financial Reporting Releases (FRRs). Accounting Series Releases dealing with financial reporting matters were codified and issued as *Financial Reporting Release No. 1.* (Only Accounting Series Releases that had continuing relevance to financial reporting were codified.) This codification (with its topical index) makes thousands of pages of material available in a concise and much more accessible format. To date, 15 additional Financial Reporting Releases have been issued.

(2) Accounting and Auditing Enforcement Releases (AAERs). This series of releases announces accounting and auditing matters related to the SEC's enforcement activities. Because of their nature, AAERs are not codified.

Staff Accounting Bulletins (SABs). The Staff Accounting Bulletins represent interpretations and practices followed by certain departments of the SEC that are responsible for reviewing the disclosure requirements of the federal securities laws. These bulletins do not constitute official rules or regulations, nor do they have the official approval of the SEC. The bulletins essentially accomplish on an informal basis what otherwise would be dealt with formally through releases. Much of the subject matter of the bulletins arises from specific questions raised by registrants. The dissemination of answers to these questions in this manner rather than solely to the company making an inquiry avoids needless repetition of inquiries pertaining to the same subject. Over 50 SABs have been issued to date. In 1981, the staff codified by topic all bulletins issued to date in *Staff Accounting Bulletin No. 40,* making the SABs substantially more easy to use.

SECURITIES ACT OF 1933

Registration

The Securities Act of 1933 prohibits sales of, or offers to sell, **securities** to the public (in interstate commerce or through the use of the mails) by an **issuer** or an **underwriter** unless the securities have been registered with the SEC. Certain exemptions to this prohibition are discussed later in the chapter. A security is defined broadly as follows:

> any note, stock, treasury stock, bond, debenture, evidence of indebtedness, certificate of interest or participation in any profit-sharing agreement, . . . transferable share, investment contract, voting trust certificate, . . . or in general any interest or instrument commonly known as a security. . . .

To avoid having a technical loophole in the law, the prohibition also applies to underwriters. An underwriter is defined as follows:

> any person who has purchased from an issuer with a view to, or offers or sells for an issuer in connection with, the distribution of any security, or participates [directly or indirectly] . . . in any such undertaking. . . .

It is important at this point to understand that registration under the 1933 Act refers only to the **actual quantity** of securities being registered and not the registration of an **entire class** of securities. This is just the opposite of the 1934 Act, which is discussed in detail later in the chapter.

Essence of registration.   Registration of a security offering under the 1933 Act begins with the filing of specified financial and nonfinancial information with the SEC using the appropriate form. The appropriate SEC form in a particular case is a legal determination. All specified financial and nonfinancial information submitted as set forth in the appropriate form is called a **registration statement.** The SEC then examines the registration statement and almost always issues a **letter of comments** (commonly referred to as a **deficiency letter**). The registrant must respond to this letter of comments to the SEC's satisfaction before it may sell the securities to the public. Responding to a letter of comments usually involves a combination of (a) direct written responses to the SEC in a letter; (b) revision of certain information in the registration statement; and (c) addition of information to the statement. The revised registration statement, called an **amended registration statement,** is filed with the SEC for reexamination. When the SEC is satisfied that the items in its letter of comments have been appropriately addressed, it permits the amended registration statement to become "effective," and the securities being offered are deemed registered under the 1933 Act and may be sold to the public.

Prospectuses.   Prospective investors in a security being registered with the SEC under the 1933 Act must be furnished a prospectus. The registration statement is divided into two basic parts:

Part I   Information required to be included in
            the prospectus.

Part II   Information not required to be included
in the prospectus.

Part I is the major part of the registration statement. It includes all required financial statements and related notes (according to the provisions of Regulation S-X), and reports by the registrant's auditors on financial statements that must have been audited. Part I also includes, among other things, such nonfinancial information as an extensive description of the registrant's business (including risk factors associated with the purchase of the securities offered) and properties, an explanation of how the proceeds are to be used, a description of any current legal proceedings, the names of the registrant's directors and officers (including their backgrounds), and the amount of remuneration of directors and officers. The financial and nonfinancial disclosures included in the prospectus should provide potential investors with an adequate basis for deciding whether to invest in the securities offered. Preliminary prospectuses, which may be distributed to potential investors before the effective date, are commonly referred to as "red herrings" because certain information on the cover is printed in red ink.

Part II of the registration statement lists all exhibits filed with the registration statement and includes specified financial statement supporting schedules and other miscellaneous information not deemed necessary for distribution to potential investors.

Regulation C.   Regulation C deals with the mechanics of registering securities under the 1933 Act. A company's legal counsel usually assumes responsibility for ensuring that the registration statement complies with Regulation C.

Unlawful representations relating to registration statements.   The 1933 Act expressly states the responsibility of the SEC with respect to its examination of registration statements as follows:

> Neither the fact that the registration statement for a security has been filed or is in effect . . . shall be deemed a finding by the Commission that the registration statement is true and accurate on its face or that it does not contain an untrue statement of fact or omit a material fact, or be held to mean that the Commission has in any way passed upon the merits of, or given approval to, such security. It shall be unlawful to make, or cause to be made, to any prospective purchaser any representation contrary to the foregoing provisions of this section [Section 23].

A statement to this effect must be made on the cover page of each prospectus. The SEC cannot evaluate the investment quality of the securities offered. This contrasts sharply with the blue sky laws of many states, which allow state regulatory commissions to prohibit the sale of securities considered potentially fraudulent, dangerously speculative, or lacking sufficient investment quality.

Exemptions from registration

Certain types of securities and securities transactions, which have no practical need for registration or for which the benefits of registration are too remote, are exempt from the registration requirements. The major categories of exemptions are discussed below.

Regulation A offerings.   Regulation A (Rules 251–263 of the 1933 Act) pertains to offerings whose total amount, together with other exempt offerings within a one-year period, does not exceed $1,500,000. If the total offering price is more than $100,000, however, a Regulation A Offering Statement (containing specified financial and nonfinancial information) must be filed with a regional or branch office of the SEC for examination. Furthermore, an offering circular (Part II of the Offering Statement) must be furnished to prospective purchasers.

Regulation D offerings.   Regulation D (Rules 501–506 of the 1933 Act) was adopted in 1982 to facilitate the capital-raising process for small companies. The amount of offerings exempted within a 12-month period is $500,000 or $5,000,000, depending on the type of company and whether it is subject to the continuous reporting requirements of the SEC. Under Regulation D, only a notice of the sale must be filed with the SEC (on Form D).

Private offerings.   The 1933 Act exempts "transactions by an issuer not involving a public offering [Section 4(2)]." Such transactions are also commonly referred to as **private placements.** This exemption is available for offerings to persons (individuals, partnerships, and corporations) having access to substantially the same information concerning the issuer that registration would provide and who can fend for themselves.[2] The fundamental consideration in determining whether this exemption applies is the potential investor's level of sophistication and such investor's access to information about the issuer. Generally, sophisticated investors have either sufficient economic power or a family or employment relationship that enables them to obtain adequate information from the issuer for purposes of evaluating the merits and risks of the investment. Private offerings are commonly made to venture capital firms and insurance companies. Because the security is not sold through a public offering, it is referred to as a **restricted security.** The restrictions are discussed in the following exemption category.

Transactions by individual investors.   The 1933 Act exempts "transactions by any person other than an issuer, underwriter, or dealer [Section 4(1)]." This section was intended to exempt only transactions between individual investors with respect to securities already issued and not distributions by issuers or acts of other individuals who engage in steps necessary to such distributions.[3] Investors who acquire an issuer's securities by means that do not involve a public offering (such as a private offering) may resell the securities to the public other than through registration only if certain conditions are met. Otherwise, the sale is considered a distribution of securities to the public because the investor is acting as a conduit for sale to the public on behalf of the issuer—that is, as an underwriter. In

---

[2] *SEC v. Ralston Purina Co.,* 346 U.S. 119 (1953).
[3] *SEC v. Chinese Consol. Benev. Ass'n.,* 120 F.2d 738 (2nd. Cir., 1941). *Certiorari* denied, 314 U.S. 618.

such cases, the resale of the security to the public must be registered. Rule 144 sets forth conditions that must be satisfied to resell restricted securities to the public other than through registration. This rule emphasizes that (a) the investor must have paid for and held the security for a reasonable period of time (a minimum of two to four years, depending on the category of the issuer), and (b) adequate current public information with respect to the issuer of the securities must be available.

Strictly intrastate issues. For intrastate issues, the security must be offered and sold only to the residents of the state in which the corporate issuer is incorporated and doing business [Section 3(11)].

Commercial paper. This category pertains to a borrowing "which arises out of a current transaction or the proceeds of which have been or are able to be used for current transactions, and which has a maturity at the time of issuance of not exceeding nine months . . . [Section 3(3)]." This category is a practical necessity; an example of this category is a bank borrowing under a 90-day note.

Securities of governments and banks. The governmental category of securities includes federal, state, and local governmental units (including municipalities) and agencies thereof [Section 3(2)].

Whether or not a security offering or transaction is exempt from registration under the 1933 Act is strictly a legal and factual determination and outside the expertise of accountants.

Forms used in registration

The SEC has devised numerous Forms to deal with the diverse companies (and their maturity) seeking to offer securities to the public. Although the general contents of a registration statement have already been described, each form has its own detailed table of contents and related instructions. (Recall that the financial statement requirements for these forms are set forth in Regulation S-X.) Two categories of Forms are used under the 1933 Act—**general forms** and **special forms.**

General forms. The SEC has three general forms:—S-1, S-2, and S-3. These three forms are set up on a tier system based on the issuer's following in the stock market. Although all three forms basically require the same information to be furnished to potential investors, the method of furnishing that information varies. Form S-1, the most widely used of the forms, is required when one of the special forms is not authorized or prescribed (or a company eligible to use Form S-2 or S-3 chooses to use Form S-1 instead). Basically, Form S-1 is used by (a) new registrants and (b) companies that are already registered under the 1934 Act but have been filing reports with the SEC for less than 36 months. All financial and nonfinancial disclosures must be included in the prospectus. (The detailed table of contents to Form S-1 appears in the Appendix to this chapter.)

To be eligible to use Forms S-2 and S-3, a company must have been subject to the reporting requirements of the 1934 Act for at least 36 months and satisfy other conditions. Form S-3 is used by large companies having a wide following in the stock market; accordingly, an additional requirement based on annual trading volume and outstanding voting stock must be met. The advantage to these forms is time and effort; that is, financial and nonfinancial information need not be included in the prospectus—it may simply be incorporated by reference to reports already filed with the SEC under the 1934 Act. Thus, these forms are effectively a simplified Form S-1.

Special forms.   The SEC has 11 special forms, five of which are commonly used. A brief description of these five forms follows:

(1) Form S-8. For securities offered to employees pursuant to employee benefit plans, such as stock option plans.
(2) Form S-11. Applicable to real estate investment trusts and real estate companies.
(3) Form S-14. For securities issued in certain business combinations and related reofferings.
(4) Form S-15. For securities issued in certain business combinations (involving a large company and a much smaller company), this streamlined form requires only an abbreviated prospectus.
(5) Form S-18. For offerings up to $7.5 million, this form gives small initial registrants a fast and simple method of raising capital in public markets because (a) the disclosure requirements are less extensive than in Form S-1, and (b) the filing may be made at an SEC regional office instead of at Washington, D.C.

Legal liability associated with a false registration statement

The Securities Act of 1933 requires that the registration statement be signed by the following persons:

(1) The principal executive officer or officers.
(2) The principal financial officer.
(3) The controller or principal accounting officer.
(4) The majority of the board of directors or persons performing similar functions [Section 6].

The 1933 Act sets forth civil liabilities for a false registration as follows:

> In case any part of the registration statement, when such part became effective, contained an untrue statement of a material fact or omitted to state a material fact required to be stated therein or necessary to make the statements therein not misleading, any person acquiring such security (unless it is proved that at the time of such acquisition he knew of such untruth or omission) may . . . sue [for recovery of losses suffered]—
>
> (1) every person who signed the registration statement;
> (2) every person who was a director of . . . the issuer . . . ;
> (3) every person who, with his consent, is named in the registration statement as being or about to become a director . . . ;

(4) every accountant, engineer, appraiser, or any person whose profession gives authority to a statement made by him, who has with his consent been named as having prepared or certified any part of the registration statement, . . . with respect to the statement in such registration statement, report, or valuation, which purports to have been prepared or certified by him;

(5) every underwriter with respect to such security [Section 11].

In addition to these civil proceedings whereby a purchaser may recover damages suffered, the 1933 Act provides for criminal penalties (monetary fines and imprisonment) if the untrue statement of a material fact or omission thereof was "willful" [Section 24].

Ramifications to outside auditors. This section of the 1933 Act has special significance to certified public accountants of companies registering securities. When securities are not registered, **gross negligence** must be proved for a company's certified public accountants to be held liable for civil damages. When a company registers securities under the 1933 Act, however, the focal point is not whether the outside auditors were grossly negligent in the performance of their duties. Instead, the issue is merely whether or not the financial statements and related notes in the registration statement **contained an untrue statement of a material fact or omitted a material fact.** Thus, the 1933 Act imposes an additional potential liability on the certified public accountants of companies registering securities. However, certain defenses are available to the outside auditors under Section 11 of the 1933 Act, that relate to having made a "reasonable investigation" and having "reasonable grounds for belief."

SECURITIES EXCHANGE ACT OF 1934

The Securities Exchange Act of 1934, which deals with the trading in (exchange of) securities, has the following two broad purposes:

(1) To require publicly held companies to disclose on a continual basis current information to their security holders (and to prospective purchasers of their securities) comparable to the information that must be disclosed in a registration statement under the 1933 Act. In this respect, the 1934 Act supplements the 1933 Act, which applies only to public offerings of securities and not to subsequent trading in such securities.

(2) To regulate the public trading markets (organized exchanges and over-the-counter markets) and the broker–dealers who operate in such markets.

Major provisions of the 1934 Act

Unlike the 1933 Act, which is a unified piece of legislation, the 1934 Act covers a wide range of areas. The major provisions of the 1934 Act are discussed in the following paragraphs.

Registration of securities exchanges. Securities exchanges (such as the New York Stock Exchange) must be registered with the SEC, which has supervisory control over such exchanges.

Registration of securities on securities exchanges. Securities exchanges cannot effect transactions in any security unless that security is registered on the exchange. The registration process involves filing a registration statement on Form 10 (or another appropriate form) with the securities exchange and with the SEC. Form 10 requires information comparable to that required in Form S-1 under the 1933 Act. A security that is traded on a securities exchange is referred to as a "listed" security. [Companies having securities registered on a securities exchange are referred to as Section 12(b) companies.]

Registration of over-the-counter securities. The over-the-counter market encompasses all securities transactions that do not take place on organized securities exchanges. In 1964, the 1934 Act was amended to require registration of securities traded in the over-the-counter market that meet certain size tests. Specifically, companies that have total assets exceeding $3 million *and* a class of equity security with 500 or more stockholders must register such security with the SEC by filing a registration statement (usually Form 10). Securities traded in the over-the-counter market are referred to as "unlisted" securities. [Companies meeting these tests are referred to as Section 12(g) companies.] Once a company meets these size tests, it is subject to all the requirements of the 1934 Act that are imposed on listed companies.

A Section 12(g) company may deregister when it has (a) less than 500 shareholders for the class of equity security and total assets of less than $3 million at the end of each of its last three fiscal years; or (b) fewer than 300 shareholders.

Filing of periodic and other reports. Issuers of securities that must be registered under the 1934 Act must file annual and quarterly reports with the SEC containing specified financial and nonfinancial information. In addition, reports describing specified important events must be filed promptly after they occur. These periodic reports are discussed in detail on pages 610–11.

Proxy regulations. For companies subject to the registration requirements of the 1934 Act, the SEC is authorized to prescribe regulations and rules governing the solicitation of proxies by management from shareholders regarding matters to be voted on by shareholders. A **proxy** is merely a document empowering one person to vote for another. Because all shareholders do not normally attend annual or special shareholders' meetings, companies typically request shareholders to sign a proxy empowering management to vote for them either as the shareholder indicates or in accordance with the recommendations of management. When soliciting proxies, a **proxy statement** containing information specified by the SEC must be furnished to the stockholders. Furthermore, preliminary proxy material must be filed with the SEC for review at least 10 days before the proposed mailing date.

Antifraud and insider trading provisions. The 1934 Act makes it unlawful for any person directly or indirectly to use deceptive or fraudulent practices or to misstate or omit any material fact in connection with the purchase or sale of a security (Section 10). Criminal fines up to $100,000 can be imposed. Persons suffering losses as a result of fraud are entitled to sue for recovery of actual losses.

Corporate "insiders" are prohibited from trading in a corporation's securities using material information that has not been disseminated to the public. Inside traders can be forced to give up their profits and be fined up to three times their profits. An insider is any person who has material nonpublic information, including any officer or director or any person who obtains such information from others. In addition, under the "short-swing profit" rule, any profit realized from any purchase and sale (or from any sale and purchase) of any such issuer's equity security within any period of less than six months by certain persons accrues to the issuer and is recoverable by the issuer, with certain exceptions. These certain persons are officers, directors, or any person who is the beneficial owner of more than 10% of any security that is registered under the 1934 Act [Section 16(b)]. Officers, directors, and such 10% security holders must report to the SEC any changes in their beneficial ownership of registered securities [Section 16(a)].

Brokers and dealers. The 1934 Act requires brokers and dealers to register with the SEC and to comply with regulations imposed on them. Certain trading practices are prohibited. Specific sections of the 1934 Act deal with unlawful representations, liability for misleading statements, and criminal penalties.

Forms used in reporting

The SEC has devised approximately 20 forms to be used by companies whose securities are registered under the 1934 Act. Because most of these forms are of a specialized nature, a complete list is not presented. By far the most commonly used forms are the following:

Form 8-K, current reports
Form 10-K, annual report
Form 10-Q, quarterly report

Regulation 12B of the 1934 Act sets forth the mechanics of reporting in the same manner that Regulation C does under the 1933 Act.

Form 8-K, current reports

Form 8-K provides certain information to investors on a reasonably current basis. A report on this form must be filed when one of the following events occurs:

(1) Changes in control of registrant.
(2) Significant acquisitions or dispositions of assets (including business combinations).
(3) Bankruptcy or receivership.
(4) Changes in registrant's certifying accountant.

(5) Other events (that the registrant deems important to its security holders).
(6) Resignation of a director.

Form 8-K reports must be filed within 15 days after the occurrence of the earliest event.

Form 10-K, annual report

Within 90 days after the end of the fiscal year, a company must file an annual report with the SEC, using Form 10-K if no other form is prescribed. Although it must be furnished to stockholders on request, this report is in addition to the company's annual report to its stockholders. Form 10-K must include substantially all nonfinancial statement disclosure requirements set forth in Regulation S-K (the major items were indicated on page 600) and the financial statement information specified in Regulation S-X (which was described on page 600).

Compared with annual report to stockholders. As part of the SEC's three-year effort to streamline its reporting requirements (1980–1982), substantially all the information called for in the 10-K annual report also must be included in the annual report sent to the stockholders. Companies may omit information from the 10-K annual report if it is included in the annual report sent to the stockholders. Of course, a copy of the annual report sent to the stockholders must be filed with the 10-K annual report, and the 10-K annual report must indicate that the omitted information is included in the annual report sent to the stockholders. (This is known as **incorporation by reference.**)

Form 10-Q, quarterly report

Within 45 days of the end of each of the first three fiscal quarters of each fiscal year, a company must file a quarterly report with the SEC on Form 10-Q. No report is necessary for the fourth quarter. Form 10-Q calls for the interim financial statements specified in Regulation S-X. These financial statements, which may be condensed, are as follows:

(1) **Balance sheets.** An interim balance sheet as of the end of the most recent fiscal quarter, and a balance sheet at the end of the preceding fiscal year.
(2) **Income statements.** Interim income statements for the most recent fiscal quarter; for the period between the end of the last fiscal year and the end of the most recent fiscal quarter (year-to-date amounts in second- and third-quarter reports); and corresponding periods of the preceding fiscal year.
(3) **Statement of changes in financial position.** Statements of changes in financial position for the period between the end of the last fiscal year and the end of the most recent fiscal quarter and for the corresponding period of the preceding fiscal year.

Detailed footnotes are not required; however, disclosures must be complete enough so that the information presented is not misleading. In this respect, companies may presume that users of the interim financial information have read or have access to the audited financial statements for the preceding fiscal year. Thus, disclosures deal primarily with events subsequent to the end of the most recent fiscal year. The interim financial information need not be audited or reviewed by an independent public accountant.

Form 10-Q also calls for a management discussion and analysis (the MDA) of the financial condition and results of operations pursuant to the nonfinancial statement disclosure requirements of Regulation S-K.

Compared with the quarterly report to stockholders. As with the rules concerning the 10-K annual report, information called for on Form 10-Q may be omitted if such information is contained in a quarterly report to the stockholders, and that a copy of the quarterly report to stockholders is filed with Form 10-Q.

REGULATION S-X: A CLOSER LOOK

In the introduction discussion of Regulation S-X (page 600), we said that this regulation sets forth not only the financial statements filed with the SEC under the various Acts but also the form and content of those financial statements. As a result of recent revisions to modernize Regulation S-X and integrate the various reporting requirements of companies, the regulation also applies to annual reports to stockholders. Accordingly, the financial statements included in Form 10-K annual report are now identical to the financial statements in annual reports to stockholders.

Because this regulation is approximately 100 pages long, a detailed discussion is beyond the scope of this book. Thus, our objective is to provide you with a general familiarity with the contents of Regulation S-X.

Regulation S-X is composed of the following 14 articles (each article has its own rules):

Article	Description of Article
1	Application of Regulation S-X
2	Qualifications and reports of accountants
3	General instructions as to financial statements
3A	Consolidated and combined financial statements
4	Rules of general application
5	Commercial and industrial companies
5A	Companies in the development stage
6	Registered investment companies
6A	Employee stock purchase, savings, and similar plans
7	Insurance companies
9	Bank holding companies
10	Interim financial statements
11	Pro forma financial information
12	Form and content of schedules

Because Articles 5A, 6, 6A, 7, and 9 have at most only limited application to most companies, they are not discussed in this chapter. The remaining articles are discussed briefly.

Article 1—Application of Regulation S-X

Article 1 specifies the nature of Regulation S-X, states the Acts to which it applies, and defines the terms used in the Regulation.

Article 2—Qualifications and reports of accountants

Article 2 discusses (1) the qualification of certified public accountants (primarily, conditions necessary for their independence), and (2) specific requirements concerning the content of a certified public accountant's report on audited financial statements included in one of the designated forms filed with the SEC.

Article 3—General instructions as to financial statements

Article 3 specifies the balance sheets, income statements, and statements of changes in financial position included in registration statements and reports filed with the SEC.

Article 3A—Consolidated and combined financial statements

This article deals with the presentation of consolidated and combined financial statements. It specifies which subsidiaries should not be consolidated and requires, in general, that all intercompany items and transactions be eliminated.

Article 4—Rules of general application

The rules of general application pertain to a variety of items regarding form, classification, and the content of notes to the financial statements. Rule 4-08, "General Notes to Financial Statements," comprises most of this article. Rule 4-08 is an extensive rule specifying certain information to be set forth in notes to the financial statements. This rule is not a duplication of FASB disclosure requirements. Instead, the requirements pertain to items not specifically addressed in pronouncements of the FASB and its predecessor organizations. Generally, preparing the additional disclosures called for by this Article is not a major task. Some examples follow.

Rule 4-08(h)—Income tax expense.   Among other things, this rule calls for a reconciliation between the amount of reported total income tax expense (benefit) and the amount computed by multiplying the pretax income (loss) by the applicable statutory federal income tax rate, showing the estimated dollar amount of each underlying cause for the difference. This disclosure requirement is not called for in any pronouncement of the FASB or its predecessor organizations.

Rule 4-08(1)—Material related party transactions.   This rule specifies the disclosures to be made regarding related party transactions.

Article 5—Commercial and industrial companies

Article 5 applies to all companies that are not required to follow Articles 5A, 6, 6A, 7, and 9. Rules 5-02 and 5-03 of Article 5 set forth the various line items and certain additional disclosures that should appear in the balance sheet, income statement, or related notes.

Rule 5-04 is a list and description of 13 financial statement supporting schedules (commonly referred to as **schedules**) that are filed in support of the basic financial statements. These schedules pertain to such things as analyses of property, plant, and equipment and analyses of valuation accounts for specified periods of time. In most cases, only four or five schedules apply. The exact form and content of the schedules are specified by Article 12.

Article 10—Interim financial statements

Article 10 deals with the form and content of presentation of interim financial statements (quarterly reports under the 1934 Act and interim financial statements in registration statements filed under the 1933 Act).

Article 11—Pro forma financial information

Article 11 specifies when pro forma financial statements must be presented. Such financial statements are required when business combinations have occurred or are probable.

Article 12—Form and content of schedules

Article 12 prescribes the form and content of the financial statement supporting schedules required by Rule 5-04 under Article 5 and certain rules in other Articles. The exact columnar headings used for each schedule are specified, along with detailed instructions on how to prepare each schedule.

SUMMARY

The Securities Act of 1933 and the Securities Exchange Act of 1934 protect investors from fraudulent acts and unethical practices by the promoters of securities and the managements of companies issuing securities. Companies subject to the registration and reporting requirements of these statutes must be familiar with a labyrinth of regulations, rules, releases, forms, and bulletins to comply with these statutes. For the disclosure of nonfinancial information, companies usually rely heavily on their legal counsel for assistance and guidance. For the disclosure of financial information, company accountants must be intimately familiar with the detailed requirements of Regulation S-X. In many respects, Regulation S-X imposes no additional reporting requirements beyond those required by generally accepted accounting principles as established in the private sector. In some areas, Regulation S-X imposes significant additional reporting requirements beyond those required under generally accepted accounting principles.

Glossary of new terms

Blue Sky Laws: State laws dealing with the purchase and sale of securities.
Exempt Offering: An offering of securities that need not be registered with the SEC because of an available statutory exemption.

Forms: Specific enumerations of the form and content of information included in registration statements and reports filed with the SEC.

Private Offering: "Transactions by an issuer not involving a public offering." (Securities Act of 1933)

Prospectus: The portion of a registration statement that must be furnished to prospective investors in connection with an offering of securities being registered with the SEC.

Proxy: A document empowering a person to vote for another person.

Proxy Statement: A statement containing specified information furnished to stockholders in connection with the solicitation of proxies for use at an annual meeting (or special meetings) of shareholders.

Registration Statement: All of the specified financial and nonfinancial information filed with the SEC (set forth according to an appropriate Form) for purposes of registering an offering of securities to the public.

Restricted Security: Securities acquired by means that did not involve a public offering.

Security: "Any note, stock, treasury stock, bond, debenture, evidence of indebtedness, certificate of interest or participation in any profit-sharing agreement, . . . transferable share, investment contract, voting trust certificate, . . . or in general any interest or instrument commonly known as a security . . ." (Securities Act of 1933)

Underwriter: "Any person who has purchased from an issuer with a view to, or offers or sells for an issuer in connection with, the distribution of any security, or participates [directly or indirectly] . . . in any such undertaking . . . "(Securities Act of 1933)

Appendix
FORM S-1: TABLE OF CONTENTS

General instructions

I. Eligibility requirements for use of Form S-1
II. Application of general rules and regulations
III. Exchange offers

Facing sheet

I. Information required in prospectus
Item
1. Forepart of the registration statement and outside front cover page of prospectus
2. Inside front and outside back cover page of prospectus
3. Summary information, risk factors, and ratio of earnings to fixed charges
4. Use of proceeds
5. Determination of offering price
6. Dilution
7. Selling security holders
8. Plan of distribution
9. Description of securities being registered
10. Interest of named experts and counsel

11. Information with respect to the registrant[4]
12. Disclosure of commission position on indemnification for securities act liabilities

II. Information not required in prospectus

13. Other expenses of issuance and distribution
14. Indemnification of directors and officers
15. Recent sales of unregistered securities
16. Exhibits and financial statement schedules
17. Undertakings

Signatures

Instructions as to summary prospectuses

Review questions

1. How does the Securities Exchange Act of 1934 differ from the Securities Act of 1933?
2. What purpose is served by the SEC's Staff Accounting Bulletins?
3. What purpose do SEC releases serve?
4. Describe the SEC's role in the formation and improvement of generally accepted accounting principles.
5. Distinguish between a registration statement and a prospectus.
6. What is the distinction between Form S-1 and Form 10-K?
7. What do Regulations A and D have in common?
8. What do Forms 8-K, 10-K, and 10-Q have in common?
9. How is Regulation C under the 1933 Act similar to Regulation 12B under the 1934 Act?
10. What is the distinction between Regulation S-X and Regulation S-K?
11. Distinguish between a proxy and a proxy statement.
12. How are financial statements that are prepared in accordance with Regulation S-X requirements different from financial statements prepared in accordance with generally accepted accounting principles?

Exercises

Exercise 17–1
SEC Promulgations

Complete the following statements:
(1) The form and content of financial statements included with filings with the SEC are set forth in _____.
(2) The pronouncements that announce the SEC's proposed revisions to its rules and regulations are called _____.

---

[4] This item specifies (a) the nonfinancial disclosure requirements contained in Regulation S-K that are to be included, and (b) the financial statement requirements of Regulation S-X that are to be included.

(3) Nonfinancial statement disclosure requirements are set forth in _____.
(4) An SEC regulation is merely a collection of _____.
(5) The SEC rules and regulations that pertain to the various sections of the 1933 Act and the 1934 Act are referred to as the _____ rules and regulations.
(6) The regulation that specifies the financial statements included in SEC filings is _____.
(7) The interpretations and practices followed by certain departments of the SEC are called _____.
(8) Accounting related releases used to be announced in _____, but now they are set forth in _____.
(9) The promulgation of the SEC that accountants deal with more than any other is _____.
(10) A list of instructions concerning what is included in a particular SEC filing is called a _____.

Exercise 17–2
1933 and 1934 Acts: Terminology

Complete the following statements:
(1) Under the 1933 Act, issuers of securities must furnish potential investors a _____.
(2) A registration statement is divided into the following two basic parts:
　　(a) Information _____.
　　(b) Information _____.
(3) A "red herring" is a _____.
(4) Stocks and bonds are _____.
(5) A person who purchases an issuer's stock with a view to distributing that stock to the public is a(n) _____.
(6) Security offerings that need not be registered with the SEC are considered _____ offerings.
(7) All the information filed with the SEC using an appropriate form under the 1933 Act is called a _____.
(8) The Securities Act of 1933 pertains to the _____ of securities.
(9) The Securities Exchange Act of 1934 pertains to _____ of issued securities.
(10) Securities acquired by means that did not involve a public offering are called _____.
(11) A document authorizing one person to vote for another person is a _____.
(12) A statement furnished to stockholders in connection with soliciting their votes is called a _____.

Exercise 17–3
1933 and 1934 Acts: Forms used in registrations and filings

Indicate the SEC form applicable to each of the following items:
(1) The most commonly used annual reporting form under the 1934 Act.
(2) The most commonly used registration form under the 1933 Act.

(3) The quarterly reporting form under the 1934 Act.
(4) The form used under the 1934 Act to report certain transactions or events that arise during the year.
(5) The form that may be used to register stock option plans, providing certain other conditions are met.
(6) The most commonly used registration form under the 1934 Act.
(7) The three general forms used under the 1933 Act.
(8) The item filed with the SEC when a Regulation A offering is involved.

Exercise 17–4
Regulation S-X: True or false

Indicate whether the following statements are true or false.
(1) Regulation S-X specifies the financial statements included in registration statements and reports filed with the SEC.
(2) Some Financial Reporting Releases explain and illustrate certain rules in Regulation S-X.
(3) Regulation S-X applies to the 1933 Act but not the 1934 Act.
(4) Some Regulation S-X rules permit the deletion of certain notes to financial statements otherwise required by generally accepted accounting principles.
(5) The form and content of financial statements included in registration statements and reports filed with the SEC are set forth in Regulation S-X.
(6) The SEC automatically amends Regulation S-X to comply with any new FASB pronouncements.
(7) Annual reports to shareholders need not present financial statements in compliance with Regulation S-X.
(8) In general, it is a major task to convert financial statements and the related footnotes (prepared in accordance with generally accepted accounting principles) to meet the requirements of Regulation S-X.
(9) Regulation S-X is a guide for preparing financial statements included in the registration statements and reports filed with the SEC—it need not be strictly followed.
(10) Regulation S-X does not specify which SEC form is used in preparing reports filed under the 1934 Act.
(11) Certain Regulation S-X rules require additional financial disclosures above and beyond disclosures normally made pursuant to generally accepted accounting principles.
(12) Changes in Regulation S-X can be announced through the issuance of a Financial Reporting Release.

Problems

Problem 17–1
Role of the SEC in relation to the FASB

Indicate whether the following statements are true or false. Discuss your reasons for your answers.

(1) The pronouncements of the Financial Accounting Standards Board must be approved by the SEC before they can be issued.

(2) The accounting related pronouncements of the SEC must be approved by the Financial Accounting Standards Board before they are issued.

(3) The SEC has given the Financial Accounting Standards Board the statutory authority to prescribe accounting principles.

(4) Publicly owned companies are subject to the financial reporting requirements of the SEC and the FASB.

(5) Privately owned companies are not subject to the financial reporting requirements of the SEC.

(6) The SEC automatically rescinds a pronouncement when the FASB issues a Statement of Financial Accounting Standards involving a particular accounting issue.

(7) When the SEC notices an emerging accounting practice that has not been addressed by the FASB, it most likely will establish accounting principles in that area until the FASB can address the issue.

(8) Unlike the FASB, the SEC can order a company subject to its reporting requirements to alter its financial statements.

Problem 17–2
Securities Act of 1933: Role of the SEC and responsibility of outside auditors

Select the best answer for each of the following items:

(1) One of the SEC's functions is to
  (a) judge the merits of the securities being offered to the public.
  (b) ascertain the wisdom of investing in securities being offered to the public.
  (c) warrant that registration statements contain all necessary financial and non-financial statement information required by the investing public to evaluate the merit of the securities being offered.
  (d) warrant that the information contained in registration statements examined and approved by the SEC is true and accurate.
  (e) none of the above.

(2) A company registers securities with the SEC under the 1933 Act. As this event concerns its outside auditors, which of the following is correct?
  (a) The SEC will defend any action brought against certified public accountants who have reported on financial statements included in a registration statement examined and approved by the SEC.
  (b) Any action brought against the auditors would have to be decided on the basis of ordinary negligence versus gross negligence.
  (c) The auditors could be held liable in the event of ordinary negligence as well as gross negligence.
  (d) The auditors could be held liable for misleading statements in the notes to the financial statements even if negligence is not involved.
  (e) None of the above.

(3) One of the major purposes of the federal security statutes is to
  (a) establish the qualifications for accountants who are members of the profession.

(b) eliminate incompetent attorneys and accountants who participate in the registration of securities offered to the public.

(c) provide a set of uniform standards and tests for accountants, attorneys, and others who practice before the Securities and Exchange Commission.

(d) provide sufficient information to the investing public who purchase securities in the marketplace.

(e) none of the above.

(4) Under the Securities Act of 1933, subject to some exceptions and limitations, it is unlawful to use the mails or instruments of interstate commerce to sell or offer to sell a security to the public unless

(a) a surety bond sufficient to cover potential liability to investors is obtained and filed with the Securities and Exchange Commission.

(b) the offer is made through underwriters qualified to offer the securities on a nationwide basis.

(c) a registration statement that has been properly filed with the Securities and Exchange Commission has been found to be acceptable and is in effect.

(d) the Securities and Exchange Commission approves of the financial merit of the offering.

(e) none of the above.

(5) A company registers securities with the SEC under the 1933 Act. As this event concerns its outside auditors, which of the following is correct?

(a) The outside auditors may disclaim any liability under the federal securities acts by an unambiguous, boldfaced disclaimer of liability on its audit report.

(b) The outside auditors must determine which SEC form the company should use in the filing.

(c) As long as the outside auditors engage exclusively in intrastate business, the federal securities laws do not apply to them.

(d) The outside auditors have primary responsibility for the nonfinancial statement portions of the registration statement as well as responsibility for the financial statement portions of the registration statement.

(e) None of the above.

Problem 17–3
1933 and 1934 Acts: Technical understanding

Select the best answer for each of the following items:

(1) Regulation A and Regulation D deal with

(a) the mechanics of registering securities under the 1933 Act.

(b) the responsibilities of outside auditors under the 1933 Act.

(c) the forms used under the 1933 Act.

(d) allowable exemptions from registration under the 1933 Act.

(e) none of the above.

(2) Concerning the relationship between the 1933 Act and the 1934 Act, which of the following is correct?

(a) Having once become subject to the reporting requirements of the 1934 Act, a company may offer securities to the public in the future without having to register such securities with the SEC under the 1933 Act.

(b) If a privately owned company having 200,000 common shares outstanding registers the sale of 50,000 new shares under the 1933 Act, then all 250,000 common shares are deemed to be registered under the 1933 Act.

(c) A company that registers securities under the 1933 Act becomes subject to the reporting requirements of the 1934 Act.

(d) If a privately owned company having 500,000 common shares outstanding registers the sale of 100,000 new shares under the 1933 Act, then only the 100,000 new shares may be registered under the 1934 Act.

(e) None of the above.

(3) Under the 1933 Act, which of the following is the most important criterion of whether a private placement to a limited number of persons or a public offering has been made?

(a) The size of the issuing corporation.

(b) The type of security offered.

(c) The prompt resale of the securities by the purchasers.

(d) Whether the company engages exclusively in intrastate business.

(e) None of the above.

(4) Which of the following is not exempt from registration under the 1933 Act?

(a) Securities offered through underwriters.

(b) Securities offered to a limited number of persons in a private placement.

(c) Securities offered only to residents of the state in which the company is located.

(d) Securities offered by a governmental unit.

(e) None of the above.

(5) Concerning the 1934 Act, which of the following is correct?

(a) A company may be subject to the reporting requirements of the 1934 Act even though it never has registered securities under the 1933 Act.

(b) A company that has been subject to the reporting requirements of the 1934 Act is always subject to such requirements unless the company becomes privately held again.

(c) A company is no longer subject to the reporting requirements of the 1934 Act if its total assets are below $3 million at the end of its last three fiscal years.

(d) A company that is no longer subject to the reporting requirements of the 1934 Act is also no longer subject to the requirements of the 1933 Act.

(e) None of the above.

Problem 17–4
Securities Exchange Act of 1934: Stock transactions by employees

New Products Corporation, incorporated in Delaware, is a manufacturing company whose securities are registered on a national securities exchange. On February 6, 19X5, one of the company's engineers disclosed to management that he had discovered a new product that he believed would be quite profitable to the corporation. Messrs. Prescott and Trout, the corporation's president and treasurer and members of its board of directors, were quite impressed with the prospects of the new product's profitability.

Trout was imbued with such confidence in the corporation's prospects that on February 12, 19X5, he purchased on the open market 1,000 shares of the corporation's common stock at $10 per share. This purchase occurred before news of the new product reached the public in late February and caused a rise in the market price to $30 per share. Prescott did not purchase any shares in February because he had already purchased 600 shares of the corporation's common stock on January 15, 19X5, for $10 per share.

On April 16, 19X5, because of unexpected expenses arising from a fire in his home, Prescott sold on the open market the 600 shares of stock he purchased in January for $35 per share. Trout continues to hold his 1,000 shares.

Required:
(1) What questions arising out of the federal securities laws are suggested by these facts? Discuss.
(2) What would be a reasonable corporate policy designed to have employees buy and sell stock on the same basis as nonemployees?

Problem 17–5
Securities Exchange Act of 1934: Public disclosures

Fudgco Corporation's sole issue of stock is traded on a national exchange. In conducting the year-end examination of its financial statements, the auditor learned that Fudgco's research department had perfected a manufacturing process that would have a positive material effect on future earnings. Fudgco did not announce the development.

When a rumor about the new process started in late January, Fudgco's president promptly telephoned financial papers in several states and announced that there was no substance to the rumor. A number of papers reported the president's denial of the rumor. Thereafter, Fudgco's stock traded in its normal narrow range. In February, relying on the information reported in the financial press, Sellinger sold a large block of his Fudgco stock at the current market price.

Fudgco's president made a public announcement about the perfection of the new process the following June. The announcement precipitated a dramatic increase in both the price and volume of trading of Fudgco's stock. Neither Fudgco nor any person with knowledge of the process engaged in trading Fudgco's stock before the public announcement of the discovery.

Required:
What questions arising out of federal securities laws are suggested by these facts? Discuss.

(AICPA adapted)

18 Troubled Debt Restructurings, Bankruptcy Reorganizations, and Liquidations

OVERVIEW OF TROUBLED DEBT RESTRUCTURINGS, BANKRUPTCY REORGANIZATIONS, AND LIQUIDATIONS

Options for financially distressed companies

Any type of economic entity (including corporations, partnerships, sole proprietorships, and municipalities) can encounter financial difficulties. Business entities in financial difficulty first usually retrench and undertake cost-cutting steps to conserve cash and reduce operating losses. Such steps may include (1) revamping the organizational structure to eliminate or consolidate functions (often resulting in the termination of a substantial number of personnel); (2) seeking wage and fringe-benefit concessions from employees; (3) seeking relaxation of restrictive union work rules; and (4) disposing of unprofitable segments. In addition, the entity may eventually need to raise additional capital, dispose of profitable segments, combine with another business, restructure its debt (outside of the bankruptcy courts); reorganize through the bankruptcy courts; or liquidate.

This chapter deals with corporations that select the last three options. The fourth option—restructuring debt (outside of the bankruptcy courts)— usually consists of extending due dates, forgiving some portion of debt, and reducing the interest rate on the debt. The fourth option gives the business a reasonable chance to continue as a viable entity and recover from the financial difficulties, thereby avoiding liquidation, at least for the time being. Although its objective is identical to that of the fourth option, the fifth option—reorganization through the bankruptcy courts—is considered a less desirable option, even though it usually results in a substantial forgiveness of debt. The sixth option—liquidation—consists of converting all noncash assets into cash, paying creditors to the extent possible, and ending the legal existence of the corporation. In discussing the options of restructuring debt and reorganizing through the bankruptcy courts, we exclude railroads and municipalities because of their special nature. We also exclude these special entities from the discussion of liquidation, because public policy dictates that these entities not be liquidated.

Purpose of bankruptcy statutes

Debt capital markets would be inhibited without some provisions for ensuring fair and equitable means of resolving rights and protecting public interests. This is the purpose of the bankruptcy laws. Distressed companies and their creditors must decide whether it is necessary to resort to the bankruptcy process. Accordingly, we now discuss the federal bankruptcy statutes.

BANKRUPTCY STATUTES

Substance of the bankruptcy statutes

Under the bankruptcy statutes, a company or an individual is placed under the protection of the court, whereby creditors (including creditors possessing security interests, unsecured creditors, tax collectors, and public utilities) are prevented from taking other legal action (such as foreclosing on loans, filing lawsuits, repossessing or seizing assets, and placing padlocks on the doors of the company's real property). When a company's rehabilitation and future viable operations are feasible, its debt is restructured under the supervision and control of the court in such a manner that the debtor may be legally freed from the payment of certain past debts. When rehabilitation and recovery are not feasible, an orderly liquidation takes place under the supervision and control of the bankruptcy court.

Federal bankruptcy statutes

Article I, Section 8 of the U.S. Constitution grants to the Congress the power to establish uniform laws throughout the United States pertaining to the subject of bankruptcies. Federal statutes pertaining to bankruptcy prevail over state laws that conflict with federal laws.

In 1978, the U.S. Congress rewrote the federal bankruptcy statutes under the Bankruptcy Reform Act of 1978. Taking effect on October 1, 1979, the new law replaced the National Bankruptcy Act of 1898. The new law established separate bankruptcy courts (adjuncts to the district courts) with special judges who supervise and review all bankruptcy petitions and proceedings.

The Bankruptcy Reform Act of 1978 consists of the following eight chapters (even-numbered chapters do not exist):

Chapter 1	General provisions
Chapter 3	Case administration
Chapter 5	Creditors, the debtor, and the estate
Chapter 7	Liquidation
Chapter 9	Adjustment of debts of a municipality
Chapter 11	Reorganization
Chapter 13	Adjustment of debts of an individual with regular income
Chapter 15	United States trustees

Regarding these eight chapters, the general provisions of Chapters 1, 3, and 5 pertain to Chapters 7, 9, 11, and 13, unless otherwise indicated. In this section, we discuss certain basic aspects of Chapters 1, 3, and 5. Chapters 9 and 13 do not pertain to corporations organized to make a profit; accordingly, they are not discussed in this chapter. (Chapter 9 applies only to municipalities that seek relief voluntarily—a municipality cannot be forced into bankruptcy proceedings against its will by its creditors.) Chapter 7 is discussed later in this chapter in the section dealing with liquidations. Chapter 11 is also discussed later in this chapter in the section dealing with bankruptcy reorganizations.

In the 1978 Act, the subject of the bankruptcy proceedings is referred to as a **debtor.** The commencement of a bankruptcy case creates an **estate.** The estate includes all of the debtor's property no matter where located (Section 541).[1]

Applicability of the bankruptcy statutes

The bankruptcy statutes apply to individuals, partnerships, corporations (all of which are collectively referred to as **persons**), and municipalities. Insurance companies and certain financial institutions (such as banks, savings and loan associations, building and loan associations, and credit unions) are excluded because they are subject to alternative regulations. Railroads may not use the liquidation provisions of Chapter 7, only the reorganization provisions of Chapter 11. Stockbrokers and commodity brokers are not eligible for the reorganization provisions of Chapter 11, only the liquidation provisions of Chapter 7 [Section 109(b)].

Voluntary petitions

An eligible corporation (that is, a corporation other than an insurance company or certain financial institutions) may file a voluntary petition with the bankruptcy courts under Chapter 7 or 11 and thereby obtain the benefits available under the statutes (Section 109). Filing a voluntary petition constitutes an **order for relief,** which has the full force and effect as if the bankruptcy court had issued an order that the debtor be granted relief under the statutes (Section 301). However, the court can dismiss a voluntary filing if it is in the best interests of creditors [Section 707 and 1112(b)].

The petition initiates bankruptcy proceedings and is an official form that must be accompanied by a summary of the debtor's property (at market or current values) and debts, including supporting schedules, all on official forms. The supporting schedules for property consist of separate schedules for real property, personal property, and property not otherwise scheduled. The supporting schedules for debts consist of separate schedules for creditors with priority (a special class of creditors explained later in the book), creditors holding security, and creditors having unsecured claims without priority. Information also must include each creditor's address (if known), when the debt was incurred, and whether the debt is contingent, disputed, or subject to setoff. In addition, the petitioner must respond to a questionnaire regarding all aspects of its financial condition and operations. Although this questionnaire is called the statement of affairs, it should not be confused with the statement of affairs that accountants prepare regarding asset values and debts owed, which is explained later in the chapter.

Involuntary petitions

Under Chapter 7 or 11, an eligible corporation may be forced into bankruptcy proceedings against its will by its creditors. One or more creditors may file an involuntary petition with the bankruptcy court. If a debtor has 12 or more creditors, at least three of them who have claims totaling a minimum

---

[1] This reference is to the Bankruptcy Reform Act of 1978. Hereafter, only the section number is provided.

of $5,000 more than the value of any lien on the property of the debtor securing such claims must sign the petition [Section 303(b)(1)]. If a company has fewer than 12 creditors, one or more creditors having such claims of at least $5,000 must sign the petition [Section 303(b)(2)]. These dollar amounts apply to both liquidation and reorganization cases.

For an involuntary petition filed under Chapter 7 or 11, the bankruptcy court enters an order for relief against the debtor only if

(1) the debtor is generally not paying its debts as they become due; or
(2) a custodian was appointed or took possession of the debtor's property within 120 days before the date of the filing of the petition. (This does not apply to a trustee, receiver, or agent appointed or authorized to take charge of less than the majority of the debtor's property for the purpose of enforcing a lien against such property) [Section 303(h)].

The first test above is an equity insolvency test; that is, the debtor's assets equitably belong to the creditors to the extent of their claims. In the second test, the appointment of a custodian presumes that the debtor cannot pay its debts as they mature.

In practice, voluntary bankruptcies occur much more frequently than involuntary bankruptcies. Regardless of whether a company enters bankruptcy proceedings voluntarily or involuntarily, it should immediately obtain the assistance of an attorney who specializes in bankruptcy proceedings.

Creditors with priority

A company entering bankruptcy proceedings can have two general classes of creditors—secured creditors and unsecured creditors. **Secured** creditors have been pledged certain of the company's assets as security on their claims. Creditors that have no right to any of the company's specific assets are **unsecured** creditors. In addition to these two general classes of creditors, the bankruptcy statutes create a special class of creditors termed **creditors with priority.** Debts with priority are listed in the order of their priority, as follows:

(1) **Administrative expenses, fees, and charges assessed against the estate.** Administrative expenses are the actual and necessary costs and expenses of preserving the estate after the petition has been filed. This includes trustee's fees, legal, accounting, and appraisal fees incurred in connection with the bankruptcy proceedings, filing fees paid by creditors in an involuntary bankruptcy petition, and expenses incurred in recovering assets that were concealed or fraudulently transferred.
(2) **Certain postfiling "gap" claims.** This category, which exists only for involuntary filings, includes unsecured claims arising in the ordinary course of the debtor's business after the involuntary filing but before the appointment of a trustee or an order of relief is entered, whichever occurs first.
(3) **Wages, salaries, and commissions.** Wages, salaries, and commissions are limited to unsecured amounts earned by an individual within 90 days before the filing date or the date of the cessation of the debtor's

business, whichever occurs first, but only up to $2,000 for each individual. This category includes vacation, severance, and sick leave pay.

(4) Employee benefit plans.   This category pertains to unsecured claims for contributions to employee benefit plans arising from services rendered by the employees within 180 days before the date of the filing of the petition or the date of the cessation of the debtor's business, whichever occurs first. The claims are limited to the number of employees covered by each such plan multiplied by $2,000, minus (a) the total amount paid to such employees as priority items in (3), above, and (b) the total amount paid by the estate on behalf of such employees to any other employee benefit plan.

(5) Deposits by individuals.   This category includes unsecured claims of up to $900 for each such individual, arising from the deposit of money before the commencement of the case in connection with the purchase, lease, or rental of property, or the purchase of services for the personal, family, or household use of such individuals, that were not delivered or provided.

(6) Taxes.   This category includes income taxes, property taxes, withholding taxes, employer payroll taxes, excise taxes, and customs duties. Most of these taxes are limited to amounts relating to a specified period of time preceding the date of the filing, usually one or three years, depending on the item.

Creditors with priority are given a statutory priority over the claims of other **unsecured creditors** with regard to payment. Later in the chapter, we illustrate this priority in a liquidation through the bankruptcy courts.

TROUBLED DEBT RESTRUCTURINGS

In troubled debt restructurings, steps are taken outside of the bankruptcy courts to give the distressed company a reasonable chance of surviving. This option is considered much more desirable than a Chapter 11 reorganization.

Advantages of restructuring versus reorganizing

One advantage of restructuring outside of the bankruptcy courts is that the restructuring can be completed in far less time than a Chapter 11 reorganization, which takes a minimum of approximately 18 months. However, of greater importance is the desire to avoid the stigma associated with being or having been subject to bankruptcy proceedings. More uncertainty is associated with Chapter 11 reorganizations concerning the distressed company's chances of survival—many companies that file for Chapter 11 reorganizations are unable to work out a successful plan of reorganization and are liquidated instead. Thus, filing for reorganization under Chapter 11 is considered the last resort, short of liquidation.

Needless to say, filing for a Chapter 11 reorganization has far greater consequences to the distressed company in terms of its impact on suppliers, competitors, customers, and employees than does a restructuring outside of the bankruptcy courts. For example, a distressed company that is restructuring may be able to obtain some credit from suppliers; when a company reorganizes under Chapter 11, suppliers usually require payment on delivery. During restructuring, competitors tend to get sales leverage from a distressed company's problems; during a Chapter 11 reorganization, competitors have that much more ammunition. (Competitors often show customers press clippings of the distressed company's financial problems.)

When a company has filed for reorganization under Chapter 11, customers have that much less assurance of the company's survival—this can be critical for a distressed company that sells products requiring the company's continued existence for purposes of providing service and stocking spare parts. Employees are more likely to look for greener pastures once a company files for reorganization under Chapter 11 because of the uncertainty associated with bankruptcy proceedings. (Personnel placement firms tend to zero in on distressed companies to hire away their employees; their chances of success increase when a company files for a Chapter 11 reorganization.)

Working out a troubled debt restructuring agreement is usually a substantial and difficult undertaking, especially when major differences exist among various groups of creditors as to the sacrifices each is willing to make. A distressed company often resorts to a Chapter 11 reorganization when it is impossible to work out a troubled debt restructuring agreement with its creditors, when its lenders refuse to lend any more money, or when suppliers start requiring payment on delivery. Although the advantages of restructuring debt outside of the bankruptcy courts are considerable, certain advantages exist in filing for reorganization under Chapter 11. These advantages are discussed later in the chapter when reorganization under Chapter 11 is discussed in detail.

Nature of troubled debt restructurings

The accounting procedures for most debt restructurings are prescribed by *FASB Statement No. 15,* "Accounting by Debtors and Creditors for Troubled Debt Restructurings." Before discussing the accounting issues and procedures in detail, we (1) define a troubled debt restructuring; (2) show transactions that may be considered troubled debt restructurings; and (3) show some ways in which a distressed company can restructure its debt.

Definition. *FASB Statement No. 15* defines a troubled debt restructuring as follows:

> A restructuring of a debt constitutes a **troubled debt restructuring** for purposes of this Statement if the creditor for economic or legal reasons related to the debtor's financial difficulties grants a concession to the debtor that it would not otherwise consider.[2]

The statement expounds on this definition as follows:

---

[2] *Statement of Financial Accounting Standards No. 15,* "Accounting by Debtors and Creditors for Troubled Debt Restructurings" (Stamford, CT: FASB, 1977), paragraph 2. Copyright by Financial Accounting Standards Board, High Ridge Park, Stamford, CT 06905, U.S.A. Reprinted with permission. Copies of the complete document are available from the FASB.

Whatever the form of concession granted by the creditor to the debtor in a troubled debt restructuring, the creditor's objective is to make the best of a difficult situation. That is, the creditor expects to obtain more cash or other value from the debtor, or to increase the probability of receipt, by granting the concession than by not granting it.[3]

Categories of transactions. The statement lists the following types of transactions that may constitute troubled debt restructurings:

(a) Transfer from the debtor to the creditor of receivables from third parties, real estate, or other assets to satisfy fully or partially a debt (including a transfer resulting from foreclosure or repossession).

(b) Issuance or other granting of an equity interest to the creditor by the debtor to satisfy fully or partially a debt unless the equity interest is granted pursuant to existing terms for converting the debt into an equity interest.

(c) Modification of terms of a debt, such as one or a combination of:

(1) Reduction (absolute or contingent) of the stated interest rate for the remaining original life of the debt.

(2) Extension of the maturity date or dates at a stated interest rate lower than the current market rate for a new debt with similar risk.

(3) Reduction (absolute or contingent) of the face amount or maturity amount of the debt as stated in the instrument or other agreement.

(4) Reduction (absolute or contingent) of accrued interest.[4]

Individual creditor agreements. The most frequently used manner of restructuring debt is the **individual creditor agreement** between a debtor and a creditor whereby the payment terms are restructured pursuant to negotiated terms. Within the last five years, dozens of large companies have restructured their debt in this manner or have at least attempted to do so. Typically, the creditors involved are banks. The most recent, widely publicized completed restructurings were those of Chrysler Corporation (which owed $4.4 billion to more than 400 banks) and International Harvester Corporation (which owed $3.4 billion to more than 200 banks).

Composition agreements. A **composition agreement** is a formal agreement between a debtor and its creditors (and among the creditors) whereby the creditors collectively agree to accept a percentage of their claims—such as 60 cents on the dollar—in full settlement of their claims. For example, a composition agreement may include only the debtor's major creditors, with all other creditors still entitled to full payment. The payment terms of the composition agreement may require immediate, partial, or full payment of the reduced amount. To the extent that payment of the reduced amount is deferred, a debtor may execute notes payable bearing interest on the deferred amount.

Composition agreements are usually negotiated when a company's filing for a Chapter 11 reorganization is imminent. As a result of the agreement, the company does not suffer the taint of having gone through a bankruptcy proceeding; a potentially lengthy and involved bankruptcy process is avoided;

---

[3] *FASB Statement No. 15*, paragraph 3.
[4] *FASB Statement No. 15*, paragraph 5.

and the creditors expect to recover more than they would in a Chapter 11 reorganization.

Conceptual issues

Troubled debt restructurings usually result in the creditors' substantial reduction of the debtor's financial obligations (required payments for principal and interest). This procedure requires a comparison of (a) the total amount owed (including unpaid interest) immediately before the restructuring, which is commonly referred to as the **carrying amount of the debt,** with (b) the **total future payments** (including amounts designated as interest) to be made pursuant to the restructuring agreement. If the carrying amount of the debt exceeds the total future payments, the debtor's liabilities must be reduced. This reduction constitutes a **forgiveness of debt.** If the debtor's total future payments exceed the carrying amount of the debt, the excess is **reported as interest expense** in future periods. This situation presents no accounting issue. The accounting issues pertain solely to the forgiveness of debt and are as follows:

(1) **How should any forgiveness of debt be measured?** The focus of this issue is primarily whether the new (post-restructuring) liability amount should be measured and reported as (a) the undiscounted total future payments to be made, or (b) the present value of total future payments. The difference between (a) or (b) and the carrying amount of the debt is the amount of the forgiveness. Obviously, the choice between (a) and (b) affects the amount of forgiveness.

(2) **How should a forgiveness of debt be classified and reported?** This issue is concerned with whether a forgiveness of debt should be considered (a) a **gain** and, therefore, reported in the **income statement,** or (b) a **capital contribution** by the creditor(s) and, therefore, credited directly to an **equity account.**

Of course, the resolution of these issues should be based on the **substance** of the restructuring, rather than its **form.** However, varying perceptions exist as to what constitutes the substance.

Conceptual issue (1):
Calculation of forgiveness of debt

In some situations, this calculation is quite simple. For example, assume a creditor that is owed $100,000 agrees to cancel $40,000 of the debt in return for the immediate payment of the remaining $60,000. Obviously, the amount of debt forgiven is $40,000. Most situations, however, are more complex. For example, assume that (1) a creditor is owed $100,000 of principal related to a delinquent loan bearing interest at 10% (for simplicity, we assume no interest is owed); and (2) the creditor agrees to be paid in full in two years with no interest to be charged. Two approaches have been advocated for such situations—one that **imputes interest** and one that **does not impute interest.** When interest is not imputed, the calculation to determine any forgiveness of debt is as follows.

Carrying amount of debt...	$100,000
Total future payments	100,000
Amount of forgiveness..	$ –0–

Under this approach, the liability reported in the balance sheet immediately after the restructuring is $100,000, and it bears a zero interest rate. No interest expense would be reported in either year.

When interest is imputed (using present value techniques), the amount of forgiveness, if any, depends on the imputed interest rate used. Assuming that the 10% pre-restructuring interest rate is appropriate, the calculation to determine any forgiveness of debt is as follows:

Carrying amount of debt.............................		$100,000
Total future payments	$100,000	
Present value factor (10%, 2 years)	0.82645	
Present value of total future payments		82,645
Amount of forgiveness...........................		$ 17,355

Under this approach, the liability reported in the balance sheet immediately after the restructuring is $82,645, and it bears interest at 10%. Interest expense of $8,264 (10% of $82,645) would be reported in year one, and $9,091 [10% of ($82,645 + $8,264)] would be reported in year two.

Rationale for not imputing interest. Arguments for not imputing interest are as follows:

(1) Troubled debt restructurings *are not* "exchanges of debt" and, therefore, *do not* require the use of present value techniques as set forth in *APB Opinion No. 21*, "Interest on Receivables and Payables," which deals with "exchanges."
(2) A creditor does not grant any forgiveness under the restructuring as long as the total future payments to be received equal or exceed the recorded investment in the receivable; that is, the **recoverability** of the recorded investment in the receivable is not affected.
(3) A reduction of the debtor's financial obligations (before the restructuring) to the amount of the recorded investment in the receivable merely changes the creditor's **future profitability** on the loan. Thus, a creditor's effective interest rate after the restructuring could vary from the pre-restructuring interest rate of 10%, for example, down to zero.

Recall from the nonimputing example that no forgiveness of debt existed because the total future payments of $100,000 were not below the $100,000 carrying amount of the debt. Thus, from the creditor's perspective, the future profitability on the loan had been reduced to zero, but the recoverability of the recorded amount of the receivable had not been affected.

Rationale for imputing interest. Arguments for imputing interest are as follows.

(1) The debtor's liability after restructuring ($82,645 in the imputing example) is reported on the same basis as the borrowings of all debtors—that is, the present value of the future cash outflows for principal and interest.
(2) The debtor's future income statements will reflect a reasonable amount of interest expense, which should enhance comparability of those statements with the debtor's past income statements and with future income statements of other companies.

An implementation issue under this approach is whether the **pre-restructuring** interest rate or a current market interest rate should be used. Most accountants feel that the debtor's obligation after the restructuring results from a modification of an existing loan. Therefore, the pre-restructuring rate should be used. Other accountants who view the debtor's obligation after restructuring as arising from the execution of a new lending agreement conclude that a current market interest rate should be used. An advantage of the pre-restructuring approach is that the interest rate is known. However, the current market rate approach involves determining the interest rate at which a debtor in a precarious financial position might be able to borrow when, in fact, no lenders may be available.

Conceptual issue (2):
Reporting forgiveness of debt

A forgiveness of debt may be reported in the income statement. In this approach, a forgiveness of debt is a **gain on restructuring,** which is **similar to a gain on extinguishment of debt.** Under *APB Opinion No. 26,* "Early Extinguishment of Debt," gain on extinguishment of debt must be reported in the income statement. Most advocates of this position agree that such a gain should be reported as an extraordinary item because the criteria of unusual and infrequent would be met.
In a second alternative, a forgiveness of debt may be reported as a **direct addition to paid-in capital.** The arguments for this approach are as follows:

(1) Because the transaction infuses capital to the debtor, in substance, the debtor has received a capital contribution from the creditor.
(2) It should make no difference whether the additional capital needed to keep the debtor in business comes from stockholders or creditors.
(3) A company in serious financial difficulty, which has probably reported substantial operating losses, should not report income on a transaction intended to assist it in eventually returning to profitable operations.

Requirements of *FASB Statement No. 15*

After considering the various viewpoints on imputing or not imputing interest, the FASB concluded that (1) interest should **not be imputed** in the calculation to determine if any forgiveness of debt exists; (2) the amount of debt forgiven should be reported as a **gain on restructuring;** and (3) such gain, if material, should be reported as an **extraordinary item,** net of its related income tax effect. Accordingly, in calculating the amount of debt forgiven, the carrying amount of the debt is compared with any one (or more) of the following that was included in the restructuring plan:

(1) The total future cash payments specified in the new terms, **not discounted** back to their present value.
(2) The fair value of the noncash assets transferred.
(3) The fair value of the equity interest granted.

To the extent that the carrying amount of the debt exceeds the relevant factor(s) listed above, a gain on restructuring is reportable.

We now define in detail certain terms used in *FASB Statement No. 15.*

(1) Carrying amount of the debt. The carrying amount of the debt is the face, or principal, amount, plus any accrued interest payable, less any unamortized discount (or plus any premium), finance charges, or debt issuance costs.[5]

(2) Total future cash payments. Total future cash payments include amounts that are designated principal and interest.[6] Thus, the labels traditionally assigned to amounts to be paid to creditors lose their significance for purposes of determining if a gain on restructuring of debt exists.

(3) Fair value. Fair value is defined as "the amount that the debtor could reasonably expect to receive . . . in a current sale between a willing buyer and a willing seller, that is, other than in a forced or liquidation sale."[7]

In most respects, this approach for calculating the amount of debt forgiven is relatively simple to apply. However, subsequent income statements reflect either no interest expense (when a forgiveness of debt is reportable) or unrealistically low interest expense (when no forgiveness of debt is reportable) until the maturity date of the restructured debt. Consequently, reported earnings are higher than the earnings reported if the company paid interest (or at least measured interest expense) at the current rate. Because of the potentially misleading inferences that can be made from subsequent income statements immediately after a complex restructuring, it is important to disclose in the notes to the financial statements of the appropriate subsequent periods the fact that reported interest expense is artificially low because the restructuring was accounted for in this manner.

Other important technical and procedural points of *FASB Statement No. 15* are the following:

(1) The date of consummation is the point in time at which the restructuring occurs.[8]
(2) The restructuring of each payable is accounted for individually, even if the restructuring was negotiated and restructured jointly.[9]

---

[5] *FASB Statement No. 15*, paragraph 13.
[6] *FASB Statement No. 15*, paragraph 16, footnote 9.
[7] *FASB Statement No. 15*, paragraph 13.
[8] *FASB Statement No. 15*, paragraph 6.
[9] *FASB Statement No. 15*, paragraph 4.

(3) When a noncash asset is transferred to a creditor in full settlement of a debt, the difference between the carrying amount of the noncash asset and its fair value is recognized as a gain or loss in the transfer of the asset. (Such gain or loss is reported in the income statement in the period of transfer as provided in *APB Opinion No. 30,* "Reporting the Results of Operations.")[10]

(4) To the extent that the total future cash payments specified in the new terms exceed the carrying amount of the debt, the difference is reported as interest expense between the restructuring date and the maturity date.[11]

(5) The "interest" method prescribed by *APB Opinion No. 21* is used to calculate the amount of the interest expense for each year between the restructuring date and the maturity date. This method causes a constant effective interest rate to be applied to the carrying amount of the debt at the beginning of each period between the restructuring date and the maturity date.[12]

(6) When a gain on restructuring has been recognized, all future cash payments are charged to the carrying amount of the payable. In other words, if a gain on restructuring is reported, then there cannot be any future interest expense with respect to that debt.[13]

(7) For determining if a gain on restructuring exists, the total future cash payments include amounts that may be contingently payable.[14]

(8) When the debtor grants an equity interest to a creditor to settle fully a payable, the equity interest is recorded in the debtor's capital accounts at its fair value, and any remaining liability in excess of this fair value is recognized as a gain on restructuring of payables.[15]

(9) When either noncash assets or an equity interest is given to a creditor in partial settlement of a payable and the payment terms of the remaining payable are modified, the fair value of the assets transferred or the equity interest granted is first subtracted from the carrying amount of the payable. The residual amount of the payable is then compared with the total future cash payments specified in the new terms to determine if a gain on restructuring exists.[16]

Illustration:
Application of *FASB Statement No. 15*

Assume that the financially distressed Never-Quit Company has consummated a troubled debt restructuring with substantially all of its unsecured creditors on August 31, 19X1. The August 31, 19X1 balance sheet of Never-Quit—before the restructuring—is shown in Illustration 18-1. We assume that all notes payable (secured and unsecured) are currently due and payable as a result of defaults under related loan agreements.

The following items are part of the restructuring. For each of these items

[10] *FASB Statement No. 15,* paragraph 14.
[11] *FASB Statement No. 15,* paragraph 16.
[12] *FASB Statement No. 15,* paragraph 16.
[13] *FASB Statement No. 15,* paragraph 17.
[14] *FASB Statement No. 15,* paragraph 18.
[15] *FASB Statement No. 15,* paragraph 15.
[16] *FASB Statement No. 15,* paragraph 19.

Illustration 18-1

NEVER-QUIT COMPANY
Balance Sheet
August 31, 19X1
(immediately before restructuring)

Assets

Current Assets:

Cash		$ 450,000
Accounts receivable	$ 650,000	
Less—Allowance for uncollectibles	(240,000)	410,000
Inventories		800,000
Total current assets...		$ 1,660,000

Noncurrent Assets:

Property, plant, and equipment	$2,700,000	
Less—Accumulated depreciation........................	(1,500,000)	1,200,000
Other assets		140,000
Total assets...		$ 3,000,000

Liabilities and Stockholders' Deficiency

Current Liabilities:

Note payable, secured by land and buildings	$ 1,000,000
Notes payable, unsecured	2,050,000
Accrued interest (all on unsecured notes)	540,000
Accounts payable...	925,000
Other accrued liabilities	75,000
Total liabilities	$ 4,590,000

Stockholders' Deficiency:

Common stock, $1 par value, 200,000 shares issued and outstanding ..	$ 200,000
Additional paid-in capital	1,850,000
Accumulated deficit	(3,640,000)
Total stockholders' deficiency	$(1,590,000)
Total liabilities in excess of stockholders' deficiency	$ 3,000,000

(except the last item), the application of *FASB Statement No. 15* is explained and the journal entry to reflect the restructuring is given. (All solutions ignore income tax effects.)

(1) Payment of cash in full settlement. Never-Quit Company owes $600,000 to 80 vendors. These vendors have collectively agreed to settle their claims fully for 40 cents on the dollar. Payment of $240,000 was made on August 31, 19X1. Because the carrying amount of the $600,000 debt exceeds the total future cash payments of $240,000, a $360,000 gain on restructuring of debt is reportable in the 19X1 income statement, recorded as follows:

Accounts payable	600,000	
Cash...		240,000
Gain on restructuring of debt		360,000
To record payment to vendors and gain on restructuring of debt.		

(2) Transfer of receivables in full settlement. The company owes $325,000 to a vendor, who has agreed to accept certain of the company's accounts receivable totaling $280,000. The company has an allowance of $100,000 recorded on the books against these receivables. The receivables were assigned to the creditor on August 31, 19X1. The company has not guaranteed the collectibility of these receivables.

Because the $325,000 carrying amount of the debt exceeds the $180,000 fair value of the assets (the net amount expected to be collectible by the debtor), a gain on restructuring of $145,000 is reportable in the 19X1 income statement, recorded as follows:

Accounts payable	325,000	
Allowance for uncollectibles	100,000	
Accounts receivable		280,000
Gain on restructuring of debt		145,000
To record transfer of assets to vendor and		
gain on restructuring of debt.		

(3) Grant of an equity interest in full settlement. The company owes $500,000 ($430,000 principal and $70,000 interest) to a financial institution, which has agreed to cancel the entire amount owed in exchange for 100,000 shares of the debtor's common stock. The market value of the common stock on August 31, 19X1 is $3.50 per share. The company issued the 100,000 shares to the creditor on this date.

Because the $500,000 carrying amount of the debt exceeds the $350,000 fair value of the equity interest granted (100,000 shares × $3.50 per share), a gain on restructuring of debt of $150,000 is reportable in the 19X1 income statement, recorded as follows:

Notes payable	430,000	
Accrued interest payable	70,000	
Common stock		100,000
Additional paid-in capital		250,000
Gain on restructuring of debt		150,000
To record grant of equity interest and		
gain on restructuring of debt.		

(4) Modification of debt terms (No contingent interest). The company owes $260,000 ($220,000 principal and $40,000 interest) to a financial institution, which has agreed to cancel $20,000 of principal and the $40,000 of accrued interest and reduce the interest rate on the remaining principal to 5% for five years, at the end of which time the note is to be paid in full.

Because the $260,000 carrying amount of the debt exceeds the $250,000 total future cash payments as specified in the terms of the agreement ($200,000 designated as a principal payment and $50,000 designated as interest payments), a gain on restructuring of debt of $10,000 is reportable in the 19X1 income statement, recorded as follows:

Notes payable	220,000	
Accrued interest payable	40,000	
Restructured debt		250,000
Gain on restructuring of debt		10,000
To record the restructuring of the debt and		
the resultant gain.		

Because a gain on restructuring of debt exists, no interest expense is reported for the next five years on this debt.

(5) Modification of debt terms (Contingent interest). The company owes a total of $750,000 ($500,000 principal and $250,000 interest) to a financial institution, which has agreed to the following:

(a) The $250,000 accrued interest is canceled.
(b) The due date of the $500,000 principal is extended six years from August 31, 19X1.
(c) The interest rate for the first three years is 5% (a reduction of 5% from the old rate).
(d) The interest rate for the following three years is 10%.
(e) If the debtor's cumulative earnings for the next six years exceed $1,000,000, then interest for the first three years must be paid at 10% instead of 5%. (The cumulative earnings will probably not exceed $1,000,000 for the next six years.)

The total minimum and maximum future payments are determined as follows:

Principal...	$500,000
Interest—years 1, 2, and 3 @ 5%	75,000
Interest—years 4, 5, and 6 @ 10%	150,000
Minimum total future payments	$725,000
Contingent interest—years 1, 2, and 3	75,000
Maximum total future payments.........................	$800,000

The $750,000 carrying value of the debt does not exceed the $800,000 total maximum future payments that may be made under the new terms. Thus, no gain on restructuring of debt is reportable in 19X1.

Notes payable	500,000	
Accrued interest payable	250,000	
Restructured debt		750,000
To record the restructuring of the debt.		

If at the end of the sixth year the cumulative earnings have not exceeded $1,000,000, then a $25,000 gain on restructuring is reported at that time. If it becomes probable during the six years that the cumulative earnings will exceed $1,000,000, then additional interest expense of $50,000 ($800,000 − $750,000 carrying amount of the debt) must be provided over the remaining life of the loan.

(6) **Combination grant of equity interest and modification of debt terms.** Never-Quit Company owes $1,080,000 ($900,000 principal and $180,000 interest) to some of its major stockholders, who have agreed to the following:

(a) Accrued interest of $80,000 is canceled.
(b) Principal of $400,000 is canceled in exchange for the issuance of 4,000 shares of 6%, $100 par value, convertible preferred stock with cumulative dividends. (We assume that the articles of incorporation were amended to approve the authorization for this new class of stock, which was issued on August 31, 19X1.)
(c) The remaining principal of $500,000 and the uncanceled interest of $100,000 bear interest at 5%, with $300,000 to be paid in six months and the remaining $300,000 to be paid in 18 months.

Because no established market price is available for the preferred stock, we assume that the fair value of the preferred stock equals the $400,000 amount of the principal canceled. This assumed fair value of the preferred stock is subtracted from the $1,080,000 carrying value of the debt to arrive at an **adjusted carrying value** of $680,000. The adjusted carrying value of $680,000 is then compared with the total future payments to determine if a gain on restructuring exists. The total future payments are $630,000 ($600,000 designated as principal and $30,000 designated as interest). Accordingly, a gain on restructuring of debt of $50,000 ($680,000 − $630,000) is reportable in the 19X1 income statement, recorded as follows:

Notes payable	900,000	
Accrued interest payable	180,000	
Preferred stock		400,000
Restructured debt		630,000
Gain on restructuring of debt		50,000

To record the restructuring of the debt.

(7) **Reclassification by secured creditor.** None of the preceding items pertains to the company's secured creditor (who is owed $1,000,000), because a secured creditor is under no economic compulsion to make concessions. Because of the preceding restructurings, however, this creditor agrees to have Never-Quit repay $960,000 of the $1,000,000 owed after August 31, 19X2, leaving only $40,000 as a current liability as of August 31, 19X1. (The interest rate was not changed.)

The August 31, 19X1 balance sheet of the Never-Quit Company, which reflects the financial terms of the restructurings, is shown in Illustration 18-2. In comparing Illustration 18-2 with Illustration 18-1, note that the stockholders' deficiency has been almost eliminated as a result of the restructuring. Although a substantial portion of the stockholders' deficiency is usually eliminated in a troubled debt restructuring, the entire deficiency need not be eliminated for the rehabilitation efforts to be successful.

Illustration 18-2

NEVER-QUIT COMPANY
Balance Sheet
August 31, 19X1
(after the restructuring)

Assets

Current Assets:

Cash		$ 210,000
Accounts receivable	$ 370,000	
Less—Allowance for uncollectibles	(140,000)	230,000
Inventories		800,000
Total current assets		$1,240,000

Noncurrent Assets:

Property, plant, and equipment	$2,700,000	
Less—Accumulated depreciation	(1,500,000)	1,200,000
Other assets		140,000
Total assets		$2,580,000

Liabilities and Stockholders' Deficiency

Current Liabilities:

Other accrued liabilities	$ 75,000
Current portion of secured note payable	40,000
Current portion of restructured debt, unsecured	300,000
Total current liabilities	$ 415,000

Long-Term Debt:

Secured note payable	$ 960,000
Restructured debt, unsecured	1,330,000
Total long-term debt	$2,290,000

Stockholders' Deficiency:

Preferred stock, 6%, $100 par value, cumulative, 40,000 shares issued and outstanding	$ 400,000
Common stock, $1 par value, 300,000 shares issued and outstanding	300,000
Additional paid-in capital	2,100,000
Accumulated deficit	(2,925,000)
Total stockholders' deficiency	$ (125,000)
Total liabilities in excess of stockholders' deficiency	$2,580,000

Never-Quit's 19X1 income statement reflects the gain on restructuring as an extraordinary item, part of the period's income but separate from income (loss) from operations. The illustration has omitted tax effects, which we address in a later section.

Nonapplicability of *FASB Statement No. 15* to quasi-reorganizations

Although a debt restructuring may eliminate most or all of the stockholders' deficiency, some companies try to eliminate the accumulated deficit by using the "quasi-reorganization" procedures provided by many state laws. Recall from intermediate accounting that adjustments made to restate (usually write down) assets in a quasi-reorganization are charged directly to equity.[17] Adjustments to restate (reduce) liabilities in a quasi-reorganization are similarly credited directly to equity. Treating such adjustments to assets and liabilities as capital transactions is desirable, because otherwise asset write-downs would be reported as capital transactions and liability reductions would be reported (per the general rule of *FASB Statement No. 15*) as noncapital (income statement) transactions.

FASB Statement No. 15 does not apply to a troubled debt restructuring that coincides with quasi-reorganization procedures if the debtor "restates its liabilities generally" in that quasi-reorganization.[18] The phrase **restates its liabilities generally** is a new term introduced into the accounting literature by *FASB Statement No. 15*. Although the pronouncement does not define the term, it means a restructuring that encompasses most of a company's liabilities, as would usually occur when restructuring is part of the quasi-reorganization plan. Although *FASB Statement No. 15* does not explain why it does not apply to these situations, we may assume that the FASB wants to allow consistent treatment for both asset and liability adjustments in quasi-reorganizations.

This explanation does not help in the more common situation in which the stockholders' deficiency resulted from several years of large operating losses—that is, not from a restatement of the assets. Regardless of what caused the accumulated deficit (whether from restating assets or from operating losses), the following question is raised: Why should the decision to eliminate the accumulated deficit using quasi-reorganization procedures (a mere formality under state law) change the perception of forgiveness of debt from an income statement gain (in *FASB Statement No. 15*) to a capital transaction? The answer evidently lies in the "fresh start" objective of a quasi-reorganization. A restructuring not involving a quasi-reorganization maintains the company's basic continuity. A quasi-reorganization results in the assumed death of the old company and the assumed creation of a new one. A "break" exists that usually destroys any pre- versus post-income statement comparability. Because of this fresh start objective, treating the forgiveness as a capital transaction makes more sense.

Tax consequences of gains on restructurings

The Internal Revenue Code treats gains on troubled debt restructurings as taxable only to the extent that such restructurings result in a positive balance in total stockholders' equity (not retained earnings). However, certain Code provisions allow the gain to be allocated to the company's assets to reduce their basis for tax reporting purposes. This allocation for income tax purposes results in deferred income taxes for financial reporting purposes, because in financial reporting, the gain must be reported as an extraordinary item net of income tax effects.

---

[17] This procedure is required pursuant to the provisions of *Accounting Research Bulletin No. 43*, Chapter 7, Section A, "Capital Accounts," paragraph 6. This position was reaffirmed in *Accounting Principles Board Opinion No. 9*, "Reporting the Results of Operations," paragraph 28.

[18] *FASB Statement No. 15*, footnote 4.

Accounting by creditors

Although this chapter is concerned with accounting by a debtor, *FASB Statement No. 15* applies to creditors as well. In most respects, accounting by a creditor is symmetrical to the accounting by a debtor. Thus, if the debtor reports a gain on restructuring, the creditor simultaneously reports an offsetting loss on restructuring of its receivables, except to the extent that such loss has already been provided for in allowances for uncollectibles or write-offs, or both.

Interestingly, the banking industry uniformly and vehemently opposed the imputed interest (discounted present value) approach of calculating the amount of debt forgiven as presented in the FASB Discussion Memorandum that preceded *FASB Statement No. 15*. This approach would have had creditors reporting much greater losses than under the "no-discount" alternative adopted by the FASB. How the banking industry's strong vocal position influenced the FASB in its deliberations is conjecture. It is interesting to note, however, that the FASB's first exposure draft on troubled debt restructurings (dated November 7, 1975 and encompassing only accounting by debtors) called for the imputed interest approach. Because of the obvious implications to creditors—that is, if a debtor reports a gain, the creditor should simultaneously report a loss—the project was expanded to include accounting by creditors as well.

Subsequent period interest expense in "no reportable gain" restructurings

As indicated in *FASB Statement No. 15* procedural points (4) and (5) (page 636), when total future payments exceed the carrying amount of the debt, the excess is reported as interest expense between the restructuring date and the maturity date using the interest method prescribed by *APB Opinion No. 21*. In such cases, the effective interest rate must be calculated. Assume the following information:

(1) Carrying amount of the debt at January 1, 19X1:

Principal owed	$1,100,000
Interest owed	33,947
	$1,133,947

(2) Cancellation of debt per restructuring agreement consummated January 1, 19X1:

Principal	$ 100,000
Interest	33,947
	$ 133,947

(3) Total future payments to be made:

Amount designated as principal (due December 31, 19X2)	$1,000,000
Amounts designated as interest (10% of $1,000,000 payable annually at year-end for two years)	200,000
	$1,200,000

Because the $1,200,000 total future payments exceed the $1,133,947 carrying amount of the debt, $66,053 interest expense ($1,200,000 − $1,133,947) is reported in the income statements during the two years following the restructuring. What interest rate is needed for the total future payments of $1,200,000 to equal the present value of the carrying amount of the debt of $1,133,947? A trial and error approach to the present value tables reveals that the effective interest rate is 3%. The present value calculations are shown below:

Designation	Total Future Payments	Present Value Factor at 3%	Present Value
Principal	$1,000,000	0.94260	$ 942,600
Interest	200,000	1.91347[a]	191,347
	$1,200,000		$1,133,947

[a] Obtained from an annuity present value table (applied to the $100,000 annual amount).

This illustration was designed so that the effective interest rate would be an even number to avoid the additional complexity of interpolating. In practice, of course, interpolating is usually necessary.

The following entries would be made for the restructuring, the recording of interest using the effective interest rate, and the payments made under the restructuring agreement:

(1) January 1, 19X1:

Notes payable	1,100,000	
Interest payable	33,947	
Restructured debt		1,133,947

To record the effect of the restructuring.

(2) December 31, 19X1:

Interest expense	34,018	
Restructured debt	65,982	
Cash		100,000

To record interest expense at 3% of $1,133,947 and the first payment of $100,000.

(3) December 31, 19X2:

Interest expense	32,035	
Restructured debt	67,965	
Cash		100,000

To record interest expense at 3% of $1,067,965 ($1,133,947 − $65,982) and the second payment of $100,000.

Restructured debt	1,000,000	
Cash		1,000,000

To record the $1,000,000 payment at its maturity date.

The entries affecting the Restructured Debt account are recorded in the following T account to illustrate how the use of the exact effective interest rate results in a zero balance after the last required payment.

		Restructured Debt	
		1,133,947	Jan. 1, 19X1
Dec. 31, 19X1	65,982		
		1,067,965	
Dec. 31, 19X2	67,965		
		1,000,000	
Dec. 31, 19X2	1,000,000		
		-0-	

BANKRUPTCY REORGANIZATIONS

Although Chapter 11 of the bankruptcy statutes is the reorganization chapter, the statutes do not define the term *reorganization*. However, we may assume from the Chapter 11 purpose and the procedures that the chapter allows that the term is intended to have a broad meaning. Basically, a **reorganization** encompasses the development of a plan—called a **plan of reorganization**— to alter the company's liability and/or equity structure so that the company has a reasonable chance of surviving bankruptcy proceedings and prospering on its own.

Most reorganization plans involve a negotiated settlement between the company and its unsecured creditors to repay debts, usually at so many cents on the dollar. Thus, the company is provided with a "fresh start," a unique opportunity in business. Approximately 10–20% of all business bankruptcy filings are Chapter 11 filings (the remainder being Chapter 7 filings). Of these Chapter 11 filings, approximately 25% emerge from Chapter 11 as viable companies; the remainder are transferred to Chapter 7 and liquidated.

Advantages of reorganizing under Chapter 11 versus restructuring outside of the bankruptcy courts

The primary advantage to a distressed company of a Chapter 11 reorganization is that it usually results in a massive reduction of the debtor's liabilities (forgiveness of debt) compared with the amount of debt forgiven in a restructuring outside of the bankruptcy courts. In addition, a considerable amount of cash is saved because interest on unsecured debt does not accrue during the period of the bankruptcy proceeding—the amount of unsecured creditors' claims is fixed at the bankruptcy filing. For example, Itel Corporation (a spectacular growth company in the 1970s) saved more than $250 million of interest related to its unsecured debt during the 32 months that it was in Chapter 11 reorganization (concluded in 1983). Furthermore, filing for reorganization under Chapter 11 places a company in sanctuary from its creditors because they cannot sue for overdue payments. As a result, the distressed company has some breathing room to develop a plan of reorganization. When recessions and high interest rates occur (as in the early 1980s), increasing numbers of companies flee to the bankruptcy courts for protection from creditors and for the opportunity to salvage the potentially productive (profitable) portions of the existing organization.

Sequence of events in a Chapter 11 filing

The typical sequence of events in a Chapter 11 filing is as follows:

(1) **Filing the petition.**   Either a voluntary or an involuntary petition can initiate bankruptcy proceedings. The company in question may prepare a statement showing asset values and amounts that would be paid to each class of creditor in the event of liquidation. As noted earlier, accountants call this a statement of affairs. We illustrate the preparation of this statement later in the chapter in connection with liquidations.

(2) **Management of the company.**   The debtor's management usually continues to control and operate the debtor's day-to-day activities. Under certain conditions and for just cause (such as fraud, incompetence, or gross mismanagement of the company) and if in the best interests of creditors, the court may appoint a trustee to manage the debtor's business [Section 1104(a)]. The appointment of a trustee in a Chapter 11 filing is **infrequent.** We discuss the duties of trustees later in the chapter in connection with liquidations, for which trustees are always appointed.

(3) **Creditors' and equity security holders' committees.**   After an order for relief has been entered, the court appoints a committee of unsecured creditors. (The court may also appoint additional committees of creditors or of equity security holders if necessary to ensure adequate representation of creditors or of equity security holders.) Such a court-appointed committee may

> (a) select and authorize [with the court's approval] the employment by such committee of one or more attorneys, accountants, or other agents, to represent or perform services for such committee [Section 1103(a)];
>
> (b) consult with the trustee or debtor in possession concerning the administration of the case;
>
> (c) investigate the acts, conduct, assets, liabilities and financial condition of the debtor, the operation of the debtor's business and the desirability of the continuance of such business, and any other matter relevant to the case or to the formulation of a plan;
>
> (d) participate in the formulation of a plan [of reorganization], advise those represented by such committee of such committee's recommendations as to any plan formulated, and collect and file with the court acceptances of a plan;
>
> (e) request the appointment of a trustee or examiner . . . if a trustee or examiner, as the case may be, has not previously been appointed . . . ; and
>
> (f) perform such other services as are in the interest of those represented [Section 1103(c)].

(4) **Plan of reorganization.**   Under Chapter 11 of the 1978 Act, a plan of reorganization may alter the legal, equitable, and contractual rights of any class of creditors' claims, secured or unsecured, or of equity interests. Such an alteration is known as **impairment** of a claim or an interest (Section 1124). In a common plan of reorganization, all unsecured creditors agree to accept payment at a percentage of their respective claims—for example, 25 cents on the dollar—with the remainder of the debt canceled.

The debtor has the exclusive right to propose a plan during the 120 days after the order for relief. At the end of this 120-day period, any party of interest—such as the trustee, committee, a creditor, or an equity security holder—may file a plan, provided certain conditions are met (Section 1121). The role of the SEC is quite limited and is as follows:

> The Securities and Exchange Commission may raise and may appear and be heard for any issue . . . but the SEC may not appeal from any judgment, order, or decree entered in the case (Section 1109).

(5) Disclosure statement.   Before acceptance of a plan of reorganization can be solicited, the debtor must furnish the plan or a summary of the plan to the various classes of creditors and equity interests, along with a written disclosure statement approved by the court as containing **adequate information** [Section 1125(b)]. Adequate information is defined as "information of a kind, and in sufficient detail, as far as is reasonably practicable in light of the nature and history of the debtor and the condition of the debtor's books and records, that would enable a hypothetical reasonable investor . . . to make an informed judgment about the plan" [Section 1125(a)(1)]. This is obviously determined on a case-by-case basis.

(6) Acceptance of plan.   Each class of creditors and equity interests then votes to accept or reject the plan of reorganization. The requirements for approval are as follows:

(a) Creditor's claims. "A class of claims has accepted a plan if such plan has been accepted by creditors . . . that hold at least **two-thirds in amount and more than one-half in number** of the allowed claims of such class . . ." [Section 1126(c)].

(b) Equity interests. "A class of interests has accepted a plan if such plan has been accepted by holders of such interests . . . that hold at least **two-thirds in amount** of the allowed interests of such class . . ." [Section 1126(d)].

(7) Confirmation of the plan by the court.   After the plan of reorganization has been submitted to the court, a hearing is held. A plan must meet 11 specific requirements to be approved by the court. The overriding requirement is that the debtor must be unlikely to be liquidated or have need for further financial reorganization after the plan is confirmed. In other words, the plan of reorganization must be feasible. Another major requirement is that each class of claims or equity interests must have accepted the plan or must not be impaired under the plan. However, a provision in the law (referred to in House Committee Reports as "cram down"), allows the court to confirm the plan (if requested by the proponent of the plan) even if each class of claims or equity interests has not accepted it. For this to occur, the plan must not discriminate unfairly and must be fair and equitable with respect to each class of claims or equity interests that is impaired or has not accepted the plan (Section 1129).

If the court does not confirm the plan of reorganization, it may, on request of a party of interest and after notice and a hearing, either dismiss the case or convert it to a Chapter 7 case (whereby the debtor is forced out of business through liquidation). Such action depends on which course of action is in the best interest of creditors and the estate (Section 1112).

(8) Discharge of indebtedness. After the court confirms the plan of reorganization, the debtor is discharged of certain indebtedness as set forth in the plan. However, if the debtor has committed certain acts, then discharge of indebtedness does not occur even though a plan has been confirmed [Section 1141(d)]. In general, discharge of indebtedness is not granted if (a) the debtor has not fully cooperated with the court (for example, by not making all properties and records available to the court's representative, failing to explain losses satisfactorily, or refusing to obey court orders); and (b) the debtor has performed certain specified acts involving the debtor's properties and records to hinder, delay, or defraud creditors (for example, concealing property, destroying records, failing to keep or preserve records, or obtaining money or property fraudulently) [Section 727(a)]. A discharge is not granted if the debtor was granted a discharge in a case commenced within six years before the filing date of the petition [Section 727(a)].

(9) Exceptions to discharge of indebtedness. Certain types of indebtedness cannot be discharged under the bankruptcy statutes. These debts, which eventually must be paid if the debtor survives Chapter 11 proceedings, are as follows:

(A) Taxes owed to the United States or any state, county, district, or municipality, and customs duties;

(B) Debts incurred in obtaining money, property, services, an extension renewal, or refinance of credit by:
(a) false pretenses, a false representation, or actual fraud, other than a statement concerning the debtor's financial condition; or
(b) use of a written statement that is materially false with respect to the debtor's financial condition on which the creditor reasonably relied and that the debtor made or published with intent to deceive;

(C) Debts that have not been duly scheduled in time for proof and allowance because a creditor had no notice or knowledge of bankruptcy proceedings;

(D) Debts for fraud or defalcation while acting in a fiduciary capacity, or larceny;

(E) Debts related to willful and malicious injury by the debtor to another entity or to the property of another entity;

(F) Fines, penalties, and forfeitures payable to and for the benefit of a governmental unit (Section 523).

Accounting issues

The accounting issues in bankruptcy reorganizations are the same as those discussed earlier for troubled debt restructurings—that is, how to calculate and report the amount of debt forgiven. After some initial confusion as to the application of *FASB Statement No. 15* to bankruptcy reorganizations,

FASB Technical Bulletin No. 81-6 was issued to clarify the matter. This bulletin states that *FASB Statement No. 15* does not apply to bankruptcy reorganizations that result in a "general restatement of the debtor's liabilities" (defined earlier as a restructuring of most of the amount of a company's liabilities).[19] Because this usually occurs in bankruptcy reorganizations, *FASB Statement No. 15* will rarely apply. Consequently, the following questions must be addressed:

(1) What is meaningful accounting for a reorganized company?
(2) What, if any, guidance is contained in promulgated accounting standards?

We first address the calculation of the amount of debt forgiven and then the reporting of such forgiveness.

Calculation of forgiveness of debt.   In reorganizations in which unsecured creditors are paid immediately at so many cents on the dollar, there is only one way to calculate the forgiveness. However, unsecured creditors may also be given cash and notes payable (and often equity securities as well). Traditionally, accountants have compared the amount owed with the fair value (discounted present value, in the case of debt) of the consideration given to determine the amount of debt forgiven. This method usually results in a much larger reported forgiveness ("gain") than would result under the *FASB Statement No. 15* approach of comparing the carrying amount of the debt (essentially the amount owed) with the undiscounted total future payments. To illustrate the dramatic difference that can occur, assume a company in bankruptcy reorganization proceedings proposes to settle with its unsecured creditors (who are owed $10,000,000) by paying $2,000,000 cash and giving $5,000,000 of 14% (assumed market rate) notes payable due in five years. The amount of debt forgiven under each approach is calculated as follows:

	Fair Value of Consideration Given Approach	Total Future Payments Approach of FASB Statement No. 15
Carrying amount of debt..................	$10,000,000	$10,000,000
Amounts to be compared with carrying amount of debt:	(fair value)	(total future payments)
Cash	$ 2,000,000	$ 2,000,000
Notes payable......................	5,000,000	5,000,000
Interest ($5,000,000 × 14% × 5 yr).........................	n/a	3,500,000
	$ 7,000,000	$10,500,000
Post-reorganization carrying value of the debt	$ 7,000,000	$10,000,000
Amount of debt forgiven ("gain")	$ 3,000,000	None
Future interest expense	$700,000/yr for the next five years	$500,000 total over the next five years

[19] *FASB Technical Bulletin No. 81-6*, "Applicability of *Statement 15* to Debtors in Bankruptcy Situations" (Stamford, CT: FASB, 1981), paragraph 3.

Most reorganization plans attempt to structure a positive stockholders' equity (though not necessarily positive retained earnings) to place the company on firmer ground for emerging from bankruptcy proceedings. To measure and report this effect is exceedingly difficult under the approach of *FASB Statement No. 15.* The pronouncement itself, if applicable, might very well be counterproductive to obtaining an agreement with the unsecured creditors concerning necessary sacrifices. (If applicable, the pronouncement requires much greater sacrifices by creditors to achieve a positive net worth.) This possibility may have been part of the FASB's rationale for exempting bankruptcy reorganizations from *FASB Statement No. 15* guidance. Another possible reason for the exemption involves the "fresh start" purpose of reorganizations under Chapter 11. Future income statements should reflect a reasonable amount of interest expense on restructured debt. This occurs under the "fair value of consideration given" approach but rarely occurs under the *FASB Statement No. 15* approach.

Imputing of interest.   The imputing of interest issue (discussed earlier in connection with troubled debt restructurings) also pertains to bankruptcy reorganizations. Unfortunately, the current accounting literature gives no explicit guidance concerning whether or not to impute interest in bankruptcy reorganizations.[20] Our inquiries to practicing accountants who are involved in bankruptcy reorganizations reveal that some companies are imputing interest under the principles of *APB Opinion No. 21,* "Interest on Receivables and Payables," and others are not.

Reporting forgiveness of debt.   Current accounting pronouncements also do not explicitly state how to report (classify) a forgiveness of debt in bankruptcy proceedings. Some practicing accountants perceive the forgiveness of debt as a "gain from extinguishment of debt" and report it as an extraordinary item, if material, pursuant to the requirements of *FASB Statement No. 4,* "Reporting Gains and Losses from Extinguishment of Debt," (paragraph 8). Practicing accountants who perceive the forgiveness of debt as a capital contribution credit it directly to paid-in capital. The latter treatment is usually found when the common stockholder accounts are adjusted on reorganization to eliminate an accumulated deficit as in quasi-reorganization accounting.

Role of accountants in bankruptcy reorganizations

Certified public accountants are commonly employed in varying capacities in bankruptcy proceedings. Many accounting firms can generate substantial fees for their services in this area. (The new bankruptcy statutes eliminated the longstanding requirement that accountants set their fees in a "spirit of

---

[20] This guidance was clear prior to the issuance of *FASB Statement No. 15,* because *FASB Interpretation No. 2,* "Imputing Interest on Debt Arrangements Made under the Federal Bankruptcy Act," extended the principles of *APB Opinion No. 21,* "Interest on Receivables and Payables," to bankruptcy reorganizations. Unfortunately, *FASB Interpretation No. 2* was expunged from the literature on the issuance of *FASB Statement No. 15* (supporting accountants who thought *FASB Statement No. 15* applied to bankruptcy reorganizations), and *FASB Technical Bulletin No. 81-6* did not reinstate it. It is not known whether this was an oversight or purposeful.

economy"; bankruptcy assistance is no longer considered charity work.) The most common capacity for outside accountants is that of rendering advice and assistance on financial projections used in developing a plan of reorganization. Both the distressed company and its creditors' committee commonly hire their own outside accountants. Occasionally, outside accountants are responsible for determining the quality of the distressed company's accounts receivable. If management is suspected of improper actions, bankruptcy judges may need to appoint outside acountants to investigate such charges. The creditors' committee often hires outside accountants to determine the following:

(1) Has the debtor made any transfers of assets that would constitute preferences to certain creditors?
(2) Has management committed any acts that would constitute fraud, deception, or bad faith?
(3) Has management committed any acts that would bar it from obtaining a discharge of certain indebtedness?
(4) In what condition are the company's books and records?

The creditors' accountants need not perform an audit of the debtor's financial statements to be of assistance in these areas. Usually, a limited special purpose examination is sufficient. Obviously, the scope of any such limited examination must be worked out with the creditors' committee.

LIQUIDATIONS

Large companies with common stock that is publicly traded on the New York Stock Exchange are seldom liquidated because they usually have adequate capital and managerial talent to deal with adverse developments. The growing trend toward diversification also works against liquidation. A large, diverse business is less apt to be affected overall by an adverse development resulting from poor management decisions in one of its industry segments. Furthermore, if management cannot deal effectively with such problems in one of its industry segments, that segment will most likely be disposed of through sale (or possibly abandonment), but the remainder of the business will continue. Consequently, liquidation is generally associated with small and moderately sized businesses. The smaller and more unseasoned a company, the more likely it is to face liquidation.

Liquidation outside of the bankruptcy courts

In some instances, liquidation may take place outside of the bankruptcy courts. In these situations, a formal **general assignment for the benefit of creditors** usually is executed, whereby the debtor's property is transferred to a designated assignee or assignees (who are often the debtor's creditors) for the purpose of converting the assets into cash and making appropriate distributions of cash to the creditors. Any assets that remain after creditors have been paid in full are returned to the debtor for ultimate distribution to its stockholders. However, if the proceeds from the conversion of assets into cash are insufficient to pay creditors in full, then the creditors have no other recourse and the stockholders receive nothing.

The possible advantages of liquidating outside of the bankruptcy court are the following:

(1) Legal fees are usually lower.
(2) The debtor can designate the assignee or assignees.
(3) There is greater flexibility in the conversion of assets into cash.

Under an involuntary proceeding, a general assignment for the benefit of creditors is considered grounds for the bankruptcy court to enter an order for relief. Accordingly, to avoid liquidation through the bankruptcy court, a general assignment must be agreed to by all of the creditors for all practical purposes. If a sufficient number of qualified creditors subsequently file an involuntary petition of bankruptcy, the general assignment for the benefit of creditors is null and void, and the bankruptcy court then supervises and controls the liquidation of the company.

Liquidation through the bankruptcy courts

After a company has filed for liquidation under Chapter 7, one of the court's first duties is to determine if the case should be dismissed. As we mentioned, the filing of a voluntary petition constitutes an **order for relief.** Dismissals of voluntary filings are infrequent. When the debtor does not dispute an involuntary petition, the court enters an order for relief against the debtor. Dismissals of uncontested involuntary filings are also infrequent. However, if the debtor disputes an involuntary petition, then a trial must be held to determine whether the case should be dismissed or an order for relief should be entered.

Role of the trustee. After an order for relief has been entered, the bankruptcy court must promptly appoint an interim trustee [Section 701(a)]. In an involuntary filing, the debtor may continue to operate the business from the filing date until an order for relief is entered, just as if the petition had not been filed [Section 303(f)]. However, the court may appoint an interim trustee during this period, if necessary, to preserve the property of the estate or to prevent loss to the estate, providing certain procedures are followed [Section 303(g)].

After an order for relief has been entered, the court must also call a meeting of the debtor's creditors (Section 341). In this meeting, the creditors (1) vote for a trustee, and (2) select a creditor's committee that consults with the trustee in connection with the administration of the estate. If the creditors are unable to select a trustee, then the interim trustee becomes the trustee [Section 702(d)]. Trustees are usually professionals, mostly practicing lawyers, who specialize in this type of work. The following duties of trustees are set forth under Section 704:

(1) Collect and reduce to money the property of the estate for which such trustee serves, and close up such estate as expeditiously as is compatible with the best interests of parties of interest.
(2) Be accountable for all property received.
(3) Investigate the financial affairs of the debtor.

(4) If a purpose would be served, examine proofs of claims and object to the allowance of any claim that is improper. . . .

(5) Unless the court orders otherwise, furnish such information concerning the estate and the estate's administration as is requested by a party of interest.

(6) If the business of the debtor is authorized to be operated, file with the court and with any governmental unit charged with responsibility for collection or determination of any tax arising out of such operation, periodic reports and summaries of the operation of such business, including a statement of receipts and disbursements, and such other information as the court requires. (Under Section 721, "the court may authorize the trustee to operate the business of the debtor for a limited period, if such operation is in the best interest of the estate and consistent with the orderly liquidation of the estate.")

(7) Make a final report and file a final account of the administration of the estate with the court.

Accounting by trustees is discussed in detail later in the chapter (pages 659–62).

Technical aspects of the duties of trustees.   The following technical aspects of the duties of the trustee should be noted:

(1) Employment of professionals.   With the court's approval, the trustee may employ attorneys, accountants, appraisers, auctioneers, or other professional persons to represent or assist the trustee in carrying out his or her duties (Section 327).

(2) Avoidance powers.   A trustee is authorized to void both **fraudulent** and **preferential** transfers made by the debtor within certain specified periods preceding the filing date. (Such transfers include the giving of a security interest in a property.) Creditors, therefore, may be required to return monies and/or properties received or may lose their security interest, or both. The section on preferences is intended to prevent a debtor from giving certain creditors preferential treatment over other creditors. The 1978 Act sets forth the conditions that must exist for a trustee to void a property transfer to a creditor. The act also sets forth certain transfers that a trustee cannot void.

(3) Setoffs.   With respect to mutual debts between the debtor and allowable claims of a creditor, the amount owed the debtor by the creditors is subtracted from or offset against the amount owed to the creditor (Section 553). (There are certain exceptions to this rule.)

Distribution of cash to creditors.   The sequence of payments to creditors is as follows:

(1) First, the proceeds from the sale of assets that have been pledged to secured creditors are applied to satisfy those claims. Note that the bankruptcy proceedings do not alter the rights of the secured creditors to the assets that have been pledged to them; these rights are only temporarily suspended.

(2) If the proceeds exceed the secured creditors' claims, such excess is available for payment to creditors with priority and unsecured creditors.

(3) If the proceeds are insufficient to satisfy the claims of the secured creditors, the secured creditors become unsecured creditors to the extent of the deficiency.

(4) The proceeds from the sale of unpledged assets are used to pay creditors with priority.

(5) After creditors with priority have been paid, payments are made to the unsecured creditors. Payments are always stated as a percentage of all allowed claims.

(6) To the extent that any creditors are not paid in full, the deficiency represents a loss.

After the final payment has been made to the unsecured creditors, the corporation is a **shell** corporation without any assets or liabilities. In most instances, the corporation then ceases its legal existence. The bankruptcy court is not authorized to grant a formal discharge of indebtedness with respect to any unpaid claims when the debtor is other than an individual [Section 727(a)(1)]. According to House Committee Reports, this change is intended to prevent trafficking in corporate shells and bankrupt partnerships.

The selling of assets and the payment of proceeds to the debtor's various creditors does not always conclude a liquidation. Trustees may file suit against former directors and officers, asking for monetary damages on the grounds of gross negligence in the management of certain aspects of the business. When a sudden collapse of a company occurs shortly after its outside auditors have issued an unqualified ("clean") audit report on the company's financial statements, serious questions may be raised concerning the performance of the audit. In such situations, the auditors may be sued for alleged breach of performance.

Role of the accountant in liquidations. Bankruptcy trustees often employ certified public accountants to assist them in preserving the assets of the bankrupt's estate. The extent of the accountant's services usually depend on the complexity of the estate. If the debtor's in-house accountants have not resigned before the bankruptcy petition is filed, they generally leave shortly thereafter. A certified public accountant can provide the following types of services to the bankruptcy trustee:

(1) Determining what accounting books and records exist at the debtor's offices.

(2) Determining the condition of the accounting records, including the filing status of all tax reports.

(3) Updating the debtor's accounting records as necessary.

(4) Preparing current-year tax reports and informational forms.

(5) Comparing creditors' claims (as filed with the court) with the debtor's books and records and with the schedule of liabilities filed with the court by the debtor.

(6) In certain instances, if fraud is suspected or known, the accountant may examine certain of the debtor's books and records in detail and submit a formal report to the trustee.

This list is not exhaustive—the accountant may be called upon to perform any service within the realm of accounting expertise.

The statement of affairs

Regardless of whether liquidation takes place outside of or through bankruptcy court, a special **statement of affairs** is prepared showing the financial condition of the company. The statement of affairs is prepared on the basis that the company is going out of business. Because the company is not considered a going concern, the historical cost basis for carrying assets loses its significance, and the amount expected to be realized in liquidation is the relevant valuation basis.

The statement of affairs provides information concerning how much money each class of creditors can expect to receive on liquidation of the company, assuming assets are converted into cash at the estimated realizable values used in preparing the statements. Thus, conventional classifications such as current assets and current liabilities lose their significance. Instead, assets are classified as to whether they are pledged with creditors or not pledged with creditors; liabilities are classified by category of creditor— namely, creditors with priority, secured creditors, and unsecured creditors. Stockholders' equity also loses its significance because companies in the process of liquidation usually have a negative net worth. The specific categories of assets and liabilities in the statement of affairs are as follows:

Assets

(1) **Assets pledged with fully secured creditors** are expected to realize an amount at least sufficient to satisfy the related debt.

(2) **Assets pledged with partially secured creditors** are expected to realize an amount below the related debt.

(3) **Free assets** are not pledged and are available to satisfy the claims of creditors with priority, partially secured creditors, and unsecured creditors.

Liabilities

(1) **Liabilities with priority** have priority under the bankruptcy statutes (explained earlier in the chapter on page 628).

(2) **Fully secured creditors** expect to be paid in full as a result of their having sufficient collateral (pledged assets) to satisfy the indebtedness.

(3) **Partially secured creditors** have collateral (pledged assets), the proceeds of which are expected to be insufficient to satisfy the indebtedness.

(4) **Unsecured creditors** have no collateral (pledged assets) relating to their indebtedness.

Contingent liabilities that are reasonably calculable and probable as to payment (the criteria under *FASB Statement No. 5*, "Accounting for Contingencies") are shown in the statement of affairs. Contingent liabilities that do not meet these criteria should be disclosed in a note to the statement of affairs.

Illustration.   The balance sheet of Fold-Up Company, which filed a voluntary bankruptcy petition on September 23, 19X5, is shown in Illustration 18-3. Additional information regarding realization follows:

(1) **Receivables.**   The notes and accounts receivable are considered to have been adequately provided for in preparing the balance sheet; thus, the company expects to realize the amounts shown.

Illustration 18-3

FOLD-UP COMPANY
Balance Sheet
September 23, 19X5

Assets

Current Assets:

Cash	$ 2,000
Notes receivable	5,000
Accounts receivable, net	25,000

Inventory:

Finished goods..	40,000
Work in process..	30,000
Raw materials..	20,000
Supplies	5,000
Prepayments	8,000
Total current assets...	$135,000

Noncurrent Assets:

Land	70,000
Building, net	110,000
Equipment, net	60,000
Deferred charges	15,000
Total assets..	$390,000

Liabilities and Stockholders' Deficiency

Current Liabilities:

10% Notes payable to bank, secured by accounts receivable	$ 35,000
Accounts payable..	246,000

Accrued liabilities:

Interest ($2,000 to bank, $6,000 to insurance company)	8,000
Salaries and wages...	7,000
Payroll taxes	2,000
Total current liabilities	$298,000

Long-Term Debt:

8% Notes payable to insurance company, secured by land and building ..	175,000
Total liabilities...	$473,000

Stockholders' Deficiency:

Common stock, no par..	$100,000
Accumulated deficit	(183,000)
Total stockholders' deficiency	$ (83,000)
Total liabilities in excess of stockholders' deficiency	$390,000

---

(2) **Finished goods.** The finished goods can be sold for $47,000; however, the company expects to incur $4,000 of direct selling and shipping costs.

(3) **Work in process.** The work in process can be completed if $3,000 of direct costs are incurred for labor. On completion, this inventory can be sold for $37,000; however, the company expects to incur $2,000 of direct selling and shipping costs.

(4) **Raw materials.** The raw materials can be converted into finished goods if $7,000 of direct costs are incurred for labor. On completion, this inventory can be sold for $19,000; however, the company expects to incur $1,000 of direct selling and shipping costs.

(5) **Supplies.** The supplies will be substantially consumed in the completion of the work in process and the conversion of raw materials into finished goods. The estimated realizable value of the remaining supplies after completion and conversion is $1,000.

(6) **Prepayments.** The prepayments are expected to expire during the liquidation period.

(7) **Land.** The land has a current market value of $90,000.

(8) **Building.** The building has a current market value of $135,000.

(9) **Equipment.** The equipment can be sold in auction for an estimated $35,000.

(10) **Deferred charges.** Deferred charges include organization costs, issuance expenses relating to the notes payable to the insurance company, and plant rearrangement costs.

(11) **Salaries and wages.** All salaries and wages were earned within the last 90 days, and no employee is owed more than $2,000.

(12) **Liquidation expenses.** The company estimates that $15,000 in court and filing fees, appraisal fees, and legal and accounting fees will be incurred in connection with the liquidation. No amounts have been provided for these expenses at September 23, 19X5.

(13) **Accounts payable.** Accounts payable include $6,000 to the company's attorneys for legal work incurred in connection with patent research and collection efforts on certain accounts receivable that have been written off. Accounts payable also include $5,000 owed to the company's certified public accountants in connection with the December 31, 19X4 audit of the company's financial statements.

A statement of affairs prepared using the above information is shown in Illustration 18-4. In reviewing Illustration 18-4, the following points should be understood:

(1) The book value column is shown only for purposes of tying into the September 23, 19X5 balance sheet, which was prepared in the conventional manner.

(2) Each asset and liability is assigned to its appropriate descriptive category. The categories themselves are the key to producing the desired information—that is, how much money can the unsecured creditors expect to receive in liquidation?

(3) Accrued interest payable is classified with the debt to which it relates, because the pledged assets are security for both the principal and the interest.

(4) Although the company has not recorded the $15,000 of estimated liquidation expenses in its general ledger at September 23, 19X5, the statement of affairs should reflect this estimate so that it is as useful as possible.

(5) Legal and accounting fees incurred in connection with matters not related to the bankruptcy are not considered debts with priority under the bankruptcy statutes.

(6) The bank is an unsecured creditor to the extent of $12,000, the amount by which the $25,000 collateral is insufficient to satisfy its $37,000 claim.

(7) The unsecured creditors are estimated to receive $149,000 of the

Illustration 18-4

FOLD-UP COMPANY
Statement of Affairs
September 23, 19X5

Book Value	Assets	Current Value	Estimated Amount Available for Unsecured Creditors	Gain or Loss on Realization
	Assets pledged with fully secured creditors:			
$ 70,000	Land	$ 90,000		$ 20,000
110,000	Building	135,000		25,000
		$225,000		
	Less—Fully secured claims (from liability side)	(181,000)	$ 44,000	
	Assets pledged with partially secured creditors:			
25,000	Accounts receivable	$ 25,000		
	(Deducted on liability side)			
	Free assets:			
2,000	Cash.	$ 2,000	2,000	
5,000	Notes receivable	5,000	5,000	
	Inventory:			
40,000	Finished goods	43,000[a]	43,000	3,000
30,000	Work in process	32,000[b]	32,000	2,000
20,000	Raw materials	11,000[c]	11,000	(9,000)
5,000	Supplies.	1,000	1,000	(4,000)
8,000	Prepayments			(8,000)
60,000	Equipment.	35,000	35,000	(25,000)
15,000	Deferred charges.			(15,000)
	Estimated amount available for unsecured creditors, including creditors with priority		$173,000	
	Less—Liabilities with priority (from liability side)		(24,000)	
	Estimated amount available for unsecured creditors		$149,000	
	Estimated deficiency to unsecured creditors (plug)		109,000	
$390,000				$(11,000)
	Total unsecured debt.		$258,000	

[a] Net of $4,000 of estimated disposal costs.
[b] Net of $3,000 of estimated labor to complete and $2,000 of disposal costs.
[c] Net of $7,000 of estimated labor to convert into finished goods and $1,000 of disposal costs.

$258,000 owed them. This figure is often expressed in terms of recovery per dollar owed. In this situation, it would be 58 cents on the dollar ($149,000/$258,000).

Once a liquidation has occurred, obviously, no accounting issues exist for the former company. An accountant performing services for a trustee

Illustration 18-4 (continued)

<table>
<tr><td colspan="3" align="center">**FOLD-UP COMPANY**
Statement of Affairs
September 23, 19X5</td></tr>
<tr><td align="center">Book
Value</td><td align="center">Liabilities and Stockholders' Deficiency</td><td align="center">Amount
Unsecured</td></tr>
<tr><td></td><td>**Liabilities with priority:**</td><td></td></tr>
<tr><td>$ -0-</td><td>Estimated liquidation expenses ....</td><td align="right">$ 15,000</td><td></td></tr>
<tr><td>7,000</td><td>Salaries and wages ....</td><td align="right">7,000</td><td></td></tr>
<tr><td>2,000</td><td>Payroll taxes ....</td><td align="right">2,000</td><td></td></tr>
<tr><td></td><td>(deducted from amount available for
   unsecured creditors on asset side).......</td><td align="right">$ 24,000</td><td></td></tr>
<tr><td></td><td>**Fully secured creditors:**</td><td></td></tr>
<tr><td>175,000</td><td>Notes payable to insurance company ....</td><td align="right">$175,000</td><td></td></tr>
<tr><td>6,000</td><td>Accrued interest on notes.....................</td><td align="right">6,000</td><td></td></tr>
<tr><td></td><td>Total (deducted on asset side) ....</td><td align="right">$181,000</td><td></td></tr>
<tr><td></td><td>**Partially secured creditors:**</td><td></td></tr>
<tr><td>35,000</td><td>Note payable to bank ....</td><td align="right">$ 35,000</td><td></td></tr>
<tr><td>2,000</td><td>Accrued interest on note.....................</td><td align="right">2,000</td><td></td></tr>
<tr><td></td><td></td><td align="right">$ 37,000</td><td></td></tr>
<tr><td></td><td>Less—Pledged accounts receivable
   (from asset side).........................</td><td align="right">(25,000)</td><td align="right">$ 12,000</td></tr>
<tr><td></td><td>**Unsecured creditors:**</td><td></td></tr>
<tr><td>246,000</td><td>Accounts payable and accruals...............</td><td></td><td align="right">246,000</td></tr>
<tr><td>(83,000)</td><td>Stockholders' deficiency</td><td></td></tr>
<tr><td>$390,000</td><td></td><td></td></tr>
<tr><td></td><td>Total unsecured debt.....................</td><td></td><td align="right">$258,000</td></tr>
</table>

in a liquidation, however, should have a basic familiarity with the liquidation process.

ACCOUNTING BY TRUSTEES

The accountability of trustees to the bankruptcy court was set forth earlier in the discussion of liquidations under Chapter 7 of the 1978 Act (see pages 652–53). The same accountability exists in reorganizations under Chapter 11 of the 1978 Act in which a trustee is appointed to operate the debtor's business. The 1978 Act sets forth specific requirements concerning the type of report(s) rendered to the courts by trustees only when the debtor's business is operated by a trustee. In most liquidation cases, normal operations cease immediately. Accordingly, we discuss accounting by trustees in liquidations separately from reorganizations (when normal operations continue).

Accounting in liquidation

When normal operations immediately cease, the preparation of an operating statement for the period covering the trustee's administration of the estate is inappropriate. This holds true even when a trustee, with the court's permission, continues the operations necessary to convert work in process (and possibly raw materials) into finished goods. Such activities by themselves do not constitute normal operations; accordingly, costs incurred in this regard are treated as bankruptcy administration costs. Because the 1978 Act does not prescribe the type of report(s) rendered by trustees when normal operations are not conducted (as was the case under the old law), each bankruptcy court establishes its own requirements. Most bankruptcy courts merely require a written explanation as to the disposition of the various assets and a statement of cash receipts and disbursements. Such a statement typically shows (1) cash balances of the debtor that were turned over to the trustee at the trustee's appointment; (2) the proceeds from the conversion of noncash assets into cash; (3) cash disbursements (which are usually limited to bankruptcy administration costs); (4) the remaining cash balance available for distribution to creditors; and (5) a summary of how the remaining cash balance should be distributed to the various classes of creditors (including creditors with priority). In most cases, only one report is rendered (called the final report). In some cases, cash is distributed to creditors on an interim basis, after an interim report proposing such a distribution is filed with and approved by the court. Some courts require the cash disbursements in summary form only, whereas others require detail by check number, payee, and purpose of disbursement.

Most trustees find it expedient to (1) open a separate checking account for each estate they administer, and (2) use the related cash receipts and disbursements records to prepare the required statement of cash receipts and disbursements. Trustees usually do not use the debtor's general ledger or any of the debtor's journals to record transactions and events. If the court or creditors desire information that relates the trustee's activity with the book balances existing when the trustee was appointed, then a **statement of realization and liquidation** can be prepared. Such a statement for Fold-Up Company is shown in Illustration 18-5. In reviewing Illustration 18-5, note that (1) the beginning balances are taken from Illustration 18-3, and (2) the activity during the assumed period that the trustee administers the estate is consistent with the estimated amounts and information provided in the data used to prepare the statement of affairs in Illustration 18-4.

In some cases, a trustee may be authorized to operate the debtor's business. This is often done when (1) a greater amount may be realized by selling the business in its entirety as opposed to a piecemeal sale, and (2) a greater amount may be realized by selling an active business as opposed to one that has been shut down. For the time that a trustee operates the debtor's business, the accounting reports rendered are the same as those required in reorganizations, which are discussed in the following section.

Accounting in reorganization

When a trustee is appointed in a Chapter 11 reorganization, the new law requires trustees to submit

> periodic reports and summaries of the operation of such business, including a statement of receipts and disbursements, and such other information as the court requires (Sections 704 and 1106).

Illustration 18-5

FOLD-UP COMPANY
Statement of Realization and Liquidation
For the Period September 23, 19X5 to May 18, 19X6

	Assets		Liabilities				Stockholders'
	Cash	Noncash	With Priority	Fully Secured	Partially Secured	Unsecured	Deficiency
Balances, September 23, 19X5 (per Illustration 18-3)	$ 2,000	$388,000	$ 9,000	$181,000	$37,000	$246,000	$ (83,000)
Cash receipts:							
Collection of note receivable and related interest	5,200	(5,000)					200
Proceeds from sale of inventory, net of $16,700 direct costs	85,800	(90,000)					(4,200)
Proceeds from sale of supplies	1,100	(5,000)					(3,900)
Proceeds from sale of equipment	35,400	(60,000)					(24,600)
Proceeds from sale of land and building, net of $181,000 withheld by title company to pay off fully secured creditor	45,500	(180,000)		(181,000)			46,500
Cash disbursements:							
Payment of bankruptcy administration costs, net of $16,700 inventory conversion and selling costs shown above	(2,000)						(2,000)
Other:							
Amortization of prepaids		(8,000)					(8,000)
Write-off of deferred charges		(15,000)					(15,000)
Release of accounts receivable to partially secured creditor		(25,000)			(25,000)		
Reclassification of residual amount to unsecured status					(12,000)	12,000	
Accrual of bankruptcy administration costs			12,600				(12,600)
Balances, May 18, 19X6	$173,000	$ -0-	$21,600	$ -0-	$ -0-	$258,000	$(106,600)
Proposed distribution	$173,000		$21,600 (100%)	$ -0-	$ -0-	$151,400 (58.7%)	

In addition to these items, the courts usually require that a balance sheet be presented whenever operating statements or summaries are furnished. In most cases, trustees find it practical to use the debtor's books and records to record transactions and events. However, the date the trustee was appointed is usually recorded so that the activity during the trustee's administration can be reported separately. Also, a distinction is usually made between (1) assets on hand and liabilities owed at the trustee's appointment, and (2) assets acquired and liabilities incurred during the trustee's administration. This distinction is necessary because trustees are responsible for (1) the acquisition and realization of new assets as opposed to only the realization of old assets; and (2) the incurrence and liquidation of new liabilities as opposed to only the liquidation of old liabilities.

When the trustee uses the debtor's books and records, the preparation of required reports and statements presents no unusual problems. In some cases, a trustee may account for some or all of the debtor's assets and operations in a new set of books. In this case, the transfer of assets to the new set of books and the accounting for subsequent operations parallels the accounting for a home office and a branch. Accordingly, the balances and activity on each set of books must be combined to the extent necessary in preparing financial reports. Traditionally, advanced accounting textbooks have included a discussion and illustration of a somewhat involved statement of realization and liquidation encompassing assets, liabilities, and operations. However, current practice favors the use of the separate conventional financial statements, and we do not present a discussion and illustration of this single comprehensive statement.

CONCLUDING COMMENTS

Most companies in serious financial difficulty never recover and must be liquidated. A company that can feasibly effect a successful recovery must show complete honesty and good faith with its creditors during this difficult period. Creditors should realize that often they can minimize their losses if a successful troubled debt restructuring can be achieved. The use of professionals in insolvency proceedings can minimize the procedural problems and help the company and its creditors to be realistic in arriving at an acceptable plan of recovery.

Not all proposed troubled debt restructurings succeed. Many are rejected as infeasible, with liquidation best serving the creditors' interests. Others are rejected as a result of evidence of management fraud, deception, or bad faith—again, liquidation best serves the creditors' interests. Consequently, an accountant furnishing assistance to a debtor or a creditors' committee must be skeptical, alert, and imaginative in carrying out this difficult assignment.

SUMMARY

The accounting issues involved with troubled debt restructurings include how to calculate whether any debt has been forgiven and how to report a forgiveness of debt. *FASB Statement No. 15* does not allow the imputing of interest in making this calculation. The total amount owed (the "carrying amount of the debt") is compared with the total amount to be paid back (the "total future payments"). If the total future payments exceed the carrying amount of the debt, the excess is reported as interest expense between the restructuring date and the maturity date. However, if the carrying amount of the debt exceeds the total future payments, a forgiveness of debt results. *FASB Statement No. 15* treats a forgiveness of debt as a gain reported as an extraordinary item, if material. As a result of these procedures, the debtor's future income statements reflect either no interest expense (when a forgiveness of debt results) or unrealistically low interest expense (when no forgiveness of debt results) until the maturity date of the debt.

In most instances, *FASB Statement No. 15* does not apply to either quasi-reorganizations or formal bankruptcy reorganizations under Chapter 11 of the bankruptcy statutes. In these situations, the amount owed is compared with the consideration given in settlement. Because the current accounting literature does not state specifically how to calculate and report a forgiveness of debt in formal reorganizations, some companies do not impute interest in making this calculation, whereas others do. Some companies treat the forgiveness of debt as a gain, whereas others treat it as a capital contribution.

Glossary of new terms

Creditors with Priority: A special class of creditors created by the bankruptcy statutes. These creditors are entitled to payment before a debtor's other unsecured creditors may be paid.

Debtor: Under the bankruptcy statutes, a debtor is the party that is the subject of a bankruptcy proceeding.

Estate: Under the bankruptcy statutes, all of a debtor's property constitutes an estate.

Impairment: The alteration of the rights of a creditor or equity holder in a bankruptcy reorganization case.

Involuntary Petition: The filing of a petition by the creditors of a company in financial distress to have the distressed company liquidated or financially reorganized under the control and supervision of the bankruptcy court.

Liquidation: The process of converting a company's assets into cash, paying off creditors to the extent possible, and ceasing operations.

Quasi-reorganization: A process outside of bankruptcy court for eliminating a deficit balance in Retained Earnings (properly called an accumulated deficit) to give the entity a "fresh start."

Reorganization: The altering of a distressed company's liability and/or equity structure under Chapter 11 of the bankruptcy statutes for purposes of financially rehabilitating the company to avoid liquidation.

Restatement of Liabilities Generally: Restructurings or modifications of debt that encompass most of the debtor's liabilities coincidentally with either a reorganization under Chapter 11 of the bankruptcy statutes or a quasi-reorganization.

Setoffs: In a bankruptcy proceeding, offsetting amounts owed to a debtor by a creditor against amounts owed to that creditor by the debtor.

Troubled Debt Restructuring: The granting of a concession by a creditor because of a debtor's financial difficulties.

Voluntary Petition: The filing of a petition with the bankruptcy court by a company in financial distress to have the company liquidated or financially reorganized under the control and supervision of the bankruptcy court.

Review questions

1. Between what two broad categories are the bankruptcy statutes divided (as they pertain to business corporations)?
2. What fundamental objectives do the bankruptcy statutes accomplish?
3. Under what conditions may an involuntary petition be filed?
4. What is meant by the term *creditors with priority*?
5. List the order of priority of creditors with priority.
6. In an involuntary bankruptcy filing, do secured creditors lose their right to their security?
7. Why do companies try to restructure their debt outside of Chapter 11 of the bankruptcy statutes if at all possible?
8. What are the advantages of filing for reorganization under Chapter 11 of the bankruptcy statutes?
9. Summarize the general procedures for determining if a gain on the restructuring of debt exists as set forth in *FASB Statement No. 15.*
10. How are material gains on the restructuring of debt reported in the income statement?
11. To what extent are the present value procedures discussed in *APB Opinion No. 21* used in determining a gain on restructuring of debt under *FASB Statement No. 15?*
12. What is the essence of a composition agreement?
13. What is meant by a *discharge of indebtedness* in a bankruptcy reorganization?
14. Which debts cannot be discharged in a bankruptcy reorganization?
15. Is a discharge of indebtedness automatic in a liquidation proceeding? in a reorganization proceeding?
16. How is the statement of affairs different from the balance sheet?
17. State two purposes for which a statement of affairs may be used.
18. Contrast the statement of affairs with the balance sheet.
19. Give four classifications of liabilities that can appear in a statement of affairs.

Discussion cases

Discussion case 18–1
Troubled debt restructuring: Theory

New Hope Company has recently completed restructuring a substantial portion of its debt with one of its major lenders, which was owed $1,000,000 of principal and $100,000 of interest as of the date the restructuring was consummated. Under the terms of the restructured debt agreement, the accrued interest of $100,000 is forgiven and the principal of $1,000,000 is to be paid two years hence, with no interest to be paid for these two years.

New Hope Company's controller has indicated to you that the company intends to value the debt owed at $826,446, which is the present value of $1,000,000 using a discount rate of 10% (the interest rate before the restructuring). This valuation results in the reporting of (1) a gain on restructuring of debt of $273,554 in the current year; (2) interest expense of $82,645 in the first year following the restructuring; and (3) interest expense of $90,909 in the second year following the restructuring. The controller gives you the following reasons why this approach best reflects the economics of the restructuring:

(1) The creditor's $1,000,000 note receivable is worth no more than what the note receivable can be sold for or discounted on a nonrecourse basis.
(2) If the creditor sold the note receivable to a financial institution on a nonrecourse basis, it certainly could not sell it for more than its present value using an interest rate commensurate with the issuing company's risk.
(3) Considering the poor financial condition of the company, a higher rate than 10% probably would be justified. However, the controller decided not to use a rate higher than 10% to be conservative in the computation of the gain on restructuring of the debt.
(4) If the value of the note receivable on the creditor's books cannot be worth more than $826,446, the excess of the carrying amount of the note payable (including accrued interest) over this amount must represent the true value of the debt forgiveness.

Required:
(1) Disregarding the requirements of *FASB Statement No. 15,* evaluate the soundness of the controller's approach.
(2) Is the controller's approach conservative? What other reason might have prompted the controller to use a low interest rate?
(3) At the end of the two years, what impact will this approach have on retained earnings? What impact will the approach set forth in *FASB Statement No. 15* have on retained earnings?

Discussion case 18–2
Troubled debt restructuring: Theory

Assume that *FASB Statement No. 15* required that income statements of periods subsequent to a troubled debt restructuring reflect interest expense related to restructured debt based on an interest rate commensurate with the risk associated with the restructured debt.

Required:
How would you determine an appropriate interest rate "commensurate with the risk"?

Discussion case 18–3
Bankruptcy reorganization: Theory

You are the controller of a company that has been attempting to work out a troubled debt restructuring at lengthy meetings with its major creditors. At the last meeting, the company's president told the creditors that if they did not agree to the restructuring plan proposed by the company, management would file for reorganization under Chapter 11 of the bankruptcy statutes.

Required:
(1) How would the accounting change as a result of restructuring the debt through the bankruptcy courts versus outside of the bankruptcy courts?
(2) What is the rationale for having different rules for the restructuring of debt in bankruptcy reorganizations?

Discussion case 18–4
Bankruptcy reorganization: Theory

Assume you are the controller for a company that, after several years of operating losses, filed for reorganization under Chapter 11 of the bankruptcy statutes. The company's plan of reorganization was confirmed 18 months after the filing, and unsecured creditors were paid 40 cents on the dollar ($30 million dollars was owed to these creditors). You want to report the $18 million amount of debt canceled in the income statement.

Required:
(1) Disregarding the accounting pronouncements, evaluate whether or not a company should report income from a bankruptcy reorganization. (Try to list arguments for and against this position.)
(2) What other options does the company have?
(3) Why might it not make much difference which way the company reports the $18 million canceled debt?

Exercises

Exercise 18–1
Bankruptcy law: Filing the petition and debts with priority—
Multiple choice

(1) Which of the entities listed below are entitled to file a voluntary bankruptcy petition under Chapter 7 or 11?
   (a) A banking corporation.
   (b) A partnership.
   (c) A corporation that manufactures consumer goods.
   (d) A corporation that provides personal services.
   (e) A municipal corporation.
   (f) A railroad.
   (g) An insurance corporation.
(2) Select the entities in (1) that may have an involuntary bankruptcy petition filed against them.
(3) In which of the following situations could an involuntary bankruptcy petition be filed?
   (a) The debtor has debts of at least $5,000.
   (b) The appropriate number of creditors required to sign the petition are owed at least $5,000.
   (c) The debtor has committed a fraudulent act.
   (d) The debtor has recently appointed a custodian.

(e) The debtor has made asset transfers that constitute a preference to one or more creditors.

(f) Wages are owed to employees for more than 90 days.

(g) The debtor is not paying its debts as they mature.

(h) The debtor has entered into discussions with its creditors to restructure its debt.

(i) The debtor's net worth is negative as a result of operating losses.

(4) Which of the following debts have priority under the bankruptcy statutes?

(a) Amounts owed to secured creditors.

(b) In an involuntary petition, amounts owed to the creditors who signed the petition.

(c) Costs of administering the bankruptcy proceedings.

(d) Debts incurred by issuing materially false statements as to financial condition.

(e) All wages owed to employees that were earned within 90 days prior to filing the bankruptcy petition.

(f) Wages of up to $2,000 per employee, no matter when earned.

(g) Taxes owed to the United States or any state or subdivision thereof.

Exercise 18–2
Bankruptcy law: Reorganization under Chapter 11—True or false

Determine if the following statements are true or false. Explain why any false statements are false.

(1) In a Chapter 11 reorganization, management usually continues to operate the business.

(2) The legal and contractual rights of any class of creditors may be altered or impaired under a plan of reorganization.

(3) A plan of reorganization must be approved by the Securities and Exchange Commission.

(4) Only a simple majority of creditors in a class of claims is required to approve a plan of reorganization.

(5) Only a simple majority in the amount of claims in a class of creditors is required to approve a plan of reorganization.

(6) The bankruptcy court usually imposes a plan of reorganization on the creditors.

(7) The rights of secured creditors are eliminated when a company files for reorganization under Chapter 11.

(8) In a reorganization under Chapter 11, the discharge provisions have no meaningful application.

Exercise 18–3
Bankruptcy law: Liquidation under Chapter 7—True or false

Determine if the following statements are true or false. Explain why any false statements are false.

(1) In involuntary filings under Chapter 7, the case is dismissed if the debtor contests the filing.

(2) In a Chapter 7 filing, the bankruptcy court usually appoints a trustee.

(3) In a Chapter 7 filing, management usually continues to operate the business until the liquidation is completed.

(4) The primary function of a trustee in Chapter 7 filings is to settle disputes between the debtor and the debtor's creditors.

(5) When a company is liquidated under Chapter 7, all unpaid debts (except those specified in the bankruptcy statutes) are discharged by the bankruptcy court.

(6) In a Chapter 7 filing, trustees have the authority to dispose of the debtor's assets.

(7) Trustees are authorized to void preferential transfers made to certain creditors.

(8) The concept of creditors with priority does not apply to Chapter 7 filings.

Exercise 18–4
Troubled debt restructuring: Modification of terms

Floter Company, which is having serious financial difficulty, executed an agreement with its bank whereby the currently due $500,000 note payable to the bank was extended for five years. The old interest rate of 10% was lowered to 4%. Interest is to be paid annually in arrears. Accrued interest of $20,000 as of the restructuring date was canceled.

Required:
(1) Determine if a gain on restructuring of debt has resulted.
(2) Prepare the journal entry related to the restructuring.

Exercise 18–5
Troubled debt restructuring: Modification of terms

Iffy Company, which is having serious financial difficulty, executed an agreement with one of its major vendors whereby the $800,000 account payable to the vendor was converted into a $600,000 note payable, all due and payable in two years. The interest rate on the note is 10%, with interest payable annually in arrears. The remaining $200,000 of the original note payable was canceled.

Required:
(1) Determine if a gain on restructuring of debt has resulted.
(2) Prepare the journal entry related to the restructuring.
(3) How would your answer be different if the due date of the note payable were four years from the restructuring date?

Exercise 18–6
Troubled debt restructuring: Modification of terms—
Use of present value concepts

Struggles Company, which is having serious financial difficulty, has entered into a restructuring agreement with a creditor that is owed $1,000,000 of principal (now due and payable) and $28,000 of interest. In the restructuring agreement, Struggles agrees to pay the principal of $1,000,000 in three years, with interest paid annually in arrears at 4%. The accrued interest of $28,000 is canceled.

Required:
(1) Determine if a gain on restructuring of debt has resulted.

(2) Determine the total amount of interest expense reported by Struggles over the next three years.
(3) Using present value tables, calculate the approximate effective interest rate.
(4) Prepare the journal entries made between the restructuring date and the maturity date, assuming all required payments are made on time.

Exercise 18–7
Troubled debt restructuring: Equity interest granted

Weathers Company, which is having serious financial difficulty, executed an agreement with one of its note holders whereby a $100,000 note payable was converted into 30,000 shares of the company's $1 par value common stock. The common stock was traded at $2 per share on the date of the agreement.

Required:
(1) Determine if a gain on restructuring of debt has resulted.
(2) Prepare the journal entry related to the restructuring.

Exercise 18–8
Troubled debt restructuring: Transfer of noncash assets

Shakey Company, which is having serious financial difficulty, executed an agreement with one of its creditors whereby a $200,000 note payable and the $25,000 related accrued interest was canceled in exchange for a parcel of land. The land had cost Shakey $100,000 and has a current appraised value of $150,000.

Required:
(1) Determine the amount of "gain on restructuring" to be reported.
(2) Prepare the required journal entry or entries.

Exercise 18–9
Bankruptcy reorganization: Settlement for cash and stock

Refresho Company's plan of reorganization under Chapter 11 of the bankruptcy statutes calls for a cash payment of $4,000,000 and the issuance of 800,000 shares of its $1 par value common stock to its unsecured creditors on a pro rata basis. These unsecured creditors are composed of vendors (owed $8,000,000) and a bank (owed $3,500,000 principal and $500,000 interest). Refresho's common stock is currently trading at $1.25 per share.

Required:
Prepare the journal entry related to this settlement.

Exercise 18–10
Bankruptcy reorganization: Settlement for cash and notes

Last-Chance Company's plan of reorganization under Chapter 11 of the bankruptcy statutes calls for a cash payment of $1,500,000 and the issuance of $2,000,000 of 14% notes payable to its unsecured creditors on a pro rata basis. These unsecured creditors are composed of vendors (owed $2,300,000) and a bank (owed $3,300,000 principal and $400,000 interest). (The 14% interest rate on the notes is considered reasonable under the circumstances.) The notes are to be paid in full in three years.

Required:
Prepare the journal entry related to this settlement.

Exercise 18–11
Statement of affairs: Calculating expected settlement amounts

The statement of affairs for Driftco Company reflects the following amounts:

	Book Value	Estimated Current Value
Assets:		
Assets pledged with fully secured creditors.................	$150,000	$180,000
Assets pledged with partially secured creditors	80,000	60,000
Free assets	220,000	150,000
	$450,000	$390,000
Liabilities:		
Liabilities with priority	$ 20,000	
Fully secured creditors	130,000	
Partially secured creditors	100,000	
Unsecured creditors	260,000	
	$510,000	

Required:
Compute the amount that each class of creditors can expect to receive if assets are converted into cash at their estimated current values.

(AICPA adapted)

Problems

Problem 18–1
Troubled debt restructuring: Modification of terms

Distresso Company, which is having serious financial difficulty, entered into an agreement with its major lender on December 31, 19X4. The amount owed to the lender was restructured as follows:

(1) Of the $2,000,000 of principal owed to the lender (all of which was currently due), 10% was canceled.
(2) Accrued interest of $300,000 was canceled.
(3) The due date on the remaining principal amount was extended to December 31, 19X8.
(4) The interest rate on the remaining principal amount was reduced from 12% to 3% for 19X5 and 19X6. For 19X7 and 19X8, the interest rate is 6%. All interest at these new rates is to be paid annually in arrears.

Required:
(1) Determine if a gain on restructuring of debt has resulted.
(2) Prepare the journal entry to record the restructuring.
(3) Calculate the total amount of interest expense, if any, reported from the restructuring date to the maturity date.

Problem 18–2
Troubled debt restructuring: Combination of equity interest granted and modification of terms

Mor-Tyme Company, which is having serious financial difficulty, entered into an agreement with holders of its notes payable on December 31, 19X5. The debt was restructured as follows:

(1) Of the total $14,000,000 of notes payable (all of which was currently due), $7,000,000 of principal was canceled in exchange for 300,000 shares of the company's $1 par value common stock. (The common stock had a market value of $20 per share on December 31, 19X5.)
(2) The remaining $7,000,000 of principal is to bear interest at 5%, payable annually in arrears. The maturity date of this $7,000,000 was extended to December 31, 19X8.
(3) Accrued interest of $350,000 was canceled.

Required:
(1) Determine if a gain on restructuring of debt has resulted.
(2) Prepare the journal entry to record the restructuring.
(3) Calculate the total amount of interest expense, if any, reported from the restructuring date to the maturity date.

Problem 18–3
Troubled debt restructuring: Combination of equity interest granted and modification of terms

Extendo Company, which is having serious financial difficulty, entered into an agreement with its bondholders on December 31, 19X1. The debt was restructured as follows:

(1) Of the total $25,000,000 in face value of bonds outstanding (which bear interest at 12%), $5,000,000 was canceled in exchange for 50,000 shares of a new class of preferred stock having a par value of $100.
(2) The maturity date of the remaining $20,000,000 of bonds was extended to December 31, 19X3.
(3) The interest rate on the $20,000,000 is 3% until maturity.
(4) Of the $2,000,000 interest payable accrued at December 31, 19X1, $1,500,000 was canceled. The remaining $500,000 was paid when the restructuring agreement was signed (at the close of business on December 31, 19X1).

Other information:

(1) The bonds were issued at a $700,000 premium eight years ago. The straight-line method of amortization had been used.

(2) The original life of the bonds was 10 years. The bonds were due in full during 19X1 as a result of a default in the interest payments.

Required:
(1) Determine if a gain on restructuring of debt has resulted.
(2) Prepare the journal entry to record the restructuring.
(3) Calculate the total amount of interest expense, if any, reported from the restructuring date to the maturity date.

Problem 18–4
Troubled debt restructuring: Combination of equity interest granted and modification of terms involving contingent interest

Contingex Company, which is having serious financial difficulty, entered into an agreement with its major lender on December 31, 19X3. The amount owed to the lender was restructured as follows:

(1) Of the $100,000,000 of principal owed to the lender (all of which was currently due), $40,000,000 was canceled in exchange for 400,000 shares of a new class of preferred stock, having a par value of $100 per share.
(2) The maturity date of the remaining $60,000,000 of principal was extended to December 31, 19X8.
(3) The interest rate on the $60,000,000 of principal was reduced to 4% from 8%, with interest payable annually in arrears.
(4) If the company's cumulative earnings before interest expense and income taxes from January 1, 19X4 through December 31, 19X8 exceed $25,000,000, then the interest rate reverts to 8% retroactive to January 1, 19X4. (As of December 31, 19X3, it is not probable that cumulative earnings during this period will exceed $25,000,000.)
(5) Accrued interest payable of $15,000,000 as of December 31, 19X3 was forgiven.

Required:
(1) Determine if a gain on restructuring of debt has resulted.
(2) Prepare the journal entry to record the restructuring.
(3) Determine the total amount of interest expense, if any, reported during the next five years, assuming that the company's cumulative earnings before interest expense and income tax expense during that period
   (a) did not exceed $25,000,000.
   (b) did exceed $25,000,000 as of September 30, 19X7.

Problem 18–5
Troubled debt restructuring: Modification of terms—
Use of present value concepts

Wobbly Company, which is having serious financial difficulty, entered into a restructuring agreement with a creditor that is owed $3,000,000 of principal (now due and payable) and $427,000 of interest. The terms of the restructuring agreement (dated January 1, 19X1) call for

(1) Cancellation of $277,000 of accrued interest, with payment of the remaining

$150,000 on signing the agreement. (This payment was indeed made at that time.)

(2) Principal payments of $1,000,000 per year beginning January 1, 19X2 (one year from now) until the loan is paid in full on January 1, 19X4.

(3) Interest to be paid annually in arrears, beginning January 1, 19X2, at 10% on the unpaid balance. (The interest rate prior to the restructuring was 14%.)

Required:
(1) Determine if a gain on restructuring of debt has resulted.
(2) Prepare the journal entry to record the restructuring.
(3) Determine the total amount of interest expense reported over the next three years.
(4) Using present value tables, calculate the approximate effective interest rate.
(5) Prepare the journal entries made between the restructuring date and the maturity date, assuming all required payments are made on time.

Problem 18–6
COMPREHENSIVE   Troubled debt restructuring

On July 1, 19X2, Firmex Company entered into a troubled debt restructuring agreement with its creditors. Data pertaining to the various classes of creditors and equity interests prior to the restructuring are as follows:

Accounts payable, unsecured..	$1,800,000
10% Note payable to bank, currently due and payable	3,000,000
Accrued interest on note payable	400,000
8% Debenture bonds (subordinated to bank loan)	2,000,000
Accrued interest on debenture bonds....................................	100,000
6% Preferred stock, $100 par value, cumulative, dividends in arrears of $90,000; 5,000 shares outstanding	
Common stock, no-par value, 200,000 shares outstanding	

The terms of the restructuring are as follows:

(1) Accounts payable of $400,000 are canceled outright. Accounts payable of $600,000 are canceled in exchange for 80,000 shares of common stock. Trading in the company's common stock was suspended on January 15, 19X2. Just before that time, the common stock was selling at $2 per share. Trading was resumed on July 2, 19X2, and the stock closed at 50 cents per share on that day. All remaining payables are to be paid within 180 days.

(2) Principal of $500,000 on the bank note, along with all accrued interest, is canceled. The due date on the remaining principal is extended to July 1, 19X5. The interest rate is reduced to 5%. However, if Firmex's cumulative earnings exceed $2,000,000 during the three years ended June 30, 19X5, then the interest rate reverts to 10% retroactively. (Currently, it appears unlikely that Firmex's earnings will exceed $2,000,000 during this period.)

(3) Principal of $1,000,000 on the debenture bonds is exchanged for a new class of 7% preferred stock. This new preferred stock, which is designated Series A, is senior to the existing preferred stock with respect to dividends and distributions in the event of liquidation. The existing preferred stock (which was issued at par) is designated Series B. All accrued interest on the debentures

is canceled. The June 30, 19X7 due date is unchanged. The interest rate on the remaining $1,000,000 of principal is reduced to 5% until maturity.

(4) The dividends in arrears on the existing preferred stock is canceled, and the future dividend rate is reduced to 3% for a period of five years.

Required:

(1) Prepare the accounting entries related to the above restructurings, assuming July 1, 19X2 is the consummation date.

(2) What entry, if any, would be made on June 30, 19X5 if Firmex's earnings do not exceed $2,000,000 from July 1, 19X2 to June 30, 19X5?

(3) Calculate the total amount of interest expense reported in the income statement for the next five years with respect to the debenture bonds.

Problem 18–7
COMPREHENSIVE   Bankruptcy reorganization

Assume that the information in Problem 18–6 pertains to a Chapter 11 bankruptcy reorganization instead of a troubled debt restructuring outside of the bankruptcy courts.

Required:

(1) Prepare the journal entries related to this plan of reorganization. Assume that it is *not* necessary to apply the provisions of *APB Opinion No. 21.*

(2) With respect to the bank note, what entry, if any, would be made on June 30, 19X5 if Firmex's earnings do not exceed $2,000,000 from July 1, 19X2 to June 30, 19X5?

(3) Calculate the total amount of interest expense reported in the income statement for the next five years with respect to the debenture bonds.

Problem 18–8
Bankruptcy reorganization: Settlement with unsecured creditors—
Use of present value concepts

Utel Corporation's plan of reorganization was confirmed by the bankruptcy court on June 30, 19X1. Under the plan, unsecured creditors (who are owed $850,000,000) are to receive the following:

Cash.	$300,000,000
12% Unsecured notes	$300,000,000
Common stock, $1 par value	10,000,000 shares

The company's investment bankers (Morgan, Stanley, and Bailey Company) have determined that the 12% unsecured notes will trade at a discount on issuance to yield a return of approximately 15%. These notes are to be paid off at $60,000,000 per year beginning June 30, 19X2 until their maturity five years from now. Interest is to be paid annually in arrears each June 30.

The company's common stock (2,000,000 shares now outstanding) traded at $1.50 per share when the company's plan of reorganization was confirmed.

Assume that *APB Opinion No. 21* applies to the 12% secured notes. Selected present value factors follow:

	Present Value Factors	
Periods	12%	15%
1	0.89286	0.86957
2	0.79719	0.75614
3	0.71178	0.65752
4	0.63552	0.57175
5	0.56743	0.49718
Five payments (annuity)	3.60478	3.35216

Required:

(1) Prepare the journal entries related to the plan of reorganization.
(2) Prepare the journal entries made for the first two years following confirmation of the plan, assuming all required payments are made on time.

Problem 18–9
Liquidation: Preparing a statement of affairs

As the Tubes Corporation's CPA, you are aware that it is facing bankruptcy proceedings. The balance sheet of the Tubes Corporation at June 30, 19X1, and supplementary data are presented below:

Assets

Cash	$ 2,000
Accounts receivable, less allowance for uncollectibles	70,000
Inventory, raw materials	40,000
Inventory, finished goods	60,000
Marketable securities	20,000
Land	13,000
Buildings, net of accumulated depreciation	90,000
Machinery, net of accumulated depreciation	120,000
Goodwill	20,000
Prepaid expenses	5,000
Total assets	$440,000

Liabilities and Equity

Accounts payable	$ 80,000
Notes payable	135,000
Accrued wages	15,000
Mortgages payable	130,000
Common stock	100,000
Accumulated deficit	(20,000)
Total liabilities and equity	$440,000

Additional information:

(1) Cash includes a $500 travel advance that has been expended.
(2) Accounts receivable of $40,000 have been pledged to bank loans of $30,000. Credit balances of $5,000 are netted in the accounts receivable total.
(3) Marketable securities consist of government bonds costing $10,000 and 500 shares Bartlett Company stock. The market value of the bonds is $10,000 and the stock is $18 per share. The bonds have accrued interest due of $200. The securities are collateral for a $20,000 bank loan.

(4) Appraised value of raw materials is $30,000 and of finished goods is $50,000. For an additional cost of $10,000, the raw materials would realize $70,000 as finished goods.

fully secured

(5) The appraised value of fixed assets is land, $25,000; buildings, $110,000; and machinery, $75,000.

(6) Prepaid expenses will be exhausted during the liquidation period.

(7) Accounts payable include $15,000 of withheld payroll taxes and $6,000 owed to creditors who had been reassured by Tubes's president that they would be paid. Unrecorded employer's payroll taxes total $500.

*15500 taxes
Payroll unsecured
6000 w/o priority*

(8) Wages payable are not subject to any limits under bankruptcy laws.

(9) Mortgages payable consist of $100,000 on land and buildings and $30,000 chattel mortgage on machinery. Total unrecorded accrued interest for these mortgages amounts to $2,400.

w Priority

(10) Estimated legal fees and expenses connected with the liquidation are $10,000.

Damages Payable

(11) Probable judgment on a pending damage suit is $50,000.

*1000 w/Priority
5000 w/o Prior*

(12) You have not rendered a $5,000 invoice for last year's audit, and you estimate a $1,000 fee for liquidation work.

Required:

(1) Prepare a statement of affairs. (The book value column should reflect adjustments that properly should have been made at June 30, 19X1 in the normal course of business.)

(2) Compute the estimated settlement per dollar of unsecured liabilities.

(AICPA adapted)

Problem 18–10
Liquidation: Preparing a statement of affairs

The Ropes Corporation is in financial difficulty because of low sales. Its stockholders and principal creditors want an estimate of the financial results of the liquidation of the assets and liabilities and the dissolution of the corporation.

ROPES CORPORATION
Postclosing Trial Balance
December 31, 19X3

	Debit	Credit
Cash	$ 1,000	
Accounts receivable	20,500	
Allowance for uncollectibles		$ 350
Inventories	40,000	
Supplies inventory	3,000	
Loco Railroad 5% bonds	5,000	
Accrued bond interest receivable	750	
Advertising	6,000	
Land	4,000	
Building	30,000	
Accumulated depreciation—building		5,000
Machinery and equipment	46,000	
Accumulated depreciation—machinery and equipment		8,000
Accounts payable		26,000
Notes payable—bank		25,000

	Debit	Credit
Notes payable—officers		20,000
Payroll taxes payable		800
Wages payable		1,500
Mortgage payable		42,000
Mortgage interest payable		500
Capital stock		50,000
Accumulated deficit	29,100	
Estimated liability for product guarantees		6,200
	$185,350	$185,350

The following information has been collected for a meeting of the stockholders and principal creditors to be held on January 10, 19X4:

(1) Cash includes a $300 protested check from a customer. The customer stated that funds to honor the check will be available in about two weeks.

(2) Accounts receivable include accounts totaling $10,000 that are fully collectible and have been assigned to the bank in connection with the notes payable. Included in the unassigned receivables is an uncollectible account of $150. The Allowance for Uncollectibles account of $350 now on the books will adequately provide for other doubtful accounts.

(3) Purchase orders totaling $9,000 are on hand for the corporation's products. Inventory with a book value of $6,000 can be processed at an additional cost of $400 to fill these orders. The balance of the inventory, which includes obsolete materials with a book value of $1,200, can be sold for $10,500.

(4) In transit at December 31 but not recorded on the books is a shipment of defective merchandise being returned by a customer. The president of the corporation authorized the return and the refund of the $250 purchase price after the merchandise had been inspected. Other than this return, the president knows of no other defective merchandise that would affect the Estimated Liability for Product Guarantees account. The merchandise being returned has no salvage value.

(5) The supplies inventory comprises advertising literature, brochures, and other sales aids, which could not be replaced for less than $3,700.

(6) The Loco Railroad bonds are recorded at face value. They were purchased in 1980 for $600, and the adjustment to face value was credited to Retained Earnings. At December 31, 19X3, the bonds were quoted at 18.

(7) The Advertising account represents the future benefits of a 19X3 advertising campaign. The account contains 10% of certain advertising expenditures. The president stated that this figure was too conservative and that 20% would be a more realistic measure of the market that was created.

(8) The land and building are in a downtown area. A firm offer of $50,000 has been received for the land, which would be used as a parking lot; the building would be razed at a cost of $12,000 to the buyer. Another offer of $40,000 was received for the real estate, which the bidder stated would be used for manufacturing that would probably employ some employees of Ropes.

(9) The highest offer received from used machinery dealers was $18,000 for all of the machinery and equipment.

(10) One creditor, whose account for $1,000 is included in the accounts payable, confirmed in writing that he would accept 90 cents on the dollar if the corporation paid him by January 10.

(11) Wages payable are for amounts earned within the last 30 days.
(12) The mortgage payable is secured by the land and building. The last two monthly principal payments of $200 each were not made.
(13) Estimated liquidation expenses amount to $3,200.
(14) For income tax purposes the corporation has the following net operating loss carryovers (the combined federal and state tax rate is 50%): 19X1, $10,000; 19X2, $12,000; and 19X3, $8,000.

Required:
(1) Prepare a statement of affairs. (The book value column should reflect adjustments that should have been made at December 31, 19X3 in the normal course of business. Assume the company has a June 30 fiscal year-end.)
(2) Prepare a schedule that computes the estimated settlement per dollar of unsecured liabilities.

(AICPA adapted)

PART FOUR Partnerships

PART

19

Partnerships: Formation and Operation

OVERVIEW OF PARTNERSHIPS

A **partnership** is an association of two or more persons who contribute money, property, or services to carry on as co-owners of a business, the profits and losses of which are shared in an agreed-upon manner. The term **person** refers to individuals, corporations, and even other partnerships. Most partners are individuals. Partnerships that comprise one or more partnerships or corporations usually are formed to combine managerial talent and financial resources to conduct a specific undertaking—for example, the design and development of a large shopping center. Such partnerships are commonly referred to as joint ventures. Regardless of whether the partners are individuals, other partnerships, or corporations, the accounting and tax issues are the same.

Chapters 19–21 deal with **general partnerships**—that is, partnerships in which each partner is personally liable to the partnership's creditors if partnership assets are insufficient to pay such creditors. In Appendix A, we briefly discuss **limited partnerships,** in which certain partners (called limited partners) are not personally liable to the partnership's creditors if partnership assets are insufficient to pay such creditors.

Introduction to the professional corporation

Traditionally, the partnership form of organization has been used by small retail establishments and businesses that are considered the professions—for example, public accounting, law, and medicine. Such professions could not incorporate under the existing laws. In the late 1960s, more and more professionals recognized that much greater tax benefits were associated with the corporate form of organization, primarily with respect to pension, profit-sharing, medical, and insurance plans. Consequently, many professional people made considerable efforts to urge legislation that would allow professional businesses to incorporate. Their efforts were so successful that each of the 50 states now has some form of legislation on the books, under the broad category of **professional corporations,** enabling professional businesses to incorporate.

Initially, the Internal Revenue Service did not recognize professional corporations as corporations for federal income tax reporting purposes. In 1969, however, after a continuous series of court defeats, the IRS issued regulations recognizing the professional corporation as a corporation for federal tax purposes. As a result of this change, many existing partnerships (as well as many sole proprietorships) have incorporated. Furthermore, substantial numbers of new businesses, which would have been conducted as either partnerships or sole proprietorships, have chosen the professional corporation form of business. Even one of the "Big 8" public accounting firms had plans in 1982 to change from a partnership to a professional corporation. (Virtually all national and regional public accounting firms have retained the partnership form of organization, however, largely because of complex compliance regulations of the professional corporation laws in each of the states in which they do business.)

The parity provisions (effective in 1984) of the Tax Equity and Fiscal Responsibility Act of 1982 eliminated most of the tax benefits available under the corporate form of organization. (The major parity provision allows sole proprietors and partners the same pension and profit sharing deductions as corporate employees.) As a result of this legislation, the mushrooming growth of the professional corporation form of business has abruptly halted. Furthermore, existing professional corporations must re-evaluate the continued use of this form of organization.

Because an accountant rendering services to a professional can expect to encounter a professional corporation as often as a partnership, a limited discussion of professional corporations is included at the end of this chapter. The advantages and disadvantages of professional incorporation must be carefully weighed against the advantages and disadvantages of either the partnership or sole proprietorship form of organization. Furthermore, the accountant can expect to be a key consultant in choosing the form of organization.

Major features of the partnership form of business

Ease of formation. Forming a partnership is a relatively simple process. The partners merely put their agreement into writing concerning who contributes assets or services, who performs which functions in the business, and how profits and losses are shared. The written document is called the **partnership agreement.**

Thus, compared with the corporate form of business, a partnership need not prepare articles of incorporation, write bylaws, print stock certificates, prepare minutes of the first meeting of the board of directors, pay state incorporation fees, or register stocks.

Potential noncontinuity of existence. Historically, the possibility that the operations of a partnership could not continue on the death or withdrawal of a partner (with the business subsequently liquidated) was considered a major disadvantage of the partnership form of organization. In practice, this problem occurs only for small partnerships. Even then, some steps can be taken to minimize the impact of the loss of a partner. For example, life insurance proceeds on the death of a partner can be used to settle with the deceased partner's estate, thus conserving the assets of the business so that the remaining partners can continue the operation. For larger partnerships, this feature usually is not significant. Some of the largest partnerships have more than 1,000 partners. Obviously, the loss of one or even several partners has minimal impact on the day-to-day operations of the business.

Difficulty in disposing of interest. An ownership interest in a partnership is a personal asset, as is the ownership of stock in a corporation. No formal established marketplace exists for the sale of a partnership interest, however, as for the sale of stock in a publicly owned corporation. Accordingly, a partner who wishes to sell or assign his or her partnership interest will have more difficulty finding a buyer than a shareholder who wishes to sell stock in a publicly owned corporation. To make this process even more difficult, the person buying a partnership interest does not have the automatic right to participate in the management of the business—the consent of the remaining partners is necessary.

Unlimited liability. If a partnership's assets are insufficient to pay its creditors, the creditors have recourse to the personal assets of any and all general partners of the partnership. This characteristic contrasts sharply with the corporate form of organization, in which the personal assets of the shareholders are insulated from the corporation's creditors. This is undoubtedly the major disadvantage of the partnership form of organization.

Mutual agency. The partnership is bound by each partner acting within the scope of partnership activities. Thus, each partner acts as an agent for the partnership in dealing with persons outside the partnership.

Sharing of profits and losses. Profits and losses are shared among the partners in any manner that the partners agree to.

Nontaxable status. Unlike a corporation, a partnership does not pay income taxes. Instead, partnerships must file with the Internal Revenue Service an information return on Form 1065, which shows the partnership's taxable income and each partner's share of such income. Each partner then reports and pays taxes on his or her share of the partnership's taxable income. These procedures eliminate the undesirable "double taxation," which is a feature of corporations—that is, the earnings of the corporation are taxed and then the dividends of the corporation are taxed. Partnership income is taxed only once, at the individual partner level.

Concluding comments. The partnership form of organization is unique. For professionals, the form of organization is simple and flexible compared with the professional corporation, which is generally considered a complex and cumbersome form of organization. The continued use of the partnership form of organization was explained by Salomon Brothers, a large, prestigious Wall Street brokerage firm, which is fiercely loyal to this form of organization even though virtually all of its Wall Street competitors (for example, Merrill Lynch & Co. and E.F. Hutton & Co.) abandoned the partnership form of organization years ago in favor of incorporation. According to Salomon Brothers, "it's a more effective way to relate to each other . . . ."[1]

Incorporating a partnership

Many existing corporations (in addition to professional corporations) began as partnerships. Obviously, at some point in the enterprise's existence, the advantages of incorporation outweighed the advantages of the partnership form of organization. When a partnership incorporates, its assets are transferred to the corporation, and the corporation assumes the partnership's

[1] "The Day Can Be Tense at Salomon Brothers, but the Money Rolls In," *The Wall Street Journal,* June 5, 1981, p. 1.

liabilities. One technical point should be noted: The corporation's board of directors is responsible for placing a value on the assets transferred to the corporation. In theory, the assets can be revalued to their current values, and this is often done. However, if the corporation ever decides to register its common stock with the Securities and Exchange Commission, the SEC will insist that assets transferred to the corporation be carried at the partnership's historical cost, adjusted for depreciation and amortization. In other words, no upward revaluation of assets on incorporation is allowed. (Presumably, a downward revaluation would be permitted if appropriate.)

FORMATION OF A PARTNERSHIP

The Uniform Partnership Act

Before discussing the partnership agreement in detail, some understanding of the laws that govern partnerships is necessary. Although each of the 50 states has laws pertaining to partnerships, most states have adopted the Uniform Partnership Act (hereafter referred to as the UPA) or a variation thereof as a means of governing partnerships. In this text, we consider the UPA the governing statute.

The UPA is reasonably comprehensive in defining the consequences of a partnership relationship. For our purposes, its more relevant sections pertain to:

(1) Relations of partners to one another.
(2) Relations of partners to persons dealing with the partnership.
(3) Dissolution and winding up of the partnership.

Some UPA sections cannot be circumvented merely by contrary provisions or omissions in the partnership agreement. For example, Section 15 of the UPA imposes joint liability on all general partners for partnership debts. If a partnership agreement contained a provision excusing certain general partners from joint liability, then that provision of the agreement would be inoperable, and creditors could seek recourse from any partner.

Other sections of the UPA apply only when a partnership agreement is silent. For example, suppose a partnership agreement is silent with respect to remuneration for partners who are active in the management of the business. If one of the active partners should claim subsequently to be entitled to remuneration for services, then the dispute would be settled against that partner in a court of law. Section 18 of the UPA expressly provides that unless otherwise stated in the partnership agreement, "no partner is entitled to remuneration for acting in the partnership interest." A partner's remuneration for managerial services would have to be provided for in the partnership agreement.

On the other hand, the UPA is not so comprehensive that it provides for every possible provision that otherwise could be included in a partnership agreement. For example, Section 27 discusses certain consequences of the sale by a partner of his or her partnership interest. Although a partner need not give the remaining partners the first opportunity to acquire the partnership interest, neither does the UPA prevent a partnership agreement from containing a clause to the effect that if a partner desires to sell any or all of his or her interest, the remaining partners must be given the right of first refusal.

A few selected sections of the Uniform Partnership Act appear in Appendix B of this chapter.

The partnership agreement

The partnership agreement is merely a written expression of what the partners have agreed to. Because state laws govern the consequences of partnership relationships, however, the partnership agreement should be prepared by an attorney who is experienced in partnership law. This is essential for the following reasons:

(1) Mandatory provisions of the UPA may be included or referred to, so that partners are aware of and somewhat familiar with partnership law.
(2) Provisions that conflict with the UPA can be avoided.
(3) Optional provisions that do not conflict with the UPA can be considered for possible inclusion.

A well-written partnership agreement should be a guide to the partners' relationship and any allowable variations from the UPA to which they have agreed. It should also minimize potential disputes among the partners.

In addition to essential legal provisions, the partnership agreement should include the following:

(1) The partnership's exact name and designated place of business.
(2) The names and personal addresses of each partner.
(3) The date on which the partnership was formed.
(4) The business purpose of the partnership.
(5) The duration of the partnership.
(6) A list of the assets contributed by each partner and the related agreed-upon valuation of those assets to the partnership.
(7) The basis of accounting to be used (for example, the accrual basis, the cash basis, or some variation of either of these methods).
(8) The partnership's accounting year-end for purposes of closing the books and dividing the profits and losses.
(9) The specific procedures for sharing profits and losses.
(10) The amounts that partners can periodically withdraw from the business and any related conditions for such withdrawals (for example, a certain amount per month or an amount up to a percentage of current-period earnings).
(11) Provisions for settling with a partner (or a partner's estate) who withdraws from the partnership through choice, retirement, or death.

An accountant can assist persons who are in the preliminary stages of forming a partnership in the following ways:

(1) By explaining the cash basis and accrual basis of accounting.

(2) By explaining and illustrating the numerous alternative methods available for sharing profits and losses and the appropriateness of each method (a significant portion of this chapter is devoted to this subject).

(3) By discussing the tax ramifications compared with other methods of organizing the business (this subject is also discussed later in the chapter).

The partnership as an entity

The business of the partnership should logically be accounted for separately from the personal transactions of the partners. Although partnerships are not separate legal entities with unlimited lives, as is the case for corporations, this does not prevent partnerships from being accounted for as separate, operating, business entities.

Although partners legally must contribute additional cash or property to the partnership to satisfy the claims of creditors, this does not mean that the partnership is inseparable from the partners. It is a common banking practice for certain top officers of corporations to guarantee personally loans made to the corporation. Thus, the fact that additional collateral for creditors exists is irrelevant.

Income tax laws do not determine sound accounting theory. They do treat partnerships as separate reporting entities, although not as separate tax-paying entities. Most partnerships are considered separate business entities in that they prepare monthly financial statements for internal use. Some of the large public accounting firms even publish annual reports, complete with financial statements, for use by their partners, employees, and other interested parties.

Applicability of generally accepted accounting principles

To study partnerships, we must make an important transition from corporate accounting (in which generally accepted accounting principles are almost always followed) to partnership accounting (in which generally accepted accounting principles need not be and often are not followed). The professional pronouncements of the AICPA and the FASB apply to businesses that present their financial statements in accordance with generally accepted accounting principles. Such businesses include (1) publicly held corporations, which must present their financial statements in accordance with generally accepted accounting principles; (2) nonpublicly held corporations, which usually present their financial statements in accordance with generally accepted accounting principles (often pursuant to requirements of loan agreements with financial institutions); and (3) partnerships and sole proprietorships that choose to present their financial statements in accordance with generally accepted accounting principles.

When a partnership does not maintain its books in accordance with generally accepted accounting principles, such a departure usually falls into one of the following categories:

(1) Cash basis instead of accrual basis. The cash basis of recording receipts and expenses is often more efficient and economical than the accrual basis.

(2) Prior-period adjustments. To achieve greater equity among the partners, prior-period adjustments are often made even though the items do not qualify as such under *FASB Statement No. 16,* "Prior Period Adjustments."

(3) Current values instead of historical cost. When the ownership of the partnership changes, it is sometimes more expedient to reflect assets at their current values than to continue to reflect them at their historical cost.

(4) Recognition of goodwill. To accommodate a partner's wishes, goodwill may be recognized on the admission or retirement of a partner, even though a business combination has not occurred.

Categories (3) and (4) are discussed and illustrated in Chapter 20 on changes in ownership.

Partners' accounts

Capital accounts. Each partner has a capital account, which is created when the partner contributes assets to the partnership. The account is increased for subsequent capital contributions and decreased for withdrawals. In addition, the account is increased for the partner's share of earnings and decreased for the partner's share of losses.

Traditionally, accountants have not attempted to maintain a balance sheet distinction between contributed capital and earnings that have been retained in the partnership, as is customary for corporations. This is primarily because the partnership's earnings do not reflect any salary expense for the partners (they are owners, not employees), and therefore they must be evaluated carefully. If the corporate form of business were used instead of the partnership form, the corporation's earnings would be lower than those reported by the partnership, because the services performed by the partners would be performed by salaried officers and employees of the corporation. Earnings under the corporate form of business would also be lower because of income tax. To avoid the implication that the earnings retained in the partnership are comparable to the retained earnings of a corporation, a Retained Earnings account is considered inappropriate for partnerships. Accordingly, the earnings or losses of a partnership are added or subtracted, respectively, to the capital accounts of the individual partners.

Drawing accounts. Typically, partners do not wait until the end of the year to determine how much of the profits they wish to withdraw from the partnership. To meet personal living expenses, partners customarily withdraw monies on a periodic basis throughout the year. Such withdrawals could be charged directly to the capital accounts of the individual partners. However, a special account called the **drawings** account is used to charge current-year withdrawals. In substance, the drawing accounts are contra capital accounts. At year-end, each partner's drawing account is closed to that partner's capital account. The maximum amount partners may withdraw during the year is usually specified in the partnership agreement.

Loan accounts. Partners may make loans to the partnership in excess of their required capital contributions. Section 18 of the UPA provides that unless otherwise agreed to by the partners, "a partner, who in aid of the partnership makes any payment or advance beyond the amount of capital which he agreed to contribute, shall be paid interest from the date of the payment or advance." Interest on partners' loans to the partnership is a bona fide borrowing expense of the business, is treated as interest expense in the general ledger, and enters into the determination of the profit or loss.

If a partnership loans money on an interest-bearing basis to a partner, the interest is recorded as interest income in the general ledger. It also enters into the determination of the profit or loss.

Recording the initial capital contributions

The following two fundamental principles are deeply rooted in partnership accounting:

(1) Noncash assets contributed to a partnership should be valued at their current values.
(2) Liabilities assumed by a partnership should be valued at their current values.

These principles achieve equity among the partners, an objective that is repeatedly stressed in partnership accounting. If these principles were not followed, the subsequent operations would not reflect the true earnings of the partnerships, and certain partners would be treated inequitably.

For example, assume a partner contributed to a partnership marketable securities with a current market value of $10,000 and a cost basis to the individual partner of $7,000. If the marketable securities were later sold by the partnership for $12,000, the recorded gain on the partnership's books would be $2,000, which is the amount of appreciation that occurred during the period that the partnership held the asset. However, if the marketable securities had been valued on the partnership's books at the partner's cost basis of $7,000, the recorded gain would be $5,000. This would result in the other partner's sharing in an additional $3,000 of profit, the appreciation that occurred before the asset was contributed to the partnership. Current values must be used to prevent such inequities. The partnership agreement normally indicates the agreed-upon valuation assigned to noncash assets contributed and liabilities assumed.

The entry to record initial capital contributions for an assumed two-person partnership is shown below using the following assumed facts:

Assets Contributed and Liabilities Assumed	Adjusted Basis[a]	Current Value
By partner A:		
Cash	$23,000	$23,000
Marketable securities	7,000	10,000
	$30,000	$33,000
By partner B:		
Cash	$ 5,000	$ 5,000
Land	15,000	20,000
Building, net	25,000	35,000
Note payable, secured by land and building	(20,000)	(20,000)
	$25,000	$40,000

Entry to record initial contributions:

Cash	28,000	
Marketable securities	10,000	
Land	20,000	
Building	35,000	
Notes payable		20,000
Capital, partner A		33,000
Capital, partner B		40,000

[a] Adjusted basis means each partner's historical cost, as adjusted for depreciation and amortization previously recorded for income tax reporting purposes.

The adjusted basis column is completely irrelevant for purposes of recording the initial capital contributions in the general ledger, but it is significant for income tax reporting. Income tax aspects are discussed later in the chapter.

METHODS OF SHARING PROFITS AND LOSSES

Section 18 of the UPA specifies that profits and losses are shared equally unless otherwise provided for in the partnership agreement. Because the sharing of profits and losses is such an important aspect of a partnership relationship, it would be rare to find a partnership agreement that did not spell out the divisions of profits and losses in detail. The formula that is used to divide profits and losses is arrived at through negotiations among the partners. Whether or not it is fair does not concern the accountant.

Profits and losses can be shared in many ways. Partners should select a formula that is sensible, practical, and equitable. Most profit and loss sharing formulas include one or more of the following features or techniques:

(1) Sharing equally or in some other agreed-upon ratio.
(2) Imputed salary allowances to acknowledge time devoted to the business.
(3) Imputed interest on capital investments to recognize capital invested.
(4) Expense sharing arrangements.
(5) Performance criteria to recognize above- or below-average performance.

Note that the computations to determine the allocation of profit and loss among the partners are made on worksheets. The only journal entry that results from this process is to close the Profit and Loss Summary account to the capital accounts of the partners, using the amounts determined from the worksheet computations.

Ratios

Under the ratio method, each partner is allocated a percentage of the profits and losses. For example, partner A is to receive 60% and partner B is to receive 40% of the profits and losses. These percentages are then expressed as a ratio. Thus, profits and losses are shared between A and B in the ratio 3:2, respectively. If the partnership of A and B had profits of $100,000, the entry to record the division of the profits would be as follows:

Profit and loss summary	100,000	
Capital, partner A		60,000
Capital, partner B		40,000

An infrequently used variation of this method is to specify one ratio for profits and a different ratio for losses. Because profit and loss years may alternate, it is extremely important that profit or loss for each year be determined accurately in all material respects whenever this variation is used.

Salary allowances and ratios

Sometimes certain partners devote more time to the business than other partners. In these cases, a frequently used method for sharing profits and losses is to provide for salary allowances, with any residual profit or loss allocated in an agreed-upon ratio. For example, assume partner A devotes all of his time to the business, and partner B devotes only one-third of her time to the business. The partners could agree to provide for salary allowances in relation to the time devoted to the business—for example, $30,000 to partner A and $10,000 to partner B. All remaining profits or losses could then be divided in the agreed-upon ratio—that is, 3:2, respectively.

Using these salary allowances and a residual sharing ratio of 3:2 for partner A and partner B, respectively, the partnership would divide $100,000 in profits in the following way:

		Allocated to	
	Total	Partner A	Partner B
Total profit	$100,000		
Salary allowances	(40,000)	$30,000	$10,000
Residual profit	$ 60,000		
Allocate 3:2	(60,000)	36,000	24,000
	$ -0-	$66,000	$34,000

The general ledger entry to divide the profits would be as follows:

Profit and loss summary	100,000	
Capital, partner A		66,000
Capital, partner B		34,000

Remember that partners are owners, not employees. Accordingly, it is not appropriate to charge a Salary Expense account and credit Accrued Salary Payable. However, some partnerships do record salary allowances in this manner. Although not technically correct, it does not affect the final profit and loss allocations. In these cases, cash distributions that relate to salary allowances are charged to Accrued Salary Payable. Any remaining credit balance in a partner's Accrued Salary Payable account at year-end is then transferred to that partner's capital account.

In the above example, the total profit was greater than the total salary allowances of $40,000. What if that were not the case? Profit of only $25,000 would be shared as follows:

		Allocated to	
	Total	Partner A	Partner B
Total profit	$ 25,000		
Salary allowances	(40,000)	$30,000	$10,000
Residual loss	$(15,000)		
Allocate 3:2	(15,000)	(9,000)	(6,000)
	$ -0-	$21,000	$ 4,000

The general ledger entry to divide the profits would be as follows:

Profit and loss summary	25,000	
Capital, partner A		21,000
Capital, partner B		4,000

Another way of handling this situation would be if the partners agreed not to use a residual sharing ratio in the event profits were less than the total salary allowances. In this case, the first $40,000 of profit would be divided in the ratio of the salary allowances. Using the above example, a profit of $25,000 would be divided as follows:

		Allocated to	
	Total	Partner A	Partner B
Total profit	$25,000		
Salary allowances—up to $40,000 in a 3:1 ratio	(25,000)	$18,750	$6,250
	$ -0-	$18,750	$6,250

Large and moderately sized partnerships usually function with an administrative hierarchy. Partnership positions within such a hierarchy have greater responsibilities than positions outside the hierarchy. To compensate the partners who assume these greater responsibilities, salary allowances commonly are used and their amounts are correlated to the various levels of responsibility within the hierarchy.

Imputed interest on capital, salary allowances, and ratios

When partners' capital investments are not equal, the profit sharing formula frequently includes a feature that recognizes the greater capital investment of certain partners. Accordingly, interest is imputed on each partner's capital investment. For example, a profit and loss sharing formula could specify that interest be imputed at 10% of each partner's average capital investment. To illustrate how this procedure is applied, assume the following profit sharing formula and average capital investments:

	Partner A	Partner B
Profit sharing formula:		
Salary allowances	$30,000	$10,000
Interest on average capital balance	10%	10%
Residual profit or loss (3:2)	60%	40%
Average capital investments	$10,000	$40,000

Profits of $100,000 would be divided as follows:

		Allocated to	
	Total	Partner A	Partner B
Total profit	$100,000		
Salary allowances	(40,000)	$30,000	$10,000
Interest on average capital investments	(5,000)	1,000	4,000
Residual profit	$ 55,000		
Allocate 3:2	(55,000)	33,000	22,000
	$ -0-	$64,000	$36,000

Based on invested capital when? Beg of yr, yr end, avg for yr? must specify.

The general ledger entry to divide the profits would be as follows:

Profit and loss summary	100,000	
Capital, partner A		64,000
Capital, partner B		36,000

Remember that the partner's capital investments are just that—they are not loans to the partnership. Accordingly, it is not appropriate to charge an Interest Expense account and an Accrued Interest Payable account. However, some partnerships do record imputed interest in this manner. This procedure is not technically correct, but it does not affect the final profit and loss allocations. In these cases, cash distributions that relate to imputed interest are charged to Accrued Interest Payable. Any remaining credit balance in a partner's Accrued Interest Payable account at year-end is then transferred to that partner's capital account.

In the above example the profit was greater than both the total of the salary allowances of $40,000 and the total of imputed interest of $5,000. A profit of only $25,000 would be divided as follows:

		Allocated to	
	Total	Partner A	Partner B
Total profit	$ 25,000		
Salary allowances	(40,000)	$30,000	$10,000
Interest on average capital investments	(5,000)	1,000	4,000
Residual loss	$(20,000)		
Allocate 3:2	20,000	(12,000)	(8,000)
	$ -0-	$19,000	$ 6,000

The general ledger entry to divide the profits would be as follows:

Profit and loss summary	25,000	
Capital, partner A		19,000
Capital, partner B		6,000

Alternatively, the partners could agree not to use a residual sharing ratio in the event profits did not exceed the total of the salary allowances and the imputed interest on average capital balances. In this case, the partners must agree on the priority of the various features. If the partnership agreement gives salary allowances priority over imputed interest on capital balances, the first $40,000 of profit would be divided in the ratio of the salary allowances, and the next $5,000 would be divided in the ratio of the imputed interest amounts. Using the profit sharing formula and data given in the preceding example, a profit of only $42,000 would be divided as follows:

		Allocated to	
	Total	Partner A	Partner B
Total profit	$42,000		
Salary allowances	(40,000)	$30,000	$10,000
Available for interest on capital	$ 2,000		
Interest on average capital investment 1:4	(2,000)	400	1,600
	$ -0-	$30,400	$11,600

In the preceding examples, interest was imputed on the average capital investments. Although this is apparently the most equitable method, using the beginning or ending capital investments are other options. Whenever this imputed interest on capital feature is used, the partnership agreement should specify whether the beginning, average, or ending capital balances should be used. Furthermore, if the partnership agreement calls for using average or ending capital investments, it should define specifically how the average or ending capital investments are determined. Only the capital account or the capital account and the drawing account of each partner may be used. For the average capital balance method, the method of computing the average must be selected—that is, using daily balances, beginning of month balances, or end of month balances.

The following assumptions and capital account activities illustrate the computation of an average capital investment.

(1) The drawing account activity is considered in arriving at the average capital investment for the year.
(2) An average capital investment for each month is used to arrive at the average capital investment for the year.

Capital, Partner X			Drawings, Partner X		
	50,000	1/1/X5	6/30/X5	6,000	
	10,000	4/1/X5	9/15/X5	6,000	
	2,000	11/15/X5	12/31/X5	6,000	

Computation:

	Monthly Averages
January	$ 50,000
February	50,000
March	50,000
April	60,000
May	60,000
June	60,000
July	54,000
August	54,000
September	51,000
October	48,000
November	49,000
December	50,000
	$636,000
Average capital investment for 19X5 ($636,000/12)	$ 53,000

Capital balances only

Many international accounting firms allocate profits and losses *solely* on the basis of capital balances. In these cases, each partner must maintain a specified capital balance, which is correlated to the level of responsibility assumed in the partnership. This method is not only easy to apply, but it can prevent certain inequities from occurring among partners if the partnership is liquidated. These potential inequities are discussed in Chapter 21, which deals with partnership liquidations.

Expense sharing arrangements

Sometimes a small partnership operates as a confederation of sole proprietorships, in that the profit sharing formula entitles each partner to all net billings generated by that partner. Expenses are then allocated to partners on the basis of total floor space, amount of billings, or some other arbitrary method. This arrangement is common when two or more sole proprietorships form a partnership, with each partner maintaining former clients. Any net billings from clients obtained after the formation of the partnership may be assigned either to the partner responsible for obtaining the client or to a common pool to be allocated to all partners on some arbitrary basis.

Performance methods

Merit measurements

Many partnerships use profit and loss sharing formulas that give some weight to the specific performance of each partner, to provide incentives to perform well. Some examples of areas in which performance criteria may be used are listed below:

(1) **Chargeable hours.**   Chargeable hours are the total number of hours that a partner incurred on client-related assignments. Weight may be given to hours in excess of a norm.

(2) **Total billings.**   The total amount billed to clients for work performed and supervised by a partner constitutes total billings. Weight may be given to billings in excess of a norm.

(3) **Write-offs.**   Write-offs consist of the amount of uncollectible billings. Weight may be given to a write-off percentage below a norm.

(4) **Promotional and civic activities.**   Time devoted to the development of future business and to the development of the partnership name in the community is considered promotional and civic activity. Weight may be given to time spent in excess of a norm or to specific accomplishments resulting in new clients.

(5) **Profits in excess of specified levels.**   Designated partners commonly receive a certain percentage of profits in excess of a specified level of earnings.

An additional allocation of profits to a partner on the basis of performance is frequently referred to as a **bonus.** As with salary allowances and imputed interest, a bonus should not be charged to an expense account in the general ledger, although some partnerships improperly do this.

Subsequent changes in methods of sharing profits and losses

If the partners subsequently agree to change the method of sharing profits and losses, equity dictates that assets be revalued to their current values at the time of the change. To illustrate, assume partners A and B shared profits and losses equally, and at a later date they agree to share profits and losses in a 3:2 ratio, respectively. Suppose also that the partnership holds a parcel of land that is carried on the books at $60,000 but now has a current value of $80,000. Partner A would receive a greater share of the profit on the land (when it is later sold) than if the land were sold before the method of sharing profits and losses was changed. This is not equitable because the land appreciated $20,000 while the profits and losses were shared equally.

An alternative to revaluing the land to its current value would be to stipulate in the new profit sharing formula that the first $20,000 of profit on the sale of that parcel of land is to be shared in the old profit and loss sharing ratio. Under this method, an entry not in accordance with generally accepted accounting principles is not recorded. However, this is not a major reason for selecting this alternative if revaluing assets is more practical.

When the profit and loss sharing formula is revised, the new profit and loss sharing formula should contain a provision specifying that the old formula applies to certain types of subsequent adjustments arising out of activities that took place before the revision date. Examples are:

(1) Unrecorded liabilities existing at the revision date.
(2) Settlements on lawsuits not provided for at the revision date, even though the liability may not have been probable as to payment or reasonably estimable at that time.
(3) Write-offs of accounts receivable existing as of the revision date.

Regardless of the fact that some of these items would not qualify as prior-period adjustments under *FASB Statement No. 16,* "Prior Period Adjustments," greater equity usually would be achieved among the partners by using the old sharing formula. Because partnerships need not follow generally accepted accounting principles, the will of the partners may prevail.

FINANCIAL REPORTING

Because partnerships are not publicly owned, their financial statements are prepared primarily for internal use. Such financial statements normally include all the financial statements that a corporation prepares, except for the statement of changes in stockholders' equity, for which a statement of changes in partners' equity is substituted.

One common reason for making partnership financial statements available to outside parties is to borrow money from financial institutions. (Under the UPA, partnerships can hold debt in the partnership name rather than in the names of its individual partners.) Financial statements made available to outside parties should be converted to the accrual basis if the cash basis is used for book purposes. (Most partnerships use the cash basis as a matter of convenience.) Because partnership earnings are not comparable to what they would have been had the business been organized as a corporation, an indication to this effect should be made in the footnotes to the financial statements.

Some accountants have suggested that a partnership's income statement should reflect an imputed amount for salaries that would have been paid to the partners had the corporate form of business been used. Presumably, such an approach would state the "true earnings" of the partnership. In our opinion, this is a somewhat futile exercise involving substantial subjectivity.

Furthermore, from a technical standpoint, consideration should also be given to (1) additional payroll taxes; (2) deductions for fringe benefits (primarily pension and profit sharing plans), which are not available to partners; and (3) income taxes. It would seem sufficient to state in a footnote that, because the partnership form of organization is used, the earnings must be evaluated carefully, because, conceptually, earnings should provide for equivalent salary compensation, return on capital invested in the partnership, retirement, and payroll-type fringe benefits.

Virtually all partnerships maintain strict confidentiality of their financial statements. International public accounting partnerships that do issue financial statements to interested parties commonly show the following:

(1) The financial statements are converted from the cash basis to the accrual basis of accounting.
(2) An imputed amount for salaries is not reflected in the income statement.
(3) A footnote to the financial statements indicates that the firm's earnings are not comparable to those of a corporation.
(4) The financial statements are prepared in accordance with generally accepted accounting principles, and the notes to the financial statements are complete as to required disclosures—for example, disclosures of accounting policies, lease commitments, and segment information.

The income statement of small partnerships commonly shows how the profit or loss is divided. The allocation can be shown immediately below net income as follows:

A & B PARTNERSHIP
Income Statement
For the Year Ended December 31, 19X1

Revenues	$1,000,000
Expenses	(900,000)
Net Income	$ 100,000

Allocation of net income to partners:

	Partner A	Partner B
Salary allowances	$30,000	$10,000
Imputed interest on capital	1,000	4,000
Residual (3:2)	33,000	22,000
Total	$64,000	$36,000

Furthermore, a small partnership's statement of changes in partners' equity is often shown *by partner* as follows:

A & B PARTNERSHIP
Statement of Changes in Partners' Equity
For the Year Ended December 31, 19X1

	Partner A	Partner B	Total
Beginning capital	$25,000	$ 85,000	$110,000
Contributions	5,000	—	5,000
Drawings	(10,000)	(15,000)	(25,000)
Net income	64,000	36,000	100,000
Ending capital	$84,000	$106,000	$190,000

INCOME TAX ASPECTS

Other than dividing the profits and losses among the partners in accordance with the profit sharing formula, accounting for the operations of a partnership presents no unusual problems. The income tax aspects of partnerships, however, are much more involved. An accountant providing services to a partnership must have a solid grasp of partnership tax concepts to serve his or her clients adequately. The following discussion will not make you an expert in partnership taxation; it will only provide a basic understanding of partnership taxation.

Equity versus basis

A partner's interest in a partnership is a personal, capital asset, which can be sold, exchanged, assigned, or otherwise disposed of. From a financial accounting viewpoint, a partner's equity in the partnership is the balance in his or her capital account net of any balance in his or her drawing account. If a partner were to sell his or her interest in the partnership, the gain or loss from a partnership accounting viewpoint would be determined by comparing the proceeds to his or her equity at the time of sale. The gain or loss from an accounting viewpoint, however, is not important. The sale is a personal transaction; therefore, any gain or loss is not reflected in the partnership's general ledger. In this respect, it is similar to the sale of stock by a shareholder of a corporation—it does not enter into the operations of the business entity. From the selling partner's viewpoint, the relevant objective is to determine the amount of the taxable gain or loss.

Contributing assets.   The tax laws are not structured around a partner's equity as recorded in the partnership general ledger. Thus, to determine the amount of gain or loss for tax purposes on the sale of a partner's interest in a partnership, we must be familiar with the concept of basis. For tax purposes, a partner's interest in a partnership is referred to as that partner's **basis.** Basis is an asset-related concept. Thus, if a partner contributed $5,000 cash to a partnership, his or her basis in the partnership is $5,000. (Coincidentally, this would be the amount credited to his or her capital account in the general ledger, but this fact is irrelevant from a tax standpoint.) If a partner contributes equipment to a partnership, then that partner's basis in the partnership increases by the adjusted basis of the equipment immediately before the contribution or transfer. The adjusted basis of the equipment is the partner's historical cost less any depreciation previously deducted for income tax reporting purposes. Thus, if equipment that cost the partner $10,000 had been depreciated $2,000 in the partner's business before the contribution or transfer, the adjusted basis would be $8,000. Accordingly, the partner's basis in the partnership would increase by $8,000.

If the equipment was completely paid for at the time of the contribution or transfer to the partnership, the amount credited to the partner's capital account in the general ledger would depend on the current value assigned to the equipment and agreed to by the partners. This current value could be more or less than the $8,000 adjusted basis. Thus, it would only be a coincidence that the credit to the partner's capital account increases by the amount of the adjusted tax basis at the time of the contribution or transfer.

No step-up or step-down in basis.   For tax purposes, any difference between the current value and the adjusted basis at the time of the contribution or transfer to a partnership is not recognized. In other words, no gain or loss must be reported. The adjusted basis of the asset (in the hands of the partner immediately before the contribution or transfer) is not stepped up or stepped down on transfer to the partnership. Accordingly, the adjusted basis of each asset contributed to a partnership merely carries over to the partnership for tax reporting purposes. To the extent that future depreciation and amortization expenses are different for book (general ledger) reporting purposes than for tax reporting purposes, the book income or loss must be adjusted (on a worksheet) to arrive at taxable income.

Contributing liabilities.   This concept of basis is slightly more involved if the contributed asset has a debt attached to it that is assumed by the partnership. Suppose the equipment had a $3,000 installment note payable attached to it, for which the partnership assumed responsibility. The con- tributing partner's basis still increases by $8,000 (the amount of the adjusted basis of the asset at the time of the contribution or transfer). The fact that the partnership has assumed responsibility for payment of the debt, however, is significant from a tax viewpoint. The tax law says the other partners (by becoming jointly responsible for the payment of this debt), in substance, have given money to this partner. Accordingly, their bases should be in- creased and the basis of the partner who contributed the liability should be decreased by the amount of money deemed to have been given con- structively to the partner. The profit and loss sharing ratio is used to determine this deemed amount. For example, if a three-person partnership shared profits equally, then the basis of the partner contributing the equipment and the related $3,000 liability would be reduced from $8,000 to $6,000 (two-thirds of $3,000) and the basis of each of the other partners would be increased by $1,000 (one-third of $3,000). This procedure is used even though the creditor could seek personal recourse from the partner who contributes the liability to the partnership.

Keeping track of each partner's basis.   Because a partner's basis cannot be determined by using the amounts recorded in the general ledger capital accounts, each partner must determine his or her own individual tax basis in the partnership on a memorandum basis outside the general ledger. In summary, each partner's tax basis can be determined when the partnership is formed by adding the first three of the following categories and subtracting the fourth category.

Cash contributed to the partnership by a partner.
Add—A partner's adjusted basis in any noncash property contributed or transferred to the partnership.
Add—A partner's share of any liabilities assumed by the partnership that were contributed by other partners.
Less—The other partners' share of any liabilities assumed by the part- nership that the partner contributed to the partnership.

Comprehensive illustration.   To further demonstrate the application of these procedures, we assume the same facts related to the formation of a partnership as in the example on page 690. In addition, we assume that partners A and B share profits and losses in a 3:2 ratio, respectively. The adjusted basis of each partner is shown below.

	Adjusted Basis		
	Partner A	Partner B	Total
Cash contributed	$23,000	$ 5,000	$28,000
Noncash assets contributed:			
Marketable securities	7,000		7,000
Land		15,000	15,000
Building		25,000	25,000
	$30,000	$45,000	$75,000
Adjustment to basis for liabilities of $20,000			
assumed by the partnership[a]	12,000	(12,000)	
Basis	$42,000	$33,000	$75,000

[a] The adjustment to each partner's basis is 60% of $20,000, because partner A assumes a 60% responsibility for the $20,000 liability contributed by partner B.

In reviewing the above illustration, one major point should be understood. Partner A's $42,000 basis plus partner B's $33,000 basis equals the partnership's basis in the assets of $75,000 for tax reporting purposes. This equality always exists. Note also that the sum of the bases of the assets immediately before the transfer ($30,000 for partner A's assets and $45,000 for partner B's assets) also equals the partnership's basis in the assets for tax reporting purposes.

Subsequent adjustments to each partner's tax basis

The personal tax basis of each partner's interest in the partnership is adjusted as subsequent partnership activity takes place. Such activities can be grouped as follows:

(1) Contributions and distributions (withdrawals).   If a partner subsequently contributes additional assets to the partnership, the tax basis of that partner's interest in the partnership increases. If the partner withdraws assets from the partnership, the tax basis of that partner's interest in the partnership decreases. (It can never be less than zero.)

(2) Profits and losses.   To the extent that there are profits, each partner's tax basis of interest in the partnership increases by that partner's share of the partnership's taxable income. To the extent that there are losses, each partner's tax basis of interest in the partnership decreases by that partner's share of the partnership's loss for tax reporting purposes.

(3) Changes in partnership liabilities.   Tax laws effectively treat partnership liabilities as personal liabilities of the partners. For example, if a partnership borrowed $1,000 from a financial institution, the partnership's assets would increase by $1,000. The same result could be produced if one of the partners were personally to borrow the $1,000 from the financial institution and then make an additional capital contribution of $1,000. The form of each transaction is different, but the substance is the same. Thus, an increase in a partnership's liabilities is treated as an additional capital contribution by the partners. This increase is shared among the partners, and each partner's basis in the partnership increases. A decrease in a partnership's liabilities is treated as a distribution of partnership assets to its partners. This decrease also is shared among the partners, and each partner's basis in the partnership decreases.

In the example given on page 701, we showed a $12,000 adjustment to the bases of partners A and B as a result of partner B contributing a $20,000 liability to the partnership. In a different approach to this adjustment, we assume that (1) instead of partner B contributing the $20,000 liability to the partnership, the partnership borrowed $20,000 from a financial institution, and (2) the partnership then distributed that $20,000 to partner B, who paid off his personal loan of $20,000. The adjustments to the basis of each of the partners are as follows:

	Adjustments to Basis	
	Partner A	Partner B
Borrowing of $20,000 by the partnership (60% to partner A and 40% to partner B)	$12,000	$ 8,000
Distribution of $20,000 to partner B		(20,000)
Net change to basis	$12,000	$(12,000)

Note that the net effect on each partner's basis is still $12,000.

The determination of a partner's tax basis in a partnership is relevant when a partner disposes of some or all of his or her partnership interest. This situation is discussed more fully in Chapter 20 on ownership changes.

Net operating loss carrybacks and carryforwards

Because partnerships are not taxable entities, they do not have net operating loss carrybacks or carryforwards. However, when a partner's share of a partnership's loss for a given year exceeds the excess of the partner's nonbusiness income over nonbusiness deductions (excluding personal exemptions as deductions), this net amount is a net operating loss that can be carried back three years and then forward seven years on the partner's individual income tax return. The excess of nonbusiness deductions (excluding personal exemptions as deductions) over nonbusiness income does not increase the net operating loss because it is not business related.

THE PROFESSIONAL CORPORATION

A complete discussion of the legal aspects and tax laws related to professional corporations is beyond the scope of this book. In general, the professional corporation form of business is available to professionals who render personal service—for example, accountants, architects, attorneys, dentists, optometrists, physicians, real estate brokers, and veterinarians. A professional corporation must act like a corporation and maintain a corporate appearance throughout its existence. For example, shareholders' and directors' meetings must be held and minutes of these meetings must be maintained. From a tax standpoint, the professional corporation is subject to tax laws that apply to corporations, including provisions related to (1) the reasonableness of compensation paid to shareholder–employees; (2) the reasonableness of accumulated earnings; and (3) the restrictions on amounts that can be deducted for pension and profit sharing plans.

Pre-1984 advantages to incorporation.   Under the partnership form of organization, only employees of the partnership can participate in fringe benefits such as pension, profit sharing, medical, and insurance plans. Because partners are not employees, they cannot participate in these plans. The tax laws do allow professionals to provide for their retirement through the use of H.R. 10 (Keogh) plans. A self-employed professional operating as a sole proprietor or a member of a partnership may take a deduction for contributions to a qualified Keogh plan. The earnings on funds invested in a qualified Keogh plan are not taxed currently. As funds from the plan are distributed during retirement years (presumably when the recipient is in a much lower income tax bracket), the distributions are reported for income tax purposes. Such contributions (limited to $7,500 prior to 1982 and $15,000 for 1982 and 1983), however, were substantially below the maximum contributions allowed for corporate employees.

By having the partnership become a professional corporation, the partners become employees of the corporation, even though they are also its shareholders. They can then participate in pension, profit sharing, medical, and insurance plans. (Pension and profit sharing plans are the major fringe benefits by far.) Thus, more pretax dollars could be set aside to earn money that is not currently taxable. (In 1982, the maximum allowable deduction for profit sharing plans was $45,475.) In summary, a partner could provide much more generously for retirement through the use of a professional corporation than through the partnership form of organization.

Enter TEFRA.   Such disparities were inequitable, and many individuals and organizations (notably the tax section of the New York State Bar Association) worked to achieve parity so that deductions for profit sharing and pension plans would be the same for all people who work, regardless of whether they are self-employed or work for a corporation. The Tax Equity and Fiscal Responsibility Act of 1982 embraced this concept. As a result, beginning in 1984, the maximum annual Keogh plan deductions were made the same as deductions for profit sharing and pension plans allowed for corporate employees. (For profit sharing plans, the maximum annual deduction is $30,000; for pension plans, the maximum annual benefit is $90,000.) As a further effort to achieve parity, the new law eliminated or changed many of the special limitations affecting Keogh plans.

Thus, the major tax factors for using a professional corporation have been eliminated. Whether this situation results in a wholesale shift back to the sole proprietorship and partnership forms of organization would be conjecture at this point. Existing professional corporations must carefully reassess whether the remaining advantages to this form of organization outweigh its disadvantages. Some tax benefits are still associated with professional corporations, such as medical and insurance plan deductions. Nontax factors also favor incorporation, such as a greater ability to insulate (in certain instances) one's personal assets from the business's creditors.

The double tax.   Recall that one disadvantage of the corporate form of business is the double taxation of earnings—that is, the corporation's earnings are taxed and then corporate dividends are taxed. This disadvantage is usually of little significance to a professional corporation. A professional corporation can enter into employment contracts with its shareholder–employees and adopt bonus plans, applying primarily to shareholder–employees, whereby salaries and bonuses can be paid to the extent necessary to eliminate any income that would be taxable at the corporate level. (Such compensation must still pass the IRS's tests of reasonableness to be allowed as a tax deduction and not deemed dividends instead of compensation.) Therefore, in the professional corporation, the double tax can be avoided or substantially mitigated.

Unlimited versus limited liability.   The incorporation of a partnership does not automatically insulate the former partners' personal assets from the corporation's creditors. Shareholder–employees are still responsible for liabilities that arise out of acts they perform (or are performed under their supervision) while rendering professional services as employees of the professional corporation. Certain states impose joint and several liability on all shareholders for professional services rendered by the professional corporation or its employees. Other states require personal participation for a shareholder of a professional corporation to be held individually liable. The ethical standards of the AICPA impose joint and several responsibility on all shareholders of a professional accounting corporation, even if wrongful acts are performed by only one or a limited number of shareholder–employees.

SUMMARY

For all practical purposes, the partnership form of organization can be accounted for as a separate entity. The primary objective of partnership accounting is to achieve equity among the partners. Because the partnership form of organization is unique, the procedures that can be used to achieve such equity are quite flexible. A solid grasp of income tax concepts and rules is required before an accountant can expect to serve a partnership properly. In addition, an accountant must be familiar with the advantages and disadvantages (tax and nontax factors) associated with professional corporations.

Appendix A
LIMITED PARTNERSHIPS

An explosive increase in the use of limited partnerships has occurred in recent years. Such partnerships are used as investment vehicles by passive investors. A limited partnership consists of a general partner and limited partners. Unlike the general partner, a limited partner's liability is limited to his or her cash investments. Furthermore, a limited partner plays no role in the management of the partnership, this being the complete responsibility of the general partner. Two types of limited partnerships have been extremely popular in recent years—real estate partnerships and research and development (R & D) partnerships.

Real estate limited partnerships

Nature of.   Real estate limited partnerships are formed by companies that package real estate investments. Such companies, which generally have real estate experience, are commonly referred to as sponsors or syndicators. These companies employ securities brokers to sell interests in the limited partnerships to individual investors. The sponsor or an affiliated company is usually the general partner. The partnership then acquires rental apartments, shopping centers, or office buildings (the most common investments). Sponsors generally receive an up-front fee, an annual management fee, and a share of the income and appreciation. The general partner controls when the property is sold. (The average life of such partnerships is 7–12 years.) It is difficult for limited partners to get their money out of the partnership until liquidation, because they cannot readily sell their interests. They must personally find a buyer. This is a major drawback for many investors.

Investing in.   Two types of syndications exist—public and private. Public partnerships must be registered with the SEC, which reviews the registration statement (as opposed to approving the offering) before interests may be sold to investors. In addition, each state has investor-eligibility requirements. Generally, an investor needs either a net worth of $75,000 (excluding one's home) or a gross income of $30,000 and a net worth of $30,000 (excluding one's home). Private partnerships (which are not registered with the SEC) account for a much bigger portion of real estate partnerships and require a much wealthier investor. In public partnerships, the minimum required investment is generally $5,000, but may be as low as $2,000 (to accommodate Individual Retirement Account investments). In private partnerships, the minimum investments generally range from $30,000 to $150,000.

Main attractions.   Real estate limited partnerships are especially attractive because special tax laws apply to them. Typically, real estate partnerships borrow from a financial institution most of the money needed to acquire the real estate. This increase in liabilities may be added to the bases of all partners (including the limited partners), even though the limited partners are not personally obligated to repay the loan if the partnership cannot repay the loan (as might happen if the project is not properly managed or the real estate declines in value). As a result, the limited partners can write off for tax purposes more than their cash investments. This feature is even more attractive because the Economic Recovery Tax Act of 1981 reduced the depreciable life for buildings from 30 years to 15 years, thereby doubling the rate at which the buildings can be depreciated. Such partnerships are commonly considered the only "true" tax shelter, because the depreciation write-off is considered a paper loss, not an economic loss. Furthermore, when the property is sold, a gain usually results for tax purposes, usually because of the 15-year depreciation life. Real estate property rarely sells for less than its depreciated cost, especially when the depreciable cost declines so quickly using a 15-year life.[2] Such gains are

---

[2] The Tax Reform Act of 1984 extended this 15-year life to 18 years (except for low-income housing).

capital gains. If the property is sold for an amount equal to its initial cost, then the resulting gain merely offsets the depreciation write-off taken to date. Because the gain is a capital gain, ordinary income has been converted into capital gain income. If the property is sold for more than its initial cost, then that portion of the gain that is attributable to selling it at more than its initial cost is a "true" capital gain.

Such investments appear to be ideal for persons with little or no real estate experience or who do not want the headaches associated with property management. Furthermore, these partnerships have done exceedingly well in recent years largely because inflation has driven property values through the roof.

Potential pitfalls.   There is an old saying in real estate that goes: The three most important considerations in selecting properties to buy are location, location, and location. What if the sponsor buys a property in an undesirable location? What if it is difficult to keep the property rented? What if the cash flow from operations does not service the debt? What if a calamity is not covered by insurance? What if the lender forecloses on the mortgage? (The lender effectively buys the property at an amount equal to the amount owed the lender at the time of foreclosure; this would terminate the tax shelter and possibly trigger a large, unexpected tax bill.) A recent concern by many investors, in light of the substantial number of properties bought by these partnerships in recent years, is whether enough investment grade properties will be available for the new offerings. Sponsors may pay too much in trying to acquire a property, because their alternative would be to return the funds to the investors and thereby lose their up-front fees (which generally are 25–30% of the amounts invested by the investors). Of course, a sponsor's past record is no guarantee of future performance.

Research and development limited partnerships

Research and development limited partnerships are used typically by start-up companies that do not have sufficient money to conduct research and development. The start-up company is the general partner, and the investors are the limited partners. The money invested by the limited partners is used for research and development of a carefully defined product.

Advantages for investors.   Investors can write off for tax purposes their share of the money spent each year on research and development (that is, their share of the partnership's loss). Thus, they obtain immediate tax deductions. If the investors had invested directly in the start-up company, the research and development expenses would not flow through to them. Instead, such expenses would just give the start-up company a net operating loss carryforward, which might not be utilized for several years.

If the product is successfully developed, the limited partners may receive cash, common stock, or royalties from the start-up company. (Typically, the start-up company has exclusive rights to the developed product.)

Advantages for start-up companies.   The owners of the start-up company generally retain all or a much greater ownership percentage in the start-up company.

Risks for investors.   Because there is no assurance that the product will be successfully developed, the limited partners have no guarantee that they will recover their investment.

Appendix B
UNIFORM PARTNERSHIP ACT

The Uniform Partnership Act has 45 sections that are separated into the following seven parts:

Part I   Preliminary provisions
Part II   Nature of partnership
Part III   Relations of partners to persons dealing with the partnership
Part IV   Relations of partners to one another
Part V   Property rights of a partner
Part VI   Dissolution and winding up
Part VII   Miscellaneous provisions

The UPA is approximately 14 pages long and can be found in law library books that contain all of the various uniform acts. Because of its length, the UPA is not set forth here in its entirety. However, two of the 45 sections are presented here to give you an idea of the content of the UPA.

Part III
Relations of partners to persons dealing with the partnership

Sec. 15. (Nature of Partner's Liability.)
All partners are liable:

(a) Jointly and severally for everything chargeable to the partnership under sections 13 and 14.
(b) Jointly for all other debts and obligations of the partnership; but any partner may enter into a separate obligation to perform a partnership contract.

Part IV
Relations of partners to one another

Sec. 18. (Rules Determining Rights and Duties of Partners.)
The rights and duties of the partners in relation to the partnership shall be determined by the following rules:

(a) Each partner shall be repaid his contributions, whether by way of capital or advances to the partnership property and share equally in the profits and surplus remaining after all liabilities, including those to partners, are satisfied; and must contribute towards the losses, whether of capital or otherwise, sustained by the partnership according to his share in the profits.
(b) The partnership must indemnify every partner in respect of payments

made and personal liabilities reasonably incurred by him in the ordinary and proper conduct of its business, or for the preservation of its business or property.

(c) A partner, who in aid of the partnership makes any payment or advance beyond the amount of capital which he agreed to contribute, shall be paid interest from the date of the payment or advance.

(d) A partner shall receive interest on the capital contributed by him only from the date when repayment should be made.

(e) All partners have equal rights in the management and conduct of the partnership business.

(f) No partner is entitled to remuneration for acting in the partnership business, except that a surviving partner is entitled to reasonable compensation for his services in winding up the partnership affairs.

(g) No person can become a member of a partnership without the consent of all the partners.

(h) Any difference arising as to ordinary matters connected with the partnership business may be decided by a majority of the partners; but no act in contravention of any agreement between the partners may be done rightfully without the consent of all the partners.

Review questions

1. Define *general partnership*.
2. How is a partnership defined?
3. Why is it advisable to use an attorney's services in preparing a partnership agreement?
4. What is the function of the partnership agreement?
5. What essential items should be set forth in the partnership agreement?
6. Must partnerships follow generally accepted accounting principles? Why or why not?
7. What common features may be structured into a profit and loss sharing formula?
8. Can partners be paid salaries?
9. What performance criteria may be incorporated into a profit sharing formula?
10. What is the function of the drawings account? Is it really necessary?
11. How are loans from a partner to a partnership accounted for on the partnership's books?
12. Why might it be appropriate to use the old profit and loss sharing formula in certain transactions instead of the new formula?
13. In what broad areas do partnerships commonly deviate from generally accepted accounting principles?
14. Should partnership financial statements be prepared so that partnership earnings are comparable to what they would have been if the corporate form of business had been used? Why or why not?
15. What is the purpose of keeping track of a partner's tax basis?
16. Define *adjusted basis*.
17. Is it possible to use a partner's capital account balance to determine that partner's tax basis? Why or why not?
18. How does the professional corporation differ from the normal corporate form of business?

19. What advantages does the professional corporation form of business have over the partnership form of business?
20. Does a shareholder of a professional corporation have limited liability?

Discussion cases

Discussion case 19–1
Selecting form of business organization

Brush and Floss, who graduated recently from dentistry school, would like to go into practice together. They have asked your advice about how to do this.

Required:
What major points would you discuss with Brush and Floss?

Discussion case 19–2
Preparing the partnership agreement

Short and Cutter have formed a partnership. They personally prepared the partnership agreement to save legal costs, but they ask you to study the agreement for completeness when you record the initial capital contributions in the general ledger.

Required:
How would you respond to this request?

Discussion case 19–3
Dividing profits and losses

Lee and Bailey, both lawyers, have decided on the partnership form of organization for their new business. They have asked your advice on how the profits and losses should be divided and have provided you with the following information:

(1) Initial capital contributions:
    Lee $20,000
    Bailey 80,000
(2) Time devoted to the business:
    Lee 75%
    Bailey 100%
(3) Personal facts:
    Lee has an excellent reputation in the community.
      Substantially all new clients will come from her efforts.
    Bailey is strong technically and is an excellent supervisor of staff lawyers who are expected to do most of the detailed legal research and initial preparation of legal documents.

Required:
How would you advise the partners to share profits and losses?

Discussion case 19–4
Recording the initial capital contributions

Trapp and Webb have agreed to form a partnership in which profits are divided equally. Trapp contributes $100,000 cash, and Webb contributes a parcel of land, which the partnership intends to subdivide into residential lots on which to build custom homes for sale. Data regarding the parcel of land are as follows:

Cost of land to Webb (acquired three years ago)	$100,000
Current market value, per most recent county property tax assessment notice	120,000
Appraised value, per recent appraisal by independent appraiser	150,000

Webb feels the land should be recorded on the partnership books at $120,000. Trapp feels the land should be recorded at $100,000 so that the tax basis to Webb carries over to the partnership. Neither feels the current appraised value is appropriate because an objective, verifiable transaction has not occurred. They have asked your advice on how to record the land.

Required:
How would you respond?

Discussion case 19–5
Selecting form of business organization

Ernest Devers has invested $600,000 in a new business venture, in which two, possibly three, former business associates will join him. He has purchased the patent rights to a revolutionary adhesive substance known as "sticko." He is considering the various forms of business organization he might use in establishing the business. You have been engaged to study the accounting and business problems he should consider in choosing either a general partnership or a corporation. Devers requests specific advice on the following aspects as they relate to one of these two forms of business organization.

(1) Personal liability if the venture is a disaster.
(2) The borrowing capacity of the entity.
(3) Requirements for operating a multi-state business.
(4) The recognition of the entity for income tax reporting purposes and major income tax considerations in selecting one of these forms of business organization.

Required:
Discuss the legal implications of each above-mentioned form of organization for each specific aspect on which Devers seeks advice.

(AICPA adapted)

Exercises

Exercise 19–1
Dividing the profit or loss: Partnership agreement is silent

The partnership of Buster and Keaton had earnings of $40,000 for the year. Buster devotes all of her time to the business, and Keaton devotes 50% of his time to the business. Buster's average capital balance was $60,000, and Keaton's average capital balance was $30,000. The partnership agreement is silent regarding the distribution of profits.

Required:
(1) Prepare a schedule showing how the profit should be divided.
(2) Prepare the entry to divide the profit.

Exercise 19–2
Dividing the profit or loss: Performance features and ratio

The partnership of Howe and Wye has the following provisions in its partnership agreement:

(1) Howe, who is primarily responsible for obtaining new clients, is to receive a 30% bonus on revenues in excess of $200,000.
(2) Wye, who is primarily responsible for administration, is to receive a 20% bonus on profits in excess of 50% of revenues, as reflected in the general ledger.
(3) All remaining profits or losses are to be divided equally.

Additional information:

Revenues for the year	$240,000
Operating expenses	110,000

130,000

Required:
(1) Prepare a schedule showing how the profit or loss should be divided for the year.
(2) Prepare the entry to divide the profit or loss for the year.

Exercise 19–3
Dividing the profit or loss: Ratio and salary allowances

The partnership of Malone and Erving shares profits and losses in a ratio of 7:3, respectively, after Erving receives a $10,000 salary allowance.

Required:
(1) Prepare a schedule showing how the profit or loss should be divided, assuming the profit or loss for the year is
   (a) $30,000.
   (b) $6,000.
   (c) $(10,000).
(2) Prepare the entry to divide the profit or loss in situations (a)–(c) of requirement (1).

Exercise 19–4
Dividing the profit or loss: Ratio, salary allowances, and imputed interest on capital

The partnership of Laurel and Hardy has the following provisions in the partnership agreement.

(1) Laurel and Hardy receive salary allowances of $12,000 and $18,000, respectively.
(2) Interest is imputed at 10% of the average capital investments.
(3) Any remaining profit or loss is shared between Laurel and Hardy in a 2:1 ratio, respectively.

Additional information:

Average capital investments:

Laurel	$100,000
Hardy	40,000

Required:
(1) Prepare a schedule showing how the profit would be divided, assuming the partnership profit or loss is
  (a) $62,000.
  (b) $37,000.
  (c) $(10,000).
(2) Prepare the entry to divide the profit or loss in situations (a)–(c) of requirement (1).

Exercise 19–5
Dividing the profit or loss: Ratio, salary allowances, and imputed interest on capital—Order of priority specified

Assume the information provided in Exercise 19–4, except that the partnership agreement stipulates the following order of priority in the distribution of profits:

(1) Salary allowances (only to the extent available).
(2) Imputed interest on average capital investments (only to the extent available).
(3) Any remaining profit in a 2:1 ratio. (No mention is made regarding losses.)

Required:
The requirements are the same as for Exercise 19–4.

Exercise 19–6
Recording initial capital contributions

On March 1, 19X7, Hatfield and McCoy formed a partnership. Each contributed assets with the following agreed-upon valuations:

	Hatfield	McCoy
Cash	$30,000	$ 70,000
Machinery and equipment	25,000	75,000
Building	—	225,000
Furniture and fixtures	10,000	—
~~Mortgage~~	(24000)	(56000)

The building is subject to a mortgage loan of $80,000, which is assumed by the partnership. The partnership agreement provides that Hatfield and McCoy share profits and losses 30% and 70%, respectively.

Required:
(1) Prepare the journal entry to record the capital contributions of each partner.
(2) (Optional) Assuming no difference exists between the agreed-upon valuation of each asset contributed and its related adjusted basis, determine the tax basis of each partner on March 1, 19X7.

(AICPA adapted)

Exercise 19–7
Puzzle: Determination of partnership net income

Kelly Quill, a partner in the Penn Partnership, has a 30% participation in partnership profits and losses. Quill's capital account had a net decrease of $60,000 during calendar year 19X4. During 19X4, Quill withdrew $130,000 (charged against her capital account) and contributed property valued at $25,000 to the partnership.

Required:
Determine the partnership net income for 19X4.

(AICPA adapted)

Exercise 19–8
Multiple choice: Theoretical understanding
of impact of salary allowance feature

Partners Hunt and Peck share profits and losses equally after each has been credited with annual salary allowances of $15,000 and $12,000, respectively. Under this arrangement, Hunt benefits by $3,000 more than Peck in which of the following circumstances?

(a) Only if the partnership has earnings of $27,000 or more for the year.
(b) Only if the partnership does not incur a loss for the year.
(c) In all profit or loss situations.
(d) Only if the partnership has earnings of at least $3,000 for the year.

(AICPA adapted)

Exercise 19–9
Determination of tax basis of each partner

Brown, Harris, and Payton have formed a partnership by combining their respective sole proprietorships. The profit and loss sharing ratio is 4:3:3, respectively. The assets and liabilities contributed to the partnership are as follows:

	Adjusted Basis	Current Value
Brown:		
Cash	$10,000	$10,000
Accounts receivable	20,000	20,000
Harris:		
Land	30,000	40,000
Payton:		
Equipment	20,000	25,000
Equipment note payable	10,000	10,000

Required:
(1) Determine the tax basis of each partner's interest in the partnership.
(2) What is the basis of each noncash asset in the hands of the partnership?
(3) Prepare the general ledger entry to record these contributions.

Exercise 19–10
Subsequent changes in tax basis of each partner

The tax basis of Boote, Gaffe, and Flubb at the beginning of their partnership year was $50,000, $35,000, and $65,000, respectively. Profits and losses are shared equally.

Additional information:

Additional cash capital contributions:	
Boote	$18,000
Gaffe	10,000
Flubb	4,000
Withdrawals during the year:	
Boote	6,000
Gaffe	12,000
Flubb	5,000
Profits for the year:	
Per the general ledger	30,000
Per the tax return	33,000

Required:
(1) Determine the tax basis of each partner at year-end, assuming no change in partnership liabilities.
(2) Determine the tax basis of each partner at year-end, assuming that the only change in liabilities during the year was a $24,000 bank loan obtained at year-end. (The $24,000 borrowed, along with $6,000 cash on hand, was used to purchase equipment costing $30,000.)

Problems

Problem 19–1
Dividing profits: Interest on capital, bonuses, and salary allowances

March and Sousa are in partnership. The activity in each partner's capital account for 19X1 is as follows:

March				Sousa			
		20,000	1/1			30,000	1/1
		8,000	2/12	3/23	5,000		
5/25	4,000			7/10	5,000		
		7,000	10/19	9/30	5,000		
12/10	2,000			12/30	5,000		
		1,000	12/30			10,000	12/31
		30,000	12/31				

A drawings account is not used. The profit for 19X1 is $50,000.

Required:
Divide the profit for the year between the partners using each of the following formulas:

(a) Beginning capital balances.
(b) Average capital balances. (Investments and withdrawals are assumed to have been made as of the beginning of the month if made before the middle of the month, and assumed to have been made as of the beginning of the following month if made after the middle of the month.)
(c) Ending capital balances.
(d) Bonus to March equal to 10% of profit in excess of $40,000; remaining profit divided equally.
(e) Salary allowances of $15,000 and $10,000 to March and Sousa, respectively; interest on average capital balances imputed at 10%; any residual balance divided equally. (Investments and withdrawals are treated as explained in part b.)

Problem 19–2
Dividing profits: Revision of profit-sharing
agreement—Prior period adjustments

The partnership of Archer, Foote, and Heale was formed in 19X5. The partnership agreement specified that profits and losses were determined on the accrual basis and were divided as follows:

	Archer	Foote	Heale
Salary allowances..............................	$15,000	$15,000	$5,000
Bonuses (percentage of profits			
in excess of $90,000)	20%	20%	
Residual profit or loss	40%	40%	20%

On January 1, 19X9, the partnership agreement was revised to provide for the sharing of profits and losses in the following manner:

	Archer	Foote	Heale
Salary allowances..............................	$20,000	$20,000	$15,000
Bonuses (percentage of profits			
in excess of $110,000)	20%	20%	10%
Residual profit or loss	35%	35%	30%

The partnership books show a profit of $145,000 for 19X9 before the following errors were discovered:

(1) Inventory at December 31, 19X7 was overstated by $7,000.
(2) Inventory at December 31, 19X8 was understated by $8,000.
(3) Inventory at December 31, 19X9 was understated by $18,000.
(4) Depreciation expense for 19X9 was understated by $5,000.

Required:
(1) Divide the profit among the partners for 19X9, assuming the partnership agreement calls for any prior years' errors to be treated as prior-period adjustments.
(2) Assuming the reported profits for 19X7 and 19X8 were $85,000 and $110,000, respectively, prepare the proper adjusting entry to correct the capital balances as of January 1, 19X9. The old profit sharing agreement is used for these items.

Problem 19–3
Combining two partnerships: Recording the initial capital contributions

The partnerships of Cooke & Coole and Walsh & Drier began business on July 1, 19X1; each partnership owns one retail appliance store. The two partnerships agree to combine as of July 1, 19X4 to form a new partnership known as Four Partners Discount Stores.

The following additional information is available:

(1) **Profit and loss ratios.** The profit and loss sharing ratios for the former partnerships were 40% to Cooke and 60% to Coole, and 30% to Walsh and 70% to Drier. The profit and loss sharing ratio for the new partnership is Cooke, 20%; Coole, 30%; Walsh, 15%; and Drier, 35%.

(2) **Capital investments.** The opening capital investments for the new partnership are to be in the same ratio as the profit and loss sharing ratios for the new partnership. If necessary, certain partners may have to contribute additional cash and others may have to withdraw cash to bring the capital investments into the proper ratio.

(3) **Accounts receivable.** The partners agreed that the new partnership's allowance for bad debts is to be 5% of the accounts receivable contributed by Cooke & Coole and 10% of the accounts receivable contributed by Walsh & Drier.

(4) **Inventory.** The opening inventory of the new partnership is to be valued by the FIFO method. Cooke & Coole used the FIFO method to value inventory (which approximates its current value), and Walsh & Drier used the LIFO method. The LIFO inventory represents 85% of its FIFO value.

(5) **Property and equipment.** The partners agree that the land's current value is approximately 20% more than its historical cost, as recorded on each partnership's books.

   The depreciable assets of each partnership were acquired on July 1, 19X1. Cooke & Coole used straight-line depreciation and a 10-year life. Walsh & Drier used double-declining balance depreciation and a 10-year life. The partners agree that the current value of these assets is approximately 80% of their historical cost, as recorded on each partnership's books.

(6) **Unrecorded liability.** After each partnership's books were closed on June 30, 19X4, an unrecorded merchandise purchase of $4,000 by Walsh & Drier was discovered. The merchandise had been sold by June 30, 19X4.

(7) **Accrued vacation.** The accounts of Cooke & Coole include a vacation pay accrual. The four partners agree that Walsh & Drier should make a similar accrual for their five employees, who will receive a two-week vacation at $100 per employee per week.

The June 30, 19X4 postclosing trial balances of the partnerships appear below.

	Cooke & Coole Trial Balance June 30, 19X4		Walsh & Drier Trial Balance June 30, 19X4	
Cash	$ 20,000		$ 15,000	
Accounts receivable	100,000		150,000	
Allowance for doubtful accounts.....		$ 2,000		$ 6,000
Merchandise inventory	175,000		119,000	
Land	25,000		35,000	
Buildings and equipment	80,000		125,000	
Accumulated depreciation		24,000		61,000
Prepaid expenses	5,000		7,000	
Accounts payable..................		40,000		60,000
Notes payable.....................		70,000		75,000
Accrued expenses		30,000		45,000
Cooke, Capital		95,000		
Coole, Capital.....................		144,000		
Walsh, Capital				65,000
Drier, Capital.....................				139,000
	$405,000	$405,000	$451,000	$451,000

Required:

(1) Prepare the journal entries to record the initial capital contribution after considering the effect of the above information. Use separate entries for each of the combining partnerships.

(2) Prepare a schedule computing the cash contributed or withdrawn by each partner to bring the initial capital account balances into the profit and loss sharing ratio.

(AICPA adapted)

Problem 19–4
Combining three sole proprietorships:
Dividing the profit for the first year of operations

Ash, Brickley, and Chimms, who are attorneys, agree to consolidate their individual practices as of January 1, 19X3. The partnership agreement includes the following features:

(1) Each partner's capital contribution is the net amount of the assets and liabilities assumed by the partnership, which are as follows:

	Ash	Brickley	Chimms
Cash	$ 5,000	$ 5,000	$ 5,000
Accounts receivable.............................	14,000	6,000	16,000
Furniture and library	4,300	2,500	6,200
	$23,300	$13,500	$27,200
Allowance for depreciation	$ 2,400	$ 1,500	$ 4,700
Accounts payable...............................	300	1,400	700
	$ 2,700	$ 2,900	$ 5,400
Capital contribution	$20,600	$10,600	$21,800

Each partner guaranteed the collectibility of receivables.

(2) Chimms had leased office space and was bound by the lease until June 30, 19X3. The monthly rental was $600. The partners agree to occupy Chimms' office space until the expiration of the lease and to pay the rent. The partners concur that the rent is too high for the space and that a fair rental value would be $450 per month. The excess rent is charged to Chimms at year-end. On July 1, the partners move to new quarters with a monthly rental of $500.

(3) No salaries are paid to the partners. The individual partners receive 20% of the gross fees billed to their respective clients during the first year of the partnership. After deducting operating expenses (excluding the excess rent), the balance of the fees billed is credited to the partners' capital accounts in the following ratios: Ash, 40%; Brickley, 35%; and Chimms, 25%.

On April 1, 19X3, Woods is admitted to the partnership; Woods receives 20% of the fees from new business obtained after April 1, after deducting expenses applicable to that new business. Expenses (excluding the excess rent) are apportioned to the new business in the same ratio that total expenses, other than bad debt losses, bear to total gross fees.

(4) The following information pertains to the partnership's activities in 19X3:
  (a) Fees are billed as follows:

Ash's clients	$ 44,000
Brickley's clients	24,000
Chimms' clients	22,000
New business:	
Prior to April 1	6,000
After April 1	24,000
Total	$120,000

  (b) Total expenses, excluding depreciation and bad debt expenses, are $29,350 including the total amount paid for rent. Depreciation is computed at the rate of 10% on original cost. Depreciable assets purchased during 19X3, on which one-half year's depreciation is taken, total $5,000.

  (c) Cash charges to the partners' accounts during the year are as follows:

Ash	$ 5,200
Brickley	4,400
Chimms	5,800
Woods	2,500
	$17,900

  (d) Of Ash's and Brickley's receivables, $1,200 and $450, respectively, proved to be uncollectible. A new client billed in March for $1,600 was adjudged bankrupt, and a settlement of 50 cents on the dollar was made.

Required:
(1) Determine the profit for 19X3.
(2) Prepare a schedule showing how the profit for 19X3 is to be divided.
(3) Prepare a statement of the partners' capital accounts for the year ended December 31, 19X3.

(AICPA adapted)

Problem 19–5
Computation of billings and determination of profits

Handy and Glover, architectural designers' and interior decorators, combined May 1, 19X8, agreeing to share profits as follows: Handy, two-thirds; Glover, one-third. Handy contributed furniture and fixtures, $3,000, and cash, $2,000; Glover contributed cash, $500.

They plan to submit monthly bills and make the following arrangements with their clients:

(1) The firm employs draftspersons who are paid on an hourly basis. Time spent on client assignments is billed to clients at their hourly rate plus 125% for overhead and profit.
(2) Partners' time on jobs is billed at $10 an hour.
(3) A 10% service fee is charged on purchases of furniture, drapes, and so on, installed on the jobs. (As an accommodation to their clients, Handy and Glover pay the vendors and charge their clients for these purchases; however, they would like to have their operating statements exclude from their revenues the amounts paid to vendors.)
(4) No service fee is charged on taxis, telephone, and other expenses identifiable to jobs and charged to clients.

Voucher register totals for May are given below:

Credits:

Vouchers payable	$3,469
Taxes withheld—Federal income	93
Taxes withheld—FICA	27
Total	$3,589

Debits:

Purchases and expenses chargeable to clients	$1,615
Partners' drawings (Handy, $100; Glover, $125)	225
General expenses	549
Salaries	1,200
Total	$3,589

The first debit column is analyzed in the voucher register as follows:

Purchases subject to 10% fee:

Client M, Job 51	$1,210	
Client H, Job 52	320	$1,530

Expenses chargeable to clients:

Client M, Job 51	$ 23	
Client M, Job 54	7	
Client H, Job 52	19	
Client L, Job 53	36	85
		$1,615

Client M has not yet authorized Handy and Glover to do job 54. The partners are confident, however, that the job will be authorized, and the above expenses, as well as charges for time spent by a draftsperson and Handy on preliminary designs, will be billed and collected. Assume it is proper to consider this an unbilled account receivable.

The payroll analysis is summarized below. Partners' time on jobs, charged to the jobs at $10 an hour, is summarized in the payroll analysis for convenience in posting costs to job sheets, although the partners are not paid for direct time on jobs.

Job	Secretary	Draftspersons	Handy	Glover
51		$ 312	$240	$300
52		276	120	230
53		304	130	320
54		48	240	
		$ 940	$730	$850
Nonbillable				
General office	$160	40		
Idle time		60		
Total payroll	$160	$1,040		

Journal entries recorded $25 depreciation on furniture and fixtures and the $54 employer's share of federal and states taxes.

There were no cash receipts other than the original investment. The cash disbursements journal shows the following totals:

Debit:
Vouchers payable $2,373
Credit:
Cash $2,358
Discount on purchases 15

Required:
(1) Compute the billings to clients for May.
(2) Prepare a worksheet for the month, showing the opening balances, the transactions for the month, and an adjusted trial balance at month-end.
(3) Divide the profit for the month.
(4) Prepare a statement of changes in partners' capital for the month.

(AICPA adapted)

Problem 19–6
Converting from cash to accrual basis

The partnership of Hatt, Hedd, and Muff engaged you to adjust its accounting records and convert them uniformly to the accrual basis in anticipation of admitting Frost as a new partner. Some accounts are on the accrual basis and others are on the cash basis. The partnership's books were closed at December 31, 19X6 by the bookkeeper, who prepared the following trial balance:

HATT, HEDD, AND MUFF
Trial Balance
December 31, 19X6

	Debit	Credit
Cash	$ 10,000	
Accounts receivable	40,000	
Inventory	26,000	
Land	9,000	
Buildings	50,000	
Accumulated depreciation—buildings		$ 2,000
Equipment	56,000	
Accumulated depreciation—equipment		6,000
Goodwill	5,000	
Accounts payable		55,000
Allowance for future inventory losses		3,000
Hatt, capital		40,000
Hedd, capital		60,000
Muff, capital		30,000
Totals	$196,000	$196,000

Your inquiries disclosed the following:

(1) The partnership was organized on January 1, 19X5 with no provision in the partnership agreement for the distribution of partnership profits and losses. During 19X5, profits were distributed equally among the partners. The partnership agreement was amended effective January 1, 19X6 to provide for the following profit and loss ratio: Hatt, 50%; Hedd, 30%; and Muff, 20%. The amended partnership agreement also stated that the accounting records should be maintained on the accrual basis and that any adjustments necessary for 19X5 should be allocated according to the 19X5 distribution of profits.

(2) The following amounts were not recorded as prepayments or accruals:

	December 31	
	19X6	**19X5**
Prepaid insurance	$700	$ 650
Advances from customers	200	1,100
Accrued interest expense		450

The advances from customers were recorded as sales in the year the cash was received.

(3) In 19X6, the partnership recorded a $3,000 provision for anticipated declines in inventory prices. You convinced the partners that the provision was unnecessary and should be removed from the books.

(4) The partnership charged equipment purchased for $4,400 on January 3, 19X6 to expense. This equipment has an estimated life of 10 years. The partnership depreciates its capitalized equipment under the double-declining balance method at twice the straight-line depreciation rate.

(5) The partners established an allowance for doubtful accounts at 2% of current accounts receivable and 5% of past due accounts. At December 31, 19X5, the partnership had $54,000 of accounts receivable, of which only $4,000 was past due. At December 31, 19X6, 15% of accounts receivable were past due, of

which $4,000 represented sales made in 19X5 that were generally considered collectible. The partnership had written off uncollectible accounts in the year the accounts became worthless, as follows:

	Account Written Off in	
	19X6	**19X5**
19X6 accounts	$ 800	
19X5 accounts	1,000	$250

(6) Goodwill was recorded on the books in 19X6 and credited to the partners' capital accounts in the profit and loss ratio in recognition of an increase in the value of the business resulting from improved sales volume. The partners agreed to write off the goodwill before admitting the new partner.

Required:
Prepare a worksheet showing the adjustments and the adjusted trial balance for the partnership on the accrual basis at December 31, 19X6. All adjustments affecting income should be made directly to partners' capital accounts. Number your adjusting entries. (Prepare formal journal entries and show supporting computations.)

(AICPA adapted)

Problem 19–7
Preparing worksheets to arrive at current trial balance

The Happ & Hazzard Company is a partnership that has not maintained adequate accounting records because it has been unable to employ a competent bookkeeper. The company sells hardware items to the retail trade and also sells wholesale to builders and contractors. As Happ & Hazzard's CPA, you prepare the company's financial statements as of June 30, 19X2.

The company's records provide the following postclosing trial balance at December 31, 19X1:

THE HAPP & HAZZARD COMPANY
Postclosing Trial Balance
December 31, 19X1

	Debit	Credit
Cash	$10,000	
Accounts receivable	8,000	
Allowance for bad debts		$ 600
Merchandise inventory	35,000	
Prepaid insurance	150	
Automobiles	7,800	
Accumulated depreciation—automobiles		4,250
Furniture and fixtures	2,200	
Accumulated depreciation—furniture and fixtures		650
Accounts payable		13,800
Bank loan payable (due January 2, 19X2)		8,000
Accrued liabilities		200
Happ, capital		17,500
Hazzard, capital		18,150
Totals	$63,150	$63,150

You collect the following information at June 30, 19X2:

(1) Your analysis of cash transactions, derived from the company's bank statements and checkbook stubs, is as follows:

Deposits:

Cash receipts from customers	$65,000
($40,000 of this amount represents collections on receivables including redeposited protested checks totaling $600)	
Bank loan, January 2, 19X2 (due May 1, 19X2, 5%)	7,867
Bank loan, May 1, 19X2 (due September 1, 19X2, 5%)	8,850
Sale of old automobile	20
Total deposits	$81,737

Disbursements:

Payments to merchandise creditors......................................	$45,000
Payment to Internal Revenue Service on Hazzard's 19X2 declaration of estimated income taxes	3,000
General expenses	7,000
Bank loan, January 2, 19X2	8,000
Bank loan, May 2, 19X2	8,000
Payment for new automobile...	7,400
Protested checks	900
Happ, withdrawals	5,000
Hazzard, withdrawals	2,500
Total disbursements	$86,800

(2) The protested checks include customers' checks totaling $600 that were redeposited and an employee's check for $300 that was redeposited.

(3) At June 30, 19X2, accounts receivable from customers for merchandise sales amount to $18,000 and include accounts totaling $800 that have been placed with an attorney for collection. Correspondence with the client's attorney reveals that one of the accounts for $175 is uncollectible. Experience indicates that 1% of credit sales will prove uncollectible.

(4) On April 1, 19X2, a new automobile was purchased. The list price of the automobile was $7,700, and $300 was allowed for the trade-in of an old automobile, even though the dealer stated that its condition was so poor that he did not want it. The client sold the old automobile, which cost $1,800 and was fully depreciated at December 31, 19X1, to an auto wrecker for $20. The old automobile was in use up to the date of its sale.

(5) Depreciation is recorded by the straight-line method and is computed on acquisitions to the nearest full month. The estimated life for furniture and fixtures is 10 years and for automobiles is three years. [Salvage value is ignored in computing depreciation. No asset other than the car in item (4) was fully depreciated prior to June 30, 19X2.]

(6) Other data as of June 30, 19X2 are the following:

Merchandise inventory	$37,500
Prepaid insurance	80
Accrued expenses	166

(7) Accounts payable to merchandise vendors total $18,750. A $750 credit memorandum was received from a merchandise vendor for returned merchandise;

the company will apply the credit to July merchandise purchases. Neither the credit memorandum nor the return of the merchandise had been recorded on the books.

(8) Profits and losses are divided equally between the partners.

Required:

Prepare a worksheet that provides, on the accrual basis, information regarding transactions for the six months ended June 30, 19X2, the results of the partnership operations for the period, and the financial position of the partnership at June 30, 19X2. (Do not prepare formal financial statements or formal journal entries, but show supporting computations when necessary.)

(AICPA adapted)

Problem 19–8
Incorporating a partnership

Salomon Sisters Manufacturing Company was dissolved as a partnership on October 31, 19X0. To obtain additional capital, a new company called the Salomon Manufacturing Corporation was incorporated in October and commenced business on November 1, 19X0.

The trial balance of Salomon Sisters Manufacturing Company at October 31, 19X0, its fiscal year-end, is as follows:

SALOMON SISTERS MANUFACTURING COMPANY
Trial Balance
October 31, 19X0

	Debit	Credit
Cash	$ 50,000	
Notes receivable	10,000	
Accounts receivable	138,000	
Allowance for doubtful accounts		$ 6,000
Inventories	60,000	
Marketable securities (bonds)	30,000	
Plant, property, and equipment	190,000	
Accumulated depreciation		70,000
Accounts payable		105,000
Accrued liabilities		22,000
Edna Salomon, Capital		62,000
Edna Salomon, Drawing	15,000	
Fran Salomon, Capital		70,000
Fran Salomon, Drawing	16,000	
Ginger Salomon, Capital		72,000
Ginger Salomon, Drawing	18,000	
Revenues		870,000
Cost of sales	500,000	
Operating expenses	250,000	
Totals	$1,277,000	$1,277,000

The following information was available and unrecorded at October 31, 19X0:

(1) A customer, Wise Company, was in bankruptcy. Under a settlement approved by the court, $4,500 of Wise Company's account is uncollectible.

(2) The doubtful accounts among notes receivable and accounts receivable, excluding that of Wise Company, were an estimated $11,000.

(3) Accrued interest on notes receivable was $500.

(4) The net realizable value of the inventory was $63,000.

(5) Marketable securities had a net current value of $21,900.

(6) The current value of plant, property, and equipment was $147,000.

(7) Profits and losses were divided equally among the three partners.

(8) Cash distributions were made to the partners as follows: Edna Salomon, $5,900; Fran Salomon, $12,900; and Ginger Salomon, $12,900. Each partner received 10,000 shares of $1 par value stock in exchange for her share of the partnership's net assets.

Required:

Using the above information, prepare a worksheet to adjust the trial balance of Salomon Sisters Manufacturing Company at October 31, 19X0 to the opening balances for Salomon Manufacturing Corporation. Prepare formal adjusting entries (and related supporting computations), the profit and loss closing entry, and the entry to reflect the closing of all the capital accounts. (Assets are valued on the new corporation's books at current values.) Ignore income taxes.

(AICPA adapted)

20 Partnerships: Changes in Ownership

OVERVIEW OF CHANGES IN OWNERSHIP

A business conducted as a partnership usually has changes in ownership during its existence. In this chapter, we discuss changes in ownership that do not result in the termination of the partnership's business activities. Such changes in ownership may be categorized as follows:

(1) Increase in number of partners
   (A) Admission of a new partner. More partners may be needed to serve clients properly, or additional capital may be required above and beyond the personal resources of existing partners.
   (B) Business combinations. Two partnerships may combine in such a manner that a pooling of interests occurs—that is, the partners of each individual partnership become partners in a larger, combined business.
(2) Decrease in number of partners
   (A) Willful or forced withdrawal. A partner may withdraw from a partnership in order to (a) engage in another line of work; (b) continue in the same line of work but as a sole proprietor; or (c) retire. In addition, a partner may be forced out of a partnership for not having performed adequately the responsibilities entrusted to him.
   (B) Death or incapacity. Aside from death, a partner may become so seriously ill that he or she cannot continue partnership duties.
(3) Purchase of an existing partnership interest. A partner may decide to sell his or her partnership interest to someone outside the partnership.

The first two categories may generate issues of how to treat each partner equitably when (1) tangible assets have current values different from book values, and (2) intangible elements exist. For simplicity, we discuss these issues separately. The third category consists entirely of personal transactions conducted outside the partnership. Because no partnership accounting issues are associated with this category, we discuss it only briefly at this point, before discussing the first two categories.

Purchase of an existing partner's interest

The purchase of an interest from one or more of a partnership's existing partners is a personal transaction between the incoming partner and the selling partners. No additional monies or properties are invested in the partnership. In this respect, it is similar to the sale of a corporation's stock by individuals. The only entry that is made on the partnership's books is an entry to transfer an amount from the selling partner's capital account to the new partner's capital account. For example, assume the following information:

(1) A and B are in partnership and share profits and losses equally.
(2) A and B have capital account balances of $30,000 each.

(3) C purchases B's partnership interest for $37,500, making payment directly to B.

The entry to record the transaction on the books of the partnership is as follows:

Capital, partner B	30,000	
Capital, partner C		30,000

The purchase price paid by C is completely irrelevant to the entry recorded on the books, regardless of why C paid more than the book value of the partnership interest. The fact that the partnership may have undervalued tangible assets or possible superior earnings power is not relevant to the accounting issues. A personal transaction has occurred, which is independent of accounting for the business of the partnership.

Alternatively, C could purchase a portion of each existing partner's interest in the partnership. For example, assume that C purchased one-third of A's interest for $12,500 and one-third of B's interest for $12,500, making payments directly to A and B. The entry to record the transaction on the books is as follows:

Capital, partner A	10,000	
Capital, partner B	10,000	
Capital, partner C		20,000

Again, the purchase of an existing partnership interest is a personal transaction between the old and the new partners.

Increase or decrease in number of partners— Methods to prevent inequities

The number of partners in a partnership may increase or decrease without the purchase of an existing partner's interest. Recall that in Chapter 19 we stated that to prevent partners from being treated inequitably as a result of revisions to the profit and loss sharing formula, either the partnership assets should be revalued to their current values or the new profit and loss sharing formula should include a special provision whereby the old profit and loss sharing formula would be used in specified instances. Because a change in ownership of a partnership produces a new profit and loss sharing formula, the same techniques to prevent inequities may be applied to situations of changes in ownership. In addition, we introduce a new method—the **bonus method**—that also may be used to prevent inequities.

TANGIBLE ASSETS HAVING CURRENT VALUES DIFFERENT FROM BOOK VALUES

Admission of a new partner

In most cases, a partner is admitted into a partnership by making a capital contribution to the partnership. In accounting and attorney partnerships, virtually all the partners admitted make substantial contributions after spending years in lower levels of the business obtaining the necessary training and experience. A capital contribution creates a new partner's interest. In substance, this is similar to a corporation issuing additional shares of its stock to new stockholders.

When a new partner is admitted, one of the three available methods of preventing an inequity must be applied. Each method, although different procedurally, produces the same result. To illustrate how each method would be applied to a situation in which a new partner is admitted into a partnership by making a capital contribution, assume the following facts:

(1) The partnership of A and B desires to admit C.
(2) The capital accounts of A and B are $25,000 each.
(3) Profits and losses are shared equally between A and B. On admission of C, profits and losses are shared equally among the three partners.
(4) All the partnership's assets have carrying values equal to their current values, except for a parcel of land that is worth $12,000 more than its book value of $100,000.
(5) Because the current value of the existing partner's equity is $62,000 ($25,000 + $25,000 + $12,000), A and B agree to admit C into the partnership on contribution of $31,000 cash.

The credit to be made to the new partner's capital account regarding the $31,000 capital contribution may be determined only after the partners agree on one of the following three methods.

Revaluing of assets method. Under the revaluing of assets method, the parcel of land merely is written up to its current value using the following entry:

Land	12,000	
Capital, partner A		6,000
Capital, partner B		6,000

Because the old partners shared profits and losses equally until C was admitted, each of their capital accounts is increased by 50% of the upward revaluation. The entry to record C's contribution is as follows:

Cash	31,000	
Capital, partner C		31,000

The revaluing of assets method is the simplest of the three methods. Although it is not in accordance with generally accepted accounting principles, this disadvantage is usually not important to the partnership form of business. If the partners agree to this method, the new partnership agreement should specify that the new partner is to receive a one-third interest in the new net assets of the partnership **after the land has been written up by $12,000,** thus receiving a full credit to his capital account for the $31,000 capital contribution.

Special profit and loss sharing provision method. Under the special profit and loss sharing provision approach, the land is carried at its historical cost. However, the new profit and loss sharing formula contains a provision that (a) acknowledges that the land's current value is $12,000 in excess of its book value at the time of C's admission, and (b) specifies that the old partners are entitled to share equally in the first $12,000 profit on the sale of the land. Assuming the land is sold for a $15,000 profit several years after C is admitted to the partnership, the profit on the sale would be divided as follows:

	Total	Partner A	Partner B	Partner C
First $12,000............................	$12,000	$6,000	$6,000	
Excess over $12,000	3,000	1,000	1,000	$1,000
	$15,000	$7,000	$7,000	$1,000

The entry to record C's contribution is the same as shown in the preceding method. If the partners agree to this method, the new partnership agreement should state that the new partner is to receive a full credit to his capital account for the $31,000 capital contribution, **with no revaluation made to the assets of the partnership.**

The bonus method. Under the bonus method, no adjustment is made to the carrying amount of the land, nor is any special provision included in the new profit and loss sharing formula because the land is worth more than its book value. When the land subsequently is sold, C will receive one-third of the *entire* profit. From an equity viewpoint, C is not entitled to one-third of the first $12,000 profit; therefore, C's capital account is reduced at his admission by the amount that will be credited to his capital account in the event the land is sold for $12,000 in excess of its current book value. Thus, one-third of $12,000, or $4,000, of C's $31,000 initial capital contribution is not credited to his capital account. Instead, the $4,000 is credited to the old partners' capital accounts. The $4,000 is shared by partners A and B in the old profit and loss sharing ratio. The entry to record C's admission into the partnership is as follows:

Cash	31,000	
Capital, partner A		2,000
Capital, partner B		2,000
Capital, partner C		27,000

Assuming the land is sold for $15,000 several years after C is admitted to the partnership, the profit on the sale would be divided as follows:

	Total	Partner A	Partner B	Partner C
Total profit	$15,000	$5,000	$5,000	$5,000

In this situation, C initially gives up part of his capital contribution, only to recover at a later date the amount given up. The old partners initially receive a bonus, but on the subsequent sale of the land, they are not allocated all of the first $12,000 profit. In this sense, "bonus" is a misnomer because it is not permanent. If the partners agree to the bonus method, the new partnership agreement should state that the new partner is to receive a one-third interest in the new net assets of the partnership of $81,000 ($50,000 + $31,000), **with no revaluation to be made to the partnership assets.**

In reviewing the three methods, the following points should be understood:

(1) If the land subsequently is sold for $112,000 (which is $12,000 more than its $100,000 book value immediately before C was admitted into the partnership), the individual capital account balances will be identical under each method. Thus, each method ensures that partners A and B share equally in the first $12,000 of profit on the sale of the land. Furthermore, each method ensures that partners A, B, and C share equally on any profit on the sale of the land in excess of $12,000.

(2) The exact method chosen depends on the personal whims of the partners. Often an incoming partner desires to have the full amount of his or her capital contribution credited to his or her capital account, if only for psychological reasons. The method agreed upon by the partners should be specified in the new partnership agreement.

(3) If the new profit and loss sharing formula includes a feature providing for imputed interest on capital investments, then the second method would result in an inequity to the old partners, because their individual capital accounts would be less than that of the new partner.

(4) The key to achieving the same result with each method is the assumption that the partnership assets actually are worth the agreed upon amounts. If they are not, then these methods do not always prevent inequities from occurring. We discuss this situation more fully below.

Because the determination of the current values of assets is so subjective, the possibility exists that the land is not really worth $12,000 more than its book value. What if shortly after C is admitted into the partnership the land is sold for only $9,000 more than its book value immediately before C was admitted? Would each method still treat each partner equitably? The answer is no. Partner C would not be treated equitably under the revaluation of assets method because he would be allocated one-third of the book loss of $3,000; he would effectively lose $1,000 of his initial $31,000 capital contribution. Partner C would not be treated equitably under the bonus method because he would not recoup all of the $4,000 bonus he initially gave to the old partners. He would recoup only $3,000 (one-third of the $9,000 book profit) and therefore lose $1,000 of his initial $31,000 capital contribution. However, under the special provision in the new profit and loss sharing method, C cannot lose any of his initial capital contribution; he is best protected under this method.

The land may actually have a current value $12,000 more than its book value immediately before C is admitted into the partnership, but then subsequently decline in value after C is admitted. The same question must be asked: Would each method treat each partner equitably? Under the special provision in the new profit and loss sharing formula, partners A and B would be treated inequitably because they would share the entire loss of value that occurred after C was admitted. From an equity viewpoint, C should share in this loss of value, and he does so only under the revaluation of assets method and the bonus method.

Obviously, each partner strives to select the method that best protects his or her personal interest. Often a conflict exists between an incoming partner and the old partners concerning which method to use. The ultimate resolution takes place through negotiation. In large partnerships—such as the national accounting firms—differences between current values and book values usually are ignored for the sake of simplicity. Of course, such partnerships usually do not have significant amounts of land and depreciable assets, which are most likely to have current values different from book values.

Business combinations

Historically, business combinations are thought of as occurring only between corporations. However, a large number of business combinations involve partnerships, especially public accounting partnerships. Business combinations in the public accounting sector range from a two-person partnership combining with a sole proprietorship to a large international firm combining with a moderately sized national firm.[1] Although *APB Opinion No. 16,* "Accounting for Business Combinations," was intended primarily for combinations among corporations, paragraph 5 of that pronouncement states that "its provisions should be applied as a general guide"[2] when two or more unincorporated businesses combine. Accordingly, business combinations among unincorporated accounting entities may be classified as either purchases or pooling of interests. Whether the substance of a combination is one or the other depends on whether or not the owners of the combining businesses continue as owners in the new, enlarged business.

If the owners of one business do not continue as owners of the enlarged business, a **purchase** has occurred. Purchases do not increase the number of partners. Thus, no change in ownership of the acquiring partnership occurs, and such transactions do not concern us here. The acquiring firm merely applies the provisions of *APB Opinion No. 16* with respect to the assets acquired. The assets of the acquiring business are not revalued to their current values.

If the owners of both businesses continue as owners of the enlarged business, a **pooling of interests** has occurred. Pooling of interests results in an increase in the number of partners; thus, the issues associated with changes in ownership exist. If the assets of either or both of the combining firms have current values different from their book values, then one of the methods of preventing inequities from occurring must be used (revaluing the assets, using a special provision in the new profit and loss sharing formula, or the bonus method). A strict application of the pooling of interests procedures does not permit the revaluing of assets of either combining firm. If the partners revalue the assets, however, they may do so and depart from generally accepted accounting principles. These three methods are

---

[1] In 1984, Price Waterhouse (the fifth largest U.S. CPA firm based on 1983 revenues) and Deloitte Haskins & Sells (the seventh largest U.S. CPA firm) began negotiating a possible merger.

[2] *Accounting Principles Board Opinion No. 16,* "Accounting for Business Combinations" (New York: AICPA, 1970), paragraph 5.

procedurally the same as when a new partner is admitted, other than through a business combination.

Decrease in number of partners

If a partnership's assets have current values different from their book values when a partner withdraws from a partnership, the partners are not treated equitably unless this difference in value is considered in settling with the withdrawing partner or his estate. In these situations, each method of preventing an inequity is available. To illustrate how each method would be applied in such a situation, assume the following facts:

(1) A, B, and C are in partnership.
(2) The capital accounts of A, B, and C are $25,000 each.
(3) Carrying values of the partnership's tangible assets equal their current values, except for a parcel of land that is worth $12,000 more than its book value.
(4) Profits and losses are currently shared equally.
(5) C decides to withdraw from the partnership.

Revaluing of assets method.   Under the revaluing of assets method, the land merely is written up to its current value using the following entry:

Land	12,000	
Capital, partner A		4,000
Capital, partner B		4,000
Capital, partner C		4,000

Each of the partners' capital accounts is increased by one-third of the upward revaluation, because the partners shared profits and losses equally until C decided to withdraw from the partnership. The entry to record C's withdrawal from the partnership is as follows:

Capital, partner C	29,000	
Payable to partner C		29,000

As indicated previously, this is the simplest of the three methods. The fact that it departs from generally accepted accounting principles may be of little concern to the partnership.

Special profit and loss sharing provision method.   Under the special profit and loss sharing provision approach, the land is carried at its historical cost. However, the new profit and loss sharing formula contains a provision that (a) acknowledges that the land's estimated current value is $12,000 in excess of its current book value, and (b) specifies that the withdrawing partner is entitled to one-third of the first $12,000 profit on the sale of the land. The entry to record C's withdrawal from the partnership is as follows:

Capital, partner C	25,000	
Payable to partner C		25,000

Effectively, a contingent liability exists with respect to the amount that is to be paid to C upon sale of the land. This method has limited application in situations involving withdrawing partners. If different appraisals of current value of partnership assets exist, this method may be a practical alternative to the other two methods, especially if such assets are expected to be sold within a relatively short period of time. Normally, however, this method is impractical, because a withdrawing partner does not want to wait until such assets are disposed of to determine his or her final settlement from the partnership.

The bonus method.   Under the bonus method, no adjustment is made to the carrying amount of the land, nor is any special provision included in the new profit and loss sharing formula because the land is worth more than its book value. Consequently, when the land subsequently is sold, A and B share all the profit. From an equity viewpoint, A and B are not entitled to one-third of the first $12,000 profit; therefore, their capital accounts are reduced at C's withdrawal by the amount that represents C's share of the $12,000 of unrealized profit. Thus, one-third of $12,000, or $4,000, is charged to the capital accounts of the old partners in their respective profit and loss sharing ratio. This bonus to C is recouped later by A and B if the land is sold for $12,000 in excess of its current book value. The entry to record the bonus and C's withdrawal from the partnership is as follows:

Capital, partner A	2,000	
Capital, partner B	2,000	
Capital, partner C		4,000
To record the bonus to the withdrawing partner.		
Capital, partner C	29,000	
Payable to partner C		29,000
To record the withdrawal of partner C.		

In this situation, A and B give up part of their capital account balances, only to recover at a later date the amounts given up. Thus, the bonus is not permanent, because it is effectively recovered later.

In reviewing each of these methods, the following points should be understood:

(1) If the land subsequently is sold for $112,000 (which is $12,000 more than its $100,000 book value immediately before C withdrew from the partnership), the settlement to C is the same under each method. Also, the capital account balances of A and B are identical under each method. Thus, each method ensures that the withdrawing partner receives one-third of the first $12,000 profit on the sale of the land. Furthermore, each method ensures that C does not share in any of the profit on the sale of the land in excess of $12,000.

(2) The real problem is obtaining reasonable assurance of the current values of partnership assets. If the agreed-upon values are overstated, then the revaluing the asset method and the bonus method result in an excess settlement to the withdrawing partner. However, under the special profit and loss sharing provision method, no such excess payment

is possible; thus, A and B are best protected under this method. If the agreed-upon values are understated, then none of the methods protects the withdrawing partner. The remaining partners share the entire increase above the agreed-upon value.

(3) If, in this situation, the land subsequently declined in value after C withdrew, then C would not be treated equitably under the special profit and loss sharing provision method, because he would be sharing in a loss that occurred after he withdrew.

In all the preceding examples, the partnership's tangible assets were undervalued. When tangible assets have current values less than their book values, the first method—whereby the assets are written down—makes the most sense. (This procedure would be in accordance with generally accepted accounting principles.) The second choice would be the bonus method. The use of the special profit and loss sharing provision method would usually be impractical.

INTANGIBLE ELEMENT EXISTS

In the preceding section, we restricted our discussion to situations in which a partnership's tangible assets have current values different from their book values. In the remaining section of this chapter, we discuss situations in which an intangible element exists with either the existing partnership or an incoming partner. In discussing these situations, we assume that all partnership tangible assets have current values equal to their book values. Although this assumption is not necessarily realistic, it allows us to concentrate on the issue of accounting for this intangible element.

The discussion of intangible elements usually has wider application than the earlier discussion of tangible assets, because most partnerships—other than those engaged in real estate development—do not have substantial investments in the types of assets that appreciate or depreciate, such as inventory, land, buildings, and equipment. The largest asset for such partnerships usually is accounts receivable.

Intangible elements usually are associated with an existing partnership. The most common intangible element is a partnership's superior earnings. Obviously, a partner's interest in such a partnership is worth more than its book value. Even when a partnership has only average earnings, a partner's interest may be worth more than its book value to an incoming partner merely because an organization exists that already has clients and the potential to develop superior earnings.

Intangible elements may also exist with an incoming partner. For example, an incoming partner may have a successful sole proprietorship business with superior earnings power. An incoming partner may individually have potential that the existing partners are willing to pay for. This is similar to situations in which corporations pay one-time bonuses to executives to induce them to work for them, or in professional sports in which a rookie may receive a one-time bonus just for signing with a particular team.

In these situations, whether the existing partnership or an incoming partner possesses the intangible element, the intangible element is referred to as **goodwill.** When goodwill exists, the accounting issue is how to compensate the partner or partners who have created or possess the goodwill.

If this is not done, the other partner(s) share unfairly in a portion of the partnership's future earnings.

The general approach to compensating the appropriate partners parallels that for situations in which tangible assets have current values different from book values—that is, we may apply the same three methods that we discussed and illustrated in the preceding section of the chapter. However, the first method is called **recording the goodwill** rather than **revaluing of assets.** Other than this descriptive change, the three methods are procedurally the same.

In the following material on the treatment of intangibles, note that the larger the partnership, the less the partners are inclined to compute the value of goodwill. For example, in the interest of simplicity, most national public accounting firms completely ignore goodwill for all changes in ownership situations. Instead, a simpler approach is adopted whereby an incoming partner initially accepts a lower than normal profit and loss sharing percentage, with that profit and loss sharing percentage being increased on a sliding scale over a period of years until the incoming partner eventually shares profits and losses equally with other partners. Such an approach has the same overall effect as the three mechanical methods of dealing with goodwill, although the exact effect on each partner would be different.

Admission of a new partner—
Existing partnership possesses goodwill

Traditionally, advanced accounting textbooks have approached the issue of goodwill by presenting a set of assumed facts regarding (1) the capital contribution made by the incoming partner; (2) the percentage interest the incoming partner receives in the partnership's net assets; and (3) whether the net assets in (2) include or exclude the value of the goodwill. Given all this information, we can determine (as if trying to solve a puzzle) which method the partners have used to compensate the partner or partners who have created or possess the goodwill. Under the valuing of the goodwill method, the value of the goodwill may then be determined and recorded on the books of the partnership. Under the bonus method, the amount of the bonus given to the old partners or the new partner may then be determined and recorded on the books of the partnership. This approach implies that (1) the value of the goodwill and/or the amount of the bonus given are derivatives of these given amounts and percentages, and (2) the partners arrive at the ownership percentages without agreeing to the value of the goodwill. This implication is completely misleading.

Although the goodwill and the amount of the bonus, or both, may be determined using this approach, the normal procedure when a partner is admitted into a partnership is obscured. The normal process, the sequence of which may vary, is as follows:

(1) The value of the existing goodwill is agreed upon between the old partners and the new partner.
(2) One of the available accounting methods designed to compensate the partner or partners who have created or possess the goodwill is selected.
(3) The profit and loss ratio is agreed upon.
(4) The capital contribution of the incoming partner is agreed upon.

Once these items are agreed upon, each partner's capital account balance may be computed (using the appropriate accounting method selected). After determining each partner's capital account balance, we may then express each partner's interest as a percentage of the partnership's net assets (as defined). Thus, the ownership percentage of each partner in the partnership's net assets is a derived amount—not the agreed upon value of the goodwill. Accordingly, in the following illustrations, the value of the goodwill will be given.

In the first illustration, the goodwill exists with the existing partnership. To illustrate the application of the three methods of compensating the old partners for the goodwill they have created, assume the following information:

(1) A and B are in partnership, sharing profits equally.
(2) C is to be admitted into the partnership.
(3) A, B, and C agree that the existing partnership will generate superior earnings of $10,000 for one year after C's admission.
(4) C contributes $30,000 cash to the partnership.
(5) Profits and losses are to be shared among A, B, and C in a ratio of 4:4:2, respectively.
(6) A and B have capital account balances of $32,500 and $27,500, respectively (for a total of $60,000), immediately before admitting C.

Recording the goodwill method. Under the recording the goodwill method, C's admission into the partnership results in the recording of the entire amount of the agreed upon goodwill in the partnership's books, as follows:

Goodwill	10,000	
Capital, partner A		5,000
Capital, partner B		5,000

To record the agreed upon value of the goodwill, shared equally between the old partners using their old profit and loss sharing ratio.

The entry to record C's capital contribution of $30,000 is as follows:

Cash	30,000	
Capital, partner C		30,000

To record C's capital contribution.

In reviewing the preceding entries, the following points should be understood:

(1) It can be stated that C has a 30% interest in the net assets of the partnership ($30,000/$100,000 total of the capital accounts).
(2) The recording of goodwill in this manner is not in accordance with generally accepted accounting principles, because the goodwill did not result from the purchase of a business.
(3) The goodwill will be amortized over a one-year period, because the partnership is expected to produce superior earnings only for one year.

(4) Because of the goodwill amortization in the year after C's admission, earnings will be $10,000 lower than if goodwill had not been recorded on the books.

(5) Effectively, $10,000 of future profits have been capitalized into the capital accounts of the old partners. In this respect, the partners have guaranteed that they alone will receive the first $10,000 of future earnings (determined without regard to the goodwill amortization expense).

(6) If $10,000 of superior earnings result in the following year, then such superior earnings completely absorb the goodwill amortization of $10,000.

(7) If the superior earnings in the following year are less than $10,000, then C effectively loses a portion of his initial capital contribution of $30,000. This is because the normal earnings of the partnership must absorb a portion of the goodwill amortization, and C cannot share in a portion of the normal earnings.

To illustrate how this method may favor the old partners over the new partner if the entire amount of the superior earnings does not materialize, assume that during the year after C's admission, only $8,000 of superior earnings materialized. These superior earnings would absorb only $8,000 of goodwill amortization. The remaining $2,000 of goodwill amortization would be absorbed by normal earnings. Thus, C would not share in $2,000 of normal earnings. Because C's profit and loss sharing percentage is 20%, he effectively loses $400 (20% of $2,000) of his $30,000 initial capital contribution.

Special profit and loss sharing provision method.   Under the special profit and loss sharing provision method, no entry is made on the partnership's books with respect to the goodwill. As under the previous method, C's capital account is credited with the full amount of his capital contribution of $30,000. It can be stated that C has a one-third interest in the partnership's net assets ($30,000/$90,000 total of the capital accounts). The new profit and loss sharing formula would stipulate that the old partners are entitled to share (in accordance with their old profit and loss sharing ratio) in the first $10,000 of earnings in excess of a specified amount, the specified amount being the expected normal earnings for the year after C's admission into the partnership.

If the superior earnings of $10,000 do not materialize during this year, then the old partners will have credited to their capital accounts only the superior earnings that do materialize. Of course, the normal earnings and any earnings above the $10,000 of superior earnings during the next year would be shared in accordance with the new profit and loss sharing ratio. This method protects the new partner's initial capital contribution of $30,000 in the event superior earnings of $10,000 do not materialize. Obviously, the old partners would prefer the previous method, under which they are assured of the first $10,000 of earnings, regardless of whether such earnings are superior earnings.

The bonus method.   Under the bonus method, no entry is made on the partnership's books with respect to goodwill. Unlike the previous two methods, C does not receive a full credit to his capital account for his capital contribution of $30,000, because he must give a bonus to the old partners. The amount of the bonus given to the old partners is C's profit and loss sharing percentage of 20% times the agreed upon value of the goodwill of $10,000. Thus, the bonus given the old partners is $2,000, which they share in their old profit and loss sharing ratio as follows:

Cash	30,000	
Capital, partner A		1,000
Capital, partner B		1,000
Capital, partner C		28,000
To record C's capital contribution and to record		
the bonus to the old partners.		

In reviewing the above entry, the following points should be understood:

(1) It can be stated that C has a 31.11% interest in the partnership's net assets ($28,000/$90,000 total of the capital accounts).
(2) By not recording goodwill on the books, generally accepted accounting principles are followed.
(3) If superior earnings of $10,000 materialize in the year following C's admission, then C shares in these superior earnings. His share is $2,000 (20% of $10,000). Consequently, he recoups the bonus he initially gave to the old partners.
(4) The bonus method compensates the old partners currently for the portion of the superior earnings that will later be credited to the new partner's capital account. Thus, if all the superior earnings materialize, the bonus is temporary.
(5) If the superior earnings in the year following C's admission are less than $10,000, then C effectively loses a portion of his initial capital contribution of $30,000. This is because he does not share in the amount of superior earnings that he thought would materialize, for which he was willing to give a bonus to the old partners.

If the entire amount of superior earnings does not materialize, the bonus method may favor the old partners over the new partner. Assume that during the year following C's admission, only $8,000 of superior earnings materialized. C's share of the $8,000 of superior earnings that did materialize would be $1,600 (20% of $8,000). Because he gave a bonus of $2,000, he only recouped $1,600 of the bonus, effectively losing $400 of his initial capital contribution of $30,000.

Approach if the value of goodwill is not given.   Assume that the partners in their negotiations agree upon an amount for the goodwill, but that they do not state this amount in the new partnership agreement. Instead, knowing the amount of agreed upon goodwill, they merely calculate the percentage that the incoming partner has in the partnership's net assets. In these situations, the accountant may determine the goodwill using the available information regarding the individual ownership percentage the new partner has in the partnership's net assets. We demonstrate the general approach using the information in our example.

If the value of the goodwill is to be recorded on the partnership's books and the new partner has a 30% interest in the net assets (tangible and intangible) of the partnership, the goodwill implicit in the transaction could be determined as follows:

(1) Divide C's $30,000 capital contribution by his 30% interest in the net assets to arrive at $100,000.
(2) Subtract from the amount determined in (1) the sum of the capital account balances of the old partners immediately before C is admitted ($60,000) plus C's capital contribution ($30,000). Thus, the goodwill would be $10,000 ($100,000 − $90,000).

Alternatively, if goodwill is not to be recorded on the partnership's books and the new partner has a 31.11% interest in the net assets (tangible assets only) of the partnership, the bonus to be given and the related goodwill implicit in the transaction could be determined as follows:

(1) Determine the total tangible net assets of the partnership including C's contribution ($60,000 + $30,000).
(2) Multiply the amount determined in (1), $90,000, by C's given ownership percentage in the partnership's net assets ($90,000 × 31.11% = $28,000).
(3) Subtract the $28,000 amount determined in (2) from C's $30,000 capital contribution to determine the $2,000 bonus that is to be given to the old partners.
(4) Dividing the $2,000 bonus by C's profit and loss sharing percentage of 20% equals $10,000—the value of the goodwill implicit in the transaction.

Admission of a new partner—
New partner possesses goodwill

Although in most situations, the existing partnership has created the goodwill, an incoming partner may possess goodwill. To illustrate the three methods of compensating an incoming partner for goodwill, assume the following information:

(1) A and B are in partnership, sharing profits equally.
(2) C is to be admitted into the partnership.
(3) A, B, and C agree that C is expected to generate superior earnings of $10,000 for one year following his admission.
(4) C contributes $30,000 cash to the partnership.
(5) Profits and losses are to be shared among A, B, and C in a ratio of 4:4:2, respectively.
(6) A and B have capital account balances of $32,500 and $27,500, respectively (for a total of $60,000), immediately before admitting C.

Recording the goodwill method. Under the recording the goodwill method, the entire amount of the agreed upon value of the goodwill is credited to C's capital account, along with his capital contribution of $30,000, as follows:

```
Goodwill .............................................   10,000
Cash ................................................   30,000
        Capital, partner C.................................          40,000
    To record the agreed upon value of the goodwill
    and C's capital contribution.
```

Compared with the situation in which the old partners created the goodwill, the roles now are reversed. The new partner will receive the first $10,000 of future earnings (determined without regard to the goodwill amortization expense), even if superior earnings do not materialize. If the superior earnings of $10,000 do not materialize, then the old partners will lose the subsequent increases to their capital accounts that they would have received. In this situation, it can be stated that C has a 40% interest in the partnership's net assets ($40,000/$100,000 total of the capital accounts).

Special profit and loss sharing provision method.   Under the special profit and loss sharing provision method, no entry is made on the partnership's books with respect to the goodwill. C would receive a credit to his capital account equal to his capital contribution of $30,000. It can be stated that C has a one-third interest in the partnership's net assets ($30,000/$90,000 total of the capital accounts). The new profit and loss sharing formula would stipulate that the new partner is entitled to receive the first $10,000 of earnings in excess of a specified amount, the specified amount being the expected normal earnings for the year after C's admission into the partnership. If superior earnings of $10,000 do not materialize during this year, then the new partner will have credited to his capital account only the superior earnings that do materialize. In this situation, this method protects the old partners' capital balances that existed when C was admitted into the partnership.

The bonus method.   Under the bonus method, no entry is made on the partnership's books with respect to goodwill. Because the new partner possesses the goodwill, the old partners give a bonus to him. The amount of the bonus given to the new partner is the total of the old partners' profit and loss sharing percentage of 80% times the agreed upon value of the goodwill, which is $10,000. Thus, the bonus given the new partner is $8,000, recorded as follows:

```
Cash ................................................   30,000
Capital, partner A .....................................    4,000
Capital, partner B .....................................    4,000
        Capital, partner C.................................          38,000
    To record C's capital contribution and to record
    the bonus given to him.
```

It can be stated that C has a 42.22% interest in the partnership's net assets ($38,000/$90,000). Compared with the situation in which the old partners created the goodwill, the roles now are reversed. The old partners will recoup the bonus they gave to the new partner only if superior earnings of $10,000 materialize. To the extent that the superior earnings are less than $10,000, then the old partners effectively will lose a portion of the balances that existed in their capital accounts immediately before C was admitted.

Approach if the value of goodwill is not given.   If the agreed-upon value of the goodwill is not available (an unusual situation), the accountant may determine this amount as long as information is available regarding the individual ownership percentage the new partner has in the partnership's net assets. We demonstrate the general approach using the information in our example.

If the value of the goodwill is to be recorded on the partnership's books and the new partner has a 40% interest in the net assets (tangible and intangible) of the partnership, the goodwill implicit in the transaction could be determined as follows:

(1) Divide the total of the old partners' capital accounts by their total interest in the net assets ($60,000/60%) to arrive at $100,000.
(2) Subtract from the amount determined in (1) the sum of the capital account balances of the old partners immediately before C is admitted ($60,000) plus C's tangible capital contribution of $30,000. Thus, the goodwill would be $10,000 ($100,000 − $90,000).

Alternatively, if goodwill is not to be recorded on the partnership's books and the new partner has a 42.22% interest in the net assets (tangible assets only), the bonus to be given by the old partners and the goodwill implicit in the transaction could be determined as follows:

(1) Determine the total net assets of the partnership, including C's tangible contribution ($60,000 + $30,000).
(2) Multiply the amount determined in (1), $90,000, by C's given ownership percentage in the partnership's net assets ($90,000 × 42.22% = $38,000).
(3) Subtract from the $38,000 amount determined in (2) C's tangible capital contribution of $30,000 to arrive at the $8,000 bonus that C receives from the old partners.
(4) Dividing the $8,000 bonus by the old partners' combined profit and loss sharing percentage of 80% equals $10,000—the value of the goodwill implicit in the transaction.

Business combinations

When two businesses combine in such a manner that the owners of each separate business continue as owners in the enlarged business (substantively, a pooling of interests) and when one of the businesses possesses goodwill, then we may apply the same three methods that have been illustrated in this section to compensate the partners of the business possessing the goodwill. Procedurally, these three methods are the same as in situations in which a new partner is admitted other than through a business combination. The mechanics are more involved, however, as the number of combining partners increases.

Decrease in number of partners

If a partnership possesses unrecorded goodwill when a partner withdraws from the partnership, the withdrawing partner is not treated equitably unless this difference in value is considered in settling with the withdrawing partner or his estate. In these situations, each of the methods of compensating the partner is available—the recording the goodwill method, the special profit and loss sharing provision method, and the bonus method. To illustrate how each of these methods would be applied in such a situation, assume the following facts:

(1) A, B, and C are in partnership, sharing profits equally.
(2) The capital accounts of A, B, and C are $40,000, $30,000, and $20,000, respectively.
(3) All the partnership's tangible assets have carrying values equal to their current values.
(4) C withdraws from the partnership.
(5) The partners agree that the partnership currently has unrecorded goodwill of $15,000.

Recording the goodwill method. Under the recording the goodwill method, goodwill is recorded on the books and shared among the partners in their profit and loss ratio, as follows:

Goodwill	15,000	
Capital, partner A		5,000
Capital, partner B		5,000
Capital, partner C		5,000
To record the agreed upon value of goodwill existing at the time of C's withdrawal from the partnership.		

The entry to record C's withdrawal is as follows:

Capital, partner C	25,000	
Payable to partner C		25,000

An alternative to recording all the goodwill is to record only C's share of the goodwill, which is $5,000. The entry is as follows:

Goodwill	5,000	
Capital, partner C		5,000

Whether all or a portion of the goodwill is recorded is irrelevant from an equity standpoint—both methods produce the same result with respect to the withdrawing partner. As previously indicated, the goodwill method is not in accordance with generally accepted accounting principles, but the partners need not follow generally accepted accounting principles. If superior earnings of $15,000 do not materialize subsequent to C's withdrawal, then the remaining partners lose a portion of their capital balances that existed at the time of C's withdrawal as a result of writing off the goodwill.

Special profit and loss sharing provision method. Under the special profit and loss sharing provision method, goodwill is not recorded on the books. Instead, C's withdrawal is conditional on the new profit and loss sharing formula between A and B, which contains a provision that C is to share in one-third of future earnings in excess of a specified level for a certain period of time. If past superior earnings have been largely dependent on C's efforts, the partnership may not be able to generate superior earnings after C withdraws. Accordingly, this method best protects the remaining partners in the event superior earnings do not materialize during the stipulated period of time after C's withdrawal.

The bonus method. Under the bonus method, the old partners give a bonus to the withdrawing partner. The bonus equals C's share of the agreed upon value of the goodwill, which is one-third of $15,000, or $5,000. The bonus is shared between the remaining partners in their respective profit and loss sharing ratio as follows:

Capital, partner A	2,500	
Capital, partner B	2,500	
Capital, partner C		5,000
To record the bonus to C on his withdrawal from the partnership.		

This method does not deviate from generally accepted accounting principles. If $15,000 of above-normal earnings do not materialize during the stipulated period of time after C withdraws, however, then the remaining partners do not recoup all of the bonus they gave to C.

Spin-off situations. A partner may withdraw from a partnership and then immediately commence business in the same line of work as a sole proprietor. In such a situation, the withdrawing partner often requests the partnership's clients and customers that he or she personally has been serving to give their future business to the newly formed sole proprietorship. When this happens, the method selected for equitably treating the withdrawing partner should be accompanied by provisions that protect the remaining partners from any loss of clients and customers as a result of the withdrawing partner forming a sole proprietorship. In other words, the remaining partners must guard against recording goodwill or paying a bonus and also losing clients or customers to the newly formed sole proprietorship.

LEGAL AND TAX ASPECTS OF CHANGES IN OWNERSHIP

Legal aspects

Although a thorough discussion of the legal aspects of a change in ownership of a partnership is properly the subject of an upper division course on business law, a brief discussion of the major legal aspects is appropriate at this point.

Section 29 of the Uniform Partnership Act (UPA) states that "the dissolution of a partnership is the change in the relation of the partners caused by any partner ceasing to be associated in the carrying on as distinguished from the winding up of the business." This definition implies that dissolution occurs only when a partner withdraws from a partnership. Section 41(1) of the UPA (which also is concerned with dissolution) refers to a partnership that admits a partner as being the "first or dissolved partnership." Accordingly, any change in ownership (whether by withdrawal of a partner, admission of a new partner, or a business combination that is in substance a pooling of interests) legally dissolves the existing partnership. Because we are dealing with changes in ownership that do not terminate the business activities of the partnership, a new partnership must be formed immediately to continue the business of the dissolved partnership.

The fact that a legal dissolution has occurred is meaningless in terms of continuity of existence; the business continues to operate just as if no change in ownership has occurred. However, a legal dissolution does have personal significance to new partners, withdrawing partners, continuing partners, and creditors of the dissolved partnership.

Admission of a partner.   With respect to an incoming partner, Section 17 of the UPA provides that "a person admitted as a partner into an existing partnership is liable for all the obligations of the partnership arising before his admission as though he had been a partner when such obligations were incurred, except that this liability shall be satisfied only out of partnership property." This provision insulates the personal assets of the new partner from creditors' claims existing at the new partner's admission.

In practice, the existing partners usually insist that an incoming partner be jointly responsible for all such pre-existing partnership debts. If the new partner agrees to this, Section 17 of the UPA may be circumvented by including a provision in the new partnership agreement to that effect. Because of the possibility of undisclosed liabilities (actual or contingent), the new partner in these situations should limit his or her responsibilities to the liabilities that are set forth in a scheduled exhibit to the partnership agreement.

Withdrawal of a partner.   With respect to a withdrawing partner, Section 36(1) of the UPA provides that "the dissolution of the partnership does not of itself discharge the existing liability of any partner." Section 36(2), however, provides that a withdrawing partner may be relieved of his or her responsibility for such debt if and only if the creditor expressly releases the partner from this responsibility by entering into an agreement to that effect between the withdrawing partner and the person or partnership continuing the business. Some court cases have held that a withdrawing partner may be liable for debts incurred after his or her withdrawal unless prior notice was given of that withdrawal. Notice usually must be given directly to persons who have dealt with the partnership. For persons who have not dealt with the partnership, a notice usually may be given by publication in a newspaper or some other appropriate manner.

Tax aspects

The general ledger entries to the capital accounts of the partners in connection with (1) the revaluation of assets; (2) valuing the goodwill; or (3) the bonus method, are not significant from a tax viewpoint. The only tax significance of such entries is the existence of unrealized gains (when partners' capital accounts increase) and unrealized losses (when partners' capital accounts decrease). In general, until the partnership interest is disposed of, such gains and losses are not reportable for tax purposes.

Withdrawal of a partner. When a withdrawing partner receives cash from either the partnership or person(s) to whom his or her partnership interest was sold, the determination of the withdrawing partner's gain or loss for income tax reporting purposes is made by comparing the proceeds to his or her basis. The proceeds are the sum of cash received plus the share of existing partnership liabilities for which he or she is relieved of responsibility. (The assumption of the partner's share of the liabilities by the remaining partners is treated as a distribution of money to the withdrawing partner.) In certain instances, some or all of the gain must be treated as ordinary income instead of as a capital gain. These situations occur when some or all of the gain on the sale or liquidation of a partnership interest is attributable to **unrealized receivables** or **substantially appreciated inventory.** Because the tax rules related to unrealized receivables and substantially appreciated inventory are complex, we do not discuss them here in detail. In general, these items are assets that if collected or sold by the partnership would be treated as ordinary income to the partnership.

For example, assume a partner is retiring from a partnership that for tax-reporting purposes reports its income on the cash basis and the partner has a gain on withdrawal. If the amount paid to the retiring partner includes an amount for his or her share of accounts receivable existing as of the retirement date (such accounts receivable not having been reported as taxable income up to that point because of the use of the cash basis), then a portion of the gain (up to the incremental amount paid because of the accounts receivable) must be treated as ordinary income. If the partner had not retired, the receivables would have been reported as ordinary income by the partnership at the time of their collection, and the retiring partner's share of such income would have been reported as ordinary income at that time. When a withdrawing partner receives some or all noncash consideration, the tax laws are even more complex; a discussion of these laws is beyond the scope of this chapter.

Admission of a partner. The procedures for determining an incoming partner's basis are the same as those illustrated in the preceding chapter on the formation of partnerships. The incoming partner's basis equals the sum of (1) the amount of cash contributed; (2) the adjusted basis of any noncash assets contributed; and (3) the share of any partnership liabilities for which he or she is jointly responsible; (4) less the old partners' share of any liabilities the new partner contributes to the partnership. As when a partnership is formed, the profit and loss sharing ratios are used to adjust each partner's basis for any liabilities relieved of or assumed.

When a partner is admitted by directly purchasing a partner's interest, the incoming partner's basis is the sum of the cash paid plus the share of any partnership liabilities for which he or she is jointly responsible. Obviously, the incoming partner's basis need not coincide with the selling partner's basis, because the amount paid is a negotiated amount. The partnership may elect to adjust the basis of the partnership assets to reflect the difference between the incoming partner's basis and the selling partner's basis. (No entries are made in the general ledger—the difference is kept on a memorandum basis.)

The amount of the increase or decrease in basis affects only the incoming partner. For example, assume that an incoming partner's basis exceeds the selling partner's basis and this difference is allocable to merchandise inventory, a building, unrealized receivables, and goodwill. In future years, the incoming partner's share of earnings is adjusted by (1) treating the amount allocable to inventory as additional cost of goods sold (as the inventory is sold); (2) treating the amount allocable to the building as additional depreciation expense; and (3) treating the amount allocable to the unrealized receivables as a reduction of revenues (as the accounts receivable are collected). Although the goodwill is assigned a basis, the incoming partner's share of the earnings would not be adjusted for the amount allocable to goodwill, because goodwill is not deductible for income tax reporting purposes.

This election to adjust the basis of the assets is much more common in small partnerships than in large partnerships because the partnership— not the individual incoming partner—must do the record keeping, and most large partnerships do not bother with this record-keeping function. If the election is made to adjust the basis of the partnership assets, the sum of the bases of each partner will equal the partnership's basis in its assets. If the election is not made, this equality will not exist, and the difference will exist until the partner disposes of his or her interest.

SUMMARY

The determination of the journal entry to reflect a change in the ownership of a partnership is to some extent an after-the-fact mechanical process using the terms and methods selected by the partners. A far more important role for the accountant when a change in ownership is contemplated is explaining and illustrating the various methods (and their ramifications) of dealing with situations in which assets have current values different from book values and/or intangible elements exist. The accountant even may assist partners in determining the amount of any goodwill by demonstrating some of the common methods that may be used to calculate goodwill. Remember that in these situations the accountant is only an advisor. It is not his or her role to select a method for determining the amount of goodwill or to select one of the three methods available for achieving equity among the partners.

Review questions

1. What is the primary objective of accounting for changes in the ownership of a partnership?
2. What three methods are available for achieving equity among partners when a change in ownership occurs?

3. Does each method of achieving equity always treat each partner equitably in every situation?
4. Under the bonus method, is the bonus temporary or permanent?
5. Is recognizing goodwill on the admission of a partner into a partnership considered to be in accord with generally accepted accounting principles?
6. Describe a business combination of two partnerships that would be, in substance, a pooling of interests.
7. Is a business combination that is in substance a purchase deemed a change in ownership with respect to the acquiring partnership?
8. How does an accountant know whether the bonus method, the special profit and loss sharing provision method, or the recording the goodwill method should be used to reflect a change in ownership?
9. Under the recording the goodwill method, substantively, what has occurred?
10. Under the bonus method, substantively, what has occurred?
11. What is the significance of a legal dissolution when a partner is admitted into a partnership? when a partner withdraws?
12. When a partner withdraws from a partnership after many years as a partner and such partner has a gain on the liquidation of his or her interest, is such gain treated as a capital gain for income tax reporting purposes?

Discussion cases

Discussion case 20–1
Admission of a partner: Evaluation of the bonus method

Konn and Ponzi are in partnership, and they are contemplating the admission of Mark into the partnership. Konn and Ponzi have proposed that Mark give a $20,000 bonus to them as a condition of admittance. Mark feels that this bonus is ridiculous considering that (1) all tangible assets have fair market values equal to their book values; (2) all partners will be devoting 100% of their time to the partnership business; (3) future profits and losses are to be shared equally; (4) Mark's capital contribution is to be 50% of the existing partnership capital of $100,000 immediately before his admission; and (5) his tax basis would be reduced by $20,000. Mark has asked you as his accountant to counsel him on this matter.

Required:
How would you respond to this request?

Discussion case 20–2
Admission of a partner: Adherence to generally accepted accounting principles

Sweaney and Brannigan are partners in the process of negotiating with Mulligan regarding his admission into the partnership. Agreement has been reached regarding the value of goodwill that the existing partnership possesses. However, the partners disagree as to whether the goodwill should be recorded on the books. Sweaney and Brannigan feel goodwill should be recognized and recorded on the books at Mulligan's admission. Mulligan feels it is improper to record goodwill because it was not bought and paid for. Furthermore, Mulligan contends that it is senseless to record goodwill, because it is not deductible for income tax purposes. They have asked you as the partnership's accountant to settle this disagreement.

Required:
How would you respond to this request?

Discussion case 20–3
Admission of a partner: Role of the accountant

Fox and Sharpe are partners contemplating the admission of Wheeler as a partner. They have requested that you, the partnership's accountant, determine how this should be done.

Required:
How would you respond to this request? Be specific about the advice you would give to the partners.

Discussion case 20–4
Admission of a partner: Role of the accountant

Keane and Witte are partners contemplating the admission of Patsy into the partnership. Keane and Witte believe the partnership possesses goodwill of $60,000, whereas Patsy believes the partnership possesses goodwill of only $20,000. As the partnership's accountant, you have been asked to determine the amount of goodwill that the partnership possesses.

Required:
How would you respond to this request?

Exercises

Exercise 20–1
Admission of a partner: Calculation of required contribution

Partners Able, Billings, and Cash share profits and losses 50:30:20, respectively. The April 30, 19X5 balance sheet is as follows:

Cash	$ 40,000
Other assets	360,000
	$400,000
Accounts payable	$100,000
Able, capital	74,000
Billings, capital	130,000
Cash, capital	96,000
	$400,000

The assets and liabilities are recorded and presented at their respective fair values. Dunn is to be admitted as a new partner with a 20% capital interest and a 20% share of profits and losses in exchange for a cash contribution. No goodwill or bonus is to be recorded.

Required:
(1) Determine how much cash Dunn should contribute.
(2) Prepare the entry to record Dunn's admission.

(AICPA adapted)

Exercise 20-2
Admission of a partner: Goodwill exists—
Recording the goodwill method

Slamm and Dunke are partners who share profits and losses equally in a highly successful partnership. The capital accounts of Slamm and Dunke have tripled in five years and currently stand at $90,000 and $60,000, respectively. Hooper desires to join the firm and offers to invest $50,000 for a one-third interest in the capital and profits and losses of the firm. Slamm and Dunke decline this offer but extend a counteroffer to Hooper of $70,000 for a one-fourth interest in the capital and profits and losses of the firm.

Required:
Assuming Hooper accepts this counteroffer and goodwill is to be recorded, prepare the entries to record the goodwill and the admission of Hooper into the partnership.

(AICPA adapted)

Exercise 20-3
Admission of a partner: Goodwill exists—The bonus method

The capital accounts for the partnership of Knight and Dey at October 31, 19X5, are as follows:

Knight, capital	$ 80,000
Dey, capital	40,000
	$120,000

The partners share profits and losses in the ratio 6:4, respectively. The partnership is in desperate need of cash, and the partners agree to admit Dawn as a partner with a one-third interest in the firm's capital and profits and losses upon his investment of $30,000. The partners have agreed to use the bonus method.

Required:
Prepare the entry to record Dawn's admission.

(AICPA adapted)

Exercise 20-4
Admission of a partner: Goodwill exists—
Recording the goodwill method and the bonus method

McCall is admitted into the partnership of Bell, Buzze, and Ring for a total cash investment of $40,000. The capital accounts and respective percentage interests in profits and losses immediately before the admission of McCall, are as follows:

	Capital Accounts	Percentage Interests in Profits and Losses
Bell	$ 80,000	60
Buzze	40,000	30
Ring...	20,000	10
	$140,000	100

All tangible assets and liabilities are fairly valued. McCall receives a one-fifth interest in profits and losses and a 20% interest in the partnership's net assets.

Required:
(1) Prepare the entry to record McCall's admission into the partnership, assuming goodwill is to be recorded.
(2) Prepare the entry to record McCall's admission into the partnership, assuming no goodwill is to be recorded.

Exercise 20–5
Admission of a partner:
Determining bonus and goodwill from interest in net assets

Ruff and Woods are partners, share profits and losses equally, and have capital balances of $30,000 and $20,000, respectively. All tangible assets have current values equal to book values. Bogey is admitted into the partnership. Determine the entry to record Bogey's admission in each of the following independent situations:

(1) Bogey contributes $10,000 cash for a 10% interest in the new net assets of the partnership of $60,000.
(2) Bogey contributes $10,000 cash for a 10% interest in the new net assets of the partnership, with Bogey to receive a credit to his capital account equal to his full cash contribution.
(3) Bogey contributes $10,000 for a one-sixth interest in the new net assets of the partnership of $60,000.
(4) Bogey purchases 10% of each existing partners' interest for a total cash payment of $10,000 to the existing partners.
(5) Bogey contributes $10,000 cash for a 20% interest in the new net assets of the partnership of $60,000.
(6) Bogey contributes $10,000 cash for a 20% interest in the new net assets of the partnership, with the old partners not to have any decrease made to their capital accounts.

Exercise 20–6
Calculation of gain on sale of partnership interests

The capital accounts of the partnership of Hale, Raines, and Snowe on June 1, 19X5, are presented below with their respective profit and loss ratios:

Hale	$200,000	1/2
Raines	150,000	1/3
Snowe	100,000	1/6
	$450,000	

On June 1, 19X5, Weathers was admitted into the partnership when she purchased for $120,000 an interest from Hale in the net assets and profits of the partnership. As a result of this transaction, Weathers acquired a one-fifth interest in the net assets and profits of the firm. Assume that implied goodwill is not to be recorded. Hale's basis just prior to the sale was $180,000.

Required:
(1) What is the gain realized by Hale on the sale of a portion of this interest in the partnership to Weathers?
(2) Is the gain calculated in (1), above, a gain for book purposes, a gain for tax purposes, or both?
(3) Prepare the entry required on the partnership's books.

Exercise 20–7
Retirement of a partner: Tangible assets overvalued and goodwill exists

Lefty, Wright, and Homer are in partnership; have capital balances of $40,000, $20,000, and $30,000, respectively; and share profits and losses in the ratio 5:3:2, respectively. Homer retires from the partnership. The partners agree that (1) the inventory is overvalued by $5,000, and (2) the partnership possesses goodwill of $30,000.

Required:
(1) Prepare the required entries assuming goodwill is to be recorded on the partnership's books. (Note: Two alternative amounts may be recorded for goodwill. Prepare entries under each alternative.)
(2) Prepare the required entries assuming goodwill is not to be recorded on the partnership's books.

Problems

Problem 20–1
Admission of a partner: Tangible assets undervalued and goodwill exists

Barr and Bell are in partnership, share profits and losses in the ratio 4:1, respectively, and have capital balances of $22,500 each. Tangible assets of the partnership have a fair value of $15,000 in excess of book value. Armstrong is admitted into the partnership for a cash contribution of $30,000. The new profit and loss sharing formula is Barr, 56%; Bell, 14%; and Armstrong, 30%. The value of the partnership's existing goodwill is agreed to be $10,000.

Required:
(1) Prepare the required entries assuming the tangible assets are to be revalued and the goodwill is to be recorded on the partnership's books.
(2) Prepare the required entries assuming the bonus method is to be used with respect to the undervalued tangible assets and the goodwill.

Problem 20–2
Retirement of a partner: Tangible assets undervalued and goodwill exists

The April 30, 19X5 balance sheet for the partnership of Green, Sanders, and Trapp is as follows. The partners share profits and losses in the ratio 2:2:6, respectively.

Assets, at cost	$100,000
Green, loan	$ 9,000
Green, capital	15,000
Sanders, capital	31,000
Trapp, capital	45,000
	$100,000

Green retires from the partnership. By mutual agreement, the assets are to be adjusted to their fair value of $130,000 at April 30, 19X5. Sanders and Trapp agree that the partnership will pay Green $37,000 cash for his partnership interest, exclusive of his loan, which is to be paid in full. No goodwill is to be recorded.

Required:
(1) Prepare the entry to record the revaluation of assets to their fair value.
(2) Prepare the entry to record Green's retirement.
(3) What is the implicit goodwill?

(AICPA adapted)

Problem 20–3
Business combination: Each partnership has undervalued tangible assets and goodwill

The partnership of A, B, C, and D has agreed to combine with the partnership of X and Y. The individual capital account and profit and loss sharing percentage of each partner are shown below:

	Capital Accounts	Profit and Loss Sharing Percentages	
		Now	Proposed
A	$ 50,000	40	28
B	35,000	30	21
C	40,000	20	14
D	25,000	10	7
	$150,000	100	70
X	$ 60,000	50	15
Y	40,000	50	15
	$100,000	100	30

The partnership of A, B, C, and D has undervalued tangible assets of $20,000, and the partnership of X and Y has undervalued tangible assets of $8,000. All the partners agree that (1) the partnership of A, B, C, and D possesses goodwill of $30,000, and (2) the partnership of X and Y possesses goodwill of $10,000. (Assume that the combined businesses will continue to use the general ledger of A, B, C, and D.)

Required:

(1) Prepare the entries required to reflect the combination, assuming tangible assets are to be revalued and goodwill is to be recorded.

(2) Prepare the entries required to reflect the combination, assuming the bonus method is to be used with respect to the undervalued tangible assets and the goodwill.

Problem 20–4
Admission of new partners; withdrawal of old partner; and division of profits

You have been engaged to prepare the June 30, 19X2 financial statements for the partnership of Grimm, Storey, and Teller. You have obtained the following information from the partnership agreement, as amended, and from the accounting records.

(1) The partnership was formed originally by Grimm and Kwitter on July 1, 19X1. At that date:

    a. Kwitter contributed $400,000 cash.

    b. Grimm contributed land, a building, and equipment with fair market values of $110,000, $520,000, and $185,000, respectively. The land and buildings were subject to a mortgage securing an 8% per annum note (interest rate of similar notes at July 1, 19X1). The note is due in quarterly payments of $5,000 plus interest on January 1, April 1, July 1, and October 1 of each year. Grimm made the July 1, 19X1, principal and interest payment personally. The partnership then assumed the obligation for the $300,000 balance.

    c. The agreement further provided that Grimm had contributed a certain intangible benefit to the partnership because of her many years of business activity in the area serviced by the new partnership. The assigned value of this intangible asset plus the net tangible assets she contributed gave Grimm a 60% initial capital interest in the partnership.

    d. Grimm was designated the only active partner at an annual salary of $24,000 plus an annual bonus of 4% of net income after deducting her salary but before deducting interest on partners' capital investments (see below). Both the salary and the bonus are to be recorded as operating expenses of the partnership.

    e. Each partner is to receive a 6% return on average capital investment; such interest is to be an expense of the partnership.

    f. All remaining profits or losses are to be shared equally.

(2) On October 1, 19X1, Kwitter sold his partnership interest and rights as of July 1, 19X1, to Teller for $370,000. Grimm agreed to accept Teller as a partner if he would contribute sufficient cash to meet the October 1, 19X1, principal and interest payment on the mortgage note. Teller made the payment from personal funds.

(3) On January 1, 19X2, Grimm and Teller admitted a new partner, Storey. Storey

invested $150,000 cash for a 10% capital interest based on the initial investments (tangible and intangible) at July 1, 19X1, of Grimm and Kwitter plus Storey's capital contribution of $150,000. At January 1, 19X2, the book values of the partnership's assets and liabilities approximated their fair market values. Storey contributed no intangible benefit to the partnership.

Similar to the other partners, Storey is to receive a 6% return on his average capital investment. His investment also entitled him to 20% of the partnership's profits or losses as defined above. For the year ended June 30, 19X2, however, Storey would receive one-half his pro rata share of the profits or losses.

(4) The accounting records show that on February 1, 19X2, the Other Miscellaneous Expenses account had been charged $3,600 for hospital expenses incurred by Grimm's eight-year-old daughter.

(5) All salary payments to Grimm have been charged to her drawing account. On June 1, 19X2, Teller made a $33,000 withdrawal. These are the only transactions recorded in the partners' drawing accounts.

(6) Presented below is a trial balance, which summarizes the partnership's general ledger balances at June 30, 19X2. The general ledger has not been closed.

	Debit	Credit
Current assets	$ 307,100	
Fixed assets	1,285,800	
Current liabilities		$ 157,000
8% mortgage note payable		290,000
Grimm, capital		515,000
Storey, capital		150,000
Teller, capital		400,000
Grimm, drawing	24,000	
Storey, drawing	-0-	
Teller, drawing	33,000	
Sales		872,600
Cost of sales	695,000	
Administrative expenses	16,900	
Other miscellaneous expenses	11,100	
Interest expense	11,700	
Totals	$2,384,600	$2,384,600

Required:

Prepare a worksheet to adjust the net income (loss) and partners' capital accounts for the year ended June 30, 19X2, and to close the net income (loss) to the partners' capital accounts at June 30, 19X2. Supporting schedules should be in good form. Amortization of goodwill, if any, is to be over a 10-year period. (Ignore all tax considerations.) Use the following column headings and begin with balances per books as shown:

	Net Income	Partner's Capital			Other Accounts	
	(Loss)	Grimm	Storey	Teller	Amount	
Description	(Dr.) Cr.	(Dr.) Cr.	(Dr.) Cr.	(Dr.) Cr.	Dr. (Cr.)	Name
Book balances at June 30, 19X2 . . .	$137,900	$515,000	$150,000	$400,000		

(AICPA adapted)

Problem 20–5
Death of a partner

The partnership agreement of Angel, Bird, Crow, Dove, and Winger contained a buy and sell agreement, among numerous other provisions, which would be operative on the death of any partner. Some provisions of the buy and sell agreement were as follows:

Article V. Buy and Sell Agreement

1. Purposes of the buy and sell agreement.

(a) The partners mutually desire that the business be continued by the survivors without interruption or liquidation on the death of one of the partners.
(b) The partners also mutually desire that the deceased partner's estate receive the full value of the deceased partner's interest in the partnership and that the estate share in the earnings of the partnership until the deceased partner's interest is fully purchased by the surviving partners.

2. Purchase and sale of deceased partner's interest.

(a) On the death of the partner first to die, the partnership shall continue to operate without dissolution.
(b) On the death of the partner, the survivors shall purchase and the executor or administrator of the deceased partner's estate shall sell to the surviving partners the deceased partner's interest in the partnership for the price and on the terms and conditions hereinafter set forth.
(c) The deceased partner's estate shall retain the deceased partner's interest until the amount specified in the next paragraph shall be paid in full by the surviving partners.
(d) The parties agree that the purchase price for the partnership interest shall be an amount equal to the deceased partner's capital account at the date of death. Said amount shall be paid to the legal representative of decedent as follows:
  (i) The first installment of 30% of said capital account shall be paid within 60 days from the date of death of the partner or within 30 days from the date on which the personal representative of the decedent becomes qualified by law, whichever date is later, and
  (ii) The balance shall be due in four equal installments, which shall be due and payable annually on the anniversary date of said death.

3. Deceased partner's estate's share of the earnings.

(a) The partners mutually desire that the deceased partner's estate shall be guaranteed a share in partnership earnings over the period said estate retains an interest in the partnership. Said estate shall not be deemed to have an interest in the partnership after the final installment for the deceased partner's capital account is paid even though a portion of the guaranteed payments specified below may be unpaid and may be due and owing.
(b) The deceased partner's estate's guaranteed share of partnership earnings shall be determined from two items and shall be paid at different times as follows:
  (i) First, interest shall be paid on the unpaid balance of the deceased partner's

capital account at the same date the installment on the purchase price is paid. The amount to be paid shall be an amount equal to accrued interest at the rate of 6% per annum on the unpaid balance of the purchase price for the deceased partner's capital account.

(ii) Second, the parties agree that the balance of the guaranteed payment from partnership earnings shall be an amount equal to 25% of the deceased partner's share of the aggregate gross receipts of the partnership for the full 36 months preceding the month of the partner's death. Said amount shall be payable in 48 equal monthly installments without interest, and the first payment shall be made within 60 days following the death of the partner or within 30 days from the date on which the personal representative of deceased becomes qualified, whichever date is later; provided, however, that the payments so made under this provision during any 12-month period shall not exceed the highest annual salary on a calendar year basis received by the partner for the three calendar years immediately preceding the date of his or her death. In the event that said payment would exceed said salary, then an amount per month shall be paid that does not so exceed said highest monthly salary, and the term over which payments shall be paid to the beneficiary shall be lengthened beyond the said 48 months to complete said payment.

Angel and Winger were both killed in an automobile accident on January 10, 19X6. The surviving partners notified the executors of both estates that the first payment due under the buy and sell agreement would be paid on March 10, 19X6, and that subsequent payments would be paid on the tenth day of each month as due.

The following information was determined from the partnership's records:

Partner	Profit and Loss Sharing Ratio	Capital Account on January 10, 19X6	Annual Salaries to Partners by Years		
			19X3	19X4	19X5
Angel	30	$25,140	$16,500	$17,000	$17,400
Bird	25	21,970	15,000	15,750	16,500
Crow	20	4,780	12,000	13,000	14,000
Dove	15	5,860	9,600	10,800	12,000
Winger	10	2,540	8,400	9,600	10,800

The partnership's gross receipts for the three prior years were:

19X3	$296,470
19X4	325,310
19X5	363,220

Required:
Prepare a schedule of the amounts paid to the Winger and Angel estates in March 19X6, December 19X6, and January 19X7. The schedule should identify the amounts attributable to earnings, and to interest in the guaranteed payments and to capital. Supporting computation should be in good form.

(AICPA adapted)

Problem 20–6
Calculation of tax basis of new partner and adjustment
to old partners' tax bases: Admission by capital contribution
into the partnership

Chipp and Putt are in partnership, share profits and losses in the ratio 3:2, respectively, and have capital balances of $60,000 and $30,000, respectively. They admit Ball into the partnership for a cash contribution of $30,000, of which $10,000 is given to the old partners as a bonus. The new profit and loss sharing percentages are Chipp, 45%; Putt, 30%; and Ball, 25%. The partnership has $12,000 of liabilities at Ball's admission. Ball became jointly responsible for these liabilities at his admission pursuant to a provision in the new partnership agreement.

Required:
(1) Calculate the tax basis of Ball's interest in the partnership.
(2) Calculate the required adjustment to the basis of each of the old partners as a result of Ball's admission.
(3) Prepare the entry required on the partnership's books.

Problem 20–7
Calculation of tax basis of new partner and determination
of old partner's proceeds and taxable gain:
Admission by purchase of existing partner's interest

Dealle and Downes are in partnership, share profits and losses equally, and have capital balances of $60,000 and $40,000, respectively. Trumpey purchases all of Downes' interest for $50,000 and agrees to be jointly responsible for all existing partnership liabilities, which total $14,000.

Required:
(1) Calculate the tax basis of Trumpey's interest in the partnership.
(2) Calculate the adjustment, if any, to Dealle's tax basis as a result of Trumpey's purchase of Downes' interest.
(3) Assuming Downes' tax basis was $47,000 when he sold his interest, determine the proceeds he received on the sale of his interest and his taxable gain, if any.
(4) Prepare the entry required on the partnership's books.

21 Partnerships: Liquidations

OVERVIEW OF PARTNERSHIP LIQUIDATIONS

The termination of a partnership's business activities is known as **liquidation.**
A partnership may be liquidated for many reasons—for example, the original
agreed-upon term of existence has expired, the business is not as successful
as expected, or the partnership is in serious financial difficulty. Although
a partnership in serious financial difficulty may attempt rehabilitation either
by filing under Chapter 11 of the Bankruptcy Reform Act of 1978 or through
a troubled debt restructuring outside of bankruptcy court, such courses of
action for partnerships do not entail any significant special problems not
already discussed for corporations. Consequently, we restrict our discussion
in this chapter to the process of liquidation.

   The liquidation process for partnerships is in several respects identical
to the liquidation process for corporations. Over a period of time, the
noncash assets of the business are converted into cash (the realization
process), creditors are paid to the extent possible, and remaining funds,
if any, are distributed to the owners (partners). Partnership liquidations,
however, are different from corporate liquidations in the following respects:

(1) Because partners have unlimited liability, any partner may be called
    upon to contribute additional funds to the partnership if partnership
    assets are insufficient to satisfy creditors' claims.
(2) To the extent that a partner does not make good a deficit balance in
    his or her capital account, the remaining partners must absorb such
    deficit balance. Such absorption of a partner's deficit balance gives
    the absorbing partners legal recourse against such partner.

The special problems created by these two situations are discussed
throughout this chapter.

   Liquidations may be categorized broadly as **lump-sum liquidations**
and **installment liquidations.**

(1) Lump-sum liquidations. In lump-sum liquidations, no distributions are
    made to the partners until the realization process is completed, when
    the full amount of the realization gain or loss is known.
(2) Installment liquidations. In installment liquidations, distributions are
    made to some or all of the partners as cash becomes available. Thus,
    cash distributions are made to partners before the full amount of the
    realization gain or loss is known.

Within each category, a variety of situations may arise concerning the ability
of the partnership and the individual partners to satisfy the claims of partnership creditors. Before discussing each situation in detail, we discuss
some general aspects of liquidations.

Procedures for minimizing inequities among partners

Sharing of gains and losses. Gains and losses incurred on the re-alization of assets may be allocated among the partners in the manner they have agreed to in the partnership agreement. If the partnership agreement is silent with respect to the sharing of gains and losses during liquidation, then the Uniform Partnership Act (UPA) treats such gains and losses in the same way as preliquidation profits and losses—that is, gains and losses are allocated in accordance with the profit and loss sharing formula. Most partnerships follow the profit and loss sharing formula in distributing gains and losses incurred during liquidation. This is the most equitable manner for the following reasons:

(1) The cumulative profit or loss of a partnership during its existence is the difference between total capital contributions and total capital with-drawals. Accordingly, the cumulative profit or loss of a partnership during its existence should include start-up periods, normal operating periods, and wind-down periods.
(2) Certain gains and losses recognized during the liquidation process actually may have occurred during normal operating periods. This would be the case when (a) land or buildings have been held for several years and appreciated in value prior to the liquidation, and (b) certain accounts receivable should have been written off as uncollectible before liquidation. The use of a method other than the profit and loss sharing formula would result in inequities among the partners.

If a partner's capital account is not sufficient to absorb his or her share of the losses incurred in liquidation, Section 18 of the UPA provides that "each partner . . . must contribute towards the losses . . . sustained by the partnership according to his share in the profits." In other words, a partner must contribute additional funds to the partnership to eliminate any deficit balance in his or her capital account created by losses incurred through normal operations or in the liquidation process. If such a partner does not have the personal resources to eliminate this deficit, the remaining partners must absorb the capital deficit, resulting in inequities to them. A basic procedure that may minimize such potential inequities is discussed in the next section.

Advance planning when the partnership is formed. Although every partnership commences business under the going concern concept, it would be unrealistic if the partners did not acknowledge the possibility that the partnership may have to be liquidated at some time. It is in the interest of each partner, therefore, to take prudent steps to minimize the possibility of inequities occurring in liquidation. Inequities among partners may arise during liquidation if a deficit balance is created in a partner's capital account (as a result of losses incurred during the conversion of noncash assets into cash), and that partner cannot contribute capital to eliminate the deficit. The partners who do not have deficit balances in their capital accounts must absorb the deficit balance of the partner who does. In other words, they must absorb losses greater than their agreed-upon profit and loss sharing percentage.

Because a partnership has no control over its partners' personal affairs, it has no assurance that its partners will have sufficient personal funds to contribute if a deficit balance is created during liquidation. Accordingly, the partnership should be operated in a manner that minimizes the possibility of a deficit balance occurring. If the partnership agreement specifies that all partners' capital balances are to be maintained in the profit and loss sharing ratio, then a partnership may incur losses on the conversion of noncash assets into cash up to the total equity of the partnership, without creating a deficit balance in any partner's capital account. This safeguard is so important that many partnerships (including most of the international accounting partnerships) require capital accounts to be maintained in the profit and loss sharing ratio. Furthermore, as cash is available for distribution to the partners (a situation that occurs only if losses during liquidation are less than the total partnership equity), such cash may be distributed to the partners in the profit and loss sharing ratio with complete assurance that no inequities will result. In such situations, the liquidation process is quite simple. Unfortunately, not all partnerships use such a provision. Partners in such partnerships needlessly expose themselves to potential inequities in the event of liquidation, making the liquidation process much more complex.

Although the potential for inequities occurring during liquidation cannot be completely eliminated, a partnership that requires capital accounts to be maintained in the profit and loss sharing ratio has taken a big step toward minimizing any potential inequities that may arise.

Rule of setoff. When a partnership has a loan outstanding **to a partner,** the partnership receivable should be subtracted, or set off, from the partner's capital account. It would not be equitable to assume the receivable is uncollectible (even though the partner may not have sufficient personal assets to repay the loan) and thereby allocate the loss among all the partners. The partner's capital account less the receivable represents the partner's true capital investment.

When a partner has a loan outstanding **to the partnership,** the loan does not rank on an equal level with other partnership liabilities. Section 40 of the UPA states that the order of payment to creditors and partners during liquidation is as follows:

    (I) Those owing to creditors other than partners.
    (II) Those owing to partners other than for capital and profits [loans].
    (III) Those owing to partners in respect of capital.
    (IV) Those owing to partners in respect of profit.

When profits and losses are closed to the partners' capital accounts at each year-end, the last two categories may be considered one amount, which is the balance in each partner's capital account. Although this section of the UPA implies that partners' loans are paid off before any cash distributions are made to partners in liquidation of their capital balances, a strict application of this order of payment could result in inequities among the partners. For example, a partner with a loan to a partnership could be repaid the loan, a deficit balance could be created in his or her capital account at a later date because of losses on the realization of assets, and the partner might not be able to make a capital contribution to eliminate that deficit balance. The other partners would have to absorb such partner's deficit balance and thus incur a greater portion of the losses during liquidation than they originally agreed to. The legal doctrine of **setoff**—whereby a deficit balance in a partner's capital account may be set off against any balance existing in his or her loan account—has been incorporated into accountants' procedures for determining which partners should receive cash as it becomes available. These procedures effectively treat the loan as an additional capital investment. The mechanical procedures, which are different in lump-sum liquidations and installment liquidations, are discussed and illustrated later in the chapter.

The statement of realization and liquidation

Because normal operations do not take place during the liquidation period, the traditional financial statements are not appropriate. Instead, the partners prefer to have a statement that provides information on the following:

(1) Gains and losses on the realization of assets, including the impact of such gains and losses on the partners' capital accounts.
(2) Payments that have been made to creditors and partners.
(3) The noncash assets still to be converted into cash.

Accordingly, accountants have devised a statement called the **statement of realization and liquidation** to provide this information. The statement is entirely historical; it reflects only the actual transactions that have occurred during the liquidation period up to the date of the statement. If the liquidation process takes place over several months, the statement is updated periodically as noncash assets are converted into cash and payments are made to creditors, partners, or both. Other than the allocation of realization gains and losses among the partners and the exercising of the right of setoff, the statement is essentially a summary of cash inflows and outflows.

Liquidation expenses

Certain costs incurred during the liquidation process should be treated as a reduction of the proceeds from the sale of noncash assets—for example, costs to complete inventory, sales commissions and shipping costs related to the disposal of inventory, escrow and title transfer fees associated with the sale of real property, and costs of removing equipment. Other liquidation costs should be treated as expenses. It is preferable to make a reasonable estimate of these expenses at the beginning of the liquidation process and record an estimated liability in the general ledger at that time, adjusting the liability as necessary during the liquidation process. Recording the estimated liability at the inception of the liquidation process minimizes the possibility of making excess cash distributions to partners. Any cash available for distribution to partners should be set aside in an amount equal to the remaining estimated liability so that it is not distributed to partners.

LUMP-SUM LIQUIDATIONS

In a lump-sum liquidation, all noncash assets are converted to cash and outside creditors are paid in full before cash is distributed to the partners. Thus, the full amount of the gain or loss on realization of assets is known before the partners receive any cash distributions. Lump-sum liquidations are rare or nonexistent, because partners liquidate their loan and capital accounts as cash becomes available for distribution. Usually, partners have personal needs for cash, and there is no sound business reason for waiting until the very last asset is converted to cash before distributing any cash to the partners. We illustrate several lump-sum liquidations for instructional purposes only.

Partnership is solvent and all partners are personally solvent

In the first three illustrations in this section, (1) the partnership is solvent (the fair value of partnership assets is sufficient to satisfy outside creditors' claims), and (2) all partners who must make capital contributions have either sufficient loans to the partnership (for purposes of exercising the right of setoff) or are personally solvent, so that the capital deficit from losses incurred during the realization process is eliminated by contributions.

Illustration:
Loss on realization does not create a deficit balance in any partner's capital account

To illustrate how the statement of realization and liquidation is prepared in a lump-sum liquidation, assume partners A and B share profits and losses in the ratio 3:2, respectively, and the balance sheet of the partnership at the beginning of the liquidation process is as follows:

A AND B PARTNERSHIP
Balance Sheet
May 31, 19X5

Cash	$ 5,000	Liabilities	$20,000
Noncash assets.............	70,000	Loan, partner B.............	3,000
		Capital:	
		partner A.................	37,000
		partner B.................	15,000
	$75,000		$75,000

Also, assume during June 19X5 that (1) the noncash assets of $70,000 are converted into $40,000 cash, resulting in a $30,000 loss, which is distributed 60% to partner A ($18,000) and 40% to partner B ($12,000); (2) outside creditors are paid in full; and (3) the remaining cash is distributed to the partners. The statement of realization and liquidation covering the entire liquidation period would be prepared as in Illustration 21-1.

In reviewing Illustration 21-1, the following points should be understood:

(1) The format of the statement does not combine the loan account of

Illustration 21-1

	A AND B PARTNERSHIP					
	Statement of Realization and Liquidation					
	June 19X5					

	Assets		Outside	Loan	Partners' Capital	
	Cash	Noncash	Liabilities	B	A(60%)[a]	B(40%)[a]
Preliquidation balances.	$ 5,000	$70,000	$20,000	$ 3,000	$37,000	$15,000
Realization of assets and						
allocation of loss.....	40,000	(70,000)			(18,000)	(12,000)
Subtotal	$45,000	$ –0–	$20,000	$ 3,000	$19,000	$ 3,000
Cash distributions:						
Outside creditors.....	(20,000)		(20,000)			
Partner's loan........	(3,000)			(3,000)		
Partners' capital......	(22,000)				(19,000)	(3,000)
Postliquidation balances	$ –0–		$ –0–	$ –0–	$ –0–	$ –0–

[a] Denotes profit and loss sharing percentage.

partner B with his capital account. The loan is a bona fide loan and not a capital investment.

(2) Cash distributions were made in accordance with the priority set forth in Section 40 of the UPA.

(3) Aside from the allocation of the loss on the realization of the noncash assets, the statement essentially presents the cash inflows and outflows that occurred during the liquidation period.

(4) We assume the liquidation process was completed within one month. Usually, it takes several months, requiring the statement to be updated periodically as noncash assets are converted into cash and cash distributions are made.

Illustration:
Loss on realization creates a deficit balance in one partner's capital account—Right of setoff exercised

Assume the information in the preceding illustration, except that partner B's loan account is $10,000 instead of $3,000 and his capital account is $8,000 instead of $15,000. The statement of realization and liquidation would be prepared as shown in Illustration 21-2.

In reviewing Illustration 21-2, the following points should be understood:

(1) The fact that partners' loans are assigned a higher priority for repayment than partnership capital accounts under Section 40 of the UPA is not significant if a partner with a loan account also has a deficit balance in his or her capital account—that is, the full amount of the loan is not paid before payments are made to partners in liquidation of their capital accounts.

(2) The $4,000 deficit in partner B's capital account after the realization loss of $30,000 on the noncash assets means that partner B must

Illustration 21-2

A AND B PARTNERSHIP					
Statement of Realization and Liquidation					
June 19X5					

	Assets		Outside	Loan	Partners' Capital	
	Cash	**Noncash**	**Liabilities**	**B**	**A(60%)**[a]	**B(40%)**[a]
Preliquidation balances.	$ 5,000	$70,000	$20,000	$10,000	$37,000	$ 8,000
Realization of assets and						
allocation of loss.....	40,000	(70,000)			(18,000)	(12,000)
Subtotal	$45,000	$ −0−	$20,000	$10,000	$19,000	$ (4,000)
Right of setoff exercised				(4,000)		4,000
Subtotal	$45,000		$20,000	$ 6,000	$19,000	$ −0−
Cash distributions:						
Outside creditors.....	(20,000)		(20,000)			
Partner's loan........	(6,000)			(6,000)		
Partners' capital......	(19,000)				(19,000)	
Postliquidation balances	$ −0−		$ −0−	$ −0−	$ −0−	

[a] Denotes profit and loss sharing percentage.

contribute $4,000 to the partnership, so that he can fully absorb his share of the loss on realization.

(3) Partner B did not contribute $4,000 to the partnership to eliminate his capital account deficit, because he could exercise the right of setoff whereby $4,000 was transferred from his loan account to his capital account.

(4) Each partner received the same amount of cash in Illustrations 21-1 and 21-2. For all practical purposes, partner B's loan account is the equivalent of an additional capital investment for liquidation purposes.

Illustration:
Loss on realization creates a deficit balance
in one partner's capital account—Right of setoff exercised
and additional capital contribution is required and made

Assume the information in the preceding illustration, except that the loss on the realization of the noncash assets is $50,000 instead of $30,000. This additional $20,000 loss will result in partner B having a capital deficit, which is not completely eliminated on his exercising the right of setoff. Assume that partner B is personally solvent and makes the required capital contribution to eliminate the remainder of his capital deficit. The statement of realization and liquidation would be prepared as shown in Illustration 21-3.

Partnership is solvent and at least one partner
is personally insolvent

In the next two illustrations, at least one partner is personally insolvent and unable to make a capital contribution to eliminate his or her capital deficit.

Illustration 21-3

	Assets		Outside	Loan	Partners' Capital	
	Cash	Noncash	Liabilities	B	A(60%)[a]	B(40%)[a]
Preliquidation balances.	$ 5,000	$70,000	$20,000	$10,000	$37,000	$ 8,000
Realization of assets and						
allocation of loss.....	20,000	(70,000)			(30,000)	(20,000)
Subtotal	$25,000	$ —0—	$20,000	$10,000	$ 7,000	$(12,000)
Right of setoff exercised				(10,000)		10,000
Subtotal	$25,000		$20,000	$ —0—	$ 7,000	$ (2,000)
Cash contribution by B..	2,000					2,000
Subtotal	$27,000		$20,000		$ 7,000	$ —0—
Cash distributions:						
Outside creditors.....	(20,000)		(20,000)			
Partner's capital......	(7,000)				(7,000)	
Postliquidation balances	$ —0—		$ —0—		$ —0—	

A AND B PARTNERSHIP
Statement of Realization and Liquidation
June 19X5

[a] Denotes profit and loss sharing percentage.

In such circumstances, the remaining partners must absorb the capital deficit of the insolvent partner in their respective profit and loss sharing ratio. If this, in turn, causes a capital deficit for an absorbing partner, then that partner must make a capital contribution to eliminate the deficit. If such partner also is personally insolvent, then his or her capital deficit must be absorbed by the remaining partners, using their respective profit and loss sharing ratio.

The absorption of a partner's deficit capital balance by other partners is a violation of the UPA, in that the partner who cannot eliminate his or her deficit capital balance has broken the terms of the partnership agreement. The other partners have legal recourse against the personal assets of the defaulting partner. This situation raises the question of how such claims against the personal assets of the defaulting partner are treated in relation to claims of personal creditors of the defaulting partner. In the next section of the chapter, we answer this question and discuss situations in which the **partnership is insolvent** and at least one partner is personally insolvent.

Illustration:
Loss on realization creates a deficit balance
in one partner's capital account—Right of setoff exercised
and additional capital contribution is required but not made

Assume partners A, B, C, and D share profits in the ratio 4:2:2:2, respectively. The partnership's balance sheet at the beginning of the liquidation process is as follows.

A, B, C, and D PARTNERSHIP
Balance Sheet
June 30, 19X5

Cash	$ 10,000	Liabilities		$157,000
Noncash assets............	290,000	Loan:		
		partner B................		10,000
		partner C		5,000
		partner D		2,000
		Capital:		
		partner A................		70,000
		partner B................		30,000
		partner C		20,000
		partner D		6,000
	$300,000			$300,000

Assume also that during July 19X5, the noncash assets realize $210,000 cash, resulting in a realization loss of $80,000, which is shared among the partners (using the profit and loss sharing ratio 4:2:2:2) as follows: A, $32,000; B, $16,000; C, $16,000; and D, $16,000. The realization loss creates a deficit in D's capital account, which is not completely eliminated through his exercising the right of setoff. D must make an additional capital contribution of $8,000, but is unable to do so. As a result, his $8,000 capital deficit must be allocated to partners A, B, and C in their profit and loss sharing ratio of 4:2:2, respectively. Assuming all cash was distributed in July 19X5, the statement of realization and liquidation would be prepared as shown in Illustration 21-4.

In reviewing Illustration 21-4, the following points should be understood:

(1) Because partner D was unable to eliminate the deficit balance in his capital account, the remaining partners had to bear a greater percentage of the realization loss than their individual profit and loss sharing percentages. For example, partner A suffered a total loss of $36,000 ($32,000 + $4,000). This represents 45% of the $80,000 total realization loss, which is greater than her stipulated profit and loss sharing percentage of 40%. Partners A, B, and C needlessly exposed themselves to this additional $8,000 loss by not employing the fundamental safeguard provision of maintaining capital accounts in the profit and loss sharing ratio.

(2) The illustration assumes that partner D was unable to make any of the required contribution. If a partial contribution had been made, then a smaller deficit balance would have had to be absorbed by the remaining partners.

(3) A partner with a deficit balance may indicate that he is unable to eliminate completely the deficit balance when it is created but that he might be able to make a capital contribution at a later date (which may or may not be specified). If partner D had indicated this, the available $220,000 cash could have been distributed to the outside creditors and the remaining partners. The partnership books then could be kept open until partner D makes a capital contribution or it subsequently is determined that he cannot make a payment after all. This procedure could result in a lengthy delay in completing the partnership liquidation.

Illustration 21-4

A, B, C, and D PARTNERSHIP
Statement of Realization and Liquidation
July, 19X5

	Assets		Outside Liabilities	Partners' Loans			Partners' Capital			
	Cash	Noncash		B	C	D	A(40%)[a]	B(20%)[a]	C(20%)[a]	D(20%)[a]
Preliquidation balances	$ 10,000	$290,000	$157,000	$10,000	$5,000	$2,000	$70,000	$30,000	$20,000	$ 6,000
Realization of assets and allocation of loss.........	210,000	(290,000)					(32,000)	(16,000)	(16,000)	(16,000)
Subtotal	$220,000	$ -0-	$157,000	$10,000	$5,000	$2,000	$38,000	$14,000	$ 4,000	$(10,000)
Right of setoff exercised...						(2,000)				2,000
Subtotal	$220,000		$157,000	$10,000	$5,000	$ -0-	$38,000	$14,000	$ 4,000	$ (8,000)
Absorption of D's capital deficit							(4,000)	(2,000)	(2,000)	8,000
Subtotal	$220,000		$157,000	$10,000	$5,000		$34,000	$12,000	$ 2,000	$ -0-
Cash distributions:										
Outside creditors	(157,000)		(157,000)							
Partners' loans	(15,000)			(10,000)	(5,000)					
Partners' capital	(48,000)						(34,000)	(12,000)	(2,000)	
Postliquidation balances	$ -0-		$ -0-	$ -0-	$ -0-		$ -0-	$ -0-	$ -0-	

[a] Denotes profit and loss sharing percentage.

No sound reason exists for keeping the partnership books open indefinitely, thereby delaying the completion of the liquidation process, merely because of partner D's uncertain financial situation. When partner D's capital account deficit was created (and not completely eliminated through exercising the right of setoff), he became liable for his deficit to the other partners. Accordingly, if partner D subsequently makes a capital contribution, he makes the payment directly to the other partners. Consequently, in situations involving lump-sum liquidations in which a partner cannot immediately eliminate his or her capital deficit, the accountant should complete the liquidation process by transferring the capital deficit to the capital accounts of the remaining partners (using their respective profit and loss sharing ratios). The partnership books may then be closed, and the liquidation process can be completed.

Illustration:
Loss on realization creates a deficit balance
in one partner's capital account—Absorption by other partners
creates deficit balance in another partner's capital account

Assume the information in the preceding illustration, except that the noncash assets are sold for only $170,000. This results in a realization loss of $120,000 instead of $80,000. The $120,000 realization loss is allocated among the partners (using the profit and loss sharing ratio 4:2:2:2) as follows: A, $48,000; B, $24,000; C, $24,000; and D, $24,000. In addition to the previously described consequences to partner D, the greater loss results in partner C being unable to absorb fully his share of partner D's deficit balance. Thus, partner C has a deficit balance that he cannot eliminate through setoff or contribution. His capital deficit, in turn, must be allocated to partners A and B in their respective profit and loss sharing ratio of 4:2. (Partners A and B have legal recourse against the personal assets of partners C and D—such recourse is discussed in the next section of this chapter.) Assuming all cash was distributed in July 19X5, the statement of realization and liquidation would be prepared as shown in Illustration 21-5.

Partnership is insolvent and at least one partner
is personally solvent

In the next two illustrations, the partnership is insolvent—that is, the loss on the realization of noncash assets is greater than the total of the partners' capital (including their loan accounts). Because unlimited liability is a feature of the partnership form of organization, creditors may seek payment from any or all of the partners as individuals.

Illustration:
Loss on realization creates a deficit balance in certain partners'
capital accounts—All partners are personally solvent

In this illustration, all the partners are personally solvent, and the partners with deficit capital balances contribute funds to the partnership to eliminate

Illustration 21-5

A, B, C, and D PARTNERSHIP
Statement of Realization and Liquidation
July 19X5

	Assets		Outside Liabilities	Partners' Loans			Partners' Capital			
	Cash	Noncash		B	C	D	A(40%)[a]	B(20%)[a]	C(20%)[a]	D(20%)[a]
Preliquidation balances....	$ 10,000	$290,000	$157,000	$10,000	$5,000	$2,000	$70,000	$30,000	$20,000	$ 6,000
Realization of assets and allocation of loss......	170,000	(290,000)					(48,000)	(24,000)	(24,000)	(24,000)
Subtotal............	$180,000	$ –0–	$157,000	$10,000	$5,000	$2,000	$22,000	$ 6,000	$(4,000)	$(18,000)
Right of setoff exercised...					(4,000)	(2,000)			4,000	2,000
Subtotal............	$180,000		$157,000	$10,000	$1,000	$ –0–	$22,000	$ 6,000	$(4,000)	$(16,000)
Absorption of D's capital deficit							(8,000)	(4,000)	(4,000)	16,000
Subtotal............	$180,000		$157,000	$10,000	$1,000		$14,000	$ 2,000	$(4,000)	$ –0–
Right of setoff exercised...					(1,000)				1,000	
Subtotal............	$180,000		$157,000	$10,000	$ –0–		$14,000	$ 2,000	$(3,000)	
Absorption of C's capital deficit							(2,000)	(1,000)	3,000	
Subtotal............	$180,000		$157,000	$10,000			$12,000	$ 1,000	$ –0–	
Cash distributions:										
Outside creditors........	(157,000)		(157,000)							
Partner's loan..........	(10,000)			(10,000)						
Partners' capital.........	(13,000)						(12,000)	(1,000)		
Postliquidation balances	$ –0–		$ –0–	$ –0–			$ –0–	$ –0–		

[a] Denotes profit and loss sharing percentage.

their capital deficits, enabling creditors to be paid in full by the partnership. Using the same preliquidation balances that are given for Illustration 21-5, assume the noncash assets of $290,000 are sold for $130,000, resulting in a realization loss of $160,000. The realization loss is shared among the partners (using the profit and loss sharing ratio 4:2:2:2) as follows: A, $64,000; B, $32,000; C, $32,000; and D, $32,000. After exercising the right of setoff, partner A has a capital balance of $6,000; partner B has a loan balance of $8,000; and partners C and D have capital deficits of $7,000 and $24,000, respectively. At this point, the available $140,000 cash may be distributed to outside creditors. Assuming partners C and D contribute funds to the partnership to eliminate their capital deficits, the $31,000 cash then may be distributed to outside creditors and partners A and B. The statement of realization and liquidation would be prepared as shown in Illustration 21-6.

In Illustration 21-6, we assumed that partners C and D made additional cash contributions to the partnership, thereby eliminating their capital deficits. Thus, the partnership could make the remaining $17,000 payment to the outside creditors. Occasionally, the creditors take legal action against some or all of the partners as individuals when creditors do not receive full satisfaction from the partnership. As a result, a partner personally may make payments to partnership creditors. Such payments should be reflected in the general ledger and on the statement of realization and liquidation as a reduction of partnership liabilities and an additional capital contribution by that partner. A partner's personal payments to creditors are in substance the equivalent of a cash contribution to the partnership that the partnership then distributes to the creditors.

Illustration:
Loss on realization creates a deficit balance in certain partners' capital accounts—Certain partners are personally insolvent

Before illustrating in detail a situation in which a partnership is insolvent and certain of its partners are personally insolvent, we discuss the following legal questions raised in such circumstances:

(1) If partnership creditors initiate legal proceedings against a partner who is personally insolvent, what would be the legal status (priority of payment) of such claims in relation to the claims of that partner's personal creditors?

(2) If a partner is personally insolvent and unable to eliminate the deficit balance in his or her capital account, thereby causing other partners to absorb that deficit balance (which is a breach of the partnership agreement entitling the wronged partners to legal recourse against the defaulting partner), what is the legal status of such claims in relation to the claims of that partner's personal creditors?

(3) If a partner is personally insolvent, to what extent may such partner's personal creditors obtain payments from the partnership?

The answers to the first two questions are found in Section 40(i) of the UPA, which states the following.

Illustration 21-6

A, B, C, and D PARTNERSHIP
Statement of Realization and Liquidation
July 19X5

	Assets		Outside	Partners' Loans			Partners' Capital			
	Cash	Noncash	Liabilities	B	C	D	A(40%)[a]	B(20%)[a]	C(20%)[a]	D(20%)[a]
Preliquidation balances......	$ 10,000	$290,000	$157,000	$10,000	$5,000	$2,000	$70,000	$30,000	$ 20,000	$ 6,000
Realization of assets and allocation of loss	130,000	(290,000)					(64,000)	(32,000)	(32,000)	(32,000)
Subtotal.............	$140,000	$ -0-	$157,000	$10,000	$5,000	$2,000	$ 6,000	$ (2,000)	$(12,000)	$(26,000)
Exercise right of setoff				(2,000)	(5,000)	(2,000)		2,000	5,000	2,000
Subtotal.............	$140,000		$157,000	$ 8,000	$ -0-	$ -0-	$ 6,000	$ -0-	$ (7,000)	$(24,000)
Distribution to outside creditors.............	(140,000)		(140,000)							
Subtotal.............	$ -0-		$ 17,000	$ 8,000			$ 6,000		$ (7,000)	$(24,000)
Contributions by C and D	31,000								7,000	24,000
Subtotal.............	$ 31,000		$ 17,000	$ 8,000			$ 6,000		$ -0-	$ -0-
Cash distributions:										
Outside creditors	(17,000)		(17,000)							
Partner's loan	(8,000)			(8,000)						
Partner's capital............	(6,000)						(6,000)			
Postliquidation balances.....	$ -0-		$ -0-	$ -0-			$ -0-			

[a] Denotes profit and loss sharing percentage.

Where a partner has become bankrupt or his estate is insolvent the claims against his separate property shall rank in the following order:
(I) Those owing to separate creditors,
(II) Those owing to partnership creditors,
(III) Those owing to partners by way of contribution.

The answer to the third question is found in Section 40(b) of the UPA, which specifies that partnership creditors have first claim on partnership assets. Consequently, these two sections of the UPA are consistent with the longstanding court procedure of **marshalling of assets,** which is summarized as follows: Partnership creditors have first priority as to partnership assets, and personal creditors of an insolvent partner have first priority as to the personal assets of such partner. Partnership creditors must exhaust partnership assets before they may receive any payments from an insolvent partner. Of course, the claims of personal creditors of an insolvent partner against the partnership are limited to the extent of the insolvent partner's credit balance in his or her capital account.

To illustrate how the marshalling of assets procedure is applied, assume the information in Illustration 21-6 with respect to partners' balances after (1) the realization loss of $160,000 is distributed; (2) the right of setoff is exercised; and (3) payment of $140,000 is made to outside creditors, leaving $17,000 owed to such creditors. At this point, the partners' accounts are as follows:

Partner	Loan Balance	Capital Balance
A		$ 6,000
B	$8,000	
C		(7,000)
D		(24,000)

Assume the personal status of each partner (exclusive of interest in or obligation to the partnership) is as follows:

Partner	Personal Assets	Personal Liabilities	Personal Net Worth (Deficit)
A	$50,000	$25,000	$25,000
B	4,000	15,000	(11,000)
C	16,000	6,000	10,000
D	20,000	33,000	(13,000)

(1) Partner D has a capital deficit and is personally insolvent. Thus, none of his personal assets is available for contribution to the partnership, because his personal creditors are entitled to all his personal assets. Consequently, his $24,000 capital deficit must be absorbed by partners A, B, and C in their respective profit and loss sharing ratio, 4:2:2. Partner A's share is $12,000; partner B's share is $6,000; and partner C's share is $6,000.

(2) Partner C had a $7,000 capital deficit, which increased to $13,000 as a result of absorbing his share of partner D's capital deficit. Partner C has a personal net worth of $10,000. Thus, he can contribute $10,000

to the partnership, leaving a $3,000 deficit, which must be absorbed by partners A and B in their respective profit and loss sharing ratio of 4:2. Partner A's share is $2,000 and Partner B's share is $1,000.

(3) Partner B had a loan balance of $8,000. However, his capital account was charged with $6,000 when partner D's capital deficit was written off and $1,000 when partner C's capital deficit was written off. Thus, $7,000 must be transferred from his loan account under the right of setoff to eliminate his capital deficit. This leaves $1,000 in his loan account, which, when distributed to him, is available to his personal creditors because he is personally insolvent.

(4) Because partner A has the largest personal net worth, let us assume that partnership creditors took legal action against her (as opposed to proceeding against partner C, who is the only other personally solvent partner from whom they could collect anything). The creditors collected the $17,000 owed them from partner A personally. Partner A had a capital balance of $6,000, which was reduced by $12,000 for her share of partner D's capital deficit and $2,000 for her share of partner C's capital deficit. This gives her a capital deficit of $8,000. Her $17,000 payment to the partnership creditors, however, is the equivalent of a capital contribution. Thus, her capital account deficit is eliminated, and she now has a positive capital balance of $9,000.

(5) This leaves the partnership with $10,000 cash, which is distributed to partner B ($1,000 in payment of his loan) and partner A ($9,000 in liquidation of her capital balance).

Illustration 21-7 summarizes the preceding sequence of events in a statement of realization and liquidation.

INSTALLMENT LIQUIDATIONS

In installment liquidations, the conversion of noncash assets into cash takes place over a period of time. As a result, the partnership realizes greater proceeds than would be possible in a quick liquidation. Because of the lengthier conversion period, cash may become available for distribution to partners long before the last noncash asset is sold. In such situations, the partners usually want cash distributed as it becomes available.

The two worst-case assumptions

If capital accounts are not maintained in the profit and loss sharing ratio, cash may not be distributed to the partners on some arbitrary basis such as the profit and loss sharing ratio, the capital balances ratio, or personal needs. Such a distribution might result in later inequities to certain partners. For example, cash may be distributed to a partner who may not be able to return such cash to the partnership if a deficit balance subsequently is created in his or her capital account as a result of future losses on the conversion of noncash assets into cash. Such partner's deficit balance would have to be allocated to partners who have credit balances, and those partners would have to bear a greater portion of the loss than their profit and loss sharing percentages. To prevent this potential inequity, accountants use two worst-case assumptions to determine which partners

Illustration 21-7

A, B, C, AND D PARTNERSHIP
Statement of Realization and Liquidation
July 19X5

	Assets Cash	Assets Noncash	Outside Liabilities	Partners' Loans B	C	D	A(40%)[a]	B(20%)[a]	C(20%)[a]	D(20%)[a]
Preliquidation balances	$ 10,000	$290,000	$157,000	$10,000	$5,000	$2,000	$70,000	$30,000	$ 20,000	$ 6,000
Realization of assets and allocation of loss	130,000	(290,000)					(64,000)	(32,000)	(32,000)	(32,000)
Subtotal	$140,000	$ -0-	$157,000	$10,000	$5,000	$2,000	$ 6,000	$ (2,000)	$(12,000)	$(26,000)
Exercise right of setoff				(2,000)	(5,000)	(2,000)		2,000	5,000	2,000
Subtotal	$140,000		$157,000	$ 8,000	$ -0-	$ -0-	$ 6,000	$ -0-	$ (7,000)	$(24,000)
Distribution to outside creditors	(140,000)		(140,000)							
Subtotal	$ -0-		$ 17,000	$ 8,000			$ 6,000		$ (7,000)	$(24,000)
Absorption of D's deficit							(12,000)	(6,000)	(6,000)	24,000
Subtotal	$ -0-		$ 17,000	$ 8,000			$ (6,000)	$ (6,000)	$(13,000)	$ -0-
Capital contribution by C	10,000								10,000	
Subtotal	$ 10,000		$ 17,000	$ 8,000			$ (6,000)	$ (6,000)	$ (3,000)	
Absorption of C's deficit							(2,000)	(1,000)	3,000	
Subtotal	$ 10,000		$ 17,000	$ 8,000			$ (8,000)	$ (7,000)	$ -0-	
Exercise right of setoff				(7,000)				7,000		
Subtotal	$ 10,000		$ 17,000	$ 1,000			$ (8,000)	$ -0-		
Capital contribution by A			(17,000)				17,000			
Subtotal	$ 10,000		$ -0-	$ 1,000			$ 9,000			
Cash distributions:										
Partner's loan	(1,000)			(1,000)						
Partner's capital	(9,000)						(9,000)			
Postliquidation balances	$ -0-		$ -0-	$ -0-			$ -0-			

[a] Denotes profit and loss sharing percentage.

should receive available cash at any particular time. These assumptions are as follows:

(1) First worst-case assumption. All noncash assets are assumed to be completely worthless. Thus, a hypothetical loss equal to the carrying values of noncash assets is assumed to have occurred. On a worksheet, the hypothetical loss is allocated to the partners' capital account balances existing at that time.

(2) Second worst-case assumption. If, as a result of the first worst-case assumption, a partner's capital account is in a deficit position (on the worksheet only), we assume that such partner is not able to make contributions to the partnership to eliminate the hypothetical deficit. (This assumption is made regardless of the partner's personal financial status.) Accordingly, the hypothetical deficit balance is allocated to the partners who have credit balances, using their respective profit and loss sharing ratio. If, in turn, this process creates a hypothetical deficit balance in another partner's capital account, then such hypothetical deficit balance is allocated (on the worksheet only) to the remaining partners who still have credit balances. This process is repeated until only partners with credit balances remain on the worksheet. Cash may then be distributed to the partners who have credit balances on the worksheet.

The result of these two assumptions is that cash is distributed only to the partners who have capital balances sufficient to absorb their share of (1) the maximum potential loss on noncash assets, and (2) any capital deficiencies that may result to other partners as a result of a maximum loss on noncash assets. In other words, payments may safely be made to such partners with full assurance that the money will not have to be returned to the partnership at some later date in the event of future realization losses.

Under this method of distributing cash to the partners, the capital accounts are brought into the profit and loss sharing ratio. Usually, this is accomplished only after several cash distributions have been made. Once the capital accounts have been brought into the profit and loss sharing ratio, cash distributions may be made in the profit and loss sharing ratio. The two worst-case assumptions need not be used for any future cash distributions, because their use would produce the same result as the profit and loss sharing ratio.

In applying the two worst-case assumptions, a partner's capital account (on the worksheet) is reduced for any loans the partnership has outstanding to such partner. Also, a partner's capital account (on the worksheet) is increased for any loan such partner may have outstanding to the partnership; this automatically provides for the hypothetical exercising of the right of setoff.

Illustration:
Loss on realization creates a deficit balance in certain partners' capital accounts—One partner is personally insolvent

To illustrate how these two worst-case assumptions are applied to an installment liquidation, assume the following.

(1) The partnership of A, B, C, and D has the same preliquidation balances as shown in Illustration 21-7.
(2) The noncash assets of $290,000 are sold as follows:

Date	Book Value	Proceeds	Loss
July 14, 19X5	$183,000	$168,000	$(15,000)
August 12, 19X5	70,000	25,000	(45,000)
September 21, 19X5	37,000	27,000	(10,000)
	$290,000	$220,000	$(70,000)

(3) Cash was distributed to outside creditors and partners as it was available.
(4) Partner D could contribute only $4,000 to the partnership during the liquidation proceedings. His remaining $2,000 capital account deficit had to be absorbed by the other partners.

The statement of realization and liquidation would be prepared as shown in Illustration 21-8. The cash distributions to partners as set forth in Illustration 21-8 were determined from Illustration 21-9, which is a supporting schedule to Illustration 21-8. In reviewing Illustrations 21-8 and 21-9, the following points should be understood:

(1) The statement of realization and liquidation reflects only the historical transactions as recorded in the general ledger. Although the statement covers the entire liquidation period, it was started when the liquidation process began and then periodically updated as noncash assets were sold and cash distributions were made.
(2) The schedule of safe payments to partners reflects the assumptions that were made at those dates when cash was available for distribution to partners. The purpose of the schedule is to determine which partners should receive the cash that is available at those dates.
(3) The payments that may be made to partners, as shown on the schedule of safe payments, are first applied as a reduction of a partner's loan and then as a reduction of his or her capital in the statement of realization and liquidation.
(4) After the first cash distribution to partners on July 14, 19X5, the capital accounts of partners A and B are in their respective profit and loss sharing ratio of 4:2. All future cash distributions to these two partners are in this 2:1 ratio.
(5) After the second cash distribution to partners on August 12, 19X5, the capital accounts of partners A, B, and C (which includes partner C's loan account balance) are in their respective profit and loss sharing ratio of 4:2:2. All future cash distributions to these three partners are in this 4:2:2 ratio.
(6) Obviously, the schedule of safe payments is prepared only after cash is available for distribution to partners. Thus, it may be used only when the partnership is solvent.

Cash distribution plan

When cash is available for distribution to partners, a schedule of safe payments to partners must be prepared using the two worst-case assumptions (except for the final payment, of course). The result of distributing cash to

Illustration 21-8

A, B, C, AND D PARTNERSHIP
Statement of Realization and Liquidation
July 1, 19X5 through September 21, 19X5

	Assets		Outside Liabilities	Partners' Loans			Partners' Capital			
	Cash	Noncash		B	C	D	A(40%)[a]	B(20%)[a]	C(20%)[a]	D(20%)[a]
Preliquidation balances	$ 10,000	$290,000	$157,000	$10,000	$5,000	$2,000	$70,000	$30,000	$20,000	$ 6,000
Realization of assets and allocation of loss	168,000	(183,000)					(6,000)	(3,000)	(3,000)	(3,000)
Subtotal	$178,000	$107,000	$157,000	$10,000	$5,000	$2,000	$64,000	$27,000	$17,000	$ 3,000
July cash distribution:										
Outside creditors	(157,000)		(157,000)							
Partner's loan	(10,000)[b]			(10,000)[b]						
Partners' capital	(11,000)[b]						(10,667)[b]	(333)[b]		
Subtotal	$ -0-	$107,000	$ -0-	$ -0-	$5,000	$2,000	$53,333	$26,667	$17,000	$ 3,000
Realization of assets and allocation of loss	25,000	(70,000)					(18,000)	(9,000)	(9,000)	(9,000)
Subtotal	$ 25,000	$ 37,000			$5,000	$2,000	$35,333	$17,667	$ 8,000	$(6,000)
Exercise right of setoff						(2,000)				2,000
Subtotal	$ 25,000	$ 37,000			$5,000	$ -0-	$35,333	$17,667	$ 8,000	$(4,000)
Cash contribution by D	4,000									4,000
Subtotal	$ 29,000	$ 37,000			$5,000		$35,333	$17,667	$ 8,000	$ -0-
August cash distribution:										
Partner's loan	(3,750)[b]				(3,750)					
Partners' capital	(25,250)[b]						(16,833)[b]	(8,417)[b]		
Subtotal	$ -0-	$ 37,000			$1,250		$18,500	$ 9,250	$ 8,000	
Realization of assets and allocation of loss	27,000	(37,000)					(4,000)	(2,000)	(2,000)	(2,000)
Subtotal	$ 27,000	$ -0-			$1,250		$14,500	$ 7,250	$ 6,000	$(2,000)
Write-off of D's deficit							(1,000)	(500)	(500)	2,000
Subtotal	$ 27,000				$1,250		$13,500	$ 6,750	$ 5,500	$ -0-
Final cash distribution:										
Partner's loan	(1,250)				(1,250)					
Partners' capital	(25,750)						(13,500)	(6,750)	(5,500)	
Postliquidation balances	$ -0-				$ -0-		$ -0-	$ -0-	$ -0-	$ -0-

[a] Denotes profit and loss sharing percentage.
[b] See Illustration 21-9.

Illustration 21-9
Supporting schedule to Illustration 21-8

A, B, C, AND D PARTNERSHIP				
Schedule of Safe Payments to Partners				
	Partner			
	A(40%)[a]	B(20%)[a]	C(20%)[a]	D(20%)[a]
Computation to determine how available cash on July 14, 19X5 should be distributed:				
Capital and loan balances at cash distribution (Per Illustration 21-8)	$64,000	$37,000	$22,000	$ 5,000
First worst-case assumption—Assume full loss on noncash assets of $107,000	(42,800)	(21,400)	(21,400)	(21,400)
Subtotal	$21,200	$15,600	$ 600	$(16,400)
Second worst-case assumption—Assume D's deficit must be absorbed by A, B, and C	(8,200)	(4,100)	(4,100)	16,400
Subtotal	$13,000	$11,500	$ (3,500)	$ -0-
Repeat second worst-case assumption—Assume C's deficit must be absorbed by A and B	(2,333)	(1,167)	3,500	
Cash to be distributed to each partner	$10,667	$10,333	$ -0-	
Computation to determine how available cash on August 12, 19X5 should be distributed:				
Capital and loan balances at cash distribution (Per Illustration 21-8)	$35,333	$17,667	$13,000	$ -0-
First worst-case assumption—Assume full loss on noncash assets of $37,000...........	(14,800)	(7,400)	(7,400)	(7,400)
Subtotal	$20,533	$10,267	$ 5,600	$ (7,400)
Second worst-case assumption—Assume D's deficit must be absorbed by A, B, and C	(3,700)	(1,850)	(1,850)	7,400
Cash to be distributed to each partner	$16,833	$ 8,417	$ 3,750	$ -0-

[a] Denotes profit and loss sharing percentage.

partners in the sequence resulting from the use of the two worst-case assumptions is to bring the capital accounts into the profit and loss sharing ratio. (As demonstrated earlier in the chapter, a partner's loan to the partnership is, in substance, part of that partner's capital investment.) Once the capital accounts are in this ratio, all future cash distributions to partners are made in the profit and loss sharing ratio.

By understanding the result of this process, we may analyze the relationship of the capital accounts at the beginning of the liquidation process to determine which partners receive cash as it becomes available. The analysis results in a **cash distribution plan.** A cash distribution plan has the advantage of informing partners at **the beginning of the liquidation process** when they will receive cash **in relation to the other partners.**

Understanding the methodology underlying the preparation of a cash distribution plan requires an intuitive understanding of the fact that when the capital accounts are not in the profit and loss sharing ratio, one or more partners have capital balances sufficient to absorb his, her, or their share of losses that exceed the partnership's net worth, whereas one or more other partners have capital balances sufficient to absorb only his, her, or their share of losses that are less than the partnership's net worth. To illustrate this fact, we present the following comparative analysis:

		Partner			
	Total	W(40%)	X(30%)	Y(20%)	Z(10%)
Actual preliquidation capital and loan balances ..	$100,000	$48,000	$33,000	$11,000	$8,000
Hypothetical capital and loan balances in the profit and loss sharing ratio of 4:3:2:1	$100,000	$40,000	$30,000	$20,000	$10,000
Percentage relationship of actual balances to hypothetical balances		120%	110%	55%	80%

Only partners W and X (because their actual balances exceed the balances that would exist if balances were kept in the profit and loss sharing ratio) could absorb their share of losses greater than the partnership capital of $100,000. On the other hand, partners Y and Z (because their actual balances are less than the balances that would exist if balances were kept in the profit and loss sharing ratio) could absorb only their share of losses that are less than the partnership capital of $100,000.

Ranking the partners. The percentage line of the analysis ranks the partners in terms of which partner could absorb the largest loss to which partner could absorb the smallest loss. The ranking in this example is W, X, Z, and Y—that is, partner W (who has the highest percentage) can absorb the largest loss, and partner Y (who has the lowest percentage) can absorb the smallest loss. This ranking can be readily proved by calculating the exact loss needed to eliminate each partner's capital and loan balance. We divide each partners' capital and loan balance by his or her profit and loss sharing percentage. Continuing with our example, this calculation is as follows:

	Partner			
	W	X	Y	Z
Actual preliquidation capital balances	$48,000	$33,000	$11,000	$8,000
Profit and loss sharing percentage.	40%	30%	20%	10%
Loss absorption potential	$120,000	$110,000	$55,000	$80,000
Ranking	1	2	4	3

Note that a loss of $120,000 would eliminate the capital and loan balance of partner W (the highest ranking partner), whereas for partner Y (the lowest ranking partner) a loss of only $55,000 would eliminate his capital and loan balance.

Ranking the partners in this manner reveals the order in which cash should be distributed to the partners as it becomes available. Distributing cash in this order brings the capital balances into the profit and loss sharing ratio on a step-by-step basis, as follows:

(1) Distribution to highest ranking partner. Distribute sufficient cash to partner W so that his capital balance is brought into the profit and loss sharing ratio with the next highest ranking partner (partner X).

(2) Distribution to two highest ranking partners. Distribute sufficient cash to partners W and X in their respective profit and loss sharing ratio of 4:3 so that their capital balances are brought into the profit and loss sharing ratio with the next highest ranking partner (partner Z).

(3) Distribution to three highest ranking partners. Distribute sufficient cash to partners W, X, and Z in their respective profit and loss sharing ratio of 4:3:1 so that their capital balances are brought into the profit and loss sharing ratio with the next highest ranking partner (partner Y).

Obviously, only the exact amount of cash distributed at each stage in this sequence needs to be determined. The calculations are shown in Illustration 21-10. In reviewing Illustration 21-10, the following points should be understood:

(1) The cash distribution plan is operable only after outside creditors have been paid in full.
(2) The schedule reflects only the order in which cash distributions to partners will be made *if* cash is available for distribution to the partners.
(3) The sequence of distributing cash in the cash distribution plan coincides with the sequence that would result if cash were distributed using the schedule of safe payments.

SUMMARY

Liquidating a partnership consists of converting the partnership's noncash assets into cash, paying cash to creditors to the extent possible, and distributing any remaining cash to the partners. In lump-sum liquidations, no distributions are made to the partners until the realization process is completed, when the full amount of the gain or loss on realization of the partnership assets is known. In these cases, cash is distributed to the partners who have credit balances in their capital and loan accounts.

In installment liquidations, distributions are made to some or all of the partners as cash becomes available; thus, cash is distributed to partners before the full amount of the gain or loss on realization of the partnership assets is known. In these cases, cash distributions are made to partners in such a manner that the capital and loan balances of the individual partners are brought into line with the profit and loss sharing ratio.

Illustration 21-10

	W, X, Y, AND Z PARTNERSHIP Schedule of Cash Distribution to Partners			
		Partner		
	W	**X**	**Y**	**Z**
Preliquidation capital and loan balances	$48,000	$33,000	$11,000	$8,000
Ranking	1	2	4	3
Step (1): Cash to be distributed to W:				
Balances, per above	$48,000	$33,000		
Balances in profit and loss ratio of 4:3 using X's actual balance as the base ...	44,000	$33,000		
	$ 4,000			
Step (2): Cash to be distributed to W and X:				
Balances, per above	$44,000	$33,000		$8,000
Balances in profit and loss ratio of 4:3:1 using Z's actual balance as the base ...	32,000	24,000		$8,000
	$12,000	$ 9,000		
Step (3): Cash to be distributed to W, X, and Z:				
Balances, per above	$32,000	$24,000	$11,000	$8,000
Balances in profit and loss ratio of 4:3:2:1 using Y's actual balance as the base ...	22,000	16,500	$11,000	5,500
	$10,000	$ 7,500		$2,500

After this distribution, all capital accounts would be in the profit and loss sharing ratio of 4:3:2:1. Accordingly, all future cash distributions would be made in this ratio.

Summary of cash distribution plan:

	W	X	Y	Z
First $4,000	$ 4,000			
Next $21,000 (4:3)	12,000	$ 9,000		
Next $20,000 (4:3:1)	10,000	7,500		$2,500
Any additional amounts (4:3:2:1)	40%	30%	20%	10%

To the extent that a partner must absorb some or all of another partner's capital account deficit, such absorbing partner has legal recourse against the personal assets of the partner who could not make good the deficit balance through setoff or contribution. The settlement of claims pursuant to such legal recourse is governed by the marshalling of assets principle. Partners may greatly minimize the possibility of having to absorb another partner's deficit balance by specifying in the partnership agreement that capital balances are to be maintained in the profit and loss sharing ratio.

Glossary of new terms

Rule of Setoff: The subtraction of a partner's deficit balance in his or her capital account from the balance of any loan outstanding to the partnership. Also, the subtraction of a partnership's loan to a partner from the partner's capital account.

Marshalling of Assets: A legal procedure whereby a partnership's creditors are given first claim on partnership assets, and personal creditors of an insolvent partner are given first claim on such partner's personal assets.

Review questions

1. How are partnership liquidations different from corporate liquidations?
2. What is the significance of maintaining partners' capital accounts in the profit and loss sharing ratio?
3. How is a deficit balance in a partner's capital account disposed of if that partner is unable to eliminate the deficit through setoff or contribution?
4. In what ratio should realization gains and losses during liquidation be shared among the partners? Why?
5. Explain how the rule of setoff is applied.
6. What is the function of the statement of realization and liquidation?
7. In what order does the UPA specify that cash distributions are to be made to creditors and partners during liquidation?
8. Is the order in Question 7 strictly followed in all situations? Why or why not?
9. Explain the marshalling of assets procedure.
10. Under what conditions may cash be distributed to partners on the installment basis instead of in a lump sum?
11. When a partnership is insolvent and some partners have positive capital account balances, whereas other partners have deficit balances, against which partners may creditors proceed personally to obtain full payment of their claims?
12. How is a partner's personal payment to partnership creditors treated on the partnership's books?

Discussion cases

Discussion case 21–1
Manner of sharing realization losses during liquidation

Highe and Lowe recently formed a partnership under the following terms:

	Highe	Lowe
Capital contributions	$80,000	$20,000
Time devoted to the business	100%	100%
Profit and loss sharing formula—		
Interest rate on capital over $20,000	10%	10%
Residual profit and loss	50%	50%

You have been hired as the partnership's accountant. While closing the partnership books for the first month of operations, Highe casually mentions to you that he feels a "good and equitable" partnership agreement was negotiated between himself and Lowe.

Required:
How would you respond to this comment?

Discussion case 21–2
Manner of sharing realization losses during liquidation

Barr, Loyer, and Willis are attempting to form a partnership in which profits and losses are shared in the ratio 4:4:2, respectively. They cannot agree on terms of the partnership agreement relating to potential liquidation. Barr feels it is a waste of time to have any provisions relating to liquidation, because the prospective partners firmly believe that the business will be successful. Loyer feels that in the event of liquidation, any realization losses should be shared in the ratio of the capital balances, because this method allows each partner to absorb losses in relation to his or her capacity to absorb such losses. Willis feels any liquidation losses should be shared equally, because if the business is not successful it will most likely be the fault of each partner. As the accountant who will be keeping the partnership's books, you have been asked to settle this dispute.

Required:
How would you respond to this request?

Discussion case 21–3
Procedures for distributing available cash to partners

The partnership of Reade and Wright is in the process of liquidation, which is expected to take several months. Reade, who is in need of cash, wants cash distributed to the partners as it is available. Wright feels no cash should be distributed to either partner until all the assets are sold and the total realization gain or loss is known. Thus, the partnership would not distribute cash to a partner and later request a capital contribution to absorb any capital deficits created by realization losses.

Required:
Evaluate the positions of each partner.

Discussion case 21–4
Procedures for distributing available cash to partners

The partnership of Banks, Cash, and Greene is in the process of being liquidated. The trial balance immediately after the sale of a portion of the noncash assets and full payment to outside creditors is as follows:

Cash	$20,000	
Note receivable from Cash	14,000	
Other assets	36,000	
Loan, Banks		$ 5,000

Capital:

Banks...		11,000
Cash..		20,000
Greene..		34,000
	$70,000	$70,000

Banks wants the available cash distributed to her to pay off her loan—she cites Section 40(b) of the UPA, which states partners' loans have priority over partners' capital. Greene wants the cash distributed to him, because he has the largest capital investment. Cash feels it should be distributed equally, which is how profits and losses are shared.

Required:
(1) Evaluate the positions of each partner.
(2) Who should receive the $20,000 available cash?

Exercises

Exercise 21–1
Lump-sum liquidation: Solvent partnership having partners' loans— All partners personally solvent

Partners Gayle, Storm, and Windham share profits and losses in the ratio 3:2:1, respectively. The partners voted to liquidate the partnership when its assets, liabilities, and capital were as follows:

Cash.........................	$ 2,000	Liabilities		$20,000
Noncash assets	78,000	Loans:		
		Gayle		5,000
		Windham		10,000
		Capital:		
		Gayle		20,000
		Storm		15,000
		Windham		10,000
	$80,000			$80,000

Assume all the noncash assets were sold for $36,000, and all cash was distributed to outside creditors and partners.

Required:
Prepare a statement of liquidation and realization.

Exercise 21–2
Lump-sum liquidation: Solvent partnership having loans to and from partners—All partners personally solvent

Partners Hurrey, Upp, and Waite share profits and losses equally. The partners voted to liquidate the partnership when its assets, liabilities, and capital were as follows.

Cash	$ 14,000	Liabilities	$ 80,000
Note receivable from		Loans:	
Waite	11,000	Hurrey.....................	4,000
Other noncash assets........	120,000	Upp	16,000
		Capital:	
		Hurrey.....................	15,000
		Upp	15,000
		Waite	15,000
	$145,000		$145,000

Assume the following:

(1) All the noncash assets of $120,000 were sold for $54,000.
(2) Waite instructed the partnership to write off the $11,000 he borrowed from the partnership.
(3) All partners could eliminate any deficits in their capital accounts through setoff or contribution, or both.
(4) All cash was distributed to outside creditors and partners.

Required:
Prepare a statement of realization and liquidation.

Exercise 21–3
Lump-sum liquidation: Solvent partnership having loans
to and from partners—Certain partners personally insolvent

Partners Buntt, Runyon, and Steele share profits and losses in the ratio 3:3:2, respectively. The partners voted to liquidate the partnership when its assets, liabilities, and capital were as follows:

Cash	$ 1,000	Liabilities	$34,000
Note receivable from Steele	9,000	Loan:	
Other noncash assets..........	75,000	Runyon.....................	15,000
		Capital:	
		Buntt	11,000
		Runyon.....................	10,000
		Steele	15,000
	$85,000		$85,000

Assume the following:

(1) All the noncash assets of $75,000 were sold for $43,000.
(2) Steele was personally insolvent and unable to contribute any cash to the partnership.
(3) Buntt and Runyon were both personally solvent and able to eliminate any deficits in their capital accounts through setoff or contribution.
(4) All cash was distributed to outside creditors and partners.

Required:
Prepare a statement of realization and liquidation.

Exercise 21–4
Lump-sum liquidation: Insolvent partnership having loans from partners—Certain partners personally insolvent

Partners Doe, Rae, Mee, and Tee share profits and losses in the ratio 5:2:2:1, respectively. The partners voted to liquidate the partnership when its assets and liabilities were as follows:

Cash	$ 15,000	Liabilities	$165,000
Noncash assets	235,000	Loans:	
		Rae	7,000
		Mee.......................	5,000
		Tee	3,000
		Capital:	
		Doe	40,000
		Rae	16,000
		Mee.......................	10,000
		Tee	4,000
	$250,000		$250,000

Assume the following:

(1) All the noncash assets were sold for $135,000.
(2) Doe contributed $5,000 to the partnership after the noncash assets were sold. He has no additional funds above and beyond what is needed to satisfy personal creditors.
(3) All other partners were personally solvent and made capital contributions as necessary to eliminate deficits in their capital accounts.
(4) All cash was distributed to outside creditors and partners.

Required:
Prepare a statement of realization and liquidation.

Exercise 21–5
Insolvent partnership and insolvent partners—Theory

Q, R, S, and T are partners sharing profits and losses equally. The partnership is insolvent and is therefore being liquidated; the status of the partnership and each partner is as follows:

Partner	Partnership Capital Balance	Personal Assets (Exclusive of Partnership Interest)	Personal Liabilities (Exclusive of Partnership Interest)
Q	$ 15,000	$100,000	$40,000
R.........................	10,000	30,000	60,000
S.........................	(20,000)	80,000	5,000
T.........................	(30,000)	1,000	28,000
	$(25,000)		

Required:
Select the correct response.

Assuming the Uniform Partnership Act applies, the partnership creditors:
a. Must first seek recovery against S because she is personally solvent and has a negative capital balance.
b. Will not be paid in full regardless of how they proceed legally because the partnership assets are less than the partnership liabilities.
c. Must share R's interest in the partnership on a pro rata basis with R's personal creditors.
d. Have first claim to the partnership assets before any partner's personal creditors have rights to the partnership assets.

(AICPA adapted)

Exercise 21–6
**Installment liquidation: Solvent partnership having partner's loan—
First cash distribution to partners**

Partners Cooke, Potter, and Walsh share profits and losses in the ratio 6:3:1, respectively. The partners voted to liquidate the partnership when its assets, liabilities, and capital were as follows:

Cash	$ 1,000	Liabilities	$35,000
Noncash assets	94,000	Loan:	
		Walsh	10,000
		Capital:	
		Cooke	30,000
		Potter	15,000
		Walsh	5,000
	$95,000		$95,000

Assume that noncash assets with a book value of $74,000 were sold for $54,000.

Required:
Determine how the cash available after this sale should be distributed.

Exercise 21–7
**Installment liquidation: Solvent partnership—
First cash distribution to partners**

Partners Diamond, Hart, and Klubnik share profits and losses in the ratio 5:3:2, respectively. The partners voted to liquidate the partnership when its assets, liabilities, and capital were as follows:

Cash..	$ 40,000	
Other assets...	210,000	
Liabilities		$ 60,000
Capital:		
Diamond		48,000
Hart		72,000
Klubnik...		70,000
	$250,000	$250,000

The partnership will be liquidated over a long period of time. Cash is to be distributed to the partners as it becomes available. The first sale of noncash assets having a book value of $120,000 realized $90,000.

Required:
Determine how the available cash should be distributed to the partners after this sale.

(AICPA adapted)

Exercise 21–8
Installment liquidation: Solvent partnership with partnership's and partner's loans—First cash distribution to partners

Partners Ho, Humm, and Knapp share profits and losses in the ratio 4:4:2, respectively. The partners voted to liquidate the partnership when its assets, liabilities, and capital were as follows:

Cash..	$ 20,000	
Note receivable from Ho	10,000	
Other assets...	170,000	
Liabilities		$ 50,000
Loan from Humm		30,000
Capital:		
Ho...		37,000
Humm		15,000
Knapp		68,000
	$200,000	$200,000

The partnership will be liquidated over a long period of time. Cash will be distributed to the partners as it becomes available. The first sale of noncash assets having a book value of $90,000 realized $50,000.

Required:
Determine how the available cash should be distributed to the partners after this first sale.

(AICPA adapted)

Problems

Problem 21–1
Lump-sum liquidation: Solvent partnership having partner's loan— All partners personally solvent

Partners A and B share profits in the ratio 3:2, respectively. The partners agreed to liquidate the partnership when the assets, liabilities, and capital were as follows:

Cash	$ 6,000	Liabilities		$27,000
Noncash assets	44,000	Loan:		
		partner B		6,000
		Capital:		
		partner A		14,000
		partner B		3,000
	$50,000			$50,000

Assume the following:

(1) Partner A agreed personally to take certain equipment having a book value of $5,000. (The partners estimated the current value of this equipment at $6,500.)
(2) Partner B agreed personally to take certain office furniture having a book value of $3,000. (The partners estimated the current value of this equipment at $2,000.)
(3) All other noncash assets were sold for $25,000.
(4) Liquidation expenses of $1,000 were incurred.
(5) Cash was distributed to outside creditors and partners.

Required:
Prepare a statement of realization and liquidation.

Problem 21–2
Lump-sum liquidation: Solvent partnership having partners' loans— Certain partners personally insolvent

Partners W, X, Y, and Z share profits and losses in the ratio 4:3:2:1, respectively. The partners agreed to liquidate the partnership when it had assets, liabilities, and capital as follows:

Cash	$ 10,000	Liabilities	$ 78,000
Noncash assets	140,000	Loans:	
		partner W..................	4,000
		partner X	3,000
		Capital:	
		partner W..................	10,000
		partner X	10,000
		partner Y	30,000
		partner Z	15,000
	$150,000		$150,000

Assume the following:

(1) The noncash assets were sold for $90,000.
(2) Partner W is personally insolvent.
(3) Partner X contributed $2,000 cash to the partnership; he had no other available funds in excess of amounts needed to satisfy personal creditors.
(4) All cash was distributed to outside creditors and partners.

Required:
Prepare a statement of realization and liquidation.

Problem 21–3
Lump-sum liquidation: Insolvent partnership having partners' loans— Certain partners personally insolvent

Partners R, S, and T share profits and losses in the ratio 3:3:2, respectively. The partners agreed to liquidate the partnership when assets, liabilities, and capital were as follows.

Cash	$ 5,000	Liabilities	$48,000
Noncash assets	85,000	Loans:	
		partner R	10,000
		partner S	3,000
		Capital:	
		partner R	11,000
		partner S	10,000
		partner T	8,000
	$90,000		$90,000

Assume the following:

(1) The noncash assets were sold for $29,000.
(2) Outside creditors of the partnership proceeded against partner T and collected from her $14,000 that the partnership was unable to pay.
(3) The partnership incurred liquidation expenses of $4,000, which were paid personally by partner S.
(4) Partner R is personally insolvent.
(5) Partners S and T (who are both personally solvent) make a personal settlement between themselves.

Required:
Prepare a statement of realization and liquidation.

Problem 21–4
Installment liquidation: Solvent partnership having partners' loans— All partners personally solvent

Partners Barker, Howle, and Wuff share profits and losses in the ratio 6:3:1, respectively. The partners decided to liquidate the partnership on June 30, 19X5, when its assets, liabilities, and capital were as follows:

Cash	$ 10,000	Liabilities	$ 42,000
Noncash assets	130,000	Loans:	
		Barker......................	4,000
		Howle	1,000
		Capital:	
		Barker......................	84,000
		Howle	5,000
		Wuff	4,000
	$140,000		$140,000

Assume the following:

(1) On July 1, 19X5, liquidation expenses were estimated at approximately $3,000. Actual liquidation expenses totaled only $2,500 and were paid as follows:

July 31, 19X5	$1,000
August 31, 19X5	1,000
September 30, 19X5	500
	$2,500

(2) Noncash assets were sold as follows:

Date	Book Value	Proceeds
July 11, 19X5	$ 30,000	$ 36,000
August 14, 19X5	40,000	28,000
September 27, 19X5	60,000	44,000
	$130,000	$108,000

(3) Partners were able to eliminate any deficits in their capital accounts through setoff or contribution as deficit balances occurred.
(4) Cash was distributed to outside creditors and partners as it was available.

Required:
Prepare a statement of realization and liquidation, including supporting schedules showing how cash was distributed to creditors and partners as it was available.

Problem 21–5
Installment Liquidation: Schedule of cash distribution

Partners Ace, Bridges, Cardell, and Decker decide to dissolve their partnership. They plan to sell the assets gradually to minimize losses. They share profits and losses as follows: Ace, 40%; Bridges, 35%; Cardell, 15%; and Decker, 10%. The partnership's trial balance as of October 1, 19X0, the date on which liquidation begins, is shown below.

	Debit	Credit
Cash	$ 200	
Receivables	25,900	
Inventory, October 1, 19X0	42,600	
Equipment (net)	19,800	
Accounts payable		$ 3,000
Ace, loan		6,000
Bridges, loan		10,000
Ace, capital		20,000
Bridges, capital		21,500
Cardell, capital		18,000
Decker, capital		10,000
	$88,500	$88,500

Required:
(1) Prepare a statement as of October 1, 19X0, showing how cash will be distributed among partners by installments as it becomes available.
(2) On October 31, 19X0, $12,700 cash was available to partners. How should it be distributed?

(AICPA adapted)

Problem 21–6
Installment liquidation: Schedule of cash distribution

On August 25, 19X5, Majors, Miners, and Sooters entered into a partnership agreement to acquire a speculative second mortgage on undeveloped real estate. They invested

$55,500, $32,000, and $12,500, respectively. They agreed on a profit and loss sharing ratio of 4:2:1, respectively.

On September 1, 19X5 the partnership purchased for $100,000 a mortgage note with an unpaid balance of $120,000. The amount paid included interest accrued from June 30, 19X5. The note principal matures at the rate of $2,000 each quarter. Interest at the annual rate of 8% computed on the unpaid balance is also due quarterly.

Regular interest and principal payments were received on September 30 and December 31, 19X5. In addition to the regular September 30 payment, the mortgagor made a lump-sum principal reduction payment of $10,000 plus a 2% penalty for prepayment. A working capital imprest fund of $150 was established, and collection expenses of $70 were paid in December.

Because of the speculative nature of the note, the partners agree to defer recognition of the discount until their cost has been fully recovered.

Required:
(1) Assuming that no cash distributions were made to the partners, prepare a schedule computing the cash balance available for distribution to the partners on December 31, 19X5.
(2) After payment of collection expenses, the partners expect to have $170,000 cash available for distribution to themselves for interest and return of principal. They plan to distribute the cash as soon as possible so that they may individually reinvest the cash. Prepare a schedule showing how the $170,000 cash should be distributed to the individual partners by installments as it becomes available.

(AICPA adapted)

Problem 21–7
Installment liquidation: Schedule of cash distribution

Partners Allen, Benny, and Chapman want you to assist them in winding up the affairs of their partnership. You gather the following information:

(1) The June 30, 19X2, trial balance of the partnership is as follows:

	Debit	Credit
Cash	$ 6,000	
Accounts receivable	22,000	
Inventory	14,000	
Plant and equipment (net)	99,000	
Note receivable—Allen	12,000	
Note receivable—Chapman	7,500	
Accounts payable		$ 17,000
Allen, capital		67,000
Benny, capital		45,000
Chapman, capital		31,500
	$160,500	$160,500

(2) The partners share profits and losses as follows: Allen, 50%; Benny, 30%; and Chapman, 20%.

The partners are considering an offer of $100,000 for the accounts receivable inventory and for plant and equipment as of June 30. The $100,000 would be paid to the partners in installments, the number and amounts of which are to be negotiated.

Required:
Prepare a cash distribution schedule as of June 30, 19X2, showing how the $100,000 would be distributed as it is available.

Problem 21-8
Installment liquidation: Schedule of cash distribution
and statement of realization and liquidation

Assume the facts in Problem 21-7, except that the partners decide to liquidate their partnership instead of accepting the offer of $100,000. Cash is distributed to the partners at the end of each month.

A summary of the liquidation transactions follows:

July:
(1) Collected $16,500 on accounts receivable; the balance is uncollectible.
(2) Received $10,000 for the entire inventory.
(3) Paid $1,000 liquidation expenses.
(4) Retained $8,000 cash in the business at month-end.

August:
(1) Paid $1,500 liquidation expenses. As part payment of his capital, Chapman accepted a piece of special equipment that he developed that had a book value of $4,000. The partners agreed that a value of $10,000 should be placed on the machine for liquidation purposes.
(2) Retained $2,500 cash in the business at month-end.

September:
(1) Received $75,000 on sale of remaining plant and equipment.
(2) Paid $1,000 liquidation expenses.
(3) No cash retained in the business.

Required:
Prepare a statement of realization and liquidation.

(AICPA adapted)

PART FIVE

Government and Nonprofit Organizations

22 Governmental Accounting: Basic Principles and the General Fund

Accounting for state and local governmental units could be the subject of an entire textbook. A major portion of this chapter, therefore, is devoted to introductory material, to give you an overall understanding of (1) the historical development and current status of accounting principles applicable to governmental units; (2) the nature of governmental operations; and (3) the current shortcomings of governmental financial reporting.

ESTABLISHMENT OF ACCOUNTING PRINCIPLES

The MFOA, *GAAFR,* and NCGA

Before 1978, the Financial Accounting Standards Board and its predecessor organizations restricted their efforts to the establishment of accounting principles for the private sector of the economy, that is, to enterprises engaged in a trade or business for a profit. To fill the void that existed with respect to the accounting principles and practices peculiar to governmental units, the National Committee on Municipal Accounting was established in 1934 through the efforts of the Municipal Finance Officers Association of the United States and Canada (MFOA). The Committee was not a permanent one, but was reestablished periodically as necessary to upgrade standards and address current problems. In 1949, the Committee's name was changed to the National Committee on Governmental Accounting (NCGA) to signify the expansion of its activities to encompass all governmental units except the federal government and its agencies. Over the years, the Committee issued numerous publications dealing with principles, practices, and procedures of accounting, budgeting, auditing, and financial reporting for state and local governmental units. In 1968, the Committee combined most of its publications issued up to that time into a publication titled *Governmental Accounting, Auditing and Financial Reporting* (referred to and cited as *GAAFR*).[1] In 1974, the American Institute of Certified Public Accountants issued an audit guide titled *Audits of State and Local Governmental Units* (referred to as the AICPA governmental audit guide and cited *ASLGU*). This audit guide not only acknowledged *GAAFR* as "an authoritative publication in the area of accounting for governmental units," but also considered the principles set forth therein to "constitute generally accepted accounting principles [except as modified in the audit guide]."[2]

It was soon evident that major improvements in financial reporting were still needed. Accordingly, the National Council on Governmental Accounting was established in 1974 as the successor to the National Committee on Governmental Accounting. Certain structural changes were made and due process procedures similar to those of the FASB were adopted.

---

[1] Published by the Municipal Finance Officers Association of the United States and Canada, 180 North Michigan Avenue, Chicago, Illinois 60601, 1968.

[2] Committee on Governmental Accounting and Auditing, "Audits of State and Local Governmental Units" (New York: AICPA, 1974), pp. 8–9. (As this book goes to print, this audit guide is in the process of being updated.)

Major improvements made. In 1979, the NCGA issued *NCGA Statement 1*, "Governmental Accounting and Financial Reporting Principles." This major pronouncement substantially upgraded the basic principles set forth in *GAAFR*. The most important revisions pertained to the manner of financial reporting. Narrative explanations and financial statements illustrate the application of the basic principles (which include the manner of financial reporting) and incorporate accounting provisions of *ASLGU*. We discuss these basic principles (grouped into seven broad categories) in detail later in the chapter. (In 1980, the AICPA issued *Statement of Position 80-2*, which amended *ASLGU* as a result of the issuance of *NCGA Statement 1*.)

GAAFR reissued but becomes a guide. In 1980, the MFOA published a revised, updated edition of *GAAFR* based on *NCGA Statement 1*. Unlike the 1968 edition of *GAAFR,* the 1980 edition is not an official pronouncement of the NCGA. It neither prescribes nor authoritatively interprets generally accepted accounting principles for governmental units. Instead, it provides detailed guidance to apply the principles in *NCGA Statement 1* to the accounting and financial reporting activities of state and local governments. Thus, NCGA Statements and Interpretations replaced *GAAFR* as the official pronouncements dealing with GAAP. *GAAFR* is widely used as a guide by state and local governmental accountants and to a lesser extent by certified public accountants.

Additional accomplishments of the NCGA. The NCGA has issued six additional statements, one of which we discuss later in the chapter. The others either deal with special topics or are beyond the scope of this and the following chapter. In addition, the NCGA started a research project to develop a conceptual framework for governmental accounting and financial reporting standards. This resulted in the 1981 issuance of *Concepts Statement 1,* which provides guidance in the future establishment of accounting and financial reporting principles for state and local governments.

FASB involvement

Because of growing concern regarding the reliability and relevance of the financial reports of governmental units in the 1970s, many people urged the Financial Accounting Standards Board to become involved in the nonbusiness sector. In response to these requests, the FASB (1) sponsored a research study dealing with the conceptual issues of financial accounting in nonbusiness organizations; (2) issued a discussion memorandum in 1978 (based on the research study); (3) held public hearings on the issues set forth in the discussion memorandum; (4) decided in 1979 to develop one or more Statements of Financial Accounting Concepts on the objectives of financial reporting by nonbusiness organizations; (5) issued in 1980 *Statement of Financial Accounting Concepts No. 4,* "Objectives of Financial Reporting by Nonbusiness Organizations"; and (6) in 1983, proposed amendments to its *Statements of Financial Accounting Concepts No. 2* and *No. 3* to apply them to nonbusiness organizations as well as business enterprises.

Statement of Financial Accounting Concepts No. 4 did not establish any new accounting standards, nor did it place the FASB in a standard-setting role for state and local governmental units. The statement outlined helpful objectives for developing improved standards for financial reporting.

Creation of GASB

The NCGA operated under several handicaps. It never had adequate financing to build and retain a sufficient staff and to support an adequate system of due process. Furthermore, its close ties to the MFOA (which primarily constitutes preparers of financial statements) gave the appearance of a lack of independence. Because of these handicaps, it seemed logical that the NCGA should be disbanded and that the FASB should assume sole responsibility for issuing reporting standards for governmental units. This alternative was opposed by governmental accounting groups.

Much discussion and committee work led to the creation in 1984 of a new standard-setting body, the Governmental Accounting Standards Board (GASB) to succeed the NCGA (which was dissolved in June 1984). The Financial Accounting Foundation (FAF), which oversees the FASB, also oversees the GASB. Its five-member board (appointed for five-year terms) includes a full-time chairman and is located in the same Stamford, CT headquarters as the FASB. To date, the GASB has issued *GASB Statement No. 1,* "Authoritative Status of NCGA Pronouncements and AICPA Industry Audit Guide." The pronouncement states that all NCGA pronouncements issued and currently in effect are considered to be generally accepted accounting principles (GAAP) until their status is changed by a subsequent GASB pronouncement. The financial reporting guidance contained in the audit guide continues in force.

The MFOA changed its name in 1984 to the Government Finance Officers Association (GFOA), because its membership includes state and county finance officers as well as municipal finance officers.

OVERVIEW: MAJOR DIFFERENCES BETWEEN GOVERNMENTAL AND PRIVATE SECTOR REPORTING

Lack of mechanism for enforcing compliance with GAAP

In the private sector, publicly owned corporations must follow accounting standards as a result of legal requirements imposed by the Securities and Exchange Commission. No comparable enforcement mechanism exists for the governmental sector. Instead, the 50 states have the sovereign right to impose accounting and financial reporting requirements on governmental units within their jurisdiction. Thus, the rule-making bodies to date, being private organizations, have had no power over state and local governmental units. The states have been inconsistent in requiring their local governmental units to follow generally accepted accounting principles. Consequently, many governmental units issue financial reports that do not comply with GAAP in one or more respects. (However, governmental units that are audited by outside certified public accountants want to comply with GAAP, because the auditors must address whether GAAP has been followed.)

The major area of accounting for which governmental units do not follow generally accepted accounting principles is that of pension plans. Numerous state and local governmental units use the "pay-as-you-go" system, which is the cash basis of accounting. The dollar amount of the unfunded liabilities pertaining to pension plans that use this system is staggering. Consequently, to the extent that the financial statements of these governmental units do not reflect liabilities for these unfunded future obligations, such financial statements are grossly misleading.

No requirement for audited annual financial statements

Many governmental units are audited annually by certified public accountants or governmental audit agencies as a result of state laws, charter provisions, or voluntary action. (Federal legislation now requires an independent audit of all recipients of general revenue sharing funds over $25,000; an annual audit is required if the amount exceeds $100,000, whereas the audit need be only every three years if the amount does not exceed $100,000.) The financial statements of many state and local governmental units, however, do not need to be audited annually. Such governmental units may issue securities to the public without the public having the benefit of audited financial statements. In the private sector, a corporation that issues securities (stocks and bonds) to the public must (1) register the sale of such securities with the Securities and Exchange Commission (unless a statutory exemption is available); (2) maintain its books in accordance with generally accepted accounting principles; and (3) have its financial statements audited annually by a certified public accountant. The MFOA has issued a pronouncement titled *Disclosure Guidelines for Offerings of Securities by State and Local Governments* that it recommends be used when offering securities to investors. As with NCGA Statements, however, compliance is voluntary.

Financial reporting

Prior to *NCGA Statement 1,* most annual financial reports served the needs of government officials more than the needs of investors and other outsiders. Such reports contained masses of detail and were therefore quite difficult for the average citizen to understand. As a result, it was almost impossible to obtain a clear picture of either the overall financial condition or operations of governmental units. General Motors, for example, could issue an annual report having 10 pages of financial statements and notes that presented an understandable picture of financial condition and operations, whereas the city of Detroit would issue an extensive financial report having over 100 pages of financial statements, notes, and supporting schedules that few people could understand.

This manner of governmental reporting was criticized in the 1970s, when several major cities and counties had widely publicized, severe, and seemingly "sudden" financial crises. In response to this serious shortcoming, *NCGA Statement 1* calls for the presentation of specified financial statements, formally called **General Purpose Financial Statements,** in governmental units' annual financial reports. Such statements give readers a summary overview of financial position and operations. Although the annual financial reports still contain masses of detail, the addition of the general purpose financial statements has been a giant step forward in financial reporting.

The specific requirements pertaining to these financial statements are presented and discussed later in the chapter.

Despite the improvements made by *NCGA Statement 1,* financial reporting by governmental units is nowhere near the level of reporting for the private sector. In a 1983 survey of over 550 governmental units (out of more than 80,000), 54% of the opinions rendered by auditors contained qualifications. The reasons for the qualified opinions were varied, with the most common being the improper accounting for fixed assets and pensions.[3]

Nature of operations

Absence of profit motive—what to measure?   The fundamental difference between the governmental sector and the private sector is that the latter is organized and operated to make a profit for its owners, whereas the former exists to provide services to its citizens substantially on a nonprofit basis. In the private sector, profit measurement is possible because a causal relationship exists between expenses and revenues. Costs and expenses are incurred to generate revenues. As a result, it is appropriate to compare these categories and determine profitability. The services of governmental units are not provided to generate revenues. Thus, revenues are not earned. They stand alone. This concept raises the following key questions:

(1) Should revenues be compared with costs?
(2) Is some other measurement base more appropriate?

NCGA Statement 1 states that revenues should not be compared with costs as in the private sector. Instead, it presumes that the only appropriate measurement base is the **flow of resources.** The source or inflow of resources (revenues and borrowings) is presented in a statement, along with the use or outflow of resources (direct operating costs, payments for servicing debt, and payments for capital additions, all of which are referred to collectively as **expenditures**). Such a statement is, in substance, a statement of changes in financial position. In governmental accounting, however, this statement is called a **statement of revenues, expenditures, and changes in fund balance.** (The format of the statement is different from that used in the private sector, and it is more detailed.) The rationale for using the flow of resources as the measurement base is the presumption that the most meaningful information concerning a governmental unit's financial operations is: What resources were given to it and how were those resources used? *NCGA Statement 1* makes governmental units accountable in this respect.

Some accountants contend that, in addition to measuring the flow of resources, revenues should be compared with costs (including depreciation expense) even though the costs do not generate revenues as in the private sector. Such a statement would provide additional information as to **whether sufficient tax revenues were raised to cover the current costs of providing services.** (In the 1970s, many governmental units had severe financial

---

[3] Cornelius E. Tierney and Philip T. Calder of Arthur Young & Company, *Governmental Accounting Procedures and Practices* (New York: Elsevier Science Publishing Company, Inc., 1983), pp. 1 and 145.

crises from providing services far beyond the tax revenues being raised, creating substantial liabilities to be borne by future taxpayers.)

Whether an operating statement comparing revenues with the costs of providing services will be a future reporting requirement is conjecture. Such a statement is an important controversial issue. However, the improved financial reporting requirements contained in *NCGA Statement 1* (particularly the requirement to show borrowings separately from revenues in the statement of revenues, expenditures, and changes in fund balance) do provide a much better picture as to whether a governmental unit is spending beyond its means.

Legal requirements. Governmental units are regulated by constitutions, charters, and statutes. Many legal provisions pertain to financial accounting areas. For example, certain activities or specified revenues must frequently be accounted for separately from all other operations. The uses of certain revenues may be limited. In some instances, a certain method of accounting— such as the cash basis—may be stipulated. We discuss the accounting ramifications of these requirements later in the chapter.

Diversity of operations. Governmental operations are tremendously diverse. *NCGA Statement 1* classifies governmental operations in three broad categories, as follows:

(1) Governmental. Operations that do not resemble commercial activities are classified in the governmental category. These operations provide primary services and are normally financed from tax revenues. Examples are education, public safety, judicial system, social services, and administration.

(2) Proprietary. Proprietary operations resemble commercial activities. Usually financed wholly or partially from user charges, these operations may be considered secondary services. Examples are utilities, public transportation, parking facilities, and recreational facilities. Proprietary operations usually have the objective of earning a profit or recovering a certain level of operating costs.

(3) Fiduciary. Fiduciary operations pertain to accounting for assets held by a governmental unit as trustee or agent. The most common example is a pension fund for public employees.

Fund accounting. Because of the legal requirements pertaining to financial accounting areas and the diversity of governmental operations, the use of a single set of accounts to record and summarize all the financial transactions of a governmental unit is neither legally possible nor practical. As a result, fund accounting, whereby certain operations are accounted for separately from other operations, is predominant in governmental accounting. *NCGA Statement 1* defines a **fund** as follows:

> A fund is . . . a fiscal and accounting entity with a self-balancing set of accounts recording cash and other financial resources, together with all related liabilities and residual equities or balances, and changes therein, which are segregated for the

> purpose of carrying on activities or attaining certain objectives in accordance with special regulations, restrictions, or limitations.[4]

Thus, from an accounting viewpoint, a governmental unit consists of all the individual funds used to account for the entity's various operations and activities.

BASIC PRINCIPLES OF *NCGA STATEMENT 1*

In reading the 12 basic principles of *NCGA Statement 1* (which we have grouped into seven broad categories), we must understand the relationship of these basic principles to the accounting principles that have been established by the FASB and its predecessor organizations. This relationship is expressed in the AICPA's governmental audit guide as follows:

> [*NCGA Statement 1's*] principles do not represent a complete and separate body of accounting principles, but rather are a part of the whole body of generally accepted accounting principles which deal specifically with governmental units.[5]

This statement means that certain accounting principles established by the FASB and its predecessor organizations may apply to governmental units even though such principles were initially intended for the private sector. Such professional pronouncements have quite limited application to most governmental funds. However, these professional pronouncements have wide application to funds that are profit oriented.

Accounting for the cost of pension plans is an area that illustrates the interrelationship between the basic principles of *NCGA Statement 1* and the professional pronouncements. *APB Opinion No. 8,* "Accounting for the Cost of Pension Plans" discusses in great detail actuarial cost methods and accounting for actuarial gains and losses. *NCGA Statement 1* contains no such detailed discussion regarding pension accounting, but it does require that expenditures for pension costs be recorded on the accrual basis of accounting. Accordingly, to follow the accrual basis of accounting for pension costs, governmental units must observe the provisions of *APB Opinion No. 8.*

Generally accepted accounting principles, compliance with legal provisions, and conflicts between legal provisions and GAAP

NCGA Statement 1 recommends that

> A governmental accounting system must make it possible both: (a) to present fairly and with full disclosure the financial position and results of financial operations of the funds and account groups of the governmental unit in conformity with generally

---

[4] Reproduced with permission from *National Council on Governmental Accounting, Statement 1,* "Governmental Accounting and Financial Reporting Principles" (Chicago: Municipal Finance Officers Association of the United States and Canada, 1979), pp. 5–6. © Copyright 1979 by the Municipal Finance Officers Association of the United States and Canada.

[5] *ASLGU,* p. 9 (as amended by SOP 80-2).

accepted accounting principles; and (b) to determine and demonstrate compliance with finance-related legal and contractual provisions.[6]

In many cases, both objectives are satisfied through the use of a separate fund for a designated activity and the preparation of separate financial statements for the separate fund. In some cases, a legal provision may specify the use of a practice that is not in accordance with generally accepted accounting principles—for example, requiring that a certain fund maintain its books on the cash basis. In these cases, the books must be maintained according to the law. For financial reporting purposes, however, the cash basis trial balance must be adjusted (on a worksheet) to arrive at a presentation in accordance with GAAP. Financial statements would then be prepared and reported according to GAAP. *NCGA Statement 1* addresses such conflicts as follows:

> Where financial statements prepared in conformity with GAAP do not demonstrate finance-related legal and contractual compliance, the governmental unit should present such additional schedules and narrative explanations in the comprehensive annual financial report as may be necessary to report its legal compliance responsibilities and accountabilities. In extreme cases, preparation of a separate legal-basis special report may be necessary.[7]

The long-range solution to this problem is to eliminate any legal provisions that conflict with generally accepted accounting principles. The NCGA has recommended this solution.

Types of funds

NCGA Statement 1 recognizes and recommends the use of eight major types of funds, categorized into three broad areas, as follows:

Governmental Funds

(1) *The General Fund*—to account for all financial resources except those required to be accounted for in another fund.
(2) *Special Revenue Funds*—to account for the proceeds of specific revenue sources (other than special assessments, expendable trusts, or for major capital projects) that are legally restricted to expenditure for specified purposes.
(3) *Capital Projects Funds*—to account for financial resources to be used for the acquisition or construction of major capital facilities (other than those financed by proprietary funds, Special Assessment Funds, and Trust Funds).
(4) *Debt Service Funds*—to account for the accumulation of resources for, and the payment of, general long-term debt principal and interest.
(5) *Special Assessment Funds*—to account for the financing of public improvements or services deemed to benefit the properties against which special assessments are levied.

Proprietary Funds

(6) *Enterprise Funds*—to account for operations (a) that are financed and operated in a manner similar to private business enterprises—where the intent of the governing body is that the costs (expenses including depreciation) of providing

---

[6] *NCGA Statement 1*, p. 4.
[7] *NCGA Statement 1*, p. 5.

goods or services to the general public on a continuing basis be financed or recovered primarily through user charges; or (b) where the governing body has decided that periodic determination of revenues earned, expenses incurred, and/ or net income is appropriate for capital maintenance, public policy, management control, accountability, or other purposes.

(7) *Internal Service Funds*—to account for the financing of goods or services provided by one department or agency to other departments or agencies of the governmental unit, or to other governmental units, on a cost-reimbursement basis.

Fiduciary Funds

(8) *Trust and Agency Funds*—to account for assets held by a governmental unit in a trustee capacity or as an agent for individuals, private organizations, other governmental units, and/or other funds. These include (a) Expendable Trust Funds, (b) Nonexpendable Trust Funds, (c) Pension Trust Funds, and (d) Agency Funds.[8]

The number of funds used by a given governmental unit depends on legal requirements and what is practical in relation to the scope of operations. The General Fund, which usually accounts for the largest part of a governmental unit's total operations, is discussed and illustrated later in the chapter. The remaining types of funds are discussed and illustrated in Chapter 23.

Basis of accounting

APB Statement No. 4, "Basic Concepts and Accounting Principles Underlying Financial Statements of Businesses," defines the accrual basis of accounting as follows:

> The effects of transactions and other events on the assets and liabilities of a business enterprise are recognized and reported in the time period to which they relate rather than only when cash is received or paid.[9]

Thus, the difference between the accrual basis and the cash basis is merely one of **timing.** The private sector initially developed the accrual basis concept to determine properly net income and financial position. Even though the profit motive is absent from most public sector operations, the concept of "recording items in the period to which they relate" can be applied. *NCGA Statement 1* recommends using the accrual basis "to the fullest extent practicable in the government environment."[10]

Certain activities in the public sector lend themselves to the use of the accrual basis of accounting. For most activities, however, it is not practicable to use the accrual basis. Instead, a combination of the accrual basis and the cash basis is more appropriate. As a result, certain items are not recorded in the period to which they relate. Although this accounting basis might be appropriately called the "combination accrual and cash basis," the NCGA chose to call it the **modified accrual basis.**

---

[8] *NCGA Statement 1,* p. 7.
[9] *Accounting Principles Board Statement No. 4,* "Basic Concepts and Accounting Principles Underlying Financial Statements of Businesses" (New York: AICPA, 1970), paragraph 35.
[10] *NCGA Statement 1,* p. 11.

Accrual basis funds.   Activities accounted for in Enterprise Funds and Internal Service Funds (proprietary funds) and Nonexpendable Trust Funds (fiduciary funds) have the objectives of profit measurement or capital maintenance. Thus, the accrual basis of accounting as conceived for private businesses is entirely suitable for these funds. Also, Pension Trust Funds (fiduciary funds) exhibit the same characteristics as pension funds established in the private sector. Thus, the accrual basis also lends itself to use with Pension Trust Funds. Accordingly, for each of these funds, revenues earned and expenses incurred may be accrued and recognized in the period to which they relate in essentially the same manner as in the private sector. For these reasons, *NCGA Statement 1* recommends the use of the accrual basis for these funds.

Modified accrual basis funds.   For all remaining funds (the five governmental funds and Expendable Trust Funds), *NCGA Statement 1* recommends the use of the modified accrual basis of accounting, which is described as follows:

> Revenues should be recognized in the accounting period in which they become **available and measurable** [emphasis added]. Expenditures should be recognized in the accounting period in which the fund liability is incurred, if measurable, except for unmatured interest on general long-term debt and on special assessment indebtedness secured by interest-bearing special assessment levies, which should be recognized when due.[11]

The reason for using the modified accrual basis of accounting for these funds may be attributed to the nature of governmental revenue sources and activities. We discuss the modified accrual basis first concerning revenues and then expenditures.

Revenues.   Fund revenues are not recognized when earned (as is done under the accrual basis); the "available and measurable" criterion is used because it is more appropriate. (Most governmental operations do not "earn" revenues.) Thus, revenues are recognized when they become **"susceptible to accrual."** The term **available** means a revenue source is "collectible within the current period or soon enough thereafter to be used to pay liabilities of the current period."[12]

The application of these revenue-related criteria results in (1) certain revenues being recognized entirely on the accrual basis; (2) certain revenues being recognized entirely on the cash basis; and (3) certain revenues being recognized partially on the cash basis and partially on the accrual basis. We discuss each of these revenue categories more fully below.

(1) Accrual basis revenues.   Many revenue sources may be accrued in essentially the same manner as is done in the private sector. Some of the most common examples are property taxes, grants, and interfund transfers:

---

[11] *NCGA Statement 1*, p. 10.
[12] *NCGA Statement 1*, p. 11.

A. **Property taxes.** Property taxes may be precisely determined for each specific property to which a legally enforceable lien attaches. Some governmental units bill property owners in advance of the fiscal year to which the property taxes relate. For control purposes, property taxes should be recorded at the time of billing. Property tax revenues, however, should be shown as deferred revenues until the start of the fiscal year to which they pertain, because the revenues do not relate to the prior fiscal year (even though the assessment date may have been in that year).

B. **Grants and interfund transfers.** Most grants from other governmental units and interfund transfers within a governmental unit are susceptible to accrual in the period to which they relate because an irrevocable commitment exists.

(2) **Cash basis revenues.** Many revenue sources may not be accrued, because governmental units cannot determine the tax receivable from individual taxpayers at each month-end. The two broad categories of such revenues are self-assessment basis revenues and such miscellaneous revenues as license and permit fees, fines, and parking meter revenues.

A. **Self-assessment basis revenues.** Self-assessment basis revenues include income taxes, sales taxes, and gross receipts taxes. The distinguishing feature of this type of revenue is that the governmental unit does not bill the taxpayer. The receivable for each revenue source at each month-end may only be estimated, because the actual amounts are unknown until taxpayer reports are received or payments are collected. It should be noted that the use of income tax withholding procedures often produces results that closely approximate the accrual basis of accounting in that tax revenues are received substantially in the period in which the income is earned by taxpayers. Even when income tax withholding procedures are used, however, the final amount to be paid to the government (or to be refunded to the taxpayer in the event of excess withholdings or estimated interim payments) is not known until several months after the year in which the taxpayer earns the income.

B. **Miscellaneous revenues.** Miscellaneous revenues include the following items:

1. **Annual business licenses.** Licenses are usually issued for new businesses at the time of payment. Because a license may not be granted, a bona fide receivable does not exist when an application is filed. Although governmental units often bill taxpayers for renewals of their annual business licenses, this billing (whether prior to or at the start of the fiscal year to which the bill pertains) is usually not relevant. The governmental unit does not know if the taxpayer will renew the license until it receives payment.

2. **Construction and home improvement permits.** Construction and home improvement permits are usually issued at the time of payment. The filing of an application does not create a bona fide receivable, because the permit may not be granted.

3. **Fines.** Most fines are collected when they are levied, which is when the amount of the fine is determined.

        4. Parking meter revenues. The amounts of parking meter revenues are not determinable until the meters have been emptied and the receipts have been counted.

(3) Partial cash and partial accrual basis revenues. This category merely applies the accrual concept to portions of revenues normally recognized on the cash basis. For example, sales taxes due from other governmental units or merchants that have not been received at the normal time of receipt should be accrued, providing the criteria of measurability and availability are met. Revenues received before their normal time of receipt that pertain to subsequent periods should be recorded as deferred revenues.

    Expenditures. By requiring expenditures to be recognized in the period in which the liability is incurred, the accrual basis is used. (This is merely a different way of saying that items should be recorded and recognized in the period to which they relate.) The strict recognition of expenditures in the period in which the liability is incurred results in the omission of prepayments and inventories from the balance sheet. Usually, these items are so minor in relation to governmental operations that such omission is an insignificant departure from generally accepted accounting principles. However, if inventory is significant, *NCGA Statement 1* recommends that it be reported in the balance sheet.[13] The manner of reporting inventory in the balance sheet is discussed later in the chapter. In Chapter 23, we discuss the two specified exceptions to the use of the accrual basis—recognizing interest on general long-term debt and special assessment indebtedness when due rather than in the period in which the interest liability arises.

    AICPA position on modified accrual basis. The AICPA governmental audit guide states the following concerning the use of the modified accrual basis of accounting for governmental funds and Expendable Trust Funds:

> Generally accepted accounting principles comprehend the use of those principles applicable in the circumstances. . . . Financial statements prepared on the modified accrual basis of accounting . . . are in conformity with generally accepted accounting principles . . . .[14]

Fixed assets and long-term liabilities

    Accounting for fixed assets. The nature of governmental operations is such that more meaningful financial reporting results if certain fixed assets are accounted for in fund accounts and all other fixed assets (referred to collectively as **general fixed assets**) are accounted for outside the funds in **account groups.** *NCGA Statement 1* recommends the following:

> Fixed assets related to specific proprietary funds or Trust Funds should be accounted for through those funds. All other fixed assets of a governmental unit should be accounted for through the General Fixed Assets Account Group.[15]

[13] *NCGA Statement 1,* p. 12.
[14] *ASLGU,* pp. 89–90.
[15] *NCGA Statement 1,* p. 8.

Fixed assets are excluded from the governmental funds because such assets do not constitute financial resources available for spending purposes. Because one of the reporting objectives of the governmental funds is to reflect the financial resources available for spending purposes, fixed assets must be excluded from governmental funds to accomplish this objective.

The General Fixed Assets Account Group is not a separate fund but merely a list of a governmental unit's general fixed assets, maintained in account form. These accounts are complemented by credit accounts showing the sources by which the assets were obtained. These accounts are said to be a "self-balancing" set of accounts. The General Fixed Assets Account Group is discussed in detail in Chapter 23.

Accounting for long-term liabilities. As with general fixed assets, more meaningful financial reporting is possible if certain long-term liabilities are accounted for in fund accounts and all other long-term debt (referred to collectively as **general long-term debt**) is accounted for outside the funds in account groups. *NCGA Statement 1* recommends the following:

> Long-term liabilities of proprietary funds, Special Assessment Funds, and Trust Funds should be accounted for through those funds. All other unmatured general long-term liabilities of the governmental unit should be accounted for through the General Long-Term Debt Account Group.[16]

Certain long-term debt is excluded from governmental funds because such debt does not require the current use of financial resources of the governmental funds. Because one of the reporting objectives of the governmental funds is to reflect those liabilities to be paid from available financial resources, these liabilities must be excluded from governmental funds to accomplish this objective. Furthermore, such debt is the liability of the governmental unit as a whole and not the liability of any specific fund. As such, it is secured by the taxing powers of the governmental unit and not by the resources available in a specific fund.

The General Long-Term Debt Account Group is also a "self-balancing" set of accounts because the list of liabilities, maintained in account form, is balanced by accounts showing (1) amounts, if any, set aside in Debt Service Funds for repayment of the General Long-Term Debt, and (2) amounts yet to be provided for repayment of the General Long-Term Debt. The General Long-Term Debt Account Group is discussed in detail in Chapter 23.

Valuation of fixed assets. With respect to the valuation of fixed assets, *NCGA Statement 1* specifies the following:

> Fixed assets should be accounted for at cost or, if the cost is not practicably determinable, at estimated cost. Donated fixed assets should be recorded at their estimated fair value at the time received.[17]

---

[16] *NCGA Statement 1*, p. 8.
[17] *NCGA Statement 1*, p. 9.

Depreciation of fixed assets. With respect to depreciating fixed assets, *NCGA Statement 1* recommends the following:

> Depreciation of general fixed assets should not be recorded in the accounts of governmental funds. Depreciation of general fixed assets may be recorded in cost accounting systems or calculated for cost finding analysis; and accumulated depreciation may be recorded in the General Fixed Assets Account Group [an optional treatment].
>
> Depreciation of fixed assets accounted for in a proprietary fund should be recorded in the accounts of that fund. Depreciation is also recognized in those Trust Funds where expenses, net income, and/or capital maintenance are measured.[18]

Commercial businesses record depreciation expense to match revenues with expenses, so that net income may be properly determined. Fixed assets accounted for in proprietary funds and certain trust funds also have the objectives of profitability or capital maintenance (cost recovery). Accordingly, depreciation expense is properly recorded in these funds, because income statements are prepared.

For all other funds, income statements are not presented, nor is a statement presented comparing revenues with costs (which would include depreciation expense). Instead, only a statement of revenues, expenditures, and changes in fund balance based on the "flow of resources" measurement base is presented. Accordingly, when a general fixed asset is acquired, it is reflected as an expenditure in the fund at the time of acquisition. Depreciation expense would not be recorded in this statement because it does not constitute a flow of resources.

The absence of depreciation expense in the statement of revenues, expenditures, and changes in fund balance should not be considered a departure from the accrual basis of accounting. *NCGA Statement 1* makes an important clarification regarding what is encompassed by the accrual basis of accounting, as follows:

> Unfortunately, the terms "accrual" and "accrual accounting" often are interpreted to mean "income determination accounting," and thus to connote the recognition of depreciation in the course of expense measurement. This misunderstanding likely has arisen because most literature centers on income determination and uses the terms "accrual" and "accrual accounting" in that context. It should be recognized, however, that depreciation and amortization are allocations, not accruals, and that "accrual" in a governmental fund accounting context does not mean that depreciation, amortization, and similar allocations should be recognized.[19]

This position is consistent with the AICPA's governmental audit guide, which does not state that the lack of depreciation expense in these funds is a departure from generally accepted accounting principles.

Budgets and budgetary accounting

Budgets. Budgets are used in the public sector for planning, controlling, and evaluating operations just as they are used in the private sector. A

---

[18] *NCGA Statement 1*, p. 10.
[19] *NCGA Statement 1*, p. 12.

budget is merely a plan of financial operations covering a specified period of time. For all governmental, proprietary, and fiduciary funds (other than Agency Funds, which are custodial in nature), *NCGA Statement 1* recommends that "an annual budget(s) should be adopted by every governmental unit."[20]

Prepared under the direction of the governmental unit's chief executive officer, the **annual** budget is submitted to the legislative body for review, possible modification, and formal adoption. For governmental funds and certain fiduciary funds, the legal significance of adopting the budget is that it serves as the statutory authorization for spending an estimated amount during the subsequent fiscal year. This authorization is referred to as an **appropriation.** For the proprietary funds and certain fiduciary funds, the formal adoption of a budget is considered to be merely the approval of a proposed operating plan, as opposed to a statutory authorization to spend a certain amount of dollars.

A **long-term** budget covers a period of several years. Long-term budgets restricted to major capital additions and improvements are referred to as **capital** budgets.

Budgetary accounting. Because legal limitations are imposed on certain of the funds (primarily the governmental funds) as to the amount that may be spent during a fiscal year, it is exceedingly important to monitor and control spending, so that expenditures do not exceed this limitation. *NCGA Statement 1* recommends, "The accounting system should provide the basis for appropriate budgetary control."[21]

NCGA Statement 1 specifies the following two areas in which budgetary accounts should be used to monitor and control spending: (1) recording the annual budget in the general ledger; and (2) recording purchase order commitments in the general ledger, which is referred to as **encumbrance accounting.**

To enhance the understanding of budgetary integration in the general ledger, we use the technique illustrated in the 1980 edition of *GAAFR* of printing budgetary account descriptions in all capital letters. As a result, we can consider all budgetary accounts as a separate trial balance from the regular general ledger accounts. We also use the same account descriptions—for budgetary and actual accounts—used in the 1980 edition of *GAAFR,* because these descriptions are now used by both the AICPA (in their official solutions to the CPA examinations) and the CPA examination review courses (in their course materials).

Recording the annual budget. The budget for the General Fund and Special Revenue Funds is recorded in the general ledger. (The annual budget pertaining to Capital Projects Funds, Special Assessment Funds, and Debt Service Funds, is recorded in the general ledger only if it would serve a useful purpose, determined on a case-by-case basis.) Assuming a governmental unit expects its General Fund revenues to exceed its General Fund appropriations for the new fiscal year, the budget is recorded in the General Fund's general ledger as follows.

[20] *NCGA Statement 1,* p. 12.
[21] *NCGA Statement 1,* p. 13.

```
ESTIMATED REVENUES CONTROL .................  1,000,000
    APPROPRIATIONS CONTROL...................                980,000
    BUDGETARY FUND BALANCE .................                 20,000
    To record the legally adopted annual
    operating budget.
```

The ESTIMATED REVENUES CONTROL account is a control account. Actual revenues are recorded in a Revenues Control account. The detail making up the ESTIMATED REVENUES CONTROL account is recorded directly in the individual subsidiary Revenue accounts at the start of the year. As a result, estimated revenues may be readily compared with actual revenues throughout the year. Although revenues cannot be "controlled" in the manner that expenditures can be controlled, a governmental unit may be able to curtail spending if it appears that revenue inflows will not be reasonably close to estimated revenues.

Likewise, the APPROPRIATIONS CONTROL account is a control account. Actual expenditures are recorded in subsidiary accounts, and total expenditures are reflected in an Expenditures Control account. The detail making up the APPROPRIATIONS CONTROL account is also recorded directly in the individual subsidiary Expenditures accounts at the start of the year. As a result, expenditures to date may be readily compared with the authorized spending limitation, revealing how much more may be spent.

The difference between a fund's assets and liabilities is the fund's equity. For governmental funds and fiduciary funds, this difference is recorded in a Fund Balance account. (For proprietary funds, which do not use budgetary accounts, Contributed Capital and Retained Earnings accounts are used.) A governmental unit's budget for the coming fiscal year may reflect an intention to increase (as in the above example) or decrease the fund balance amount existing at the beginning of the year. Most governmental units (with the notable exception of the federal government) try to accumulate a reasonable "surplus" in the Fund Balance account in case unforeseen adverse events occur. In recording the budget in the general ledger, the difference between the debit to ESTIMATED REVENUES CONTROL and the credit to APPROPRIATIONS CONTROL is credited (as in the above example) or debited to BUDGETARY FUND BALANCE.

Recording the budget in the general ledger does not affect the year-end balance in the Fund Balance account because the budget entry is reversed at year-end as part of the normal closing process.

Encumbrance accounting. As stated earlier, expenditures are recognized when the fund liability is incurred, which is usually when goods are received or services are rendered. Many expenditures involve the issuance of purchase orders, whereby goods are received or services are rendered at a later date. Outstanding purchase orders are commitments for future expenditures. To monitor and control spending properly, governmental units must keep track of the amount of outstanding purchase orders. This is accomplished by recording the amount of each purchase order (including the amount of contracts entered into) in the general ledger at the time of issuance. For example, assuming a purchase order for $50,000 is issued, the following budgetary entry would be made.

```
ENCUMBRANCES CONTROL ........................  50,000
    FUND BALANCE RESERVED FOR
        ENCUMBRANCES ............................          50,000
    To record encumbrances for purchase
    orders issued.
```

The ENCUMBRANCES CONTROL account may be thought of as an "expenditure-to-be" account. At a later date, when the goods or services are received, the entry is reversed, and the expenditure is recorded. Assume in the above example that the actual cost of the goods received under the purchase was $49,000. The following entries would be made:

```
FUND BALANCE RESERVED FOR ENCUMBRANCES.....  50,000
    ENCUMBRANCES CONTROL ......................          50,000
    To cancel encumbrances of $50,000 upon
    receipt of materials and rendering of
    services totaling $49,000.

Expenditures control ....................................  49,000
    Vouchers payable....................................          49,000
    To record expenditures of $49,000 for
    goods and services which were previously
    encumbered for $50,000.
```

Like the APPROPRIATIONS CONTROL account, the ENCUMBRANCES CONTROL account is a control account. Each encumbrance is recorded in the subsidiary Expenditures accounts. As a result, the remaining amount that may be legally spent at a given time is readily determined by subtracting expenditures to date and encumbrances outstanding from appropriations. This calculation can be done at the control level or at the detail level using the subsidiary accounts.

Illustration 22-1 shows what a subsidiary ledger might look like at the departmental level. Note that the format indicates the spendable amount remaining at the end of each month. (Only two months' activities are illustrated.) If an encumbrances column were not included, the department supervisor might erroneously conclude that $94,000 ($100,000 appropriations − $6,000 expenditures) was available for spending at July 31, 19X1. This figure is incorrect because purchase orders outstanding at July 31, 19X1 total $7,000.

Illustration 22-1
Example of a department's subsidiary ledger account

Department No. 34				
Date	Appropriation	Expenditures	Encumbrances	Remaining Spendable Amount
July 1, 19X1	$100,000			$100,000
July 19X1.............		$ 6,000	$ 7,000	(13,000)
July 31, 19X1	$100,000	$ 6,000	$ 7,000	$ 87,000
August 19X1		11,000	(3,000)	(8,000)
August 31, 19X1........	$100,000	$17,000	$ 4,000	$ 79,000

Thus, of the $94,000 not yet spent at July 31, 19X1, $7,000 is earmarked for the outstanding purchase orders. This leaves only $87,000 available for spending at July 31, 19X1. The objective of the procedure, of course, is to prevent spending more than has been authorized (appropriated).

From the preceding discussion and analysis, you should realize that only the debit entry recording the encumbrance is used in controlling spending. The credit to the FUND BALANCE RESERVED FOR ENCUMBRANCES account serves no control function other than to provide a credit for double-entry bookkeeping. Thus, it is merely a contra account.

Encumbrances outstanding at year-end. When encumbrances are outstanding at year-end, the encumbrance budgetary accounts must be closed. To illustrate, assume a governmental unit has outstanding at year-end $5,000 of encumbrances. The following journal entry would be made:

FUND BALANCE RESERVED FOR ENCUMBRANCES....... 5,000
    ENCUMBRANCES CONTROL   5,000
    To close out encumbrances outstanding
    at year-end by reversing the entry that previously
    recorded them.

[handwritten margin note: BUDGET'S CONTROL ITEMS IN LARGE TYPE]

Governmental units generally honor purchase orders and commitments outstanding at year-end. In such cases, *NCGA Statement 1* requires that encumbrances outstanding at year-end be disclosed as a reservation of the Fund Balance account (similar to an appropriation of retained earnings for a private corporation). This requires an additional journal entry, as follows:

Unreserved fund balance 5,000
    Fund balance reserved for encumbrances   5,000
    To record *actual* fund balance reserve account
    to indicate the portion of year-end fund
    balance segregated for expenditure upon
    vendor performance.

Thus, if a fund had a year-end total fund balance of $75,000, the fund balance would be presented in the balance sheet as follows:

FUND EQUITY
    Fund balance:
        Reserved for encumbrances .... $ 5,000
        Unreserved...   70,000
        Total Fund Balance $75,000

From this presentation, financial statement readers know that $5,000 of the $75,000 total fund balance has been earmarked for encumbrances outstanding at year-end. Thus the uncommitted amount available for spending in the following year is $70,000.

At the start of the new year, the preceding two $5,000 journal entries would be reversed to reestablish budgetary control over encumbrances outstanding in the normal manner. These reversing entries are as follows:

Fund balance reserved for encumbrances	5,000	
Unreserved fund balance		5,000
To reverse appropriation of fund balance		
made at the end of the prior year.		

ENCUMBRANCES CONTROL	5,000	
FUND BALANCE RESERVED FOR ENCUMBRANCES...		5,000
To reestablish budgetary control over		
encumbrances outstanding at the end of		
the prior year which will be honored		
during the current year.		

Budgetary comparisons—GAAP basis. A financial reporting requirement of *NCGA Statement 1* is the preparation of "budgetary comparison statements or schedules" (as appropriate) in which budgeted data are compared with actual data for the year. Recall that under GAAP reporting, encumbrances outstanding at year-end are not reported in the statement of revenues, expenditures, and changes in fund balance. They would become expenditures in the following year and be reported as expenditures in that year. To present a meaningful comparison of actual expenditures with the budgeted expenditures, the budgeted expenditures must be prepared on a basis consistent with GAAP. To do this, amounts must be included in the following year's budget for encumbrances outstanding at the current year-end. Thus, it can be said that **encumbrances outstanding at the end of the current year "lapse," but then they are "rebudgeted" and "reappropriated" in the following year.** Without this procedure, the following year's expenditures would include amounts relating to the encumbrances outstanding at the end of the prior year, but no amount would appear in the following year's budget for these expenditures, resulting in a meaningless comparison.

To illustrate this comparison process, we assume the following data:

(1) For 19X1, a governmental unit expects routine expenditures of $500,000 and also the purchase of a new fire truck for $30,000. Thus, it budgets $530,000 for 19X1 expenditures.
(2) Actual spending occurs according to budget, except that the fire truck is received in early 19X2 instead of 19X1.
(3) The governmental unit expects routine expenditures of $500,000 for 19X2. It also "reappropriates" or "rebudgets" an additional $30,000 to cover the fire truck for 19X2. Thus, the total budget for 19X2 expenditures is $530,000.
(4) Actual spending for 19X2 occurs according to budget.

The budgetary comparison (on a GAAP basis) is as follows.

| | GAAP Basis of Comparison | | |
	Budget	Actual	Variance Favorable (Unfavorable)
19X1:			
Expenditures..........	$530,000	$500,000	$30,000
19X2:			
Expenditures..........	530,000	530,000	-0-

Budgetary comparisons—Non-GAAP "budgetary" basis. Most governmental units do not prepare their annual operating budgets on a basis consistent with GAAP. Thus, the following year's budget does not include amounts to honor the encumbrances outstanding at year-end. Instead, **the authorization to honor the encumbrances outstanding merely carries over to the following year.** This manner of budgeting is commonly referred to as the **non-GAAP "budgetary" basis.** To make a valid comparison to the budgeted data, the expenditures pertaining to the current-year budget must be combined with the encumbrances outstanding at year-end. Using the information in the preceding example, but assuming the non-GAAP "budgetary" basis of budgeting, the budgetary comparison would be as follows:

| | Non-GAAP "Budgetary" Basis of Comparison | | |
	Budget	Actual	Variance Favorable (Unfavorable)
19X1:			
Expenditures and encumbrances	$530,000	$530,000	$-0-
19X2:			
Expenditures and encumbrances	500,000	500,000	-0-

When the annual operating budget is prepared on the non-GAAP "budgetary" basis, encumbrances and expenditures must be separated by year of appropriation. This is because current-year expenditures that resulted from encumbrances outstanding at the end of the prior year are not reported as current-year expenditures in the budgetary comparison statements. (They are reported, instead, as encumbrances in the prior year's budgetary comparison statement.) In our example dealing with the fire truck, the Expenditures—19X1 account (or Expenditures Control—Prior Year) would be charged in 19X2 when the fire truck was received.

When the budgetary comparison statement is presented on the non-GAAP "budgetary" basis, *NCGA Statement 1* still requires the presentation of a statement of revenues, expenditures, and changes in fund balance (not involving budgetary comparisons) on a GAAP basis.

Regardless of whether (a) encumbrances outstanding at year-end lapse and are reappropriated in the following year's budget, or (b) the spending authority carries over to the following year, the year-end closing entries pertaining to the encumbrances and reserving a portion of the fund balance are identical.

Financial reporting

As discussed earlier in the chapter, the financial reporting requirements of *NCGA Statement 1* substantially upgraded former reporting practices. *NCGA Statement 1* recommended that financial statements be presented in the governmental unit's annual financial report using a "reporting pyramid" concept. The "pyramid" consists of four levels of financial information, each of which provide more detailed information than the previous level. Illustration 22-2 shows how this reporting pyramid might appear.

The reporting pyramid includes the following levels of financial information:

(1) Combined financial statements—Overview (General purpose financial statements). The financial statements in the first level present the overall financial position and operating results of a governmental unit as a whole. They are referred to as the "General Purpose Financial Statements." Level 1 contains

> (1) Combined Balance Sheet—All Fund Types and Account Groups.
> (2) Combined Statement of Revenues, Expenditures, and Changes in Fund Balance—All Governmental Fund Types.
> (3) Combined Statement of Revenues, Expenditures, and Changes in Fund Balances—Budget and Actual—General and Special Revenue Fund Types (and similar governmental fund types for which annual budgets have been legally adopted).
> (4) Combined Statement of Revenues, Expenses, and Changes in Retained Earnings (or Equity)—All Proprietary Fund Types.
> (5) Combined Statement of Changes in Financial Position—All Proprietary Fund Types.
> (6) Notes to the financial statements.
> (Trust Fund operations may be reported in (2), (4), and (5), as appropriate, or separately.)[22]

The combined balance sheet in (1) shows data for each fund type and account group in columnar format. The combined statement in (2) shows data only for each fund type. Both statements may present a total column, which may or may not reflect interfund and similar eliminations. If a total column is presented, it is described as "memorandum only." For the combined statements in (3), (4), and (5), a total "memorandum only" column is used. Illustrations of the financial statements in (1), (2), and (4) are presented in the Appendix to this chapter (pages 838–42).

(2) Combining statements by fund type. In preparing combined financial statements for the first reporting level, individual funds of a given type must be combined. The financial statements in level 2 present the individual funds that have been combined, along with a total column that ties into the appropriate column of the combined financial statements in level 1. (Note that this level would be completely bypassed if a governmental unit had no more than one fund for each type of fund.)

(3) Individual fund and account group statements. Level 3 presents data for (1) individual funds not shown in level 2, and (2) individual funds for which additional detailed information is provided—such as

---

[22] *NCGA Statement 1,* p. 19.

Illustration 22-2
The Financial Reporting Pyramid

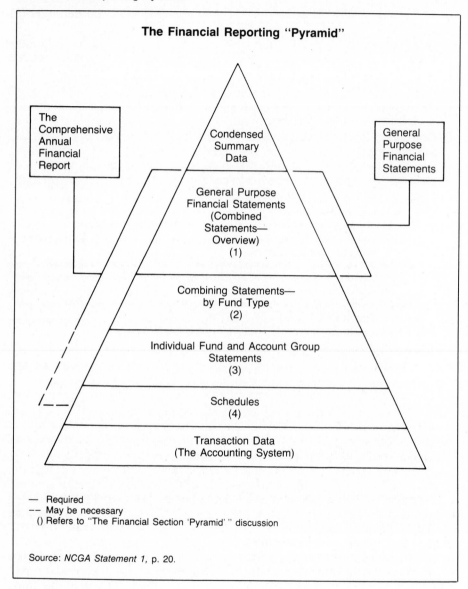

The Financial Reporting "Pyramid"

Condensed Summary Data

General Purpose Financial Statements (Combined Statements— Overview) (1)

Combining Statements— by Fund Type (2)

Individual Fund and Account Group Statements (3)

Schedules (4)

Transaction Data (The Accounting System)

The Comprehensive Annual Financial Report

General Purpose Financial Statements

— Required
-- May be necessary
() Refers to "The Financial Section 'Pyramid' " discussion

Source: *NCGA Statement 1*, p. 20.

budgetary and prior-year comparative data. Illustrations of individual fund and account group financial statements are presented later in the chapter and in Chapter 23.

(4) Schedules. Level 4 primarily presents data in connection with demonstrating legal compliance for finance-related matters. Other useful information may also be presented at this level.

In presenting operating statements at any level in the reporting pyramid and for any fund or fund type, *NCGA Statement 1* recommends that such statements incorporate changes in fund balance or retained earnings (as appropriate).[23]

In addition to financial statements and notes required for adequate disclosure, governmental units generally include in their annual reports substantial statistical tables and data covering such items as population, number of employees, assessed values, and principal taxpayers.

Classification and terminology

NCGA Statement 1 recommends the following classification reporting practices:

> Interfund transfers and proceeds of general long-term debt issues [that are not recorded as fund liabilities] should be classified separately from fund revenues and expenditures or expenses.
>
> Governmental fund revenues should be classified by fund and source. Expenditures should be classified by fund, function (or program), organization unit, activity, character, and principal classes of objects.
>
> Proprietary fund revenues and expenses should be classified in essentially the same manner as those of similar business organizations, functions, or activities.[24]

Classifying proceeds of general long-term debt separately from fund revenues is a substantial improvement over the former practice of showing such proceeds as revenues. Such proceeds must be shown under a separate section of the operating statement of the recipient fund called Other Financing Sources. Reporting interfund transfers separately from fund revenues and expenditures or expenses is also a substantial improvement over the former practice of showing these items as revenues and expenditures or expenses.

Types of interfund transactions. In *NCGA Statement 1,* interfund transactions are divided into the following four types: (a) quasi-external transactions, (b) reimbursements, (c) loans or advances, and (d) transfers. Only category (c) requires no further explanation.

Quasi-external transactions. These interfund transactions are reported as revenues, expenditures, or expenses in the particular funds, because the transactions would be treated as such if they were conducted between a fund and an organization external to the governmental unit. An example would be a city's electric utility (which would be accounted for in an Enterprise Fund) supplying electricity to the city. The city's General Fund would report expenditures, but the Enterprise Fund would report revenues in the same amount. The theory here is that the General Fund would have recorded an expenditure if it had been supplied the electricity by a private utility.

Reimbursements. Transactions in which a fund (Fund A, for example) reimburses another fund (Fund B, for example) for expenditures or expenses

---

[23] *NCGA Statement 1,* p. 22.
[24] *NCGA Statement 1,* p. 15.

it (Fund B) incurs are reimbursements. The reimbursing fund (Fund A) would report expenditures or expenses, and the reimbursed fund (Fund B) would reduce its expenditures or expenses. This prevents the double reporting of expenditures or expenses and ensures that these items are reported in the correct fund.

Transfers.   All interfund transactions that do not fit into one of the other three categories are called transfers. Transfers fit into the following two categories:

(1) **Residual equity transfers.**   Residual equity transfers are **nonrecurring** or **nonroutine** transfers of equity between funds made in connection with the formation, expansion, contraction, or discontinuance of a fund. Because such transfers are of a nonoperating nature, they are reported **outside the operating statements** as direct additions to or subtractions from the fund equity accounts (Fund Balance, Contributed Capital, or Retained Earnings, as appropriate).
(2) **Operating transfers.**   Operating transfers are made in connection with the **normal operation** of the recipient fund. Accordingly, they are reported **within the operating statements** of the affected funds but under a separate category called Other Financing Sources (Uses).[25]

Examples of the various types of interfund transactions are given later in the chapter and in Chapter 23, where we present a detailed discussion of the individual funds and the related operating statements.

THE GENERAL FUND

Nature and scope of activities

The **General Fund** accounts for all revenues and expenditures of a governmental unit that are not accounted for in one of the special purpose funds. Because all other funds are special purpose funds, most activities and current operations of governmental units are financed from the General Fund. For instance, general government administration, public safety, judicial system, health, sanitation, welfare, and culture-recreation are usually accounted for in this fund.

Normally, more types of revenues flow into this fund than any other fund. For instance, property taxes, sales taxes, income taxes, transfer taxes, licenses, permits, fines, penalties, and interest on delinquent taxes commonly flow into the General Fund. In addition, the General Fund may receive monies from other governmental units; such receipts are classified by *NCGA Statement 2* as follows:

> A *grant* is a contribution or gift of cash or other assets from another government to be used or expended for a specified purpose, activity, or facility. *Capital grants* are restricted by the grantor for the acquisition and/or construction of fixed (capital) assets

---

[25] *NCGA Statement 1*, p. 16.

[which would be accounted for in a Capital Projects Fund]. All other grants are *operating grants*.

An *entitlement* is the amount of payment to which a state or local government is entitled as determined by the federal government (e.g., the Director of the Office of Revenue Sharing) pursuant to an allocation formula contained in applicable statutes. A *shared revenue* is a revenue levied by one government but shared on a predetermined basis, often in proportion to the amount collected at the local level, with another government or class of government.[26]

The General Fund often engages in a variety of transactions with other funds, as described on pages 831–32.

Comprehensive illustration:
Journal entries and financial statements

The June 30, 19X1 balance sheet for Emerson City's General Fund is shown in Illustration 22-3.

Before proceeding with assumed transactions for the subsequent fiscal year, the following points should be understood with regard to Illustration 22-3:

(1) Omission of prepayments and supplies inventory. Because we assume that these items are insignificant at June 30, 19X1, they are excluded from the balance sheet.

(2) Fund balance—Reserved for encumbrances. The Fund Balance—Reserved for Encumbrances account signifies that a portion of the fund's assets has been earmarked for liquidation of outstanding purchase orders.

---

[26] Reproduced with permission from *National Council on Governmental Accounting, Statement 2,* "Grant, Entitlement, and Shared Revenue Accounting and Reporting by State and Local Governments" (Chicago: Municipal Finance Officers Association of the United States and Canada, 1979), p. 1. © Copyright 1979 by the Municipal Finance Officers Association of the United States and Canada.

Illustration 22-3

EMERSON CITY Balance Sheet—General Fund June 30, 19X1	
Assets	
Cash	$57,000
Property taxes receivable—delinquent	32,000
Less: Allowance for estimated uncollectible taxes—delinquent	(9,000)
Total Assets	$80,000
Liabilities and Fund Equity	
Vouchers payable	$26,000
Fund balance:	
Reserved for encumbrances	$20,000
Unreserved	34,000
Total Fund Balance	$54,000
Total Liabilities and Fund Equity	$80,000

(3) Fund balance—Unreserved. The $34,000 Unreserved Fund Balance account signifies that the fund has $34,000 of uncommitted assets available for spending purposes in the following fiscal year.

Assumed transactions and related journal entries for the fiscal year July 1, 19X1 through June 30, 19X2 are discussed in the following paragraphs.

(1) Adoption of the budget. The city council approved and adopted the budget for the year. The budget contained the following amounts:

Estimated revenues	$700,000
Authorized expenditures (including $20,000 pertaining to encumbrances existing at June 30, 19X1, which has been "reappropriated")	670,000
Estimated operating transfer in from the city-owned electric utility, which is accounted for in an Enterprise Fund	55,000
Authorized operating transfer out to the Library Debt Service Fund	75,000

As explained earlier, the adoption of the budget for the General Fund involves the use of budgetary accounts, as follows:

ESTIMATED REVENUES CONTROL	700,000	
ESTIMATED OTHER FINANCING SOURCES CONTROL	55,000	
APPROPRIATIONS CONTROL.....................		670,000
ESTIMATED OTHER FINANCING USES CONTROL...............................		75,000
BUDGETARY FUND BALANCE		10,000
To record the legally adopted annual operating budget.		

(2) Property taxes. Property taxes for the period July 1, 19X1 through June 30, 19X2 were levied in the amount of $500,000. Emerson estimated that $12,000 of this amount would be uncollectible. During the year, $484,000 was collected ($21,000 of which pertained to delinquent taxes of the prior fiscal year), and $8,000 of prior-year delinquent balances was written off as uncollectible. A $16,000 allowance for uncollectibles was considered necessary as of June 30, 19X2. Property taxes unpaid at the end of the fiscal year become delinquent.

As explained earlier, the accrual basis of accounting is usually appropriate for property taxes. In this case, the city's fiscal year coincides with the period to which the property taxes relate; accordingly, the property tax levy is appropriately recorded on the first day of the new fiscal year. In recording the property taxes, the estimated uncollectible amount is netted against the revenues, and the use of a Bad Debts Expense account is avoided. A Bad Debts Expense account would be inappropriate, because the General Fund has expenditures, not expenses. At the end of the fiscal year, remaining property tax receivables and the related allowance for uncollectible accounts are transferred to accounts that designate these items as relating to delinquent taxes. Thus, tax levies of the following fiscal year may be separated from the delinquent taxes.

Property taxes receivable—current.....................	500,000	
Allowance for uncollectibles—current................		12,000
Revenues control		488,000
To record the property tax levy.		

Cash	484,000	
Property taxes receivable—current.................		463,000
Property taxes receivable—delinquent..............		21,000
To record the collection of property taxes.		

Allowance for uncollectibles—delinquent................	8,000	
Property taxes receivable—delinquent..............		8,000
To write off accounts determined to be uncollectible.		

Revenues control	3,000	
Allowance for uncollectibles—current................		3,000
To increase the allowance for uncollectibles— current from $12,000 to $15,000.[a]		

(32000 +
11000 -

Property taxes receivable—delinquent...................	37,000	
Allowance for uncollectibles—current...................	15,000	
Property taxes receivable—current.................		37,000
Allowance for uncollectibles—delinquent............		15,000
To transfer the fiscal year-end balances to the delinquent accounts.		

delinquent txs are simply not current.

[a] The Allowance account now totals $16,000 ($1,000 remains from the beginning of the year balance).

(3) Revenues other than property taxes. The total estimated revenues for the year include an estimated **entitlement** from the federal government of $22,000. We assume these funds are used for purposes normally financed through the General Fund. The amount is assumed to be susceptible to accrual; the actual amount received midway through the year is $23,000. Revenues of $181,000 are collected from sales taxes, business licenses, permits, and miscellaneous sources. Because these revenues are not susceptible to accrual, they are accounted for on the cash basis.

(not same as operating xfer in)

Entitlement receivable	22,000	
Revenues control		22,000
To record entitlement from the federal government.		

Cash	23,000	
Entitlement receivable		22,000
Revenues control		1,000
To record collection of entitlement.		

Cash	181,000	
Revenues control		181,000
To record revenues accounted for on the cash basis.		

(4) Encumbrances relating to the prior year. The goods and services relating to the purchase orders outstanding at June 30, 19X1 were received. The invoices totaled $19,000. Recall that budgetary control must be re-established over encumbrances existing at the end of the prior fiscal year. Accordingly, the following entries are made on the first day of the new fiscal year:

```
Fund balance reserved for encumbrances ................ 20,000
     Unreserved fund balance ...........................          20,000
     To reverse appropriation of fund balance made at June
     30, 19X1 relating to encumbrances outstanding
     at June 30, 19X1 that will be honored during
     the current year.

ENCUMBRANCES CONTROL .......................... 20,000
     FUND BALANCE RESERVED FOR
          ENCUMBRANCES ..............................          20,000
     To re-establish budgetary control over encumbrances
     outstanding at June 30, 19X1.
```

Recall that the encumbrances budgetary accounts are closed out at year-end. Thus, the preceding entry is also merely a reversing entry. The entries pertaining to the receipt of the goods or services ordered are then recorded in the normal manner, as follows:

```
FUND BALANCE RESERVED FOR ENCUMBRANCES..... 20,000
     ENCUMBRANCES CONTROL ......................          20,000
     To cancel encumbrances of $20,000 upon receipt of
     goods and services totaling $19,000.

Expenditures control .................................. 19,000
     Vouchers payable..................................          19,000
     To record expenditures of $19,000 for goods and
     services which were previously encumbered for
     $20,000.
```

(5) Expenditures and encumbrances initiated during the current year. Purchase orders totaling $115,000 were issued during the current year. Goods and services relating to $103,000 of these purchase orders were received; invoices totaling $102,000 were received and approved. Additional expenditures of $526,000 (which did not involve the use of purchase orders) were incurred. Of the total expenditures for the year, $36,000 pertained to the purchase of supplies inventories. The city uses the "purchases" method of accounting for supplies purchases whereby expenditures are charged on acquisition.[27]

---

[27] *NCGA Statement 1* also sanctions the use of the "consumption" method of accounting for inventories, whereby expenditures for the year are based on actual usage. Under this method, inventories on hand at year-end are reported in the balance sheet (*NCGA Statement 1*, p. 12). The manner of reporting significant amounts of inventory in the balance sheet is discussed later in the chapter.

```
ENCUMBRANCES CONTROL ........................   115,000
    FUND BALANCE RESERVED FOR
        ENCUMBRANCES .............................            115,000
    To record encumbrances on purchase orders issued.

FUND BALANCE RESERVED FOR ENCUMBRANCES...   103,000
    ENCUMBRANCES CONTROL ....................            103,000
    To cancel encumbrances of $103,000 upon receipt of
    goods and services totaling $102,000.

Expenditures control .....................................   102,000
    Vouchers payable.....................................            102,000
    To record expenditures of $102,000 for goods and
    services which were previously encumbered for
    $103,000.

Expenditures control .....................................   526,000
    Vouchers payable.....................................            526,000
    To record expenditures for items not previously
    encumbered.
```

(6) Disbursements (other than interfund). Cash disbursements totaled $631,000.

```
Vouchers payable.....................................   631,000
    Cash ...........................................            631,000
    To record cash disbursements other than interfund
    disbursements.
```

(7) Interfund transactions. The operating transfer of $55,000 to be received from the Electric Utility Enterprise Fund and the operating transfer of $75,000 to be made to the Library Debt Service Fund may be recorded on the first day of the fiscal year, because the amounts are susceptible to being accrued.

```
Due from electric utility enterprise fund...................   55,000
    Other financing sources control......................            55,000
    To record operating transfer to be received from the
    Electric Utility Enterprise Fund.

Other financing uses control ...........................   75,000
    Due to library debt service fund ....................            75,000
    To record operating transfer to be made to the Library
    Debt Service Fund.
```

The following entries assume the payments were made in accordance with the authorized amounts.

```
Cash ...................................................   55,000
    Due from electric utility enterprise fund...............            55,000
    To record receipt of operating transfer from the Electric
    Utility Enterprise Fund.
```

Due to library debt service fund	75,000	
Cash		75,000

To record payment of operating transfer to the Library
Debt Service Fund.

The Capital Projects Fund pertaining to the construction of a new library was terminated during the year when the construction was completed. A residual equity balance of $2,500 was transferred to the General Fund. This nonrecurring transfer may not be reflected in the operating statement of the General Fund, because it is not an operating transfer but a **residual equity transfer.** Residual equity transfers are recorded as adjustments directly to the Fund Balance account.

Cash	2,500	
Unreserved fund balance		2,500

To record residual equity transfer from the Library Capital
Projects Fund.

During the year, the city's central printing department, which is operated as an Internal Service Fund, rendered billings for services to the General Fund in the amount of $11,000. Of this amount, $9,000 was paid during the fiscal year. These billings qualify for treatment as **quasi-external transactions.** Accordingly, they are treated as expenditures in the General Fund (and as revenues in the Internal Services Fund).

Expenditures control	11,000	
Due to central printing internal service fund		11,000

To record as expenditures services acquired from the
Central Printing Internal Service Fund.

Due to central printing internal service fund	9,000	
Cash		9,000

To record payment made to Central Printing Internal
Service Fund.

The General Fund preclosing trial balances after recording the preceding items are shown in Illustration 22-4.

(8) Closing entries. The closing entries at June 30, 19X2 are as follows:

APPROPRIATIONS CONTROL	670,000	
ESTIMATED OTHER FINANCING USES CONTROL	75,000	
BUDGETARY FUND BALANCE	10,000	
ESTIMATED REVENUES CONTROL		700,000
ESTIMATED OTHER FINANCING SOURCES		
CONTROL		55,000

To reverse the entry previously made to record the
legally adopted annual operating budget.

(Reversing entries)

Illustration 22-4

EMERSON CITY Preclosing Trial Balances—General Fund June 30, 19X2		
	Debit	Credit
Actual (nonbudgetary) accounts:		
Cash	87,500	
Property taxes receivable—delinquent	40,000	
Allowance for estimated uncollectibles—delinquent		16,000
Vouchers payable		42,000
Due to Internal Service Fund.............................		2,000
Unreserved fund balance		56,500
Revenues control		689,000
Expenditures control......................................	658,000	
Other financing sources control...........................		55,000
Other financing uses control	75,000	
Totals...	860,500	860,500
Budgetary accounts:		
ESTIMATED REVENUES CONTROL	700,000	
ESTIMATED OTHER FINANCING SOURCES CONTROL	55,000	
APPROPRIATIONS CONTROL............................		670,000
ESTIMATED OTHER FINANCING USES CONTROL		75,000
BUDGETARY FUND BALANCE		10,000
ENCUMBRANCES CONTROL	12,000	
FUND BALANCE RESERVED FOR ENCUMBRANCES.....		12,000
Totals...	767,000	767,000

Revenues control	689,000	
Other financing sources control........................	55,000	
Appropriations control		658,000
Other financing uses control		75,000
Unreserved fund balance		11,000
To close *actual* revenues, expenditures, and other financing sources and uses accounts into Unreserved Fund Balance.		
FUND BALANCE RESERVED FOR ENCUMBRANCES...	12,000	
ENCUMBRANCES CONTROL		12,000
To close encumbrances outstanding at year-end by reversing the entry that previously recorded them.		
Unreserved fund balance	12,000	
Fund balance reserved for encumbrances		12,000
To record *actual* fund balance reserve account to indicate the portion of the year-end fund balance segregated for expenditure upon vendor performance.		

The financial statements for the fiscal year ended June 30, 19X2 are shown in Illustrations 22-5 and 22-6.

Illustration 22-5

EMERSON CITY Balance Sheet—General Fund June 30, 19X2	
Assets	
Cash	$ 87,500
Property taxes receivable—delinquent	40,000
Less: Allowance for estimated uncollectible taxes—delinquent	(16,000)
Total Assets	$111,500
Liabilities and Fund Equity	
Vouchers payable	$ 42,000
Due to Internal Service Fund	2,000
Total Liabilities	$ 44,000
Fund balance:	
Reserved for encumbrances	$ 12,000
Unreserved	55,500
Total Fund Balance	$ 67,500
Total Liabilities and Fund Equity	$111,500

Manner of classifying expenditures

The operating statement for Emerson City classifies expenditures by **character**
and **function.** Character refers to the fiscal period that the expenditures
are presumed to benefit. Virtually all of Emerson City's expenditures were
presumed to benefit the current fiscal year. Note that even the expenditures
relating to encumbrances existing at June 30, 19X1 (although initially ap-
propriated and ordered during the preceding fiscal year) benefit the year
in which the goods and services are incurred. Thus, no separate categorization
of these expenditures is needed. Other major categories of character classification are "Capital Outlay" (which benefits primarily future periods) and
"Debt Service" (which benefits the period encompassing the useful life of
the related fixed assets acquired or constructed with the proceeds of the
borrowing).

Note that the operating statement shows a minor amount for the capital
outlay category and no debt service category. In Chapter 23, which covers
the other types of funds, the capital outlay category is also encountered
in Capital Projects Funds and Special Assessment Funds (in which the
amounts are usually not minor); the debt service category is encountered
in Debt Service Funds and Special Assessment Funds.

When desirable, the major functions may be subdivided into **activities**
and **objects.** For example, the sanitation function could be subdivided into
sewage treatment and disposal, garbage collection, garbage disposal, and
street cleaning. Alternatively, the sanitation function could be subdivided
into employee salaries, contracted services, materials, and supplies. These
other ways of classifying expenditures may be presented in the financial
statements, in supporting schedules to the financial statements, or in notes
to the financial statements.

Illustration 22-6

EMERSON CITY
Statement of Revenues, Expenditures, and
Changes in Fund Balance—Budget and Actual—General Fund
For the Fiscal Year Ended June 30, 19X2

	Budget[b]	Actual	Variance Favorable (Unfavorable)
Revenues:			
Property taxes	$488,000	$485,000	$ (3,000)
Intergovernmental grant	22,000	23,000	1,000
Sales taxes[a]	130,000	124,000	(6,000)
Licenses and permits[a]	45,000	38,000	(7,000)
Miscellaneous[a]	15,000	19,000	4,000
Total Revenues	$700,000	$689,000	$(11,000)
Expenditures:			
Current:			
General government[a]	$103,000	$101,000	$ 2,000
Public safety[a]	215,000	220,000	(5,000)
Sanitation[a]	50,000	49,500	500
Health[a]	40,000	41,500	(1,500)
Welfare[a]	70,000	62,700	7,300
Education[a]	185,000	176,300	8,700
Subtotal	$663,000	$651,000	$ 12,000
Capital outlay	7,000	7,000	—
Total Expenditures	$670,000	$658,000	$ 12,000
Excess of Revenues over Expenditures	$ 30,000	$ 31,000	$ 1,000
Other Financing Sources (Uses):			
Operating transfers in	$ 55,000	$ 55,000	—
Operating transfers out	(75,000)	(75,000)	—
Total Other Financing Sources (Uses)	$ (20,000)	$ (20,000)	—
Excess of Revenues and Other Sources over Expenditures and Other Uses	$ 10,000	$ 11,000	$ 1,000
Fund balance—July 1, 19X1	54,000	54,000	—
Residual equity transfer from Capital Projects Fund	—	2,500	2,500
Fund balance—June 30, 19X2	$ 64,000	$ 67,500	$ 3,500

[a] These assumed amounts were not given in the transactions and journal entries.
[b] The budget includes $20,000 relating to encumbrances existing at June 30, 19X1, which amount has been "rebudgeted" during the current year. As a result, actual expenditures (including amounts relating to encumbrances existing at June 30, 19X1) may be meaningfully compared with the budget column.
Note: Because it has been prepared in accordance with generally accepted accounting principles, the budget is presented in this statement for budgetary comparison purposes, as required under NCGA Statement 1.

Manner of reporting inventory

We assumed in Emerson City's financial statements that the supplies inventories were insignificant at each balance sheet date. Accordingly, they were not reported in the balance sheets. When supplies inventories are significant, NCGA Statement 1 calls for such inventory to be reported in the balance sheet. Because **supplies inventory is not an asset that is available for spending in the succeeding fiscal year,** the entry reflecting the supplies inventory must indicate clearly that the portion of the fund balance designated unreserved is not affected and is therefore available for spending in the succeeding fiscal year. The journal entries to reflect significant amounts of supplies inventories are different under the "purchases" method and the "consumption" method.

The purchases method. Recall that under the purchases method, all supplies acquired are immediately charged to Expenditures when received— a periodic or perpetual inventory system does not exist under the purchases method. Accordingly, the Expenditures account may not be adjusted in reporting significant amounts of supplies inventory in the balance sheet. The entry, which takes place entirely in balance sheet accounts, is as follows:

Inventory of supplies xxx
    Fund balance reserved for inventory of supplies   xxx
  To report supplies inventory in the balance sheet.

Note that the portion of the fund balance that is designated unreserved is not affected. If the amount of supplies inventory changes from one balance sheet date to the next, the above two accounts are adjusted accordingly.

The consumption method. Under the consumption method, expenditures are charged based on **usage,** whether a perpetual or a periodic inventory system is used. Under a **perpetual** system, supplies inventories are automatically reported in the balance sheet because supplies are charged to an Inventory of Supplies account when acquired and then transferred to the Expenditures account as used. Under a **periodic** system, inventories are charged to the Expenditures account as they are acquired, but an entry is made at year-end to adjust the Inventory of Supplies account and the Expenditures account, so that the Expenditures account reflects usage instead of purchases. For example, assume that under a periodic system, $50,000 of supplies were acquired during the year but only $40,000 of supplies were used. The entry to adjust the Inventory of Supplies account and the Expenditures account at year-end would be as follows:

Inventory of supplies 10,000
    Expenditures   10,000
  To adjust the Expenditures account to reflect actual
  usage for the year.

If the amount of supplies inventory changes from one balance sheet date to the next, the Unreserved Fund Balance account and the Fund Balance Reserved for Inventory of Supplies account are adjusted accordingly.[28]

---

[28] *NCGA Statement 1* sanctions an alternative practice under the "consumption" method, which is to establish a reserve for inventory only if "minimum amounts of inventory must be maintained and thus are not available for use (expenditure)" (*NCGA Statement 1,* p. 32).

SUMMARY

Accounting for state and local governmental units requires a familiarity with the pronouncements of the National Council on Governmental Accounting. Because of the diverse nature of governmental operations and the extensive legal provisions of a financial nature, operations are accounted for in separate funds and account groups as opposed to a single set of books. Because of the absence of a profit motive in most governmental operations, the use of an income statement is inappropriate; accordingly, most governmental operations are presented in a statement of revenues, expenditures, and changes in fund balance, which shows in detail the sources and uses of fund resources. A modified accrual basis of accounting is used when the accrual basis is not practical. Budgetary accounts assist in controlling and monitoring spending on an interim basis.

Glossary of new terms

Appropriation: "A legal authorization granted by a legislative body to make expenditures and to incur obligations for specific purposes. An appropriation is usually limited in amount and as to the time when it may be expended."[29]

Budgetary Accounts: "Accounts used to enter the formally adopted annual operating budget into the general ledger as part of the management control technique of formal budgetary integration."[29]

Encumbrances: "Commitments related to unperformed (executory) contracts for goods or services."[29]

Expenditures: "Decreases in net financial resources."[29]

Fund: "A fiscal and accounting entity with a self-balancing set of accounts recording cash and other financial resources, together with all related liabilities and residual equities or balances, and changes therein, which are segregated for the purpose of carrying on specific activities or attaining certain objectives in accordance with special regulations, restrictions, or limitations."[29]

Fund Balance: "The fund equity of governmental funds and Trust Funds."[29]

General Fixed Assets: "Fixed assets used in operations accounted for in governmental funds. General fixed assets include all fixed assets not accounted for in proprietary funds or in Trust and Agency Funds."[29]

General Fixed Asset Account Group: "A self-balancing group of accounts set up to account for the general fixed assets of a government."[29]

General Long-Term Debt: "Long-term debt (other than special assessment bonds) expected to be repaid from governmental funds."[29]

General Long-Term Debt Account Group: "A self-balancing group of accounts set up to account for the unmatured general long-term debt of a government."[29]

Operating Transfers: "All interfund transfers other than residual equity transfers . . . ."[29]

Quasi-External Transactions: "Interfund transactions that would be treated as revenues, expenditures, or expenses if they involved organizations *external* to the governmental unit."[29]

Residual Equity Transfers: "Nonrecurring or nonroutine transfers of equity between funds."[29]

[29] Source: *GAAFR*, 1980 edition, Appendix B.

Appendix: ILLUSTRATIONS OF SELECTED GENERAL PURPOSE FINANCIAL STATEMENTS

Illustration 22-7

not all fixed assets in fund (bridge, road, etc.)

Not adding

NAME OF GOVERNMENT
COMBINED BALANCE SHEET—ALL FUND TYPES AND ACCOUNT GROUPS
December 31, 19X2

Assets	Governmental Fund Types					Proprietary Fund Types		Fiduciary Fund Type	Account Groups		Totals (Memorandum Only)	
	General	Special Revenue	Debt Service	Capital Projects	Special Assessment	Enterprise	Internal Service	Trust and Agency	General Fixed Assets	General Long-term Debt	19X2	19X1
Cash	$255,029	$101,385	$10,889	$434,100	$232,185	$279,296	$29,700	$216,701	—	$ —	$1,559,285	$1,232,930
Investments, at cost or amortized cost	65,000	37,200						1,239,260			1,341,460	1,116,524
Receivables (net, of allowances for uncollectibles):												
Taxes, including interest, penalties, and liens	61,771	2,500						580,000			647,799	230,435
Accounts	8,300	3,300		100		24,130					35,830	43,850
Special assessments			3,528		646,035						646,035	462,035
Notes						2,350					2,350	1,250
Loans								35,000			35,000	35,000
Accrued interest	50	25			350			2,666			3,091	4,280
Due from other funds	12,000					2,000	12,000	11,189			37,189	51,220
Due from other governments	30,000	75,260		640,000							745,260	116,800
Advance to internal service fund	55,000										55,000	65,000
Inventory, at cost	7,200	5,190				23,030	40,000				75,420	48,670
Prepaid expenses						1,200					1,200	740
Restricted assets: Cash and investments, at cost or amortized cost						306,753					306,753	417,268
Fixed assets (net)						5,769,759	103,100		6,913,250		12,786,109	10,864,206
Amount available in debt service funds										12,572	12,572	5,010
Amount to be provided for retirement of general long-term debt										1,687,428	1,687,428	854,990
Total Assets	$494,350	$224,860	$14,417	$1,074,200	$878,570	$6,408,518	$184,800	$2,084,816	$6,913,250	$1,700,000	$19,977,781	$15,550,208

Liabilities

											Total	(Prior)
Vouchers and accounts payable	$118,261	$32,454	$—	$29,000	$20,600	$116,471	$15,000	$5,200	$—	$—	$336,986	$179,973
Contracts payable	57,600	18,300	—	69,000	50,000	26,107	—	—	—	—	221,007	503,724
Judgments payable	—	2,000	—	22,600	11,200	—	—	—	—	—	35,800	15,500
Accrued general obligation interest	—	—	—	—	—	14,000	—	—	—	—	14,000	14,100
Other accrued expenses	—	—	—	—	10,700	3,009	—	4,700	—	—	18,409	18,713
Payable from restricted assets:												
Construction contracts	—	—	—	—	—	64,749	—	—	—	—	64,749	145,643
Accrued interest	—	—	—	—	—	48,000	—	—	—	—	48,000	75,150
Revenue bonds	—	—	—	—	—	64,060	—	—	—	—	64,060	44,000
Deposits	—	—	—	—	—	—	—	680,800	—	—	680,800	55,500
Due to other taxing units	—	—	—	—	—	—	—	—	—	—	—	200,000
Due to other funds	24,189	2,000	—	1,000	—	—	10,000	—	—	—	37,189	51,220
Deferred revenues	49,500	1,396	1,845	—	556,200	—	—	—	—	—	608,941	412,951
Advance from general fund	—	—	—	—	—	—	55,000	—	—	—	55,000	65,000
General obligation bonds payable	—	—	—	—	—	700,000	—	—	—	1,700,000	2,400,000	1,610,000
Revenue bonds payable	—	—	—	—	—	1,798,000	—	—	—	—	1,798,000	1,846,000
Special assessment bonds payable	—	—	—	—	555,000	—	—	—	—	—	555,000	420,000
Total Liabilities	$249,550	$56,150	$1,845	$121,600	$1,203,700	$2,834,396	$80,000	$690,700	$—	$1,700,000	$6,937,941	$5,657,474

Fund Equity

											Total	(Prior)
Contributed capital	$—	$—	$—	$—	$—	$1,370,666	$95,000	$—	$—	$—	$1,465,666	$815,000
Investment in general fixed assets	—	—	—	—	—	—	—	—	6,913,250	—	6,913,250	5,174,250
Retained earnings:												
Reserved for revenue bond retirement	—	—	—	—	—	129,155	—	—	—	—	129,155	96,975
Unreserved	—	—	—	—	—	2,074,301	9,800	—	—	—	2,084,101	1,998,119
Fund balance:												
Reserved for encumbrances	38,000	46,500	—	941,500	75,000	—	—	—	—	—	1,101,000	410,050
Reserved for inventory	7,200	5,190	—	—	—	—	—	—	—	—	12,390	10,890
Reserved for advance to internal service fund	55,000	—	—	—	—	—	—	—	—	—	55,000	65,000
Reserved for loans	—	—	—	—	—	—	—	50,050	—	—	50,050	45,100
Reserved for endowments	—	—	—	—	—	—	—	160,865	—	—	160,865	119,035
Reserved for employees' retirement system	—	—	—	—	—	—	—	1,426,201	—	—	1,426,201	1,276,150
Reserved for debt service	—	—	12,572	—	(400,130)	—	—	—	—	—	(387,558)	(258,950)
Unreserved:												
Designated for subsequent years' expenditures	50,000	—	—	—	—	—	—	—	—	—	50,000	50,000
Undesignated	94,600	117,020	—	11,100	—	—	—	(243,000)	—	—	(20,280)	91,115
Total retained earnings/fund balance	$244,800	$168,710	$12,572	$952,600	$(325,130)	$2,203,456	$104,800	$1,394,116	$—	$—	$4,660,924	$3,903,484
Total Fund Equity	$244,800	$168,710	$12,572	$952,600	$(325,130)	$3,574,122	$104,800	$1,394,116	$6,913,250	$—	$13,039,840	$9,892,734
Total Liabilities and Fund Equity	$494,350	$224,860	$14,417	$1,074,200	$878,570	$6,408,518	$184,800	$2,084,816	$6,913,250	$1,700,000	$19,977,781	$15,550,208

Source: Adapted with permission from the Government Finance Officers Association, 1980 *Governmental Accounting, Auditing, and Financial Reporting (GAAFR)* (Chicago: Municipal Finance Officers Association of the United States and Canada, 1980), pp. 126–27. © Copyright 1980 by the Municipal Finance Officers Association of the United States and Canada.

Illustration 22-8

NAME OF GOVERNMENT
COMBINED STATEMENT OF REVENUES, EXPENDITURES, AND CHANGES IN
FUND BALANCES—ALL GOVERNMENTAL FUND TYPES AND EXPENDABLE TRUST FUNDS
For the Year Ended December 31, 19X2

	Governmental Fund Types					Fiduciary Fund Type	Totals (Memorandum Only)	
	General	Special Revenue	Debt Service	Capital Projects	Special Assessment	Expendable Trust	19X2	19X1
Revenue:								
Taxes and special assessments	$ 846,800	$ 189,300	$49,362	$ —	$ 86,000	$ —	$1,171,462	$1,117,694
Licenses and permits	103,000	—	—	—	—	—	103,000	96,500
Intergovernmental	186,500	831,366	41,500	1,250,000	—	—	2,309,366	1,256,000
Charges for services	91,000	79,100	—	—	—	—	170,100	160,400
Fines and forfeits	33,200	—	—	—	—	—	33,200	26,300
Miscellaneous	18,000	71,359	2,500	3,750	20,664	150	116,423	106,750
Total Revenues	$1,278,500	$1,171,125	$93,362	$1,253,750	$ 106,664	$ 150	$3,903,551	$2,763,644
Expenditures:								
General government	$ 121,805	$ —	$ —	$ —	$ —	$ —	$ 121,805	$ 134,200
Public safety	258,395	480,000	—	—	—	—	738,395	671,300
Highways and streets	85,400	417,000	—	—	—	—	502,400	408,700
Sanitation	56,250	—	—	—	—	—	56,250	44,100
Health	44,500	—	—	—	—	—	44,500	36,600
Welfare	46,800	—	—	—	—	—	46,800	41,400
Culture and recreation	40,900	256,450	—	—	—	—	297,350	286,400
Education	509,150	—	—	—	—	2,370	511,520	512,000
Capital projects	—	—	—	1,625,500	308,265	—	1,933,765	1,075,035
Debt service:								
Principal retirement	—	—	60,000	—	—	—	60,000	60,000
Interest and fiscal charges	—	—	25,800	—	19,569	—	45,369	35,533
Total Expenditures	$1,163,200	$1,153,450	$85,800	$1,625,500	$ 327,834	$ 2,370	$4,358,154	$3,305,268
Excess (Deficiency) of Revenues over Expenditures	$ 115,300	$ 17,675	$ 7,562	$ (371,750)	$(221,170)	$(2,220)	$ (454,603)	$ (541,624)

Other financing sources (uses):

Proceeds of general obligation bonds	$ —	$ —	902,500	$ —	$ —	$ 902,500	$ 105,000
Operating transfers in	—	—	64,500	10,000	2,530	77,030	89,120
Operating transfers out	(74,500)	—			—	(74,500)	(87,000)
Total Other Financing Sources (Uses)	$ (74,500)	$ —	$ 967,000	$ 10,000	$ 2,530	$ 905,030	$ 107,120
Excess (Deficiency) of Revenues and Other Financing Sources over Expenditures and Other Uses	$ 40,800	$ 17,675	$ 595,250	$(211,170)	$ 310	$ 450,427	$ (434,504)
Fund Balance at Beginning of Year	202,500	151,035	357,350	(113,960)	26,555	628,490	1,062,994
Increase in Reserve for Inventory	1,500	—	—			1,500	—
Fund Balance at End of Year	$ 244,800	$ 168,710	$ 952,600	$(325,130)	$26,865	$1,080,417	$ 628,490

Source: Adapted with permission from the Government Finance Officers Association, 1980 Governmental Accounting, Auditing, and Financial Reporting (GAAFR) (Chicago: Municipal Finance Officers Association of the United States and Canada, 1980), p. 128. © Copyright 1980 by the Municipal Finance Officers Association of the United States and Canada.

Illustration 22-9

NAME OF GOVERNMENT
COMBINED STATEMENT OF REVENUES, EXPENSES AND CHANGES IN
RETAINED EARNINGS/FUND BALANCES—ALL PROPRIETARY FUND TYPES
AND SIMILAR TRUST FUNDS
For the Year Ended December 31, 19X2

	Proprietary Fund Types		Fiduciary Fund Types		Totals (Memorandum Only)	
	Enterprise	Internal Service	Pension Trust	Nonex-pendable Trust	19X2	19X1
Operating revenues:						
Charges for services	$ 672,150	$88,000	$ —	$ —	$ 760,150	$ 686,563
Interest	—	—	28,460	2,480	30,940	26,118
Contributions	—	—	160,686	—	160,686	144,670
Gifts	—	—	—	45,000	45,000	—
Total operating revenues	$ 672,150	$88,000	$ 189,146	$ 47,480	$ 996,776	$ 857,351
Operating expenses:						
Personal services	$ 247,450	$32,500	$ —	$ —	$ 279,950	$ 250,418
Contractual services	75,330	400	—	—	75,730	68,214
Supplies	20,310	1,900	—	—	22,210	17,329
Materials	50,940	44,000	—	—	94,940	87,644
Heat, light, and power	26,050	1,500	—	—	27,550	22,975
Depreciation	144,100	4,450	—	—	148,550	133,210
Benefit payments	—	—	21,000	—	21,000	12,000
Refunds	—	—	25,745	—	25,745	13,243
Total operating expenses	$ 564,180	$84,750	$ 46,745	$ —	$ 695,675	$ 605,033
Operating income	$ 107,970	$ 3,250	$ 142,401	$ 47,480	$ 301,101	$ 252,318
Nonoperating revenues (expenses):						
Operating grants	$ 55,000	$ —	$ —	$ —	$ 55,000	$ 50,000
Tap fees	22,000	—	—	—	22,000	20,000
Interest	3,830	—	—	—	3,830	3,200
Rent	5,000	—	—	—	5,000	5,000
Interest and fiscal charges	(78,888)	—	—	—	(78,888)	(122,408)
Total nonoperating revenues (expenses)	$ 6,942	$ —	$ —	$ —	$ 6,942	$ (44,208)
Income before operating transfers	$ 114,912	$ 3,250	$ 142,401	$ 47,480	$ 308,043	$ 208,110
Operating transfers in (out)	—	—	—	(2,530)	(2,530)	(2,120)
Net income	$ 114,912	$ 3,250	$ 142,401	$ 44,950	$ 305,513	$ 205,990
Retained earnings/fund balances at beginning of year	2,088,544	6,550	1,040,800	139,100	3,274,994	3,069,004
Retained earnings/fund balances at end of year	$2,203,456	$ 9,800	$1,183,201	$184,050	$3,580,507	$3,274,994

Source: Adapted with permission from the Government Finance Officers Association, 1980 *Governmental Accounting, Auditing, and Financial Reporting (GAAFR)* (Chicago: Municipal Finance Officers Association of the United States and Canada, 1980), p. 131. © Copyright 1980 by the Municipal Finance Officers Association of the United States and Canada.

Review questions

1. What was the role of the National Council on Governmental Accounting?
2. What has been the role of the FASB and its predecessor organizations in the development of generally accepted accounting principles peculiar to state and local governmental units?

3. Must all state and local governmental units prepare their financial statements in accordance with NCGA pronouncements?
4. What major steps has the NCGA taken toward improving governmental financial reporting?
5. What are some unique features of the governmental sector compared with the private sector?
6. Explain the relationship between revenues and expenditures.
7. What is meant by *fund accounting?*
8. Name the eight major types of funds recommended by *NCGA Statement 1.*
9. Are general fixed assets and general long-term debt accounted for in funds? Explain.
10. When is it appropriate to depreciate fixed assets of a governmental unit?
11. Is the modified accrual basis of accounting in accordance with generally accepted accounting principles? Why or why not?
12. What is meant by *budgetary accounting?*
13. What are the two major types of interfund transfers?
14. Explain the difference between an *expenditure* and an *encumbrance.*

Discussion cases

Discussion case 22–1
Modified accrual basis of accounting

As an accountant for the city of Roseville, you assist the city manager in answering questions raised at city council meetings. At one meeting, a taxpayer asks why the city (which has a June 30 fiscal year-end) uses the modified accrual basis of accounting for its General Fund instead of the accrual basis, which is required for public corporations in the private sector. Furthermore, the taxpayer would like to know "the magnitude of the misstatement at the end of the recently concluded fiscal year as a result of not using the accrual basis." Assume the city has an income tax, a sales tax, a property transfer tax, a property tax, and annual business licenses.

Required:
Respond to these questions.

Discussion case 22–2
Comparison with private sector

Cheryl Jackson is executive vice-president of Intel Industries, Inc., a publicly held industrial corporation. Jackson has just been elected to the city council of Sun City. Before assuming office as a member of the city council, she asks you as her CPA to explain the major differences in accounting and financial reporting for a large city compared with a large industrial corporation.

Required:
(1) Describe the major differences in the purposes of accounting and financial reporting and in the types of financial reports of a large city and a large industrial corporation.

(2) Why are inventories often ignored in accounting for local governmental units? Explain.

(3) Under what circumstances should depreciation be recognized in accounting for local governmental units? Explain.

(AICPA adapted)

Exercises

Exercise 22–1
True or false: Theory and basic principles of *NCGA Statement 1*

Indicate whether the following statements are true or false.

T (1) For governmental funds, the measurement base is the flow of resources.

F (2) For governmental funds, capital maintenance is measured instead of net income.

T (3) The operating statement for governmental funds is essentially a source and use of funds statement.

T (4) When legal provisions conflict with generally accepted accounting principles, legal provisions prevail in financial reporting.

F (5) When legal provisions conflict with generally accepted accounting principles, two sets of books must usually be maintained.

F (6) Basis of accounting refers to what is being measured rather than to when items are recognized.

T (7) In revenue recognition under the modified accrual basis, "available" means collectible within the current period or soon enough thereafter to be used to pay current-period liabilities.

T (8) Recording depreciation in governmental funds would inappropriately mix expenditures and expenses.

F (9) The practice of not recording depreciation in the governmental funds is a departure from generally accepted accounting principles.

T (10) General long-term debt is secured by the general credit and revenue-raising powers of a governmental unit.

F (11) General long-term debt is a General Fund liability.

T (12) Operating transfers between funds affect the results of operations in both governmental and proprietary funds.

F (13) Quasi-external transactions are reported outside the operating statement of the affected funds.

T (14) Residual equity transfers are capital transfers between funds.

T (15) The proceeds from the sale of general fixed assets are reported as a source of financial resources.

Exercise 22–2
Multiple choice: Revenues

(1) For the five governmental funds, revenues are recognized
   (a) In the period to which they relate.
   (b) When they become susceptible to accrual.
   (c) When earned.
   (d) When the related expenditures are recognized.
   (e) None of the above.

(2) For the five governmental funds, revenues are
   (a) Matched against the cost of providing services.
   (b) Generated by expenditures.
   (c) Earned.
   (d) Reported in a quasi-income statement.
   (e) None of the above.

(3) Under the modified accrual method of accounting, which of the following would be a revenue susceptible to accrual?
   (a) Income taxes.
   (b) Business licenses.
   (c) Sales taxes.
   (d) Property taxes.
   (e) Parking meter receipts.
   (f) None of the above.

(4) At the end of the fiscal year, a governmental unit increased its allowance for uncollectible accounts relating to property tax receivables. The entry resulted in a charge to
   (a) Unreserved fund balance.
   (b) ENCUMBRANCES CONTROL.
   (c) Bad debts expense.
   (d) Revenues control.
   (e) ESTIMATED REVENUES CONTROL.
   (f) APPROPRIATIONS CONTROL.

(5) A city's General Fund budget for the forthcoming fiscal year shows estimated revenues in excess of appropriations. The initial effect of recording the budget results in an increase in
   (a) Taxes receivable.
   (b) Unreserved fund balance.
   (c) ENCUMBRANCES CONTROL.
   (d) Retained earnings.
   (e) BUDGETARY FUND BALANCE.
   (f) None of the above.

Exercise 22–3
Multiple choice: Expenditures and encumbrances

(1) Under the modified accrual basis, expenditures (other than the exceptions set forth in *NCGA Statement 1*) are recognized
   (a) When the liability is incurred.
   (b) When paid.
   (c) When the related revenues are recognized.
   (d) When the goods or services are ordered or contracted for.
   (e) None of the above.

(2) Expenditures are defined as
   (a) The cost of providing services.
   (b) Costs incurred to generate revenues.
   (c) An outflow of resources.
   (d) Amounts arising from encumbrances.
   (e) None of the above.

(3) When a fire truck is received by a governmental unit, it should be recorded in the general fund as a(n)
- (a) Appropriation.
- (b) Encumbrance.
- (c) Expenditure.
- (d) Expense.
- (e) Fixed asset.
- (f) Transfer to the General Fixed Assets Account Group.

(4) When supplies are ordered out of the General Fund, they should be recorded as a(n)
- (a) Appropriation.
- (b) Encumbrance.
- (c) Expenditure.
- (d) Estimated expenditure.
- (e) Reduction of the fund balance.

(5) Which of the following terms refers to an actual cost rather than an estimate in reporting for the five governmental funds?
- (a) Appropriation.
- (b) Encumbrance.
- (c) Expenditure.
- (d) Expense.
- (e) None of the above.

(6) Wages that have been earned by the employees of a governmental unit but not paid should be recorded in the General Fund as an
- (a) Appropriation.
- (b) Encumbrance.
- (c) Expenditure.
- (d) Expense.
- (e) None of the above.

Exercise 22–4
Multiple choice: Budgetary accounting

(1) Which of the following is a budgetary account in governmental accounting?
- (a) Fund balance reserved for encumbrances.
- (b) Unreserved fund balance.
- (c) APPROPRIATIONS CONTROL.
- (d) Estimated uncollectible property taxes.
- (e) Expenditures control.

(2) Authority granted by a legislative body to make expenditures and to incur obligations during a fiscal year is the definition of an
- (a) Appropriation.
- (b) Authorization.
- (c) Encumbrance.
- (d) Expenditure.
- (e) None of the above.

(3) The actual general ledger account Fund Balance—Reserved for Encumbrances is a(n)
- (a) Liability in substance.

    (b) Budgetary account.
    (c) Contra account.
    (d) Appropriation of the fund balance.
    (e) None of the above.
(4) An encumbrance could not be thought of as a(n)
    (a) Commitment.
    (b) Contingent liability.
    (c) Future expenditure.
    (d) An eventual reduction of the fund balance.
    (e) Liability of the period in which the encumbrance was created.
(5) Which of the following General Fund accounts would be credited when a purchase order is issued?
    (a) APPROPRIATIONS CONTROL.
    (b) ENCUMBRANCES CONTROL.
    (c) Estimated expenditures.
    (d) Vouchers payable.
    (e) Fund balance.
    (f) None of the above.

Exercise 22–5
Fill-in statements: Terminology

Fill in the blanks in the following statements.
(1) Under the modified accrual basis of accounting, revenues are recognized in the accounting period in which they become _measurable_ and _available_.
(2) For the five governmental funds, expenditures are recognized in the period in which the fund liability is _incurred_.
(3) Commitments related to unperformed contracts for goods and services are called _encumbrances_.
(4) The use of financial resources of a fund are broadly referred to as _expenditures_.
(5) _Acct_ _groups_ are used to establish accounting control and accountability for a governmental unit's general fixed assets and general long-term debt.
(6) Accounts used to control and monitor spending on an interim basis are called _funds_.
(7) Items that are not accounted for in any fund are _inventory_ _fixed_ _assets_ and _____.
(8) Reporting encumbrances outstanding at year-end as a reservation (or appropriation) of the fund balance indicates that a portion of the fund balance has been segregated for _payment_ upon vendor performance.
(9) Encumbered appropriations may or may not _lapse_ at year-end.
(10) To honor in 19X2 encumbrances outstanding at the end of 19X1, the governmental unit may allow encumbrances to _lapse_, in which case it would be necessary to _rebudget_ for these items in 19X2. Alternatively, the governmental unit could not let the encumbrances _lapse_, thereby allowing the spending authority to _be extend_ to 19X2.

Exercise 22–6
Fill-in statements: Financial presentation and reporting

Fill in the blanks in the following statements.

(1) The three major categories of funds are _____, _____, and _____.

(2) Proprietary fund revenues and expenses are recognized on the _____ _____.

(3) For the five governmental funds, the _____ _____ basis of accounting is used.

(4) The first level of reporting in the financial reporting pyramid presents _____ _____ financial statements.

(5) In the operating statement, revenues are classified by _____.

(6) In the operating statement, expenditures are classified by _____ and _____. In addition, expenditures may be classified further by _____ and _____.

(7) A type of interfund transfer that is classified within the operating statement is a(n) _____ _____.

(8) A type of interfund transfer that is classified outside the operating statement (as a direct adjustment to the fund balances) is a(n) _____ _____ _____.

(9) A transaction in which one fund performs services for another fund and bills that fund is a _____ _____.

(10) Budgetary comparison statements may be presented on a _____ basis or on a _____ basis.

Exercise 22–7
True or false: Budgeting practices and GAAP reporting

Indicate whether the following statements are true or false.

(1) To honor encumbrances outstanding at year-end, a governmental unit must rebudget (or reappropriate) these items in the following year.

(2) Expenditures incurred in 19X2 relating to encumbrances outstanding at the end of 19X1 must be reported as expenditures in 19X2 under GAAP reporting regardless of whether the encumbrances outstanding were rebudgeted (or reappropriated) in 19X2.

(3) If a governmental unit does not reappropriate or rebudget for encumbrances outstanding at year-end, the budgeting is not done on a basis consistent with GAAP reporting.

(4) Encumbrances outstanding at year-end that will be honored in the following year because the spending authority is carried over to the following year (that is, no rebudgeting or reappropriating occurred) cannot be reported as expenditures in the following year under GAAP reporting.

(5) If encumbrances outstanding at year-end lapse and these items are rebudgeted (or reappropriated) in the following year, the governmental unit must cancel the unfilled purchase orders and reissue them in the following year.

(6) Under GAAP reporting, encumbrances are never reported in the statement of revenues, expenditures, and changes in fund balance.

(7) The manner of budgeting determines whether the budgetary comparison statement of revenues, expenditures, and changes in fund balance is prepared on a GAAP basis or a non-GAAP "budgetary" basis.

(8) *NCGA Statement 1* allows expenditures related to prior-year encumbrances to be reported as adjustments to the fund balance in the manner of a prior-period adjustment.

Exercise 22–8
Budgetary control

The following balances are included in the subsidiary records of Tylersville's fire department at May 31, 19X2:

Appropriations—supplies	$33,000
Expenditures—supplies	27,000
Encumbrances—supply orders	2,000

Required:
Determine how much the fire department has available for additional purchases of supplies.

Problems

Problem 22–1
General fund: Preparing transaction and closing journal entries—
Fundamentals

The City of Saragosa had the following activities pertaining to its General Fund for the fiscal year ended June 30, 19X6.
(1) **Adoption of the budget.** Revenues were estimated at $1,000,000, and authorized expenditures were $950,000. (Assume no encumbrances were outstanding at June 30, 19X5.)
(2) **Property taxes.** Property taxes were billed in the amount of $800,000, of which $25,000 was expected to be uncollectible. Collections were $750,000. A $22,000 allowance for uncollectibles is deemed adequate at year-end. All uncollected property taxes at year-end are delinquent.
(3) **Other revenues.** Cash collections of $210,000 were received from sales taxes, licenses, fees, and fines.
(4) **Purchase orders.** Purchase orders totaling $300,000 were issued to vendors and contractors during the year. For $270,000 of these purchase orders and contracts, billings totaling $268,000 were received. Cash payments totaling $245,000 were made.
(5) **Payroll and other operating costs.** Expenditures for payroll and other operating costs not requiring the use of purchase orders and contracts totaled $631,000. Cash payments of $590,000 were made on these items.

Required:
(1) Prepare the journal entries relating to the above items.
(2) Prepare the year-end closing entries assuming that encumbrances outstanding at year-end will be honored in the following year.

(3) Prepare the entry or entries that must be made on the first day of the following fiscal year.

Problem 22–2
General fund: Preparing transaction and closing journal entries and a statement of revenues, expenditures, and changes in fund balance

Funn City had the following events and transactions for its fiscal year ended June 30, 19X2:
(1) The budget for the year was approved. It provided for (a) $620,000 of estimated revenues; (b) $565,000 of expenditures; (c) $40,000 for servicing general long-term debt (principal and interest); and (d) $30,000 to establish a central printing department that will provide services to all city departments. (The $30,000 will not be repaid to the General Fund.)
(2) Items (c) and (d) in (1), above, were expended in accordance with authorizations.
(3) Property taxes totaling $450,000 were levied, of which $8,000 was estimated to be uncollectible. Property tax collections totaled $405,000. At year-end, the estimated allowance for uncollectibles was increased from $8,000 to $12,000. Unpaid taxes at year-end become delinquent.
(4) City income taxes, sales taxes, business licenses, and fines totaled $162,000.
(5) Bonds backed by the full faith and credit of the city were issued at par for $200,000 to finance an addition to city hall. (Construction is to begin in July 19X2.)
(6) Some equipment accounted for in the General Fixed Assets Account Group was sold for $11,000. This transaction was not included in the budget.
(7) A Special Assessment Fund was short $3,000 as a result of changes to contracts issued in connection with certain street improvements being charged to certain property owners. Authorization was given during the year to transfer funds to this fund to make up the shortage. The amount was not budgeted and will not be repaid.
(8) The city received a $500,000 donation from the estate of a wealthy citizen to be used only for the acquisition of open space for parks.
(9) Purchase orders and contracts totaling $280,000 were entered into. For $255,000 of this amount, invoices for goods and services totaling $254,000 were rendered. (Assume that no encumbrances were outstanding at June 30, 19X1.)
(10) Payroll and other operating costs not involving the use of purchase orders and contracts totaled $282,000.
(11) Cash disbursements (other than to other funds) totaled $507,000.

Required:
(1) Prepare the General Fund entries for these items.
(2) Prepare the closing entries at June 30, 19X2 assuming that encumbrances outstanding at year-end will be honored in the following year.
(3) Prepare a statement of revenues, expenditures, and changes in fund balance for the year ended June 30, 19X2 for the General Fund that compares budgeted amounts with actual amounts. (Assume that the General Fund had a total fund balance of $100,000 at June 30, 19X1.)

Problem 22–3
COMPREHENSIVE Preparing transaction and closing journal entries and a budgetary comparison statement on a GAAP basis
(Several interfund transactions)

The City of Sludge Falls had the following items and transactions pertaining to its General Fund for the fiscal year ended June 30, 19X3:

(1) The budget for the year was as follows:

Estimated revenues	$800,000
Authorized expenditures (including $55,000 reappropriated for encumbrances outstanding at June 30, 19X2, which lapsed)............	725,000
Authorized operating transfers to other funds..........................	50,000

(2) Property taxes were levied totaling $550,000. Of this amount, $10,000 was estimated to be uncollectible. Collections during the year were $535,000, of which $12,000 pertained to property tax levies of the prior year that had been declared delinquent at the end of the prior year. All remaining property tax receivables at the beginning of the current year totaling $4,000 were written off as uncollectible.

(3) The estimated revenues for the year include an entitlement from the federal government for $34,000. During the year, $36,000 was received.

(4) City income taxes, sales taxes, licenses, permits, and miscellaneous revenues totaled $222,000.

(5) Purchase orders and contracts totaling $370,000 were entered into during the year. For $330,000 of this amount, invoices totaling $328,000 for goods and services were rendered. Assume that the city generally allows encumbrances outstanding at year-end to lapse but reappropriates amounts in the following year to honor the encumbrances.

(6) Encumbrances outstanding at the beginning of the year totaled $55,000. The goods and services relating to these encumbrances were received along with invoices totaling $53,000.

(7) Payroll and other items not involving the use of purchase orders and contracts totaled $280,000. (This amount excludes interfund billings.)

(8) Cash disbursements (other than to other funds) totaled $740,000.

(9) Interfund transactions consisted of the following:
   a. The Central Printing Internal Service Fund was discontinued pursuant to authorization given by the legislative body at the beginning of the year. It was estimated then that the capital balance of the fund at the time of discontinuance would be $25,000. The actual amount transferred to the General Fund during the year when the fund was discontinued was $17,000.
   b. A transfer of $30,000 was made to the Electric Utility Enterprise Fund to make up its operating deficit, which was initially estimated to be $35,000.
   c. A transfer of $15,000 was made to a Special Assessment Fund to finance a portion of certain street improvements. (This transfer was equal to the amount authorized to be transferred.)
   d. The Electric Utility Enterprise Fund rendered billings to the city totaling $26,000 for electricity supplied to the city by the Enterprise Fund. Cash disbursements to this fund during the year in payment of such billings totaled $22,000.

(10) Assume the city uses the purchases method of accounting for acquisitions of supplies inventory, which totaled $32,000 during the year and is part of the

$328,000 amount in (5), above. Assume the supplies inventory is insignificant at June 30, 19X3.

Required:
(1) Prepare General Fund journal entries only for the above items.
(2) Prepare the closing entries at June 30, 19X3 for the General Fund.
(3) Prepare a statement of revenues, expenditures, and changes in fund balance for the year ended June 30, 19X3 that compares budgeted amounts with actual amounts. (Assume the fund balance at the beginning of the year was $100,000.)

Problem 22–4
General fund: Reconstructing transaction and closing journal entries; preparing a budgetary comparison statement on a GAAP basis

The following data were obtained from the general ledger for the General Fund of the City of Dreamsville after the general ledger had been closed for the fiscal year ended June 30, 19X6:

	Balances June 30, 19X5	Fiscal 19X5–19X6 Charges Debit	Fiscal 19X5–19X6 Charges Credit	Balances June 30, 19X6
Cash	$180,000	$ 955,000	$ 880,000	$255,000
Taxes receivable	20,000	809,000	781,000	48,000
Allowance for uncollectible taxes	(4,000)	6,000	9,000	(7,000)
	$196,000			$296,000
Vouchers payable	$ 44,000	813,000	822,000	$ 53,000
Due to Internal Service Fund . . .	2,000	7,000	10,000	5,000
Due to Debt Service Fund	10,000	60,000	100,000	50,000
Fund balance reserved for				
encumbrances	40,000	40,000	47,000	47,000
Unreserved fund balance	100,000	47,000	88,000	141,000
	$196,000	$2,737,000	$2,737,000	$296,000

Additional information:
(1) The budget for fiscal 19X5–19X6 provided for estimated revenues of $1,000,000, appropriations of $905,000 (including $40,000 pertaining to encumbrances outstanding at June 30, 19X5), and $100,000 to be transferred to a debt service fund.
(2) Expenditures totaled $832,000, of which $37,000 pertained to encumbrances outstanding at June 30, 19X5.
(3) Purchase orders issued during 19X5–19X6 totaled $170,000.
(4) The city does not use delinquent accounts for delinquent taxes.

Required:
(1) Using the given data, reconstruct the original detailed journal entries that were required to record all transactions for the fiscal year ended June 30, 19X6, including the recording of the current year's budget. (Hint: Use T accounts.)
(2) Prepare the year-end closing entries from the entries you have reconstructed.
(3) Prepare a budgetary comparison statement of revenues, expenditures, and changes in fund balance for the current year.

(AICPA adapted)

Problem 22–5
General fund: Reconstructing transactions, preparing closing entries, and preparing a statement of revenues, expenditures, and changes in fund balance (Optional: Preparing a budgetary comparison statement on a non-GAAP "budgetary" basis)

The following summary of transactions was taken from the accounts of the Happy Times School District General Fund *before* the books had been closed for the fiscal year ended June 30, 19X5.

	Postclosing Balances June 30, 19X4	Preclosing Balances June 30, 19X5	
Actual accounts:			
Cash	$400,000	$ 630,000	230 000
Property taxes receivable—delinquent	150,000	180,000	30 000
Allowance for uncollectibles—delinquent	(40,000)	(80,000)	(40 000)
Expenditures control	—	2,842,000	
Expenditures control—prior-year	—	58,000	
	$510,000	$3,630,000	
Vouchers payable	$ 80,000	$ 408,000	328 000
Due to other funds	210,000	62,000	148 000
Fund balance reserved for encumbrances	60,000	—	60 000
Unreserved fund balance	160,000	220,000	60 000
Revenues from property taxes control	—	2,800,000	
Miscellaneous revenues control	—	140,000	
	$510,000	$3,630,000	
Budgetary accounts:			
ESTIMATED REVENUES CONTROL		$3,000,000	
ENCUMBRANCES CONTROL		91,000	
		$3,091,000	
APPROPRIATIONS CONTROL		$2,980,000	
BUDGETARY FUND BALANCE		20,000	
FUND BALANCE RESERVED FOR ENCUMBRANCES		91,000	
		$3,091,000	

Additional information:
(1) The property tax levy for the year ended June 30, 19X5 was $2,870,000. Taxes collected during the year totaled $2,810,000, of which $100,000 pertained to delinquent balances as of June 30, 19X4. Of the June 30, 19X4 delinquent balances, $30,000 was written off as uncollectible. Unpaid taxes become delinquent at the end of the fiscal year.
(2) Encumbrances outstanding at each year-end are always honored in the following year. However, the encumbrances are not rebudgeted or reappropriated in the following year. The spending authority merely carries over to the following year. On May 2, 19X5, commitment documents were issued for the purchase of new textbooks at a cost of $91,000. Only this encumbrance is outstanding at June 30, 19X5. Other purchase orders issued during the year totaled $850,000, with invoices having been rendered for $847,000.
(3) An analysis of the transactions in the Vouchers Payable account for the year ended June 30, 19X5 follows.

Balance, June 30, 19X4..	$	80,000
Expenditures pertaining to the prior year's budget...................		58,000
Expenditures pertaining to the current year's budget		2,700,000
Cash disbursements		(2,430,000)
Balance, June 30, 19X5..	$	408,000

(4) During the year, the General Fund was billed $142,000 for services performed on its behalf by other city funds.

Required:
(1) Using the data presented above, reconstruct the original detailed journal entries that were required to record all transactions for the fiscal year ended June 30, 19X5, including the recording of the current year's budget. (Hint: Use T accounts.)
(2) Prepare the closing entries at June 30, 19X5.
(3) Prepare a statement of revenues, expenditures, and changes in fund balance for fiscal 19X4–19X5 (GAAP basis).
(4) (Optional) Prepare a budgetary comparison statement for fiscal 19X4–19X5 (non-GAAP "budgetary" basis).

(AICPA adapted)

Problem 22–6
CHALLENGER   Preparing adjusting and closing entries;
Preparing balance sheet and budgetary comparison
statement on a GAAP basis (Non-General Fund transactions
improperly recorded in General Fund)

The General Fund trial balances of the Three R's School District at June 30, 19X7 are as follows:

THREE R's SCHOOL DISTRICT
General Fund Trial Balances
June 30, 19X7

	Debit	Credit
Actual accounts:		
Cash	$ 60,000	
Taxes receivable—current year	31,800	
Allowance for uncollectibles—current-year taxes		$ 1,800
Inventory of supplies (June 30, 19X6)	10,000	
Buildings	1,300,000	
Bonds payable		500,000
Vouchers payable		12,000
Operating expenses:		
Administration	24,950	
Instruction	601,800	
Other..	221,450	
Capital outlays (equipment)	22,000	
Debt service (interest)...............................	30,000	
State grant revenue.................................		300,000
Revenues from tax levy, licenses, and fines.............		1,008,200
Fund balance reserved for inventory....................		10,000
Unreserved fund balance		470,000
Totals	$2,302,000	$2,302,000

	Debit	Credit
Budgetary accounts:		
ESTIMATED REVENUES CONTROL..................	$1,007,000	
APPROPRIATIONS CONTROL		$1,000,000
BUDGETARY FUND BALANCE......................		7,000
Totals	$1,007,000	$1,007,000

Additional information:

(1) The recorded allowance for uncollectible current-year taxes is considered sufficient. Unpaid taxes become delinquent at year-end.

(2) During the year, the local governmental unit gave the school district 20 acres of land for a new grade school and a community playground. The unrecorded estimated value of the land donated was $50,000. In addition, a state grant of $300,000 was received, and the full amount was used in payment of contracts pertaining to the construction of the grade school. Purchases of classroom and playground equipment costing $22,000 were paid from general funds of the school district.

(3) On July 1, 19X2, a 5%, 10-year serial bond issue in the amount of $1,000,000 for constructing school buildings was issued. Principal payments of $100,000 must be made each June 30, along with interest for the year. All payments required through June 30, 19X7 have been made.

(4) Outstanding purchase orders for operating expenses not recorded in the accounts at year-end were as follows:

Administration	$1,000
Instruction	1,400
Other...	600
Total	$3,000

The school district honors encumbrances outstanding at each year-end and reappropriates amounts in the following year's budget. No encumbrances were outstanding at June 30, 19X6.

(5) Appropriations for the year consisted of the following:

Current:	
Administration	$ 25,200
Instruction	600,000
Other...	222,300
Capital outlay	22,500
Debt service:	
Principal	100,000
Interest	30,000
	$1,000,000

(6) The physical inventory of supplies at year-end totaled $12,500. Supplies are charged to expenditures at the time of receipt under the purchases method. The school district reports the amount of supplies inventory on hand in its balance sheet at each year-end. (The $2,500 increase in the supplies inventory was budgeted for in the current year.)

Required:
(1) Prepare the appropriate adjusting entry to eliminate the activities and accounts that the school district should be accounting for in separate funds or account groups outside the General Fund. (It is not necessary to prepare the entries that would be made in these other funds or account groups to account properly for these items.)
(2) Prepare any adjusting entries to accounts that are properly part of the General Fund.
(3) Prepare the closing entries relating to the General Fund.
(4) Prepare a balance sheet at June 30, 19X7.
(5) Prepare a statement of revenues, expenditures, and changes in fund balance for the year ended June 30, 19X7, comparing budgeted amounts with actual amounts. (The beginning fund balance amount must be "forced" as if a correcting entry had been made at June 30, 19X6.)

(AICPA adapted)

Problem 22–7
CHALLENGER   Preparing budgetary comparison statements from selected data: GAAP basis versus non-GAAP "budgetary" basis

The following information is given for Nap-Town Township:

Fund Balance at December 31, 19X1 (GAAP basis):	
Reserved for encumbrances	$ 30,000
Unreserved	70,000
Total Fund Balance	$100,000
Budgeted items for 19X2:	
Estimated revenues...	$500,000
Appropriations (including $30,000 rebudgeted for encumbrances outstanding at December 31, 19X1)	480,000
Actual amounts for 19X2:	
Revenues..	503,000
Expenditures (including $29,000 relating to encumbrances outstanding at December 31, 19X1)	473,000
Encumbrances outstanding at December 31, 19X2......................	5,000

Required:
(1) Prepare a budgetary comparison statement of revenues, expenditures, and changes in fund balance for 19X2 on a GAAP basis.
(2) Prepare a budgetary comparison statement of revenues, expenditures, and changes in fund balance for 19X2 on a non-GAAP "budgetary" basis. (You now have to assume that the $30,000 relating to encumbrances outstanding at December 31, 19X1 was not rebudgeted for in 19X2.) Note: The ending fund balance in the actual column must agree with the total fund balance that would be reported in the balance sheet. However, the beginning fund balance in the actual column is the $70,000 unreserved fund balance at December 31, 19X1 (the fund balance on a non-GAAP "budgetary" basis). Accordingly, you must reconcile to the December 31, 19X2 fund balance on a GAAP basis.

Problem 22–8
Additional requirement for Problem 22–6 (to be assigned only after Chapter 23 has been covered)

Required:
Prepare the entries that would be made in the other funds and account groups to account properly for the items that should not be accounted for in the General Fund.

23 Governmental Accounting: Special Purpose Funds and Account Groups

In Chapter 22, we discussed the General Fund. In this chapter, we discuss the remaining seven types of funds used for governmental accounting, the General Fixed Asset Account Group, and the General Long-Term Debt Account Group. Concerning the number of funds to be used by a governmental unit, *NCGA Statement 1* says:

> Only the minimum number of funds consistent with legal and operating requirements should be established . . . since unnecessary funds result in inflexibility, undue complexity, and inefficient financial administration.[1]

Certain revenues, functions, or activities of government often must be accounted for in a designated fund separate from all others. In some situations, greater accounting control may be obtained through the use of a separate fund, even though it is not required by law. In most cases, the type of fund to be used to account for the specific revenues, functions, or activities is readily determinable. In a few instances, selecting the most appropriate type of fund requires greater scrutiny.

Certain transactions or events require entries in one or more funds or account groups. For example, the decision to build a new civic center to be financed through the issuance of general obligation bonds eventually results in entries being made in a Capital Projects Fund, a Debt Service Fund, the General Fixed Assets Account Group, the General Long-Term Debt Account Group, and in some cases, the General Fund.

SPECIAL REVENUE FUNDS

Special Revenue Funds account for "the proceeds of specific revenue sources (other than special assessments, expendable trusts, or for major capital projects) that are legally restricted to expenditure for specified purposes."[2] Special Revenue Funds may be used for such small activities as the maintenance of a municipal swimming pool or such gigantic operations as a state highway system. The distinguishing feature of a Special Revenue Fund is that its revenues are obtained primarily from tax and nontax sources not directly related to services rendered or facilities provided for use. In other words, revenues are *not* obtained primarily from direct charges to the users of the services or facilities. Conceptually, therefore, Special Revenue Funds are the opposite of *most* Enterprise Funds, which recover the majority of their operating costs from charges to users.

NCGA Statement 1 requires the use of Enterprise Funds when the costs

---

[1] Reproduced by permission from *National Council on Governmental Accounting, Statement 1,* "Governmental Accounting and Financial Reporting Principles" (Chicago: Municipal Finance Officers Association of the United States and Canada, 1979), p. 8. © Copyright 1979 by the Municipal Finance Officers Association of the United States and Canada.

[2] *NCGA Statement 1*, p. 7.

of providing goods or services are recovered primarily from user charges. In addition, **under certain circumstances,** which we discuss later, Enterprise Funds may be used for activities that do not recover their costs primarily from user charges. The following activities could be accounted for in either Special Revenue Funds or Enterprise Funds, depending on the individual facts, circumstances, and operating policies: off-street parking facilities, transportation systems, turnpikes, golf courses, swimming pools, libraries, and auditoriums.

Special Revenue Funds may derive their revenues from one or several sources, commonly (1) specified property tax levies, (2) state gasoline taxes, (3) licenses, (4) grants, and (5) shared taxes from other governmental units (including federal revenue sharing).

Unless legal provisions specify to the contrary, Special Revenue Funds are accounted for using the same accounting principles, procedures, and financial statements shown for the General Fund in Chapter 22. As explained there, when a governmental unit has more than one fund of a given type, combining financial statements are prepared for financial reporting purposes, showing each individual fund of that type and a total column (the second level of reporting within the "reporting pyramid" concept). This is also the case for the other funds discussed in this chapter.

CAPITAL PROJECTS FUNDS

Capital Projects Funds account for

> financial resources to be used for the acquisition or construction of major capital facilities (other than those financed by proprietary funds, Special Assessment Funds, and Trust Funds).[3]

Examples of major capital facilities are administration buildings, auditoriums, civic centers, and libraries. These funds do not account for the purchase of fixed assets having comparatively limited lives, such as vehicles, machinery, and office equipment, which are normally budgeted for and acquired through the General Fund or a Special Revenue Fund and recorded as expenditures.

Capital Projects Funds do not account for the fixed assets acquired— only for the acquisition of the fixed assets. The fixed assets acquired are accounted for in the General Fixed Asset Account Group, which we discuss later in the chapter. Furthermore, Capital Projects Funds do not account for the repayment and servicing of any debt obligations issued to raise monies to finance the acquisition of capital facilities. Such debt and related servicing is accounted for in the Long-Term Debt Account Group and a Debt Service Fund, both of which we discuss later in the chapter.

Capital Projects Funds are categorized as governmental funds. Recall that the measurement basis for governmental funds is sources and uses (and balances) of financial resources. Accordingly, the same financial statements that are used for the General Fund are used for Capital Projects Funds. Likewise, the modified accrual basis of accounting is used.

[3] *NCGA Statement 1*, p. 7.

Establishment and operation of Capital Projects Funds

Capital Projects Funds are usually established on a project-by-project basis, because legal requirements may vary from one project to another. Most capital facilities are financed through the issuance of general obligation bonds, the liability for which is recorded in the General Long-Term Debt Account Group. In many cases, some portion is financed by the General Fund or a Special Revenue Fund. Such transfers are **operating transfers,** which we discussed in the preceding chapter. The General Fund or Special Revenue Fund debits an account called Other Financing Uses Control, and the Capital Project Fund credits Other Financing Sources Control. Federal and state grants are another major source of funds, the accounting for which is prescribed in *NCGA Statement 2.*

Major capital facilities are usually constructed by contracted labor. Because encumbrance accounting procedures alone are usually deemed sufficient for control purposes, recording the budgeted amounts in the general ledger is usually considered unnecessary. Construction costs incurred are charged to expenditures. At the end of each year, expenditures are closed out to the Unreserved Fund Balance account, as are any amounts recorded in accounts pertaining to bond proceeds and operating transfers in for the year. Each Capital Project Fund is terminated upon completion of the project for which it was created. Any residual equity balance should be disposed of in accordance with legal provisions (usually as a residual equity transfer to either a Debt Service Fund or the General Fund).

At the completion of the project, the cost of the facility is recorded as a fixed asset in the General Fixed Assets Account Group. Until then, any costs incurred are shown as Construction Work in Progress in the General Fixed Assets Account Group. Generally, the year-end closing entry in the Capital Projects Fund triggers the recording of an amount in the General Fixed Assets Account Group equal to the credit to the Expenditures account. (We explain more fully later in the chapter (page 892) that *NCGA Statement 1* makes optional recording in the General Fixed Assets Account Group certain types of improvements constructed through Capital Projects Funds.)

Illustration:
Journal entries and financial statements

Assume that Emerson City established a Capital Projects Fund during the fiscal year ended June 30, 19X2 for the construction of a new city hall. Assumed transactions pertaining to the establishment and operation of the fund, along with the related journal entries, are as follows:

(1) Establishment of the fund and sale of bonds.   The new city hall is expected to cost $5,000,000. The city obtained a **capital grant** from the state government of $1,500,000, of which $600,000 was contributed at the inception of the project. The remaining $900,000 is deemed to be susceptible to accrual. The General Fund contributes $500,000, of which $200,000 was contributed at the inception of the project. The remaining $3,000,000 was obtained from the sale of general obligation bonds at par.

```
Cash .........................................   800,000
Grant receivable ..............................   900,000
Due from general fund .........................   300,000
    Revenues control ...........................              1,500,000
    Other financing sources control.................              500,000
    To record amounts received and due from the
    state government and the General Fund.

Cash .........................................  3,000,000
    Other financing sources control.................            3,000,000
    To record the sale of general obligation bonds.
```

Recall that the bond liability must also be recorded in the General Long-Term Debt Account Group. That entry would be

```
Amount to be provided for
    payment of bonds..............................  3,000,000
        Bonds payable ............................            3,000,000
```

Observe that the entry normally made in the private sector for the issuance of bonds (debiting Cash and crediting Bonds Payable) is effectively made through the combination of the two preceding entries. The debit to Cash is made in the Capital Projects Fund, and the credit to Bonds Payable is made in the General Long-Term Debt Account Group.

(2) **Construction-related activity.** A construction contract for $4,600,000 is authorized and signed. During the year ended June 30, 19X2, billings of $2,700,000 were rendered, and payments totaling $2,200,000 were made.

```
ENCUMBRANCES CONTROL .....................  4,600,000
    FUND BALANCE RESERVED FOR
        ENCUMBRANCES ..........................            4,600,000
    To record encumbrance on construction contract.

FUND BALANCE RESERVED FOR
    ENCUMBRANCES .............................  2,700,000
        ENCUMBRANCES CONTROL .................            2,700,000
    To cancel part of encumbrance for project contract
    with general contractor for completions to date.

Expenditures control..............................  2,700,000
    Contracts payable.............................            2,700,000
    To record actual expenditures to date on contract
    with general contractor for completions to date.

Contracts payable................................  2,200,000
    Cash .......................................            2,200,000
    To record payments to contractor.
```

In addition to the preceding construction contract, $390,000 was incurred for the services of architects and engineers. Of this amount, $310,000 was paid. (For simplicity, we assume that encumbrance accounting procedures were not used.)

Expenditures control	390,000	
Vouchers payable.............................		390,000
To record fees for architects and engineers.		

Vouchers payable................................	310,000	
Cash		310,000
To record payment of architect and engineering fees.		

(3) Closing entries.   The appropriate closing entries at June 30, 19X2 are as follows:

Revenues control	1,500,000	
Other financing sources control.....................	3,500,000	
Expenditures control............................		3,090,000
Unreserved fund balance		1,910,000 — *difference*
To close out actual revenues, other financing sources, and expenditures into unreserved fund balance.		

FUND BALANCE RESERVED FOR ENCUMBRANCES	1,900,000	
ENCUMBRANCES CONTROL		1,900,000
To close encumbrances outstanding at year-end by reversing the entry that previously recorded them.		

Unreserved fund balance	1,900,000	
Fund balance reserved for encumbrances		1,900,000
To record *actual* fund balance reserve account to indicate the portion of year-end balance segregated for expenditure upon contractor performance.		

now dealing with Gen'l fixed asset Group at end of yr.

In addition to the preceding closing entries, the partially completed capital facility must be reflected in the General Fixed Assets Account Group at June 30, 19X2. These accounts are discussed in detail later in the chapter. For now, you should know that the following entry would be made:

Construction work in progress	3,090,000	
Investment in general fixed assets from capital projects—		
General obligation bonds (60%)		1,854,000
State grants (30%)		927,000
General fund revenues (10%)		309,000
To record city hall construction in progress.		

Financial statements. The financial statements that would be prepared for the fiscal year ended June 30, 19X2 as a result of the preceding journal entries are shown in Illustrations 23-1 and 23-2.

Completion of project in following year. Assume the project is completed in the following fiscal year. A cost overrun of $5,000 was made up by a transfer in from the General Fund. The journal entries that would be made during the fiscal year ended June 30, 19X3 begin on page 867.

Illustration 23-1

EMERSON CITY Capital Projects Fund—City Hall Balance Sheet June 30, 19X2	
Assets	
Cash	$1,290,000
Grant receivable..	900,000
Due from general fund	300,000
Total Assets	$2,490,000
Liabilities and Fund Equity	
Vouchers payable	$ 80,000
Contracts payable	500,000
Total Liabilities	$ 580,000
Fund balance:	
Reserved for encumbrances	$1,900,000
Unreserved	10,000
Total Fund Balance	$1,910,000
Total Liabilities and Fund Equity	$2,490,000

Illustration 23-2

EMERSON CITY Capital Projects Fund—City Hall Statement of Revenues, Expenditures, and Changes in Fund Balance For the Fiscal Year Ended June 30, 19X2	
Revenues:	
Intergovernmental—state grant.......................................	$ 1,500,000
Expenditures:	
Capital outlay	(3,090,000)
Revenues under Expenditures	$(1,590,000)
Other Financing Sources:	
Proceeds of general obligation bonds.................................	$ 3,000,000
Operating transfer in from general fund	500,000
Total Other Financing Sources.......................................	$ 3,500,000
Excess of Revenues and Other Sources over Expenditures	$ 1,910,000
Fund Balance, July 1, 19X1	-0-
Fund Balance, June 30, 19X2	$ 1,910,000

(1) Reestablishment of budgetary control over outstanding encumbrances. Budgetary control must be reestablished over outstanding encumbrances on July 1, 19X2. This is done by reversing the prior year-end closing entries related to encumbrances.

ENCUMBRANCES CONTROL	1,900,000	
FUND BALANCE RESERVED FOR		
ENCUMBRANCES		1,900,000
To reestablish budgetary control on remainder of		
construction contract.		

Fund balance reserved for encumbrances	1,900,000	
Unreserved fund balance		1,900,000
To reverse appropriation of fund balance made at		
June 30, 19X2 relating to encumbrances		
outstanding at June 30, 19X2 that will be		
honored during the current year.		

(2) Cash receipts. All receivables were collected, and the $5,000 needed to pay for the cost overrun was received from the General Fund.

Cash	900,000	
Grant receivable		900,000
To record collection of grant receivable.		

Cash	305,000	
Due from general fund		300,000
Other financing sources control.................		5,000
To record collection of amounts received from		
the General Fund.		

(3) Construction-related activity. The contractor submitted bills for the remainder of the contract. Additional engineering services totaled $15,000. All liabilities were paid.

FUND BALANCE RESERVED FOR		
ENCUMBRANCES	1,900,000	
ENCUMBRANCES CONTROL		1,900,000
To cancel remainder of encumbrance for project		
contract with general contractor upon		
completion of contract.		

Expenditures control.............................	1,900,000	
Contracts payable............................		1,900,000
To record expenditures relating to billings on		
remainder of contract.		

Contracts payable................................	2,400,000	
Cash		2,400,000
To record payments to contractor.		

Expenditures	15,000	
Vouchers payable		15,000
To record fees for engineering services.		

Vouchers payable	15,000	
Cash		15,000
To record payment of engineering fees.		

(4) Closing entry. The appropriate closing entry at June 30, 19X3 is as follows:

Other financing sources control.....................	5,000	
Unreserved fund balance	1,910,000	
Expenditures control		1,915,000
To close out other financing sources and expenditures into unreserved fund balance.		

In addition to the preceding closing entry, the fully completed capital facility would be reflected in the General Fixed Assets Account Group at June 30, 19X3 as a result of the following entry in these accounts:

Buildings	5,005,000	
Construction work in progress		3,090,000
Investment in general fixed assets from capital projects—		
General obligation bonds (60%)		1,146,000
State grants (30%)		573,000
General fund revenues (10% of $5,000,000 plus $5,000)		196,000
To record completed city hall in the General Fixed Assets Account Group.		

Financial statements for year ended June 30, 19X3. Because all liabilities were paid by June 30, 19X3 and no assets remained, a balance sheet at June 30, 19X3 is not necessary. The operating statement for the year ended June 30, 19X3 is shown in Illustration 23-3.

Other procedural matters

The preceding example illustrated a project cost overrun, which was made up from the General Fund. Such situations are common. The source of additional monies to pay for cost overruns is specified by legal requirements or operating policy.

All the money necessary to pay for the capital improvements is usually raised at or near the inception of the project, but contractors are paid as work progresses. Excess cash, therefore, may be temporarily invested in high-quality, interest-bearing securities. In such cases, the interest income on the investments may be either credited to revenues—to be available to

Illustration 23-3

EMERSON CITY Capital Projects Fund—City Hall Statement of Expenditures and Changes in Fund Balance For the Fiscal Year Ended June 30, 19X3	
Expenditures:	
Capital outlay	$(1,915,000)
Other Financing Sources:	
Operating transfer in from general fund	5,000
Excess of Expenditures over Other Sources........................	$(1,910,000)
Fund Balance, July 1, 19X2	1,910,000
Fund Balance, June 30, 19X3	$ -0-

the Capital Projects Fund in the event of cost overruns—or transferred to the related Debt Service Fund.

DEBT SERVICE FUNDS

For discussion purposes, long-term debt of governmental units may be categorized as follows:

(1) Special assessment bonds.   Special assessment bonds are issued to finance certain public improvements. The bonds are shown as liabilities of Special Assessment Funds, because their repayment and servicing comes from monies raised by those funds.

(2) Revenue bonds.   Revenue bonds are issued to finance the establishment or expansion of activities accounted for in Enterprise Funds. These bonds are shown as liabilities of the Enterprise Funds, because their repayment and servicing can only come from monies generated from the operations of those funds.

(3) General obligation bonds serviced from Enterprise Funds.   General obligation bonds also are issued to finance establishment or expansion of activities accounted for in Enterprise Funds. They bear the full faith and credit of the governmental unit. When such bonds are to be repaid and serviced from monies generated from an Enterprise Fund's operations, the bonds should be shown as liabilities of the Enterprise Fund and as a contingent liability of the General Long-Term Debt Account Group. (We discuss these bonds more fully later in the chapter.)

(4) All other long-term debt.   All long-term debt not fitting into one of the three preceding categories is shown as a liability of the General Long-Term Debt Account Group.

Debt Service Funds are created for the fourth category of long-term debt. Remember that the General Long-Term Debt Account Group is not a fund but merely a self-balancing group of accounts that keep track of all unmatured long-term debt in the fourth category above. Debt Service Funds account for the matured portion of and the payment of principal and interest on such long-term debt. Although notes payable are occasionally encountered, substantially all long-term debt of governmental units consists of one of the following two major types of bonds:

(1) Term bonds. Term bonds are bonds whose principal is repaid in a lump sum at their maturity date. Such a lump-sum payment is usually made possible through the accumulation of money in the Debt Service Fund on an actuarial basis over the life of the bond issue ("sinking fund"). Term bonds are less prevalent than they used to be.

(2) Serial bonds. The principal of serial bonds is repaid at various pre-determined dates over the life of the issue. **Regular** serial bonds are repaid in equal annual installments. **Deferred** serial bonds are also repaid in equal annual installments, but the first serial payment is delayed a specified number of years. **Irregular** serial bonds are repaid in other than equal principal repayments.

On the date that a principal payment relating to general long-term debt is to be made, a liability is established in the Debt Service Fund for the amount of the payment. Simultaneously, the amount of the debt as recorded in the General Long-Term Debt Account Group is reduced by a like amount. Thus, liabilities recorded in the General Long-Term Debt Account Group are effectively transferred at their maturity dates to a Debt Service Fund for their liquidation.

The only unusual feature of Debt Service Funds is the method of accounting for interest on the general long-term debt. Interest is not reflected as a liability of the Debt Service Fund **until the date it is due and payable.** This use of the cash basis of accounting is the major exception to the accrual of expenditures in the period to which they relate. As a result, interest for the period from the last payment date to the end of the fiscal year is not reflected as a liability at the end of the fiscal year. This is because governmental units generally budget for interest on the cash basis instead of the accrual basis.

Debt Service Funds are categorized as governmental funds. Accordingly, the modified accrual basis of accounting is used, and the financial statements used for the General Fund are also used for Debt Service Funds.

Establishment and operation of Debt Service Funds

The legal provisions of a specific debt issue may require the establishment of a separate Debt Service Fund solely for that debt issue. In other cases, several debt issues may be accounted for using a single Debt Service Fund. Concerning the appropriateness of recording budgeted amounts in the general ledger, *NCGA Statement 1* states:

> it would not be necessary [to record the budget] in controlling most Debt Service Funds, where the amounts required to be received and expended are set forth in bond indentures or sinking fund provisions and few transactions occur each year.[4]

Encumbrance accounting is not appropriate because contracts are not entered into and purchase orders are not issued.

[4] *NCGA Statement 1*, p. 14.

Debt Service Funds may obtain their revenues from one or several sources. The most common source is property taxes. A separate rate is levied for each bond issue or group of bond issues. In these situations, the revenues are recognized on the accrual basis. (The accounting procedures are identical to those used by the General Fund in accounting for property taxes.) Revenues obtained from sources such as shared sales taxes are customarily recorded at the time of receipt. When monies are to be transferred from the General Fund, a receivable from the General Fund may be recorded at the start of the fiscal year for the amount authorized to be transferred to the Debt Service Fund. Such transfers are **operating transfers,** and the General Fund debits the Other Financing Uses Control account, and the Debt Service Fund credits Other Financing Sources Control. Payments made for principal and interest are recorded as expenditures.

Governmental units commonly use designated fiscal agents to make the payments to the bondholders. In such cases, monies are transferred from the Debt Service Funds to the fiscal agents, who submit reports and canceled coupons (if used) to the governmental unit. The fee charged for such services is recorded as an expenditure of the Debt Service Fund.

The operation of Debt Service Funds pertaining to issues of **regular** serial bonds essentially involves collecting revenues and transferring monies to the fiscal agent. Significant accumulations of monies requiring investment do not occur. In these cases, the journal entries to record the revenues, the expenditures, and the closing of the books parallel those used in the General Fund. Accordingly, an illustration of journal entries and financial statements for this type of Debt Service Fund is not presented.

When **deferred** serial bonds and **term** bonds are involved, the operation of Debt Service Funds is more complex. Accumulated monies must be invested, and bond premiums and discounts may exist on such investments. Actuarial computations are used to determine additions and earnings. The journal entries and financial statements for a Debt Service Fund pertaining to term bonds are illustrated in the following section.

Illustration:
Journal entries and financial statements—Term bonds

Assume Emerson City established a Debt Service Fund on October 1, 19X1 for an 8%, $400,000 general obligation bond issue due in 20 years (the proceeds of which will be used to construct a new civic center). Interest is to be paid semiannually on March 31 and September 30. For simplicity, we assume that all required additions to the fund will come from the General Fund. Assumed transactions pertaining to the operation of the fund for the fiscal year ended June 30, 19X2, along with related journal entries, are as follows:

Transaction or Event	Journal Entry		
The required fund transfer from the general fund is recorded on October 1, 19X1.	Due from general fund..... Other financing sources control	25,000	 25,000
The required fund transfer is received from the general fund.	Cash .... Due from general fund...	25,000	 25,000

An investment of $8,500 is made.	Investment 8,500	
	Cash	8,500
Cash is transferred to the fiscal agent for the March 31, 19X2 interest payment.	Cash with fiscal agent 16,000	
	Cash	16,000
Interest of $16,000 and the fiscal agent's fee of $100 is charged as an expenditure on the interest due date (March 31, 19X2).	Expenditures control........ 16,100	
	Interest payable.........	16,000
	Accrued liability	100
Interest is paid by the fiscal agent, and the fiscal agent's fee is paid.	Interest payable........... 16,000	
	Accrued liability 100	
	Cash with fiscal agent ...	16,000
	Cash	100
Interest earned on investments is accrued at June 30, 19X2.	Interest receivable......... 450	
	Revenues control	450
The fiscal year-end closing entry is made.	Other financing sources control 25,000	
	Revenues control 450	
	Expenditures control.....	16,100
	Fund balance reserved for debt service	9,350

Financial statements. The financial statements that would be prepared for the fiscal year ended June 30, 19X2 as a result of the preceding journal entries are shown in Illustrations 23-4 and 23-5. In reviewing the financial statements, the following points should be understood:

(1) A liability for interest for the period April 1, 19X2 through June 30, 19X2 is not reflected in the statement of financial position at June 30, 19X2 in accordance with the modified accrual basis of accounting. This interest will be shown as an Expenditure in the following year when the September 30, 19X2 interest payment is due and payable.

(2) If all required additions are made on time and earnings on investments earn the rate assumed in the actuarial calculations, then $400,000 will be accumulated in the Debt Service Fund by the maturity date of the bonds (19¼ years from June 30, 19X2).

Illustration 23-4

EMERSON CITY	
Debt Service Fund—Civic Center	
Balance Sheet	
June 30, 19X2	
Assets	
Cash..	$ 400
Investments..	8,500
Interest receivable	450
Total Assets	$9,350
Fund Equity	
Fund balance reserved for debt service...................................	$9,350[a]

[a] The actuarial requirement at June 30, 19X2 is $9,300.

Illustration 23-5

EMERSON CITY Debt Service Fund—Civic Center Statement of Revenues, Expenditures, and Changes in Fund Balance For the Fiscal Year Ended June 30, 19X2	
Revenues:	
Interest on investments	$ 450
Expenditures:	
Interest on bonds..	$ 16,000
Fiscal agent's fees..	100
Total Expenditures...	$ 16,100
Revenues under Expenditures	$(15,650)
Other Financing Sources:	
Operating transfer in from general fund	25,000
Excess of Revenues and Other Sources over Expenditures	$ 9,350[a]
Fund Balance, July 1, 19X1	-0-
Fund Balance, June 30, 19X2	$ 9,350

[a] The actuarial requirement for the year was $9,300.

no investment here, but they do accrue interest receivable.

(3) At the maturity date of the bonds, the entire $400,000 is recorded as a liability in the Debt Service Fund by debiting the Expenditures account and crediting Bonds Payable. Simultaneously, this debt is removed from the General Long-Term Debt Group of Accounts.

(4) Making all required additions and earning interest at rates at least equal to the actuarially assumed interest rate is critical to the accumulation of the $400,000 required to redeem the bonds. If a lower interest rate is actually earned, then additional monies must be contributed to the fund to make up the shortage. To the extent that earnings exceed the actuarially assumed rate, future contributions may be reduced accordingly.

(5) The following essential disclosures for Debt Service Funds pertain to term bonds: (a) the actuarially computed amount that should exist in the Fund Balance account as of the statement of financial position date, and (b) the actuarially computed amount of earnings that should have been earned during the current fiscal year.

SPECIAL ASSESSMENT FUNDS

Some government activities involve constructing public improvements that benefit a specific geographical area rather than the community as a whole. The most common examples are residential streets, sidewalks, street lighting, and sewer lines. In these cases, governmental units usually charge all or most of the costs of the improvements directly to the owners of the properties benefited. Special Assessment Funds account for all such construction activities, including (1) any borrowings made to finance the improvements, including the retirement and servicing of the debt, and (2) collections to be made from property owners who bear the ultimate responsibility for paying for the improvements. Thus, Special Assessment Funds may be thought of as "combination Capital Projects–Debt Service Funds."

Because Special Assessment Funds are categorized as governmental funds, the modified accrual basis of accounting is used, and the financial statements used for the General Fund are used for Special Assessment Funds.

Establishment and operation of Special Assessment Funds

Special Assessment Funds are established on a project-by-project basis. As with Capital Projects Funds, recording the budget in the general ledger usually serves no useful purpose if construction is contracted out rather than performed by a governmental unit's internal work force. Encumbrance accounting procedures alone are sufficient for control purposes.

In most cases, monies are collected from the appropriate property owners in installments over a period of years. In some cases, the General Fund contributes monies for part of the improvements. Such transfers are **operating transfers,** and the General Fund debits the Other Financing Uses Control account, and the Special Assessment Fund credits Other Financing Sources Control.

Although construction may be started after all the necessary money has been collected, it is more common to: (a) borrow money (usually by issuing bonds); (b) use the borrowed funds to pay for the improvements; (c) collect monies in installments from property owners in succeeding years; and (d) use the monies collected from the property owners in these succeeding years to make principal and interest payments on the borrowings. In these cases, the borrowings are generally serial bonds, which may be either special assessment bonds or general obligation bonds. The former may be repaid only from assessments made against the applicable properties benefited, whereas the latter bear the full faith and credit of the governmental unit. To pay for the interest on outstanding bonds, the assessment payers are charged interest in installments.

Manner of recording interest expense and interest income.   As with general long-term debt, NCGA Statement 1 calls for the recognition of interest on special assessment indebtedness **when due** rather than in the period to which the interest relates. For practical reasons, interest revenues on special assessment levies may also be recorded when due rather than accrued as earned, providing this interest approximately offsets the interest on special assessment indebtedness that is recorded when due. However, if such treatment causes the reported financial position or operating results to differ significantly, the statement requires these items to be recognized on the accrual basis.[5]

Special reporting situation.   Because special assessment bonds payable are reported as a liability of Special Assessment Funds (with Bonds Payable credited instead of Other Financing Sources Control), an unusual

[5] NCGA Statement 1, pp. 12 and 27.

reporting result occurs in the statement of revenues, expenditures, and changes in fund balance that is different from the reporting for the other four governmental funds. The operating statement for the initial year of operations (the year in which the improvements are made) reports expenditures (an outflow of resources) but no inflow of resources. After the initial year of operations, as installment collections are received from property tax owners, revenues (an inflow of resources) are reported; however, the primary use of these monies (to repay principal on the borrowings) is not reported as an expenditure. The result of this manner of reporting is a fund deficit at the end of the initial year of operations (expenditures exceed revenues). In subsequent years (when revenues exceed expenditures), the deficit eventually is eliminated. To prevent misleading inferences (for example, that the governmental unit is spending beyond its means), disclosure is necessary in the notes to the financial statements explaining why the fund is reporting a deficit and how future collections on assessments will eliminate that deficit.

How can expenditures alone be reported in the initial year of operations? In other words, how can there be an outflow of resources without a corresponding inflow of resources from which to pay for the expenditures? The answer lies in the definition of inflows and outflows of resources used in governmental accounting. Inflows and outflows of money are not inflows and outflows of resources unless they influence the fund balance. By initially crediting Bonds Payable (instead of Other Financing Sources Control), the borrowings do not affect the fund balance, and therefore, are not considered an inflow of resources.

The unusual reporting results for Special Assessment Funds have been discussed at length in recent years; some accountants have proposed that Special Assessment Funds be eliminated altogether, and others have proposed that special assessment bonds be reported as a special category of General Long-Term Debt. (In the latter case, the Special Assessment Funds would credit Other Financing Sources Control, and no unusual reporting would result.) This is an area of potential future change.

Termination of the fund.   After all installment receivables have been collected and the bonds payable have been paid off, the fund is terminated. At that point, the Fund Balance account should have a nominal balance. A positive balance in the Fund Balance account should be disposed of in accordance with legal requirements. For example, the balance could be transferred to the General Fund (which would record the transfer as a **residual equity transfer** by crediting its Fund Balance account), or it could be refunded to the appropriate property owners. If the Fund Balance account will apparently have a deficit balance at the maturity date of the bonds, additional assessments must be made or a contribution must be obtained from the General Fund (which would treat the transfer as an **operating transfer**).

As explained more fully later in the chapter (page 892), *NCGA Statement 1* makes optional the recording in the General Fixed Assets Account Group virtually all types of improvements constructed through Special Assessment Funds.

Illustration:
Journal entries and financial statements

Assume Emerson City established a Special Assessments Fund for certain residential street improvements during the fiscal year ended June 30, 19X2. Assumed transactions pertaining to the establishment and operation of the fund, along with related journal entries, are as follows:

(1) Establishment of the fund and sale of assessment bonds. Improvements are estimated to cost $400,000. The General Fund will contribute $50,000 and the remaining $350,000 will be collected from certain property owners in five equal installments of $70,000 per year beginning October 1, 19X1. Interest at 9% is to be charged on deferred assessments and is to be paid semiannually. On October 1, 19X1, special assessment bonds bearing interest at 8%, with interest payable semiannually, were issued at par in an amount equal to the deferred installment payments of $280,000.

Special assessments receivable—current	70,000	
Special assessments receivable—deferred	280,000	
Revenues control...................................		70,000
Deferred revenues..................................		280,000
To record levy of assessments.		

Note that the deferred portion cannot be reported as revenues at this time because the amount (although measurable) is not "available" to pay current-period liabilities.

Due from general fund.................................	50,000	
Other financing sources control		50,000
To record amount due from General Fund.		

Cash...	120,000	
Special assessments receivable—current		70,000
Due from general fund..............................		50,000
To record collection of current assessments		
receivable and all of the city's share of the cost.		

Cash...	280,000	
Special assessment bonds payable		280,000
To record sale of special assessment bonds at par.		

(2) Construction-related activity. A construction contract for $395,000 is authorized and signed. During the year, billings of $360,000 were rendered, and payments of $330,000 were made. (The entries in this section are identical to entries that would be made for purchase orders issued or contracts entered into in the General Fund.)

ENCUMBRANCES CONTROL...........................	395,000	
FUND BALANCE RESERVED FOR		
ENCUMBRANCES		395,000
To record encumbrances on construction contract.		

| FUND BALANCE RESERVED FOR ENCUMBRANCES ... | 360,000 | |
| ENCUMBRANCES CONTROL .... | | 360,000 |

To reverse portion of original encumbrances entry
related to billings received under the construction
contract.

| Expenditures control .... | 360,000 | |
| Contracts payable .... | | 360,000 |

To record expenditures relating to billings approved to
date.

| Contracts payable .... | 330,000 | |
| Cash... | | 330,000 |

To record payments to contractor.

(3) Interest-related entries. Interest on special assessment indebtedness and special assessment levies is recorded when due rather than accrued, because such interest expenditures approximately offset such interest revenues, having no significant effect on the financial statements. We assume all required interest collections and payments are made on time.

| Expenditures control .... | 11,200 | |
| Cash... | | 11,200 |

To record first semiannual interest payment on
April 1, 19X2. *(on bond from spec. assessment fund*

| Cash.. | 12,600 | |
| Revenues control................................ | | 12,600 |

To record first semiannual interest collection on
April 1, 19X2.

(4) Closing entries. The appropriate closing entry at June 30, 19X2 is as follows:

nothing transferred to gen't asset corp fund—

Revenues control.......................................	82,600	
Other financing sources control	50,000	
Unreserved fund balance...............................	238,600	
Expenditures control		371,200

To close actual revenues, other financing sources, and
expenditures into unreserved fund balance.

this fund stays off til spec. assessment pd off.

| FUND BALANCE RESERVED FOR ENCUMBRANCES ... | 35,000 | |
| ENCUMBRANCES CONTROL .... | | 35,000 |

To close encumbrances outstanding at year-end by
reversing the entry that previously recorded them.

Note: Because the Fund Balance account has a deficit balance, it is legally impossible to appropriate any of the fund balance at year-end for encumbrances outstanding, even though they will be honored next year. (Appropriate disclosure must be made in the notes to the financial statements.)

If the governmental unit's practice is to reflect such capital improvements in its General Fixed Assets Account Group, the following entry would be made in these accounts at June 30, 19X2:

Construction work in progress 360,000
    Investment in general fixed assets from special
      assessments.................................... 360,000
    To record street improvements construction in progress.

Financial statements.   The financial statements prepared for the fiscal year ended June 30, 19X2 as a result of the preceding journal entries are shown in Illustrations 23-6 and 23-7.

Illustration 23-6

EMERSON CITY
Special Assessment Fund—Project No. 36
Balance Sheet
June 30, 19X2

Assets

Cash	$ 71,400
Special assessments receivable—deferred	280,000
Total Assets	$ 351,400

Liabilities and Fund Deficiency

Contracts payable	$ 30,000
Special assessment bonds payable..................................	280,000
Deferred revenues..	280,000
Fund deficiency	(238,600)[a]
Total Liabilities and Fund Deficiency............................	$ 351,400

[a] The fund deficiency will be eliminated as the deferred revenues are reported as revenues in future years.

Illustration 23-7

EMERSON CITY
Special Assessment Fund—Project No. 36
Statement of Revenues, Expenditures, and
Changes in Fund Balance
For the Fiscal Year Ended June 30, 19X2

Revenues:	
Special assessments...	$ 70,000
Interest on assessments	12,600
Total Revenues	$ 82,600
Expenditures:	
Capital outlay	$ 360,000
Debt service—interest..	11,200
Total Expenditures..	$ 371,200
Revenues under Expenditures	$(288,600)
Other Financing Sources:	
Operating transfer in from general fund	50,000
Revenues and Other Sources under Expenditures	$(238,600)
Fund Balance, July 1, 19X1	-0-
Fund Balance (Deficiency), June 30, 19X2	$(238,600)

Other procedural matters

In the preceding example, interest was charged to assessment payers in excess of the interest rate of the special assessment bonds to build up a nominal balance in the Fund Balance account in the event that costs incurred exceed $400,000. When bonds are issued at a premium or a discount, the premium or discount is amortized over the life of the bonds as offsets or additions, respectively, to the Interest Expenditure account.

In the example, we also assumed that all the construction was performed by one contractor. In practice, several contractors may be involved. Furthermore, contracts may be entered into at various dates other than at the inception of the project. Because all the money necessary to pay for improvements is usually raised at or near the inception of the project and contractors are paid as work progresses, excess cash may be temporarily invested in high-quality, interest-bearing securities.

Installment receivables that are delinquent should be transferred to a Special Assessments Receivable—Delinquent account. It may be necessary to foreclose on properties when property owners are unable or refuse to pay.

ENTERPRISE FUNDS

According to *NCGA Statement 1,* Enterprise Funds account for

> operations (a) that are financed and operated in a manner similar to private business enterprises—where the intent of the governing body is that the costs (expenses, including depreciation) of providing goods or services to the general public on a continuing basis be financed or recovered primarily through user charges; or (b) where the governing body has decided that periodic determination of revenues earned, expenses incurred, and/or net income is appropriate for capital maintenance, public policy, management control, accountability, or other purposes.[6]

The most common type of activity accounted for in an Enterprise Fund is the public utility providing water services, electricity, or natural gas. Other activities commonly accounted for in Enterprise Funds are off-street parking facilities, recreational facilities (principally golf courses and swimming pools), airports, hospitals, and public transit systems. The language of *NCGA Statement 1* is so broad that a governmental unit may establish an Enterprise Fund for almost any activity regardless of the extent of financing obtained from user charges. In practice, however, only a small percentage of governmental units use Enterprise Funds for activities that recover less than 50% of their costs from user charges, with public transit systems probably being the most common.

Because Enterprise Funds evaluate operations from a profit and loss perspective, the accounting principles and procedures used in private industry for comparable activities lend themselves to Enterprise Fund use. Accordingly, the accrual basis of accounting is used, depreciation expense is recorded, and earnings are closed out at year-end to a Retained Earnings account. The following financial statements are used.

[6] *NCGA Statement 1,* p. 7.

(1) A Balance Sheet (which includes all the fund's assets and liabilities).
(2) A Statement of Revenues, Expenses, and Changes in Retained Earnings (or Equity).
(3) A Statement of Changes in Financial Position (most commonly prepared using a cash flow format).

Although evaluated from a profit and loss perspective, the activities accounted for in Enterprise Funds are not engaged in to maximize profits, as in the private sector. Instead, the intent is to raise sufficient revenues to either (1) recover costs to break even, or (2) generate profits so that capital is effectively raised to finance expansion of operations.

Establishment and expansion of Enterprise Funds

Some of the more common ways of establishing an operation to be accounted for as an Enterprise Fund or expanding the operations of an existing Enterprise Fund are as follows:

(1) **Contribution from the General Fund.**   An interfund transfer from the General Fund is categorized as a **residual equity transfer.** Accordingly, the General Fund debits its Unreserved Fund Balance account, and the Enterprise Fund credits an account called Contributed Capital. Contributed Capital accounts are similar to the capital stock accounts used by private corporations in that both reflect the value of assets contributed. Thus, Enterprise Funds do not use a Fund Balance account. Contributed Capital accounts are normally shown by the source of the contribution, for example, Contributed Capital from Municipality.

(2) **Loan from the General Fund.**   When the General Fund makes a loan, it debits an account called Advance to Enterprise Fund and credits Cash. The Enterprise Fund debits Cash and credits Advance from General Fund (a liability account). If interest is paid on the advance, then the Enterprise Fund has interest expense and the General Fund has interest revenue.

(3) **Issuance of revenue bonds.**   Revenue bonds are issued by an Enterprise Fund and are repayable, with interest, only from the earnings of the operations accounted for in the Enterprise Fund. (If the bonds also have a security interest in the fixed assets of the Enterprise Fund, then they are called mortgage revenue bonds.) Revenue bonds require accounting entries only in the Enterprise Fund. Bond indenture agreements frequently restrict the use of bond proceeds to specific capital projects; therefore, the bond proceeds are deposited in a separate checking account called, for example, Construction Cash. Using a separate account provides greater accounting control to ensure that the proceeds are spent only on authorized projects. The offsetting credit is to Revenue Bonds Payable.

(4) **Issuance of general obligation bonds.**   General obligation bonds are issued by a governmental unit with its full faith and backing. The proceeds are transferred to the Enterprise Fund, which uses the cash in accordance with the bond indenture agreement. General obligation bonds fall into the following two categories, based on the source of their repayment and payment of related interest.

A. **Repayable from earnings of the enterprise.** When the governmental unit intends to repay the principal and related interest from Enterprise Fund earnings, NCGA *Statement 1* recommends that such debt be reflected as a liability in the Enterprise Fund. This position conforms with the AICPA's governmental audit guide, which states:

> General obligation bonds being repaid by enterprise funds should be carried as liabilities of the enterprise fund to reflect the intention of retirement out of resources of that fund. . . . The existence of the bonds should be included in a note to the statement of general long-term debt to reflect the contingent liability for payment of these bonds.[7]

B. **Repayable from taxes and general revenues.** When the bonds and related interest are to be repaid from taxes and general revenues of the governmental unit, the bond liability is shown as a liability of the General Long-Term Debt Account Group. The Enterprise Fund treats the monies received as a contribution and credits the Contributed Capital from Municipality account. Thus, a liability is not reflected in the Enterprise Fund.

Unique features of financial statements

Because the financial statements of Enterprise Funds are similar to those of private enterprises engaged in comparable activities, typical transactions, related journal entries, and a complete set of illustrative financial statements are not presented. Instead, we discuss the unique features of Enterprise Fund financial statements, and then illustrate a balance sheet of a water utility. (The balance sheet has certain unique classification features.)

(1) **Contributed capital accounts.** As mentioned previously, Enterprise Funds use Contributed Capital accounts instead of capital stock accounts.
(2) **Restricted assets.** Assets that are restricted as to use are shown separately. The most common examples are:
  A. **Construction cash.** Construction cash is not available for normal operating purposes and must be identified as usable only for its designated purpose—for example, expansion of plant.
  B. **Customer deposits.** For public utilities that require their customers to make deposits to ensure payment of final statements, the deposits constitute restricted assets that are not available for normal operations. When such deposits are invested in allowable investments, the investments should also be shown as restricted assets.
  C. **Debt-related accumulations.** Some bond indenture agreements require that certain amounts of cash provided from operations be set aside in separate accounts for retirement and servicing of bonds. In some cases, monies must be set aside to cover potential future losses.
(3) **Appropriation of retained earnings.** When monies relating to debt retirement and servicing of bonds have been set aside pursuant to

---

[7] *Audits of State and Local Governmental Units*, p. 79.

bond indenture agreements, it may be necessary to appropriate a portion of retained earnings. The appropriation indicates that a portion of the retained earnings is not available for normal operations, internal expansion, or cash transfers to the General Fund; that is, cash that might otherwise be used for such purposes has been set aside for other purposes. This practice is at variance with customary practice in private industry, where showing the restricted assets separately is deemed sufficient disclosure.

Technically, at any balance sheet date, the appropriation should equal only the amounts set aside to cover: (a) future interest expense; (b) future principal payments (above and beyond amounts deemed to have been generated from operatons to date); and (c) potential future losses.

(4) Depreciation expense. For public utilities, depreciation expense is usually a major expense because of the large capital investment required. Depreciation expense is customarily shown on a separate line of the income statement.

(5) Income taxes. Because governmental units do not pay income taxes, no income tax expense is shown in the statement of revenues and expenses.

(6) Payments to the General Fund. Payments to the General Fund in lieu of taxes are **quasi-external transactions,** which we discussed in Chapter 22. Accordingly, such payments are recorded as **expenses** in the Enterprise Fund and as **revenues** in the General Fund. Payments to the General Fund not in lieu of taxes but for the purpose of financing General Fund expenditures are **operating transfers.** Accordingly, such payments are recorded as **operating transfers out** by the Enterprise Fund and as **operating transfers in** by the General Fund.

(7) Inverted balance sheet format. Some governmental utilities use an inverted format for their balance sheets. Under this presentation, fixed assets, long-term debt, and capital balances are shown before current items to emphasize the relative importance of the investment in fixed assets and the related financing sources. However, the conventional format, which places current items first, is still more prevalent than the inverted format. A utility fund balance sheet using the conventional format is shown in Illustration 23-8 (pages 884–85).

INTERNAL SERVICE FUNDS

Various departments of a governmental unit usually require common services. Each department may hire people to perform these services or it may contract with outside vendors. It is usually cheaper, however, for the governmental unit to establish one or more separate operations to provide these services to its various departments. Internal Service Funds account for each of these separate operations in a manner that charges the total cost of an operation to the various user departments. Internal Service Funds commonly are established for: (1) motor pool operations; (2) central purchasing and stores; (3) maintenance services; (4) printing and reproduction services; and (5) data-processing services. The primary distinction between an Internal Service Fund and an Enterprise Fund is that the former **provides services to departments within a governmental unit or to related governmental units,** whereas the latter provides services primarily to the general public.

The objective of an Internal Service Fund is to recover the total cost of an operation from billings to the various user departments. Generally, billings are not set at levels intended to generate significant profits—only to recover costs or generate a slight profit. The accounting principles and procedures used in private industry also lend themselves to use with Internal Service Funds, even though billings are not made to independent parties. Accordingly, the accrual basis of accounting is used, depreciation expense is recorded, and any earnings are closed out at year-end to a Retained Earnings account. The following financial statements are used:

(1) A Balance Sheet.
(2) A Statement of Revenues, Expenses, and Changes in Retained Earnings (or Equity).
(3) A Statement of Changes in Financial Position.

Merely because all costs are recovered through billings, it does not automatically follow that the services are being provided at a lower cost than would be incurred if the Internal Service Fund were not used. This determination may only be made by comparing the total cost incurred with amounts that would have been incurred if the Internal Service Fund had not been established.

Establishment and operation of Internal Service Funds

Internal Service Funds are normally established by contributions or advances from the General Fund. Contributions are credited to a Contributed Capital account (which is considered the equivalent of a private corporation's capital stock accounts). This type of interfund transfer is a **residual equity transfer;** accordingly, the General Fund debits its Fund Balance account. Advances are credited to an Advance from General Fund account (a liability account); the General Fund debits Advance to Internal Service Fund (a receivable account). Cash is then used to purchase materials, parts, supplies, and equipment as needed to fulfill the objectives of the fund.

A significant managerial accounting issue is that of developing a cost accounting system for charging the various user departments for the costs of the operation as reflected in the statement of revenues and expenses. When billings exceed costs, some or all of the retained earnings may need to be transferred to the General Fund. When billings are below cost, an accumulated deficit may be made up through additional charges to the user departments or a transfer from the General Fund. These interfund transfers must be substantively evaluated as to whether they are **operating transfers** or **residual equity transfers.** As discussed in the preceding chapter, **nonrecurring** or **nonroutine** transfers are considered **residual equity transfers,** and all other transfers are treated as **operating transfers.**

Illustration 23-8

EMERSON CITY			
Water Fund			
Balance Sheet			
June 30, 19X2			

Assets

Current Assets:			
Cash....................................		$ 330,000	
Customers' accounts receivable, less			
$185,000 allowance for uncollectible			
accounts		2,490,000	
Due from other funds		55,000	
Unbilled accounts receivable		670,000	
Inventories of materials and supplies		240,000	
Prepaid expenses		34,000	
Total Current Assets..................			$ 3,819,000
Restricted Assets:			
Customers' deposits:			
Cash.................................	$ 23,000		
Investments	512,000	$ 535,000	
Revenue bond construction account:			
Cash.................................		188,000	
Revenue bond current debt			
service account:			
Cash.................................	$ 10,000		
Investments	1,130,000	1,140,000	
Revenue bond future debt service			
reserve account:			
Cash.................................	$ 70,000		
Investments	1,200,000	1,270,000	
Total Restricted Assets			3,133,000
Property, plant, and equipment:			
Land		$ 1,511,000	
Buildings		4,477,000	
Improvements other than buildings		38,870,000	
Machinery and equipment		18,440,000	
Construction in process		2,900,000	
		$66,198,000	
Less: Accumulated depreciation		(12,450,000)	53,748,000
Total Assets			$60,700,000

Illustration:
Journal entries and financial statements

Assume Emerson City established a Central Printing and Reproduction Fund during the fiscal year ended June 30, 19X2. Assumed transactions pertaining to the establishment and operation of the fund, along with related journal entries, are as follows:

(1) Establishment of the fund. The fund was established by a contribution of $40,000 from the General Fund. The operation is conducted in a facility leased on a month-to-month basis from a privately owned company.

Illustration 23-8 (continued)

EMERSON CITY		
Water Fund		
Balance Sheet		
June 30, 19X2		

Liabilities and Fund Equity

Current Liabilities (payable from current assets):

Vouchers payable.....................................	$ 1,347,000	
Accrued wages and taxes	73,000	
Accrued interest payable on advance from municipality ...	26,000	
Advance from municipality	50,000	
Total.......................................		$ 1,496,000

Current Liabilities (payable from restricted assets):

Customer deposits	$ 535,000	
Construction contracts payable	172,000	
Accrued revenue bond interest payable	400,000	
Revenue bonds payable	1,000,000	
Total.......................................		2,107,000
Total Current Liabilities		$ 3,603,000

Liabilities Payable after One Year:

Revenue bonds payable	$28,000,000	
Advance from municipality	650,000	
Total.......................................		28,650,000
Total Liabilities..............................		$32,253,000

Fund Equity:

Contributions:

Contributions from municipality	$ 5,000,000	
Contributions from subdividers.......................	7,880,000	
Total Contributions		$12,880,000

Retained Earnings:

Reserved for revenue bond future debt service		
reserve account.................................	$ 1,270,000	
Unreserved.....................................	14,297,000	
Total Retained Earnings		15,567,000
Total Fund Equity		$28,447,000
Total Liabilities and Fund Equity		$60,700,000

Cash...	40,000	
Contributed capital—General Fund		40,000
To record contribution from the General Fund.		

(2) Purchase and depreciation of equipment. Equipment costing $30,000 was acquired on July 3, 19X1. The equipment is assigned a 10-year life and no salvage value.

Equipment	30,000	
Vouchers payable.................................		30,000
To record purchase of equipment.		

Operating expenses control	3,000	
Accumulated depreciation.......................		3,000
To record depreciation expense.		

(3) Purchase and use of supplies inventory. Supplies costing $65,000 were acquired. A physical inventory taken on June 30, 19X2 was valued at $11,000.

Inventory of supplies	65,000	
Vouchers payable..................................		65,000
To record purchase of supplies.		

Operating expenses control	54,000	
Inventory of supplies		54,000
To record cost of supplies used.		

Note that inventories are accounted for in the same manner as in a private corporation.

(4) Incurrence of operating expenses and payment of liabilities. Various operating expenses were incurred. Of these expenses, $7,000 represented charges from the city's electric utility (an Enterprise Fund).

Operating expenses control	67,000	
Vouchers payable..................................		60,000
Due to electric utility fund.........................		7,000
To record operating expenses.		

Vouchers payable.....................................	138,000	
Due to electric utility fund............................	5,000	
Cash		143,000
To record partial payment of liabilities.		

(5) Billings and collections. Total billings to the city's various departments were $125,000. Of this amount, $9,000 pertained to services performed for the city's electric utility and $5,000 pertained to services performed for the city's central garage (an Internal Service Fund).

Due from general fund.................................	111,000	
Due from electric utility fund..........................	9,000	
Due from central garage fund	5,000	
Operating revenues control........................		125,000
To record billings to departments for services rendered.		

Cash..	110,000	
Due from general fund.............................		102,000
Due from electric utility fund......................		5,000
Due from central garage fund		3,000
To record partial collection of amounts due from other funds.		

Because closing entries would be identical to those made for a private enterprise, they are not shown.

Financial statements. The balance sheet and operating statement that would be prepared for the fiscal year ended June 30, 19X2 are shown in Illustrations 23-9 and 23-10.

Illustration 23-9

EMERSON CITY
Central Printing and Reproduction Fund
Balance Sheet
June 30, 19X2

Assets	
Cash	$ 7,000
Due from general fund	9,000
Due from electric utility fund	4,000
Due from central garage fund	2,000
Inventory of supplies	11,000
Equipment	30,000
Accumulated depreciation	(3,000)
Total Assets	$60,000
Liabilities and Fund Equity	
Vouchers payable	$17,000
Due to electric utility fund	2,000
Total Liabilities	$19,000
Contributed capital	$40,000
Retained earnings:	
Unreserved	1,000
Total Fund Equity	$41,000
Total Liabilities and Fund Equity	$60,000

Illustration 23-10

EMERSON CITY
Central Printing and Reproduction Fund
Statement of Revenues, Expenses, and
Changes in Retained Earnings
For the Year Ended June 30, 19X2

Operating revenues:		
Charges for services		$125,000
Operating expenses:		
Supplies	$54,000	
Salaries and wages	42,000	
Lease expense	18,000	
Utilities	7,000	
Depreciation	3,000	124,000
Net Income		$ 1,000
Retained Earnings, July 1, 19X1		-0-
Retained Earnings, June 30, 19X2		$ 1,000

Note: A statement of changes in financial position would also be prepared. Because it would be similar to that prepared for a private corporation, it is not shown here.

FIDUCIARY OPERATIONS

AGENCY AND TRUST FUNDS

Agency and Trust Funds are created to account for money and property received but not owned.

Agency Funds

Agency Funds act as conduits for the transfer of money. Money deposited with such a fund is generally disbursed shortly after receipt to authorized recipients, such as other governmental funds, other governmental units, and private corporations. Common examples of Agency Funds are as follows:

(1) **Tax collection funds.**   When overlapping governmental units collect tax revenues from the same source, it is usually more practical and economical for only one of the governmental units to collect the taxes and then distribute the taxes collected to the various taxing authorities. Counties commonly collect all property taxes and then distribute amounts collected to the various cities, school districts, water districts, and any other special districts.

(2) **Employee benefit funds.**   When governmental employees have premiums on medical and dental insurance plans withheld from their paychecks, withholdings are deposited in such funds. Periodically, the governmental unit makes a lump-sum payment to an insurance company. (The alternative to using employee benefit funds is to set up liabilities in the appropriate funds.)

Trust Funds

Most Trust Funds involve investing and using money in accordance with stipulated provisions of trust indenture agreements or statutes. Common examples of Trust Funds include the following:

(1) **Public employee pension and retirement systems.**   These Trust Funds account for employer and employee retirement contributions, the investment of such contributions, and the payments to retired employees.

(2) **Nonexpendable Trust Funds.**   These funds account for **endowments,** the money and property given to a governmental unit. The principal must be preserved intact; only the Trust Fund income may be expended or completely used in the course of operations.

(3) **Expendable Trust Funds.**   These funds also account for endowments. However, the principal does not have to be preserved intact; the trust principal and income may be expended or completely used in the course of operations. State and federal grant programs that establish a continuing trustee relationship are to be accounted for in this type of fund under the requirements of *NCGA Statement 2.*

Classification for accounting measurement purposes

NCGA Statement 1 states

> Each Trust Fund is classified for accounting measurement purposes as either a governmental fund or a proprietary fund. Expendable Trust Funds are accounted for in essentially the same manner as governmental funds. Nonexpendable Trust Funds and Pension Trust Funds are accounted for in essentially the same manner as proprietary funds. Agency Funds are purely custodial (assets equal liabilities) and thus do not involve measurement of results of operations.[8]

Nonexpendable Trust Funds and Pension Trust Funds would use the **accrual basis of accounting** and present operations using a statement of revenues, **expenses,** and changes in fund balance. On the other hand, Expendable Trust Funds would use the **modified accrual basis of accounting** and present operations using a statement of revenues, **expenditures,** and changes in fund balance. Agency Funds are effectively on the cash basis. Because Agency Funds do not have operating statements, a statement of changes in assets and liabilities is prepared to report the changes in the governmental unit's custodial responsibilities.

Establishment and operation of Agency and Trust Funds

Agency Funds have no unusual operating characteristics or unique accounting issues. Usually, cash is the only asset, which is completely offset by liabilities to the authorized recipients. Thus, it has no Fund Balance account. Because cash disbursements are made frequently, on many occasions throughout the year these funds have no assets or liabilities at all. For all these reasons, we do not illustrate journal entries and financial statements for Agency Funds.

Public employee pension and retirement trust funds have the same operating characteristics and accounting issues as private pension and retirement plans that are funded with a trustee. Accordingly, journal entries and financial statements for these funds are not illustrated. As mentioned in the preceding chapter, a major shortcoming of many such trust funds is the lack of a sound actuarial basis in accounting for contributions to meet retirement payments.

For state and federal grant programs accounted for in **expendable Trust Funds,** no significant accounting issues exist. As the creators of trusts, donors of **nonexpendable Trust Funds** have the right to specify in the trust agreement the accounting treatment to be accorded specific items. Such instructions prevail over generally accepted accounting principles. In the absence of specific accounting instructions, the governing authority is state statutes, which usually conflict with generally accepted accounting principles in several respects. For example, most state statutes require gains and losses on the sale of trust investments to be credited or charged, respectively, to trust principal instead of to trust income. For nonexpendable

---

[8] *NCGA Statement 1,* p. 6.

trusts, separate trust funds may be established for the principal and for the income generated by the principal. (The latter fund is essentially treated as a Special Revenue Fund.) In the following section, we illustrate journal entries and financial statements for this type of fund.

Illustration:
Journal entries and financial statements

Assume that Emerson City received $100,000 from a citizen, who specifies that the principal amount should remain intact. Earnings on the principal are to be used for park beautification projects. Assumed transactions pertaining to the establishment and operation of these funds, along with related journal entries, are as follows:

Endowment Principal
Nonexpendable Trust Fund

Transaction or Event	Journal Entry		
The endowment principal fund is established.	Cash	100,000	
	Operating revenues control ..		100,000
Investment of cash.	Investments	96,000	
	Cash		96,000
Accrual of interest on investments.	Interest receivable	8,000	
	Operating revenues control ..		8,000
Amortization of bond discount on investments.	Investments	700	
	Operating revenues control ..		700
Collection of interest on investments.	Cash	4,500	
	Interest receivable		4,500
To reflect liability to Endowment Revenues Fund.	Operating transfers out control	8,700	
	Due to endowment revenues fund.....................		8,700
To close operating revenues and operating transfer out control accounts.	Operating revenues control	108,700	
	Operating transfers out control		8,700
	Fund balance reserved for endowments		100,000
Payment of part of amount due to Endowment Revenues Fund.	Due to endowment revenues fund........................	7,500	
	Cash		7,500

Endowment Revenues
Expendable Trust Fund

Transaction or Event	Journal Entry		
To reflect revenues earned by and payable from Endowment Principal Fund.	Due from endowment principal fund........................	8,700	
	Other financing sources control...................		8,700
Receipt of part of amount due from Endowment Principal Fund.	Cash	7,500	
	Due from endowment principal fund		7,500
Payment of administrative expenses.	Expenditures control	300	
	Cash		300

Costs incurred on park beautification projects are paid.	Expenditures control .... Cash	6,300 6,300

To close other financing sources and expenditures into Fund Balance Reserved for Endowments.	Other financing sources control .... Expenditures control .... Fund balance reserved for endowments	8,700
		    6,600
		
		    2,100

Financial statements. The balance sheets and statements of revenues, expenses, and changes in fund balance that would be prepared at June 30, 19X2 for each of these funds are shown in Illustrations 23-11, 23-12, and 23-13.

Illustration 23-11

EMERSON CITY Endowment Trust Funds Balance Sheets June 30, 19X2		
	Principal Fund (Nonexpendable)	Revenue Fund (Expendable)
Assets:		
Cash..	$ 1,000	$ 900
Due from endowment principal fund		1,200
Investments	96,700	
Interest receivable..............................	3,500	
Total Assets	$101,200	$2,100
Liabilities and Fund Equity:		
Due to endowment revenues fund	$ 1,200	
Fund balances:		
Reserved for endowments	$100,000	$2,100
Total Fund Balance	$100,000	$2,100
Total Liabilities and Fund Equity	$101,200	$2,100

Illustration 23-12

EMERSON CITY Endowment Principal Fund (Nonexpendable) Statement of Revenues, Expenses, and Changes in Fund Balance For the Year Ended June 30, 19X2	
Operating revenues:	
Gifts	$100,000
Interest income...	8,700
Total revenues	$108,700
Operating expenses	-0-
Income before Operating Transfers..................................	$108,700
Operating transfers out...	(8,700)
Net Income	$100,000
Fund Balance, July 1, 19X1	-0-
Fund Balance, June 30, 19X2	$100,000

Illustration 23-13

EMERSON CITY Endowment Revenues Fund (Expendable) Statement of Revenues, Expenditures, and Changes in Fund Balance For the Year Ended June 30, 19X2	
Revenues..	$ -0-
Expenditures:	
Park beautification	$ 6,300
Administrative	300
Total Expenditures......................................	$ 6,600
Revenues under expenditures	$(6,600)
Other Financing Sources:	
Operating transfer in	8,700
Excess of Revenues and Other Financing Sources over Expenditures	$ 2,100
Fund Balance, July 1, 19X1	-0-
Fund Balance, June 30, 19X2	$ 2,100

GENERAL FIXED ASSETS ACCOUNT GROUP

The General Fixed Assets Account Group is created to account for a governmental unit's fixed assets that are not accounted for in an Enterprise Fund, an Internal Service Fund, or a Trust Fund. This group of accounts is not a fund, but rather a self-balancing group of accounts. For each asset recorded in the group of accounts, there is a corresponding offsetting credit descriptive of the source of the asset. A statement of general fixed assets classified by type of asset is the basic financial statement for this group of accounts. This statement may be supplemented with: (1) a statement showing these assets broken down by function, activity, or department; and (2) a statement showing the changes in the account balances for the year. A typical statement of general fixed assets classified by type of account and source is shown in Illustration 23-14.

As mentioned previously, not all improvements constructed through Capital Projects Funds and Special Assessment Funds must be recorded in the General Fixed Assets Account Group. According to *NCGA Statement 1:*

> Reporting public domain or "infrastructure" fixed assets—roads, bridges, curbs and gutters, streets and sidewalks, drainage systems, lighting systems, and similar assets that are immovable and of value only to the governmental unit—is optional.[9]

In practice, only a small percentage of governmental units capitalize and report "infrastructure" fixed assets in their general fixed assets.

Accounting procedures

Most high dollar general fixed assets originate from Capital Projects Funds. Most of the equipment shown in this account group originates from expenditures made through the General Fund and Special Revenue Funds.

---

[9] *NCGA Statement 1*, p. 9.

Illustration 23-14

EMERSON CITY Statement of General Fixed Assets June 30, 19X2	
General Fixed Assets:	
Land	$ 1,300,000
Buildings	12,900,000
Improvements other than buildings	1,100,000
Equipment	450,000
Construction work in progress	3,600,000[a]
Total General Fixed Assets	$19,350,000
Investment in General Fixed Assets From:	
Capital Projects Funds—	
General obligation bonds	$15,300,000
Federal grants	1,000,000
State grants	800,000
County grants	600,000
General Fund Revenues	560,000
Special Revenue Fund Revenues	310,000
Gifts	180,000
Special Assessments	600,000
Total Investment in General Fixed Assets	$19,350,000

[a] This is work in progress in all of the Capital Projects Funds and Special Assessment Funds.

When such assets are constructed or acquired, these three classes of funds debit Expenditures. At the same time or at the end of the fiscal year, entries are made in the General Fixed Assets Account Group debiting the appropriate asset category and crediting the appropriate source investment accounts. Entries to record construction work in progress in the General Fixed Assets Account Group were shown earlier in the chapter (pages 865 and 878). Typical entries to record items in the other accounts are as follows:

Buildings	3,500,000	
Construction work in progress		2,150,000
Investment in general fixed assets from capital projects funds—general obligation bonds		1,350,000
To record cost of community center building, which was started in the prior fiscal year and completed during the current fiscal year.		
Equipment	47,000	
Investment in general fixed assets from general fund revenues		47,000
To record equipment purchased through the General Fund.		

General fixed assets acquired through purchase or construction are recorded at cost. Assets arising from gifts or donations are recorded at their estimated current fair values at the time of donation. On abandonment, the entry is reversed. On sale, the entry is reversed, and the sales proceeds are recorded as revenues (usually in the fund that initially acquired the asset). As discussed in the preceding chapter, accumulated depreciation may be reflected for general fixed assets in the General Fixed Assets Account Group at the option of the governmental unit. Depreciation expense, however, may not be reported in the operating statements of the governmental funds.

In 1982, *NCGA Statement 5,* "Accounting and Financial Reporting Principles for Lease Agreements of State and Local Governments," was issued. This pronouncement expounds on accounting for lease agreements and requires that *FASB Statement No. 13,* "Accounting for Leases," be followed.

GENERAL LONG-TERM DEBT ACCOUNT GROUP

The General Long-Term Debt Account Group presents a governmental unit's debt that (1) has a maturity date of more than one year at the time of issuance; and (2) is not properly shown in proprietary funds (Enterprise Funds and Internal Service Funds), Special Assessment Funds (see the list below), or Trust Funds. Such debt is shown as a liability in this account group until its maturity date, when the liability is effectively transferred to the appropriate Debt Service Fund. For governmental purposes, "long-term debt" includes the portion of long-term debt that is due and payable in the coming fiscal year.

As previously discussed, the General Long-Term Debt Account Group does not include the following types of long-term debt:

(1) Revenue bonds of Enterprise Funds, which are recorded as liabilities of the applicable Enterprise Funds.
(2) General Obligation Bonds to be repaid and serviced from Enterprise Fund operations, which are recorded as liabilities of the applicable Enterprise Funds. (The contingent liability must be disclosed in a footnote.)
(3) Special Assessment Bonds, which are recorded as liabilities of Special Assessment Funds.

When general long-term debt is created, an entry is made in the General Long-Term Debt Account Group crediting a descriptive liability account—for example, Serial Bonds Payable—and debiting an offsetting account called Amount to Be Provided for Payment of Bonds (Serial or Term). As money accumulates in the Debt Service Fund, the Amount to Be Provided for Payment of Bonds account is reduced to that extent, and an account called Amount Available for Payment of Bonds is debited to signify the availability of these monies. (The proceeds are recorded in the appropriate fund authorized to use the borrowings.) For financial reporting purposes, a statement of general long-term debt is used. A typical statement of general long-term debt is shown in Illustration 23-15.

Accounting procedures

Typical entries that would be made in the General Long-Term Debt Account Group are as follows.

Illustration 23-15

EMERSON CITY Statement of General Long-Term Debt June 30, 19X2		
Amount Available and to Be Provided for the Payment of General Long-Term Debt:		
Term Bonds—		
Amount available in Debt Service Funds	$ 196,000	
Amount to be provided	204,000	
		$ 400,000
Serial Bonds—		
Amount available in Debt Service Funds	$ 14,000	
Amount to be provided	2,386,000	
		2,400,000
Total Amount Available and to Be Provided		$2,800,000
General Long-Term Debt Payable:		
Term Bonds payable		$ 400,000
Serial Bonds payable		2,400,000
Total General Long-Term Debt Payable		$2,800,000

Note: Footnote disclosure is required for the contingent liability that exists for general obligation bonds recorded in Enterprise Funds or Special Assessment Funds.

Amount to be provided for payment of bonds (serial or term)	3,500,000	
Bonds payable (serial or term)		3,500,000
To record the issuance of bonds for the new community center.		
Amount available in debt service fund	100,000	
Amount to be provided for repayment of serial bonds		100,000
To record increase in assets available for retirement of serial bonds.		
Serial bonds payable	100,000	
Amount available in debt service fund		100,000
To transfer liability to Debt Service Fund.		

SUMMARY ILLUSTRATION

Illustration 23-16 presents a summary of the individual fund and account group statements required under NCGA Statement 1.

Review questions

1. When would a Special Revenue Fund be used instead of the General Fund?
2. For what type of bonds does the Debt Service Fund function as a sinking fund?
3. What is the relationship between a Capital Projects Fund and the General Fixed Assets Account Group?

Illustration 23-16
Summary of required individual fund and account group financial statements per *NCGA Statement 1*

Fund Type or Account Group	Basis of Accounting	Statement Title						
		Balance Sheet	Revenues, Expenditures, and Changes in Fund Balance	Revenues, Expenses, and Changes in Retained Earnings	Changes in Financial Position	Changes in Assets and Liabilities	General Fixed Assets	General Long-Term Debt
Government Funds:								
General Fund[a]	Modified accrual	X	X					
Special Revenue Funds[a]	Modified accrual	X	X					
Capital Projects Funds[a]	Modified accrual	X	X					
Debt Service Funds	Modified accrual	X	X					
Special Assessment Funds[a]	Modified accrual	X(2)	X					
Proprietary Funds:								
Enterprise Funds	Accrual	X(1)		X	X			
Internal Service Funds	Accrual	X(1)		X	X			
Fiduciary Funds:								
Trust Funds—								
Pension trusts	Accrual	X(1)		X	X			
Nonexpendable	Accrual	X(1)		X	X			
Expendable	Modified accrual	X	X					
Agency	Modified accrual	X				X		
Account Groups:								
General Fixed Assets	N/A						X	
General Long-Term Debt	N/A							X

[a] Encumbrance accounting normally is used.
(1) The balance sheet would include fixed assets and long-term liabilities of this fund.
(2) The balance sheet would include long-term liabilities of this fund.
Note: Budgetary comparisons must be made for funds for which an annual budget has been adopted. For funds *that budget in accordance with GAAP*, the budgetary comparison is made in the individual fund Statement of Revenues, Expenditures, and Changes in Fund Balance. For funds *that do not budget in accordance with GAAP*, the individual fund operating statement may not include budgetary data. Instead, a "schedule" comparing the legally adopted budget with the actual data on the budgetary basis is required in addition to the individual fund operating statement.

4. In what way are Enterprise Funds and Internal Service Funds similar to commercial operations?
5. What significance may be attributed to the fact that the billings of an Internal Service Fund exceed its costs and expenses?
6. What is the distinction between an Agency Fund and a Trust Fund?
7. What is the distinction between improvements made by a Capital Projects Fund and improvements made by a Special Assessment Fund?
8. May we say that a Special Assessment Fund is a combination Capital Projects Fund, Debt Service Fund, and Long-Term Debt Account Group?
9. Does the General Fixed Assets Account Group include all fixed assets of a governmental unit? Why or why not?
10. What is the difference in meaning of the term *long-term debt* as used in the General Long-Term Debt Account Group and as used in private industry?
11. Does the General Long-Term Debt Account Group include all long-term debt? Why or why not?
12. What is the relationship between the Debt Service Fund and the General Long-Term Debt Account Group?

Exercises

Exercise 23–1
Multiple choice: Differentiation of types of funds—Activities

(1) Recreational facilities run by a governmental unit and financed on a user-charge basis most likely would be accounted for in which fund?
   (a) General Fund.
   (b) Trust Fund.
   (c) Enterprise Fund.
   (d) Capital Projects Fund.
   (e) Special Revenue Fund.

(2) The activities of a municipal golf course that receives most of its revenues from a special tax levy should be accounted for in which fund?
   (a) Capital Projects Fund.
   (b) Special Assessment Fund.
   (c) Special Revenue Fund.
   (d) General Fund.
   (e) Enterprise Fund.

(3) A data-processing center established by a governmental unit to service all agencies within the unit should be accounted for in which fund?
   (a) Capital Projects Fund.
   (b) Internal Service Fund.
   (c) Agency Fund.
   (d) Trust Fund.
   (e) Enterprise Fund.

(4) The activities of a municipal employees' retirement and pension system should be recorded in which fund?
   (a) General Fund.
   (b) Special Assessment Fund.
   (c) Internal Service Fund.

(d) Agency Fund.

(e) Trust Fund.

(5) Receipts levied to finance sidewalk improvements would be accounted for in which fund?

(a) Special Revenue Fund.

(b) General Fund.

(c) Special Assessment Fund.

(d) Capital Projects Fund.

(e) Both (c) and (d).

(6) A city collects property taxes for the benefit of the local sanitary, park, and school districts and periodically remits collections to these units. This activity should be accounted for in a(n)

(a) Agency Fund.

(b) General Fund.

(c) Internal Service Fund.

(d) Special Assessment Fund.

(e) None of the above.

(AICPA adapted)

Exercise 23–2
Multiple choice: Differentiation of types of funds—Activities

(1) The operations of a public library receiving the majority of its support from property taxes levied for that purpose should be accounted for in a(n)

(a) General Fund.

(b) Special Revenue Fund.

(c) Enterprise Fund.

(d) Internal Service Fund.

(e) None of the above.

(2) The proceeds of a federal grant to help finance the future construction of an adult training center should be recorded in a

(a) General Fund.

(b) Special Revenue Fund.

(c) Capital Projects Fund.

(d) Special Assessment Fund.

(e) None of the above.

(3) The receipts from a special tax levy to retire and pay interest on general obligation bonds issued to finance the construction of a new city hall should be recorded in a

(a) Debt Service Fund.

(b) Capital Projects Fund.

(c) General Fund.

(d) Special Revenue Fund.

(e) None of the above.

(4) The lump-sum monthly remittance to an insurance company for hospital-surgical insurance premiums collected as payroll deductions from employees should be recorded in a(n)

(a) General Fund.

(b) Agency Fund.

(c) Special Revenue Fund.

Agency & Trust funds are Fiduciary funds

(d) Internal Service Fund.

(e) None of the above.

(5) The activities of a central motor pool that supplies and services vehicles for the use of municipal employees on official business should be accounted for in a(n)

(a) Agency Fund.

(b) General fund.

(c) Internal Service Fund.

(d) Special Revenue Fund.

(e) None of the above.

(6) To provide for the retirement of general obligation bonds, a city invests a portion of its general revenue receipts in marketable securities. This investment activity should be accounted for in a(n)

(a) Trust Fund.

(b) Enterprise Fund.

(c) Special Assessment Fund.

(d) Special Revenue Fund.

(e) None of the above.

(AICPA adapted)

Exercise 23–3
Multiple choice: Understanding the interrelationship among the funds and account groups—Fixed assets

(1) A new fire truck was purchased out of a city's General Fund. An entry is also required in a(n)

(a) Internal Service Fund.

(b) Capital Projects Fund.

(c) Special Revenue Fund.

(d) General Fixed Assets Account Group.

(e) None of the above.

(2) A city sells an unused fire station that previously was accounted for in its General Fixed Assets Account Group. An entry is also required in a

(a) General Fund.

(b) Special Revenue Fund.

(c) Trust Fund.

(d) Special Assessment Fund.

(e) None of the above.

(3) A city built a new city hall, the construction of which was accounted for in a Capital Projects Fund. Entries relating to the new building are also required in a(n)

(a) General Fixed Assets Account Group.

(b) Special Assessment Fund.

(c) Internal Service Fund.

(d) General Fund.

(e) None of the above.

(4) A city made certain public improvements properly accounted for in a Special Assessment Fund. Entries relating to the improvements are also required in a(n)

(a) General Fixed Assets Account Group.

(b) Internal Service Fund.
(c) Special Revenue Fund.
(d) Capital Projects Fund.
(e) None of the above.

(5) A city's water utility, which is accounted for in an Enterprise Fund, acquired some new fixed assets. An entry is also required in a(n)
(a) General Fixed Assets Account Group.
(b) Internal Service Fund.
(c) General Fund.
(d) Agency Fund.
(e) None of the above.

(6) A city's central purchasing and stores department is properly accounted for in an Internal Service Fund. When fixed assets are acquired for this department, accounting entries are required in a(n)
(a) General Fixed Assets Account Group.
(b) Internal Service Fund.
(c) General Fixed Assets Account Group and an Internal Service Fund.
(d) General Fund and the General Fixed Assets Account Group.
(e) Enterprise Fund.
(f) Enterprise Fund and the General Fixed Assets Account Group.

Exercise 23-4
Preparing journal entries: Understanding the interrelationship among the funds and account groups—Fixed assets

Required:
For each transaction discussed in Exercise 23–3, prepare the journal entry or entries (without amounts) required in the applicable funds and account groups.

Exercise 23-5
Multiple choice: Understanding the interrelationship of the funds and account groups—Long-term debt

(1) A transaction in which a municipal electric utility issues bonds (to be repaid from its own operations) requires accounting recognition in a(n)
(a) General Fund.
(b) Debt Service Fund.
(c) Enterprise and Debt Service Funds.
(d) Enterprise Fund, a Debt Service Fund, and the General Long-Term Debt Account Group.
(e) None of the above.

(2) The liability for general obligation bonds issued for the benefit of a municipal electric company and serviced by its earnings should be recorded in a(n)
(a) Enterprise Fund.
(b) General Fund.
(c) Enterprise Fund and the General Long-Term Debt Account Group.
(d) Enterprise Fund and disclosed in a footnote in the statement of General Long-Term Debt.
(e) None of the above.

(3) The liability for special assessment bonds that carry a secondary pledge of a municipality's general credit should be recorded in a(n)
   (a) Enterprise Fund.
   (b) Special Revenue Fund and the General Long-Term Debt Account Group.
   (c) Special Assessment Fund and the General Long-Term Debt Account Group.
   (d) Special Assessment Fund and disclosed in a footnote in the statement of General Long-Term Debt.
   (e) None of the above.

(4) A transaction in which a municipality issues general obligation serial bonds to finance the construction of a fire station requires accounting recognition in the
   (a) General Fund.
   (b) Capital Projects and General Funds.
   (c) Capital Projects Fund and the General Long-Term Debt Account Group.
   (d) General Fund and the General Long-Term Debt Account Group.
   (e) None of the above.

(5) Several years ago, a city established a sinking fund to retire an issue of general obligation bonds. This year, the city made a $50,000 contribution to the sinking fund from general revenues and realized $15,000 in revenue from sinking fund securities. The bonds due this year were retired. These transactions require accounting recognition in the
   (a) General Fund.
   (b) Debt Service Fund and the General Long-Term Debt Account Group.
   (c) Debt Service Fund, the General Fund, and the General Long-Term Debt Account Group.
   (d) Capital Projects Fund, a Debt Service Fund, the General Fund, and the General Long-Term Debt Account Group.
   (e) None of the above.

(AICPA adapted)

Exercise 23–6
Preparing journal entries: Understanding the interrelationship among the funds and account groups—Long-term debt

Required:
For each of the transactions discussed in Exercise 23–5, prepare the journal entry or entries (without amounts) required in the applicable funds and account groups.

Exercise 23–7
Multiple choice: Determining financial statements, basis of accounting, and accounts used

(1) Which financial statement is recommended for governmental funds?
   (a) A statement of revenues, expenses, and changes in retained earnings.
   (b) A statement of costs of providing services.
   (c) A statement of cash receipts and disbursements.
   (d) A statement of revenues, expenditures, encumbrances, and changes in fund balance.

(e) A statement of revenues, expenditures, and changes in fund balance.

(f) A statement of changes in financial position.

(2) Which financial statement is recommended for proprietary funds? (Choose from the statements listed in the preceding question.)

(3) A statement of changes in financial position is prepared for which fund?

(a) General Fund.

(b) Special Revenue Fund.

(c) Capital Projects Fund.

(d) Special Assessment Fund.

(e) Debt Service Fund.

(f) None of the above.

(4) Which of the following funds or account groups uses the accrual basis of accounting?

(a) Agency Fund.

(b) Special Revenue Fund.

(c) General Long-Term Debt Account Group.

(d) Debt Service Fund.

(e) Internal Service Fund.

(5) Which of the following funds uses the modified accrual basis of accounting?

(a) Enterprise Fund.

(b) Debt Service Fund.

(c) Internal Service Fund.

(d) Nonexpendable Trust Fund.

(e) None of the above.

(6) Which of the following funds records depreciation expense?

(a) Capital Projects Fund.

(b) Agency Fund.

(c) Special Assessment Fund.

(d) Internal Service Fund.

(e) Debt Service Fund.

(f) None of the above.

(7) Which of the following funds does not have a fund balance?

(a) Agency Fund.

(b) Special Revenue Fund.

(c) Special Assessment Fund.

(d) Capital Projects Fund.

(e) None of the above.

(8) An Expenditures account does not appear in which fund?

(a) Capital Projects Fund.

(b) Debt Service Fund.

(c) Special Assessment Fund.

(d) Special Revenue Fund.

(e) Internal Service Fund.

(f) None of the above.

(9) Encumbrances accounts would not be used in which of the following funds?

(a) Special Revenue Fund.

(b) Capital Projects Fund.

(c) Special Assessment Fund.

(d) Internal Service Fund.

(e) None of the above.

Exercise 23–8
Preparing journal entries
relating to general long-term debt

The following transactions occurred during Bondsville County's fiscal year ended June 30, 19X2:

(1) On October 1, 19X1, general obligation term bonds having a face value of $1,000,000 and an interest rate of 8% were issued. Interest is payable semiannually on April 1 and October 1. The $980,000 proceeds were used for the construction of a new courthouse.
(2) On January 1, 19X2, the county transferred $16,000 from the General Fund to a Debt Service Fund for sinking fund purposes.
(3) The Debt Service Fund immediately invested this money, and by June 30, 19X2, the county's fiscal year-end, $1,000 of interest had been earned on these investments.
(4) On March 27, 19X2, $40,000 was transferred from the General Fund to the Debt Service Fund to meet the first interest payment.
(5) On April 1, 19X2, the Debt Service Fund made the required interest payment of $40,000. (A fiscal agent is not used.)

Required:
Prepare the journal entries that would be made in all of the appropriate funds and account groups for these transactions.

Problems

Problem 23–1
Capital projects fund

On August 1, 19X2, the City of Roses authorized the issuance of 6% general obligation serial bonds having a face value of $8,000,000. The proceeds will be used to construct a new convention center that is estimated to cost $8,300,000. Over the last several years, the Unreserved Fund Balance account in the city's General Fund has been approximately $300,000 greater than is prudently needed. Accordingly, this excess accumulation will be used to pay for the remainder of the construction cost. A Capital Projects Fund, designated the Convention Center Construction Fund, was established to account for this project.

The following transactions occurred during the fiscal year ended June 30, 19X3:

(1) On August 4, 19X2, the city deposited $300,000 (its share of the financing) into the Convention Center Construction Fund.
(2) On September 5, 19X2, a construction contract was entered into with Antonio Construction Company in the amount of $8,100,000.
(3) On December 1, 19X1, one-half of the authorized bond issue was sold at 101. The bond premium was properly transferred to a Debt Service Fund.
(4) On October 7, 19X2, a payment of $180,000 was made out of the General Fund to Bloom Architectural Company. This payment was for the design of the Convention Center, which was authorized in the city's 19X1–19X2 annual operating

budget for the General Fund. (This $180,000 for architect's fees was part of the $8,300,000 total estimated cost of the Convention Center.) The Expenditures Control account was charged on the books of the General Fund. (No interfund payment was made.)

(5) On April 30, 19X3, Antonio Construction Company submitted a billing of $2,100,000 for work completed to date. Only $1,900,000 was paid.

(6) On June 1, 19X3, the first semiannual interest payment on the bonds was made. (Principal payments are deferred until December 1, 19X4.)

(7) On June 20, 19X3, the city was awarded an irrevocable federal grant totaling $1,000,000 to help finance the cost of the Convention Center. Payment will be received within 60 days. The city had applied for this grant in May 19X1, with slight expectation of receiving it. Accordingly, it obtained authorization for a bond issue of $8,000,000 instead of $7,000,000.

Additional information:

(a) The city intends to use a Special Revenue Fund to account for the operations of the Convention Center upon completion of the project.

(b) The city does not record budgets for capital projects in Capital Projects Funds.

Required:

(1) For the above transactions, prepare the entries that should be made in the Convention Center Construction Fund for the year ended June 30, 19X3.

(2) Prepare the appropriate closing entries at June 30, 19X3.

(3) Prepare a balance sheet at June 30, 19X3.

(4) Prepare a statement of revenues, expenditures, and changes in fund balance for the year ended June 30, 19X3.

Problem 23-2
Debt service fund and general long-term debt account group
(Journal entries only)

Surf City had the following transactions during its fiscal year ended June 30, 19X4:

(1) General obligation serial bonds having a face value of $100,000 matured during the year and were redeemed. (Money was transferred from the General Fund to the Debt Service Fund to redeem this debt.)

(2) Total interest paid on serial bonds during the year was $80,000. (Money was transferred from the General Fund to the Debt Service Fund to pay this interest.)

(3) General obligation term bonds having a face value of $500,000 were issued for $505,000. The proceeds are for construction of a new fire station, which is expected to cost $500,000. The $5,000 premium, which will not be used for construction purposes, was properly transferred to the Debt Service Fund.

(4) A cash transfer of $10,000 was made from the General Fund to a Debt Service Fund in connection with a sinking fund requirement pertaining to general obligation term bonds.

(5) Special Assessment bonds having a face value of $400,000 were issued at par. The proceeds are for construction of residential street improvements.

(6) General obligation serial bonds having a face value of $800,000 were issued at par. The proceeds will provide working capital for the General Fund.

Required:

Prepare journal entries for each of the above transactions in all appropriate funds or account groups. Use the following headings for your workpaper:

Transaction Number	Journal Entries	Amount Dr.	Cr.	Fund or Account Group

Problem 23-3
Debt service fund: Preparing a statement of revenues, expenditures, and changes in fund balance from selected information— No journal entries involved

The following information relating to the city of Fudgeville's Debt Service Fund is provided for the year ended December 31, 19X2:

Interest:
Interest owed at December 31, 19X1 (none past due)................... $ 160,000
Interest payments made at due dates during 19X2...................... 700,000
Interest owed at December 31, 19X2 (none past due)................... 130,000
Cash received from the General Fund to pay interest 700,000
Property Taxes:
Property tax assessments made in 19X2 (to be collected
  by an Agency Fund) 566,000
Agency Fund property tax collections disbursed
  to the Debt Service Fund....................................... 550,000
Allowance for uncollectible accounts:
December 31, 19X1 4,000
December 31, 19X2 5,000
Accounts written off during 19X2 (from 19X1 assessments) 2,000
Property tax receivables:
December 31, 19X1 26,000
December 31, 19X2 40,000
Long-Term Debt:
Cash received from the General Fund to pay for the
  retirement of debt principal 400,000
General long-term debt that matured during 19X2
  and was paid off 1,000,000
Miscellaneous:
Gain on sale of investments 11,000
Interest on investments 50,000
Fund balance, December 31, 19X1 (all reserved for
  debt service) 621,000

Required:

Prepare a statement of revenues, expenditures, and changes in fund balance for 19X2. (Hint: Use T accounts for calculations pertaining to property tax revenues.)

Problem 23-4
Special assessment fund

You are engaged to audit the city of Crebitsville as of June 30, 19X2. You find the following accounts, among others, in the General Fund for the fiscal year ended June 30, 19X2.

Special Cash

Date	Reference	Dr.	Cr.	Balance
Aug. 1, 19X1	CR 58	301,800		301,800
Oct. 1, 19X1	CR 60	80,000		381,800
Dec. 1, 19X1	CD 41		185,000	196,800
Feb. 1, 19X2	CD 45		9,000	
June 1, 19X2	CR 64	51,000		238,800
June 30, 19X2	CD 65		167,000	71,800

Construction in Progress—Ledger Street Lighting Project

Date	Reference	Dr.	Cr.	Balance
Dec. 1, 19X1	CD 41	185,000		185,000
June 30, 19X2	CD 65	167,000		352,000

Bonds Payable

Date	Reference	Dr.	Cr.	Balance
Aug. 1, 19X1	CR 58		300,000	300,000
June 1, 19X2	CR 64		50,000	350,000

Premium on Bonds

Date	Reference	Dr.	Cr.	Balance
Aug. 1, 19X1	CR 58		1,800	1,800

Assessment Income

Date	Reference	Dr.	Cr.	Balance
Oct. 1, 19X1	CR 60		80,000	80,000

Interest Expense

Date	Reference	Dr.	Cr.	Balance
Feb. 1, 19X2	CD 45	9,000		9,000
June 1, 19X2	CR 64		1,000	8,000

The accounts resulted from the project described below:

On July 1, 19X1, the city council authorized the Ledger Street Lighting Project, a serial bond issue of $350,000 to permit deferral of assessment payments. Interest is 6% (payable on February 1 and August 1), with four equal principal payments to be made starting one year after issuance. According to the terms of the authorization, the property owners were assessed 80% of the estimated cost of construction and the balance was supplied by the City on October 1, 19X1. On October 1, 19X1, the first of five equal annual assessment installments was collected from the property owners. The deferred assessments were to bear interest at 10% from October 1, 19X1.

A construction contract for $500,000 was signed on August 1, 19X1; the project should be completed by October 31, 19X2.

Required:
(1) Prepare the journal entries that should have been made in a Special Assessment Fund for the Ledger Street Lighting Project for the year ended June 30, 19X2.
(2) Prepare the closing entries that should have been made in the Special Assessment Fund at June 30, 19X2.
(3) Prepare a balance sheet for the Special Assessment Fund at June 30, 19X2.
(4) Prepare a statement of revenues, expenditures, and changes in fund balance for the Special Assessment Fund for the fiscal year ended June 30, 19X2.

(5) Prepare the entries that should have been made in the General Fund during the fiscal year ended June 30, 19X2.

(6) Prepare the correcting entry to be made in the General Fund at June 30, 19X2, assuming a Special Assessment Fund is established at June 30, 19X2 as a result of your work.

(AICPA adapted)

Problem 23–5
Enterprise fund (Journal entries only)

The following activities pertain to Enterprise Funds:

(1) City A contributed $1,000,000 to a newly established Enterprise Fund formed to provide off-street parking facilities.

(2) City B established an Enterprise Fund to account for its municipal golf course, which would be built using the proceeds of $3,000,000 of general obligation bonds and be repaid from golf course earnings. The bonds were issued at a premium of $50,000.

(3) City C established an Enterprise Fund to account for its municipal swimming pools to be built using the proceeds of $2,000,000 of general obligation serial bonds to be repaid from taxes and general revenues. The bonds were issued at a discount of $25,000.

(4) City D operates a water utility in an Enterprise Fund. To expand operations, the city issued $5,000,000 of revenue bonds at a premium of $40,000.

(5) City E operates an electric utility in an Enterprise Fund, which made a $500,000 payment in lieu of taxes to the city's General Fund.

(6) City F operates an airport in an Enterprise Fund, which made a $600,000 payment to the city to finance General Fund expenditures.

(7) City G discontinued its municipal golf course, which was accounted for in an Enterprise Fund. The land was sold to a residential home developer. All outstanding liabilities were paid, and the remaining $750,000 cash was disbursed to the General Fund. (The Enterprise Fund had $300,000 in its Capital Contribution from Municipality account and $450,000 in its Retained Earnings account just before the disbursement.)

(8) City H operates a public transit system in an Enterprise Fund. The transit system usually recovers approximately 60% of its costs and expenses from user charges. During the current year, the Enterprise Fund received an $800,000 subsidy from the General Fund.

(9) City I operates an electric utility in an Enterprise Fund. During the year, the city redeemed $500,000 of its electric utility's revenue bonds.

(10) City J operates a gas utility in an Enterprise Fund. During the year, the city redeemed $1,000,000 of its general obligation serial bonds, which were issued many years ago to finance expansion of the gas utility. The bonds were to be repaid from taxes and general revenues.

Required:
For each transaction, prepare the necessary journal entries for all the funds and account groups involved. Use the following headings for your workpaper:

Transaction Number	Journal Entries	Amount Dr.	Cr.	Fund or Account Group

Problem 23–6
Internal service fund

The city of Hope had the following transactions relating to its newly established Central Printing Internal Service Fund during the fiscal year ended June 30, 19X1:

(1) A contribution of $100,000 was received from the General Fund to establish the Internal Service Fund.

(2) Machinery and equipment costing $80,000 was purchased and paid for by the Internal Service Fund. These items were placed in service on January 4, 19X1 and have an estimated useful life of 10 years. (All machinery and equipment in the General Fixed Assets Account Group is depreciated using a 10-year life.)

(3) Materials and supplies of $18,000 were ordered using purchase orders. For $14,000 of these purchase orders, the materials and supplies were received at a cost of $14,300. Payments totaling $9,500 were made on these billings.

(4) Total billings for the year were $60,000. Of this amount, $7,000 was billed to the city's water utility, which is operated in an Enterprise Fund. The remaining amount was billed to various departments in the General Fund. Of these billings, $32,000 was collected from the General Fund and $5,500 was collected from the water utility.

(5) Salaries and wages totaling $49,000 were paid.

(6) The city's electric utility, which is operated as an Enterprise Fund, billed the Internal Service Fund $900. Of this amount, $700 was paid.

(7) Materials and supplies on hand at June 30, 19X1 were counted and costed at $3,800.

(8) A subsidy of $5,000 was received from the General Fund near the end of the fiscal year in recognition of the fact that the first year of operations was a start-up year at a loss. In addition, $10,000 was received from the General Fund near the end of the fiscal year as a temporary advance to be repaid (without interest) during the following fiscal year.

Required:

(1) Prepare the appropriate journal entries for the above transactions in the Internal Service Fund.

(2) Prepare the year-end closing entry.

(3) Prepare a balance sheet at June 30, 19X1.

(4) Prepare a statement of revenues, expenses, and changes in retained earnings for the year ended June 30, 19X1.

Problem 23–7
Agency fund (Journal entries only)

In compliance with a newly enacted state law, Wheeler County assumed the responsibility of collecting all property taxes levied within its boundaries as of July 1, 19X5. A composite property tax rate per $100 of net assessed valuation, which was developed for the fiscal year ended June 30, 19X6, is presented below:

Wheeler County General Fund	$ 6
Carr City General Fund	3
Trane Township General Fund	1
	$10

All property taxes are due in quarterly installments and, when collected, are distributed to the governmental units represented in the composite rate. To administer collection and distribution of such taxes, the county has established a Tax Agency Fund.

Additional information:

(1) To reimburse the county for estimated administrative expenses of operating the Tax Agency Fund, the Tax Agency Fund deducts 2% from the tax collections each quarter for Carr City and Trane Township. The total amount deducted is remitted to the Wheeler County General Fund.

(2) Current-year tax levies collected by the Tax Agency Fund are as follows:

	Gross Levy	Estimated Amount to Be Collected
Wheeler County	$3,600,000	$3,500,000
Carr City	1,800,000	1,740,000
Trane Township	600,000	560,000
	$6,000,000	$5,800,000

(3) Because of an error in the original computation of its current gross tax levy and the estimated amount to be collected, $10,000 was charged back to Trane Township.

(4) As of September 30, 19X5, the Tax Agency Fund has received $1,440,000 in first-quarter payments. On October 1, this fund made a distribution to the three governmental units.

Required:

For the period July 1, 19X5, through October 1, 19X5, prepare journal entries to record the transactions described above for the following funds:

Wheeler County Tax Agency Fund
Wheeler County General Fund
Carr City General Fund
Trane Township General Fund

Use the following format:

Accounts	Wheeler County Tax Agency Fund Debit	Credit	Wheeler County General Fund Debit	Credit	Carr City General Fund Debit	Credit	Trane Township General Fund Debit	Credit

(AICPA adapted)

Problem 23–8
COMPREHENSIVE—ALL FUNDS AND ACCOUNT GROUPS
Preparing journal entries for typical transactions

The Village of Happyville had the following transactions for the year ended December 31, 19X3.

(1) Property taxes were levied in the amount of $500,000. Of this amount, $100,000 is a special levy for the servicing and retirement of serial bonds issued 15 years ago for the construction of a fire station. It was estimated that 2% of the total amount levied would be uncollectible.

(2) The village received its share of state sales taxes on gasoline. The $33,000 share can be used only for street improvements and maintenance. During the year, the village spent $31,000 for this purpose. (The village used its own work force.)

(3) On March 31, 19X3, general obligation bonds bearing interest at 6% were issued in the face amount of $500,000. The proceeds were $503,000, of which $500,000 was authorized to be spent on a new library. The remaining $3,000 was set aside for the eventual retirement of the debt. The bonds are due in 20 years, with interest to be paid on March 31 and September 30 of each year.

(4) A construction contract in the amount of $490,000 was entered into with Booker Construction Company to build the new library. Billings of $240,000 were submitted, of which $216,000 was paid.

(5) On September 30, 19X3, the interest due on the library bonds was paid using money from the General Fund.

(6) On November 30, 19X3, the fire station serial bonds referred to in (1) above were paid off ($60,000), along with interest due at that time ($36,000).

(7) Assessments were levied totaling $100,000 for a residential street lighting project; the village contributed $7,000 out of the General Fund as its share. Of the $100,000 assessed, $10,000 was collected, with the remaining $90,000 to be collected in succeeding years.

(8) On July 31, 19X1, 8% special assessment bonds having a face value of $90,000 were issued at par; the proceeds will be used for the street lighting project. Interest is paid annually each July 31.

(9) A General Fund transfer of $8,000 was made to establish an Internal Service Fund to provide for a central purchasing and stores function.

(10) During the year, the Internal Service Fund purchased various supplies at a cost of $6,500. Of this amount, $4,400 was billed to the city's various departments at $5,500.

(11) A Capital Projects Fund having a fund balance of $2,000 was terminated. The cash was sent to the General Fund as required.

(12) A local resident donated marketable securities with a market value of $80,000 (the resident's cost was $44,000) under the terms of a trust agreement. The principal is to remain intact. Earnings on the principal are to be used for college scholarships to needy students. Revenues earned during 19X3 totaled $7,500, of which $7,000 was disbursed for scholarships.

(13) The village water utility billed the General Fund $6,600.

(14) A new fire truck costing $22,000 was ordered, received, and paid for. The old fire truck (which cost $8,000) was sold for $1,500.

Required:

For each transaction, prepare the necessary journal entries for all of the appropriate funds and account groups involved. Use the following headings for your workpaper:

Transaction Number	Account Titles and Explanation	Amount Dr.	Amount Cr.	Fund or Account Group

24 Accounting for Nonprofit Organizations

OVERVIEW OF ACCOUNTING FOR NONPROFIT ORGANIZATIONS

In preceding chapters, we were concerned with one type of nonprofit organization—governmental units. In this chapter, we focus on the remaining types of nonprofit organizations, which increasingly represent a significant segment of the U.S. economy. Billions of dollars, representing voluntary contributions and millions of hours of donated services, flow into these organizations annually. We consider the following organizations:

(1) Colleges and universities
(2) Hospitals
(3) Voluntary health and welfare organizations (for example, United Way and the American Heart Association)
(4) Other miscellaneous nonprofit organizations (for example, labor unions, political parties, private foundations, professional and religious organizations)

We do not include in our discussion the types of entities that operate essentially as commercial enterprises for the direct economic benefit of members or shareholders—for example, employee benefit and pension plans, mutual insurance companies, mutual banks, credit unions, trusts, and farm cooperatives.

Many nonprofit organizations have grown in size and influence and have developed from individually operated organizations to organizations of national and international scope. Along with this growth has come an increasing awareness of the nature and importance of the roles of nonprofit organizations and the need for improved accounting standards and reporting practices. Many constituencies need full knowledge of an organization's activities and how well the organization is meeting its goals. **Constituencies** include governing boards, creditors, donors and prospective donors, granting agencies, oversight committees of federal, state, and local legislative bodies, regulatory governmental agencies, national headquarters of organizations with local chapters, and accrediting agencies.

In this chapter, we introduce the generally accepted accounting principles that apply specifically to nonprofit organizations. In addition to the individual treatment of selected types of nonprofit organizations, our presentation compares the various types of nonprofit organizations, emphasizing differences in fund structure, revenue recognition, investment valuation, and the content and format of financial statements. This approach facilitates a broad understanding of nonprofit organizations as a group.

THE DEVELOPMENT OF GENERALLY ACCEPTED ACCOUNTING PRINCIPLES FOR NONPROFIT ORGANIZATIONS

Early development

Statements of generally accepted accounting principles promulgated by the Financial Accounting Standards Board and its predecessor bodies generally have applied only to business enterprises. For example, *Accounting Research Bulletin No. 43,* which is a 1953 restatement and revision of all Accounting Research Bulletins issued up to that time and which is still in force, states that

> except where there is a specific statement of a different intent by the committee, its opinions and recommendations are directed primarily to the business enterprises organized for profit.[1]

The early development of accounting principles specifically for nonprofit organizations was largely undertaken by nonprofit industry groups outside the accounting profession. Accounting manuals representing a codification of industry practices and the delineation of reporting problems were developed by colleges and universities, religious organizations, hospitals, country clubs, museums, and voluntary health and welfare organizations. The manuals provided guidance in accounting for specific types of nonprofit organizations. Not surprisingly, this piecemeal process, representing a compilation of practices, resulted in the development of inconsistencies among the industry manuals.[2]

Development of the audit guides

Increased public awareness of the nonprofit sector of our economy in the 1960s largely precipitated the increased recognition by the accounting profession of the shortcomings of the industry-developed manuals. The accounting profession developed and issued the following three audit guides in the early 1970s: *Audits of Voluntary Health and Welfare Organizations; Hospital Audit Guide;* and *Audits of Colleges and Universities.* This latter guide codified a number of practices followed by colleges and universities and also eliminated some practices that were generally considered questionable. These three guides provided the substantial authoritative support required for all generally accepted accounting principles. The audit guide for colleges and universities states

> This audit guide is published for the guidance of members of the Institute (AICPA) in examining and reporting on the financial statements of colleges and universities. It represents the considered opinion of the Committee on College and University Accounting and Auditing and as such contains the best thought of the profession

---

[1] *Accounting Research and Terminology Bulletins,* Final Edition (New York: AICPA, 1961), Introduction, paragraph 5.

[2] Malvern J. Gross, Jr., "Nonprofit Accounting: The Continuing Revolution," *Journal of Accountancy,* June 1977, p. 67.

as to the best practices in this area of financial reporting. Members should be aware that they may be called upon to justify departures from the Committee's recommendations.[3]

The audit guides were restricted to three types of nonprofit organizations—colleges and universities, hospitals, and voluntary health and welfare organizations. The AICPA has subsequently amended (a) the audit guide for colleges and universities by issuing *Statement of Position 74-8* and (b) the audit guide for hospitals by issuing *Statements of Position 78-1, 78-7,* and *81-2.* These amendments have not substantially modified the contents of the audit guides.

Closing the gap

In 1974, the accounting advisory committee to the Commission on Private Philanthropy and Public Needs issued a report summarizing the accounting and reporting principles of several types of philanthropic organizations. The committee concluded that

> Present financial reporting to the public by philanthropic organizations requires substantial improvement. . . .
>
> In the committee's opinion, private philanthropy cannot achieve its full potential without completely open, understandable financial reporting based on uniform principles. The committee is concerned that if private philanthropy does not do a more effective job of financial reporting, regulatory bodies will increasingly assume responsibility to regulate philanthropic organizations. Inadequate reporting, including the absence of uniform accounting principles will encourage governmental intervention and may lead to decisions regarding philanthropic goals being made more by government and less by the contributor.[4]

In 1975, soon after this report, the AICPA Accounting Standards Division established a subcommittee to develop a set of recommendations of accounting principles and reporting practices for nonprofit organizations that were not covered by an existing audit guide. The final pronouncement, *Statement of Position 78-10,* was issued in 1978 without an effective date. Because this statement concerns standards of financial accounting and reporting, the recommendations are subject to the ultimate disposition of the Financial Accounting Standards Board. The subcommittee's purpose in making the recommendations was to urge the FASB to promulgate standards that would be in the public interest. Until acted upon by the FASB, compliance with the provisions of *SOP 78-10* is voluntary. In 1981, the AICPA's Accounting Standards Division issued an audit and accounting guide titled *Audits of Certain Nonprofit Organizations. Statement of Position 78-10* is part of this publication as an appendix (pp. 55–171). (The first 54 pages give guidance to auditors in examining and reporting on the applicable organizations—no accounting principles are prescribed nor is *SOP 78-10* amended or superseded.)

In 1979, the FASB announced plans to extract the specialized accounting

---

[3] *Audits of Colleges and Universities,* 2nd edition (New York: AICPA, 1975), inside cover.
[4] Malvern J. Gross, Jr., "Report on Nonprofit Accounting," *Journal of Accountancy,* June 1975, pp. 56–57. Copyright © 1975 by the American Institute of Certified Public Accountants, Inc.

principles and practices set forth in existing AICPA SOPs and Guides and issue them as FASB Statements, after appropriate due process. As an interim measure, the Board issued in 1979 *FASB Statement No. 32*, "Specialized Accounting and Reporting Principles and Practices in AICPA Statements of Position and Guides on Accounting and Auditing Matters," which accords the status of "preferable accounting principles" to the special accounting and reporting practices set forth in *SOP 78-10,* the Industry Audit Guides discussed in this chapter, and certain other SOPs and Guides when applying *APB Opinion No. 20*, "Accounting Changes"—that is, when justifying a change in accounting principle.[5]

On the horizon

The development of a set of uniform generally accepted accounting principles for nonprofit organizations based on a logically conceived and developed conceptual framework is apparently gaining momentum. In May 1978, the FASB published a research report titled *Financial Accounting in Nonbusiness Organizations: An Exploratory Study of Conceptual Issues.* Under the broad scope of the study, government is considered a type of nonbusiness organization. The report's author, Robert N. Anthony, states its purpose as follows:

> This study attempts to identify the problems that would be involved in arriving at one or more statements of objectives and basic concepts of financial reporting of nonbusiness organizations. It identifies certain issues that need to be addressed in arriving at such statements and the principal arguments, pro and con, that are advanced in connection with each issue. *It does not recommend how any of these issues should be resolved.*[6]

In the early 1980s, the FASB issued a document titled "Objectives of Financial Reporting by Nonbusiness Organizations." The statement does not establish any new accounting standards. Its purpose is to set forth objectives to help in the development of improved standards for financial reporting.

CHARACTERISTICS OF NONPROFIT ORGANIZATIONS

Nonprofit organizations are diverse, varying in size, scope, geographical influence, and objectives. Most of them, however, share certain common characteristics. We consider these characteristics now to provide an important frame of reference within which to explain current and prospective accounting and reporting practices of these units as a group.

---

[5] *FASB Statement No. 32,* "Specialized Accounting and Reporting Principles and Practices of AICPA Statements of Position and Guides on Accounting and Auditing Matters" (Stamford, CT: FASB, 1979), paragraphs 2 and 10.

[6] Robert N. Anthony, *Financial Accounting in Nonbusiness Organizations: An Exploratory Study of Conceptual Issues* (Stamford, CT: FASB, 1978), p. 7. Copyright by Financial Accounting Standards Board, High Ridge Park, Stamford, CT 06905, U.S.A. Reprinted with permission. Copies of the complete document are available from the FASB.

Objectives of nonprofit organizations

The objective of nonprofit organizations is to provide various types of services to their membership or to society as a whole. Often, the fees charged to the users of their services are less than the expenditure incurred to provide the services. For example, many hospitals and private colleges and universities cannot meet operating expenditures through patient fees and student tuition. The difference must be provided by such private and public funding as federal and state governments, philanthropic organizations, and individuals. Such providers perceive the nonprofit organization as a public service agency accomplishing goals for the public good.

In contrast, an important objective of a business enterprise is to generate a satisfactory amount of income in relation to its resource or equity base. The emphasis is on income, and success is generally measured by the ability of the business enterprise to achieve acceptable rates of profitability, the benefits from which accrue to specific equity interests. Of course, nonprofit organizations are not owned by an individual proprietor or investor but by the organization's membership or the general public.

The financial viability of a business organization is judged by its ability to meet its maturing obligations and to retain and attract new capital through earnings. The nonprofit organization is also judged by its ability to meet its commitments and obligations, but unlike business, the second concern is with the nature of the resource inflows and any restrictions on their use. Nonprofit organizations that generate their resources principally from services as opposed to gifts are considered more financially viable. They are less vulnerable to changes in donor attitudes and other external factors beyond their control. The greater the restrictions on the use of resources, the more difficult it is for the organization to meet new objectives.

The traditional matching concept used to determine net income does not apply to a nonprofit organization as it does to a business enterprise. For many of the activities of nonprofit organizations, no essential causal relationship exists between the incurrence of an expense and the generation of revenue. For example, no direct relationship generally exists between contributions, grants and governmental appropriations, and the services provided by the nonprofit organization. Such resource inflows are not *earned*, in the general definition of the term. The difference, then, between revenue and expense does not have the same meaning to the nonprofit organization as it does to the business enterprise.

Reporting emphasis

The financial statements of nonprofit organizations disclose information about the flows of funds, solvency, and liquidity, like those of business enterprises. Nonprofit organizations, however, place greater emphasis on the nature of resource inflows and the degree of resource transferability. Anthony states

> An important distinction in some [nonprofit] organizations is between hard money (e.g., revenues from services rendered) and soft money (e.g., annual gifts); the higher the proportion of hard money, the firmer the financial foundation.[7]

[7] *Financial Accounting in Nonbusiness Organizations*, p. 49.

Regarding resource transferability, he states

> Resource transferability refers to the organization's freedom to use resources for various purposes; the greater the proportion of resources that is restricted to specified uses, the more difficult it is to change direction or to meet new needs.[8]

Nonprofit organization financial statements must also disclose compliance with a number of spending mandates, such as conditions of grants, gifts, and bequests. The unit must provide assurance that the resources have been used for the intended purposes. Externally imposed spending mandates provide the rationale for fund accounting and reporting.

FRAMEWORK OF ACCOUNTING FOR NONPROFIT ORGANIZATIONS

Objectives and user needs

The accounting and financial reporting of nonprofit organizations must be adapted to the objectives of the organization and the needs of the financial information users. Clearly, the organization's accounting system must ensure compliance with all external restrictions and all internal designations by the governing board (for example, funds designated for student loans, construction, and future equipment acquisitions). As mentioned earlier, the necessity to comply with spending mandates is the rationale for fund accounting. Fund accounting permits financial resources to be classified for accounting and reporting purposes in accordance with their intended use, as directed either by the externally imposed restrictions or by the governing board.

An essential accounting differentiation exists between externally imposed spending mandates and designations internally imposed by the governing board. The governing board may change the designation of unrestricted funds at a later date. This information is obviously important to a user assessing the unit's resource transferability.

The framework of the accounting system

The assets, liabilities, fund balances, and changes in the fund balances of a nonprofit organization may be classified into the following six basic self-balancing fund groups:

(1) Current Funds (restricted and unrestricted)
(2) Land, Building, and Equipment Funds (sometimes called Plant Funds)
(3) Endowment and Similar Funds
(4) Agency Funds
(5) Annuity and Life Income Funds
(6) Loan Funds

Illustration 24-1 compares, in a necessarily general manner, the types of funds used in nonprofit organizations as recommended by the audit

---

[8] *Financial Accounting in Nonbusiness Organizations*, p. 49.

Illustration 24-1
Overview of fund structure

Colleges and Universities	Hospitals	Voluntary Health and Welfare	Other Nonprofit
Current Unre- stricted Fund	Unrestricted Fund	Current Unre- stricted Fund	Current Unre- stricted Fund
Current Restricted Fund	Specific Purpose Fund	Current Restricted Fund	Current Restricted Fund
Plant Funds Group	Plant Replacement and Expansion Fund	Land, Building, and Equipment Fund	Land, Building, and Equipment Fund
Endowment and Similar Funds	Endowment Fund	Endowment Fund	Endowment Fund
Agency Funds	Agency Funds	Agency Funds	Agency Funds
Annuity and Life Income Funds			Annuity and Life Income Funds
Loan Funds	Loan Funds		Loan Funds

guides and *Statement of Position 78-10.* More useful comparisons are developed later in the chapter.

COLLEGES AND UNIVERSITIES

Colleges and universities provide educational services, including teaching and research. They may be public institutions, profit-oriented institutions, and private, nonprofit institutions. Financial statements for public institutions reflect generally accepted accounting principles used for governmental units and those specified by *Audits of Colleges and Universities.* Financial statements for profit-oriented units reflect generally accepted accounting principles for businesses and also those specified by the audit guide. Our study focuses primarily on nonprofit institutions, and we give primary attention to these organizations.

As Illustration 24-1 shows, colleges and universities use the following seven fund types: Current Unrestricted Funds, Current Restricted Funds, Plant Funds, Endowment and Similar Funds, Agency Funds, Annuity and Life Income Funds, and Loan Funds.

Current Funds

The **Current Funds Group,** consisting of resources expendable for operating purposes, includes the asset, liability, and activity accounts necessary to record daily operations. For example, expenditures for instruction, research, extension programs, and auxiliary enterprise activities would be accounted for in the Current Funds Group (unrestricted and restricted). Within the group, unrestricted funds that have not been designated by the trustees for loan, investment, or plant purposes may be expended for operating purposes. For example, the trustees may transfer unrestricted funds to a quasi-endowment fund, in which such funds serve as endowments until some other more suitable purpose is determined. The trustees may decide

Current Restricted / restricted for certain uses

to transfer funds to supplement governmental appropriations for loan funds, to plant funds for expansion or rehabilitation, or for debt retirement. Similarly, the trustees may return any balances of designated funds appearing in other fund groups to unrestricted current funds.

Restricted current funds are also available for operating purposes, but they are restricted by donors or other outside agencies as to the specific purpose for which they may be expended. Restricted current funds are augmented through gifts, endowment income, contracts, grants and appropriations received from private organizations or governments (for research, public service, or other restricted purposes), and income and gains from investments of restricted current funds.

The unrestricted current funds subgroup for colleges and universities includes revenues from the following sources:

(1) **Student tuition and fees.**
(2) **Government appropriations,** including all unrestricted amounts receivable or made available by government sources. *largest single fund (75%) at Coyc.*
(3) **Contributions and private grants,** including all unrestricted gifts and bequests.
(4) **Endowment income,** consisting of unrestricted income from endowment and similar funds.
(5) **Expired term endowments,** consisting of any term endowment funds that become unrestricted during the reporting period. Unrestricted annuity and life income fund balances that mature during the reporting period may be included in this subgroup. *for a specific pd. of time.*
(6) **Auxiliary enterprises,** consisting of revenues from activities conducted primarily to provide facilities or services to staff, faculty, and students— for example, residence halls, food services, college unions, college stores, and other services. *Often operate at a net loss.*
(7) **All revenues not included elsewhere,** for example, income and gains and losses from investments of unrestricted current funds.

Revenues for restricted current funds are recognized only to the extent that they were expended for the intended purpose. Revenue sources for restricted funds include restricted governmental appropriations, the expended portion of specific research or other program grants or contracts from government agencies, restricted gifts to the extent expended for the specific purpose, and expended restricted income of endowment and similar funds. Illustration 24-2 is a partial balance sheet showing the content and presentation of the Current Funds Group for a university.

The activity statement for a college or university discloses the revenues, expenditures, and fund transfers only for the Current Funds Group. Illustration 24-3 (pages 924–25) presents such a statement, showing unrestricted, restricted, and total columns for the current year, and a total column for the preceding year. The statement reflects only transfers to other funds that the trustees have directed from current revenues.

Current Funds Group expenditures include all expenses defined by generally accepted accounting principles **except depreciation.** Unlike most other nonprofit organizations, colleges and universities **do not depreciate exhaustible fixed assets.** The audit guide states the following.

Illustration 24-2

<table>
<tr><td colspan="3" align="center">ANDOVER UNIVERSITY
Balance Sheet—Current Funds
June 30, 19X1
With Comparative Figures at June 30, 19X0</td></tr>
<tr><td align="center">Assets</td><td align="center">19X1</td><td align="center">19X0</td></tr>
<tr><td colspan="3">Current Funds:</td></tr>
<tr><td colspan="3">Unrestricted:</td></tr>
<tr><td>Cash ....</td><td>$ 210,000</td><td>$ 110,000</td></tr>
<tr><td>Investments, at cost ....</td><td>450,000</td><td>360,000</td></tr>
<tr><td>Accounts receivable, less allowance of $20,000 in 19X1;</td><td></td><td></td></tr>
<tr><td>$35,000 in 19X0...................................</td><td>228,000</td><td>175,000</td></tr>
<tr><td>Inventories, at lower of cost (first-in, first-out)</td><td></td><td></td></tr>
<tr><td>or market......................................</td><td>90,000</td><td>80,000</td></tr>
<tr><td>Prepaid expenses and deferred charges ....</td><td>28,000</td><td>20,000</td></tr>
<tr><td>Total Unrestricted............................</td><td>$1,006,000</td><td>$ 745,000</td></tr>
<tr><td colspan="3">Restricted:</td></tr>
<tr><td>Cash ....</td><td>$ 145,000</td><td>$ 101,000</td></tr>
<tr><td>Investments, at cost ....</td><td>175,000</td><td>165,000</td></tr>
<tr><td>Accounts receivable, less allowances of $10,000 in both</td><td></td><td></td></tr>
<tr><td>years..</td><td>68,000</td><td>160,000</td></tr>
<tr><td>Unbilled charges ....</td><td>72,000</td><td>-0-</td></tr>
<tr><td>Total Restricted ....</td><td>$ 460,000</td><td>$ 426,000</td></tr>
<tr><td>Total Current Funds ....</td><td>$1,466,000</td><td>$1,171,000</td></tr>
<tr><td colspan="3" align="center">Liabilities and Fund Balances</td></tr>
<tr><td colspan="3">Current Funds:</td></tr>
<tr><td colspan="3">Unrestricted:</td></tr>
<tr><td>Accounts payable.....................................</td><td>$ 125,000</td><td>$ 100,000</td></tr>
<tr><td>Accrued liabilities ....</td><td>20,000</td><td>15,000</td></tr>
<tr><td>Students' deposits ....</td><td>30,000</td><td>35,000</td></tr>
<tr><td>Due to other funds ....</td><td>158,000</td><td>120,000</td></tr>
<tr><td>Deferred revenue.....................................</td><td>30,000</td><td>20,000</td></tr>
<tr><td>Fund Balance ....</td><td>643,000</td><td>455,000</td></tr>
<tr><td>Total Unrestricted............................</td><td>$1,006,000</td><td>$ 745,000</td></tr>
<tr><td colspan="3">Restricted:</td></tr>
<tr><td>Accounts payable.....................................</td><td>$ 14,000</td><td>$ 5,000</td></tr>
<tr><td>Fund Balance ....</td><td>446,000</td><td>421,000</td></tr>
<tr><td>Total Restricted ....</td><td>$ 460,000</td><td>$ 426,000</td></tr>
<tr><td>Total Current Funds ....</td><td>$1,466,000</td><td>$1,171,000</td></tr>
</table>

Source: Adapted from *Audits of Colleges and Universities*, 2nd ed., Exhibit A, p. 60. Copyright © 1975 by the American Institute of Certified Public Accountants, Inc.

The reason for this treatment is that these statements present expenditures and transfers of current funds rather than operating expenses in conformity with the reporting objectives of accounting for resources received and used rather than the determination of net income. Depreciation allowance, however, may be reported in the balance sheet and the provision for depreciation reported in the statement of changes in the balance of the investment-in-plant subsection of the plant funds group.[9]

[9] *Audits of Colleges and Universities*, pp. 9–10.

The following sections illustrate the accounting for Current Funds Group transactions.

Illustration:
Unrestricted current funds subgroup transactions

The following journal entries pertain to financial events and transactions of Andover University's Unrestricted Current Funds for the year ended June 30, 19X2.

(1) Student tuition and fees billed for the year were $8,000,000, which was used for educational and general purposes. Prior experience shows that $100,000 of this billing will be uncollectible. At year-end, $800,000 remains uncollected.

Cash..	7,200,000	
Accounts receivable	800,000	
Expenditures—Instruction	100,000	
Revenue—Student tuition and fees...............		8,000,000
Allowance for bad debts		100,000

(2) Unrestricted government appropriations for the year amounted to $5,000,000, all of which have been collected.

Cash..	5,000,000	
Revenue—Government appropriations		5,000,000

(3) Unrestricted gifts and private grants received during the period amounted to $50,000.

Cash..	50,000	
Revenue—Gifts and private grants		50,000

(4) Unrestricted income from endowment and similar funds amounted to $185,000.

Cash..	185,000	
Revenue—Endowment income		185,000

(5) Auxiliary enterprise revenue included $175,000 from student residence halls; $200,000 from cafeterias; and $750,000 from the college store sales. All billed amounts have been collected except for $50,000 in student residence fees. Of this amount, an estimated $5,000 will be uncollectible.

Cash..	1,075,000	
Accounts receivable	50,000	
Expenditures—Auxiliary enterprises	5,000	
Revenue—Auxiliary enterprises		1,125,000
Allowance for bad debts		5,000

Illustration 24-3

ANDOVER UNIVERSITY
Statement of Current Funds Revenues, Expenditures, and Other Changes
For the Year Ended June 30, 19X4
With Comparative Figures for 19X3

	19X4			19X3
	Unrestricted	Restricted	Total	
Revenues:				
Educational and general:				
Student tuition and fees	$2,600,000		$2,600,000	$2,300,000
Government appropriations	1,300,000		1,300,000	1,300,000
Government grants and contracts	35,000	$ 425,000	460,000	595,000
Gifts and private grants	850,000	380,000	1,230,000	1,190,000
Endowment income	325,000	209,000	534,000	500,000
Total educational and general	$5,110,000	$1,014,000	$6,124,000	$5,885,000
Auxiliary enterprises	2,200,000		2,200,000	2,100,000
Expired term endowment	40,000		40,000	
Total Revenues	$7,350,000	$1,014,000	$8,364,000	$7,985,000
Expenditures and mandatory transfers:				
Educational and general:				
Instruction and departmental research	$2,820,000	$ 300,000	$3,120,000	$2,950,000
Organized activities related to instructional departments	140,000	189,000	329,000	350,000
Sponsored research		400,000	400,000	500,000
Extension	130,000		130,000	125,000
Libraries	250,000		250,000	225,000
Student services	200,000		200,000	195,000
Operation and maintenance of plant	220,000		220,000	200,000
General administration	200,000		200,000	195,000
General institutional expense	250,000		250,000	250,000
Student aid	90,000	125,000	215,000	180,000
Educational and general expenditures	$4,300,000	$1,014,000	$5,314,000	$5,170,000

Mandatory transfers for:			
Principal and interest	250,000		250,000	250,000
Renewals and replacements	70,000		70,000	70,000
Total Educational and General	$4,620,000	$1,014,000	$5,634,000	$5,490,000
Auxiliary enterprises:			
Expenditures	$1,830,000		$1,830,000	$1,730,000
Mandatory transfers for:			
Principal and interest	90,000		90,000	50,000
Renewals and replacements	100,000		100,000	80,000
Total Auxiliary Enterprises	$2,020,000		$2,020,000	$1,860,000
Total Expenditures and Mandatory Transfers	$6,640,000	$1,014,000	$7,654,000	$7,350,000
Net Increase in Fund Balances	$ 710,000	$ -0-	$ 710,000	$ 635,000

(6) Term endowment funds that are now available for unrestricted use amount to $300,000.

Cash..	300,000	
Revenue—Endowment income		300,000

(7) Purchases of materials and supplies amounted to $800,000 for the year. A perpetual inventory is used. Purchases of $150,000 remain unpaid at year-end.

Materials and supplies inventory	800,000	
Cash..		650,000
Vouchers payable		150,000

(8) Operating expenditures are incurred and assigned as shown in the following journal entry. Note that $2,250,000 of these expenditures are unpaid vouchers payable at year-end.

Expenditures—Instruction	3,500,000	
Expenditures—Research	1,200,000	
Expenditures—Academic support	3,000,000	
Expenditures—Student services....................	380,000	
Expenditures—Operation and maintenance of plant	1,120,000	
Expenditures—Institutional support	500,000	
Cash..		7,450,000
Vouchers payable		2,250,000

(9) Use of materials and supplies is assigned as shown in the following journal entry:

Expenditures—Instruction	300,000	
Expenditures—Research	150,000	
Expenditures—Academic support	50,000	
Expenditures—Student services....................	25,000	
Expenditures—Institutional support	120,000	
Materials and supplies inventory		645,000

(10) The university's student aid committee granted student tuition and fee reductions of $200,000.

Expenditures—Student aid	200,000	
Accounts receivable		200,000

(11) The trustees have specified that certain Current Fund revenues must be transferred to meet the debt service provisions relating to the university's institutional properties, including amounts set aside for debt retirement, interest, and required provisions for renewal and replacement. For this year, these mandatory transfers total $550,000.

Transfers—Plant funds.............................	550,000	
Cash..		550,000

(12) Auxiliary enterprises expenditures amount to $650,000.

Expenditures—Auxiliary enterprises	650,000	
Vouchers payable (Cash)		650,000

(13) Closing entries are not illustrated. Revenues, expenditures, and transfers are merely closed to the Fund Balance account.

Illustration:
Restricted current funds subgroup transactions

The following journal entries pertain to financial events and transactions of Andover University's Restricted Current Funds for the year ended June 30, 19X2.

(1) Restricted gifts in the amount of $100,000 were received from the Wollaston Foundation to be used for student aid.

Cash	100,000	
Fund balance[10]		100,000

(2) A $750,000 federal government grant was received for library acquisitions in science and engineering.

Cash	750,000	
Fund balance...................................		750,000

(3) Federal government contracts were awarded to certain academic departments to develop training programs and instructional institutes for child care and development. These contracts amounted to $1,500,000 and included a provision for reimbursement to the university of indirect costs of $75,000. The contract payments were collected.

Cash	1,500,000	
Fund balance...................................		1,500,000
Fund balance....................................	75,000	
Cash		75,000

The latter entry transfers the indirect cost recovery to the Unrestricted Current Fund. The Unrestricted Current Fund would acknowledge receipt of the payment with the following entry:

Cash	75,000	
Revenue—General		75,000

(4) Expenditures incurred were for: student aid, $85,000; instruction (library acquisitions), $700,000; training programs and instructional institutes, $1,425,000. At year-end, 10% of the expenditures remain unpaid.

---

[10] Subsidiary accounts would usually show the sources, purposes, and applications of restricted resources.

Expenditures—Student aid	85,000	
Expenditures—Instruction	700,000	
Expenditures—Instruction	1,425,000	
Cash		1,989,000
Vouchers payable		221,000
Fund balance.....................................	2,210,000	
Revenue—Student aid..........................		85,000
Revenue—Instruction..........................		2,125,000

(5) Closing entries are not illustrated. (Because total revenues equal total expenditures, these accounts offset each other in the closing entry.)

Land, building, and equipment funds

Colleges and universities include investment in plant within a Plant Funds Group, which accounts for both unexpended and expended resources. The Plant Funds Group consists of:

> (1) funds to be used for the acquisition of physical properties for institutional purposes but unexpended at the date of reporting; (2) funds set aside for the renewal and replacement of institutional properties; (3) funds set aside for debt service charges and for the retirement of indebtedness on institutional properties; and (4) funds expended for and thus invested in institutional properties.[11]

Illustration 24-4 discloses in more detail the nature of the funds flows for the accounts in the Plant Funds Group.

Illustration 24-5 is a partial balance sheet for a university's Plant Funds Group. In reviewing this illustration, the following points should be noted:

(1) The first two funds are, in effect, Unexpended Plant Funds. Frequently, they are summarized or combined and disclosed as unexpended funds for financial reporting purposes.
(2) Unexpended Plant Funds include both externally and internally designated funds.
(3) The Investment in Plant Fund is, in effect, the Expended Plant Fund. The resources are carried at cost, and because colleges and universities do not depreciate their assets, no contra asset account exists for accumulated depreciation. This fund's residual equity is referred to as Net Investment in Plant, not Fund Balance.

The following sections illustrate accounting for Plant Funds Group transactions.

Illustration:
Plant funds group transactions

The following journal entries pertain to transactions of Andover University's Plant Funds Group for the year ended June 30, 19X2. First, we illustrate Unexpended Plant Fund activities.

[11] *Audits of Colleges and Universities,* p. 44.

Illustration 24-4
Plant funds group for colleges and universities: Subgroup funds flows

Unexpended Plant Funds	
Inflows	**Outflows**
Bond sales proceeds	Disbursements
Private donations	Investment losses
Restricted government appropriations	Return of unrestricted amounts to
Income and gains from the investment of	unrestricted current funds
unexpended funds	Transfers: Investment in plant
Transfers from other fund groups	

Renewals and Replacement Funds	
Inflows	**Outflows**
Mandatory and voluntary transfers from	Investment losses
current funds	Return of unrestricted amounts to
Income and gains from the investment of	unrestricted current funds
funds	Expenditures not capitalized
	Capitalized expenditures for renewals and
	replacements

Retirement of Indebtedness Funds	
Inflows	**Outflows**
Transfers from current funds for principal	Payments on principal and interest
and interest payments	Trustees fees and expenses
Income and gains from the investment of	Investment losses
funds	
Gifts, grants, and government appro-	
priations restricted to debt retirement	
Transfers from other fund groups as	
directed by donors (e.g., expired term	
endowments, annuity and life income	
funds)	

Investment in Plant	
Inflows	**Outflows**
Current fund equipment replacements	Disposal
Gifts of plant assets	Abandonment
Transfers from unexpended plant and	Sale of plant assets
renewals and replacement funds	
Debt retirement	

(1) A major fund-raising drive for new laboratory equipment generated $300,000 cash and $250,000 in marketable securities.

Cash	300,000	
Marketable securities	250,000	
Fund balance—Restricted		550,000

(2) The university received a federal grant of $1,000,000 for the construction of a new classroom wing for the science department. The grant requires the university to match the government appropriation.

Illustration 24-5

<table>
<tr><td colspan="3" align="center">**ANDOVER UNIVERSITY**
Balance Sheet—Plant Funds
June 30, 19X1
With Comparative Figures at June 30, 19X0</td></tr>
<tr><td align="center">**Assets**</td><td align="center">**19X1**</td><td align="center">**19X0**</td></tr>
<tr><td>**Plant Funds:**</td><td></td><td></td></tr>
<tr><td>Unexpended:</td><td></td><td></td></tr>
<tr><td>Cash ....</td><td>$ 275,000</td><td>$ 410,000</td></tr>
<tr><td>Investments, at cost...........................</td><td>1,285,000</td><td>1,590,000</td></tr>
<tr><td>Due from unrestricted current funds.................</td><td>150,000</td><td>120,000</td></tr>
<tr><td>Total Unexpended ....</td><td>$ 1,710,000</td><td>$ 2,120,000</td></tr>
<tr><td>Renewal and Replacement:</td><td></td><td></td></tr>
<tr><td>Cash ....</td><td>$ 5,000</td><td>$ 4,000</td></tr>
<tr><td>Investments, at cost...........................</td><td>150,000</td><td>286,000</td></tr>
<tr><td>Deposits with trustees ....</td><td>100,000</td><td>90,000</td></tr>
<tr><td>Due from unrestricted current funds.................</td><td>5,000</td><td>-0-</td></tr>
<tr><td>Total Renewal and Replacement ....</td><td>$ 260,000</td><td>$ 380,000</td></tr>
<tr><td>Retirement of Indebtedness:</td><td></td><td></td></tr>
<tr><td>Cash ....</td><td>$ 50,000</td><td>$ 40,000</td></tr>
<tr><td>Deposits with trustees ....</td><td>250,000</td><td>253,000</td></tr>
<tr><td>Total Retirement of Indebtedness...............</td><td>$ 300,000</td><td>$ 293,000</td></tr>
<tr><td>Investment in Plant:</td><td></td><td></td></tr>
<tr><td>Land...</td><td>$ 500,000</td><td>$ 500,000</td></tr>
<tr><td>Land improvements ....</td><td>1,000,000</td><td>1,110,000</td></tr>
<tr><td>Buildings ....</td><td>25,000,000</td><td>24,060,000</td></tr>
<tr><td>Equipment ....</td><td>15,000,000</td><td>14,200,000</td></tr>
<tr><td>Library books...................................</td><td>100,000</td><td>80,000</td></tr>
<tr><td>Total Investment in Plant ....</td><td>$41,600,000</td><td>$39,950,000</td></tr>
<tr><td>Total Plant Funds ....</td><td>$43,870,000</td><td>$42,743,000</td></tr>
<tr><td colspan="3" align="center">**Liabilities and Fund Balances**</td></tr>
<tr><td>**Plant Funds:**</td><td></td><td></td></tr>
<tr><td>Unexpended:</td><td></td><td></td></tr>
<tr><td>Accounts payable ....</td><td>$ 10,000</td><td>$ -0-</td></tr>
<tr><td>Fund Balances:</td><td></td><td></td></tr>
<tr><td>Restricted ....</td><td>1,510,000</td><td>1,860,000</td></tr>
<tr><td>Unrestricted ....</td><td>190,000</td><td>260,000</td></tr>
<tr><td>Total Unexpended ....</td><td>$ 1,710,000</td><td>$ 2,120,000</td></tr>
<tr><td>Renewal and Replacement:</td><td></td><td></td></tr>
<tr><td>Fund Balances:</td><td></td><td></td></tr>
<tr><td>Restricted ....</td><td>$ 25,000</td><td>$ 180,000</td></tr>
<tr><td>Unrestricted ....</td><td>235,000</td><td>200,000</td></tr>
<tr><td>Total Renewal and Replacement ....</td><td>$ 260,000</td><td>$ 380,000</td></tr>
<tr><td>Retirement of Indebtedness:</td><td></td><td></td></tr>
<tr><td>Fund Balances:</td><td></td><td></td></tr>
<tr><td>Restricted ....</td><td>$ 185,000</td><td>$ 125,000</td></tr>
<tr><td>Unrestricted ....</td><td>115,000</td><td>168,000</td></tr>
<tr><td>Total Retirement of Indebtedness..............</td><td>$ 300,000</td><td>$ 293,000</td></tr>
<tr><td>Investment in Plant:</td><td></td><td></td></tr>
<tr><td>Notes payable ....</td><td>$ 790,000</td><td>$ 810,000</td></tr>
<tr><td>Bonds payable..................................</td><td>2,200,000</td><td>2,400,000</td></tr>
<tr><td>Mortgages payable.............................</td><td>400,000</td><td>200,000</td></tr>
<tr><td>Net investment in plant ....</td><td>38,210,000</td><td>36,540,000</td></tr>
<tr><td>Total Investment in Plant ....</td><td>$41,600,000</td><td>$39,950,000</td></tr>
<tr><td>Total Plant Funds ....</td><td>$43,870,000</td><td>$42,743,000</td></tr>
</table>

Source: Adapted from *Audits of Colleges and Universities*, 2nd ed., Exhibit A, pp. 62–63. Copyright ©
1975 by the American Institute of Certified Public Accountants, Inc.

```
Cash ..........................................  1,000,000
    Fund balance—Restricted......................              1,000,000
```

(3) The university's governing board directed a transfer from Unrestricted Current Funds for the construction of the new classroom wing for the science department. The $1,000,000 transfer complied with the government's building grant.

```
Cash ..........................................  1,000,000
    Fund balance—Restricted......................              1,000,000
```

(4) The addition to the science department building was completed during the year and cost the university $2,500,000. A mortgage was signed for $500,000.

```
Cash ..........................................    500,000
    Mortgage payable.............................                500,000

Construction in progress.........................  2,500,000
    Cash ........................................              2,500,000

Mortgage payable[12] .............................    500,000
Fund balance—Restricted..........................  2,000,000
    Construction in progress.....................              2,500,000
```

(5) Income from pooled investments totaled $25,000.

```
Cash ..........................................     25,000
    Fund balance—Unrestricted....................                 25,000
```

(6) A planned expansion of the university's sports stadium was abandoned because of cutbacks in available federal funds. The governing board directed the return of $400,000 to Unrestricted Current Funds.

```
Fund balance—Unrestricted........................    400,000
    Cash[13] ....................................                400,000
```

(7) Expenses of $20,000 were incurred in connection with fund-raising activities for the new science department classroom wing and laboratory equipment.

```
Fund balance—Unrestricted........................     20,000
    Cash ........................................                 20,000
```

Now we cover Renewals and Replacement Fund activities.

(1) Income from pooled investments totaled $15,000.

```
Cash ..........................................     15,000
    Fund balance—Unrestricted....................                 15,000
```

---

[12] This entry transfers the building cost and mortgage to the Investment in Plant Fund account.
[13] The Unrestricted Current Fund would credit the Transfers—Unexpended Plant Fund account.

(2) The governing board transferred cash to the Renewals and Replacements Fund for equipment replacement in the science department, $80,000.

Cash[14]	80,000	
Fund balance—Unrestricted		80,000

(3) Replacement equipment was purchased for the science department for $78,000.

Fund balance—Unrestricted[15]	78,000	
Cash		78,000

The Retirement of Indebtedness Fund has the following activity:

(1) Income earned from pooled investments amounts to $10,000.

Cash	10,000	
Fund balance—Unrestricted		10,000

(2) The governing board transferred $250,000 to the Retirement of Indebtedness Fund for interest and principal payments on debt. The debt payments were made.

Cash	250,000	
Fund balance—Unrestricted		250,000
Fund balance—Unrestricted	250,000	
Cash		250,000

The Investment in Plant Fund has the following activity:

(1) Completed science building is transferred from the Unexpended Plant Fund [see transaction (4), Unexpended Plant Fund].

Building (science)	2,500,000	
Mortgage payable		500,000
Net investment in plant		2,000,000

(2) Replacement equipment is transferred from the Renewals and Replacement Fund [see transaction (3), Renewals and Replacement Fund].

Equipment (science)	78,000	
Net investment in plant		78,000

(3) Mortgage payable is reduced [see transaction (2), Retirement of Indebtedness Fund].

Mortgage payable	250,000	
Net investment in plant		250,000

---

[14] The Unrestricted Current Fund would charge the Transfers—Plant Funds Renewals and Replacements account.

[15] This entry transfers the equipment cost to the Investment in Plant Fund account.

(4) The university received an art collection and several rare books for its library. The appraised values were $325,000 for the art collection and $200,000 for the rare books.

Valued collections—Art	325,000	
Valued collections—Rare books	200,000	
Net investment in plant		525,000

(5) The laboratory equipment that was replaced was sold for $30,000. The recorded value of the equipment was $55,000.

Net investment in plant[16]	55,000	
Equipment (science)		55,000

Endowment and similar funds

For most nonprofit organizations, the Endowment Funds Group includes **endowment funds** and **term endowment funds.** College and university trustees also designate **quasi-endowment funds,** and therefore the funds group title is Endowment and *Similar* Funds.

Endowment funds are established by donors that have stipulated that the principal is nonexpendable. The income generated from the endowment usually may be expended by current operating funds. *Term endowment* fund principal becomes expendable at some specified time or after a designated event. These funds are then available for operating needs. *Quasi-endowment* funds are internally designated by the board of trustees rather than externally restricted. The board of trustees may expend the principal at any time.

Legal restrictions in the endowment instrument determine the accounting for each fund's principal, income, and investments. Each endowment is accounted for as a separate fund, but the resources are generally pooled for investment purposes unless restrictive covenants limit investments to certain types of securities.

Illustration:
Endowment and similar funds group transactions

The following journal entries pertain to transactions of Andover University's Endowment and Similar Funds Group.

(1) The Quincy family established an Endowment Fund, the income from which should be used to maintain the university's rare books collection. This permanent endowment does not restrict the investment of the funds.

Cash	350,000	
Fund balance—Endowment		350,000

(2) The university's board of trustees directed the accounting officer to

---

[16] The sales proceeds could be accounted for by the Unrestricted Current Fund or by the Unexpended Plant Funds, depending on the disposition of the funds.

establish a quasi-endowment fund of $200,000. The income is to be used to maintain the campus theater. No restrictions were imposed on the investment of the funds. The transfer was made from Unrestricted Current Fund.

Cash	200,000	
Fund balance—Endowment[17]		200,000

(3) The Coulomb Corporation established an Endowment Fund in the amount of $150,000, the income from which will augment a professorial chair in electrical engineering. The endowment instrument stipulates that all income and investment gains are expendable for salary augmentation for five years. At the end of the fifth year, the principal is to be used to replace equipment in the engineering laboratories.

Cash	150,000	
Fund balance—Term endowment		150,000

(4) Investment earnings from pooled investments totaled $19,500, received as shown:

Cash	19,500	
Fund balance—Endowment		6,500
Fund balance—Term endowment		8,000
Fund balance—Quasi-endowment		5,000

(5) Salary augmentation payments for the professorial chair in electrical engineering amount to $6,500.

Fund balance—Term endowment[18]	6,500	
Cash		6,500

Agency funds

An **Agency Fund** accounts for assets that are not the university's property. The university is simply a fiscal agent. For example, a university may act as fiscal agent for the assets of student government and of faculty and staff organizations. The net assets of such a fund would appear as a liability, because the university has no equity in the fund.

---

[17] Unrestricted Current Fund:

Transfers—Endowment and similar funds	200,000	
Cash		200,000

[18] Restricted Current Fund:

Cash	6,500	
Fund balance—Endowment fund		6,500

Then, as expended:

Fund balance—Endowment fund	6,500	
Revenue—Instruction		6,500

Illustration:
Agency fund transactions

The following journal entries pertain to Andover University's Agency Fund transactions.

(1) Student government fees collected during the registration process are deposited in the student government fund.

Cash	25,000	
Fund balance—Agency (liability)		25,000

(2) Income earned from student government fund investments amounted to $2,000.

Cash	2,000	
Fund balance—Agency		2,000

(3) Authorized disbursements for the period amounted to $7,500.

Fund balance—Agency	7,500	
Cash		7,500

(4) Fund maintenance charges were $350.

Fund balance—Agency	350	
Cash		350

Annuity funds

A university's **Annuity Funds Group** consists of assets contributed to it with the stipulation that the university, in turn, promises to pay a certain sum, periodically, to a designated individual, usually for the remainder of his or her life. On the death of the designated individual, the unexpended assets of the Annuity Fund are transferred to the university's unrestricted fund, restricted fund, or endowment fund, as specified by the donor.

At the date of the contribution, the assets are accounted for at their fair market value, an Annuities Payable account is credited for the current value of the liability (based on life expectancy tables), and the balance is credited to the annuity Fund Balance account.

Investment income and gains or losses are credited or charged to the liability account. Annuity payments are charged to the liability. The liability and the fund balance are periodically adjusted to record the actuarial gain or loss due to recomputation of the liability based on revised life expectancy.

Illustration:
Annuity funds group transactions

The following journal entries show Andover University's Annuity Funds Group transactions.

(1) Phyllis Sims donated $250,000 to the university with the stipulation that she receive $20,000 per year for the rest of her life. Thereafter, the principal should be used to provide student aid. The actuarial value of the annuity is $85,000.

Cash	250,000	
Annuities payable		85,000
Fund balance—Annuity		165,000

(2) Net investment gains for the period were $24,000, and investment income was $14,000.

Cash	38,000	
Annuities payable		38,000

(3) Payments to annuitant were $20,000.

Annuities payable	20,000	
Cash		20,000

(4) Recorded the periodic adjustment for the actuarial gain due to recomputation of the liability based on revised life expectancies of all annuitants.

Annuities payable	53,500	
Fund balance—Annuity		53,500

(5) Annuitant Josh Gaylord died. The annuity was transferred to the Endowment Funds Group according to the provisions of the gift instrument.

Annuities payable	1,500	
Fund balance—Annuity	23,000	
Cash		24,500

Life income funds

The essential difference between Annuity Funds and Life Income Funds is that for the latter the principal remains intact, and all income is distributed to the beneficiary. Annuity Fund distributions are fixed, whereas Life Income Fund distributions reflect all fund earnings.

Illustration:
Life income funds group transactions

The following journal entries show Andover University's Life Income Funds Group transactions.

(1) Gerald Baumann established a Life Income Fund, which specified that at his death the principal is to be transferred to the Unrestricted Current Fund group and used at the discretion of the board of trustees.

Cash	50,000	
Investments	150,000	
Fund balance—Life income		200,000

(2) Income earned on investments amounted to $15,000.

Cash	15,000	
Income payable		15,000

(3) Life Income Fund distributions amounted to $15,000.

Income payable	15,000	
Cash		15,000

(4) The Erika Meagher Life Income Fund was transferred to Endowment Funds in accordance with the provisions of the gift instrument.

Fund balance—Life income[19]	100,000	
Cash		100,000

Loan funds

Loan Funds are usually established to provide loans to students, faculty, and staff of colleges and universities, to nursing students and staff of hospitals, and to students and staff of other nonprofit organizations. Loan Funds are generally revolving, that is, repayments of principal and interest are loaned to other individuals. Illustration 24-6 shows sources and uses of Loan Funds.

Notes receivable are carried at face value, less an allowance for doubtful notes. Provisions for doubtful notes are charged directly to the Loan Fund equity account. All other transactions that affect the fund equity account are also credited or charged directly to that account.

---

[19] Endowment Fund:

Cash	100,000	
Fund balance—Endowment fund		100,000

Illustration 24-6
Sources and uses of loan funds

Sources	Uses
Gifts, bequests, and government advances	Loans written off
Interest on loan notes	Deductions to provide appropriate allowances for uncollectible loans
Income from endowment funds	Interfund transfers
Interfund transfers	Refunds to grantors
Income, gains, and losses on investment of Loan Funds	Administrative and collection costs

Illustration:
Loan fund transactions

The following journal entries show Andover University's Loan Fund transactions.

(1) A fund-raising drive for student loan funds generated $750,000.

```
Cash ............................................... 750,000
        Fund balance—Loan .............................          750,000
```

(2) The board of trustees directed the use of $200,000 of Unrestricted Current Funds for low interest real estate loans to the faculty.

```
Cash[20] ............................................ 200,000
        Fund balance—Loan .............................          200,000
```

(3) Loans to students and faculty totaled $500,000. An allowance for uncollectible loans was established for 1% of this amount.

```
Notes receivable .................................... 500,000
        Cash .........................................          500,000

Fund balance—Loan ................................... 5,000
        Allowance for doubtful loans ..................          5,000
```

(4) Excess cash of $400,000 was invested in marketable securities.

```
Investments ......................................... 400,000
        Cash .........................................          400,000
```

(5) Investment income earned amounted to $8,000.

```
Cash ................................................ 8,000
        Fund balance—Loan .............................          8,000
```

(6) Certain notes having a face amount of $25,000 proved to be uncollectible and were written off.

```
Allowance for doubtful loans ........................ 25,000
        Notes receivable .............................          25,000
```

(7) Administrative and collection costs for the period amounted to $4,000.

```
Fund balance—Loan ................................... 4,000
        Cash .........................................          4,000
```

---

[20] Unrestricted Current Funds:
```
    Transfer—Endowment fund ............................................ 200,000
        Cash............................................................          200,000
```

Illustration 24-7

ANDOVER UNIVERSITY Balance Sheet—Loan Funds and Endowment and Similar Funds June 30, 19X1 With Comparative Figures at June 30, 19X0		
Assets	**19X1**	**19X0**
Loan Funds:		
Cash	$ 30,000	$ 20,000
Investments, at cost	100,000	100,000
Loans to students, faculty, and staff, less valuation		
allowance of $10,000 in 19X1; $5,000 in 19X0	550,000	382,000
Due from unrestricted current funds	3,000	-0-
Total Loan Funds	$ 683,000	$ 502,000
Endowment and Similar Funds:		
Cash	$ 100,000	$ 101,000
Investments, at cost	13,900,000	11,800,000
Total Endowment and Similar Funds	$14,000,000	$11,901,000
Liabilities and Fund Balances		
Loan Funds:		
Fund balances:		
U.S. government grants refundable	$ 50,000	$ 33,000
University funds:		
Restricted	483,000	369,000
Unrestricted	150,000	100,000
Total Loan Funds	$ 683,000	$ 502,000
Endowment and Similar Funds:		
Fund balances:		
Endowment	$ 7,800,000	$ 6,740,000
Term endowment	3,840,000	3,420,000
Quasi-endowment	2,360,000	1,741,000
Total Endowment and Similar Funds	$14,000,000	$11,901,000

Source: Adapted from *Audits of Colleges and Universities*, 2nd ed., Exhibit A, p. 61. Copyright © 1975 by the American Institute of Certified Public Accountants, Inc.

Illustration 24-7 is a partial balance sheet for Andover University, disclosing Loan Funds and Endowment and Similar Funds Groups. Loan Fund equities disclose restricted and unrestricted (trustee-designated) balances; Endowment and Similar Funds balances are separated into pure endowment, term endowment, and quasi-endowment funds. This disclosure is clearly important to the balance sheet user who attempts to assess transferability.

HOSPITALS

As providers of health services, hospitals may be voluntary nonprofit, government owned, or owned by investors and operated on a proprietary basis. The term **hospital** extends to teaching hospitals, extended care facilities, and nursing homes.

Hospitals use the following six different types of funds: Unrestricted Fund, Specific Purpose Fund, Plant Replacement and Expansion Fund, Endowment Fund, Agency Funds, and Loan Funds. Because significant differences exist in Current Funds and Plant Fund accounting between hospitals and universities, we focus our attention on the Unrestricted Fund, Specific Purpose Fund, and Plant Replacement and Expansion Funds of voluntary nonprofit hospitals.

Unrestricted and specific purpose funds

Hospitals do not use a current funds group. For operating purposes, they employ an Unrestricted Fund, which comprises unrestricted assets and liabilities, including property, plant and equipment, accumulated depreciation, and related liabilities. Assets designated by the governing board are also included in this fund. Revenue sources for the Unrestricted Fund include

(1) Revenue from daily patient services.
(2) Revenue from nursing services. Charges for use of operating rooms, recovery rooms, delivery and labor rooms, central services, and supply and emergency services.
(3) Revenue from other professional services, including charges for laboratory, blood bank, radiology, and pharmacy services.
(4) Other revenues, including nonmedical services, income transfers from specific purpose funds, endowment funds, plant funds, and gains on disposal of assets.

Hospitals account for property, plant and equipment, and related liabilities as part of Unrestricted Funds. The *Hospital Audit Guide* argues that segregation in a separate fund implies the existence of restrictions on the use of the assets. Third party restricted resources held for future investment in fixed assets, however, are accounted for in a restricted fund—Plant Replacement and Expansion Fund.

Unlike colleges and universities, hospitals record depreciation. The American Hospital Association supports the depreciation of hospitals but recommends that depreciation calculations be based on replacement cost. This treatment does not conform to generally accepted accounting principles, but hospitals may use this information for internal management purposes in planning and controlling their operations.

Hospitals use a Specific Purpose Fund, which is similar to the restricted current funds subgroup in that it accounts for resources externally restricted by donors or other outside agencies as to the specific purpose for which they may be expended. It differs from the restricted current funds subgroup in that it does not ultimately expend the resources for the specific purpose. The spending unit is the Unrestricted Fund. Interfund transfers are effected from the Specific Purpose Fund to the Unrestricted Fund as the resources are expended. In hospital accounting, similar treatment may be found in accounting for plant and endowment funds; the expending fund is the Unrestricted Fund.

Illustration:
Unrestricted funds transactions

The following journal entries pertain to the financial events and transactions of Charleston Memorial Hospital's Unrestricted Fund for the year ended June 30, 19X1:

(1) Gross billings[21] to patients for the year were assigned as shown in the following entry:

Accounts receivable	4,050,000	
Revenues—Daily patient services		3,000,000
Revenues—Other nursing services		750,000
Revenues—Other professional services		300,000

Typically, more detailed revenue accounts are maintained by specific revenue producing segments (for example, Daily Patient Services: Cardiac Unit).

(2) Adjustments to gross revenue include contractual adjustments with third party payers, $500,000, and approved charity adjustments, $200,000.

Charity service	200,000	
Contractual adjustments	500,000	
Accounts receivable		700,000

(3) Collection of accounts receivable totaled $3,350,000.

Cash	3,350,000	
Accounts receivable		3,350,000

(4) Inventory acquisitions, including materials and supplies, amounted to $700,000. One-fourth of the approved invoices remain unpaid at year-end.

Materials and supplies inventory	700,000	
Cash		525,000
Vouchers payable		175,000

(5) Use of the materials and supplies inventory is assigned as shown in the following entry.

---

[21] Generally, hospitals bill their patients at standard rates, even though collectibility is questionable. This procedure provides management with more useful information and also facilitates the calculation and support of reimbursement claims submitted to third party payers (such as Medicare, Medicaid, and Blue Cross).

Expenses—Nursing services[22]	190,000	
Expenses—Other professional services	75,000	
Expenses—General services	300,000	
Expenses—Fiscal services	10,000	
Expenses—Administrative services	5,000	
Materials and supplies inventory................		580,000

(6) Salaries and wage expenses incurred for the year total $2,200,000. Of this amount, $176,000 is accrued at year-end.

Expenses—Nursing services	1,000,000	
Expenses—Other professional services	700,000	
Expenses—General services	300,000	
Expenses—Fiscal services	150,000	
Expenses—Administrative services	50,000	
Cash		2,024,000
Accrued salaries and wages		176,000

(7) Other operating expenses processed through the voucher system are assigned as shown, including $18,000 of approved but unpaid vouchers at year-end.

Expenses—Nursing services	75,000	
Expenses—Other professional services	50,000	
Expenses—General services	30,000	
Expenses—Fiscal services	25,000	
Expenses—Administrative services	20,000	
Cash		182,000
Vouchers payable.............................		18,000

(8) The provision for estimated uncollectible accounts is $125,000.

Provision for uncollectible accounts	125,000	
Allowance for uncollectible accounts		125,000

(9) Depreciation expense for the year is $350,000. This provision is based on historical cost, which conforms with generally accepted accounting principles. Hospitals may compute depreciation expense based on replacement cost for internal management purposes.

Expense—Depreciation[23]	350,000	
Accumulated depreciation......................		350,000

(10) Interfund transfers for the year to the Unrestricted Fund are recorded as shown.[24]

[22] In practice, hospitals maintain detailed expense control accounts and even more detailed subsidiary accounts for managerial control purposes.

[23] Generally, for reporting purposes, depreciation is not charged to the functional areas (for example, Expenses—Nursing Services). For internal management purposes, depreciation is charged to subsidiary expense accounts by cost center.

[24] Receipts of restricted resources by the Specific Purpose, Plant Renewal and Replacement, and Endowment

All cash expended thru gen't fund.

Cash	945,000
Revenue[25]—Other revenue: Transfers from specific purpose fund..........................	320,000
Revenue—Other revenue: Transfers from plant renewal and replacement fund	500,000
Revenue—Other revenue: Transfers from endowment fund	125,000

(11) Closing entries are not shown. Revenues, expenses, charity services, contractual adjustments, and the provision for uncollectibles are merely closed to the Fund Balance account.

Illustration 24-8 presents a complete balance sheet for a hospital, using the layered format employed by most hospitals. In reviewing Illustration 24-8, the following points should be understood:

(1) The fund layers are basically divided into unrestricted funds and restricted funds. The hospital's unrestricted funds are further divided into current and noncurrent portions.
(2) Summary totals for the assets and equities of all funds are not provided. Totals of assets and equities are provided, however, for the two basic divisions—unrestricted and restricted.
(3) Expended funds for property, plant, and equipment are classified as noncurrent and part of unrestricted funds. Board-designated funds for replacement and expansion might be presented in the balance sheet in the following format:

	19X1	19X0
Total current assets	$ 1,814,000	$ 1,453,000
Replacement and expansion fund (board-designated), including securities and accrued interest receivable......................	$ 1,570,000	$ 1,780,000
Property, plant, and equipment	$11,028,000	$10,375,000

Externally restricted funds for replacement and expansion would, of course, be classified as restricted.

Illustration 24-9 is an activity statement for a hospital. Hospitals prepare this Statement of Revenues and Expenses, which shows in detail only the

---

funds are credited directly to the respective Fund Balance. All subsequent earnings from investments of these resources are also credited to Fund Balance. When the Unrestricted Fund expends resources for the designated purpose, the affected restricted fund charges Fund Balance and credits Cash or an interfund payable. The Unrestricted Fund acknowledges receipt of the transfer by a charge to Cash and a credit to Other Revenue—Transfers.

[25] The following entries would be recorded by the other funds reflecting transfers to the Unrestricted Fund:

Specific Purpose Fund:		
Fund balance	320,000	
Cash		320,000
Plant Renewal and Replacement Fund:		
Fund balance	500,000	
Cash		500,000
Endowment Fund:		
Fund balance	125,000	
Cash		125,000

Illustration 24-8

CHARLESTON MEMORIAL HOSPITAL
Balance Sheet
June 30, 19X1
With Comparative Figures at June 30, 19X0

Assets	19X1	19X0
Unrestricted Funds		
Current:		
Cash	$ 133,000	$ 33,000
Receivables	$ 1,382,000	$ 1,269,000
Less estimated uncollectibles and allowances	(160,000)	(105,000)
	$ 1,222,000	$ 1,164,000
Due from restricted funds	215,000	-0-
Inventories (lower of cost or market)	176,000	183,000
Prepaid expenses	68,000	73,000
Total Current Assets	$ 1,814,000	$ 1,453,000
Other:		
Cash	$ 143,000	$ 40,000
Investments	$ 1,427,000	$ 1,740,000
Property, plant, and equipment	$11,028,000	$10,375,000
Less accumulated depreciation	(3,885,000)	(3,600,000)
Net Property, Plant, and Equipment	$ 7,143,000	$ 6,775,000
Total	$10,527,000	$10,008,000

Liabilities and Fund Balances

	19X1	19X0
Unrestricted Funds		
Current:		
Notes payable to banks	$ 227,000	$ 300,000
Current installments of long-term debt	90,000	90,000
Accounts payable	450,000	463,000
Accrued expenses	150,000	147,000
Advances from third party payers	300,000	200,000
Deferred revenue	10,000	10,000
Total Current Liabilities	$ 1,227,000	$ 1,210,000
Deferred revenue, third party reimbursement	$ 200,000	$ 90,000
Long-term debt:		
Housing bonds	$ 500,000	$ 520,000
Mortgage note	1,200,000	1,270,000
Total Long-term Debt	$ 1,700,000	$ 1,790,000
Fund Balance	$ 7,400,000	$ 6,918,000
	$10,527,000	$10,008,000

activities of the Unrestricted Fund. Restricted Funds flows are included in the Statement of Changes in Fund Balances, which is linked with the revenue and expense statement. In addition, a Statement of Changes in Financial Position is prepared for the Unrestricted Fund.

VOLUNTARY HEALTH AND WELFARE ORGANIZATIONS

Voluntary health and welfare organizations provide a broad scope of public services in the areas of health, social welfare, and community services. Their principal sources of revenue are public contributions and government

Illustration 24-8 (continued)

Assets	19X1	19X0
Restricted Funds		
Specific Purpose Funds:		
Cash..	$ 1,260	$ 1,000
Investments......................................	200,000	70,000
Grants receivable...................................	90,000	-0-
Total Specific Purpose Funds......................	$ 291,260	$ 71,000
Plant Replacement and Expansion Funds:		
Cash..	$ 10,000	$ 450,000
Investments......................................	800,000	290,000
Pledges receivable, net of estimated uncollectibles......	20,000	360,000
Total Plant Replacement and Expansion Funds.......	$ 830,000	$1,100,000
Endowment Funds:		
Cash..	$ 50,000	$ 33,000
Investments......................................	6,100,000	3,942,000
Total Endowment Funds	$6,150,000	$3,975,000
Liabilities and Fund Balances		
Restricted Funds		
Specific Purpose Funds:		
Due to unrestricted funds.............................	$ 215,000	$ -0-
Fund Balances:		
Research grants....................................	$ 15,000	$ 30,000
Other...	61,260	41,000
	$ 76,260	$ 71,000
Total Specific Purpose Funds......................	$ 291,260	$ 71,000
Plant Replacement and Expansion Funds:		
Fund Balances:		
Restricted by third party payers	$ 380,000	$ 150,000
Other...	450,000	950,000
Total Plant Replacement and Expansion Funds.......	$ 830,000	$1,100,000
Endowment Funds:		
Fund Balances:		
Permanent endowment.............................	$4,850,000	$2,675,000
Term endowment..................................	1,300,000	1,300,000
Total Endowment Funds	$6,150,000	$3,975,000

Source: Adapted from *Hospital Audit Guide*, 4th ed., Exhibit A, p. 40. Copyright © 1982 by the American Institute of Certified Public Accountants, Inc.

grants. These organizations generally use five of the seven fund types discussed earlier—Current Unrestricted Fund; Current Restricted Fund; Land, Building, and Equipment Fund; Endowment Fund; and Agency Funds.

Investments in plant and unexpended donor-restricted resources for fixed assets are accounted for in a restricted Land, Building, and Equipment Fund. Depending on the procedures followed by the organization, the fixed assets may be carried in the Current Unrestricted Fund.

Illustration 24-10 is a complete balance sheet for a voluntary health and welfare organization. This balance sheet closely resembles that of colleges and universities and certain other nonprofit organizations. It is perhaps interesting to note that the balance sheet includes the designations of

Illustration 24-9

CHARLESTON MEMORIAL HOSPITAL		
Statement of Revenues and Expenses		
For the Year Ended December 31, 19X4		
With Comparative Figures for 19X3		
	19X4	**19X3**
Patient Service Revenues..............................	$8,500,000	$8,000,000
Less—Allowances and uncollectible accounts	(1,777,000)	(1,700,000)
Net Patient Service Revenues........................	$6,723,000	$6,300,000
Other Operating Revenue (including $100,000 and		
$80,000 from specific purpose funds)	184,000	173,000
Total Operating Revenues	$6,907,000	$6,473,000
Operating Expenses:		
Nursing services	$2,200,000	$2,000,000
Other professional services	1,900,000	1,700,000
General services.....................................	2,100,000	2,000,000
Fiscal services.......................................	375,000	360,000
Administrative services	350,000	335,000
Interest expense	50,000	40,000
Depreciation expense	300,000	250,000
Total Operating Expenses	$7,275,000	$6,685,000
Loss from Operations	$ (368,000)	$ (212,000)
Nonoperating Revenues:		
Unrestricted gifts and bequests.......................	$ 228,000	$ 205,000
Unrestricted income from endowment funds	170,000	80,000
Income and gains from board-designated funds	54,000	41,000
Total Nonoperating Revenues	$ 452,000	$ 326,000
Excess of Revenues over Expenses	$ 84,000	$ 114,000

Source: Adapted from *Hospital Audit Guide,* 4th ed., Exhibit B, p. 42. Copyright © 1982 by the American Institute of Certified Public Accountants, Inc.

board-restricted fund equities. Of course, this would be more fully disclosed in the notes to the financial statements.

Voluntary health and welfare organizations must prepare two activity statements. The Statement of Support, Revenue, Expenses, and Changes in Fund Balances (Illustration 24-11, pages 950–51) is like the activity statement prepared by colleges and universities with some important differences. First, the voluntary health and welfare statement uses the term **support** to designate charitable contributions and gifts. Thus, revenue represents amounts earned by the organization. Second, the voluntary health and welfare statement shows expenses segregated by program and by supporting services. The latter discloses the organization's management and fund-raising costs. The second activity statement for voluntary health and welfare organizations (Illustration 24-12, page 952) simply presents an analysis of program and supporting service costs by natural expense classification.

Voluntary health and welfare organizations obtain most of their resources from contributions. They also receive substantial amounts of donated services. Often large amounts of money are invested in various types of securities.

Contributions, donated services, and investments also pertain to colleges and universities, hospitals, and other miscellaneous nonprofit organizations included in *Statement of Position 78-10,* but generally to a much lesser extent. Accordingly, we discuss these important topics in a comparative context that includes all nonprofit organizations. Before doing so, however, we discuss briefly the financial statements used by other miscellaneous nonprofit organizations included in *Statement of Position 78-10.*

OTHER MISCELLANEOUS NONPROFIT ORGANIZATIONS

Other miscellaneous nonprofit organizations included in *Statement of Position 78-10* use the same financial statements used by voluntary health and welfare organizations, with the following exceptions:

(1) The Statement of Functional Expenses (shown in Illustration 24-12) is not appropriate and is **not used.**
(2) When the organization does not receive support, the activity statement is more appropriately called a Statement of Revenues, Expenses, and Changes in Fund Balance. (The word "support" is deleted.)

ACCOUNTING FOR CONTRIBUTIONS, DONATED SERVICES, AND INVESTMENTS (ALL NONPROFIT ORGANIZATIONS)

Accounting for unrestricted contributions

As shown in Illustration 24-13 (pages 954–55), unrestricted contributions of cash, gifts, grants, bequests, and endowment income are usually recognized when received. If the contribution applies to a future period, amounts should be credited to a Deferred Revenue account.

Pledges represent a primary source of income for many nonprofit organizations. Through the use of the installment method—small amounts committed over an extended period—organizations benefit by increased contributions over the long run.

Pledges that will likely be collected should be recorded as assets and valued at their net realizable value. Given past experience, many nonprofit organizations can predict collectible portions of pledges with considerable accuracy. Colleges and universities may account for pledges at their net realizable value, with appropriate credits to unrestricted revenues, deferred income, current restricted funds, plant funds, and so on, or they may disclose the total number of time periods over which the pledges are collected and related restrictions, if any, in footnotes to the financial statements.

Illustration:
Pledge disclosure and accounting for a pledge
collected over several years

Pledge revenue should be recognized in the year in which the pledge or installment of the pledge is received. The donor's intention determines its future accounting. For example, beginning this year, several donors have

Illustration 24-10

<table>
<tr><th colspan="3">THE CAPISTRANO FOUNDATION
Balance Sheets (All Funds)
December 31, 19X2 and 19X1</th></tr>
<tr><th>Assets</th><th>19X2</th><th>19X1</th></tr>
<tr><td colspan="3">**Current Fund—Unrestricted**</td></tr>
<tr><td>Cash</td><td>$2,207,000</td><td>$2,530,000</td></tr>
<tr><td>Investments:</td><td></td><td></td></tr>
<tr><td>For long-term purposes</td><td>2,727,000</td><td>2,245,000</td></tr>
<tr><td>Other</td><td>1,075,000</td><td>950,000</td></tr>
<tr><td>Pledges receivable less allowance for uncollectibles</td><td>475,000</td><td>363,000</td></tr>
<tr><td>Inventories of educational materials, at cost</td><td>70,000</td><td>61,000</td></tr>
<tr><td>Accrued interest, other receivables, and prepaid expenses</td><td>286,000</td><td>186,000</td></tr>
<tr><td>Total</td><td>$6,840,000</td><td>$6,335,000</td></tr>
<tr><th colspan="3">Liabilities and Fund Balances</th></tr>
<tr><td>Accounts payable</td><td>$ 148,000</td><td>$ 139,000</td></tr>
<tr><td>Research grants payable</td><td>596,000</td><td>616,000</td></tr>
<tr><td>Contributions designated for future periods</td><td>245,000</td><td>219,000</td></tr>
<tr><td></td><td>$ 989,000</td><td>$ 974,000</td></tr>
<tr><td>Fund Balances:</td><td></td><td></td></tr>
<tr><td>Designated by the governing board for:</td><td></td><td></td></tr>
<tr><td>Long-term investments</td><td>$2,800,000</td><td>$2,300,000</td></tr>
<tr><td>Purchases of equipment</td><td>100,000</td><td>-0-</td></tr>
<tr><td>Research purposes</td><td>1,152,000</td><td>1,748,000</td></tr>
<tr><td>Undesignated, available for general activities</td><td>1,799,000</td><td>1,313,000</td></tr>
<tr><td></td><td>$5,851,000</td><td>$5,361,000</td></tr>
<tr><td>Total</td><td>$6,840,000</td><td>$6,335,000</td></tr>
<tr><th colspan="3">Assets</th></tr>
<tr><td colspan="3">**Current Fund—Restricted**</td></tr>
<tr><td>Cash</td><td>$ 3,000</td><td>$ 5,000</td></tr>
<tr><td>Investments</td><td>71,000</td><td>72,000</td></tr>
<tr><td>Grants receivable</td><td>58,000</td><td>46,000</td></tr>
<tr><td></td><td>$ 132,000</td><td>$ 123,000</td></tr>
<tr><th colspan="3">Liabilities and Fund Balances</th></tr>
<tr><td>Fund Balances:</td><td></td><td></td></tr>
<tr><td>Professional education</td><td>$ 84,000</td><td>$ -0-</td></tr>
<tr><td>Research grants</td><td>48,000</td><td>123,000</td></tr>
<tr><td></td><td>$ 132,000</td><td>$ 123,000</td></tr>
</table>

agreed to give a total of $25,000 a year for four years for normal operating expenses. Therefore, only $25,000 should be recorded as revenue in the current year, as shown in the following entry:

```
Pledges receivable .....................................  100,000
    Allowance for uncollectible pledges .................          5,000
    Pledge revenue.....................................          25,000
    Deferred pledge revenue ...........................          70,000
```

In subsequent years, the following entries would be posted.

Illustration 24-10 (continued)

Assets	19X2	19X1
Land, Building, and Equipment Fund:		
Cash	$ 3,000	$ 2,000
Investments	177,000	145,000
Pledges receivable less allowance for uncollectibles	32,000	25,000
Land, buildings and equipment, at cost less accumulated		
depreciation of $296,000 and $262,000	516,000	513,000
Total	$ 728,000	$ 685,000
Liabilities and Fund Balances		
Mortgage payable, 10% due in 19XX	$ 32,000	$ 36,000
Fund Balances:		
Expended	$ 484,000	$ 477,000
Unexpended—restricted	212,000	172,000
	$ 696,000	$ 649,000
Total	$ 728,000	$ 685,000
Assets		
Endowment Fund:		
Cash	$ 4,000	$ 10,000
Investments	1,944,000	2,007,000
	$1,948,000	$2,017,000
Liabilities and Fund Balances		
Fund Balance	$1,948,000	$2,017,000
	$1,948,000	$2,017,000

Source: Adapted from the *Audits of Voluntary Health and Welfare Organizations,* Exhibit C, pp. 46–47. Copyright © 1974 by the American Institute of Certified Public Accountants, Inc.

Cash	25,000	
Pledges receivable		25,000
Deferred pledge revenue	23,333	
Pledge revenue		23,333

Of course, if the amounts are material, the provisions of *APB Opinion 21* concerning the valuation of the pledge receivable would apply.

Accounting for donated services

Donated services represent a significant resource used to carry on many nonprofit organizations' activities. However, accounting recognition is seldom given to the imputed value of these services. The principal problem is measuring their value. *Statement of Position 78-10* suggests that donated services should be reported as an expense (and, of course, as revenue) when all the following circumstances exist:

(1) The services performed are significant and essential to the organization and would be performed by salaried personnel if volunteers were not available, and the organization would continue this program or activity if volunteers were not available.

(2) The organization controls the employment and duties of the donors of

Illustration 24-11

THE CAPISTRANO FOUNDATION
Statement of Support, Revenue, Expenses, and Changes in Fund Balances
For the Year Ended December 31, 19X2
With Comparative Totals for 19X1

	Current Funds		Land, Building, and Equipment Fund	Endowment Fund	Total (All Funds)	
	Unrestricted	Restricted			19X2	19X1
Public Support and Revenue:						
Public support:						
Contributions (net of estimated uncollectible pledges of $95,000 in 19X2 and $80,000 in 19X1)	$3,764,000	$162,000		$ 2,000	$3,928,000	$3,976,000
Contributions to building fund			$ 72,000		72,000	150,000
Special events (net of direct costs of $81,000 in 19X2 and $73,000 in 19X1)	104,000				104,000	92,000
Legacies and bequests	92,000			4,000	96,000	129,000
Received from federated and nonfederated campaign (which incurred related fund-raising expenses of $38,000 in 19X2 and $29,000 in 19X1)	275,000				275,000	308,000
Total Public Support	$4,235,000	$162,000	$ 72,000	$ 6,000	$4,475,000	$4,655,000
Revenue:						
Membership dues	$ 17,000				$ 17,000	$ 12,000
Investment income	98,000	$ 10,000			108,000	94,000
Realized gain on investment transactions	200,000			$ 25,000	225,000	275,000
Miscellaneous	42,000				42,000	47,000
Total revenue	$ 357,000	$ 10,000		$ 25,000	$ 392,000	$ 428,000
Total Public Support and Revenue	$4,592,000	$172,000	$ 72,000	$ 31,000	$4,867,000	$5,083,000

Expenses:

Program services:						
Research	$1,257,000	$155,000	$ 2,000		$1,414,000	$1,365,000
Public health education	539,000		5,000		544,000	485,000
Professional education and training	612,000		6,000		618,000	516,000
Community services	568,000		10,000		578,000	486,000
Total Program Services	$2,976,000	$155,000	$ 23,000	$ -0-	$3,154,000	$2,852,000
Supporting services:						
Management and general	$ 567,000		$ 7,000		$ 574,000	$ 638,000
Fund raising	642,000		12,000		654,000	546,000
Total Supporting Services	$1,209,000		$ 19,000	$ -0-	$1,228,000	$1,184,000
Total Expenses	$4,185,000	$155,000	$ 42,000	$ -0-	$4,382,000	$4,036,000
Excess (Deficiency) of Public Support and Revenue over Expenses	$ 407,000	$ 17,000	$ 30,000	$ 31,000		
Other Changes in Fund Balances:						
Property and equipment acquisitions from unrestricted funds	(17,000)		17,000			
Transfer of realized endowment fund appreciation	100,000			(100,000)		
Returned to donor		(8,000)				
Fund Balances, Beginning of Year	5,361,000	123,000	649,000	2,017,000		
Fund Balances, End of Year	$5,851,000	$132,000	$696,000	$1,948,000		

Source: Adapted from *Audits of Voluntary Health and Welfare Organizations*, Exhibit A, pp. 42–43. Copyright © 1974 by the American Institute of Certified Public Accountants, Inc.

Illustration 24-12

THE CAPISTRANO FOUNDATION
Statement of Functional Expenses
For the Year Ended December 31, 19X2
With Comparative Totals for 19X1

	Program Services					Supporting Services			Total Expenses	
	Research	Public Health Ed'cn	Prof. Ed'cn & Training	Community Services	Total	Mgmt. and Gen'l	Fund Raising	Total	19X2	19X1
Salaries	$ 45,000	$291,000	$251,000	$269,000	$ 856,000	$331,000	$368,000	$ 699,000	$1,555,000	$1,433,000
Employee health and retirement benefits	4,000	14,000	14,000	14,000	46,000	22,000	15,000	37,000	83,000	75,000
Payroll taxes, etc.	2,000	16,000	13,000	14,000	45,000	18,000	18,000	36,000	81,000	75,000
Total Salaries and related Expenses	$ 51,000	$321,000	$278,000	$297,000	$ 947,000	$371,000	$401,000	$ 772,000	$1,719,000	$1,583,000
Professional fees	$ 1,000	$ 10,000	$ 3,000	$ 8,000	$ 22,000	$ 26,000	$ 8,000	$ 34,000	$ 56,000	$ 53,000
Supplies	2,000	13,000	13,000	13,000	41,000	18,000	17,000	35,000	76,000	71,000
Telephone and telegraph	2,000	13,000	10,000	11,000	36,000	15,000	23,000	38,000	74,000	68,000
Postage and shipping	2,000	17,000	13,000	9,000	41,000	13,000	30,000	43,000	84,000	80,000
Occupancy	5,000	26,000	22,000	25,000	78,000	30,000	27,000	57,000	135,000	126,000
Equipment rental	1,000	24,000	14,000	4,000	43,000	3,000	16,000	19,000	62,000	58,000
Local transportation	3,000	22,000	20,000	22,000	67,000	23,000	30,000	53,000	120,000	113,000
Conferences and conventions	8,000	19,000	71,000	20,000	118,000	38,000	13,000	51,000	169,000	156,000
Printing and publications	4,000	56,000	43,000	11,000	114,000	14,000	64,000	78,000	192,000	184,000
Awards and grants	1,332,000	14,000	119,000	144,000	1,609,000				1,609,000	1,448,000
Miscellaneous	1,000	4,000	6,000	4,000	15,000	16,000	21,000	37,000	52,000	64,000
Total Expenses before Depreciation	$1,412,000	$539,000	$612,000	$568,000	$3,131,000	$567,000	$650,000	$1,217,000	$4,348,000	$4,004,000
Depreciation of buildings and equipment	2,000	5,000	6,000	10,000	23,000	7,000	4,000	11,000	34,000	32,000
Total Expenses	$1,414,000	$544,000	$618,000	$578,000	$3,154,000	$574,000	$654,000	$1,228,000	$4,382,000	$4,036,000

Source: Adapted from *Audits of Voluntary Health and Welfare Organizations*, Exhibit B, pp. 44–45. Copyright © 1974 by the American Institute of Certified Public Accountants, Inc.

the services. The organization can influence the activities of the volunteers (including control over the volunteers' time, location, duties, and performance) in a way comparable to the control it would exercise over employees with similar responsibilities.

(3) The organization has a clearly measurable basis for the amount to be recorded.

(4) The program services of the reporting organization are not principally intended for the benefit of the organization's members.[26]

Essentially, an employee–employer relationship must exist, and objective measurement or valuation of the services must be possible. These circumstances are most often met only by organizations operated by religious groups. In such cases, the value of the services is determined by subtracting the amounts paid to or on behalf of the religious personnel from the amount of compensation that would be paid to lay persons.

Illustration:
Accounting for donated services

The value of the unpaid teaching services of the sisters at St. Theresa School was $900,000 for the year. The following entry would be posted:

```
Contributed services (expenses) ........................ 900,000
    Contributed services (support and revenue) ..........          900,000
```

The following disclosure would be made in the footnotes to the financial statements:

> Support arising from contributed services of certain religious personnel have been recognized in the accompanying financial statements. The computation of the value of the contribution of those services represents the difference between the stipends and other amounts paid to or on behalf of the religious personnel and the comparable compensation that would be paid to lay persons if lay persons occupied those positions. No computation is made for positions that can only be held by religious personnel.

Of course, there is no net effect on the operating excess because the amount recorded as expense is offset by an equal amount of revenue. The disclosure, however, has enhanced the comparability of the financial statements, especially when an organization that relies significantly on donated services is compared with another organization that pays market prices for the same services.

Accounting for restricted contributions

Accounting practice for the recognition of restricted contributions is not uniform. In fact, it varies considerably among the four groups of nonprofit organizations discussed in this chapter.

---

[26] *Statement of Position 78-10*, "Accounting Principles and Reporting Practices for Certain Nonprofit Organizations" (New York: AICPA, 1978), p. 23.

Illustration 24-13
Accounting recognition of donated items

	Accounting Treatment			
Donated Item	Colleges and Universities	Voluntary Health and Welfare Organizations	Hospitals	Other Nonprofit Organizations
Unrestricted:				
Cash, gifts, grants, bequests, endowment fund income	Unrestricted current fund revenue (marketable securities may be carried at market value)	Current fund unrestricted support revenue (marketable securities may be carried at market value)	Unrestricted nonoperating revenue	Unrestricted current fund revenue and support (marketable securities should be carried at market value)
Personal services[a]				
Pledges[b]	May be disclosed in notes to the financial statements or as unrestricted current fund revenue			If period designated by donor extends beyond the balance sheet date, should be deferred support or deferred revenue
Supplies, materials, facilities, etc.	Unrestricted current fund revenue		Unrestricted operating revenue	Unrestricted current fund revenue; record at fair value; facilities should be in revenue and expense
Plant, property, and equipment	Plant fund balance (not revenue)	Land, building, and equipment fund support revenue	Unrestricted fund balance (not revenue)	Plant fund; considered capital addition and not support and revenue
Restricted:				
Cash, gifts, bequests, endowment fund, personal services, pledges	Appropriate restricted fund balance; if expended for operating purposes, transfer at time of expenditure to	Current fund restricted support revenue	Appropriate restricted fund balance; when restriction is met or lapses, unrestricted nonoperating revenue	Restricted current fund; revenue and support to the extent that expenses are incurred for the purpose specified by the

Funds restricted to acquisition of supplies, materials, etc.	current restricted fund revenue. Pledges may be disclosed in footnote and accounted for when received		Specific purpose restricted fund balance; when restriction is met, unrestricted operating revenue	donor or grant during the period; deferred revenue or support until restrictions are met
Funds restricted to acquisition of property, plant, and equipment	Restricted plant fund balance; originally, to unexpended plant fund balance; when expended, transfer to investment in plant fund balance	Land, building, and equipment fund restricted support revenue	Plant replacement and expansion. Restricted fund balance; when restriction is met, transfer directly to unrestricted fund balance	Capital additions that are restricted for acquisition of plant assets should be treated as deferred capital support in the balance sheet until they are used for the indicated purpose. Once used, the amounts should be reported as capital additions in the statement of activity
Endowments	Endowment fund balance; when term endowments lapse, if unrestricted, recognize as unrestricted current fund revenue	Endowment fund restricted support revenue	Endowment restricted fund balance; when term endowments lapse, report as nonoperating revenue if unrestricted	

[a] Employer–employee relationship is necessary for formal accounting recognition. This relationship is usually found only in religious groups.
[b] If applicable to future periods, deferred revenue may be credited.
Source: William W. Holder, "Revenue Recognition in Not-for-Profit Organizations," *The CPA*, November 1976, p. 18.

One approach, currently used only by voluntary health and welfare organizations, permits the recognition of revenue immediately upon receipt of a restricted contribution. The recognition of revenue is required without regard to whether the contribution had been used or the restrictions met. Of course, a contribution specified by the donor for use in a future period is recorded as deferred revenue. This approach implies that the critical event for revenue recognition is the donation and not the expenditure.

Hospitals and colleges and universities do not recognize revenue at the date of receipt; rather, the contribution is credited to an appropriate Fund Balance account. When the restrictions are met or lapse, the amount is transferred to unrestricted nonoperating revenue for hospitals and to current restricted fund revenue for colleges and universities. The legal rationale for this approach is that revenue is not earned until the restriction imposed by the donor has been met.

All other nonprofit organizations use a third approach whereby revenue is recognized upon expenditure of restricted *or* unrestricted funds, and unexpended amounts are credited to deferred revenue and not to a Fund Balance account. *Statement of Position 78-10* states:

> If a donor restricted a contribution . . . to be used for a specific program service, and the organization subsequently . . . incurred expenses for that particular program service, the . . . obligation imposed by the restriction should be deemed to have been met even if unrestricted funds were used. Management should not avoid recognizing the restricted contribution as support in that period simply because it chose to use dollars attributed to unrestricted funds at the time the expense was incurred . . .
>
> . . . current restricted gifts, grants, bequests, and other income should be accounted for as revenue and support in the statement of activity to the extent that expenses have been incurred for the purpose specified by the donor or grantor during the period. The balances should be accounted for as deferred revenue or support in the balance sheet outside the fund balance section until the restrictions are met.[27]

Accounting for investments

Investments in debt and equity securities represent a significant portion of total resources for many nonprofit organizations. Within these organizations, most investments are held by the unexpended plant funds, endowment funds, annuity funds, and life income funds.

Valuation. The audit guides and *Statement of Position 78-10* provide a variety of possible methods for valuing equity and debt securities. Colleges and universities generally report their investments at cost, with market values scheduled in the notes to the financial statements. The investments may be reported at current market values, however, provided the same method is used for all investments of all funds.

Most hospitals carried their investments at cost with market prices noted in the financial statements. In 1978, *Statement of Position 78-1* on accounting by hospitals for certain marketable equity securities was issued by the

---

[27] *Statement of Position 78-10,* paragraphs 60 and 62. Copyright © 1978 by the American Institute of Certified Public Accountants, Inc.

Accounting Standards Division of the AICPA. *Statement of Position 78-1* amends the *Hospital Audit Guide* to recommend that nonprofit hospitals apply the provisions of *FASB Statement No. 12,* which states that marketable securities should be carried at the lower of aggregate cost or market. The American Hospital Association recommends that investments be carried at their current market values, thereby providing for the recognition of holding gains and losses. Such a treatment does not conform with current generally accepted accounting principles.

Voluntary health and welfare organizations may carry their investments at cost or market. *Statement of Position 78-10* for other nonprofit organizations sets forth the following valuation rules:

> (1) Marketable debt securities, when there is both the ability and intention to hold the securities to maturity, should be reported at amortized cost, market value, or the lower of amortized cost or market value;
> (2) Marketable equity securities and marketable debt securities that are not expected to be held to maturity should be reported at either market value or the lower of cost or market value.[28]

Of course, when using the market value method for investments, unrealized gains or losses should be reported in the same way that realized gains and losses are reported using the cost method.

Interfund sales.   Transfers of investments between funds occur when restrictions lapse or when the assets are sold by the receiving fund. In these cases, the investments should be transferred at their fair market values, and gains or losses should accrue to the fund making the transfer. The market value is the basis for the fund receiving the investments.

Investment pools.   Nonprofit organizations frequently pool the investments of their various funds. Pooling provides several advantages, including increased investment flexibility, enhanced protection of fund principal through broad diversification, and, in some cases, lower investment costs.

Nonprofit organizations commonly use both pooled and nonpooled investments. Provisions in a gift instrument may prohibit participation in pooled investment schemes. In some instances, several pools are used so that different investment objectives may be accommodated. For example, certain endowment funds may be invested in one investment pool to obtain a high rate of investment income and protection of principal. Other funds could be placed in investment pools with a goal of capital appreciation.

Implementation of investment pooling requires careful attention to an accounting system that ensures equitable determination of principal, allocation of realized and unrealized gains or losses, and income. The method most generally in use and one specified in the audit guides and *Statement of Position 78-10* is the **market value unit method.**

The market value unit method assigns to individual participating funds units in the investment pool. The number of units assigned to a participating

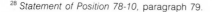

Basic Example for almost any kind of Investment Trust.

---

[28] *Statement of Position 78-10,* paragraph 79.

fund is calculated on the basis of the market value of the total assets of the pool when the specific fund enters the pool. This method is similar to the method used with open-end investment trusts or mutual funds.

Illustration: Investment pool transactions.

(1) Four funds of Andover University form an investment pool and contribute cash as shown in the following schedule:

Quasi-endowment fund	$ 20,000
Endowment fund	30,000
Unrestricted fund	40,000
Plant fund group	10,000
	$100,000

An arbitrarily determined value per unit is selected. Subsequently, value per unit is determined by dividing the current market value of all net assets in the investment pool by the number of outstanding units.

Fund	Unit Value	Units	Market Value
Quasi-endowment fund	$10	2,000	$ 20,000
Endowment fund	10	3,000	30,000
Unrestricted fund	10	4,000	40,000
Plant fund group	10	1,000	10,000
		10,000	$100,000

(2) During the first quarter, the board of trustees authorizes the withdrawal of $10,000 of the quasi-endowment fund's investment in the pool. Calculation of the number of units withdrawn is as follows:

$$\text{Units Withdrawn} = \frac{\text{Amount Withdrawn}}{\text{Market Value per Unit}} = \frac{\$10,000}{\$10} = 1,000 \text{ units}$$

Market value per unit is from the previous valuation date. After the withdrawal, the investment pool contains the following funds:

Fund	Unit Value	Units	Market Value
Quasi-endowment fund	$10	1,000	$10,000
Endowment fund	10	3,000	30,000
Unrestricted fund	10	4,000	40,000
Plant fund group	10	1,000	10,000
		9,000	$90,000

The following funds made additional investments to the investment pool during the second quarter.

Plant fund group	$15,000
Life income funds group	30,000

The value per unit of funds currently in the investment pool is calculated as follows:

$$\text{Market Value per Unit} = \frac{\text{Total Market Value}}{\text{Units Outstanding}} = \frac{\$108{,}000}{9{,}000} = \$12$$

The units allocated to each additional investment are determined by dividing the amount of each additional investment by the corresponding current unit value:

Fund	Addition	Units
Plant funds group	$15,000	1,250
Life income funds group	30,000	2,500

Immediately after this transaction, the fund includes the following:

Fund	Unit Value	Units	Market Value
Quasi-endowment fund	$12	1,000	$ 12,000
Endowment fund	12	3,000	36,000
Unrestricted fund	12	4,000	48,000
Plant fund group	12	2,250	27,000
Life income funds group	12	2,500	30,000
		12,750	$153,000

Income distributions, including gains or losses on sales of investments, is allocated by dividing the total income available by the total units.

SUMMARY

Accounting and reporting practices among nonprofit organizations are not uniform. This situation is generally explained by the diversity of their objectives and the manner in which accounting principles for these units have been developed.

Operating funds

Fund accounting is used by all nonprofit organizations, but the framework of the funds differs among them. All nonprofit organizations use a fund or fund group for operations, similar to the General Fund of governmental units. However, the structure and content of operating funds varies between them.

Accounting for land, building, and equipment

Colleges and universities as well as voluntary health and welfare organizations use separate funds to account for land, buildings, and equipment and other capital assets because such assets are not considered part of the current operating funds. (For colleges and universities, both expended and unexpended resources are accounted for within the Plant Funds Group.)

In contrast, accounting for hospitals and the nonprofit organizations included in *Statement of Position 78-10* is different. These organizations account for property, plant, and equipment and related liabilities as part of unrestricted funds. (Donor-restricted resources held by hospitals for future investments in fixed assets are accounted for in a restricted fund.) In some cases, however, it may be more appropriate for the nonprofit organizations included in *Statement of Position 78-10* to account for property, plant, and equipment and related liabilities in a restricted fund.

Valuation of land, buildings, and equipment

Plant asset acquisition accounting is the same for all nonprofit organizations. Plant assets are recorded at cost, and donated assets are recorded at their estimated fair market values at the date of the gift. Museums, art galleries, botanical gardens, libraries, and similar entities have inexhaustible collections, the values of which probably represent the most significant assets of the organization. However, it is often impractical to assign any value, cost, or estimated fair market value to these collections. In these cases, the plant assets need not be capitalized, and the caption "collections" must appear on the balance sheet with a reference to a note that describes the collections.

Depreciation

Generally, nonprofit organizations depreciate exhaustible fixed assets. The mechanics of depreciation and its presentation in the financial statements are similar to those used for business enterprises. However, colleges and universities do not depreciate exhaustible fixed assets.

Accounting for unrestricted and restricted contributions

In most cases, unrestricted contributions of cash, gifts, grants, bequests, and endowment income are recognized when received. If the contribution applies to a future period, amounts should be credited to a Deferred Revenue account. Accounting recognition is seldom given to the imputed value of donated services. *Statement of Position 78-10* outlines conditions that essentially require an employer–employee relationship and objective measurement of the services before accounting recognition is given to donated services. Accounting practice for the recognition of restricted contributions is also not uniform. In fact, it varies considerably among the four groups of nonprofit organizations.

Very little difference exists in structure and content of Endowment Funds, Agency Funds, Annuity Funds, Life Income Funds, and Loan Funds. Colleges and universities show the greatest differences when compared with all other nonprofit organizations. For example, colleges and universities include trustee-designated funds in the Endowment Funds Group; hence, the fund title Endowments and Similar Funds. The Endowment Funds of the other nonprofit organizations include only externally restricted funds.

Illustration 24-14
Summary of required financial statements

	Colleges and Universities	Hospitals	Health and Welfare	All Other
Balance sheet	X	X	X	X
Statement of Activity:				
Statement of Current Funds, Revenues, Expenditures, and Other Changes ...	X			
Statement of Revenues and Expenses		X[a]		
Statement of Support, Revenue, Expenses, and Changes in Fund Balances			X	X[c]
Statement of Functional Expenses			X	
Statement of Changes in Financial Position		X[a]		X
Statement of Changes in Fund Balances		X[b]		

[a] Unrestricted funds only.
[b] Unrestricted funds and restricted funds.
[c] If no "support" is received, delete "Support" from the title.

Financial statements

Illustration 24-14 summarizes the required financial statements for the four types of nonprofit organizations in this chapter.

Glossary of new terms

Agency Fund: Funds received and held by an organization as fiscal agent for others.[29]

Annuity Fund: A fund that includes gifts of money or other property given to an organization on the condition that the organization bind itself to make periodic stipulated payments that terminate at a specified time to the donor or other designated individuals.

Deferred Revenue and Support: Revenue or support received or recorded before it is earned, that is, before the conditions are met, in whole or in part, for which the revenue or support is received or is to be received.[29]

Endowment Funds: The fund in which a donor has stipulated in the donative instrument that the principal is to be maintained inviolate and in perpetuity and only the income from the investments of the fund may be expended.[29]

Expendable Funds: Funds that are available to finance an organization's program and supporting services, including both unrestricted and restricted amounts.[29]

Fund: An accounting entity established for the purpose of accounting for resources used for specific activities or objectives in accordance with special regulations, restrictions, or limitations.[29]

[29] Definitions taken directly from *Statement of Position 78-10.*

Fund Group: A group of funds of similar character, for example, operating funds, endowment funds, annuity funds, and life income funds.[29]

Investment Pool: Assets of several funds pooled or consolidated for investment purposes.[29]

Loan Funds: Resources restricted for loans. When both principal and interest on the loan funds received by an organization are loanable, they are included in the loan fund group. If only the income from a fund is loanable, the principal is included in endowment funds, while the cumulative income constitutes the loan fund.[29]

Market Value Unit Method: A method of allocating realized and unrealized gains (or losses) and income to participating funds in an investment pool.

Pledge: A promise to make a contribution to an organization in the amount and form stipulated.[29]

Quasi-endowment Funds: Funds that the governing board of an organization, rather than a donor or other outside agency, has determined are to be retained and invested. The governing board has the right to decide at any time to expend the principal of such funds.[29] Also called designated funds.

Renewal and Replacement Funds: A fund within the Plant Fund group of colleges and universities that represents unexpended resources held for renewal and replacement of plant assets.

Resource Transferability: The nonprofit organization's freedom to use resources for various purposes.

Restricted Funds: Funds for which use is restricted by outside agencies or persons as contrasted with funds over which the organization has complete control and discretion.[29]

Revenues: Gross increases in assets, gross decreases in liabilities, or a combination of both from delivering or producing goods, rendering services, or other earning activities of an organization during a period, for example, dues, sale of services, ticket sales, fees, interest, dividends, and rent.[29]

Support: The conveyance of property from one person or organization to another without consideration, for example, donations, gifts, grants, or bequests.[29]

Term Endowment: A fund that has all the characteristics of an endowment fund, except that at some future date or event, it will no longer be required to be maintained as an endowment fund.[29]

Unexpended Plant Fund: A fund within the Plant Fund group of colleges and universities that represents unexpended resources for the acquisition of plant assets.

Unrestricted Funds: Funds that have no external restrictions on their use or purpose—that is, funds that can be used for any purpose designated by the governing board, distinguished from funds restricted externally for specific purposes (for example, for operations, plant, or endowment).[29]

Review questions

1. Compare the objectives of nonprofit organizations with those of business organizations.

[29] Definitions taken directly from *Statement of Position 78-10*.

2. Discuss why nonprofit organizations place greater emphasis on the nature of resource inflows and the degree of resource transferability.
3. Financial statements of nonprofit organizations distinguish between restricted and unrestricted funds. Why is this separation important?
4. Many nonprofit organizations recognize depreciation expense even though income is not a stated objective. What are some arguments in support of this practice?
5. Argue against the recognition of depreciation for nonprofit organizations.
6. How do nonprofit organizations account for pledges?
7. Compare the accounting and reporting of fixed assets by hospitals and colleges and universities.
8. Explain why contributed services are generally not given accounting recognition.
9. Describe how accounting for quasi-endowments differs among the various nonprofit organizations.
10. What common characteristics are shared by governmental units and the nonprofit organizations discussed in this chapter?
11. Outline the historical development of generally accepted accounting principles for nonprofit organizations.
12. Identify the differences in the content of current operating funds that exist among the various nonprofit organizations.
13. Describe the differences in accounting for restricted revenue among colleges, hospitals, voluntary health and welfare organizations, and other nonprofit organizations.
14. Why do voluntary health and welfare organizations use a financial statement that discloses their functional expenses?

Discussion cases

Discussion case 24–1
Defining user needs and meaningful financial statements

The Stecca Foundation is a nonprofit health and welfare organization concerned with public nutrition. Its program services include research, public education, and professional education and training.

The governing board has asked certain public accounting firms to submit proposals to review the foundation's accounting system—including its internal controls—and to perform an audit of its financial statements for the current year. The organization has never been audited. The governing board is acting in compliance with new state legislation that requires audits of all health and welfare organizations by public accountants.

Your accounting firm is submitting a proposal. In reviewing the foundation's most recent financial statements, you discover that they were prepared on a cash basis and that the activity statement is simply a cash receipts and disbursements statement. The balance sheet discloses only one asset—cash—and a fund balance. The organization owns a significant amount of fixed assets, including a large office building and other real properties.

Required:
Prepare the part of the proposal that sets forth your recommended changes in the organization's financial reporting system. Your recommendations should represent a careful delineation of user needs, internal and external, and how the statements and system should be designed to meet these particular needs.

Discussion case 24–2
Responding to the issue of depreciation expense for a nonprofit organization

The board of the Stecca Foundation has reviewed your proposals concerning the organization's financial reporting system and has asked you to expand on certain proposal recommendations.

The recommendation that generated the most concern from the board members concerned the accounting for depreciation expense. Arguments centered on the belief that income is not an objective and no causal relationship exists between depreciation and revenue.

Required:
Defend your recommendation that depreciation expense be recognized in the accounts and included in the financial statements.

Discussion case 24–3
Accounting for donated services

Andersson Medical Services is a voluntary medical service organization that renders limited medical assistance to the elderly residing in several cities in the western United States. The organization receives funding from United Way, other philanthropic organizations, and various government agencies. The medical and lay staff—including doctors, registered nurses, medical technicians, and lay persons who assist the medical staff—are all volunteers.

Peter Karppinen, the organization's director, wishes to consult with you concerning the possible inclusion of the value of donated services in his organization's financial statements. Apparently, his current accountant feels that "it simply cannot be done."

During the conversation, Karppinen develops several points that he believes represent sufficient support for including donated services in the financial statements. First, he argues that the fair value of the services of the doctors, nurses, and medical technicians is readily determinable. Second, the inclusion of the donated services would show more accurately the amount of services rendered to its various programs, which, in his opinion, would assist him in obtaining additional funding, especially from philanthropic organizations. He also argues that the inclusion of the value of donated services may assist him in competing more effectively for matching grants, because he can argue that the organization's matching contribution is the value of its human resources.

Required:
Respond to Peter Karppinen in writing, outlining current accounting practices concerning accounting for donated services and carefully develop the essential rationale for the current accounting practice.

Exercises

Exercise 24–1
Transactions: Current funds group of a university

(1) Student tuition and fees billed were $1,500,000. Prior experience shows that $150,000 will prove uncollectible.
(2) Unrestricted gifts and bequests received during the period amounted to $135,000.
(3) Restricted income from endowment and similar funds amounted to $100,000. The contributions are to be used for student aid.
(4) Collections on accounts receivable were $1,350,000. Accounts receivable of $100,000 were written off.
(5) The university student aid committee granted student tuition and fee reductions of $225,000.
(6) Restricted fund expenditures for student aid amounted to $45,000.
(7) The board of trustees directed the transfer of $125,000 to the Plant Funds Group for the future expansion of the library.

Required:
Prepare journal entries for the above transactions.

Exercise 24–2
Transactions: Unrestricted funds for a hospital

(1) Patient services revenue was billed for the period as follows:

Daily patient services	$3,750,000
Other nursing services	1,500,000
Other professional services	2,000,000

(2) Accounts receivable valuation was adjusted for estimated uncollectible accounts, $320,000 (debit Contractual Adjustments).
(3) Provision for estimated retroactive adjustments by third party payers (for example, Blue Cross) amounted to $430,000.
(4) Transfers from specific purpose funds amounted to $150,000 (credit Other Operating Revenue).
(5) Depreciation expense for the period is $300,000. The governing board directed the transfer of $310,000 to the Plant Renewal and Replacement Fund.
(6) Additions to the voucher register for the period amounted to $5,300,000, with charges to the following account controls and their respective subsidiary accounts:

Nursing services	$2,300,000
Other professional services	1,000,000
General services	1,000,000
Fiscal services	700,000
Administrative services	300,000

(7) Nonoperating revenue received for the period is as follows:

Unrestricted gifts and bequests	$150,000
Unrestricted income from endowments	135,000

Required:
Prepare journal entries for the above transactions.

Exercise 24–3
Transactions: Unrestricted, restricted, and plant funds for religious school

(1) Tuition and fees billed for the period amounted to $955,000. An estimated 1% of this amount will be uncollectible.
(2) The period's fund-raising drive for unrestricted pledges generated $245,000 in pledge receivables. One-half the pledges apply to the next operating period; doubtful pledges amount to $10,000.
(3) Depreciation for the period was $282,000, which was allocated as follows:

Instruction and student activities	$175,000
Auxiliary activities	80,000
Summer school and other programs	15,000
General administration	12,000

(4) Restricted contributions received for special instruction and financial aid for students totaled $220,000. By the end of the period, $100,000 had been spent for such purposes from unrestricted resources.
(5) The fair value of unpaid professional services rendered by religious personnel was $115,000. The provisions of *Statement of Position 78-10* had been met.

Required:
Prepare journal entries for the above transactions.

Exercise 24–4
Transactions: Plant funds group—Colleges and universities

(1) The university's annual fund-raising drive generated $150,000 for new equipment.
(2) The university received a federal grant of $750,000 for the construction of a new library.
(3) The city provided a $100,000 grant for a planned expansion of the sports stadium. An alumni fund drive generated $125,000 for the expansion.
(4) The university's board of trustees directed the transfer of $600,000 from Unrestricted Current Funds for the construction of the new library.
(5) The library building was completed during the year and cost the university $1,500,000. A mortgage was signed for $150,000.
(6) New microfilm projectors were stolen from the university library. The projectors had a recorded value of $8,500.
(7) Income received from the pooled investments of unexpended amounts were held by the following funds:

Unexpended Plant Fund	$10,125
Plant Renewal and Replacement Fund	6,700
Retirement of Indebtedness	3,500

(8) The board of trustees directed the following cash transfers from Unrestricted Current Funds.

Unexpended Plant Fund	$25,000
Plant Renewal and Replacement Fund	30,000
Retirement of Indebtedness	55,000

Required:
Prepare journal entries for the above transactions.

Exercise 24–5
Transactions: Endowment fund of a university

(1) Cash of $1,000,000 was received to endow a professorial chair in business ethics.

(2) The cash received for the endowed chair was used to purchase units in several investment pools.

(3) An individual donated marketable securities that had cost him $125,000 and that had a current market value of $225,000. The income from these securities is to be used for student aid.

(4) The board of trustees directed the transfer of $250,000 from the Unrestricted Current Fund. The money will be invested in high-grade corporate bonds and the income used for student aid.

(5) The $250,000 from the Unrestricted Current Fund is invested in corporate bonds.

(6) The sole owner of a small shopping center donated her entire equity interest in the shopping center to the university, directing that the net income be used for the maintenance of the university's sports stadium. The gift instrument specified that the distributable income of the center would be determined, in part, after depreciation had been calculated based on replacement cost. The estimated fair value of the shopping center at the endowment date was $4,500,000.

(7) Income received from pooled investments amounted to $85,000. This amount is to be distributed as follows:

Endowments	$65,000
Term endowments	10,000
Quasi-endowments	10,000
	$85,000

(8) Income received from unpooled investments amounted to $15,000, allocable to the Endowments Fund.

(9) Shopping center income, paid out as dividends, amounted to $875,000.

(10) Income transfers to the Restricted Current Fund amounted to $800,000. Amounts still due to the Restricted Current Fund at year-end amounted to $165,000.

Required:
Prepare journal entries for the above transactions.

Exercise 24–6
Accounting for revenues: Colleges and universities

For the 19X5 fall semester, San Luis College billed its students $2,300,000 for tuition and fees. The net amount realized was only $2,100,000 because of the following revenue reductions.

Refunds for class cancellations and student withdrawals	$ 50,000
Tuition reductions granted to faculty members' families....................	10,000
Scholarships and fellowships	140,000

Required:
How much should San Luis College report for the period for Unrestricted Current Funds revenues from tuition and fees?

(a) $2,100,000
(b) $2,150,000
(c) $2,250,000
(d) $2,300,000

(AICPA adapted)

Exercise 24–7
Accounting for revenues: Colleges and universities

During the years ended June 30, 19X4 and 19X5, Cabrillo University conducted a cancer research project financed by a $2,000,000 gift from an alumnus. The entire amount was pledged by the donor on July 10, 19X3, although he paid only $500,000 at that date. The gift was restricted to the financing of this particular research project. During the two-year research period, related gift receipts and research expenditures were as follows:

	Year Ended June 30	
	19X4	**19X5**
Gift receipts	$1,200,000	$ 800,000
Cancer research expenditures.....................	900,000	1,100,000

Required:
How much gift revenue should Cabrillo report in the restricted column of its statement of current funds revenues, expenditures, and other changes for the year ended June 30, 19X5?

(a) $0
(b) $800,000
(c) $1,100,000
(d) $2,000,000

(AICPA adapted)

Exercise 24–8
Accounting for contributions and fund classifications: Hospitals

During the year ended December 31, 19X4, Foothills Hospital received the following donations, stated at their respective fair values:

Employee services from members of a religious group	$100,000
Medical supplies from an association of physicians (these supplies were restricted for indigent care, and were used for such purpose in 19X4)......	30,000

Required:
How much revenue (operating and nonoperating) from donations should Foothills report in its 19X4 statement of revenues and expenses?

(a) $0
(b) $30,000
(c) $100,000
(d) $130,000

(AICPA adapted)

Exercise 24–9
Accounting for contributions and fund classifications: Hospitals

On July 1, 19X4, Good Shepherd Hospital's governing board designated $200,000 for expansion of out-patient facilities. The $200,000 will be expended in the fiscal year ended June 30, 19X7.

Required:
In Good Shepherd's June 30, 19X5 balance sheet, this cash should be classified as a $200,000

(a) Restricted current asset.
(b) Restricted noncurrent asset.
(c) Unrestricted current asset.
(d) Unrestricted noncurrent asset.

(AICPA adapted)

Exercise 24–10
Accounting for contributions and fund classifications: Hospitals

El Camino Hospital's property, plant, and equipment (net of depreciation) consist of the following:

Land	$ 500,000
Buildings	10,000,000
Movable Equipment	2,000,000

Required:
What amount should be included in the restricted fund grouping?

(a) $0
(b) $2,000,000
(c) $10,500,000
(d) $12,500,000

(AICPA adapted)

Problems

Problem 24–1
Transactions and preparation of financial statements: Country club

The balance sheet for Parrville Country Club for the fiscal year ended March 31, 19X1 is presented below:

PARRVILLE COUNTRY CLUB
Balance Sheet
March 31, 19X1

Assets
Current Assets:

Cash	$	45,000
Investments—at market		290,000
Accounts receivable, less allowances of $25,000		70,000
Inventories		25,000
Prepaid expenses		20,000
Total Current Assets	$	450,000

Property and Equipment—at cost:

Land and land improvements	$1,010,000
Buildings	1,330,000
Furniture, fixtures, and equipment	275,000
	$2,615,000
Less—Accumulated depreciation	(860,000)
	$1,755,000

Other Assets:

Deferred charges	$	52,000
Beverage license		40,000
	$	92,000
Total Assets		$2,297,000

Liabilities and Membership Equity
Current Liabilities:

Accounts payable and accrued expenses	$	62,000
Deferred revenues—initiation fees		15,000
Due to resigned members		16,000
Taxes		20,000
Total Current Liabilities	$	113,000

Membership Equity:

Proprietary certificates, 500 at $1,500 each	$	750,000
Cumulative excess of income over expenses		1,434,000
		$2,184,000
Total Liabilities and Membership Equity		$2,297,000

Transactions for the year ended March 31, 19X2 were as follows:

(1) Members were billed as follows for the year.

Initiation fees	$ 83,000
Annual dues	660,000
Restaurant and bar charges	155,550
Greens fees	160,000
Tennis and swimming fees	93,250
Locker and room rentals	51,000
Golf cart rentals	21,500

(2) Pro shop cash sales for the year were as follows:

Golf cart rentals to guests	$5,500
Miscellaneous	3,500

(3) Collections on accounts receivable totaled $1,150,000 for the year. Uncollectible accounts amounted to $4,200.

(4) Additions to the voucher register for the year totaled $1,165,500, charged as follows:

Greens	$245,000
House expenses	160,000
Restaurant and bar	120,500
Tennis courts and swimming pool	70,000
General and administrative expenses	560,000
Dues to resigned members	10,000

(5) Vouchers paid during the year amounted to $1,150,000.

(6) Capital additions funded by short-term notes:

Land improvements	$150,000
Golf carts	200,000
Office machines	50,000

Payments on these notes for the year were $230,000, providing principal reductions of $200,000 and interest of $30,000.

(7) Received from the bank the proceeds of a $350,000 short-term loan dated March 31, 19X2.

Additional information:

(1) Accrued expenses at March 31, 19X2 should be $70,000. The necessary adjustment should provide for the following charges:

House expenses	$3,000
Restaurant and bar expenses	3,500
General and administrative expenses	1,500

(2) Deferred revenues—Initiation Fees should have a $25,000 balance at March 31, 19X2.

(3) The market value of the investments at March 31, 19X2 was $315,000. No investment transactions were made during the year.

(4) Depreciation for the year was assigned as follows:

Buildings	$120,000
Furniture, fixtures, and equipment	23,500

Depreciation should be allocated to program services and general and administrative expenses as follows:

Greens expenses	$ 3,500
House expenses	81,500
Restaurant and bar expenses	45,000
Tennis courts and swimming pool expenses	12,000
General and administrative expenses	1,500

(5) Inventories and prepaid expenses should have the following balances at March 31, 19X2:

Inventories	$20,000
Prepaid expenses	18,000

These adjustments should be assigned to program services and general and administrative expenses in the following manner:

House	$3,000
Restaurant	2,500
General and administrative	1,500

Required:
(1) Prepare journal entries for the above transactions.
(2) Prepare a balance sheet and a detailed Statement of Revenues, Expenses, and Changes in Cumulative Excess of Revenue over Expenses for the year ended March 31, 19X2.

Problem 24–2
Transactions and preparation of activity statement: Sports club

In 19X0, a group of merchants in Sunnyview City organized the Committee of 100 to establish the Bay View Sports Club, a nonprofit sports organization for the city's youth. Each of the committee's 100 members contributed $1,000 toward the club's capital, and, in turn, received a participation certificate. In addition, each participant agreed to pay dues of $200 per year for the club's operations. All dues have been collected in full for the fiscal year ended March 31. Members who have discontinued their participation have been replaced by an equal number of new members through a transfer of the participation certificates. The club's April 1, 19X4 trial balance follows:

	Debit	Credit
Cash	$ 9,000	
Investments (market value equals cost)	58,000	
Inventories	5,000	
Land	10,000	
Building	164,000	
Accumulated depreciation—building		$130,000
Furniture and equipment	54,000	
Accumulated depreciation—furniture and equipment		46,000
Accounts payable		12,000
Participation certificates (100 at $1,000 each)		100,000
Cumulative excess of revenue over expenses		12,000
	$300,000	$300,000

Club transactions for the year ended March 31, 19X5 were as follows:

(1) Collections of dues from participants amounted to $20,000.
(2) Snack bar and soda fountain sales receipts totaled $28,000.
(3) Interest and dividends received were $6,000.
(4) Additions to the voucher register were as follows:

House expenses	$17,000
Snack bar and soda fountain expenses	26,000
General and administrative expenses	11,000

(5) Vouchers paid totaled $55,000.
(6) Assessments for capital improvements not yet incurred, $10,000 (assessed on March 20, 19X5; none collected by March 31, 19X5; deemed 100% collectible during the year ended March 31, 19X6).
(7) Unrestricted bequests received amounted to $5,000.

Additional information:
(1) Investments are valued at market, which amounted to $65,000 at March 31, 19X5. No investment transactions were made during the year.
(2) Depreciation for the year was as follows:

Building	$4,000
Furniture and equipment	8,000

This depreciation was allocated as follows:

House expenses	$9,000
Snack bar and soda fountain expenses	2,000
General and administrative expenses	1,000

(3) A physical inventory at March 31, 19X5, revealed that $1,000 worth of supplies remained in the snack bar and soda fountain.

Required:
(1) Prepare journal entries for the above transactions.
(2) Prepare the appropriate activity statement for the year ended March 31, 19X5.

Problem 24–3
Transactions analysis and preparation of statement of changes in fund balances: University current funds

A partial balance sheet for St. Juliann University at the end of its fiscal year (July 31, 19X4) is as follows:

St. Juliann University
Balance Sheet—Current Funds
July 31, 19X4

Assets
Current Funds:
  Unrestricted:
    Cash $200,000

Accounts receivable—student tuition and fees, less $15,000
allowance for doubtful accounts 360,000
Prepaid expenses 40,000
Total Unrestricted $600,000

Restricted:
Cash .... $ 10,000
Investments 210,000
Total Restricted $220,000
Total Current Funds $820,000

Liabilities and Fund Balances
Current Funds:
Unrestricted:
Accounts payable $100,000
Due to other funds 40,000
Deferred revenue—tuition and fees 25,000
Fund balance... 435,000
Total Unrestricted $600,000

Restricted:
Accounts payable .... $ 5,000
Fund balance... 215,000
Total Restricted $220,000
Total Current Funds $820,000

The following financial events and transactions occurred during the fiscal year ended July 31, 19X5:

(1) Cash collected from student tuition totaled $3,000,000. Of this amount, $362,000 was outstanding at July 31, 19X4; $2,500,000 was for current-year tuition; and $138,000 was for tuition applicable to the semester beginning in August 19X5.

(2) Deferred revenue at July 31, 19X4 was earned during the year ended July 31, 19X5.

(3) July 31, 19X4 accounts receivable that were not collected during the year ended July 31, 19X5, were declared uncollectible and were written off against the allowance account. At July 31, 19X5, the Allowance for Doubtful Accounts was an estimated $10,000.

(4) During the year, an unrestricted grant of $60,000 was awarded by the state. This state grant was payable to St. Juliann sometime in August 19X5.

(5) During the year, unrestricted cash gifts of $80,000 were received from alumni. St. Juliann's board of trustees allocated $30,000 of these gifts to the student loan fund.

(6) During the year, investments costing $25,000 were sold for $31,000. Restricted fund investments were purchased for $40,000. Investment income of $18,000 was earned and collected during the year.

(7) Unrestricted general expenses of $2,500,000 were recorded in the voucher register. At July 31, 19X5, the unrestricted Accounts Payable balance was $75,000.

(8) The restricted Accounts Payable balance at July 31, 19X4 was paid.

(9) The $40,000 due to other funds at July 31, 19X4 was paid to the Plant Fund as required.

(10) One-quarter of the prepaid expenses at July 31, 19X4, which pertain to general education expenses, expired during the current year. No additions to prepaid expenses were made during the year.

Required:
(1) Prepare general journal entries for the foregoing transactions for the year ended July 31, 19X5. Number each entry to correspond with the indicated transaction number. Organize your answer as follows:

| Entry | | Current Funds | | | |
| | | Unrestricted | | Restricted | |
No.	Account	Dr.	Cr.	Dr.	Cr.

(2) Prepare a statement of changes in fund balances for the year ended July 31, 19X5.

(AICPA adapted)

Problem 24–4
Transactions analysis and preparation of statement
of revenue and expense: Hospitals

Children's Hospital had the following financial events and transactions pertaining to its unrestricted fund for the year ended June 30, 19X2:

(1) Gross billings to the patients for the year were as follows:

Daily patient services	$2,500,000
Other nursing services	750,000
Other professional services	300,000
	$3,550,000

(2) Adjustments from gross revenues were as follows:

Contractual adjustments with third party payers	$500,000
Approved charity and free care adjustments	175,000
Discounts and allowances to hospital staff	7,800

(3) Collections of accounts receivable totaled $2,000,000.
(4) Inventory acquisitions, including materials and supplies, amounted to $350,000. One-fifth of the approved invoices remain unpaid at year-end. The hospital uses a perpetual inventory system.
(5) Use of materials and supplies from inventory was assigned as follows:

Nursing services	$190,000
Other professional services	75,000
General services	235,000
Fiscal services	6,000
Administrative services	2,500

(6) The following salary and wage expenses were incurred for the year:

Nursing services	$990,000
Other professional services	550,000
General services	175,000
Fiscal services	120,000
Administrative services	25,000

(7) Other operating expenses processed through the voucher system were as follows:

Nursing services	$65,000
Other professional services...	35,000
General services	17,500
Fiscal services	6,500
Administrative services..	3,500

(8) The provision for estimated uncollectible accounts was $154,000.
(9) Depreciation of buildings and equipment was as follows:

Buildings	$185,000
Equipment...	120,000

The depreciation of the building is based on appraisals by qualified appraisers. Appraisals were necessary several years ago because historical records were destroyed before the hospital prepared its first set of accrual basis financial statements.

(10) Interfund transfers for the year to the Unrestricted Fund were as follows:

Specific purpose fund...	$110,000
Plant renewal and replacement fund	300,000
Endowment fund	45,000

(11) Other data are as follows:

	June 30	
	19X1	19X2
Accrued general services expenses	$35,000	$23,000
Prepaid administrative services expenses	10,000	18,500

Required:
Prepare the appropriate journal entries, post to T accounts, and draft a Statement of Revenues and Expenses for the Unrestricted Fund.

Problem 24–5
Transactions analysis and preparation of statement of current funds revenues, expenditures, and transfers: Colleges and universities

Lerner College had the following financial events and transactions pertaining to its current funds group for the year ended June 30, 19X2:

Unrestricted Current Funds:

(1) Student tuition and fees billed for the year amounted to $2,345,000. Prior experience shows that 2% of this billing will be uncollectible.
(2) Unrestricted government appropriations collected amounted to $750,000.
(3) Operating expenditures were incurred and assigned as follows.

Instruction	$1,600,000
Research	350,000
Academic support	700,000
Student services	65,000
Operation of plant	450,000
Institutional support	130,000

(4) Several term endowments amounting to $300,000 became available for un-restricted use.

(5) Unrestricted gifts and bequests received during the period amounted to $50,000.

(6) Auxiliary enterprise income amounted to $225,000. Auxiliary enterprise expenditures for the year were $85,000.

(7) Use of the materials and supplies inventory was charged as follows:

Instruction	$34,500
Research	18,000
Academic support	22,000
Student services	15,000
Institutional support	12,000

(8) The student aid committee granted student tuition and fee reductions of $23,000.

(9) Unrestricted income from Endowment and Similar Funds amounted to $47,500.

(10) Mandatory transfers to other funds included the following:

Principal and interest	$250,000
Renewals and replacements	100,000

(11) Other data are as follows:

	June 30	
	19X1	**19X2**
Prepaid expenses and deferred charges	$32,000	$28,500
Accrued expenses	11,000	20,000

These expenses are allocated in the following proportions:

Instruction	15%
Research	10
Academic support	25
Student services	30
Institutional support	20

Restricted Current Funds:

(1) Restricted gifts of $55,000 were received from a foundation to be used for student aid.

(2) A federal government grant of $800,000 was received for library acquisitions.

(3) Expenditures were incurred for student aid, $52,000, and instruction (library acquisitions), $750,000.

Required:

Prepare the appropriate journal entries, post to T accounts, and draft a statement of Current Funds Revenues, Expenditures, and Transfers for Lerner College for the year ended June 30, 19X2.

Problem 24–6
Transactions analysis: University current funds

A partial balance sheet of Studyville University is shown below.

STUDYVILLE UNIVERSITY
Partial Balance Sheet
June 30, 19X0

Assets

Current funds:

Unrestricted:

Cash	$210,000
Accounts receivable—student tuition and fees, less $9,000 allowance	
for doubtful accounts	341,000
State appropriations receivable	75,000
Total Unrestricted	$626,000

Restricted:

Cash	$ 7,000
Investments	60,000
Total Restricted	$ 67,000
Total Current Funds	$693,000

Liabilities and Fund Balances

Current funds:

Unrestricted:

Accounts payable	$ 45,000
Deferred revenues	66,000
Fund balance..	515,000
Total Unrestricted	$626,000

Restricted:

Fund balance..	$ 67,000
Total Restricted	$ 67,000
Total Current Funds	$693,000

The following financial events and transactions occurred during the fiscal year ended June 30, 19X1:

(1) On July 7, 19X0, a $100,000 gift was received from an alumnus. The alumnus requested that one-half the gift be used for the purchase of books for the university library and the remainder be used for the establishment of a scholarship fund. The alumnus further requested that the income generated by the scholarship fund be awarded annually as a scholarship to a qualified disadvantaged student. On July 20, 19X0, the board of trustees resolved that the funds of the newly established scholarship fund would be invested in savings certificates. On July 21, 19X0, the savings certificates were purchased.

(2) Revenue from student tuition and fees for the year ended June 30, 19X1 amounted to $1,900,000. Of this amount, $66,000 was collected in the prior year and $1,686,000 was collected during the year ended June 30, 19X1. In addition, at June 30, 19X1, the university had received $158,000 cash, representing fees for the session beginning July 1, 19X1.

(3) During the year ended June 30, 19X1, the university collected $349,000 of the outstanding accounts receivable at the beginning of the year. The balance was determined to be uncollectible and was written off against the allowance account. At June 30, 19X1, the allowance account was increased by $3,000.

(4) During the year, interest charges of $6,000 were earned and collected on late student fee payments.

(5) During the year, the state appropriation was received. An additional unrestricted appropriation of $50,000 was made by the state but had not been paid to the university as of June 30, 19X1.

(6) An unrestricted gift of $25,000 cash was received from alumni of the university.

(7) During the year, investments of $21,000 were sold for $26,000. Investment income of $1,900 was received.

(8) During the year, unrestricted operating expenses of $1,777,000 were recorded. At June 30, 19X1, $59,000 of these expenses remained unpaid.

(9) Restricted current funds of $13,000 were spent for authorized purposes during the year.

(10) The accounts payable at June 30, 19X0 were paid during the year.

(11) During the year, $7,000 interest was earned and received on the savings certificates purchased in accordance with the board's resolution in Item (1).

Required:

(1) Prepare journal entries to record the above transactions for the year ended June 30, 19X1. Number each journal entry to correspond with the transaction described above.

Organize your answer sheet as follows:

	Current Funds				Endowment Fund	
	Unrestricted		Restricted			
Accounts	Dr.	Cr.	Dr.	Cr.	Dr.	Cr.

(2) Prepare a statement of changes in fund balances for the year ended June 30, 19X1.

(AICPA adapted)

Problem 24–7
Transactions: University current funds group; recording transactions in ledger accounts; preparing special trial balance

Hathaway University uses the following funds:

Unrestricted Current Funds	Restricted Current Funds
Unexpended Plant Fund	Investment in Plant
Endowment Fund	Student Loan Fund
Annuity Fund	

The following financial events and transactions occurred during 19X1:

January 1:

Hathaway University, which previously held no Endowment Funds, received five gifts as a result of an appeal for funds. The campaign closed December 31, and all gifts received are recorded as of January 1. Gifts are as follows:

(a) From A. Newsom, $10,000, the principal to be held intact and the income to be used for any purpose that the university's board of trustees should indicate.

(b) From B. Goode, $20,000, the principal to be held intact and the income to be used to endow scholarships for worthy students.

(c) From C. Parrish, $30,000, the principal to be held intact and the interest to be loaned to students only. All income is to be loaned again; all losses from student loans are to be charged against income.

(d) From D. Klassen, $200,000. During the donor's lifetime, semiannual payments of $2,500 are to be made to the donor. After Klassen's death, the fund should be used to construct or purchase a residence hall for students. Because Klassen is seriously ill, no present value of the annuity is established.

(e) From E. Twigg, 1,000 shares of Datatron, Inc. common stock, which had a market value on this date of $150 per share. Such shares are to be held for not more than five years, and all income received from them is to be held intact. At any date during this period, designated by the board of trustees, all assets are to be liquidated and the proceeds used to build a student infirmary.

(f) The board of trustees consolidated the Newsom and Goode funds into a Merged Investments account (in the proportion of their principal accounts) and purchased $25,000 Intercontinental Gas and Electric Company bonds at par. Interest rate is 10%; interest dates are January 1 and July 1.

(g) The cash of the Parrish fund is used to purchase $30,000, 9% bonds of the Marrelli Corporation at par plus accrued interest. Interest dates are April 1 and October 1.

(h) The $200,000 cash of the Klassen fund is used to purchase $200,000, 8% U.S. Treasury notes at par. Interest dates are January 1 and July 1.

July 1:

(i) All interest has been received as stipulated on bonds owned, and $4,000 dividends are received on the Datatron stock.

(j) Payment is made to Klassen in accordance with the terms of the gift. A cash loan is authorized from the Endowment Fund to cover overdraft created.

(k) Intercontinental Gas & Electric Company bonds with a $20,000 par value are sold at 102. No commission was involved.

(l) Loan was made to M. Brinkman, $300, from the Parrish student loan fund.

October 1:

(m) Notice is received of the death of D. Klassen. There is no liability to the estate.

(n) A scholarship award of $200 was made to P. Dulles from the Goode scholarship fund.

(o) U.S. Treasury notes at $200,000 par held by the Klassen fund were sold at 101 and accrued interest. The Endowment Fund loan was repaid.

(p) Interest due on bonds is received.

December 31:

(q) M. Brinkman paid $100 principal and $5 interest on her student loan.

(r) The board of trustees purchased a building suitable for a residence hall for $250,000, using the available funds from the Klassen gift as part payment and giving a 20-year mortgage payable for the balance.

Required:

Record the transactions in appropriate ledger accounts, keying them to the given transaction letters. Classify your accounts into suitable groups by funds to facilitate the preparation of a balance sheet. Do not prepare a formal balance sheet, but complete a trial balance that discloses the self-balancing funds, including all accounts used in your ledger, even though they do not have balances.

(AICPA adapted)

PART SIX Unrelated Areas

25 Estates and Trusts

OVERVIEW OF ESTATES AND TRUSTS

In this chapter, we consider the role accountants play in the administration of estates and trusts. Before proceeding into this subject, however, we discuss briefly the role accountants may play in estate planning, which takes place before an individual dies.

Estate planning

People commonly make plans for the orderly transfer of their property upon death to relatives, other persons, organizations, or trusts to be set up for the benefit of relatives. Such planning is known as **estate planning.** Accountants often work closely with attorneys in estate planning. The attorney's role centers around preparing wills, and in many cases, trust agreements (which are discussed in detail later in the chapter). The accountant's role consists of suggesting planning techniques consistent with the objective of minimizing transfer costs (federal estate taxes, state inheritance taxes, and fees and expenses). In this capacity, an accountant often determines expected transfer costs under various options. An accountant may also play an important role in advising his or her client on accounting matters pertaining to trusts that are to be established.

Participation by accountants in estate planning, however, is usually limited to cases in which individuals are wealthy or moderately wealthy. The Tax Reform Act of 1976 substantially overhauled the federal estate and gift tax laws, and an estimated 98% of all estates became exempt from estate and gift tax laws. However, inflation was lowering this percentage. Furthermore, certain inequities were perceived to exist still. To address these two areas, further changes were enacted in the Economic Recovery Tax Act of 1981, and an estimated 99.5% of all estates are now exempt from estate and gift tax laws. An accountant participating in estate planning must have substantial expertise in estate and gift taxes—a complex area of the tax laws. A detailed discussion of these laws and the use of planning techniques to minimize transfer costs is properly the subject matter of a tax course. However, a brief discussion of the estate and gift tax laws is included later in the chapter.

The trust feature of estate planning

Frequently, a will contains a provision for the establishment of a trust, whereby certain designated property of the decedent's estate is to be transferred to a **trustee** when the person dies. The trustee holds legal title to the property and administers the property for the benefit of one or more other persons, who are called **beneficiaries.** Thus, the trustee serves in a position of trust with respect to the beneficiaries. This is a fiduciary relationship, and the trustee is commonly referred to as a **fiduciary.** (Recall another type of fiduciary relationship discussed in Chapter 18 in connection with companies in bankruptcy proceedings.) The person creating the trust is referred to as the **trustor** (also known as the **grantor, donor, creator,** and **settlor**). The legal document creating the trust is the **trust agreement.** Trust beneficiaries are of the following two classes:

(1) Income beneficiary.   An income beneficiary is entitled to the income earned by the trust's assets, which are referred to as the trust **principal,** or **corpus.**

(2) Principal beneficiary.   A principal beneficiary is entitled to the principal, or corpus, of the trust, which is distributed according to the terms of the trust agreement (usually at the specified termination date of the trust). A principal beneficiary is also known as a **residuary beneficiary** or **remainderman.**

The income and principal beneficiaries may or may not be the same person. A common arrangement is to name one's spouse as the income beneficiary for his or her remaining life and name one's children as the principal beneficiaries. Another common arrangement is to name one's minor children as both income and principal beneficiaries, with some or all of the income to be used for their support and the principal to be distributed to them when they reach a specified age.

The basic accounting problem

Regardless of whether the income and principal beneficiaries of a trust are the same person or persons, it is necessary to account for the separate interests of each class. The manner of accomplishing this task is the subject of this chapter. The requirement of correct separate accounting for the interests of each class is the reason for the special theories and techniques for accounting for the administration of estates and trusts by fiduciaries. Otherwise, quite simple record-keeping procedures would be adequate.

Accounting for the separate interests of each class of beneficiaries is even more difficult because there is a built-in clash of interests between the two classes. When the principal and income beneficiaries are not the same person or persons, the clash revolves around who gets what. When the principal and income beneficiaries are the same person or persons, the clash concerns the timing of distributions. Frequently, disputes between these interests lead to litigation.

Although a trust may be established by a transfer of property to the trustee during the transferor's lifetime (known as an *inter vivos* trust), we deal solely with trusts that are created by a gift made in the will of a decedent (known as a **testamentary trust**). Thus, we must consider the administration of a decedent's estate in connection with the establishment of a trust.

Relationship between an estate and a testamentary trust

All the states have enacted some form of legislation concerning the administration of trusts. State statutes pertaining to trusts are operative, in most cases, only to the extent that they do not conflict with the terms of a trust agreement. Twenty states have adopted the Revised Uniform Principal and Income Act (of 1962) either in its entirety or with modifications; accordingly, we base our discussion on this act. Under this act, testamentary trusts are deemed to be created at the time of a person's death, even though the property to be placed in trust usually is not actually distributed to the trustee until some time after the person dies.[1] Property to be placed in trust becomes subject to the trust at the time of death; the rights of the income beneficiary are also established at the time of death. Therefore, the interests of the income beneficiary of the trust must be accounted for separately from the interests of the principal beneficiary of the trust **during the period of the estate administration,** as well as after the property is actually transferred to the trustee. (Some trust agreements simplify matters by specifying that the rights of the income beneficiary do not begin until the assets are actually transferred to the trustee.)

For accounting purposes, we treat the estate and the trust as separate accounting entities. (Conceptually we view each of these entities as comprising two accounting entities—a "principal entity" and an "income entity.") For tax reporting purposes, estates and trusts both are treated as taxable entities. However, they are not legal entities in the sense that corporations are legal entities.

PRINCIPAL VERSUS INCOME

When a testamentary trust is established, every transaction must be analyzed to determine if it relates to principal or income. An incorrect determination has important legal consequences to a fiduciary. If it is later determined that income has been overstated and the fiduciary cannot recover the amount of an overpayment from the income beneficiary, then the fiduciary must make up the deficiency. In turn, if the error was made by the accountant or was based on the bad advice of the fiduciary's legal counsel, then these persons may be professionally responsible to the fiduciary.

Manner of analyzing transactions

Reference to the trust agreement. In determining whether a transaction pertains to principal or income, **generally accepted accounting principles are not the point of reference.** The trustor may create his or her own definition of income. In other words, the trustor may specify the receipts that are to be income and the receipts that are to be principal. Likewise, the trustor may specify disbursements that are to be treated as charges against income and disbursements that are to be treated as reductions of the principal. Accordingly, all transactions must be analyzed as to the decedent's intent.

Because the decedent is not available, the first step is to determine if the decedent's intent is expressed in the trust agreement. Unfortunately, a common shortcoming of estate planning is that trust agreements usually do not explain in detail the treatment to be accorded specific types of receipts and disbursements. Many potential problems can be avoided if

---

[1] Revised Uniform Principal and Income Act, U.L.A. Volume 7A, Section 4 (St. Paul, MN: West Publishing Company).

the decedent's personal accountant, who should have a knowledge of his or her client's properties, participates in the preparation of the trust agreement sections that pertain to accounting matters.

Reference to state laws. If the treatment of an item cannot be resolved by referring to the trust agreement, the second step is to find out what the state law is on the subject. Again, generally accepted accounting principles are not the point of reference. The Revised Uniform Principal and Income Act specifically addresses the principal versus income treatment of several items. Much of the impetus for revising the original Uniform Principal and Income Act (of 1931) resulted from the development of new forms of investment property, the treatment of which was not specified in state statutes. The treatment accorded many items specifically dealt with in the act produces income results that would be obtained if generally accepted accounting principles were applied. For numerous other items, however, the treatment produces results that are quite contrary to generally accepted accounting principles. For example, the act provides that the following items be treated as increases and decreases, respectively, to the trust principal instead of to income:

(1) Gains and losses on the sale of corporate securities.
(2) Gains and losses on the sale of rental property.
(3) Bond discounts (with certain exceptions) and bond premiums.

We present the general thrust of the act's accounting requirements later in the chapter. Section 5 of the act calls for income during the administration of an estate to be determined in the same manner that income is to be determined by a trustee in administering a trust. Thus, the act applies to estates as well as trusts.

Reference to case law. If the treatment of an item is not covered in state law, the third step is to determine if the courts have encountered and ruled on the same problem. If so, the answer is found in case law. If the answer cannot be found in case law, then the fiduciary may petition the court for a determination.

Accountant's role in analyzing transactions. When the treatment to be accorded an item is not clearly set forth in the trust agreement or state statutes, the accountant does not determine whether an item pertains to principal or income. This is the function of the fiduciary, the fiduciary's legal counsel, or the courts. The accountant's role would be expanded, of course, when the trust agreement specifies that income is to be determined in accordance with generally accepted accounting principles. Such cases are the exception and not the rule.

Manner of record keeping

Because the interests of the principal beneficiary and the income beneficiary must be accounted for separately, it is necessary to identify the assets and transactions pertaining to principal and those pertaining to income.

Conceptually, we may view the assets and transactions pertaining to principal as belonging to a separate accounting entity and do likewise for the assets and transactions pertaining to income. Thus, a trust may be viewed as comprising two entities, each with a self-balancing set of books.

One method of record keeping is physically to maintain separate journals and general ledgers for each conceptual entity. An alternate method is to use one set of books for both entities but to use separately identified columns in the journals and separately identified accounts in the general ledger for principal and income. This technique allows separate trial balances to be prepared for each conceptual entity, just as if two general ledgers were used. In practice, this technique is quite simple to work with, largely because cash is usually the only type of asset common to both principal and income. Regardless of which method is used, it is not necessary to use one bank account for cash pertaining to principal and another bank account for cash pertaining to income, unless the trust agreement requires it. When only one set of books is used, the separation of the total cash balance is reflected in the general ledger through a Principal Cash ledger account and an Income Cash ledger account. One set of books is generally used in practice. We illustrate this manner of record keeping later in the chapter.

Cash basis versus accrual basis

At the beginning and the end of the income beneficiary's rights.   In most respects, the Revised Uniform Principal and Income Act provides for the use of the accrual basis in determining at the time of the person's death the assets that are to be treated as part of the trust principal. The purpose, of course, is to establish a reasonably fair and practical starting point to determine income for the income beneficiary. Specifically, the following items are to be included as part of trust principal at the time of death:

(1) Amounts due but not paid at the time of death [Section 4(a)].
(2) Pro-rations of amounts not due at the time of death that pertain to periodic payments, including rents, interest, and annuities [Section 4(b)].
(3) Corporate distributions declared for which the date of record precedes the person's death [Section 4(e)].

The cash basis is specified for all other items [Section 4(c)]. In a somewhat parallel manner, the act provides in most respects for the use of the accrual basis on termination of an income interest, to effect a reasonably fair and practical cutoff of the income beneficiary's interest [Sections 4(d) and (e)].

Accounting periods between the beginning and the end of the income beneficiary's rights.   For accounting periods between the beginning and the end of the income beneficiary's rights, the accrual basis in most respects does not fit in with the underlying objective of the fiduciary, which is to account for the **flow of assets in and out of his or her control.** Accordingly, with one major exception, the cash basis is considered more appropriate for such accounting periods. However, the accrual basis offers much better measuring results when determining the income of a business in which principal is invested.

At the end of the estate administration.   When the income rights of the income beneficiary are established at the time of the person's death, the end of the estate administration is not relevant to the income and principal beneficiaries. Using the accrual basis is therefore unnecessary at the end of probate administration. Of course, if the trust agreement provides that income rights do not start until the end of the estate administration, then accrual techniques would be appropriate.

ACCOUNTING FOR ESTATES

Probate administration

When a person dies, his or her property and liabilities (collectively referred to as the **estate**) must be administered, regardless of whether the person died with a will (referred to as having died **testate**) or without a will (referred to as having died **intestate**). Each state has laws concerning the affairs of decedents, commonly known as **probate law** or the **law of decedent estates.** A Uniform Probate Code exists, but only two states have adopted it. Accordingly, uniformity among the states in this area is negligible. The objectives of probate laws are to (1) discover and make effective the decedent's intent in the distribution of his or her property; (2) gather and preserve the decedent's property; and (3) provide for an efficient and orderly system of making payments of estate debts and distributions in the course of liquidating estates. If the decedent does not have a will, property is distributed according to state inheritance tax laws.

Under the probate laws, the affairs of decedents must be administered by fiduciaries who are subject to the control of the state **probate courts** (referred to in a few of the states as **surrogate courts** or **orphans' courts**). The following two terms are used for estate fiduciaries:

(1) Executor.   An executor is named in the decedent's will to serve as the decedent's personal representative in administering his or her estate and is appointed by the court to serve in that capacity.

(2) Administrator.   An administrator is appointed by the court when (a) a person dies intestate; (b) a person does not name anyone in his or her will; (c) the person named in the decedent's will refuses to serve as executor; or (d) the court refuses to appoint the person named in the will.

The title to a decedent's property is subject to the possession of the fiduciary and the control of the court, even though title passes at the time of death to the person or persons to whom the property is to be distributed. In short, the probate court serves as guardian of the estate. If a person dies testate, his or her will has no legal effect until it has been "probated." **Probate** is the act by which the court determines if the will submitted to it meets the statutory requirements concerning wills. If the court so determines, then it issues a certificate or decree that enables the terms of the will to be carried out. The will is said to have been "admitted to probate."

Basically, an estate fiduciary must (1) take an inventory of the decedent's assets; (2) settle the claims of the decedent's creditors; (3) prepare and file the applicable income, estate, and inheritance tax returns; (4) distribute the remaining assets as gifts as provided for in the will; and (5) make the appropriate accountings to the court.

Gift terminology

A gift of personal property by means of a will is called a **legacy.** The recipient of a legacy is called a **legatee.** Legacies are classified as follows:

(1) Specific legacies.   A specific legacy is a gift of specified noncash items. For example, "my automobile to my son, Harvey."
(2) Demonstrative legacies.   A demonstrative legacy is a gift of cash for which a particular fund or source is designated from which payment is to be made. For example, "$1,000 to my sister, Christine, out of my savings account."
(3) General legacies.   A general legacy is a gift of cash for which no particular fund or source is designated from which payment is to be made. For example, "$2,000 to my brother Chad."
(4) Residual legacies.   A residual legacy is a gift of all personal property remaining after distribution of specific, demonstrative, and general legacies. For example, "the balance of my personal property to my wife, Ann Marie."

If the balance of the estate assets after payment of estate liabilities, taxes, and administrative expenses is insufficient to make good all of various types of legacies, then the legacies are deemed to be null and inoperative in the reverse of the above order (referred to as the process of **abatement**).

A gift of real property by means of a will is called a **devise.** The recipient of a devise is called a **devisee.** Devises are classified as specific, general, or residual devises. Estate assets to be transferred to a trustee pursuant to the establishment of a testamentary trust may be any type of legacy or devise. The most common type of legacy given to a trustee is a residual legacy, which we illustrate later in the chapter.

Inventory of decedent's property

The estate fiduciary's first major task in administering the estate is to take an inventory of the decedent's property. Each item must then be valued at its current market value for federal estate and state inheritance tax purposes (using state inheritance tax or private appraisers, as required), and the appropriate tax forms must be filed. (We discuss these in more detail in the following section.) In addition, the estate fiduciary must submit to the probate court an inventory of the decedent's property that is subject to probate administration. Not all items included for estate tax and state inheritance tax purposes are subject to probate administration. Many states allow real property to pass directly to the beneficiaries (or to the trustee, in the case of real property placed in trust), thus bypassing probate administration. Likewise, many states allow certain types of personal property—such as personal effects, clothing, household items, and a limited amount of cash—to pass directly to beneficiaries outside of probate. State probate law must be consulted to determine which items are subject to probate administration; an attorney's services are usually used for this. Although required only by some states, a separate schedule should list the items not subject to probate administration, if only for the record.

In general, the following items are subject to probate administration:

(1) Cash in checking and savings accounts, cash in a safety deposit box, and cash on hand.
(2) Investments in stocks and bonds.
(3) Interest accrued on bonds through the date of the person's death.
(4) Dividends declared on stocks prior to the person's death.
(5) Investments in businesses and partnerships.
(6) Life insurance proceeds that name the estate as the beneficiary.
(7) Notes and accounts receivable, including interest accrued through the date of the person's death.
(8) Accrued rents and royalties receivable.
(9) Advances to those named in the will as beneficiaries, including interest accrued through the date of death.
(10) Unpaid wages, salaries, and commissions.
(11) Valuables, such as jewelry and coin collections.
(12) Real estate not specifically exempted (the most common exemption is property held in joint tenancy, because all rights in such property immediately pass to the surviving tenant at the time of death).

Even though other items may be includible for federal estate tax and state inheritance tax purposes, the fiduciary's accountability to the probate court includes only the items subject to probate administration. The fiduciary must take control of these items for estate preservation purposes.

Payment of estate liabilities

The liabilities of the estate must be paid before any distributions are made to beneficiaries. Probate laws usually require the estate fiduciary to publish promptly notices in newspapers for a certain period of time calling for persons having claims against the decedent to file them within a specified period of time or be barred forever. The estate fiduciary is responsible for determining the validity of claims filed. If the estate assets are insufficient to pay all liabilities, payment must be made in accordance with the priority provided for in state law. This general order of priority is as follows:

(1) Funeral expenses.
(2) Estate administration expenses.
(3) Allowances for support of the decedent's spouse and dependent children for a specified period of time.
(4) Expenses of the deceased's last illness.
(5) Wages owed to employees of the decedent.

(6) Debts owed to the federal, state, or local government that have priority under federal or state law.

(7) Lien claims.

(8) All other debts.

Tax matters

The estate fiduciary is responsible for preparing and filing tax returns for the decedent and the decedent's estate.

Decedent's final income tax return.   A final income tax return must be filed for the decedent, covering the period from the date of the decedent's last income tax return to the date of death. Any taxes owed are paid from estate assets.

Taxation of estate income.   An estate is a taxable entity, which comes into being at the time of the person's death. Estate income taxes must be filed annually on federal Form 1041 (U.S. Fiduciary Income Tax Return) until the estate is terminated upon discharge of the fiduciary by the probate court. The gross income of an estate is computed in the same manner as that of an individual. In addition to deductions for expenses relating to the generation of income, a deduction is allowed for net income currently distributable to beneficiaries. As a result, the estate is taxed only on the remaining net income not currently distributable. The beneficiaries, in turn, are taxed on the currently distributable net income. The tax rates that apply to estates are those that apply to married individuals filing separately.

You should understand that the concept of estate income for tax reporting purposes differs in many respects from the concept of estate income for fiduciary reporting purposes. Accordingly, working paper adjustments to fiduciary book income amounts are usually necessary to arrive at gross income and deductions for income tax reporting purposes.

State inheritance taxes.   Most states impose an inheritance tax on the value of property to be distributed to each individual heir. This tax is based on the **right to receive or inherit** property; thus, the burden of taxation falls on the recipient of the property. Although the taxes are paid to the state out of the estate assets, the estate fiduciary either seeks reimbursement from the individual heirs (when noncash assets are distributed) or reduces proportionately the amount to be distributed to each individual heir (when cash is distributed). The tax rates and allowable exemptions are based on the relationship of the heir to the decedent, with tax rates increasing and exemptions decreasing as the relationship becomes more distant. It is quite common, however, for wills to provide specifically that state inheritance taxes be paid out of the residue of the estate, so that the entire burden of taxation falls on the heirs who receive the residue.

Federal estate taxes.   Unlike state inheritance taxes, the federal estate tax is based on the **right to give** property. The burden of taxation, therefore, falls entirely on the estate and not on each individual heir. Of course, this merely reduces the amount of the residue of the estate that otherwise would be distributed to heirs. (Some state probate codes require the federal estate tax to be borne by each heir, as with the state inheritance taxes.) Assuming a decedent has made no gifts during his or her lifetime, estate taxes are calculated in the following manner:

(1) The total value of the decedent's property is determined at the time of death, or if the estate fiduciary elects, at a date six months after death. Property sold within six months of the person's death is valued at its selling price. (Recall that the gross estate for federal estate tax purposes is usually greater than the probate estate.)
(2) Deductions from the gross estate determined in (1), above, to arrive at the **taxable estate** are
   a. Liabilities of the estate.
   b. Administrative expenses, including funeral expenses, court costs, and attorney fees.
   c. Casualty and theft losses during the administration of the estate.
   d. A marital deduction (a term used to describe a transfer between spouses that is exempt from transfer taxes). The marital deduction is unlimited; thus, any amount may be used.
   e. Charitable contributions.
(3) The estate tax rates are then applied to the taxable estate to arrive at the **gross estate tax.** The estate tax rates are graduated from 18% on taxable estates of $10,000 to a maximum of 55% (scheduled to drop to 50% in 1988) on taxable estates in excess of $2,500,000.
(4) Certain specified credits—such as state death taxes (with limitations) and the unified transfer tax credit—are subtracted from the gross estate tax to arrive at the **net estate tax.**

The unified transfer tax credit is the equivalent of an exemption. The following table shows the amount of the unified transfer tax credit and the related exemption equivalent through 1987.

	Unified Transfer Tax Credit	Exemption Equivalent
1985	$121,800	$400,000
1986	155,800	500,000
1987	192,800	600,000

Accordingly, a single individual may transfer a taxable estate of $600,000 in 1987 and incur no federal estate tax.

Because a surviving spouse may take a marital deduction for any amount (a provision enacted as part of the Economic Recovery Tax Act of 1981), all federal estate taxes otherwise payable can be deferred until the death of that surviving spouse. This change was made largely because many surviving spouses of farmers had to sell a portion of their farms to pay estate taxes. Thus, for the first time, the tax law treats a married couple as a single economic unit.

To use the unified credit fully, the marital deduction amount chosen generally is small enough to leave a taxable estate equal to the exemption equivalent of the unified transfer tax credit. For example, assume that (1)

Henry Steele passed away in 1987; (2) his gross estate is $3,700,000; and (3) all deductions other than the marital deduction are $100,000. With a marital deduction amount of $3,000,000, the taxable estate is $600,000, resulting in a gross estate tax of $192,800. However, because the unified transfer tax credit for 1987 is $192,800, no net estate tax is payable. The unified transfer tax credit can also be used on the death of Steele's surviving spouse. Thus, the exemption equivalent of $600,000 (for 1987) is really $1,200,000 for a married couple.

The calculation of estate taxes is substantially more complicated when the decedent has made gifts during his or her lifetime. One of the major changes in the Tax Reform Act of 1976 was to unify the previously separate estate and gift tax rate schedules into a combined transfer tax system, so that lifetime transfers and transfers at death are no longer taxed at different rates. The unified transfer tax credit is labeled as such because it also may be applied against gift taxes due on lifetime gifts. The amount of any unused credit is then applied against the gross estate tax.

The opening entry

Once an inventory of the decedent's property that is subject to probate administration has been compiled, the opening entry for the "principal entity" of the estate is made. The entry consists of debits to the various assets and a credit to an Estate Principal account. The Estate Principal account is merely a balancing account that facilitates the double-entry bookkeeping system. It does not reflect the "net worth" of the estate, inasmuch as the decedent's liabilities are not recorded as part of the opening entry. Liabilities are recorded in the books when they are paid, and such payments are eventually reflected as reductions to the Estate Principal account. This manner of accounting reflects the fiduciary's role, which is to **administer the decedent's assets,** rather than attempting to establish and account for the net worth of the estate. As expected, no opening entry pertains to the "income entity."

Transactions pertaining to principal

Transactions pertaining to principal are recorded by debiting or crediting the appropriate asset account and crediting or debiting, respectively, an account that is descriptive of the transaction. Transactions pertaining to principal may be grouped as follows:

(1) Transactions That Increase Principal:
    a. Assets subsequently discovered
    b. Gains on disposition of principal assets
(2) Transactions That Decrease Principal:
    a. Losses on disposition of principal assets
    b. Payments of debts and certain taxes
    c. Payment of funeral expenses
    d. Payment of administrative expenses
    e. Distributions of gifts

(3) **Transactions That Do Not Affect Principal:**
    a. Disposition of principal assets at their carrying values
    b. Receipts of amounts to be given to legatees (which are reflected as liabilities until paid)
    c. Disbursements of amounts held for legatees, as described in (3)b
    d. Payments of amounts chargeable to a beneficiary (which are reflected as receivables until collected)

The nonasset accounts that are debited or credited in categories 1 and 2 are nominal or temporary accounts that are eventually closed to the Estate Principal account. (Some finer points concerning principal transactions are discussed later in the chapter.)

Transactions pertaining to income

The accounting techniques used for the principal entity are also used for the income entity. An income asset account is debited or credited, and the other half of the entry is to an account that substantively explains the transaction. Initially, the income entity has no assets. Revenues, expenses, and distributions to income beneficiaries are closed periodically to an Estate Income account, which accumulates undistributed earnings.

A detailed discussion of the various types of income transactions and charges made against income is delayed until after the illustration of estate accounting. For simplicity, the illustration limits income transactions to interest on savings and bond investments, cash dividends on corporate stock investments, and interest on a partnership investment.

Illustration:
The opening entry and subsequent transactions

Richard Howes died testate on March 27, 19X1, with the following provisions in his will:

(1) The decedent's residence and household items are left to his wife, Yvonne Howes, who assumes the mortgage on the residence.
(2) Cash of $150,000 is to be given to the decedent's wife, Yvonne Howes.
(3) All the corporate stocks are to be given to the decedent's alma mater, Stewart University, to be used for scholarships in accounting.
(4) The decedent's automobile is to be given to Brian Howes, the decedent's brother.
(5) The residual balance of the estate is to be placed in trust with the following terms:
    (a) Trustee: Dana Point Bank
    (b) Income beneficiary: Yvonne Howes, wife of the decedent, for the remainder of her natural life.
    (c) Principal beneficiaries: Crystal and Cherice Howes, the only two children of the decedent. The principal is to be distributed at the later of: (a) the date of death of Yvonne Howes, or (b) when both Crystal and Cherice Howes reach the age of 25. (If Yvonne Howes dies before both children reach the age of 25, then the children

succeed her as income beneficiaries until they both reach the age of 25.)

(d) The accrual basis is to be used in determining principal at the time of death.

(6) State inheritance taxes are to be paid out of the residue of the estate and not by the individual heirs, except for the case of the automobile given to Brian Howes.

(7) The decedent's personal financial advisor, Jack Cass, is named executor of the estate.

The estate of Richard Howes consists of the following items, each listed at its current value:

Assets Subject to Probate Administration:

Cash (including checking and savings accounts)	$	70,000
U.S. government and corporate bonds—face value, $350,000;		
cost, $341,000		337,000
Corporate stocks—cost, $38,000		63,000
Life insurance (payable to the estate)		100,000
Investment in partnership of Howes, George, and White:		
Capital account balance at date of death,		
net of drawings	$84,000	
Share of profits from close of preceding		
partnership accounting period to date of		
death	14,000	
Share of partnership goodwill deemed to exist at		
date of death (calculated according to the		
terms of the partnership agreement)	22,000	120,000
Accrued interest receivable on bonds		10,000
Accrued interest receivable on savings accounts		2,000
Dividends declared on corporate stocks		1,000
Automobile		7,000
Total		$ 710,000

Assets Not Subject to Probate Administration:

Residence and household items		240,000
Duplex rental unit (cost, $75,000), subject to secured loan of		
$55,000		110,000
Total Estate Assets		$1,060,000

Liabilities to Be Paid out of Probate Estate:

Outstanding balance on credit cards	$	1,100
Medical expenses pertaining to illness		3,700
State and federal income taxes for the period January 1,		
19X1 to March 27, 19X1		5,500
Total	$	10,300

Liabilities Not to Be Paid out of Probate Estate:

Mortgage on residence		30,000
Mortgage on duplex rental unit		55,000
Total Estate Liabilities	$	95,300

In reviewing the items making up the estate, note that we have assumed that the decedent's residence, household items, and the duplex rental unit are not subject to probate administration of the state probate law. Consequently, the residence and household items pass immediately to the decedent's surviving spouse outside probate, and the duplex rental unit passes immediately to the trustee outside of probate. None of these items is accounted for in the administration of the estate. Accounting for the depreciable assets of a trust (such as the duplex rental unit used in this illustration) is discussed and illustrated later in the chapter.

The opening entry in the estate books follows.

Principal cash	70,000	
Investment in bonds	337,000	
Investment in stocks	63,000	
Life insurance receivable	100,000	
Investment in partnership of Howes, George, and White	120,000	
Accrued interest receivable on bonds	10,000	
Accrued interest receivable on savings accounts	2,000	
Dividends declared on corporate stocks	1,000	
Automobile	7,000	
Estate principal		710,000

No liabilities are recorded, because the accounting concerns the administration of estate assets.

Assumed transactions and related journal entries pertaining to activities completed by the executor during the administration of the estate from March 27, 19X1 to June 30, 19X2 are as follows:

Transaction	Entry		
(1) Subsequent discovery of a checking account.	Principal cash	700	
	Asset subsequently discovered		700
(2) Receipt of life insurance proceeds.	Principal cash	100,000	
	Life insurance receivable		100,000
(3) Receipt of proceeds from liquidation of investment in partnership, along with interest to date of receipt.	Principal cash	120,000	
	Income cash	4,000	
	Investment in partnership		120,000
	Interest income		4,000
(4) Receipt of interest on bonds.	Principal cash	10,000	
	Income cash	18,000	
	Accrued bond interest receivable		10,000
	Interest income		18,000
(5) Receipt of interest on savings accounts.	Principal cash	2,000	
	Income cash	6,000	
	Accrued interest receivable on savings accounts		2,000
	Interest income		6,000

Transaction	Entry		
(6) Receipt of cash dividends on corporate stocks. (Receipts pertaining to dividends declared during the estate administration accrue to the legatee.)	Principal cash	4,000	
	Accrued dividends receivable		1,000
	Liability to Stewart University		3,000
(7) Payment of credit card, medical, and income tax liabilities.	Debts of decedent	10,300	
	Principal cash		10,300
(8) Payment of funeral and administrative expenses.	Funeral and administrative expenses	11,000	
	Principal cash		11,000
(9) Payment of $49,300 inheritance taxes, $300 of which is to be borne by Brian Howes, who received the decedent's automobile.	Inheritance taxes	49,000	
	Receivable from legatee, Brian Howes	300	
	Principal cash		49,300
(10) Distribution of automobile as gift (a specific legacy) and collection of related inheritance taxes from legatee.	Principal cash	300	
	Legacies distributed	7,000	
	Receivable from legatee, Brian Howes		300
	Automobile		7,000
(11) Distribution of corporate stocks as gift (specific legacy) to Stewart University, along with dividend receipts pertaining to dividends declared and received during the estate administration.	Legacies distributed	63,000	
	Liability to Stewart University ...	3,000	
	Investment in stocks		63,000
	Principal cash		3,000
(12) Sale of a portion of the bonds to raise cash. (Current value at Howes' death was $9,600.)	Principal cash	9,800	
	Investment in bonds		9,600
	Gain on sale of principal asset		200
(13) Distribution of cash (general legacy) to Yvonne Howes.	Legacies distributed	150,000	
	Principal cash		150,000
(14) Payment of income taxes relating to estate income.	Estate income tax expense	4,600	
	Income cash		4,600
(15) Payment of administration expenses pertaining to income.	Administration expenses	300	
	Income cash		300
(16) Distributions to income beneficiary of trust.	Distributions to income beneficiary	18,000	
	Income cash		18,000

We assume that no estate taxes are owed because of the use of the unlimited marital deduction. If estate taxes had been paid, the entry would appear as follows.

Estate taxes... xxx
    Principal cash xxx

Illustration:
Charge and discharge statements

Continuing with our illustration, the only remaining task for the estate fiduciary is to submit an accounting to the probate court with a request to distribute the residual balance of the estate to the trustee, Dana Point Bank. Trial balances for the principal entity and the income entity as of June 30, 19X2 are presented in Illustration 25-1. Charge and discharge statements, which portray the activity of these entities through June 30, 19X2, are shown in Illustration 25-2. The charge and discharge statements are usually accompanied by supporting schedules—such as the detail of the decedent's debts paid and the detail of legacies distributed. Because they are quite simple, such schedules are not presented.

Illustration:
Closing entries for the estate

Assuming the probate court authorizes the distribution of the residual Howes estate assets to the trustee, the entries to record the distributions and close the estate books are shown on page 1001.

Illustration 25-1

ESTATE OF RICHARD HOWES Trial Balance—Principal June 30, 19X2		
	Debit	Credit
Cash	$ 93,200	
Investments in bonds	327,400	
Estate principal..		$710,000
Asset subsequently discovered............................		700
Gain on sale of principal asset...........................		200
Debts of decedent	10,300	
Funeral and administrative expenses	11,000	
Inheritance taxes	49,000	
Legacies distributed......................................	220,000	
Totals	$710,900	$710,900

ESTATE OF RICHARD HOWES Trial Balance—Income June 30, 19X2		
	Debit	Credit
Cash	$ 5,100	
Interest income...		$28,000
Estate income tax expense	4,600	
Administrative expenses...................................	300	
Distributions to income beneficiary	18,000	
Totals	$28,000	$28,000

Illustration 25-2

ESTATE OF RICHARD HOWES		
Jack Cass, Executor of the Estate		
Charge and Discharge Statements		
March 27, 19X1–June 30, 19X2		

First, as to Principal:

I charge myself as follows:

Assets per inventory	$710,000	
Assets discovered	700	
Gain on asset realization	200	$710,900

I credit myself as follows:

Debts of decedent paid	$ 10,300	
Funeral and administrative expenses paid	11,000	
Inheritance taxes paid	49,000	
Legacies distributed	220,000	(290,300)

Balance of the estate:

Principal cash	$ 93,200	
Investment in bonds	327,400	$420,600

Second, as to Income:

I charge myself as follows:

Interest received on bonds	$ 18,000	
Interest received on savings accounts	6,000	
Interest received on partnership investment	4,000	$ 28,000

I credit myself as follows:

Estate income taxes paid	$ 4,600	
Administrative expenses paid	300	
Distributions made to income beneficiary	18,000	(22,900)

Balance of the estate:

Income cash		$ 5,100

Transaction	Entry		
(17) Distribution of residual estate assets of principal entity to Dana Point Bank, trustee.	Legacies distributed	420,600	
	Principal cash		93,200
	Investment in bonds		327,400
(18) Distribution of residual estate assets of income entity to Dana Point Bank, trustee.	Distribution to trustee for income beneficiary	5,100	
	Income cash		5,100
(19) Closing of nominal accounts of principal entity into estate principal.	Asset subsequently discovered	700	
	Gain on sale of principal asset	200	
	Estate principal	710,000	
	Debts of decedent		10,300
	Funeral and administrative expenses		11,000
	Inheritance taxes		49,000
	Legacies distributed		640,600
(20) Closing of nominal accounts of income entity.	Interest income	28,000	
	Estate income tax expense		4,600
	Administrative expenses		300
	Distributions to income beneficiary		18,000
	Distribution to trustee for income beneficiary		5,100

ACCOUNTING FOR TRUSTS

Accounting for trusts is identical to accounting for estates, except that a Trust Principal account is used instead of Estate Principal for the principal entity, and a Trust Income account is used instead of Estate Income for the income entity to accumulate undistributed earnings. The nature of the transactions is different, of course. An estate fiduciary is concerned primarily with cleaning up the affairs of a decedent and making proper distributions of estate property. A trustee, on the other hand, is concerned primarily with prudently managing a pool of assets in accordance with the powers granted to him or her by the trust agreement. This task usually involves buying and selling trust assets. Trustees must make periodic accountings to the principal and income beneficiaries and the probate court. A charge and discharge statement similar to the one illustrated for estates is used. Upon termination of the life of the trust, the trustee distributes the assets of the trust principal to the remainderman, makes a final accounting to the court, and requests to be discharged.

Using the illustration from the preceding section, the entries to record the receipt of the gifts from the estate of William Howes are as follows:

Principal entity:

Principal cash	93,200	
Investment in bonds.................................	327,400	
Trust principal		420,600

Income entity:

Income cash	5,100	
Trust income		5,100

Transactions pertaining to principal

We have summarized the general thrust of the accounting requirements of the Revised Uniform Principal and Income Act regarding principal transactions. Some finer points of principal transactions are as follows:

(1) The costs of investing and reinvesting principal assets are charged against principal.
(2) The costs of preparing property for rental or sale are charged against principal.
(3) Taxes levied on gains or profits allocated to principal are charged against principal.
(4) The costs incurred in maintaining or defending any action to protect the trust or trust property or ensure title to any trust property are charged against principal.
(5) Extraordinary repairs or costs incurred in making capital improvements paid for out of principal may be recouped from income through depreciation charges.
(6) Trustee's fees and costs relating to the periodic accounting to the court of jurisdiction (court costs, attorney fees, and accounting fees, for example) are shared equally between principal and income.

(7) Liquidating dividends are considered to be principal.
(8) Stock dividends go to principal, not income.

Transactions pertaining to income

As mentioned earlier, under the Revised Uniform Principal and Income Act, interest and cash dividends are considered income transactions. The act also includes the following as income: rents, loan prepayment penalties, lease cancellation charges, lease renewal fees, and the net profits of any business in which principal is invested. Losses of any business in which principal is invested are charged to principal, because no provision exists for loss carryforward or carryback into any other calendar or fiscal year for purposes of calculating net income. Profits and losses of such businesses are to be determined using generally accepted accounting principles.

Among other things, the act includes as charges against income interest expense on trust liabilities (such as a mortgage on a trust rental property), property taxes, insurance premiums, ordinary repairs, depreciation expenses (including depreciation charges pertaining to extraordinary repairs), income taxes attributable to trust income, a share of trustee fees and costs relating to periodic accounting to the court, and any other ordinary expense incurred in connection with the administration, management, or preservation of trust property. (Depreciation and unusual charges are discussed in detail in the following paragraphs because of the unique manner in which journal entries are recorded.)

Depreciation. Under the act, depreciation is mandatory and results in preserving the estate principal for the principal beneficiaries. However, under many state statutes, depreciation is provided at the discretion of the trustee. When depreciation is to be provided, a portion of the income entity's revenue flow must go to the principal entity. Because we view the trust as comprising two entities, the accounting entries to record depreciation produce results as if the principal entity had sent a bill to the income entity for the use or consumption of the depreciable asset. The entries are as follows:

	Income Entity		Principal Entity	
(1) To record depreciation:				
Depreciation expense	1,000			
Due to principal		1,000		
Due from income			1,000	
Accumulated depreciation				1,000
(2) To record payment:				
Due to principal	1,000			
Income cash		1,000		
Principal cash			1,000	
Due from income				1,000

In estate planning, whether or not to provide depreciation should be thoroughly explored. Depreciation charges may deprive an income beneficiary of income necessary to maintain the standard of living intended by the decedent. Depreciation makes no sense if the properties are appreciating in value, as is the case with many rental properties. If depreciation is to be provided, it should be computed based on the current value of the property when it becomes subject to the trust.

Unusual charges against income.   The Revised Uniform Principal and Income Act states:

> If charges against income are of unusual amount, the trustee may by means of reserves or other reasonable means charge them over a reasonable period of time and withhold from distribution sufficient sums to regularize distributions [Section 13(b)].

This provision is somewhat ambiguous and open-ended. Under the "by means of reserves" approach, the trustee must anticipate and estimate expected unusual charges before they are incurred. Charges are then made against income over a reasonable period of time prior to their incurrence, resulting in the buildup of a "reserve," or estimated liability. The cash distributable to the income beneficiary during these periods is limited; thus, funds accumulate from which to make the expenditure when it actually arises. Under the "by other reasonable means" option, the trustee can possibly have the principal entity make the expenditure when it arises but record the expenditure as a deferred charge, which is subsequently amortized against income.

The entries under each approach for an unusually large expenditure, such as the painting of an apartment building exterior, are as follows:

	Income Entity	Principal Entity
(1) Accumulation Method:		
(a) Periodic charge.		
Estimated painting expense	1,000	
Estimated future liability	1,000	(no entry)
(b) Actual payment.		
Estimated future liability	5,000	(no entry)
Income cash	5,000	
(2) Amortization Method:		
(a) Actual payment.		
Painting of building		5,000
Principal cash	(no entry)	5,000
(b) Periodic amortization.		
Painting expense	1,000	
Due to principal	1,000	

| Due from income .... (no entry) | 1,000 | |
| Painting of building............... | | 1,000 |

SUMMARY

The fundamental function of estate and trust fiduciaries is to administer assets under their control rather than attempting to determine the net worth of an estate or trust. Accordingly, accounting for estates and trusts involves accounting for assets rather than accounting for net worth. As a result, special bookkeeping practices and accountability statements are used for estates and trusts that are quite unlike those found in commercial enterprises. Furthermore, the cash basis of accounting suffices in most instances.

Generally accepted accounting principles have virtually no application to estates and trusts. Trust income (including trust income during the administration of an estate) is determined according to the terms and provisions of the trust agreement. If the trust agreement is silent on the treatment to be accorded an item, then state statutes control. An accountant rendering services to a trust must recognize that his or her role is a passive one when it comes to determining the treatment to be accorded items that are not clearly set forth in the trust agreement or state statutes. Decisions on such matters should be referred to legal counsel or the courts. In most cases, an accountant rendering services to an estate or trust must also have expertise in estate, inheritance, and trust taxation.

Glossary of new terms

Administrator: A person appointed by the court to administer the affairs of a decedent when an executor is not appointed.

Demonstrative Legacy: A gift of cash for which a particular fund or source is designated from which payment is to be made.

Devise: A gift of real property.

Devisee: The recipient of a devise.

Estate Planning: The making of plans for the orderly transfer of one's property on death as desired, with a view toward minimizing transfer costs.

Executor: A person who is named in a will to serve as the decedent's personal representative in administering the estate and who is appointed by the court to serve in that capacity.

General Legacy: Gifts of cash for which no particular fund or source is designated.

Income Beneficiary: The party to a trust who is entitled to the income earned on trust assets.

***Inter Vivos* Trust:** A trust created during a person's life.

Intestate: A term used to refer to having died without a will.

Legacy: A gift of personal property.

Legatee: The recipient of a legacy.

Principal Beneficiary: The party to a trust who is entitled to the trust principal.

Probate: The act by which a probate court determines if a decedent's will meets the statutory requirements concerning wills.

Probate Court: Courts in the state court system that have jurisdiction over the affairs of decedents.

Remainderman: The party to a trust who is entitled to the trust principal.

Residual Legacy: A gift of all personal property remaining after distribution of specific, demonstrative, and general legacies.

Testamentary Trust: A trust that comes into being on a person's death, pursuant to provisions in the decedent's will.

Testate: A term used to refer to having died with a will.

Trust: An arrangement in which property is transferred to a person, called a trustee, who holds title to the property but administers the property for the benefit of other parties, who are called the beneficiaries.

Trustee: That party to a trust who takes title to trust property and administers the property for the benefit of others.

Trustor: The party to a trust agreement who created the trust. (Also referred to as a settlor, grantor, donor, or creator.)

Specific Legacy: A gift of specified noncash items.

Review questions

1. What role do generally accepted accounting principles play in determining trust income? Explain.
2. How do we determine whether a transaction pertains to principal or income?
3. What is the nature of the relationship between a trust income beneficiary and a trust principal beneficiary?
4. What are legacies and devises?
5. Are estate liabilities recorded in the opening entry for an estate? Why or why not?
6. An estate fiduciary may have to deal with what four types of taxes?
7. Under the Revised Uniform Principal and Income Act, when do the rights of income beneficiaries begin?
8. When is the accrual method used in accounting for estates and trusts?
9. What is the function of probate administration?
10. State the major tasks of an estate fiduciary.
11. Describe the accountant's role with respect to distinguishing principal and income transactions.
12. Must assets and transactions pertaining to income be accounted for in separate general ledgers? Explain.

Discussion cases

Discussion case 25–1
Estate planning

Your client, Vann Wheeler, has asked your advice on accounting matters with respect to his attorney's preparation of a testamentary trust agreement. Vann wants all his residential rental property holdings placed in trust for the benefit of his wife (as income beneficiary) and his children (as principal beneficiaries).

Required:
On what points should you advise your client? (Assume you are located in a state that has adopted the Revised Uniform Principal and Income Act without modification.)

Discussion case 25-2
Role of the accountant

An attorney who is an acquaintance of yours has suggested that you attend a meeting that may lead to some work for you. At the meeting, you are informed that: (1) Moe Grasser died approximately one year ago; (2) the attorney is serving as the executor of the estate; (3) the residual balance of the estate is to be placed in trust; and (4) the trustee is Maureen Grasser, Moe's widow. Mrs. Grasser describes the nature of the trust assets as bonds, residential rental properties, and the stock of a wholly owned corporation, which continues to operate. She requests that you become the accountant for the trust and, in that capacity, do the following:

(1) Maintain the books and records.
(2) Make all accounting decisions.
(3) Prepare the fiduciary income tax returns.
(4) Prepare the annual financial statements.

Required:

How would you respond to this request? Elaborate on the points you should discuss with Mrs. Grasser.

Exercises

Exercise 25-1
Estates: True or false

Indicate whether the following statements are true or false. Explain any false answers.

(1) An estate is a taxable entity.
(2) An estate is a legal entity.
(3) The probate estate is usually smaller than the estate for federal estate tax purposes.
(4) One function of an estate fiduciary is to account for the estate in a manner that continually reflects the estate's net worth.
(5) Federal estate taxes are effectively borne by the residual beneficiaries of the estate.
(6) State inheritance taxes are based on the right to give away one's property.
(7) The Estate Principal account reflects the net worth of the estate at a given point in time.
(8) Accounting for estates revolves around the administration of the decedent's assets.
(9) The probate court essentially serves as the guardian of the estate.
(10) A legacy is a gift of real property.

Exercise 25-2
Estates: Fill-in statements

For the following items, fill in the missing word.

(1) An estate fiduciary who is named in a decedent's will is called a(n) _____.

(2) An estate fiduciary who is appointed by the probate court when no person is named in a decedent's will is called a(n) _____.

(3) A gift of personal property is called a _____.

(4) A gift of real property is called a _____.

(5) The four types of legacies are _____, _____, _____, and _____.

(6) A person who dies without a will is said to have died _____.

(7) A person who dies with a will is said to have died _____.

(8) State laws dealing with the affairs of decedents are commonly known as _____ _____.

(9) Federal estate taxes are based on the right to _____ property.

(10) State inheritance taxes are based on the right to _____ property.

Exercise 25–3
Trusts: True or false

Indicate whether the following statements are true or false. Explain any false answers.

(1) When the income beneficiary and the principal beneficiary are the same person, no built-in clash of interests exists as in trusts in which these beneficiaries are not the same person.

(2) The rights of an income beneficiary begin when assets are actually transferred to the trustee.

(3) In trust accounting matters, the terms of the trust agreement prevail over generally accepted accounting principles.

(4) When the accounting treatment of an item is not clearly specified in the trust agreement, reference is made to generally accepted accounting principles.

(5) The Revised Uniform Principal and Income Act of 1962 is somewhat outdated because it is based on generally accepted accounting principles in effect at that time.

(6) When reference must be made to state laws to distinguish trust principal from trust income, it is the accountant's role to interpret those laws concerning accounting matters.

(7) The Revised Uniform Principal and Income Act specifies the use of the accrual basis for many items at the commencement of a trust.

(8) Accounts and transactions pertaining to trust income must be accounted for in a separate ledger to prevent commingling of accounts and transactions with that of trust principal.

(9) If the answer to an accounting question cannot be found by referring to the trust agreement, state law, or case law, then reference is made to generally accepted accounting principles.

(10) Trustors may specify their own definition of net income, even if this definition is contrary to state laws pertaining to trust principal and income.

Exercise 25–4
Trusts: Fill-in statements

For the following items, fill in the missing word.

(1) The person creating a trust is commonly called the _____.

(2) Trusts established pursuant to the provisions of a will are called _____ trusts.

(3) Trusts established during a person's life are called _____ trusts.

(4) The party taking title to trust assets is called the _____.

(5) The two classes of trust beneficiaries are the _____ beneficiaries and the _____ beneficiaries.

(6) Another term for trust principal is trust _____.

(7) The basis of accounting that is used in most respects when an income beneficiary's rights are established is the _____ basis.

(8) Depreciation is _____ under the Revised Uniform Principal and Income Act.

(9) When the accounting treatment of an item is in doubt, the first place to look is the _____ _____.

(10) The _____ basis of accounting is used during the administration of a trust but not at the beginning and end of an income beneficiary's rights.

Exercise 25–5
Estates: Preparing journal entries

Carl McDonald died on May 12, 19X1, with a provision in his will for the establishment of a testamentary trust. His estate had the following assets subject to probate administration:

	Current Value
Cash in checking and savings accounts	$ 42,000
Investment in U.S. government bonds	387,000
Coin collection	11,000
Bond interest receivable	6,500
Total	$446,500

The estate fiduciary had the following receipts and disbursements from May 12, 19X1 to January 20, 19X2:

(1) Personal liabilities totaling $2,200 were paid.

(2) Funeral expenses of $1,800 were paid.

(3) Federal estate taxes of $37,000 were paid.

(4) State inheritance taxes of $14,000 were paid. Of this amount, $400 is to be borne by the legatee receiving the coin collection, and $1,100 is to be borne by the legatee (Children's Hospital) that is to receive $25,000 cash.

(5) Administrative expenses of $3,300 were paid.

(6) A note receivable of $2,000 was discovered in September 19X1.

(7) The note receivable in (6) was collected in December 19X1, along with $150 interest.

(8) Interest on bonds was received totaling $22,000.

(9) Bonds having a current value of $60,500 at McDonald's death were sold for $58,800.

(10) The coin collection was distributed to the specified legatee, and the legatee reimbursed the estate for the inheritance taxes at that time.

(11) Cash of $23,900 was distributed to Children's Hospital ($25,000 specified in the will – $1,100 state inheritance taxes).

(12) Estate income taxes for the period May 12, 19X1 to December 31, 19X1 totaling $3,800 were paid.

(13) Cash of $10,000 was distributed to the income beneficiary of the trust, Wendy McDonald.

Required:
(1) Prepare the opening and subsequent transaction journal entries for the estate.
(2) Prepare closing journal entries as of January 20, 19X2.

Exercise 25–6
Trusts: Preparing journal entries

Following are the 19X3 transactions of a trust that has investments in corporate bonds and an apartment house:

(1) Rental receipts totaled $38,500.
(2) Property taxes of $1,400 were paid.
(3) Mortgage payments of $15,500 were made. Of this amount, $14,900 pertained to interest and $600 pertained to principal. (Assume that the mortgage liability is reflected as a liability in the trust general ledger only on a memorandum basis.)
(4) Normal operating costs of the apartment totaling $7,300 were paid.
(5) The exterior of the apartment building was painted in January 19X3 for $2,100, and payment was made at that time. The apartment exterior is painted approximately every seven years. [Assume that this qualifies as an "unusual amount," as that term is used in Section 13(b) of the Revised Uniform Principal and Income Act.]
(6) The annual depreciation charge on the apartment is $4,500.
(7) Bond investments having a face value of $50,000 matured during the year and were redeemed. (These bonds had a current value of $48,800 when they became subject to the trust.)
(8) Federal trust income taxes pertaining to the prior year were paid totaling $450.
(9) Estimated federal trust income tax payments for the current year were paid totaling $1,850.
(10) The $2,200 trustee's fee for the year was paid.
(11) Interest receipts on bond investments totaled $14,400.
(12) Cash distributions totaling $9,000 were made to the income beneficiary.

Required:
(1) Prepare the trust transaction journal entries for the year.
(2) Prepare the year-end closing entries.

Problems

Problem 25–1
Estates: Preparing charge and discharge statements

The will of Clay Potter, deceased, directed that his executor, Raney Waters, liquidate the entire estate within two years of the date of Potter's death and pay the net proceeds and income, if any, to the Childrens Town Orphanage. Potter, who never married, died February 1, 19X4 after a brief illness.

An inventory of the decedent's property subject to probate administration was prepared, and the fair market value of each item was determined. The preliminary inventory, before the computation of any appropriate income accruals on inventory items, follows:

	Fair Market Value
First National Bank checking account	$ 6,000
$60,000 of 8% City of Hope school bonds, payable January 1 and July 1, maturity date of July 1, 19X8	59,000
2,000 shares of Crocker Corporation capital stock........................	220,000
Term life insurance, beneficiary—estate of Clay Potter....................	20,000
Personal residence ($75,000) and furnishings ($15,000)	90,000

During 19X4, the following transactions occurred:

(1) The interest on the City of Hope bonds was collected. The bonds were sold on July 1 for $59,000, and the proceeds and interest were paid to the orphanage.
(2) The Crocker Corporation paid cash dividends of $1 per share on March 1 and December 1, as well as a 10% stock dividend on July 1. All dividends were declared 45 days before each payment date and were payable to stockholders of record as of 40 days before each payment date. On September 2, Waters sold 1,000 shares at $105 per share, and paid the proceeds to the orphanage.
(3) Because of a depressed real estate market, the personal residence was rented furnished at $300 per month commencing April 1. The rent is paid monthly, in advance. Real estate taxes of $900 for calendar year 19X4 were paid. The house and furnishings have estimated lives of 45 and 10 years, respectively. The part-time caretaker was paid four months' wages totaling $500 on April 30 for services performed, and he was released.
(4) The First National Bank checking account was closed; the $6,000 balance was transferred to an estate bank account.
(5) The term life insurance was paid on March 1 and deposited in the estate bank account.
(6) The following disbursements were made:
   (a) Funeral expenses, $2,000.
   (b) Final illness expenses, $1,500.
   (c) April 15 income tax remittance, $700.
   (d) Attorney's and accountant's fees, $12,000.
(7) On December 31, the balance of the undistributed income, except for $1,000, was paid to the orphanage. The balance of the cash on hand derived from the estate principal was also paid to the orphanage on December 31.

Required:
Prepare Charge and Discharge Statements, separating principal and income, together with supporting schedules, on behalf of the executor for the period February 1, 19X4 through December 31, 19X4. The following supporting schedules should be included:

(1) Original Principal of Estate
(2) Gain or Loss on Disposal of Estate Assets
(3) Funeral, Administration, and Other Expenses
(4) Debts of Decedent Paid

(5) Legacies Paid or Delivered
(6) Assets (Corpus) on Hand, December 31, 19X4
(7) Income Collected
(8) Expenses Chargeable to Income
(9) Distributions of Income   (AICPA adapted)

Problem 25–2
Estates: Preparing charge and discharge statements

Art Fern died in an accident on May 31, 19X1. His will, dated February 28, 19X0, provided that all just debts and expenses be paid and that his property be disposed of as follows:

(1) Personal residence is devised to Arless Fern, widow. (Real property is not subject to probate administration in the state in which the deceased resided.)
(2) U.S. Treasury bonds and Carson Company stock is to be placed in trust. All income to go to Arless Fern during her lifetime, with right of appointment on her death.
(3) Landers Company mortage notes are bequeathed to Carol Fern Sellers, daughter.
(4) A bequest of $10,000 cash goes to Wayne Fern, son.
(5) Remainder of estate is to be divided equally between the two children.

The will further provided that during the administration period, Arless Fern was to be paid $800 a month out of estate income. Estate and inheritance taxes are to be borne by the residue. Wayne Fern was named executor and trustee.

An inventory of the decedent's property was prepared. The fair market value of all items as of Fern's death was determined. The preliminary inventory, before the computation of any appropriate income accruals on inventory items, is as follows:

Personal residence property	$145,000
Jewelry—diamond ring	9,600
York Life Insurance Company—term life insurance policy on life of Art Fern; beneficiary, Arless Fern, widow	120,000
Granite Trust Company—8% savings account, Art Fern, in trust for Philip Sellers (grandchild), interest credited January 1 and July 1; balance May 31, 19X1	400
Fidelity National Bank—checking account; balance May 31, 19X1	141,750
$200,000 U.S. Treasury bonds, 10%; interest payable March 1 and September 1	200,000
$10,000 Landers Company first mortgage notes, 12%, 19X5; interest payable June 30 and December 31	9,900
800 shares Carson Company common stock	64,000
700 shares Mity Manufacturing Company common stock	70,000

The executor opened an estate bank account, to which he transferred the decedent's checking account balance. Other deposits, through July 1, 19X2, were as follows:

Interest collected on bonds:	
$200,000 U.S. Treasury—	
September 1, 19X1	$10,000
March 1, 19X2	10,000

Dividends received on stock:

800 shares Carson Company—

June 15, 19X1, declared May 7, 19X1, payable to holders of record May 27, 19X1	800
September 15, 19X1	800
December 15, 19X1..	1,200
March 15, 19X2	800
June 15, 19X2	800
Net proceeds of June 19, 19X1 sale of 700 shares of Mity Manufacturing Company	68,810
Interest collected on Landers Company first mortgage notes— June 30, 19X1	600

Payments were made from the estate's checking account through July 1, 19X2 for the following items:

Funeral expenses...	$ 2,000
Assessments for additional 19X0 federal and state income tax ($1,700) plus interests ($110) to May 31, 19X1......................................	1,810
19X1 income taxes of Art Fern for the period January 1, 19X1 through May 31, 19X1, in excess of estimated taxes paid by the decedent..........	9,100
Federal and state fiduciary income taxes, fiscal year ended June 30, 19X1 ($75) and June 30, 19X2 ($1,400).....................................	1,475
State inheritance taxes	28,000
Monthly payments to Arless Fern: 13 payments of $800	10,400
Attorney's and accountant's fees	25,000
Payment of interest collected on Landers Company mortgage notes that accrues to legatee	600

The executor waived his commission. However, he wanted his father's diamond ring in lieu of the $10,000 specific legacy. All parties agreed to this in writing, and the court's approval was secured. All other specific legacies were delivered by July 15, 19X1.

Required:

Prepare Charge and Discharge Statements for principal and income, and supporting schedules, to accompany the attorney's formal court accounting on behalf of the executor of the Estate of Art Fern for the period May 31, 19X1 through July 1, 19X2. The following supporting schedules should be included:

 (1) Original Capital of Estate
 (2) Gain on Disposal of Estate Assets
 (3) Loss on Disposal of Estate Assets
 (4) Funeral, Administration, and Other Expenses
 (5) Debts of Decedent Paid
 (6) Legacies Paid or Delivered
 (7) Assets (Corpus) on Hand, July 1, 19X2
 (8) Proposed Plan of Distribution of Estate Assets
 (9) Income Collected
(10) Distribution of Income

(AICPA adapted)

Problem 25–3
Trusts: Treatment of disputed items

You have been assigned by a CPA firm to work with the trustees of a large trust in the preparation of the first annual accounting to the court. The income beneficiaries and the remaindermen cannot agree on the proper allocation of the following items on which the trust agreement is silent:

(1) Costs incurred in expanding the garage facilities of an apartment house owned by the trust and held for rental income.
(2) Real estate taxes on the apartment house.
(3) Cost of casualty insurance premiums on the apartment house.
(4) A 2-for-1 stock split of common stock held by the trust for investment.
(5) Insurance proceeds received as the result of a partial destruction of an office building that the trust owned and held for rental income.
(6) Costs incurred by the trust in the sale of a tract of land.
(7) Costs incurred to defend title to real property held by the trust.

Required:
Locate a copy of the Revised Uniform Principal and Income Act in your library. Indicate the allocations between principal and income to be made for each item, using the act as the point of reference. Be sure to quote the applicable section of the act. (The purpose of this problem is to force you to search out items in the act as is necessary in actual practice.)

(AICPA adapted)

Problem 25–4
Trusts: Preparing journal entries and charge and discharge statements

The postclosing combined trial balance for the principal entity and the income entity of a trust as of December 31, 19X3 is as follows:

	Debit	Credit
Principal cash	$ 3,500	
Income cash	800	
Investments in bonds	123,400	
Investment in S & W Corporation common stock	86,200	
Duplex rental unit	95,000	
Accumulated depreciation on duplex rental unit		$ 12,000
Trust principal		296,100
Trust income		800
Totals	$308,900	$308,900

Following are the 19X4 trust transactions:

(1) Rental receipts were $11,500.
(2) Property taxes of $1,000 were paid.
(3) Mortgage payments of $6,500 were made. Of this amount, $5,800 pertained to interest and $700 pertained to principal. (The mortgage liability of $57,500 on the duplex at December 31, 19X3 is recorded in the trust general ledger on a memorandum basis.)

(4) Normal operating costs of the duplex rental unit totaling $600 were paid.

(5) New carpeting was installed in both units of the duplex in January 19X4 at a cost of $1,800, with payment being made at that time. (New carpeting is installed approximately every 10 years.)

(6) The annual depreciation charge on the duplex is $2,000. (Of the $95,000 value assigned to the duplex when it became subject to the trust, $15,000 was assigned to land, and $80,000 was assigned to the building, carpets, and drapes. The $80,000 is depreciated over 40 years.)

(7) Bond investments having a face value of $25,000 matured during the year and were redeemed. (These bonds had a $25,500 current value when they became subject to the trust.)

(8) Bonds having a face value of $20,000 were purchased in the open market for $19,000 on July 1, 19X4. The maturity date of the bonds is June 30, 19X9.

(9) Interest receipts on bond investments totaled $9,800.

(10) S & W Corporation declared a 10% stock dividend on April 1, 19X4. The trust held 200 shares of S & W Corporation's common stock prior to this declaration. (The market price of S & W Corporation's common stock increased $30 per share during 19X4.)

(11) Cash dividends of $3,300 on S & W Corporation's common stock were received.

(12) The $1,500 trustee's fee for the year was paid.

(13) Attorney's and accountant's fees for periodic judicial accounting totaling $1,200 were paid.

(14) Cash distributions totaling $8,000 were made to the income beneficiary.

(15) "Due to" and "due from" accounts are settled at year-end.

Required:

(1) Prepare the trust transaction journal entries for the year.

(2) Prepare the year-end closing entries.

(3) Prepare Charge and Discharge Statements for the year for trust principal and trust income.

26 Installment Sales, Franchises, and Consignments

Certain businesses conduct operations in a manner that demands special or delayed revenue recognition practices. In this chapter, we discuss accounting for installment sales, business franchises, and consignments.

ACCOUNTING FOR INSTALLMENT SALES

In some sales transactions in which credit is granted, the terms provide for the collection of the sales price in installments over an extended period of time. Such sales are commonly referred to as **installment sales.** The terms and conditions of installment sales may vary widely, as follows:

(1) Collection period. A collection period of from one to three years is common for installment sales in the retail furniture and appliance businesses. For the retail land sales business, the collection period may be as long as 10 or 15 years.
(2) Cash down payment. Some installment sales require a fairly high cash down payment (ranging from 20–40% of the sales price), forcing the buyer immediately to have a material equity in the purchased item. On the other hand, some installment sales require only a nominal cash down payment, such as 5% of the sales price.
(3) Seller's recourse in the event of default. If the buyer defaults on payment of the receivable, the seller's only recourse may be to repossess the item. In other cases, the seller may have recourse against other assets of the purchaser.

Accordingly, installment sales usually produce more uncertainty than noninstallment sales regarding the ability and willingness of the buyer to make full payment. Furthermore, the ability and willingness of the buyer to make full payment may change over the extended period of collection. For some installment sales, this uncertainty is so great that no reasonable basis exists for estimating the degree of collectibility of the receivable. In such cases, prudence dictates that a more conservative approach be used to report such transactions than that used for credit sales in which collection of the sales price is reasonably assured. Two methods may be used to effect a more conservative treatment—the **installment method** and the **cost recovery method.**

The installment method

Under the installment method, a sale is recorded, but the gross profit on the sale is recognized in the income statement only in proportion to the payments received on the purchase price. In this way, recognition of the gross profit is delayed (through the use of deferral accounts), and the receivable is carried at a conservative value over the credit period. (The unrecognized deferred gross profit at any point in time is shown in the balance sheet as an offset to the receivable.)

Theoretically, the gross profit should be reduced by direct selling expenses (such as commissions) when determining the amount of profit to be deferred. Practice varies in this respect. (In *FASB Statement No. 66,* "Accounting for Sales of Real Estate," the illustrations dealing with the recognition of profit on retail land sales under the installment method treat selling expenses as a reduction of gross profit.[1]) The matching concept may also be used as an argument in favor of subtracting a pro rata portion of general and administrative expenses from the gross profit. The conventional installment method, however, treats these expenses as period costs for reasons of conservatism and simplicity, thereby avoiding the need to make complex and arbitrary allocations.

Whether or not an individual installment sale should be accounted for under the installment method is a judgmental decision based on the terms and conditions of the sales contract. *APB Opinion No. 10—1966,* "Omnibus Opinion," states that the installment method of accounting is inappropriate "unless the circumstances are such that the collection of the sales price is not reasonably assured."[2]

Thus, the selection of the installment method cannot be an arbitrary decision—the use of the method must be justified to be in accordance with generally accepted accounting principles. In practice, the installment method is not widely used for installment sales for financial reporting purposes. For income tax reporting purposes, however, use of the installment method for installment sales is quite widespread. Income tax aspects are discussed more fully later in the chapter.

In addition to sales of manufactured products, the installment method (or the cost recovery method, which is discussed on page 1028) may have to be used in the following two special areas:

(1) Sales of Real Estate. This topic is dealt with in *FASB Statement No. 66.* Briefly, if certain specified criteria are not met (some of which set forth minimum amounts or down payment levels), the installment method is mandatory. (In certain situations, the cost recovery method may be used instead of the installment method.)[3]

(2) Franchise Fee Revenues. This topic is dealt with in *FASB Statement No. 45.* Briefly, the installment method or the cost recovery method is mandatory when the franchise fee revenue is to be paid over an extended period and no reasonable basis exists for estimating the collectibility of the receivable.[4] (The wording in *FASB Statement No. 45* is slightly different from that in *APB Opinion No. 10,* but it is substantively the same criterion.)

---

[1] *FASB Statement No. 66,* "Accounting for Sales of Real Estate" (Stamford, CT: FASB, 1982), p. 62.
[2] *APB Opinion No. 10,* "Omnibus Opinion" (New York: AICPA, 1966), paragraph 12.
[3] *FASB Statement No. 66,* paragraphs 22 and 47.
[4] *FASB Statement No. 45,* "Accounting for Franchise Fee Revenue" (Stamford, CT: FASB, 1981), paragraph 6.

Illustration:
The installment method

To illustrate the application of the installment method of accounting and the related financial statement presentation, we assume the following facts for a sale that may be properly accounted for under the installment method:

(1) Sales price $100,000
(2) Cost of goods sold. . . . . $ 60,000
(3) Gross profit . . . . $ 40,000
(4) Gross profit percentage ($40,000/$100,000) 40%
(5) Sales date . . . . January 1, 19X1
(6) Payment terms:

Cash down payment at date of sale $10,000
Installment payments of $2,500 per month over 36 months,
  beginning January 31, 19X1 and ending December 31,
  19X3 . . . . $90,000
Annual interest rate to be charged on outstanding balance 10%

(7) All monthly payments, along with interest on the unpaid balance, are made on time. Accordingly, cash collections are as follows:

	19X1	19X2	19X3	Total
Down payment	$10,000			$ 10,000
Installment payments	30,000	$30,000	$30,000	90,000
Total.	$40,000	$30,000	$30,000	$100,000
Interest on average unpaid balance:				
10% of $75,000.	$ 7,500			$ 7,500
10% of $45,000.		$ 4,500		4,500
10% of $15,000.			$ 1,500	1,500
				$ 13,500

The journal entries that would be recorded for this transaction for 19X1, 9X2, and 19X3 are as follows:

19X1:

Cash 10,000
Installment receivables—19X1 90,000
    Installment sales 100,000
  To record installment sale.

Cost of installment sales. 60,000
    Inventory 60,000
  To relieve inventory for goods sold on the install-
  ment basis.

Deferral of gross profit (an income statement account)...	36,000	
Deferred gross profit—19X1 (a contra asset		
account)		36,000

To defer the recognition of gross profit on installment
sale (40% of $90,000). (The Deferral of Gross
Profit account is closed to retained earnings at year-
end along with the other income statement accounts.)

Cash	37,500	
Installment receivables—19X1		30,000
Interest income		7.500

To record collections on installment receivable,
along with related interest on average outstanding
balance.

Deferred gross profit—19X1	12,000	
Recognition of deferred gross profit (an income		
statement account)		12,000

To recognize gross profit based on cash collected
on sales price (40% of $30,000).

19X2:

Cash	34,500	
Installment receivables—19X1		30,000
Interest income		4,500

To record collections on installment receivable,
along with related interest on average outstanding
balance.

Deferred gross profit—19X1	12,000	
Recognition of deferred gross profit		12,000

To recognize gross profit based on cash collected
on sales price (40% of $30,000).

19X3:

Cash	31,500	
Installment receivables—19X1		30,000
Interest income		1,500

To record collections on installment receivable,
along with related interest on average outstanding
balance.

Deferred gross profit—19X1	12,000	
Recognition of deferred profit		12,000

To recognize gross profit based on cash collected
on sales price (40% of $30,000).

The financial statements for 19X1, 19X2, and 19X3 would reflect the
following accounts and amounts as a result of these journal entries.

Income statement

	19X1	19X2	19X3
Installment sale	$100,000		
Cost of installment sale	(60,000)		
Gross profit	$ 40,000		
Less—Deferral of gross profit	(36,000)		
Add—Recognition of deferred gross profit	12,000	$12,000	$12,000
Gross profit recognizable	$ 16,000	$12,000	$12,000
Interest income	7,500	4,500	1,500

Balance Sheet

	December 31,		
	19X1	19X2	19X3
Installment receivable	$ 60,000	$30,000	
Less—Deferred gross profit	(24,000)	(12,000)	
Installment receivable, net of deferred gross profit	$ 36,000	$18,000	

Financial statement presentation

In presenting accounts relating to installment sales accounted for under the installment method in the financial statements, the following finer points require discussion.

Installment sales and regular sales. If a company has sales that are not accounted for under the installment method, then such sales and their related cost of goods sold and gross profit would be shown in the income statement separately from the accounts relating to the installment sales accounted for under the installment method. This presentation may be made (a) vertically, by showing the regular sales, cost of sales, and gross profit either above or below the accounts relating to the sales accounted for under the installment method; or (b) horizontally, by showing one column for regular sales, another column for installment sales accounted for under the installment method, and a total column. The vertical presentation is generally used in comparative-year financial statements. Likewise, in the balance sheet, normal trade receivables would be shown separately from installment sale receivables.

Classification of deferred gross profit. In the preceding illustration, we showed the Deferred Gross Profit account as a deduction from installment receivables in the balance sheet. The Deferred Gross Profit account is substantively an asset valuation allowance. Under the provisions of *APB Opinion No. 12—1967,* "Omnibus Opinion," asset valuation allowances must be shown as deductions from the assets to which they relate.[5] *FASB Statement No. 66,* "Accounting for Sales of Real Estate," also requires this presentation for real estate sales accounted for under the installment method.[6]

---

[5] *APB Opinion No. 12,* "Omnibus Opinion" (New York: AICPA, 1967), paragraph 3.
[6] *FASB Statement No. 66,* paragraph 60.

(These pronouncements disallow the previously accepted alternative presentation of showing the deferred gross profit as a deferred credit immediately above the stockholders' equity section.)

Classification of installment receivables as current assets.   A company that uses an operating cycle of more than one year as the basis for classifying current assets and current liabilities on its balance sheet classifies installment receivables as current assets under the provisions of *ARB No. 43* (dealing with the definition of working capital), provided the installment sales "conform generally to normal trade practices and terms within the business."[7] In such cases, a company will often show: (a) parenthetically in the balance sheet, the amount of installment receivables maturing within one year, or (b) in the notes to the financial statements, the maturity of the installment receivables by year. A company that uses a one-year time period as the basis for classifying current assets and current liabilities on its balance sheet must separate the installment receivables into current and noncurrent portions. Likewise, the related deferred gross profit must be separated into current and noncurrent portions.

Defaults and repossessions

A seller customarily retains a security interest in items sold on the installment basis to be able to repossess them if and when purchasers default on their payments. Repossessed items become part of the used goods inventory. In many cases, reconditioning costs are incurred to increase the salability of the repossessed item. When repossession occurs, the seller must (1) write off the balance of the unpaid installment receivable; (2) eliminate the balance in the Deferred Gross Profit account; and (3) assign a value to the repossessed item. At first, we might conclude that the carrying value of the receivable (the installment receivable net of the related deferred gross profit) should be the amount to be assigned to the repossessed item. Under this approach, no gain or loss is reported at the time of the repossession. If accounting is to be a mirror of economic events, however, such an approach cannot be justified. The amount to be assigned to the repossessed item must be related to its current value, which may be quite different from the carrying value of the receivable. When the current value of the repossessed item is above or below the carrying value of the receivable, a gain or loss, respectively, should be reported at the time of repossession.

To illustrate the entry required when the current value of a repossessed item is below the carrying value of the receivable, assume the following facts at the time of repossession:

Installment receivable	$30,000
Deferred gross profit	(12,000)
Carrying value	$18,000
Current value of the repossessed item	$16,000

---

[7] *Accounting Research Bulletin No. 43*, "Restatement and Revision of Accounting Research Bulletins" (New York: AICPA, 1953), Chapter 3, paragraph 4.

The journal entry to reflect the repossession is as follows:

Inventory—repossessed items............................	16,000	
Deferred gross profit	12,000	
Loss on repossession	2,000	
Installment receivable		30,000
To record repossession of inventory sold on the install-		
ment basis.		

Note that if the current value of the repossessed item had been $20,000 (instead of $16,000), a gain of $2,000 on repossession would have been reported instead of a loss of $2,000.

The key element in determining whether a gain or loss has resulted is the current value of the repossessed item. Two generally accepted approaches are used to determine the current value of repossessed items. The first approach is to estimate the selling price of the repossessed item and subtract from the estimated selling price (a) a normal gross profit margin on used items of this type, and (b) anticipated reconditioning costs, if any. The merit of this approach is that it results in a valuation that should theoretically equal the amount the seller would have been willing to pay in the open market for the item in the condition found.

Under the second approach, which is a variation of the first approach, estimated selling costs and anticipated reconditioning costs, if any, are subtracted from the estimated selling price to determine the current value. Thus, estimated selling costs are substituted for a normal gross profit margin in the subtraction process. The second approach produces the **net realizable value** of the repossessed item. This valuation is slightly higher than under the first method. We prefer the first method primarily because financial statement users normally expect inventory reported in the balance sheet to generate a contribution margin—not just recover the carrying value and the estimated selling costs. The first method also gives a more conservative valuation. Under both approaches, reconditioning costs incurred are charged to the assigned current value.

Other installment sales considerations

Detailed record keeping.   Considering that the gross profit rate varies from year to year, the accounting system must segregate the installment receivables and deferred gross profit by years. In our illustration of the installment method, we assumed a perpetual inventory system. A company that uses a periodic inventory system must maintain sufficient inventory records that the cost of installment sales may be determined apart from the cost of regular sales.

Imputation of interest.   If the terms of the installment sale provide for no interest to be paid on the outstanding installment receivable or for an unreasonably low interest rate, then a reasonable interest rate must be imputed using the provisions of *APB Opinion No. 21,* "Interest on Receivables and Payables." For instance, if we changed the assumed facts in the preceding illustration so that no separate interest payments were required, then it would be necessary to determine how much of the $100,000 sales price actually represents interest. The remainder would then be reported as the sales price. The amount determined to be interest would then be amortized to income over the credit period. Assuming no separate interest payments are required and that $11,000 is determined to be the amount of the imputed interest, the installment sale would be recorded as follows:

Cash	10,000	
Installment receivable	90,000	
Deferred interest income (a contra asset account)		11,000
Installment sales		89,000
To record installment sale.		

Because a portion of the purchase price is allocated to interest, the gross profit is reduced from $40,000 to $29,000.

Trade-ins.   When a trade-in is accepted as part payment, the item traded in should be valued in inventory at its current value. As with repossessions, the current value is the estimated selling price of the item, less: (a) estimated reconditioning costs, and (b) a normal gross profit margin on used items of this type (which normally is more than sufficient to cover estimated reselling costs). This value should be used regardless of the actual amount allowed to the customer on the trade-in. If the amount allowed to the customer exceeds the current value of the trade-in, the excess should be treated as a reduction of the sales price. (Some companies may keep track of overallowances on trade-ins by using a contra sales account called Overallowances on Installment Sales.) In determining the gross profit to be recognized, the current value of the trade-in is treated as equivalent to a cash down payment. To illustrate, assume the following facts:

Sales price of item sold	$10,500
Cost of installment sale	6,300
Gross profit	$ 4,200
Trade-in allowance granted	$ 1,100
Cash down payment	1,000
Installment payments to be made	8,400
	$10,500
Estimated reconditioning costs of item traded in	$120
Estimated selling price of item traded in after reconditioning	$900
Normal gross profit margin on used items of this type	20%

The current value assigned to the trade-in and the amount of the overallowance are calculated as follows.

Trade-in allowance granted			$1,100
Less—Current value of item traded in:			
Estimated selling price of item traded in		$900	
Less—Estimated reconditioning costs	$120		
Gross profit to be realized on resale			
(20% of $900)	180	(300)	(600)
Overallowance given on item traded in			$ 500

The entries to record the sale and the related cost of goods sold (assuming a perpetual inventory system) are as follows:

Cash	1,000	
Inventory—trade-ins	600	
Installment receivables	8,400	
Installment sales ($10,500 − $500 overallowance)		10,000

| Cost of installment sales | 6,300 | |
| Inventory—new | | 6,300 |

Because a $500 overallowance was given on the trade-in, the gross profit on the sale is reduced from $4,200 to $3,700. The amount of gross profit that is immediately recognizable is 16% of $3,700, or $592. The 16% was derived by dividing the sum of the $1,000 cash down payment and the $600 value assigned to the item traded in by the $10,000 recorded sales price.

Income tax aspects

Sections 453, 453A, and 453B of the Internal Revenue Code deal with the use of the installment method. For sales of personal property regularly sold or otherwise disposed of on the installment plan (that is, by dealers in personal property), dealers **may elect to use** the installment method of reporting for all such sales. For casual sales of personal property by non-dealers and sales of real estate, the installment method is the normal method of reporting such sales; however, the taxpayer **may elect not to use** the installment method and thereby report the entire gross profit in the year of sale. The installment method is not applicable to sales at a loss.

As stated earlier, many companies having installment sales use the installment method only for income tax reporting purposes. In such cases, a company has deferred income tax credits reported in its balance sheet. Companies that present classified balance sheets (showing current assets and current liabilities) must follow the provisions of *APB Opinion No. 11*, "Accounting for Income Taxes," which requires that deferred income tax credits be classified in the same way as the related installment receivables.[8]

---

[8] *APB Opinion No. 11*, "Accounting for Income Taxes" (New York: AICPA, 1967), paragraph 57. (In 1980, the FASB issued *FASB Statement No. 37*, "Balance Sheet Classification of Deferred Income Taxes," which amends paragraph 57 of *APB Opinion No. 11*. This amendment is a clarification, and it does not change the requirements of paragraph 57 as it pertains to classifying deferred income tax credits relating to installment receivables.)

Accordingly, if a company (1) uses an operating cycle longer than one year as the basis for classifying current assets and current liabilities on its balance sheet, and (2) classifies all its installment receivables as current assets, then all related deferred income tax credits are to be classified among current liabilities. If a company uses a one-year period as the basis for classifying current assets and current liabilities on its balance sheet, then that portion of the deferred income tax credits relating to the installment receivables due within one year should be classified among current liabilities. For example, if 23% of the total installment receivables were classified as current, then 23% of the deferred income tax credits related to the installment receivables would be classified as current.

The cost recovery method

APB Opinion No. 10 also sanctions the use of the cost recovery method for installment sales.[9] Far more conservative than the installment method, the cost recovery method allows no recognition of gross profit until cash collections on the sales price equal the cost of the goods sold. All collections in excess of the seller's cost of the goods sold then cause the recognition of profit equal to the amount of cash collected. Because most practicing accountants and academicians consider the cost recovery method too conservative, it is rarely encountered in practice.

The accounts used under the cost recovery method are the same as those previously illustrated for the installment method. The amounts are different from those previously shown only because the gross profit is recognized at a much later date under the cost recovery method. Accordingly, we do not illustrate the detailed journal entries. Using the assumed information given in the illustration of the installment method, the income statement under the cost recovery method would be as follows:

Income statement

	19X1	19X2	19X3
Installment sale	$100,000		
Cost of installment sale	(60,000)		
Gross profit	$ 40,000		
Less—Deferral of gross profit	(40,000)		
Add—Recognition of deferred gross profit		$10,000	$30,000
Gross profit recognizable	$ -0-	$10,000	$30,000
Interest income	7,500	4,500	1,500

Summary

Under the installment method, gross profit is recognized to the degree that collections on the sales price relate to the total selling price. The installment method may be used only when collection of the sales price is not reasonably assured. Deferred gross profit is reported as a deduction from the installment receivable. In the event of a default and repossession, a gain or loss is reported, determined by comparing the carrying value of the receivable

---

[9] *APB Opinion No. 10*, footnote 8 to paragraph 12.

with the current value of the repossessed item. The current value of the repossessed item is its estimated selling price less a normal gross profit margin for used goods of that type and any anticipated reconditioning costs. An allowable alternative approach to determining current value is to use the item's net realizable value. The value assigned to an item received on a trade-in is its current value, determined in the same manner as in cases of repossession. An overallowance on a trade-in is subtracted from the selling price.

ACCOUNTING FOR THE BUSINESS FRANCHISE

The business franchise industry now generates in excess of $300 billion in sales, accounting for approximately one-third of all U.S. retail trade. It is a dynamic industry, beginning with gas stations, continuing with hotels, motels, hamburgers, real estate, brake repair, and most recently evolving into home computer stores, business brokerages, dental centers, vision centers, and photo finishing stores.

Although the business franchise does not generate new generally accepted accounting principles, it does present certain unique conditions that require the careful application of current principles. Furthermore, the accounting and reporting problems presented by these conditions relate to the franchisor, not the franchisee.

Distinguishing features of a franchise

Business franchises are distinguished from other business arrangements in the following ways:

a. The relation between the franchisor and franchisee is contractual, and an agreement, confirming the rights and responsibilities of each party, is in force for a specified period.

b. The continuing relation has as its purpose the distribution of a product or service, or an entire business concept, within a particular market area.

c. Both the franchisor and franchisee contribute resources for establishing and maintaining the franchise. The franchisor's contribution may be a trademark, a company reputation, products, procedures, manpower, equipment, or a process. The franchisee usually contributes operating capital as well as the managerial and operational resources required for opening and continuing the franchised outlet.

d. The franchise agreement outlines and describes the specific marketing practices to be followed, the contribution of each party to the operation of the business, and sets forth certain operating procedures that both parties agree to comply with.

e. The establishment of the franchised outlet creates a business entity that will, in most cases, require and support the full-time business activity of the franchisee. (There are numerous other contractual distribution arrangements in which a local business person becomes the "authorized distributor" or "representative" for the sale of a particular good or service, along with many others, but such sale usually represents only a portion of the person's total business.)

f. Both the franchisee and franchisor participate in a common public identity. This identity is achieved most often through the use of common trade names or trademarks and is frequently reinforced through advertising programs designed to promote the recognition and acceptance of the common identity within the franchisee's market area.[10]

In addition to these distinctions, we must also understand the legal and operational relationships between the franchisor and franchisee. The following provisions are commonly found in franchise agreements:

(1) Rights to use trademark, trade name, processes, and so on, are transferred to the franchisee.
(2) Initial franchise fee amount and terms of payment.
(3) The continuing franchise fee amount and terms of payment. The amount of the fee is usually based on a percentage of the franchisee's gross revenues.
(4) Services to be provided by the franchisor initially and on a continuing basis. The services may include personnel training, operating manuals, bookkeeping and financial services, and quality control programs.
(5) Provisions for acquisition of inventory, supplies, and equipment from franchisor or a designated supplier.
(6) Provisions for cancellation, reacquisition, or acquisition of the franchise.

The franchise is thus a contractual agreement between two parties, the franchisor and franchisee, the ultimate purpose of which is to expand the distribution channels of the franchisor's products, services, or both. Clearly, franchising is a marketing strategy that provides the franchisor with the necessary capital for expansion and a shift in investment risk. Specific provisions of the agreement establish certain rights; the amount and terms of payment of an initial franchise fee; the amount and terms of payment of continuing franchise fees; the nature of the franchisor's commitment; provisions for the acquisition of inventory, supplies, and equipment from the franchisor; and cancellation, reacquisition, and acquisition of the franchise.

The franchisor's accounting and reporting problems arise from the unique and frequently complex provisions of the franchise agreement. These provisions must be carefully analyzed to ensure appropriate applications of generally accepted accounting principles.

The franchisor's accounting and reporting problems focus on such matters as (1) when to recognize revenue (a timing problem), (2) separating the various kinds of revenue (a classification problem), (3) the collectibility of the receivable representing the franchisee's unpaid portion of the initial franchise fee (a valuation problem), (4) accounting for costs, and (5) disclosing to financial statement users information that is unique or significant to franchisors (a disclosure problem).

Revenue recognition

The franchisor generates revenue from the sale of the initial franchise; the sale of fixtures, equipment, inventory, and supplies to the franchisee; and continuing fees charged the franchisee based on the operation of the

---

[10] *FASB Statement No. 45*, "Accounting for Franchise Fee Revenue" (Stamford, CT: FASB, 1981), pp. 11–12. Copyright by Financial Accounting Standards Board, High Ridge Park, Stamford, CT 06905, USA. Reprinted with permission. Copies of the complete document are available from the FASB.

franchise. Essentially, the initial franchise fee represents consideration for establishing the franchise relationship and for such services as site selection, architectural and design assistance, shop or store layout, training, and staff assistance when the franchise business is opened.

The revenue recognition problem concerns the initial franchise fee, which is payment for certain intangible rights and services. No discrete time occurs at which "title passes" and revenue is recognized, as occurs with the sale of inventory, equipment, and so on. The franchise agreement may specify that the initial fee is to be paid completely or partially in cash; it may be paid completely or partially on the date the agreement is signed, on the date the franchisee commences business, or periodically thereafter. The fee may or may not be refundable under the terms of the agreement. In the 1960s, franchisors commonly recognized the initial fee revenue at the date the agreement was signed, even though significant costs had yet to be incurred by the franchisor.

Because questionable accounting practices were employed during the 1960s, the American Institute of Certified Public Accountants issued an accounting industry guide, *Accounting for Franchise Fee Revenue.* This guide promulgated a concept of revenue recognition for franchisors called **substantial performance.** Because authoritative guidance is now provided by *FASB Statement No. 45,* the guide was withdrawn by the AICPA. (The provisions of *FASB Statement No. 45* are not significantly different from the guide.) In accordance with *FASB Statement No. 45,* substantial performance by the franchisor represents the consummation of the transaction and is evidenced when

> (a) the franchisor has no remaining obligation or intent—by agreement, trade practice, or law—to refund any cash received or forgive any unpaid notes or receivables; (b) substantially all of the *initial services* of the franchisor required by the franchise agreement have been performed; and (c) no other material conditions or obligations related to the determination of substantial performance exist.[11]

Substantial performance has been interpreted by the profession as the point at which the franchisee begins operations. Most franchisors have rendered the required services by that time. Of course, recognizing substantial performance at this time also results in a more conservative determination of income than would occur at the date the franchise agreement is signed.

Recognition of revenue at any other time—earlier or later—carries with it the burden of demonstrating that the alternative time best reflects income for the franchisor. Some franchise arrangements clearly support a time other than when the franchisee begins operations.

It is important to observe that although in most cases the conditions for substantial performance are met when the franchisee commences operations, certain conditions may require careful judgment. This could be the case, for example, if the franchisor has little business experience, particularly in franchise operations. Little or no relevant experience or, for that matter, a poor record of franchise operations may require a more conservative interpretation of substantial performance. Similar concerns

---

[11] *FASB Statement No. 45,* paragraph 5.

would be appropriate if an experienced franchisor develops a new and different franchise venture or expands an existing franchise operation into a new geographic area.

Other revenue recognition methods may be used in certain franchise accounting situations, including (1) recognition of revenue over the life of the contract, (2) percentage of completion, and (3) installment and cost recovery. If the first method is appropriate, revenue would be recognized ratably over the life of the contract. For example, if the initial fee amounted to $150,000 and the franchise life were 15 years, the franchisor would recognize $10,000 of the initial fee as revenue each year for 15 years. In this instance, the initial fee would be viewed as a prepayment for use of the franchise over the franchise period. However, most franchise agreements show little or no indication that the initial franchise fee includes compensation for any intangible benefits associated with membership in the franchise system.[12] This method would be particularly difficult to defend if the franchisor incurred significant costs for initial services and if adequate continuous fees were charged over the life of the contract. However, if the evidence shows that the initial fee includes significant compensation for intangible rights conveyed to a franchisor—and this would be more clearly evidenced when large fees are charged for franchise renewals—this method may be preferable to substantial performance.

Although percentage of completion is generally associated with construction accounting, the method may be applied to other situations. A particular strength of the method is that it recognizes effort spent and, hence, revenue earned between the date of the franchise agreement and the date the franchisee begins business. Of course, judgment must be used in estimating the cost of services performed over the total expected cost of services. When the initial fee is for initial services only, this method generally provides results similar to those of the substantial performance method.

Installment sales and cost recovery methods may be used only under exceptional circumstances. In essence, no reasonable basis exists for estimating the degree of collectibility of the receivable. (For a complete discussion of this subject, see pages 1019–29.)

Frequently, the initial franchise fee includes charges to the franchisee for fixtures, equipment, and inventory. In these cases, the relevant portion of the fee pertaining to these items should be separated, and the revenue and related costs should be matched when title passes, even if it occurs before the opening date of the franchise.

Collectibility of the receivable

After it has been concluded that substantial performance has occurred and the initial franchise fee has been separated into charges for fixtures, equipment, and inventory, the next important accounting question concerns the collectibility of the receivable. The following circumstances in franchise accounting make this process especially difficult.

---

[12] Charles H. Calhoun III, "Accounting for Initial Franchise Fees: Is It a Dead Issue?" *Journal of Accountancy,* February 1975, p. 61.

1. Unpaid franchise notes may be significant to the individual franchisee and payment may depend upon the franchisee's future operations, or current or prospective capitalization, or a combination thereof.
2. The franchisee may be inexperienced in business with a consequent effect on his credit standing.
3. The franchise agreement, which is important as a basis for making collection estimates, may require interpretation by legal counsel as to uncertainties.
4. The credit standing of guarantors or other indirect sources of credit to the franchisee may require investigation.[13]

The first two circumstances raise basic concerns in estimating the collectibility of the receivable. In the first case, if little or no cash has been paid by the franchisee and reliance is based solely on the success of future operations, the uncertainty of collection may indeed be quite high because the franchisee has nothing at risk. In the second instance, the probability of failure may be quite high because inexperience is a major contributor to business failure. The likelihood that the franchisor will repurchase the franchise should also be carefully assessed. This requires study of the franchise agreement and recent behavior of the franchisor. Obviously, if the probability of repurchase is high, it is less likely that the receivable will be collected.

Accounting for franchise costs

The matching concept requires that costs directly related to revenues be reported in the accounting period in which the revenue transaction occurred. The concept presumes a cause-and-effect relationship between revenue and expense. Other costs that are not directly associated with the revenue transaction are generally expensed when incurred.

Franchisors are likely to encounter different circumstances when trying to match costs and revenues. Costs and revenues may exhibit irregular and nonrecurring patterns, and because we are dealing with services and intangibles, the sources of revenues may not be as readily identifiable. This is especially true for transactions involving initial franchise fees. Some costs may be incurred before or after the revenue is recognized.

Generally, franchisors should defer direct costs and relate them to specific franchise sales for which revenue has not yet been recognized. Indirect costs that are regular and recurring, and that are incurred regardless of the level of sales, should be expensed as incurred. Costs that exceed anticipated revenues less estimated additional costs should not be deferred.

Illustration:
Accounting for the franchise

John David enters the 4-wheel drive vehicle parts sales business at the retail level by signing a franchise agreement with Specialty 4-Wheel Drive Parts, Inc. The franchisor provides David with assistance in site selection,

---

[13] Committee on Franchise Accounting and Auditing of the American Institute of Certified Public Accountants, *Accounting for Franchise Fee Revenue,* an AICPA Industry Accounting Guide (New York: AICPA, 1973), pp. 9–10. Copyright © 1973 by the American Institute of Certified Public Accountants, Inc.

shop layout, equipment and building fixtures, inventory, operating manuals, personnel training, and advertising.

The franchise agreement includes provisions for an initial franchise fee as payment for site selection assistance, shop layout, shop equipment and building fixtures, initial inventory, use of operating manuals, and training of personnel. The initial fee is $150,000, of which $20,000 is payable when the agreement is signed, and $130,000 is payable in five non-interest-bearing notes of $26,000 each, one note to be paid on each anniversary date of the opening. The agreement also includes a provision for a continuing franchise fee of $10,000 per year in return for David's use of Specialty's accounting system and advertising and the right to purchase parts.

Assumed transactions and related journal entries pertaining to activities completed by Specialty in the first year of the franchise agreement are shown in Illustration 26-1.

Illustration 26-1
Accounting for the franchise

Transactions	Entry		
1. Franchisor incurred direct costs related to the franchise prior to the store opening.	Deferred franchise expenses . . . . Accounts payable	12,000	12,000
2. The franchise agreement was signed. The credit ratings of all franchisees entitle them to borrow at the current interest rate of 15%. The present value of an ordinary annuity of five annual receipts of $26,000 each, discounted at 15%, is $87,156.	Cash . . . . Notes receivable . . . . . . Discount on notes receivable ($130,000 − $87,156) Equipment sales . . . . . Sales (inventory) . . . . Unearned franchise fee revenue	20,000 130,000	42,844 65,000 15,000 27,156
The following additional information pertains to equipment and inventory sold to the franchisee:	Cost of equipment sold . . Cost of goods sold . . . . Inventory	35,000 8,000	43,000
Sales Price Cost Equipment and fixtures . . . . $65,000 $35,000 Inventory. 15,000 8,000			
3. The store was opened.	Unearned franchise fee revenue . . . . Franchise fee revenue	27,156	27,156
	Franchise expenses . . . Deferred franchise expenses	12,000	12,000
4. The continuing franchise fee was received.	Cash . . . . Continuing franchise fee revenue	10,000	10,000

Disclosure

In addition to customary disclosure requirements, franchisors must disclose relevant information pertaining to franchising. In this regard, *FASB Statement No. 45* states:

> *Significant commitments and obligations:* The nature of all significant commitments and obligations resulting from franchise agreements, including a description of the services that the franchisor has agreed to provide . . . that have not yet been substantially performed, shall be disclosed.
>
> *Use of installment or cost recovery method:* If no basis for estimating the collectibility of specific franchise fees exists, the notes to the financial statements shall disclose whether the installment or cost recovery method is being used to account for the related franchise fee revenue. Furthermore, the sales price of such franchises, the revenue and related costs deferred (both currently and on a cumulative basis), and the periods in which such fees become payable by the franchisee shall be disclosed. Any amounts originally deferred but later recognized because uncertainties regarding the collectibility of franchise fees are resolved also shall be disclosed.
>
> *Segregation of franchise revenues:* Initial franchise fees shall be segregated from other franchise fee revenue if they are significant. If it is probable that initial franchise fee revenue will decline in the future because sales predictably reach a saturation point, disclosure of that fact is desirable. Disclosure of the relative contribution to net income of initial franchise fees is desirable if not apparent from the relative amounts of revenue.
>
> *Franchisor-owned outlets:* Revenue and costs related to franchisor-owned outlets shall be distinguished from revenue and costs related to franchised outlets when practicable. That may be done by segregating revenue and costs related to franchised outlets. If there are significant changes in franchisor-owned outlets or franchised outlets during the period, the number of (a) franchises sold, (b) franchises purchased during the period, (c) franchised outlets in operation shall be disclosed.[14]

Summary

Franchising, which is an important part of our economy, presents certain inherent accounting and reporting problems. Because of its unique nature, current generally accepted accounting principles must be carefully applied.

The accounting and reporting problems confronted by the franchisor are (1) determining when to recognize revenue (a timing problem), (2) properly separating the various kinds of revenue (a classification problem), (3) estimating the collectibility of the receivable representing the franchisee's unpaid portion of the initial franchise fee (a valuation problem), (4) accounting for costs, and (5) disclosing important information unique to the franchise.

The initial fee revenue is recognized when conditions of substantial performance are met. Generally, such conditions are satisfied when the franchisee commences operations. When the initial franchise fee includes charges for equipment, inventory, and so on, these amounts must be segregated from the initial franchise fee and separately stated.

The receivables must be carefully valued. When little or no cash has been paid by the franchisee, the risk of noncollection is quite high because the franchisee has risked nothing. The franchisee's lack of business experience must also be considered in the estimation process.

---

[14] *FASB Statement No. 45,* paragraphs 20–23.

Direct costs should be deferred and related to the specific franchise sale, and indirect costs should be expensed as incurred. Costs should not be deferred when they exceed anticipated revenues, less estimated additional costs.

ACCOUNTING FOR CONSIGNMENTS

Manufacturers and distributors who market their products through dealers cannot always enter into agreements that require the dealers to purchase their products outright when the items are shipped. Instead, an owner may enter into a **consignment agreement,** whereby the owner ships inventory to a dealer but retains title until the dealer sells it. Inventory of an owner in the possession of another is called **consigned inventory.** The owner may not report any profit on the transaction because a sale has not yet occurred.

In legal terms, the owner is called the **consignor,** and the dealer is called the **consignee.** The rights and duties of each party are usually set forth in the consignment agreement. For example, the consignee typically must give the consignor's property reasonable care and make periodic accountings (or notifications of sales) to the consignor. (You may want to refer to a law textbook covering consignments for a more detailed discussion of the relationship between a consignor and a consignee and the corresponding rights and duties of these parties.)

In perspective

Consignments are infrequently used in marketing products largely because of the now common use of **flooring plan** lines of credit offered to dealers by financial institutions (including finance subsidiaries of manufacturers). Briefly, the usual features of these flooring plans include the following:

(1) Dealers borrow money from financial institutions to purchase certain individual inventory items from manufacturers or distributors.
(2) The borrowings are secured by the individual items purchased.
(3) Borrowings to purchase an individual inventory item must be repaid when the dealer sells the item or within a specified period of time, whichever occurs first.
(4) The manufacturer or distributor agrees to pay a portion of the dealer's financing costs under the flooring plan.

Automobiles, recreational vehicles, farm machinery, major home appliances, and television sets are almost always carried by dealers under flooring plans rather than under consignment agreements. In the publishing and record industries, it is common practice to sell inventory to retail outlets under terms that allow the retail outlets to return the inventory if they do not sell it—a practice that, in substance, is the equivalent of a consignment. For these industries, allowances for sales returns are established when sales to the retail outlets are recorded.

Responses to our inquiries have led us to conclude that consignments are limited to cases in which (1) a dealer is not financially strong enough to enter into flooring arrangements with financial institutions; (2) the salability of a new product is in doubt, and dealers are reluctant to devote floor space to it (this was the case with microwave ovens several years ago); and (3) a manufacturer is attempting to rekindle interest in a product that had a poor image when originally introduced.

Accounting procedures

The procedures used to account for consignments should reflect the substance of the consignment agreement. Not only has the use of consignments declined considerably over the years, but the terms and substance of consignment agreements have changed. We first discuss the traditional arrangements between a consignor and a consignee and then a new arrangement, which we call the modern arrangement.

The traditional arrangement. Traditionally, the substance of consignment agreements has been that the consignee merely acts as the consignor's agent, for which the consignee earns a commission on sale of the consigned inventory. When the consignee made credit sales, the resultant receivable was the property of the consignor, with the consignor bearing any collection loss. (Sometimes, the consignee guaranteed the collectibility of the receivable, in which case the consignee was referred to as a *del credere* agent.) As called for in the consignment agreement, the consignee periodically rendered an accounting to the consignor. Such a report—known as an **account sale**—showed the sales made for the consignor's account less the commission on the sales earned by the consignee and any other charges incurred by the consignee to be borne by the consignor. Typically, the consignee remitted a check to the consignor for the net amount on this report when it was submitted. Under this traditional arrangement, the accounting procedures resulted in the consignor reporting in the income statement (1) sales at the amount for which the consignee sold the consigned inventory to the ultimate customer; (2) the consignor's cost of the inventory sold; (3) the commission expense (paid to the consignee); and (4) any freight or other incidental costs incurred. The consignee's income statement reflected only commission revenues and selling expenses not reimbursable by the consignor. Responses to our inquiries have led us to believe that this type of arrangement is no longer widely used, if at all. Accordingly, we do not illustrate the related accounting procedures.

The modern arrangement. The substance of most consignment arrangements currently consists of a purchase of the consigned inventory by the consignee from the consignor—when the consignee sells the consigned inventory to the ultimate customer. At that time, the consignee pays the consignor an agreed-upon amount. (Often the consignor bills the consignee at the time of shipment so that the consignee can make ready payment; the consignor does not record the billing as a sale, however, until the consignee notifies the consignor that the consigned inventory has been sold.) On receipt of consigned inventory, the consignee makes only a memorandum entry—the purchase is recorded when the consignee sells the consigned inventory. Furthermore, when the consignee sells on credit, the resultant receivable is the property of the consignee—there is no continuing involvement by the consignor. Under this arrangement, the accounting procedures result in both the consignor and the consignee reporting sales and cost of goods sold.

Illustration:
The modern arrangement

Assume that a manufacturer ships inventory with a manufacturing cost of $1,000 to a dealer at an agreed upon billing price of $1,500. The manufacturer pays $30 for shipping charges. The dealer later sells the inventory for $1,800 and notifies the consignor of the sale and makes payment. Illustration 26-2 shows the journal entries that would be recorded on the books of the consignor and the consignee.

In reviewing Illustration 26-2, the following points should be understood:

(1) The consigned inventory remains on the consignor's books until the consignee notifies the consignor that the consigned inventory has been sold, which causes the consignee to purchase the consigned inventory from the consignor.

Illustration 26-2
Consignment journal entries

Consignor's Books (the manufacturer)			Consignee's Books (the dealer)		
Shipment of inventory to dealer on consignment:					
Finished goods on consignment	1,000		Memorandum entry only		
Inventory—finished goods		1,000			
Payment of freight costs on shipment to consignee:					
Finished goods on consignment	30		No entry		
Cash		30			
Sale of inventory by consignee:					
No entry			Cash	1,800	
			Sales		1,800
			Purchases	1,500	
			Accounts payable (to consignor)		1,500
Notification of sale to consignor and payment of billing price:					
Cash	1,500		Accounts payable	1,500	
Sales		1,500	Cash		1,500
Cost of consignment goods sold	1,030				
Finished goods on consignment		1,030			

(2) The consignee made payment to the consignor at the time of notification, although sometimes, payment is made shortly after notification.

Summary

A consignment is a transfer of possession of inventory from its owner (called the consignor) to another party (called the consignee). Because the transfer is not an outright sale, no profit is recorded by the owner at the time of the transfer. Instead, profit is recorded by the consignor when the consignee sells the inventory to the ultimate customer. Under the modern arrangement, a sale is recorded between the consignor and the consignee (at a billing price agreed upon in advance) when the consignee sells the inventory.

Glossary of new terms

Consignee: The party holding possession of inventory—but not ownership—in a consignment arrangement.

Consignment: A transfer of possession of inventory from an owner (the consignor) to another party (the consignee) to facilitate the sale of inventory.

Consignor: The owner of inventory in a consignment arrangement.

Continuing Franchise Fee: Consideration for the continuing rights granted by the franchise and for general or specific services during its life.[15]

Franchise Agreement: A contract between a franchisor and a franchisee that specifies the legal and operational relationship between them. Some common provisions found in franchise agreements are (a) rights transferred by the franchisor; (b) the amount and terms of payment of initial franchise fees; (c) amount or rate and terms of payment of continuing franchise fee or royalty; (d) services to be rendered by the franchisor initially and on a continuing basis, (e) acquisition of inventory, supplies, or equipment, and terms of payment; and (f) cancellation, reacquisition, or acquisition of franchise.

Initial Franchise Fee: Consideration for establishing a franchise relationship and providing some initial services. Occasionally, the fee includes consideration for initially required equipment and inventory, but those items usually are the subject of separate consideration.[15]

Substantial Performance: Substantial performance for the franchisor means that (a) the franchisor has no remaining obligation or intent—by agreement, trade practice, or law—to refund any cash received or forgive any unpaid notes or receivables; (b) substantially all of the *initial services* of the franchisor required by the franchise agreement have been performed; and (c) no other material condition or obligation related to the determination of substantial performance exists.[15]

Review questions

1. What basic condition must exist for the installment method to be used for financial reporting purposes?

[15] Definition quoted from *FASB Statement No. 45*, Appendix A.

2. How are selling expenses for an installment sale treated when the sale is recorded under the installment method for financial reporting purposes?
3. How is deferred gross profit relating to installment sales reported in the balance sheet?
4. Define *current value* as it is used in connection with defaults and repossessions occurring on installment sales.
5. How are overallowances on trade-ins reported when reporting installment sales?
6. Summarize the major features distinguishing a business franchise from other business arrangements.
7. Accounting practice specifies the nature of the disclosures required in the financial reports of franchisors. Identify the required disclosures.
8. List some common provisions specified in franchise agreements.
9. Conceivably, continuing franchise fees could be less than the incremental costs associated with these fees. How would this condition affect the recognition of the initial franchise fee?
10. Describe the four principal accounting problems associated with franchises.
11. Describe the concept of substantial performance as used in franchise accounting.
12. Identify the approaches for revenue recognition, other than substantial performance, and discuss the conditions under which they could be used.
13. In what principal ways does a franchisor generate revenue?
14. What factors should be considered in valuing receivables?
15. Describe the accounting for costs associated with franchises.
16. Explain why a consignment may not be recorded as a sale.
17. How has the use of consignments changed over the years?
18. Explain the differences in the consignor's income statement under the traditional arrangement and under the modern arrangement.
19. How do we determine whether to account for consignments under the traditional arrangement or under the modern arrangement?

Discussion case

Discussion case 26–1
Installment sales: Theory—Classification of deferred gross profit

The Lanza Company has recently allowed customers to purchase items on the installment basis. In preparing the year-end financial statements, the company is considering separating the Deferred Gross Profit account into the following categories: (1) an allowance for uncollectibles, shown as an offset to the installment receivables; (2) a Deferred Income Taxes account, shown immediately below its long-term debt; (3) an Unrealized Profit account, shown immediately above stockholders' equity.

Required:
Evaluate the theoretical soundness of this approach. (Ignore the presentational requirements of the professional pronouncements.)

Exercises

Exercise 26–1
Installment sales: Determining year-end balance
of Deferred Gross Profit account

McCormick Corporation, which began business on January 1, 19X1, appropriately uses the installment method for financial reporting purposes. The following data were obtained for 19X1 and 19X2:

	19X1	19X2
Installment sales	$350,000	$420,000
Cost of installment sales	280,000	315,000
General and administrative expenses	35,000	42,000
Cash collections on installment sales in:		
19X1	150,000	125,000
19X2		200,000

Required:
Determine the balance in the Deferred Gross Profit control account at December 31, 19X2.

(AICPA adapted)

Exercise 26–2
Installment sales: Determining gain or loss on repossession

The Sills Company appropriately uses the installment method for financial reporting purposes. In 19X4, a customer who purchased merchandise in 19X2 defaulted. At the date of the default, the balance of the installment receivable was $12,000, and the repossessed merchandise had a fair value of $8,200. Data for 19X2 are as follows:

Installment sales	$700,000
Cost of installment sales	560,000
General and administrative expenses.....................................	70,000

Required:
Assuming the repossessed merchandise is recorded at its current value, determine the gain or loss on repossession.

(AICPA adapted)

Exercise 26–3
Installment sales: Determining gain or loss on repossession

The Price Company repossessed equipment in 19X3 that it had sold for $60,000 on the installment basis in 19X1. The company appropriately used the installment method for financial reporting purposes. At the time of the repossession, the installment receivable was $40,000, and the deferred gross profit was $12,000.

The company expects to resell the repossessed item for $30,000 (after it incurs reconditioning costs of $400). The company's normal gross profit margin on sales of used equipment of this type is 10%. The company also expects to incur a 3% sales commission on the resale. The customer was granted a trade-in allowance of $1,500 when the equipment was initially sold; of this amount, $600 was determined to be an overallowance.

Required:
(1) Determine the gain or loss at the time of repossession.
(2) Prepare the journal entry to be made at the time of repossession.

Exercise 26–4
Installment sales: Trade-in and over-allowance

Recondo Company sold equipment to a customer on the following terms:

(a) Sales price	$75,000
(b) Cash down payment	2,000
(c) Allowance granted on item traded in	3,000
(d) Installment payments over 30 months.................................	70,000

The manufacturing cost of the equipment sold is $54,500. Assume the use of the installment method is appropriate. The estimated selling price of the item traded in (after expected reconditioning costs of $300) is $3,500. The company's normal profit margin on the sale of used items of this type is 20%.

Required:
Prepare the journal entries to be made at the time of the sale. (Assume a perpetual inventory system is used.)

Exercise 26–5
Installment sales: Determining installment receivables and current portion of installment receivables from amount of deferred income taxes

The Birchwood Company sells household furniture. Customers who purchase furniture on the installment basis make payments in equal monthly installments over a two-year period, with no down payment required. Birchwood's gross profit on installment sales equals 60% of the selling price of the furniture.

For financial accounting purposes, sales revenue is recognized when the sale is made. For income tax purposes, however, the installment method is used. There are no other book and income tax accounting differences, and Birchwood's income tax rate is 50%.

Birchwood's December 31, 19X1, balance sheet includes a deferred tax credit of $30,000 arising from the difference between book and tax treatment of the installment sales, of which $14,000 is classified as a current liability.

Required:
(1) Determine the total amount of installment accounts receivable at December 31, 19X1.

(2) Determine the amount of installment receivables that should be classified as current assets.

(AICPA adapted)

Exercise 26–6
Franchises: Revenue recognition

On January 1, 19X3, David Catton signed an agreement to operate a franchise of Herbie's Hot Dogs, Inc., for an initial franchise fee of $40,000. Of this amount, $15,000 was paid when the agreement was signed, and the balance is payable in five annual payments of $5,000 each beginning January 1, 19X4. The agreement provides that the down payment is not refundable and no future services are required of the franchisor. Catton's credit rating indicates that he can borrow money at 15% for a loan of this type.

Required:
Prepare the appropriate journal entry for the franchisee to record the acquisition of the franchise on January 1, 19X3.

(AICPA adapted)

Exercise 26–7
Franchises: Revenue recognition

On December 31, 19X2, Annie's Pizza, Inc., signed an agreement authorizing Alamande Company to operate as a franchise for an initial franchise fee of $50,000. Of this amount, $20,000 was received when the agreement was signed, and the balance is due in three annual payments of $10,000 each beginning December 31, 19X3. The agreement provides that the down payment (representing a fair measure of the services already performed by Annie) is not refundable and substantial future services are required of Annie's Pizza. Alamande's credit rating is such that collection of the note is reasonably certain. At December 31, 19X2, the present value of the three annual payments discounted at 14% (the implicit rate for a loan of this type) is $23,220.

Required:
Prepare the appropriate journal entry for Annie's Pizza, Inc. on December 31, 19X2, the date the agreement was signed.

(AICPA adapted)

Exercise 26–8
Consignments: Determining proper year-end inventory amounts

Cotter Company is a manufacturer that markets its products through dealers, sometimes using consignment arrangements. At December 31, 19X1, Cotter and one of its dealers, Pinn Company, took a physical count of inventory in their possession. The amounts were $1,000,000 for Cotter and $50,000 for Pinn. The following additional information is available.

(1) Of the $50,000 of inventory counted by Pinn, $8,000 of this amount represents the billing price of inventory on consignment from Cotter. (Cotter's manufacturing cost is $6,000.)

(2) On December 30, 19X1, Pinn sold inventory that it had obtained from Cotter on consignment at a billing price of $2,500. Cotter's manufacturing cost was $2,000. Pinn notified Cotter of this sale on January 6, 19X2.

(3) At December 31, 19X1, inventory in transit between Cotter and Pinn that is being shipped on consignment at a billing price of $1,400 has a manufacturing cost of $1,000.

Required:
Determine the correct amount of inventory to be reflected in each company's balance sheet at December 31, 19X1.

Problems

Problem 26–1
Installment sales: Basic journal entries

The Noss Company, which reports on a calendar year-end, sold equipment on October 1, 19X1 to a customer on the following terms:

(a) Sales price $80,000
(b) Cash down payment $8,000
(c) Installment payments over 24 months, beginning October 31, 19X1 .... $72,000
(d) Annual interest rate charged on outstanding balance (to be paid
   each month) 10%

The manufacturing cost of the equipment is $50,000. Assume the use of the installment method is appropriate and that all payments are made on time.

Required:
(1) Prepare the appropriate journal entries for 19X1, 19X2, and 19X3. (Assume a perpetual inventory system is used.)
(2) Prepare an income statement for 19X1, 19X2, and 19X3 using the amounts from the journal entries in (1).

Problem 26–2
Installment sales: Default and repossession

The Rodney Company sold equipment on July 1, 19X1 to a customer on the following terms:

(a) Sales price $50,000
(b) Cash down payment $2,000
(c) Installment payments over 48 months, beginning July 31, 19X1 .... $48,000
(d) Annual interest rate charged on outstanding balance (to be paid
   each month) 10%

The manufacturing cost of the equipment is $30,000. The company appropriately used the installment method to report the transaction. The purchaser defaulted on its November 30, 19X2 payment, and the company repossessed the equipment on December 20, 19X2. The estimated selling price of the repossessed equipment (after expected reconditioning costs of $300) is $23,000. The company's normal profit margin on the sale of used items of this type is 20%.

Required:
(1) Prepare the journal entries made at the time of the sale. (Assume a perpetual inventory system is used.)
(2) Prepare the journal entry made at the time of the repossession.

Problem 26–3
Installment sales: Determining realizable gross profit and interest income (Equal installment payments include interest)

On July 1, 19X1, Berry Computers, Inc. sold computer equipment with a book value of $15,000 to Hacker, Inc. for $20,000. Because the collection of the sales price was questionable, Berry retained title to the equipment until Hacker made the last payment. Hacker made a down payment of $2,000 and signed an 8% note due in eight equal quarterly payments of $2,457 each, including interest, beginning September 30, 19X1. During July 19X1, Berry incurred $750 selling expenses in the sale of this equipment. Assume that (1) the 8% interest rate is reasonable, (2) all payments are made in accordance with the agreement, and (3) the installment method is appropriate for financial reporting purposes.

Required:
Prepare a schedule of all income and expenses for the above transaction for the year ended June 30, 19X2. (Ignore income taxes.)

(AICPA adapted)

Problem 26–4
Installment sales: Determining year-end balance in Gross Profit account and dealing with a repossession

The Furillo Company uses the installment method for financial reporting purposes. Selected data follow:

	December 31,	
	19X4	**19X5**
Installment receivables—19X3	$100,000	$ 70,000
Installment receivables—19X4	280,000	230,000
Installment receivables—19X5		420,000
Deferred gross profit—19X3	37,000	
Deferred gross profit—19X4	112,000	
Installment sales—19X5		600,000
Cost of installment sales—19X5		390,000
Initial down payments made on 19X5 installment sales		110,000

On October 1, 19X5, the company repossessed equipment that it had sold in 19X4 for $15,000, of which $6,000 had been collected. The company credited Installment Receivables—19X4 and debited Inventory—Repossessed Equipment for the unpaid balance. The current value of the equipment at the repossession date was $4,500.

Required:
(1) Calculate the year-end balances in the Deferred Profit accounts. (Do each year separately.)
(2) Make the appropriate adjustment needed for the repossession.
(3) Prepare a partial income statement for 19X5.

Problem 26–5
Franchises: Revenue recognition

Chucky's, Inc. sells fast-food franchises to independent operators throughout the United States. The contract with the franchisee generally includes the following provisions:

(a) The franchisee is charged an initial fee of $100,000. Of this amount, $50,000 is payable when the agreement is signed, and a $10,000 non-interest-bearing note is payable at the end of each of the five subsequent years.
(b) The initial franchise fee collected by Chucky's is refunded and the remaining obligation canceled if, for any reason, the franchisee fails to open the franchise.
(c) In return for the initial franchise fee, Chucky's agrees to (1) assist the franchisee in selecting the location for the business, (2) negotiate the lease for the land, (3) obtain financing and assist with building design, (4) supervise construction, (5) establish accounting and tax records, and (6) provide expert advice, over a five-year period, on such matters as employee and management training, quality control, and promotion.
(d) In addition to the initial franchise fee, the franchisee must pay to Chucky's a monthly fee of 2% of sales. This fee is a payment for menu planning, recipe innovations, and the privilege of purchasing ingredients from the franchisor at or below prevailing market prices.

The management of Chucky's estimates that the value of the services rendered to the franchisee when the contract is signed amounts to at least $20,000. All franchisees to date have opened their locations at the scheduled time, and none has defaulted on any of the notes receivable.

The credit ratings of all franchisees would entitle them to borrow at the current interest rate of 16%. The present value of an ordinary annuity of five annual receipts of $10,000 each, discounted at 16%, is $32,743.

Required:
(1) Discuss the alternatives that Chucky's might use to account for the initial franchise fee. Evaluate each by applying generally accepted accounting principles to this situation, and give illustrative entries for each alternative.
(2) Given the nature of Chucky's agreement with its franchisees, when should revenues be recognized? Discuss the question of revenue recognition for both

the initial franchise fee and the additional monthly fee of 2% of sales, and give illustrative entries for both types of revenue.

Problem 26–6
Franchises: Revenue recognition and disclosure

Dunker's, Inc. has established franchised outlets that bake and sell various types of donuts. Mugsy Kupper entered into an agreement for a Dunker's franchise on March 10, 19X1, for a term of 10 years. The agreement included the following provisions:

(a) An initial franchise fee of $100,000 is to be paid as follows: $20,000 cash at the opening of the store; the balance in eight non-interest-bearing notes of $10,000 each, one note to be paid on each anniversary date of the opening.
(b) The initial franchise fee includes charges for store equipment, fixtures, and inventory. The cost of the equipment and fixtures to Dunker's is $15,000; the estimated salable value is $20,000. The cost of the inventory and supplies to Dunker's is $5,500, and the estimated wholesale price to the franchisee is $7,000.
(c) Continuing fees are ½% of gross revenue. These fees are for the right to use the Dunker's trademark for the duration of the franchise, the privilege of buying inventory and supplies at or below recognized market prices, advertising, quality control visitations, use of the Dunker's accounting and reporting system for franchisees, and management assistance.
(d) Incremental costs associated with the initial franchise fee are $32,000, which does not include the costs of equipment, fixtures, and inventory. Minor costs associated with the franchise are not accrued. The estimated annual continuing costs are $275.

Additional information:
The store opened for business on June 30, 19X2. Store revenues for the six months ended December 31, 19X2 amounted to $500,000. The credit rating of the franchisee would entitle him to borrow at the current interest rate of 15%.

Required:
(1) Prepare a schedule that shows the income recognized by Dunker's, Inc., in regard to the franchise, through December 31, 19X2. The schedule should disclose fully the nature of the revenue and expense items.
(2) Prepare a disclosure statement included in Dunker's annual report. Assume that Dunker's only has this one franchise agreement.

Problem 26–7
Consignments: Preparing journal entries

Rangette Company is an appliance distributor. In December 19X1, the following events occurred between the company and one of its dealers, Buttons Company:

(1) Inventory costing $100,000 was shipped to Buttons at a total billing price of

$150,000. Of these amounts, inventory costing $7,000 was shipped on consignment at a billing price of $10,000.

(2) Rangette incurred shipping costs of $1,100 on inventory shipped to Buttons. Of this amount, $100 pertained to goods shipped on consignment.

(3) Rangette received remittances of $135,000 from Buttons. Of this amount, $8,000 pertained to the sale of consigned inventory by Buttons. The manufacturing cost for all inventory totaled $90,000, of which $6,000 pertained to the consigned inventory sold.

(4) Rangette received notification from Buttons that inventory on consignment at a billing price of $3,300 was sold by Buttons, but the remittance was not made to Rangette until January 19X2. (Rangette's manufacturing cost was $2,200.)

Required:

Prepare the journal entries recorded on each company's books for these transactions.

Index

12–2 Income tax expense recorded by parent, $16,000

12–3 Income tax expense recorded by parent, $20,000

12–4 Income tax expense recorded by parent, $42,000

12–5 Income tax expense recorded by investor, $3,000

12–6 (1a) Consolidated primary EPS, $1.62
(1b) Consolidated primary EPS, $1.65

12–7 (1a) Consolidated primary EPS, $0.81
(1b) Consolidated primary EPS, $0.83

12–8 (1a) Consolidated primary EPS, $1.62
Consolidated fully diluted EPS, $1.40
(1b) Consolidated primary EPS, $1.67
Consolidated fully diluted EPS, $1.43

13–2 (1) Net income, $72,000
19X2 translation adjustment, $157,000

13–3 (1) Net income, $203,000
Transaction gain from remeasurement, $219,000

13–4 (1) Net income, $18,600
19X6 translation adjustment, $(4,740)

13–5 (1) Net income, $13,600
Transaction gain from remeasurement, $1,000

14–1 Vendor A, July 31, 19X1 transaction gain, $200
Customer A, July 30, 19X1 transaction loss, $125

14–2 Vendor A, July 15, 19X1 transaction gain, $2,000
Customer A, July 10, 19X3 transaction gain, $100

14–3 Dec. 31, 19X1, two $2,000 adjustments
Jan. 15, 19X2, two $800 adjustments

14–4 June 30, 19X3, two $1,500 adjustments
July 30, 19X3, two $500 adjustments

14–5 Capitalized cost of equipment, $481,000

14–6 June 30, 19X1 transaction gain, $24,000
Dec. 31, 19X1 transaction gain, $36,000

15–1 (1) Reportable segments, B, C, D, E, and G

15–2 Consolidated operating profit, $99,200
Consolidated assets, $164,200

15–3 (1) Consolidated operating profit, $444,000
Consolidated assets, $1,934,000
(2) Consolidated operating profit, $455,600
Consolidated assets, $1,934,000

15–4 Consolidated operating profit, $717,600
Consolidated assets, $1,176,600

15–6 Income from continuing operations, $1,140,000

Loss from discontinued operations, $810,000
Net income, $270,000

16–1 First-quarter income tax expense, $200,000
Second-quarter income tax expense, $220,000

16–2 First-quarter bonus expense, $14,000 or $8,000
Second-quarter bonus expense, $5,000 or $4,000

16–3 (3) Revised estimated annual tax rate, 49.09%
Second-quarter income tax expense, $197,540

There are no key figures for Chapter 17.

18–1 (1) Gain on restructuring, $176,000
18–2 (1) Gain on restructuring, $300,000
18–3 (1) Gain on restructuring, $440,000
18–4 (2a) Future interest expense, $-0-
(2b) Future interest expense, $9,000,000
18–5 (3) Future interest expense, $323,000
(4) Approx. effective interest rate, 5%
(5) 19X1 interest expense, $163,850
18–6 (2) Gain on restructuring, $375,000
(3) Future interest expense, $150,000
18–7 (2) No entry required
(3) 5% of the face amount
18–8 (1) Discount, $19,773,720
Gain on restructuring, $254,773,720
(2) First-year interest expense, $6,033,942
18–9 (1) Deficiency to unsecured creditors, $18,200
18–10 (1) Deficiency to unsecured creditors, $10,250

19–1 (1e) March's profit, $27,675
Sousa's profit, $22,325
19–2 (1) Archer's profit, $54,250
(2) Credit Archer's capital, $3,800
19–3 (1) Credit Cooke's capital, $99,000
Credit Walsh's capital, $80,000
(2) Coole to contribute $900
Walsh to withdraw $4,550
19–4 (1) 19X3 profit, $88,300
(2) Partner A's share of profits, $35,840
19–5 (1) Total billings, $5,463
(2) Net income, $2,035
Total assets, $8,580
19–6 Capital balances (adjusted): Hatt, $40,870; Hedd, $60,242
19–7 19X1 profit, $18,672
Total debits in adjusted trial balance, $77,067